EX LIBRIS

475-4946

Name Bal Bamra.

CONTEMPORARY CANADIAN BUSINESS LAW

PRINCIPLES & CASES

FOURTH EDITION

CONTEMPORARY CANADIAN BUSINESS LAW

PRINCIPLES & CASES

FOURTH EDITION

JOHN A. WILLES

Q.C., B.A., M.B.A., L.L.B., LL.M.
Barrister-at-Law
Professor in Industrial Relations and Business Law
Queen's University

McGRAW-HILL RYERSON LIMITED

Toronto   Montreal   New York   Auckland   Bogotá   Caracas
Lisbon   London   Madrid   Mexico   Milan   New Delhi   Paris
San Juan   Singapore   Sydney   Tokyo

CONTEMPORARY CANADIAN BUSINESS LAW:
PRINCIPLES & CASES
Fourth Edition

1 2 3 4 5 6 7 8 9 0 RRD 3 2 1 0 9 8 7 6 5 4

SPONSORING EDITOR: Kelly Smyth
SUPERVISING EDITOR: Lenore Gray
PROOFREADER: Shirley Corriveau
INDEX: Christopher Blackburn
PAGINATION: Pages Design
COVER & TEXT DESIGN: Jack Steiner Graphic Design
COVER PHOTOGRAPH: J.A. Kraulis/Masterfile

Canadian Cataloguing in Publication Data

Willes, John A.
    Contemporary Canadian business law : principles & cases

4th ed.
Includes bibliographical references and index.
ISBN 0-07-551656-X

1. Commercial law — Canada — Cases.   I. Title

KE919.W55 1994   346.71'07   C93-095576-5
KF887.W55 1994

TABLE OF CONTENTS

PREFACE TO THE FOURTH EDITION

The fourth edition of Contemporary Canadian Business law represents a further evolutionary change in the text to incorporate not only the changes in the law since the last edition, but to also incorporate new areas of law that reflect some of the more recent concerns of society. The purpose of the text, nevertheless, has remained the same: to provide an exposition of those areas of the law that affect organizations that carry on business in Canada.

The fourth edition contains a new chapter on environmental law and revised chapters where the law has changed since the third edition was published. These revisions include the new bankruptcy legislation and new developments in the Charter of Rights area, as well as expanded topics in tort law, contracts, intellectual property, and international business law. With respect to international business law, the text now includes the UNCITRAL rules for international contract dispute resolution.

The function of the text is to provide a general overview of the legal principles and concepts that are of interest to business persons and to assist the reader in the recognition of potential legal problems. The breadth of topics, however, limits the treatment of the law to only the most general statements of what are often complex and specialized areas of the law, and the text is therefore in no way intended to be used as a substitute for the advice of legal counsel.

As was the case with the previous editions, I am indebted to many. The changes in the fourth edition represent a composite of the suggestions that were submitted by users, reviewers, students, and a number of university instructors and practitioners who kindly reviewed the manuscript. Special thanks in this regard go to Deborah J. Meredith of the University of British Columbia, Elaine F. Geddes of the University of Alberta, Ken Thornicroft of Memorial University, Bill Fitzgerald of Mohawk College, Lian Smith of Grant MacEwan College, and Laura Bechard of Lakeland College. We would also like to thank Steven Enman of Acadia University, Ivan Ivankovich of the University of Alberta, K.G. Gwynne-Timothy of the University of Toronto, Paul Atkinson of Sir Sandford Fleming College, Fran Smyth of Seneca College, John Peace of the law firm Peace, Marshall, Burns, and William H. White of the law firm Haney, White, Jenkins and Duncan.

I would also like to thank my son John and daughter-in-law Carol, both members of the legal profession, for some of the new case problems and the selection of the new judicial decisions contained in the fourth edition. Their comments and suggestions for text revisions were also most helpful. Very special thanks must once again go to my wife Fran, who took time out from her own busy schedule to prepare my manuscript for publication, and to attend to the many administrative matters associated with the publication process. Finally, I would also like to express my thanks to my editors Kelly Smyth and Dennis Bockus for their patience and assistance in bringing the work to the point of publication, and to Jennifer Mix, Ann Byford, Lenore Gray and the College Division staff at McGraw-Hill Ryerson for transforming the manuscript to the published text form.

John A. Willes, Q.C.,
Queen's University,
September 1993.

ACKNOWLEDGEMENTS

ALL ENGLAND LAW REPORTS material reproduced by permission of Butterworths Legal Medical and Scientific Publishers, London, England.

Canada Law Book Ltd., Law Publishers, 240 Edward Street, Aurora, Ontario, for DOMINION LAW REPORTS and CANADIAN PATENT REPORTER.

ENGLISH REPORTS, Stevens & Sons Ltd., London, William Green & Sons, Edinburgh.

Maritime Law Book Ltd., publishers of the ALBERTA REPORTS, the ATLANTIC PROVINCE REPORTS, the MANITOBA REPORTS (2d), the NATIONAL REPORTER, the NEW BRUNSWICK REPORTS (2d), the NEW-FOUNDLAND & PRINCE EDWARD ISLAND REPORTS, the NOVA SCOTIA REPORTS (2d), and the SASKATCHEWAN REPORTS.

SUPREME COURT REPORTS material reproduced by permission of the Minister of Supply and Services Canada.

The Law Society of Upper Canada for ONTARIO LAW REPORTS and ONTARIO WEEKLY NOTES, ONTARIO REPORTS and ONTARIO WEEKLY REPORTER.

LAW REPORTS and WEEKLY LAW REPORTER material reproduced by permission of The Incorporated Council of Law Reporting for England and Wales.

WESTERN WEEKLY REPORTS, MARITIME PROVINCES REPORTS, CANADIAN BANKRUPTCY REPORTS (New Series), PERSONAL PROPERTY SECURITY ACT CASES, and BRITISH COLUMBIA LAW REPORTS reproduced by permission of the Carswell Company Ltd.

Newsome and Gilbert, Limited, Toronto, Ontario, for printed law forms. Reproduced with their permission.

A.C. (App. Cas.)	Law Reports Appeal Cases	(U.K.)
A. & E.	Adolphus and Ellis Reports	
All E.R. (All E. Rep.)	All England Reports	(U.K.)
Alta. L.R.	Alberta Law Reports	
App. Cas.	Appeal Cases	
Atk.	Atkyn's Chancery Reports	
Atl.	Atlantic Reports	
B.&C.	Barnewall & Cresswell Reports	(U.K.)
B.C.L.R.	British Columbia Law Reports	
Black.W. (Bl.W.)	William Blackstone Reports	(U.K.)
B.&S.	Best and Smith Reports	(U.K.)
C.B.R.	Canadian Bankruptcy Reports	
Ch.	Law Reports Chancery	(U.K.)
Ch. App.	Law Reports Chancery Appeal	(U.K.)
Ch.D.	Law Reports Chancery Division	(U.K.)
CLLC	Canadian Labour Law Cases	
Co. Rep.	Coke Reports	(U.K.)
C.&P/Car. & P	Carrington & Payne's Nisi Prius Reports	
C.P.	Law Reports Common Pleas	(U.K.)
C.P.D.	Law Reports Common Pleas Division	(U.K.)
C.P.R.	Canadian Patent Reporter	
Cranch	Cranch's United States Supreme Court Reports	
De G.F. & J.	De Gex Fisher & Jones Chancery Reports	
De G.M. & G.	De Gex Macnaughten & Gordon's Bankruptcy Reports	
D.L.R.	Dominion Law Reports	
E.R.	English Reports (a reprint series)	(U.K.)
Exch.	Law Reports Exchequer	(U.K.)
Ex. C.R.	Exchequer Court Reports	
F.	Federal Reporter	(U.S.A.)
Godb.	Godbolt Reports	(U.K.)
Hare	Hare Reports	(U.K.)
H.&C.	Hurlstone & Coltman Reports	(U.K.)
H.L. Cas.	Clark's House of Lords Cases	(U.K.)
Ill. App.	Illinois Appellate Court Reports	(U.S.A.)
J.&H.	Johnson & Hemming Reports	(U.K.)
Jur. N.S.	Jurist Reports, New Series	
K.B.	Law Reports King's Bench	(U.K.)
L.R.C.P.	Law Reports Common Pleas	(U.K.)
L.R. Exch.	Law Reports Exchequer Court	(U.K.)
L.R.H.L.	Law Reports House of Lords	(U.K.)
Mod.	Modern Reports	(U.K.)
M.P.R.	Maritime Provinces Reports	
M. & W.	Meeson & Welsby's Exchequer Reports	
My.&Cr.	Mylne & Craig Reports	(U.K.)
N.B.R.	New Brunswick Reports	
N.E.	North Eastern Reporter	(U.S.A.)
Nfld.R.	Newfoundland Reports	
N.S.R.	Nova Scotia Reports	

N.Y.	New York Reports	(U.S.A.)
O.L.R.	Ontario Law Reports	
O.R.	Ontario Reports	
O.W.N.	Ontario Weekly Notes	
P.E.I.R.	Prince Edward Island Reports	
Popham (Pop.)	Popham Reports	(U.K.)
P.(Pac.)	Pacific Reporter	(U.S.A.)
P.P.S.A.C.	Personal Property Security Act Cases	
Q.B.	Law Reports Queen's Bench	(U.K.)
Q.B.D.	Law Reports Queen's Bench Division	
S.C.R.	Supreme Court Reports	
Sty.	Style Reports	(U.K.)
T.L.R.	Times Law Reports	
W.L.R.	Weekly Law Reports	(U.K.)
W.W.R.	Western Weekly Reports	
Y.B.	Year Book	(U.K.)

TABLE OF CASES

CONTEMPORARY CANADIAN BUSINESS LAW

PRINCIPLES & CASES

FOURTH EDITION

PART I

Introduction to the Law

THE LEGAL ENVIRONMENT OF BUSINESS

In Canada, one would expect that any individual or group of individuals would be free to establish and carry on a business activity in any manner that they see fit. However, this is not the case. Modern business operates in an exceedingly complex legal environment. Laws govern the formation of many types of business organizations, the products they may manufacture or sell, the conditions under which the employees of a business may work, and the relationships between customers and competitors, and indeed, between the business owners themselves. These laws present a complicated web of rules and regulations for the business person. They may ensnare the unwary as well as those who deliberately ignore them.

Very briefly, business law may be divided into a number of general areas. These include tort law, which represents an area of the law largely concerned with injury to others. These injuries may arise as a result of the negligent production of goods causing injury to the consumer, careless professional service causing physical or economic loss, unsafe operating premises, or injury to others in a myriad of other ways either directly or through the actions of employees. While tort law in a business context is concerned with injuries to others arising out of the conduct of business, a second major area of the law is concerned with the basis of most business activity. This is contract law, and represents perhaps the law that has the greatest application in the day-to-day operations of a business organization. The law facilitates the purchase and sale of goods, the employment of staff, the reduction of risk (through insurance contracts), and some forms of organization of the business itself. Special contractual relationships and laws that control these and other business relationships include bailment, labour law and employment, negotiable instruments, consumer protection, and the law relating to restrictive trade practices.

Because a knowledge of the law relating to business organizations, their formation and operation, is important in order to determine the appropriate vehicle by which to conduct business activities, a knowledge of partnerships and corporations is also essential. Important, as well, is a knowledge of how premises are acquired for business operations. Land law, which covers the purchase or leasing of premises or the financing of the purchase of land and buildings, sets out the rules for these business activities. The final areas of the law of interest to business include the securing of debt in credit transactions, bankruptcy law, international trade, environmental law, and the protection of intellectual and industrial property. Persons engaged in business must have at least a rudimentary knowledge of these areas of the law in order to function effectively in a business environment.

Many of these laws simply reflect behavioural norms that fair-minded people would expect as treatment of them by others, but some laws go much further in the sense that they are designed to enforce or control policy.

Legislation that requires the licensing of the various professions or laws that control the possession or use of certain goods, such as drugs or explosives, are examples of the latter policies.

It is important for all business persons to be aware of the areas of the law that affect them in the conduct of their business activities. This is not only from the point of view of knowing their rights at law, but to ensure their own compliance with all relevant legislation. However, understanding a law often requires an appreciation of how and why the law was passed. In many cases, the historical background provides the clues. In other cases, new technological changes required a legislative response. Chapter 1 provides a historical setting for the law, its different classifications, and its enforcement as a part of the stage-setting for a closer examination of the law and how it impacts on business. The second chapter introduces the constitution and our Charter of Rights and Freedoms. The third and final chapter in this part of the text takes an in-depth look at the legal system and the legal profession. A historical perspective is established for each of these topics, since each is largely the product of an evolutionary process.

CHAPTER

1

The Law and the Legal System

The Nature of Law
The Role of Law
The Development of Law
The Rise of the Courts and the Rule of Law

Sources of Law
  The Common Law and Equity
  Statute Law
  Administrative Law
Classification of Laws
Summary
Discussion Questions

THE NATURE OF LAW

The law holds a special fascination for most people. This is perhaps partly due to the fact that the law has become so all-pervasive that we are constantly reminded of its presence, but it cannot be the only reason. It is also of interest because it reflects the society in which we live. It determines the rights and freedoms of the individual, and the extent to which these privileges may be enjoyed. The law at any given point in time represents the values and concerns of the people in the jurisdiction from which it arose, and to examine the historical development of the laws of a society is much like an examination of the society itself, for the two are inextricably intertwined. In effect, the law touches so many facets of human endeavour that it would be difficult to imagine how a modern society might exist without it. It has become, in fact, the very essence of society. This, in itself, is reason enough to justify the study of its principles and application.

The word "law" has been applied to so many rules, principles, and statements that it is probably incapable of exact definition. Legal philosophers have agonized over the meaning of the term and have wrestled with its sources and nature since the earliest of times. Part of the difficulty in reaching a precise definition is the nature of law itself. It is very much a concept rather than an object or thing that has clearly defined limits or parameters. Simple definitions, however, may be attempted, bearing in mind that the definition may not be precise or all-encompassing.

Irwin Dorfman, a prominent lawyer, explained the term very simply in a speech to the Canadian Bar Association in 1975. He defined the law as "merely a set of rules that enable people to live together and respect each other's rights."[1] This definition covers much of the law that affects interpersonal relationships, and in particular, the common law (which is simply the recorded judgements of the courts). Modern society has prompted others to offer definitions of the law,

---

1. Statement by Irwin Dorfman, President, Canadian Bar Association, at the annual meeting of the association, August 1975, at Halifax, Nova Scotia.

3

each in an attempt to explain the nature and purpose of the law as succinctly and precisely as possible. Salmond, for example, described the law as the "body of principles recognized and applied by the state in the administration of justice." [2]

Oliver Wendell Holmes, the distinguished American jurist, once described the law as "a statement of circumstances in which the public force will be brought to bear through the Courts."[3] Blackstone, in his famous *Commentaries on the Law of England,* defined the law as "a rule of civil conduct, prescribed by the supreme power in a state, commanding what is right, and prohibiting what is wrong." [4]

Each of these definitions implies that something will happen if an individual does not obey the rules. In Irwin Dorfman's definition of the law, he mentions respect for the "rights" of others. To understand the operation or application of the law then, it is necessary to know what constitutes a **right,** and to distinguish this right from that which constitutes a **privilege.** When we say we have the "right" to do something, we are saying, in essence, that we may do the particular act with impunity, or with the force of the state behind us. Because rights are closely associated with duties, our right to do an act usually imposes a duty on others not to interfere with our actions. What the law does is to set out our rights and duties in order that everyone will know what they are, and to whom they apply. In a similar fashion, the law sets out actions that are not rights and duties, but privileges.

Privileges are actions that may be taken by an individual under specific circumstances and that may be withdrawn or curtailed by the state. Rights enjoyed by individuals often become privileges as a result of social pressure or public policy. Occasionally, rights may also become privileges out of a desire on the part of the legislators to increase the flow of funds to the public coffers through licence fees. Statutes relating to the ownership and operation of automobiles are examples of laws of this nature.

THE ROLE OF LAW

The law represents a means of social control, and a law in its most basic form is simply an obligatory rule of conduct.[5] **The law**, in contrast to a single law, consists of the body of rules of conduct laid down by a sovereign or governing body to control the actions of individuals in its jurisdiction. It is normally enforced by sanctions. The law develops to meet the needs of the people in a free society and changes with their changing needs. For this reason, the law tends to respond to the demands of a free society, rather than shape its nature. Laws, however, may arise in other ways as well.

Laws established and enforced by legislators that are not in response to the demands of the majority of citizens of the state may be introduced to shape or redirect society in ways that legislators perceive as desirable. Laws of this type represent a form of social engineering that frequently restricts individual rights and freedom, and very often transfers individual rights and powers to the governing body. Laws of this nature represent a growing proportion of Canadian law, but this form of legislation is not a recent phenomenon.

2. Williams , G., *Salmond on Jurisprudence,* 11th ed. (London: Sweet & Maxwell Ltd., 1954), p. 41.

3. Corley, R.N., and Black, R.L., *The Legal Environment of Business,* 2nd ed. (New York: McGraw-Hill Book Company, 1968), p. 4.

4. Lewis, W.D., *Blackstone's Commentaries on the Law of England* (Philadelphia: Rees, Welsh & Company, 1897), Book 1, s. 2, para. 44.

5. Osborn, P.G., *The Concise Law Dictionary*, 4th ed. (London: Sweet & Maxwell Ltd., 1954), p. 194.

Laws that legislatures have attempted to impose on society to alter the behaviour of the majority normally prove to be ineffective unless enforced by oppressive penalties or complete government control of the activity. In a business context, compulsory, provincially operated automobile insurance schemes in a number of provinces in Canada represent examples of legislation of the latter kind. It tends to be of a confiscatory nature in the sense that the government, by decree, transfers the right to engage in the activity to itself and virtually excludes all private sector insurers. Provinces with this type of legislation have decided that as a matter of public policy the government should engage in the activity for the public good, and without interference or competition from the private sector. In a free society, the only way that a governing body may implement such a policy is through laws that establish an insurance system that, in a variety of ways, excludes all others from engaging in the activity.

The desirability of this type of legislation, which impinges on the freedom of the individual and alters the rights and behaviour patterns of those living in the jurisdiction, has been the subject of much debate amongst legal philosophers for centuries. The basis of much of this debate is rooted in political philosophy rather than in the law as such. It does, however, illustrate how the law may be used to implement public policies that may not represent the particular desires or wishes of the people, but rather the desires of those in a position of political power at a given point in time.

While social control very broadly represents the role of law in a society, the law itself may be subdivided into a number of functions that are essentially subsets of its principal role. Laws must, first of all, be the vehicle by which disputes between individuals are settled. Some of the earliest laws were simply procedural rules outlining the manner in which parties would deal with each other in the settlement of their dispute by combat. The sole purpose of these laws was to ensure some degree of fairness in the combat and a minimum of disruption in the lives of others not directly involved in the dispute. In this sense, the law served a second function: it established rules of conduct for individuals living in close association with others. Such rules direct the energies of individuals in an orderly fashion and minimize conflict between persons engaged in similar activities, or in activities which have the potential for conflict. In the distant past these were rules that determined which hunter was entitled to the game where more than one party was responsible for bringing the animal down. A classic example of a modern application of this type of law would be the "rules of the road" under the various Highway Traffic Acts. These rules dictate where and how a motor vehicle may be driven, in order to facilitate the orderly flow of traffic and to minimize the risk of accident or injury to those who drive motor vehicles.

The third major function of the law is to provide protection for individuals in a society. Self-preservation is of paramount importance to any person, and the law represents a response to this desire or need. Individuals in the earliest societies realized they were dependent upon one another for much of their security. Some of the first laws therefore related to the protection of individuals from intentional or careless assaults by others. These laws soon expanded to include the protection of possessions as well, and established the concepts of individual freedom and property rights. The development of these laws can best be understood by an examination of law in its historical context.

THE DEVELOP-MENT OF LAW

The origins of some of our most basic laws and principles are lost in antiquity. Records of early civilizations make reference to a great many laws similar to those that stand today on our statute books or in our common law as the law of the land. Even then, the early writings no doubt simply recorded what had then been long-standing rules or customs. By using logic and an understanding of human nature, one may speculate on how the law evolved in early times.

The earliest laws were handed down by word of mouth from generation to generation long before the first words were recorded on parchment or on clay tablets. These early laws, or rules of behaviour, probably had their origins as rules of conduct established to maintain orderly relationships in the families of early human-kind. Later on, they were perhaps expanded to govern conduct between families in a tribe as families began living in close proximity to one another.

The concentration of families in a relatively small area, however, was not without its disadvantages. Disruptive behaviour in a village affected a far greater number of individuals than it would in an isolated family setting, and the need to curb activities of this nature took on a new importance. During this period, early attempts to control disruptive behaviour took the form of the selection of individuals, usually family elders (or the strongest members of the community), to hear disputes and recommend non-disruptive, or at least controlled methods of settlement. The disputants were required to accept their decision as the binding resolution of the conflict. Initially, this group decided each dispute on its merits, but gradually some consistency emerged as similar disputes were decided on the basis of the previous decisions. At this point, rules of behaviour for the entire community began to take on meaning. In the beginning, these decisions were imposed by the community if they were considered just and equitable. However as the decision-makers assumed more responsibility for the orderly operation of the affairs of the village, so, too, did they acquire the power to impose their decisions on disputants. With the establishment of a governing body or a sovereign with the power to impose a decision on an individual in the interests of the community good, the law, as an instrument of social control, took form.

These changes did not happen in any significant way until the village form of living gave way to the establishment of the city and the city state. The city arose with the development of trade and the production of goods and services by individuals for others. This was first in the form of barter and later by way of some medium of exchange. In any event, the concentration of activity in a relatively small area gave the individual an identification with the community, and a desire to act in a concerted way in the solution of common problems. The answer was usually to form some sort of organization or government to deal with these matters and to direct the efforts of the community as a whole. The formation of these formal bodies, with the authority to decide how individuals in the community should conduct themselves in their dealings with others, and with the power to enforce their decisions, created the first state-legislated laws.

Needless to say, these laws developed gradually over a relatively long period of time, and at different rates among different peoples. The earliest known written laws were undoubtedly accepted as the officially sanctioned rules of behaviour long before they were formally recorded. In some cases, when a tribe or race reached the stage of the city state and became rich and weak from "easy living," it would then be plundered by less-civilized tribes. The invaders would then adopt the new city life and much of its form of organization. The laws of the city state, necessary for order and tranquillity, would often be adopted as well by the invaders. Then, as a tribe or a race, they would move directly from a relatively lawless behavioural system directed by custom to a society governed by law. In other cases, the law was imposed upon less-developed tribes or races by the invading armies of city states. The Roman Empire was a notable example of a state that spread the rule of law over much of Western Europe and the Middle East and established the first legal institutions in many of those parts of the world.

THE RISE OF THE COURTS AND THE RULE OF LAW

The law, without some system of determining its application or imposing its sanctions, has little more than a persuasive effect on human behaviour. The rise of the city state brought with it the establishment of the mechanism for law enforcement. The inhabitants of large communities (and later, the city states) were quick to realize that disputes between individuals would increase as the population's density increased. At first, these communities established tribunals or other bodies officially authorized to hear disputes. With the aid of the society, these tribunals could force restitution or undertake vengeance; however, they lacked sufficient power to compel the use of their system. Eventually, by the process of requiring certain formalities that must be undertaken before vengeance, and by providing the inducement of monetary compensation as a remedy, the state ultimately became powerful enough to force everyone to use the tribunal or court. At this stage, because of its negative effect on the community, vengeance itself became a crime.[6]

Of particular importance in the development of the courts was the nature of their decisions. For the most part, the law relating to relationships between individuals, and the rights and responsibilities of one to another, was gradually established in the form of consistent decisions, first by tribunals, and later by the courts. As a result, the judgements of the courts preceded the law. The correctness of these early decisions, or judgements, was usually based upon either a religious foundation (if the head of the state held his or her position by some divine right), or the approval of the assembled citizens of the community. Consistency in the decisions handed down by these courts in similar cases eventually created the body of rules known as the law.

In England, the early courts and the law were imposed on the inhabitants by a number of successive invaders. Following the Roman conquest of England in 43 B.C., the country was subject to *lex romana* (Roman law) and its administrative machinery. In theory at least, in those areas under Roman control, the law was uniform in nature and application. This lasted throughout the period of Roman occupation.

The disintegration of the Roman Empire and the invasion of England by the Germanic tribes produced a decentralized system of government under a king. This system divided the land into shires and counties, each with its own government and, to varying degrees, freedom from royal interference. The shires were further divided into smaller communities called hundreds, administrative units about the size of a township. Within these units were the boroughs or local communities.

---

6. *Hemmings and Wife et al. v. The Stoke Poges Golf Club, Ltd. et al.,* [1920] 1 K.B. 720.

In the pre-Norman period, the law in each of these shires developed according to local custom or need. It was not until after 1066 that the trend was reversed. At that time, the only laws that were common throughout the land were the small number of written laws, relating to general crimes, that several of the kings had pronounced as law. These laws frequently set out the penalty in monetary terms, with a part of the money to be paid to the king by the perpetrator of the crime, and the balance to be paid to the injured party or the party's next of kin. These laws were enforced by a relatively weak central government, called a witenage-mot, that governed the country along with the king.

The Norman Conquest in 1066 brought with it a more centralized system of administration and, shortly thereafter, the establishment of a central judicial system. The Conquest had very little effect on English custom, but it did have a considerable effect on the administration of the country. The power of the shires was brought under the control of the king, and the right of the **shire court** or **county court** to hear cases concerning land and certain criminal cases (known as **pleas of the Crown**) was transferred to the king's justices.

The establishment of a central judiciary under King Henry II to hear the more serious cases was an important factor in the development of the common law in England. After 1180, justices of the royal court travelled regularly throughout the country to hear cases. On their return to London, they discussed their cases with one another or exchanged notes on their decisions. Amongst themselves they gradually developed what later became a body of law common throughout the land.

During the twelfth and thirteenth centuries, the administration of justice became more centralized, and the king's justices began keeping their own records after 1234. Early decisions were largely based on local custom. However, this gradually changed as the judges based their decisions more upon the written records of the court, and less upon what was alleged to be local custom. After 1272, written records of decisions were maintained to assist the fledgling legal profession. Although the records were sparse during the early period following 1272, they improved over the next three centuries to the point where they were useful as statements of the common law. Better case reports, and their consolidation in the years that followed, developed the body of law known as the **common law of England.** The discovery and subsequent settlement of English colonies in North America established the common law in Canada and the United States. Today, these principles represent a large and flexible body of law that is adaptable and responsive to the needs of our society.

SOURCES OF LAW

The Common Law and Equity

The **common law** represents an important source of law in Canada. It is sometimes referred to as "case law," because that is where statements of the common law may be found. Another reason is to distinguish it from the second major source of law: **statute law.**

In common law provinces, and in those countries with common law systems, the law (except statute law) is not found in a code, but in the recorded judgements of the courts. These judgements were not always recorded, but in 1290, during the reign of Edward I, the *Year Books* were commenced. These books provided reports of the cases, but in the early years, reasons for the decisions were seldom included. With the introduction of printing in England in 1477, the *Year Books* were improved, and printed copies became available to the legal profession. The reporting of cases in the form of law reports took place in the sixteenth century, and from that point on, the decisions of the judges were reported without a break by various law reporters. Judicial reasoning and the principles applied by the judges were readily available by way of these reports, and the common law could be determined from them through the **doctrine of** *stare decisis.*

Stare decisis ("to let a decision stand" or "to stand by a previous decision") is the theory of **precedent** in common law. In its application, the doctrine means that a judge must apply the previous decision of a similar case to the one before the court if the facts of the two cases are the same, providing such decision was (1) from the judge's own court; (2) from a court of equal rank; or (3) from a higher (or superior) court.

The need for certainty in the law (in the sense that it must be clear in its meaning and predictable in its application) was quickly realized by judges. The adoption of the theory of precedent provided a degree of stability to the common law without sacrificing its flexibility; although at times the courts became so reluctant to move from previous decisions that their application of the law made no sense at all to the case at hand. Fortunately, judges have been adaptable in their formulation of the law. Over the years they have maintained the common law as a blend of predictable yet flexible principles, capable of conforming to the changing needs of society. This has been due, in part, to a reluctance on the part of the judiciary to accept precedent as a hard and fast rule. The facts of any two cases are seldom precisely the same. Differences in the facts or circumstances are sufficient to permit a judge to decide that a particular obsolete precedent should not apply to the case before the court if the application of such a precedent would produce an unsatisfactory result. In this fashion, the courts have gradually adapted the common law to changing times.

The adaptability of the common law has enabled it to absorb, over a long period of time, many legal principles, customs, and laws from other legal systems and sources. The law of England before the Norman Conquest was, for the most part, local in both form and application. It consisted of a mixture of early customs, a few remnants of early Roman law, and the laws and customs brought to England by the Anglo-Saxon invaders. Decisions were handed down by judges based upon local custom, which prior to the Conquest was the only precedent available. The Norman Conquest brought with it a central system for the administration of justice and, through this centralized system, the incorporation of the customs and laws from all parts of the country into the common law.

Other laws were also incorporated into the common law as the courts in England expanded their jurisdiction. Originally, the church had jurisdiction over religion, family and marriage, morals, and matters relating to the descent of personal property of deceased persons. The law relating to these matters was initially administered by ecclesiastic courts, but cases concerning some of these church-administered areas of the law gradually found their way before judges of the civil courts. After the Reformation (during the years 1534–1538) much of the ecclesiastic courts' jurisdiction passed to the royal courts. In dealing with cases that had previously fallen within the province of the ecclesiastic courts, the judges naturally looked at the decisions of those courts in reaching their own decisions. As a result, many of the rules of **canon** or **church law** became a part of the common law.

In much the same fashion, a substantial part of the law relating to commerce and trade was incorporated into the common law. Early merchants belonged to guilds, as did the artisans. Customs of the various trades gradually developed into a body of rules that were similar throughout much of Western Europe, and disputes that arose between merchants were frequently settled by the application of these rules.

Initially, most of the merchants sold their wares and goods at fairs and markets, and any disputes which arose were settled by the senior merchants, whose decisions were final and binding. Later, decision-making became somewhat more formal, and the decisions more uniform. Gradually, rules of law relating to commercial transactions began to emerge, as the decisions of the guild courts became firmly established and consistent in their application by the merchant guilds. These courts had jurisdiction only over their members, so for a long period of time, the body of law known as the **law merchant** was within the exclusive domain of the merchant guilds. Eventually, merchants who were not guild members began to trade, and when disputes arose, they appealed to the courts of the land for relief. The judges in dealing with these disputes, applied the law merchant. By way of their decisions the large body of law relating to commerce gradually became a part of the common law.

Other rules of law were incorporated into the common law by more direct means. The law relating to land tenure, which had its roots in feudal law, was introduced by the Normans following the Conquest in 1066, and the courts thereafter were obliged to apply these rules in dealing with land disputes.

Even customs or practices which have developed over time have found their way into the common law. The courts have often recognized long-standing practices in determining the rights of parties at law, and, in this fashion, have established the custom or practice as a part of the common law.

The last important source of law administered by the common law courts was the body of law called **equity**. The rules of equity are not, strictly speaking, a part of the common law, but, rather, a body of legal principles that take precedence over the common law where the common law and rules of equity conflict. The rules of equity developed largely because the common law in England had become rigid in its application by the fifteenth century, and litigants often could not obtain a satisfactory remedy from the courts. To obtain the kind of relief desired, they would frequently petition the king. The king, and later his chancellor, heard these cases and made in each case what was called an equitable decision; one which was not necessarily based upon the law, but one which the king considered to be fair. The ideas of fairness which the king expressed as the basis for his decisions gradually took on the form of principles or rules, which he applied in other cases which came before him. Over time, these became known as principles of equity. These principles were later followed by the chancellor, and later still by the Court of Chancery (the Chancellor's Court). Eventually, they took on the form of rules of law. In the late nineteenth century, the Court of Chancery and the common law courts merged, and the rules of equity became a part of the body of law that the courts could apply in any civil case coming before them. As a result, a judge may apply either the common law rules or the principles of equity to a case before the court, and, where the common law might be inappropriate, the equitable remedy is usually available to ensure a fair and just result. How these laws are administered is the subject matter of the next two chapters.

Statute Law

Statutes are laws that are established by the governing bodies of particular jurisdictions and have their root in the Latin word *statutum,* meaning "it is decided." Governments are vested with the power to make laws, either under the terms of a written constitution, such as that of Canada or the United States, or as a result of long-standing tradition, such as in England.

Statutes are the product or end result of a legislative process. Under this process, the wishes of the people, as interpreted by the members of a provincial legislature or the Parliament of Canada are brought forward for debate in the legislative assembly. They then finally become law if the majority of the legislators believe that the law is necessary. The process provides time for study and amendment of the proposals and, in the case of the Parliament of Canada, a thorough examination not only by the House of Commons but by the Senate as well. It is by this democratic process that statute laws are created.

A statute law has its beginnings in a **bill,** which is essentially a proposed law presented to a legislative body (such as the House of Commons or a provincial legislature). The bill then requires a **motion** (or decision) to have the bill read a first time and printed for circulation. Members of the legislature are then given a period of time to read the bill and prepare for the debate of its contents before it is brought forward again. Some time later, the bill comes before the legislature (or House) for a second reading. The bill is then debated in principle.

If the bill passes the second reading, it is then sent to a committee of the House or legislature for study on a clause by clause basis. The committee is made up of a number of members of the legislature appointed to examine the proposed legislation and amend it if necessary. Any member of the committee may propose amendments, as the bill must be passed one clause at a time in committee. Once the bill (perhaps in amended form) has been passed by the committee, the Chair of the Committee reports the bill in final form to the legislature.

The report of the bill may then be subject to further debate and amendment before the bill is given a third reading. If passed (in the sense that a motion to have the bill read a third time is carried by a majority vote) the bill is then sent to the Senate at the federal level. It must then be approved by a similar process at the Senate level. The Senate may also initiate bills, but if it does so, it must send the bill to the House of Commons where the process is repeated.

Once a bill has been passed by the House of Commons and Senate (at the federal level) or the provincial legislature, it must received **royal assent** by the Governor-General (federally) or the Lieutenant-Governor (provincially). Royal assent is largely automatic, as it has never been refused at the federal level. This, however, has not been the case with respect to provincial bills, as on numerous occasion in the past royal assent has been refused.

A bill does not become law until it receives royal assent, but in some cases the government may not wish to implement the law (or parts of it) until some time in the future. In these cases, the bill will not become law until a point in time when it is **proclaimed** or becomes effective.

Properly passed, and within the jurisdiction of a legislature, a statute affects the residents of that province, or in the case of a federal statute, all residents of Canada. Each year, the federal government and the provinces publish the statutes and amendments to statutes passed in that year. At regular intervals these statutes are collected together and published in their updated or amended form as the **revised statutes** of a province or the federal government. For example, the federal government collected together all of the statutes in effect on a date in 1985, arranged them in alphabetic order by name and reproduced them. They were designated as the *Revised Statutes of Canada, 1985* (R.S.C. 1985). The previous revision had been made in 1970, fifteen years before.

Provinces also revise their statutes at regular intervals. For example, Alberta and Ontario are provinces that revise their statutes at ten year intervals. These are designated as the *Revised Statutes of Alberta* and *Revised Statutes of Ontario,* respectively. These designations always include the year of revision; e.g., R.S.A. 1980 or R.S.O. 1990 to indicate the year of revision.

As noted previously, when a statute is properly enacted within the legislative jurisdiction of a provincial or the federal government, it will, when declared to be law, apply to all those persons within that jurisdiction. Statute law can be used to create laws to cover new activities or matters not covered by the common law, or to change or abolish a common law rule or right. Statutes may also be used to codify the common law by collecting together in one written law the common law rules or principles relating to a specific matter.

The particular advantage of statute law over the common law is the relative ease by which the law may be changed. The common law is generally very slow to respond to changing societal needs. It follows a gradual, evolutionary pattern of change, rather than a quick response. Statute law, on the other hand (in theory at least), may be quickly changed in response to the demands of the public. The disadvantage of statute law is that it will be strictly interpreted by the courts. Unless it is very carefully drafted, it may not achieve its intended purpose. Occasionally, a badly drafted statute only serves to compound the problems that it was intended to solve, and may require additional laws to respond to the problems it created. In spite of the potential problems inherent in statute law, the general direction of the law appears to be toward more (rather than less) statute law to deal with social change.

In contrast to the rest of Canada, the Province of Quebec has codified much of the law that is normally found in the common law of other provinces. As a result, this body of law, which is known as the **Civil Code,** may be consulted in the determination of rights and duties. These same rights and duties would ordinarily be found in the common law in other jurisdictions. This particular method of establishing the law of a jurisdiction is not a new or novel approach. It is simply an alternate method of setting out the law that has a long history. The first codification of law of major significance took place under the direction of the Roman emperor Justinian, who ordered a compilation of all the laws of Rome dating back to the time of Cicero. The collection of the laws was an enormous task that took seven years to compete, and on completion in A.D. 534 became the famous **Corpus Juris Civilis.** This body of law formed the basis of the law in a large part of continental Europe for the next 1200 years. It was not until the eighteenth century that major revisions were made.

Frederick the Great of Prussia directed the preparation of a new code during his reign, but it was not adopted until 1794, some eight years after his death. Shortly thereafter, France (under Napoleon), began a codification of French law in 1804. It was this code that influenced the codification of the law in Spain, Italy, Belgium, and by way of colonization, much of South America, the state of Louisiana, and the Province of Quebec. The 1900 codification of the law in Germany, which replaced Frederick the Great's Prussian code, found favour as a model for many other countries, the most notable being Japan, Switzerland, and Greece. Quebec, however, continued to follow a civil code based upon the French model. More recently, the province completed a thorough review of its code, and produced a new Quebec Civil Code which up-dated much of the code through the recognition of modern business practices. The new code came into effect in 1993.

The codification of the common law in England was never seriously considered, even though it was urged by such respected English writers as Sir Francis Bacon. Nor did the idea find much favour in the United States or the common law provinces of Canada. Codification of some parts of the common law in all three countries, however, has taken place. England codified the common law as it stood in 1882 with respect to bills of exchange and negotiable instruments, and in 1890, codified the law with respect to partnership. The common law relating to the sale of goods was codified in 1893, but after that, the process lost its impetus. Since then, no major effort has been made to codify other branches of mercantile law except to modify or settle matters of difficulty relating to particular issues.

The American Bar Association, during the late nineteenth century and early twentieth century, proposed a number of uniform statutes relating to commercial practices in an effort to eliminate the differences that existed in state legislation, but their efforts were unsuccessful. It was not until after World War II that there was sufficient interest in codification to produce the United States Uniform Commercial Code. This code, which relates to commercial law practices, was first drafted in 1952, and, following a number of amendments, eventually was adopted by all states by 1975. Unfortunately, the goal of true conformity of legislation, as envisaged by the Bar Association, was not realized. Not all of the states adopted the entire code, and some altered the code to suit their own particular needs. Substantial conformity, however, was achieved in the United States, at least with respect to a number of areas of commercial law.

Proponents of codification have long argued that the advantage of this method over the common law is certainty. According to their argument, if the law is written down, it is there for all to see and know. In theory, the judge decides a dispute by reference to the appropriate part of the code. However, if no specific article covers the dispute, then the decision is based upon general principles of law set out in the code. The particular difficulty with the code is that it might be interpreted differently in some cases by different judges. Unless some uniformity exists between judges in deciding similar cases, one of the important advantages of the code is lost. To avoid this, judges in Quebec, and those countries with civil codes, do consider the decisions of other judges who have decided similar cases when they apply the law.

Administrative Law

A growing part of statute law is an area of law called **administrative law**. The primary focus of this body of law is directed toward the **regulations** made under statute law and enforced by administrative bodies. While legislation usually creates laws, or repeals old laws, it may also create agencies or **administrative tribunals** to regulate activities or do specific things. The activities of these tribunals and agencies are said to be administrative acts, and the body of law that relates to their activities is administrative law.

Administrative law is not a new area of the law, but rather an area of law that has increased substantially in size and importance since World War II. In early times in England, Parliament would authorize the king and his officials to carry out such activities as the collection of taxes, the maintenance of the armed forces, and the operation of the courts. In the beginning, the king and his officials carried out these duties, but gradually a public service was established to perform these tasks. In this fashion, Parliament did not directly supervise the activity, but merely authorized it and set out guidelines for the officials to follow in the performance of their duties. Today, Parliament and the provincial legislatures use this method to regulate many activities that fall within their legislative jurisdiction. Examples of some of the activities under the control of regulatory agencies include the sale of securities by public companies, labour relations, employment standards, aeronautics, broadcasting, the sale and consumption of alcoholic beverages, land use, and a wide variety of commercial activities.

The process is usually quite uniform. In most cases, a statute is passed to create a board or commission to supervise an activity, but the governing act will only set out broad policy guidelines for the regulation of the activity by the body created. To enable the tribunal to carry out the particular public policy goals of the statute it is generally permitted to establish its own procedures and rules. These may either be approved by the government as an **Order in Council,** or by the minister in charge of the tribunal, depending upon the importance attached to the regulations.

The regulations of administrative tribunals represent a body of **subordinate** legislation that governs activities subject to supervision by an agency or board. These regulations, together with the decisions of the tribunals, form a part of the body of law that is known as **administrative law.** The general trend of governments at all levels to exercise greater control over the activities of citizens within their respective jurisdictions has resulted in a proliferation of boards and agencies, often acting in conflict with one another. The net result of this trend has been the creation of a large and unwieldy bureaucracy at provincial and federal levels of government, and a substantial restriction of the freedom of the individual in a tangled web of regulations. In recent years, complaints from the public concerning the actions of the many boards and tribunals prompted governments to study the need for so many administrative agencies. However, to date nothing has been done to reduce the size of this bureaucracy. Given the nature of the public service in Canada, and the propensity of governments at all levels to create more laws rather than reduce their number, it is unlikely that government regulation of the individual will diminish significantly in the foreseeable future.

**CLASSIFICA-
TION OF LAWS**

Statute law and the common law may be classified in two broad, general categories. The first is **substantive law,** and includes all laws that set out the rights and duties of individuals. The second broad classification is **procedural law.** This area of the law includes all laws that set out the procedures by which individuals may enforce their substantive law rights or duties.

To illustrate these two classifications of law we might note an old observation of the law relating to assault that says, "your right to swing your arm stops just short of your neighbour's nose." Put another way, you owe a duty to your friends not to injure them if you swing your arm in their presence. If you should strike one of your friends through your carelessness, your friend has a right for redress for the injury which you cause. This right is a **substantive right,** and it represents a part of the substantive law. To enforce the right, your friend would institute legal proceedings to obtain redress for the injury, and the steps taken would be part of the procedural law.

Substantive law may be further subdivided into two other types of law: **public law** and **private law.** Public law deals with the law relating to the relationship between the individual and the government (or its agencies). The Criminal Code and the Income Tax Act are two examples of this kind of law at the federal level, and the various Highway Traffic Acts are examples of similar public laws at the provincial level. Under these statutes, if an individual fails to comply with the duties imposed, it is the Crown that institutes proceedings to enforce the law.

Private law concerns the relationship between individuals, and includes all laws relating to the rights and duties that the parties may have, or may create between themselves. Much of the common law is private law, but many statutes also represent private law. The law of contract is private law. Such statutes as the Partnerships Act[7] and the Sale of Goods Act[8] are examples of private law as well. Legal rights, if private law in nature, must be enforced by the injured party.

For example, Anderson is digging a trench alongside a sidewalk and is placing the excavated soil on the walkway. While walking along the sidewalk, Brown complains to Anderson that the soil is blocking his way. Anderson is angered by Brown's complaint and strikes him with his shovel. In this situation, Anderson has violated s. 265 of the Criminal Code[9] by striking Brown with the intention of causing him injury. The Criminal Code is a public law, and it is the Crown that will take action against Anderson for his violation of the law.

Anderson, in this example, also owes a duty to Brown not to injure him (a private law duty). If Anderson injures Brown, as he did in this case, Brown has a common law right to recover from Anderson the loss that he has suffered as a result of Anderson's actions. Brown's right at common law is a private law matter, and Brown must take steps himself to initiate legal proceedings to enforce his right against Anderson.

In this case, both the Crown in the enforcement of the Criminal Code, and Brown in taking legal action against Anderson, use procedural law to enforce their rights.

---

7. Partnerships Act, R.S.O. 1990, c. P5.

8. Sale of Goods Act, R.S.O. 1990, c. S1.

9. Criminal Code, R.S.C. 1985, c. C-46 s. 265, as amended.

Private law is sometimes referred to as civil law to distinguish private laws of a non-criminal nature from public laws (principally the Criminal Code). Unfortunately, this has caused some confusion in Canada, because most of the private law in the Province of Quebec has been codified, and the law there is referred to as the Civil Code. While both the common law and the Code deal with private law, care must be taken to note the distinction between the two bodies of law when reference is made to civil law.

SUMMARY

The law is the principal means by which the state maintains social control, and the system of courts is the vehicle used for its enforcement. The first laws were not laws as such, but family behavioural rules, and later, religious and non-religious taboos. These were enforced, first, by the family elders, and later by the community. As the community became stronger, it gradually assumed more and more of the duties of law-making and, with the development of the early city states, law-making and enforcement took on an organized character. As the power of the state increased, so, too, have the areas of human endeavour that the state has brought under its control.

The law that we have today has evolved over a long period of time, and now represents a very complex system consisting of the common law, statute law, and a subordinate type of law called administrative law. These laws may be classified as either substantive law or procedural law, with the former setting out rights and duties, and the latter, as the name indicates, setting out the procedure for the enforcement of the substantive law rights.

DISCUSSION QUESTIONS

1. Why is the word "law" so difficult to define in a precise manner?
2. What is the difference between a "right" and a "privilege"?
3. Why are "rights" and "duties" often considered together when one thinks of laws?
4. Could a society exist without laws? If not, why not?
5. "Advanced civilizations are generally characterized by having a great many laws or statutes to control the activities of the citizenry." Comment on the validity of this statement.
6. Explain the common law system, and how it relates to the function of the courts.
7. Why is the doctrine of *stare decisis* an important part of the common law system?
8. How does the common law differ from the principles of equity? From statute law?
9. How does a legislature establish a new law? Explain the procedure.
10. Define substantive law, and explain how it differs from procedural law.
11. Describe the difference between the common law and the civil code of the Province of Quebec. What are the relative merits of each system?
12. "The supremacy of the state was reached when it managed to exercise a sufficient degree of control over the individual to compel him or her to use the state judicial system rather than vengeance to settle differences with others." Why was it necessary for the state to require this of the individual?
13. How does a "regulation" made under a statute differ from other "laws"?
14. Identify the following laws as "public" or "private": Highway Traffic Act; Criminal Code; Sale of Goods Act; Liquor Control Act; Income Tax Act; Immigration Act; Customs and Excise Act.
15. Explain how the enforcement of a public law differs from the enforcement of rights under private law.

CHAPTER 2

The Canadian Constitution

INTRODUCTION   Most countries have found some form of written authority, setting out both the fundamental rights and freedoms of their citizens and the law-making powers of the various legislative bodies of the state. This document is generally referred to as a **constitution.** It represents a source of law in the sense that it not only establishes certain legal rights, but also law-making authority. A constitution, however, may not always be contained in a single document. The "constitution" of Great Britain, for example, consists of a large number of proclamations, statutes, legal decisions, and traditions. These, over many centuries, have come to establish the fundamental rights of individuals and to represent the source of a number of limits on the legislative authority of the British Parliament. These sources of law or rights are nevertheless very fragile, as they might conceivably be overridden by Parliament (the supreme law-making authority) or ignored by the courts. Strong public support for these traditions requires both the government and the courts to give them greater force and effect than they would otherwise possess.

In contrast to this type of constitution, the United States of America has a formal written document setting out the rights and freedoms of the individual (the Bill of Rights) and the powers that may be exercised by the executive, legislative, and judicial branches of government. The written constitution is the supreme law of the United States, and every law enacted must be in conformity with the constitution, otherwise it is invalid.

The Constitution of the United States divides legislative authority between the federal government and the state legislatures. Also, by allocating certain powers to the **executive** (the president), the **Congress** (the House of Representatives and the

Senate), and the **judiciary** (the courts), it imposes a number of limitations on the exercise of power by any one law-making authority. The constitution of each of the 50 states is organized in a similar fashion. This division of powers among the three branches of government is an attempt to limit the exercise of power by any one branch to those powers granted to it in the constitution. Any encroachment by one branch upon the constitutional function or powers of another branch would be **unconstitutional,** that is to say, invalid, if so determined by the court. This system of checks and balances in the United States is known as the **doctrine of separation of powers.**

A second principle of constitutional law is also utilized in the United States to ensure that the exercise of power by each branch of government is maintained within the confines of its jurisdiction as set out in the constitution. This principle is known as the **doctrine of judicial review.** It permits the courts to review the laws passed by the legislative branch or to examine the actions of the executive, and to declare them invalid if they are found to be beyond the authority or powers of the issuing body under the Constitution. The final authority on questions of constitutionality is in the hands of the United States Supreme Court, the highest court in the land for the determination of these issues.

The Constitution of the United States makes no precise reference to the Supreme Court as the "chief interpreter" or the body with the final word on the question of constitutionality. However, this role of the courts was confirmed in the early U.S. case of *Marbury v. Madison.*[1] In that case, the court asserted the right to declare an act by another branch of government unconstitutional. It did so on the basis that the Supreme Court was the only body that the framers of the constitution could have intended to act as the final arbiter of the document, since it was the only body with both a degree of permanence and freedom from direct political pressure. As a result, the U.S. Supreme Court has continued to play this role to this day. It has also served as a model for the role of the courts in connection with the Canadian constitution.

The Canadian constitution is also a formal written document that sets out the rights and freedoms of Canadians (the Canadian Charter of Rights and Freedoms) and the powers of the federal government and the provinces. As noted earlier, in Chapter 1, the Canadian constitution establishes the jurisdiction of each level of government to pass laws, and empowers the courts to determine the validity of the laws if their constitutionality should be challenged. However, unlike the Constitution of the United States, which imposes an elaborate system of checks and balances on the different branches of government, the Canadian constitution recognizes the supremacy of the legislative bodies for passing certain laws within their sphere of jurisdiction. This is notwithstanding the possibility that they might thereby violate certain rights and freedoms set out in the constitution. This particular distinction is examined in greater detail in the review of the specific sections of the Charter of Rights and Freedoms set out in this chapter.

THE CANADIAN CONSTITUTION

Historical Background

In 1982, Canada finally evolved into a full-fledged, independent nation. In effect, it had been so since 1867, when the **British North America Act** was passed by

---

1. *Marbury v. Madison* (1803), 1 Cranch 137.

the British Parliament; but the Canadian "constitution" remained a British statute, and any changes in it could only be made by the British Parliament. This final tie with the United Kingdom was severed when the British Parliament passed the **Canada Act,**[2] granting Canada complete control over its own law-making powers. At the same time, a Canadian Charter of Rights and Freedoms was enacted, which might be described as "the supreme law" of the country. Both Parliament and the provincial legislatures are obliged to respect it in the drafting of any future laws. The Charter is entrenched in the constitution.[3] It basically consists of the Canadian Charter of Rights and Freedoms, the recognition and affirmation of aboriginal treaty rights, certain commitments to equalization payments, an amending formula, and those provisions of the British North America Act in effect at the time of its patriation.

A Canadian Charter of Rights and Freedoms had been the goal of many Canadian politicians for many years prior to 1982, but the division of powers between federal and provincial governments under the British North America Act,[4] 1867, precluded the establishment of a charter than would bind both levels of government. Indeed, the act establishing the legislative powers of the two levels of government was itself beyond their reach, and only capable of amendment by the British Parliament.

Nevertheless, in an attempt to recognize the fundamental rights and freedoms that Canadian citizens enjoyed, in 1960, the Parliament of Canada enacted the **Canadian Bill of Rights.**[5] A number of provinces introduced similar legislation thereafter, as well. While these statutes recognized the fundamental rights and freedoms of individuals and groups, the statutes themselves were only ordinary statutes. They could be overridden, changed, or altered at any time by the government, or indeed by any other statute a particular government might enact. These statutes, then, offered no real protection for rights and freedoms. What was clearly required was some method of entrenching these rights in a constitution applicable throughout the country that would take precedence over any other legislation.

The constitutional process began in October of 1980, when the federal government established a Special Joint Committee of the Senate and the House of Commons to study a prepared constitution that would embody the British North America Act and a Charter of Rights for Canadians. This committee travelled throughout the country to hear the views and submissions of interested groups and individuals. In 1981, the committee made its recommendations to the federal government. Immediately thereafter, the federal and provincial governments met, and, through some difficult bargaining, produced a Charter of Rights acceptable to the federal government and all of the provinces except Quebec. More debate followed in Parliament, and, with the addition of a further clause to the Charter, a resolution was passed that would request the British Parliament to pass legislation establishing a Canadian constitution with an incorporated Canadian Charter of

---

2. The Canada Act, 1982 (U.K.), c. 11 Royal Assent, March 29, 1982.

3. The Constitution Act, 1982 includes the Charter of Rights and Freedoms as Part I.

4. The British North America Act, 1867, 30-31 Vict. c. 3 (U.K.) became the Constitution Act, 1867, by virtue of the Canada Act, 1982, and a part of the Canadian constitution.

5. Canadian Bill of Rights, R.S.C. 1970 Appendix III as amended.

Rights and Freedoms. As a result, in early 1982, Canada acquired its own constitution in the form of the **Constitution Act, 1982.**[6]

The "constitution" of Canada is essentially divided into two major parts, the first being a Canadian Charter of Rights and Freedoms, and the second containing an amending formula, some additional changes in the powers of government, and what was previously the contents of the British North America Act, 1867, as amended. This new constitution not only entrenches the basic rights and freedoms of the citizens of Canada, but establishes the organization and jurisdiction of the federal and provincial governments.

THE CANADIAN CHARTER OF RIGHTS AND FREEDOMS

The Canadian Charter of Rights and Freedoms sets out the basic rights and freedoms of all Canadians. For the most part, many of these have been the same basic freedoms and democratic and legal rights Canadians have enjoyed for many years. Now they are entrenched in the constitution, which may only be repealed or amended by an Act of Parliament consented to by at least two-thirds of the provinces that together contain at least 50% of the country's population. This restriction makes the constitution very difficult to change and, in a sense, provides a level of protection to these rights and freedoms. However, this does not mean that the rights set out in the Charter are clear and absolute, because the Charter itself states in Section 1:

Guarantee of Rights and Freedoms

1. The Canadian Charter of Rights and Freedoms guarantees the rights and freedoms set out in it, subject only to such reasonable limits prescribed by law as can be demonstrably justified in a free and democratic society.

As a consequence of this provision in the Charter, the rights set out may be limited or proscribed wherever Parliament or a provincial legislature can justify legislation placing a limit or restriction on the exercise of a right or freedom. This limitation may be necessary, in some cases, so that rights or freedoms of a single individual will not be exercised to the detriment of the public generally. For example, the Charter permits freedom of expression, but should an individual be allowed the unbridled freedom to defame others with impunity? Surely not. Some restriction on the freedom of expression is necessary if a person's reputation is to be protected as well. For this reason, the law must attempt to balance these rights.

Apart from this general qualification upon the rights and freedoms in the Charter, the Charter specifically permits Parliament or provincial legislatures to pass legislation that conflicts with or overrides fundamental freedoms, legal rights, and certain equality rights, by way of a "notwithstanding clause."[7] This allows statutes to be enacted to meet special situations without the necessity of a constitutional amendment. In each case, the legislation would automatically expire at the end of a five-year period, unless specifically renewed.

Fundamental Freedoms

The fundamental freedoms enshrined in the Charter are those which in the past were established under British tradition, custom, and law. The Charter describes them this way:

---

6. The Constitution Act, 1982 proclaimed in force April 17, 1982. *Canada Gazette,* Vol. 116, p. 1808.

7. See: Canadian Charter of Rights and Freedoms s. 33.

Fundamental Freedoms

2. *Everyone has the following fundamental freedoms:*

   (a) freedom of conscience and religion;

   (b) freedom of thought, belief, opinion, and expression, including freedom of the press and other media of communication;

   (c) freedom of peaceful assembly; and

   (d) freedom of association.

Democratic Rights

Similarly, democratic rights, which include the right to vote and the right to stand for election, are contained in the Charter. For the protection of the public, a limit is placed on the duration that a legislative assembly may continue without an election. This time period is limited to five years, except in time of war, invasion, or insurrection.

Democratic Rights

3. *Every citizen of Canada has the right to vote in an election of members of the House of Commons or of a legislative assembly, and to be qualified for membership therein.*

4. *(1) No House of Commons and no legislative assembly shall continue for longer than five years from the date fixed for the return of the writs at a general election of its members.*

   (2) In time of real or apprehended war, invasion, or insurrection, a House of Commons may be continued by Parliament, and a legislative assembly may be continued by the legislature beyond five years, if such continuation is not opposed by the votes of more than one-third of the members of the House of Commons or the legislative assembly, as the case may be.

5. *There shall be a sitting of Parliament and of each legislature at least once every twelve months.*

Under s. 3, the right to vote is restricted by other legislation, governments having established "reasonable and justifiable" conditions that must be met, such as age and mental competence. Minors, for example, are not entitled to vote, nor are persons who are mentally incompetent and confined to an institution. Similarly, persons who must remain politically non-partisan by virtue of their office (such as judges) may not seek election to a legislative assembly.

Mobility Rights

An important right enshrined in the Charter is found in s. 6, which provides that Canadian citizens are free to remain in, enter, or leave Canada, and to move freely within the country. Canadians have always assumed that they enjoyed these rights, but in the past, some Canadian citizens have had these rights restricted in times of national emergency. For example, during World War II, Canadian citizens of Japanese ancestry were stripped of their citizenship and interned in special camps during hostilities with Japan. The purpose of this provision in the

Charter is to prevent a reoccurrence of this type of treatment of Canadian citizens and to permit free movement throughout Canada. Mobility rights essentially grant to every permanent resident the right to take up residence anywhere in the country and to move for the sake of earning a livelihood in any province, as well. The Charter provides:

Mobility Rights

6. (1) Every citizen of Canada has the right to enter, remain in, and leave Canada.

(2) Every citizen of Canada and every person who has the status of a permanent resident of Canada has the right

(a) to move to and take up residence in any province; and

(b) to pursue the gaining of a livelihood in any province.

(3) The rights specified in subsection (2) are subject to

(a) any laws or practices of general application in force in a province other than those that discriminate among persons primarily on the basis of province of present or previous residence; and

(b) any laws providing for reasonable residency requirements as a qualification for the receipt of publicly provided social services.

(4) Subsections (2) and (3) do not preclude any program or activity that has as its object the amelioration in a province of conditions of individuals in that province who are socially or economically disadvantaged, if the rate of employment in that province is below the rate of employment in Canada.

Legal Rights

Of equal importance to the right to move freely about the country is the right to enjoy life without interference by the state. This broad right, which includes the right to life, liberty, and the security of the person, is supported by the right to be free from unreasonable search and seizure, and freedom from arbitrary detention or imprisonment. Accompanying this later right is the right to be informed, on arrest or detention, of the reasons for the arrest, and the right to retain and instruct a lawyer promptly after the arrest or detention has been made. The arrest itself must be for an alleged act or omission that at the time would constitute an offence under Canadian or international law, or where the person is considered to be a criminal, according to the general principles of law recognized by the community of nations.

In cases where the state has reasonable grounds for the arrest, the accused is entitled to be brought to trial within a reasonable time. In addition, the accused person is presumed innocent until proven guilty according to a fair and impartial public hearing of the matter. To ensure fairness at trial, accused persons are entitled to have the services of an interpreter if they do not speak the language in which the trial is conducted, or if they are deaf. The trial itself must be conducted in a fair manner, and an accused person must not be compelled to testify against himself or herself. In addition, whether found innocent or guilty, no one must be tried a second time for the same offence. Where a person is found guilty, the punishment for the offence must not constitute cruel or unusual treatment.

The legal rights in the Charter also provide that, pending trial, a person should not be denied reasonable bail unless the denial can be justified. Moreover, the Charter provides that persons who give evidence at a trial that would incriminate them may not have that evidence used against them in any other proceedings, except where they have committed perjury or given contradictory evidence.

The specific sections of the Charter that relate to these legal rights are as follows:

Legal Rights

7. *Everyone has the right to life, liberty, and security of the person and the right not to be deprived thereof, except in accordance with the principles of fundamental justice.*

8. *Everyone has the right to be secure against unreasonable search or seizure.*

9. *Everyone has the right not to be arbitrarily detained or imprisoned.*

10. *Everyone has the right on arrest or detention*
    (a) to be informed promptly of the reasons therefor;
    (b) to retain and instruct counsel without delay and to be informed of that right; and
    (c) to have validity of the detention determined by way of habeas corpus *and to be released if the detention is not lawful.*

11. *Any person charged with an offence has the right*
    (a) to be informed without unreasonable delay of the specific offence;
    (b) to be tried within a reasonable time;
    (c) not to be compelled to be a witness in proceedings against that person in respect of the offence;
    (d) to be presumed innocent until proven guilty according to law in a fair and public hearing by an independent and impartial tribunal;
    (e) not to be denied reasonable bail without just cause;
    (f) except in the case of an offence under military law tried before a military tribunal, to the benefit of trial by jury where the maximum punishment for the offence is imprisonment for five years or a more severe punishment;
    (g) not be found guilty on account of any act or omission unless, at the time of the act or omission, it constituted an offence under Canadian or international law or was criminal according to the general principles of law recognized by the community of nations;
    (h) if finally acquitted of the offence, not to be tried for it again and, if finally found guilty and punished for the offence, not to be tried or punished for it again; and
    (i) if found guilty of the offence and if the punishment for the offence has been varied between the time of commission and the time of sentencing, to the benefit of the lesser punishment.

12. *Everyone has the right not to be subjected to any cruel and unusual treatment or punishment.*

13. *A witness who testifies in any proceedings has the right not to have any incriminating evidence so given used to incriminate that witness in any other proceedings, except in a prosecution for perjury or for the giving of contradictory evidence.*

> *14. A party or witness in any proceedings who does not understand or speak the language in which the proceedings are conducted or who is deaf has the right to the assistance of an interpreter.*

Most of these rights are not new, as they existed in the past in the form of precedent or practice followed by the courts, or have their roots in statute law, some dating back as far as the English Magna Carta (in 1215).[8] The federal government had included many of these rights in the Canadian Bill of Rights in 1960. However, by enshrining these rights in the constitution, not only must the state and its law enforcement agencies respect them, but they may not be taken away except through the difficult amendment process which must be followed to effect constitutional change.

Equality Rights

Equality rights in the Charter complement the legal rights of Canadians by providing that every individual is equal before the law. He or she has the right to equal protection and benefit without discrimination on the basis of race, creed, colour, religion, sex, age, national or ethnic origin, or any mental or physical disability.

This section of the Charter also permits "affirmative action" programs or laws designed to improve the conditions of disadvantaged individuals or groups, and laws which might otherwise be precluded by the Charter as providing special rights or benefits for one group and not others. The enforcement of this section was originally held in abeyance for a period of three years following patriation of the constitution to permit the federal government and the provinces to review their legislation to ensure conformity with this provision in the Charter. The specific wording of the equality section reads as follows:

Equality Rights

> *15.(1) Every individual is equal before and under the law and has the right to the equal protection and equal benefit of the law without discrimination based on race, national or ethnic origin, colour, religion, sex, age, or mental or physical disability.*

> *(2) Subsection (1) does not preclude any law, program or activity that has as its object the amelioration of conditions of disadvantaged individuals or groups including those that are disadvantaged because of race, national or ethnic origin, colour, religion, sex, age, or mental or physical disability.*

Language Rights

The Canadian Charter of Rights and Freedoms confirms that the two official languages in Canada are English and French. It confirms also the right of the individual to communicate with the federal government in either official language. It also establishes the right to receive federal government services in either

---

8. The English Magna Charta (or Magna Carta), which was proclaimed by King John of England in 1215, became the foundation of the fundamental rights and freedoms of the individual.

language, where there is a significant demand for services in that language. The Charter requires neither the public nor the public service to be bilingual, but, instead, it ensures that the federal government will provide its services in both languages. New Brunswick is the only officially bilingual province, but Quebec and Manitoba residents are entitled to use either language in their courts or their legislatures (under the British North America Act, 1867, in the case of Quebec, and The Manitoba Act, 1870, in the case of Manitoba).[9] The remaining provinces are free to offer their services in a language other than English if they so desire, as they do not specifically fall under the official languages provisions of the Charter.

Official Languages of Canada

16.(1) *English and French are the official languages of Canada, and have equality of status and equal rights and privileges as to their use in all institutions of the Parliament and government of Canada.*

(2) *English and French are the official languages of New Brunswick, and have equality of status and equal rights and privileges as to their use in all institutions of the legislature and government of New Brunswick.*

(3) *Nothing in this Charter limits the authority of Parliament or a legislature to advance the equality of status or use of English and French.*

17.(1) *Everyone has the right to use English or French in any debates and other proceedings of Parliament.*

(2) *Everyone has the right to use English or French in any debates and other proceedings of the legislature of New Brunswick.*

18.(1) *The statutes, records, and journals of Parliament shall be printed and published in English and French, and both language versions are equally authoritative.*

(2) *The statutes, records, and journals of the legislature of New Brunswick shall be printed and published in English and French, and both language versions are equally authoritative.*

19.(1) *Either English or French may be used by any person in, or in any pleading in or process issuing from, any court established by Parliament.*

(2) *Either English or French may be used by any person in, or in any pleading in or process issuing from, any court of New Brunswick.*

20.(1) *Any member of the public in Canada has the right to communicate with, and to receive available services from, any head or central office of an institution of the Parliament or government of Canada in English or French, and has the same right with respect to any other office of any such institution where*

(a) *there is a significant demand for communication with and services from that office in such language; or*

(b) *due to the nature of the office it is reasonable that communication with and services from that office be available in both English and French.*

(2) *Any member of the public in New Brunswick has the right to communicate with, and to receive available services from, any office of an institution of the legislature or government of New Brunswick in English or French.*

9. These statutes have now become the Constitution Act, 1867, and the Manitoba Act, 1870 [33 Vict. c. 3 (Can.)]. They both represent a part of the Canadian constitution.

21. *Nothing in sections 16 to 20 abrogates or derogates from any right, privilege, or obligation with respect to the English and French languages, or either of them, that exists or is continued by virtue of any other provision of the Constitution of Canada.*

22. *Nothing in sections 16 to 20 abrogates or derogates from any legal or customary right or privilege acquired or enjoyed either before or after the coming into force of this Charter with respect to any language that is not English or French.*

Minority Language Educational Rights

Minority English or French language groups in a province where the official language is other than their own language are granted special rights or guarantees under the Charter, so as to have their children educated in their own language. These sections of the Charter set three criteria as a means of determining the right to this type of education. These are:

(1) the mother tongue of either parent or the children,

(2) the previous language of education received by the children in the family, and

(3) whether numbers warrant the establishment of publicly funded educational facilities in that language.

Minority Language Educational Rights

23.(1) *Citizens of Canada*

    (a) *whose first language learned and still understood is that of the English or French linguistic minority population of the province in which they reside, or*

    (b) *who have received their primary school instruction in Canada in English or French and reside in a province where the language in which they received that instruction is the language of the English or French linguistic minority population of the province.*

(2) *Citizens of Canada of whom any child has received or is receiving primary or secondary school instruction in English or French in Canada, have the right to have all their children receive primary and secondary school instruction in the same language.*

(3) *The right of citizens of Canada under subsections (1) and (2) to have their children receive primary and secondary school instruction in the language of the English or French linguistic minority population of a province*

    (a) *applies wherever in the province the number of children of citizens who have such a right is sufficient to warrant the provision to them out of public funds of minority language instruction; and*

    (b) *includes, where the number of those children so warrants, the right to have them receive that instruction in minority language educational facilities provided out of public funds.*

The right of access on the basis of mother tongue, as provided in s. 23(1)(a), is subject to s. 59 of the Constitution Act, 1982, which is not a part of the Charter. Section 59 provides that the application of this criterion will not apply to the Province of Quebec until it is so authorized by the legislature of that province. As a consequence, only citizens or their children who have been educated in English have a constitutional right to demand that they or their children be educated in English in the Province of Quebec until such time as its government authorizes s. 23(1)(a) as applicable.

ENFORCEMENT OF RIGHTS UNDER THE CHARTER

A charter of rights and freedoms is of no value to anyone unless some means are provided for the enforcement of the rights granted under it. To provide for enforcement, the Charter itself states that persons who believe their rights or freedoms under the Charter have been infringed upon may apply to a court of law for a remedy that would be appropriate in the circumstances. For example, a person accused of a crime and denied bail, unless good cause exists for denial of bail, would be entitled to a bail order on application to a proper court. Similarly, any restriction placed upon a person's religious activity by a public servant would, perhaps, constitute a denial of religious freedom, and the person so affected could apply to a competent court for an order preventing such a restriction. With both of these examples, it is important to note that the rights are not absolute, and, if the actions of the public servant were found to be justified, the courts might not provide the relief requested. To carry the bail example further: if an accused person represents a clear danger to the public if released pending trial, the denial of bail in the first instance may be justified, and the court may very well agree that the denial was a reasonable decision for the purpose of protecting the public.

The particular wording of the enforcement sections of the Charter is as follows:

Enforcement

24.(1) *Anyone whose rights or freedoms, as guaranteed by this Charter, have been infringed or denied may apply to a court of competent jurisdiction to obtain such remedy as the court considers appropriate and just in the circumstances.*

(2) *Where, in proceedings under subsection (1), a court concludes that evidence was obtained in a manner that infringed or denied any rights or freedoms guaranteed by this Charter, the evidence shall be excluded if it is established that, having regard to all the circumstances, the admission of it in the proceedings would bring the administration of justice into disrepute.*

With respect to enforcement of rights under the Charter, it is also important to realize that the Charter would appear to apply only to governments and not to private individuals. This does not mean, however, that private individuals may infringe on the freedoms of others; action can be taken against them under other laws. What the Charter does is protect individual rights and freedoms from unreasonable restriction or interference by governments or persons acting on their behalf.

If a government passes legislation that encroaches on the individual rights or freedoms set out in the Charter, then the individual affected must take steps to have a court decide if the statute has affected a particular right guaranteed under the Charter. This is necessary because all statutes passed by a legislature or Parliament are presumed to be valid until determined otherwise by the courts. This means that the individual must bring the matter before the court for a decision. It is then up to the government to show that the statute or law in question is not invalid but a reasonable limitation on the right or freedom which "can be demonstrably justified in a free and democratic society," as provided in s. 1 of the Charter. If the government cannot satisfy the court that the limits imposed by the statute are reasonable and necessary, the court may very well decide that the statute is invalid.

For example, in 1985, a Canadian citizen who was returning to Canada had with him a magazine that a customs officer at the border seized under the Customs Act. The statute, which empowered the customs office to prohibit entry of immoral material, was challenged by the citizen, on the basis that the law was an unreasonable restriction on the freedom of expression. The government could not satisfy the court that the law was a reasonable limit on the freedom, and the court ruled the provision in the statute invalid because it violated the Charter of Rights and Freedoms.

During the past decade, the Supreme Court of Canada has had an opportunity to assess existing legislation in the light of the Charter of Rights and Freedoms. By 1992, the Court had rendered over 200 decisions, many of which struck down existing laws which offended the Charter. In a business context, the Court declared that a law banning Sunday shopping for religious reasons violated s. 1 of the Charter,[10] but upheld a law which required a "common pause day."[11] The Supreme Court also stated that picketing by striking workers constitutes freedom of expression under s. 2 (b) of the Charter, but may be restricted.[12] In 1989, the Court held that a provincial government ban on advertising directed at children was permissible under s. 2 of the Charter,[13] but struck down a sign law which permitted only the French language on business signs as the law was a violation of the fundamental freedom of expression and communication.[14] An important decision in 1990 held that an official under the Combines Act (now the Competition Act) could order a company to produce documents, and the demand would not violate the s. 8 Charter rights of the company.[15] The same year, the Court decided that tax officials also had the right to demand the production of documents by a taxpayer.[16]

Since the establishment of the Charter in 1982 the Supreme Court of Canada has ruled on many other statutes in addition to those that affect business activity.

---

10. *R. v. Big M. Drug Mart Ltd.*, [1985] 1 S.C.R. 295; 18 D.L.R. (4th) 321.

11. *R. v. Edwards Books and Art Ltd.*, [1986] 2 S.C.R. 713; 35 D.L.R. (4th) 1.

12. *Retail Wholesale and Department Store Union Local 580 v. Dolphin Delivery,* [1986] 2 S.C.R. 573; 33 D.L.R. (4th) 174.

13. *Irwin Toy Ltd. v. Quebec (Attorney General),* [1989] 1 S.C.R. 927.

14. *Devine v. Quebec (Attorney General),* [1988] 2 S.C.R. 790; 55 D.L.R. (4th) 641.

15. *Thompson Newspapers Ltd. v. Canada* (Director of Investigation & Research, Restrictive Trade Practices Commission, [1990] 1 S.C.R. 425.

16. *R. v. McKinlay Transport Ltd.,* [1990] 1 S.C.R. 627; 68 D.L.R. (4th) 568.

Many decisions were related to the Charter provisions of equality rights, and the fundamental freedoms of religion, expression, media rights, and assembly, and a significant number dealt with the application of Charter rights to the Criminal Code. While it is difficult to clearly define the attitude of the Supreme Court toward the Charter, the Court has tended to stress the rights of the individual over collective rights in many of its decisions. It has also in some cases restricted or delineated the legislative and other activities of governments and its agencies.[17] While many of the decisions have required the Court to decide if legislation (or a part thereof) offends the Charter, a more recent decision of the Court (1992)[18] has expressed the intent of the Court to "read into" legislation words or provisions that the legislature did not include either deliberately or by error. While it is unclear at the present time if the court will use this approach extensively in the future, it does raise the question of the propriety of an unelected judiciary assuming the functions of an elected government.

Overall, the Charter of Rights and Freedoms has not had a major impact on business firms and their relationship to the state. It has, however, set certain parameters for governments and their boards and agencies in their dealings with business activities. Today, these governments and bodies must be more aware of the rights of the individual in both the legislative and administrative activities that they conduct.

PROTECTION OF OTHER SPECIAL AND GENERAL RIGHTS AND FREEDOMS

The rights and freedoms set out in the Charter are intended to be the basic or minimum rights entrenched or guaranteed for all citizens. The Charter also recognizes that other rights and freedoms exist which all individuals, or certain of them, may enjoy. Among the groups assigned special rights are the aboriginal or native peoples. These groups were granted a number of freedoms and rights under treaties they entered into with the government in the past. The Charter recognizes these rights, in a sense, by stating that it will not interfere with or limit special rights previously acquired, or that may be acquired in future through land settlement claims. The constitution also recognizes and affirms past treaties made with the aboriginal or native peoples of Canada.

The protection which the Charter offers native peoples is stated as follows:

General

25. *The guarantee in this Charter of certain rights and freedoms shall not be construed so as to abrogate or derogate from any aboriginal, treaty, or other rights or freedoms that pertain to the aboriginal peoples of Canada including*

    (a) any rights or freedoms that have been recognized by the Royal proclamation of October 7, 1763; and

    (b) any rights or freedoms that may be acquired by the aboriginal peoples of Canada by way of land claims settlement.

---

17. *McKinney v. University of Guelph,* [1990] 3 S.C.R. 229; 76 D.L.R. (4th) 545.

18. *Schachter v. Canada,* [1992] 2 S.C.R. 679; 93 D.L.R. (4th) 1; see also *Haig and Birch v. Canada* (1992), 5 O.R. (3d) 245, (C.A.) under s. 3 Canada Human Rights Code.

The framers of the Charter also recognized that a Charter of Rights could not include all of the rights Canadians possessed at the time the Charter came into effect. They realized that while many of these rights or freedoms were not included in the Charter, they were, nevertheless, important rights and freedoms. In their view, the Charter should ensure that its specific guarantee of certain rights and freedoms would not deny Canadians these other freedoms and rights. Consequently, the Charter simply entrenches the fundamental or basic rights and freedoms.

Those not specifically entrenched, however, may be infringed upon by governments, as they would not have the special protection of the Charter. For example, unlike the Constitution of the United States, which enshrines the right to own property, the Canadian Charter of Rights and Freedoms does not. Canadian citizens at the present time have the right to own property, but property rights remain outside the Charter. Consequently, governments may at any time impose limits on this right, or could theoretically abolish the right entirely if they so desired.

> 26. *The guarantee in this Charter of certain rights and freedoms shall not be construed as denying the existence of other rights or freedoms that exist in Canada.*

The multicultural heritage or character of the country is also recognized in the Charter. In an effort to avoid the blending or merger of cultures, the document provides that it should be interpreted to preserve or enhance cultural differences, rather than promote the development of a "melting pot" of peoples.

This directive is contained in s. 27 of the Charter:

> 27. *This Charter shall be interpreted in a manner consistent with the preservation and enhancement of the multicultural heritage of Canadians.*

Another important general right that cannot be overridden by Parliament or by provincial legislatures is the equality right of men and women under the Charter. Equality rights are included in s. 15 of the Charter, but as a further guarantee of equality of rights, the Charter also provides a clause which states:

> 28. *Notwithstanding anything in this Charter, the rights and freedoms referred to in it are guaranteed equally to male and female persons.*

Finally, the Charter preserves the right of state-funded religious schools to select teachers and students adhering to a particular religious faith without offending the equality provisions of the Charter. In effect, the Charter states that the establishment and operation of these schools will not be adversely affected by the specific rights and freedoms granted in the Charter. This recognition of the rights of certain religious or separate schools is found in s. 29:

> 29. *Nothing in this Charter abrogates or derogates from any rights or privileges guaranteed by or under the Constitution of Canada in respect of denominational, separate, or dissentient schools.*

The remainder of the Charter deals with governments and their powers. It specifically provides in s. 30 that the Charter applies to the territories as well as the provinces, and stipulates (in s. 31) that the legislative powers of the various bodies or authorities are not changed by the Charter.

> *30. A reference in this Charter to a province or to the legislative assembly or legislature of a province shall be deemed to include a reference to the Yukon Territory and the Northwest Territories, or to the appropriate legislative authority thereof, as the case may be.*
>
> *31. Nothing in this Charter extends the legislative powers of any body or authority.*

This latter section states that the powers divided between the federal government and the provincial legislatures under the British North America Act remain unchanged. Moreover, the legislative authority of each is subject to the limitation imposed upon its powers by the Charter. In effect, the Charter defines those rights and freedoms that both levels of governments must respect in their respective legislative jurisdictions. The application of the Charter is clearly defined in s. 32:

Application of Charter

> *32.(1) This Charter applies*
>
> > *(a) to the Parliament and government of Canada in respect of all matters within the authority of Parliament including all matters relating to the Yukon Territory and Northwest Territories; and*
> >
> > *(b) to the legislature and government of each province in respect of all matters within the authority of the legislature of each province*
>
> *(2) Notwithstanding subsection (1), section 15 shall not have effect until three years after this section comes into force.*

The reason for the three-year delay in the implementation of s. 15 of the Charter was to permit the various levels of government time to examine their laws for provisions that might be contrary to the Charter, and to amend them to recognize the entrenched right of citizens. This period expired on April 17, 1985.

Legislatures that wish to retain laws that might limit rights and freedoms, or to pass new laws that conflict with the Charter, are permitted to do so, provided that the legislature or government specifically states in the law that it is doing so notwithstanding the specific provisions in the Charter to the contrary. The "notwithstanding" clause that allows a legislature to override the Charter would permit it to enforce the law. However, the law would automatically expire five years after it was enacted, unless the legislature declared it re-enacted at that time for a further five years. This provision requires the legislature (or federal government) to review, at regular intervals, all legislation encroaching on the Charter rights and freedoms. The Charter would, however, permit some specific policy that the government believed should take precedence over the fundamental rights of individuals. In effect, it would put political pressure on the legislature to justify the law to the public at large at election time. It would also ensure that the elected representatives of the people, rather than the courts, have the final say on matters of public policy. It would not, however, permit a provincial legislature to opt out of the Charter, as a provincial legislature may not pass a law that would permit it to exempt all of its legislation from the Charter. It may only use the "notwithstanding" clause to exempt a specific law from the Charter with respect to a specific right or freedom protected by the Charter. However, s. 33 political decisions are unlikely to be taken unless the legislators believe that they have public support for their proposals. To act otherwise, they would risk being thrown out of power at the next election by irate electors. Nevertheless, the power is there, and in some circumstances a legislature may even disregard the Charter by using its power under s. 33 of the constitution to override the constitutional rights of persons by a statute effective for a period of five years.

For example, the Province of Quebec language law (Bill 101) was held by the Supreme Court of Canada to offend the Charter of Rights and Freedoms with respect to the languages that businesses in that province might use on their signs and establishments. When Bill 101 was held to be unconstitutional with respect to this provision, the province passed new legislation that would require French language only on exterior business signs. In doing so, the province invoked s. 33 of the Charter that allowed the legislature to have the new statute override the Charter rights of the business persons for a period of five years.

> 33.(1) *Parliament or the legislature of a province may expressly declare in an Act of Parliament or of the legislature, as the case may be, that the act or a provision thereof shall operate notwithstanding a provision included in section 2 or sections 7 to 15 of this Charter.*
>
> (2) *An Act or a provision of an Act in respect of which a declaration made under this section is in effect shall have such operation as it would have but for the provision of this Charter referred to in the declaration.*
>
> (3) *A declaration made under subsection (1) shall cease to have effect five years after it comes into force or on such earlier data as may be specified in the declaration.*
>
> (4) *Parliament or a legislature of a province may re-enact a declaration made under subsection (1).*
>
> (5) *Subsection (3) applies in respect of a re-enactment made under subsection (4).*

The final section of the Charter (s. 34) cites the Charter as the Canadian Charter of Rights and Freedoms.

Citation

34. This part may be cited as the Canadian Charter of Rights and Freedoms.

GOVERNMENT POWERS UNDER THE CONSTITUTION

Canada's constitution not only sets out the rights and freedoms of individuals, but also delineates the legislative powers of the federal government and the provinces in much the same way as they were before the constitution was adopted.

Part of Canada's constitution was originally in the form of an English statute, the British North America Act, 1867.[19] This particular statute created the governing bodies at the federal and provincial levels, and also divided and assigned the legislative jurisdiction or powers between the two levels of government. English statute law also gave Canadian citizens the right to enjoy the basic rights and

---

19. The British North America Act, 1867, and amendments, when patriated by the Canada Act, 1982, cited together became the Constitution Acts, 1867 to 1981.

freedoms traditionally possessed by their English counterparts. In 1982, the division of powers in the British North America Act, 1867, were embodied in the constitution by the Canada Act, 1982.[20]

Under the Canadian constitution, the jurisdiction of the provinces over nonrenewable natural resources was confirmed. The provinces were also given certain rights to levy indirect taxes on these resources. Section 92 specifies the exclusive authority of the provinces to make laws pertaining to such matters as property and civil rights (heading 13); matters of a local or private nature in a province (heading 16); the incorporation of companies (heading 11); the licensing of certain businesses and activities (heading 9); the solemnization of marriage (heading 12); and local works and activities (heading 10).

Section 91 gives the federal government exclusive jurisdiction over the regulation of trade and commerce (heading 2); criminal law (heading 27); bankruptcy and insolvency (heading 21); navigation and shipping (heading 10); bills of exchange and promissory notes (heading 18); and a wide variety of other activities, totalling 31 in all. Most important, s. 91 gives the federal government residual powers over all matters not expressly given to the provinces. Also, it is under this particular power that the federal government has assumed authority over relatively recent technological developments such as communications, radio, television, aeronautics, and nuclear energy.

While s. 91 and s. 92 appear to clearly divide the authority to make laws, the nature of the wording of the two sections has raised problems. For example, would the regulation of a particular provincial commercial practice constitute regulation of trade and commerce under s. 91, or would it be property and civil rights under s. 92? More particularly, would the construction of a pipeline from an oil well in the bed of a river be navigation and shipping, and, hence, a federal matter, or would it be a local work or undertaking and within the jurisdiction of the province? These are the kinds of problems associated with the interpretation of this statute. Because the legislative jurisdictions of the federal government and the provincial legislatures are not always clear and precise, overlaps tend to occur. When legislation passed by one legislative body appears to encroach on the jurisdiction of another level of government, the matter of constitutionality must be answered by the courts.

SUMMARY

The Canadian Charter of Rights and Freedoms was designed to recognize the basic or minimum rights and freedoms that citizens are entitled to enjoy in a free and democratic country such as Canada. These freedoms are the fundamental freedoms of conscience, religion, thought, belief, opinion and expression, and peaceful assembly and association. The rights are democratic rights, mobility rights, legal rights, equality rights, aboriginal rights, and certain official language rights. In addition, the Charter recognized that these are not the only rights and freedoms, since other rights and freedoms are available to Canadian citizens and may be limited or enlarged upon by governments.

20. The Canada Act, 1982, (U.K.), c. 11.

The rights and freedoms recognized by the Charter are not absolute or inviolate, however, as they may be limited by governments if the limitations can be justified in a free and democratic society. Governments may also limit rights and freedoms by passing "notwithstanding" laws permitting encroachment on specific rights or freedoms in the Charter. These laws automatically expire at the end of five years, unless re-enacted by the government.

The constitution of Canada includes not only the Charter of Rights and Freedoms, but the British North America Act, 1867, and amending legislation passed thereafter. The constitution then, includes not only the rights and freedoms of individuals, but the powers and authority of the federal and provincial governments as well.

DISCUSSION QUESTIONS

1. The Canadian Charter of Rights and Freedoms has been described as being "supreme" law, or law which is "entrenched." Why, or in what sense, is this the case?

2. Why is it only now important for Canadian citizens to have a Canadian Charter of Rights and Freedoms?

3. On what basis are Charter fundamental rights and freedoms open to restriction by Parliament or the provincial legislatures?

4. Does the Canadian Charter of Rights and Freedoms permit the Supreme Court of Canada to override the will of Parliament or a provincial legislature? If so, in what way?

5. On what grounds can the democratic right to stand for election to a legislature be denied to certain persons?

6. What is the purpose of the "notwithstanding" clause (s. 33) in the Canadian Charter of Rights and Freedoms? Can you think of a situation where a government might wish to introduce legislation that would employ the clause?

7. Someone is accused of stealing an automobile. What would this person's rights be under the Canadian Charter of Rights and Freedoms?

8. If changing social attitudes or values were to dictate a change in the Canadian Charter of Rights and Freedoms, how would this be accomplished?

9. A government official denies a group of people the right to conduct a religious service on a property that they have purchased for that purpose. What are their rights in this case? How might the official justify such a decision?

10. Discuss the extent to which language rights can be enforced as they pertain to the two official languages in Canada.

11. What impact does the Canadian Charter of Rights and Freedoms have on rights and freedoms not mentioned specifically in the Charter? Could these "other rights and freedoms" be curtailed or extinguished by governments?

12. Explain the apparent conflict between the exception to equality rights in s. 15(2) and the affirmation of equality rights in s. 28 of the Canadian Charter of Rights and Freedoms. How might governments circumvent s. 28 if they wished to introduce affirmative action legislation?

13. In what way does the Constitution Act, 1982, affect the legislative jurisdiction of the Parliament of Canada and the provincial legislatures? How are questions of jurisdiction decided?

**JUDICIAL
DECISION**

**Charter of
Rights —
Freedom of
Commercial
Expression**

The Attorney General of Quebec v. La Chaussure Brown's Inc. et al., [1988] 2 S.C.R. 712.

This decision on December 15, 1988, by the Supreme Court of Canada represents an example of a charter case in which a number of business firms were charged for violating the Quebec provincial statute requiring public signs, commercial advertising, and firm names on shops and establishments to be in the French language only. The business firms challenged the validity of the provincial statute on the basis that it violated their freedom of expression as guaranteed under s. 2(b) of the Charter of Rights and Freedoms.

The Supreme Court of Canada held that the provincial statute violated s. 2(b) and ruled that it was unconstitutional, and hence invalid. A side issue, but nevertheless an important one, was whether the guarantee of freedom of expression in the charter extended to commercial expression, such as advertising and business names. The Supreme Court of Canada dealt with the issue in the following manner:

> ... There is no historical basis for a guarantee of freedom of commercial expression in pre-*Charter* jurisprudence, in which recognition was given, on the basis of the division of powers and the "implied bill of rights", to freedom of political expression. Freedom of expression appears in both the Canadian *Charter* and the Quebec *Charter* under the heading of "Fundamental Freedoms"; there is nothing fundamental about commercial expression. A guarantee of freedom of expression which embraces commercial advertising would be the protection of an economic right, when both the Canadian *Charter* and the Quebec *Charter* clearly indicate that they are not concerned with the protection of such rights. The American decisions recognizing a limited First Amendment protection for commercial speech must be seen in the context of a constitution that protects the right of property, whereas that right was deliberately omitted from the protection afforded by s. 7 of the Canadian *Charter*. This Court, in refusing to constitutionalize the right to strike, has recognized that the Canadian *Charter* does not extend to economic rights or freedoms. To extend freedom of expression beyond political expression, and possibly artistic and cultural expression, would trivialize that freedom and lead inevitably to the adoption of different justificatory standards under s. 1 according to the kind of expression involved. The terms of s. 1, as interpreted and applied by the courts, do not permit of such differential application. Freedom of commercial expression, and in particular commercial advertising, does not serve any of the values that would justify its constitutional protection. Commercial advertising is manipulative and seeks to condition or control economic choice rather than to provide the basis of a truly informed choice. As the American experience shows, the recognition of a limited protection for commercial expression involves an evaluation of regulatory policy that is better left to the legislature. Academic criticism of the American approach to commercial speech and judicial expression of misgivings concerning it provide sufficient reason for declining to follow it.
>
> It is apparent to this Court that the guarantee of freedom of expression in s. 2(b) of the Canadian *Charter* and s. 3 of the Quebec *Charter* cannot be confined to political expression, important as that form of expression is in a free and democratic society. The pre-*Charter* jurisprudence emphasized the importance of political expression because it was a challenge to that form of expression that

most often arose under the division of powers and the "implied bill of rights", where freedom of political expression could be related to the maintenance and operation of the institutions of democratic government. But political expression is only one form of the great range of expression that is deserving of constitutional protection because it serves individual and societal values in a free and democratic society.

The post-*Charter* jurisprudence of this Court has indicated that the guarantee of freedom of expression in s. 2(*b*) of the *Charter* is not to be confined to political expression. In holding, in *RWDSU v. Dolphin Delivery Ltd., [1986] 2 S.C.R. 573,* that secondary picketing was a form of expression within the meaning of s. 2(*b*) the Court recognized that the constitutional guarantee of freedom of expression extended to expression that could not be characterized as political expression in the traditional sense but, if anything, was in the nature of expression having an economic purpose. Although the authority canvassed by McIntyre J. on the importance of freedom of expression tended to emphasize political expression, his own statement of the importance of this freedom clearly included expression that could be characterized as having other than political significance, where he said of freedom of expression at p. 583: "It is one of the fundamental concepts that has formed the basis for the historical development of the political, social and educational institutions of western society."....

.... In order to address the issues presented by this case it is not necessary for the Court to delineate the boundaries of the broad range of expression deserving of protection under s. 2(*b*) of the Canadian *Charter* or s. 3 of the Quebec *Charter.* It is necessary only to decide if the respondents have a constitutionally protected right to use the English language in the signs they display, or more precisely, whether the fact that such signs have a commercial purpose removes the expression contained therein from the scope of protected freedom.

In our view, the commercial element does not have this effect. Given the earlier pronouncements of this Court to the effect that the rights and freedoms guaranteed in the Canadian *Charter* should be given a large and liberal interpretation, there is not sound basis on which commercial expression can be excluded from the protection of s. 2(*b*) of the *Charter.* It is worth noting that the courts below applied a similar generous and broad interpretation to include commercial expression within the protection of freedom of expression contained in s. 3 of the Quebec *Charter.* Over and above its intrinsic value as expression, commercial expression which, as has been pointed out, protects listeners as well as speakers plays a significant role in enabling individuals to make informed economic choices, an important aspect of individual self-fulfillment and personal autonomy. The Court accordingly rejects the view that commercial expression serves no individual or societal value in a free and democratic society....

CHAPTER 3

The Judicial System

INTRODUCTION

In a complex modern society, such as in Canada or the United States, the courts play an important role in the lives of the citizens. First and foremost, the courts decide disputes between individuals, and between individuals and the state. This is the role that generally comes to mind when the function of the courts in society is considered. However, the courts have other very important functions to perform as well. The courts are the chief interpreters of the constitution and, in this capacity, decide if legislation passed by either the federal government or the provincial legislatures exceeds their respective powers or violates the rights and freedoms of individuals. In this sense, the courts are the guardians of these rights and freedoms, and through their interpretation of the constitution may enlarge or restrict its provisions.

For example, s. 2(b) of the Canadian Charter of Rights and Freedoms provides for freedom of expression, including freedom of the press. Section 1 permits a government to establish a limit on the exercise of this freedom if the limit is "demonstrably justified in a free and democratic society." If the government passed a law prohibiting the publication in a newspaper of any literary review of certain kinds of literature, would this violate freedom of the press under s. 2(b) of the Charter? This would be a matter for the court to decide, as it would be necessary to establish the validity of the legislation in terms of whether the law represented a reasonable limit on the freedom of the press, as provided in s. 1 of the Charter. If the court decided that the law represented a reasonable limit, then the fundamental freedom would be diminished by that interpretation. If the court ruled that the law was an unreasonable limitation, then it would be invalid, and the court would have preserved the freedom in its broader sense. How the courts interpret the provisions of the Charter has a profound effect on the rights and freedoms that an individual will, in reality, enjoy. Consequently, the Supreme Court of Canada, which has the ultimate say in how the provisions of the Charter may be interpreted, is expected to take great care and deliberation in reviewing challenged legislation that touches these rights and freedoms.

The courts are also responsible for deciding the legislative jurisdiction of the federal and provincial governments under the Constitution Act. This is not a new role for the courts, as the court has been charged with this duty since the original British North America Act was passed in 1867. Again, the Supreme Court of Canada has the last word in deciding the question of whether a government has exceeded its legislative powers under the constitution. Where the Supreme Court rules that a law is beyond the powers of the particular legislative body, the law is a nullity and unenforceable.

Much of the law relating to business concerns only disputes between individuals. However, as the regulatory powers of governments at both the federal and provincial levels intrude to a greater degree into areas of business activity previously untouched by government, the need for judicial review of legislation in the light of the Charter becomes more important. For this reason, the courts may, in a sense, also be considered the guardian of business rights and freedoms as well.

In a business context, the courts are generally called upon to interpret contracts between individuals and business firms in order to determine the rights and duties of each of the parties. Also, where a person or business is injured through the negligence of other persons, the courts will play an important role in establishing the responsibility for the loss and the compensation payable. For example, if a construction firm carelessly constructs a wall of a building and it falls upon a passerby, the injured person may take legal action against the construction firm for its negligence in the construction of the wall. The court will hear the dispute and decide if the firm is liable for the injuries to the person. If liability is found, the court will also establish the amount of the loss payable as compensation.

DEVELOPMENT OF THE LAW COURTS

The legal system as we know it today evolved over a long period of time. The system developed gradually as the law developed. It was not until the state was strong enough to require resort to the courts and the rule of law that the courts assumed an important place in the social system.

THE UNITED STATES JUDICIAL SYSTEM

The Canadian and American judicial systems had their beginnings in England. While two North American jurisdictions have since evolved in slightly different ways, they are both an outgrowth of the English court system, and consequently share the same heritage. In both Canada and the United States courts were established in the colonies as a part of the British Colonial administrative structure.

These courts applied British law to the cases that came before them during the colonial period.

A significant change took place in court procedure as a result of the United States War of Independence. The war severed both political and legal ties with England, but the law, and much of the legal system, remained in the former colonies. Pennsylvania, for example, continued to call its civil trial court the Court of Common Pleas, and the law which the court dispensed was the common law. Most states at the time of the War of Independence adopted English common law as it stood in 1776, with appropriate modifications to meet local needs and conditions. States which joined the union later, however, brought with them a different legal background. Louisiana, for example, had a French legal history, and followed the French Civil Code for non-criminal matters. The United States judicial system after the War of Independence became a dual system with two sets of courts: state and federal.

State and Federal Courts

The Constitution of the United States established as federal jurisdiction such matters as questions of law arising out of the Constitution, any Act of Congress, and any treaty between another country and the United States. It also included admiralty and maritime cases, certain cases involving citizens residing in different U.S. states (where the sum of money exceeded $10,000), disputes between a United States citizen and a citizen of another country, and disputes which involved the United States as a party.

The federal court system formed to hear these cases includes essentially three general types of courts and a number of special courts. The judges of all these courts are appointed by the President of the United States on the advice of, and with the consent of, the Senate.

The lowest of the federal courts is the **District Court.** It is a trial court where a litigant brings an action for the first time to be heard by either a single judge, or by a panel of two or three (and occasionally more) judges, depending upon the nature of the case. These courts are called District Courts because the country, under the federal court system, is divided into districts, with each of the less populous states forming a district, and the more populous states, such as New York, containing more than one district.

Appeals from the decision of the District Court may be made to a **Federal Court of Appeals**, although some matters may be appealed directly to the Supreme Court of the United States. The country is divided into 11 areas for appeal purposes, each with an Appeals Court that is usually presided over by a panel of three judges, although the number may vary. These areas are called "circuits" even though the judges no longer travel the circuit as they once did. The Courts of Appeals hear appeals from District Courts, and also review the orders of federal administrative agencies.

The final court of appeal is the **United States Supreme Court,** which, at present, consists of nine justices. The Supreme Court is an appellate court for cases that have been reviewed by the federal Courts of Appeals, or occasionally by one of the highest state Court of Appeals. Appeal to the Supreme Court is discretionary, and the Court will only hear an appeal if it concludes that the issue in dispute is of sufficient importance to warrant a hearing.

A number of other federal courts also exist. These include the United States **Tax Court,** the **Customs Court** (that deals with customs disputes), the **Court of Claims** (that hears claims against the federal government), and the **Court of Customs and Patent Appeals** (which is essentially an appeal court to hear appeals from the Customs Court, and decisions of the Patent and Trademark Office). A number of other specialized courts such as Military Courts and Territorial Courts form the remaining part of the federal court system.

At the state level, some variation exists, but in every state a system of trial and appeal courts has been established to hear legal disputes that fall within the jurisdiction of the particular state. The names of the courts vary, as do the methods of selecting or appointing the judiciary. In some states judges are elected; in others, they are appointed by the state governor. The trial courts are usually divided into two classes: one to hear minor cases, such as small debt disputes, and a second to hear more serious matters. **Justices of the Peace** frequently preside over the first class of courts, which are sometimes called **Municipal Courts** or **Small Claims Courts.**

The second class of trial court, which has jurisdiction to hear the more important cases, is usually called the **County Court, District Court,** or sometimes, the **Superior Court.** In some states, this court may hear appeals from a Small Claims Court, as well as hear the trials of more important civil matters. Some states may also have special courts to hear particular kinds of disputes, such as probate cases or criminal trials.

In addition to its trial courts, each state has an Appeals Court that is usually called the Supreme Court of the state. This court is normally presided over by from five to seven justices. A number of states have an Intermediate Appeal Court as well. Where an Intermediate Appeal Court exists, the right to appeal to the Supreme Court of the state is usually discretionary, with only the more important legal issues receiving a second review.

THE JUDICIAL SYSTEM IN CANADA

The Historical Development of Canadian Courts

Canada did not experience the wrenching changes brought about by the War of Independence in the United States. Instead, the Canadian system of courts gradually changed as the country moved from a colonial status to that of a dominion. After 1663, the law in what is now Quebec, Ontario, Prince Edward Island, and part of Nova Scotia consisted of the Customs of Paris which had been declared the law of New France by the Conseil Superieur of France. The Seven Years' War, however, resulted in the capture by England of the first colonies in 1758 and 1759, and the imposition of English law in New France. France formally surrendered to England what is now Quebec, Cape Breton, and Prince Edward Island by the Treaty of Paris in 1763, and the law administered by the new civil courts established in 1764 was English law. **The Quebec Act**[1] of 1774 made a further change in the legal system by introducing a Court of King's Bench, and a significant change in the law — the criminal law in the new British Province of Quebec was declared to be English law, but the civil law was to be based upon "Canadian" law. Canadian law in Quebec was essentially the Customs of Paris

---

1. Quebec Act, 14 Geo. III, c. 83.

that had been introduced in 1663, and Quebec, as a result, continued to follow this law until 1866, when a new Quebec Civil Code was compiled and put into effect.

When the United States War of Independence officially ended in 1783, more than 10 000 United Empire Loyalists left the United States and moved into the western part of Quebec. The new settlers did not understand, nor did they like, French civil law. Initially, in response to their demands, the western part of Quebec (which is now Ontario) was divided into four districts where English law would apply. Each new district had a **Court of General Sessions** to hear minor criminal cases, a civil **Court of Common Pleas** to hear common law matters, and a **Prerogative Court** to deal with wills and intestacy. In 1791, the Canada Act[2] created two separate provinces: the Province of Upper Canada (now Ontario) with its own governor, executive council, and elected house of assembly; and the Province of Lower Canada (now Quebec) which continued as it had before.

The first act passed by the new House of Assembly for the Province of Upper Canada was a **Property and Civil Rights Act.** This act provided that English law (as it existed on October 15, 1792), would be the law of the province in all matters concerning property and civil rights. The law in amended form is still in force.[3] The following year, the courts were reorganized by the replacement of the Prerogative Courts in each district with a **Surrogate Court.** A Probate court was also established to hear appeals in cases concerning wills and intestacy on a province-wide basis.

In 1794, the **Judicature Act**[4] was passed. The effect of this act was to abolish the former Court of Common Pleas, and replace it with the Court of King's Bench. The new court had jurisdiction over both civil and criminal matters for the entire province. The judges of the new court were also different from the old (all of the new judges having been members of the Bar of either Upper Canada, England, or some other English jurisdiction). A later act provided for the appointment of judges "during the period of their good behaviour," and required an address from both the council and the Assembly to remove a judge from office.[5]

The Court of Chancery was established in 1837 for the Province of Upper Canada, and was composed of the chancellor (who was also the governor) and a vice-chancellor. All judicial powers were exercised by the vice-chancellor who handled all of the legal work. In 1849, the office of chancellor became a judicial office, and a second vice-chancellor was appointed.

The courts were again changed in 1849, this time by the creation of a Court of Common Pleas. Its jurisdiction was concurrent with that of the Court of Queen's Bench, and in 1856 the procedure of the two courts was modernized and unified. In the same year, a new Appeal Court for Upper Canada was established — the Court of Error and Appeal. This court consisted of all of the judges of the Courts of Queen's Bench, Common Pleas, and Chancery sitting together as an appeal body at Toronto. This particular court later became the Court of Appeal. The British North America Act, 1867, did not change the composition of these courts,

2. Canada Act, 31 Geo. III, c. 31.

3. Property and Civil Rights Act, R.S.O. 1990, c. P-29.

4. Judicature Act, 34 Geo. III, c. 2.

5. An Act to Render the Judges of the court of King's Bench in This Province Independent of the Crown, 4 Wm. IV,

but simply changed the name from Upper Canada to Ontario.[6] The names of the courts in the other provinces also remained unchanged upon joining Confederation. The courts in most of the older provinces had developed along lines similar to those of Ontario, although legislation that brought about the change was passed at different times, and with some variation.

In the later part of the nineteenth century, changes that took place in the structure of the courts in England soon appeared in Canada. The many Law Reform Acts that were passed in England between 1873 and 1925 were reflected in a number of changes in Canadian law and its judicial system. The western Prairie Provinces were influenced not only by law reform in England, but also by other Canadian provinces in the establishment of their court systems. When Ontario introduced its own law reform legislation (in 1881, 1909, and 1937) that reorganized the Supreme Court into two parts (a High Court of Justice as a trial court, and a Court of Appeal to hear appeals), a number of other provinces followed suit.[7]

Law reform in Canada has been an evolutionary process. The general trend has been toward a streamlining of the judicial process, with a gradual reduction in formal procedure. Although much variation exists from province to province, a provincial judicial system generally consists of a Small Claims or Small Debts Court, a County or District Court (some provinces), a Superior or Supreme Court, and a Court of Appeal. In those provinces where a Court of Appeal as a separate court does not exist, the Supreme Court is empowered to hear appeals from courts of original jurisdiction. Criminal cases are usually heard by both Supreme Court and County Court judges. In addition, each province has a **Provincial** or **Magistrate's Court** (presided over by either a provincial judge or magistrate) for the purpose of hearing minor criminal matters and cases concerning violations of non-criminal provincial statutes.

In 1982, the introduction of the Charter of Rights and Freedoms created a new role for the courts, that of chief interpreter of the rights and freedoms of the individual. Prior to this time, the role of the courts in constitutional matters was for the most part limited to the determination of the validity of provincial or federal statutes under s. 91 and s. 92 of the British North America Act. However, with the advent of the new constitution, this role has expanded. The court is now the body charged not only with the responsibility to determine the jurisdiction of the law-making bodies, but with the responsibility to determine if statutes offend the Charter of Rights and Freedoms as well. In a very real sense, the Supreme Court of Canada had become the ultimate interpreter of the constitution.

The Structure of the Judicial System

In Canada, there are many different courts at the present, each with a different jurisdiction. In this context, **jurisdiction** means the right or authority of a court to hear and decide a dispute. Jurisdiction may take a number of different forms. Usually the court must have the authority to deal with cases of the particular type

6. British North America Act, 1867, 30 Vict., c. 3, as amended.

7. See the Judicature Act, 9 Edw. VII, c. 5, as an example of the New Brunswick Acts of the General Assembly.

brought before it, in addition to authority over either the parties or the property in dispute. With respect to the first type of jurisdiction, the authority of the court may be **monetary** or **geographic** in the sense that the court has been authorized to hear cases concerning money up to a set amount, or to hear cases concerning land within the particular county or area where the land is situated. In the case of jurisdiction over the parties to a dispute, the court must have the authority or power to compel their attendance or to impose its decision on them.

Courts of law may be placed in two rather general classifications. The first group are called **courts of original jurisdiction.** These are courts before which a dispute or case is heard for the first time by a judge, and where all the facts are presented to enable the judge to render a decision. Courts of original jurisdiction are sometimes referred to as **trial courts,** where both civil and criminal cases are first heard.

Courts which fall into the second group are called **courts of appeal.** These courts, as their name implies, hear appeals from the decisions of courts of original jurisdiction. Courts of appeal are superior or "higher" courts in that their decisions may overrule or vary the decisions of the "lower" or trial courts. Their principal function is to review the decisions of trial courts where one of the parties to the action in the lower court believes that the trial judge made an erroneous decision. They do not normally hear evidence, but instead hear argument by counsel for the parties concerning the decision of the trial court. Usually an appeal alleges that the judge hearing the case at trial erred in the application of the law to the facts of the case. Sometimes the appeal is limited to the amount of damages awarded, or in a criminal case, to the severity of the penalty imposed. On occasion, an appeal court may find that the judge at trial failed to consider important evidence in reaching his or her decision, in which case the appeal court may send the case back to the lower court for a new trial.

Federal Courts

In Canada, each province has a number of courts of original jurisdiction and at least one appeal court. In addition, the federal court system also exists to deal with matters that fall within the exclusive jurisdiction of the federal government. The **Federal Court Trial Division** hears disputes between provincial governments and the federal government, actions against the federal government, admiralty, patent, trade mark, copyright, taxation matters, and appeals from federal boards, tribunals, and commissions. In some cases, the court has exclusive jurisdiction to hear the dispute, and in others, the jurisdiction is concurrent with that of the superior provincial courts in order that a person may sue in either the Federal Court or the appropriate provincial court. A trial decision of the Federal Court may be appealed to the **Federal Court of Appeal,** and with leave, to the **Supreme Court of Canada.**

At the federal level, the Supreme Court of Canada is maintained to hear important appeals from the appeal courts of the various provinces, as well as those from the Federal Court of Appeal.

Provincial Courts

There is no uniform system of courts in the provinces, as each province has the authority to establish its own system and to assign to each court a specific jurisdiction. Fortunately, however, most of the provinces have established courts somewhat similar in jurisdiction. Bearing this in mind, and the fact that variation in names and powers do exist, the following list represents what might be considered to be typical of the court systems found in a province.

TABLE 1   Criminal Appeals*

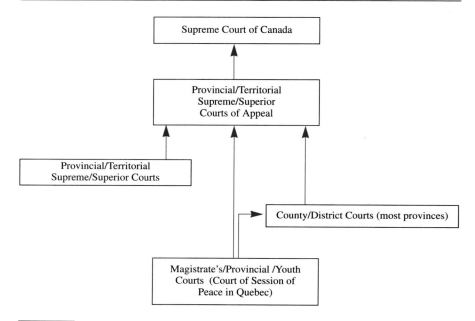

* Court names, and in some cases, appeal routes, differ for some provinces.

Criminal Courts

Magistrate's or Provincial Court

A **Magistrate's Court** or **Provincial Court** is a court of original jurisdiction that is presided over by a provincially appointed magistrate or judge. This court generally deals with criminal matters, although many provinces have empowered the court to hear cases involving the violation of provincial statutes and municipal by-laws where some sort of penalty is imposed.

The Provincial or Magistrate's Court initially deals with all criminal cases, either as a court with jurisdiction to dispose of the matter (as in cases involving less serious offences where the court has been given absolute jurisdiction), or where the accused has the right to elect to be tried by a magistrate or provincial

court judge. It will also hold a preliminary hearing of the more serious criminal cases to determine if sufficient evidence exists to have the accused tried by a higher court. All provinces except Quebec have a Magistrate's Court or Provincial Court. The Quebec counterpart of the Magistrate's Court is the **Court of Sessions of the Peace.**

County Court or District Court

The County Court or District Court is a court that usually has both civil and criminal jurisdiction. As the name implies, these courts are organized on a county or district basis, and have jurisdiction to hear cases which arise within their geographic area. All provinces except British Columbia, Ontario, Nova Scotia, and Quebec have courts of this kind. The County Court at "General Sessions of the Peace" hears criminal cases of a more serious nature than those that fall within the absolute jurisdiction of the Magistrate's or Provincial Court. For many of these offences, the accused may elect to be tried by the judge alone, or by a judge and jury. County Courts, however, do not have jurisdiction to hear cases involving the most serious crimes: treason, piracy, murder, or rape.

The County Court may also act as an appeal court to hear appeals from the decisions of the Magistrate's or Provincial Court in cases concerned with minor offences. These minor offences are known as **summary conviction offences.**

Provincial Supreme Court

Each province has a Supreme Court or Superior Court empowered to hear the most serious criminal cases. Ontario calls this court the Ontario Court, General Division. In many provinces, justices of the court periodically travel throughout the province to hear these cases (usually at the county courthouse) at sessions of the Supreme Court called assizes. In some provinces, the court follows the English custom of presenting the judge with a pair of white gloves at the beginning of the session, if no criminal cases are scheduled to be heard.

Youth Courts

Youth Courts are particular courts designated in each province to deal with cases where young persons are accused of committing criminal offences. Under the **Young Offenders Act,**[8] a young person is defined as a person 12 years of age or more and under 18 years of age. Persons over this age limit are treated as adults and would be tried in the ordinary courts if accused of a criminal offence.

Youth Courts are presided over by judges who have the powers of a justice or magistrate of a summary conviction court. They may, if the young person is found guilty, impose a fine, order compensation or restitution, direct the youth to perform community service work, commit the youth to custody, or provide an absolute discharge — depending upon what is believed to be in the best interest of the young person. In some instances, the case may be transferred to ordinary courts. Unlike other courts, the names of young persons and the offences they have committed may not be published by the press or media, and, under certain circumstances, the public may be excluded from the hearing.

---

8. Young Offenders Act, R.S.C. 1985 c. Y-1.

Family Courts

Family Courts, while not criminal courts in the ordinary sense, have jurisdiction to deal with domestic problems and the enforcement of federal and provincial legislation that relates to family problems. Most of the cases in Family Court are related to non-support of family members, or family relationships that have deteriorated to the point where the actions of one or more members of a family have become a serious threat to others. Family Courts are usually presided over by a magistrate or provincial court judge in those provinces where they have been established; in others, where separate courts do not exist, family disputes or legislation relating to family matters fall under the jurisdiction of the County or Supreme Court.

Criminal Courts of Appeal

In addition to the County Court, which in some provinces hears appeals in minor criminal cases, each province has a Court of Appeal to review the convictions of accused persons by the Youth Court, County Court, Supreme Court, or Magistrate's (or Provincial) Court. A panel of judges presides over the Appeal Court, and the decision of the majority of the judges hearing the appeal decides the case. The final Court of Appeal in criminal matters is the Supreme Court of Canada. It will hear appeals from the decisions of provincial Courts of Appeal; however, neither the accused nor the Crown generally may appeal to the Supreme Court of Canada as a matter of right. Instead, they must obtain leave to appeal. A right to appeal, however, does exist in the case of an indictable offence if the decision of the provincial Court of Appeal on a question of law was not unanimous.

Civil Courts

Most provinces have a number of civil courts to deal with disputes that arise between individuals or between individuals and the government. Some courts have limited jurisdiction and hear only special kinds of disputes; others hear only appeals from inferior courts. Although most civil courts of original jurisdiction permit cases to be heard by both a judge and jury, in some courts, such as Small Claims Courts, cases are heard by a judge sitting alone. Courts of Appeal are always non-jury courts.

Small Claims Court

Small Claims Courts have jurisdiction to hear cases where the amount of money involved is relatively small. In those provinces that have a Small Claims Court (Nova Scotia and Prince Edward Island do not), usually the court's jurisdiction is limited to hear only those cases where the amount of money involved is less than $10 000. In some provinces, the Small Claims Court is limited to a much smaller monetary limit; although at the time of writing a number of jurisdictions are seriously considering raising their monetary limits.

Small Claims Courts are usually informal courts that may be presided over by a county court judge in a number of provinces, and by a magistrate (as a part of the Provincial Court) in others. In Nova Scotia, the "court" is presided over by an

adjudicator. The cases the courts hear are usually small debt or contract disputes, and damage cases, such as claims arising (in some provinces) out of minor automobile accidents. Litigants in Small Claims Court frequently present their own cases, and court costs are usually low. The right to appeal a Small Claims Court decision is sometimes restricted to judgements over a specific amount, and where an appeal exists, it is usually to a single judge of the Court of Appeal of the province.

County Court or District Court

All provinces (except British Columbia, Ontario, Nova Scotia, and Quebec) have County or District Courts to hear disputes concerning monetary amounts in excess of the jurisdiction of the Small Claims Courts. These courts are also subject to specified upper monetary limits in most provinces, although restrictions are by no means universal. Both Alberta and Newfoundland, for example, have no upper monetary limits on cases that their County Courts may hear. County Courts are presided over by a federally appointed judge. Most cases may be heard by a judge and jury if the parties so desire. Appeals from the County Court are usually made to the Court of Appeal of the province.

TABLE 2   Civil Appeals*

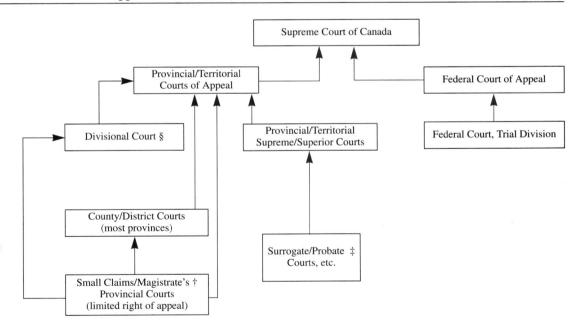

* Some provinces do not have all of the courts shown on this chart.

† Appeal routes vary from province to province with respect to Small Claims Courts.

‡ Special courts, such as Probate or Surrogate, usually have disputes litigated in the Supreme Court of the province.

§ Ontario only. The Divisional Court is a unique court in that it can conduct both trials and certain types of appeals.

Provincial Supreme Court

Each province has a Supreme or Superior Court to hear civil disputes in matters that are beyond or outside the jurisdiction of the lower courts. Ontario calls its Superior Court the Ontario Court, General Division. The provincial Supreme Court has unlimited jurisdiction in monetary matters, and is presided over at trial by a federally appointed judge. As shown in Table 3 which follows, although the Supreme Court of each province (or territory) is similar in jurisdiction, no one designation applies to all of these courts.

TABLE 3   Trial Level

Jurisdiction	*Designation of Court*
Alberta	Court of Queen's Bench of Alberta
British Columbia	Supreme Court of British Columbia
Manitoba	Court of Queen's Bench for Manitoba
New Brunswick	Supreme Court of New Brunswick, Queen's Bench Division
Newfoundland	Supreme Court of Judicature for Newfoundland, Trial Division
Northwest Territories	Supreme Court of Northwest Territories
Nova Scotia	Supreme Court of Nova Scotia, Trial Division
Ontario	Ontario Court, General Division
Prince Edward Island	Supreme Court of Prince Edward Island
Quebec	Superior Court
Saskatchewan	Court of Queen's Bench of Saskatchewan
Yukon Territory	Territorial Court

Appeal Level

Jurisdiction	*Designation of Court*
Alberta	Court of Appeal of Alberta
British Columbia	Court of Appeal of British Columbia
Manitoba	Court of Appeal of Manitoba
New Brunswick	Supreme Court of New Brunswick, Appeal Division
Newfoundland	Supreme Court of Judicature for Newfoundland, Court of Appeal
Northwest Territories	Court of Appeal of the Northwest Territories
Nova Scotia	Supreme Court of Nova Scotia, Appeal Division
Ontario	Ontario Court of Appeal
Prince Edward Island	Supreme Court of Prince Edward Island
Quebec	Court of Appeal
Saskatchewan	Court of Appeal of Saskatchewan
Yukon Territory	Court of Appeal

Cases in the Supreme Court (both jury and non-jury) may be heard by judges who travel throughout the province to the various court houses (the assizes), or in specified cities where the court sits without a jury on a regular basis. An appeal from a decision of the Supreme Court is to the Appeal Court of the province.

In the Yukon and Northwest Territories, territorial ordinances have established Trial Courts equivalent to the provincial Supreme Courts: the Territorial Court and the Supreme Court of the Northwest Territories. An unusual feature of these two courts may be found in the Rules of Procedure that apply to each. The Territorial Court of the Yukon has adopted the Rules of Procedure of the Supreme Court of British Columbia, and the Supreme Court of the Northwest Territories follows the Rules of Procedure of the Court of Queen's Bench of Alberta.

Surrogate or Probate Court

The Surrogate Court (or Probate Court, as it is called in New Brunswick and Nova Scotia) is a special court established to hear and deal with wills and the administration of the estates of deceased persons. The provinces of Newfoundland, Quebec, British Columbia, and Prince Edward Island do not have special courts to deal with these matters, but, instead, have placed them under the jurisdiction of their Supreme Courts. In provinces that do have Surrogate or Probate Courts, the presiding judge is usually the same judge appointed as the county or district court judge.

Civil Courts of Appeal

Provincial Court of Appeal

Each province (or territory) has an Appeal Court, although (as indicated in Table 3) no one designation applies to all of these courts. The lines of appeal in civil cases are not always as clear-cut as those in criminal matters. Sometimes the right of appeal from an inferior court does not go directly to the Appeal Court of the province or the territory. In Ontario, for example, an appeal from a decision of the Small Claims Court (where the amount is above a certain minimum) would be appealed to a single judge of the Divisional Court, which is a part of the Ontario Court. Supreme Court trial judgements, however, would be appealed to the provincial Court of Appeal or the Appeal Division of the provincial Supreme Court, as the case may be. County or District Court decisions in those provinces where they exist usually have an appeal route to the Court of Appeal for the province.

Supreme Court of Canada

The Supreme Court of Canada is the final and highest Appeal Court in Canada. It hears appeals from the provincial Appeal Courts, but the right to appeal is restricted. In civil cases, **leave (or permission) to appeal** must be obtained before a case may be heard by the Supreme Court of Canada, and normally the issue or legal point must be of some national importance before leave will be granted. The Court also hears appeals from the Federal Court, and it is the body that finally determines the constitutionality of statutes passed by both the federal and provincial governments.

THE JUDICIAL SYSTEM IN ACTION

Essentially there are three bodies that enforce the law in Canada. These are: (1) the criminal court; (2) the civil court; and (3) the administrative tribunal.

Criminal Court Procedure

As the name implies, the criminal court is concerned with the enforcement of the criminal law. A criminal court is often the same court that deals with civil law matters, or it may be a court organized to deal exclusively with law of a criminal of quasi-criminal nature. The Provincial Court (Criminal Division) in Ontario, or the Magistrate's Court in most other provinces, is frequently the court with jurisdiction to deal with criminal matters of a minor nature, or to act as a court where a preliminary hearing of a more serious criminal offence would be held.

In a criminal case involving a minor or less serious offence, the Crown brings the case before the court by way of the **summary conviction rules of procedure.** In a serious case, it will bring the case by way of **indictment.** In either situation, the case is first heard in the Provincial Court (Criminal Division), or in the Magistrate's Court. These courts have absolute or elective jurisdiction to dispose of the case if the matter is minor in nature. When the offence is of a more serious nature, the court will conduct a **preliminary hearing** to determine whether the Crown has sufficient evidence to warrant a full hearing of the case by a superior court.

The procedure of the Magistrate's or Provincial Court tends to be very informal. The normal procedure at the hearing is to have the charge which the Crown has placed before the court read to the accused. The **accused** is then asked how he (or she) **pleads**. If the accused admits to the commission of the offence, a plea of guilty is entered, and the court will then hear evidence from the Crown to confirm the act and the circumstances surrounding it. A **conviction** will then be lodged against the accused, and a penalty imposed.

If a plea of not guilty is entered by the accused, the Crown is then obliged to proceed with its evidence to show that, in fact, the criminal act was committed *(actus reus)* by the accused, and that the accused had intended to commit *(mens rea)* the crime. Witnesses are normally called by the Crown to identify the accused as the person who committed the act and to establish this evidence. Counsel for the accused (the defence) then has the opportunity to **cross-examine** the witnesses.

On completion of the Crown's evidence, the defence counsel may ask the judge or magistrate to dismiss the case if the Crown has failed to prove beyond any reasonable doubt that the accused committed the crime. If the judge does not accept the defence counsel's motion, then the defence may proceed to introduce evidence to refute the Crown's case. This, too, is usually done by calling witnesses, although, in this instance, they testify on the accused's behalf. Where defence witnesses are called, they are open to cross-examination by the Crown counsel.

Once all of the evidence has been presented to the court, both parties are entitled to sum up their respective cases and argue any legal points that may apply to the case. The judge or magistrate then determines the accused either not guilty or guilty of the crime, and his or her decision, with reasons, is recorded as his or her **judgement.**

In the case of a preliminary hearing, the proceedings will normally end at the conclusion of the Crown's evidence (which will not necessarily be all of the evidence, but only that part which the Crown believes will be necessary to establish sufficient evidence to warrant a further hearing). The case would then be referred to the court with jurisdiction to try the matter in full if the presiding judge concludes that the case should go on to a full trial.

Civil Court Procedure

Civil cases follow a much different procedure. Before a civil case may proceed to trial, the parties must exchange a number of documents called **pleadings** that set out the issues in dispute and the facts surrounding the conflict.

Civil cases may begin in a number of ways, depending upon the court and the relief sought. In many provinces, usual procedure in a simple dispute is for the **plaintiff** (the injured party) to issue a **writ of summons** against the defendant alleging the particular injury suffered by the plaintiff, and notifying the defendant that the plaintiff intends to hold the defendant responsible for the injury set out in the claim. The writ of summons is usually prepared by the plaintiff's lawyer, and taken to the court's office, where the writ is issued by the court. It is then served personally on the defendant, usually by the Sheriff or someone from that office.

Once the defendant receives the writ, he or she must notify the court's office that a defence will follow. This is done by filing a document called an **appearance.**

The next step in the proceedings is for the plaintiff to provide the defendant (and the court) with details of the claim and the facts that the plaintiff intends to prove when the case comes to trial. This document is called a **statement of claim.** In some provinces (Ontario and Nova Scotia, for example), a civil action is usually commenced by the issue of this pleading.

The defendant, on receipt of the statement of claim, must prepare a **statement of defence** setting out the particular defence that the defendant has to the plaintiff's claim, and if necessary, the facts that he or she intends to prove at trial to support the defence. The statement of defence is filed with the court and served upon the plaintiff. If the defendant also has a claim against the plaintiff, the defendant will file a pleading called a **counter-claim,** which is essentially a statement of claim. Where a counter-claim is filed, the roles of parties change, and the defendant on his or her counter-claim becomes the plaintiff by counter-claim; the plaintiff, the defendant by counter-claim.

On receipt of the defendant's statement of defence the plaintiff may wish to respond. In this case the response to the statement of defence will be set out in a document called a **reply** that is filed and served on the defendant. If the defendant has served the plaintiff with a counter-claim, then the plaintiff (who at this point is also the defendant by counter-claim) will usually file a **statement of defence to counter-claim,** which will set out his or her defence. This usually ends the exchange of documents, and the pleadings are then noted closed.

Occasionally, a pleading may not contain sufficient information to enable the opposing party to properly prepare a response. If this should be the case, a further document called a **demand for particulars** may be served to obtain the necessary information.

Once the pleadings have been closed, either party may set the action down on the list for trial by filing and serving **a notice of trial** on the other party. In some instances, where a jury may be appropriate, a **jury notice** may also be served.

This indicates that the party serving the notice intends to have the case heard by a judge and jury.

To clarify points in the statement of claim and the statement of defence, the parties may also hold examinations under oath, called **examinations for discovery.** The transcript of this evidence is often used later at the trial. In Ontario, in an effort to encourage the parties to resolve their differences, a **pretrial** is held whereby the parties (or their counsel) briefly present their cases to a judge. The judge then provides the parties with an indication of how the court might decide the case if a full trial of the issue was held.

At trial, the case follows a procedure that differs from that of a criminal action. In a civil matter, the counsel for the plaintiff usually begins the case with an **opening statement** that briefly sets out the issues and the facts that the plaintiff intends to prove. Witnesses are called, and evidence is presented to prove the facts in the claim. All witnesses may be subject to cross-examination of defence counsel.

On the completion of the plaintiff's case, counsel for the defendant may ask the judge to dismiss the plaintiff's case if the evidence fails to establish liability on the defendant's part. Again, if the judge does not agree with the defendant, the action will proceed, and the defendant must enter evidence by way of witnesses to prove that the plaintiff's claim is unfounded. Defence witnesses, like the plaintiff's witnesses, may be subject to cross-examination.

Witnesses may be of two kinds: **ordinary witnesses** who testify as to what they saw, heard, or did (direct evidence), and **expert witnesses** who are recognized experts on a particular subject and give opinion evidence on matters that fall within their area of special knowledge. A medical expert testifying as to the likelihood of a plaintiff suffering permanent physical damage as a result of an injury would be an example of this type of expert witness.

Courts will generally insist that only the "best evidence" available be presented to the court, so, for this reason, a court will not normally allow hearsay evidence. **Hearsay evidence** is evidence based upon what a person has heard someone else say, but that is not within that person's own direct knowledge. Because the statements would not be open to challenge on cross-examination, the courts will not usually admit such evidence. Consequently, a party wishing to have the particular evidence placed before the court would be obliged to bring the person with the direct knowledge before the court to testify about it.

When all of the evidence has been entered, counsel argue the relevant points of law and sum up their respective cases for the judge. The judge will then render a decision, which, with his or her reasons, represents the **judgement.**

If either of the parties believe that the trial judge erred in some manner (such as in the application of the law, or the admission of certain evidence), an appeal may be lodged with the appropriate Appeal Court. A **notice of appeal** must be served within a relatively short time after the trial judgement is handed down. Then an **appeal book** containing all material concerning the appeal is prepared by counsel for the Appeal Court. The Appeal Court will review the case, and, if it finds no errors, it will **affirm** the decision of the Trial Court and **dismiss the appeal**. On the other hand, if it should find that the Trial Court erred in reaching its decision, it may **admit the appeal** and **reverse the decision** of the Trial Court, **vary the decision,** or send the case back for a **new trial.**

Very recently, a number of provinces have made efforts to streamline the litigation process. Ontario, for example, has attempted to remove some of the unnecessary steps in the pleadings process. The province has eliminated archaic terms and the use of Latin terminology, and has placed a greater onus on legal counsel to expedite trial matters. It has also restructured the court system by the elimination of the County Court and the establishment of an administrative system to streamline the court process to the trial stage. Nova Scotia has eliminated its County Court as well in an effort to simplify its court system.

Court Costs

Court costs represent a part of the expense that litigants incur when they bring their dispute before the court for resolution. Most of these costs are imposed to help defray the expense of maintaining court offices and the services that they provide, such as the acceptance and recording of pleadings, the issue of certificates, and the preparation of copies of court documents. The service of certain pleadings by court officers, such as the Sheriff, would also constitute court costs. The fees of counsel according to a fixed schedule or tariff are also considered to be a part of the court costs. These fees usually represent only a portion of the actual fee that the client must pay for the legal services rendered. While these costs must be paid initially by the plaintiff (and defendant), the plaintiff usually asks the court to order the defendant to pay these costs along with the damages or relief requested in the action. Conversely, the defendant may ask the court to dismiss the plaintiff's claim and order the plaintiff to pay the defendant's cost of defending the action.

Court costs and counsel fees are awarded at the discretion of the court. However, judges will usually award the successful party to the litigation the cost that that party has incurred, plus a counsel fee that the court may fix in amount or that may be calculated according to a tariff or schedule. Costs awarded on this basis are frequently referred to as "costs on a party and party basis." In some cases, such as where the plaintiff had an indefensible claim and the defendant insisted on proceeding with the case even though no valid defence was put forward, the court may award costs on a "solicitor and client" basis. In this case, the court would be ordering the unsuccessful party to pay the plaintiff's entire legal expenses associated with the court action. In cases where the plaintiff's claim was entirely unfounded, the court might make a similar award to the defendant who was obliged to defend the unfounded claim. In both of these situations the court is, in effect, compensating the party who was obliged to undertake court action in a case where the matter should have been resolved outside the court, and in a sense, punishing the party who caused the unnecessary litigation. In most cases, however, the courts will only award costs on a party and party basis, because the action merits a judgement or determination of issues that the parties are unable to resolve themselves.

The Law Reports

The common law, as noted in Chapter 1, consists of the recorded judgements of the courts. Each time a judge hands down a decision, the decision constitutes a part of the body of common law. Most of these decisions simply confirm or apply existing common law principles. However, where a common law principle is applied to a new or different situation, the decision of the court is usually published and circulated to the legal profession. These published decisions are called **law reports.**

Judicial decisions have been reported in England for hundreds of years, the first series being the *Year Books,* which were very sketchy reports of the judges' decisions. The reporting of cases was variable for many years, and the accuracy of the reports was dependent to no small degree on the skill of the reporter. The early reports themselves varied from an account of the cases heard during a part of a single year, to many volumes, spanning several decades. It was not until the nineteenth century that the reporting of English cases was rationalized, and a council set up to oversee the reporting and publishing of the cases. The council also collected many of the older, important cases, and reproduced them in a series called the *English Reports* (E.R.).

In Canada, judicial decisions have been reported for many years in a number of different series covering different parts of the country. Cases decided in the maritime provinces, for example, may be found in the *Maritime Reports.* These represent a series separate from those of Quebec, Ontario, and Western Canada. Quebec cases, due to the different nature of Quebec law, have a distinct and separate use from those in the common law provinces. They are seldom referred to as precedent outside of that province.

Ontario has maintained its own law reporting in a number of different series of reports, the most important today being the *Ontario Reports.* Western Canada cases are found in the *Western Weekly Reports,* and its predecessor series, the *Western Law Reports.*

In addition to these various regional series, a comprehensive national series is also available in the form of the *Dominion Law Reports* (D.L.R.) that document cases from all parts of Canada. A second national series that reports only Supreme Court of Canada decisions is the *Supreme Court Reports* (S.C.R.). The *Supreme Court Reports,* however, are limited to the decisions of a single court, but nevertheless, a most important one.

Specialized series of reports are also available. These usually deal with particular types of cases or courts. For example, criminal matters are covered by the *Canada Criminal Cases* (C.C.C.), bankruptcy by the *Canadian Bankruptcy Reports* (C.B.R.), and patent matters in the *Canadian Patent Reporter* (C.P.R.).

The cases are cited as authority for the statements of the law contained therein. In order that a legal researcher may readily find the report and read the statement of the law, a concise method of case identification has been developed by the legal profession. This involves the writing of a case reference in a particular manner.

Cases are usually cited in terms of the names of the parties to the action, followed by the year in which the case was decided, the volume and name of the report, and finally, the page in the report where the case may be found. For example, the case of *Wilson v. Taylor* that was decided by the court in November of 1980, was reported in volume 31 of the second series of the *Ontario Reports* at page 9. The case would be cited as follows: *Wilson v. Taylor* (1980), 31 O.R. (2d) 9.

The names of all law reports are referred to by their initials, or some other short form. In the above example, the second series of the Ontario Reports is written as shown. If the series is produced on an annual basis rather than by volume number, the citation would be written with the year in square brackets followed by the abbreviation of the report series. Viz: [1937] 1 D.L.R. 21 where the volume of the law report is the first of the 1937 *Dominion Law Reports* for that year, and the case reported at page 21.

If a particular case is reported in several different reports, or subsequently appealed to a higher court, the case citation may list all of the reports in which the case may be found, together with information as to the disposition of the case to show if it was affirmed, reversed, or appealed. Thus, in the case of *Read v. J. Lyons and Co.*, the trial was reported in [1944] 2 All E.R. 98, appealed to the Court of Appeal where the judgement was reversed, and reported in [1945] 1 All E.R. 106. The case was then appealed to the House of Lords, where it was reported in [1947] A.C. 156. The appeal was dismissed by the House of Lords, affirming the Court of Appeal decision. The case, as a result, might be reported in the following manner:

Read v. J. Lyons and Co., [1944] 2 All E.R. 98; reversed, [1945] 1 All E.R. 106; C.A. affirmed, [1947] A.C. 156.

Canada also has a series of summarized cases called the *Canadian Abridgement.* This series has organized judicial decisions on a topical basis to aid legal practitioners in their research. Cases on each topic are briefly described in the abridgement to enable the researcher to assess the application of the cases to his or her particular legal problem. Once the appropriate cases are determined, the researcher may then turn to the appropriate law report series where the full reports of the judicial decisions would be found.

Data banks of law reports have also been developed to enable legal researchers to examine court decisons more efficiently. These data banks cross-reference cases in a number of different ways to permit computer accessible searches on a fee for service basis. While these searches may be made on a topic basis, the data banks normally record the individual cases using the standard citation method.

ADMINISTRATIVE TRIBUNALS

Administrative tribunals are often boards or commissions charged with the responsibility of regulating certain business activities. These tribunals are established under specific legislation, and their duties and responsibilities are set out in the statute, along with the power to enforce those provisions in the law that affect persons or businesses that fall under the legislation. For example, administrative tribunals regulate the radio and television industry, telephone companies, and the securities market. They also regulate certain aspects of business practices such as labour relations where employees wish to be represented by a trade union.

Administrative tribunals have only the powers granted to them under the legislation that they are directed to enforce. In most cases, where their decisions affect the rights of parties, the tribunal is expected to hold a hearing, where the parties affected may attend and present their case. The hearing is usually less formal than a court hearing. Nevertheless, the tribunal must conduct the hearing in such a way that the parties are treated fairly and have a full opportunity to present their case to the tribunal before a decision is made. If a tribunal fails to treat a party in a fair manner, then recourse may be had to the courts, where the decision of the tribunal may be "quashed" or rendered a nullity.

While many administrative tribunals are permanent bodies, legislation may provide for the establishment of **ad hoc tribunals** to deal with disputes that fall under the legislation. Most ad hoc administrative tribunals tend to be boards of arbitration, established to deal with specific disputes between parties, and are frequently found in the area of labour relations. Such boards are usually constituted with one nominee selected by one interested party, and a second by the other party to the dispute. A neutral third party who acts as chairperson is then selected by the two nominees to complete the tribunal. In some cases, only a single, neutral arbitrator may be appointed. For example, under the **Ontario Labour Relations Act**,[9] the Minister of Labour may appoint a single arbitrator to hear and decide a labour dispute arising out of a collective agreement if either the employer or the union request the Minister to do so.

In addition to regulatory tribunals, tribunals are sometimes used as alternatives to the courts to deal with a wide variety of disputes between individuals. The advantages associated with these bodies are the speed at which hearings may be held, the informality of the proceedings, and the lower cost of obtaining a decision. Given the high cost of resolving disputes in the courts, business contracts often contain clauses that provide for alternative methods of resolving disputes between the parties. The usual method is by arbitration, whereby the parties agree that if any dispute arises between them, they will refer the dispute to an arbitrator and that they will be bound by the arbitrator's award or ruling on the dispute.

An arbitration is conducted much like a court, but the process tends to be less formal. The process normally begins with the selection of an arbitrator or the establishment of an arbitration board. Unlike a court, the parties choose their own arbitrator. If a board of arbitration is to be established, the parties each nominate a member of the board, and the nominees select an impartial chairperson who is usually knowledgeable in that area of business.

Once the arbitrator is selected or the board of arbitration established, an informal hearing is held where each of the parties present their side of the dispute, or their evidence. Often the parties will make written submissions to the arbitrator. Depending upon the nature of the dispute, the hearing may be conducted in the same manner as a court, with witnesses called to give evidence, and legal counsel conducting the case for each of the parties. When all of the evidence has been submitted to the arbitrator or board of arbitration, the arbitrator or board will then make a decision that will be binding on the parties. In the case of a board of arbitration, the decision of the majority is generally the decision of the board.

Most provinces[10] have passed legislation to provide for the establishment of arbitration boards, and to give arbitrators or arbitration boards the power to require witnesses to give evidence under oath, to conduct their own procedure, and to provide for the enforcement of their awards. The parties themselves are expected to bear the cost of the arbitration.

---

9. Labour Relations Act, R.S.O. 1990, c. L-2, s. 46.
10. See for example, Arbitration Act, R.S.B.C. 1979 c. 18 (B.C.); Arbitration Act, R.S.S. 1978 c. A-24 (Sask.); Arbitration Act, R.S.N.S. 1989 c. 19 (N.S.); Arbitration Act, R.S.O. 1990 c. 25 (Ont.)

In Canada, recent private sector developments patterned after similar systems in the United States provide various kinds of civil litigants with an alternative to the courts as a means of resolving their disputes. For example, one such organization, called **The Private Court,** offers arbitration by experts in a number of fields as a means of dispute resolution that avoids the costly and formal court system. The "court" consists of a panel of experienced persons (lawyers for the most part) in various fields of law who will hear disputes in much the same manner as an administrative tribunal, then render a decision that the parties agree will be binding upon them. The private court procedure involves a two step process, with the first step being a settlement conference under the auspices of the "court." If the conference does not result in a settlement, then the parties move to a second step consisting of a streamlined discovery and trial, and finally, an award.[11]

THE JUDICIAL APPOINTMENT PROCESS

Judges who sit on the Supreme Court of Canada, the Federal Court, the Tax Court, Provincial Supreme or Superior Courts, and the judges of District and County Courts are appointed by the federal government. Provincial and Magistrate Court judges (including small claims courts in some provinces) are appointed by provincial governments.

Approximately 850 judges are federally appointed, and these persons, once appointed, are expected to devote their full time to their judicial duties. Of the 850, about 45 are judges of the Supreme Court of Canada, the Federal Court, and the Tax Court.

The present process for appointing judges to the Supreme and Superior Courts of a province, and provincial, district or county courts was established in late 1985. At that time the federal government decided that a more consultative process should be established, whereby the qualifications of potential candidates for appointment would be examined initially at the provincial or territorial level, and then federally. The new procedure is rather complex in the sense that it is essentially a four-step process. The process includes the Federal Commissioner for Judicial Affairs, the provincial or territorial Committee, the Minister of Justice, and the Governor-in-Council.

The Federal Commissioner for Judicial Affairs, who is responsible for all matters concerning the judiciary, is also responsible for the recruitment of new judges. The office of the Commissioner has the duty to solicit and maintain a record of persons suitable for appointment to judicial positions in order that vacancies on the various courts may be filled within a reasonable time by qualified persons.

The Commissioner is the first step in the process. He conducts a preliminary screening of potential nominees to make certain that they have been members in good standing in their respective provincial or territorial law associations for a period of no less than ten years. All potential candidates must, as a prerequisite, be qualified lawyers who have either been in the practice of law for at least ten years, or possess at least a total of ten years as a practitioner and a provincial judge or magistrate.

---

11. The Private Court is a Toronto based organization.

Following this preliminary step in the process, the Commissioner submits the candidate's name to the provincial or territorial committee where the candidate resides for further review and assessment. The committee is a permanent committee that consists of five members: one person nominated by the Federal Minister of Justice, a person nominated by the provincial or territorial Attorney General, a federally appointed judge, nominated by the Chief Justice of the provincial Supreme Court, a person nominated by the provincial board of the Canadian Bar Association, and a person nominated by the provincial or territorial law society. The persons nominated by the Attorney General and the Minister of Justice would normally be persons other than practising lawyers in order that the public would have some input into the selection process.

The committee examines the professional and other qualifications of the persons whose names are submitted to it by the Commissioner and will either assess the candidate as qualified or not qualified, along with the reasons for the determination. Persons who are assessed as not qualified have the right to be informed of the reasons if they so desire, and may respond to correct any misinformation or mistakes that might have affected the committee's decision.

The names of qualified persons will then be reported to the Commissioner for Federal Judicial Affairs who will add all the names to the list of qualified persons that the office maintains.

The third step in the process takes place when a vacancy occurs on a court. The Minister of Justice will usually select a person who has been screened by the committees in advance or in contemplation of an appointment, but the Minister may exercise his or her discretion by submitting a name for assessment. It should be noted that the Minister retains the overriding authority to recommend an appointment to the Governor-in-Council without assessment, but this is unlikely to occur except in unusual circumstances. The usual practice is for the Minister to consult with the Chief Justice and the Attorney General of the province where a vacancy exists in order to determine the type of qualifications required to fill the appointment.

Except for the position of Chief Justice of a Provincial Supreme or Superior Court (which is recommended by the Prime Minister), the Minister of Justice will put forward the recommended name of the person to the Governor-in-Council for appointment to the judicial vacancy on the court. The Governor General on the advice of Cabinet performs the fourth and final step in the process by approving the recommendation and appointing the person as a judge of the particular court.

The four-step appointment process also applies in modified form to the appointment of judges of the Federal Court and of the Tax Court, but does not apply to the Supreme Court of Canada.

Judges of the courts, once appointed, are largely independent in the performance of their duties and may only be removed from the bench for serious misconduct. Complaints against a judge may be made to the Canadian Judicial Council, a body composed of all provincial Chief Justices and Chief Judges. The Council is presided over by the Chief Justice of Canada and investigates complaints and has the power to discipline judges who act improperly. In the case of serious misconduct, the Council may recommend to the Minister of Justice that the judge be removed from office. The actual removal, however, may only take place through a process whereby both the Senate and the House of Commons request the Governor General to do so. This process is known as a "joint address to the Governor General."

THE LEGAL PROFESSION

The legal profession has a long and noble history which dates back to early Roman times. In England, attorneys were not necessary to plead cases before the Anglo-Saxon courts, as the parties to a dispute presented their own cases. By Norman times, however, a person who was old or infirm was permitted to appoint an attorney to act for him, if he agreed to be bound by the attorney's acts. This gradually changed over the next century to the point where the king's justices permitted any person to bring an action in the king's court by an attorney. The attorney, at that time, required no formal training the law.

The first legislation regulating persons who might practise as attorneys was passed in 1402.[12] This statute required anyone who wished to practise before the courts to be first examined by the justices of the king's court, and if found to be fit, to have his name put on a **Roll.** Only those persons whose names appeared on the Roll were entitled to practise law as attorneys. If an attorney failed to carry out his duties properly, his name could be struck from the Roll and he would be barred from appearing before the king's court forever.

Persons who became familiar with proceedings in the chancellor's court were called **solicitors** because the special proceedings in the chancellor's court were begun by a petition soliciting some form of equitable relief from the court.

Attorneys and solicitors continued to be examined by the judges and the chancellor (or his senior master) for almost three centuries. By 1729, however, the examination process had become so perfunctory that complaints were made to the courts that some solicitors and attorneys were not "learned in the law." To remedy this situation, legislation was passed that required both solicitors and attorneys to serve a five-year apprenticeship with a practising attorney or solicitor before taking the examination for admission to practise alone.

As early as the fourteenth century practitioners in England banded together in societies for the purpose of jointly purchasing and owning law manuscripts and law books, and to establish premises where they could maintain their libraries and live during the time when the courts were in session. These establishments were known as **inns.** The inns were governed by senior members who, by tradition, dined together at a high table on a bench. Consequently, these senior members acquired the name **benchers.**

As part of their training at the inns, junior members were expected to attend after-dinner lectures and engage in "practice" moots. A **barra,** or bar similar to the bar found in the courts, was usually set up in the hall. When an apprentice was considered to be sufficiently experienced, the benchers would allow the apprentice to plead his case from the bar. The apprentice's **call to the bar** was recognition by the profession that he had acquired the necessary skill to act as a **barrister.** Once the apprentice had been called to the bar he would then be permitted to plead cases in the courts (although until 1846 the Court of Common Pleas would only allow practitioners who held the degree of serjeant to plead

---

12. Punishment of an Attorney Found in Default, 4 Hen. IV, c. 18.

before it). The training of apprentices unfortunately declined during the late eighteenth century and early nineteenth century to the point where the four Inns of Court decided (in 1852) to establish a law school to provide instruction and to conduct examinations of apprentices before the students could be called to the bar. Formal training has been required since that time for the legal profession in England.

When the **Law Society Act** was passed in Upper Canada in 1793,[13] the tradition of the Inns of Court, including the titles, was followed by the then fledgling legal profession. Similar legislation in the other colonies adopted the same traditions. The small number of lawyers in North America did not, however, permit the division of the profession (barristers and solicitors) as it existed in England. From the beginning, lawyers in the North American colonies combined both avenues of practice into one. Formal training continued to be patterned after the English model, and for many years, formal legal training was possible in some provinces by apprenticeship and examination by the provincial bars. Over time, however, legal training gradually shifted to the universities where courses in law were offered. At first these courses were part of general university programs; later they became part of the curriculum of university law schools.

McGill University in Montreal, Quebec, established a law school in 1848, and claims to be the oldest university with a law faculty. Many other universities established law schools shortly thereafter, and by the late nineteenth century, law schools existed in New Brunswick, Quebec, Ontario, Nova Scotia, and Manitoba. One of the most famous, and one of the oldest, Osgoode Hall Law School, dates from 1797. However, it did not grant an academic law degree until the benchers of the Law Society of Upper Canada transferred the formal teaching function to degree-granting institutions (including its own school) in 1957.

Formal training of the legal profession in most common law provinces now requires a law degree as well as some form of apprenticeship to be served in the office of a practising solicitor or barrister for a specified period of time.

Legal training in the Province of Quebec requires a knowledge of the Civil Code, and this training is now provided by Quebec universities. The training in civil law is quite different in terms of approach and content. Even the terminology used to describe certain members of the legal profession differs from that used in the common law provinces. Much of the work normally considered a part of a solicitor's practice in other provinces is performed in Quebec by **notaries**, and the "trial work" is conducted by **avocats.**

THE ROLE OF THE LEGAL PROFESSION

The legal profession in each province is governed by legislation which limits the right to practice law to those persons admitted to practice pursuant to the legislation. This legislation is designed to ensure that persons who offer legal services to the public are properly trained to do so. The legislation also provides for control of the profession, usually through a provincial law society or association that is charged with the responsibility of administering the governing act. The law society or association enforces rules of conduct, and usually has the power to discipline or disbar members who fail to comply with the rules or the standards of competence set for the profession.

---

13. Law Society Act, 37 Geo. III, c. 13.

The legal profession provides a wide variety of services to the public by advising and assisting the public with their legal problems. Those members of the profession who undertake to provide service to business persons practise their profession in the relatively broad and loosely defined area of "business law." This area of the law includes legal work associated with the formation and financing of business organizations, the broad range of activities engaged in by business organizations generally, and in the many specialized areas of law such as intellectual and industrial property, real property, labour relations, taxation, and security for debt. Large law firms who offer their services to business firms tend to have members of the firm who specialize in particular areas of the law that affect business, while the smaller law firms may either specialize in one or a few areas of business law. Many small firms engage in a wide variety of legal work, and call upon the services of other lawyers who specialize in a particular area of business law when a client has a particularly difficult problem in that area of the law.

The role of the legal profession in a business transaction is usually to advise a client of the legal implications of the course of action proposed by the client and, if the client decides to undertake the matter, to act on behalf of the client to protect his or her interests and give effect to the action undertaken. For example, if a client wishes to enter into a contract with another business person to sell certain assets, the lawyer will advise the client of the nature of the sale agreement required, the tax implications of the sale, and perhaps the need for any special licence or permit required to sell the assets if the buyer resides abroad and the assets are goods subject to export restrictions. The lawyer will also either prepare the agreement of sale, or review the sale agreement if it is prepared by the other party's lawyer, to make certain that it protects the rights of the client and gives effect to the client's wishes in the sale. In the event that the other party fails to complete the transaction, a lawyer will advise the client of his or her rights under the agreement and, if retained to do so, will take the necessary legal action on behalf of the client to enforce the agreement.

Apart from advising clients on the legal implications of business transactions, firms frequently engage lawyers to assist in the negotiation of collective agreements with the labour unions that represent the firm's employees. Collective agreements are enforceable contracts that set out the terms and conditions of employment under which the employees will work, and often require much discussion before the agreement is reached. Lawyers who specialize in labour relations are frequently called upon to assist organizations of employees (**unions**) in their negotiations as well. Both employers and unions call upon members of the legal profession to process disputes arising out of collective agreements at the stage where the dispute is brought before an arbitrator or arbitration board for a determination.

Some law firms specialize in the area of patents, trade marks, and copyright law, and these firms assist inventors and firms that develop new products to establish patent protection for their products or processes. They also assist businesses with trade names or trade marks by attending to the necessary legal work associated with the protection of the name or mark.

In large financial centres, many law firms specialize in providing advice and assistance in the incorporation of firms, the mergers of firms, and legal work associated with the financing of take-overs. This is often complex work, as it frequently involves not only expertise in the area of securities (bonds, debentures, shares) but also taxation and to some extent public policy related to restrictive trade practices.

SUMMARY

The legal system is the vehicle by which the law is enforced. However, this was not always the case. The development of the legal system has been evolutionary in nature. The earliest courts were not courts as we know them today, but simply meetings of the community. Community pressure to support a decision was common until the Norman Conquest of England in 1066. After the Conquest, the gradual centralization of power began, and with it, the courts' increased authority to demand that the parties comply with their decisions. Courts established special procedures which the parties were required to follow if they wished to be heard, and these special procedures in turn gave rise to the legal profession. Modern courts in Canada and the United States still retain many of the traditions and names of the English courts, even though the kinds of cases that they hear are quite different today.

While the judicial process appears to be cumbersome and complex, much of the procedure is designed to ensure that justice is done. Safeguards in the form of rules of evidence and judicial review form an important part of the mechanism designed to eliminate arbitrary or unfair decision-making. As a result, the legal systems in Canada, the United States, and the United Kingdom represent a system that is fair to all.

DISCUSSION QUESTIONS

1. "In a free and democratic society, the courts perform the important role of guardians of the rights and freedoms of the individual. While important, this is far from being the only part they play in society." How do the courts perform this important role? What other functions do they have in society?
2. Discuss the importance of an independent judiciary.
3. What is a court of original jurisdiction? How does it differ from a court of appeal?
4. Explain the differences between a Small Claims Court and a Magistrate's Court.
5. On what basis is it possible to justify the right of the court to declare unconstitutional a law enacted by a legislature?
6. How does a criminal case differ from a civil action?
7. In criminal proceedings, what obligation rests on the Crown in order to obtain a conviction?
8. What is the purpose of "pleadings" in a civil case?
9. How does "direct" evidence differ from "opinion" evidence? How do these kinds of evidence differ from "hearsay" evidence?
10. Describe the role performed by legal counsel in the adminstration of justice.
11. Distinguish between a "barrister" and a "solicitor."
12. On what basis might an appeal be heard from a judgement of the court of original jurisdiction?
13. Where a judgement is reviewed by a Court of Appeal, what type of decisions might the court make?
14. If a provincial government passed a law prohibiting any person from expressing any criticism of any elected government official, on penalty of imprisonment, how might the law itself be challenged?

PART II

The Law
of Torts

TORT LAW DEFINED

The term *tort* is a legal term derived from the Latin word *tortus* meaning a "wrong." Its use in law is to describe a great many activities that result in damage to others with the exception of a breach of trust, a breach of duty that is entirely contractual in nature, or a breach of a merely equitable obligation.[1] The term has been used in English law for many hundreds of years to characterize a wrong committed by one person against another, or against the person's property or reputation, either intentionally or unintentionally. It also generally covers cases where a person causing an injury has no lawful right to do so. Unfortunately, the term is not capable of precise definition, because the area of the law that it encompasses is so broad that to determine its limits with any degree of precision would be an impossible task. We can, however, identify many of the more important areas of tort law and examine those which have a direct bearing on ordinary personal and business activities.

THE DEVELOPMENT OF TORT LAW

Some of the earliest laws made by the community or the early judges pertained to actions that are now the subject of tort law. Indeed, most of our more familiar criminal law was once tort law, and many criminal actions today still have a concurrent tort liability attached to

them. Assault causing bodily harm, for example, is an act covered by the Criminal Code, where the Crown would proceed against the person who committed the assault. Under tort law, the victim of the assault would also have the right to seek redress from the accused for the injury by way of civil proceedings for assault and battery.

In the past, no distinction was made between acts that were criminal, and acts that were civil in nature. Both were treated as torts in the sense that compensation would be due to the victim or the victim's family. This is not so today. Because so many torts in the past have now become crimes, modern legal writers, particularly those in the United States, distinguish the two classes by referring to crimes as "public wrongs" or "wrongs against society," and the remainder of tort law as "private wrongs" or "wrongs against the individual."

The earliest tort cases tended to reflect the injuries that a plaintiff of that era might suffer: violent assault and battery, the seizure of one's goods, or the slander of one's name. Today, the scope of the law of torts has broadened to the point where it encompasses a great many areas of human endeavour. Yet, for all of its applications to modern-day activity, many of the principles and concepts date back to much simpler earlier times when the courts first saw the need to remedy a wrong.

Tort law, by and large, is an attempt by the courts to cope with the changes that take place in society, and to balance as best they can individual freedom of action with protection or compensation for the inevitable injury to

---

1. Osborn, P.G., *The Concise Law Dictionary*, 4th ed. (London: Sweet & Maxwell, 1954), p. 334.

others that the exercise of such freedom occasionally produces. The development of the law of torts is essentially the development of the principles and legal fictions used by the courts to effectively maintain some sort of equilibrium between these two individual desires in an ever-increasingly complex society.

Tort situations might arise in the course of a number of business activities. It would, for example, arise where a business person negligently produces a product that injures the user or consumer. It would also occur where a surgeon carelessly performs an operation on a patient, causing the patient further unnecessary pain and suffering or permanent injury.

While many areas of the law affect business, the law of torts and the law of contract are two major areas of importance in terms of rights of the parties arising out of business transactions or business activity. As a very general rule, contract law applies to business activities where the parties have voluntarily agreed to their rights and responsibilities which the courts will enforce through civil action. In the case of tort law, a party affected

by a business activity which causes injury need not necessarily be associated in the business transaction or activity, and in many cases may be a complete stranger to the transaction, but, nevertheless, injured by it. In this instance, tort law may provide a remedy, and in a sense, has a much broader application than contract law.

Many common business torts relate to carelessness resulting in injury or loss to a client or customer, but some torts may arise out of deliberate acts. For example, for a person to deliberately enter on the private property of a landowner is the tort of trespass, and to deliberately threaten and then strike someone a blow with your fist would be an assault and battery. Because business persons are often responsible for the actions of their employees in the course of carrying out their duties, liability for any tort committed by an employee in the course of business may fall on the employer as well. In the chapters in this part of the text, the law of torts and its impact on business activity is explored under the general headings of intentional and unintentional torts.

CHAPTER 4

Intentional Interference

INTENTIONAL INTERFERENCE WITH THE PERSON

Interference with the person in tort law includes both willful and unintentional interference; but for ease in distinguishing between the two, we shall look at each separately. The principal forms of willful or intentional interference are the torts of assault and battery and false imprisonment. These torts are ancient, and represent breaches of the "king's peace" as well as intentional injury to the person. Today, assault and battery constitute criminal offences under the Criminal Code[1] in both serious and less serious forms, a distinction that has been carried forward for these particular torts since the thirteenth century. Similarly, false imprisonment is an offence under the Criminal Code when it takes the form of kidnapping or abduction.[2] It remains a tort in those instances where persons are restrained without their consent. Needless to say, the Crown is concerned with the criminal aspects of these torts, but the individual must normally look to the civil courts for compensation for the injury caused to the person.

Most victims of violent tort do not seek redress for their injuries, however, because the persons who cause the injuries seldom have sufficient financial assets to make civil action worthwhile to recover the damages. In view of this fact, some governments have recognized that victims of crime are for all practical purposes left without compensation for their injuries. Consequently, in some provinces, boards (usually called Criminal Compensation Boards) have been established to review cases of criminal injury. They have the power to award compensation to the victims of these and other types of physical violence to

---

1. Criminal Code, R.S.C. 1985, c. C-46 s. 265-278, as amended.
2. Criminal Code, R.S.C. 1985, c. C-46, s. 279-286.

persons. Compensation is paid from a fund established by the province, and in this sense is a quite different procedure from court action.

Assault and Battery

Assault and battery are torts that rarely arise in ordinary business relationships. They do, however, arise in some instances where employees act improperly in dealing with unruly patrons of food and drink establishments, or in professions where dealing with people in a physical manner occurs.

Assault and battery are frequently considered to be a single tort, but in fact each term refers to a separate tort. **Assault** originally referred to a threat of violence, and **battery** to the application of force to the person. The distinction between the two torts has become blurred by the passage of time, and today, judges occasionally refer to the application of force as an assault. This evolutionary change is understandable, since an assault usually occurs before the application of force, or accompanies it. The distinction is still important, however, because not every application of force by one person on another is a battery within the meaning of the law. For example, two people passing in a dark and narrow hall may accidentally collide with one another, yet neither are injured or bruised in any way from the contact. Technically, each would have applied force to the other, but each act was not intended to cause harm, and this would distinguish the unintentional act from a battery. For the battery in this case to be actionable, it must be something more than the mere application of force. The force must be applied with the intention of causing harm; where it does not cause harm, it must be done without consent, in anger, or accompanied by a threat of injury or violence in order to constitute a tort.[3]

An assault, however, need not be accompanied by the application of force to be actionable. In an early case, a man hammered on a tavern door with a hatchet late one night and demanded entry. When the plaintiff told him to stop, he struck at her with the hatchet but missed. He caused her no harm, but was held to have made an actionable assault.[4] In a more modern case involving a plea of self-defence, the defendant was driving his car close to the rear of the plaintiff's vehicle. After the two cars stopped, the plaintiff got out of his car and shook his fist at the defendant. The plaintiff's actions were held to be an assault.[5]

In some cases, a battery need not be violent. It is sufficient for it to be any situation that involves the touching of a person without consent in such a way that the recipient of such action is injured. In a number of recent cases, surgeons have been found liable for battery where they failed to inform their patients of the risks involved in operations,[6] or where they used experimental techniques without fully explaining the risks to the patients.[7]

The damages that a court may award in assault and battery cases are designed to compensate the plaintiff for the injury suffered. But in many cases, particularly

---

3. *Cole v. Turner* (1705), 6 Mod. 149, 87 E.R. 907.

4. *De S and M v. W De S* (1348), Year-Book. Liber Assisarum, folios 99, pl. 60.

5. *Bruce v. Dyer,* [1966] 2 O.R. 705; affirmed, [1970] 1 O.R. 482.

6. *Reibl v. Hughes* (1977), 16 O.R. (2d) 306.

7. *Zimmer et al. v. Ringrose* (1978), 89 D.L.R. (3d) 646.

where the attack on the plaintiff is vicious and unprovoked, the court may award **punitive** or **exemplary damages** as well. The principal thrust of these awards is to deter the defendant from any similar actions in the future, and to act as a general deterrent for the public at large.

In some cases of assault and battery, a defendant may raise the defences of **provocation** or **self-defence,** but each defence is subject to particular limitations imposed by the courts. Generally, the defence of provocation will only be taken into consideration in determining the amount of punitive damages that may be awarded to the plaintiff. As a defence, it would not absolve the defendant from liability. Self-defence, on the other hand, may be a complete defence if the defendant can satisfy the court that he or she had a genuine fear of injury at the hands of the plaintiff, and that he or she only struck the plaintiff as self-protection from a threatened battery. Normally, the courts also require the defendant to establish that the amount of force used by the defendant was reasonable and necessary under the circumstances.[8]

In the case of *MacDonald v. Hees* (1974), 46 D.L.R. (3d) 720, the judge described the manner in which the parties to an alleged assault must present their cases before the court, and the onus on the defendant who raises "self-defence" as justification for the assault (battery):

> In an action for assault, it has been, in my view, established that it is for the plaintiff to prove that he was assaulted and that he has sustained an injury thereby. The onus is upon the plaintiff to establish those facts before the jury. Then it is upon the defendant to establish the defences, first, that the assault was justified and, secondly, that the assault even if justified was not made with any unreasonable force and on those issues the onus is on the defence.

Assault and battery are obviously torts that have a criminal side as well. The state has an interest in preserving the peace and protecting its citizens from injury. As a consequence, the Crown may take steps to charge a person who commits an assault or battery. The nature of the criminal charge, however, depends to some extent on the type of assault and the severity of the injury inflicted.

Assault and battery under the Criminal Code usually occurs outside the ordinary business relationship, but occasionally an employee of a business may assault a customer. The employee may be personally liable for the tort, but at common law, the employer may also be held liable for the actions of his or her employees in the ordinary course of business. This is known as **vicarious liability.** However, in an instance where an employee assaults a customer in the course of business, it is important to note the difference between the criminal and civil consequences. While the employer may be liable for the actions of the employee in the case of a tort committed by the employee in the ordinary course of business, only the employee will be liable for the criminal consequences of the act unless the employer had in some way directed or authorized the commission of the offence by the employee, or the employer was aware of the propensity of the employee to commit violent acts.

False Imprisonment

False imprisonment is another type of intentional interference with the person that Canadian courts will recognize as a tort. As an actionable civil wrong, it represents

---

8. *Veinot v. Veinot* (1978), 81 D.L.R. (3d) 549.

any restraint or confinement of the individual by a person who has no lawful right to restrict the freedom of another. It most often arises where a shopkeeper seizes and holds a person suspected of taking goods from his or her shop, only to discover later that an innocent person has been apprehended. In such cases, the imprisonment need not involve the actual physical restraint if the shopkeeper makes it clear to the suspect that any attempt to leave the premises will result in the embarrassment of seizure, or pursuit accompanied by calls for help.

The law, as a matter of public policy, usually views the restraint of one individual by another with disfavour, and the defences available to the defendant are meagre. The Criminal Code permits ordinary citizens to seize persons who have committed a criminal offence (such as shoplifting) and hold them without warrant until a police officer can take the offender into custody. This provision of the Criminal Code (s. 494) provides:

> *494.(1) Any one may arrest without warrant*
>> *(a) a person whom he finds committing an indictable offence; or*
>> *(b) a person who, on reasonable grounds, he believes*
>> *(i) has committed a criminal offence, and*
>> *(ii) is escaping from and freshly pursued by persons who have lawful authority to arrest that person.*
>
> *(2) Any one who is*
>> *(a) the owner or a person in lawful possession of property, or*
>> *(b) a person authorized by the owner or by a person in lawful possession of property, may arrest without warrant a person whom he finds committing a criminal offence on or in relation to that property.*
>
> *(3) Any one other than a peace officer who arrests a person without warrant shall forthwith deliver the person to a peace officer. R.S., c.C-34, s.449; R.S., c.2 (2nd Supp.), s.5.*

As a general rule, a person may restrain another where the person apprehended is in the process of committing a crime, or where a person attempting to seize the criminal mistakenly apprehends the wrong person. In the latter case, however, the person falsely seizing the innocent person must have reasonable and probable grounds for believing that the innocent person had committed an offence and was escaping custody; otherwise, it would be no defence to a claim of false imprisonment.[9] Peace officers, of course, may mistakenly restrain innocent persons without committing the tort of false imprisonment or false arrest, provided they had reasonable grounds for believing the person was an offender at the time of the restraint.[10]

False imprisonment is also a criminal offence in the form of **forcible confinement.** Under the Criminal Code, anyone, who without lawful authority confines, imprisons, or forcibly seizes another person may be prosecuted for the offence. If found guilty, that person would be liable to imprisonment for a term of up to ten years.[11] If forcible confinement is alleged, the lack of resistance is not a defence

---

9. Criminal Code, R.S.C. 1985, c. C-46, s. 494.

10. Criminal Code, R.S.C. 1985, c. C-46, s. 495.

11. Criminal Code, R.S.C. 1985, c. C-46, s. 279.

unless the accused can successfully prove that the failure to resist was not caused by threats, duress, the use of force, or the exhibition of force. In the ordinary business situation where a shopkeeper apprehends a person suspected of shoplifting or theft, the shopkeeper would probably not be subject to criminal charges if the shopkeeper immediately called the police to take charge of the suspect, and the suspect was later found not guilty of the alleged offence that led to the confinement.

INTENTIONAL INTERFERENCE WITH A PERSON'S REPUTATION

The law of tort that relates to the interference with a person's reputation is called **defamation**. Defamation may take the form of either **libel** or **slander**. Slander generally consists of false statements or gestures that injure a person's reputation. Libel takes the form of printed or published slander. Defamatory statements that slandered a person's good name or reputation were originally dealt with as moral matters by the old ecclesiastic courts, but with the passage of time, fell under the jurisdiction of the common law courts. Before the introduction of printing, defamation took the form of slander. This was largely a "localized" injury, but with the invention of printing, the extent of the injury changed both in terms of geographical limits and permanency. The printed word was capable of widespread circulation, and thus spread the scandal over a larger area. In addition, it provided a permanent record of the defamation that would remain long after slanderous statements would normally be forgotten. The criminal aspects of the printed defamation (libel) originally fell within the jurisdiction of the English Court of the Star Chamber, where the person who published a libel was punished both criminally as well as civilly for the tort. When the Star Chamber Court was abolished in 1641, the jurisdiction fell to the common law courts.

Generally, in a defamation action the plaintiff must establish that the defendant's statements have seriously injured his or her reputation; otherwise, the court will award only nominal damages. If the defendant's statements are true, the plaintiff will not succeed, as the truth of the statements will constitute a good defence to the plaintiff's claim.

Qualified and **absolute privilege** are also recognized by the court as defences to a claim for defamation. Absolute privilege, as the name implies, protects the speaker of the words absolutely, regardless of their truth or falsity, and even if they are made with malicious intent. This defence is limited, however, to those cases where it is in the public's interest to allow defamatory statements to be made. Consequently, statements made in Parliament, before a Royal Commission, in court, at coroners' inquests, and in any proceeding of a quasi-judicial nature[12] are not subject to an action for defamation by a person injured by the statements.

In some instances, a qualified privilege may apply where the defendant can show that the statements were made in good faith and without malicious intent, even though the facts that he or she believed to be true at the time were subsequently proven to be false. The most common example of this situation would be where A provides a letter of reference containing derogatory statements (which A believes to be true, and which A honestly believes are a fair assessment) of B. The justification for these exceptions is based upon the importance of allowing

---

12. *Voratovic v. Law Society of Upper Canada* (1978), 20 O.R. (2d) 14.

free speech on matters of public importance, and balancing this intent with the protection of the individual's reputation.[13] Some provinces now have legislation dealing with the action of libel and slander; to some extent, this legislation has modified the common law.[14]

Defamation has a criminal element as well. Under the Criminal Code, defamatory libel arises where a matter is published without lawful excuse or justification that is likely to injure the reputation of any person by exposing the person to hatred, contempt, or ridicule, or that is designed to insult the person concerned. Publishing includes not just newspapers but any exhibition in public of the material, causing it to be read or seen, and includes books, pamphlets, or other printed matter. Persons who publish a defamatory libel that they know to be false may be charged with the offence and, if found guilty, would be subject to imprisonment for a term of up to five years.

Publishers of newspapers as a group are most concerned with this aspect of the law, and usually take care to avoid defamatory libel in material that they include in their newspapers. Defences to an allegation of defamatory libel may include the publication for the public benefit of matters that in themselves are true, and fair comment of fair reporting in good faith of lawful public meetings. As a general rule, the publisher of a newspaper is in the same position as the writer of the material, and in order to establish the defence of fair comment, the newspaper must be able to say that the comment represents the honest opinion of the newspaper.[15]

Cartoons which often ridicule or satirize political figures are also subject to defamation law, but most newspapers may successfully defend against libel claims in these cases on the basis of fair comment, as a person's political life may be open to a much greater degree of criticism and comment than their private life.[16]

INTENTIONAL INTERFERENCE WITH LAND AND CHATTELS

Intentional interference with land and chattels are matters that relate to property law, but also contain an element of tort liability. The two principal classes of torts that relate to property law are **trespass** to land and **conversion** of goods. In both of these cases (as with assault and battery and false imprisonment), there is an element of intention associated with the act of interference.

Trespass to Land

The law relating to trespass to land represents one of the oldest actionable torts. It is the act of entering on the land of another without the express or implied consent of the person in lawful possession. It is also trespass if a person, once given permission to enter on the lands, refuses to leave when requested to do so.[17] This tort is relatively broad in its application to interference with the land as well. For example, the acts of tunnelling under another's land without permission or lawful

---

13. *Stopforth v. Goyer* (1979), 23 O.R. (2d) 696.
14. See, for example, Libel and Slander Act, R.S.O. 1990, c. L-12.
15. *Cherneskey v. Armadale Publishers Ltd.,* [1979] 1 S.C.R. 1067.
16. *Vander Zalm v. Times Publishers et al.* (1980), 18 B.C.L.R. 210 (B.C.C.A.).
17. *"The Six Carpenters Case"* (1610), 8 Co. Rep. 146a, 77 E.R. 695.

right, erecting a wall or fence on another's land, or stringing wires or lines over another's land all constitute trespass. Even things can trespass. Trespassing trees, overhanging eaves, and the like are common sources of dispute among urban neighbours. Involuntary entry on the lands of another, however, would not constitute trespass, as the act of entry would be unintentional.[18]

In a recent case,[19] the court described the law of trespass in the following terms:

> *Prima facie*, every invasion of property, be it ever so minute and negligible, is a trespass and therefore unlawful. Such trespass may not amount to crime since "breaking the close" simpliciter is not a criminal offence. Nonetheless, entry into the premises of another without either consent or specific legal authorization has always been tortious and unlawful. It is an interference with the common law right to peaceful enjoyment of one's property that has been recognized at least since *Semayne's Case* (1604), 5 Co. Rep. 91a, 77 E.R. 194 [at 195] (K.B.), where it was said: "that the house of everyone is to him as his castle and fortress, as well as for his defence against injury and violence, as for his repose."

In one British Columbia case, a building contractor, during the course of construction of a large building, inserted a large number of steel rods under the adjacent property to shore-up the walls of the new structure. The eight metre long rods caused no physical damage to the neighbouring property, but were installed without the neighbours consent, and without attempting to contact the property owner to obtain consent. The court found the contractor liable for trespass and awarded the neighbouring property owner general damages in the amount of $500 and exemplary damages in the amount of $47 500, because the contractor had made no effort to obtain the consent of the landowner.[20]

Much of the law relating to trespass is well settled due to its long period of existence, but occasionally new forms of technology give rise to new claims in trespass. In England, for example, the invention and use of aircraft resulted in actions for trespass by property owners,[21] but the control of this activity by statute and government regulatory bodies have, for all intents and purposes, removed it from the realm of actionable trespass.

Conversion and Willful Damage to Goods

The intentional interference with the goods of another constitutes the torts of conversion or trespass to goods. Conversion is the wrongful taking of the goods of another or, where the goods lawfully come into the possession of the person, the willful refusal to deliver up the goods to the lawful owner. For the tort of conversion to exist, the lawful owner must be denied possession and enjoyment of the goods, and the defendant must retain the goods without colour of right. The remedy granted by the courts is usually monetary damages equal to the value of the goods.

---

18. *Smith v. Stone* (1647), Style 65, 82 E.R. 533.

19. Reference Pursuant to s. 27(1) of the Judicature Act [1985] 2 W.W.R. 193.

20. *Austin v. Rescon Construction (1984) Ltd.* (1987), 18 B.C.L.R. (2d) 328, 45 D.L.R. 324 (C.A.).

21. *Pickering v. Rudd* (1815), 4 Camp. 219, but see *Bernstein v. Skyviews & Gen.,* [1977] 2 All E.R. 902 for current view that trespass limited to the landowner's useable air space above the property.

The second form of trespass to goods involves the willful damage to the goods while they are in the possession of the owner. (For example, the deliberate smashing of the windshield of a person's automobile while it is parked in a parking lot, or the deliberate act of killing a farmer's livestock.) Both of these torts normally have a criminal element attached to them, and while a great many of these cases reach the criminal courts, the widespread use of insurance to protect against loss of goods through conversion or willful damage has reduced the number of tort actions that might otherwise come before the courts. The two torts, nevertheless, remain as actionable wrongs.

BUSINESS-RELATED TORTS AND CRIMES

The conduct of business activities in a free enterprise economy involves competition between business firms for customers. While the vast majority of business firms compete with each other on a fair and equitable basis, occasionally some will engage in improper practices that cause injury to others. These improper practices often take the form of untrue statements about competitors or the goods or services they provide to the public. In other cases, they may involve improper attempts to acquire the trade secrets of others. They may, as well, involve agreements to restrict trade between businesses to the detriment of the public. Most of these improper practices were originally (and have remained) actionable torts at common law, but others have become the subject matter of legislation such as the Competition Act and, in some cases, been made offences under the Criminal Code. It should be noted, however, that not all business-related torts and crimes are committed by persons engaged in business. Consumers may attempt to obtain goods under false pretences from business firms, or may attempt to injure the reputation of a firm by making untrue or false statements about the firm or its dealings. These consumer-related activities would also be actionable torts and, in some cases, criminal offences as well.

Perhaps the most common business-related tort an unscrupulous business person might commit is the slander of goods. The **slander of goods** involves making a statement alleging that the goods of a competitor are in some way defective or shoddy, or are injurious to the health of the consumer. Statements of this nature, if untrue, could cause injury to the competitor, and would be actionable at law. This tort is not limited to business persons; consumers who make untrue and unfounded statements of this nature would also commit the tort of slander of goods.

A similar tort is **slander of title.** This arises where a person makes an untrue statement about the right of another to the ownership of goods. It may take the form of statements that the competitor or seller has improperly acquired the goods put up for sale. For example, the allegation might be that the goods were stolen, improperly imported, or produced in violation of the copyright or patent rights of the rightful owner. The allegation might also be that the seller is passing off his or her goods as those of another well-known manufacturer in violation of that manufacturer's trade mark or trade name.

Untrue allegations of any of these aspects of the title of the seller to the goods would constitute the tort slander of title, and would be actionable at law. However, if, in fact, the goods were produced and sold in violation of the copyright or patent of the true owner, their production would in itself constitute an actionable right by the copyright or patent owner. Patent and copyright law in

Canada gives the inventor or creator the exclusive right to production of the work for the life of the patent or copyright, and any unauthorized production of the work would entitle the true owner to bring an action against the unauthorized producer. Similarly, the production of goods and their presentation to the market as being the goods of another well-known producer (such as packaging the goods in the same distinguishing guise as the well-known producer or marking the goods with the same trade mark) is also actionable, as it constitutes plagiarism or passing-off, and, in effect, trading on the good will that belongs to another. Patents, trade marks, and copyright are controlled by statute, and under each of these acts the penalty for improper dealing with the property rights of the owner is usually an award of money damages and an accounting for profits lost as a result of the violation. These topics are dealt with in detail in Chapter 33 of the text, but, for the purpose of studying business torts and crimes, it is sufficient here to note that such improper activities are actionable at law.

Improper dealings with a competitor's employees may also constitute an actionable tort. For example, if a business person were to attempt to acquire trade secrets by offering money or some inducement to a competitor's employee, the competitor would have a right of action for the loss suffered against both the employee and the firm or person who offered the inducement. The remedies in these cases are usually money damages against the employee for **breach of confidence** (along with the right to dismiss the employee for the breach) and an injunction against the other business to prevent it from using the improperly acquired trade secret.

In a broader context, there are some signs that the courts are attempting to enforce a form of corporate or commercial morality by applying the confidentiality rules to corporate dealings. For example, in one case where two companies were exploring the possibility of a joint venture to develop a mining property, one of the participants revealed information of a confidential nature about an adjacent property purchase it was considering. The second company then used the information for its own benefit after the discussions ceased, and purchased the adjacent property. In the litigation that followed, the court held that the use of the confidential information constituted a breach of confidentiality, and ordered the company to transfer the property to the party who had discussed its own purchase of it in confidence.[22]

Agreements in restraint of trade, such as combinations or conspiracies to eliminate competition, to fix prices, to restrict the output of goods in order to enhance the price of the goods or services to the public, or to prevent the entry of others into the market are treated as "business crimes" under the Competition Act, and, if proven, are subject to penalty. As with criminal law, in these cases the Crown enforces the law, rather than the injured party, because these activities are treated as contrary to the public interest generally. The Competition Act, and the various offences that fall under it, are examined at some length in Chapter 23.

If one business firm induces another to break or sever a business relationship, it may have committed an actionable tort. For example, if a firm induces a manufacturer to sever its contract to supply a competitor, on the threat of ceasing to

---

22. *Lac Minerals Ltd. v. International Corona Resources Ltd.,* [1989] 2 S.C.R. 574.

deal with the manufacturer itself, the action would constitute an attempt to inter-fere with the business contract between the manufacturer and the competitor. The competitor could take action against the firm for its interference. This type of interference, if proven, would also be in violation of the Competition Act, which establishes the activity as a punishable offence.

Two final torts that fall within the realm of business activity are the tort of **deceit** (arising from fraudulent misrepresentation) and the tort, **fraudulent con-version of goods.** Deceit as a tort may arise where one person induces another to enter into a contract by way of false statements. To constitute fraudulent misrep-resentation, the statements made must be of a material nature, and must be made with the intention of deceiving the other party. In addition, the plaintiff must have relied on the misrepresentation. The statements themselves must be known to be false or made recklessly, without caring as to their truth or falsity, and must be relied upon by the other party. If proven, fraudulent misrepresentation consti-tutes the tort of deceit, and would permit the injured party to rescind the contract made as a result of misrepresentation (provided that the party does so promptly on discovery of the fraud). For the tort of deceit, the injured party would also be entitled to damages for any loss suffered, and perhaps to punitive damages as well.

Fraudulent conversion of goods is also a tort, and usually arises where the person has obtained goods under false pretenses. It differs from the theft of goods (which is the taking of goods without the owner's consent) in the sense that the goods are voluntarily delivered by the owner to the person who obtains them through the fraud. For example, a person may obtain goods on credit by posing as the agent or employee of a well-known customer of the seller, or by the presenta-tion of a cheque as payment for the goods, where the cheque is drawn on a non-existent bank account. Fraudulent conversion of goods is also a criminal offence.

Some provincial governments, in response to business and consumer groups, have introduced consumer protection legislation meant to control a number of "unfair" business practices that sometimes take advantage of consumer ignorance or inexperience. For example, the provinces of Saskatchewan and Ontario have established by statute a list of business practices recognized as "unfair practices." Any business engaging in them would be subject to penalty. The injured customer would also be free to rescind any agreement made as a result of the unfair prac-tice. Many of the unfair practices listed also relate to torts (such as fraudulent misrepresentation), but some, such as contracts imposing onerous payment terms on the buyer, become "actionable" by way of the complaint procedure set out in the statute. Although these laws are concerned with consumer protection, they are also designed to protect honest and ethical business persons from unfair competi-tion by the few firms that take advantage of consumer inexperience or ignorance. Consumer protection legislation is examined in greater detail in Chapter 22.

Many business torts also may be considered business crimes, and are subject to prosecution under the Criminal Code. These offences include fraudulent prop-erty transfers, and fraud itself, obtaining goods under false pretenses, importing prohibited articles, falsifying books and records, theft, extortion, charging crimi-nal rates of interest (over 60 percent), and theft. Ethical business persons do not engage in these criminal activities in the conduct of their business. Charges against business persons under these provisions of the Criminal Code, while not uncommon, are relatively rare, given the large amount of business activity that takes place in Canada.

SUMMARY

Tort law is concerned with the injury that one person causes to another, or to his or her property. As a result, tort law is not limited to a specific type of injury or activity. Tort law includes the intentional injury to another in the form of assault and battery, the intentional restraint of a person in the form of false imprisonment, and injury to a person's reputation in the form of libel and slander.

Injury to a person's reputation is called defamation, and may take the form of slander (verbal defamatory statements) or libel (published statements of a defamatory nature). Both are torts, but libel is the more serious of the two due to the permanency of its nature.

Trespass to land is a form of intentional injury involving either the unlawful entrance upon the land of another or willful damage to the land in some fashion (such as tunnelling under it). Trespass may also include the willful damage to goods where the act is done deliberately. If the goods are simply retained and the owner is denied possession, the tort is conversion. Any denial of the true owner's title, or any dealing with the goods without colour of right that would deny the true owner possession also constitutes conversion.

Business torts, which involve unfair practices or statements by unethical business persons, are generally actionable at law, but many are now subject to special statutes designed to deal specifically with the improper acts.

DISCUSSION QUESTIONS

1. Distinguish between the civil and criminal aspects of intentional torts such as assault and battery or false imprisonment.
2. How does an "assault" differ from a "battery"? Must both have a violent element?
3. Under what circumstances might a person accused of assault and battery raise self-defence as justification?
4. Explain the circumstances under which the tort of false imprisonment might arise.
5. Distinguish between slander and libel. Why is libel generally considered to be more serious in the eyes of the law?
6. Define qualified and absolute privilege, and explain the circumstances where each might be claimed.
7. How does the tort "trespass to land" arise? Must damage occur for the tort to be actionable?
8. Explain the difference between conversion and theft of goods.
9. Explain "slander of title." How does this differ from ordinary tort law related to defamation?
10. Explain the rationale behind the law that condemns as a tort any third-party interference with the performance of contracts made between other persons.
11. Define: passing-off, plagiarism, slander of goods.
12. Give an example of "involuntary entry on the lands of another."
13. Does false imprisonment always have a criminal aspect to it? Explain.
14. To what extent, if any, does libel differ from the publication of a slanderous statement made by a person other than the publisher?

MINI-CASE PROBLEMS

1. A, a lawyer, who was also a professional boxer, was travelling by train from Winnipeg to Regina. He was sitting next to a woman, who, during the course of a conversation, said: "Professional boxers should be charged with assault and battery each time they engage in a prize fight." As a lawyer, how should he respond to her statement?

2. The house in which X resided was located on a busy street, where, from time to time, vandals had broken into his garage and stolen tools and equipment he had stored there. One evening, just at dusk, he saw someone enter his garage. He quickly rushed out to the garage, closed the door, locked it, then called the police. When the police arrived, X discovered that he had locked the municipal building inspector in the garage. Discuss the legal position of X and the building inspector.

JUDICIAL DECISIONS

Assault — Self-defence Justification

Bruce v. Dyer, [1966] 2 O.R. 705.

The defendant attempted to pass the plaintiff's car on the highway on a number of occasions, but on each attempt, the plaintiff increased his vehicle's speed to prevent the defendant from re-entering the traffic lane.

After the defendant had followed the plaintiff for some 16 km, the plaintiff stopped his car on the paved portion of the highway, blocking the defendant's passage. The plaintiff then got out of his car and, gesturing with his fist, walked back to the defendant's car. The defendant got out of his car, and when the parties met, the defendant struck the plaintiff on the point of his chin, causing a serious fracture to his diseased jaw. The plaintiff brought an action against the defendant for damages for assault.

FERGUSON, J.:

The question for decision, therefore, is whether Dr. Dyer is liable in damages for the assault suffered by the plaintiff.

The law concerning assault goes back to earliest times. The striking of a person against his will has been, broadly speaking, always regarded as an assault. It has been defined in the 8th American Edition of *Russell on Crime* as "An attempt or offer with force and violence to do a corporal hurt to another". So an attempted assault is itself an assault; so an attempt to strike another is an assault even though no contact has been made.

Usually, when there is no actual intention to use violence there can be no assault. When there is no power to use violence to the knowledge of the plaintiff there can be no assault. There need not be in fact any actual intention or power to use violence, for it is enough if the plaintiff on reasonable grounds believes that he is in danger.

When the plaintiff emerged from his vehicle waving his fist, I think the defendant had reasonable grounds for believing that he was about to be attacked and that it was necessary for him to take some action to ward it off.

In *Salmond on Torts,* 8th ed., p. 373, the following passage appears based on *R. v. St. George* (1840), 9 Car. & P. 483, 173 E.R. 921:

"There need be no actual intention or power to use violence, for it is enough if the plaintiff on reasonable grounds believes that he is in danger of it."

More modern cases point out that, even if it later appears that no violence was intended, it is sufficient if the defendant or a reasonable man think that it is intended.

Bruce had not only emerged from his vehicle shaking his fist, in addition he blocked the defendant's passage on the road. In my opinion, that blocking action on his part was an assault ....

If the plaintiff in the case at bar had left his auto in some place where subsequently it had blocked the defendant's way, I have no doubt that the proper remedy would be an action on the case, but when, as here, he drove his car to a position on the roadway to block the defendant's vehicle, he took active steps to block the defendant and so committed an assault upon him. The defendant was then justified in defending himself from the assault thus imposed upon him: *Re Lewis* (1874), 6 P.R. (Ont.) 236, where Gwynne, J., illustrates when the action is one for assault or on the case. When a person is assaulted he may do more than ward off a blow, he may strike back: *R. v. Morse* (1910), 4 Cr. App. R. 50.

The right to strike back in self-defence proceeds from necessity. A person assaulted has a right to hit back in defence of himself, in defence of his property or in defence of his way. He has, of course, no right to use excessive force and so cannot strike back in defence of his way if there is a way around. Here, however, the evidence is that the traffic from the rear was such that it would have been a highly dangerous manoeuvre for the defendant to emerge into it, and the *Highway Traffic Act,* at all events, prohibits proceeding off the pavement and on to the shoulder for the purpose of passing. The defendant was effectively blocked for the time being at least.

The law requires that the violence of defence be not disproportionate to the severity of the assault. It is, of course, a fact that severe damage was done to the plaintiff. In my opinion, the plea of self-defence is still valid. The defendant struck one blow only. The law does not require him to measure with nicety the degree of force necessary to ward off the attack even where he inflicts serious injury. This is not a case of "beating up". The defendant was highly provoked by the plaintiff's conduct which was quite unjustified in my view. The plaintiff knew the condition of his own physical state and one would have thought that he would have, for that reason alone, refrained from such highly provocative conduct. He invited the treatment he received.

Tort — Defamation — Test for "Fair Comment" Defence

Vander Zalm v. Times Publishers, Bierman et al. (1980), 18 B.C.L.R. 210.
The plaintiff, a minister in the British Columbia government, was depicted in a newspaper cartoon removing the wings from flies. The plaintiff brought an action against the newspaper alleging that the cartoon was defamatory as it depicted him as a cruel person. The newspaper, in its defence, argued that it was making "fair" comment about the minister. At the trial of the case, the plaintiff was successful. The newspaper then appealed. The appeal court commented on the defence of "fair comment" in the following manner:

NEMETZ C. J. B.C.:

The three elements of the defence of fair comment are well known. First, the matter must be recognizable to the ordinary reasonable man as a comment upon true facts, and not as a bare statement of fact. Secondly, the matter commented upon must be one of the public interest. There must, in short, be a public nexus between the matter and the person caricatured. In a case such as this, the cartoonist may not intrude upon the private life of a public man, no matter how interesting such an intrusion may be to the public, nor may he expose a private person to unsought publicity. Finally, as explained by Diplock J. (as he then was) in *Silken v. Beaverbrook Newspapers,* [1958] 1 W.L.R. 743 at 747, [1958] 2 All E.R. 516, and by the Supreme Court of Canada in *Cherneskey v. Armadale Publishers Ltd.,* [1979] 1 S.C.R. 1067, 24 N.R. 271, the comment must be "fair" in that it must, to quote Martland J. in *Cherneskey* at p. 1073, "represent an honest expression of the real view of the person making the comment". At the trial of this action, the availability of the defence turned on this last element.

[The judge then went on to conclude that the cartoon represented comment on a matter of considerable public interest by a minister of the government in his public capacity and not in his personal capacity.]

The next question that arises is whether the comment was "fair". In charging the jury in the *Silken* case, supra, Lord Diplock explained the test in this way [p. 747]:

"I have been referring, and counsel in their speeches to you have been referring, to fair comment, because that is the technical name which is given to this defence, or, as I should prefer to say, which is given to the right of every citizen to comment on matters of public interest. But the expression 'fair comment' is a little misleading. It may give you the impression that you, the jury, have to decide whether you agree with the comment, whether you think it is fair. If that were the question you had to decide, you realize that the limits of freedom which the law allows would be greatly curtailed. People are entitled to hold and to express freely on matters of public interest strong views, views which some of you, or indeed all of you, may think are exaggerated, obstinate or prejudiced, provided — and this is the important thing — that they are views which they honestly hold. The basis of our public life is that the crank, the enthusiast, may say what he honestly thinks just as much as the reasonable man or woman who sits on a jury, and it would be a sad day for freedom of speech in this country if a jury were to apply the test of whether it agrees with the comment instead of applying the true test: was this an opinion, however exaggerated, obstinate or prejudiced, which was honestly held by the writer?"

The question, then, is this: Did the comment made by the cartoon represent the honest opinion of Mr. Bierman? At the end of the cartoonist's examination-in-chief, the following exchange took place:

"MR. FARQUAHAR: Now, you have testified as to what you intended the cartoon to say about the Minister of Human Resources, did that represent your honest opinion of the Minister of Human Resources at the time you prepared the cartoon?"

"MR. BIERMAN: Yes, sir."

Now, as I have already stated, what the cartoonist intended the cartoon to say, as quoted above, coincides, in my opinion, with what the ordinary and reasonable person would take the cartoon as saying; namely, it is a comment of the nature Mr. Bierman described, concerned solely with the plaintiff in his ministerial capacity. I conclude from the whole of Mr. Bierman's testimony that that indeed represents an honest expression of his real view. No question arises as to credibility since it is obvious that the learned trial judge did not disbelieve the cartoonist, and no issue arose in this regard. Having these factors before us, is the defence of fair comment available? I think it is. As, in the circumstances of this case, it is my respectful view that the cartoon represents fair comment on a matter of public interest, I would, therefore, allow the appeal and dismiss the action.

CASE PROBLEMS FOR DISCUSSION

Case 1

At his wife's request, Smith purchased a picnic basket at a hardware store in a nearby shopping mall. The basket was not wrapped by the sales clerk at the conclusion of the transaction. Smith carried his new basket with him to a supermarket located in the same mall, where he intended to purchase a quantity of grapefruit.

At the produce counter he could not find grapefruit on display, and inquired of the clerk if the store had any in stock. The clerk offered to check in the storage room for him. While he waited for the clerk to return, Smith picked a quantity of grapes from a display case and ate them. A few moments later, the clerk returned to inform him that all the fruit had been sold.

As Smith left the store, he was seized by the store owner and requested to return to the owner's office. Smith obediently followed him back inside the store. Once inside the owner's office, the owner accused Smith of theft; then, without further explanation, telephoned the police.

When the police officer arrived, the store owner informed him that Smith was a thief and that he had apprehended him just outside the store. Smith admitted stealing the grapes, then to his surprise, he discovered that the owner had apprehended him because he (the owner) thought Smith had stolen the picnic basket.

Both the supermarket and the hardware store sold similar baskets; even on close examination, the products appeared identical. With the aid of the sales clerk at the hardware store, Smith was able to convince the police officer that he had purchased the basket which he had in his possession.

He later decided to bring an action against the owner of the supermarket for false imprisonment.

Discuss the issues raised in this case and determine the respective arguments of the parties. Render a decision.

Case 2

The plaintiff, a nurse, was injured in a motor vehicle accident and was taken to a local hospital. She was examined by the defendant, who could find no physical injury other than a few minor bruises. She was discharged from the hospital the next day when she admitted that she "felt fine." Within 24 hours after her release, she returned to the hospital. She complained to the defendant of painful headaches and remained in hospital for a month. During her second stay in hospital she was examined by three neurosurgeons who could find nothing wrong with her.

On her release from the hospital, she instituted legal proceedings against the parties responsible for her automobile accident, and her solicitor requested a medical opinion from the defendant to support her case.

In response to the solicitor's request, the defendant wrote two letters that were uncomplimentary and suggested that the plaintiff had not suffered any real physical injury. In addition, the defendant had indicated on the plaintiff's medical records that the plaintiff was suffering from hypochondriasis.

After her discovery of the uncomplimentary letters and medical reports, the plaintiff brought an action against the defendant for libel.

Examine the arguments that might be raised in this case and identify the defences (if any) to the plaintiff's claim. Render a decision.

Case 3

Gretel was shopping at a large shopping centre and, while walking through the crowded mall area, she saw a youth pushing his way through the crowd in what appeared to be an attempt to escape from a man in a dark blue uniform, who was following him.

At that time, Gretel was standing near the exit from the building. When the youth finally broke through the crowd and attempted to leave the building, she stepped in front of him to block his path. The youth collided with Gretel, and the two parties fell to the floor.

Gretel seized the fallen youth by the arm as he attempted to stand up and tried to pull him back down to the floor. The youth then struck Gretel a blow on the side of the head with his fist, causing her to lose consciousness.

The youth, as it turned out, was hurrying through the crowd in an attempt to catch a bus, and the older man, who was following him through the crowd, was his father. The youth's father was employed as a security guard at the shopping centre and was leaving work for the day.

Explain this incident in terms of tort law and tort liability.

Case 4

Wilson stored his power lawn-mower in his neighbour's garage. In return for the privilege, he allowed his neighbour to use the lawn-mower to cut his own lawn.

Wilson's lawn was relatively small; nevertheless, he did not enjoy cutting grass or using his lawn-mower. He complained bitterly each time he used the machine and, on one occasion, told his neighbour that, if he sold his house, he would buy a condominium so that he would not be required to mow a lawn again. On another occasion, he indicated to another friend that, if he should buy a condominium, he would "take great pleasure in giving his lawn-mower to his neighbour."

After several years, Wilson's employment required him to take up residence in another city. At the time of his departure, he advised his neighbour that he had leased an apartment in the other city. He made no mention of his lawn-mower.

The neighbour continued to use Wilson's lawn-mower for the balance of the summer and, when Wilson did not return to retrieve his lawn-mower by late autumn, the neighbour used the machine as a trade-in on a snow-blower for his own use.

The next spring, Wilson returned for his power lawn-mower. When he discovered that his neighbour had disposed of it, he brought an action against him for its value.

Discuss the rights of the parties in this case. Explain the nature of the action that Wilson could bring in the court and render a decision.

Case 5

A university operated a tavern on its premises for the benefit of its students. One student, who attended the tavern with some friends for the purpose of celebrating the end of the Fall semester, became quite drunk. The tavern bartenders realized that the student was quite drunk around 11:00 p.m. and refused to serve him any additional alcoholic beverages. They also requested him to leave the premises. The student, however, remained and drank two additional beers that were purchased for him by his friends.

Some time later, around 12:00 a.m., one of the bartenders noticed the student drinking and instructed the tavern bouncer to ask the student to leave. The bouncer did so, but the student refused, and the bouncer took the student by the arm and escorted him to the door. Along the hallway to the door the student was abusive and resisted leaving, but the bouncer managed to eject him from the building.

A few minutes later, the student returned to the tavern and slipped by the door man for the alleged purpose of obtaining an explanation as to why he had been ejected. About eight feet from the door, he was apprehended by the bouncer and once again expelled from the tavern, but not without some resistance in the form of pushing and shoving and abusive language on the part of the student. In the course of ejection, the student fell against the door and smashed a glass pane in the door, which caused severe lacerations to his hand. The injury to the student's hand required medical treatment and took several months to heal.

The student brought an action against the university and the bouncer, claiming damages and claiming as well that the injury he received caused him to fail his mathematics course in the semester that followed the accident.

Discuss the issues raised in this case and the various arguments that each party might raise. Render a decision.

Case 6

The Silver Sports and Recreation League was a mixed hockey league which operated under Canadian Amateur Hockey Association rules. Under the rules, no bodily contact was permitted by the players.

During the course of a semi-final play-off game between the Silver Lake Lions and the Calabogie Cats in the Silver Lake Municipal Arena, April, the star centre of the Silver Lake Lions was attempting to regain control of the puck in her own end of the ice when Bertha, a defence player of the Calabogie Cats, collided with her from behind, driving her into the boards. As a result of the collision, April suffered a serious injury to her neck and spine.

Immediately after the collision, the referee, who had witnessed the collision, stopped the game and awarded a "match penalty" against Bertha on the basis that she had deliberately attempted to injure April. According to the referee, Bertha and April were both skating towards the puck, with April ahead of Bertha. Upon reaching the puck, April stopped abruptly. Bertha, in the process of stopping, raised her hockey stick to a horizontal position in front of her body just before she collided with April from behind. The blow from the horizontally held hockey stick prevented Bertha's body from striking April, but the impact of the hockey stick propelled April into the boards.

The linesman, who also witnessed the incident, reported that from his point of view, Bertha had pushed April from behind either to move her away from the puck or to avoid a more violent collision. The impact, however, in his opinion only caused April to lose her balance and it was her loss of balance that resulted in her fall against the boards.

April subsequently instituted legal proceedings against Bertha for her injuries.

Discuss the various legal arguments that each party might raise, and render, with reasons, a decision.

CHAPTER

5

Unintentional Interference with the Person or Property

THE CONCEPT
OF TORT
LIABILITY

Early Concepts: Strict Liability

The basic premise upon which tort liability is founded is that individuals living in a civilized society will not (and should not) intentionally cause injury to one another or their property. This particular assumption is based upon the public policy that every person is entitled to protection of their person; if anyone should commit a deliberate act injuring them or their property, then the injured party should be entitled to redress from the person causing the injury. The torts of assault and battery and false imprisonment are notable examples of deliberate acts that injure others, and ones that the courts will recognize as actionable torts.

Initially, under tort theory, only deliberate direct injury was open to action, and the application of the law was equally direct in its application. If a person intentionally caused injury to another, compensation according to a fixed amount (based upon a prescribed schedule) was payable.[1] No consideration was given to the actual loss suffered by the plaintiff; the only concern of the court was that a direct injury had occurred. In effect, the early courts imposed **strict liability** in dealing with deliberate acts causing injury to others — no inquiry was made into the circumstances surrounding the event.

---

1. For example, during the late sixth and early seventh centuries, a detailed Tariff of Compensations was established which fixed the amount to be paid for wrongs or injuries. If an ear was lacerated, the price of the injury was 6 shillings. See Attenborough, F.L., *The Laws of The Earliest English Kings* (Cambridge, England: University Press, 1922), pp. 2–17.

Over time, the courts gradually moved away from the strict liability approach to torts and considered other factors as well. Some torts, however, have remained subject to strict liability. Today, any person who maintains a potentially dangerous animal or thing on his or her land may be held strictly liable for any damage it may occasion should it escape. This may be the case even where the landowner takes every precaution to protect others from injury, and where the escape of the dangerous animal or chattel is not due to any act or omission on the landowner's part. For example, in order to have a supply of water for the purpose of operating his mill, Rylands built a water reservoir on land that he occupied. He employed engineers and contractors to construct the reservoir and, when the reservoir was completed, began filling it with water. Unknown to Rylands, the land under the reservoir was a part of a coal mine that was being worked by Fletcher. Water from the reservoir found its way into the old shafts and passageways in large quantities and flooded areas of the mine some distance away where Fletcher was working. Fletcher sued Rylands for damages. The court held in this case that Rylands was liable for the damage caused to Fletcher even though Rylands did nothing to deliberately harm Fletcher. The court, in reaching its decision, stated that anyone who accumulates anything non-natural on his land or uses it in a non-natural way which might injure his neighbour does so at his peril, and if it should escape through no fault of his own, he should nevertheless be liable.[2]

This form of liability, which is neither based upon intent nor negligence, remains largely because the conduct, while not wrongful or improper, is so inherently dangerous or so unusual that any risk associated with it should be borne entirely by the individual wishing to proceed with it upon his or her property. The same principle is sometimes applied where one person controls the activity of another to such an extent that the act of one may be attributed to the other. In these cases, the courts carry the liability for the tort back to the person who (in a sense) initiated the act, and in this manner impose liability on a person not directly associated with the tortious act.

At common law, an employer is usually considered to be **vicariously liable** for the torts of the firm's employees, provided that the torts are committed by the employees in the course of the employer's business. The reasoning of the courts on this rule is that employees may not have the financial means to compensate for the damage they might cause, but their employers probably would, if only through insurance coverage. Additionally, because the employee's tort is committed during the course of the employer's business, the employer should have some responsibility for the loss as he or she is presumably directing or controlling the employee at the time. Similarly, all partners in a partnership are vicariously liable for the torts committed by a partner in the conduct of partnership business. In a similar vein, provincial statute law has imposed a vicarious liability on the owner of a motor car, where the driver of the vehicle is negligent in its operation.

The imposition of liability on persons not directly associated with a tort reflects a departure from the tort theory that the individual who injures another should bear the loss. It also reflects a move from the former laissez-faire policy to a new social policy that recognizes that some satisfactory method must exist for

---

2. See: *Rylands v. Fletcher* (1868), L.R. 3 H.L. 330.

the distribution of what is essentially a social loss among those best able to bear it. The modern concept of insurance is, for the most part, responsible for this shift in tort liability and represents a further extension of this philosophy. Similar examples may be found in other rights and statutes that deal with specific areas of tort, such as the various Workers' Compensation Acts. These acts essentially spread the risk of loss to workers injured in employment-related accidents to all employers in an effort to reduce the burden that would otherwise fall on the individual or the injured worker's employer.

Unintentional Torts and the Duty Not to Injure

A second important tort liability concept gradually developed to cover injuries suffered by persons who were not intentionally injured, but were injured nevertheless by the actions or inaction of others. Initially, the liability for unintentional injury was established for persons with specific trades, callings, or professions where their careless conduct or performance of their professed skills injured another. The early cases were generally decided on the basis that the skilled person had failed to carry out the skilled work in accordance with the level of skill that the person professed to possess. While these cases imposed a duty of care on persons with particular skills, the actions were not in negligence as such since the modern concept of duty and negligence did not emerge until the nineteenth century in tort law. What they did do, however, was to eventually shift the preoccupation of the courts from the defendant's deliberate action to both inaction and action where the intention to injure was not present. This particular shift in tort law broadened the scope for recovery to include not only deliberate acts which injure, but all acts where the cause of injury could be directly attributed to the defendant.

The enlarged area of liability was essentially a response by the courts to the changing needs of society. The early torts were related to a more violent era, where the individual's concern was for the safety of his or her person and redress for violent attacks by others. However, as society became more civilized, the need for protection from violence lessened. The more sophisticated human endeavours associated with the advances in civilization, nevertheless, brought with them new forms of injury requiring some form of control. In the light of these changes, the courts took their first steps to enlarge tort liability. This move on the part of the courts introduced a number of new elements as well. The plaintiff, while no longer limited to cases of deliberate injury, was obliged to establish a duty on the part of the defendant not to injure, and also to satisfy the courts that the proximate cause of the injury was directly related to the **breach of duty** on the part of the defendant.

Proximate Cause and the Duty of Care

By the early eighteenth century, the courts considered the conduct of the defendant in cases where the injury to the plaintiff was unintentional. If the evidence indicated that the defendant's actions had shown a careless disregard for others, then the defendant's conduct would be considered culpable. The plaintiff, however, was obliged to establish that the defendant's careless acts were the proximate cause of the injury. The difficulty with both of these elements of tort is obviously the question of degree. Clearly, the defendant should not be expected to answer for every careless act, not should the cause of the injury, no matter how remote, be traceable to the defendant, regardless of intervening factors. **Proximate cause** and conduct were difficult problems for the court because both often represented difficult value judgements.

Proximate cause is perhaps the most difficult element to determine since it is very much a matter that must be decided on a case-by-case basis. Essentially, the act that the plaintiff alleges is the cause of the injury must be related in a relatively direct way to the act of the defendant without intervening events. Any break in the chain of events running from the defendant's act to the plaintiff's injury will normally defeat the plaintiff's claim that the proximate cause was the defendant's act. For example, where a person slips on a neighbour's icy sidewalk and breaks a leg, the neighbour may be liable for injury if the neighbour's failure to remove the ice was the proximate cause of the injury. However, if the injured person is being transported to a hospital to have the broken leg treated, and along the way is severely injured when the ambulance is involved in an accident with another vehicle, the neighbour's negligence cannot be said to be the proximate cause of the injuries suffered as a result of the motor vehicle accident. The intervening event of driving the person to the hospital is sufficient to break the direct link between the neighbour's action (or inaction) and the traffic accident.

The concept of a **duty of care** on the part of the defendant is no less easy a matter to determine. As an element of tort liability, the duty not to injure must be more than simply a moral obligation — it must be a duty that the person causing the injury owes to the injured party. This is sometimes referred to as the **right-duty relationship** in tort law. Generally, under this relationship, the duty not to injure must be owed to the party who suffers the injury; in turn, the injured party must have a legal right that has been violated by the act or omission of the other. For example, a taxi driver owes a duty of care to his passengers, and the passengers have a right to safe transportation to their destination. A breach of the duty of care by the driver that results in an injury to the passengers would violate their right to safe transportation and be actionable as a tort.

Much of the law relating to negligence is based upon the concept of duty of care; to this end the courts have extended their investigation of the circumstances surrounding a tort by attempting to determine the foreseeability of the defendant's actions.

The Concept of Foreseeability: The Reasonable Person

Foreseeability as an element of tort liability was a particularly difficult concept for the courts to apply due to its nebulous nature. Foreseeability was essentially a standard that had to be determined before damages for an unintentional act could flow, yet it had to be flexible enough to be applicable to a wide variety of actions. The courts eventually seized upon a mythical person, the **reasonable person**, as a standard, and measured the actions of the negligent person against what might be the actions of the reasonable person in the same situation. The reasonable person was presumed to possess normal intelligence and would exercise reasonable care in his or her actions toward others. Because the assumption of some risk is a part of daily living, the reasonable person was expected to assume such risks, but was considered to do so only after taking reasonable precautions to avoid injuring others. This became the standard that determined the foreseeability aspect of negligence. Tort liability was (and still is) determined by asking the question: Would a reasonable person in similar circumstances have foreseen the injury to the plaintiff as a consequence of his or her actions? An affirmative answer would place the defendant at fault; a negative answer would render the defendant blameless.

It should be noted children may be held liable for the torts they commit, provided they have the degree of maturity to appreciate the nature of their acts. Obviously a very small child of tender years would not be held liable in tort, but children in their early teens, depending upon the extent of their maturity and level of understanding may very well be held responsible for their actions.

The concept of the reasonable person permitted the courts to deal with a great many torts where the unintentional acts of a person caused injury to others. It also permitted the courts to establish broad guidelines for the standard of care that a person could reasonably expect to meet in the conduct of activities that had a potential for injury to others. Nevertheless, this tort concept is by no means easy to apply, as parties in tort actions frequently possess widely divergent views on whether a reasonable person would or would not foresee the result of his or her actions, given the circumstances surrounding the case. The particular advantage of the tort concept lies in the flexibility that it gives the courts in responding to social change. In spite of the growing complexity of modern civilization, the test remains relevant as the standard can vary with the passage of time; the reasonable person acquires the degree of sophistication dictated by society itself.

Negligence

The difference between intentional and unintentional interference with the person is essentially a matter that relates to the state of mind of the person causing the interference. Intentional interference generally involves a conscious mental decision to act in a violent manner towards another; it may or may not involve a verbal threat of violence (or assault) before the actual battery takes place. In most cases, unintentional interference with the person is simply an omission on the part of the party causing the injury, or a thoughtless act that injures another. Persons are found liable in negligence more often for their acts than for their omissions, and rarely does a person have a legal duty to act positively. Rather, the duty is usually defined as a duty to refrain from acting negatively. In either case, there is no *mens rea* or deliberate decision on the part of the person causing the interference to injure the other party. Unintentional interference with the person generally falls under the broad heading of negligence, but, while this distinction between negligence and intentional interference is settled today (at least with respect to assault and negligence), it was not always so. As late as 1951 the courts were still attempting to distinguish the two forms of interference.[3]

The number of ways that a person may unintentionally interfere with the person or the property of another are myriad. The negligent operation of a motor vehicle that causes injury or death to a pedestrian, the careless manufacture of a

---

3. *Eisener v. Maxwell*, [1951] 3 D.L.R. 345.

food product that poisons or injures a consumer, or the careless performance of an operation by a surgeon that disables or kills the patient are examples that come to mind. All of these cases have something in common. In each case, one party owes a duty of care not to injure the other in the performance of the act in question. Where a breach of the duty occurs, tort liability (assuming no intervening or extenuating circumstances exist) may follow. In the determination of liability, the essential ingredients are:

(1) the defendant owes the plaintiff a duty not to injure;
(2) the defendant's actions constitute a breach of that duty;
(3) the plaintiff suffers some injury as a direct result of the defendant's actions.

The duty of care varies, depending upon the nature of the activity. The particular duty of care may vary from slight (in the case of the occupier's duty toward a trespasser) to very high (in the case of a person handling explosives). In each case, the duty owed is a matter to be determined by the courts, and is generally subject to the test of foreseeability, and the standard of the "reasonable person." Whether the defendant has acted in breach of the duty (once the duty and the breach thereof have been established) is a question of fact to be determined from the evidence submitted in the case. Because the principles that apply in the determination of the standard for a duty of care apply to both interference with persons and their property, the more important standards for the specific activities may be discussed together, without differentiation between persons or property.

Res Ipsa Loquitur

One of the particular difficulties that sometimes faces a person injured by the negligence of another is proving the negligent act. In some cases, the injured party is unaware of how the injury occurred, or what the act of the other party was that resulted in the loss. For example, a passenger on an aircraft has a right to expect a safe flight from the departure point to the passenger's destination. However, if the aircraft should crash on landing and the passenger is seriously injured, can the passenger, as a plaintiff, reasonably be expected to satisfy the courts that certain specific acts of the pilot constituted negligence? Only the pilot or the flight crew would know the circumstances that led to the crash causing injury to the passengers. This dilemma of the injured plaintiff first came before the courts in an English case[4] in the mid-nineteenth century, when a person standing in the street was injured by a barrel of flour that fell from the upper level of a shopkeeper's building. The person sued the shopkeeper for his injuries, but could do nothing more than relate the facts of the case available to him and plead *res ipsa loquitur* (the thing speaks for itself). The court accepted this line of reasoning and ruled that since the plaintiff had established that he was injured by the defendant's barrel of flour, it was now up to the defendant to satisfy the court that he was not negligent in the handling of the barrel.

---

4. *Byrne v. Boadle* (1863), 2 H. & C. 722, 159 E.R. 299.

Since this decision, the rule or principle of *res ipsa loquitur* has been applied in a wide variety of negligence cases where the plaintiff has been unable to ascertain the particular circumstances surrounding the injury inflicted. For the rule to apply, however, the cause of the injury must be something that is exclusively in the care and control of the defendant at the time of the injury. Also the circumstances surrounding the accident must be unusual in the sense that they constitute events that do not ordinarily occur if proper care has been taken by the defendant. If the plaintiff is in a position to satisfy the courts on these two points, the burden of proof then shifts to the defendant to show no negligence; otherwise the defendant will be held liable for his or her apparent actions.

Contributory Negligence and *Volenti Non Fit Injuria*

A further development in tort law relating to negligence occurred when the courts expanded their examination of the circumstances surrounding a tort to include the actions of the injured party. One of the earliest defences raised by a defendant in a negligence case was the argument that the injuries suffered by the plaintiff were due in some measure to the plaintiff's own carelessness, or to the plaintiff's voluntary assumption of the risk of injury by undertaking the activity resulting in the injury. Initially, both of these defences, if accepted by the courts, would allow the defendant to escape liability even in those cases where the defendant was, for the most part, responsible for the loss or injury suffered by the plaintiff.

The voluntary assumption of risk (***volenti non fit injuria***) has remained as a valid defence where a defendant is able to satisfy the court that the plaintiff voluntarily assumed the risk of the injury that occurred. To some extent this was a reflection of the early laissez-faire individualism prevalent in the nineteenth century that was based upon the premise that the law should not protect those who were capable of protecting their own interests, and in particular, should not protect those who were prepared to assume the risk of loss or injury on a voluntary basis.

Contributory negligence, on the other hand, underwent a number of largely unsuccessful efforts by the courts to relieve the hardship in cases where the plaintiff was responsible in only a very minor way for the injury or loss sustained. Eventually, it became clear that the problem could only be solved by legislation. In 1924, the Province of Ontario passed legislation[5] that required the courts to determine the degree of responsibility of each of the parties in a tort action, and to apportion the damages accordingly. The rest of the provinces soon followed suit with similar legislation to provide a general framework for the apportionment of loss in contributory negligence cases in all jurisdictions. These statutes say that where harm is contributed by two or more parties, loss is apportioned according to the degree of fault.

Negligence law remains a major area of tort law, notwithstanding its relatively short history, and is an important part of the law of torts dealing with unintentional interference with individuals and property. There are, however, a number of other principles and doctrines which relate to the law of torts. The development of these particular principles and concepts and the defences that may apply to

---

5. Contributory Negligence Act, 1924, 1924 (Ont.), c. 32.

them may be best illustrated by an examination of the specific areas of tort law to which they generally apply.

Duty of Care of Professionals

In general, the person who professes to be a professional must maintain the standard of proficiency or exercise the degree of care in the conduct of his or her duties that the profession normally imposes on its members. This does not mean that the professional person will not make mistakes, nor does it mean that the results will always be perfect. In many professions, the work of the professional requires much skill and judgement, often more closely resembling an "art" than an exact "science." Consequently, a successful malpractice suit against a member of a profession must measure the performance or duty of the particular practitioner with that prescribed by the profession in general, and must show in the evidence that the practitioner failed to meet that standard.[6] This is not always an easy thing to do. However, in many cases the professional's performance is so far below the standard set for the profession that the determination of the duty of care and the breach thereof are not difficult.[7] For example, in the course of a tonsillectomy, a surgeon used a number of sponges that did not have strings or tapes attached for easy retrieval from the child's throat. The attending nurse did not do a sponge count before and after the operation. On completion of the surgery, the anaesthetist present suggested that all of the sponges may not have been removed. The surgeon made a cursory search in the child's throat with his forceps and, when he found none, did nothing more to determine the number used. The child suffocated and died as a result of a sponge left in its throat.

At trial, the evidence submitted indicated that the surgeon had performed the operation carefully by using the proper techniques and suture. The evidence also indicated that it was not a common practice to use sponges with tapes attached, although some hospitals followed this practice. The surgeon's search at the end of the operation was also a normal practice.

The action in negligence brought against the surgeon was dismissed by the trial judge on the basis that the surgeon had followed the same practices as any other careful practitioner. On appeal, however, the court viewed the matter in a slightly different light. It concluded that the surgeon had a duty to make a thorough, rather than routine, search when a fellow professional informed him that he might not have removed all the sponges. Because he did not employ all of the safeguards available to him, his failure to do so constituted negligence.[8]

In the case of *Kangas v. Parker and Asquith,* [1976] 5 W.W.R. 25, the court was called upon to consider the standard of care imposed upon professionals. The judge in that case described the standard by reference to other common law decisions in the following manner:

> The medical man must possess and use that reasonable degree of learning and skill ordinarily possessed by practitioners in similar communities in similar cases and it is the duty of the specialist who holds himself out as possessing special skill and

---

6. *Karderas v. Clow,* [1973] 1 O.R. 730.

7. *McCormick v. Marcotte,* [1972] S.C.R. 18; 20 D.L.R. (3d) 345.

8. *Anderson v. Chasney,* [1950] 4 D.L.R. 223; affirming [1949] 4 D.L.R. 71; reversing in part, [1948] 4 D.L.R. 458.

knowledge to have and exercise the degree of skill of an average specialist in the field. Vide: *McCormick v. Marcotte*, [1972] S.C.R. 18, 20 D.L.R. (3d) 345.

In *Rann v. Twitchell* (1909), 82 Vt. 79 at 84 appears the following comment:

> He is not to be judged by the result nor is he to be held liable for an error of judgment. His negligence is to be determined by reference to the pertinent facts existing at the time of his examination and treatment, of which he knew, or in the exercise of due care, should have known. It may consist in a failure to apply the proper remedy upon a correct determination of existing physical conditions, or it may precede that and result from a failure to properly inform himself of these conditions. If the latter, then it must appear that he had a reasonable opportunity for examination and that the true physical conditions were so apparent that they could have been ascertained by the exercise of the required degree of care and skill. For, if a determination of these physical facts resolves itself into a question of judgment merely, he cannot be held liable for his error.

Lord Hewat C.J. in *Rex v. Bateman* (1925), 41 T.L.R. 557 at 559, 19 Cr. App. R. 8, clearly and succinctly stated the desired standard of care as follows:

> If a person holds himself out as possessing special skill and knowledge and he is consulted as possessing such skill and knowledge by or on behalf of a patient, he owes a duty to the patient to use due caution in undertaking the treatment. If he accepts the responsibility and undertakes the treatment and the patient submits to his direction and treatment accordingly, he owes a duty to the patient to use diligence, care, knowledge, skill and caution in administering the treatment ... The law requires a fair and reasonable standard of care and competence.

In each of these case comments to which the judge referred in his judgement, the common thread is the duty of the professional to maintain the standard of skill that the profession itself has fixed for its members. The standard generally is that of the competent and careful "reasonable person" trained to exercise the skills of the profession. Here the level of competence to be maintained is that of the average member of the profession, rather than the skill level of the most highly skilled member of the professional group.

In most cases, the duty of care of the professional is owed to the client or patient that engages the services of the professional. The relationship is usually one of contract, and the contract will normally specify the services to be performed by the professional. The professional person has an obligation to perform the services set out in the contract in accordance with the standards of the profession. Even if the contract does not specifically set out the standard, or if a lower standard is agreed, the contract normally must specifically refer to the lower standard, otherwise the standard of the profession would probably apply.

Architects in the design of buildings must consider the safety of the occupants. Similarly, engineers in the design and construction of buildings, bridges, roads, and equipment must also consider the loads, stresses, and use of the structures or equipment in the performance of their services. For example, if an engineer designs a bridge without consideration for the weight of traffic that would travel over the bridge, and the bridge collapses, the engineer may be negligent in the performance of his or her professional duty, and liable for the loss or injury that results.

A duty of care on the part of a professional may arise in other ways as well. For example, it may arise out of a **fiduciary relationship**, where a relationship of **trust** is established between the parties. The text examines this relationship in depth in later chapters, but it is sufficient to say here that where a fiduciary relationship is established, the professional has a duty to put the interests of the client before those of his or her own, and to take care that the services are performed in accordance with accepted standards for the profession. By way of illustration, if a professional accountant agrees to audit the financial records of a religious or charitable organization without charging a fee, no contract would exist, but the accountant would nevertheless have a duty to perform the audit in accordance with the standards of the profession. If the audit was performed carelessly, and the organization suffered a loss, the accountant may be liable for breach of the fiduciary duty of care arising out of the relationship between the two parties.

Professional negligence extends beyond carelessness in carrying out duties, and extends as well to statements made and information provided to clients. Lawyers, accountants, and others (such as brokers) who provide advice or information must ensure that they are not negligent in this regard as **negligent misstatements** or **negligent misrepresentation** may constitute a breach of duty of care on the part of the professional. The courts in the past were reluctant to impose this type of liability on those who provided advice or information except in certain kinds of cases such as where a fiduciary relationship existed or where the contract between the parties provided for the provision of the information. The restriction on the scope of liability was deliberately limited because the courts had no wish to impose virtually unlimited liability on professionals for words negligently expressed. However, by 1964, the scope of liability was extended significantly by the case of *Hedley Byrne & Co. Ltd. v. Heller & Partners Ltd.*[9]

In that case, an advertising agency requested its own bank to determine that a client was in sound financial condition. The bank made enquiries of the client's bank and replied in the affirmative, advising that the client's bank had issued a disclaimer of responsibility when it provided the information. The information proved to be false, and as a result, the agency suffered a financial loss. The agency then brought an action against the client's bank claiming negligence. While the bank successfully avoided liability on the basis of its disclaimer of responsibility, the court held that an action could lie for negligent misstatements or negligent misrepresentation where a plaintiff could prove that it relied upon the skill or expertise of the person or party that made the negligent statement or representation.

The courts subsequent to the *Hedley Byrne* case have delineated the limits of liability for negligent misrepresentation. In the case of *Haig v. Bamford* (1976), 72 D.L.R. (3d) 68, the Supreme Court of Canada decided that the test for liability to third parties for negligent misrepresentation by auditors would be actual knowledge of the limited class that would use or rely on the information.

Normally, a professional is only responsible in tort to the patient or client. However, in recent cases, the courts have held some professionals liable to third

---

9. [1964] A.C. 465.

parties where the professional's expertise or skill was intended to be relied upon by the third party, and the professional was aware of this fact. Accountants, in particular, have been subject to this extended tort liability. This is partly because they are generally aware that their financial statements will be relied upon by third parties, and partly because securities legislation in most jurisdictions imposes a liability on the accountant to third parties if the third party purchases securities based upon negligently prepared financial statements published in a prospectus. Liability to third parties is not unlimited, however, as the professional accountant is generally responsible only to those third parties whom the accountant can reasonably expect to rely on the information provided. Liability for negligently prepared financial information is not necessarily limited to the professional accountant third party relationship. It appears to be applicable to all persons and institutions engaged in providing financial advice.[10]

A recent case in England[11] has suggested that a three-fold test be used to determine liability for economic loss caused by negligent misrepresentation. The test would consider (1) whether the harm was foreseeable, (2) whether there was a relationship between the parties of sufficient proximity, and (3) that in terms of public policy and the circumstances it would be just and reasonable to impose the duty on the party making the statement.

Should the Canadian courts adopt this test, the effect would be a limiting of the liability for negligent misrepresentation for accountants and auditors to a more restricted group who might use or rely upon the information.

While the courts have traditionally held professional persons responsible for their acts of negligence, persons engaged in business activities where some expertise or special knowledge or skill is required may also be held responsible for losses others suffer as a result of their careless acts or omission. For example, insurance agents, even though they are agents of companies selling insurance, may be held liable for clients' losses, if when requested to do so, they fail to provide proper coverage for the contemplated loss. In one instance, a husband and wife contacted an insurance agent for coverage for the wife's business, financed by the husband. The agent negligently arranged for insurance in the husband's name only. When the wife suffered a loss she thought would be covered by the policy, she discovered that her business was not covered by the insurance. In the court action that followed, the agent was held liable for the loss the wife suffered, because he had failed in his duty to make proper arrangements for coverage of the wife's interest.[12]

Occupier's Liability

The owner or occupier of land is not subject to the ordinary rules of negligence with respect to persons entering on land or buildings for reasons that are largely historical. After the Norman Conquest of England, occupiers of land were subject

---

10. See, for example, *Hedley Byrne & Co. Ltd. v. Heller & Partners Ltd.,* [1964] A.C. 465; *Goad v. Canadian Imperial Bank of Commerce,* [1968] 1 O.R. 579 (bankers); *Haig v. Bamford,* [1974] 6 W.W.R. 236 (accountants); *Cari-Van Hotel Ltd. v. Globe Estates Ltd.,* [1974] 6 W.W.R. 707 (real estate appraisers); *Surrey Credit Union v. Willson et al.* (1990), 73 D.L.R. (4th) 207 (auditors).

11. *Caparo Industries v. Dickman,* [1990] 2 A.C. 605, 1 All E.R. 568. See also *Surrey Credit Union v. Willson* (1990), 49 B.C.L.R. (2d) 102 for a recent Canadian Case on this issue.

12. *Knowles et al. v. General Accident Assurance Co. of Canada, et al.* (1984), 49 O.R. (2d) 52.

to certain rules of land law that imposed specific duties according to the kind of person entering on the land. Today, the duty of care, in ascending order of importance, applies to: (1) trespassers, (2) licensees, (3) invitees.

The lowest or least duty of care is required for **trespassers.** The trespasser entering on the occupier's land does so without permission, and consequently, at a certain risk to his or her person. Historically, the only obligation on the part of the occupier of land has been to avoid deliberately injuring the trespasser. Recent developments in the law, however, have imposed additional obligations on the landowner. This is so, particularly where small children are concerned. Persons who install swimming pools on their property, or who construct dangerous structures on their premises in neighbourhoods where small children live, have a special duty to protect the children from harm or injury, as the courts consider swimming pools and dangerous premises to be "attractive nuisances."[13] Some provinces have included this special duty in their legislation. The province of Alberta, for example, under its Occupier's Liability Act,[14] provides that where an occupier of land knows or has reason to know that a child may trespass on the property, the occupier has a duty to take reasonable care that the child will be safe from any existing dangers. In the case of a swimming pool, this would mean that the occupier would be obliged to fence the pool and take any other precautions necessary to prevent small children from gaining access to the pool area.

Trespassers to property (other than small children) are generally considered to assume all risks of injury when they enter on the lands of another. Consequently, the occupier of the land need not take steps to warn them of any dangers that exist on the property, unless the dangers may be considered to be traps or devices deliberately set to injury the unwary. However, if an occupier of land is aware that trespassers use the land and takes no steps to prohibit such use, the occupier risks the chance of being considered to have consented to the use, and thereby has a duty to warn the trespasser of any dangers that might exist. In an Ontario case, an occupier of land was held liable for the injuries to the operator of a snowmobile after the operator had trespassed on the lands of the occupier, because the occupier allowed a particular danger to exist with the full knowledge that people used the private road, albeit as trespassers. The Supreme Court of Canada reasoned that the occupier of the land had consented by implication to the use of the land by the operators of snowmobiles. The plaintiff, by reason of the occupier's failure to take steps to prohibit his use, had become a licensee and was entitled to a warning of any unusual or hidden dangers.[15]

The standard that the court adopted was essentially the test of **common humanity**. In the case, the court accepted with approval an English House of Lords description of the test that was summarized as follows:

> It does not follow that the occupier never owes any duty to the trespasser. If the presence of the trespasser is known to or reasonably to be anticipated by the occupier, then the occupier has a duty to the trespasser, but it is a lower and less onerous duty than the one which the occupier owes to a lawful visitor. Very broadly stated, it is a duty to treat the trespasser with ordinary humanity.

---

13. *Corporation of the City of Glasgow v. Taylor,* [1922] 1 A.C. 44.

14. Occupier's Liability Act, R.S.A. 1980, c. 0-3.

15. *Veinot v. Kerr-Addison Mines Ltd.* (1974), 51 D.L.R. (3d) 533.

The court went on to indicate the points that a judge should consider by also adopting with approval the test applied in another English Court of Appeal case where the judge stated the test in the following words:

> The long and short of it is that you have to take into account all the circumstances of the case and see then whether the occupier ought to have done more than he did. (1) You must apply your common sense. You must take into account the gravity and likelihood of the probable injury. Ultra-hazardous activities require a man to be ultra-cautious in carrying them out. The more dangerous the activity, the more he should take steps to see that no one is injured by it. (2) You must take into account also the character of the intrusion by the trespasser. A wandering child or a straying adult stands in a different position from a poacher or a burglar. You may expect a child when you may not expect a burglar. (3) You must also have regard to the nature of the place where the trespass occurs. An electrified railway line or a warehouse being demolished may require more precautions to be taken than a private house. (4) You must also take into account the knowledge which the defendant has, or ought to have, of the likelihood of trespassers being present. The more likely they are, the more precautions may have to be taken.

At common law, the second type of person who may enter upon the lands of another is the **licensee.** Licensees normally enter on the land with either the express or implied consent of the owner, and usually for their own benefit. For example, a person requesting permission to cross the property of a landowner in order to launch a boat on a lake would be a licensee, since the entry on the lands would be for the boat owner's own benefit. At common law, the duty of the occupier of the land toward the licensee would be to protect the licensee from any concealed dangers of which the occupier had knowledge, and that were in the area where the licensee might be.

An **invitee** is owed the highest duty of care of any of the three classes of persons who enter on the lands of others. An invitee, as the name suggests, is a person who is invited to enter on the lands, usually for the benefit of the occupier. Customers of a store and patrons of a theatre, for example, are normally classed as invitees even though a specific invitation is not given. The shopkeeper is usually considered to have offered an invitation to the public at large to enter the shop premises for business purposes, unless the shopkeeper has clearly indicated otherwise. The particular duty owed the invitee is to warn or protect the invitee from any unusual dangers of hazards of which the occupier is aware or ought to be aware. The standard applied would likely be that of the "reasonable person" in the event of injury to an invitee as a result of a hazard that the occupier was not aware of, but that the occupier might have discovered had he or she been more diligent.

In 1957, the United Kingdom codified its law pertaining to occupier's liability.[16] In so doing, it abolished the common law distinction between invitees and licensees, referring to both as "visitors" to the premises. By the new statute, the higher standard of care owed an invitee was extended to both invitees and licensees, obliging the occupier to take reasonable care to protect such persons from injury. Later, in 1973, the Province of Alberta introduced an Occupier's

---

16. Occupier's Liability Act, 1957, 5 & 6 Eliz. 2 c. 31.

Liability Act patterned after the United Kingdom statute.[17] The Alberta statute also eliminated the difference between licensees and invitees. In addition, it expressly stated that the occupier owed no duty of care to a trespasser except the duty not to deliberately injure the trespasser by willful or reckless conduct. As noted previously, a special exception was made for child trespassers who might enter on the premises. Otherwise, the ordinary trespasser assumed all risks of injury when trespassing on the property of another. The Province of British Columbia codified its law relating to occupiers of land in 1974,[18] and, in its statute, also abolished the difference between licensees and invitees. Some five years later, Ontario introduced similar legislation.[19] In each of these provinces, the higher standard of care that at common law applied to invitees now applies to both invitees and licensees. In those jurisdictions, the occupier is bound to take reasonable care to protect such persons from injury. In the remaining provinces, the distinction remains, as does the standard of care that the occupier of the land is expected to maintain with respect to each.

The liability imposed on the occupier does not mean that the invitee (or licensee for that matter) is not required to act in a careful manner, once warned of existing dangers. For example, if a patron of a hotel is warned by prominent signs that the floor of the hotel lobby is hazardous because it has just been waxed, a lack of care in crossing the floor that results in an injury to the patron may not entitle the patron to recover from the hotel owner. The courts normally expect the invitee to act in a reasonable and prudent manner when warned of a particular danger or hazard.

Manufacturers' Liability for Defective Products

Before the Industrial Revolution, goods were normally made by craftsmen serving the local population. The Industrial Revolution permitted the mass production of goods and their distribution over a wide area. This in turn established a manufacturer remoteness from the ultimate consumer in the distribution system. Under the law of contract, the seller of goods (as an implied condition in the sale agreement) provides that the goods sold are of merchantable quality and reasonably fit for the use intended. If a purchaser buys such goods by description and the goods contain a defect, the law allows the purchaser to recover any loss from the vendor. While this aspect of the law of contract will be dealt with in greater detail in subsequent chapters, it is sufficient to say at this point that the law of contract provides a remedy to the purchaser or the person for whom the goods were intended if the goods prove to be defective or cause some injury.

The limitation imposed by the law of contract is that it does not provide a remedy for the user or the consumer of the goods if that person is not the purchaser. This particular shortfall of the law was eventually remedied by the law of torts in the United States. The case involved the sale of a motor car that contained a defect in its construction resulting in an injury to the purchaser. The purchaser sued the manufacturer, rather than the seller of the car, and was met by the

17. Occupier's Liability Act, S.A. 1973, c. 79.
18. Occupier's Liability Act, S.B.C. 1974, c. 60.
19. Occupiers' Liability Act, R.S.O. 1990, c. 0-2.

defence that the manufacturer owed a duty of care only to the immediate purchaser, i.e., the retailer. The court, however, ruled that the duty of care extended beyond the immediate purchaser to the plaintiff, who was the ultimate user of the goods.[20]

English and Canadian courts discussed the duty of care of manufacturers in a number of cases,[21] but it was not until the case of *M'Alister (or Donoghue) v. Stevenson*[22] came before the courts that the issue of the responsibility of manufacturers was established. In that case, a friend of the injured plaintiff purchased a bottle of ginger-beer from a shop, and gave it to the plaintiff. The plaintiff, on consuming part of the contents, became seriously ill. She alleged that the bottle of ginger-beer, unknown to the shopkeeper and the purchaser, contained a decomposed snail that had contaminated the contents. The bottle was made from an opaque glass that prevented a visual examination of the contents by a purchaser and bore the label of the defendant manufacturer. The plaintiff brought an action claiming negligence on the part of the manufacturer. The manufacturer denied that the plaintiff could sue on such a claim, which rested on the assumption that it owed a duty of care toward the consumer, since the consumer was not a purchaser of the product. The House of Lords recognized the right of the plaintiff to bring such an action, thus establishing that the manufacturer had a duty not to injure the consumer of its product.

In the cases that have followed the *M'Alister (or Donoghue) v. Stevenson* decision, the courts have held that where there is physical injury to persons or damage to property, the manufacturer will be liable to the ultimate consumer where it can be shown that the manufacturer was negligent in the manufacture of the goods,[23] or where the goods had some danger associated with them, and that the producer failed to adequately warn the consumer of the danger.[24] In the United States, the liability of the manufacturer is not limited to cases where negligence may be proven, but in many cases has been held to be strict. Accordingly, in the United States, for certain types of goods the manufacturer may be held liable for any injury, regardless of the efforts made by the manufacturer to prevent faulty products from reaching the consumer.[25]

Nuisance

The tort **nuisance** has been applied to a great many activities that cause injury to landowners or occupiers, and because of its wide use, it is now, to some extent, incapable of precise definition. In practice, it generally refers to any interference with a person's enjoyment of their property, and includes such forms of interference as noise, vibration, smoke, fumes, and contaminants of all sorts that may affect the use of land. Unlike some torts, nuisance is very much dependent upon

---

20. See, for example, *Heaven v. Pender* (1883), 11 Q.B.D. 503; *Le Lievre v. Gould,* [1893] 1 Q.B. 491.
21. See, for example, *Heaven v. Pender* (1883), 11 Q.B.D. 503; *Le Lievre v. Gould,* [1893] 1 Q.B. 491.
22. *M'Alister (or Donoghue) v. Stevenson,* [1932] A.C. 562.
23. *Arendale v. Canada Bread Co. Ltd.,* [1941] O.W.N. 69; *McMorran v. Dominion Stores Ltd. et al.* (1977), 14 O.R. (2d) 559.
24. *Austin v. 3M Canada Ltd.* (1975), 7 O.R. (2d) 200, but see also, *Lem v. Barotto Sports Ltd. et al.* (1977), 69 D.L.R. (3d) 276.
25. See, for example, *Escola v. Coca-Cola Bottling Co. of Fresno* (1944), 150 P. (2d) 436.

the circumstances surrounding the interference, or the degree of interference, rather than the fact that the interference occurred.

The courts have long recognized that in the case of nuisance they must essentially balance the reasonable use of land by one person with the decrease in enjoyment that the reasonable use of the property produces for that person's neighbour, and in some cases, the community as a whole. To be actionable then, the interference must be such that it results in a serious decrease in the enjoyment of the neighbour's property, or that it causes specific damage to the land. What is a reasonable use of land is usually determined by an examination of the uses of land in the immediate vicinity. For example, if individuals insist on making their residence in an area of a city where heavy manufacturing activity is carried on, they must expect the reasonable use of adjoining property to include the emission of noise, and perhaps odours, smoke, and dust.

Where a nuisance is determined, the remedies available to the party subjected to the nuisance would be damages and, at the court's discretion, an **injunction** ordering the defendant to cease the activity causing the interference. Where the nuisance is such that its restraint would be detrimental to the community as a whole, the court, in balancing the two interests, will normally place the interests of the community before those of the individual, and will limit the landowner's remedy to damages. For example, where the issuance of an injunction would have the effect of closing down a mine or smelter upon which the community depends for its very existence, the public interest would dictate that the remedy take only the form of monetary compensation.[26] On the other hand, where the interference is localized, the courts have often considered an injunction to be appropriate as well.[27]

In the case of *Segal et al v. Derrick Golf & Winter Club* (1977), 76 D.L.R. (3d) 746, the court dealt with a complaint by the owners of property located adjacent to a golf course that members of the golf club were interfering with their enjoyment of their property by driving golf balls into their yards. The property owners complained to the court that the careless golfing was a nuisance, and sought court assistance to have it stopped. The judge in reviewing the law of nuisance stated that the nuisance was essentially interference with the occupier's beneficial interest and enjoyment of the property. He described the law as it applied to this case in the following manner:

> That there has been interference with the plaintiff's pleasure, comfort and enjoyment of their land is clearly established. They are unable to use and enjoy their backyard during the golfing season. Their fears for the safety of their children and for their own safety are well-founded and their home will continue to receive damage from hard-driven golf balls. Their inconvenience is serious and substantial.
>
> As I have previously stated, this interference was entirely foreseeable from the layout of the 14th hole. The defendant as owner and operator of the golf-course has known of this interference at least since 1972, and has permitted it to continue although it was and is within its power to prevent it by control and supervision which it has over the players using the course.

26. *Black v. Canada Copper Co.* (1917), 12 O.W.N. 243.
27. *Russell Transport Ltd. v. Ontario Malleable Iron Co. Ltd.,* [1952] 4 D.L.R. 719.

In the circumstances, the defendant as occupier of the golf course is liable for the private nuisance to the plaintiffs.

The current concern for the environment, and the difficulty in determining the sources of pollution in a precise manner, have prompted all levels of government to establish legislation for the purpose of controlling the sources of many of the more common environmental nuisances that interfere with the use and enjoyment of property. The statutes have for the most part replaced actions for nuisance as a means of controlling pollution, but on an individual basis, where the cause of the pollution is isolated and identified by a landowner, an action for nuisance may still be used to stop the offending activity.

It should be borne in mind that as a tort, nuisance applies to many activities that are not environmental in nature. For example, picketers unlawfully carrying picket signs at the entrances to a hotel have been declared a nuisance by the courts.[28] Similarly, while awaiting the opening of a theatre, a queue of patrons who habitually blocked the entrance to an adjoining shopkeeper's premises were held to be a nuisance.[29] These are simply two of the many kinds of nuisances that the courts may recognize as interference with the enjoyment of property.

Because nuisance generally involves a public policy decision, much of the legislation relating to property use at the municipal level is directed to this particular problem. Local zoning laws attempt to place industrial uses and residential uses of land some distance apart. This is to permit the users maximum freedom in the respective uses of their properties, and to minimize the interference of one with the other that might take the form of nuisance. The larger problems of industrial nuisances and the environment are also the subject of increasing control by senior levels of government rather than the courts. The right of the individual to redress for interference with the enjoyment of property, nevertheless, still remains for many nuisances which are not subject to statutory regulation.

GENERAL TORT DEFENCES

Liability does not always rest on a person who causes injury or damage to another person or to his or her property. Certain persons have the lawful right in the course of carrying out the duties of their work or office to interfere with others, or, in some cases, to cause them injury or inconvenience. For example, a police officer, in pursuit of a person believed to have committed a criminal offence, may trespass on the property of a third party in the course of the pursuit. A customs officer may search the luggage of a Canadian citizen returning to Canada from abroad and may prohibit the entry of goods that may not be lawfully brought into the country. Similarly, goods smuggled into Canada illegally are forfeited to the Crown and may be seized by customs officers or the police. All of these acts would normally be actionable at law if done by an ordinary citizen under different circumstances, but persons such as police officers and customs officers possess these special rights or powers by the nature of their office. Ordinary citizens nevertheless may have defences that would excuse them from liability in cases where they are accused of committing a tort against another. Some of the more common defences follow.

---

28. *Nipissing Hotel Ltd. v. Hotel & Restaurant Employees and Bartenders International Union* (1962), 36 D.L.R. (2d) 81.

29. *Lyons, Sons & Co. v. Gulliver*, [1914] 1 Ch. 631.

Act of God

A good defence in the instance of property damage might arise where the defendant can establish that the resulting loss was caused by an **act of God.** For example, assume lightning struck a person's house and set it on fire, and the fire spread to the neighbour's house. If the neighbour claimed compensation for the damage, the person whose house was struck by lightning might argue that the cause of the fire was an act of God, and therefore beyond personal control. In this instance, assuming that there were no unusual circumstances (such as the storage of large quantities of explosive or highly inflammable substances in the residence), the defence of act of God may prevent the neighbour from recovering for the property loss resulting from the spread of the fire.

Waiver

The defence of **waiver** may be raised by a defendant, if the defendant can satisfy the court that the injured party specifically waived his or her right to claim against the defendant for the particular injury that did occur. Waivers are usually in writing and, to be effective, must cover the injury contemplated by the parties at the time. However, because the circumstances surrounding the injury are often different from those contemplated at the time the waiver is given, a waiver is not always effective as a means of avoiding liability.

Release

Sometimes, where damage or injury in a tortious situation has occurred, the injured party may **release** the person who caused the injury or damage. They may do so either because the person has paid compensation for the injury or damage, or because the injured party has decided not to claim for the tort. When a proper release is given under circumstances where the injured party is fully aware of the nature and extent of the loss or damage suffered, such a person may not normally take action against the released party at a later time. If the injured party should do so, the released party may raise the release as a defence to the tort action.

Statute of Limitations

Persons who are injured or who suffer a loss as a result of the tortious acts of another must take steps to bring a claim before the court within a reasonable time after the loss or injury occurs. To delay for a long period of time places the defendant at a disadvantage, as records may be destroyed, witnesses may die or move elsewhere, and memories of the event may fade. Consequently, a person with a right of action is expected to pursue the claim without undue delay. At common law, judges may refuse to hear a case where the plaintiff fails to bring a claim before the court within a reasonable length of time, if the defendant can satisfy the court that he or she has been prejudiced by the unreasonable delay. The barring of this relief is known as the **doctrine of laches.**

While the common law doctrine may still be applied, the limitation period for tort actions is now largely covered by statute law. In most provinces, specific laws have been passed stating the time within which different claims must be brought before the courts, otherwise claimants lose their right to do so. Limitation periods are calculated from the time when a victim could reasonably been expected to discover the loss.[30] The time limits vary from relatively short periods for certain specified torts (two years, in some provinces, for motor vehicle accidents and claims of defamation) to a general maximum of six years for tort claims without specified time limits. Subject to certain exceptions, if a person fails to institute a tort action within the period fixed by the statute, the defendant may raise as a successful defence the fact that the claim is **statute-barred** by the legislation, and thereby avoid liability.

TORT REMEDIES

Once liability for a tort has been established, the court will provide the injured party with a suitable remedy for the damage or injury suffered. The general approach is to attempt to place the injured party in the same position that the party would have been in had the tort not been committed. For this reason, the courts have fashioned a variety of different remedies, each designed to compensate for specific losses.

The most common remedy is **money damages.** Often, the loss suffered by a person in a negligence case is the loss of or damage to property. In these instances, an award of money damages may be sufficient to undo the harm done by the tort. For example, if a person negligently operated an automobile in a manner that caused $1000 damage to another person's automobile, a judgement of the court that obliged the negligent person to pay the injured party $1000 (plus court costs) would cover the cost of having the damaged automobile repaired to its previous condition. In this way, the injured party would be returned to the same position as before the tort incident.

Torts that cause physical injury to persons are often compensated for by money damages, as the injury often results in medical expenses, the loss of wages, and many other identifiable costs that usually flow from the sudden incapacity of the injured party. An award of money damages to cover these specific costs or losses suffered by the injured party is referred to as **special damages**. These may be determined from invoices or calculated (for example, in the case of lost wages). In a typical motor vehicle accident where an innocent party is seriously injured, special damages might include: ambulance expenses, hospital charges, the fees of medical practitioners attending to the injuries, the cost of drugs and therapy, lost wages, rehabilitation costs, and the cost of repairs to the injured party's automobile. To this would be added a sum intended to compensate the injured party for pain and suffering, for future health problems that might arise from the injuries suffered, and for any permanent incapacity resulting from the accident.[31] These losses are referred to as **general damages**; the monetary amount to cover them may be estimated by the court, based upon the evidence of expert witnesses at the trial.

If a tort does not result in a monetary loss to the person whose rights have been infringed by the act, such as where a person trespasses on the land of another without inflicting physical damage to the property, a court may sometimes

---

30. *City of Kamloops v. Nielsen et al.,* [1984] 2 S.C.R. 2.
31. See, for example, *Andrews v. Grand & Toy Alberta Ltd. and Anderson,* [1978] 2 S.C.R. 229 where the various components were noted and a cap placed on the amount for pain and suffering.

award **nominal damages** in the amount of one dollar. This is done by the court to emphasize to the trespasser that the property owner's right to exclusive possession had been affected by the trespass. In most of these cases, however, the cost to the injured party of bringing the case before the court is significantly higher than one dollar, as court costs and legal fees must also be paid to have the matter decided by the court. In keeping with the concept of compensation for the loss suffered, courts will usually order the trespasser to pay not only the nominal damages of one dollar, but the plaintiff's court costs as well. On this basis, the cost to the defendant might very well be substantial, even though the tort committed caused no actual damage to the "injured" party.

Where a tort is intentionally committed for the purpose of injuring another, or with reckless disregard for the other party, a court may award the injured party **punitive** or **exemplary damages.** For example, where one person assaults another, or spreads malicious lies about another individual, punitive damages may be awarded by the court to punish the wrongdoer. The award of punitive damages runs contrary to the concept of compensation for the injury suffered. However, because one person may sometimes cause injury to another in a vindictive or malicious manner, punitive damages are awarded as a deterrent to further similar behaviour, as well as to compensate for the injury suffered.

Where the tort committed is of an ongoing nature, such as trespass to land, pollution of a person's water supply, or interference in any way with an individual's exercise of lawful rights, the court may issue an injunction as a remedy, to prevent further occurrences of the tort. An **injunction** is a court order directed to a person (or persons) ordering the person named to cease doing the act described in the order. Failure to comply with the injunction, or continuation of the prohibited act, is considered to be **contempt of court.** It may be punished by a fine or jail sentence, if the court finds the person concerned ignored the court order.

In cases where a person has wrongfully retained goods that belong to another, the retention of the goods may constitute the tort **conversion.** When this occurs, the owner of the goods usually wishes to regain possession of the property, rather than receive an award of money damages equal to their value. Common law courts in such cases may issue **an order of replevin** that directs the sheriff or bailiff of the county or district to take possession of the goods until their ownership can be determined by the court. An order of replevin is a remedy often granted in addition to money damages, where the owner has requested court assistance to recover goods and to obtain compensation for the loss of use of the goods while they were wrongfully retained.

SUMMARY

The law of torts is one of the oldest areas of law. It is concerned with injury caused by one person to another, or to property, where the courts have determined that a duty exists not to injure. Unintentional injury to a person, where a duty not to injure is owed, is a tort. Most torts of this nature fall under the general classification of negligence, which includes not only the unintentional injury to the person, but injury to property as well.

Injury to the property of another through carelessness is actionable in tort if a duty is owed not to damage the property. While trespass to land normally is a willful act and an actionable tort, unintentional interference with the enjoyment of the lands of another constitutes the tort of nuisance. Landowners or occupiers of land, however, owe a duty not to injure persons who enter on their land, but the extent of the duty differs between trespassers, licensees, and invitees. The manufacturers of goods also owe a duty not to injure the users of their products and are subject to a very high duty of care.

The courts have developed a number of principles and doctrines applicable to both old and new forms of tort. Two important principles, the concept of a duty of care and the standard of the "reasonable person," have made the law flexible in its application. In addition, the development of "foreseeability" as a test for tort liability has been an important advancement in the law. In tort cases, the courts usually attempt to compensate the injured party for the loss suffered insofar as monetary damages permit. However, in cases where injury is caused by the deliberate acts of one party the courts may award punitive damages as well.

DISCUSSION QUESTIONS

1. Distinguish between a moral obligation not to injure and a duty not to injure. Why is this distinction important?
2. Why do the courts impose strict liability for damage in certain instances?
3. Explain the concept of duty of care as it relates to liability in a tort action.
4. Why are the concept of duty of care and the concept of "the reasonable person" important in a case where negligence is alleged?
5. Explain the concept or doctrine of proximate cause in tort law.
6. How are the concept of the reasonable person and the concept of foreseeability related?
7. Identify and explain the essential ingredients of unintentional tort liability.
8. Does strict liability apply to manufacturers of goods where the goods are defective and cause injury or damage?
9. What is the duty of care of an occupier of land to a trespasser? To an invitee?
10. Describe the standard of care imposed upon a professional person.
11. In some cases, the courts consider the public interest as an important aspect of a nuisance action. Why is this so? Give an example.
12. Is "nuisance" simply another name for negligence? If not, why not?
13. Does a professional person have any responsibility to a person other than the one who engages the professional's services?
14. Define *res ipsa loquitur.*
15. Why was it necessary for the common law provinces to introduce contributory negligence legislation?
16. Is the defence of *volenti non fit injuria,* in effect, the defence of waiver?
17. In what way (or ways) does occupier's liability legislation change the common law liability of occupiers of land towards others?

MINI-CASE PROBLEMS

1. X, a trained and licensed plumber, carelessly installed a steam heater in Y's house, and, as a result, Y was seriously burned when a heater pipe exploded. Z, a qualified medical practitioner who treated Y at the hospital, prescribed an improper medication as treatment for the burn that aggravated the injury. This obliged Y to undergo an expensive skin graft operation to correct the condition. Discuss the responsibility of X and Z to Y.
2. At dusk, one evening, as X was hauling a load of rock in his truck, he saw a large piece of rock fall from the truck onto the travelled portion of the roadway.

X continued on his way without stopping. Y, who was travelling in her automobile along the same road some time later, collided with the rock and damaged her automobile. Discuss the liability of X.

3. Would your decision in Question 2 be any different:
   (a) If X was unaware that the piece of rock fell from his truck?
   (b) If Y was travelling along the road at a high rate of speed?
   (c) If Y noticed the rock in her driving lane and swerved to the other side of the road to avoid it, thereby colliding with Z, who was travelling in the opposite direction?

JUDICIAL DECISIONS

The duty of care is central to the principles of law relating to negligence. Manufacturers' liability for defective products at common law was for the most part described in terms of this duty in the classic case that follows. A part of the court's decision is set out here for two reasons: first, to illustrate how a judge applies the common law to a fact situation, and second, to provide an example of a judicial decision that, as one noted earlier in the text, constitutes a part of the body of common law.

The second judicial decision in this chapter illustrates the law relating to *volenti non fit injuria*. In the case, the judge examines the duty of the municipality to protect the user of a tennis court from injury, given that the user was aware of the condition of the court surface. The judge reviews the authorities and concludes that the user was aware of the condition of the tennis court and had voluntarily assumed the risk of injury by playing on it.

Negligence — Duty of Care — Manufacturers' Liability

M'Alister (or Donoghue) v. Stevenson, [1932] A.C. 562.

The plaintiff and a friend entered a shop in Paisley, Scotland, where the friend purchased a bottle of ginger-beer manufactured by the defendant and gave the same to the plaintiff. The glass bottle was opaque and the contents could not be inspected before opening. The plaintiff consumed part of the bottle. Then, when she emptied the remainder of the contents into her glass, discovered the remains of a decomposed snail.

She became violently ill following the incident and brought an action for damages against the manufacturer on the grounds of negligence.

LORD MACMILLAN:

The law ... concerns itself with carelessness only where there is a duty to take care and where failure in that duty has caused damage. In such circumstances carelessness assumes the legal quality of negligence and entails the consequences in law of negligence. What, then, are the circumstances which give rise to this duty to take care? In the daily contacts of social and business life human beings are thrown into, or place themselves in, an infinite variety of relations with their fellows; and the law can refer only to the standards of the reasonable man in order to determine whether any particular relation gives rise to a duty to take care as between those who stand in that relation to each other. The grounds of action may be as various and manifold as human errancy; and the conception of legal responsibility may develop in adaptation to altering social conditions and standards. The criterion of judgment must adjust and adapt itself to the changing circumstances of life. The categories of negligence are never closed. The cardinal principle of liability is that the party complained of should owe to the party complaining a duty to take care, and that the party complaining should be able to prove that he has suffered damage in consequence of a breach of that duty. Where there is room for diversity of view, it is in determining what circumstances will establish such a relationship between the parties as to give rise, on the one side, to a duty to take care, and on the other side to a right to have care taken.

To descend from these generalities to the circumstances of the present case I do not think that any reasonable man or any twelve reasonable men would hesitate to hold that, if the appellant establishes her allegations, the respondent has exhibited carelessness in the conduct of his business. For a manufacturer of aerated water to store his empty bottles in a place where snails can get access to them, and to fill his bottles without taking any adequate precautions by inspection or otherwise to ensure that they contain no deleterious foreign matter, may reasonably be characterized as carelessness without applying too exacting a standard. But, as I have pointed out, it is not enough to prove the respondent to be careless in his process of manufacture. The question is: Does he owe a duty to take care, and to whom does he owe that duty? Now I have no hesitation in affirming that a person who for gain engages in the business of manufacturing articles of food and drink intended for consumption by members of the public in the form in which he issues them is under a duty to take care in the manufacture of these articles. That duty, in my opinion, he owes to those whom he intends to consume his products. He manufactures his commodities for human consumption; he intends and contemplates that they shall be consumed. By reason of that very fact he places himself in a relationship with all the potential consumers of his commodities, and that relationship which he assumes and desires for his own needs imposes upon him a duty to take care to avoid injuring them. He owes them a duty not to convert by his own carelessness an article which he issues to them as wholesome and innocent into an article which is dangerous to life and health. It is said that liability can only arise where a reasonable man would have foreseen and could have avoided the consequences of his act or omission. In the present case the respondent, when he manufactured his ginger-beer, had directly in contemplation that it would be consumed by members of the public. Can it be said that he could not be expected as a reasonable man to foresee that if he conducted his process of manufacture carelessly he might injure those whom he expected and desired to consume his ginger-beer? The possibility of injury so arising seems to me in no sense so remote as to excuse him from foreseeing it. Suppose that a baker, through carelessness, allows a large quantity of arsenic to be mixed with a batch of his bread, with the result that those who subsequently eat it are poisoned, could he be heard to say that he owed no duty to the consumers of his bread to take care that it was free from poison, and that, as he did not know that any poison had got into it, his only liability was for breach of warranty under his contract of sale to those who actually bought the poisoned bread from him? Observe that I have said "through carelessness," and thus excluded the case of a pure accident such as may happen where every care is taken. I cannot believe, and I do not believe, that neither in the law of England or in the law of Scotland is there redress for such a case. The state of facts I have figured might well give rise to a criminal charge, and the civil consequences of such carelessness can scarcely be less wide than its criminal consequences. Yet the principle of the decision appealed from is that the manufacturer of food products intended by him for human consumption does not owe to the consumers whom he has in view any duty of care, not even the duty to take care that he does not poison them.

It must always be a question of circumstances whether the carelessness amounts to negligence, and whether the injury is not too remote from the carelessness. I can readily conceive that where a manufacturer has parted with his product and it has passed into other hands it may well be exposed to vicissitudes which may render it defective or noxious, for which the manufacturer could not in any view be held to be to blame. It may be a good general rule to regard responsibility as ceasing when control ceases. So, also, where between the manufacturer and the user there is interposed a party who has the means and opportunity of examining the manufacturer's product before he re-issues it to the actual user. But where, as in the present case, the article of consumption is so prepared as to be intended to reach the consumer in the condition in which it leaves the manufacturer, and the manufacturer takes steps to ensure this by sealing or otherwise closing the container so that the contents cannot be tampered with, I regard his control as remaining effective until the article reaches the consumer and the container is opened by him.

Dangerous Premises — Awareness — *Volenti Non Fit Injuria*

Burrough v. Town of Kapuskasing (1987), 60 O.R. (2d) 727.

In this case the plaintiff, Burrough, was a tennis player. He used the tennis courts owned by the town on a regular basis. During a tournament, his right toe lodged in a crack in the cement playing surface and he was severely injured when he fell to the ground. He brought an action against the municipality for damages. The town was aware of the dangerous condition of the tennis court surface, as was the plaintiff, who regularly used the court. The issue in the case was whether the plaintiff had voluntarily assumed the risk by continuing to use the tennis court knowing of its state of disrepair. The judge considered the town's defence of *volenti non fit injuria* in the following manner:

DESMARAIS, D.C.J.:

(3) *Is the plaintiff precluded from succeeding by virtue of the application of s. 4(1) of the Occupiers' Liability Act?*

Section 4(1) reads as follows:

> 4(1) *The duty of care provided for in subsection 3(1) does not apply in respect of risks willingly assumed by the person who enters on the premises,* but in that case the occupier owes a duty to the person to not create a danger with the deliberate intent of doing harm or damage to the person or his property and to not act with reckless disregard of the presence of the person or his property.

(Emphasis mine.)

Section 4(1) is essentially a codification of the common law defence of *volenti non fit injuria.*

The nature of the defence is defined in 34 Hals., 4th ed., p. 51, para. 62:

> Where a plaintiff relies on the breach of a duty to take care owed by the defendant to him it is a good defence that the plaintiff consented to that breach of duty, or, *knowing of it, voluntarily incurred the whole risk entailed by it.* In such a case the maxim *volenti non fit injuria* applies.

(Emphasis mine.)

In para. 63 of Halsbury, the application of the defence is defined as follows:

> In order to establish the defence, the plaintiff must be shown not only to have perceived the existence of danger but also to have appreciated it fully and voluntarily accepted the risk. The question whether the plaintiff's acceptance of the risk was voluntary is generally one of fact, and the answer to it may be inferred from his conduct in the circumstances.

The issue therefore is whether the plaintiff knew of the dangers involved and notwithstanding that knowledge, voluntarily incurred the whole risk entailed by it.

In *Letang v. Ottawa Electric R. Co.,* [1926] 3 D.L.R. 457, [1926] 3 W.W.R. 88, [1926] A.C. 725, a decision of the Privy Council of the House of Lords, Lord Shaw of Dunfermline, speaking on behalf of the court, quoted with approval Bowen L.J. in *Thomas v. Quartermaine* (1887), 18 Q.B.D. 685 at pp. 696–7, as follows:

> The maxim, be it observed, is not "*scienti*" *non fit injuria*, but "*volenti*". It is plain that mere knowledge may not be a conclusive defence ... The defendant in such circumstances does not discharge his legal obligation by merely affecting the plaintiff with knowledge of a danger ... Knowledge is not a conclusive defence in itself. But when it is a knowledge under circumstances that leave no inference open but one, viz., that the risk has been voluntarily encountered, the defence seems to me complete.

In the case at bar I am satisfied that the defendant has satisfied the onus upon it to show that the plaintiff was aware of the risk, i.e., had knowledge of the deteriorated state of the courts and that notwithstanding same he voluntarily encountered that risk.

Schroeder J.A. in *Such v. Dominion Stores Ltd.,* [1963] 1 O.R. 405 at p. 410, 37 D.L.R. (2d) 311, said the following:

> Under the rule in *Indermaur v. Dames, supra,* the duty resting upon the defendant occupier of property is to prevent damage from unusual danger which he knows or ought to know. It is a valid defence if he has clearly and sufficiently warned the invitee of the existence of that unusual danger. In this case a specific warning to the plaintiff would have been wholly superfluous, since the plaintiff on his own admission was completely aware of the condition that existed. Moreover the defendant has clearly established that the plaintiff freely and voluntarily with full knowledge of the nature and extent of the risk he ran impliedly agreed to incur it. Thus the defendant is entitled to invoke and rely upon the maxim *volenti non fit injuria.* While it may be sufficient for the defendant to show that the plaintiff incurred the risk *sciens,* it has nevertheless established that he also incurred it *volens.*

The circumstances referred to in the *Such v. Dominion Stores* case also existed in this case. It is clear from the evidence that the plaintiff knew of the danger the cracks in the courts presented. He was affixed with this knowledge for some time and notwithstanding this knowledge of the potential danger, he voluntarily assumed the risk involved.

The plaintiff made use of the premises knowing that their state of disrepair represented a danger and further, doing so in a highly competitive manner. The plaintiff was one of the best 12 players in the Town of Kapuskasing. His approach to the game was primarily to be competitive. Because of this approach he would, of his own admission, dedicate his entire attention to the competition at hand and ignore whatever potential dangers may exist. He played the game actively and intensely. He was familiar with the courts on Riverside Dr. playing most of his games at that location. I am satisfied therefore that he voluntarily or willingly assumed whatever risks there were in engaging in the game of tennis on the premises in question at that time. The plaintiff is an intelligent man who was knowledgeable in the game. He knew the dangerous condition of the courts but notwithstanding same he participated in an intense and highly competitive match. He had the choice not to play but he did and he lost.

The plaintiff's claim is therefore dismissed.

CASE PROBLEMS FOR DISCUSSION

Case 1

Henry operated a small food stand at an open-air market where farmers in close proximity to one another had set up makeshift stalls or tables to display their produce. To protect themselves from the hot sun, most had erected canvas or cloth canopies over their tables. The stand operated by Henry was located in the midst of the covered stalls.

For the purpose of cooking a particular delicacy that he sold, Henry had placed a tiny propane-fuelled stove on his table-top and used it to boil a pot of oil. While he was serving a customer, a youth about 16 years old turned up the flame on the burner, and the oil immediately caught fire. In a frantic attempt to put out the fire, Henry seized the flaming pot and flung it from his food stand. The youth was splashed with flaming oil and was seriously burned when his clothes caught fire.

The pot of burning oil landed in a nearby farmer's stall and set fire to the canopy that he had placed over it. The farmer kicked the flaming pot out of his stall and into a neighbouring stall where it set fire to a quantity of paper that was used for food packaging.

Before the fire was finally extinguished, three stalls had been destroyed, and both the youth and Henry hospitalized with serious burns.

Discuss the rights and liabilities of the parties involved in this incident.

Case 2

Basil, aged 14, lived in a large metropolitan city, but spent his summer vacations with his parents at a cottage in a remote wilderness area of the province. On his fourteenth birthday, his father presented him with a pellet rifle and provided him with instruction on the safe handling of the weapon. The father specified that the gun was only to be used at the cottage. Basil used the pellet rifle to rid the cottage of area rodents during his vacation.

On their return to the city, Basil's father stored the weapon and the supply of pellets in his workshop closet. He warned Basil that he must not touch the rifle until the next summer, but did not lock the cabinet in which the weapon was stored.

One day, when Basil was entertaining a few friends at his home, he mentioned his summer hunting activities. At the urging of his friends, he brought out the pellet gun for examination. Basil demonstrated the ease with which the magazine could be filled, and how the weapon operated. He then emptied the magazine and allowed his friends to handle it. The gun was returned to him and, as he was replacing it in the cabinet, the weapon discharged. He was unaware that a pellet had remained in the weapon, and that he had accidentally charged the gun when he handled it. The pellet struck one of his friends in the eye, and an action was brought against Basil and his parents for negligence.

Discuss the liability (if any) of Basil and his parents, and the defences (if any) that might be raised. Render a decision.

Case 3

Smith lived in a residential area some distance from where he worked. One morning, he found himself late for work because his alarm clock failed to wake him at the usual time. In his rush to leave his home, Smith backed his automobile from his garage after only a cursory backward glance to make certain the way was clear. He did not see a small child riding a tricycle along the sidewalk behind his car, and the two came into collision. The child was knocked from the tricycle by the impact and was injured.

The child's mother, at the front door of her home (some 70 m away), heard the child scream and saw the car back over the tricycle. She ran to the scene of the accident, picked up the child, and carried him home. Smith called an ambulance, and the child was taken to the hospital and treated for a crushed leg.

The mother brought a legal action against Smith for damages resulting from the shock of seeing her child struck by Smith's car. An action was also brought on behalf of the child for the injuries suffered.

Discuss the validity of the claims in this case, and identify the issues and points of law that are raised by the actions of Smith. How would you decide the case?

Case 4

Thompson operated an ice-cream truck owned by Smith. During the summer months Thompson travelled throughout the residential areas of a large city selling ice-cream products. Thompson's principal customers were children, and Thompson would drive along the streets ringing a series of bells attached to his truck to signal his arrival in the area.

Alberta, a five-year-old child, and her brother were regular customers of Thompson. On the day in question the two children heard the bells that signalled the approach of Thompson's ice-cream truck. Martha, Alberta's mother, was talking to her husband on the telephone at the moment that the ice-cream truck arrived. In response to the cries of her two small children for money to buy ice-cream, she gave them enough money to buy an ice-cream bar each. The children ran across the street to where the truck was parked, and each ordered a different ice-cream product. Thompson served Alberta first, and then turned to serve her brother. At that instant, Alberta ran into the street, with the intention of returning home, and was struck by a car driven by Donaldson.

Alberta was seriously injured as a result of the accident and an action for damages was brought against Thompson, the operator of the ice-cream truck, Smith, the owner of the truck, and Donaldson, the owner and driver of the automobile.

Discuss the basis of the action on Alberta's behalf against the owners and drivers of the vehicles, and determine the basis of the liability of each party under the law of torts. Render a decision.

Case 5

Sampson operated a bowling alley in a commercial area that was adjacent to a residential area. Many small children used the parking lot near the bowling alley as a playground, and Sampson was constantly ordering the children off the premises for fear that they might be injured by motor vehicles.

One young boy, about six years old, was a particular nuisance in that he would climb to the flat roof of the bowling alley by way of a fence at the back of the building. Sampson ordered the child off the roof on several occasions, but to no avail. The child continued to climb on the roof at every opportunity in spite of Sampson's instructions to the contrary.

On one occasion, when Sampson was away from the premises, the child climbed to the roof and, while running about, tripped and fell to the ground. The fall seriously injured the child, and an action was brought on his behalf against Sampson.

Discuss the liability of Sampson, and his defences, if any. Render a decision.

Case 6

On a clear September day, Smith walked across a parking lot adjacent to his home for the purpose of buying a newspaper at a convenience store in a shopping plaza. He purchased the newspaper and left the store, but before he had walked more than one or two paces, his foot struck a raised portion of a sidewalk slab, and he fell heavily to the concrete.

Smith was unable to work for a month as a result of his injuries, and he brought an action for damages against the tenant who operated the convenience store and the owner of the shopping plaza.

When the case came to trial, the evidence established that the maintenance of the sidewalk outside the store was the sole responsibility of the owner of the shopping plaza, but the owner had not inspected the sidewalk for some months. The sidewalk, while not in disrepair, had been slightly heaved by the previous spring frost. It presented an uneven surface upon which the patrons of the plaza were forced to walk. Many of the concrete slabs were raised from 1/2 to 1 1/4 cm, but some protruded above abutting slabs by as much as 4 cm. The particular slab which caused Smith's fall protruded approximately 3 cm.

The tenant who occupied the milk store was aware of a "certain unevenness of the slabs," but did not realize that it was hazardous.

Discuss the liability (if any) of the defendant and render, with reasons, a decision.

Case 7

Alex carried on a relatively successful business as a manufacturer of a cleaning product that was well received by the users. After several years of slow but steady growth in sales, his accountant suggested that he expand the business by the incorporation of a company and the sale of shares to acquire the capital necessary for a new plant and equipment.

A company was eventually incorporated, but instead of selling shares to acquire the necessary capital to expand the business, Alex decided to arrange a $200 000 loan from his banker. To do so, however, Alex required the accountant to prepare financial statements for the company to deliver to the bank.

Preparing the financial statements, the accountant failed to notice that the existing plant building was not acquired by the corporation, but retained by Alex, and simply leased to the company on an annual-lease basis. The accountant had included the land and building (which had a value of $250 000) as an asset of the corporation on the financial statements, without checking with Alex to determine whether the land was transferred. When the error was discovered later, during negotiations with the bank, the bank insisted that Alex guarantee the loan as a principal debtor and use the land and building as additional security for the loan.

A few weeks later, Alex decided that it would be necessary to acquire additional capital to complete the expansion program. He contacted a private investor with a view to selling her shares in the corporation. The investor was interested in the financial status of the corporation, and Alex informed her that the corporation had borrowed $200 000 from the bank for the purpose of expanding the business. He also suggested that the investor contact either his accountant or the bank for information on the corporation's assets and financial position. The investor contacted the bank and requested copies of the statements that the accountant had prepared. A bank employee, who was unaware that the statements were in error, gave them to the investor without comment.

On the strength of the financial statements, the investor invested $50 000 in shares of the corporation. Some months later, she discovered that the corporation did not own the land or buildings, and that the financial statements were in error.

Advise the investor of her legal position and her rights (if any) against Alex, the accountant, and the bank.

Case 8

Kamikazi Ski Lodge Limited operated a ski resort in a mountainous ski area. While the company offered a number of runs suitable for skiers of all levels of competence, it maintained one particularly fast and adventurous run on a slope that required a relatively high degree of proficiency to successfully ski its course. In its advertising brochure the company warned potential patrons of the lodge that they should not attempt the run unless they had considerable experience. The company also required all guests to sign a guest registration form at the time of check-in at the lodge. The form provided as follows:

"Guests assume all risks associated with their use of the owner/operator's lodge and facilities. The owner/operator, its employees, and agents shall not be liable for any loss or injury incurred by any guest, however caused. Registration as a guest shall constitute a waiver of all claims that the guest may have against the owner/operator or its employees for any injury or loss suffered while on the premises."

Each year the lodge held a special challenge competition on its most difficult slope that required the contestants to travel down the slope in large rubber inner tubes rather than on skis. The competition was appropriately described as the "$500 Kamikazi Challenge Race," and was open to all contestants on the payment of a $15 race registration fee. Contestants were also required to sign an entry form at the time of payment which provided:

"Contestant recognizes that the Kamikazi Challenge is a dangerous undertaking that could result in injury. The contestant assumes all risk and responsibility for any or all injuries suffered while engaged in the competition."

Two days before the competition, Crocker, a novice skier who was a guest at the lodge, paid his entry fee and signed the entry form without bothering to read it. He had been drinking prior to the point in time that he entered the contest, but did not appear to be drunk or unaware of his actions.

Later that day, the contestants (including Crocker) were shown a videotape of the previous year's race. The tape described the race and provided footage of incidents that involved contestants being thrown from their inner tubes, as well as those who managed to remain in their inner tubes to the end of the race.

On the day of the contest, Crocker appeared at the starting point for the race in an obviously drunken state. His speech was slurred, and he had difficulty standing on the slope. Nevertheless, he managed to obtain his inner tube from the lodge employees in charge of the race and prepared for the start of the race. At the starting gun, he threw himself into the inner tube and managed thereafter to more or less successfully navigate the slope. He placed among the five finalists, suffering only a cut above one eye when he was thrown from his inner tube on one occasion.

Before the final run, he took a large drink of brandy that had been offered to him by a spectator. The race operator noticed Crocker drinking brandy, and asked him if he was in any condition to compete in the final race. Crocker replied that he was, and the final race began.

Part way down the slope, Crocker failed to negotiate a sharp turn, and was thrown from his inner tube and into a rock gully. His injuries rendered him a quadriplegic, and he brought an action against the resort for damages.

Discuss the liability of the lodge, and speculate, with reasons, as to how the case might be resolved.

Case 9

Kevin B. and a companion spent the most part of a Saturday afternoon and evening drinking alcoholic beverages at Kevin's home. Around 10:00 p.m., they decided to visit a local tavern where they had arranged to meet some friends. The two drove in Kevin's automobile to the tavern that was located on a highway some 5 km away. Kevin was obviously quite drunk when he arrived at the tavern, and the next two hours he continued to drink beer.

At closing time, the bartender informed the group (who were all quite drunk by then) that they must leave the premises. Kevin and his companion did so, and drove from the tavern parking lot, with Kevin behind the wheel, and his companion attempting to direct him into the traffic. When the way appeared to be clear for Kevin to enter his traffic lane, his friend said: "O.K.! Clear to go!" Kevin accelerated into the traffic, but was unable to control the automobile, and it careened across the centre line of the highway and into the path of an on-coming vehicle.

The collision destroyed the two automobiles, killed the driver of the other vehicle, and permanently crippled both Kevin's friend and the passenger in the other automobile. The estimated loss suffered by those injured in the accident was $1 900 000. Apart from some cuts, bruises, and a broken arm, Kevin suffered no serious effects from the accident. Blood tests taken shortly after the accident indicated that Kevin's blood-alcohol level was almost three times the legal limit.

Advise the parties of their rights in this case, and indicate how the liability, if any, would be determined.

PART III

The Law of Contract

INTRODUCTION

A contract may be defined as an agreement made between two or more persons that is enforceable at law.[1] It is not something that is tangible (although in some cases evidence of its existence may take that form) — it is a legal concept. It comes into existence, in a legal sense, when the parties have established all of the elements that make it enforceable. Until they have done so, no enforceable agreement exists. This part of the text, consisting of nine chapters, will examine the nature of each of these elements.

Contract law differs from the law of torts and many other areas of law in a rather remarkable way: if the parties comply with the principles laid down for the creation of an enforceable contract, they are free to create specific rights and duties of their own that the courts will enforce. In some respects, they create their own "law" that they are obliged to follow. How these concepts were developed is largely a matter of history, although as a body of law, the law of contract is not old. Its development parallels the rise of the mercantile class in England and North America, but it did not reach a position of importance until the nineteenth century. The next 100 years, however, saw the growth of contract law to the point where it became one of the most important areas of the common law. Today, contract law forms the basis of most commercial activity.

HISTORICAL DEVELOPMENT OF THE LAW OF CONTRACT

The law of contract is essentially an area of law relating to business transactions. Until the rise of the merchant class in England, business transactions as we know them today were not common. Under the feudal system, each manor was relatively self-sufficient, and such trade as did exist was frequently by barter or by purchase at a local fair or market. Transactions were usually instantaneous, in the sense that goods changed hands as soon as the exchange was agreed upon. Disputes that arose between merchants were promptly settled by the merchants themselves, and later by way of the rules set down by their guilds. Disputes arising out of the informal contracts or agreements that did reach the courts most often fell within the jurisdiction of the ecclesiastic courts on the basis that a breach of a solemn promise was a moral issue to be dealt with by the church. Minor cases (the equivalent of our breach of contract), however, were occasionally handled by manor courts, where damages were sometimes awarded for breach of the promise.

The establishment of England as a trading nation in the seventeenth century brought with it the need for a legal response to trade disputes. As a consequence, the seventeenth century saw the development of the **bargain theory** of a contract, whereby each party to the agreement derived some benefit from the

---

1. Osborn, P.G., *The Concise Law Dictionary,* 4th ed. (London, England: Sweet & Maxwell, 1954).

agreement in return for a promise to do or give something in return. This benefit-detriment approach formed the basis of modern contract. From that point on in time, the law developed rapidly as it responded to the changes taking place in society. The decline of the feudal system and the rise of the merchant class saw a change in the economic order that required new methods of dealing with the changing activities of the people. The development of the law of contract was essentially a response to those needs, rather than a gradual evolution of older common law.

An Introduction to the Legal Relationship

THE ELEMENTS OF A VALID CONTRACT

The creation of a binding contract that the courts will enforce requires the contracting parties to meet a number of requirements that are prescribed by the law of contract. While these requirements are not numerous, they must nevertheless be met before the agreement creates rights and duties that may be enforceable at law. These requirements are referred to as the elements of a valid contract, and consist of:

(1) an intention to create a legal relationship,
(2) offer,
(3) acceptance,
(4) consideration,
(5) capacity to contract,
(6) legality.

In addition to the six basic elements, certain types of contracts must be in writing, or take on a special form, to be enforceable. But in general, all contracts must have these six elements present to be valid and binding. Contracts must also be free from any vitiating elements such as mistake, misrepresentation, or undue influence. These elements are examined in the text following an examination of the basic elements. In this chapter, the first three elements are examined, to identify the rules applicable to the establishment of these requirements for a contract.

THE INTENTION TO CREATE A LEGAL RELATIONSHIP

The concept of a contract as a bargain or agreement struck by two parties is based upon the premise that the end results will be a meeting of the parties' minds on the terms and conditions that will form their agreement with each other. Each will normally agree to do, or perhaps refrain from doing, certain things in return for the promise of the other to do certain things of a particular nature. In the process of reaching this meeting of the minds, the parties must establish certain elements of the contract itself.

Negotiations relating to the agreement must, of necessity, have a beginning. If the agreement, by definition, consists of promises made by the parties, then one of the essential elements of an agreement must be a **promise.** Obviously, not all promises can be taken as binding on the party making them. Some may be made by persons with no intention of becoming legally obligated to fulfill them. This type of promise cannot be taken as the basis for a contract. The first requirement, then, for a valid contract, must be the **intention** on the part of the promisor to be bound by the promise made. This intention to create a legal relationship is an essential element of a valid contract. It is generally presumed to exist at law in any commercial transaction where the parties are dealing with one another at arm's length.

The intention to create a legal relationship is a **presumption at law** because the creation of the intention would otherwise be difficult to prove. Presuming that the party intended to be bound by the promise shifts the onus to prove otherwise, if the intention did not exist. If the intention is denied, the courts will usually use the conduct of the party at the time that the statements were made as a test, and assess such conduct and statements from the point of view of the "reasonable person."

The reason for the presumption that strangers who make promises to one another intend to be bound by them is essentially an approach that permits the courts to assume that the promises are binding, unless one or both of the parties can satisfy the courts that they were not intended to be so. The law, nevertheless, recognizes certain kinds of promises or statements as ones that are normally not binding, unless established as such by the evidence. For example, promises made between members of a family would not normally be considered to be an enforceable contract. Also, generally speaking, advertisements in newspapers, magazines, and other written media are not normally taken as enforceable promises that are binding on the advertiser.

The basis for these two exceptions is for the most part obvious. Members of a family frequently make promises to one another that they would normally not make to strangers. Advertisers, on the other hand, in the presentation of their goods to the public, are permitted to describe their products with some latitude and enthusiasm, provided, of course, that they do not mislead the prospective purchaser. While these two groups are not normally subject to the presumption that their promises represent an intention to create a legal relationship, they may, nevertheless, be bound by their promises if the party accepting their promises can convince a court that the promisor intended to be bound by the promise.

An early example of this point was an English case[1] which involved a manufacturer of a pharmaceutical product that advertised the product as a cure for influenza. The company had promised in its advertisement that it would pay £100 to anyone who used the product according to the prescribed directions and later contracted the illness. The advertisement also contained a statement to the effect that it intended to be bound by its promise, and that to show its good faith it had

---

1. *Carlill v. Carbolic Smoke Ball Co.,* [1893] 1 Q.B. 256.

deposited £100 for this purpose with a particular banking institution. When a person who had purchased and used the product according to the instructions later fell ill with influenza and claimed the £100, the company demurred, on the basis that it did not intend to create a legal relationship by simply advertising its product. The court held, however, that it had, by its words in the advertisement, clearly expressed the intention to be bound, and it accordingly could not later avoid or deny it.

The rule that can be drawn from this case is that while an advertiser is not normally bound by the claims set out in an advertisement, if a clear intention to be bound by them is expressed, then the courts will treat the promise as one made with an intention to create a legal relationship.

As a general rule, the courts view an advertisement (or for that matter, any display of goods) as a mere *invitation to do business,* rather than an intention to enter into a contract with the public at large. The purpose of the advertisement or display is merely to invite offers that the seller may accept or reject. This particular point becomes important in determining when a contract is made where goods are displayed for sale in a self-serve establishment. The issue was decided in an English case where the court held that the display of goods in a self-serve shop was not an offer to sell the goods to the patron of the shop, but merely an invitation to the public to examine the goods and, if the patron desired, to offer to purchase the goods. The possession of the goods by the prospective purchaser was of no consequence, as the offer to purchase and the acceptance of the offer by the seller did not take place until the seller dealt with the goods at the check-out counter. It was at this point in time that the contract was made — not before.[2]

OFFER AND ACCEPTANCE

The Nature of an Offer

The second element of a binding contract deals with promises made by the parties. Only a promise made with the intention of creating a legal relationship may be enforced. But in the normal course of negotiations a person seldom makes such a promise unless some **condition** is attached to it, requiring the other party (the **promisee**) to do some act or give a promise in exchange. Consequently, such a promise is only tentative until the other party expresses a willingness to comply with the condition. The tentative promise made subject to a condition is therefore not binding on the offering party (the **promisor** or **offeror**) until the proposal is accepted. It is only when a valid **acceptance** takes place that the parties may be bound by the agreement. These two additional requirements constitute the second and third elements of a valid contract: offer and acceptance.

Communication of an Offer

If the analysis of the negotiations is carried further, an obvious observation can be made. An offer must be communicated by the offeror to the other party (the **offeree**) before the offer is capable of being accepted. From this observation flows the first rule for offer and acceptance: *An offer must be communicated by the offeror to the offeree before acceptance may take place.*

---

2. *Pharmaceutical Society of Great Britain v. Boots Cash Chemists (Southern) Ltd.,* [1952] 2 All E.R. 456.

This rule may appear to be self-evident, but an offer is not always made directly to the offeree by the offeror. In some cases the parties may deal with each other by letter, telegraph, telex, fax, or a variety of other means of communication. Then it is important for the offeror to know when the offeree becomes aware of the offer. This is so because an offer is not valid until it is received by the offeree, and the offeror is not bound by the offer until such time as it is accepted. This means that identical offers that cross in the mail do not constitute a contract, even though there is an obvious meeting of the minds of the parties as evidenced by their offers. The essential point to make here is that no person can agree to an offer of which he or she is unaware.

If the acceptance, for example, takes place before the offer is made, the offeror is not bound by the promise. This is particularly true in the case of offers of **reward**. For example, Jones returns from work one evening to discover his prize dog missing. The next morning, on his way to work, he places an advertisement in the local newspaper offering a $50 reward for the return of his lost dog. Later that morning, his neighbour, Smith, finds the dog on the street, and returns the animal to Mrs. Jones, who is home at the time. Mrs. Jones calls Mr. Jones and tells him the dog has been returned, but it is too late for Jones to remove the advertisement from the newspaper. That afternoon, Smith discovers the offer of reward in the newspaper and claims the $50 from Jones because he found and returned his lost dog.

In this case, Jones' offer was not communicated to Smith until after Smith had fully performed what was required of him under the terms of the offer of reward. Smith, therefore, cannot accept the offer, because he returned the dog without the intention of creating a contract. His act was **gratuitous**, and he cannot later claim the right to payment. This concept will be examined more closely with respect to another element of a contract, but for the present, it may be taken as an example of the communication rule.

If the negotiation process is examined closely, another rule for offer and acceptance can be drawn from it. A person who makes an offer frequently directs it to a specific person, rather than to the public at large. A seller of goods may wish to deal with a specific person for a variety of sound reasons. For example, a seller of a prize dog may wish to sell it only to a person who would appreciate and care for the animal, or a seller of a specific type of goods may wish to sell the goods only to those persons trained in the use of the goods if some danger is attached to their use. Hence, we have the general rule that *only the person to whom an offer is made may accept the offer.*[3] If an offer is made to the public at large, this rule naturally does not apply; for the offeror is, by either words or conduct, implying in such an offer that the identity of the offeree is not important in the contract.

Acceptance of an Offer

While both an offer and its acceptance may be made or inferred from the words or the conduct of the parties, the words or conduct must conform to certain rules that have been established before the acceptance will be valid. These rules have been

---

3. *Cudney v. Lindsay* (1878), 3 App. Cas. 459.

formulated by the courts over the years as a result of the many contract disputes that came before them. At present, the major rules for acceptance are now well settled.

The first general rule for acceptance where a response is necessary is simply the reverse of the rule for offers. It states that *the acceptance of the offer must be communicated to the offeror in the manner requested or implied by the offeror in the offer.* The acceptance must take the form of certain words or acts in accordance with the offer that will indicate to the offeror that the offeree has accepted the offer. These words or conduct need not normally be precise, but they must convey the offeree's intentions to the offeror in the manner contemplated for acceptance. The rationale behind this general rule is that the offeror is entitled to some indication from the offeree of the offeree's intention to enter into the agreement, failing which the offeror may then take steps to revoke the offer and make it to someone else.

For example, if a person who writes a letter to a seller of a particular product states in the letter that she wishes to purchase a given quantity of the goods at a stipulated price, and requests that they be sent to her, the letter would constitute an offer to purchase. The acceptance would take place when the seller acted in accordance with the instructions for acceptance set out in the letter. It would not be necessary for the seller to write a reply conveying acceptance of the offer, because the offer contemplates acceptance by the act of sending the goods to the offeror. The acceptance would be complete when the seller did everything required by the terms of the offer contained in the letter.

This particular issue was raised in the case mentioned previously, where a pharmaceutical product was offered to the public at large as a cure and prevention for influenza. One of the arguments raised by the manufacturer was the fact that the plaintiff had not communicated her acceptance of the offer before using the product. Hence, no contract existed. The court disposed of this argument by saying that if the terms of the offer intimate a particular mode of acceptance to make the promise binding, it is sufficient for the offeree to comply with the indicated mode of acceptance. Notification to the offeror of the acceptance would then be unnecessary.[4]

In the case of an offer requiring some expression of acceptance by written or spoken words, a number of specific rules for acceptance have been set down. If acceptance is specified to be by oral means, the acceptance would be complete when the acceptance is communicated by the offeree either by telephone, or when the offeree meets with the offeror and speaks the words of acceptance directly to the offeror. With this form of acceptance there is no question about the communication of the words of acceptance. It takes place when the words are spoken.

The time of acceptance, however, is sometimes not as clear-cut with other modes of acceptance, and the courts have been called upon to decide the issues as the particular modes of acceptance came before them. In the case of an offer that invites acceptance by post, the rule that has been established is that the *acceptance of the offer takes place when the letter of acceptance, properly addressed and the postage paid, is placed in the postbox or post office.*[5] The reasoning

---

4. *Carlill v. Carbolic Smoke Ball Co.,* [1893] 1 Q.B. 256.
5. *Household Fire and Carriage Accident Ins. Co. v. Grant,* [1878] 4 Ex.D. 216.

behind this decision is sensible. The offeree, in preparing a letter of acceptance and delivering it to the post office, has done everything possible to accept the offer when the letter moves into the custody of the postal system. The postal system, as the agent of the addressee, is responsible for delivery from that point on. If the acceptance should be lost while in the hands of the post office, the contract would still be binding, as it was formed when the letter was posted. The offeror, by not specifying that acceptance would not be complete until the letter is received, assumes the risk of loss by the post office and any uncertainty that might accompany this specified mode of acceptance.

The courts have also held that where an offer does not specifically state that the mail should be used for acceptance, but where it is the usual or contemplated mode of acceptance, then the posting of the letter of acceptance will constitute acceptance of the offer.[6]

A somewhat similar rule also applies to the telegraph as a mode of acceptance. The acceptance is complete when the telegram of acceptance is delivered to the telegraph office for transmission to the offeror.[7] For all other modes of communication, the acceptance would not be complete until the offeror was made aware of the acceptance. The widespread use of fax machines and computers will undoubtedly produce some additional changes in the law. However, for the most part, this new technology provides for virtually instant communication of offers and their acceptance, at least with respect to the terms.

A number of other rules also apply to acceptance in addition to the rules relating to the time and place. Of particular importance is the nature of the acceptance itself. When an offer is made, the only binding acceptance would be one that clearly and **unconditionally** accepted the offeror's promise, and complied with any accompanying condition imposed by the offeror. Anything less than this would constitute either a **counter-offer,** or an **inquiry.** If an acceptance is not unconditional, but changes the terms, then it would have the effect of rejecting the original offer. It would represent, in itself, an offer that the original offeror could then either accept or reject. For example, Smith writes a letter to Jones in which he offers to sell Jones his automobile for $3000 cash. Jones writes a letter of reply in which she "accepts" Smith's offer, but states that she will buy the automobile on the payment of $1000 cash and give Jones a promissory note for $2000 to be payable $200 per month over a 10-month period.

In this example, Smith's offer is to sell his automobile for a cash payment of $3000. Jones has expressed her willingness to purchase the automobile, but has changed the offer by altering the payment provision from $3000 cash to $1000 cash and a promissory note for $2000. The change in terms represents for Smith (who now becomes the offeree) a counter-offer that he must accept or reject. The counter-offer submitted by Jones has the effect of terminating the original offer that was made by Smith. If Smith should reject the counter-offer, Jones may not accept the original offer unless Smith wishes to revive it.

The desirable approach for Jones to follow in a situation where some aspect of the offer is unacceptable to her would be to **inquire** if Smith would be willing

---

6. *Henthorn v. Fraser,* [1892] 2 Ch. 27.

7. *Cowan v. O'Connor* (1888), 20 Q.B.D. 640.

to modify the terms of payment before a response is made to the offer in a definite manner. In this fashion, she might still retain the opportunity to accept the original offer if Smith should be unwilling to modify his terms of payment.

A somewhat different matter is a rule stating that **silence** cannot be considered to be acceptance unless a pre-existing agreement to this effect has been established between the parties. The rationale for this rule is obvious. The offeree should not be obligated to refuse an offer, nor should the offeree be obliged to comply with an offer made to him simply because he has failed to reject it. The only exception to this rule would be where the offeree has clearly consented to be bound by this type of arrangement.

The question of whether a pre-existing agreement exists that would make silence acceptance is not always answerable in a definitive way. In some cases, persons may conduct themselves in such a way that, even though they remain silent in terms of acceptance, they lead the offeror to believe that acceptance has been made of the offer. This is particularly true where a person offers to perform a service with the intention of receiving payment for the service, and the offeree stands by in silence while the service is performed, with full knowledge that the offeror expects payment.

For example, in the case of *Saint John Tug Boat Co. Ltd. v. Irving Refinery Ltd.* (1964), 49 M.P.R. 284, the court quoted authorities for the common law rules which stated:

> 1. Liabilities are not to be forced upon people behind their backs any more than you can confer a benefit upon a man against his will.
>
> 2. But if a person knows that the consideration is being rendered for his benefit with an expectation that he will pay for it, then if he acquiesces in its being done, taking the benefit of it when done, he will be taken impliedly to have requested its being done: and that will import a promise to pay for it.

What the court was saying here, in essence, is that a person cannot be forced to refuse an offer presented on the basis that silence will constitute acceptance. However, if offerees so conduct themselves that their actions would lead a reasonable person to believe that they had assented to terms of the offer, then the offerees may not stand by and watch the offeror perform a benefit for them if it is clear that the offeror expects to be compensated for the work performed. Under these circumstances, offerees would have an obligation to immediately stop the offeror from performing, or reject the offer.

It is important to note that this exception to the silence rule would normally apply to those situations where the offeree's actions constitute some form of acquiescence. It would not apply, for example, where sellers send unsolicited goods to householders, because no acquiescence could take place before the delivery of the goods, at least in terms of communication of the interest to the seller.

Recent consumer protection legislation in a number of provinces has reinforced this common law rule. The legislation generally provides that members of the public shall not be obliged to pay for unsolicited goods delivered to them, nor should they be liable for the goods in any way due to their loss or damage while in their possession. Neither the common law nor the legislation, however, affect a pre-existing arrangement whereby silence may constitute acceptance of a subsequent offer. This is a common characteristic of most book and video "clubs." These clubs operate on the basis that a contract will be formed and the book or video will be delivered to the offeree if the offeree fails to respond to the offeror within a specific period of time after the offer has been made. Contracts of this nature are generally binding, because silence is considered acceptance due to the pre-existing agreement governing the future contractual relationship of the parties.

Acceptance, while it must be unconditional and made in accordance with the terms of the offer, may take many forms. The normal method of accepting an offer is to state or write, "I accept your offer," but acceptance may take other forms as well. For example, it may take the form of an affirmative nod of the head and a handshake. At an auction sale, it may take the form of the auctioneer dropping his hammer and saying, "sold," to the person making the final offer.

Where a particular method of accepting the offer is specified, the offeree must, of course, comply with the requirements. If the offeror has stated in an offer that acceptance must *only* be made by telegraph, then the offeree, if he or she wishes to accept, must use this form of communication to make a valid acceptance. Offerors usually do not impose such rigid requirements for acceptance, but often suggest that a particular method of communication would be preferred. In these cases, *if a method other than the method mentioned in the offer is selected, the acceptance would only be effective when it was received by the offeror.*[8]

Offers that require offerees to complete their part of the contract as a mode of acceptance form a special class of contracts called **unilateral agreements.** These agreements usually do not call for the communication of acceptance before the contract is to be performed, but rather signify that the offer may be accepted by the offeree completing his or her part of the agreement. Once completed, the offeror would then perform his or her part. On the surface, there would appear to be a danger with this mode of acceptance. If the offeror should withdraw the offer before the offeree has fully performed the acceptance, then no contract would exist, and any expense or inconvenience incurred by the offeree would not be recoverable. To remedy this situation, the courts have held that where an offeree is obliged to perform his or her part of the contract in order to accept the offer, then the offeror will not be permitted to withdraw the offer so long as the offeree is in the course of performing his or her part. This approach, however, assumes that the offeror has not expressly reserved the right to withdraw the offer at any time during the offeree's act of acceptance. The offer of reward for the return of a lost animal would be an example of a contract where the offer would be accepted by the act of the offeree.

Lapse of an Offer

Until an offer is accepted, no legal rights or obligations arise. Offers are not always accepted. Even in cases where the offeree may wish to accept, events may occur or conditions may change that will prevent the formation of the agreement. The death of either party, for example, will prevent the formation of the contract, because the personal representative of the deceased normally may not complete the formalities for offer and acceptance on behalf of the deceased. When an

---

8. *Henthorn v. Fraser,* [1892] 2 Ch. 27.

offeree dies before accepting an offer, the offer **lapses**, because the deceased's personal representative cannot accept an offer on behalf of a deceased person. By the same token, acceptance cannot be communicated to a deceased offeror, as the personal representative of the offeror would not be bound by the acceptance, except under special circumstances where the offeror has bound them to the offer. The same rule would hold true in the case of the bankruptcy of either of the parties, or if a party should be declared insane before acceptance is made.

An offer will also lapse as a result of a direct or indirect response to the offer that does not accept the offer unconditionally and in accordance with its terms. If the offeree rejects the offer outright, it lapses and cannot be revived except by the offeror. Similarly, any change in the terms of the offer in a purported acceptance will cause the original offer to lapse, as the modified acceptance would constitute a counter-offer.

Offers may also lapse by the passage of time, or the happening of a specified event. Obviously, an offer that must be accepted within a specified period of time or by a stipulated date will lapse if acceptance is not made within the period of time or by the particular date. An offer may also lapse within a reasonable time if no time of acceptance has been specified. What constitutes a reasonable time, needless to say, will depend upon the circumstances of the transaction and its subject-matter. An offer to sell a truckload of perishable goods would have a much shorter "reasonable" time for acceptance than an offer to sell a truckload of non-perishable goods that are not subject to price or market fluctuation.

As a general rule, where an offer is made by a person in the company of another and where no time-limit for acceptance is expressed, the offer is presumed to lapse when the other party departs without accepting the offer, unless the circumstances surrounding the offer would indicate otherwise.

Revocation of an Offer

Revocation, as opposed to lapse, requires an act on the part of the offeror in order to be effective. Normally the offeror must communicate the revocation to the offeree before the offer is accepted, otherwise the notice of revocation will be ineffective. With an ordinary contract, as a general rule, an offeror may revoke the offer at any time prior to acceptance, even where the offeror has gratuitously agreed to keep the offer open for a specified period of time. If the offeree wishes to make certain that the offeror will not revoke the offer, the method generally used is called an **option**. An option is a separate promise that obliges the offeror to keep the offer open for a specified period of time, either in return for some compensation, or because the promise is made in a formal document under seal. (The effect of the seal on a document will be examined in the next chapter, as will the effect of compensation paid to an offeror in return for the promise. However, for the present it is sufficient to note that either of these two things will have the effect of rendering the promise to keep the offer open for a specified period of time irrevocable.)

A second aspect of revocation of an offer is that it need not be communicated in any special way to be effective. The only requirement is that the notice of revocation be brought to the attention of the offeree before the offer is accepted. This does not mean, however, that the same rules apply to revocation as apply to acceptance where some form of communication other than direct communication is used. Because the offeree must be aware of the revocation before it is effective, the courts have held that the posting of a letter revoking an offer previously made does not have the effect of revoking the offer. The notice of revocation is only effective when it is finally received by the offeree.[9] The same rule would apply to a telegraph message.

The question of whether indirect notice of revocation will have the effect of revoking an offer is less clear. For example, Anderson offers to sell her car to Burton and promises to keep the offer open for three days. On the second day, Andrews sells her car to Coulson. The sale of the car would clearly be evidence of Andrews' intention to revoke the offer to sell to Burton. If a mutual friend of Burton and Coulson told Burton of the sale of the car to Coulson, would this indirect notice prevent Burton from accepting the offer? This very question arose in an English case in which an offer had been made to sell certain property and the offeree was given a number of days to accept. Before the time had expired, the offeror sold the property to another party, and a person not acting under the direction of the offeror informed the offeree of the sale. The offeree then accepted the offer (within the time period for acceptance) and demanded conveyance of the property. The court held in this case that the offeree was informed of the sale by a reliable source, and this knowledge precluded acceptance of the offer by him.[10]

The judge in the case described the situation in the following manner:

> If a man makes an offer to sell a particular horse in his stable, and says, "I will give you until the day after tomorrow to accept the offer," and the next day goes and sells the horse to somebody else, and receives the purchase-money from him, can the person to whom the offer was originally made then come and say, "I accept," so as to make a binding contract, and so as to be entitled to recover damages for the non-deliver of the horse? If the rule of law is that a mere offer to sell property, which can be withdrawn at any time, and which is made dependent on the acceptance of the person to whom it is made, is a mere *nudum pactum,* how is it possible that the person to whom the offer has been made can by acceptance make a binding contract after he knows that the person who has made the offer has sold the property to some one else? It is admitted law that, if a man who makes an offer dies, the offer cannot be accepted after he is dead, and parting with the property has very much the same effect as the death of the owner, for it makes the performance of the offer impossible. I am clearly of the opinion that, just as when a man who has made an offer dies before it is accepted it is impossible that it can then be accepted, so when once the person to whom the offer was made knows that the property has been sold to some one else, it is too late for him to accept the offer, and on that ground I am clearly of opinion that there was no binding contract for the sale of this property....[11]

The essential point to note, in cases where notice of revocation is brought to the attention of the offeree by someone other than the offeror or the offeror's agent, is the reliability of the source. The offeror must, of course, prove that the offeree had notice of the revocation before the offer was accepted. The onus

9. *Byrne & Co. v. Leon Van Tienhoven & Co.* (1880), 5 C.P.D. 344; *Henthorn v. Fraser,* [1892] 2 Ch. 27.

10. *Dickinson v. Dodds* (1876), 2 Ch.D. 463.

11. Ibid.

would be on the offeror to satisfy the court that the reliability of the source of the knowledge was such that a reasonable person would accept the information as definite evidence that the offeror had withdrawn the offer. Cases of indirect notice, consequently, turn very much on the reliability of the source when the notice comes from some source other than the offeror or the offeror's agent. The case cited represents only an example of how a court may deal with the problem of indirect notice, rather than a statement of the common law on this issue.

SUMMARY

The law of contract, unlike many other laws, does not set out the rights and duties of the parties. Instead, it permits the parties to establish their own rights and duties by following a series of principles and rules for the formation of a contract. A contract is essentially an agreement that is enforceable at law. As such, it must contain all of the elements of a true agreement. It must, first of all, be a "meeting of the minds of the parties," and an intention on the part of both parties to create a legal relationship must be present. There must also be an offer of a promise by one party subject to some condition, and the offer must be properly accepted by the other party. If the offer is not properly accepted, no contract will exist, and the offer may be terminated or replaced by a counter-offer. If nothing is done to accept the offer it will lapse, or the offeror may withdraw it. In either case, if validly done, no contract will exist. If an unconditional acceptance has been properly made in accordance with the terms of the offer, and before the offer lapses or is withdrawn, then the parties will be bound by the agreement they have made, and their promises will be enforced by the courts. Offer, acceptance, and an intention to create a legal relationship represent three very important elements of a contract. There are other elements that the parties must establish to have a valid contract. These represent the subject-matter of the following chapters.

DISCUSSION QUESTIONS

1. "The parties to a contract, if they do things right, create their own rights and duties." Is this a valid observation?
2. Why is an intention to create a legal relationship an important element of a valid contract?
3. Explain why communication of an offer must take place before the offer may be accepted. Why is this important?
4. Describe the "rules" for acceptance, and explain why such "rules" are necessary.
5. Under what circumstances would "silence" be acceptance?
6. Explain the term *counter-offer,* and describe how it might arise.
7. Is an advertisement containing an offer of a reward for a lost pet a valid offer? How does it differ from an advertisement of goods for sale?
8. Describe four instances where an offer might lapse before acceptance.
9. Explain the rationale behind the rule that states that an offer by mail invites acceptance by mail, and that the acceptance is complete when a properly addressed letter of acceptance is dropped in a post office letter-box.
10. What condition must be met before revocation of an offer is effective?
11. Describe the burden placed upon the offeror by the courts when the offeror has alleged that indirect notice of revocation was received by the offeree.
12. How does acceptance of a unilateral agreement differ from that of an ordinary agreement?

MINI-CASE
PROBLEMS

1. X placed a "for sale" sign on his lawn-mower, and displayed the machine at the front of his house. The sign read: "Lawn-Mower for Sale — $50." Y and Z both arrive at X's house and wish to acquire the machine. Y is the first to meet X and says: "I accept your offer. Here is my $50." Z then states: "Here is $51. I will take your mower." Must X sell the mower to Y?

2. D offered to sell his automobile to E for $5000 cash. E responded to D's offer by saying: "I will buy your automobile for $5000. I will pay you $2500 now, and $2500 in one week's time." Have D and E formed a binding agreement?

3. The president of A Co. wrote a letter to B Co. offering to sell B Co. a large quantity of steel at a specific price. B Co. did not respond to the letter, but A Co. sent a "sample load" of one tonne that B Co. used in its manufacturing process. A month later, A Co. sent the quantity of steel specified in its letter along with an invoice at the price specified. Is B Co. bound to accept and pay for the steel?

**JUDICIAL
DECISIONS**

The *Pharmaceutical Society of Great Britain v. Boots Cash Chemists (Southern) Ltd.* is a case that delineates when offer and acceptance takes place under conditions where goods are placed on display in a self-serve establishment. The judge notes that the mere display of goods does not amount to an offer to sell, but rather to invite offers that the seller may then either accept or reject. The judge gives various examples of when an offer might be considered to take place. He concludes that offer and acceptance takes place at the self-serve check-out, where the seller may accept or reject the offer at that time.

The *Carlill v. Carbolic Smoke Ball Co.* case illustrates an offer to the public-at-large and the conditions under which an advertisement may be taken to be an offer. The judge states that the advertisement must clearly indicate by its wording that the advertiser intends it to be an offer, otherwise it remains an invitation to do business. The judge discusses the point of communication of acceptance of such an offer, and concludes that no communication is necessary, as it invites acceptance by the offeree acting in accordance with the terms of the offer.

**Offer —
Acceptance —
Time of an
Offer — Time of
Acceptance**

Pharmaceutical Society of Great Britain v. Boots Cash Chemists (Southern) Ltd., [1952] 2 Q.B. 795.

The defendants operated a self-serve drug store. Some drugs which were classed as "poison" under government legislation were displayed on self-serve shelves, but the sales were recorded by a qualified pharmacist at the check-out counter. The defendant was charged with selling poisons contrary to the act by failing to have a registered pharmacist supervise the sale of the product. The case turned on when and where the sale took place.

> LORD GODDARD, C.J. (after reviewing the evidence):
>
> The question which I have to decide is whether the sale is completed before or after the intending purchaser has passed the scrutiny of the pharmacist and paid his money, or, to put it in another way, whether the offer which initiates the negotiations is an offer by the shopkeeper or an offer by the buyer.
>
> I think that it is a well-established principle that the mere exposure of goods for sale by a shopkeeper indicates to the public that he is willing to treat but does not amount to an offer to sell. I do not think I ought to hold that that principle is completely reversed merely because there is a self-service scheme, such as this, in operation. In my opinion it comes to no more than that the customer is informed that he may himself pick up an article and bring it to the shopkeeper

with a view to buying it, and if, but only if, the shopkeeper than expresses his willingness to sell, the contract for sale is completed. In fact, the offer is an offer to buy, and there is no offer to sell; the customer brings the goods to the shopkeeper to see whether he will sell or not. In 99 cases out of a 100 he will sell and, if so, he accepts the customer's offer, but he need not do so. The very fact that the supervising pharmacist is at the place where the money has to be paid is an indication to the purchaser that the shopkeeper may not be willing to complete a contract with anybody who may bring the goods to him.

Ordinary principles of common sense and of commerce must be applied in this matter, and to hold that in the case of self-service shops the exposure of an article is an offer to sell, and that a person can accept the offer by picking up the article, would be contrary to those principles and might entail serious results. On the customer picking up the article the property would forthwith pass to him and he would be able to insist upon the shopkeeper allowing him to take it away, though in some particular cases the shopkeeper might think that very undesirable. On the other hand, if a customer had picked up an article, he would never be able to change his mind and to put it back; the shopkeeper could say, "Oh no, the property has passed and you must pay the price."

It seems to me, therefore, that the transaction is in no way different from the normal transaction in a shop in which there is no self-service scheme. I am quite satisfied it would be wrong to say that the shopkeeper is making an offer to sell every article in the shop to any person who might come in and that that person can insist on buying any article by saying "I accept your offer." I agree with the illustration put forward during the case of a person who might go into a shop where books are displayed. In most book-shops customers are invited to go in and pick up books and look at them even if they do not actually buy them. There is no contract by the shopkeeper to sell until the customer has taken the book to the shopkeeper or his assistant and said "I want to buy this book" and the shopkeeper says "Yes." That would not prevent the shopkeeper, seeing the book picked up, saying: "I am sorry I cannot let you have that book; it is the only copy I have got and I have already promised it to another customer." Therefore, in my opinion, the mere fact that a customer picks up a bottle of medicine from the shelves in this case does not amount to an acceptance of an offer to sell. It is an offer by the customer to buy and there is no sale effected until the buyer's offer is accepted by the acceptance of the price. The offer, the acceptance of the price, and therefore the sale, take place under the supervision of the pharmacist.

Offer to Public at Large — Acceptance — Notice to Offeror

Carlill v. Carbolic Smoke Ball Co., [1893] 1 Q.B. 256.

The defendants were manufacturers of a medical preparation called the "carbolic smoke ball." To sell their product they inserted an advertisement in a number of newspapers which read:

"100£ reward will be paid by the Carbolic Smoke Ball Company to any person who contracts the increasing epidemic influenza, colds, or any disease caused by taking cold, after having used the ball three times daily for two weeks according to the printed directions supplied with each ball. 100£ is deposited with the Alliance Bank, Regent Street, shewing our sincerity in the matter.

During the last epidemic of influenza many thousand carbolic smoke balls were sold as preventives against this disease, and in no ascertained case was the disease contracted by those using the carbolic smoke ball.

One carbolic smoke ball will last a family several months, making it the cheapest remedy in the world at the price, 10s., post free. The ball can be refilled at a cost of 5s. Address, Carbolic Smoke Ball Company, 27, Princes Street, Hanover Square, London.

The plaintiff purchased and used the preparation according to the instructions and was then attacked by influenza. She brought an action against the defendant for the £100 reward.

Lindley, L.J.:

The first observation I will make is that we are not dealing with any inference of fact. We are dealing with an express promise to pay 100£ in certain events. Read the advertisement how you will, and twist it about as you will, here is a distinct promise expressed in language which is perfectly unmistakable — "100£ reward will be paid by the Carbolic Smoke Ball Company to any person who contracts the influenza after having used the ball three times daily for two weeks according to the printed directions supplied with each ball."

We must first consider whether this was intended to be a promise at all, or whether it was a mere puff which meant nothing. Was it a mere puff? My answer to that question is No, and I base my answer upon this passage: "100£ is deposited with the Alliance Bank, shewing our sincerity in the matter." Now, for what was that money deposited or that statement made except to negative the suggestion that this was a mere puff and meant nothing at all? The deposit is called in aid by the advertiser as proof of his sincerity in the matter — that is, the sincerity of his promise to pay this 100£ in the event which he has specified. I say this for the purpose of giving point to the observation that we are not inferring a promise; there is the promise, as plain as words can make it.

Then it is contended that it is not binding. In the first place, it is said that it is not made with anybody in particular. Now that point is common to the words of this advertisement and to the words of all other advertisements offering rewards. They are offers to anybody who performs the conditions named in the advertisement, and anybody who does perform the condition accepts the offer. In point of law this advertisement is an offer to pay 100£ to anybody who will perform these conditions, and the performance of the conditions is the acceptance of the offer....

But then it is said, "Supposing that the performance of the conditions is an acceptance of the offer, that acceptance ought to have been notified." Unquestionably, as a general proposition, when an offer is made, it is necessary in order to make a binding contract, not only that it should be accepted, but that the acceptance should be notified. But is that so in cases of this kind? I apprehend that they are an exception to the rule, or, if not an exception, they are open to the observation that the notification of the acceptance need not precede the performance. This offer is a continuing offer. It was never revoked, and if notice of acceptance is required — which I doubt very much, for I rather think the true view is that which was expressed and explained by Lord Blackburn in the case of *Brogden v. Metropolitan Ry. Co.* — if notice of acceptance is required, the person who makes the offer gets the notice of acceptance contemporaneously with his notice of the performance of the condition. If he gets notice of the acceptance before his offer is revoked, that in principle is all you want. I, however, think that the true view, in a case of this kind, is that the person who makes the offer shews by his language and from the nature of the transaction that he does not expect and does not require notice of the acceptance apart from notice of the performance.

It appears to me, therefore, that the defendants must perform their promise....

CASE PROBLEMS FOR DISCUSSION

Case 1

Jones lived in Calgary, Alberta, and owned a cottage on Vancouver Island. Percy, who lived in Victoria, British Columbia, was interested in purchasing the cottage owned by Jones. On September 10th, he wrote a letter to Jones offering to purchase the cottage and lot for $75 000. Jones received the letter on September 15th, and sent Percy a telegram offering to sell the cottage to him for $78 000.

Percy did not respond to the telegram immediately, but on a business trip to Calgary on September 22nd, he spoke to Jones about the cottage in an effort to determine if Jones might be willing to reduce the price. Jones replied that the price was "firm" at $78 000.

When Percy returned to Victoria, he sent a letter to Jones accepting his offer to sell the cottage at $78 000. The letter was posted at 11:40 a.m. on September 23rd, but, through a delay in the mail, was not delivered to Jones in Calgary until 4:20 p.m. on September 28th.

In the meantime, when Jones had not heard from Percy by September 26th he offered to sell the cottage to Johnson, who had expressed an interest in purchasing the cottage some time before. Johnson accepted the offer, and the two parties executed a written purchase agreement in Johnson's office on the morning of September 27th.

Identify the various rights and liabilities that developed from the negotiations set out above.

Case 2

McKay operated a large farm on which he grew a variety of vegetables for commercial canners. He would also grow a smaller quantity for sale to local retailers and wholesalers as fresh produce. On August 5th, Daigle approached McKay and offered to purchase 100 bushels of tomatoes from him at a fixed price per bushel. McKay stated that the price was acceptable to him, but he was uncertain as to whether his crop would be sufficient to make up the 100 bushels. He told Daigle he could definitely supply 80 bushels, and that he would be in a position to tell Daigle by the next week if the additional 20 bushels would be available. Daigle nodded approval and left.

A few days later, McKay discovered that crop failures in other parts of the province had pushed tomato prices substantially above the price offered by Daigle. McKay's crop, however, was abundant, and he discovered that he had 120 bushels when the crop was harvested.

At the end of the week, Daigle called to determine if McKay could supply him with 100 bushels, or only 80. McKay refused to supply Daigle with any tomatoes, and informed him that it was his intention to sell the crop elsewhere.

Discuss the negotiations between the parties, and determine the rights (if any) and liabilities (if any) of the parties. Assume that Daigle brought an action against McKay. Discuss the nature of the action and render, with reasons, a decision.

Case 3

Armstrong wrote a letter to Bishop on May 2nd offering to sell him 200 tonnes of scrap mica at $180 per tonne. Bishop received the letter on May 3rd. A few weeks later, Bishop checked the price of mica, and discovered that the market price had risen to $185 per tonne. On May 22nd, Bishop wrote Armstrong, accepting the offer. Armstrong did not receive Bishop's letter until May 30th. Armstrong refused to sell the mica to Bishop at $180 per tonne, but expressed a willingness to sell at the current market price of $187 per tonne.

Bishop instituted legal proceedings against Armstrong for breach of the contract that he alleged existed between them.

Discuss the rights (if any) and the liabilities (if any) of the parties, and render a decision.

Case 4

The Clear Fruit Juice Company purchased a quantity of a special variety of apple that Ely grew in his orchards. The apple was of a type that kept well in winter storage, and the company would market a part of the apples purchased as fresh fruit and process the remainder into apple juice that it sold under a private brand name. The company purchase represented approximately 50 percent of Ely's total harvest each year.

Initially, the Clear Fruit Juice Company and Ely entered into a formal, written purchase agreement for each year's crop. However, over time the agreement became less formal. Eventually it consisted at first of a telephone order for the "usual supply," and later to an arrangement whereby Ely would deliver the normal quantity to the company each year, and in due course would receive payment at the going market price for the crop. This latter arrangement carried on for a period of about 10 years.

In the last year, the president of the Clear Fruit Juice Company fell seriously ill and retired. He had been responsible for the original contracts with Ely, and had made the later informal arrangements for the supply of apples. For many years, the two men had been good friends. The new president of the company moved to the area from a subsidiary corporation, and was not aware of the arrangement between Ely and the company. He decided that for the current year he would purchase the company's apple requirements from another orchard.

Over the course of the summer, Ely heard rumours that an orchard some miles distant had acquired a contract to supply his variety of apple to the company, but he did nothing to investigate the matter further. In the fall of the year, he delivered his usual supply in large pallet boxes to the company, and placed them in the storage yard. No employees were in the yard at the time, but Ely did not find the fact unusual, as that was typically the case when he made his deliveries in the past. He was not concerned about identification of the crop as each pallet box bore his name and address as well as the variety and quantity.

The yard foreman noticed the apples in the supply yard some time later on the day of delivery, and informed the plant manager. The plant manager did nothing about the apples until the next day, when he informed the company president. The company president decided to write a letter to Ely requesting him to take back his apples, but it was Friday, so he left the letter until Monday of the next week. Ely received the letter on the Wednesday, some six days after delivery of the fruit to the company.

During the six-day period the apples had remained in the hot sun and had deteriorated from the exposure. Ely refused to take back the apples, and the company refused to pay for them.

Advise the parties of their rights in this case, and determine the probable outcome if Ely should bring an action against the company for the value of the goods.

Case 5

On February 2nd, Brown, who lived in Kingston, wrote a letter to Jones, offering to sell his (Brown's) snowmobile for $1000. The letter was delivered to Jones at his home in Brockville, some 80 km from Kingston, on February 6th.

On February 3rd, Brown met his friend Black on the main street of Kingston. During their conversation, Black expressed an interest in buying Brown's snowmobile. He offered Brown $1000 for the machine, but Brown said only that he would "give the offer some thought," and promised to advise Black of his decision. Brown did not tell Black of his offer to sell the machine to Jones.

On February 4th, while in Toronto on business, Black sent a telegram to Brown, offering to buy the snowmobile for $1100, if Brown would deliver the machine, on February 10th, to his farm, located some 16 km north of Kingston. Brown received the telegram the same day and, that evening, wrote and mailed a letter to Jones, revoking his offer to sell the snowmobile.

On February 7th, Jones wrote a letter to Brown accepting his offer to sell the snowmobile and enclosed a cheque for $1000 as payment in full. On February 8th, Jones received Brown's letter revoking the offer.

Brown had business at a small village north of Kingston on February 8th, and, since his trip would take him past Black's farm, he decided to deliver the snowmobile on his way to the village. Brown unloaded the machine at Black's farm, but, finding no one at home, left the keys to the machine and a note in Black's mail-box. The note stated that he had left the machine behind the garage.

On February 9th, Brown received the letter of acceptance Jones had mailed to him on February 7th. Brown immediately telephoned Jones to tell him that he had sold the machine to Black, but Jones was out of town on a business trip. Brown left the message with Jones's wife and, on February 10th, returned by mail the cheque that Jones had sent him with the letter of acceptance.

Later on February 10th, Brown received a telephone call from Black, who had just returned from Toronto, requesting delivery of the snowmobile. When Brown explained that the machine had been delivered on February 8th, Black stated that he had seen snowmobile tracks in the yard, but the machine was not behind the garage. Brown then requested Black to call in the police to investigate the theft.

On February 13th, the police located the machine in the possession of Smith, age 17, and an arrest was made. Unfortunately, the machine had been badly damaged while in Smith's possession. The estimate of the damage was $300.

Discuss the issues raised in this case. Describe the rights of the parties (if any) and the possible outcome of any litigation if legal action should be taken to enforce the rights of the parties.

Case 6

The Garden Book Company advertised in a local newspaper the publication of its latest book on growing flowers. The advertisement indicated that orders would be taken by mail at a price of $30 per copy, but the book would be available at all book stores as well.

In response to the advertisement, Laurel Bush sent her cheque for $30 to the Garden Book Company, and requested in her letter that the company send her a copy of the book by return mail. Laurel mailed her letter on February 19th. On February 21st, Laurel noticed the same book on sale at a local book store at a price of $9.95. She purchased a copy, then went home and immediately wrote a letter to the Garden Book Company revoking her offer to purchase the book, and requested a return of her $30 cheque. Laurel mailed her letter at 4:20 p.m. on February 21st.

The Garden Book Company received Laurel's letter of February 19th on February 22nd, and mailed her a letter the same day which acknowledged her order and advised her that the book would be sent to her by courier within a few days. The Garden Book Company received Laurel's letter of February 21st on February 23rd. The company ignored her second letter, and delivered the book to the courier on February 25th.

Discuss the rights of the parties in this case. Identify and explain the legal principles and rules applicable, and indicate in your answer how the case would be decided if the matter came before the court.

Case 7

The Golden Lake Mining Company decided to dispose of two of its undeveloped mining properties ("A" and "B") and authorized the company president to find a buyer. On September 10th, the president wrote a letter to the East Country Exploration Corporation offering to sell the properties "en bloc" for $500 000.

On September 16th, East Country Exploration Corporation replied by mail to the letter in which it expressed an interest in the purchase of property "A" at a price of $275 000 if Golden Lake Mining was prepared to sell the properties on an individual basis.

On September 22nd, the president of Golden Lake Mining replied by fax that he would prefer to sell both properties, but if he could not find a buyer for the two parcels within the next few weeks, the Company might consider selling the properties on an individual basis.

On September 30th, the East Country Exploration Corporation made an inquiry by fax to determine if Golden Lake Mining had decided to sell the properties on an individual basis. The president of Golden Lake responded with a fax which stated: "Still looking for a buyer for both properties."

Following this response, East Country Exploration decided to examine property "B," and sent out its two geologists to do a brief exploratory evaluation. On October 6th they reported back to say that they had examined property "B" and found some surface evidence of what might be a potentially economic ore body worth between 5 and 15 million dollars. East Country Exploration then prepared a letter accepting the offer of Golden Lake Mining to sell properties "A" and "B" for $500 000. The letter was mailed on October 9th.

On October 10th the president of Golden Lake Mining Company found a buyer for the "B" property at a price of $300 000, and signed a sale agreement the same day. He then wrote a letter to East Country Exploration in which he accepted their offer to buy the "A" property for $275 000. The president of Golden Lake Mining received the October 9th letter of East Country Exploration on October 11th.

Discuss the issues raised in this case, and indicate in your answer how the case might be decided if it was brought before the court.

Requirement of Consideration

CONSIDERATION

Nature of Consideration

The **bargain theory** of contract suggests that a contract is essentially an agreement between parties where each gets something in return for his or her promise. If this is the case, then every promise by an offeror to do something must be conditional. The promise must include a provision that the offeree, by conveying acceptance, will promise something to the offeror. The "something" that the promisor receives in return for the promisor's promise is called **consideration** — an essential element of every simple contract.

Consideration can take many forms. It may be a payment of money, the performance of a particular service, a promise not to do something by the promisee, the relinquishment of a right, the delivery of property, or a myriad of other things, including a promise in return for the promise. However, in every case, the consideration must be something done with respect to the promise offered by the promisor. Unless a promisor gets something in return for his or her promise, the promise is merely **gratuitous.** Generally, consideration for a promise must exist for the contract to be legally binding.

There are, however, certain exceptions to this rule; but they are few in number, most dating back to times before the concept of modern contract was developed. It has long been a rule of English law that a gratuitous offer of a service, if accepted, must be performed with care and skill, otherwise the promisor will be liable for any loss suffered as a result of careless performance or negligence. This liability, however, would not flow from any breach of contract, but, rather from the tort committed.

A second major exception, dating back to the days of the law merchant, remains today as a part of our legislation dealing with negotiable instruments. A person may be liable on a promissory note, or other negotiable instrument, to a subsequent endorser, even though no consideration exists between them. Under the same body of law, a party who endorses a bill of exchange (e.g., a cheque) to enable another to negotiate it may be held liable on the bill, even though no consideration was given as a result of the endorsement.

A modern-day exception to the rule concerns the promise of a donation to a charitable organization. If the rule relating to consideration is strictly applied to a promise of a donation to charity, the agreement would not be enforceable, as the promise would be gratuitous. This is because the donor would receive nothing in return for the promise made. While this is the usual situation where a donation to a charity is concerned, the courts have made exceptions in some cases. If the charity can show that it undertook a specific project on the strength of the donor's pledge, then the promise may be enforced. This, of course, would only be applicable where the donor's promised donation was such that it represented a substantial part of the funds necessary for the project. For example, in a city in Manitoba, the YMCA, while soliciting donations for the construction of a new building, obtained a substantial pledge from one person. The amount of the pledge prompted the YMCA to commit itself in contract to erect and equip the new building. After construction was underway, the pledgor refused to honour his promise of payment, and the YMCA sued for the amount. The pledgor's defence was that the promise was unenforceable due to a lack of consideration, but the court ruled otherwise. The charity satisfied the court that it would not have begun the project without the particular pledge, and had incurred liability on the strength of the promise of funds. The court decided that this was sufficient consideration for the promised donation.[1]

If the promised donation is not significant, the courts will not enforce the gratuitous promise. In the case of *Governors of Dalhousie College v. Boutilier*,[2] the university solicited funds for the maintenance and the construction of new facilities. Mr. Boutilier promised a donation, but died before the payment was made. When his estate refused to pay the pledge, the university sued to obtain the amount promised. The amount pledged, however, was small in comparison with the total funds contributed. As a result, the court refused to enforce the pledge against the estate on the basis that the university had not relied on the specified subscription of Mr. Boutilier when it undertook the repairs and new construction.

Seal as Consideration

A final, major exception to the requirement for consideration in a contract is a device that was used by the courts to enforce promises long before modern contract law emerged. This particular device is the use of a **seal** on a written contract. In the past (as early as the thirteenth century), a written agreement would be enforced by the court if the promisor had placed his seal on the document. The original purpose of the seal was to prove the authenticity of the agreement, leaving the promisor free to prove the document fraudulent if the seal was not present. As time passed, the document became a formal agreement that the courts would

---

1. *Sargent v. Nicholson* (1915), D.L.R. 638.
2. *Governors of Dalhousie College v. Boutilier,* [1934] 3 D.L.R. 593.

enforce if the seal was present. The general thinking of the judges of the day was that any person who affixed a seal to a document containing a promise to do something had given the matter considerable thought, and the act of affixing the seal symbolized the intention to be bound by the agreement. In a sense, the promisor, by affixing the seal to the written promise, was formalizing his intention to be bound. This particular method of establishing an agreement, and this ritual, distinguished the formal contract from the ordinary or simple contract that may or may not be in writing.

Originally, the person entering into the agreement would affix a seal (a wax impression of his or her family crest or coat of arms) to the document, then place a finger on the impression and express the intention to be bound by the promise. This formal act gave the document its validity. Over time, the act became less formal. Today, most formal legal documents that require a seal either have the seal printed on the form, or have a small gummed wafer attached to the form by the party who prepares the document before it is signed by the promisor. The binding effect of a formal contract under seal, however, persists today. The courts will not normally look behind a contract under seal to determine if consideration exists, because the agreement derives its validity from its form (i.e., the signature plus the seal).

In spite of its ancient roots, the contract under seal is a useful form of contract today. For example, where parties wish to enforce a gratuitous promise, the expression of the promise in writing with the signature of the promisor and a seal affixed is the usual method used.

Many formal agreements still require a special form and execution under seal to be valid. For example, in some provinces where the Registry System applies to land transfers, the various Short Forms of Conveyances Acts require a conveyance of land to be in accordance with a particular form, as well as signed, sealed, and delivered to effect the transfer of the property interest to the grantee. A power of attorney in some provinces must also be executed under seal to authorize an attorney to deal with a grantor's land.

Some legal entities execute formal documents by way of a seal. A corporation, for example, can only act through its agents to carry out its objects. For many kinds of simple contracts it may be bound by its properly authorized agent without the use of the corporate seal. To be bound by a formal contract, in some provinces, those corporations that have corporate seals must have the corporate seal affixed by the agent. It should be noted, however, that not all corporations are required to have seals. Under some business corporations' statutes (such as the Canada Business Corporations Act) formal documents need only be signed by the proper officers of the corporation. The general trend has been to eliminate the need for business corporations to use seals to execute documents such as contracts.

Tenders

The **tender** in contract law, as it relates to the formation of a legal relationship, differs from the ordinary offer. Tenders are frequently used by business firms, government organizations, and others with a view to establishing a contractual relationship for the supply of goods or services or the construction of buildings, machinery, or equipment. Municipalities commonly use the tender method in the acquisition of supplies or services as a means of fairly opening competition to all firms in the municipality (and elsewhere). The tendering process generally uses the seal to render an offer irrevocable, and often uses the payment of a money deposit as a special type of consideration.

The tender process usually involves the advertisement of the particular needs of the firm to potential suppliers of the goods or services, either by way of newspapers or by direct mail contact. This step in the process is known as **calling for tenders,** and has no binding effect on the firm that makes the call. It is merely an offer to negotiate a contract. In most cases it represents an invitation to persons or business firms to submit offers that the firm calling for the tenders may, at its option, accept or reject. The firm making the call is not bound to accept the lowest offer nor, for that matter, any of the offers.

As a general rule, unless provided to the contrary in the call for tenders, an offer made in response to the call may be revoked at any time before acceptance. To avoid this, the call for tenders frequently requires offerors to submit their offers as irrevocable offers under seal. In this manner the offer may not be revoked, and will stand until such time as it is either accepted or it expires. Businesses and organizations calling for tenders may also require the offerors to provide a money deposit as well to ensure that the successful offeror will execute the subsequent contract that is usually required to formalize the agreement between the parties. When a deposit has been submitted with the tender under seal, a failure or refusal on the part of the successful bidder to enter into the formal contract and perform it according to its terms would result in forfeiture of the deposit, as well as entitle the party who made the call to take legal action.

For example, in the case of *The Queen in Right of Ontario v. Ron Engineering and Construction Eastern Ltd.*[3], a call for tenders was made and the defendant submitted a tender along with the required deposit. Later, the defendant was notified that it was the successful bidder. The defendant, however, discovered an error in the tender that would result in a loss for the defendant if the contract was performed. The defendant then refused to enter into a formal contract to perform the work. In the litigation that followed, the court held that the call for tenders stipulated that the deposit would be forfeited if the successful bidder refused to execute the formal contract. The defendant had agreed to these terms, and as a result, the defendant was not entitled to a return of the deposit money.

Adequacy of Consideration

In general, the courts are not concerned about the adequacy of consideration because they are reluctant to become involved as arbiters of the price or value that a person receives for a promise. Apart from the requirement that the consideration be legal, their main concern is with the presence or absence of consideration, rather than whether the promisor received proper compensation for his or her promise. In some cases, however, the courts will look more closely at the adequacy of the consideration. If the promisor can satisfy the court that the promise was made under unusual circumstances (such as where an error occurred that

---

3. *The Queen in Right of Ontario v. Ron Engineering and Construction Eastern Ltd.* (1981), 119 D.L.R. (3d) 267.

rendered the consideration totally inadequate in relation to the promise made), the courts may intervene. For example, Able writes a letter to Baker offering to sell his car to Baker for $3500. Baker refuses the offer, but makes a counter-offer to Able to purchase the car for $3000. Able sends a wire in return, rejecting Baker's offer to purchase and offering to sell his car for $3200. In sending the wire, the telegraph office mistakenly shows the price as $3.20, instead of $3200. If Baker should "snap up" the offer, he could not enforce Able's promise to sell, because the courts would reject his claim on the basis of the obvious error in the offer. Able, after offering his car for sale for $3500 and rejecting an offer for $3000, would not then offer to sell the car for a nominal consideration of $3.20.

If the error, however, was in Able's original letter in which he intended to sell the car for $3500, but inadvertently offered it to Baker for $3000 and Baker accepted the offer, he would probably be bound by the contract. In this case, the courts would have no way of determining Able's intention at the time the offer was made, and would not inquire into the adequacy of the consideration.

To be valid, consideration must also be something of value that the person receives in return for the promise is made. It cannot be something that the person has received before the promise is made, nor can it be something that a person is already entitled to receive by law, or under another enforceable agreement. In the first case, if a person has already received the benefit for which the promise is offered, nothing is received in return for the promise. The consideration is essentially **past consideration**, which is no consideration at all, and the promise is gratuitous. The consideration offered must be something that the promisee will give, pay, do, or provide, either at the instant the promise is made (present consideration), or at a later date (future consideration).

For example, A cuts B's lawn while B is on vacation, and on B's return, B promises to give A $10 for his kind act. In this case, A's act of cutting B's lawn was gratuitous, and past consideration for B's later promise of payment. If B fails to pay the $10, no contract exists for A to enforce because no consideration can be shown except the past gratuitous act.

However, if B requested A to cut his lawn while he was on vacation, and promised A $10 if he did so, when B returned he would be obliged to pay the $10 because the consideration would be future consideration, and the contract enforceable when A cut the lawn.

In the second case, the consideration that the promisee agrees to provide in return for the promise must not be something that the promisee is already bound to do at law or under another agreement. In both instances it would not constitute a benefit that the promisor would receive in return for the promise, and it would not constitute valuable consideration. If a person already has a duty to do some act, provide some service, or pay something to the promisor, then the promisor receives nothing from the promisee in return for the promise, other than that which he or she is already entitled to receive. There is no consideration given in return for the promise; again, the promise would be gratuitous. For example, Smith enters into a contract with Jones to construct a house for her on her property for $90 000. Smith underestimates the cost of constructing the house and, when the house is partly finished, he refuses to proceed with the construction unless Jones agrees to pay him an additional $10 000. If Jones agrees to pay the additional amount, and Smith completes the construction, Jones is not bound by the promise if she should later decide to withhold the $10 000. Smith is already under a duty to construct the house for Jones, and Jones receives nothing in return for her promise to pay the additional amount of money to Smith.[4] Her promise is gratuitous and unenforceable by Smith.

Quite apart from the aspect of lack of consideration, the enforcement of a contract of the kind illustrated in this example would be contrary to public policy. If this type of contract were enforceable, it would open the door to extortion — in the sense that an unethical contractor could threaten to cease operations at a critical stage in the construction, unless additional funds were made available to complete the remainder of the contract.

As noted earlier, the consideration in a contract must be *legal*. If Able should promise Baker $1000 on the provision that Baker murders Charlie, and later Able fails to pay Baker the $1000 when Charlie is murdered, the courts would not enforce Able's promise. Public policy dictates that the contract must be lawful in the sense that the promises do not violate any law or public policy. For this reason, an ordinary business contract containing a clause requiring the buyer to resell goods at a fixed or minimum price would be unlawful under the Competition Act. It would be illegal, as well as unenforceable.

QUANTUM MERUIT

Occasionally a person may request goods or services of another, and the goods will be provided or the services rendered without mention of the price. In effect, no mention of consideration is made. No remedy was available for the unfortunate seller or tradesperson in this kind of situation until the seventeenth century. Prior to that date, an unpaid seller could not recover for the goods by way of an action of debt because the sum certain had not been agreed to for the debt. Nor could the tradesperson recover by way of ***assumpsit***, because the recipient of the goods or service had not made an express promise to pay. The law simply did not provide a remedy. By the seventeenth century, the courts had come to recognize this problem. They determined that by requesting the goods or the service the parties had made an agreement, whereby the goods would be supplied or the service rendered in return for the implied promise of payment of a reasonable price for the goods (***quantum valebant***) or a reasonable price for the services rendered (***quantum meruit***). Because contracts of this type frequently involve the supply of goods as well as services (such as where an electrician is called to replace a faulty light switch or a plumber replaces a worn faucet) the term *quantum meruit* has come to be used to cover both situations.

If the parties agree upon a price for the services or goods at any time after the services have been performed or the goods supplied, the agreed price will prevail, and the contract will become an agreement for a fixed price. If the parties cannot agree upon a reasonable price, then the courts will decide what is reasonable,

---

4. The courts in the United States have, on occasion, taken a slightly different approach in cases of this type. Because the contractor is free to abandon the contract at any time and compensate the owner for any damages that he might suffer, some American courts have held that the promise to pay an additional amount constitutes a part of a new contract between the parties. This is because the original contract is executory and there is consideration on the part of both parties to terminate it and replace it with a new agreement. See, for example, *Pittsburgh Testing Laboratory v. Farnsworth & Chambers Co. Inc.* (1958), 251 F. (2d) 77. And also see *Owens v. City of Bartlett* (1974), 528 P. (2d) 1235 for a discussion of the exception as well. Most American courts, however, would probably follow the consideration rule.

based upon the price of the goods or the service in the area where the contract was made. As a general rule, the rate charged for similar goods or services by other suppliers of goods and services in the immediate area will be treated by the courts as a reasonable price. If the price charged for the service or goods is comparable to the "going rate" charged by similar suppliers, then the court will fix the contract price accordingly.

For example, a homeowner may call a plumber to fix a leak in a water pipe. No price for the service call is mentioned, but the plumber responds to the call and repairs the broken pipe. The plumber later submits an account for $200 for the work done. If the homeowner considers the account excessive, then recourse may be had to the courts to have a reasonable price fixed for the work done. However, if the parties agreed upon $200 as the price at any time after the request for the service was made by the homeowner, the price of $200 would stand.

THE DEBTOR-CREDITOR RELATIONSHIP

Under the law of contract, a debt paid when due ends the debtor-creditor relationship, as the debtor has fully satisfied his or her obligations under the contract. Similarly, the creditor has no rights under the contract once the creditor has received payment in full. The law relating to consideration applies where the debtor and creditor agree that the amount payable on the due date should be less than the full amount actually due. At first glance, it would appear that this common business practice is perfectly proper. The creditor, if he agrees to accept a lesser sum than the amount due, should be free to do so, and his promise should be binding upon him. Unfortunately, this practice runs counter to the doctrine of consideration. Unless the parties bring themselves within an exception to this rule, the creditor's promise is simply gratuitous and unenforceable.

Under the doctrine of consideration, where a creditor agrees to accept a lesser sum than the full amount of the debt on the due date, there is no consideration for the creditor's promise to waive payment of the balance of the debt owed. To recover this amount the creditor can, if desired, sue for payment of the balance immediately after receiving payment of the lesser sum.

The difficulties that the application of this principle raise for the business community are many, and the courts, as a result, have attempted to lessen the impact or harshness of the law in a number of ways. The most obvious method of avoiding the problem of lack of consideration would be for the parties to include the promise to take a lesser sum in a written document that would be under seal and signed by the creditor. The formal document under seal would eliminate the problem of lack of consideration entirely. A second method would be for the creditor to accept something other than money in full satisfaction of the debt. For example, the debtor could give the creditor his automobile or his stamp collection as payment in full, and the courts would not inquire into the adequacy of the consideration.[5] Payment of the lesser sum in full satisfaction of the debt before the due date would also be consideration for the creditor's promise to forgo the balance, since the payment before the time required for payment would represent a benefit received by the creditor. A final exception to the consideration rule arises where the lesser sum is accepted as payment in full by the creditor under

---

5. *Pinnels' Case* (1602), 5 Co. Rep. 117a; 77 E.R. 237.

circumstances where a third party makes the payment in settlement of the creditor's claim against the debtor. For example, Able is indebted to Baker for $1000. Charlie, Able's father, offers Baker $900 as payment in full of his son's indebtedness. If Baker accepts Charlie's payment as settlement of the $1000, she cannot later sue Able for the remaining $100, as it would be a fraud on the stranger (Charlie) to do so.[6]

The difficulties that this particular rule for consideration raises in cases where indebtedness has been gratuitously reduced have been resolved in part by legislation in some jurisdictions.[7] In all provinces west of Quebec, statute law (such as the Mercantile Law Amendment Act in Ontario) provides that a creditor who accepts a lesser sum in full satisfaction of a debt will not be permitted to later claim the balance once the lesser sum has been paid. The eastern common law provinces, however, remain subject to the requirement of consideration, and the parties must follow one of the previously mentioned methods of establishing or avoiding consideration if the debtor is to avoid a later claim by the creditor for the balance of the debt.

The relationship between an individual creditor and debtor, however, must be distinguished from an arrangement or a bona fide scheme of consolidation of debts between a debtor and his or her creditors. This differs from the isolated transaction in that the creditors agree with each other to accept less than the full amount due them. Each of the creditors promise the other creditors to forgo a portion of the claim against the debtor (and forbear from taking legal action against the debtor to collect the outstanding amount) as consideration for their promise to do likewise.

It is also important to note that an agreement between a creditor and debtor, whereby the creditor agrees to accept a lesser sum when the amount owed is in dispute, does not run afoul of the consideration rule. If there is a genuine dispute concerning the amount owed, and the creditor accepts a sum less than the full amount claimed, the consideration that the creditor receives for relinquishing the right to take action for the balance is the debtor's payment of a sum that the debtor honestly believes he does not owe the creditor.

GRATUITOUS PROMISES CAUSING INJURY TO ANOTHER: EQUITABLE OR PROMISSORY ESTOPPEL

A gratuitous promise is, by definition, a promise that the promisor has no legal obligation to perform. Occasionally, when the recipient of such a promise relies on the promise to his or her detriment, the following social question arises: Should the promisor, having misled the promisee, be required to compensate the promisee for his or her loss? After all, it was the promisor's conduct or promise that induced the promisee to act to his or her detriment.

It is a settled point of law that once a fact is asserted to be true (even if it is later proved otherwise) and another person relies on it to his or her detriment, that statement of fact cannot be denied by the person who made the assertion. This particular concept is known as **estoppel**. The essential characteristics of estoppel are the expression of a fact as being true and the reliance on that statement by the other party. In the late nineteenth century, the doctrine of equitable estoppel was

---

6. For a discussion of this point see the dictum of Willes, J., in *Cook v. Lister* (1863), 13 C.B. (N.S.) 543 at p. 595; 143 E.R. 215.

7. See, for example, Ontario: Mercantile Law Amendment Act, R.S.O. 1990, c. M-10, s. 16.

developed by the English courts as a defence to a promisor's claim against a promisee where the promisee suffered some injury by the promisee's reliance on a gratuitous promise made by the promisor.[8]

In the case of *Central London Property Trust, Ltd. v. High Trees House, Ltd.,*[9] Lord Denning applied the concept of equitable estoppel to a case where a landlord had gratuitously reduced the rent on a long-term lease because it was not possible for the tenant to lease the apartments in the building during the war years. At the end of the war, the receiver for the debenture holders claimed against the tenant for the full amount of the rent. There was clearly no consideration given for the promise to reduce the rent. Lord Denning was of the opinion that the tenant had relied on the promise to its detriment, and that the full rent should not be payable for the entire period when the difficult conditions existed. Lord Denning described the principle of estoppel in another case in the following terms:

> The principle, as I understand it, is that where one party has, by his word or conduct, made to the other a promise or assurance which was intended to affect the legal relations between them and to be acted on accordingly, then, once the other party has taken him at his word and acted on it, the one who gave the promise or assurance cannot afterwards be allowed to revert to the previous legal relations as if no such promise or assurance had been made by him, but he must accept their legal relations subject to the qualification which he himself has so introduced, even though it is not supported in point of law by any consideration but only by his word.[10]

Lord Denning's view of equitable or promissory estoppel as a defence was approved in a second case that followed closely on the heels of the High Trees case.[11]

As a result, its use has continued as an effective defence against a claim relating to the enforcement of contractual rights where the promisee has relied upon a gratuitous promise to his or her detriment.[12]

SUMMARY

Consideration is an essential requirement for any contract not under seal. If the promise is gratuitous, the promise must be made in writing and under seal to be enforceable. Consideration must be legal, and must have some value in the eyes of the law. The courts, however, will not consider the adequacy of the consideration unless it is grossly inadequate given the circumstances surrounding the transaction. Since consideration is the price that a person receives for his or her promise, the consideration must move from the promisee to the promisor. In cases where the consideration is not specified, and a request is made for goods or services, the consideration will be determined by the courts at a reasonable price.

8. *Hughes v. Metropolitan Railway Co. et al.* (1877), 2 App. Cas. 439; *Birmingham and District Land Co. v. London & North Western Railway Co.* (1888), 40 Ch. D. 268.

9. *Central London Property Trust, Ltd. v. High Trees House, Ltd.,* [1947] K.B. 130.

10. *Combe v. Combe,* [1951] 2 K.B. 215.

11. *Ledingham v. Bermejo Estancia Co.,* [1947] 1 All E.R. 749. Equitable estoppel was also recognized as an appropriate defence in a Canadian case before the High Trees decision. See *Pierce v. Empey,* [1939] S.C.R. 247.

12. *Owen Sound Public Library Board v. Mial Developments Ltd. et al.* (1980), 26 O.R. (2d) 459; *Bojtar v. Parker* (1980), 26 O.R. (2d) 705.

The courts have permitted the injurious reliance on the part of a party to be used as a defence in cases where a plaintiff attempts to enforce an original agreement that had been altered by a gratuitous promise. In cases involving promises of donations to charitable organizations, gratuitous promises have been enforced where the promise was such that it induced the charity to act to its detriment on the strength of the promise.

DISCUSSION QUESTIONS

1. Explain the nature of "consideration" as it applies to a contract.
2. Must consideration always be present to render a promise enforceable?
3. Does a contract under seal require consideration? If not, why not?
4. Consideration may be "present" or "future." How do these forms of consideration differ?
5. A creditor's promise to accept the lesser sum as payment in full for a larger debt is considered gratuitous at common law. Why is this so?
6. How have the common law courts, in some cases, permitted a debtor to enforce a creditor's gratuitous promise to reduce a debt?
7. In what way does the Mercantile Law Amendment legislation in some provinces alter the common law rules for gratuitous reduction of debt?
8. What conditions must be established to put forward a claim of *quantum meruit?*
9. In what way does an agreement on the price for services made after the services have been performed affect the right of the person who performed the service to claim *quantum meruit?*
10. Explain promissory estoppel. What are its uses in a contract setting?

MINI-CASE PROBLEMS

1. X offered to deliver a parcel for Y to a downtown shop, as he would pass the shop on his way to work. Y agreed and gave X the parcel. The next day, Y told X he would give him $5 for delivering the parcel. X accepted Y's offer, but, later, Y refused to pay the $5. What are X's rights?
2. A, a wealthy widow, was approached by a women's group for a money donation that the group intended to use to construct a women's centre in the community. A offered to donate an amount that would cover 25 percent of the cost of the proposed building.

   If the group commenced construction based upon A's promise, could A later refuse to pay?

JUDICIAL DECISIONS

The case of *Foakes v. Beer* illustrates the importance of consideration in a contract where the contract is not under seal. The agreement is discussed by the judge in terms of a promise and consideration for the promise. The judge asks the question: What consideration did Mrs. Beer receive for a promise not to claim interest? The judge finds no consideration, and enforced the judgement as to interest. Note also that the judge discusses the distinction between an ordinary agreement and one under seal.

The case of the *Governors of Dalhousie College v. Boutilier* deals with a gratuitous promise of a donation to an educational institution, and whether the promise might be enforced. The judge points out that the promised donation was for no specific building or project, and nothing was done by the college on the strength of the promise that obligated the college or caused it to incur liability. The judge concludes that the promise is not enforceable.

In the case of *Gloge Heating & Plumbing v. Northern Construction Co. Ltd.* the issue in the case is whether a company that discovers an error in its tender may withdraw the tender without incurring liability for the damage that it causes to others. In this case, Gloge made an error in its tender to Northern. Northern accepted a contract at a price based upon Gloge's tender to do certain work. When Gloge refused to do the work, Northern hired another company at a substantial loss. The court held Gloge responsible for the loss.

**Offer —
Acceptance —
Consideration —
Contract Not
Under Seal**

Foakes v. Beer (1884), 9 App. Cas. 605.

Mrs. Beer had successfully sued Dr. Foakes for the sum of £2090 and recovered judgement. Dr. Foakes and Mrs. Beer entered into a written agreement whereby Foakes would immediately pay £500 and the balance over five years if Mrs. Beer would take no proceedings on the judgement. The money was paid, and, after receipt of payment, Mrs. Beer took action against Dr. Foakes for interest on the funds. No interest had been mentioned in the agreement.

EARL OF SELBORNE, L.E.:

...the question remains, whether the agreement is capable of being legally enforced. Not being under seal, it cannot be legally enforced against the respondent, unless she received consideration for it from the appellant, or unless, though without consideration, it operates by way of accord and satisfaction, so as to extinguish the claim for interest. What is the consideration? On the face of the agreement none is expressed, except a present payment of £500, on account and in part of the larger debt then due and payable by law under the judgment. The appellant did not contract to pay the future instalments of £150 each, on the times therein mentioned; much less did he give any new security, in the shape of negotiable paper, or in any other form. The promise de futuro was only that of the respondent, that if the half-yearly payments of £150 each were regularly paid, she would "take no proceedings whatever on the judgment." No doubt if the appellant had been under no antecedent obligation to pay the whole debt, his fulfilment of the condition might have imported some consideration on his part for that promise. But he was under the antecedent obligation; and payment at those deferred dates, by the forbearance and indulgence of the creditor, of the residue of the principal debt and costs, could not (in my opinion) be a consideration for the relinquishment of interest and discharge of the judgment, unless the payment of the £500, at the time of signing the agreement, was such a consideration. As to accord and satisfaction, in point of fact there could be no complete satisfaction, so long as any future instalment remained payable; and I do not see how any mere payments on account could operate in law as a satisfaction ad interim, conditionally upon other payments being afterwards duly made, unless there was a consideration sufficient to support the agreement while still unexecuted. Nor was anything, in fact, done by the respondent in this case, on the receipt of the last payment, which could be tantamount to an acquittance, if the agreement did not previously bind her.

The distinction between the effect of a deed under seal, and that of an agreement by parol, or by writing not under seal, may seem arbitrary, but it is established in our law; nor is it really unreasonable or practically inconvenient that the law should require particular solemnities to give to a gratuitous contract the force of a binding obligation. If the question be (as, in the actual state of the law, I think it is), whether consideration is, or is not, given in a case of this kind, for a promise by the creditor to relinquish, after certain further payments on account, the residue of the debt, I cannot say that I think consideration is given, in the sense in which I have always understood that word as used in our law.

Gratuitous Promise of Gift — Consideration — Enforceability

Governors of Dalhousie College v. Boutilier, [1934] 3 D.L.R. 593.
Boutilier promised to donate the sum of $5000 to the university for the general improvement of the institution. The promise of a donation was made as a result of a subscription campaign by the university. Boutilier died without making the payment and the university brought an action against his estate.

CROCKET, J.:

So far as the signed subscription itself is concerned, it is contended in behalf of the appellant that it shows upon its face a good and sufficient consideration for the deceased's promise in its statement that it was given in consideration of the subscription of others. As to this, it is first to be observed that the statement of such a consideration in the subscription paper is insufficient to support the promise if, in point of law, the subscriptions of others could not provide a valid consideration therefor. I concur in the opinion of Chisholm, C.J., that the fact that others had signed separate subscription papers for the same common object or were expected so to do does not of itself constitute a legal consideration....

The doctrine of mutual promises was also put forward on the argument as a ground upon which the deceased's promise might be held to be binding. It was suggested that the statement in the subscription of the purpose for which it was made, *viz*: "of enabling Dalhousie College to maintain and improve the efficiency of its teaching, to construct new buildings and otherwise to keep pace with the growing need of its constituency" constituted an implied request on the part of the deceased to apply the promised subscription to this object and that the acceptance by the college of his promise created a contract between them, the consideration for the promise of the deceased to pay the money being the promise of the college to apply it to the purpose stated.

I cannot think that any such construction can fairly be placed upon the subscription paper and its acceptance by the college. It certainly contains no express request to the college either "to maintain and improve the efficiency of its teaching" or "to construct new buildings and otherwise to keep pace with the growing need of its constituency," but simply states that the promise to pay the $5,000 is made for the purpose of enabling the college to do so, leaving it perfectly free to pursue what had always been its aims in whatever manner its Governors should choose. No statement is made as to the amount intended to be raised for all or any of the purposes stated. No buildings of any kind are described. The construction of new buildings is merely indicated as a means of the college keeping pace with the growing need of its constituency and apparently to be undertaken as and when the Governors should in their unfettered discretion decide the erection of any one or more buildings for any purpose was necessary or desirable.

It seems to me difficult to conceive that, had the deceased actually paid the promised money, he could have safely relied upon the mere acceptance of his own promise, couched in such vague and uncertain terms regarding its purpose as the foundation of any action against the college corporation.

So far as I can discover, there is no English or Canadian case in which it has been authoritatively decided that a reciprocal promise on the part of the promisee may be implied from the mere fact of the acceptance by the promisee of such a subscription paper from the hands of the promisor to do the thing for which the subscription is promised. There is no doubt, of course, that an express agreement by the promisee to do certain acts in return for a subscription is a sufficient consideration for the promise of the subscriber. There may, too, be circumstances proved by evidence, outside the subscription paper itself, from which such a reciprocal promise on the part of the promisee may well be implied, but I have not been able to find any English or Canadian case where it has actually been so decided in the absence of proof that the subscriber has himself either expressly requested the promisee to undertake some definite project or personally taken such a part in connection with the projected enterprise that such a request might be inferred therefrom....

To hold otherwise would be to hold that a naked, voluntary promise may be converted into a binding legal contract by the subsequent action of the promisee alone without the consent, express or implied, of the promisor. There is no evidence here which in any way involves the deceased in the carrying out of the work for which the promised subscription was made other than the signing of the subscription paper itself.

Contract — Tender in Error — Right to Withdraw — Reliance on Tender

Gloge Heating and Plumbing Ltd., v. Northern Construction Co. Ltd. (1986), 27 D.L.R. (4th) 264.

Gloge submitted a tender to do certain mechanical work for Northern Construction. Northern Construction entered into a construction contract to do work on the strength of Gloge's bid. Gloge later discovered the bid was too low, and refused to do the work. Northern was obliged to have the work done by another company but the cost was much higher. Northern Construction then brought an action against Gloge for the amount of its loss.

Irving, J.A.:

.... The owner duly accepted Northern's tender and awarded it the work. Gloge refused to perform the mechanical subcontract, so that Northern was required to make alternative arrangements by employing a subsidiary at an increase of $341,299 in the mechanical subcontract price.

The appellant Gloge has submitted:

A That it was free to withdraw its tender at any time before Northern accepted that tender by awarding the subcontract to Gloge, and had done so.

B Northern failed in a duty it owed to alert Gloge that its tender was sufficiently low that it must be erroneous.

C That Northern could not purport to accept Gloge's tender after it knew that the tender was erroneous because of *bona fide* mathematical mistakes.

The latter two arguments can be disposed of summarily. Gloge had purposely delayed submitting its tender until minutes before the deadline for submitting tenders. Thus Northern had no real opportunity to analyze Gloge's tender, or to make any meaningful comparison with other mechanical tenders. Accordingly, the evidence does not persuade us — nor did it persuade the trial judge — that Northern ought to have known of error in Gloge's tender. Furthermore, Northern had only minutes to submit its own tender after receiving Gloge's tender. Although it learned afterwards (on September 23rd) about the error in Gloge's tender, it was then too late for Northern to assist Gloge without the owner's consent which was not forthcoming.

The real issue raised before us is Gloge's first submission — was Gloge free to withdraw its bid, and did it do so? In our view, the decisions in *The Queen in right of Ontario et al. v. Ron Engineering & Construction Eastern Ltd. (1981),* 119 D.L.R. (3d) 267, [1981] 1 S.C.R. 111, 35 N.R. 40, and *Calgary v. Northern Construction Co. Division of Morrison-Knudsen Co., Inc. et al.* (1985), 42 Alta. L.R. (2d) 1, 67 A.R. 95, provide the answer.

Applying the analysis of Estey J. in *Ron Engineering*, Northern made an offer to Gloge to submit a tender for the mechanical subcontract; Gloge accepted the offer by submitting its tender on September 19, 1980, and contract A (as described by Estey J.) was made.

As Estey J. stated in *Ron Engineering* [at pp. 274-5]:

> The tender submitted by the respondent brought contract A into life. This is sometimes described in law as a unilateral contract, that is to say a contract which results from an act made in response to an offer, as for example in the simplest terms. "I will pay you a dollar if you will cut my lawn". No obligation to cut the lawn exists in law and the obligation to pay the dollar comes into being upon the performance of the invited act. Here the call for tenders created no obligation in the reposndent or in anyone else in or out of the construction world. When a member of the construction industry responds to the call for tenders, as the respondent has done here, that response takes the form of submission of a tender, or a bid as it is sometimes called. The significance of the bid in law is that it at once becomes irrevocable if filed in conformity with the terms and conditions under which the call for tenders was made and if such terms so provide. There is no disagreement between the parties here about the form and procedure in which the tender was submitted by the respondent and that it complied with the terms and conditions of the call for tenders. Consequently, contract A came into being. The principal term of contract A is the irrevocability of the bid, and the corollary term is the obligation in both parties to enter into a contract (contract B) upon the acceptance of the tender.

Was Gloge's tender revocable after close of tender? Gloge knew that Northern would select a mechanical tender and rely on it, and Gloge also knew that the tenders of the general contractors to the owner would be irrevocable for the time set out in the contract documents. Perhaps these facts of themselves might justify holding the Gloge tender to be irrevocable. But, in addition, the trial judge accepted certain expert evidence given at the trial by two witnesses who had been in the construction industry for many years. That evidence demonstrated that it was normal and standard practice for general contractors to accept last minute telephone tenders from subcontractors, and that it was understood and accepted by those in the industry that while such tenders could be withdrawn prior to close of tendering, if not so withdrawn, that such tenders must remain irrevocable for the same term that the general contractors' tenders to the owner are irrevocable.

This industry practice is eminent common sense. Without such accepted practice the tendering system would become unenforceable and meaningless. Estey J. observed in *Ron Engineering* [at p. 273]:

> I share the view expressed by the Court of Appeal that the integrity of the bidding system must be protected where under the law of contracts it is possible so to do.

Applying the industry practice to this case, Gloge could not withdraw its tender to Northern after tenders had closed, and its tender was irrevocable for the same period as Northern's. Accordingly, Gloge was obligated to perform the work when Northern awarded it the subcontract, and is liable for failing to do so.

We observe that Gloge's conduct after its tender error was discovered is consistent with the industry practice already described. Gloge did not take the position with Northern that it had the right to withdraw its bid. Instead, it sought Northern's assistance in attempt to persuade the owner to consent to the substitution of a higher mechanical tender to replace Gloge's.

In the result, the judgement at trial is affirmed. The appeal is dismissed with costs to be calculated on the same basis as ordered by the trial judge.

Appeal dismissed.

CASE PROBLEMS FOR DISCUSSION

Case 1

Able and Baker were good friends for many years. Able wished to make a gift to Baker of a house he owned that was subject to two mortgages held by a third party. In order to avoid the gift tax legislation in force at the time, the parties agreed that Able would convey the property to Baker and take back an interest-free mortgage equal to the difference between the two existing mortgages and the value of the property. The third mortgage would be forgiven each year in an amount equal to the permissible tax-free gift allowed each year under the Gift Tax Act. The gift transaction was a lawful method of disposing of the property, and Baker accepted the gift of the property. Baker moved into the house and made the payments on the first two mortgages for a number of years; then, after a difference of opinion on another matter, Able demanded payment of the third mortgage. Baker refused to pay, and Able sued Baker for the amount owed.

Discuss the respective positions of the parties to the transaction and render a decision.

Case 2

Hansen and Brown owned cottage lots that abutted each other along a line at right angles to a lake front. Nothing marked the boundary between the two lots, and neither landowner could recall with any degree of accuracy where the lot line actually lay. The parties had mentioned a survey of the lots on several occasions, but nothing had been done to fix the boundaries.

One summer, when both Hansen and Brown were vacationing at their respective cottages, Brown noticed a large diseased limb on a tall tree that was growing at a point approximately equidistant from each cottage. As he was concerned that the limb might fall on his cottage, Brown suggested to Hansen that he do something about the situation. To this suggestion Hansen replied: "That tree is growing on your lot, and it is up to you to cut the limb. If it should fall my way and damage the roof of my cottage, I would look to you for the repairs."

Brown decided to cut down the entire tree instead of just the diseased limb. He did so with some reluctance because the elimination of the tree would remove the only protection Hansen had from the hot afternoon sun.

Hansen did not object to the cutting of the tree at the time. Some time later, however, when a survey that he had requested revealed that the tree had been entirely on his side of the property line between the two cottage lots, he brought an action against Brown for damages.

Identify the defences that might be raised by Brown, and explain how the courts might decide this case.

Case 3

On a cold evening in January, the furnace in Smith's home failed to operate properly, causing the water pipes to freeze and later burst, flooding his basement. Smith made a hurried telephone call to Brown, a plumber, when he discovered the water in his basement, and asked him if he could come over immediately and fix the leaking pipes.

Brown agreed to do so, and arrived about an hour later, only to find that Smith had discovered the leak and fixed it himself. Brown left immediately, and the next day he submitted an account to Smith for $45 for services rendered. Smith refused to pay Brown's account.

If Brown should sue Smith on the account, explain the arguments that might be raised by each of the parties, and indicate how the case might be decided.

Case 4

Nuptial Creations carried on business as a custom manufacturer of wedding dresses and accessory products. The company offered a standard line of dresses that it sold through its own retail establishments. The prices for the basic dress line were available to prospective purchasers, but the final price was dependent upon the amount of lace, beading, and changes that a customer requested in the product.

For her wedding, Marie D selected a particular dress design that carried a basic price of $1200. She requested a number of changes in the design that included a great deal of beadwork, requiring time-consuming hand application. No price was quoted by the company for the custom dress at the time that Marie D requested that it be made for her.

Some time later, when the dress was finished and ready for delivery, Marie D went to the shop and enquired as to the price. She was informed by a salesperson that the completed dress would probably cost "around $2000." Nevertheless she accepted the dress, with the complaint that she was surprised at the cost.

Two weeks later, the company submitted an account to Marie D for $2368 for the dress. Marie refused the pay the account.

Advise the parties of their rights, and if legal action should be taken, discuss the way in which the case might be resolved.

Case 5

A service club in a small community decided to raise funds for the purchase of a special wheelchair that it intended to donate to a disabled child. The wheelchair was of a special design, and made only on special order. The estimated purchase price was $5600.

Donations were solicited throughout the community, and a total of $2100 was raised toward the purchase price. The club, unfortunately, found it difficult to solicit further donations, as the $2100 represented the contributions of nearly every family in the community.

A meeting of the club members was held to discuss ways and means of raising the further $3500. After some discussion, one member stood up and promised to "match dollar for dollar every additional contribution received, if the club can raise a further $1750."

The next day, the local newspaper reported the club member's pledge, and the publicity produced a large number of donations to the fund. By the end of the week, the donations totalled $3700, of which $1600 had been donated that week. The club immediately place an order for the special wheelchair, confident that the additional $150 could be raised by the club members.

A few weeks later, the club was advised that the wheelchair was ready for delivery, and that the price would be $5300 instead of the $5600 originally quoted. The club was delighted to receive the news that the wheelchair would only cost $5300, and immediately notified the club member who had promised to match the contributions.

When the member was advised that the $1600 donated, together with his matching pledge, would be sufficient (along with funds previously collected) to pay for the wheelchair, he responded: "I promised to match dollar for dollar only if the club could raise a further $1750. Since it did not do so, I have no intention of matching the donations."

Discuss the position at law of the parties in this case, and explain how this matter might be determined if each party exercised his (or its) legal rights (if any).

Case 6

Anderson and Bacon were good friends as well as neighbours. When Anderson was about to leave for a three-week vacation at his cottage, he asked Bacon to "keep an eye on" his house, and if anything should happen, to call him on the telephone. Bacon agreed to do so.

By the end of the second week of Anderson's vacation, Bacon noticed that Anderson's lawn and yard were in need of a "cut and trim." He spent most of his weekend mowing Anderson's lawn and weeding the garden.

When Anderson returned, he was so pleased to discover that Bacon had kept his grounds in such good order that he promised Bacon a 1967 silver dollar that he knew Bacon required for his coin collection. Bacon was delighted with Anderson's offer, and readily accepted. Anderson promised to deliver the dollar as soon as he could remove it from his safety deposit box at the bank.

A few days later, before Anderson had picked up the silver dollar from his bank, the two friends had a violent disagreement on politics, and Anderson vowed that he would never give Bacon the silver dollar.

Bacon brought an action against Anderson, claiming he was entitled to the coin.

Discuss the legal issues raised in this case, and identify the particular points of law that the parties must address in their arguments. Render a decision.

Case 7

A holiday tour company offered white water raft trips involving a relatively short 50 km journey down a swift river. The price of the trip, including overnight hotel and meals, was advertised at $250. Jack and Jill, in response to the advertisement, entered into a verbal arrangement with the operator of the tour to join in on a journey, and agreed to appear at the designated hotel the evening before the date of the excursion.

At the hotel, they met the president of the tour company and paid him the tour price. The next morning, as Jack and Jill assembled their gear with the nine other passengers, a representative of the company spoke to the participants, and instructed each of them to sign a form entitled "Standard Release." The form stated that the operator of the tour was "not responsible for any loss or damage suffered by any passenger for any reason, including any negligence on the part of the company, its employees, or agents."

Jack and Jill were reluctant to sign the release, but when they were informed by the tour representative that they would not be allowed on the raft unless they signed it, they did so. When the release was signed, the representative gave each of them a life jacket with a 10 kg buoyancy rating. After they donned the life jackets, they were allowed to climb aboard the raft.

During the course of the journey, the raft overturned in very rough water, and Jack and two other persons drowned.

An investigation of the accident by provincial authorities indicated that the life jacket Jack had been wearing was too small to support the weight of a person his size. The investigation also revealed that, due to the swiftness of the river at the place where the accident occurred, a more suitable life jacket would probably not have saved Jack's life.

Jill survived the accident, and brought an action against the tour company under the provincial legislation that permitted her to institute legal proceedings on behalf of her deceased husband.

Discuss the issues raised in this case, and indicate the arguments that might be raised by each party.

Render a decision.

Case 8

Speedy Delivery Service Ltd. had been engaged by the Big Bank as its regular courier for documents and other bank correspondence for both local and long distance deliveries. The parties had an on-going agreement for services under which Speedy's maximum liability to the Bank for any matter arising out of their relationship was limited to $100 000. Speedy also held business insurance in the amount of $10 000 000 from which it could claim indemnification should any claim be made against Speedy by the bank or by any other party with which Speedy did business. A term of its insurance policy required Speedy to make an immediate report to the insurer if it suspected that there may be a claim made against it.

A few days after Speedy had made a delivery of documents to one of Big Bank's branches, a letter arrived from the bank stating that the documents had been lost. Apparently the Speedy driver had placed the documents in the usual outside receptacle at the branch which was used for deliveries after the branch has closed, but he could not remember whether he had properly secured the receptacle afterwards. The bank's letter stated that bank employees were trying to locate the missing documents and that they related to an important mortgage transaction which was to have been finalized that week. The letter further stated that there would be losses to the bank if the documents could not be found, but, in any event, the bank would further advise Speedy at a later date of its progress.

Speedy heard nothing more from the bank about the documents and assumed that they had been located. Almost three years later the bank wrote to Speedy stating that it was suing for its damages for the lost documents in the amount of $100 000. When Speedy refused to pay, the bank threatened to bring legal action.

Discuss the legal issues raised in this case and the arguments which all of the parties, including the insurance company, will rely on.

CHAPTER 8

Legal Capacity to Contract

THE MINOR OR INFANT

Not everyone is permitted to enter into contracts that would bind them at law. Certain classes of promisors must be protected as a matter of public policy, either for reasons of their inexperience and immaturity, or their inability to appreciate the nature of their acts in making enforceable promises. The most obvious class to be protected is the group of persons of tender age called **minors** or **infants**. An infant at common law is a person under the age of 21 years, but in most provinces this has been lowered to 18 or 19 years of age by legislation.

Public policy dictates that minors should not be bound by their promises; consequently, they are not liable on most contracts that they might negotiate. The rule is not absolute, however, because in many cases, a hard and fast rule on the liability of a minor would not be in his or her best interest. For example, if a minor could not incur liability on a contract for food or clothing, the hardship would fall on the minor, rather than the party with full power to contract, as no one would be willing to supply an infant with food, shelter, or clothing on credit.[1] The law, therefore, attempts to balance the protection of the minor with the need to contract by making only those contracts for necessary items enforceable against a minor.

Enforceability and the Right of Repudiation

The enforceability of any contract for non-necessary goods will depend to some extent on whether the contract has been fully executed by the minor, or whether it has yet to be performed. If the contract made by the minor has been fully performed (and consequently, fully executed) then the minor may very well be

---

1. *Zouch v. Parsons* (1765), 3 Burr. 1794, 97 E.R. 1103.

bound by the agreement, unless he or she can show that he or she had been taken advantage of by the merchant, or can return all the goods purchased to the other party. For example, a minor purchases a gift for a friend, and pays the merchant the full purchase price. The contract at this point has been fully performed (executed) by both parties. If the minor some time later wishes to repudiate the contract, the court would not allow the minor to do so unless the minor could convince the court that the merchant had taken advantage of the minor by charging the minor an excessively high price. The minor would also be obliged to return the goods in order to succeed in the court action. If the contract has not been fully performed, then the agreement (if for a non-necessary item) may be voidable at the minor's option. This rule would probably apply as well to a necessary item, if the minor has not taken delivery of the goods. For example, if a minor orders a clothing item from a mail order house, and then repudiates the contract before delivery is made, the minor would probably not be bound by the agreement, even though the item is a necessary.

The adult with full capacity to contract is bound in every case by the contract negotiated with an infant, since the adult person has no obligation to do business with an infant unless the adult wishes to do so. Any business firm or merchant that decides to enter into a contract with a minor assumes the risk (in the case of a contract for a non-necessary) that the minor might repudiate the agreement.

A minor or infant of tender age is normally under the supervision of a parent or guardian, and the need to contract in the infant's own name is limited. The older minor, however, is in a slightly different position, with a need in some cases to enter into contracts for food, clothing, shelter, and other necessaries. For this latter group, the law provides that an infant will be bound by contracts for necessaries, and will be liable for a reasonable price for the goods received or the services supplied. The effect of this rule is to permit a merchant to provide necessaries to an infant or minor, yet limit the infant's liability to a reasonable price. This is eminently fair to both contracting parties: the merchant is protected because the minor is liable on the contract; the infant is protected in that the merchant may only charge the infant a reasonable price for the goods.

The unusual aspect of the law relating to minors is the criteria used by the courts to determine what is a necessary for a minor. The courts will examine the social position of the infant in deciding the question. Such an approach smacks of different standards for different minors, and has its roots in a number of older English cases.[2] Nevertheless, it remains as the law today. Other requirements, which are perhaps of more concern to a modern day merchant, are that the goods supplied to the minor are actually necessary, and that the minor is not already well supplied with similar goods. Since the merchant in each case has the onus of proving these facts, some care is obviously essential on the part of merchants supplying goods of this nature to infants. The entire issue becomes rather obscure when the merchant must also distinguish between what constitutes a necessary, and what might be a luxury, bearing in mind the minor's station in life.

In many cases, contracts of employment or apprenticeship are contracts considered to be beneficial to minors, and are enforceable against them. Although

---

2. *Ryder v. Wombwell* (1868), L.R. 3 Ex. 90; reversed L.R. 4 Ex. 32; *Nash v. Inman,* [1908] 2 K.B. 1.

some educational ventures that involve minors may not be considered by the courts as being beneficial, many are held enforceable, even when the educational aspect is unusual. In the case of *Roberts v. Gray*,[3] an infant entered into a contract with a professional billiard player to take part in a world tour as his playing opponent. He later repudiated the contract before the tour was scheduled to take place, and the adult contracting party took action against him for breach of contract. The court held that the infant was bound by the contract because the experience of playing billiards with a professional would be valuable instruction for a minor who wished to make billiards his career.

The Effect of Repudiation

The general rule relating to contracts that have not been fully performed (executory contracts) for non-necessary goods or services is that the minor or infant may repudiate the contract at any time at his or her option. This rule applies even when the terms of the contract are very fair to the infant. Once the contract has been repudiated, the minor is entitled to a return of any deposit paid to the adult contractor. However, where the minor has purchased the goods on credit and taken delivery, the minor must return the goods before the merchant is obliged to return any monies paid. Any damage to the goods that is not a direct result of the minor's deliberate act is not recoverable by the merchant: the merchant may not deduct the "wear and tear" to the goods from the funds repayable to the infant. The reasoning of the courts in establishing this rule is that the merchant should not be permitted to recover under the law of torts what the merchant cannot recover by the law of contract.[4] However, if the minor deliberately misrepresents the use intended for the goods, and the goods are damaged, then the merchant may be entitled to recover the loss by way of an action for tort.[5]

In a New Brunswick case,[6] a merchant sold an automobile to a minor. The minor acquired possession of the automobile and agreed to pay for the vehicle on an installment basis over a period of time. Shortly after obtaining possession of the car, the infant was involved in an accident, and the vehicle was seriously damaged. The infant repudiated the contract and the merchant took legal action against the infant in tort for the damage to the automobile in the amount of the unpaid balance of the purchase price. The judge dismissed the tort action against the infant, in the following words:

> While an infant may be liable in tort generally, he is not answerable for a tort committed in the course of doing an act directly connected with, or contemplated by, a contract which, as an infant, he is entitled to avoid. An infant cannot, through a change in the form of action to one *ex delicto,* be made liable for the breach of a voidable contract.
>
> The plaintiff, when selling the car, clearly contemplated the defendant would drive it. The conditional sale contract provided the car was to be at the defendant's risk and placed no restriction on the manner in which it should be driven. That the

---

3. [1913] 1 K.B. 520.

4. *Jennings v. Rundall* (1799), 8 T.R. 335, 101 E.R. 1419; *Dickson Bros. Garage & U Drive Ltd. v. Woo* (1957), 10 D.L.R. (2d) 652; affirmed 11 D.L.R. (2d) 477.

5. *Burnhard v. Haggis* (1863), 3 L.J.C.P. 189; *Ballett v. Mingay,* [1943] K.B. 281.

6. *Noble's Ltd. v. Bellefleur* (1963), 37 D.L.R. (2d) 519.

plaintiff had in mind the possibility of physical damage resulting from the driving of the car is evidenced by the stipulation in the contract that the defendant would procure and maintain insurance against all physical damage risks.

The amount of the damages which the plaintiff claimed was the equivalent of the deferred balance of the purchase-price less the financing charge. The action was framed in tort, but the real purpose was to recover under the contract. As at the time of its destruction the car was being used in a manner contemplated by the parties to the conditional sale agreement, any claim against the plaintiff in tort, founded on his negligent driving, must fail.

Fraudulent Misrepresentation as to Age

The protection extended to a minor under the rules of contract may not be used by a minor to perpetrate a fraud on an unsuspecting merchant. On the other hand, an adult entering into a contract with a minor where the minor has represented himself as having attained the age of majority will not be permitted to hold the minor to the contract. The mere fact that a minor misrepresents his or her age does not generally alter the fact that the minor cannot be bound in a contract for non-necessaries.[7]

In contracts for non-necessary goods where the minor has falsely represented that he or she is of full age when, in fact, the infant is not, the merchant may be entitled to recover the goods on the basis of the minor's fraud. Additionally, where a minor attempts to use age incapacity to take advantage of merchants, the criminal law relating to obtaining goods under false pretenses may also be applicable. What the law attempts to do in providing protection to the minor is to impose only a limited liability toward others, based upon what is perceived as being in the best interests of the minor. The treatment of minors is, in a sense, a matter of equity. Where a minor has attempted to use age minority in a manner that is contrary to public policy, the courts will either provide the other contracting party with a remedy for the loss caused by the infant, or prevent the infant from avoiding liability under the contract.

Ratification and Repudiation

Where the minor has entered into a contract of a continuing or permanent nature under which the minor receives benefits and incurs obligations (such as engaging in a partnership, or purchasing non-necessary goods on a long-term credit contract), the contract must be **repudiated** by the minor within a reasonable time after attaining the age of majority. Otherwise the contract will become binding on the minor for the balance of its term.

The reverse is true for contracts for non-necessary items purchased by a minor, when the contract is not of a continuing nature. The infant must expressly **ratify** (acknowledge and agree to perform) such a contract on attaining the age of majority in order to be bound by it. For example, a minor enters into a contract to purchase a sailboat in the fall of the year. The minor gives the merchant a deposit to hold the boat until spring, and promises to pay the balance at that time. The contract would be voidable at the infant's option, and the infant would be free to

---

7. *Jewell v. Brood* (1909), 20 O.L.R. 176.

ignore the contract or repudiate it at any time before reaching the age of majority. If the minor wished to be bound by the transaction, the infant would be obliged to ratify it after attaining the age of majority.

Statutory Protection of Minors

Statute law has modified the common law on the question of ratification to some extent. The provinces of New Brunswick, Newfoundland, Nova Scotia, Ontario, and Prince Edward Island have all passed legislation requiring the ratification to be in writing before it will be binding on the infant. British Columbia has carried the matter one step further in its protection of minors: an infant cannot ratify a contract of this nature in any fashion that would render is enforceable by the adult contracting party. This legislation also has the effect of rendering contracts for non-necessaries and debt contracts "absolutely void." This particular term, however, is open to question as to whether it will only be applied to the liability of the minor, or to both the minor and the other contracting party if the issue should be raised. If the adult contracting party fails to perform the contract, the question arises: Is the contract absolutely void and is the infant deprived of a remedy, or would the words "absolutely void" be construed to mean void as against the minor? The question remains unresolved at the present time, but given the intent of the legislation, an interpretation that would deprive the minor of a right of action would appear to be counter to the intention of the statute.

Minors Engaged in Business

Contracts of employment, if they are lawful and contain terms that are not onerous, are generally binding on minors. Since agreements of this type are generally contracts of indefinite hiring, the minor need only give reasonable notice to terminate, and the infant would be free of all obligations imposed by the agreement. A minor engaging in business as a sole proprietor, or in a partnership, is in quite a different situation. That is because the law generally does not support the thesis that an infant must, of necessity, engage in business activity as a principal.

The rules relating to contracts engaged in by an infant merchant are, for the most part, consistent with those for minors in general. Since it is not necessary for an infant to engage in business, any attempt to purchase business equipment, even if the equipment is necessary for the business, will probably be treated by the courts as a contract for non-necessaries. This renders the contract voidable at the option of the minor, and, if the minor has not taken delivery of the goods, it may permit the minor to repudiate the contract and obtain a refund of any deposit paid. Similarly, if a minor has taken delivery of goods on credit, the minor may return the goods and cancel the obligation. Where the goods are accidentally damaged while in the minor's possession, the minor will not normally be liable for the damage. However, if the minor has sold the goods, the minor will be required to deliver up any monies received.

In the case of a sale of goods by an infant merchant, the infant merchant cannot be obliged to perform the contract if he or she does not wish to do so, as this type of contract is also voidable at the infant's option. If the infant merchant received a deposit or part-payment with regard to a sale of goods or services, the infant would not be required to deliver the goods, but would, of course, be required to return the deposit.

These general rules for contracts engaged in by infant merchants are also consistent with the general rules for the enforcement of infant contracts. Even though they tend to place hardship on adults dealing with minors, public policy, nevertheless, dictates protection of the minor over the rights of persons of full contracting age. With freedom to contract, an adult is under no obligation to deal with an infant merchant any more than there is an obligation on the adult merchant to deal with an infant customer. Since the opportunity to take advantage of the infant's inexperience in business matters exists in both cases, unfair treatment is avoided by the extension of infant protection rule to the infant merchant as well.

In the case of a minor joining a partnership, the protection afforded the minor is again consistent with the general public policy concerning infants' contracts. A partnership agreement involving a minor in a contract for non-necessaries is voidable by the minor, even though the adult parties remain bound. Since the contract is a continuing contract, the infant must repudiate it promptly on or before reaching the age of majority if the infant wishes to avoid liability under it.[8] If a minor continues to accept benefits under the contract after reaching the age of majority, the minor will be bound by the contract, even though he or she did not expressly ratify it. Ratification will be implied from the action of taking benefits under the contract.

Should the minor repudiate the partnership agreement, the minor would not be liable for any debts incurred by the partnership during minority. It would also appear that a minor would not be entitled to withdraw any contribution to the partnership until the debts of the partnership had been settled.[9]

The Parent-Infant Relationship

Parents are not normally liable at common law for the debts incurred by their infant children. This rule, however, has been modified to some extent by family law legislation in some provinces (such as Ontario). This legislation obligates parents to support a child under the age of 16 years, and renders parents jointly and severally liable with the child for any necessaries supplied to the child by merchants. The minor may, as the parent's "agent of necessity," pledge the parents' credit to obtain the necessaries of life, and the parents will be bound by the minor's actions. Apart from this statutory requirement, there are a number of other circumstances under which parents may become liable for the debts of their infant children. In some cases, a parent may have appointed the child to act as his or her agent to purchase goods on credit. In these situations, a true agency situation would exist in which the parent, as principal, would be liable for payment. However, if the child were to later purchase goods on credit for his or her own use, and the parents continued to pay the merchant, the parents would be bound to pay the debts of the infant in the future. This is because the parents implied by their conduct that they would continue to honour the debts incurred. In such cases,

---

8. *Hilliard v. Dillon,* [1955] O.W.N. 621. Should the minor repudiate the partnership agreement, he would not be liable for any debts incurred by the partnership during his minority. It would also appear that he would not be entitled to withdraw his contribution to the partnership until the debts of the partnership had been settled.

9. See, for example, the Partnerships Act, R.S.O. 1990, c. P-5, s. 44.

the parents must specifically state to the merchant that they do not intend to be bound by any subsequent purchases of their infant child if they wish to avoid liability for future purchases negotiated by the minor.

DRUNKEN AND INSANE PERSONS

The courts treat drunken and insane persons in much the same way as infants with respect to the capacity to contract. Those persons who have been committed to a mental institution cannot normally incur any liability in contract. Persons who suffer mental impairment from time to time are subject to a number of special contract rules.

In general, persons who suffer from some mental impairment caused either as a result of some physical of mental damage, or as a result of drugs or alcohol, will be liable on any contract for necessaries negotiated by them, and they will be obliged to pay a reasonable price for the goods or services. In this respect, the law makes no distinction between infants and persons suffering from some mental disability. The merchant involved would be entitled to payment even if the merchant knew of the insane or drunken state of the purchaser. Again, public policy dictates that it is in the best interests of the drunken or insane person to be entitled to obtain the necessaries of life from merchants, and to be bound by such contracts of purchase.

Contracts for non-necessary items, however, are treated in a different manner from contracts for necessaries. If a person is intoxicated or insane when entering into a contract for what might be considered a non-necessary item or service, and the person's mental state renders him incapable of knowing or appreciating the nature of his actions (and if he can establish by evidence that he was in such a condition, and the other contracting party knew he was in that condition), then the contract may be voidable by him when he becomes aware of the contract on his return to a sane or sober state.

It is important in the case of an intoxicated or insane person that the contract be repudiated as soon as it is brought to the person's attention after his or her return to sanity or sobriety. If the contract is not repudiated promptly, and all of the purchased goods returned, the opportunity to avoid liability will be lost. Similarly, any act that would imply acceptance of the contract while sane or sober would render the contract binding. For example, Able attended an auction sale while in an intoxicated state. Everyone at the sale, including the auctioneer, was aware of his condition. When a house and land came up for auction, Able bid vigorously on the property, and was the successful bidder. Later, when in a sober state, he was informed of his purchase, and he affirmed the contract. Immediately thereafter he changed his mind, and repudiated the contract on the basis that he was drunk at the time, and the auctioneer was aware of his condition.

When the case came before the court, the court held that he had had the opportunity to avoid the contract when he became sober, but instead, he affirmed it. Having done so, he was bound by his acceptance, and he could not later repudiate the contract.[10]

The effect of the affirmation renders the contract binding, and the insane or intoxicated person would be liable for breach of contract if the agreement was

---

10. *Matthews v. Baxter* (1873), L.R. 8 Ex. 132.

later rejected. If the contract concerned goods or services, the injured party would be entitled to monetary damages for the loss suffered. In the case of a contract concerning land, the equitable remedy of specific performance would be available to force the person to complete the transaction.

ENEMY ALIENS

An **alien** is a person residing in Canada who is not a Canadian citizen. An alien is not restricted in the right to contract except for a few special laws in some provinces that are applicable to certain kinds of contracts.[11] An **enemy alien**, on the other hand, is a person who, in time of war, has a permanent residence or business in the country that is the declared enemy of Canada. Once hostilities are declared, all contracts between enemy aliens and residents of Canada are generally void and illegal as a matter of public policy. Nationality is not necessarily the determining factor in deciding if a person is an enemy alien. A Canadian citizen living in the enemy country and carrying on a business there would probably be classed as an enemy person with respect to any contract entered into with a resident of Canada.[12] Where the curtailment of the enemy alien's activities would not be in the public interest, the Crown will often grant the enemy alien the right to continue business operations in Canada as if the person or corporation were an alien friend. However, where this is done, strict controls relating to dealing with the enemy country are usually imposed. In some cases, contracts of a continuing nature that existed at the time hostilities began may be suspended if it can be shown that the suspension is in the public interest. Again, permission of the Crown would probably be required if the contract required any contact between a resident of Canada and the enemy alien.

CORPORATIONS

A corporation is a creature of statute, and as such may possess only those powers that the statute may grant it. Corporations formed under Royal Charter or letters patent are generally considered to have all the powers to contract that a natural person may have. The statute that provides for incorporation may specifically give the corporation these rights as well. The legislature need not give a corporation broad powers of contract if it does not wish to do so; indeed, many special-purpose corporations do have their powers strictly controlled or limited. Many of these corporations are created under a special act of a legislature or Parliament for specific purposes. If they should enter into a contract that is beyond their limitations the contract will be void, and their action *ultra vires*. While this may appear to be harsh treatment for an unsuspecting person who enters into a contract with a "special act" corporation that acts beyond the limits of its powers, everyone is deemed to know the law; and the statute creating the corporation and its contents, including the limitations on its contractual powers are considered to be public knowledge, and familiar to everyone.

Business corporations in most provinces are usually incorporated under legislation that gives the corporations very wide powers to contract; in many

---

11. For example, in some provinces, an alien may not be permitted to engage in certain kinds of professional work, such as law, until a licence to practise (which may be restricted to Canadian citizens) is obtained.
12. *Porter v. Freudenberg,* [1915] 1 K.B. 857; *Daimler Co. v. Continental Tyre and Rubber Co. (Great Britain) Ltd.,* [1916] 2 A.C. 307.

cases, all the power of a mature natural person. This is not, however, always the case. A corporation, in its articles of incorporation, may limit its own powers for specific reasons, and, depending upon the legislation under which it was incorporated, the limitation may bind third parties. A full discussion of the effect of these limitations on the capacity of a corporation to contract is reserved for Chapter 17, "Corporation Law."

LABOUR UNIONS

A labour union is an organization with powers that vary considerably from province to province. Originally, a union was an illegal organization, since its object was restraint of trade, but legislation in the nineteenth century changed the status of the union to a legal one. An agreement that a labour union negotiates with an employer would not normally be enforceable were it not for specific legislation governing its negotiation and enforcement. Apart from a brief period in Ontario when the courts had the authority to enforce collective agreements,[13] the courts have not normally been concerned with labour "contracts." The reason for this may be found in the law itself. The legislation in most provinces, and at the federal level, provides for the interpretation and enforcement of collective agreements by binding arbitration rather than the courts. In addition, the legislation in all provinces specifically provides that a labour union certified by the Labour Relations Board has the exclusive authority to negotiate a collective agreement for the employees it represents. The capacity of a labour union in this regard is examined in detail in Chapter 19, "Labour Law."

BANKRUPT PERSONS

A person who has been declared bankrupt has a limited capacity to contract. Until a bankrupt person receives a **discharge,** he or she may not enter into any contract except for necessaries. All business contracts entered into before bankruptcy become the responsibility of the **trustee in bankruptcy,** and the bankrupt, on discharge, is released from the responsibility of the contracts and all related debts, except those relating to breach of trust, fraud, and certain orders of the court. To protect persons who may not realize that they are dealing with an undischarged bankrupt, the Bankruptcy Act[14] requires the undischarged bankrupt to reveal the fact that he or she is an undischarged bankrupt before entering into any contract involving more than $500.

SUMMARY

Not everyone has the capacity at law to enter into a contract that the courts will enforce. Minors or infants, as a general rule, are not liable under any contract they may make; but in the interests of the minor, the courts will hold the minor liable in contracts "for necessaries." **Necessaries** generally include food, shelter, clothing, employment, and education, but do not include contracts negotiated by an infant or minor engaged in business as a proprietor. All contracts, other than contracts for necessaries, are voidable at the infant's option.

---

13. Collective Bargaining Act, 1943, S.O. 1943 (Ont.), c. 4.
14. Bankruptcy Act, R.S.C. 1985, c. B-3 as amended by S.C. 1992 c. 27.

Other persons may also lack the capacity to contract. Enemy aliens during hostilities are neither permitted to enter into, nor enforce, contracts with others. Intoxicated persons and insane persons are bound to pay a reasonable price for necessaries contracted for while in a drunken or insane state. However, they will not generally be liable for other contracts if they can show that they were drunken or insane at the time of making the contract, and the other party was aware of it. They must, however, repudiate the contract promptly on becoming sane or sober. Bankrupt persons are prohibited from entering into contracts (except for necessaries) until they are discharged by the courts.

Corporations and labour unions, because of their nature, may be subject to certain limitations in their capacity to contract. The limitations are based, in part, on their activities, with the rights and powers in respect to their contracts or collective agreements clearly delineated by statute. Apart from the restrictions placed upon these groups, and certain limitations on a few others (such as native peoples living on reservations), the courts recognize all persons that have reached the age of majority as persons with full capacity to contract.

DISCUSSION QUESTIONS

1. Explain the reasoning behind the common law rules that limit the capacity of certain persons to bind themselves in contract.
2. Why do the courts make certain exceptions to the general rule concerning the capacity of infants to bind themselves in contract?
3. If an adult entered into a contract without realizing that he was dealing with an infant, would the adult be in a position to enforce the agreement? Would your answer to this question apply under all circumstances?
4. How do the courts generally view a contract for the payment of tuition fees between a minor and an educational institution? Does this differ from the common law that relates to a contract for apprenticeship for a minor?
5. Where a minor or infant is engaged in business, how are the courts likely to view business contracts entered into by the minor?
6. Under what conditions or circumstances would an "agency of necessity" arise?
7. How does the capacity to contract of a minor differ from the capacity to contract of an insane or drunken person?
8. What are the limits on the powers of a "special act" corporation to bind itself in contract?
9. How does the law limit the capacity of a bankrupt person to enter into a binding contract?

MINI-CASE PROBLEMS

1. X, age 17, purchased a bicycle on credit for the purpose of transportation to and from her place of employment. She made no payments on the bicycle, and the seller brought an action against her for the debt. Discuss the issues raised in this case, and render a decision.
2. D, while in a drunken state, engaged a taxi to carry him home. He could not remember where he lived, but after having the driver take him to several wrong addresses, he finally recognized his residence, and had the driver deliver him to the door. Once there, he discovered that he had no money. What are the rights of the taxi driver?

**JUDICIAL
DECISIONS**

The *Nash v. Inman* case that follows illustrates the principle of infant liability for necessaries. The case deals with the issue of whether an infant is liable for what would normally be a necessary item if the infant is already well supplied with it. The judge concludes near the end of the judgement that when the infant or minor already has a sufficient supply, the purchase of additional "necessaries" would not constitute a purchase of a necessary item, and the sale would be voidable at the infant's option.

The *Gregson v. Law and Barry* case deals with the question of misrepresentation by an infant as to age. The infant or minor in this situation swore affidavits that she was of the age of majority (when in fact she was not) in order to sell some property. The infant then attempted to recover the property. The judge deals with the right of an infant to avoid a contract she made as a result of her fraud, and concludes that the court should not assist her to recover the land she sold by fraud. The judge did this by dismissing her legal action.

**Capacity to
Contract —
Infants —
Necessaries**

Nash v. Inman, [1908] 2 K.B. 1.

The defendant was an infant university student who purchased 11 fancy suits when he already had an ample supply of clothes. The plaintiff tailor brought an action for the price of the clothes when the infant refused to pay for the goods.

FLETCHER MOULTON, L.J.:

I think that the difficulty and at the same time the suggestion of hardship to the plaintiff in such a case as this disappear when one considers what is the true basis of an action against an infant for necessaries. It is usually spoken of as a case of enforcing a contract against the infant, but I agree with the view expressed by the Court in *Rhodes v. Rhodes,* in the parallel case of a claim for necessaries against a lunatic, that this language is somewhat unfortunate. An infant, like a lunatic, is incapable of making a contract of purchase in the strict sense of the words; but if a man satisfies the needs of the infant or lunatic by supplying to him necessaries, the law will imply an obligation to repay him for the services so rendered, and will enforce that obligation against the estate of the infant or lunatic. The consequence is that the basis of the action is hardly contract. Its real foundation is an obligation which the law imposes on the infant to make a fair payment in respect of needs satisfied. In other words the obligation arises *re* and not *consensu.* I do not mean that this nicety of legal phraseology has been adhered to. The common and convenient phrase is that an infant is liable for goods sold and delivered provided that they are necessaries, and there is no objection to that phraseology so long as its true meaning is understood. But the treatment of such actions by the Courts of Common Law has been in accordance with that principle I have referred to. That the articles were necessaries had to be alleged and proved by the plaintiff as part of his case, and the sum he recovered was based on a quantum meruit. If he claimed anything beyond this he failed, and it did not help him that he could prove that the prices were agreed prices. All this is very ancient law, and is confirmed by the provinces of s. 2 of the Sale of Goods Act, 1893 — an Act which was intended to codify the existing law. That section expressly provides that the consequence of necessaries sold and delivered to an infant is that he must pay a reasonable price therefor.

The Sale of Goods Act, 1893, gives a statutory definition of what are necessaries in a legal sense, which entirely removes any doubt, if any doubt previously existed, as to what that word in legal phraseology means. [The Lord Justice read the definition.] Hence, if an action is brought by one who claims to enforce against an infant such an obligation, it is obvious that the plaintiff in order to prove his case must shew that the goods supplied come within this definition.

... the plaintiff has to shew, first, that the goods were suitable to the condition in life of the infant; and, secondly, that they were suitable to his actual requirements at the time — or, in other words, that the infant had not at the time an adequate supply from other sources. There is authority to shew that this was the case even before the Act of 1893. In *Johnstone v. Marks* this doctrine is laid down with the greatest clearness, and the ratio decidendi of that case applies equally to cases since that Act. Therefore there is no doubt whatever that in order to succeed in an action for goods sold and delivered to an infant the plaintiff must shew that they satisfy both the conditions I have mentioned. Everything which is necessary to bring them within s. 2 it is for him to prove.

Passing on from general principles, let me take the facts of the present case. In my opinion they raise no point whatever as to the duty of the judge as contrasted with the duty of the jury arising from the peculiar character of the action. We have only to follow the lines of the law consistently administered by this Court for many more years than I can think of, an example of which as applied to the case of the supply of necessaries to an infant is given by the decision of the Court of Exchequer Chamber in the case of *Ryder v. Wombwell.*

The issue in that case was whether certain articles were suitable to the condition in a life of the defendant, the infant; and the Court of Exchequer Chamber thought that no jury could reasonably find that those articles were suitable to the condition of that defendant, and therefore they said that the judge — not by reason of any peculiar rule applicable to actions of this kind, but in the discharge of his regular duties in all cases of trial by a jury — ought not to have left the question to the jury because there was no evidence on which they could reasonably find for the plaintiff. We have before us a similar case, in which the issue is not only whether the articles in question were suitable to the defendant's condition in life, but whether they are suitable to his actual requirements at the time of the sale and delivery; and how does the evidence stand? The evidence for the plaintiff shewed that one of his travellers, hearing that a freshman at Trinity College was spending money pretty liberally, called on him to get an order for clothes, and sold him within nine months goods which at cash prices came to over 120£, including an extravagant number of waistcoats and other articles of clothing, and that is all that the plaintiff proved. The defendant's father proved the infancy, and then proved that the defendant had an adequate supply of clothes, and stated what they were. That evidence was uncontradicted. Not only was it not contradicted by any other evidence, but there was no cross-examination tending to shake the credit of the witness, against whose character and means of knowledge nothing could be said. On that uncontradicted evidence the judge came to the conclusion, to use the language of the Court in *Ryder v. Wombwell,* that there was no evidence on which the jury might properly find that these goods were necessary to the actual requirements of the infant at the time of sale and delivery, and therefore, in accordance with the duty of the judge in all cases of trial by jury, he withdrew the case from the jury and directed judgment to be entered for the defendant. In my opinion he was justified by the practice of the Court in so doing, and this appeal must be dismissed.

Capacity to Contract — Infants — Fraud on Part of Infant

Gregson v. Law and Barry (1913), 5 W.W.R. 1017.

An infant made a transfer of land to a person who was unaware of her infancy in return for the market value of the property. In the affidavits accompanying the deed, the infant swore that she was of full age. She later repudiated the conveyance, and brought an action for a return of the property.

MURPHY, J.:

In this action I am forced to hold on the evidence that the plaintiff well knew when she executed the final deed to Law that, being a minor, she could not legally do so, and that, with such knowledge, she proceeded to complete and execute the same, including the making of the acknowledgment and representing herself to be of full age. No hint of the true condition of things was given to Law, and I hold this was done knowingly, and that therefore the plaintiff is now coming into court to take advantage of her own fraud. Whilst, apparently, it is true to say that being an infant she could not be made liable on a contract thus brought about, it is, I think, an altogether different proposition to say the court will actually assist her to obtain advantages based entirely on her own fraudulent act.

The authorities cited in argument show in fact, I consider, that infants are no more entitled than adults to gain benefits to themselves by fraud, or at any rate establish the proposition that the courts will not become active agents to bring about such a result.

The action is dismissed.

CASE PROBLEMS FOR DISCUSSION

Case 1

Alice, a young woman 17 years of age, saw an advertisement in a magazine that offered a 24-piece set of silver flatware for sale on the following terms: "$100 payable with order, and monthly payments of $50 each, payable over a three-year term."

The advertisement was accompanied by a coupon setting out the terms of payment and requiring the purchaser to provide his or her name and address and signature in the space provided.

Alice completed the coupon and mailed it, together with a cheque for $100, to the seller. A few weeks later, the 24-piece set of silverware arrived by post.

Alice made a number of payments according to the terms of the agreement, then decided that she did not wish to continue with the agreement. A week before her eighteenth birthday, she wrote to the seller and repudiated the contract, but did not offer in return the silverware because she had lost several of the teaspoons.

The seller and Alice then engaged in a protracted round of correspondence in which the seller demanded a return of the silverware and the retention of all money paid as the price of her release from the agreement. Alice refused to return the silverware. She maintained that she was entitled to a return of the payments as she was a minor at the time she entered into the agreement.

The seller, some 10 months later, brought an action against Alice for the balance of the purchase price.

Discuss the defences (if any) that Alice might raise in this case, and render a decision.

Case 2

Hamish, a university student and a football enthusiast, travelled with his university football team to watch a game played at an out-of-town university. After the game, he visited a local bar with some friends and drank a great deal. He was quite drunk when he stumbled into the hotel where he had arranged accommodation, but managed to sign the hotel register and find his way to his room.

The next morning, he awoke late and discovered that he had only a few minutes to catch the bus back to the university. He raced from the hotel, and arrived at the bus stop just before the bus was ready to leave. Some time later, he discovered the key to the hotel room in his pocket, and realized that he had not paid for his room.

In a few days' time, Hamish received a statement from the hotel for $175. He thought that this rate for the room was excessive, and refused to pay the account on the basis that he was intoxicated at the time. The hotel then brought an action against him for the rental of the room.

Discuss the rights of the parties, and the issues that might be raised in this case. Render a decision.

Case 3

Sharp had operated a small wholesale grocery business for a number of years with limited success. Eventually, he found himself seriously in debt as a result of a number of unfortunate purchases of goods that spoiled before he could find a market for them, and he made a voluntary assignment in bankruptcy.

A few weeks later, while still an undischarged bankrupt, he purchase $600 worth of farm produce on credit from a farmer who was unaware of the fact that he was an undischarged bankrupt. Sharp sold part of the goods at a profit to a friend, and kept the remainder of the food for his own use.

When Sharp failed to pay the farmer, the farmer instituted legal proceedings to collect the $600.

Explain the rights of the farmer in this case, and render a decision.

Case 4

Jones entered into a rental agreement with Cross-Moto-Cycle for a one-month lease of a motorcycle by misrepresenting his age as being 20 when, in reality, he was only 17 years of age. The agreement that Jones signed prohibited the use of the motorcycle in any race or contest, and required Jones to assume responsibility for any damage to the machine while it was in his possession.

A week after Jones acquired the machine, he made arrangements to enter a motorcycle race that was to be held in a nearby city. On his way to the race, he lost control of the motorcycle on a sharp turn in the road, and the machine was badly damaged in the ensuing accident.

Jones refused to pay for the rental and the damage on the basis that he had not attained the age of majority, and was not liable on the contract.

Discuss the rights of Cross-Moto-Cycle, and comment on its likelihood of success if it should take legal proceedings against Jones.

Case 5

Linda and John, aged 17 and 18 respectively, entered into a partnership agreement to carry on business as a local parcel delivery service. The business was to be operated under the name "L & J Parcel Delivery." In order to conduct the business, the two partners purchased a small truck on credit from a local truck dealer. The purchase agreement for the truck was signed "L & J Parcel Delivery" by John, who negotiated the purchase.

Linda purchased a motorbike on credit from a local dealer for the two-fold purpose of (1) delivering parcels, and (2) transportation to and from her home to the place of business of L & J Parcel Delivery, a distance of some 8 km. She had informed the seller that the motorbike would be used by L & J Parcel Delivery and for personal transportation, but signed the purchase agreement in her own name only.

A few days before Linda's eighteenth birthday, John and Linda decided to cease their business operations. A substantial part of the purchase price remained owing to the sellers of both the truck and the motorbike, and with the intention of avoiding liability on the two purchase agreements, Linda repudiated the contracts and the partnership agreement. Over the next few months, John and Linda retained possession of the truck and motorbike, while they argued between themselves and with the two sellers as to responsibility for the payment of the balance of the purchase price on each vehicle. Finally, after three months of fruitless discussion and argument, the sellers each brought an action against John and Linda for payment of the debts.

Discuss the rights of the parties and the issues that might be raised in the case. Render a decision.

Case 6

Jane Poore watched a television commercial for Dealer Bob's Furniture and Appliance Warehouse, offering great sale prices and no payment for one year on approved credit. In response to the advertisement, Jane went to Dealer Bob's Store and purchased a washer and dryer, a microwave oven, and a new bed. She also applied for their delayed payment credit terms and provided the bank account number of her niece, who was also named Jane Poore, for the store's credit staff to check. Jane's niece had, on other occasions, lent Jane money for certain purchases she needed to make. On the basis of its investigation, the store agreed to extend their advertised credit terms to delay any payment on Jane's purchases for one year. The store then delivered the items to Jane's apartment. Dealer Bob's later sold Jane's debt to a financing company at a discounted price and assigned it the right to collect her payments in due course.

Several weeks later Jane found herself in need of money and offered to sell her car to her brother for $5000. The brother paid Jane $2500 and promised to pay the remainder in a few months.

Within a month Jane found herself in dire financial circumstances and was forced to declare bankruptcy. Over a period of time the trustee in bankruptcy was able to liquidate some of Jane's assets and pay off most of her debts. However, a number of months after Jane had declared bankruptcy, her brother paid her the balance owing on the car. Jane did not report this payment to the trustee nor did she turn over the funds to him.

Some time later, Jane obtained a discharge from her bankruptcy. Shortly thereafter, the finance company which had purchased Jane's debt from Dealer Bob's and which had not yet been paid out of Jane's assets, contacted Jane and demanded payment in full. In a letter to Jane it stated that it had been made aware through members of Jane's family that she had received sums of money after her bankruptcy which had not been turned over to the trustee for the payment of her creditors.

Discuss the legal positions of Jane and the finance company and the nature of any action which may be taken. What issues will be raised by each and what is the likely outcome?

CHAPTER 9

Requirement of Legality

**ENFORCEABIL-
ITY OF AN
ILLEGAL
AGREEMENT**

Agreements that offend the public good are not enforceable. If parties enter into an agreement that has an illegal purpose, it may not only be unenforceable, but illegal as well. Under these circumstances, the parties may be liable to a penalty or fine for either making the agreement, or attempting to carry it out. However, certain contracts are only rendered void by public policy in general, or by specific statutes. In these cases, the law has simply identified certain contractual activities that it will not enforce if the parties fail to comply with the statute or the policy. In other cases, the law declares certain activities to be not only illegal, but the contract pertaining thereto void, or absolutely void. As a result of these various combinations, the absence of legality does not always neatly classify contracts as those that are unlawful, and those that are void, since an overlap exists.

**LEGALITY
UNDER
STATUTE LAW**

An illegal contract, if considered in a narrow sense, includes any agreement to commit a crime, such as an agreement to rob, assault, abduct, murder, obtain goods under false pretences, or commit any other act prohibited under the Criminal Code.[1] For example, an agreement by two parties to commit the robbery of a bank would be an illegal contract, and subject to criminal penalties as a conspiracy to commit a crime, even if the robbery was not carried out. If one party refused to go through with the agreement, the other party would not be entitled to take the matter to the courts for redress because the contract would be absolutely void and unenforceable.

    Another type of agreement that would be unenforceable would be an agreement relating to the embezzlement of funds by an employee where the employee,

---

1. Criminal Code, R.S.C. 1985, c. C-46, as amended.

when the crime is discovered, promises the employer restitution in return for a promise not to report the crime to the police. The victim of the theft is often not aware that the formation of an agreement to accept repayment of the funds in return for a promise to not report the matter is improper. The contract would accordingly be unenforceable.

A statute that affects certain kinds of contracts and that, in part, is criminal law is the Competition Act.[2] This statute renders illegal any contract or agreement between business firms that represents a restraint of competition. The act covers a number of business practices that are contrary to the public interest, the most important being contracts or agreements that tend to fix prices, eliminate or reduce the number of competitors, allocate markets, or reduce output in such a way that competition is unduly restricted. The act applies to contracts concerning both goods and services, and attempts to provide a balance between freedom of trade and the protection of the consumer. The formation of mergers or monopolies that would be against the public interest may also be prohibited under the act, and all contracts relating to the formation of such a new entity would also be illegal. Similarly, any agreement between existing competitors that would prevent new competition from entering the market would be prohibited by the act, and the agreement would be illegal.

Statute law, other than criminal law, may also render certain types of contracts illegal and unenforceable. Some statutes (such as worker's compensation legislation, land-use planning legislation in some provinces,[3] and wagering laws[4]) render any agreement made in violation of the act void and unenforceable. In contrast to illegal contracts, void contracts usually carry no criminal penalties with them. The contract is simply considered to be one that does not create rights that may be enforced. For example, under the land use control legislation in Ontario[5] any deed, purporting to convey a part of a lot that a landowner owns and requiring consent of the planning authority for the severance, is void unless consent to sever the parcel is obtained from the planning authority and endorsed on the deed. With respect to gambling, the courts have long frowned upon gamblers using the courts to collect wagers and, as a matter of policy, have treated wagering contracts as unenforceable except where specific legislation has made them enforceable.

One type of contract that contains an element of wager, which is not treated as being illegal or void, is the contract of insurance. An insurance transaction, while it bears a superficial resemblance to a wager, is essentially an attempt to provide protection from a financial loss that the insured hopes will not occur. This is particularly true in the case of life insurance. In this sense, it is quite different from placing a wager on the outcome of a football game or a horse race, where the gambler hopes to be the winner.

What distinguishes the contract of insurance from a simple wager is the insurable interest of the party taking out the insurance. Since the insured is presumed

---

2. Combines Investigation Act, R.S.C. 1985, c. C-34. Renamed the Competition Act by 1986 S. Can. c. 26.

3. For example, the Planning Act, R.S.O. 1990, c. P-13.

4. The Gaming Act, R.S.O. 1990, c. G-2, s. 3, however, permits bets on cards, dice, or other games to be recoverable if the amount of money involved does not exceed $40. It does not apply to other kinds of wagers.

5. The Planning Act, R.S.O. 1990, c. P-13, s. 49, provides that any subdivision and sale of land that violates the act is void in the sense that no property interest passes.

to have an interest in the insured event not happening (particularly if the insurance is on his or her life) this type of wager assumes an air of legitimacy. The provincial legislatures have recognized this difference and passed legislation pertaining to insurance contracts that render them valid and enforceable, provided that an insurable interest exists, or that the provisions of the act permit the particular interest to be insured. The importance of this type of agreement as a risk-spreading or risk-reducing device for business and the public in general far outweighs the wager element in the agreement. Public policy has, on this basis, generally legitimated insurance contracts by legislative enforcement.

One type of contract that the courts treat as illegal is a contract between an unlicensed tradesperson, or professional, and a contracting party. If the jurisdiction in which the tradesperson or professional operates requires the person to be licensed in order to perform services for the public at large, then an unlicensed tradesperson or professional may not enforce a contract for payment for the services if the other party refuses to pay the account. In most provinces, the licensing of professionals is on a province-wide basis, and penalties are provided where an unlicensed person engages in a recognized professional activity. The medical, legal, dental, land surveying, architectural, and engineering professions, for example, are subject to such licensing requirements in an effort to protect the public from unqualified practitioners. The same holds true for many trades, although, in some provinces, these are licensed at the local level.

Where a licence to practice is required, and the tradesperson is unlicensed, it would appear to be a good defence to a claim for payment for the defendant to argue that the contract is unenforceable on the tradesperson's part because he or she is unlicensed.[6] However, where the unlicensed tradesperson supplies materials as well as services, the defence may well be limited only to the services supplied and not to the value of the goods. In a recent case,[7] the Supreme Court of Ontario held that an unlicensed tradesperson may recover for the value of the goods supplied, because the particular by-law licensing the contractor did not contain a prohibition on the sale of material by an unlicensed contractor. It should be noted, however, that the reverse does not apply. If the tradesperson fails to perform the contract properly, and the injured party brings an action against the tradesperson for breach of contract, the tradesperson cannot claim that the contract is unenforceable because he or she does not possess a licence. The courts will hold the tradesperson liable for the damages that the other party suffered.[8]

These various forms of illegality and their impact on a contract were described by the court in the following manner:

> The effect of illegality upon a contract may be threefold. If at the time of making the contract there is an intent to perform it in an unlawful way, the contract, although it remains alive, is unenforceable at the suit of the party having that intent; if the intent is held in common, it is not enforceable at all. Another effect of illegality is to prevent a plaintiff from recovering under a contract if in order to prove his rights under it he has to rely upon his own illegal act; he may not do that even though he can show that at the time of making the contract he had no intent

---

6. *Kocotis v. D'Angelo* (1958), 13 D.L.R. (2d) 69.

7. *Monticchio v. Torcema Construction Ltd. et al.* (1979), 26 O.R. (2d) 305.

8. *Aconley and Aconley v. Willart Holdings Ltd.* (1964), 49 W.W.R. 46.

to break the law and that at the time of performance he did not know that what he was doing was illegal. The third effect of illegality is to avoid the contract *ab initio* and that arises if the making of the contract is expressly or impliedly prohibited by statute or is otherwise contrary to public policy.[9]

LEGALITY AT COMMON LAW: PUBLIC POLICY

There are a number of different circumstances at common law under which a contract will not be enforceable. Historically, these are activities that were contrary to public policy, and remain so today. Contracts designed to obstruct justice, injure the public service, or injure the state are clearly not in the best interests of the public. They are illegal as well as unenforceable. An agreement, for example, that is designed to stifle prosecution, or influence the evidence presented in a court of law, is contrary to public policy.[10]

In a similar fashion, contracts that tend to promote unnecessary litigation of a speculative nature are void, and at common law are contrary to public policy. The reasoning behind this rule is that a solicitor-client relationship based upon a splitting of the proceeds of litigation would tend to promote unnecessary lawsuits, since the client would have virtually nothing to lose by the undertaking. The lawyer, as well, having a personal interest in the outcome of the legal proceedings, may be inclined to promote an action knowing full well that it is not bona fide. Both attitudes represent something that would not be in the best interests of the public or the profession, hence the prohibition on contracts that would tend to abuse the legal process. Two points, however, should be noted with respect to this rule. First, it is not improper for a lawyer to assist a poor person who cannot afford legal assistance by providing legal services, even though the suit may not be successful. The important distinction is that the assistance is made available in a disinterested manner, and not for a percentage of the outcome.[11] Second, the need for legal assistance to maintain an action is now, to some extent, provided by provincial legal aid, and is available to those persons who are unable to afford legal counsel on their own. This second fact, in particular, may reduce the need for a member of the legal profession to undertake, on behalf of a client, a case that may be speculative with respect to outcome and with respect to his or her fees. Some states in the United States, however, do permit members of their bar to carry on litigation for clients in return for a percentage of the outcome. In Canada, legislation (and proposed legislation) in some provinces permits the legal profession to undertake litigation on a contingent fee basis in an effort to improve public access to the courts. The expectation is that persons with limited incomes who do not qualify for legal aid may retain counsel on a contingency fee basis.

Contracts prejudicial to Canada in its relations with other countries would also be void on the grounds of public policy. An example of a contract of this type would be an agreement between a resident of Canada and an enemy alien during a period when hostilities had been declared between the two countries.

Public policy and the Criminal Code also dictate that any contract that tends to interfere with or injure the public service would be void and illegal. For example, an agreement with a public official, whereby the official would use his or her

---

9. *Archbolds (Freightage) Ltd. v. S. Spanglett Ltd.,* [1961] 1 Q.B. 374.

10. *Symington v. Vancouver Breweries and Riefel,* [1931] 1 D.L.R. 935.

11. *Harris v. Brisco* (1886), 17 Q.B.D. 504.

position to obtain a benefit for the other party in return for payment, would be both illegal and unenforceable.

Another class of contract that would be contrary to public policy is a contract involving the commission of a tort, or a dishonest or immoral act. In general, agreements of this nature that encourage or induce others to engage in an act of dishonesty or immoral conduct will be unenforceable.

Contracts for debts where the interest rate charged by the lender is unconscionable are contrary to public policy. Where a lender attempts to recover the exorbitant interest from a defaulting debtor, the courts will not enforce the contract according to its terms, but may set aside the interest payable, or, in some cases, order the creditor to repay a portion of the excessive interest to the debtor.[12]

The law with respect to contracts of this nature is not clear as to what constitutes an unconscionably high rate, as there is often no fixed statutory limit for contracts where this issue may arise. Interest rates fall within the jurisdiction of the federal government, and, while it has passed a number of laws controlling interest rates for different types of loans, the parties in many cases are free to set their own rates. To prevent the lender from hiding the actual interest rate in the form of extra charges, consumer protection legislation now requires disclosure of true interest rates and the cost of borrowing for many kinds of consumer loan transactions. For others, the courts generally use, as a test, the rate of interest that a borrower in similar circumstances (and with a similar risk facing the lender) might obtain elsewhere.[13] To charge an interest rate in excess of 60% would also violate the Criminal Code, and render the creditor liable to criminal action as well.

CONTRACTS IN RESTRAINT OF TRADE

Contracts in restraint of trade fall into three categories:

(1) agreements contrary to the Competition Act (which were briefly explained earlier in this chapter),
(2) agreements between the vendor and purchasers of a business that may contain an undue or unreasonable restriction on the right of the vendor to engage in a similar business in competition with the purchaser, and
(3) agreements between an employer and an employee that unduly or unreasonably restrict the right of the employee to compete with the employer after the employment relationship is terminated.

Of these three, the last two are subject to common law public policy rules that determine their enforceability. The general rule in this respect states that all contracts in restraint of trade are *prima facie* void and unenforceable. The courts will, however, enforce some contracts of this nature, if it can be shown that the restraint is both reasonable and necessary and does not offend the public interest.

Restrictive Agreements Concerning the Sale of a Business

When a vendor sells a business that has been in existence for some time, the goodwill, which the vendor has developed is a part of what the purchaser acquires and pays for. Since goodwill is something that is associated with the good name

---

12. *Morehouse v. Income Investments Ltd.* (1966), 53 D.L.R. (2d) 106.
13. *Miller v. Lavoie* (1966), 60 D.L.R. (2d) 495; *Scott v. Manor Investments,* [1961] O.W.N. 210.

of the vendor, and represents the propensity of customers to return to the same location to do business, its value will depend in no small part on the vendor's intentions when the sale is completed. If the vendor intends to set up a similar business in the immediate vicinity of the old business, the "goodwill," which the vendor has developed, will probably move with the vendor to the new location. The purchaser, in such a case, would acquire little more in the sale than a location and some goods. The purchaser would not acquire many of the vendor's old customers, and consequently, may not value the business at more than the cost of stock and the premises. On the other hand, if the vendor is prepared to promise the purchaser that he or she will not establish a new business in the vicinity, nor engage in any business in direct competition with the purchaser of the business, the goodwill of the business will have some value to both parties. The value, however, is in the enforceability of the promise of the vendor not to compete or do anything to induce the customers to move their business dealings from the purchaser after the business is sold.

The difficulty with the promise of the vendor is that it is *prima facie* void as a restraint of trade. The courts, however, recognize the mutual advantage of such a promise with respect to the sale of a business. If the purchaser can convince the courts that the restriction is reasonable and does not adversely affect the public interest, then the restriction will be enforced. It is important to note, however, that the court will not rewrite an unreasonable restriction to render it reasonable. It will only enforce a reasonable restriction, and nothing less.

The danger that exists with restrictions of this nature is the temptation on the part of the purchaser to make the restriction much broader than necessary to protect the goodwill. If care is not taken in the drafting of the restriction, it may prove to be unreasonable, and will then be struck down by the courts. If this should occur, the result will be a complete loss of protection for the purchaser, as the courts will not modify the restriction to make it enforceable. For example, Victoria operates a drugstore in a small town and enters into a contract with Paul, whereby Paul will purchase Victoria's business if Victoria will promise not to carry on the operation of a drugstore within a radius of 160 km of the existing store for a period of 30 years.

In this case, the geographical restrictions would be unreasonable. The customers of the store, due to the nature of the business, would be persons living within the limits of the town, and perhaps within a few kilometres' radius. No substantial number of customers would likely live beyond a 10 km radius. Similarly, the time limitation would be unreasonable, as a few years would probably be adequate for the purchaser to establish a relationship with the customers of the vendor. The courts, in this instance, would probably declare the restriction unenforceable; with the restriction removed, the vendor would be free to set up a similar business in the immediate area if she wished to do so.

Agreements of this nature might be severed if a part of the restriction is reasonable, and a part overly restrictive. In a classic case on this issue, a manufacturer of arms and ammunition transferred his business to a limited company. As a part of the transaction, he promised that he would not work in or carry on any other business manufacturing guns and ammunition (subject to certain exceptions), nor would he engage in any other business that might compete in any way with the purchaser's business for a period of 25 years. The restrictions applied on a worldwide basis. The court, in this case, recognized the global nature of the business and held that the restriction preventing the vendor from competing in the arms and ammunition business anywhere in the world was reasonable, and the restriction enforceable. However, it viewed the second part of the restriction (which prevented the vendor from engaging in any other business) as overly restrictive, and severed it from the contract on the basis that the two promises were separate.[14]

An unenforceable restriction may only be severed if the agreement's meaning will remain the same after the severance. This rule, the "blue pencil rule," was once applied by English courts in a number of cases concerning restraint of trade where the unreasonable restriction was reduced to a reasonable covenant by the elimination of a few words.[15] This approach was rejected in later cases,[16] however, and is now limited to "blue pencilling" an entire or severable unreasonable restriction, leaving the remainder of the restrictions intact. Even this practice would appear to be limited to restraint of trade restrictions contained in agreements between the vendors and purchasers of a business.[17]

In the case of *Stephens v. Gulf Oil Canada Ltd. et al.* (1974), 3 O.R. (2d) 241, the judge discussed the freedoms that the courts attempt to balance in dealing with public policy as it relates to restraint of trade. The judge in the case outlined the policies in terms of "freedom," and the way in which the courts have reconciled the differences. He described the process in the following words:

> As usual in all such cases it is necessary to choose between or to reconcile, according to principle, important public policies that may be or appear to be in conflict with one another. Here, these policies are:
>
> Freedom under the law — Freedom of a person to conduct himself as he wishes subject to any restraint imposed upon him by the law.
>
> Freedom of commerce — The right of a person or firm to establish the business of his choice assuming that he has the capital and ability to do so, to enter a market freely, to make contracts freely with others in the advancement and operation of his business and to gain such rewards as the market will bestow on his initiative.
>
> Free competition — The right of business to compete for supplies and customers on the basis of quality, service and price, and the right of the public at large, whether industrial consumers or end users, to a choice in the market of competing goods and services of competitive quality and at prices established by competition.
>
> It will at once be apparent that these public policy principles are inherent in the private enterprise economy which depends for its proper working on a free competitive market. The market under this concept will determine what is produced, who produces it, who obtains the product or service and at what price.
>
> It must be recognized, however, that the Canadian economy is not universally a free market economy; it is a mixed economy, substantial areas of which are subject to regulation by Governments or public agencies in accordance with federal or

---

14. *Nordenfelt v. Maxim Nordenfelt Guns & Ammunition Co. Ltd.,* [1894] A.C. 535.

15. *Goldsoll v. Goldman,* [1915] 1 Ch. 292.

16. *Putsnam v. Taylor,* [1927] 1 K.B. 637.

17. *Mason v. Provident Clothing Co.,* [1913] A.C. 724; *E.P. Chester Ltd. v. Mastorkis* (1968), 70 D.L.R. (2d) 133.

provincial statutes. In these areas there may exist to a greater or lesser degree, economic or social controls which replace in whole or in part the free market operations in those areas. There, market forces as the main influence in economic decision-making may be replaced by state agencies or officials who in accordance with valid statutes may determine questions of entry, production, distribution and price. Inroads are thus made on the three public policy principles which I have mentioned. But in the areas of the economy not so regulated, the private enterprise competitive market system prevails. This is the fundamental mechanism whereby economic resources are allocated to their most productive uses and economic efficiency is encouraged, inefficiency penalized and waste controlled.

It will also be apparent that the public policy in relation to freedom of commerce, particularly freedom of contract, may and frequently does, come into conflict with the public policy in relation to free competition. For example, an agreement between two or more suppliers to deny supplies of an essential commodity or service to a new entrant to a market may foreclose that market to the newcomer and so destroy his right to establish or expand the business of his choice.

Such conflicts are nowadays ordinarily adjusted, if public policy requires it, by appropriate legislation. But it is also open to the common law Courts to do so by the development of jurisprudence....

Restrictive Agreements Between Employees and Employers

The law distinguishes restrictive agreements concerning the sale of a business from restrictive agreements made between an employer and an employee. In the latter case, an employer, in an attempt to protect business practices and business secrets, may require an employee to promise not to compete with the employer upon termination of employment. The legality of this type of restriction, however, is generally subject to close scrutiny by the courts, and the criteria applied differ from that which the law has established for contracts where a sale of a business is concerned.

The justification for the different criteria is based upon the serious consequences that may flow from a restriction of the employee's opportunities to obtain other employment and to exercise acquired skills or knowledge. In general, the courts are reluctant to place any impediment in the way of a person seeking employment. As a consequence, a restrictive covenant in a contract of employment will not be enforced unless serious injury to the employer can be clearly demonstrated. This reluctance of the courts stems from the nature of the bargaining relationship at the time the agreement is negotiated between the employer and the employee. The employee is seldom in a strong bargaining position vis-à-vis the employer when the employment relationship is established. Also, the employment contract is often an agreement on the employer's standard form that the employee must accept or reject at the time. Public policy recognizes the unequal bargaining power of the parties by placing the economic freedom of the employee above that of the special interests of the employer.

In some cases, however, the special interests of the employer may be protected by a restrictive covenant in a contract of employment. The courts have held, for example, that when an employee has access to secret production processes of the employer, the employee may be restrained from revealing this information to others after the employment relationship is terminated.[18] The same view is taken where the employee has acted on behalf of the employer in his or her dealings with customers, and then later uses the employer's customer lists to solicit business for a new employer.[19] The courts will not, however, prevent an employee from soliciting business from a previous employer's customers under ordinary circumstances, nor will the courts enforce a restriction that would prevent a person from exercising existing skills and ordinary production practices acquired while in the employment relationships after the relationship is terminated.[20]

In contrast, contracts of employment, containing restrictions on the right of employees to engage in activities or business in competition with their employer while the employment relationship exists, are usually enforceable. This is provided that they do not unnecessarily encroach on the employees' personal freedom and that they are reasonable and necessary. The usual type of clause of this nature is a "devotion to business" clause in which the employees promise to devote their time and energy to the promotion of the employer's business interests, and to refrain from engaging in any business activity that might conflict with it.

A second type of restriction sometimes imposed by an employer is one requiring the employee to keep confidential any information of a confidential nature concerning the employer's business that should come into the employee's possession as a result of the employment. An employee subject to such a covenant would conceivably be liable for breach of the employment contract (and damages) if he or she should reveal confidential information to a competitor that results in injury or damage to the employer. Restrictionsof this type are frequently framed to extend beyond the termination of the employment relationship, and, if reasonable and necessary, they may be enforced by the courts.[21] The particular reasoning behind the enforcement of these clauses is not based upon restraint of trade, but rather upon the duties of the employee in the employment relationship. The employer has a right to expect some degree of loyalty and devotion on the employee's part in return for the compensation paid to the employee. Actions on the part of the employee that cause injury to the employer represent a breach of the employment relationship, rather than a restraint of trade. It is usually only when the actual employment relationship ceases that the public policy concerns of the court come into play with respect to restrictive covenants.[22]

With some types of employment, where the service offered to the public by the employer is essential for the public good, the courts will generally take into consideration the potential injury to the public-at-large if a restrictive covenant in an employment contract is enforced. For example, if a medical clinic employs a medical specialist under a contract of employment prohibiting the specialist from practising medicine within a specified geographic area if the specialist should leave the employ of the employer, the courts might refuse to enforce the restriction

18. *Reliable Toy & Reliable Plastics Co. Ltd. v. Collins*, [1950] 4 D.L.R. 499.

19. *Fitch v. Dewes*, [1921] 2 A.C. 158; *Western Inventory Service Ltd. v. Flatt and Island Inventory Service Ltd.* (1979), 9 B.C.L.R. 282.

20. *Herbert Morris Ltd. v. Saxelby*, [1916] 1 A.C. 688.

21. *Reliable Toy & Reliable Plastics Co. Ltd. v. Collins*, [1950] 4 D.L.R. 499.

22. An interesting restrictive covenant concerning pension rights may be found in the case of *Taylor v. McQuilkin et al.* (1968), 2 D.L.R. (3d) 463.

even if it is reasonable, if the court concluded that enforcement would deprive the community of an essential medical service.

In the case[23] upon which this example was based, the court considered the criteria it would use to decide the question of enforceability of a restrictive covenant. The words of the judge are as follows:

> I find that the defendant signed the agreement, ex. 3, being well aware of the restrictive covenant therein and that he was under no duress or at any disadvantage in so doing. The agreement was supported by the mutual promises of the plaintiffs and in any event, it was under seal. Were it not for other aspects of this case, I would hold that it was binding on the defendant and the plaintiffs were entitled to the injunction which they seek.
>
> The first other aspect of the matter which, in my view, renders the covenant unenforceable is the public interest....
>
> In my view, the public interest is the same as public policy.
>
> In the *Harvard Law Review,* vol. 42 (1929), p. 76, Professor Winfield, then of St. John's College, Cambridge, England, at p. 92, defines public policy as: "a principle of judicial legislation or interpretation founded on the current needs of the community." He goes on to say that public policy may change not only from century to century but from generation to generation and even in the same generation.
>
> This author goes on to say at p. 97 that in ascertaining what is public policy at any time, one guide that Judges are certain to employ whenever it is available is statutory legislation in *pari materia.*
>
> It will, therefore, be opposite to consider how statute law in the Province of Ontario affects medical care for the residents of this Province....
>
> Now the beneficial purpose of this legislation is to provide the widest medical care for the residents of the Province. Clearly this is in the public good. And I think it follows that the public are entitled to the widest choice in the selection of their medical practitioners.
>
> In the light of this modern development, ex. 26 at the trial may have some special significance where in May, 1971, a resolution of the council of the Ontario Medical Association was passed as follows:
>
> "RESOLVED that the Ontario Medical Association disapproves the concept of restrictive covenants in the contracts of one physician with another."
>
> A further feature to be considered is whether a restrictive covenant between medical people tends to further limit the right of the public to deal with a profession which has a strong monopoly position. I believe that it does and I think that to widen that monopoly would be injurious to the public.

SUMMARY

The legality of the subject matter of a contract determines its validity and enforceability. Legality is generally determined on the basis of public policy or public interest; any agreement contrary to these considerations may be illegal or void. Contracts or agreements to commit a criminal offence are clearly illegal, and as such are unenforceable. So, too, are agreements between businesses that restrain competition contrary to the Competition Act. Agreements that violate

---

23. *Sherk et al. v. Horowitz,* [1972] 2 O.R. 451.

specific laws are generally treated in this legislation as being either void or illegal. Other contracts in restraint of trade at common law may be simply unenforceable in a court of law. Some contracts, such as loan agreements that require the borrower to pay an unconscionable rate of interest, may only be enforceable in part; and others, which tend to offend the public good, such as agreements that injure the public service or obstruct justice, will not be enforceable at all. Some restraint of trade agreements that are beneficial to the parties and do not offend public policy may be enforced where the restrictions can be shown to be reasonable and necessary.

DISCUSSION QUESTIONS

1. Distinguish between "illegal" and "void" with respect to contract law.
2. What is the basis upon which the requirement of legality of a contract is determined?
3. Explain the risk assumed by an unlicensed tradesperson when entering into a contract to perform a service that may only be performed by a person possessing a license.
4. Identify the three major classes of contracts considered to be in restraint of trade.
5. Explain the rationale behind the passage of the Competition Act.
6. Under what circumstances would a restrictive covenant in the contract for the sale of a business be enforceable? Why is this so, when contracts in restraint of trade are contrary to public policy?
7. Why are courts reluctant to enforce restrictive covenants in contracts of employment? Under what circumstances would such a covenant be enforceable?
8. Indicate the purpose of a devotion to business clause in a contract of employment, and explain the conditions under which this type of clause would be enforceable.
9. Discuss the application of public policy or the "public interest" to contracts of employment containing a covenant that would limit the ability of an employee to compete with the employer in a given area for a period of time.
10. An employee is caught stealing money from her employer, confesses to the theft, and agrees to repay the money taken. The employer, in response, promises not to report the incident to the police. Discuss the validity or enforceability of the employer's promise.

MINI-CASE PROBLEMS

1. A and B agree to carry on a business in partnership as hardware merchants. A and B agree that if either party wishes to end the partnership he must not carry on a similar business within 80 km for a period of 10 years. A leaves the business a year later and sets up a competing hardware business across the street from their old shop, which B continues to operate. Advise B and A.
2. X and Y are marathon runners. X challenges Y to a 42 km race and offers to pay Y $100 if Y should win the race. Y wins the race and X refuses to pay the $100. Can Y successfully sue X for the money?

JUDICIAL DECISIONS

The three judicial decisions in this chapter deal with different aspects of legality. In the case of *Mack v. Edenwold Fertilizer Services Ltd.* the judge is called upon to decide if a contract that relates to an illegal agreement is enforceable in view of the fact that it has as its subject matter a legal purpose (the payment of interest). The judge notes that it is related to an illegal contract and it is necessary to refer to the illegal contract to determine the amount payable under the "legal" contract.

The court's conclusion is that the second contract is tainted with the illegality of the first agreement and is unenforceable.

The *J.G. Collins Insurance Agencies Ltd. v. Elsley* case represents an exception to the general public policy rule with respect to restraint of trade, and concerns the enforcement of a restrictive covenant in a contract for the sale of a business. The judge states that the courts recognize that some restraint may be legitimately imposed to protect the goodwill purchased as a part of the business. He also reviews the "reasonableness" of the restriction, outlines the test to be applied, and raises the important consideration of equality of bargaining power between the parties at the time the contract is made. Finally, the judge concludes that the restrictive covenant is reasonable and enforceable.

The third case, *Baker et al. v. Lintott,* illustrates a slightly different restrictive covenant situation in that it involves the protection of the public as a factor in deciding if a covenant is reasonable and enforceable. The judge is asked to consider if a reduction in the choice of medical practitioners in a given area would render a restrictive covenant unreasonable. He concludes that to reduce the number by one would not adversely affect the medical services offered to the public, as there would be an adequate choice remaining. The judge finds the restrictive covenant enforceable.

Illegal Contract — Second Agreement Not Illegal in Itself — Relationship

Mack v. Edenwold Fertilizer Services Ltd., [1987] 5 W.W.R. 469.

The plaintiff and defendant entered into a contract for the purchase of fertilizer. The supplier agreed to back-date the contract to the previous year to enable the plaintiff to claim an expense deduction on his income tax for that year. The contract was not fully performed by the defendant and the parties entered into a second agreement whereby the defendant would pay interest to the plaintiff on the money paid for the fertilizer. When the defendant later refused to pay the interest, the plaintiff took legal action for payment of the interest.

At trial the plaintiff was successful in enforcing the contract. The defendant then appealed the decision.

VANCISE, J.A. (orally):

The narrow issue on this appeal [from case reported at [1986] 3 W.W.R. 731, 46 Sask. R. 137] is whether a subsequent agreement to pay interest on a sum of money due and owing under an illegal contract is an independent transaction capable of being enforced at law.

The trial judge found that a contract to purchase fertilizer entered into between the appellant as vendor and the respondent as purchaser, which was backdated to a different fiscal year, for the unlawful purpose of defrauding the Department of National Revenue, was illegal and unenforceable in accordance with the principles enunciated in *Zimmermann v. Letkeman,* [1978] 1 S.C.R. 1097, [1977] 6 W.W.R. 741, 79 D.L.R. (3d) 508, 17 N.R. 564 [Sask.]. He found, however, that two agreements made subsequent to the illegal and unenforceable contract were separate transactions which transactions were enforceable by reason that no assistance was required from the illegal transaction to enforce payment of interest. In so doing, he relied on *Clark v. Hagar* (1893), 22 S.C.R. 510 [Ont.].

In our opinion, the undertaking by the appellant to pay interest was a modification of the illegal contract to purchase fertilizer. The undertaking to pay interest was not an independent or separate transaction which could be enforced without reference to the contract. Indeed, in order to calculate the amount of interest payable on the amount owing from time to time, it was necessary to know the dates the fertilizer purchased under the illegal contract was delivered to the respondent. The public policy considerations as enunciated in *Zimmermann v. Letkeman,* which dictate that the main contract is illegal and unenforceable, apply equally to the modification of the agreement by undertaking to pay interest. The comments of Bayda J.A. [now C.J.S.] in *Thompson v. Biensch,* [1980] 6 W.W.R. 143, 3 Sask. R. 353 at 360, dealing with the tainting of a document which bears no illegality on its face, in this case the undertaking to pay interest, to an illegal transaction to which it is tied, are equally applicable to this case.

In the result, the appeal is allowed and the action dismissed with no costs to either party throughout.

Contract in Restraint of Trade — Reasonableness of Covenant in Restraint of Trade Where Vendor Becomes Employee of Purchaser of Business

J.G. Collins Insurance Agencies Ltd. v. Elsley (1976), 70 D.L.R. (3d) 513.
The defendant sold an insurance business and agreed to work for the purchaser as his sales manager. At that time, the defendant signed a covenant whereby he would not compete with the plaintiff as a general insurance agent for a period of five years within a given area.

The defendant left the employ of the plaintiff and set up his own business within the five-year period and within the defined area.

EVANS, J.A. (after reviewing the evidence and the trial judgement):

The general rule is that clauses restraining the scope of a man's future business activities, whether contained in agreements of employment or of sale of a business, must be reasonable both as between the parties and with reference to the public interest. Otherwise such a clause is unenforceable as being in restraint of trade and contrary to public policy. Public policy is not a fixed and immutable standard but one which changes to remain compatible with changing economic and social conditions. The old doctrine that any restraint on trade was void as against public policy must be balanced against the principle that the honouring of contractual obligations, freely entered into by parties bargaining on equal footing, is also in the public interest. These competing principles of public policy are frequently in conflict in the commercial world and the question whether a particular non-competition agreement is void and unenforceable is one of law to be determined on a consideration of the character and nature of the business, the relationship of the parties, and the relevant circumstances existing at the time the agreement was entered into.

Courts recognize that some restraints must be imposed, otherwise the purchaser of a business could not with safety buy the goodwill of the business unless the vendor could be enjoined from setting up next door in competition. A similar problem would arise in certain employer and employee situations where, because of the confidential nature of the relationship, the employee has access to computer lists, trade secrets or other matters in which the purchaser or the employer has a proprietary interest.

The modern and authoritative position is stated in the recent decision of the Privy Council in *Stenhouse Australia Ltd. v. Phillips,* [1974] 1 All E.R. 117. That appeal involves consideration of a clause in an employment contract prohibiting an employee from soliciting clients of his former employer, an insurance broker, within a defined area and for a specified time following termination of his employment. It was pointed out that the success of an insurance agency depends a great deal on its relationship with its clients which may have taken some time to develop and to build up and yet it is recognized that such relationship is a fairly tenuous connection which, because of its comparative fragility, makes the risk of solicitation of clients by a former employee more serious. These factors demonstrate the very real need of protection by way of injunctive restraint of an insurance broker's proprietary interest in its customer lists. In the above decision Lord Wilberforce at p. 122 stated:

"...the employer's claim for protection must be based on the identification of some advantage or asset inherent in the business which can properly be regarded as, in a general sense, his property, and which it would be unjust to allow the employee to appropriate for his own purposes, even though he, the employee, may have contributed to its creation. For while it may be true that an employee is entitled — and is to be encouraged — to build up his own qualities of skill and experience, it is usually his duty to develop and improve his employer's business for the benefit of his employer. These two obligations interlock during his employment; after its termination they diverge and mark the boundary between what the employee may take with him and what he may legitimately be asked to leave behind to his employers."

Adopting the above reasons, as I do, there can be no doubt in the present case that the plaintiff had a substantial proprietary interest which he was entitled to have protected. At the time of purchase of the business, both parties recognized that goodwill represented by the customer lists had an economic value and that this business connection was a substantial asset. The defendant moved from owner-vendor to manager and ostensible owner of the business that had been his originally without any break in time or in his relationship with the customers. I am satisfied, as was the trial Judge, that the covenant against competition is not invalid as an unreasonable restraint of trade and any challenges to the covenant on that ground cannot succeed.

Turning to a consideration whether the present covenant is wider than is necessary to protect the plaintiff's proprietary right, it must be pointed out at the outset that the defendant is not precluded from carrying on his life insurance and real estate business. The plaintiff only seeks to restrain him from enticing away the plaintiff's general insurance customers. The burden of establishing the validity of the restrictive covenant is on the plaintiff, and tests it has to meet have been defined by Birkenhead, L.C., in these words (*McEllistrim v. Ballymacelligott Co-operative Agricultural & Dairy Society, Ltd.,* [1919] A.C. 548 at p. 562):

"A contract which is in restraint of trade cannot be enforced unless (a) it is reasonable as between the parties, (b) it is consistent with the interests of the public."

Before submitting the present covenant to the above tests it must be made clear that there is a distinction to be drawn between a restrictive covenant in a vendor and purchaser agreement and that contained in an employment contract. Those given in the context of employment are more rigorously examined than those in sale transactions. The learned trial Judge in drawing this distinction quoted from *Attwood v. Lamont,* [1920] 3 K.B. 571 at p. 589 (C.A.), where Lord Justice Younger stated: "An employer is not entitled by a covenant taken from his employee to protect himself after the employment has ceased against his former servant's competition per se, although a purchaser of goodwill is entitled to protect himself against such competition on the part of his vendor."

In cases dealing with sale transactions, the Courts have been reluctant to interfere with restrictive covenants contained in agreements entered into by businessmen having a presumed equality of bargaining power. On the other hand, such clauses in employment agreements are carefully scrutinized and are frequently held unenforceable on the ground that they extend beyond the interest which the employer is properly entitled to protect.

The present case does not fit neatly into either a sale or an employment category as it involves both. It was argued on behalf of the appellant that the background association between the parties with respect to the purchase and sale of the defendant's business should be disregarded and that the Court should limit its consideration only to the restrictive covenant contained in the employment contract. I am not in agreement with that submission. To take such a narrow view would be to ignore the realities of the situation in which the sale and the employment contract are inextricably bound together. Their combined effect provided the defendant with an unusual opportunity over a period of 17 years to acquire an intimate knowledge of the plaintiff's customers and of their insurance needs. The additional fact that the business was carried on under their joint names and that the plaintiff took a relatively inactive part in the business meant that to the customers the defendant, for all practical purposes, was *their* agent for *their* general insurance requirements. The proof of this situation is demonstrated by ex. 10, a list of approximately 200 former customers of the plaintiff who advised that they were transferring their insurance business to the defendant. Some of those transfers involved customers whose business and goodwill the defendant had originally sold to the plaintiff. In my view these facts are all relevant in determining the reasonableness of this particular restrictive covenant.

The generally accepted test as to which employees may be restrained is set out by Lord Parker in *Herbert Morris, Ltd., v. Saxelby,* [1916] 1 A.C. 688 at p. 709, as those employees who will acquire not merely knowledge of customers, but in addition, influence over them:

"A restraint is not valid unless the nature of the employment is such that customers will either learn to rely upon the skill or judgment of the servant or will deal with him directly and personally to the virtual exclusion of the master with the result that he will probably gain their custom if he sets up business on his own account." (Cheshire and Fifoot, *Law of Contract,* 8th ed. 1972, p. 369.)

There is no doubt that the present defendant falls into the category of a confidential employee. The defendant's name which had been sold to the plaintiff along with the goodwill of the business appeared in the new firm name under which the business was conducted. The defendant continued throughout the period of his employment to carry on his own real estate and life insurance business from an office at which sales of general insurance for the plaintiff were effected and premiums paid. He had access to customer files and because of his day-to-day supervision of the business had personal contact with the customers and was in a position to influence them. When the defendant terminated his employment he took with him two insurance salesmen and an insurance clerk formerly employed by the plaintiff. I think it fair to say that to the staff and the general public the defendant was the key man in the plaintiff's general insurance business.

I agree with the trial judge that the plaintiff has established special circumstances which justify the non-competition clause and that it does not afford him more protection than is needed to protect and preserve his general insurance business.

Whether a particular clause is to be held invalid as being too wide in its area of restriction or because it extends for a period of time which is too lengthy must depend on the circumstances. The degree of confidentiality, the length of association, the status of the former employee in the organization and his business connections in the particular area are relevant factors. Viewed in that aspect a time period of five years is not unreasonable *inter partes* and is consonant with public policy. Normally, fire insurance policies are written for a three-year term while auto policies expire after one year and it would be extremely difficult for the plaintiff to supervise and protect himself against the activities of the defendant in switching policies within those periods. The area covered in the covenant in effect covers the present City of Niagara Falls and cannot be considered too broad as far as geographical boundaries are concerned. In fact the defendant does not seriously question the area of restriction but submits that the restriction should apply, if at all, only to those customers which the plaintiff had at the time the defendant terminated his employment. It is true that in some cases involving an employer-employee relationship a general covenant against engaging in certain business in a given area has been held invalid on the ground that it would cover persons who had never been customers of the employer or persons who had become such only after the termination of the employment: *New Method Cleaners & Launderers Ltd. v. Hartley,* [1939] 1 D.L.R. 711, [1939] 1 W.W.R. 142, 46 Man. R. 414. However, in the present case a different standard of reasonableness must be applied. The plaintiff and the defendant were competent and successful businessmen, each of whom stood to gain by their agreement. There was no inequality of bargaining power between them. Against that background, the non-competition covenant which the plaintiff seeks to enforce in the present City of Niagara Falls for the protection of legitimate proprietary interest in his general insurance business does not appear unreasonable and in my view is a legal and enforceable obligation and entitles the plaintiff to the injunctive relief sought.

The covenant having been breached, the plaintiff's entitlement to damages has been established.

Restraint of Trade — Public Interest

Baker et al. v. Lintott (1981), 141 D.L.R. (3d) 571.

KERANS, J.A.:

This is an appeal from the dismissal of an action on a restrictive covenant. The appellant and plaintiffs are the partners of the Medicine Hat Medical Arts Clinic, a firm of medical practitioners in the City of Medicine Hat. In 1978 the respondent, who is a family practitioner, joined the partnership and made a covenant with his partners that he would not, if he left the clinic, practice medicine for two years within a radius of 25 miles of the City of Medicine Hat. Effective July 31, 1980, he quit the firm and opened an office in Medicine Hat in defiance of his covenant. The clinic sued for a declaration that the covenant was valid and asked for injunctive relief as well as damages. However, counsel agreed to defer the issue of assessment of damages.

The governing rule is that such a covenant is valid and enforceable if it is reasonable between the parties and not contrary to public policy. The learned trial judge, in a carefully reasoned judgment, found that the term was reasonable *inter partes.* He also found as a fact that it did not deprive Medicine Hat of adequate health care in a global sense and was not therefore contrary to public policy in that way.

However, he then took note of the fact that, just before the respondent and defendant executed his covenant, thirteen of the seventeen family practitioners in Medicine Hat were associated with the clinic and that effectively the community had not seventeen but only five choices when it came to the selection of a family practitioner. He was of the view that, in this day, adequate health care includes a reasonable level of choice, particularly of family practitioners who are the point of entry, so to speak, into the health care delivery system. He found that the limitation of choice which had existed in Medicine Hat, and which this covenant tended to maintain, was not reasonable and was contrary to public policy. It was in respect of this finding that an appeal was made.

Assuming, without deciding, that two doctors in partnership do not offer a choice of medical service to the community; and assuming, without deciding, that a reasonable number of choices is part of an adequate health care in this day, we are unable to agree that the choice left to the community was here unreasonably restricted. We must remind ourselves that, were there no clinic, there would presumably yet be many associations among doctors, and therefore much fewer than seventeen choices. Here there were five. We are not persuaded that this number is so inordinately low that public policy requires nullifying the agreement before us only because it *might* help to perpetuate the situation particularly where, as here, the history after the signing of the covenant and up to trial is that the proportion of non-clinic to clinic doctors was rising.

We are agreed that the covenant is valid and enforceable. In the circumstances, however, where only about nine months remain in the period of restriction, we would exercise a discretion not to give injunctive relief.

In the result, the appeal is allowed. There will be an order declaratory that the covenant is valid and enforceable and the parties may proceed to an assessment of damages.

The appellant will have costs here and at trial.

CASE PROBLEMS FOR DISCUSSION

Case 1

A company owned a parcel of land upon which it wished to have a commercial building constructed. An architect was engaged to design the building, and a contractor was contacted to carry out the construction. Contracts were signed with both.

Before the construction was completed, it was discovered that the building violated a municipal by-law that required certain safety features to be included in the building. Neither the architect nor the contractor were aware of the by-law at the time they entered into their respective agreements with the company.

The safety features required by the by-law could be incorporated in the building at a cost of approximately $10 000, but the contractor refused to do so unless he was paid for the work as an "extra" to the contract price. The company refused to do so, and withheld all payment to the contractor on the basis that the construction contract was illegal. The contractor then instituted legal proceedings against the company.

Explain the nature of the contractor's claim, and the defence raised by the company. Discuss the issue of responsibility in the case. Render a decision.

Case 2

The Suburban Medical Centre was founded in 1971 as a medical clinic by eight physicians and surgeons. In 1987, the clinic advertised in the medical press for an obstetrician. Harvey, a medical specialist, answered the advertisement. Following an interview, Harvey was employed by the clinic, and signed an employment contract that contained the following clause:

> Should the employment of the Party of the Second Part by the Parties of the First Part terminate for any reason whatsoever, the Party of the Second Part COVENANTS AND AGREES that he will not carry on the practice of medicine or surgery in any of its branches on his own account, or in association with any other person or persons, or corporation or in the employ of any such person or persons or corporations within the said City of Suburbia or within ten kilometres of the limits thereof for a period of five years (5) thereafter.

Harvey proved to be a difficult, but hard-working employee, and after some years an argument arose between Harvey and one of the founders of the clinic. As a result of the argument, Harvey resigned. He immediately set up a practice in the same city. The clinic continued to operate without the services of Harvey, and later brought an action for damages and an injunction against him.

Discuss the factors the courts should consider in deciding this case. Render a decision.

Case 3

The Allen Laundry, a corporation that manufactured laundry equipment and also operated a laundry in a particular city, employed Murphy in its laundry operation. Shortly after Murphy was hired, he was requested to enter into a written employment contract that contained a clause whereby he agreed, in return for the wages paid to him, that he would not engage in the laundry business anywhere in Canada for a period of three years after leaving the Allen Laundry. Murphy was employed by the corporation for six years, during which time he normally worked in the laundry operation but occasionally made sales trips to other provinces to sell laundry equipment. At the end of the sixth year, he tendered his resignation to the corporation, and a few months after he left its employ, purchased a laundry business in the same city.

Allen Laundry took legal action to enforce the agreement that Murphy had signed.

Discuss the issues raised in this case, and render a decision.

Case 4

In 1975, Herbert entered into the employ of TOPE Limited as an electrical engineer. He was employed to design electronic testing equipment, which the company manufactured. At the time he was hired, he signed a written contract of indefinite hiring as a salaried employee. The contract contained a clause whereby he agreed not to disclose any confidential company information. The contract also required him to agree not to seek employment with any competitor of the company if he left the employ of TOPE Limited.

Herbert was requested to develop a dwell tachometer suitable for sale to home mechanics through a particular hardware store chain under the chain's brand name. He produced a prototype in less than a week, and went to the president's office to discuss the development and production of the equipment.

During the course of the discussion, Herbert and the company president became involved in a heated argument over manufacturing methods. At the end of the meeting, the president suggested that Herbert might begin a search for employment elsewhere, as his job would be terminated in three months' time.

The next morning, Herbert went to the president's office once more, ostensibly to discuss the dwell tachometer. Instead, Herbert informed the president as soon as he entered the room that he no longer intended to work for the firm. He complained that the company had never given him more than a two-week vacation in any year, and that he often worked as much as 50 hours per week, with no overtime pay for the extra hours worked. In a rage, he smashed the dwell tachometer prototype on the president's desk, breaking it into a dozen small pieces. He then left the room.

The following week, Herbert accepted employment with a competitor of TOPE Limited to do a type of work similar to that which he had done at his old firm. He immediately developed a dwell tachometer similar in design to the previous model, and suggested to the management of his new employer that they consider the sale of the equipment through the same hardware chain that TOPE Limited had contemplated for its product. The competitor was successful in obtaining a large order for dwell tachometers from the hardware chain a short time later.

TOPE Limited presented its new product to the hardware chain a week after the order had been given to the competitor, and only then discovered that Herbert had designed the equipment for that firm. The hardware chain had adopted the competitor's product as its own brand and was not interested in purchasing the product of TOPE Limited, in view of its apparent similarity in design.

TOPE Limited had expected a first year's profit of $21 000 on the dwell tachometer if they obtained the contract from the hardware chain.

Discuss the nature of the legal action (if any) that TOPE Limited might take against Herbert, and indicate the defences (if any) that Herbert might raise if TOPE Limited should do so.

Case 5

Samuels was a qualified journeyman electrician who was employed by a municipal public utilities commission on a full-time basis. On weekends and evenings, he occasionally assisted friends who were constructing their own homes by installing their electrical wiring for them. In most cases he did he installation work gratuitously, but from time to time he would be given a sum of money in appreciation of his services.

One day, while on vacation at his summer cottage, a neighbouring cottage-owner who was renovating his cottage approached Samuels and inquired if he might be interested in taking on the job of rewiring the cottage. Samuels thought about the offer, then agreed to do so, and a price was agreed upon. Samuels would do the work and supply the materials (estimated at $950) for $1400.

A few days later, Samuels purchased the necessary materials, and proceeded to rewire the cottage. Upon completion of the job, Samuels presented his account for $1550, which represented the cost of materials at $1100 and his labour at $450.

Samuels' neighbour refused to pay the account, insisting that the agreed price was $1400. Samuels' argument was that the $950 price quoted was only an estimate, and subject to change. The only firm part of his quote, he maintained, was his labour charge of $450.

The two parties continued to argue over the price for several months, and eventually Samuels instituted legal proceedings to collect the account.

Identify and discuss the legal issues that might arise in this case and could affect Samuels' right to recover payment. If you were called upon to act as counsel for the defendant, what inquiries would you make?

Case 6

Peter Able was a computer scientist with over 25 years experience in the computer field. For the last 5 years of his 12 years with a large computer manufacturer, his mandate was to develop "next generation" computer hardware. He was, in essence, responsible for most of the "high tech" research in the area of data reading technology in the company. He was also a recognized international authority in this highly specialized area of research.

A competitor offered Peter a position in its firm to carry out the same type of research, as it, too, was interested in producing next generation data reading equipment. Peter accepted the position, and began working for his new employer.

Peter's previous employer then sought an injunction to prevent Peter from engaging in any work for the competitor that was similar to the work he had carried on at his previous place of employment.

The above employment scenario raises a number of significant legal and public policy issues. Identify and discuss these issues, and in your answer indicate how the courts attempt to deal with them.

CHAPTER 10

The Requirements of Form and Writing

**FORMAL
AND SIMPLE
CONTRACTS**

Under the law of contract there are two general classes of contracts. A contract deriving its validity from the form that it takes is referred to as a **formal contract,** or, sometimes (under English law), a **covenant.** The second class of contract is the informal or **simple contract,** which may be implied, oral, or written. These two classes of contracts evolved in different ways under early English law, with the formal contract being the older of the two. It is important to bear in mind that both forms of contract were not normally matters that the early king's justices felt should fall under their jurisdiction. As a consequence, agreements in the nature of mutual promises were either under the jurisdiction of the ecclesiastic courts or the early local, or communal, courts. A breach of an agreement, then, took on the character of a breach of a promise that, if solemnly made, was considered to be a breach of faith, and hence, a religious matter. Promises that bore no solemn or ritualistic aspect presumably fell under the jurisdiction of local or communal court for consideration. In any event, the king's courts did not concern themselves with the forerunners of modern contracts until the thirteenth century, when the royal court began to expand its jurisdiction.

Contractual disputes between merchants of a business-related nature were normally resolved by the merchants themselves in accordance with the rules established by the various merchant guilds. Later they were resolved by the courts that largely adopted the merchant rules in rendering a decision. By the end of the thirteenth century, covenants in writing (except for debt), if under the seal of the promisor, were enforced by the king's courts on the basis that the impression of the seal was an expression of the promisor's intention to be bound by the promise made. While these early agreements were not the same as modern contracts, the use of a seal has continued to the present day.

In most provinces, many kinds of agreements must still be made under seal to be enforceable. An example of a modern formal "covenant" would be a **power of attorney.** This is a formal document frequently used to empower a person to deal with the land of another. At common law, the grant of the power must be made under the seal to be valid. Another formal "covenant" is a deed of land under the Registry System in a number of provinces in Eastern Canada. To be valid, the deed must be in writing, and signed, sealed, and delivered in order to convey the property interest in the land to the grantee. Apart from these, and a number of other special types of agreements that must be in a specific form and under seal, the formal agreement has been largely replaced by the second type of agreement, the informal contract.

Informal contracts developed along a distinctly different route. In English law, the informal agreement, like the formal agreement, was initially enforced by the church or communal courts if some formality was attached to the agreement to render it morally binding. In this respect, the actions of the parties assumed immense proportions in determining the question of enforceability. The handshake, for example, rendered a promise binding; in this respect, the informal agreement and the early formal agreement were similar. At that time, the ceremonial aspects surrounding the agreement were important determinants of enforceability.

In the early cases, the courts would enforce the duties promised by persons in particular trades or professions if they improperly carried out their duties. No action would lie, however, if they simply did nothing to fulfill their promises, because there could be no trespass if a person did nothing. This early deficiency was remedied in part by the application of the action of deceit (also a tort) in the early sixteenth century. This provided a remedy where one party had fully performed, but where the other refused to do so. If neither party had performed there was still no remedy. It was not until the seventeenth century that the courts were finally prepared to enforce executory promises by way of a writ of assumpsit. From that point on, the theory of consideration and the modern concept of contract developed rapidly, and with them the enforceability of the informal contract by common law, rather than the law of tort. Today, the informal or simple contract does not depend upon a prescribed form for its enforceability. Had it not been for a statute passed in 1677,[1] no simple contract would have been required to be evidenced in writing under any circumstances to be enforceable at law.

THE STATUTE OF FRAUDS

The particular statute that imposed the requirement of writing for certain informal contracts was the **Statute of Frauds** — an act that was passed by the English Parliament and introduced to Canada and the United States while both were colonies. The law still remains as a statute in parts of the United States, and in most common-law provinces, even though it has been repealed in England.[2] The Statute of Frauds was originally passed following a period of political upheaval in England. It was ostensibly designed to prevent perjury and fraud with respect to leases and agreements concerning land. The statute went further than perhaps was intended at the time, and encompassed, as well, a number of agreements that, today, are simple contracts in nature.

---

1. "An Act for Prevention of Frauds and Perjures," 29 Car. II, c. 3.

2. See, for example, the Statute of Frauds, R.S.O. 1990, c. S-20, s. 4.

In most provinces, this particular section of the act now provides:

No action shall be brought whereby to charge any executor or administrator upon any special promise to answer damages out of his own estate, or whereby to charge any person upon any special promise to answer for the debt, default or miscarriage of any other person, or to charge any person upon any agreement made upon consideration of marriage, or upon any contract or sale of lands, tenements or hereditaments, or any interest in or concerning them, or upon any agreement that is not to be performed within the space of one year from the making thereof, unless the agreement upon which the action is brought, or some memorandum or note thereof, is in writing and signed by the party to be charged therewith or some person thereunto by him lawfully authorized.

The effect of the law was that none of the following could be brought in a court of law unless they were in writing and signed by the party to be charged (or an authorized agent): an agreement or contract concerning an interest in land, a special promise by an executor or administrator to settle any claim out of his or her own personal estate, a guarantee agreement, an agreement made in consideration of marriage,[3] and a contract that could not be performed within a year.

The law did not prohibit or render void these particular agreements if they did not comply with the statute — the law simply rendered them unenforceable by way of the courts. The agreement continued to exist, and, while rights could not be exercised to enforce the agreement, it was possible to appeal to the courts in the event of breach under certain circumstances. For example, if a party had paid a deposit to the vendor in an unwritten agreement to buy land, the vendor's refusal to convey the land would entitle the prospective purchaser to treat the agreement as at an end and recover his or her deposit. The courts, however, would not enforce the agreement, since it would not be evidenced in writing and signed by the vendor. The agreement was caught by the statute, but once it was repudiated the purchaser could bring an action to recover the deposit.

The justification for the statutory requirement is obvious. Each of the five particular kinds of contracts at the time were agreements that were either important enough to warrant evidence in writing to clearly establish the intention of the particular promisors to be bound by the agreement, or the nature of the agreement was such that some permanent form of evidence of the terms of the agreement would be desirable for further reference.

The application of the law to each of these contractual relationships produced a number of responses by the courts to avoid the hardships imposed by the law. Each response was an attempt to assist innocent parties who were unaware of the implication of the lack of evidence in writing of their agreement.

Contracts by Executors and Administrators

The protection that the act provides to the executor or administrator of an estate from a claim that the executor promised to answer for a debt or default out of his or her own estate is perhaps the most justifiable reason for the continued existence of the statute. An executor or administrator undertakes to collect, care for, and

3. This particular type of contract has been removed from the statute in some provinces. See, for example, the Family Law Act, R.S.O. 1990, c. F-3, s. 88.

distribute the assets of a deceased person, and essentially to keep the assets of the deceased's estate separate from his or her own personal funds. However, an executor might be tempted to personally pay outstanding debts of the deceased's estate should the state of affairs of the estate render prompt payment inopportune. This temptation might stem from a concern to protect the good name of the deceased, or it might simply provide the executor with immediate relief from persistent creditors. In any event, it is important to note that an executor has no obligation to pay the debts of the estate out of personal funds. However, should an executor decide to do so, such an intention must be clearly indicated in writing as the statute requires.

Assumed Liability: The Guarantee

The second legal agreement that the statute embraces is an agreement whereby a person agrees to answer for the debt, default, or tort of another. One particular type of agreement of this nature, which requires a memorandum to be in writing and bear the signature of the party to be charged, is the **guarantee**. This relationship always involves at least three parties: a principal debtor, a creditor, and a third party, the guarantor. The guarantor's role in a guarantee agreement is to provide a promise of payment in the form of a **contingent liability**. If the principal debtor does not make payment when the debt falls due, the creditor may then look to the guarantor for payment. The guarantor is never the party who is primarily liable. The guarantor's obligation to pay is always one that arises if and when the principal debtor defaults. The consideration for the guarantor's promise is usually based upon the creditor's act or promise to provide to the principal debtor goods on credit or funds, in circumstances where the creditor would not ordinarily do so. Because of the unique relationship between the parties, the guarantee must be in writing to be enforceable. The province of Alberta has added an additional procedural step which a guarantor in certain circumstances must follow in order to be bound by his or her promise. Under the Alberta **Guarantees Acknowledgement Act**[4] the guarantee must not only be in writing, but it must be made before a notary public, who must signify in writing that the guarantor understands the obligation. The statute does not apply to corporations that act as guarantors, nor does the statute apply to guarantees given in the sale of land or interests in chattels.

The legal nature of the guarantee was succinctly described by the court in the case of *Western Dominion Investment Co. Ltd. v. MacMillan*[5] where the judge said:

> Reduced to its simplest terms a guaranty is the promise of one man to pay the debt of another if that other default. In every case of guaranty there are at least two obligations, a primary and a secondary. The secondary — the guaranty — is based upon the primary, and is enforceable only if the primary default. It is so completely dependent upon the unchanged continuance of that primary, that if any, even the slightest, unauthorized changes are made in the primary, as, e.g., by extension of time for payment, or by reducing the chances of enforcing payment, as, e.g., by

4. R.S.A. 1990 c. G-12.

5. [1925] 1 W.W.R. 852.

releasing any part of the securities, the secondary thereby falls to the ground. In other words, the secondary is not only collateral to, but is exactly co-extensive with the primary, as the primary existed when the secondary came into existence. Lastly, if the secondary obligor pays the debt he is entitled, as of right, to step into the creditor's shoes.

If a principal debtor fails to make payment when required to do so, the creditor may call upon the guarantor to pay. The guarantor is then liable for payment of the principal debtor's indebtedness. If the guarantor pays the obligation, the guarantor may demand an assignment of the debt. Once the debt is paid, the guarantor possesses the rights of the creditor, and may demand payment from the debtor if he or she should choose to do so.

The distinction between a guarantee and a situation where a person becomes a principal debtor by a direct promise of payment is important. If the promise to pay is not conditional upon the default of the principal debtor, but a situation where both parties become principal debtors, then the agreement need not be in writing or signed to be enforceable. By the same token, the third party can request the creditor to release the principal debtor from the debt and promise to assume payment of the indebtedness personally. This transaction would also be outside the statute because the agreement would simply be to substitute principal debtors.

A guarantee agreement between parties is not a simple arrangement, because the guarantor's potential liability is of a continuous nature. Consequently, the requirement that the guarantee be reduced to writing and signed by the guarantor is not unreasonable. As with any agreement extending over a long period of time, memories become hazy, facts may be forgotten, and interpretations may change. Far from being onerous, the requirement of evidence of the agreement in writing makes good sense. As a result, the courts have not attempted to circumvent the statute with respect to guarantees to avoid injustice. One form of relief that the courts have employed in guarantee cases, however, relates to agreements made between the creditor and principal debtor subsequent to the guarantee agreement. If these two parties alter the security that the guarantor may look to in the event of default, or alter the debt agreement without the consent of the guarantor, the alteration may release the guarantor. Where the change in the agreement is detrimental to the guarantor, the courts will normally not enforce the guarantee if the principal debtor should later default.

Assumed Liability: Tort

A second promise of a somewhat similar nature to the guarantee is also covered by this particular section of the Statute of Frauds. Any agreement whereby a third party promises to answer for the tort of another must be in writing and be signed by the party to be charged, otherwise the promise will not be enforceable. This is not unlike the guarantee, but it applies where a third party promises to compensate a person who is injured by the tortious act of another, rather than by the person's failure to pay a debt. For example, Thompson, Jr., a young man aged 16 years, carelessly rode his bicycle on the sidewalk and collided with Varley. The collision caused injuries to Varley and placed her in the hospital. Thompson, Sr., Thompson's father, promised to compensate Varley for her injuries, if Varley would promise not to sue Thompson, Jr. If Varley wishes to enforce the promise of Thompson, Sr., she must insist that Thompson, Sr. put his promise in writing and sign it. Otherwise it would be caught by the Statute of Frauds, and would be unenforceable against Thompson, Sr.

Consideration of Marriage

A further type of contract to which the statute applies is an agreement made in consideration of marriage. This was perhaps of greater importance at the time that the statute was passed than today. The act in some provinces still requires that any promise of payment of money or property settlement, conditional upon or in consideration of marriage taking place, be evidenced in writing and signed to be enforceable. It is important to note, however, that in this section the statute does not refer to promises of marriage between individuals who intend to marry. But rather, it refers to collateral promises such as may be included in a pre-nuptial agreement concerning property to be brought into the marriage, or to a promise made by a third party to pay a sum of money if the marriage takes place. In this sense, the promise takes on a business-like character that would obligate the promisor to fulfill the agreement when the conditions set out in the agreement were met. In most provinces, family law reform legislation deals specifically with agreements between the parties. For all practical purposes the Statute of Frauds, where applicable, would probably be limited to the third party type of agreement.

Contracts Concerning Interests in Land

Of the remaining two kinds of agreements subject to the statute, the requirement of writing for contracts concerning the sale (or other dealing with land) has given the courts the most concern. The vagueness of the wording initially gave rise to much litigation. This forced the courts to struggle with an interpretation that would limit the application of the statute to those cases concerned specifically with the sale or other disposition of interests in land. The courts gradually excluded: agreements that did not deal specifically with the land itself, agreements concerned with the repair of buildings, and contracts for "room and board." A great many other agreements that were remotely concerned with the disposition of land were also held to be outside the statute. For those cases encompassed by the statute, it was necessary to devise ways and means to prevent the law itself from being used to perpetrate a fraud on an unsuspecting party by way of an unwritten agreement.

The most important relief developed by the courts to avoid the effect of the statute was the **doctrine of part performance**. This concept allowed the courts, on the basis of equity, to enforce an unwritten agreement concerning land. The doctrine, unfortunately, is quite limited in its application. A party adversely affected by a failure to place the agreement in writing must be in a position to meet four criteria to successfully avoid the statute:

(1) The acts performed by the party alleging part performance must be demonstrated to be acts that refer only to the agreement of the lands in question, and to no other.

(2) It must be shown that to enforce the statute against the party who partly performed for the lack of a written memorandum would perpetrate a fraud and a hardship on the person.

(3) The agreement must relate to an interest in land.

(4) The agreement itself must be valid and enforceable apart from the requirement of writing, and verbal evidence must be available to establish the existence of the agreement.[6]

To meet these four criteria is seldom an easy task. For example, Anderson enters into a verbal agreement with Baxter to purchase Baxter's farm for $100 000. Anderson gives Baxter $100 in cash to "bind the bargain," and takes possession of the buildings and property. Anderson removes an old barn on the premises and makes extensive repairs to the house. After Anderson has completed the repairs, Baxter refuses to proceed with the transaction. He raises the absence of a written agreement as a defence.

To meet the first criterion, the payment of $100 cash will not qualify, as it was not an act that would solely relate to this particular transaction (it could represent payment of rent). The acts of removing the old barn and repairing the house, however, might meet this requirement. A person would not normally undertake activities of this nature unless the person believed that he or she had some interest in the land. Therefore, the purchaser's acts would refer to such a contract, and to no other, under the circumstances.

The second criterion would also be met by Anderson's expenditure of time and expense in making renovations and removing the barn. These actions would represent acts that a person would only perform in reliance on the completion of the unwritten agreement. They would constitute a detriment or loss if the agreement was not fulfilled. To allow the landowner to refuse to complete the transaction at that point would constitute a fraud on the purchaser and represent unjust enrichment of the vendor.

The third criterion would be met by the nature of the agreement itself: it constitutes a contract for an interest in land, and one that equity would enforce by way of an action for specific performance.

The last criterion would be one that the purchaser might be able to prove by showing the court that the agreement, apart from the requirement of writing, contained all of the essential components of a valid agreement. This might be done by way of the evidence of witnesses who were present at the time of the making of the agreement, and who might be in a position to establish the terms.

An example of how the courts regard the doctrine of part performance was illustrated in the case of *Brownscombe v. Public Trustee of Alberta*.[7] The judge in that case described the event and the law as follows:

> In 1932 when Canada and the world in general were in a severe business depression, the plaintiff, whose home was in Prince George, B.C., and who was then 16 years of age, applied to the late Robert Marcel Vercamert at the latter's home, not far from Rockyford in Alberta, for work. The said Vercamert, a bachelor, somewhat severely crippled by heart trouble and able to do but little work on the farm where he lived and which he conducted, took the plaintiff into his home. On the evidence I find that plaintiff worked faithfully for his employer with but little

---

6. See *Rawlinson v. Ames,* [1925] 1 Ch. 96 at p. 114; *Brownscombe v. Public Trustee of the Province of Alberta* (1969), 5 D.L.R. (3d) 673.

7. (1969) 5 D.L.R. (3d) 673.

financial reward for a considerable number of years. I find that on a number of occasions when the plaintiff thought of leaving Vercamert's employ he was dissuaded by the latter's promised assurance that on his demise the farm would go to plaintiff by will. In January 1961, Vercamert died intestate and this action is the result.

The contract relating to land is within s. 4 of the Statute of Frauds, and there is no memorandum in writing. Therefore, part performance is necessary for the plaintiff to succeed on his claim for specific performance. Per Cranworth, L.C., in *Caton v. Caton* (1866), L.R. 1 Ch. App. 137 at p. 147: Part performance will afford relief from the operation of the statute "...in many cases ... when to insist upon it would be to make it the means of effecting instead of preventing fraud". However, not all acts done in pursuance of the unenforceable contract will constitute part performance in law. They may be found to relate only to a contract of service as in *Maddison v. Alderson* (1883), 8 App. Cas. 467, and *Deglman v. Guaranty Trust Co. of Canada and Constantineau*, [1954] 3 D.L.R. 785, [1954] S.C.R. 725, except where such acts are "unequivocally referable in their own nature to some dealing with the land which is alleged to have been the subject of the agreement sued upon...": Per Duff, J., in *McNeil v. Corbett* (1907), 39 S.C.R. 608 at p. 611, approved by the Supreme Court of Canada in *Deglman*. The issue for decision by this Court is whether the acts relied upon by the appellant over the period 1932 to 1961 are acts which are "unequivocally referable in their own nature to some dealing with the land which is alleged to have been the subject of the agreement sued on", as stated by Duff, J. (as he then was), in *McNeil v. Corbett* (1907), 39 S.C.R. 608, and approved by this Court in *Deglman v. Guaranty Trust Co. of Canada and Constantineau*, [1954] 3 D.L.R. 785, [1954] S.C.R. 725.

It is clear that not all the acts relied on as testified to by the appellant and his wife can be regarded as "unequivocally referable in their own nature to some dealing with the land", but in my view the building of the house on the lands in question in the years 1946 and 1947 at the suggestion of Vercamert almost, if not wholly, at the appellant's expense was, as the learned trial Judge found "unequivocally referable" to the agreement which the appellant alleged had been made and inconsistent with the ordinary relationship of employee or tenant.

Long-Term Contracts

The last type of agreement to which the statute applies is an agreement that is not to be performed within the period of one year from the date it is made. The logic behind the requirement that a contract of this nature be evidenced by a written memorandum is readily apparent. Any agreement that is not to be performed within a relatively short space of time is subject to the frailties of human memory and the risk of misinterpretation at a later date. The requirement of writing makes a great deal of sense; but, nevertheless, by its arbitrary nature, it may cause hardship as well. To overcome this drawback, the courts have limited its application to those agreements that cannot be fully performed by either party within the space of one year, and to those contracts that do not permit termination on reasonable or express notice within the one-year period. Since many contracts are written in such a way that they run for an indefinite period of time, the courts have generally treated them as if they were potential short-term agreements in order to avoid difficulty. The reasoning behind this approach is that even though the agreement might conceivably run for more than one year, it might also be terminated within the one-year period if one of the parties so desires. As a result, contracts for an indefinite period of time, even though not in writing, are generally enforceable if termination is possible within the one-year period.

REQUIREMENTS FOR THE WRITTEN MEMORANDUM

To comply with the statute, evidence of the contract in writing need not be embodied in a formal document. It is essential, however, to include in the written document all of the terms of the contract.

The first requirement is that the parties to the agreement be identified either by name or description, and that the terms of the agreement be set out in sufficient detail that the contract may be enforced. For example, an agreement may consist of an exchange of letters that identify the parties, contain the offer made, describe the property as well as the consideration paid, or to be paid, and include a letter of acceptance. The two documents taken together would constitute the written memorandum. The final requirement is that the written memorandum be signed by the party to be charged. It is important to note that only the party to be charged need sign the memorandum. The party who wishes to enforce the agreement need not be a signatory, since the statute requires only that it be signed by the party to be charged.[8]

Of importance, where written agreements are concerned, is the **parol evidence rule**, which limits the kind of evidence that may be introduced to prove the terms of a contract. By this rule, no evidence may be adduced by a party that would add new terms to the contract, or change or contradict the terms of a clear and unambiguous written agreement. Evidence may only be admitted to rectify or explain the terms agreed upon, or to prove some fact such as fraud or illegality that may affect the enforceability of the agreement.

The application of the rule is not arbitrary, however, and the courts have accepted a number of different arguments that allow parties to circumvent the effect of the rule. The argument that a **condition precedent** exists is an example. A condition precedent, as the name implies, is an event that must occur before the contract becomes operative. The parties frequently place this term in the written agreement, but they need not do so. If the condition is agreed to by the parties, or in some cases, if it can be implied, then the written agreement will remain in a state of suspension until the condition is satisfied. If the condition cannot be met, then the contract does not come into existence, and any money paid under it may usually be recovered.

For example, Allan and Brewster discuss the purchase of Brewster's car by Allan. Allan agrees to purchase the car for $3000 if she can successfully negotiate a loan from her banker. Allan and Brewster put the agreement in writing. However, they do not include in the agreement the term that the purchase is conditional upon Allan obtaining a loan for the purchase. While the parol evidence rule does not permit evidence to be admitted to add to the contract, the court will admit evidence to show that the agreement would not come into effect until the condition was met. The distinction here is that the evidence relating to the condi-

---

8. *Daniels v. Trefusis*, [1914] 1 Ch. 788; *McLean v. Little*, [1943] O.R. 202.

tion precedent does not relate to the contract terms, but, rather, to the circumstances under which the written agreement would become enforceable.

A second exception to the parol evidence rule is the application of the **doctrine of implied term.** Occasionally, in the writing of an agreement, the parties may leave out a term that is usually found in contracts of the type the parties negotiated. If the evidence can establish that the parties had intended to put the term in, and that it is a term normally included in such a contract by custom of the trade, or normal business practice, the courts may conclude that the term is an implied term. They could then enforce the contract as if it contained the term. Generally, the type of term that will be implied is one that the parties require in the contract in order to implement the agreement. It must be noted, however, that if the term conflicts in any way with the express terms of the agreement, the parol evidence rule will exclude it. Similarly, an express term may be incorporated in a written agreement by reference if (a) the agreement is a "standard form" type of contract, and (b) the term is expressed before the agreement is concluded. For example, in a parking lot a large sign, which states that the owner will not be responsible for any damages to a patron's vehicle, may be binding upon the patrons. This may be the case even though the limitation is not expressly stated on the ticket, but is referred to in small print on the back.

A third important exception to the parol evidence rule is the **collateral agreement.** A collateral agreement is a separate agreement that the parties may make that has some effect on the written agreement, but that is not referred to in it. One of the difficulties with the collateral agreement is that it usually adds to, or alters, the written contract. If it were allowed at all times, it would effectively circumvent the parol evidence rule. For this reason, the courts are reluctant to accept the argument that a collateral agreement exists, unless the parties can demonstrate that it does, in fact, exist as a separate and complete contract with its own consideration. The application of this criteria usually defeats the collateral agreement argument because the collateral agreement seldom contains separate consideration from that of the written agreement. However, in those cases where a separate agreement does exist, the courts will enforce the collateral agreement even though it may conflict to some extent with the written one.

With all of these exceptions to the parol evidence rule, one element is common. In each case, the modifying term precedes, or is concurrent with the formation of the written agreement. Any verbal agreement made by the parties after the written agreement is effected may alter the terms of the written contract[9] or cancel it.[10] The parol evidence rule will not exclude evidence of the subsequent agreement from the court. The reason for this distinction is that the subsequent agreement represents a new agreement made by the parties that has as its subject-matter the existing agreement.

It is not uncommon for business persons to enter into either verbal or written negotiations with a view to making a formal contract. During these negotiations the parties may reach agreement upon a sufficient number of key issues to agree **in principle** to proceed with a formal contract. This agreement would embody the

9. *Johnson Investments v. Pagratide,* [1923] 2 D.L.R. 985.
10. *Morris v. Baron and Co.,* [1918] A.C. 1.

issues agreed upon in principle but not include the details yet to be agreed upon. If a final agreement is reached and reduced to writing in its formal form, the negotiations would be complete. However, the parties sometimes do not proceed beyond the agreement in principle stage, and one party or the other may attempt to enforce the agreement in principle on the basis that an enforceable contract had been reached. The formal written agreement in their view would be merely the fine-tuning of the existing agreement.

Where one party alleges an enforceable agreement exists, the courts are generally obliged to determine the stage at which the parties intended to be bound by their negotiations. In the case of *MacLean v. Kennedy* (1965), 53 D.L.R. (2d) 254, the court noted that two principles of law must be kept in mind in dealing with this type of case:

> It appears to be well settled by the authorities that if the documents or letters relied on as constituting a contract contemplate the execution of a further contract between the parties, it is a question of construction whether the execution of the further contract is a condition or term of the bargain or whether it is a mere expression of the desire of the parties as to the manner in which the transaction already agreed to will in fact go through.
>
> The second principle of law to be kept in mind is that the material terms of the contract must not be vague, indefinite or uncertain. This principle has been variously stated.
>
> If an oral agreement is vague, indefinite or uncertain, it would appear that this fact may be taken into account in deciding whether the execution of a formal agreement is a condition or term of the oral agreement. At least this would seem to follow from certain observations of Meredith, C.J. in *Stow v. Currie* (1910), 21 O.L.R. 486 at pp. 493 and 494, and of Clute, J., at p. 496. In *Stow v. Currie,* the uncertain agreement was written, not oral, but it was held that it was intended to be subject to a new and formal agreement, the terms of which were not expressed in detail, and one reason for so holding was its uncertainty in certain respects.

SALE OF GOODS ACT

A second important statute that contains a requirement of writing is the *Sale of Goods Act.*[11] The particular requirement of writing was originally a part of the Statute of Frauds, and had remained there for several hundred years. After 1893, when separate legislation concerning the sale of goods was passed in England, the requirement of writing was removed from the Statute of Frauds and embodied in the new act. The provincial legislatures in Canada copied the English legislation and varied the value of the goods to which the requirement of evidence of the agreement in writing applied. The legislation fortunately provided, as well, a number of activities on the part of the parties that would permit them to enforce the agreement, even though the contract was not evidenced by a written memorandum. These activities include the payment of a deposit, acceptance of delivery of part of the goods, or the giving of "something in ernest" (such as a trade-in) to bind the bargain. Because the parties normally comply with one of the exceptions, where the contract of sale is not in writing, the requirement does not pose a hazard for most buyers and sellers. Of more importance today is the consumer protection legislation applicable to many kinds of contracts. This legislation often

---

11. All provinces (except Quebec) have legislation pertaining to the sale of goods.

requires certain types of sales contracts to be in writing. It also imposes penalties for the failure to provide consumers with a written purchase agreement, disclosing information concerning the sale and any credit terms.

SUMMARY

Formal and informal contracts developed along distinctive lines. Each has a different legal history. Formal contracts generally derive their validity from the form that they take. They may be required to effect particular transactions. All formal contracts are evidenced by writing, and most are subject to the requirement that they be signed, sealed, and delivered, before they become operative.

Informal contracts may be written, oral, or, in some cases, implied. However, certain informal contracts (those subject to the Statute of Frauds) must be evidenced by a memorandum in writing setting out their terms, and must be signed by the party to be charged before they are enforceable by a court of law.

Written contracts are subject to a number of rules, principles, and doctrines that have developed to mitigate the hardship that is sometimes imposed by the statute. A notable example of one of these special rules is the doctrine of part performance, which may be applied in some cases where land is sold without written evidence of the transaction.

Not all of the rules, however, are designed to prevent hardship. Written agreements are also subject to the parol evidence rule, which excludes evidence of any prior or concurrent agreement that might add to, or contradict, the terms of the written agreement in question. Exceptions to this rule, nevertheless, exist in the form of conditions precedent, implied terms, and genuine collateral agreements. All may take either a written or oral form. Additionally, agreements made subsequent to a written agreement may alter or terminate the contract, even though the subsequent agreement is verbal in nature.

Special requirements for consumer contracts have been established by legislation in many provinces in recent years. These statutes usually require certain kinds of transactions to be in writing. While ostensibly designed to require the seller to disclose information concerning the sale to the buyer, the statutes also require the written memorandum to contain specific information, otherwise fines or penalties may be imposed upon the seller. The contract of sale and the legislation pertaining thereto are examined at length in Chapters 21 and 22.

DISCUSSION QUESTIONS

1. Explain the effect of the Statute of Frauds on the law of contract.
2. What are the legal implications of failing to comply with the requirements of writing under the Statute of Frauds?
3. Distinguish a guarantee from an indemnity. How does the Statute of Frauds affect these two relationships?
4. Why is the requirement of writing justified in the case of a contract that cannot be performed in less than one year?
5. What exceptions from the Statute of Frauds have the courts established for contracts that do not require immediate performance?
6. Describe the minimum requirements for a written memorandum under the Statute of Frauds.
7. Explain the doctrine of part performance and the rationale behind the establishment of the doctrine as a means of avoiding the Statute of Frauds.

8. How does the parol evidence rule affect evidence related to a contract in writing?
9. Explain the effect of a collateral agreement and the doctrine of implied term on a written agreement subject to the parol evidence rule.
10. Explain the rationale behind the general common law rule stating that an agreement in writing may be terminated by a subsequent verbal agreement. Is this always the case, or is it subject to exception?

MINI-CASE PROBLEMS

1. X enters into a verbal agreement with Y to purchase Y's farm for $150 000. X pays Y a deposit of $1000 cash. What are X's rights if Y later refuses to go through with the agreement?
2. How would your answer to the problem in question 1 differ, if X refused to fulfill his part of the agreement?
3. A offers to buy B's sailboat for $10 000, provided that he can obtain a loan of $5000 from his banker. A and B put the agreement in writing, but the agreement does not mention the loan. If A cannot borrow the $5000, can B sue A for failing to comply with the agreement of purchase?

JUDICIAL DECISIONS

Contracts in writing are usually considered by the courts to represent the entire agreement between the parties. Evidence of additional terms or agreements made before the contract is reduced to writing are normally excluded by the parol evidence rule if they add to or contradict the terms of the written agreement. However, the court will sometimes read implied terms into an agreement, or will correct agreements through the process known as **rectification**. In the *Bank of Montreal v. Vancouver Professional Soccer Ltd.* case, the bank attempted to have an agreement rectified to reflect the bank's understanding of a written agreement, when the other parties did not agree with the change or the bank's interpretation of the agreement. In the judgement, the court outlines the circumstances where rectification will be granted as a remedy. It also notes that care must be taken with rectification to ensure that it will not impose terms or an agreement on a party that the party did not make. The court in this instance concluded that the terms that the bank wished to include through rectification were not terms agreed upon by the other parties to the agreement and dismissed the appeal.

The *Gallen et al. v. Allstate Grain Co. Ltd.* case provides an example of how the courts apply the parol evidence rule where one party alleges that a separate verbal statement of one party should constitute a collateral warranty to a written agreement. The judge outlines eight circumstances where the rule applies. He also points out that the collateral warranty might stand alone if it does not contradict the written agreement. The judge concludes that the verbal statement is a collateral warranty and that it is not at variance with the written agreement. His decision is that the verbal warranty is binding on the defendant, and that the defendant is in breach of the warranty.

Contracts — Parol Evidence Rule Collateral Warranty

Gallen et al. v. Allstate Grain Co. Ltd. et al. (1984), 9 D.L.R. (4d) 496 (B.C.).
Allstate Grain Co. Ltd. was engaged in the purchase and sale of seed grains and sold the plaintiff, Gallen, buckwheat seeds. The seller assured the buyer that weeds wouldn't grow amongst the grain. The written purchase agreement subsequently entered into stated that the seller gave no warranty as to the germination of the seeds "or any other matter pertaining to the seed." The agreement also stated that the seller was in no way responsible for the crop.

The seeds were planted, but the crop was destroyed by weeds. The purchaser sued the seller on the basis that the defendant's verbal statement was a collateral warranty. The trial judge found in favour of the plaintiff. The defendant then appealed the trial decision.

LAMBERT, J.A.:

The parol evidence rule is not only a rule about the admissibility of evidence. It reaches into questions of substantive law. But it is a rule of evidence, as well as a body of principles of substantive law, and if the evidence of the oral representation in this case was improperly admitted, the appeal should be allowed.

The rule of evidence may be stated in this way: Subject to certain exceptions, when the parties to an agreement have apparently set down all its terms in a document, extrinsic evidence is not admissible to add to, subtract from, vary or contradict those terms.

So the rule does not extend to the cases where the document may not embody all the terms of the agreement. And even in cases where the document seems to embody all the terms of the agreement, there is a myriad of exceptions to the rule. I will set out some of them. Evidence of an oral statement is relevant and may be admitted, even where its effect may be to add to, subtract from, vary or contradict the document:

(a) to show that the contract was invalid because of fraud, misrepresentation, mistake, incapacity, lack of consideration, or lack of contracting intention;

(b) to dispel ambiguities, to establish a term implied by custom, or to demonstrate the factual matrix of the agreement;

(c) in support of a claim for rectification;

(d) to establish a condition precedent to the agreement;

(e) to establish a collateral agreement;

(f) in support of an allegation that the document itself was not intended by the parties to constitute the whole agreement;

(g) in support of a claim for an equitable remedy, such as specific performance or rescission, on any ground that supports such a claim in equity, including misrepresentation of any kind, innocent, negligent or fraudulent; and

(h) in support of a claim in tort that the oral statement was in breach of a duty of care.

I do not consider that I am setting out an exhaustive list. I am only showing that appropriate allegations in the pleadings will require that the evidence be admitted.

So, if it is said that an oral representation, that was made before the contract document was signed, contains a warranty giving rise to a claim for damages, evidence can be given of the representation, even if the representation adds to, subtracts from, varies or contradicts the document, if the pleadings are appropriate, and if the party on whose behalf the evidence is tendered asserts that from the factual matrix it can be shown that the document does not contain the whole agreement. The oral representation may be part of a single agreement, other parts of which appear in the document. (The one-contract theory.) Alternatively, the document may record a complete agreement, but there may be a separate collateral agreement with different terms, one of which is the oral representation. (The two-contract theory.)

On the basis of the pleadings in this case, I do not doubt that the evidence was properly admitted on the question of whether the document constituted a record of the whole agreement.

I should add that I can see very little residual practicality in the parol evidence rule, as a rule of evidence, in cases tried by a judge alone.

Is the oral representation a warranty? A warranty is one of the terms that may form a part of a contractual relationship and affect the scope of the relationship. It may be either a representation as to the existence of a present fact ("This car has travelled only 10 000 kms."); or it may be a promise to bear the risk of the loss that will flow from a failure of a fact to occur in the future ("This car is guaranteed rust-proof.")

It is not necessary to distinguish, in this case, between conditions, warranties, and other contractual terms that may give rise to claims in damages. But what must be done in this case is to distinguish between a warranty, where the breach gives rise to a claim for damages, and a bare and innocent misrepresentation, which may give rise to a claim in equity for rescission, but does not give rise to a claim for damages.

The distinction does not turn on whether the recipient of the representation acted on it. The distinction turns on whether the representation became a part of the contractual relationship between the maker and the recipient. That, in turn, depends on the intention of the parties, as derived from objective evidence, including but not limited to, evidence that tends to show whether the representation was intended to be acted upon and was in fact acted upon.

Mr. Justice Seaton, whose reasons I have seen in draft form, has set out six factors listed in Halsbury as aids in determining whether a statement is a warranty or a bare representation. The six factors are only straws in the wind, but, to the extent that they are helpful, I think that the second factor, namely, that the recipient makes it clear that he regards the matter as so important that he would not contract without the assurance, and the third factor, namely, that the maker is stating a matter that should be within his knowledge and of which the recipient is known to be ignorant, both apply on the facts of this case, and both tend to show a warranty rather than a bare representation.

More helpful than Halsbury, in my opinion, are the reasons of Mr. Justice Robertson in *Yorke v. Duval,* [1953] 3 D.L.R. 820, 9 W.W.R. (N.S.) 523, a decision of this court. They contain two guides for determining whether a pre-contractual representation is a warranty. First, at p. 821 D.L.R., p. 524-5 W.W.R., Mr. Justice Robertson said that the way to decide is to look at the contract in the light of all the surrounding circumstances, and that one of the first things to look to is to what extent the accuracy of the statement — the truth of what is promised — would be likely to affect the substance and foundation of the adventure which the contract is intended to carry out. Then, second, at p. 822 D.L.R., p. 525 W.W.R., Mr. Justice Robertson said that the essence of a warranty is that it becomes plain by the words and actions of the parties that it is intended that, in the purchase, the responsibility of the soundness will rest upon the vendor.

That seems to me to put the question squarely. What the trier of fact is trying to find out is this: who was to bear the risk that the statement might be wrong, the person who made it, or the person who acted on it? If it must be taken to have been intended, and understood, when said, to form a part of the contractual relations between the parties, then it is a warranty.

As was said by Mr. Justice Robertson in *Yorke v. Duval,* in the end it is a question of fact as to whether what was said was a warranty or just a statement. I will return to that question of the fact in this case in Part VII of these reasons.

The trial judge said: "It is clear on the law that the exclusionary clause in the contract will not avail the defendant, Allstate, if such a warranty is made out of the evidence. Is it so made out?"

For the reasons I have set out in Parts V and VI, I think that it is a considerable oversimplification of the law to say that an exclusionary clause will not avail the defendant if a collateral warranty is made out on the evidence. Sometimes it will, sometimes it would not; the court must strive to reach the true contractual intention of the parties, guided, in the case of contradiction, by the strong presumption in favour of the document.

But even if the trial judge oversimplified the law, he considered the right question on the evidence, namely: Is a warranty made out as a matter of fact? I do not think that he misdirected himself on the principles to be applied in answering that question of fact. It involved a nice question of judgment and an assessment of the testimony and demeanour of the witnesses. Mr. Justice Paris concluded that Mr. Nunweiler's statement regarding weed control constituted a warranty. There is ample evidence to support that conclusion, much of it referred to by Mr. Justice Paris in his reasons. I do not think that it is open to me to consider that matter afresh, or, if I were to reach a different conclusion on the facts than Mr. Justice Paris, to substitute my view of the facts for his.

Once it has been decided that the oral representation was a warranty, then, in my opinion,

(a) evidence accepted on the basis that there would be a subsequent ruling on admissibility, becomes admissible;

(b) the oral warranty and the document must be interpreted together, and, if possible, harmoniously, to attach the correct contractual effect to each;

(c) if no contradiction becomes apparent in following that process, then the principle in *Hawrish, Bauer* and *Carman* has no application; and

(d) if there is a contradiction, then the principle in *Hawrish, Bauer* and *Carman* is that there is a strong presumption in favour of the written document, but the rule is not absolute, and if on the evidence it is clear that the oral warranty was intended to prevail, it will prevail.

Since, in my opinion, there is no contradiction in this case between the specific oral warranty and the signed standard form Buckwheat Marketing Agreement, 1980, I have concluded that the warranty has contractual effect and that the defendant, Allstate Grain Co. Ltd., is liable to the plaintiffs for breach of that warranty.

But if it were correct, in this case, to conclude that the oral representation and the Buckwheat Marketing Agreement, 1980 contradicted each other, then, on the basis of the facts found by the trial judge and his conclusion that the oral representation was intended to affect the contractual relationship of the parties, as a warranty, I would have concluded that, in spite of the strong presumption in favour the document, the oral warranty should prevail.

I would dismiss the appeal.

Contracts in Writing — Rectification

Bank of Montreal v. Vancouver Professional Soccer Ltd. (1987), 15 B.C.L.R. (2d) 34.

The plaintiff bank and the defendant corporation entered into an agreement to refinance the team's debt. The debt was guaranteed by a number of guarantors and by $1 250 000 in commercial letters of credit to support the guarantees. Each would be liable for a percentage of the debt, less the amount received by the bank from the commercial letters of credit. The loan agreement was signed by the owners.

Reorganization of the team resulted in a release of three guarantors from their guarantees (which the bank agreed to do). An agreement prepared by the bank to this effect was signed by the team owners. At this point, however, the bank realized that the agreement reduced the guarantees and letters of credit to below 120% of the loan value. When the team owners refused to change the agreement, the bank applied to the courts for rectification of the written agreement to include the terms that the bank believed had been part of the verbal agreement.

At trial, the judge rejected the request for rectification, and the bank appealed.

McLachlin, J.A.:

The trial judge held that the case for rectification had not been made out because the bank had failed to establish that it and the defendants ever were in agreement on the matters sought to be added by rectification. In my opinion, he was correct in so holding.

Where the contracting parties have agreed on one set of terms and their agreement is later embodied in a document containing different terms, rectification may be available: Treitel, *The Law of Contract*, 4th ed. (1975), pp. 202-203. The remedy is concerned only with defects in the recording, not the making of the contract, a principle expressed succinctly in the maxim: "Courts of equity do not rectify contracts; they may and do rectify instruments": *Mackenzie v. Coulson* (1869), L.R. 8 Eq. 368 at 375.

Before rectification can be obtained, the applicant must establish:

1. that the written instrument does not reflect the true agreement of the parties;
2. that the parties shared a common continuing intention up to the time of signature that the provision in question stand as agreed rather than as reflected in the instrument.

See *Joscelyne v. Nissen,* [1970] 2 Q.B. 86 at 98-99, [1970] 2 W.L.R. 509, [1970] 1 All E.R. 1213 (C.A.); *Frederick E. Rose (London) Ltd. v. William H. Pim Junior & Co.,* [1953] 2 Q.B. 450 at 451, [1953] 3 W.L.R. 497, [1953] 2 All E.R. 739 (C.A.).

The standard of proof of these elements is a stringent one because of the danger of imposing on a party a contract which he did not make. While it may not be so high as the criminal onus of proof beyond a reasonable doubt (see *Joscelyne v. Nissen*, supra: *Peter Pan Drive-In Ltd. v. Flambro Realty Ltd.* (1978), 22 O.R. (2d) 291., 93 D.L.R. (3d) 221, affirmed 26 O.R. (2d) 746, 106 D.L.R. (3d) 576 (C.A.)), terms such as "certainty" (*Rose v. Pim,* supra) and "convincing proof" (*Joscelyne v. Nissen*) are appropriate.

In the case on appeal, these requirements are not met. The bank contends that the letter of 21st February 1983 reflects the agreement of the parties and submits that the subsequent formal documentation should be amended to conform to that letter. But that letter does not refer to the issue of how the letters of credit supplied by the guarantors were to affect their several liabilities in the event the letters were called. Nor does the letter deal with what was to happen if some of the guarantors were released. The evidence indicates that these matters were not discussed or considered at the time. In these circumstances, the bank has not discharged the burden upon it of establishing a common continuing intention in favour of the terms for which rectification is sought.

The bank submitted additionally that the second term sought, that relating to the release of three of the guarantors and assumption of their portion of the security by the remaining guarantors, was the subject of informal agreement in the fall of 1983. Assuming that such an agreement could be established, the doctrine of rectification would not be applicable because that agreement was never embodied in a formal instrument adhered to by the parties, the plaintiff having refused to sign the document drafted to reflect the new state of affairs. In short, there is nothing to rectify.

I am satisfied that the case for rectification, which was the only issue in the judgment appealed from, is not made out. Nor do I consider it appropriate, given the course this matter has followed, to consider the matter on some different legal basis, as counsel for the bank invited us to do.

I would dismiss the appeal.

CASE PROBLEMS FOR DISCUSSION

Case 1

Reid owned a car and travel trailer that he wished to sell. The trailer was outfitted with a stove and refrigerator as built-in equipment. Reid had added a small television set and antenna as a part of the equipment, but the television set was not built into the trailer.

Calder expressed an interest in the car and trailer, and also examined the equipment. Reid advised Calder that the price was $8600 and that the television set would be $100 extra if Calder wished to buy it as well. Calder indicated that he wished to do so.

Reid prepared a written purchase agreement that itemized the car and trailer, but simply referred to the appliances as "equipment." The contract price was $8600, and the agreement called for a deposit of $100. Both parties signed the agreement, and Calder gave Reid a deposit cheque in the amount of $200.

Reid changed his mind about the sale of the television set. Shortly before Calder was due to return for the car and trailer, Reid telephoned to say that he was selling only what was specified in the written agreement.

Explain Calder's rights (if any) in this case.

Case 2

Simon, a professional engineer, entered into an agreement with Easy Exploration Co. whereby he agreed to spend a year in Peru in search of a number of different kinds of minerals. The verbal agreement was made on September 7th, and Simon was to begin work for the company the following week on September 10th. The contract was to terminate on September 10th of the following year. Easy Exploration Co. offered to prepare a formal agreement for Simon's signature before he departed on September 10th.

On September 9th, Easy Exploration Co. decided to cancel its exploration program. They notified Simon that there was no need for him to sign the employment contract as his services would not be required.

Discuss Simon's rights (if any), and Easy Exploration's position at law.

Case 3

Amber, a young musician, obtained a position with an orchestra. As a result, she wished to acquire a musical instrument of better quality. The conductor of the orchestra accompanied Amber to Smith's Music Supply, where Amber selected a relatively expensive violin on the conductor's recommendation. Smith agreed to accept Amber's present violin in trade, but was reluctant to extend credit to Amber for the $1000 difference between the value of the two instruments.

To enable Amber to acquire the violin, the conductor agreed to guarantee the indebtedness if Smith would take a chattel mortgage (a type of security in which the debtor has possession but the creditor holds the title to the property or goods) on Amber's rather old automobile. It was also agreed that Amber would insure the violin against loss or damage, and Smith would hold a chattel mortgage on the violin as well.

A few months later, Amber was late for rehearsal as a result of engine trouble with her automobile. When she explained her problem to the conductor, the conductor suggested that she find something more reliable as transportation.

After the rehearsal, Amber arranged to sell her automobile and purchase a motorcycle of equal value. In order to effect the transaction, Amber arranged with Smith to have the automobile released from the chattel mortgage, and a chattel mortgage placed on the motorcycle.

On her way to rehearsal the next day, Amber was involved in an accident in which both the motorcycle and the violin were destroyed. As a result of the accident, she was hospitalized and unable to work.

The payments to Smith fell into arrears, and, in spite of repeated requests for payment, Amber failed to comply. Eventually, Smith called upon the conductor to honour his guarantee and pay the balance of the debt owed.

At that point, the conductor discovered that Amber had not insured the violin and that the property secured by the chattel mortgage no longer existed.

The conductor refused to make payment, and Smith took legal action against him to enforce the guarantee.

Explain the positions of the parties at law, and render a decision.

Case 4

Clement entered into a verbal agreement with Calhoun to purchase Calhoun's farm for $140 000. In the presence of his friend Saunders, Clement gave Calhoun $500 in cash "to bind the bargain." The farm adjoined the farm that Clement already owned. Immediately after the deal was made, both he and Saunders proceeded to remove an old fence that separated the two farms.

A few days later, Clement plowed a large field on his "new" farm, and Saunders cut down a few trees. Later that day, he prepared a cheque in the amount of $139 500, and took it to the farmhouse where Calhoun was still living.

Calhoun met Clement at the door and said that he had changed his mind. He did not wish to move off the land and had decided not to sell the farm.

Discuss Clement's rights (if any) in this case. Explain the possible outcome if Clement should decide to take legal action against Calhoun.

Case 5

Slippery Silica Mining Corporation entered into a contract with Highgrade Transport Company to haul its ore from its mine to a railway terminal, a distance of some 50 km. The contract called for the hauling of approximately 60 t a week for a one-year period. Because Slippery Silica Mining Corporation was a very small company, Highgrade Transport requested that Wilson and Rose, its two principal shareholders, personally guarantee the payment required under the terms of the contract.

In due course, Wilson and Rose provided a written guarantee of payment. It bore their signatures and that of their witness, Sheila Drew, a young woman who worked in their office as a receptionist and typist. The guarantee was not under seal, so the owner of the transport company immediately drove down to the mine office to have the two owners affix seals to the document.

At the mine office, the owner of the transport company met Sheila, who informed him that both Wilson and Rose were away for the day. When he told her the purpose of his visit, she took a box of red legal seals from her desk and offered them to him with the comment, "I don't think they would mind if you put on the seals yourself."

The owner of the transport company took two red seals and affixed them next to the signatures of Wilson and Rose on the guarantee. Then he left the office with the document.

Some time later, the mining company fell into arrears in its payments under the contract. The transport company notified Wilson and Rose that it intended to look to them for payment under their guarantee.

Discuss the issues raised in this case, and determine the legal position of the parties.

Case 6

Karl and Wilbur were older men who each lived alone on small farms on the same township concession lot. Karl worked on engines in his spare time, and was owed some money by Wilbur for a tractor repair. Karl's health was poor and he told Wilbur he wanted to retire. He told Wilbur that he had a mortgage on his farm for $30 000, and that he was prepared to sell his farm to Wilbur for $50 000. Wilbur did not have access to such money, but by the end of the conversation, Karl and Wilbur agreed that Wilbur would make Karl's mortgage payments, and in four and a half years, when a $25 000 GIC that Wilbur owned came due, Wilbur would pay Karl $24 500 (the $20 000 balance plus some interest) in cash.

Wilbur made the next three monthly trips to the bank, at the end of December, January and February, paying the appropriate $750 on each trip. Karl died on March 1st, having remained in the house over those previous three months. During that time the men had discussed Karl's impending move to the town, and the planting that Wilbur expected to do once the frost was out of the ground. In the first week of March, Karl's executor told Wilbur he knew of the deal, but that it was "off." He offered Wilbur a cheque for $250, which represented a refund of Wilbur's payments to the bank, less the money Wilbur owed to Karl for tractor repairs. Wilbur refused the cheque, wrote his own cheque to the executor for $2000 in payment of his repair bill, and told him that he would sue to enforce the deal as "the deal was really good for me, and you want to hold out for more cash." The property, independently appraised, was worth $67 000.

Assess the likelihood of Wilbur succeeding in obtaining an order of specific performance, compelling the sale on the agreed terms.

CHAPTER 11

Failure to Create an Enforceable Contract

INTRODUCTION

In their negotiations, the parties may meet all of the essentials for the creation of a binding agreement, but, nevertheless, they may occasionally fail to create an enforceable contract. Offer and acceptance, capacity, consideration, legality of object, and an intention to create a legal relationship all must be present, together with the requirements of form and writing under certain circumstances. But even when these elements are present, the parties may not have an agreement that both may enforce until they also show that they both meant precisely the same thing in their agreement. There are essentially four situations of this general nature that could arise and render the agreement unenforceable.

MISTAKE

If the parties in their negotiations are mistaken as to some essential term in the agreement, they may have failed to create a contract. **Mistake**, at law, however, does not mean the same thing to both the layperson and the legal practitioner. Mistake from a legal point of view has a relatively narrow meaning. It generally refers to a situation where the parties have entered into an agreement in such a way that the contract does not express their true intentions. This may occur in cases where the parties have formed an untrue impression concerning an essential element, or where they have failed to reach a true meeting of the minds as to a fundamental term in the agreement. For example, if Ann offers to sell her car to Burt for $1800, then realizes that her car is worth $1900, the courts would probably not allow Ann to avoid the agreement on the basis of mistake. Because Ann made the offer to Burt, and then later alleged that she had made a mistake as to the value of the subject-matter, the courts would have no real way of knowing Ann's true state of mind at the time the offer was made. On the other hand, if the consideration is clearly out of line and the mistake is obvious, the courts may not allow the other party to "snap up" the bargain.[1] When the mistake, however, is due to the party's own negligence, the contract, under certain circumstances, may be binding.[2]

Mistake of Law

Until very recently, a mistake could take the form of a mistake of law or a mistake of fact. Recovery of money paid under a mistake of law was often difficult, because everyone was (and is) presumed to know the law. As a consequence, recovery was only possible if the statute provided for recovery of the money paid, or there were some other conditions related to the mistake that permitted the court to direct the repayment of the money. For example, a rent restriction law prohibited the collection of a rental premium by the landlord for leasing premises to a tenant. In a case where the tenant paid the premium then later applied to the courts to recover the premium on the basis of a mistake of law, the court held that the collection of the premium was illegal but the restriction applied only to the landlord, and allowed the tenant to recover the premium.[3]

By 1989, the Supreme Court of Canada decided that money paid under a mistake of law should not be distinguished from mistake of fact. In essence, the difference should be abolished. In the case of *Air Canada et al. v. British Columbia* [4] the court stated:

> Where an otherwise constitutional or intra vires statute or regulation is applied in error to a person to whom its true construction it does not apply, the general principles of restitution for money paid under mistake should be applied, and subject to available defences and equitable considerations, the general rule should favour recovery. No distinction should be made between mistakes of fact and mistakes of law.

Mistake of Fact

Mistake of fact may take many forms, and, for many of these, the courts do provide relief. As a general rule, if the parties are mistaken as to the **existence** of the subject-matter of the contract, then the contract will be void.[5] For example, Alice offers to sell Beverley her canoe, and Beverley accepts the offer. Unknown to both Alice and Beverley, the previous day a fire had completely destroyed the boat house in which Alice had stored her canoe. The subject-matter did not exist at the time that Alice and Beverley made the contract. The contract is void due to a mistake as to the existence of the subject-matter. In essence, there was no canoe to sell at the time the parties made their agreement. The same rule might well apply if the canoe had been badly damaged in the fire and was no longer usable as a canoe. Under the common law, the courts would not require the purchaser to accept something different from what she had contracted to buy.

---

1. *Hartog v. Colin & Shields,* [1939] 3 All E.R. 566; *Imperial Glass Ltd. v. Consolidated Supplies Ltd.* (1960), 22 D.L.R. (2d) 759.
2. *Timmins v. Kuzyk* (1962), 32 D.L.R. (2d) 207; *Hydro Electric Comn. of Township of Nepean v. Ontario Hydro* (1980), 27 O.R. (2d) 321.
3. *Kiriri Cotton Co. Ltd. v. Dewani,* [1960] All E.R. 177.
4. *Air Canada et al. v. British Columbia et al.,* [1989] 1 S.C.R. 1161 at 1167.
5. *Barrow, Lane, & Ballard Ltd. v. Phillips & Co.,* [1929] 1 K.B. 574.

A second type of mistake of fact applies where there is a mistake as to the **identity** of one of the contracting parties. This is essentially an extension of the rule for offer and acceptance stating that only the person to whom an offer is made may accept the offer. With a mistake of fact of this nature the courts will generally look at the offer to determine if the identity of the person in question is an essential element of the contract. If the identity of the party is not an essential element of the agreement, then the agreement may be enforceable.[6] However, if one party to the contract does not wish to be bound in an agreement with a particular contracting party, and is misled into believing that he or she is contracting with someone else, the contract may be voidable when the true facts are discovered.[7]

For example, Able Engineering may wish to engage the services of a soil testing company to do a site inspection for it. Able Engineering used the services of soil testing company 'B' in the past and found their services to be unsatisfactory. On this occasion they request soil testing company 'C' to do the work.

Unknown to Able Engineering, soil testing company 'B' has purchased company 'C,' and all work of company 'C' is directed to company 'B.' Company 'B' accepts the offer. When Able Engineering becomes aware of the acceptance by 'B' company it may successfully avoid the contract on the basis of mistake as to the identity of the contracting party, if the identity of the party is an important element in the contract.

Mistake may also occur when one of the parties may be mistaken as to the true nature of a written contract. However, this is a very narrow form of mistake that represents an exception to the general rule that a person will be bound by any written agreement that he or she signs. The important distinction here is that the circumstances surrounding the signing of the written document must be such that the person signing the document was led to believe that the document was of a completely different nature from what it actually was. Had the person known what the agreement really was, he or she would not have signed it. This exception is subject to a number of constraints. It has a very limited application, because a person signing a written agreement is presumed to be bound by it. A failure to examine the written agreement does not absolve a person from any liability assumed under it. Nor is a person absolved from liability if the party is aware of the nature of the agreement as a whole, but remains ignorant of a specific term within it.[8] To avoid liability, a person must be in a position to establish that the document was completely different in nature from the document described, and that due to some infirmity or circumstances he or she was obliged to rely entirely on another person to explain the contents. The person must also establish that it was not possible to obtain an independent opinion or assistance before signing the written form and he or she was not in any way careless. This particular exception, which represents a form of mistake, is a defence known as ***non est factum*** (it is not my doing).

It is important to note, however, that the Supreme Court of Canada has

---

6. *Ellyatt v. Little*, [1947] O.W.N. 123.

7. *Said v. Butt*, [1920] 3 K.B. 497; *Boulton v. Jones* (1857), 2 H & N 564, 157 E.R. 232. *Cundy v. Lindsay* (1878), 3 App. Cas. 459.

8. *Sumner v. Sapkas* (1955), 17 W.W.R. 21.

essentially limited this defence to a very narrow group of contracting parties. In the *Marvco Color Research Limited v. Harris case,*[9] the Supreme Court held that if a person was careless in signing a document, the defence of *non est factum* would not be available to the person. This was the case even if the person had some infirmity, such as a reading difficulty or partial blindness.

The narrowness of this defence may be illustrated by the following example. An elderly person with failing eyesight and no opportunity to get legal or other advice on a document is induced to sign that document. The person believed it to be a letter of reference, when in fact it was a guarantee. Under these conditions the person may be able to avoid liability under it. However, first she must show that she was not careless, but obliged to rely upon the person presenting it for her signature. She must also prove that it was described to her as being a completely different document. The infirmity that made a personal examination and understanding of the document impossible must, of course, also be established to the satisfaction of the court, which will require evidence to prove that the party was not otherwise careless in signing the document. Once this is done, the court may decide that the party would not be bound by the document.[10]

An additional point to note here is the true nature of the document. The signed document must be completely different in nature from the document that the party believed he or she was signing, for a plea of *non est factum* to succeed. If, however, the document is not of a different nature, but, rather, the same type of document as described, differing only in degree, then a defence of *non est factum* would be unsuccessful. The party would have been aware of the true nature of the agreement at the time of signing, and no mistake as to the nature of the document would have existed.[11] The justification for this rule of law is obvious. Public policy dictates that a person should be bound by any agreement signed; the excuse that it was not read before signing is essentially an admission of carelessness or negligence on the part of the signor. The courts are not prepared to offer relief to those persons who are so careless in the management of their affairs that they are unwilling to take the time to read the terms and conditions that are contained in an agreement. There are, however, persons who, as a result of advanced years, some infirmity, or simply the lack of knowledge, are unable to read the written agreement. It is this group that the courts are prepared to assist if, through their reliance on another, they have been misled as to the true nature of the agreement that they have signed. Even here, the disadvantaged persons are expected to assume some responsibility for their own protection. If the opportunity for independent advice is available, and they refuse to avail themselves of it, the courts will probably treat their actions as careless and not permit them to avoid the contract. For example, where a person heard the contract read aloud, and then later pleaded *non est factum*, the claim was rejected and the contract enforced.[12]

---

9. *Marvco Color Research Limited v. Harris,* [1982] 2 S.C.R. 774.
10. *W.T. Rawleigh Co. v. Alex Dumoulin,* [1926] S.C.R. 551; *Commercial Credit Corp. v. Carroll Bros. Ltd.* (1971), 16 D.L.R. (3d) 201.
11. *Dorsch v. Freeholders Oil Co.,* [1965] S.C.R. 670.
12. *Prudential Trust Co. Ltd. v. Forseth,* [1960] S.C.R. 210.

Unilateral and Mutual Mistake

Mistake may take one of two forms insofar as the parties are concerned. The mistake may be made by only one party to the agreement, in which case it is called **unilateral mistake**. Or it may occur that both parties are unaware of the mistake, and the mistake is a **mutual mistake.** In the case of unilateral mistake, usually one of the parties is mistaken as to some element of the contract, and the other is aware of the mistake. Cases of this nature closely resemble misrepresentation — one of the parties is aware of the mistake, and either allows the mistake to exist or actively encourages the false assumption by words of conduct. The major difficulty with this form of mistake is establishing a general rule for its application. The best that might be said here is that the courts tend to treat contracts as being unenforceable where a party makes or accepts an offer that he knows the other party thinks or understands to be materially different from what he, himself, makes or accepts.

Unilateral mistake may arise, for example, where a seller, offering to sell a particular product to a buyer, knows that the buyer believes the offered product is something different from what it is. In this case, if the court is satisfied that the seller was aware of the buyer's mistake, but allowed it to go uncorrected, the court may permit the buyer to rescind the agreement.

Mutual mistake, on the other hand, is generally the easiest to deal with. It encompasses common forms of mistake, such as mistake as to the existence of the subject-matter or mistake as to its identity. Only the latter sometimes presents problems. When it does so, the courts frequently decide that a mistake has occurred and the contract is therefore unenforceable.[13] Cases of this sort tend to place a hardship on the plaintiff, because the courts, in effect, reject the plaintiff's interpretation of the contract. Nevertheless, if a reasonable interpretation is possible, it may be accepted by the court in an effort to maintain the agreement.

The nature of mistake and the differences between its various forms was discussed by the court in the case of *McMaster University v. Wilchar Construction Ltd. et al.*[14] The judge described mistake in the following terms:

> The distinction between cases of common or mutual mistake and, on the other hand, unilateral mistake, must be kept in mind. In mutual or common mistake, the error or mistake, in order to avoid the contract at law, must have been based either upon a fundamental mistaken assumption as to the subject-matter of the contract or upon a mistake relating to a fundamental term of the contract. There, the law applies the objective test as to the validity of the contract. Its rigour in this aspect has been designed to protect innocent third parties who have acquired rights under the contract.
>
> Normally a man is bound by an agreement to which he has expressed assent. If he exhibits all the outward signs of agreement, at law it will be held that he has agreed. The exception to this is in the case where there has been fundamental mistake or error in the sense above stated. In such case, the contract is void *ab initio*. At law, in unilateral mistake, that is when a mistake of one party relating to the contract is known to the other party, the Courts will apply the subjective test and

---

13. See *Raffles v. Wichelhaus* (1864), 2 H.&C. 906, 159 E.R. 375 for an example of a case of mutual mistake which the court found insoluable insofar as an interpretation of the interest was concerned.

14. *McMaster University v. Wilchar Construction Ltd. et al.,* [1971] 3 O.R. 801.

permit evidence of the intention of the mistaken party to be adduced. In such case, even if one party knows that the other is contracting under a misapprehension, there is, generally speaking, no duty cast upon him to disclose to the other circumstances which might affect the bargain known to him alone or to disillusion that other, unless the failure to do so under the circumstances would amount to fraud. This situation, of course, must be distinguished from the case in which the mistake is known to or realized by both parties prior to the acceptance of the offer.

The law also draws a distinction between mistake simply nullifying consent and mistake negativing consent. Error or mistake which negatives consent is really not mistake technically speaking in law at all, as it prevents the formation of contract due to the lack of consensus and the parties are never *ad idem*. It is rather an illustration of the fundamental principle that there can be no contract without consensus of all parties as to the terms intended. This is but another way of saying that the offer and the acceptance must be coincident or must exactly correspond before a valid contract results.

A promisor is not bound to fulfil a promise in a sense in which the promisee knew at the time that the promisor did not intend it. In considering this question, it matters not in what way the knowledge of the meaning is brought to the mind of the promisee, whether by express words, by conduct, previous dealings or other circumstances. If by any means he knows there was no real agreement between him and the promisee, he is not entitled to insist that the promise be fulfilled in a sense to which the mind of the promisor did not assent.

A special form of relief is available in the case of mistake in a written agreement that renders performance impossible. This is known as **rectification.** It is sometimes used to correct mistakes or errors that have crept into a written contract, either when a verbal agreement has been reduced to writing, or when a written agreement has been changed to a formal agreement under seal. In each of these cases, if the written agreement does not conform with the original agreement established by the parties, the courts may change the written words to meet the terms of the original agreement. The purpose of this relief is to "save" the agreement that the parties have made. It is not intended to permit alteration of an agreement at a later date to suit the wishes or interpretation of one of the parties. It is, essentially, a method of correcting typographical errors, or errors that have crept into the writing through the omission of a word or the insertion of the wrong word in the agreement.

To obtain rectification, however, it is necessary to convince the courts through evidence that the original agreement was clear and unequivocal with regard to the term that was later changed when reduced to writing. The courts must also be convinced that there were no intervening negotiations or changes in the interval between the establishment of the verbal agreement and the preparation of the written document. It would also be necessary to establish that neither party was aware of the error in the agreement at the time of signing.[15] For example, A Co. and B Co. enter into an agreement by which A Co. agrees to supply a large quantity of fuel oil to B Co.'s office building at a fixed price. The building is known municipally as 100 Main St. When the agreement is reduced to writing, the address is set out in error as 1000 Main St., an address that does not exist.

---

15. *Paget v. Marshall* (1884), 54 L.J. Ch. 575.

After the contract is signed, B Co. discovers that it could obtain fuel oil at a lower price elsewhere. It attempts to avoid liability on the basis that A Co. cannot perform the agreement according to its terms. In this case, A Co. may apply for rectification to have the written agreement corrected to read 100 Main St., the address that the parties had originally agreed would be the place of delivery.

MISREPRESENTATION

Misrepresentation is a statement or conduct that may be either **innocent** or **fraudulent** and that induces a person to enter into a contract. Normally, a person is under no obligation to make any statement that may affect the decision of the other party to enter into the agreement. Any such statement made, however, must be true. Otherwise it may constitute misrepresentation if it is material (important) to the contract. Additionally, the law recognizes a small group of contractual relationships where the failure to disclose all material facts may also amount to misrepresentation. Misrepresentation does not, however, render a contract *void ab initio*. Misrepresentation, whether innocent, fraudulent, or by means of non-disclosure, will only render the agreement voidable at the option of the party misled by the misrepresentation. In every instance, it is important that the injured party cease accepting benefits under the agreement once the misrepresentation is discovered. Otherwise the continued acceptance of benefits may be interpreted as a waiver of the right to rescind the contract. Exceptions have been made to this general rule by both statute law[16] and recent cases concerning fraudulent misrepresentation.[17] However, the behaviour of the injured party, once the misrepresentation is discovered, is still of paramount importance.

The false statement must be a **statement of fact** and not a mere expression of **opinion**. Whether the fact is material or not is determined on the basis of whether the innocent party to the negotiations would have entered into the agreement had he or she known the true fact at the time. If the innocent party did not rely on the particular fact, or was aware of the falsity of the statement made, then he or she cannot avoid the contract on the basis of misrepresentation by the other party. **Rescission** is only possible where the innocent or injured party relied on the false statement of fact made by the other party.

Misrepresentation seldom arises out of a term in a contract. It is generally something, that takes place before the contract is signed, and that induces a party to enter into the agreement. Misrepresentation must be of some material fact, and not simply a misstatement of a minor matter that does not go to the root of the contract. If the parties include the false statement as a term of the contract (such as a statement as to quality or performance), then the proper action, if the statement proves to be untrue, is an action for a breach of contract, rather than misrepresentation.

Innocent Misrepresentation

Innocent misrepresentation is the misrepresentation of a material fact that the party making the statement honestly believes to be true, but is discovered to be false after the parties enter into the contract. If the statement can be shown by the

---

16. See, for example, insurance legislation in each province that does not permit the insurer to avoid liability on a policy where the insured failed to disclose a material fact many years before a claim is made on the policy.

17. See, for example, *Siametis et al. v. Trojan Horse (Burlington) Inc. et al.* (1979), 25 O.R. (2d) 120.

injured party to be a statement of a material fact that induced him to enter into the agreement, then he may treat the contract as voidable and bring an action for **rescission**. If the injured party acts promptly, the courts will normally make every effort to put the parties back in the same position that they were in before the contract was made. For example, ABC Co. and XYZ Co. enter into negotiations for the purchase of a building lot that ABC Co. owns. The president of XYZ Co. asks the president of ABC Co. if the land is suitable for the construction of a small apartment building. The president of ABC Co. (who had inquired from the municipality some months before and determined that the land was indeed suitable and approved for the proposed use) answers: "Yes." Unknown to ABC Co., the lands had subsequently been rezoned for single-family dwellings, and the construction of apartment buildings was prohibited. XYZ Co., on the strength of the ABC Co.'s statement, enters into an agreement to purchase the lot. A short time later, before the deed is delivered, XYZ Co. discovers that the land is not zoned for multiple-family dwellings and refuses to proceed with the contract. In this case, XYZ Co. would be entitled to rescission of the agreement on the basis of ABC Co.'s innocent misrepresentation. At the time that the ABC Co.'s statement was made, the land was not zoned for the use intended by XYZ Co. Even though the president of ABC Co. honestly believed the land to be properly zoned at the time that he made the statement, it was untrue. Since XYZ Co. had relied on ABC Co.'s statement, and it was material to the contract, the courts would probably provide the relief requested by XYZ Co. and rescind the contract. The courts would probably order ABC Co. to return any deposit paid by XYZ Co., but would not award punitive damages.[18]

A classic statement on the common law related to innocent misrepresentation was pronounced in the case of *Newbigging v. Adam*.[19] The court described innocent misrepresentation and the remedies available in the following words:

> If we turn to the question of misrepresentation, damages cannot be obtained at law for misrepresentation which is not fraudulent, and you cannot, as it seems to me, give in equity any indemnity which corresponds with damages. If the mass of authority there is upon the subject were gone through, I think it would be found that there is not so much difference as is generally supposed between the view taken at common law and the view taken in equity as to misrepresentation. At common law it has always been considered that misrepresentations which strike at the root of the contract are sufficient to avoid the contract on the ground explained in *Kennedy v. Panama, New Zealand, and Australian Royal Mail Company;* but when you come to consider what is the exact relief to which a person is entitled in a case of misrepresentation it seems to me to be this, and nothing more, that he is entitled to have the contract rescinded, and is entitled accordingly to all the incidents and consequences of such rescission. It is said that the injured party is entitled to be replaced *in statu quo*. It seems to me that when you are dealing with innocent misrepresentation you must understand that proposition that he is to be replaced *in statu quo* with this limitation — that he is not to be replaced in exactly the same position in all respects, otherwise he would be entitled to recover damages, but is to be replaced in his position so far as regards the rights and obligations which have been created by the contract into which he has been induced to enter.

18. *Derry v. Peek* (1889), 14 App. Cas. 337; *Alessio v. Jovica* (1973), 42 D.L.R. (3d) 243.
19. *Newbigging v. Adam* (1887), 34 Ch. D. 582.

Fraudulent Misrepresentation

Unlike innocent misrepresentation, where a party honestly believes a fact to be true when the fact is stated, **fraudulent misrepresentation** is a statement of fact that, when made, is known to be false. It is made with the intention of deceiving the innocent party. If a party makes a false statement recklessly, without caring if it is true or false, it may also constitute fraudulent misrepresentation. In each case, however, the statement must be of a material fact and must be made for the purpose of inducing the other party to enter into the agreement.[20]

In the case of fraudulent misrepresentation, the innocent party must prove fraud on the part of the party making the false statement. This is because the action is based upon the tort **deceit**, as well as a request for the equitable remedy of rescission. Rescission is limited to those cases where the courts may restore the parties to the position they were in before entering into the contract. However, this is not the case with tort. If the innocent party is able to prove fraud on the part of the party making the statement, then the courts may award punitive damages against that party committing the tort as punishment for the act. This remedy would be available in all cases where fraud may be proven, even where it would not be possible to restore the injured party to the same position that he was in before the contract was established. As with innocent misrepresentation, the injured party must refrain from taking any benefits under the agreement once the fraud is discovered. The continued acceptance of benefits may prevent a future action for rescission. Usually the parties must act promptly to have the agreement rescinded, because the remedy would not be available if a third party should acquire the title to any property that may have been the subject-matter of the agreement.

Insofar as the tortious aspect of the misrepresentation is concerned, prompt action by the innocent party is usually also important in order to avoid any suggestion that that party had accepted the agreement notwithstanding the fraud. Delay does not always preclude relief, however, as the courts have awarded damages under certain circumstances even after the passage of a lengthy period of time.[21]

The requirement for a tort action for deceit may not be an easy matter to establish. In the case of *Charpentier v. Slauenwhite*[22] the defendant, Mrs. Slauenwhite, made certain false statements concerning water supply to a property. The plaintiff brought an action in tort for the alleged deceit, and the court in its judgement described the requirements for maintaining a successful deceit action as follows:

> First in order to sustain an action of deceit, there must be proof of fraud, and nothing short of that will suffice. Secondly, fraud is proved when it is shown that a false representation has been made, (1) knowingly, or (2) without belief in its truth, or (3) recklessly, careless whether it be true or false. Although I have treated the second and third as distinct cases, I think the third is but an instance of the second, for one who makes a statement under such circumstances can have no real belief in the truth of what he states.

20. *Derry v. Peek* (1889), 14 App. Cas. 337.

21. *Siametis et al. v. Trojan Horse (Burlington) Inc. et al.* (1979), 25 O.R. (2d) 120.

22. *Charpentier v. Slauenwhite* (1971), 3 N.S.R. (2d) 42.

Occasionally, a party injured by the false statements of the other contracting party may not be able to satisfy the court that the statements consituted fraudulent misrepresentation. In these instances the court may provide only the contract remedy of rescission if the statements represent an innocent misrepresentation. For example, in one case, a purchaser in response to an advertisement of a model 733 BMW automobile for sale, contacted the seller and was assured that it was a model 733. The vehicle was a 728 model that did not meet Canadian safety standards. Nor were parts readily available, as it was a European model. The purchaser brought an action for fraudulent misrepresentation against the seller, but the court found the statements of the seller to be innocent misrepresentation and awarded only rescission of the contract.[23]

Misrepresentation by Non-Disclosure

Generally a party is under no duty to disclose material facts to the other contracting party. However, the law does impose a duty of disclosure in certain circumstances where one party to the contract possesses information that, if undisclosed, might materially affect the position of the other party to the agreement. This duty applies to a relatively narrow range of contracts called contracts of **utmost good faith**. It also applies to cases where there is an active concealment of facts, or where partial disclosure of the facts has the effect of rendering the part disclosed as false. With respect to this latter group, the courts will normally treat the act of non-disclosure, or act of partial disclosure, as a fraud or an intention to deceive. In contracts of "utmost good faith" the failure to disclose, whether innocent or deliberate, may render the resulting contract voidable.

Contracts of utmost good faith, fortunately, constitute a rather small group of contracts. The most important are contracts of insurance, partnership, and those where a relationship of special trust or confidence exists between the contracting parties. The courts have indicated that the class of contracts that may be identified as being of utmost good faith are not limited, but they have generally been reluctant to expand the class.[24] This is perhaps due in part to the fact that the duty of disclosure, in many cases, has been dealt with by statute, rather than the common law.[25]

Contracts of insurance, in particular, require full disclosure by the insurance applicant who knows essentially everything about the risk that he or she wishes to have insured, while the insurer knows very little. The reasoning behind the law under these circumstances is that an obligation rests on the prospective insured to reveal all material facts. This is, first, to enable the insurer to determine if it wishes to assume the risk, and second, to have some basis upon which to fix the premium payable for the risk assumed. This is particularly important in the case of life insurance, where the insurer relies heavily on the insured's statement as to his or her health record in determining insurability and the premium payable. Even here, limits have been imposed on innocent non-disclosure. Most provinces have

---

23. *Ennis v. Klassen* (1990), 66 M.R. (2d) 117 (C.A.).

24. See, for example, *Hogar Estates Ltd.* in *Trust v. Shelbron Holdings Ltd. et al.* (1979), 25 O.R. (2d) 543; *Laskin v. Bache & Co. Inc.*, [1972] 1 O.R. 465.

25. See, for example, consumer protection legislation and recent securities legislation in most provinces.

legislation for particular kinds of insurance that limit the insurer's right to avoid liability on a contract of insurance for non-disclosure beyond a fixed period of time.

Partnership agreements, and all other contracts representing a fiduciary relationship, are similarly subject to the rules requiring full disclosure of all material facts in any dealings that the parties may have with each other. In all of these circumstances, withholding information of a material nature by one party would entitle the innocent party to avoid liability under the agreement affected by the non-disclosure.

The question of non-disclosure of material facts arose in the case of *Re Gabriel and Hamilton Tiger-Cat Football Club Ltd.*[26] The issue was whether an employment contract was one that fell within the definition of a contract of this special type because the club failed to reveal the length of the playing season. The judge explained the nature of a contract of utmost good faith by saying:

> ...there is a limited class of contract in which one of the parties is presumed to have means of knowledge which are not accessible to the other and is, therefore, bound to tell him everything which may be supposed likely to affect his judgment. They are known as contracts *uberrimae fidei,* and may be voided on the ground of non-disclosure of material facts. Contracts of insurance of every kind are in this class. There are other contracts, though not contracts *uberrimae fidei,* in the same sense, which impose a duty of full disclosure of all material facts by the parties entering into them. Contracts for family settlements and arrangements fall into this category. I am dealing here with a contract of personal service. The House of Lords in *Bell et al. v. Lever Bros. Ltd. et al.,* [1932] A.C. 161, refused to extend the duty of disclosing material facts to contracts for service.

UNDUE INFLUENCE

The law of contract assumes that the parties to a contract have freely assumed their respective duties under the agreement. However, such is not always the case. Occasionally, a party entering into an agreement may be so dominated by the power or influence of another that the person is unable to make a free and deliberate decision to be bound by his or her own act. In essence, **undue influence** occurs where the party is so dominated by another that the decision is not his or her own. A contract obtained under these circumstances would be voidable, if the dominated party acts to avoid the contract as soon as he or she is free of the dominating influence.

Undue influence must be established before the courts will allow a contracting party to avoid the agreement. Where no special relationship exists between the parties, the party alleging undue influence must prove the existence of such influence. In certain cases, however, where a special relationship exists between the parties, a rebuttable presumption of undue influence is deemed to exist. These cases are limited to those relationships of trust or good faith and frequently have a confidential aspect to them. These special relationships include solicitor-client, medical doctor-patient, trustee-beneficiary, parent-child, and spiritual advisor-parishioner relationships. In all of these relationships, if undue influence is alleged, the onus shifts to the dominant party to prove that no undue influence

---

26. *Gabriel v. Hamilton Tiger-Cat Football Club Ltd.* (1975), 57 D.L.R. (3d) 669.

affected the formation of the contract. The onus is usually satisfied by showing the courts that the fairness of the bargain or the price (if any) paid for the goods or service was adequate; that a full disclosure was made prior to the formation of the agreement; and that the weaker party was free to seek out the advice of others, and to seek out independent legal advice, if appropriate. If the presumption cannot be rebutted by evidence, then the contract is voidable by the weaker party, and the courts will grant rescission. Again, prompt action is necessary to obtain relief from the courts. If the weaker party fails to take steps promptly on being free on the undue influence, or ratifies the agreement either expressly or by inaction for a long period of time, the right to avoid the agreement may be lost, and the agreement will be binding.

The presumption of undue influence does not apply to the husband-wife relationship. Consequently, undue influence must be proven by the party raising the allegation. The relationship, however, is treated in a slightly different manner from one where the relationship is deemed to exist and where the presumption applies. The courts in the case of the husband-wife relationship normally look at the degree of domination of the subordinate party by the dominant party, and the fairness or unfairness of the bargain struck between them, in deciding the question of enforceability.

For example, A convinces his wife (who is inexperienced in business matters) to convey to him a valuable property that she owns in exchange for some worthless company shares that he holds. If A's wife does so, and later discovers that the shares are worthless, she may be able to convince a court that the contract should be rescinded. To do so, however, she must establish undue influence on the part of A. If she can satisfy the court that the transaction was unfair, and that A so dominated her judgement that the decision was not her own, the court may provide relief.

A common business situation that frequently gives rise to an allegation of undue influence is related to the requirement made by banks for a married person to guarantee his or her spouse's indebtedness. No presumption of undue influence exists in these cases. However, banks often require an assurance that the spouse has had independent legal advice before signing a guarantee of the married partner's loan to avoid any later claim that the guarantee is unenforceable on the basis of undue influence.[27]

DURESS

The last basis for avoiding a contract is, fortunately, a rare business occurrence. Nevertheless, it is grounds for rescission. If a person enters into a contract under a threat of violence, or as a result of actual violence to his or her person or to a family member (or a close relative),[28] the contract may be avoided on the basis of **duress.** The threat of violence, however, must be made to the person, and not simply directed toward the person's goods or chattels. Again, it is important that the victim of the violence take steps immediately on being free of the duress to avoid the contract. Otherwise the courts are unlikely to accept duress as a basis for avoiding the agreement.

---

27. See, for example, *Bank of Montreal v. Stuart,* [1911] A.C. 120.
28. *Kaufman v. Gerson,* [1904] 1 K.B. 591.

SUMMARY

The parties may comply with all of the essentials for the creation of a valid contract, but if there is not a true meeting of the minds, or if some mistake occurs that affects the agreement in an essential way, the contract may be either void or voidable. If a mistake should occur as to the existence of the subject-matter, the identity of a contracting party, or in some cases, the nature of the agreement, then the agreement may be unenforceable. If a party is induced to enter into a contractual relationship as a result of innocent misrepresentation of a material fact by a party, then the contract may be voidable at the option of the injured party when the misrepresentation is discovered. If the misrepresentation is made deliberately, and with the intention of deceiving the other party, then the party making the fraudulent misstatement may also be liable in tort for deceit. A contract may also be voidable if a party enters into the agreement as a result of undue influence or duress. In each case, the victim must take steps to avoid the agreement as soon as he or she is free of the influence or threat. In all cases where the contract is voidable, if the party continues to take benefits under the agreement, or affirms the agreement after becoming aware of the defect, misrepresentation, undue influence, or duress, the right to rescind the contract may be lost.

DISCUSSION QUESTIONS

1. In what way(s) would mistake in its legal context differ from what one would ordinarily consider to be mistake?
2. How does unilateral mistake differ from mutual mistake?
3. What effect does mistake, if established, have on an agreement that the parties have made?
4. Explain the difference between mistake and misrepresentation.
5. Distinguish innocent misrepresentation from fraudulent misrepresentation.
6. What obligation rests upon a person who, having made an innocent misrepresentation, discovers the error?
7. Why do the courts consider non-disclosure to be misrepresentation under certain circumstances? Identify the circumstances where this rule would apply.
8. Explain the rationale behind the rule that a person who applies for insurance from an insurer must disclose all material facts concerning the subject matter of the insurance.
9. The presumption of undue influence applies to contracts made by individuals in specific types of relationships. Why is this so?
10. What obligation rests on the "dominant party" in a contract where the presumption of undue influence applies, if the other party alleges undue influence?
11. How does undue influence differ from duress?
12. Identify the situations where duress may be raised as a legal means for avoiding a contract.

MINI-CASE PROBLEMS

1. A and B entered into a verbal agreement whereby A would sell an automobile to B for $6500. B drew up a written agreement (which A and B signed) that set out the price as being $6000. A failed to notice the change at the time of signing the agreement. What advice would you give A?
2. How would your answer to question 1 differ if A was illiterate and B read the contract aloud to him, stating the price to be $6500, instead of the $6000 price set out in the written agreement?

**JUDICIAL
DECISIONS**

The *Siametis et al. v. Trojan Horse* case represents an example of a business transaction in which the purchaser of a business relied upon the fraudulent statements of the seller. The judge in the case discusses the elements of fraud by reference to a number of cases. He notes that in the case of proven fraudulent misrepresentation, the injured party is entitled not only to rescission of the contract, but damages for the fraud (the tort deceit). He refers to the statement of Lord Atkin as to the right to the damages and the determination of the amount that should be awarded. The judge at the end of the decision concludes that the entire loss suffered by the buyer (including money spent on improvements) should be covered by the damages.

The *Vukomanovic v. Cook Bros. Transport* case illustrates the principle that a person will be bound by the contract that he or she signs, even where the person is aware of errors in the contract. In this situation, the plaintiff noticed the errors in delivery dates, but did not bring the errors to the attention of the other contracting party. Instead, the plaintiff chose to rely on the verbal representations made by the other party prior to the preparation of the contract. The judge, however, concluded that if a party was aware of errors in the dates for performance before entering into the agreement, the party could not later object to the other party performing the contract in accordance with the dates set out in the written agreement.

**Contracts —
Fraudulent
Misrepresentation
— Damages**

Siametis et al. v. Trojan Horse (Burlington) Inc. et al. (1979), 25 O.R. (2d) 120.

The plaintiffs purchased a restaurant business based upon fraudulent statements and information provided by the defendants. The fraud was not discovered until some months after the plaintiffs had operated the business and expended funds of their own in an attempt to make the business profitable.

The plaintiffs brought an action against the defendants for damages as well as rescission of the contract.

LERNER, J.:

It has long been recognized that where a party is found to be guilty of participating in a fraudulent scheme, he is not entitled to excuse his own illegality and fraud by establishing that the victim of the fraud in fact suffered no injury. In *Scheuerman v. Scheuerman* (1916), 52 S.C.R. 625, 28 D.L.R. 223, 10 W.W.R. 379, a husband had put property in his wife's name to delay or hinder a creditor until a certain debt for the payment of which he was being pressed had been discharged. The intention of both parties was that the property be in the wife's name to conceal the fact that the husband was the owner, thus protecting it from proceedings by the creditor who already held a judgement. This debt was subsequently satisfied so that the creditor's claim was not defeated by the fraud. The wife's refusal to convey the property to her husband subsequently was upheld by the Supreme Court of Canada. In the *Scheuerman* case Idington, J., stated at pp. 628-9 S.C.R., p. 25 D.L.R.:

"Many authorities have been cited which I have, in deference to the argument and divided opinion below, fully considered. But from none of them can I extract authority for the proposition of law that when a man has, out of the sheer necessity to prove anything upon which he can hope to rest the alleged claim of trust, to tell of an illegal purpose as the very basis of his claim, that he may yet be entitled to succeed. I find cases where the man has, accidentally as it were, or incidentally, to the relation of his story told that which he might if skilfully directed both in pleading and in giving evidence have avoided telling, yet has told enough to disclose that he was far from being always guided by the law or morality in his intentions, and still entitled to succeed because he had in fact established, by the untainted part of his story as it were, enough to entitle him to succeed without reliance upon that which was illegal or immoral.

"This is not respondent's case, but the other kind of case I have just referred to is."

In the same judgement, Brodeur, J., stated, at p. 641 S.C.R., p. 233 D.L.R.: "The general principle is that fraud vitiates all contracts," and at pp. 642-3 S.C.R., p. 234 D.L.R.:

"The courts should never help any person who has acted with a fraudulent intent, and the same rule should apply whether a transfer is made for the purpose of defeating subsequent creditors or when it is made with the purpose of defeating existing creditors who may exercise their right upon the increased value of the property."

The plaintiff could not have discovered the fraud by examining the statements, including the Trojan Horse statement, for the first year's business. A cheat may not escape even if the fraud could be uncovered by a more sophisticated purchaser. That Siametis may have been a foolish and unwise purchaser did not absolve the deceivers; Fleming, *Law of Torts,* 4th ed. (1971), at p. 560.

Once the fraud was proved, the onus was upon the vendors to satisfy the Court that the fraudulent misrepresentation was not an inducement for execution by Siametis of the offer to purchase, ex. 2. In *Barron v. Kelly* (1918), 56 S.C.R. 455, 41 D.L.R. 590, it was stated by Anglin, J., at p. 482 S.C.R., p. 609 D.L.R.:

"Fraudulent misrepresentation in a matter *prima facie* material and likely to operate as an inducement having been shown by the plaintiff, the onus of satisfying the court that it did not in fact so operate is certainly cast upon the defendants."

If the misrepresentation is fraudulent, the case for relief is overwhelming. The person deceived is entitled to damages and rescission: Waddams, *The Law of Contracts* (1977), p. 248. The problem here is whether Siametis is entitled to both or only to damages.

In *McConnel v. Wright,* [1903] 1 Ch. 546, Lord Collins, M.R., pointed out the distinction between damages for breach of contract and damages for fraud or deceit. At p. 554, he stated concerning an action for fraud:

"It is not an action for breach of contract, and, therefore, no damages in respect of prospective gains which the person contracting was entitled by his contract to expect to come in, but it is an action of tort — it is an action for a wrong done whereby the plaintiff was tricked out of certain money in his pocket; and therefore, prima facie, the highest limit of his damages is the whole extent of his loss, and that loss is measured by the money which was in his pocket and is now in the pocket of the company."

In *Doyle v. Olby (Ironmongers) Ltd. et al.,* [1969] 2 Q.B. 158 at p. 166, Lord Denning, M.R., preferred and adopted the statement of Lord Atkin in *Clark et al. v. Urquhart,* [1930] A.C. 28 at pp. 67-8, wherein Lord Atkin stated:

"I find it difficult to suppose that there is any difference in the measure of damages in an action of deceit depending upon the nature of the transaction into which the plaintiff is fraudulently induced to enter. Whether he buys shares or buys sugar, whether he subscribes for shares, or agrees to enter into a partnership, or in any other way alters his position to his detriment, in principle, the measure of damages should be the same, and whether estimated by a jury or a judge. I should have thought it would be based on the actual damage directly flowing from the fraudulent inducement. The formula in *McConnel v. Wright,* [1903] 1 Ch. 546, may be correct or it may be expressed in too rigid terms."

Lord Denning was of the opinion that Lord Collins' statement in *McConnel, supra,* was too rigid and he then went on to state, at p. 167:

"I think that Lord Collins did express himself in too rigid terms. He seems to have overlooked consequential damages. On principle the distinction seems to be this: in contract, the defendant has made a promise and broken it. The object of damages is to put the plaintiff in as good a position, as far as money can do it, as if the promise had been performed. In fraud, the defendant has been guilty of a deliberate wrong by inducing the plaintiff to act to his detriment. The object of damages is to compensate the plaintiff for all the loss he has suffered, so far, again, as money can do it. In contract, the damages are limited to what may reasonably be supposed to have been in the contemplation of the parties. In fraud, they are not so limited. The defendant is bound to make reparation for all the actual damages directly flowing from the fraudulent inducement. The person who has been defrauded is entitled to say:

'I would not have entered into this bargain at all but for your representation. Owing to your fraud, I have not only lost all the money I paid you, but, what is more, I have been put to a large amount of extra expense as well as suffered this or that extra damages.'

"All such damages can be recovered: and it does not lie in the mouth of the fraudulent person to say that they could not reasonably have been foreseen. For instance, in this very case Mr. Doyle has not only lost the money which he paid for the business, which he would never have done if there had been no fraud: he put all that money in and lost it: but also he has been put to expense and loss in trying to run a business which has turned out to be a disaster for him. He is entitled to damages for all his loss, subject, of course to giving credit for any benefit that he has received. There is nothing to be taken off in mitigation: for there is nothing more that he could have done to reduce his loss. He did all that he could reasonably be expected to do."

The measure of damages in a case such as this was stated simply in the inimitable style of Lord Denning, *Doyle v. Olby,* supra, at p. 167, where he stated:

"The person who has been defrauded is entitled to say:

'I would not have entered into this bargain at all but for your representation. Owing to your fraud, I have not only lost all the money I paid you, but, what is more, I have been put to a large amount of extra expense as well as suffered this or that extra damages.'"

All such damages can be recovered and the defrauders cannot plead that the damages could not reasonably have been foreseen.

Siametis is entitled to damages for all of his loss "subject to allowances for any benefit that he has received."

Errors in Written Agreement — Failure to Inform Other Party at the Time

Vukomanovic v. Cook Bros. Transport Ltd. and Mayflower Transit Co. Ltd. (1987), 65 Nfld. R. 181.

The plaintiff entered into a contract with the defendant to have his household goods moved from Calgary, Alberta to St. John's, Newfoundland. The contract was entered into by the parties in January of 1985. The contract specified a February 25th loading date and a March 22nd delivery date. The goods were in fact loaded on January 25th. The plaintiff noticed the errors in the dates on the written agreement. He had been advised that delivery would take "approximately four weeks." He did not inform the defendant of the error in the contract at the time. The goods, however, were delayed in delivery, and were not delivered until March 14th. The plaintiff was obliged to stay at a motel for the period February 22nd to March 14th, due to the late delivery. He then brought an action for damages against the moving companies.

STEELE, J.:

[11] Counsel for the plaintiff takes the position that the defendants or their agents made a mistake in preparing the dates on the bill of lading and erroneously showed the loading date as February 25th and a delivery date of March 22, 1985. He maintains that the goods were in fact loaded on the transfer truck January 25th and that the delivery date was February 22nd and not March 22nd. To support his position, counsel for the plaintiff points out that the plaintiff's goods were in actuality loaded on January 25th; that the form "Household Goods Descriptive Inventory" bears the date January 25, 1985; that the plaintiff accepted his position with the Provincial Government on the agreement his work was to commence February 1, 1985; that other estimates from other moving companies in Calgary indicate a loading date of either January 25 or January 26, 1985 and, finally, in his letter to the Department of Mines and Energy he indicated he would be ready to load his goods on the transfer truck on or about January 25 or January 26, 1985.

[12] Counsel for the defendant transportation companies both argue that the bill of lading shows the delivery date to be March 22nd and, although loading may have been January 25th, the plaintiff signed the bill of lading without making any alterations to the dates and, perhaps of more importance, without even mentioning to the driver that the dates were incorrect. It appears that other agents of the defendants may have been involved in the move but at all times the delivery date of March 22, 1985 was accepted as correct by the defendants.

[13] The question posed by counsel for the plaintiff is whether the dates appearing on the bill of lading are the correct dates and the bill of lading representing the true contract between the parties or, whether an error was made by the defendants whereby the delivery date ought to have been February 22nd as per an oral agreement that preceded the signing of the bill of lading.

[20] In the case at hand there is no allegation or suggestion that the defendants or their agents in Calgary were guilty of misrepresentation, fraud, deceit or for that matter any improper or irregular conduct. It is possible that somehow, perhaps by inadvertence, the incorrect dates were put on the bill of lading but, certainly, at most the charge can be only that of inadvertence. It was never established how the defendants got the dates that appeared on the bill of lading. Cook attempted to explain how the dates could only have come from the plaintiff. However, in view of what subsequently occurred I hardly think it matters. The plaintiff was presented with the bill of lading at the time of loading and by his own evidence he examined it carefully. As I have already indicated, he was fully aware of the dates already filled in on the bill of lading showing the loading date as February 25th and a delivery date of March 22nd. The plaintiff says that he was not concerned by the delivery date shown as both he and the driver signed the bill of lading on January 25th. In my view it was the plaintiff who carelessly or neglectfully failed to bring the matter to the attention of the driver. He did nothing. By signing the bill of lading that indicated a delivery date of

March 22nd the plaintiff quite unintentionally misled the defendants into believing that March 22nd was the proper delivery date. For that carelessness or neglect he can hardly now blame the defendants. The defendants or their agents in Calgary were innocent of any negligence, carelessness or wrongdoing and it was the failure of the plaintiff to bring the alleged irregularity to the attention of the driver that ultimately resulted in the goods not reaching St. John's until March 13th. The plaintiff's error was in assuming that if the goods were picked up on January 25th, they would be delivered within four weeks and that, therefore, the delivery date of March 22nd was meaningless. That was the crucial mistake and for that error assume his loss.

[21] Without again reviewing the evidence, I should also state I am satisfied the defendants acted reasonably once they became aware of the plaintiff's predicament. Cook made every effort to cooperate and cannot be faulted. Unfortunately for the plaintiff it was the time of year when the carriage of household goods are at its lowest level and it simply was not possible to expedite the move.

[22] The plaintiff's claim is dismissed.

CASE PROBLEMS FOR DISCUSSION

Case 1

Schuster owned two volumes of a rare edition of Chaucer's *The Canterbury Tales.* One volume was in excellent condition. The second volume was in poor shape, but nevertheless intact. Schuster sold both volumes to MacPherson, a rare book merchant.

MacPherson loaned the two volumes to a local library for a rare book display. Unknown to MacPherson only the volume in excellent condition was put on display with a collection of other rare books. The second copy was placed in a display designed to show how rare books might be repaired, but the book was placed in such a position that neither its title nor its contents could be determined.

A week after the books had been returned to their owner, Holt, a collector of rare books, telephoned MacPherson to determine if he had a copy of *The Canterbury Tales* for sale. MacPherson replied that he did, but it was "not in top shape." Holt then asked if the copy had been on display at the library, and MacPherson said, "Yes."

Holt informed MacPherson that she had seen the display of books at the library, and would be interested in purchasing the volume. A price was agreed upon, and Holt sent a cheque to MacPherson for the agreed amount.

MacPherson sent the volume that was in poor condition to Holt by courier. On its receipt, Holt complained that the volume was not the same one that had been on display at the library. MacPherson maintained that it was, and refused to return Holt's money.

Holt brought an action against MacPherson for a return of the money that she had paid MacPherson.

Indicate the nature of Holt's claim, and express an opinion as to the outcome of the case.

Case 2

Chamberlain carried on business as a used-furniture dealer. He would occasionally purchase all of the furnishings in a person's home if the person was leaving the country or moving a long distance.

Mrs. Lyndstrom, an elderly widow, indicated to Chamberlain that she intended to sell her home and furniture, as she was planning to move into her daughter's home to live with her. Chamberlain expressed an interest in purchasing her furniture, so an appointment was arranged for Chamberlain to examine the contents of the Lyndstrom home.

When Chamberlain arrived, Mrs. Lyndstrom took him to each room and indicated the furniture that she intended to sell. Chamberlain listed the different items by groups, such as "all chairs and table in kitchen," or "bedroom suite in front bedroom." When they reached the living-room, Mrs. Lyndstrom said, "all the furniture in here," and Chamberlain recorded, "all furniture in living-room." Chamberlain offered $3500 for the lot when the list was complete. Mrs. Lyndstrom agreed, and Chamberlain added to the bottom of the list: "Agreed price of all above furniture, $3500." Both signed the document.

The next day, Chamberlain arrived with a truck to pick up the furniture and a cheque for $3500. As he was about to have the grand piano moved from the living-room, Mrs. Lyndstrom informed him that he was to take only the furniture, not the piano. Chamberlain protested that the piano was included. However, Mrs. Lyndstrom argued that a piano was not furniture, but a musical instrument.

Explain how this matter might be resolved.

Case 3

Corgi was the breeder of prize-winning pedigree dogs that often sold for very high prices. Reynolds, a wealthy businessman who had recently retired, decided to purchase a prize-winning dog. His intention was to enter the animal in the various dog shows that were held from time to time across the country.

Reynolds knew very little about dogs. He explained to Corgi that he wished to purchase a young dog that was already a prize-winning specimen of the breed. Corgi took Reynolds to a fenced run where several young dogs were caged. He pointed to one dog that he said, in his opinion, had the greatest potential, and that it had already won a prize at a local dog show. Corgi pointed to a red ribbon pinned to the opposite wall of the kennel building, and explained that it was a first prize ribbon that the dog had won. Reynolds did not bother to examine the ribbon.

Reynolds purchased the dog for $1000 and took it home. His neighbour later saw the dog in Reynolds' backyard. He instantly recognized it as the dog that had recently won the first prize ribbon in the children's pet show at the neighbourhood park. When he told Reynolds where he had last seen the dog, Reynolds telephone Corgi immediately and demanded his money back.

Corgi refused to return Reynolds' money or take back the dog, and Reynolds threatened to take legal proceedings against him. Reynolds was unable to do so immediately, however, as he was called out of town on a family matter the next day. He was obliged to leave the dog with his neighbour during his absence. Reynolds advised the neighbour to take care of the animal as if it were his own.

Reynolds was out of town for several weeks. During that time, his neighbour entered the dog in a dog show sponsored by a kennel club. The dog won first prize in its class for its breed. On Reynolds' return, the neighbour advised him of his success. The two men decided to enter the dog in another dog show that was scheduled to be held in a nearby city.

At this second show, the dog placed only third in its class, and Reynolds was disappointed. He returned home and immediately took legal action against Corgi.

Discuss the basis of Reynolds' claim and the defences (if any) of Corgi. Render, with reasons, a decision.

Case 4

Gordon was an avid golfer who played golf every weekend during the summer months, and practised in his backyard on weekday evenings.

One evening, while practising putting in his yard, he became annoyed at his lack of success. He struck the ball a much harder blow than usual, so much so that the ball travelled over the fence, and continued through his neighbour's picture window. Gordon immediately went to his neighbour's home and offered his apologies for shattering the glass, but refused to pay for the damage. When his neighbour demanded payment, he refused.

The neighbour became angry at his refusal and called the police. A police officer arrived on the scene almost immediately. He suggested that Gordon provide his neighbour with a written undertaking to pay for the damage. Gordon did so reluctantly, and signed the paper.

A week later, the neighbour presented Gordon with an account for replacement of the window that amounted to $425. Gordon refused to make payment, and the neighbour brought an action against him for his breach of the agreement.

Discuss the possible success of the neighbour's action and indicate the defence (if any) that Gordon might raise. What alternate action might the neighbour have taken?

Case 5

A general contractor invited sub-contractors to submit bids for mechanical work in the construction of a large office building. Several written bids were received by the contractor, as well as a telephone call from a sub-contractor who responded with a bid about 12% below the lowest bid price of the written submissions. All written bids were within 1% of each other.

The sub-contractor who submitted the telephone bid checked his estimates the day following the telephone call. He discovered that he had made an error in his calculations, and immediately called the contractor to withdraw his bid. Unfortunately, the contractor was out of town, and the sub-contractor could not reach him at his office. However, he left a message with the contractor's secretary to the effect that his bid was in error, and that his bid price for the contract would be 13% above the figure quoted on the telephone.

The contractor, while out of town, prepared his contract price for the construction of the building, using the original telephone bid price for the mechanical work. He was awarded the construction contract. When he returned to the office, his secretary informed him of the sub-contractor's error.

The sub-contractor refused to enter into a written contract or to perform the mechanical work at the original price. The contractor was obliged to get the work done by the sub-contractor who had submitted the next lowest bid. When the contract was fully performed, the contractor brought an action against the telephone bidder for the difference between the contract price quoted on the telephone and the actual cost incurred in having the work done.

Discuss the arguments that might be raised by the parties in this case. Render a decision.

Case 6

Able attended an auction sale of race horses at a well-known and respectable racing stable. Prior to the sale, Able, who was interested in acquiring a particular horse, examined the animal's lineage, breeding history, and veterinary records, as well as the horse itself. At the time of the sale, the horse appeared to be ill, and Able asked the vendor's veterinarian about its health. The veterinarian replied that she thought the horse was suffering from a cold. On the basis of this information, Able entered the bidding on the sale of the horse, and was the successful bidder at a price of $9000. The conditions of the sale were that the purchaser assumed all risks and responsibility for the horse from the instant of the sale, when the title to the animal was deemed tổ pass.

Able took the horse to his own stable and informed his veterinarian that the horse was ill with a cold. Without examining the horse, the veterinarian prescribed some medicine for it. The medicine did not appear to help the horse. It remained ill for two weeks, becoming increasingly more feeble, as the time passed. Sixteen days after the horse had been purchased, it died. An autopsy revealed that the cause of death was rabies.

Able brought an action for a return of the purchase money paid for the horse. At the trial, expert witnesses for the plaintiff and defendant disagreed as to when the horse might have contracted the disease, but both agreed that it could possibly have had the disease at the time of the sale. Both also agreed that rabies was a disease most difficult to detect in its early stages of development. Neither the purchaser nor the vendor had any suspicion that the horse had contracted rabies, because of the rarity of the disease among horses vaccinated against it. For some reason, the horse Able had purchased was not vaccinated against rabies.

Identify the issues raised in this case. Indicate how it might be decided.

Case 7

Mary McDonald was an 86-year-old widow who lived in her own home. She complained frequently about the high cost of maintenance of her home and the high property taxes she paid. Mrs. McDonald eventually felt it was necessary to cancel her fire insurance to reduce her household expense. However, she handled all her own business affairs, as well as maintaining herself in her home.

Mary's daughter was a real estate agent, and aware of her mother's concern about her property. On a summer day, she drove to her mother's home and informed her that she had some papers at the lawyer's to protect her. The two women went down to the lawyer's office, where the lawyer advised Mary McDonald that the document was the deed to the property and required her signature. Mary briefly glanced at the document and said: "Where do I sign?"

Some months later, the municipal tax bill arrived and Mary McDonald was surprised to see that the property was in her daughter's name. She immediately brought a legal action against her daughter to have the property transferred back into her own name.

Discuss the arguments that the parties might raise in this case and render a decision.

Case 8

Tower Installation Co., by way of a newspaper advertisement, learned of an invitation to bid on the engineering work for an electric power transmission tower line that a hydro-electric corporation wished to have erected in a remote area of the province. The advertisement indicated that the right-of-way had been laid out, and preliminary site preparation was in the process of completion. Engineers from Tower Installation Co. visited the site before making a bid. They noticed that many downed trees and branches cluttered the right-of-way throughout the entire length of the proposed line. The engineers assumed that the downed trees and branches were part of the preliminary site preparation.

The proposed contract stipulated that the successful bidder would be "responsible for the removal of standing trees and brush in those areas where they had not been cleared, and the final site preparation." The proposal also stated that the bidders must inform themselves of all aspects of the site and the work to be done. Tower Installation Co. submitted its bid to perform the required work based upon its examination of the site and the proposed contract terms.

Some three months later, the contract was awarded to The Tower Installation Co. It immediately sent its engineers and work crews to the construction site to begin work. To the surprise of the engineers, the downed trees and branches still remained on the site, as no further work had been done since the site was visited before. The company engineers complained to the electric corporation, but were told that they should have enquired about the logs and downed trees before making their bid on the work.

The Tower Installation Co. proceeded with the contract and completed it in accordance with its terms. The company, however, lost two million dollars as a result of the extra work required to clear the downed trees and branches from the right-of-way.

Tower Installation Co. took legal action against the electric power corporation for the amount of its loss on the contract.

Discuss the basis of the claim in this case and the possible defences of the corporation. Render a decision.

Case 9

Efficient Management Inc. offered to purchase the shares of Clean Management Ltd. from its shareholders, A and B. Efficient Management Inc. also agreed to lease premises from shareholder A under a long-term lease.

Under the share purchase agreement, Efficient Management Inc. agreed to purchase all of the outstanding shares which were owned 50% by A and 50% by B. The total price payable for the shares was $2, being $1 for all of the shares of A and $1 for all of the shares of B. Efficient Management Inc. also agreed to repay to A and B loans that they had made to their corporation, Clean Management Ltd., in the amount of $450 000. The purchase agreement provided that Clean

Management had accounts receivable outstanding in the amount of $350 000 which A and B warranted were all in good standing and could be collected by Clean Management Ltd. from its customers within 60 days.

Under the terms of the agreement, Efficient Management Inc. agreed to pay $100 000 as a deposit on the signing of the agreement and the balance of the money in 90 days. The shares of Clean Management Ltd. were to be delivered at the time of signing on payment of the $1 to each shareholder. The agreement was signed on May 1 and the $100 000 paid. A and B signed over their shares on the same day and each received $1 as payment in full.

By June 30, Efficient Management Inc. had collected only $225 000 of the accounts receivable, and the balance had to be considered uncollectible. At that time they informed A and B that they expected them to provide the company with the remaining $125 000 that A and B had warranted were collectable accounts. A and B did not pay the balance owing.

On July 31 the accountant at Efficient Management Inc. inadvertently sent A and B a cheque for the $350 000 balance owing under the agreement. When the error was discovered, the company claimed repayment for A and B of the $125 000. A and B refused to do so, and Efficient Management Inc. instituted legal proceedings against A and B to recover the $125 000, or in the alternative, to set off rent owing to A against the amount unpaid.

Outline the nature and basis of the claim against the shareholders, and any defences that A and B might raise. Render a decision.

CHAPTER 12

The Extent of Contractual Rights

PRIVITY OF CONTRACT

Once a valid contract has been negotiated, each party is entitled to performance of the agreement according to its terms. In most cases, the contract calls for performance by the parties personally. However, the parties may either attempt to confer a benefit on the third party by way of contract, or attempt to impose a liability on a third party to perform a part of the agreement.

At common law, the rule relating to third party liability is relatively clear. Apart from any statutory obligation or obligation imposed by law, a person cannot incur liability under a contract to which he or she is not a party. By this rule, parties to an agreement may not impose a liability on another who is not a party to the contract except in those circumstances where the law imposes liability. For example, under the law of partnership, a partner (in the ordinary course of partnership business) may bind the partnership in contract with a third party. The remaining partners, although not parties to the agreement, will be liable under it and obligated to perform. The law provides in such a case that the partner entering the contract acts as the agent of all of the partners and negotiates the agreement on their behalf as well.

Under certain circumstances a person may acquire liability under a contract negotiated by others if the person accepts land or goods that have conditions attached to them as a result of a previous contract. In this case, the person would not be a party to the contract, but, nevertheless, would be subject to liability under it. This situation, however, may be distinguished from the general rule on the basis that the person receiving the goods or the property accepts them subject to the conditions negotiated by the other parties. This person must also be fully aware of the liability imposed at the time that the goods or property are received. The acceptance of the liability along with the goods or property resembles, in a sense, a subsidiary agreement relating to the original agreement under which one of the original contracting parties retains rights in the property transferred.

For example, Alton owns a large charter power boat that she wishes to sell, but that she presently leases to Chambers for the summer. Burrows enters into a contract with Alton to purchase the boat, aware of the lease that runs for several months. Burrows intends to make a gift of the boat to his son. As a part of the contract he requires delivery by Alton to his son of the ownership papers pertaining to the vessel. If Burrows' son accepts the ownership of the boat, aware of the delay in delivery, he would probably be required to respect the contract and accept the goods under the conditions imposed by the contract between Alton and his father.[1]

An important exception to the privity of contract rule concerns contracts that deal with the sale, lease, or transfer of land. In general, the purchaser of land takes the land subject to the rights of others who have acquired prior interests in the property or rights of way over the land. The purchaser, however, is usually aware of the restrictions before the purchase is made. With the exception of some tenancies, all restrictions running with land and all rights of third parties must be registered against the land in most jurisdictions. Consequently, the person acquiring the land has notice of the prior agreements at the time of the transfer of title. Actual notice of an unregistered contract concerning the land may also bind the party, depending upon the jurisdiction and the legislation relating to the transfer of interests or land. Apart from this limited form of restriction or liability imposed by-law, a person who is not a party to a contract may not normally incur liability under it.

The second part of the rule relating to third parties concerns the acquisition of rights by a person who is not a party to a contract, but upon whom the parties agree to confer a benefit. The principle of consideration, however, comes into play if the third party attempts to enforce the promise to which he or she was not a contracting party. When the principle of consideration is strictly applied, it acts as a bar to a third party claiming rights under the contract. This is so because the beneficiary gives no consideration for the promise of the benefit. Only the person who is a party to the agreement and gives consideration for the promise would have the right to insist on performance.

The strict enforcement of the rule had the potential for abuse at common law whenever a party to a contract who had the right to enforce the promise was unable or unwilling to do so. To protect the third party, the courts of equity provided a remedy in the form of the **doctrine of constructive trust.** Under this equitable doctrine, the contract is treated as conferring a benefit on the third party. As well, the promisor is obliged to perform as the **trustee** of the benefit to be conferred on the third party beneficiary. Under the rules of trust, the trustee, as a party to the contract, has the right to sue the contracting party required to perform. However, if the trustee refuses or is unable to take action, the third party beneficiary may do so by simply joining the trustee as a party defendant.

For example, A and B enter into an agreement that will provide a benefit for C, who is not a party to the agreement. Under the privity of contract rule, C, who is not a party to the agreement, could not enforce the promise to confer the benefit. Only the person who gave consideration for the promise could enforce the agreement. However, if that person refuses to take court action, C would be entitled to

---

1. See, for example, *Lord Strathcona Steamship Co. v. Dominion Coal Co.*, [1926] A.C. 108.

do so. The reasoning here is that if the trustee of the benefit refused or was unable to act to enforce the promise, this in turn affected C's rights as beneficiary of the trust. This would also be the case if the trustee, once in possession of the funds or benefit refused to confer the benefit, on the beneficiary.

A formal contract under seal also represents an exception to the general rule concerning privity of contract. If the formal agreement is addressed to the third party and contains covenants that benefit the third party, the delivery of the agreement to the third party would enable that person to maintain an action against the promisor to enforce the rights granted under the agreement, should the promisor fail or refuse to perform.

Since rights are frequently conferred on third parties in certain types of contracts, the legislation governing these types of contracts generally provides the third party with the statutory right to demand performance directly from the contracting party. This is without regard for consideration or the common law rule concerning privity of contract.[2] The right of a beneficiary under a contract of life insurance is a notable example of the legislative establishment of third party rights to a benefit under such a contract. Without statutory assistance (and assuming that a trust cannot be ascertained) the doctrine of privity of contract would apply and the beneficiary would be unable to collect from the insurance company. This is so because under the privity of contract rule a person not a party to a contract would not acquire rights under the agreement. This rule also applies to the liability of outside parties. Unless the person can be shown to be liable by way of some statutory or common law rule, a person who is not a party to a contract cannot be liable under it.

The acquisition of rights and the assumption of liabilities by third parties may, nevertheless, be expanded at common law to include parties who are closely related to the agreement and aware of the terms. In a number of cases, the courts have held that a party who receives a benefit under a contract may take advantage of implied terms within it,[3] or be subject to the liabilities that were negotiated.[4]

From a practical point of view, another route is available whereby a third party may acquire a right against another. By the law of contract, only the purchaser under a contract of sale would have a right of action if the goods purchased proved to be unfit for the use intended. While under the law of torts, if the user or consumer can establish a duty on the part of the manufacturer not to injure the consumer, and if injury ensues as a result of use by the third party, a right of action would lie against the manufacturer. This would be the case even though no contractual relationship existed. The availability of these alternate remedies to third parties has eased the pressure for changes in the privity of contract rule, and perhaps slowed the move toward broadening the exceptions to it. Apart from the use of the law of torts, the general trend seems to be to provide for specific cases in legislation or by alternate remedies, rather than to alter the basic concept of privity of contract.

2. See, for example, the Insurance Act, R.S.O. 1990, c. I-8, ss. 164-169.

3. *Shanklin Pier Ltd. v. Detel Products Ltd.,* [1951] 2 K.B. 854.

4. *Pyrene Co. Ltd. v. Scindia Navigation Co. Ltd.,* [1954] 2 Q.B. 402; *Anticosti Shipping Co. v. Viateur St.-Armand,* [1959] S.C.R. 372.

A similar agreement that attempts to confirm a right on a party would be the type of situation where a third party might attempt to enforce rights or benefits under an agreement to which the third party is not a party but a beneficiary. This issue arose in the case of *Shanklin Pier Ltd. v. Detel Products Ltd.*,[5] where a warranty had been given that certain paint substituted for the type specified was suitable for the purpose intended. The contract was negotiated by the painting contractor and the paint supplier. However, when the paint proved to be unsuitable, the third party owner of the painted pier attempted to enforce the warranty.

The judge discussed the issue in the following manner:

> This case raises an interesting and comparatively novel question whether or not an enforceable warranty can arise as between parties other than parties to the main contract for the sale of the article in respect of which the warranty is alleged to have been given.
>
> The defence, stated broadly, is that no warranty such as is alleged in the statement of claim was ever given and that, if given, it would give rise to no cause of action between these parties. Accordingly, the first question which I have to determine is whether any such warranty was ever given.

His Lordship reviewed the evidence about the negotiations which led to the acceptance by the plaintiffs of two coats of D.M.U. in substitution for the paint originally specified, and continued:

> In the result, I am satisfied that, if a direct contract of purchase and sale of the D.M.U. had then been made between the plaintiffs and the defendants, the correct conclusion on the facts would have been that the defendants gave to the plaintiffs the warranties substantially in the form alleged in the statement of claim. In reaching this conclusion, I adopt the principles stated by Holt, C.J. in *Crosse v. Gardner* and *Medina v. Stoughton* that an affirmation at the time of sale is a warranty, provided it appear on evidence to have been so intended.
>
> Counsel for the defendants submitted that in law a warranty could give rise to no enforceable cause of action except between the same parties as the parties to the main contract in relation to which the warranty was given. In principle this submission seems to me to be unsound. If, as is elementary, the consideration for the warranty in the usual case is the entering into of the main contract in relation to which the warranty is given, I see no reason why there may not be an enforceable warranty between A and B supported by the consideration that B should cause C to enter into a contract with A or that B should do some other act for the benefit of A.

Where employees negligently perform their duties under a contract made between their employer and a customer of the firm, the customer may have the opportunity to bring an action in tort against both the employer and the employees. If a duty of care was owed by the employees to the customer, it would appear that the court may consider the employees personally liable to the customer for their tort. In the case of *London Drugs v. Kuehne & Nagel International Ltd.*[6] a customer entered into a storage contract with a warehouse operator for the storage of a transformer. Employees of the warehouse operator negligently damaged the

5. *Shanklin Pier Ltd. v. Detel Products Ltd.,* [1951] 2 K.B. 854.

6. *London Drugs Ltd. v. Kuehne & Nagel International Ltd.* (1992), 73 B.C.L.R. (2d) 1 (S.C.C.).

transformer in the course of moving it. The customer bought an action for damages in contract and tort for negligence against both the warehouse operator and the employees. The court decided that both the employees and the warehouse operator were liable for the loss, but allowed the employees who were not party to the contract between the warehouse operator and the customer to limit their liability to the amount agreed upon in the contract. On the basis of this case, it would appear that employees who are not parties to their employer's contract may nevertheless use the contract's provisions to limit their liability in tort.

ASSIGNMENT OF CONTRACTUAL RIGHTS

Novation

A third party may, of course, wish to acquire rights or liability under a contract by direct negotiation with the contracting parties. Should this be the case, the third party may replace one of the parties to the contract by way of a process called **novation**. This process does not conflict with the privity of contract rule because the parties, by mutual consent, agree to terminate the original contract and establish a new agreement. In this agreement the third party (who was outside the original agreement) becomes a contracting party in the new contract and subject to its terms. The old agreement terminates, and the original contracting party, now replaced by the third party, becomes free of any liability under the new agreement. By the same token, the original contracting party, being no longer a contracting party, is subject to the privity of contract rule.

The legal nature of novation involves a number of elements that must be present to establish a complete novation. These were set out by the court in the case of *Re Abernethy-Lougheed Logging Co.; Attorney-General for British Columbia v. Salter*[7] where the requirements were noted as follows:

> ...three things must be established: First, the new debtor must assume the complete liability; second, the creditor must accept the new debtor as a principal debtor, and not merely as an agent or guarantor; third, the creditor must accept the new contract in full satisfaction and substitution for the old contract; one consequence of which is that the original debtor is discharged, there being no longer any contract to which he is a party, or by which he can be bound.
>
> All these matters are in our law capable of being established by external circumstances; by letters, receipts, and payments and the course of trade or business."
>
> In other words, in the absence of an express agreement the intention of the parties may be inferred from external circumstances including conduct.

The process of novation, as a means of transferring contractual rights to a third party, is a useful method of avoiding the privity of contract rule. However, in modern business practice, it is not only cumbersome but inappropriate for certain kinds of transactions, where the third party may only be interested in a particular aspect of the transaction. For example, A Co. sells goods to B Co. on credit. A Co. may not wish to have its funds tied up in a large number of credit transactions. It may wish to have access to its money to finance its own business. C Co. is prepared to buy B Co.'s promise to pay from A Co., but if novation is the only method of transfer of these rights, all parties would be obliged to consent.

---

7. *Re Abernethy-Lougheed Logging Co.; Attorney-General For British Columbia v. Salter*, [1940] 1 W.W.R. 319.

Assuming B Co. is willing to surrender its rights against A Co. in the contract of sale, a new agreement between B Co. and C Co. would have to be formed. In this contract C Co. would be obliged to give some consideration for B Co.'s promise to pay, or the contract would have to be under seal. Novation would clearly be an unwieldy tool for such a simple business transaction.

Equitable Assignments

There was a difficulty at common law that prevented the development of a simpler, more streamlined method of bringing a third party into a contractual relationship. This was the fact that, originally, the common law courts would only recognize rights in contracts between parties as personal rights that were not subject to transfer. These particular rights, called **choses in action** (in contrast to **choses in possession**, which are goods and things of a physical nature), were treated differently by the court of equity. Equity recognized the need for flexibility in the transfer of rights under contracts and business agreements. It would enforce rights that had been transferred to a third party if all of the parties could be brought before the court. If the court could be satisfied that a clear intention to assign the rights had been intended by the parties to the agreement, the contract would be enforced. While this process, too, was cumbersome, it nevertheless permitted the assignee a right to enforce it against the promisor.

Equity did not normally permit an assignee to bring an action on an assignment in the assignee's own name. Rather it imposed a duty on the assignee to attach his or her name to the action. This step was normally necessary in order to have all parties before the court, and to prevent a further action in the common law courts by the assignor against the debtor at a later date. The presence of the assignor, while sometimes inconvenient, was necessary since equitable assignments need not take any particular form. They may be either oral or written. The only essential part of the assignment was that the debtor be made aware of the fact that the assignment had been made to the third party. If this was done, any other evidence surrounding the assignment or the original agreement would be available to the court by way of evidence at trial.

Under the rules of equity, an assignment did not bind the debtor or promisor until notice had been given to him of the assignment. From that point on, the assignment was effective, and he was obliged to comply with it. The assignment, however, was subject to any rights that existed between the debtor and the assignor, for the assignee took the assignment subject to any defences to payment that existed between the original parties to the contract.

Certain contracts were recognized as unassignable in both the common law courts and the courts of equity. Any contract that required the personal service or personal performance by a party to the contract could not be performed by a third party to the agreement. For example, if a person engaged an artist to paint her portrait, the artist who was engaged would be required to do the painting. The only procedure enabling a third party to perform would be novation, which would require all parties to consent to the change. In some circumstances the courts did permit a modified form of personal performance to take place where the contract did not specifically state that only the contracting party could perform. In these contracts, the party to the contract remains liable for the performance according to the terms of the agreement. However, the actual work done, or performance, is carried out by another person under a separate agreement with the contractor. This type of performance is known as **vicarious performance,** and involves two or more contracts. The first contract is the contract between the parties in which the contractor agrees to perform certain work or services. The contractor, in turn, enters into a second contract. This may be a contract of employment with one of the contractor's employees, or it may be a contract with an independent contractor to have the actual work done. In all cases, the primary liability rests with the contractor if the work is done improperly. The unsatisfied party to the contract would not sue the person who actually performed the work, but would sue the contractor. The contractor, in turn, would have the right under the second contract to take action against the party who actually performed the work, if the work was done negligently.

These contracts conflict neither with the privity of contract rule nor with the rules relating to novation and the assignment of contractual rights. Both contracts remain intact, and the third party does not acquire rights under the second contract. The only difference is that the actual performance of the work in one contract is done by a party to the second contract.

As a general rule, most contracts for the performance of work or service may be vicariously performed if there is no clear understanding that only the parties to the contract must perform personally. Most parties to business transactions do not contemplate that the other party to the agreement will personally carry out the work, nor in many cases would the parties consider it desirable. Consequently, by customs of the trade in most business fields, the contracts may be vicariously performed. Only in the case of professionals, entertainers, and certain other specialized activities where special skills or talents are important would personal service be contemplated.

Statutory Assignments

By the middle of the nineteenth century, the need for a more streamlined method of transferring contractual rights (other than novation, vicarious performance, and equitable assignments) became apparent. Business frequently assigned contractual rights, but when difficulties arose, the practice of the courts of equity to require all parties to be present often proved inconvenient. This was particularly so if the assignor had made a complete assignment of all rights to the assignee, and the dispute concerned only those events that transpired after the assignment had been made. To eliminate these difficulties, the law was altered by an English statute in 1873[8] to give the assignee of a chose in action a right to institute legal proceedings in the assignee's own name if the assignee could satisfy four conditions:

(1) the assignment was in writing and signed by the assignor,
(2) the assignment was absolute,
(3) express notice of the assignment was given in writing to the party charged, the title of the assignee taking effect from the date of the notice, and

---

8. The Supreme Court of Judicature Act, 36 & 37 Vict., c. 66, s. 25(6). Similar legislation was passed in most common law provinces of Canada.

(4) the title of the assignee was taken subject to any equities between the original parties to the contract.[9]

Essentially, the change in the law did nothing more than permit the assignee to bring an action in the assignee's own name to enforce a contractual right that had been assigned absolutely, and to provide the form in which notice of the assignment should take. In effect, however, it enormously increased the efficiency by which assignments could be made. In all other respects, the rights and duties of the parties remained much the same as those for equitable assignments that the courts of equity had enforced before the statutory change.

The statutory requirement of written notice of the assignment was a beneficial change in procedure. In the past, the notice for equitable assignments could be either written or oral. Indeed, in many cases where the debtor was illiterate, the creditor saw no need to prepare a written notice, only to be obliged to explain it to the debtor on delivery. The alteration, however, reflected the changes that had taken place in society and the relative rarity of illiteracy, particularly in the business community, by the end of the century. It also had the added advantage of fixing the time at which the title in the assignee is established as far as enforcement of the debt is concerned. Until the written notice is received by the debtor, any payment could properly be made to the creditor. If the assignee was tardy in delivering the notice of the assignment, the payment of the debt to the original creditor would discharge the debtor. The assignee would then be obliged to recover the money from the assignor. Conversely, any payment made to the original creditor after the debtor received notice of the assignment would be at the debtor's risk, for the assignee would be entitled to payment of the full amount owing from the time the notice was given. If the debtor failed to heed the notice, the debtor could conceivably be obliged to pay the amount over again to the assignee, if he was unable to recover it from the original creditor.

In the event that a creditor has assigned the same debt to two different assignees, by either accident or design, the assignee first giving notice to the debtor would be entitled to payment, provided that he or she had no notice of any prior assignment. Thus, if the first assignee delays giving notice to the debtor, and the second assignee of the same debt gives notice to the debtor without knowledge of the prior assignment, and is paid by the debtor, the debtor is discharged from any obligation to pay the first assignee.

Some risk is involved from the assignee's point of view when an assignment takes place, because the assignee takes the contract as it stands between the parties at the time of the assignment. While the assignee can usually obtain some assurance as to the amount owing on the debt, the risk that the debtor-promisor may have some defence to payment, or some **set-off**, is always present. The assignee gets the same title that the assignor had. If the assignor obtained the title or rights by fraud, undue influence, duress, or some other improper means, the debtor may raise this as a defence to any claim for payment. While the assignee would not be liable in tort for any deceit, the defence would allow the debtor to avoid payment, as the contract would be voidable against both the assignor and assignee. The same rule would also apply if the assignor became indebted to the

---

9. See, for example, Conveyancing and Law of Property Act, R.S.O. 1990, c. C-34, s. 54(1).

debtor on a related or unrelated matter before the notice of the assignment was made. The debtor, in such circumstances, would be entitled to deduct the assignor's debt from the amount owing by way of set-off. He or she would be obliged to pay the assignee only the difference between the two debts. If the assignor's obligation was greater than the amount of the debt assigned, then the assignee would be entitled to no payment at all. He or she would not, however, be liable to the debtor for the assignor's indebtedness.

Assignments by Law

In addition to the provision made for the assignment of ordinary contractual rights by which the parties must prepare a document in writing and give notice, there are a number of other statutory assignments that come into effect on the death or bankruptcy of an individual. Certain other statutory rights also come into play in some cases where a person is incapable of managing his or her own affairs. Under all of these circumstances, some other person assumes all of the contractual rights and obligations of the individual, except for those requiring personal performance. For example, when a person dies, all of the assets of the deceased, and all contractual rights and obligations by operation of law, are assigned to the executor named in the deceased's will or to the administrator appointed if the person should die intestate. Similarly, when a person makes a voluntary assignment in bankruptcy or is adjudged bankrupt, a trustee is appointed. The trustee acquires an assignment of all contractual rights of the bankrupt for the purpose of preservation and distribution of the assets to the creditors. The rights and duties of both the executor and trustee are governed by statute, as are the rights and duties of persons similar appointed under other legislation to handle the affairs of incapacitated persons or corporations.[10]

Negotiable Instruments

The assignment of contractual rights must be distinguished from the assignment of negotiable instruments, such as promissory notes and cheques. Negotiable instruments are subject to special legislation called the Bills of Exchange Act that governs the rights of the parties and assignees. Assignments under the Bills of Exchange Act are examined in some detail in Chapter 25 of this text. However, for the purpose of assignments generally it is important to note that these instruments are subject to a different set of assignment rules.

SUMMARY

The general common law rule with respect to contractual rights and liabilities states that no person may acquire rights or liability under a contract to which he or she is not a party. By novation, a party may replace another in a contract and become bound if all parties consent. The contract, however, is a new agreement and the replaced party no longer has rights or liability under the agreement. In some cases, parties may acquire rights if they are in a position to establish that a

---

10. For example, the public trustee in the case of a person committed to a mental institution.

constructive trust for their benefit was created by a contract. Apart from these exceptions, the common law rule applies to all contracts, unless of course, a statute specifically provides a right to a third party.

Rights under a contract may also be performed by another under vicarious performance, unless the contract calls for personal performance. At law, rights may be assigned either by an equitable assignment or by a statutory assignment. In each case, notice of the assignment must be given to the promisor before the assignment is effective. Even then, the assignee receives only as good a title to the right as the assignor had. Any defence that the promisor or debtor is entitled to raise to resist or avoid a payment demand by the assignor may be raised against the assignee.

Where parties are no longer capable of dealing with their own affairs, due to death, incapacity, or bankruptcy, statute laws assign their contract rights to others to manage.

DISCUSSION QUESTIONS

1. Explain the importance of the privity of contract rule in contract law.
2. What are the major exceptions to the privity of contract rule? Why are these exceptions necessary?
3. Define novation and explain its role in the assignment of contractual rights.
4. How is an equitable assignment of a contract made?
5. Discuss vicarious performance as an exception to the assignment of contractual rights. Why is this the case?
6. Explain the requirements that must be met in order to make a proper statutory assignment of contractual rights.
7. What risk does an assignee take when a contract assignment is made?
8. Indicate the rights and duties of a debtor when notice of assignment of the debt is received.
9. Under what circumstances would a debtor be entitled to "set-off" a debt against a claim for payment that the debtor has against another debtor?
10. Must a person always consent to a statutory assignment before it is effective?

MINI-CASE PROBLEMS

1. C, a contractor, enters into a contract with D to construct a house for him. C engages E, a plumber, to install the plumbing in the house. If E installs the plumbing negligently, what are D's rights?
2. X owes Y $500. Some time later, X sells Y her canoe for $200, but Y makes no payment for it. Y assigns the $500 debt that X owes him to Z. Notice is given by Z to X that Z is now the assignee of the debt, and Z is to be paid the $500. What are X's rights? What are Z's rights?

JUDICIAL DECISION

The judicial decision in this chapter deals with the right of the parties to a contract to impose the terms of the contract on a third party who is not a party to the agreement. The judge in this case notes that parties may confer a right on a third party by way of a trust, but no trust is created by the contract. The judge concludes that some consideration must be presented in the contract if the parties wish to hold the third party, Messrs. Dew, to the terms of their agreement. The judge concludes that no consideration is present in the contract, and consequently, they cannot enforce the agreement against the third party.

**Contracts —
Third Parties —
Enforcement of
Rights**

Dunlop Pneumatic Tyre Co. Ltd. v. Selfridge & Co., Ltd., [1915] A.C. 847.

An agreement between the manufacturer and the purchaser of tires included a term that stipulated that the purchaser must resell the tires at not less than a set price. The tires were resold to a second purchaser, Dew. Dew resold the tires at less than the stipulated price. The plaintiff took action for breach of agreement.

VISCOUNT HALDANE, L.C.:

My Lords, in the law of England certain principles are fundamental. One is that only a person who is a party to a contract can sue on it. Our law knows nothing of a jus quaesitum tertio arising by way of contract. Such a right may be conferred by way of property, as, for example, under a trust, but it cannot be conferred on a stranger to a contract as a right to enforce the contract in personam. A second principle is that if a person with whom a contract not under seal has been made is to be able to enforce it, consideration must have been given by him to the promisor or to some other person at the promisor's request. These two principles are not recognized in the same fashion by the jurisprudence of certain Continental countries or of Scotland, but here they are well established. A third proposition is that a principal not named in the contract may sue upon it if the promisee really contracted as his agent. But again, in order to entitle him so to sue, he must have given consideration either personally or through the promisee, acting as his agent in giving it.

My Lords, in the case before us, I am of opinion that the consideration, the allowance of what was in reality part of the discount to which Messrs. Dew, the promisees, were entitled as between themselves and the appellants, was to be given by Messrs. Dew on their own account, and was not in substance, any more than in form, an allowance made by the appellants. The case for the appellants is that they permitted and enabled Messrs. Dew, with the knowledge and by the desire of the respondents, to sell to the latter on the terms of the contract of January 2, 1912. But it appears to me that even if this is so the answer is conclusive. Messrs. Dew sold to the respondents goods which they had a title to obtain from the appellants independently of this contract. The consideration by way of discount under the contract of January 2 was to come wholly out of Messrs. Dew's pocket, and neither directly nor indirectly out of that of the appellants. If the appellants enabled them to sell to the respondents on the terms they did, this was not done as any part of the terms of the contract sued on.

No doubt it was provided as part of these terms that the appellants should acquire certain rights, but these rights appear on the face of the contract as jura quaesita tertio, which the appellants could not enforce. Moreover, even if this difficulty can be got over by regarding the appellants as the principals of Messrs. Dew in stipulating for the rights in question, the only consideration disclosed by the contract is one given by Messrs. Dew, not as their agents, but as principals acting on their own account.

The conclusion to which I have come on the point as to consideration renders it unnecessary to decide the further question as to whether the appellants can claim that a bargain was made in this contract by Messrs. Dew as their agents; a bargain which, apart from the point as to consideration, they could therefore enforce. If it were necessary to express an opinion on this further question, a difficulty as to the position of Messrs. Dew would have to be considered. Two contracts — one by a man on his own account as principal, and another by the same man as agent — may be validly comprised in the same piece of paper. But they must be two contracts, and not one as here. I do not think that a man can treat one and the same contract as made by him in two capacities. He cannot be regarded as contracting for himself and for another uno flatu.

My Lords, the form of the contract which we have to interpret leaves the appellants in this dilemma, that, if they say that Messrs. Dew contracted on their behalf, they gave no consideration, and if they say they gave consideration in the shape of a permission to the respondents to buy, they must set up further stipulations, which are neither to be found in the contract sued upon nor are germane to it, but are really inconsistent with its structure. That contract has been reduced to writing, and it is in the writing that we must look for the whole of the terms made between the parties. These terms cannot, in my opinion consistently with the settled principles of English law, be construed as giving to the appellants any enforceable rights as against the respondents.

CASE PROBLEMS FOR DISCUSSION

Case 1

Adams was a naturalist who made a wildlife film that he hoped to use in conjunction with lectures to be given to conservation and hiking groups throughout the country. He engaged Basso, a well-known musician in his community, to prepare the musical background for the film. Adams paid Basso $1000 for his work. However, unknown to Adams, Basso had given the work to another musician, Smith, and paid him $500 for his efforts.

Adams used the film on one of his lecture tours, and the newspaper reviews without exception declared the film to be the highlight of his performance. Many of the reporters commented favourably about the beautiful musical background to the film.

Some months later, while on a second lecture tour, a musician in the audience recognized Smith's musical style. He mentioned to Adams how much he enjoyed listening to the musical accompaniment that the musician had provided. Adams was annoyed when he discovered that the background music had not been played by Basso, but by another. On his return home, he confronted Basso with the evidence. Basso admitted that he had been too busy to do the musical background.

Discuss the outcome of the case if Adams should decide to take legal action against Basso.

Case 2

Personalized Performance Garage advertised "personalized service" for its customers. A large sign at the front of the garage depicted the owner of the establishment placing a check mark in a box on a work order that read "personally inspected and repaired by a certified A-1 Mechanic."

Smith was impressed with the advertisement and the prospect of obtaining careful repair of her expensive automobile. She delivered the automobile for a minor engine adjustment, and inquired if the owner did provide personal service. In response to her question, the owner replied, "I look at every one."

Smith left the car at the garage and returned home. About an hour later, she received a telephone call from the garage owner who informed her that he had fixed the engine, but the automobile had a leak in its radiator. Smith requested that the leak be repaired as well.

Some time later, Smith went to the garage and was informed that the car was "ready." She paid her account and drove away in the automobile. A few blocks away the vehicle broke down, because the radiator had not been filled with coolant after it had been repaired.

The garage refused to repair the damage. They informed Smith that the radiator had been repaired by another repair shop that specialized in radiator repairs. It was apparently not a custom of the trade for ordinary mechanics to repair radiators in view of the special skill and equipment involved.

Discuss the rights of the parties in this case.

Case 3

Sly operated a used-car business. He sold Fox an automobile that he indicated was in good condition and suitable for use by Fox as a taxi. In the course of this discussion, Sly stated that, in his opinion, the vehicle was "hardly broken in" as the odometer registered only 26 000 km.

Sly suggested that Fox test drive the car to satisfy himself as to its condition. Fox did so and, on his return from a short drive, agreed to purchase the automobile for $5000. Fox signed a purchase agreement whereby he would pay for the car by monthly installments over a three-year period.

On the completion of the transaction, Sly immediately sold the purchase agreement to the Neighbourhood Finance Company for $4500. Fox was duly notified in writing of the assignment.

A week later, the automobile broke down. When the vehicle was examined by a mechanic, Fox was informed that most of the running gear and the engine were virtually worn out. Unknown to both Sly and Fox, the previous owner had driven the automobile 226 000 km and the odometer, which registered only six digits (including tenths of kilometres), was now counting the third time over.

When Fox discovered the condition of the automobile, he refused to make payments to the finance company.

Discuss the rights of the parties in this transaction.

Case 4

White sold his snowmobile to Brown for $1000. Under their agreement Brown was to pay White $100 per month over a 10-month period, commencing on March 1st of that year. Before the first payment was due, White, became indebted to Brown for $500. White then assigned the $1000 debt agreement to Black. Notice of this assignment was given to Brown. When he discovered that he was to make all payments under the agreement to Black, he informed Black that he would not make a payment until August. He would then make only the five remaining payments under the agreement and consider the debt fully satisfied.

Discuss the rights of Brown and Black, and the reasoning behind Brown's response to the notice.

Case 5

Riggs owned a yacht named *The Satanita* and wished to enter it in an 80 km race that had been arranged by a yacht club to which he belonged.

The entry form that Riggs signed contained a clause stating that while sailing in the race he agreed to be bound by the sailing rules of the racing association and by all the rules and by-laws of the club to which he belonged.

Some time before, the racing association had published a series of rules that were attached to the entry form. One of the rules provided: "If a yacht should by negligence damage another yacht, the yacht owner shall forfeit any prize and pay for the damage caused to the other yacht."

During the race, Riggs carelessly sailed *The Satanita* into the side of another yacht and caused it to sink. He later refused to pay for the damage caused.

The owner of the other vessel brought an action against Riggs for the value of the lost yacht. His claim was based on the agreement attached to the entry form that provided that Riggs must pay for the damage.

Assess the plaintiff's claim and indicate the arguments that Riggs might raise in his defence. Render a decision.

What alternate action would be open to the owner of the sunken yacht?

Case 6

On August 4th, ABC Company entered into an agreement with R A Company. By this agreement R A Company would assign to ABC Company its right to payment under a contract it had with XYZ Company. This would settle its indebtedness for certain services rendered by ABC Company.

Under the terms of the contract between XYZ Company and R A Company, XYZ Company was obliged to make monthly payments in the amount of $5000 over a three-year term. Johnson, a trustee, would collect the payments and forward them to R A Company. R A Company assigned the right to these payments to ABC Company on August 4th. On the same day they gave written notice to Johnson that, as trustee, he was to make all future payments to ABC Company.

On August 10th, R A Company gave a general assignment of its accounts receivable to its bank as security for a loan. The bank notified XYZ Company in writing on December 27th that it held a general assignment of the accounts receivable of R A Company, and that all future payments of the company should be made to the bank. Included with the notice was a written request from R A Company for payment in full to the bank if XYZ Company could possibly manage it, even though the contract only called for monthly payments.

When XYZ Company received the notice, the president of the company contacted R A Company by telephone, and asked if payment should not be made to Johnson, rather than to the bank. The response of R A Company was: "Pay the bank." On this advice, XYZ Company paid the balance of the money to the bank.

A month later, when no payment had been received, Johnson contacted XYZ Company and was informed that the money had been paid to the bank. He immediately notified ABC Company of the fact. ABC Company then instituted legal proceedings against XYZ Company for payment under the contract.

Discuss the legal issues raised in this case and the respective arguments of the parties. Render a decision.

Case 7

Black wished to purchase Green's farm. After lengthy negotiation, the two parties drew up and signed an agreement of purchase and sale for the farm with the assistance of and in the presence of Green's real estate agent, Simms. The agreement that the parties signed was a standard, preprinted form used by all local real estate agents that contained a clause which was an irrevocable direction by the vendor of the land, Green, to the purchaser, Black, to deduct from the sale price and pay the real estate agent's commission directly to Simms, on the closing day of the transaction. The preprinted form had printed on it a black circle which looked like a seal and had the word "Seal" written under it. Also, above the line for Green's signature were printed the words "In witness whereof I have hereunto set my hand and seal." Beside Green's signature line was a place for a witness to sign the agreement. Immediately above this place appeared the preprinted words "Signed, sealed and delivered in the presence of." Green and Black each had lawyers looking after the details of the transaction and each gave a copy of the agreement to their respective lawyers. Shortly before the closing of the sale, Green's lawyer prepared some final paperwork and had Green sign several important documents. Among them was a direction to Black and Black's lawyer to make the cheque for the full amount of the purchase price payable to Green. On closing, Black's lawyer presented to Green's lawyer a cheque made payable to Green for the full purchase price of the farm. Green's lawyer later turned over the cheque to Green.

After the closing, Simms contacted Green to request delivery of his commission cheque. Green replied that neither he nor his lawyer had received a cheque for Simms from Black's lawyer on closing and suggested that Simms contact Black himself since that was the arrangement. When Simms called Black, Black stated that as far as he was concerned he had paid for the farm and didn't owe anyone any more money.

Discuss the legal issues raised here and the respective arguments, rights, and liabilities of the parties. Render a decision.

CHAPTER 13

Performance of Contractual Obligations

**THE NATURE
AND EXTENT OF
PERFORMANCE**

A contract that contains all of the essential requirements for a binding agreement, and that does not contain an element enabling a party to avoid the agreement, must be performed by the parties in accordance with its terms. Performance must always be exact and precise in order to constitute a discharge of a contractual obligation. Anything less than complete compliance with the promise would render the party in default liable for **breach** of the contract. For example, a party entered into a contract to supply a quantity of canned fruit packed 30 cans to the case and, on delivery, supplied some of the goods in cases containing 24 cans. The failure to supply the goods in the correct size of case entitled the buyer to reject the goods, even though the total number of cans was correct.[1]

If the performance of the promises of the parties is complete, the contract is said to be **discharged.** If, however, one of the parties does not fully perform the promise made, then the agreement remains in effect until the promise is fulfilled or the agreement is discharged in some other way. Whether the performance is complete or not must be determined by comparing the promise made, with the act performed. The act of offering to perform the promise is called **tender of performance** and may take one of two general forms: **tender of payment** or **tender of performance of an act.**

---

1. *Re An Arbitration Between Moore & Co. Ltd. and Landauer & Co.,* [1921] 2 K.B. 519.

Tender of Payment

If a promisor simply agrees to purchase goods from a seller, performance would be made when payment is offered to the seller at the required time and place fixed for delivery under the contract. The sum of money offered in payment at that time must be in accordance with the terms of the agreement. If the form of payment is not specified, then currency, which is known as **legal tender**, must be offered to the seller. Legal tender may not be refused when offered in payment providing that it is the exact amount. Unless specified in the agreement, a personal cheque, credit card, bill of exchange, or other form of payment may be rejected by the seller. This would constitute a failure to perform by the buyer. For this reason, buyers will often include in a purchase agreement that payment may be by personal cheque or some other form of payment in lieu of legal tender.

The importance of the rule for tender was underscored by the court in the case of *Blanco v. Nugent*,[2] where the plaintiff made a tender conditional upon the defendant executing a transfer of certain property to the plaintiff. The court rejected the plaintiff's action and noted the requirements for a valid tender in the following words:

> In order to support a plea of tender, there must be evidence of an offer of the specific sum, unqualified by any circumstance whatever: *Brady v. Jones* (1823), 2 Dow & Ry KB 305. The condition here sought to be imposed — that the defendant execute a transfer to the plaintiff — is entirely unwarranted and vitiates the tender.

And at p. 387:

> The tender was bad for the further reason that Mr. McFadden did not tender the exact amount payable, but tendered a larger amount and asked for change. The amount tendered ought to be the precise amount that is due. If the debtor tenders a larger amount and ... requires change it is not a good tender.

In the case of a debt owing, once the debtor tenders payment to the creditor in the proper amount of legal tender at the required time and place, the tender of payment is complete. If the creditor is unwilling to accept payment, the debtor need not attempt payment again. Once a proper tender of payment is made, interest ceases to run on the debt. While the debtor is not free of the obligation to pay, the debtor need only hold the amount of the debt until the creditor later demands payment, then pay over the money. If he or she should be sued by the creditor, or if the creditor attempts to seize an asset of the debtor, the debtor may prove the prior tender and pay the money into court. The courts, in such circumstances, will normally penalize the creditor with costs for causing the unnecessary litigation or action.

Where the contract concerns the purchase and sale of land, the purchaser, on the date fixed for closing the transaction, has an obligation to seek out the seller and offer payment of the full amount in accordance with the terms of the contract. Once this is done, any refusal to deliver up the deed to the land would probably entitle the purchaser to bring an action in court for **specific performance**. By this action, if the purchaser can satisfy the court that he or she was ready and willing to close the transaction and was prepared to pay the required funds, the purchaser may obtain an order from the court ordering the seller to deliver up the land.

_____

2. *Blanco v. Nugent*, [1949] 1 W.W.R. 721.

Tender of Performance

The seller's performance is not by tender of money, but by the tender of an act. For the sale of goods, the seller must be prepared to deliver the goods to the buyer at the appointed time and place, and in accordance with the specifications set out in the agreement. If the buyer refuses to accept the goods when the tender is made, the seller need not tender the goods again. He or she may simply institute legal proceedings against the buyer for breach of the contract. If the contract concerns land, the equitable remedy of specific performance may be available to the seller.

The remedy of specific performance is a discretionary remedy. To obtain this relief, the seller must show that he or she was prepared to deliver the title documents for the property to the purchaser as required under the agreement. It must also be shown that on the closing date the seller attempted to transfer the deed, but the purchaser was unwilling to accept it. Unless the purchaser had a lawful or legitimate reason to refuse the tender of performance by the seller, the courts may order the payment of the funds by the purchaser and require the purchaser to accept the property. In this respect, the tender of performance of a seller of land differs from the seller of goods. Apart from this difference, the tender itself remains the same. The seller must do everything required in accordance with the promise made, if the seller wishes to succeed against the purchaser for breach of contract.

A variation of this situation arose in a case[3] where a company agreed to sell to the defendant the entire quantity of a specific type of scrap metal that the company produced at its manufacturing plant during a one-year period. Later the defendant refused to perform the agreement. The plaintiff argued that the agreement constituted a contract, but the defendant submitted that the agreement was only an agreement to sell, and not an agreement on the defendant's part to buy. The court dismissed the defendant's argument with the words:

> The case appears to me clearly to fall within the class referred to by Cockburn, C.J., in *Churchward v. The Queen* (1865), L.R. 1 Q.B. 173, at p. 195: "Although a contract may appear on the face of it to bind and be obligatory only upon one party, yet there are occasions on which you must imply — although the contract may be silent — corresponding and correlative obligations on the part of the other party in whose favour alone the contract may appear to be drawn up. Where the act done by the party binding himself can only be done upon something of a corresponding character being done by the opposite party, you would there imply a corresponding obligation to do the things necessary for the completion of the contract ... If A covenants or engages by contract to buy an estate of B, at a given price, although that contract may be silent as to any obligation on the part of B to sell, yet as A cannot buy without B selling, the law will imply a corresponding obligation on the part of B to sell: *Pordage v. Cole* (1607), 1 Wm. Saund. 319 i (85 E.R. 449).

A contract may, of course, involve performance in the form of something other than the delivery of goods or the delivery of possession of land. It might, for example, require a party to carry out some work or service. In this case, the other contracting party must permit the party tendering performance to do the required work. Any interference with the party tendering performance of the act might entitle that party to treat the interference as a breach of contract.

---

3. *Canada Cycle & Motor Co. Ltd. v. Mehr* (1919), 48 D.L.R. 579.

DISCHARGE BY MEANS OTHER THAN PERFORMANCE

Contracts may be discharged in a number of other ways in addition to performance. The law itself, under certain circumstances, may operate to terminate a contract, or the parties themselves may agree to end the contract before it is fully performed. Often, the parties may specifically provide in the agreement that the contract may be terminated at any time on notice, or on the happening of a subsequent event. The contract may also provide that the contract does not operate unless some condition precedent occurs. In addition, the parties may, by mutual agreement, decide to terminate the contract and replace it with a revised agreement, or simply decide before either has fully performed that the contract should be discharged.

Many other methods of discharge may also be possible. The parties could replace the existing agreement with a substituted agreement. This can be done either by a material alteration of the terms, or by accord and satisfaction. (The latter is a means by which one party offers different goods in satisfaction of a promise made under the agreement, and the buyer is prepared to accept the different goods as a substitute for the goods originally requested.) Each of these, in turn, has a different effect on the obligation of the parties to perform their specific promises in the agreement.

Termination as a Right

An **option to terminate** is a method of discharging an agreement that is usually effected by either party giving notice to the other. The option frequently has a time-limit attached to the notice. At the expiry of the notice period, the agreement comes to an end. Agreements that contain a notice or option to terminate often provide for some means of compensating the party who has partly performed at the time the notice is given, but this is not always the case.

The right to terminate, if exercised in accordance with the specific terms of the agreement, may entitle a party to terminate the agreement without liability for any loss suffered by the other. For example, Arnold and Brown enter into a contract whereby Brown agrees to sell Arnold a new automobile. As part of the contract, Arnold reserves the right to cancel the agreement, without incurring liability, **on notice** to Brown at any time before Brown has the car ready for delivery. After Brown receives the automobile from the factory, but before he services it in preparation for delivery, Arnold notifies Brown of his intention to cancel the order. In this instance, Arnold would not be obliged to purchase the car — under the terms of the contract, the notice would have the effect of terminating the agreement, and Arnold would be free of any liability under it. Brown, who had assumed the risk of Arnold's cancellation, would have no rights against Arnold, but he would also no longer be liable to deliver an automobile to Arnold.

External Events

Express Terms

If a contract is discharged upon the occurrence of a particular event, the circumstance that gives rise to the termination is called a **condition subsequent.** It is not uncommon to make provision in contracts of a long-term or important nature for events that might arise to prevent the performance of the agreement by one party or both. These are sometimes referred to as *force majeure* clauses. They may either specifically or generally set out the circumstances under which the contract may be terminated. (In Roman law, the term is interpreted to mean a major force in the nature of an act of God.) *Force majeure* usually indicates an unforeseen and overpowering force affecting the ability of a party to perform the contract (such as war, insurrection, natural disasters, etc.); although the parties may indicate in their contract that the interference need not be that serious to constitute discharge. Since the parties making the contract are free to insert whatever clauses they are prepared to mutually agree upon, either or both of the parties may set out a large number of circumstances that, if any one should occur, would discharge the agreement.

Implied Terms

In certain fields, conditions subsequent are sometimes implied in contracts by the courts from customs of the trade. For example, common carriers, who are normally liable for any ordinary loss or damage to goods carried, may be exempted from liability if the loss is due to an **act of God** or some other event that could not have been prevented by the carrier.[4] Partial destruction of the goods would not discharge the carrier from its obligation to deliver, however, but the carrier would not be liable for the damage caused by the act of God. If the goods are inherently dangerous and self-destruct while in the possession of the carrier, the carrier would also be absolved from any liability. Indeed, if dangerous goods were deliberately mislabelled by the shipper, the carrier might have a right of action against the shipper for any damage caused by the goods. Rather than relying on implied terms, most carriers take the added precaution of making the terms express by including them on their bills of lading.

Implied Terms and the Doctrine of Frustration

Where performance is rendered impossible due to circumstances not contemplated by the parties at the time the agreement was entered into, and through no fault of their own, the agreement may be said to be **frustrated** and thereby discharged. This particular doctrine has been applied to a number of different situations, the simplest being one where the agreement could not be performed because of the destruction of something essential to the performance of the contract. For example, Allen, a theatre owner, enters into a contract with Black to provide the premises for a concert that Black wishes to perform. Before the date of the concert, the theatre burns to the ground. Allen, as a result of the fire, is unable to perform her part of the contract through no fault of her own. In this case, the courts would assume that the contract was subject to an implied term that the parties would be excused from performance if an essential part of the subject-matter should be destroyed without fault on the part of either party.[5]

Where the contract involves the sale of goods, the Sale of Goods Act in most provinces provides that the destruction of specific goods (through no fault of either the buyer or seller) before the title to the goods passes to the buyer will void the contract. This particular section of the act represents a codification of the

---

4. See, for example, *Nugent v. Smith* (1875), 1 C.P.D. 423.

5. *Taylor v. Caldwell* (1863), 3 B. & S. 826, 122 E.R. 309.

doctrine of implied term with respect to the sale of goods. It would apply in most cases where specific goods are destroyed before the title to the goods passes to the buyer.

The **doctrine of frustration** is also applicable in cases where the personal services of one of the parties is required under the terms of the agreement, but through death or illness, the party required to provide the personal service is unable to do so. For example, Albert enters into a contract with Roberts, whereby Roberts agrees to perform at Albert's theatre on a particular date. On the day before the performance, Roberts falls ill with a severe case of influenza and is unable to perform. In this case, the courts would include as an implied term the continued good health of the party required to personally perform. The occurrence of the illness has the effect of discharging both of the parties from the contract.[6]

A third and somewhat different application of the doctrine may apply in cases where the event that occurs so alters the circumstances under which the agreement is to be performed that performance will be virtually impossible for a promisor. Many of these cases arose during the First and Second World Wars, where goods were diverted for war purposes. In these cases the hostilities were not contemplated by the parties. Therefore, to impose the contract after hostilities ceased would, in effect, be imposing an entirely different agreement on the parties.[7]

Although less common, the doctrine may also apply to cases where the performance of the agreement is based upon the continued existence of a particular state of affairs. However, the state of affairs changes to prevent the performance of the agreement. For example, Adams Construction Co. enters into a contract with Bullock to erect a particular type of building on lands owned by Bullock. Before a building permit can be obtained, the zoning of the land is changed to prevent the construction of the type of building contemplated by the parties. In this case, the actions of the municipality, over which the parties have no control, render performance impossible. As a result, the courts would probably find that the contract had been frustrated.

While the courts may be prepared to find that a contract has been frustrated as a result of unforeseen circumstances, they will not relieve a party from performing simply because performance turned out to be more onerous or expensive than expected at the time the agreement was made. Nor will they provide relief in cases where the performance has been rendered impossible by the deliberate act of a promisor in an effort to avoid the agreement. For example, Baxter Co. enters into an agreement with the local municipality whereby it agrees to spray the road allowances alongside all rural roads with a particular herbicide to control the growth of weeds. The company later discovers that the herbicide costs twice the price that it contemplated at the time that it made the agreement. As a result it can only perform its part of the agreement at a loss. The company then sells its spraying equipment and claims that it cannot perform the contract. Under the circumstances, the Baxter Co. would be liable to the municipality for breach of contract, as the courts would not allow the company to avoid the contract on the basis of self-induced frustration.

---

6. *Robinson v. Davidson* (1871), L.R. 6 Ex. 269.

7. *Morgan v. Manser,* [1948] 1 K.B. 184.

When an event occurs that renders performance impossible, or changes the conditions under which the contract was to be performed to such an extent that the parties would have provided in the contract for its discharge in such circumstances, the courts will treat the agreement as frustrated and relieve both parties from any further performance after the frustrating event occurs. The frustrating event in the eyes of the courts would have the effect of bringing the contract to an end automatically. This was a reasonable conclusion for the courts to reach, but in some of the early cases the rule worked a hardship on one of the parties.

Initially, the courts let the loss fall on the parties as at the time the event occurred. If rights had accrued to a party at the time of the event, they could still be enforced.[8] This was later modified to provide that if the contract was wholly executory by one party, and if the other party had paid money under the agreement, but received no benefit for it, the money could be recovered on the basis that no consideration had been received for the payment.[9]

In the case of *Cahan v. Fraser*[10] the court described the impact of frustration at common law on a contract:

> The rights of the parties fall to be determined at the moment when impossibility of further performance supervened, that is, at the moment of dissolution ... The effect of frustration is that while the parties are relieved from any further performance under it, it remains a perfectly good contract up to that point, and everything previously done in pursuance of it must be treated as rightly done.
>
> The same event which automatically renders performance of the consideration for the payment impossible not only terminates the contract as to the future, but terminate the right of the payee to retain the money which he has received only on the terms of the contract performance....
>
> The payment for the option in *Goulding's case*, [1927] 3 D.L.R. 820, was an "out and out" payment, that is, there was no provision for its return or for its application on the purchase-price if the option were exercised. An "out and out" payment cannot be recovered in the event of frustration...
>
> In the case at bar the sums paid were not "out and out" but were to be applied on to the purchase-price; the payment was originally conditional. The condition of retaining it was eventual performance. Accordingly, when that condition failed, the right to retain the money must simultaneously fail....

The unsatisfactory state of the common law prompted the English Parliament to pass a Frustrated Contracts Act in 1943.[11] This legislation permits a court to apportion the loss somewhat more equitably. This is done by providing for the recovery of deposits and/or advances and the retention of part of the funds to cover expenses, where a party has only partly performed the contract at the time the frustrating event occurs. The legislation also permitted a claim for compensation where one party, by partly performing the contract, had conferred a benefit on the other party.

However, a party who has received no benefit and paid no deposit under the contract will not be obliged to compensate the other party to the contract for any

---

8. *Chandler v. Webster*, [1904] 1 K.B. 493.

9. *Fibrosa Spolka Akcyjna v. Fairbairn Lawson Combe Barbour, Ltd.*, [1943] A.C. 32.

10. *Cahan v. Fraser*, [1951] 4 D.L.R. 112.

11. Law Reform (Frustrated Contracts) Act, 1943, 6 & 7 Geo. VI, c. 40.

work done prior to the frustrating event. Under these circumstances the act does not protect the party who undertakes to perform or must perform a contract without the benefit of a deposit.

Seven provinces, Alberta,[12] Manitoba,[13] New Brunswick,[14] Newfoundland,[15] Ontario,[16] British Columbia,[17] and Prince Edward Island,[18] subsequently passed legislation somewhat similar to the English Act. The remainder of the provinces remain subject to the common law. This legislation, however, does not apply to an agreement for the sale of specific goods under the Sale of Goods Act, where the goods have perished without fault on the part of the seller (or buyer) and before the risk passes to the purchaser. Nor does it apply to certain types of contracts such as insurance contracts, or those contracts that are expressly excluded by the act.[19]

Condition Precedent

The parties may also provide in their agreement that the contract does not come into effect until certain conditions are met or events occur. These conditions, if they must occur before the contract is enforceable, are called **conditions precedent.**

Often, when a condition precedent is agreed upon, the agreement is prepared and signed; only the performance is postponed pending the fulfillment of the condition. Once fulfilled, performance is necessary to effect discharge. If the condition is not met, it then has the effect of discharging both parties from performance. It may be argued that an agreement cannot exist until the condition is satisfied, in which case the agreement only then comes into effect. But regardless of the position adopted, the condition is the determining factor with respect to the termination of the agreement or the establishment of contractual rights between the parties.

The case of *Turney et al. v. Zhilka*[20] provides an example of a condition precedent in a contract. It supplies a description of how the courts apply this legal principle in a case involving the sale of land, where the sale was subject to a condition that the property could be annexed to a village and the village council would approve a plan of subdivision proposed for the parcel of land in question. The agreement provided that the transaction was to be performed (i.e., the deed given) 60 days after the plan of subdivision was approved. However, the agreement did not specify which party was to satisfy the condition. The purchaser in the case then attempted to hold the vendor liable for the non-performance. The court discussed the nature of the condition in the following terms:

---

12. Frustrated Contracts Act, R.S.A. 1980, c. F-20.
13. Frustrated Contracts Act, R.S.M. 1987, c. F-190.
14. Frustrated Contracts Act, R.S.N.B. 1973, c. F-24.
15. Frustrated Contracts Act, R.S.Nfld. 1990, c. F-26.
16. Frustrated Contracts Act, R.S.O. 1990, c. F-34.
17. Frustrated Contracts Act, R.S.B.C. 1979, c. 144.
18. Frustrated Contracts Act, R.S.P.E.I. 1988, c. F-16.
19. See, for example, the Frustrated Contracts Act, R.S.A. 1980, c. F-20, ss. 3 and 4.
20. *Turney et al. v. Zhilka*, [1959] S.C.R. 578.

The date for the completion of the sale is fixed with reference to the performance of this condition — "60 days after plans are approved". Neither party to the contract undertakes to fulfil this condition, and neither party reserves a power of waiver. The obligations under the contract, on both sides, depend upon a future uncertain event, the happening of which depends entirely on the will of a third party — the Village Council. This is a true condition precedent — an external condition upon which the existence of the obligation depends. Until the event occurs there is no right to performance on either side. The parties have not promised that it will occur. In the absence of such a promise there can be no breach of contract until the event does occur. The purchaser now seeks to make the vendor liable on his promise to convey in spite of the non-performance of the condition and this to suit his own convenience only. This is not a case of renunciation or relinquishment of a right but rather an attempt by one party, without the consent of the other, to write a new contract. Waiver has often been referred to as a troublesome and uncertain term in the law but it does at least presuppose the existence of a right to be relinquished.

Operation of Law

A contract may be discharged by the operation of law. For example, Anderson, a Canadian citizen and resident, and Black, a resident and citizen of a foreign country, enter into a partnership agreement. Shortly thereafter, hostilities break out between the two countries. The contract between Anderson and Black would be dissolved, as it would be unlawful for Anderson to have any contractual relationship with an enemy. Similarly, if Anderson and Black entered into a partnership to carry on a type of business in Canada that was subsequently declared unlawful, the agreement between Anderson and Black would be discharged.

Specific legislation also discharges certain contracting parties from contracts of indebtedness. The Bankruptcy and Insolvency Act,[21] for example, provides that an honest but unfortunate bankrupt debtor is entitled to a discharge from all debts owed to his or her creditors when the bankruptcy process is completed. The Bills of Exchange Act provides that a bill of exchange that is altered in a material way without the consent of all of the parties liable on it has the effect of discharging all parties, except the person who made the unauthorized alteration and any subsequent endorsers.[22] A holder, in due course, however, would still be entitled to enforce the bill according to its original tenor if the alteration is not apparent.[23]

The law also comes into play when a person allows a lengthy period of time to pass before attempting to enforce a breach of contract. At common law, in cases where a party fails to take action until many years later, the courts will sometimes refuse to hear the case. The reasoning here is that the undue and unnecessary delay would often render it impossible for the defendant to properly defend against the claim. Undue delay in bringing an action against a party for failure to perform at common law is known as **laches**. Under this doctrine, a court may refuse to hear a case not brought before it until many years after the right of action arose. It is important to note, however, that the doctrine only bars a right of

---

21. Bankruptcy and Insolvency Act, R.S.C. 1985, c. B-3 as amended by S.C. 1992, c. 27.

22. Bills of Exchange Act. R.S.C. 1985 c. B-4, s. 144(1).

23. Bills of Exchange Act. R.S.C. 1985 c. B-4, s. 144(2).

action; it does not void the agreement. In effect, it denies a tardy plaintiff a remedy when a defendant fails to perform.

While the doctrine of laches still remains, all of the provinces have passed legislation stating the time-limits for bringing an action before the courts following a breach of an agreement. These statutes, which are usually called Limitations Acts,[24] provide that actions not brought within the specified time-limits will be statute-barred, and the courts will not enforce the claim or provide a remedy. As with laches, the statutes do not render the contracts void — they simply deny the injured party a judicial remedy. The contract still exists, and, if liability should be acknowledged (such as by part-payment of a debt or part-performance), the contract and a right of action may be revived.

Merger may also discharge an agreement. For example, A Co. and Brown enter into an informal written agreement, whereby A Co. agrees to sell Brown a parcel of land. If the informal written agreement is later put into a formal agreement under seal and is identical to the first except as to form, then a merger of the two takes places, and the informal agreement is discharged. The delivery of a deed on the closing of a real estate transaction normally has the same effect on an agreement of purchase and sale (relating to the same parcel of land), although there are a number of exceptions to this general rule.

Agreement

Waiver

Often, the parties to an agreement may wish to voluntarily end their contractual relationship. If neither party has fully performed their duties, they may mutually agree to discharge each other by waiver. In the case of a waiver, each party agrees to abandon his or her right to insist on performance by the other. As a result, there is consideration for the promises made by each party. However, if one of the parties has fully performed the agreement, it would be necessary to have the termination agreement in writing and under seal in order for it to be enforceable. For example, Alford and Brown enter into an agreement whereby Brown agrees to drive Alford to a nearby town. Upon arrival at their destination Alford will pay Brown $10. Alford and Brown may mutually consent to terminate their agreement at any time before they reach their destination, and the mutual promises will be binding. However, as soon as they reach the destination, Brown would have fully performed his part of the contract. If Brown chose to waive his rights under the agreement after they reached their destination (after he had fully performed his part of the contract), his promise to do so would be gratuitous. He would be required to sign and seal a written promise to that effect before it would be enforceable by Alford.

Novation

The parties may also discharge an existing agreement by mutually agreeing to a change in the terms of the agreement or to a change in the parties to the agreement. Both of these changes require the consent of all parties and have the effect of replacing the original agreement with a new contract. A substituted agreement

---

24. See, for example, Limitations Act, R.S.O. 1990, c. C-15.

differs from merger in several ways. In the case of merger, the terms and the parties to the agreement remain the same — only the form of the agreement changes. The parties are simply replacing a simple agreement with a written one, or replacing a written agreement with a particular type of formal agreement dealing with the same subject-matter (e.g., replacing an agreement for the sale of land under seal with a deed for the same land). On the other hand, a substituted agreement may involve a change in the parties to the agreement, or a change of a material nature in the terms of the contract. For example, Appleby, Ballard, and Crawford enter into an agreement. Appleby later wishes to be free of the contract, and Donaldson wishes to enter the agreement and replace Appleby. This may be accomplished only with the consent of all parties. The arrangement would be a novation situation where Appleby would be discharged from her duties under the agreement with Ballard and Crawford, and the parties would establish a new contract between Ballard, Crawford, and Donaldson.

Material Alteration of Terms

A **material alteration** of the terms of an existing agreement has the effect of discharging the existing agreement and replacing it with a new one containing the material alteration. The alteration of the terms of the existing agreement must be of a significant nature before the contract will be discharged by the change. As a general rule, the change must go to the **root** of the agreement before it constitutes a material alteration. A minor alteration, or a number of minor alterations, would not normally be sufficient to create a new contract unless the overall effect of the changes completely altered the character of the agreement. For example, if a highway transportation company places an order to purchase a truck of a standard type with a truck sales dealer, then later decides to have the vehicle equipped with a radio and a special brand of tires, the changes would constitute only a variation of terms of the agreement. If, however, the transport company should decide to change its order after acceptance to a special-bodied truck of a different size and with different equipment, the changes would probably be sufficient to constitute a discharge of the first contract, and the substitution of a new one. The nature of the agreement (i.e., the purchase of a truck) would still be the same, but the subject-matter would be altered to such an extent by the changes that it would represent a new contract.

Substitute Agreement

If it is the intention of the parties to discharge an existing contract by a substitute agreement, the substitution may effect the discharge, even if it is unenforceable in itself. This situation is likely to arise where the parties enter into a written contract to comply with the Statute of Frauds, and then later agree to discharge the written agreement by a subsequent one. The statute simply requires agreements to be in writing to be enforceable, but does not require compliance with the statute to dissolve such a contract. Consequently, if the parties, by way of a subsequent mutual agreement, agree to discharge an existing contract and replace it with a verbal agreement that is rendered unenforceable by its non-compliance with the Statute of Frauds, the subsequent agreement will discharge the prior one, but will be unenforceable with respect to the remainder of its terms.[25]

---

25. See, for example, *Morris v. Baron*, [1918] A.C. 1.

Breach of Contract

The last method of discharge is by **breach of contract**. This act gives rise to a right of action by the party affected by the breach. It is the court's disposal of the action that serves as a discharge of the agreement and its replacement with a **judgement.** In addition, the breach of contract by one party in certain circumstances will have the effect of discharging the injured party from any further performance under the agreement. Discharge of a contract by breach covers a wide range of activities and remedies. It is examined in detail in the next chapter.

SUMMARY

The usual method of discharging a contract is by performance. To constitute a discharge, however, the performance must exactly match the one required under the terms of the agreement. Anything short of full and complete performance will not discharge the contract. The parties may also provide in the agreement that it may be terminated at the option of one or both of the parties, or they may provide that the agreement will automatically terminate on the occurrence of a particular event.

Where events occur that were not contemplated by the parties and that render the promises of one or both of the parties impossible to perform, the courts may treat the contract as frustrated, and exempt both parties from further performance. Specific legislation in the form of a Frustrated Contracts Act (in some provinces) attempts to equitably distribute the loss where performance is rendered impossible. In the remainder of the provinces, the common law rules apply.

Some contracts are discharged by the operation of law on the happening of particular events that are set out in the statutes or provided for at common law. In other cases, the failure to enforce rights under a contract may result in what amounts to a discharge of the agreement by the **extinguishment** of the right to enforce performance.

The parties may also, by mutual agreement, decide to discharge a contract either by waiver or by the substitution of a new agreement for the existing contract.

A final method of discharge that arises out of a breach of the contract has special consequences that are dealt with in the following chapter.

DISCUSSION QUESTIONS

1. What is meant by "performance" with respect to contract law?
2. Outline the nature of a valid tender. How does it relate to performance?
3. Describe the effect of a valid tender of payment of a debt.
4. Distinguish performance from specific performance.
5. What are the usual consequences that flow from a failure or refusal to perform a valid contract?
6. How might "custom" affect the performance of a valid contract?
7. Explain the nature and purpose of a *force majeure* clause in a contract. Illustrate your answer with an example.
8. Other than by performance, in what ways might a contract be discharged?
9. Describe the effect of a material alteration on the enforceability of a contract.
10. What are the implications at common law where an unanticipated event renders performance of a contract impossible? Has this been altered by Frustrated Contracts legislation in some provinces?

11. Distinguish between a void and a frustrated contract.
12. Does performance by one party terminate a contract?
13. Explain the effect of a condition precedent on the obligation of the parties to perform a contract subject to the condition.

MINI-CASE PROBLEMS

1. X agreed to lease her automobile to Y for the month of July in return for the payment of $300. Before the end of June, X was involved in an automobile accident and the automobile severely damaged. What are the rights and obligations of X and Y?

2. A agreed to purchase B's snow-shoes from him for $100 on the Saturday of the next week. On the required date, A went to B's home with 10 000 pennies and demanded the snow-shoes. B refused to deliver them. Discuss the rights and obligations of the two parties.

JUDICIAL DECISIONS

The *Fibrosa* judicial decision was an important case that brought to the attention of the U.K. government the need for legislation to deal with frustrated contracts. One of the difficulties with contracts that become impossible to perform due to external events concerns the common law rule that the loss as a result of the frustration will lie where it falls at the time. The judge in this case examines this rule in terms of consideration (a failure of consideration) for the benefits received. In the last paragraph he concludes that monies paid (i.e. the deposit) would be recoverable when the consideration for the payment (the delivery of the machinery) becomes impossible, as there was a total failure of consideration for the payment.

The *Farnel v. Main Outboard* case discusses the question of what constitutes performance of a contract. In the case, the contract was for "winterizing the engine" of the plaintiff's boat. Water was left in the engine block, and the block cracked as a result of the water freezing. The judge decides the case by examining the performance of the contract by the defendant. He concludes that the promise to winterize the boat was more than a promise to exercise ordinary care. It represented a promise to put the boat engine in a condition that would allow it to survive the winter. The fact that the defendant followed the normal winterizing procedure did not release that company from the responsibility to the plaintiff to prepare the boat engine in such a way that it would survive the winter.

Frustration of Contract — Failure of Consideration

Fibrosa Spolka Akcyjna v. Fairbairn Lawson Combe Barbour, Ltd., [1943] A.C. 32.

The respondents agreed to sell the appellants certain machinery before the outbreak of World War II. Partial payment was made, but before delivery of the goods, the country was occupied by the enemy and the contract could not be performed by the respondents. The appellants demanded a return of the deposit.

Lord Russell of Killowen:

My Lords, that which has been described during the argument of this case, and at other times, as "the rule in *Chandler v. Webster*" should, I think, rather be called the rule (to put it shortly) that in cases of frustration loss lies where it falls, or (at greater length) that where a contract is discharged by reason of supervening impossibility of performance payments previously made and legal rights previously accrued according to the terms of the contract will not be disturbed, but the parties will be excused from liability further to perform the contract. I say this because, as I read the judgement of the Master of the Rolls in *Chandler v. Webster,* he does not purport to be framing any new rule, or laying down any new law. He thought that the case which he was deciding was one which, on its facts, was governed by a rule already established by the authorities.... We must examine the rule as it exists in the law of England, and determine whether the appellants are entitled to be repaid the 1000£. If *Chandler v. Webster* was rightly decided, they would clearly not be so entitled.

It is to be observed that the doubt as to the correctness of the rule only arises in cases in which one of the parties to the contract has paid over to the other party the whole or part of the money payable by him as the consideration for what he is to receive as the consideration moving from the other party. If no such money has been paid the rule must apply, for I know no principle of English law which would enable either party to a contract which has been frustrated to receive from the other compensation for any expense, or indemnity from any liability, already incurred in performing the contract. Nor could moneys paid before frustration be recovered if the person making the payment has received some part of the consideration moving from the other party for which the payment was made. In such a case the rule would still apply.

But I am of opinion that this appeal should succeed because of another aspect of the matter. In the present case the appellants, before frustration, paid in advance a part of the price of the machines. We heard an elaborate argument as to what was the exact consideration moving from the respondents for that part of the contract which stipulated for payment of part of the price in advance. I am not aware of any justification for splitting up the consideration in this way, and assigning a consideration for each separate provision of a contract. Under the contract here in question the consideration moving from the respondents was either the delivery of the machines at Gdynia, or the promise to deliver the machines at Gdynia. I think that the delivery was the consideration, but in whichever way the consideration is viewed, it is clear that no part of the consideration for which part of the price of the machines was paid ever reached the appellants. There was a total failure of the consideration for which the money was paid. In those circumstances, why should the appellants not be entitled to recover back the money paid, as money had and received to their use, on the ground that it was paid for a consideration which has wholly failed? I can see no reason why the ordinary law, applicable in such a case, should not apply. In such a case the person who made the payment is entitled to recover the money paid. That is a right which in no way depends upon the continued existence of the frustrated contract. It arises from the fact that the impossibility of performance has caused a total failure of the consideration for which the money was paid. In his judgement in *Chandler v. Webster* the Master of the Rolls states that the right to recover moneys paid for a consideration which has failed only arises where the contract is "wiped out altogether," by which expression I understand him to mean is void ab initio. This is clearly a misapprehension on the part of the learned judge. The money was recoverable under the common indebitatus count, as money received for the use of the plaintiff. The right so to recover money paid for a consideration that had failed did not depend on the contract being void ab initio. There are many such cases in the books in which the contract has not been void ab initio, but the money paid for a consideration which has failed has been held recoverable. Thus, as one example, money paid as a deposit on a contract of sale which has been defeated by the fulfilment of a condition is recoverable: *Wright v. Newton.* It was submitted by the respondents, but without argument, that money paid for a consideration which had failed was recoverable only when the failure was due to the fault of the other party to the contract, but, on the authorities, this submission is clearly ill-founded. *Chandler v. Webster* was, accordingly, in my opinion, wrongly decided. The money paid was recoverable, as having been paid for a consideration which had failed. The rule that on frustration the loss lies where it falls cannot apply in respect of moneys paid in advance when the consideration moving from the payee for the payment has wholly failed, so as to deprive the payer of his right to recover moneys so paid as moneys received to his use, but, as I understand the grounds on which we are prepared to allow this appeal, the rule will (unless altered by legislation) apply in all other respects.

Farnel v. Main Outboard Centre Ltd. (1987), 50 Man. R. (2d) 13.

The plaintiff owned a boat with an inboard/outboard engine, and requested the defendant company to "winterize the engine" before the onset of cold weather. The defendant allegedly did so, but water left in the cooling system froze in the cold weather and cracked the engine block and exhaust manifold. The boat owner took legal action against the company for breach of contract and the negligent performance of the work. The trial judge dismissed the action, but the boat owner appealed the decision.

TWADDLE, J.J.A.:

[1] This appeal involves the question: What is the duty of a boat marina owner who agrees to winterize a boat engine?

[2] The plaintiff is a boat owner. In October 1984 he asked the defendant to winterize the inboard/outboard engine of his boat. The defendant did the work it thought necessary and invoiced the plaintiff for its services. Before winter's end, the boat was taken to the workshop of another company where unrelated work on the power trim unit was to be undertaken. The mechanic who was to do that work noticed that the top of the exhaust manifold and the engine block were cracked....

[11] A contract for the performance of a service often obligates the performer to do no more than exercise reasonable care in performing it. Sometimes, however, a contractor warrants more than careful performance. There may be an implied term that the product of a contractor's services will be reasonably fit for the purpose for which it is required: see *Greaves & Co. (Contractors) Ltd. v. Boynham Meikle and Partners*, [1975] 3 All E.R. 99. Alternatively, there may be expressed in the language of the contract a term which, when properly construed, imposes an obligation greater than the exercise of care. Each contract must be considered separately.

[12] A promise to winterize a boat engine is more than a promise to exercise care in doing so. It is a promise to put the engine in a condition in which it will survive the winter without damage due to water left in it. The promise is not, of course, a promise to remove water retained within the engine as a result of a defect unknown to the person engaged in the winterization. The promisor may raise the defect as a defence. If the water remained in the engine because of a defect, the existence of which could not have been detected by the promisor in the ordinary course of winterization, he will not be liable. It may be that, once

facts consistent with such a defence are proved, the onus of showing that the damage resulted from the promisor's fault will revert to the owner as a shift in the evidentiary burden, but that does not arise in this case.

[13] In the case at bar, the defendant raised only two defences. It said that it had drained all of the water from the engine and that, in any event, it had not been negligent. No explanation was offered as to how there could have been water in the engine if the defendant had performed its contract. The defendant did suggest that mud, from the river water which cooled the engine, might have accumulated within the engine causing a blockage. That may be so, but the defendant was aware of that possibility and cranked the engine over to eliminate water which might be trapped behind blockage. The finding of the learned trial judge that the cause of the engine cracking was the freezing of water within the engine can mean only one thing in the circumstances: the defendant did not drain all the water from the engine.

[14] As the defendant did not fulfill its contractual obligation, the fact that it followed the normal and proper winterizing procedure does not relieve it of liability. The absence of negligence is irrelevant....

[17] In the result, I would set aside the judgment appealed from and substitute judgment for the plaintiff in the amount of $2,552.27.

CASE PROBLEMS FOR DISCUSSION

Case 1

Taylor owned and operated a large gravel truck. He entered into a contract with Road Construction Contractors to haul gravel for them at a fixed price per load for a period of six months, commencing May 1st. On April 24th, he appeared at the construction site with his truck. When he examined the distance he would be required to haul the gravel, he realized that he had made a contract that he could only perform at a substantial loss.

He approached one of the partners of the firm with which he had contracted, and informed him that he could not perform the agreement. The partner persuaded Taylor not to be hasty in his decision, but to wait until the next day, when he could discuss the matter with the other partners. Taylor agreed to wait and left his truck in the contractor's garage overnight.

During the night, a fire at the garage destroyed Taylor's truck and some of the contractor's equipment that had also been stored in the garage.

Analyze the events that occurred in this case, and discuss the legal position of both parties.

Case 2

Hamish, an experienced painting contractor, entered into an agreement with Mr. McPhail to paint the McPhail residence both inside and out for $2200. Mrs. McPhail selected the colours, and Hamish proceeded with the work. During the time Hamish was painting the interior of the house, Mrs. McPhail constantly complained that he was either painting too slowly and interfering with her house cleaning, or painting too fast and splattering paint on the wood trim. Hamish, at no time, responded to her remarks.

By the fifth day, Hamish had painted all of the house except the eavestroughs and down-spouts. As he was climbing the ladder to begin painting the eavestroughs, Mrs. McPhail appeared and warned him not to drop paint on her prize azaleas.

At that point, Hamish turned and, without a word, climbed down from the ladder and left the premises.

The next day, he presented his account for $2200 to Mr. McPhail. When Mr. McPhail refused to make payment, Hamish instituted legal proceedings to collect the amount owing.

Discuss the nature of the claim, and indicate the defence (if any) which Mr. McPhail might raise. Render a decision.

Case 3

Potter owned a farm that had a rather odd-shaped land formation at its centre. Gill, a road contractor, suspected that the land formation might contain a quantity of gravel. He entered into a purchase agreement with Potter to purchase the farm for $280 000. On the offer to purchase Potter deleted the words "or cheque" and insisted that he be paid only in cash.

Before the date fixed for Gill and Potter to exchange the deed and money, Potter heard rumours that Gill wished to buy the farm because it contained a "fortune in gravel." Potter accused Gill of trying to steal his land by offering him only a fraction of its true worth. He instructed his lawyer not to prepare the deed. In actual fact, the $280 000 was slightly more than the value of most similar farms in the area.

On the date fixed for closing, Gill arranged with the bank for $280 000 in cash. He drove to Potter's farm with the money in a brief case. At the gate, he met Potter who refused to allow him entry. Pointing to the brief case, Gill said that he had the money and wanted the deed. Potter refused, so Gill returned to the city.

Discuss the actions of Gill and Potter in this case. Determine the rights and obligations of each if Gill should institute legal proceedings to enforce the contract. Render a decision.

Case 4

Hansen admired a sports car that Ross owned and wished to sell. Hansen informed Ross that he would buy the automobile if he could obtain a loan from the bank to cover a part of the $7000 asking price. Ross agreed to hold the car until Hansen could check with his bank.

Hansen discussed a loan with his bank manager. The manager stated that he would be prepared to make a $5000 loan, but due to the nature of the purchase, he must first get approval from the regional office. He indicated that this was usually just a formality, and he did not anticipate any difficulty in obtaining approval for the loan.

Hansen then entered into a written agreement with Ross to purchase the sports car, with payment to be made in 10 days' time. Both parties signed the agreement, and Hansen paid Ross a $100 deposit. Ross retained the sports car pending payment of the balance.

A few days later, the bank manager telephoned Hansen to say that he had encountered a problem with the loan approval. The most he could lend would be $4000. As a result of the reduction in the loan amount, Hansen found himself $1000 short of cash.

Advise Hansen of this position at law. Indicate how the case might be decided if Ross wished to enforce the agreement.

Case 5

The Metro Mallards Baseball Club was concerned about the practice of "reselling" tickets to its games by persons who would appear at the entrances of the baseball stadium just before game time and offer tickets for sale to ticketless patrons at premium prices. These persons, who are known as "scalpers," would purchase a quantity of tickets in advance of the games with the intention of selling them at a profit, a practice which the club wished to curtail. The practice was also prohibited under provincial laws.

In an effort to stop the resale of tickets (except through authorized agents) the club printed its tickets with the following terms on the back of each ticket:

> This ticket is a personal, revocable license to enter the stadium and view the game described on the front side hereof, and shall not be resold to any other person without the express consent in writing of the issuer or its authorized agents. Management shall have the right to refuse admission to the stadium to anyone in possession of this ticket on return of the stated purchase price.
>
> The issuer, on notice to the person in possession of this ticket, may revoke at any time the license represented by this ticket and recover the same without compensation if the person in possession attempts to resell the ticket.

The notice was included in very fine print on the back of each ticket, along with the usual clauses related to liability for injury and cancellation of game matters.

John Doe and Jane Doe purchased a number of tickets with the intention of reselling them at the stadium before a game. They were not aware of the change in the printed information on the back of each ticket.

At the stadium, an employee of the club noticed John and Jane Doe attempting to sell their tickets. She immediately confronted them, and demanded that they turn over their tickets to her. John and Jane Doe refused to do so, and a nearby police officer was called over to the scene. John and Jane Doe denied that they were attempting to sell at a profit the tickets they had in their possession. The club employee then pointed out the terms on the back of the tickets to the police officer, and after reading the notice, the police officer suggested to John and Jane Doe that it might be advisable for them to surrender their tickets. John and Jane Doe did so, but only on the condition that the police officer hold the tickets until they could obtain legal advice. The officer agreed to do so.

Advise John and Jane Doe. In your answer clearly identify the legal principles that would be applied in this case to determine the rights of the parties.

Case 6

Community Clipper Airlines Ltd. was a small airline that operated a scheduled service to a number of remote northern communities in the province. In addition, it operated a charter service that consisted for the most part of flying hunting and fishing enthusiasts to tourist camps located on otherwise inaccessible northern lakes.

On a day late in September, the dispatcher received a radio telephone request from the operator of a remote tourist camp, requesting an aircraft to fly in and pick-up two late season fishermen who must return to their offices for work the next day. The dispatcher passed the flight instructions to one of the charter pilots, "Red Baron."

The pilot checked the aircraft, a four-passenger, single engine, wheel and float-equipped craft, then called the weather office for a weather briefing. The weather office reported marginal flying weather until 4:00 p.m. that day. The forecast for the period after 4:00 p.m. indicated rain and fog conditions in the area of the airport, and in the area generally. The weather was expected to close all of the neighbouring airports as well, but remain clear in the area of the tourist camp.

The tourist camp was approximately two hours flying time from the airport, and given that the time was then 11:00 a.m., "Red Baron" decided to make the flight. She arrived at the tourist camp at approximately 1:00 p.m., but the fishermen had not yet packed their bags and fishing tackle for the trip. "Red Baron" warned the two fishermen that the weather was deteriorating, and they must leave immediately, otherwise they would be unable to land at the airport. One of the fishermen was particularly slow at getting his equipment and clothes packed, and in spite of her urging, the fisherman was not ready to leave until almost 2:00 p.m. At 2:05 p.m. the plane flew from the camp with the two fishermen and their gear.

The weather, although still appropriate for flying, held until the aircraft was within approximately 20 minutes flying time of the airport. At that point the aircraft encountered rain and deteriorating visibility. The pilot advised the two passengers that she might not be able to proceed to the airport if the weather became worse. Undaunted, the passengers urged her to proceed on rather than fly back to the camp, as they were obliged to make flight connections at the airport in order to be at their offices the next morning.

With some misgivings and warning about the weather, "Red Baron" continued on. She contacted the airport, and was informed that rain and fog had closed the runways, but the lake approach might still be possible since a very slight on-shore breeze was keeping the lake from being totally closed-in.

"Red Baron" elected to try the lake approach rather than turn back. Visibility was poor in the rain, and fog patches obscured parts of the lake. Due to the weather, she decided to land some distance out in the lake, then taxi to the dock area. She made a careful approach, but after successfully landing on the water, collided with a floating log. The log damaged the aircraft, and caused it to flip forward and begin to sink.

A rescue boat was dispatched to the aircraft immediately, and the pilot and passengers were rescued from the cold water. While not seriously injured, the passengers suffered bruises, some minor lacerations, and exposure. They were kept in hospital overnight, and released the next day to return home.

If the passengers instituted legal proceedings against the airline, discuss the possible arguments and legal principles each side would raise. Render, with reasons, a decision.

CHAPTER 14

Breach of Contract

THE NATURE OF BREACH OF CONTRACT

The express or implied refusal to carry out a promise made under a contract is a form of discharge. When the refusal occurs, it creates new rights for the injured party that entitle the party to bring an action for the damages suffered as a result of the breach. Under certain circumstances, a breach of contract may also permit the injured party to treat the agreement as being at an end, and to be free from any further duties under it. The courts may either grant compensation for the injury suffered as a result of the non-performance, or, in some cases, issue an order requiring performance according to the terms of the contract by the party who committed the breach.

Express Repudiation

Breach of contract may be either express or implied. Where a party to a contract expressly repudiates a promise to perform, either by conduct or by a form of communication, the repudiation is said to be an **express breach.** For example, A Co. and Baxter enter into a contract under which A Co. agrees to sell Baxter a truckload of firewood. They agree to make delivery at Baxter's residence on September 1st, but A Co. later refuses to deliver the firewood on that date. In this case, A Co. has committed an express breach of contract by its refusal to deliver the goods on the date fixed in the agreement. The company's breach of the agreement would give Baxter a right of action against it for damages for breach of the contract.

Repudiation of a promise before the time fixed for performance is known as **anticipatory breach.** If the repudiated promise represents an important condition in the agreement, then the repudiation of the promise would entitle the other party to treat the agreement as at an end. The injured party, however, has an alternate remedy available. The injured party may also treat the contract as a continuing agreement. He or she may wait until the date fixed for performance by the other party, notwithstanding the express repudiation, and then bring an action for non-performance at that time. If the injured party should elect to follow the latter course, presumably with the hope that the party who repudiated the agreement might experience a change of mind, the injured party must assume the risk that the agreement may be discharged by other means in the interval. For example, Maxwell and the Fuller Co. enter into a contract for the purchase of a new car that the Fuller Co. has on display in its showroom. Maxwell is to take delivery of the car at the end of the month. Before the end of the month, the Fuller Co. sales manager advises Maxwell that the company does not intend to sell the car, but plans to keep it as a display model. Maxwell does nothing to treat the contract as at an end. He continues to urge Fuller Co. management to change its mind. The day before the date fixed in the agreement for delivery, the car is destroyed in a fire at the Fuller Co.'s showroom. The destruction of the specific goods would release both Maxwell and the Fuller Co. from their obligations under the agreement. As a consequence, Maxwell would lose his right of action for breach of contract.

Generally, a breach of contract that takes the form of express repudiation would entitle the injured party to a release from his or her promise of performance under the contract. But if the promises are such that each party must perform independently of the other, the injured party may not be entitled to treat the contract as at an end. For example, Russell and Hall, two farmers, enter into an agreement. Russell agrees to cut Hall's hay, and Hall consents to harvest Russell's wheat crop for him in return. The parties agree that the value of each service is approximately equal, and if both services are performed they will cancel each other out in terms of payment. If Russell should later refuse to cut Hall's hay crop, Hall is not necessarily released from his agreement to harvest Russell's wheat crop. However, he would be entitled to bring an action against Russell for damages arising out of the breach.

Similarly, if the repudiated promise has been partly fulfilled, the party injured by the repudiation may not be entitled to avoid the contract unless the repudiation goes to the very root of the agreement. If the repudiated promise is one that has been substantially performed before repudiation, the injured party is usually bound to perform the agreement in accordance with its terms, subject only to a deduction for the damages suffered as a result of the breach by the other party.

The particular rule of law that may be applied in cases where a contract has been substantially performed before the breach occurs is known as the **doctrine of substantial performance.** It is frequently employed by the courts to prevent the injured party from taking unfair advantage of the party who commits a breach after his promise has been largely fulfilled. For example, Smith enters into an agreement with Bradley Construction Co. to have them erect a garage on her premises. Payment is to be made in full by Smith upon completion of the construction. Bradley Construction purchases the materials and erects the garage. When the garage has been completed, save and except for the installation of some small trim boards, Bradley Construction leaves the job to work on another more important project. Because the agreement had been substantially completed by

Bradley Construction before it repudiated the contract, Smith could not treat the contract as at an end. She would be required to perform her part of the agreement, but would be entitled to deduct from the contract price the cost of having the construction completed by some other contractor. The doctrine of substantial performance would prevent Smith from taking unfair advantage of Bradley Construction, and from obtaining benefit from that company's breach that would be disproportionate to the injury that she suffered as a result of the breach.

Similarly, in an English case[1] where the court was required to consider defects that would cost approximately £56 to complete a £750 contract, the court held that the work done excluding the defects (which amounted to 92% completion) was sufficient to constitute substantial performance. In the later case of *Bolton v. Mahadeva*[2] the judge accepted the reasoning in the previous case and made clear in the judgement that the court not only considers the nature of the defects but also the percentage of the work completed in arriving at a conclusion as to the application of the doctrine of substituted performance. In that case the judge stated:

> In considering whether there was substantial performance I am of opinion that it is relevant to take into account both the nature of the defects and the proportion between the cost of rectifying them and the contract price. It would be wrong to say that the contractor is only entitled to payment if the defects are so trifling as to be covered by the *de minimis* rule.

A rule somewhat similar to the doctrine of substantial performance is also applicable in cases of express repudiation, where the repudiation is of a subsidiary promise, rather than an essential part of the agreement. These subsidiary promises are referred to as **warranties** where a sale of goods is concerned. They do not permit a party to avoid the agreement as a result of the repudiation or non-performance by the other party. The general thrust of this rule is similar to that of the doctrine of substantial performance. If the repudiated promise does not go to the root of the agreement, or is not a **condition** (an essential term), then the parties should both be required to fulfill their obligations under the agreement. Appropriate compensation would go to the injured party for the incomplete performance of the other.

This approach is consistent with the general policy of the courts to uphold the contract, whenever it is just and reasonable to do so.

Implied Repudiation

The most difficult form of anticipatory breach to determine is **implied repudiation** of a contract. This occurs where the repudiation must be ascertained from the actions of a party, or implied from statements made before the time fixed for performance. For example, where a party acts in a manner indicating that he might not perform on the specified date, the other party to the agreement is faced with a dilemma. To assume from the actions of a party that performance will not be forthcoming in the future is hazardous; yet to wait until the date fixed for performance may only exacerbate the problem if the performance does not take place.

---

1. *Hoenig v. Isaacs,* [1952] 2 All E.R. 176.
2. *Bolton v. Mahadeva,* [1972] 1 W.L.R. 1009

The same problem exists where a party is required to perform over a period of time, or where a seller promises to deliver goods to a buyer from time to time in accordance with the terms of a contract. In each of these cases, a failure to perform in accordance with the contract initially may not permit the other party to treat the substandard performance as a breach. Continued failure to meet the requirements, however, may permit the injured party to be free of the agreement. This would occur if the failure on the part of the other party falls so short of the performance required in the agreement that performance of the promise as a whole becomes impossible.

Where a party infers from the circumstances that performance will be below standard in the future, or where the party decides, on the basis of incomplete information, that performance may not take place as required, it becomes risky indeed to treat the contract as at an end. For example, A Co. enters into a contract with B Co. to clear snow from B Co.'s premises during the winter months. After the first snowfall is cleared, A Co. complains bitterly about the poor contract that it made with B Co. A week later, and before the next snowfall, B Co. president is informed by Carter, a business acquaintance, that he has just purchased A Co.'s snow removal equipment. B Co. assumes that A Co. has no intention of performing the snow removal contract, so it enters into a contract with D Co. for snow removal for the balance of the winter.

The next evening, a snowstorm strikes the area, and B Co. president discovers that both A Co. and D Co. drivers are at his door arguing over who has the right to remove the snow. A Co. had sold its old snow removal equipment and purchased a new and larger snowblower. It had no intention of repudiating the contract.

The dilemma of B Co. in this example illustrates the hazard associated with the determination of repudiation where the intention of a party must be inferred from the party's conduct. In this case, B Co.'s own actions placed it in a position where it was now in breach of the contract.

Fundamental Breach

Occasionally, where the performance by a party is so far below that required by the terms of the contract, it may be treated as a **fundamental breach** of the agreement. Fundamental breach permits the party injured by the breach to be exonerated from performance, even though the contract may specifically require performance by the party in the face of a breach. This particular doctrine was developed by the courts in a line of English and Canadian cases that dealt with contracts containing exemption clauses. In part, the doctrine was a response by the courts to the problems that have arisen as a result of the unequal bargaining power between buyers and sellers in the marketplace. In the past, contract law was based upon the premise that the agreement was freely made between two parties with equal bargaining power, or at least equal knowledge of the terms of the agreement and their implications. The shift of marketing power in favour of sellers permitted them to insert exemption clauses in standard form contracts. These clauses protect sellers from the risks of liability for defects, price changes, and the obligation to comply with implied warranties and other terms designed to protect the buyer.

Exemption clauses usually require the buyer to perform, even though the seller may avoid performance or substitute performance of a different nature by way of the exemption clause. While the courts will normally enforce exemption clauses (except where the clauses are excluded by legislation), they construe them strictly, and against the party who inserts them in the agreement. Even so, if the breach on the part of the party who seeks to hide behind an exemption clause is so serious as to constitute non-performance of a fundamental term of the agreement, the courts may not allow that party to use the clause to avoid liability. For example, a person purchased a new truck from a seller of trucks under a contract containing a broadly worded exemption clause. The buyer discovered that the truck had many defects and was so difficult to drive as to be unsuitable. The court held that the seller had delivered a truck that was totally different from that which the buyer had contracted for, and the buyer was entitled to rescind the contract.[3] The court, in that particular case, decided that the buyer was entitled to a vehicle that was relatively free from defects and reasonably fit for the use intended. The truck turned out to be wholly unsatisfactory, and the court decided that the delivery of such a vehicle by the seller constituted a repudiation of the agreement. The failure to deliver a vehicle that the parties had contracted for constituted a fundamental breach of the agreement. Notwithstanding the exemption clause, the buyer was entitled to treat the contract as at an end.

Canadian courts have frequently employed the doctrine of fundamental breach to provide relief from onerous exemption or disclaimer clauses, although its articulation has taken on many forms. In an early case it was expressed as a "failure of consideration"[4] and as a "failure to deliver what was ordered."[5] As the concept continued to develop, the term became "the foundation upon which the contract was built"[6] and, finally, the "doctrine of fundamental term or fundamental breach." The doctrine permits the buyer to ignore the exemption clause entirely when the court determines that the seller's performance was totally different from that which the parties contemplated.[7]

More recently, the Supreme Court of Canada has thrown the doctrine of fundamental breach into confusion with respect to exemption clauses by stating that, where a fundamental breach occurs, the effect of the exemption clause does not depend upon a rule of law, but upon the construction of the contract.[8] By this statement, the Court presumably meant that where a fundamental breach occurs, the application of the exemption clause would not automatically be excluded by a rule of law, because no such rule exists. Instead, the ability of the party to rely on the clause would depend upon the wording of the whole contract. For example, in a case where a person leased a machine for breaking land, and the machine proved to be completely unsuited for the purpose, the person was entitled to repudiate the contract. However, he was not entitled to incidental and consequential

---

3. *Cain et al. v. Bird Chevrolet-Oldsmobile Ltd. et al.* (1976), 69 D.L.R. (3d) 484.

4. *Canada Foundry Co. Ltd. v. Edmonton Portland Cement Co.,* [1918] 3 W.W.R. 866.

5. *Schofield v. Emerson-Brantingham Implement Co.* (1918), 43 D.L.R. 509.

6. *Arrow Transfer Co. Ltd. v. Fleetwood Logging Co. Ltd.* (1961), 30 D.L.R. (2d) 631.

7. *Cain et al. v. Bird Chevrolet-Oldsmobile Ltd. et al.* (1976), 69 D.L.R. (3d) 484; *Murray v. Sperry Rand Corp. et al.* (1979), 5 B.L.R. 284.

8. *Beaufort Realties (1964) Inc. and Belcourt Construction (Ottawa) Ltd. v. Chomeday Aluminium Co. Ltd.* (1980), 116 D.L.R. (3d) 193.

damages, because these were specifically excluded in the contract in the event of breach by the lessor of the equipment.[9]

A problem for an injured party may arise in cases where that party continues to hold the agreement in effect after the other contracting party has failed to properly perform an important part of the promise. The effect of the delay may change a condition into a mere warranty. This has important implications for the parties to a contract because of the nature and effect of these terms. Generally, the essential terms of the contract constitute **conditions.** If they are not performed, conditions may entitle the other party to treat the contract as being at an end. **Warranties,** on the other hand, are generally minor promises or terms that may be express or implied and are collateral to the object of the agreement. A breach of a warranty usually does not permit the injured party to treat the contract as being at an end; it only entitles the injured party to sue for damages. However, if a party should refuse to perform a condition or important term that would entitle the other party to avoid performance, and that party does not act at once to do so, the condition may become a mere warranty. The same holds true if the party injured by the breach of the condition continues on with the contract and accepts benefits under it. Then the condition becomes a **warranty ex post facto.** In effect, the injured party's actions constitute a waiver of the right to avoid the agreement. The injured party will be obliged to perform with only the right to damages as compensation for the breach by the other party.[10]

For example, a purchaser of a parcel of land wishes to avoid the purchase of the land and recover the deposit paid, because the vendor of the land did not have the deed available on the date fixed for closing the transaction. Unless the purchaser can satisfy the court that the purchase monies had been paid or tendered, the court may treat the purchaser's failure to show the ability to complete the contract as the purchaser's default or his rejection of the contract. The court may refuse to assist the purchaser in the recovery of the deposit paid.

In the case of *Zender et al. v. Ball et al.,*[11] similar to the example above, the judge described the purchaser's position as follows:

> ...ordinarily a want of title would entitle the purchaser to commence an action for rescission and the return of all moneys paid. However, the purchaser is only entitled to rescind on the neglect or refusal of his vendor to deliver a registrable conveyance on the date fixed by the contract if he has tendered or paid all his purchase money or otherwise performed his part of the contract. The purchaser cannot recover, at law, his deposit where he has constructively or expressly abandoned the contract, wrongfully repudiated, or unequivocally manifested his inability to carry out his part of the contract and the vendor is willing to complete. The deposit, under the terms of the contract, is in the nature of a guarantee or security for the performance of a contract and is not merely a part payment of the purchase price. To permit a purchaser to recover his deposit on his default, where he has abandoned or wrongfully repudiated the contract, would be to permit him to take advantage of his own wrong. Ordinarily, a demand by the purchaser for the return of his deposit from the defaulting vendor is an election to rescind and specific performance is no longer available.

9. *Borg-Warner Acceptance Canada Ltd. v. Wyonzek,* [1981] 4 W.W.R. 193 (Sask.).
10. *Couchman v. Hill,* [1947] 1 K.B. 554.
11. *Zender et al. v. Ball et al.* (1974), 5 O.R. (2d) 747.

REMEDIES

The Concept of Compensation for Loss

A breach of contract gives the party injured by the breach the right to sue for compensation for the loss suffered. Loss or injury as a result of the breach must be proven. If this is done, the courts will attempt to place the injured party in the same position as he or she would have been in had the contract been properly performed. Compensation may take the form of monetary damages, or it may, in some circumstances, include the right to have the contract promise, or a part of it, performed by the defaulting promisor. It may also take the form of *quantum meruit*, a quasi-contract remedy.

The usual remedy for a breach of contract is **monetary damages.** The reason that the courts usually award compensation in this form is that most contracts have as their object something that can be readily translated into a monetary amount in the event of non-performance. For example, Fuller offers to sell Brown 60 crates of apples at $5 per crate. On the date fixed for delivery, Fuller delivers the apples to Brown, but Brown refuses to take delivery. Fuller later sells the apples to Caplan, but the price by then has fallen to $4 per crate. Fuller has suffered a loss of $1 per crate, or $60 in total, as a result of Brown's breach of the contract. If Fuller should sue Brown for breach of contract, the courts would probably award Fuller damages in the amount of $60 to place Fuller in the same position that he would have been in had Brown carried out his part of the agreement. This basic principle of damages is sometimes referred to as the principle of ***restitutio in integrum,*** which originally meant a restoration to the original position. However, this is not what the common law courts attempt to do. In the case of a breach of contract, they attempt to place the injured party in the same position as if the contract had been performed. *Restitutio in integrum* was originally a principle in the old courts of equity. It was applied in cases where it was desirable to place the parties in the position they were in before the agreement had been formed. Today, the term is usually used by the courts to mean to make the party whole, or to compensate for the loss suffered.

The Extent of Liability for Loss

While damages may be readily determined in the event of a breach of a simple contract, some contracts may be such that a breach or failure to perform may have far-reaching effects. This is particularly true where a contract may be only a part of a series of contracts between a number of different parties, and the breach of any one may adversely affect the performance of another. A manufacturer of automobiles, for example, depends heavily upon the supply of components from many subcontractors, while the manufacturer's assembly plant performs the function of merging the various parts into the finished product. The failure of any one supplier to provide critical parts could bring the entire assembly process to a standstill and produce losses of staggering proportions. Fortunately, automobile manufacturers usually take precautions to prevent the occurrence of such a state of affairs. However, the example illustrates the fact that a breach of contract may have ramifications that extend beyond the limits of the simple contract.

Since a party may generally be held liable for the consequences of his or her actions in the case of a breach of contract, it is necessary to determine the extent of the liability that might flow from the breach. At law, it is necessary to draw a line at some point that will end the liability of a party in the event of a breach of contract. Beyond this line, the courts will treat the damages as being too remote. An early English case[12] involved a contract between a milling firm and a common carrier to deliver a broken piece of machinery to the manufacturer to have a replacement made. The mill was left idle for a lengthy period of time because the carrier was tardy in the delivery of the broken mill part to the manufacturer. The miller sued the carrier for damages resulting from the undue delay. In determining the liability of the carrier, the court formulated a principle of remoteness that identified the damages that may be recovered as *those that the parties may reasonably contemplate as flowing from such a breach.* The case, in effect, established two rules to apply in cases where a breach of contract occurs. The first identifies the damages that might obviously be expected to result from a breach of the particular contract as contemplated by a *reasonable person.* The second "rule" carries the responsibility one step further, and includes *any loss that might occur from special circumstances relating to the contract that both parties might reasonably be expected to contemplate at the time the contract is made.*

These two "rules" for the determination of remoteness in the case of a breach of contract were enunciated in 1854. With very little modification they were used as a basis for establishing liability for over a century. More recently, however, the two rules were rolled into a single one that states: *"...any damages actually caused by a breach of any kind of contract is recoverable, providing that when the contract was made such damage was reasonably foreseeable as liable to result from the breach."*[13]

This particular rule would hold a person contemplating a breach liable for any damages that would reasonably have been foreseen at the time that the contract was formed. However, the person would only be liable for those damages that would be related to the knowledge available to the party that might indicate the likely consequences of the contemplated breach.

In rare instances, the compensation may also be extended to cover damage in the nature of mental stress where it is associated with the transaction and where the actions of the party in breach compound the problems of the injured party. In the case of *Vorvis v. Insurance Corporation of British Columbia,* [14] the Supreme Court of Canada indicated that under certain circumstances in cases of breach of contract, aggravated damages for mental suffering may be appropriate. The court, however, characterized such damages as compensatory rather than punitive, and stated that the award would hinge upon whether the party in breach should have reasonably expected that mental suffering would result from the breach. Nevertheless, the court emphasized that an injured plaintiff is normally entitled only to have what the contract provided for, or the equivalent in compensation for the loss.

The Duty to Mitigate Loss

In the case of breach, the injured party is not entitled to remain inactive. The prospective plaintiff in an action for damages must take steps to mitigate the loss

---

12. *Hadley et al. v. Baxendale et al.* (1854), 9 Ex. 341, 156 E.R. 145.

13. *C. Czarnikow Ltd. v. Koufos,* [1966] 2 W.L.R. 1397 at p. 1415.

14. *Vorvis v. Insurance Corporation of British Columbia,* [1989] 1 S.C.R. 1085.

suffered. Otherwise the courts may not compensate the injured party for the full loss. If the party fails to take steps to reduce the loss that flows from a breach, then the defendant, if he or she can prove that the plaintiff failed to mitigate, may successfully reduce the liability by the amount that the plaintiff might otherwise have recovered, had it not been for the neglect. For example, Ashley enters into a contract with Bentley for the purchase of a case of strawberries. The purchase price is fixed at $10, but when Bentley delivers the case of berries, Ashley refuses to accept delivery. If Bentley immediately seeks out another buyer for the strawberries and sells them for $5, Bentley would be entitled to claim the actual loss of $5 from Ashley. On the other hand, Bentley may do nothing after Ashley refuses to accept delivery of the berries, and, as a result, the berries become worthless. Then a claim against Ashley for the $10 loss suffered by Bentley may be reduced substantially, if Ashley can successfully prove that Bentley did nothing to mitigate the loss.

It should also be noted that if Ashley refused to accept the berries, and Bentley sold them to Carter for $10, Bentley would still have a right to action against Ashley for breach of contract. Bentley, however, would only be entitled to nominal damages under the circumstances, because he suffered no actual loss.

The question arises: to what lengths must a person go in order to mitigate a loss? In the case of *Asamera Oil Corp. Ltd. v. Sea Oil & General Corp. et al.*[15] the Supreme Court of Canada reviewed the requirements:

> We start of course with the fundamental principle of mitigation authoritatively stated by Viscount Haldane, L.C., in *British Westinghouse Electric & Mfg. Co., Ltd. v. Underground Electric R. Co. of London, Ltd.,* [1912] A.C. 673 at p. 689:
>
> "The fundamental basis is thus compensation for pecuniary loss naturally flowing from the breach; but this first principle is qualified by a second, which imposes on a plaintiff the duty of taking all reasonable steps to mitigate the loss consequent on the breach, and debars him from claiming any part of the damage which is due to his neglect to take such steps. In the words of James L.J. in *Dunkirk Colliery Co. v. Lever* (1898), 9 Ch.D. 20, at p. 25. 'The person who has broken the contract is not to be exposed to additional cost by reason of the plaintiffs not doing what they ought to have done as reasonable men, and the plaintiffs not being under any obligation to do anything otherwise than in the ordinary course of business.'
>
> "As James L.J. indicates, this second principle does not impose on the plaintiff an obligation to take any step which a reasonable and prudent man would not ordinarily take in the course of his business. But when in the course of his business he has taken action arising out of the transaction, which action has diminished his loss, the effect in actual diminution of the loss he has suffered may be taken into account even though there was no duty on him to act."

Liquidated Damages

At the time the contract is entered into, the parties may attempt to estimate the damages that might reasonably be expected to flow from a breach of contract, and they may insert the estimate as a term. The courts will generally respect the agreement, provided that the estimate is a genuine attempt to estimate the loss.

---

15. *Asamera Oil Corp. Ltd. v. Sea Oil & General Corp. et al.* (1978), 89 D.L.R. (3d) 1.

Usually the clause takes the form of a right in the seller to retain a deposit as **liquidated damages** in the event that the buyer refuses to complete the contract. However, the parties may occasionally insert a clause that requires a party in default to pay a fixed sum. If the amount is unreasonable in relation to the damage suffered, the sum may be treated as a **penalty** rather than liquidated damages, and the courts will not enforce the clause. Similarly, if a party has paid a substantial portion of the purchase price at the time the contract is entered into, and the contract contains a clause that entitles the seller to retain any payments made as liquidated damages, a failure to perform by the buyer would not entitle the seller to retain the entire part-payment. The seller, instead, would only be entitled to deduct the actual loss suffered form the partial payment and would be obliged to return the balance to the purchaser. The reasoning of the courts behind this rule is that punitive damages will not be awarded for an ordinary breach of contract. Only in cases where the actions of a party are reprehensible will a party be penalized. In the case of contract, the circumstances would probably be limited to those relating to contracts negotiated under fraud or duress.

The distinction between a part-payment and a deposit arose in the case of *Stevenson v. Colonial Homes Ltd.*[16] A purchaser of cottage building materials had paid a "deposit" of $1000 under a contract that provided that if the purchaser failed to complete the contract the deposit would be forfeited. The $1000 deposit in this case represented a substantial part of the purchase price, and the purchaser attempted to recover a part of it when default did occur. The purchaser argued that the payment was a part-payment and not a deposit.

In the case, the court reviewed the law as it related to liquidated damages by saying:

> Whether or not the appellant is entitled to the return of the $1,000, in the view I take of the case, depends upon whether the $1,000 was paid as a deposit or whether it was part payment of the purchase price.
>
> A useful summary of the law upon this point is to be found in the judgment of Finnemore, J., in *Gallagher v. Shilcock,* [1949] 2 K.B. 765 at pp. 768-9:
>
> "The first question is whether the [money] which the plaintiff buyer paid on May 17 was a deposit or merely a pre-payment of part of the purchase price.... When money is paid in advance, it may be a deposit strictly so called, that is something which binds the contract and guarantees its performance; or it may be a part payment — merely money pre-paid on account of the purchase price; or, again it may be both: in the latter case, as was said by Lord Macnaghten in *Soper v. Arnold* (1889), 14 App. Cas. 429, 435: 'The deposit serves two purposes — if the purchase is carried out it goes against the purchase-money — but its primary purpose is this, it is a guarantee that the purchaser means business.' If it is a deposit, or both a deposit and prepayment, and the contract is rescinded, it is not returnable to the person who pre-paid it if the rescission was due to his default. If, on the other hand, it is part-payment only, and not a deposit in the strict sense at all, then it is recoverable even if the person who paid it is himself in default. That, I think, follows from *Howe v. Smith,* 27 Ch.D. 89, and from *Mayson v. Clouet,* [1924] A.C. 980, a case in the Privy Council. As I understand the position, in each case the question is whether the payment was in fact intended by the parties to be a deposit in the strict sense or no more than a part-payment: and, in deciding this

16. *Stevenson v. Colonial Homes Ltd.,* [1961] O.R. 407.

question, regard may be had to the circumstances of the case, to the actual words of the contract, and to the evidence of what was said."

As was stated by Lord Dunedin in *Mayson v. Clouet,* at p. 985: "Their Lordships think that the solution of a question of this sort must always depend on the terms of the particular contract." The contract between the appellant and the respondent should be critically examined to see if from it can be drawn the intention of the parties as to whether the $1,000 was to be a deposit or a part payment of purchase price only.

SPECIAL REMEDIES

Specific Performance

In rare cases, where monetary damages would be an inadequate compensation for breach of contract, the courts may decree specific performance of the contract. The decree of **specific performance** is a discretionary remedy that has its origins in the English Court of Chancery. The remedy requires the party subject to it to perform the agreement as specified in the decree; a failure to comply with the decree would constitute contempt of court. Unlike an ordinary monetary judgement, the decree of specific performance carries with it the power of the courts to fine or imprison the wrongdoer for failure to comply with the order.

Specific performance is generally available as a remedy when the contract concerns the sale of land. The unique nature of land is the reason why the courts will enforce the contract, as no two parcels of land are exactly the same. Even then, the courts expect the injured party to show that the fault rests entirely on the party in breach before the remedy will be granted. The plaintiff (the injured party) must satisfy the court that he or she was willing and able at all times to complete the contract, and did nothing to prompt the refusal to perform by the party in breach. To satisfy this particular onus, the plaintiff must usually make a tender of either the money or the title documents as required under the contract. This must be done strictly in accordance with the terms of the contract on the day, and at the time and place fixed for performance. The plaintiff must also satisfy the court that the other party refused to perform at that time. If the court is satisfied on the evidence presented that the plaintiff did everything necessary to perform, and that the other party was entirely at fault for the breach, it may issue a decree of specific performance that would require performance of the contract by the party in breach.

Specific performance may apply to either a vendor or a purchaser in a land transaction. The courts may order performance by either a defaulting seller or buyer in the contract. The remedy of specific performance may also be available in a case where the contract has a "commercial uniqueness" or has as its subject-matter a chattel that is rare and unique.[17] But for most contracts that involve the sale of goods, monetary damages would normally be the appropriate remedy. Moreover, the courts will not grant specific performance of a contract of employment or any contract that involves the performance of personal services by an individual. The principal reason for not doing so is that it will not enforce promises that it would be obliged to continually supervise.

---

17. *Re Wait,* [1927] 1 Ch. 606.

Injunction

A remedy similar to specific performance may also be available in the case of a breach of contract where the promise that the party refuses to perform is a promise to forbear from doing something. The difference between this remedy, known as an **injunction,** and a decree of specific performance is that the injunction usually orders the party to refrain from doing something that the party promised that he or she would not do. On the other hand, a decree of specific performance usually requires the party to do a positive act.

Like a decree of specific performance, an injunction is an equitable remedy, and may be issued only at the discretion of the court. Its use is generally limited to the enforcement of "promises to forbear" contained in contracts. However, the courts are sometimes reluctant to grant the remedy in contracts of employment if the effect of the remedy would be to compel the promisor to perform the contract to his or her detriment. For example, Maxwell and Dixon enter into an agreement. Maxwell agrees to work exclusively for Dixon for a fixed period of time, and to work for no one else during that time. If Maxwell should repudiate her promise and work for someone else, Dixon may apply for an injunction to enforce Maxwell's promise not to work for anyone else. If the injunction should be granted, it would enforce only the negative covenant, and not Maxwell's promise to work exclusively for Dixon. In other words, Maxwell need not remain in the employ of Dixon, but because of the injunction, she would not be permitted to work for anyone else. It should be noted, however, that if circumstances were such that Maxwell did not have independent means, and was obliged to work for Dixon in order to support herself, the courts may not issue an injunction. The reasoning here is that the injunction, in effect, would constitute an order of specific performance of the entire contract. Usually contracts containing a negative promise limit the party to the acceptance of similar employment, rather than employment of any kind. By placing only a limited restriction on the employee's ability to accept other employment, the plaintiff may argue that the defendant is not restricted from other employment, but only employment of a similar nature. Therefore, the employee would not be restricted to working only for the plaintiff.

In other types of contracts, an injunction may be issued to enforce a negative covenant if the covenant is not contrary to public policy. It may be granted, for example, in the case of a contract for the sale of a business to enforce a covenant made by the vendor, where the vendor agrees not to compete with the purchaser within a specific geographic area for a specified period of time. It may also be available to enforce a negative covenant with respect to the use of premises or equipment. For example, Dawson may enter into an agreement with Ballard to allow Ballard the use of certain premises for business purposes. In turn, Ballard promises that he will not operate the business after a certain hour in the evening. If Ballard should continue to operate the business past the stipulated hour, Dawson may be entitled to an injunction to enforce Ballard's negative covenant. It is important to note, however, than an injunction, like a decree of specific performance, is discretionary. The courts will not issue an injunction unless it is fair and just to do so.

Quantum Meruit

In some cases, where a contract is repudiated by a party, and the contract is for services, or goods and services, the remedy of ***quantum meruit*** may be available as an alternative for the party injured by the repudiation. *Quantum meruit* is not a remedy arising out of the contract, but, rather, it is a remedy based upon quasi-contract. In the case of *quantum meruit,* the courts will imply an agreement from a request for goods and services. They will also require the party who requested the service to pay a reasonable price for the benefit obtained.

Quantum meruit may be available as a remedy where the contract has only been partly performed by the injured party at the time the breach occurred. To succeed, however, the injured party must show that the other party to the contract repudiated the contract, or did some act to make performance impossible. The breach by the party cannot be of a minor term, but must be of such a serious nature that it would entitle the party injured by the breach to treat the contract as at an end. *Quantum meruit* is not normally available to the party responsible for the breach. However, under the doctrine of substantial performance, the party may be entitled to recover for the value of the work done. Similarly, *quantum meruit* would not apply where a party had fully performed his or her part of the contract at the time the breach occurred. The appropriate remedy in that case would be an action for the price if the party in breach refused or failed to pay. *Quantum meruit* would also be inapplicable where the contract itself required complete performance as a condition before payment might be demanded.

The distinction between the two remedies is also apparent in the approach the courts may take to each. In the case of an ordinary breach of contract, the remedy of monetary damages is designed to place the injured party in the position that the party would have been in had the contract been completed. This is not so with *quantum meruit.* Where a claim of *quantum meruit* is made, the courts will only be concerned with compensation to the party for work actually done. The compensation will be the equivalent of a reasonable price for the service rendered. This may differ substantially from the price fixed in the repudiated agreement. It is not designed to place the injured party in the same position that the injured party would have been in had the other party not broken the agreement.

SUMMARY   Breach of contract is the express or implied refusal by one party to carry out a promise made to another in a binding contract. Express or implied repudiation before the date fixed for performance is called anticipatory breach. If the refusal to perform is such that it goes to the root of the agreement, and is made before the agreement has been fully performed by the other party, the injured party may be released from any further performance and may sue for the damages suffered. However, if the party who refused to complete the contract has substantially performed the agreement, the doctrine of substantial performance may apply, and the injured party may only obtain damages for the deficient performance.

The remedies available in the case of breach are: (1) monetary damages; (2) specific performance; (3) an injunction; and (4) the quasi-contract remedy of *quantum meruit.*

Specific performance and the injunction are equitable remedies that may be awarded only at the discretion of the court. They are normally only awarded to enforce contract clauses where it is fair and just to do so. These circumstances are usually limited to contracts concerning land, commercial uniqueness, and rare chattels in the case of specific performance, and to the enforcement of a negative promise, in the case of an injunction. In most other cases, monetary damages are adequate compensation. As an alternative to damages, if the contract has not been fully performed by a party, the remedy of *quantum meruit* may be available. *Quantum meruit,* however, only entitles the party to a reasonable price for the service or the work done. It is not designed to put the party in the position the party would have been in had the contract been performed.

DISCUSSION QUESTIONS

1. Explain the difference between express and implied repudiation of a contract. Give an example of each.
2. What are the rights of one party to a contract when informed by the other party to the contract that performance will not be made?
3. In a situation where a contract is expressly repudiated, what are the dangers associated with waiting until the time for performance to determine if breach will actually occur?
4. How does the doctrine of substantial performance affect the rights of a party injured by repudiation when the contract is not fully performed?
5. Explain the doctrine of fundamental breach as it applies to a contract situation.
6. Does repudiation of a subordinate promise permit the party affected by the repudiation to avoid the obligation to perform the contract itself?
7. Describe the concept of damages as it applies to common law contracts.
8. What does *restitutio in integrum* mean?
9. What tests are applied by the courts to determine the remoteness of a damage claim for breach of contract?
10. Apart from money damages, what other remedies are available from the courts in cases involving a breach of contract? Under what circumstances would these remedies be granted?
11. Explain why mitigation of loss by the injured party is important where a breach of contract occurs.
12. Under what circumstances would a contractor be entitled to partial payment where the work was not fully performed?

MINI-CASE PROBLEMS

1. X engaged Y to repair his lawn-mower. Y dismantled the machine. However, before he had time to carry out the repairs, X informed him that he had purchased a new mower and did not require the repairs on the old machine. Discuss the rights and duties of the parties.
2. D agreed to make certain alterations to an expensive dress that E had purchased. A violent storm caused the roof of D's shop to leak, and the dress was stained by the rain entering the building. D offered to have the dress professionally cleaned to remove the water stains, but E refused and attempted to remove the stains herself. Her attempt was unsuccessful, and the dress was ruined. Advise D and E.

**JUDICIAL
DECISIONS**

The case of *Hadley v. Baxendale* that follows contains the classic statement with respect to damages arising out of a contract. It represents the common law rule today, even though the case itself was decided over a hundred and thirty years ago. The judge states the rule with respect to damages at the beginning of his judgement. Then he notes that in special circumstances damages would be recoverable where the potential injury in the event of breach is communicated to the other contracting party at the time the contract is entered into. Also recoverable would be those damages that might reasonably be considered to flow from the breach.

Borg-Warner Acceptance Canada Ltd. v. Wyonzek is a case that illustrates a fundamental breach situation. The judge concludes that the equipment was inadequate for the type of work that the supplier knew that it was required to perform. Consequently, this represented a fundamental breach of the lease agreement by the supplier. The judge in the case also examines the exclusion clause in the contract that was designed to overcome the consequences of fundamental breach. He notes that it refers to representations and warranties, but nowhere does the clause refer to fundamental breach. However, the contract clause does say that the lessor was not liable for special, incidental, or consequential damages. The judge then concludes that while the lessor is liable for damages for fundamental breach, the lessor would not be liable for incidental damages, as these would be caught by the exclusion clause.

Page One Records, Ltd. v. "The Troggs" illustrates how the court deals with the enforcement of a restrictive covenant in an agreement. The restrictive covenant in the case made the plaintiffs (Page One Records) the exclusive agents and managers of The Troggs. The restriction prevented The Troggs or anyone else from managing their affairs. The judge reviewed the facts and concluded that the restriction, if enforced by an injunction, would compel The Troggs to deal only through the plaintiffs if they wished to engage in their professional activities. The judge concluded that the agreement tied The Troggs so closely to the plaintiffs that it made their relationship something like a partnership or joint venture, whereby the management services of the plaintiffs were of a personal service nature.

The judge in the case notes that the contracts for personal services are not enforced by the courts by way of injunctions. The reasoning is that injunctions force the parties to remain in the personal relationship, something that the courts would not be prepared to have them do. The judge also notes that this case differs from the *Warner Bros.* case in that the artiste in that case could engage in other activities (other than film work) if she wished to do so. This was not the case with The Troggs, as their contract tied them exclusively to the plaintiffs. He then dismissed the motion for the injunction.

**Breach of
Contract —
Quantum of
Damages**

Hadley et al. v. Baxendale et al. (1854), 9 Exch. 341, 156 E.R. 145.
The plaintiffs were millers who operated a steam-powered mill. The crankshaft of the engine cracked, and it was necessary to obtain a new part from the engine manufacturer. A common carrier contracted to deliver the old part to the manufacturer the next day if he received the part before noon. The old part was accordingly

delivered to the carrier, but through neglect was not delivered to the engine manufacturer for some time.

The plaintiffs instituted legal proceedings against the carrier for the loss suffered as a result of the delay.

Alderson, B.:

> Now we think the proper rule in such a case as the present is this: — Where two parties have made a contract which one of them has broken, the damages which the other party ought to receive in respect of such breach of contract should be such as may fairly and reasonably be considered either arising naturally, i.e., according to the usual course of things, from such breach of contract itself, or such as may reasonably be supposed to have been in the contemplation of both parties, at the time they made the contract, as the probable result of the breach of it. Now, if the special circumstances under which the contract was actually made were communicated by the plaintiffs to the defendants, and thus known to both parties, the damages resulting from the breach of such a contract, which they would reasonably contemplate, would be the amount of injury which would ordinarily follow from a breach of contract under these special circumstances so known and communicated. But, on the other hand, if these special circumstances were wholly unknown to the party breaking the contract, he, at the most, could only be supposed to have had in his contemplation the amount of injury which would arise generally, and in the great multitude of cases not affected by any special circumstances, from such a breach of contract. For, had the special circumstances been known, the parties might have specially provided for the breach of contract by special terms as to the damages in that case; and of this advantage it would be very unjust to deprive them. Now the above principles are those by which we think the jury ought to be guided in estimating the damages arising out of any breach of contract.

Borg-Warner Acceptance Canada Ltd. v. Wyonzek, [1981] 4 W.W.R. 193 (Sask.).

The defendant leased a land-breaking machine from the plaintiff under a three-year lease. The machine did not perform satisfactorily, and the defendant refused to make payments, claiming fundamental breach. The plaintiff then sued for the amount owing under the lease.

Cameron, J.:

> The first issue I propose to deal with is the allegation by the defendant of "fundamental breach of the contract."
>
> The notion of fundamental breach has been a vexing one; its essence, application, and consequence have bedevilled the courts, particularly as to the effect of exclusion clauses in a contract in respect of which there has been a fundamental breach.
>
> Two issues arise:
> (a) Was there, in the circumstances here, a fundamental breach; and
> (b) If so, what is the effect of the exclusion clauses?
>
> ...Whatever its limitations or subtle shades of its essence, the doctrine, with all its imperfections, is embedded in Canadian law and at least for the purposes at hand may be sufficiently if not exhaustively nor perfectly stated thus: A

fundamental breach is one going to the very root of the contract; where one party fails to perform the very purpose for which the contract is designed so as to deprive the other of the whole or substantially the whole of the benefit which the parties intended should be conferred and obtained, such breach goes to the very root of the contract and the party not in default is absolved from performing his end of the contract.

The contract here, to the extent it is embodied in the commercial lease contract, was for the letting by the plaintiff to the defendant of "one Madge Rotary Land Breaker serial No. 75-009", sold to the plaintiff by Thompson. The machine being let is thus described by reference to its descriptive name, a rotary land breaker, its serial number to identify it specifically and its manufacturer. It was obviously a substantial machine; its price was $47 000, it was to be let for approximately $63 000 over a three-year term. It was a new machine and by virtue of its description was known to be a heavy duty, diesel-powered land breaker.

Can it be fairly said that the plaintiff performed the very purpose for which the contract was designed; that the defendant got what the parties bargained for and derived the whole or substantially the whole of the benefit contemplated by the contract? Or was there, in what the plaintiff delivered, really no performance at all or something altogether different from what the contract contemplated?

What the defendant got and what the parties intended he should get under the contract for $63 000 clearly are two very different things. I need not refer at length to the problems associated with the machine, the lack of power of its engine, its consistent overheating, its malfunctioning in several major ways and the fact it worked only 50 hours and worked only 10 to 15 acres of land, that unsatisfactorily, before being abandoned.

...In all of the circumstances I have concluded that there was a fundamental breach in the failure by the plaintiff to perform its prime obligation under the contract, namely, supplying to the defendant a new diesel-powered Madge Rotary Land Breaker, well tested, in working condition. It did not do this. Its performance was altogether different than that contemplated, thus depriving the defendant of substantially the whole of the benefit which it was the intention of the parties that he should obtain under the contract. It is, in my view, a breach that goes to the very root of the contract and entitles the defendant to refuse to perform his obligations subject to the exclusion clauses.

So the question arises: What is the effect of the exclusion clauses? ...I am of the view, therefore, notwithstanding a series of other Canadian cases to the contrary, that there is no rule of law providing that a party guilty of a fundamental breach of contract cannot rely on an exemption clause inserted in the contract to protect him. So in this case I must turn to consider whether despite the fundamental breach, the exclusion clauses operate to relieve the plaintiff of what would otherwise be the consequence of the fundamental breach. This is a matter of the construction of the contract as a whole.

These are the key parts of the exclusion clauses:

Clause 4(A) and 4(B) provide, inter alia, as follows:

"Lessor has made no *representation* or *warranty,* express or implied as to any matter whatsoever, including the condition of the equipment.

"There are no *implied warranties* of merchantability or fitness for a particular purpose.

"Lessee leases the equipment 'as is'.

"If the equipment is not properly installed, does not operate as *represented* or *warranted* by supplier, or is unsatisfactory for any reason, lessee shall make any claim on account thereof solely against supplier...

"Lessor may include, as a condition of its purchase order, that supplier agree that all *warranties, agreements* and *representations* if any which may be made by supplier to lessee or lessor may be enforced by lessee in its own name.

"Lessor hereby agrees to assign to lessee, solely for the purpose of making and prosecuting any said claim, all of the rights which lessor has against supplier for breach of *warranty* or other *representations* respecting the equipment.

"...the equipment shall be presumed to be in an undamaged condition when received by lessee unless...".

In considering the effect and the extent of these clauses I ought to have regard to the usual rules of construction including these:

(a) Each of the clauses, in case of ambiguity, is to be interpreted contra proferentem;
(b) General words of exclusion will cover liability for serious breaches only in the clearest circumstances;
(c) The clauses have to be interpreted consistently with the main object of the contract.

I am, of course, to have regard for the contract as a whole.

The exclusion clauses here speak in the main of *representations* and *warranties*. There is no reference to conditions, including any fundamental condition, nor to the consequences of fundamental breach. The words are largely general words of exclusion going to representations and warranties. Clearly damage to the equipment is not included but what else is included or excluded is not altogether clear. Ambiguity exists.

I note the words pick up considerably in strength and clarity when they refer to incidental or consequential damage. In this respect they are precise and clear. "In no event shall lessor be liable for special, incidental or consequential damages whatsoever and howsoever caused."

Looking at the clauses and the contract as a whole, I am by no means satisfied that they were intended to give exemption from the consequences of fundamental breach. Indeed, I think they cannot be said to have this effect and I have concluded therefore that they are of no assistance to the plaintiff. Brownridge J.A. in *Western Tractor,* supra, quotes with approval [at p. 224] the passage from *Yeoman Credit Ltd. v. Apps,* [1962] 2 Q.B. 508, [1961] 2 All E.R. 281 at 289-90 (C.A.):

"There may be, as in *Pollock & Co. v. Macrae* [supra] and in the present case, an accumulation of defects which, taken singly, might well be within an exception clause, but which taken en masse, constitute such a non-performance, or repudiation, or breach going to the root of the contract, as disentitles a party to take refuge behind an exemption clause intended to give protection only in regard to those breaches which are not inconsistent with and not destructive of the whole essence of the contract."

I think that is the situation here.

For the foregoing reasons I hold that there was a fundamental breach of the contract, going to its very root, entitling the defendant to repudiate, and that the exclusion clauses were never intended to be applicable to such a breach. In the circumstances I find that the defendant repudiated the contract, as he was entitled to, and is entitled to recover the amount he paid thereunder.

What I have before me to decide is whether in principle the defendant is entitled to damages in consequence of the fundamental breach of the contract. As I have observed earlier, the exemption clause in respect of damages is very clear in its meaning and effect, far more so than any other of the exclusion clauses. It says in clear, unambiguous terms "In no event shall lessor be liable for special, incidental or consequential damages, whatsoever or howsoever caused". I cannot see that the defendant should not be bound by this clause, nor do I see an inconsistency in holding him bound by this clause and at the same time affording the plaintiff no relief from the consequences of fundamental breach by reason of the other exclusionary clauses.

Accordingly, I find that the defendant is not entitled to the incidental damages he claims.

In conclusion, the plaintiff's claim is dismissed and the defendant shall have judgement against the plaintiff for $21 641.89.

The machine, of course, belongs to the plaintiff and it may do as it wishes with the machine.

Injunctions — Breach of a Restrictive Covenant

Page One Records, Ltd. and Another v. Britton and Others (trading as "The Troggs") and Another, [1967] 3 All E.R. 822.

"The Troggs," a group of four musicians, entered into written agreements with Page One Records, Ltd. and another, whereby the latter parties would manage the affairs of The Troggs as their agents for a period of five years. A clause in the agreement provided that The Troggs would not hire any other person to manage their affairs, nor would they act as their own managers during the five year period.

In the year that followed, The Troggs became a successful musical group. They then repudiated the contracts entered into the year before. The managers and agents brought an action for an injunction against The Troggs to enforce the clause in their agreements that prohibited The Troggs from hiring another agent or managing their own affairs.

STAMP, J.:

...this present case, in my judgement, fails on the facts at present before me on a more general principle, the converse of which was conveniently stated in the judgement of BRANSON, J., in *Warner Brothers Pictures Inc. v. Nelson* (7). BRANSON J., stated the converse of the proposition and the proposition, correctly stated, is, I think, this, that where a contract of personal service contains negative covenants, the enforcement of which will amount either to a decree of specific performance of the positive covenants of the contract or to the giving of a decree under which the defendant must either remain idle or perform those positive covenants, the court will not enforce those negative covenants.

In the *Warner Brothers* case (8) BRANSON, J., felt able to find that the injunction sought would not force the defendant to perform her contract or remain idle. He said:

"It was also urged that the difference between what the defendant can earn as a film artiste and what she might expect to earn by any other form of activity is so great that she will in effect be driven to perform her contract. That is not the criterion adopted in any of the decided cases. The defendant is stated to be a person of intelligence, capacity and means, and no evidence was adduced to show that, if enjoined from doing the specified acts otherwise than for the plaintiffs, she will not be able to employ herself both usefully and remuneratively in other spheres of activity, though not as remuneratively as in her special line. She will not be driven, although she may be tempted, to perform the contract, and the fact that she may be so tempted is no objection to the grant of an injunction."

So it was said in this case, that if an injunction is granted The Troggs could, without employing any other manager or agent, continue as a group on their own or seek other employment of a different nature. So far as the former suggestion is concerned, in the first place, I doubt whether consistently with the terms of the agreements which I have read, The Troggs could act as their own managers (9); and, in the second place, I think that I can and should take judicial notice of the fact that these groups, if they are to have any great success, must have managers. Indeed, it is the plaintiffs' own case that The Troggs are simple persons, of no business experience, and could not survive without the services of a manager. As a practical matter on the evidence before me, I entertain no doubt that they would be compelled, if the injunction were granted on the terms that the plaintiffs seek, to continue to employ the first plaintiff as their manager and agent and it is, I think, on this point that this case diverges from the *Lumley v. Wagner* case (10) and the cases which have followed it, including the *Warner Brothers* case (11): for it would be a bad thing to put pressure on The Troggs to continue to employ as a manager and agent in a fiduciary capacity one, who, unlike the plaintiff in those cases who had merely to pay the defendant money, has duties of a personal and fiduciary nature to perform and in whom The Troggs, for reasons good, bad or indifferent, have lost confidence and who may, for all I know, fail in its duty to them.

On the facts before me on this interlocutory motion, I should, if I granted the injunction, be enforcing a contract for personal services in which personal services are to be performed by the first plaintiff. In *Lumley v. Wagner* (10), LORD ST. LEONARDS, L.C., in his judgement, disclaimed doing indirectly what he could not do directly; and in the present case, by granting an injunction I would, in my judgement, be doing precisely that. I must, therefore, refuse the injunction which the first plaintiff seeks....

(7) [1936] 3 All E.R. 160 at p. 165; [1937] 1 K.B. 209 at p. 217.

(8) [1936] 3 All E.R. at p. 167; [1937] 1 K.B. at p. 219.

(9) Cf. p. 823, letter I, ante.

(10) [1843-60] All E.R. Rep. 368; (1852), 1 De G.M. & G. 604.

(11) [1936] 3 All E.R. 160; [1937] 1 K.B. 209.

CASE PROBLEMS FOR DISCUSSION

Case 1

Hatfield owned a large farm on which he grew grain. His combine was inadequate in relation to the acreage of grain that he harvested annually. As a result, on several occasions his crops had been adversely affected by rain and poor weather conditions. He reasoned that a larger machine could reduce the time spent harvesting by as much as two-thirds and, thereby, reduce the chances of bad weather affecting his harvest.

At an agricultural exhibition, he examined a new self-propelled combine that was advertised as capable of harvesting grain at three times the speed of his old equipment. The machine was much larger and more powerful than his old combine and appeared to be of the correct size for his farm.

On his return home, he contacted the local dealer for the combine. After explaining his needs, he was assured by the dealer that the size he was considering would be capable of harvesting his crop in one-third of the time taken by his older model. He placed an order for the combine, with delivery to be made in early July, well before he would require the equipment.

The machine did not arrive until the beginning of the harvest, and Hatfield immediately put the machine into service. Unfortunately, the machine was out of adjustment, and Hatfield was obliged to call the dealer to put it in order. The equipment continued to break down each time Hatfield operated it at the recommended speed. In spite of numerous attempts by the dealer to correct the problem, the equipment could not be operated at anything more than a very slow speed without a breakdown. Hatfield found that despite the large size of the equipment, his harvest time was no faster. When the harvest was completed, he returned the machine and demanded his money back.

The equipment dealer refused to return his money. He pointed to a clause in the purchase agreement that Hatfield had signed, which read: "No warranty or condition, express or implied, shall apply to this agreement with respect of fitness for the use intended or as to performance, except those specifically stated herein."

The only reference in the agreement to the equipment stated that it was to be a "new model XVX self-propelled combine."

Advise Hatfield of his rights (if any).

Case 2

Mrs. Field listed her home for sale with a local real estate agent. The agent introduced Mr. Smith to Mrs. Field as a prospective purchaser. After Mr. Smith had inspected the house, the agent obtained a written offer to purchase from him. The offer provided that he would purchase the house for $160 000 if Mrs. Field could give him vacant possession of the premises on September 1st, some three weeks' hence. The offer was accompanied by a deposit in the amount of $1000.

Mrs. Field accepted the offer in writing, then proceeded to lease an apartment under a two-year lease. She moved her furniture to the new premises immediately, and vacated her home in preparation for closing. A few days before the date fixed for delivery of the deed, Mrs. Field was informed by one of her new neighbours (who was a friend of Mr. Smith) that Mr. Smith's employer intended to transfer him to a new position in another city some distance away.

Discuss the rights and obligations (if any) of the parties in this case. Suggest a course of action that Mrs. Field might follow.

Case 3

Trebic was a skilled cabinet-maker of European extraction. Moldeva, who had emigrated to Canada from the same country, requested him to build a set of kitchen cupboards "in the old country style." The two men discussed the general appearance desired, then Trebic drew up a list of materials that he required to construct the cupboards. Moldeva obtained the necessary lumber and supplies for Trebic, then took his family on a vacation.

On his return, Moldeva found the work completed, and admired the craftsmanship and design that Trebic had exhibited in the making of the cabinets. Trebic had carefully carved the "old country designs" on the trim boards. He had skillfully constructed the drawers and cabinets using wooden dowels, rather than nails, again in accordance with "old country" tradition. In the execution of this skill he had used only hand tools, and then only the tools used by old country craftsmen in the cabinet-making trade. In every detail, the cabinets were "old country style."

When Moldeva indicated that he was completely satisfied with the cabinets, Trebic submitted his account in the amount of $1600. The sum represented 80 hours work at $20 per hour, the normal rate charged by skilled cabinet-makers in the area.

Moldeva, who was a building contractor himself, objected to the amount of Trebic's account. He stated that carpenters in his shop could manufacture kitchen cabinets of the general size and shape of those made by Trebic in only a few days' time. He offered Trebic $400 as payment in full.

Trebic refused to accept the $400 offer and brought an action against Moldeva on the $1600 account.

Discuss the possible arguments of the parties. Render a decision.

Case 4

Andrews, a skilled carpenter, agreed to construct a garage for Henderson for a contract price of $800. Henderson was to supply the plans and materials.

Andrews constructed the garage according to the plans. When the building had been framed, he discovered that the siding boards that Henderson had purchased were of poor grade lumber. The boards could only be made to fit with a great deal of hand labour and cutting.

Andrews complained to Henderson and demanded that he provide siding boards that were of "construction grade" lumber. Henderson refused to do so. An argument followed in which Andrews refused to complete the work until Henderson provided suitable materials.

At the time of the argument, the foundation, the roof, and the walls had been erected. The work that remained included the installation of the wall siding, the doors and windows, and the trim.

Discuss the rights of the parties, and the nature of the claims and defences of each. Indicate the possible outcome, if the case should come before the courts.

Case 5

Casey purchased a used motorcycle from Oscar for $350. Oscar stated that the motorcycle was a 1982 model. He offered it "as is," since it was not operating and required repairs. Casey, who was 17 years of age, believed that he could put the machine in good running condition for an estimated cost of $150 (for parts). He agreed to the purchase.

At the time of the sale, Oscar told Casey that the machine was old and not in good working order. He was not familiar with motorcycles and had not examined the machine to determine what was wrong with it. He had acquired it as a part of a "trade" from a person who had purchased his snowmobile. He understood that parts were available for the machine, as it was a relatively popular model.

Casey took the machine home and attempted to purchase the necessary parts. At that time he discovered that the motorcycle was a 1980 model instead of a 1982 model. While the two motorcycles were almost identical in appearance, the cost of parts for the 1980 model was approximately double the price of those for the 1982 model. Also, the parts were very difficult to obtain. However, Casey found a few essential parts at a local motorcycle shop. He managed to put the machine in adequate running condition for driving to and from his home to his work at a nearby office building.

Less than two weeks later, the machine broke down, and Casey attempted to return the machine to Oscar. However, Oscar refused to return Casey's purchase money or to accept the return of the machine. At this point, Casey told Oscar that he was only 17 years of age, and that he intended to repudiate the sale. Oscar was surprised to hear that Casey was only 17 years old, but still refused to return the money or accept the machine.

Casey did nothing about the matter for another week. Then he managed to make a few temporary repairs to the motorcycle in order to use it to travel to work. That week he also reached the age of majority in the province where he resided. He continued to use the machine for another two weeks, then it broke down once again, and could only be repaired at great expense.

Casey then brought an action against Oscar for the return of the price he had paid for the machine.

Discuss the basis of Casey's claim and the arguments that each party might raise in this case. Render a decision.

Case 6

Valentino entered into a contract with TV Production Company to perform the leading role in a television play the company wished to produce. The contract called for the actor to devote his time exclusively to the play until taping was complete, a period of some four weeks. His compensation was to be $20 000. Three days after the contract was signed, Valentino notified the company that he did not intend to perform the role, and that the company should find a new leading actor for the production.

The company attempted to find a substitute for Valentino, but after an exhaustive search could find no one suitable. As a consequence, they were obliged to abandon their plans for the production. During the three-day period after signing Valentino, the company incurred liability of $36 500, under contracts they had entered into for services and commitments made in anticipation of his starring in the production. They also incurred the sum of $2500 in expenses paid to find a substitute, when Valentino refused to perform.

The company instituted legal proceedings against Valentino to recover the total expenses incurred as a result of his repudiation. In response, Valentino offered a settlement of $2500 to cover expenses incurred in their search for a substitute actor.

Discuss the arguments of the parties and render a decision.

Case 7

Ms. Marshall, a successful young businesswoman, wished to purchase an automobile that would not only provide her with basic transportation to and from her home to her place of employment, but would have a sporty appearance. She also wanted a vehicle with sufficient power to enable her to engage in rally racing.

She visited a local dealer in imported automobiles, and enquired about a sports sedan displayed on the premises. The salesman on duty informed her that the vehicle was a used car that had been driven only 12 000 km. It had been purchased the year before as a new car by a customer who then traded it in on a similar model of the current year's production. To the salesman's knowledge, it was a "good car." Since it had a turbo-charged engine, the policy of the company was to sell it "as is," without a warranty of any kind.

After a careful inspection of the car, Ms. Marshall asked the salesman to start the engine, in order for her to determine the condition of the turbo-charger. The salesman did so, and, after running the engine for a few moments at various engine speeds, he shut it down. He offered Ms. Marshall a test drive, but at that point she noticed a coolant leak at the engine water pump. The salesman examined the pump. He then stated that the water pump would be repaired or replaced if necessary, if she wished to buy the car. Ms. Marshall said she would think about the purchase overnight and contact the salesman the next day if she was still interested.

Ms. Marshall returned the next day. She informed the salesman that she was prepared to purchase the automobile if the dealer would repair the water pump and take $500 less than the advertised price of $14 000. With some reluctance, the dealer agreed to sell the car to her, and a written agreement of sale was prepared that contained the following terms:

9. It is expressly agreed that used goods are not warranted by the dealer as to year, make, model, or otherwise, unless so stated in writing.

10. The dealer agrees to make the following repairs to the vehicle as a part of this sale:

(1) repair or replace water pump, as necessary.

Ms. Marshall was anxious to use the car in a local car rally the following day. She enquired if she might take the car immediately, then return it early the next week to have the water pump dealt with at that time. The dealer agreed, but cautioned her not to drive the car too hard until the pump was fixed. He also told her not to worry if she heard a slight "popping" noise from the pump.

Ms. Marshall paid for the car, then drove it home, a distance of some 16 km. Along the way she heard was she described as a "clangy" or "tinny" noise from the engine. However, she was not concerned about it, believing it to be the noise the dealer had described to her.

The next morning, when she attempted to start the car, the engine made a number of "clangy" sounds, then stopped. A mechanic who came to her home in response to her call examined the engine and informed her that the noise came from the engine bearings. He indicated that the engine had been seriously damaged and could cost up to $2000 to repair.

Ms. Marshall immediately informed the automobile dealer that she wished to have her money back. When the dealer refused, she brought an action for rescission of the agreement. At the trial, an expert testified that the problem was indeed a breakdown of the engine bearings, something that could occur in only a few minutes if insufficient oil was supplied to them. There was no evidence to indicate that the damage was in any way related to the water pump.

Discuss the nature of Ms. Marshall's claim, and the possible defences to it. Render a decision.

Case 8

On September 1st, Rothwell entered into an agreement to purchase "A's Restaurant." The purchase price was $375 000, with a down payment of $75 000. The balance was payable December 1st, when Rothwell was to take possession of the business. In anticipation of his start in the restaurant business, Rothwell quit his job and enrolled in a three month community college course on restaurant management.

On November 1st, the owner of the restaurant notified Rothwell that she had received another offer to purchase the restaurant for $450 000, and intended to sell the business to the offeror. Rothwell objected to the restaurant owner's actions, and threatened to take legal action against her if she proceeded with the proposed sale.

A few days later, the restaurant owner did in fact enter into an agreement to sell the business to Polonek, the new purchaser, for the purchase price of $450 000. The closing date of the transaction was to be December 1st. She then mailed a cheque to Rothwell for the $75 000 she had received from him previously as his deposit.

Rothwell immediately returned the cheque and insisted that the restaurant owner proceed with the sale of the restaurant to him in accordance with their agreement.

On November 28th, the local newspaper contained an announcement of the opening of a new restaurant in a large office building across the street from "A's Restaurant." The office building housed most of the customers of "A's Restaurant," and the new restaurant could be expected to take about 70% of the lunch customers and 40% of the dinner customers from "A's Restaurant."

The announcement came as a surprise to all parties. Polonek immediately wrote a letter to the owner of "A's Restaurant" in which he indicated that he did not intend to proceed with the transaction unless the owner reduced the purchase price to $150 000. Rothwell was out of town on other business on November 28th, and did not become aware of the new competitor until December 1st, the proposed closing date for his purchase of the restaurant.

Advise each of the parties of their legal position in this case. Assuming that each party exercised their rights at law, indicate how the issues raised in the case would be resolved by a court.

Case 9

A commercial vegetable grower decided to grow a variety of open-pollinated cabbage as a market garden crop, based upon the success that his relative (who was also a commercial grower) had with the variety several years before. He purchased seeds for the cabbage variety from the catalogue of a commercial seed supplier.

The seeds were planted according to proper planting instructions and cultivated in accordance with accepted agricultural practices. Weather conditions were "normal" throughout the growing season, but in spite of this, the seeds produced a very poor crop.

The grower informed the seed supplier that the crop had failed, even though he had used proper growing techniques, and demanded that the seed company compensate him for his loss. The seed company rejected his complaint and noted the seed purchase contract term which stated:

> The vendor warrants seeds only as to variety named and makes no warranty express or implied as to quality or quantity of crop produced from the seed supplied. Any responsibility of the vendor is limited to the price paid for the seed by the purchaser.

When the seed company refused to entertain his complaint, the grievor decided to take legal action to recover his loss.

Discuss the basis for the grievor's action, and the defence, if any, of the seed company. Render a decision.

Case 10

Complex Software Corporation produced sophisticated software programs for computer-assisted product development. Complex Software was engaged by Turbine Engines Ltd. to develop software that would enable its engineers to develop the most efficient blade design and angles for its large turbines that were used in hydro-electric power generators. Turbine Engines provided the engineering data necessary to develop the program, and Complex Software prepared the software.

The software was tested by both Complex Software and Turbine Engines using a simple turbine with known design and performance characteristics as a model. The software appeared to work properly, and Turbine Engines used the program to design a new multi-stage turbine engine.

Unknown to Turbine Engines, the striking of certain computer keys in a particular sequence had the effect of cancelling out the safety factor to be built into the turbine blades. The key sequence was not the sequence used in the test, but a technician used the particular key sequence in designing the new model turbine blades. As a result, when the new turbine was tested in a high-speed operational mode, the blades disintegrated and destroyed the engine.

Turbine Engines brought a legal action against Complex Software claiming $850 000 damages as its loss in the construction of the faulty prototype turbine.

Discuss the various arguments that may be raised by the parties in this case, and prepare a decision as if you were the judge. Outline your reasoning in reaching your decision.

PART IV

Forms of Business Organization

INTRODUCTION

Business organizations may take on many forms that represent legal relationships at law. Many of these organizations, from a conceptual point of view, are based upon the law of contract. For example, the agency and the partnership are, for the most part, special contracts, while the corporation, another special form of organization, is an entity that contracts with third parties through agents.

Apart from the form that a business itself may take, most of its activities are conducted by way of the law of contract. The organization buys and sells goods, hires employees, acquires premises, advertises its wares, reduces risk, and generally carries on its business operations through the medium of contract. The law relating to all of these activities will be examined in detail in the chapters that follow, but the important point to note is that the law of contract forms a basis for the law in most cases. The special features of the law merely relate to the particular nature of the relationship that arises out of the contract in each situation.

FORMS OF BUSINESS ORGANIZATION

A business organization may be established to carry out a particular project or venture, produce a certain product or product line, or provide a service to the public or a part thereof. In the classic view, a business begins when an entrepreneur identifies a particular need in a community for a product or service and proceeds to satisfy the need. The business is often established in a small way in the beginning. Then it grows, if the entrepreneur has accurately assessed the market, until the business, through investment and the development of new or better products or services, becomes a large business entity. In doing so the business entity may begin as a **sole proprietorship**, expand to include others and become a **partnership**, then continue to develop and take on the form of a **corporation.** This developmental sequence of a business organization, needless to say, is not the only way that large firms may develop. Large organizations are often created to carry on business activities that have been established by larger organizations. Not infrequently, businesses that require a large amount of capital for their establishment generally begin their existence as large organizations. In these cases, the organizations do not pass through different forms of organization. Nevertheless, the classic type of business growth pattern remains as one of the most common patterns of development. It illustrates the number of forms of organization that a business may take during the period of its progression from a small entrepreneurial venture to a large corporate organization. The purpose of this part of the text is to examine some of the more general laws that affect the nature of the firm, as it passes through the various stages of development from its beginning to its final stage.

Sole Proprietorship

The **sole proprietorship** represents the simplest form of business organization as far as the law is concerned. The sole proprietor, as the owner of the business, owns all of the assets, is entitled to all of the profits, and is responsible for all of the debts. The sole proprietor also makes all of the decisions in the operation of the business and is directly responsible for its success or failure. The major disadvantages of the sole proprietorship are usually the limited ability to raise capital and the management skill limitations of the proprietor who must assume responsibility for all aspects of the business.

One of the important requirements for a sole proprietorship is the registration or the licensing of the business. Persons who offer to the public services of a professional nature must generally be licensed to practise the particular skill in a province before they may carry on a professional practice. The legislation governing professions such as medicine, dentistry, law, architecture, and others is usually provincial. It must be complied with before the practice may be established. Many semi-professional and skilled trade activities are also subject to provincial licensing or registration. Municipalities often impose their own registration or licensing of certain businesses in an effort to protect or control the activity. Skilled trades, the operation of taxis, and many other service-oriented businesses frequently require municipal licences to operate within the confines of the municipality.

In spite of the organizational disadvantages of the sole proprietorship, the freedom that it allows the individual in the operation of the business frequently makes it the most attractive form of business organization for a new small enterprise. The flexibility of the operation during the formative period is often as important as the speed by which decision may be made. However, as the business becomes larger, the need for new and varied management skills may require a change in the form of the organization.

Partnerships

From a progressive point of view, the second phase that a small business may enter is that of the **partnership**. A partnership differs in a number of ways from a sole proprietorship, but it, too, is essentially a simple form of business organization. The increase in the number of proprietors to two or more provides additional management expertise in the operation of the firm, and usually additional capital as well. Lending institutions, if they are in a position to look to the assets of several proprietors, are generally more willing to extend credit in larger amounts to a partnership than to a sole

proprietorship. In addition, partners usually possess a greater interest in the success of the business than do employees. An overall advantage of the partnership is that the introduction of new proprietors may substantially increase the chances for growth and development of the enterprise. The partnership form is not without risk, however, as the partnership is responsible for the carelessness or poor judgement of each partner in his or her conduct of partnership business.

Corporations

The **corporation,** unlike the sole proprietorship or partnership, is a separate entity that has a legal existence of its own. If it is organized to carry on a business, it is the corporation that "owns" the business — not the people who own shares in it. It is also the corporation that earns the profit and bears the responsibility for any losses. The shareholders cannot bind the corporation in contract, nor are they directly responsible to its creditors for its debts.

The corporate form is useful because it represents a vehicle that may be used to amass the large amounts of capital necessary to set up and carry on business activities that require capital in excess of that which a partnership or sole proprietorship can acquire. Its continuous existence and ability to bring together the necessary expertise to undertake large and complex business activities have also contributed to its widespread use as the appropriate form for most large-scale business enterprises.

Agencies

An **agency** is a particular form of business organization that is subject to its own rules of law. In the strict sense, it is not a form of business organization like a partnership or corporation, although the agency business itself may take on either form as a method of organization. It is essentially a service relationship that operates as an extension of other organizations to carry out their business activities. It is also a relationship that may exist between individuals within an organization. The law of agency, because of its application to so many other forms of business organization, is examined in detail in the next chapter.

CHAPTER 15

Law of Agency

THE ROLE OF AN AGENT

The law of agency is concerned with the relationship that arises when one individual (a **principal**) either expressly or impliedly uses the services of another (the **agent**) to carry out a specific task on his or her behalf. The relationship may arise through an express agreement, conduct, or necessity, but in every case the relationship involves three parties: the principal, the agent, and a third party. The purpose of the agency relationship is to enable the principal to accomplish some particular purpose, usually the formation of a contract with the third party. If the law has been properly complied with, the end result will be the accomplishment of the task without direct dealings between the principal and the third party.

Agents are generally engaged in business activities that involve the negotiation of contracts, but agents may also be used for many other purposes. For example, a lawyer may be engaged as an agent to perform certain legal services on behalf of a client, or a real estate agent may be engaged to bring a buyer and seller together, but with no authority to bind the principal (the seller) in contract. Still, the most common use of an agent is to bind the principal in contract with a third party.

HISTORICAL DEVELOPMENT OF THE LAW OF AGENCY

The law of agency has its roots in the law relating to tort, contract, quasi-contract, and equity. Some evidence indicates that agency existed in the early medieval period. However, agents were not widely used during that period because it was seldom necessary for a person to engage another to perform a service in a community that was small and mostly self-sufficient. It was only with the growth of trade and the rise of the mercantile class that the use of agents became important and widespread.

During the late eighteenth century, and throughout the nineteenth century, the rapid growth of industry and commerce created the need for a common law response to the problems that the rapid industrial change had brought about. The law of contract was a part of this response, and with it, the law of agency was refined. In their respective spheres of influence, both the common law courts and equity moulded the concepts and ideas that now form the basis of modern agency law. The law of agency itself was distinguished from the law of employment by means of a subtle blend of maritime and mercantile law, tort, contract, and trust concepts that the courts modified and merged into the present-day body of law. These rules of law relating to agency may be divided into a number of distinct categories, where each refers to a particular aspect of the agency relationship.

THE NATURE OF THE RELATIONSHIP

By definition, an **agent** is a person who is employed to act on behalf of another. If the act of an agent is done within the scope of the agent's authority, the act will bind the principal.[1] A great many agents are independent business people who may be employed by a number of principals at any one time to act for each in a variety of different business transactions. The employment of an agent should not be viewed merely as the ordinary relationship of employer-employee.

The general rules of contract normally apply to an agency relationship. An infant, for example, may be a principal, but any contract negotiated on the infant's behalf (except a contract for necessities) would remain voidable at the infant's option, even if the agent was of full age. Since the agent is simply a conduit by which a contract may be effected between the principal and a third party, the capacity of the agent is to some extent unimportant. An agent, however, must not be insane. An agent may still be a minor and, despite this minority, may negotiate a binding agreement on behalf of a principal who possesses full capacity to contract. The agency agreement between the principal and agent, nevertheless, is subject to the ordinary rules of contract. If one of the parties is an infant, it may be voidable at the option of the infant, even though the other party may be bound.

Agency by Express Agreement

The principal-agent relationship may arise as a result of an express agreement, which may be either oral or in writing. The relationship may also be inferred from the actions of the principal, in which case it is sometimes called **agency by conduct** or **agency by estoppel.** A third type of agency that may arise in certain circumstances is referred to as an **agency of necessity.**

Agency that arises out of an express agreement is contractual in nature, and is subject to the ordinary rules of contract with respect to its formation and performance. While it may be oral and binding under most circumstances, it must comply with the Statute of Frauds if the agreement cannot be fully performed within a year. The agreement must also comply with any special requirements for formal contracts, if the agent, as a part of his or her duty, is expected to execute such a document on behalf of the principal. For example, suppose that Anderson engages Baker as her agent to sell a parcel of land for her and to execute a conveyance of the land to the purchaser. Baker must be empowered to do so by a grant of the power under seal, if the provincial law requires the document

---

1. Osborn, P.G., *The Concise Law Dictionary*, 4th ed. (London: Sweet & Maxwell, 1954), p. 22.

Anderson would be expected to sign to be made under seal. The particular document under seal that would authorize the execution of the conveyance would be a **power of attorney** — a legal document that would appoint the agent as the principal's attorney for the purpose of conveying the land.

The advantage of a written agency agreement is that the terms and conditions of the agency, and in particular the duties of the principal and the agent, are set out in a document for future reference. Not every agency agreement requires this formality, since a verbal agreement is perfectly adequate in many cases. For example, if Martin requests Thomas to purchase an item for him from the local hardware store, an agency relationship would be created whereby Thomas would be authorized to act as Martin's agent in the purchase from the shopkeeper. A written agreement would not normally be required for this simple agency task.

The ordinary agency relationship extends beyond the agreement between the principal and the agent. It usually involves a second contract with a third party. The two contracts are separate, but in the case of the contract negotiated by the agent and the third party, if the agent acts within the scope of his or her authority, the rights and duties under the agreement become those of the principal and the third party. The agent, in effect, drops from the transaction once the agreement is executed, and has neither rights nor liabilities under it.

Duties of the Parties

A point to note with respect to agency is the nature of the relationship between the principal and the agent. Unlike many contractual relationships, the parties in an agency relationship must act in good faith in their dealings with each other. Under agency law, the principal has a duty to pay the agent either the fee fixed or a reasonable fee for the services rendered. The principal must also indemnify the agent for any reasonable expenses that the agent properly incurs in carrying out the agency agreement. At common law, the agent is entitled to payment immediately on the completion of the service. However, it is customary for the parties to fix the time for payment at some later date, usually when the accounts have been settled.

The agent has a number of obligations toward the principal. First, the agent must obey all lawful instructions of the principal and keep confidential any information given to him by the principal. Secondly, the agent must keep in constant contact with the principal and inform the principal of any important developments that might occur as negotiations progress. This is a particularly important duty on the part of the agent, for the law holds that any notice to an agent is notice to the principal, and the principal is therefore deemed to know everything that is communicated to the agent by the third party.

If an agent possess special skills or the competence to perform the act required under the agency agreement, then the agent must maintain the standard required for that skill in the performance of his or her duties. The agent may be liable to the principal if the agent fails to maintain that standard, and if the failure results in a loss to the principal. The agent normally may not, except with the express permission of the principal, delegate agency duties to a sub-agent. The principal is entitled to rely on the special skills and judgement of the agent alone. While there are certain exceptions to this rule, generally, a principal is entitled to personal service by the agent.

Where an agent is authorized to receive funds or goods on behalf of the principal, the agent has a duty to account for the goods or the money. To fulfill this obligation, the agent must keep records of the money received and keep the funds separate from his or her own. The usual practice of agents in this regard is to place all funds in a trust account, or a special account identified as the principal's, and to remit money to the principal at regular intervals. If the agent is entitled to deduct an earned commission from the funds received under the terms of the agency agreement or by custom of the trade, then the deduction is usually made at the time that the balance of the account is remitted to the principal.

The agency relationship is a relationship of the utmost good faith. The agent is obliged to always place the principal's interest above his or her own. To fulfill this duty, the agent must bring to the principal's attention any information that the agent receives that might affect the principal. Also, when the agent engages in any activity on behalf of the principal, the agent must act only in the best interest of the employer. For example, an agent must endeavour to obtain the best price possible for goods that he or she sells for the principal, or, if engaged to purchase goods, the agent must seek out the lowest price that can be found in the marketplace. In both cases, the agent must act in the best interests of the principal, and seek the most favourable price, rather than the quickest commission.

An agent has a duty only to the principal and not to any third party with whom the agent negotiates. The agent may not act for both parties without the express consent of the principal and the third party. If the agent should obtain a commission or benefit from the third party without disclosing the fact to the principal, the agent would not be entitled to claim a commission from the principal.[2] For example, Newsome enters into an agency agreement with Wilson to sell his business, and agrees to pay Wilson a commission if he is successful. Wilson, without Newsome's knowledge or permission, enters into an agreement with Bray to find Bray a business and to be paid a commission if he is successful. Wilson negotiates the sale of Newsome's business to Bray and collects a commission from both Newsome and Bray. In this case, there would be no enforceable commission contract, as Wilson would be liable to Newsome for the return of any commission paid for his actions. Similarly, if Newsome engaged Wilson to sell a quantity of goods for him, and Wilson sold the goods to Bray as if they were his own and at a higher price than that reported to Newsome, Newsome would be entitled to recover the secret profit made by Wilson in the transaction.[3]

The courts generally take a very strong position against agents who place their own interests above those of their principal. In the case of *Andrews v. Ramsay & Co.*[4] a dishonest agent colluded with the purchaser to acquire land that the agent was authorized to sell at a price lower than what a purchaser might otherwise pay for it. When the collusion was discovered, the vendor (principal) refused to pay the agent the commission on the sale. The judge commented:

> It seems to me that this case is only an instance of an agent who has acted improperly being unable to recover his commission from his principal. It is impossible to

2. *S.E. Lyons Ltd. v. Arthur J. Lennox Contractors Ltd.,* [1956] O.W.N. 624; *Andrews v. Ramsay & Co.,* [1903] 2 K.B. 635; *McPherson v. Watt* (1877), 3 App. Cas. 254.

3. *Fullwood v. Hurley,* [1928] 1 K.B. 498; *Industries & General Mortgage Co. v. Lewis,* [1949] 2 All E.R. 573.

4. *Andrews v. Ramsay & Co.,* [1903] 2 K.B. 635.

say what the result might have been if the agent in this case had acted honestly. It is clear that the purchaser was willing to give 20£ more than the price which the plaintiff received, and it may well be that he would have given more than that. It is impossible to gauge in any way what the plaintiff has lost by the improper conduct of the defendants. I think, therefore, that the interest of the agents here was adverse to that of the principal. A principal is entitled to have an honest agent, and it is only the honest agent who is entitled to any commission. In my opinion, if an agent directly or indirectly colludes with the other side, and so acts in opposition to the interest of his principal, he is not entitled to any commission. That is, I think, supported both by authority and on principle; but if, as is suggested, there is no authority directly bearing on the question, I think that the sooner such an authority is made the better.

Agency by Conduct

Agency may arise in ways other than by express agreement. A person may, by actions, convey the impression to another that he or she has conferred authority on a particular person to act as an agent in specific matters. In this case, an agency relationship may be created by **conduct**. If a person permits this state of affairs to occur, and the agent enters into a contract with a third party on the person's behalf, the person may not be permitted to later deny it. In this instance, the person may be said to have created an agency relationship by **estoppel**. The authority of the agent under these circumstances would not be real, but apparent. The binding effect of the agent's actions, however, would be real if the principal led the third party to believe that the agent had the authority to act on his or her behalf.[5]

Agency by estoppel arises most often from a contractual relationship wherein the principal has adopted a contract negotiated by another. As a result the principal has given the third party the impression that the contract was one of agency. For example, a person may engage another to make cash purchases of goods on his or her behalf on a number of occasions. The same person may be engaged at some later time to purchase goods on credit without the authority of the person for whom they were intended. If the principal adopts the contract by paying the account, the third party seller would be led to believe that the agent had the authority to pledge the principal's credit. This would be inferred from the principal's conduct of settling the account. Unless the principal makes it clear to the seller that the agent does not have authority to pledge his or her credit, the principal may be estopped from denying the agent's authority to pledge credit in the future.[6] The failure to act would in effect "clothe the agent with apparent authority" to act on behalf of the principal. There are other instances where apparent authority may exist apart from the situation where the conduct of the principal creates the agency relationship. A wife, for example, is presumed at common law to have the authority to purchase goods and services for household use as her husband's agent.[7] This particular presumption at law arises out of cohabitation as a rebuttable presumption only, rather than a right at law. The presumption may be

---

5. *Reid and Keast v. McKenzie Co.* (1921), 61 D.L.R. 95; *Agnew v. Davis* (1911), 17 W.L.R. 570.

6. *Reid and Keast v. McKenzie Co.* (1921), 61 D.L.R. 95; *Agnew v. Davis* (1911), 17 W.L.R. 570.

7. *Miss Gray Ltd. v. Earl Cathgart* (1922), 38 T.L.R. 562, but see also for example Family Law Act, R.S.O. 1990, c. F-3.

rebutted by the husband in several ways. He may establish one of the following: that notice was given to the shopkeepers that they were not to supply goods on credit; that the wife was provided with an adequate cash allowance to make the purchases and directed to purchase no goods on credit; that the household was already adequately supplied with such goods; or possibly that the goods were extravagant, in light of the husband's station in life and income. Under family law reform legislation in many provinces, the common law obligation of a husband to provide support for his wife and family has been substantially changed. This may also affect this common law presumption. However, if the wife had pledged the husband's credit previously, and if the accounts had been paid by the husband without giving notice to the shopkeepers that future purchases were not to be on credit, the husband may be bound by his conduct on his wife's future credit purchases.

Agency by conduct may result in liability for the principal if the principal fails to notify third parties that the agency relationship has terminated. Until such time as the third party becomes aware of the termination of the agency relationship, the third party is entitled to assume that the agency continues to exist and that the agent has authority to bind the principal. Again, the authority of the agent would only be apparent, because the termination of the agency relationship would have the effect of ending the agent's real authority. The third party may, nevertheless, hold the principal liable on a contract negotiated by the agent on the basis of the agent's apparent authority.[8]

An agent may also possess the implied authority to bind the principal in circumstances where the agency agreement expressly withholds real authority to do so from the agent. When an agent is engaged to perform a particular service, the agent customarily has the authority to engage in other forms of contract on behalf of the principal. If a principal engages an agent to perform a particular service, any restriction on the agent's authority must be brought to the attention of the third party, otherwise the principal may be bound if the agent should exceed his or her actual authority and negotiate a contract within what may be described as the agent's implied authority. For example, a retailer has the implied authority to sell goods placed in his or her possession. If a principal sends goods to a retailer on the express agreement that they must not be sold before a particular time, a sale by the retailer before that time would be binding on the principal. This is so because a retailer is normally clothed with the authority to sell goods in the retailer's possession without restriction as to time of the sale. The agent in this instance would be liable to the principal for breach of the agency agreement by selling the goods, but this would not affect the validity of the sale to the third party.

An example of a case where agents bound their principal on the basis of apparent authority arose in the case of *Reid & Keast v. McKenzie Co. Ltd.*[9] In this instance agents were authorized to enter into contracts on the principal's contract form, subject to a proviso that the agents inform the third parties that the contracts would not come into effect until the principal had approved samples of the

8. *Trueman v. Loder* (1840), 11 Ad. & E. 589, 113 E.R. 539.

9. *Reid & Keast v. A.E. McKenzie Co. Ltd.*, [1921] 3 W.W.R. 72.

product. An agent failed to so inform the third parties, and the outcome of the case turned on the agent's apparent authority. The judge described the case as follows:

> The defendants admit that they sent [the agent] out armed with the forms of the contracts actually entered into. They admit also that he had authority to get the plaintiffs to sign these contracts, and that he had authority to sign them on behalf of the defendants, subject to this: that he must stipulate that the contracts were not to come into effect until the company had approved of the samples. He represented to the plaintiffs that he had authority to enter into these contracts on behalf of the defendants. As evidence of that authority he produced the contract forms. He did not mention, as the trial Judge has found, the limitations on his authority which had been verbally given to him, but which did not appear on the forms.
>
> The arming of the agent with the defendants' contract forms and the sending him out to have these forms executed by the plaintiffs was, in my opinion, a clear holding out by the defendants that he had their authority to make the contracts. The defendants were, therefore, bound by the contract entered into by Thompson, as the plaintiffs had no notice of the limitations which had been placed upon his authority.

Agency by Operation of Law

Agency may also arise by operation of law. In certain circumstances it may be necessary for a person to act as an agent (such as in an emergency), where it is impossible to obtain authority to perform the particular acts from the property owner. With modern day communications, the circumstances under which an agency of this nature may arise are limited. Nevertheless, in an emergency, certain persons at common law may act as **agents of necessity** on behalf of others and bind them in contract. For example, a ship-master at common law is presumed to have the power to bind the ship-owner in contract in the event of an emergency if it is necessary to do so to preserve the ship and its cargo. However, this right would only arise if the ship-master was unable to communicate with the owner, and if it was necessary to do so to secure the safety of the ship. The same right at law would permit the ship-master to sell or otherwise deal with the cargo in an emergency, even though no express authorization would be given by the owner of the cargo to do so.

A wife may also be an agent of necessity at common law. If a husband fails to maintain his family as he is required to do by law, then his wife may, as an agent of necessity, pledge his credit in order to purchase necessaries. In most provinces, special legislation has been passed that sets out a husband's obligation to support his family. But in some provinces, family law changes in the form of legislation have altered the common law obligation of a husband to support his wife and family. In so doing, they may have altered the common law right of a wife to act as an agent of necessity. At the present time, the trend in support obligation appears to spread the obligation over the entire family, rather than place the full burden on the husband. As a result of this type of legislation, the question is unclear as to whether the credit of one person may be pledged by an agent of necessity when the obligation rests on other members of the family as well.[10]

---

10. For example, in some jurisdictions, self-supporting children may be responsible for the maintenance of their parents, and both spouses may be jointly responsible for the support of each other and their dependent children: Family Law Act, R.S.O. 1990, c. F-3.

The common law limits the circumstances under which a person may act as an agent of necessity. The courts have recognized a number of instances where an agency of necessity may arise, such as in a true emergency. However, the relationship is generally limited to those cases where a pre-existing legal relationship exists between the principal and the agent of necessity. For example, in one case, a railway carrying perishable goods sold the goods to avoid total loss, because a labour strike prevented the railway from making delivery. The court in that instance ruled that the railway acted as an agent of necessity, since a true emergency existed, and the owner could not be reached for authority to act.[11]

However, the court will not normally find an agency of necessity where no pre-existing relationship can be shown. In an eighteenth century case, a man found a dog and maintained it until its master came to retrieve it. The court would not hold that the man was an agent of necessity and entitled to compensation for the expense of caring for the animal, because no pre-existing legal relationship could be shown between the agent and the owner.[12] The rationale of the court in reaching this conclusion was that no person should be entitled to force an obligation upon another unless express or implied consent has been given.

RATIFICATION OF CONTRACTS BY A PRINCIPAL

A principal may in certain circumstances wish to take advantage of a contract that an agent negotiated on his or her behalf, and that the agent clearly had no authority to make. The process of acceptance of a contract of this type is called **ratification.** If properly done, it has the effect of binding the principal in contract with the third party as of the date it was negotiated by the agent.

A principal may ratify a contract if the principal was in existence at the time the agent made the contract and was identified in the agreement as the principal. This particular rule generally applies to corporations rather than to individuals, since corporations have a particular time at which they come into existence. Unless the legislation under which a corporation is created permits the adoption of pre-incorporation contracts,[13] the corporation may not ratify a contract made before it was created. In addition, the subject-matter of the contract must be something that the principal would have been capable of doing at the time the contract was made by the agent, and at the time of ratification. Again, this rule would have direct application to corporations rather than individuals. Corporations in some jurisdictions are limited to the objects for which they are incorporated. If the subject-matter of the contract should be something that the corporation is not permitted to do, the subsequent change of the objects clause (to permit the corporation to undertake a particular activity) would still not permit the corporation to ratify the contract, unless statutory authority permitted the ratification.[14]

Ratification in every case must be made within a reasonable time after the agent enters into the contract and the principal becomes aware of its existence. Effective ratification must be of the whole agreement, and not simply of the

---

11. *Sims & Co. v. Midland Railway Co.,* [1913] 1 K.B. 103. See also *Hastings v. Village of Semans,* [1946] 3 W.W.R. 449; *Campbell v. Newbolt* (1914), 20 D.L.R. 897.

12. *Binstead v. Buck* (1776), 2 Black., W. 1117, 96 E.R. 660.

13. See for example, the Canada Business Corporations Act, R.S.C. 1985, c. 44, s. 14 (2).

14. *McKay v. Tudhope Anderson Co., Ltd.* (1919), 44 D.L.R. 100.

favourable parts. The ratification, however, need not be expressly stated. It may be implied from the conduct of the principal. The principal, for example, may accept benefits under the contract, or perform the promises made on the principal's behalf to signify ratification. The principal's silence would not normally constitute acceptance. However, in circumstances where the agent has exceeded his or her authority in negotiating the contract, a refusal to promptly repudiate the agreement on becoming aware of it may imply acceptance.

In each case, ratification of the contract by the principal dates the time of acceptance back to the date on which the contract was made. It does not run from the date of ratification. As a result of this rule, the actions of the third party may be altered by the subsequent ratification of the contract by the principal. The law on this particular point is unclear at the present time. In an English case, the court held that repudiation by the third party, before ratification, was ineffective if the principal subsequently ratified.[15] However, this decision has been questioned in Canada and reversed in the United States. The law in the United States presently seems to state that withdrawal from the agreement by the third party, or the institution of legal proceedings against the agent for breach of warranty of authority, would prevent later ratification of the agreement by the principal.[16] The position in Canada appears to fall somewhere between the two extremes. Some case-law suggests that the principal may not ratify if the ratification would adversely affect parties other than the third party,[17] and others follow the English law.[18]

The English common law on this point has been described by the courts in the following manner:

> The rule as to ratification by a principal of acts done by an assumed agent is that the ratification is thrown back to the date of the act done, and that the agent is put in the same position as if he had had authority to do the act at the time the act was done by him. Various cases have been referred to as laying down this principle, but there is no case exactly like the present one.... The rule as to ratification is of course subject to some exceptions. An estate once vested cannot be divested, nor can an act lawful at the time of its performance be rendered unlawful, by the application of the doctrine of ratification.[19]

THIRD PARTIES AND THE AGENCY RELATIONSHIP

In an ordinary agency relationship between principal, agent, and third party, the agent (if negotiating a contract within the scope of his or her authority) will bind the principal. The performance of the contract will be by the principal and the third party. The agent must clearly indicate to the third party that he is acting only as an agent, and will usually identify the principal for whom he acts. This is normally done by the agent signing the principal's name on the agreement and adding his own, together with words to indicate that his signature is that of an agent only. For example, an agent may sign as follows: "Mary Smith per Jane

---

15. *Bolton Partners v. Lambert* (1889), 41 Ch.D. 295; *Pickles and Mills v. Western Assurance. Co.* (1902), 40 N.S.R. 327.

16. See for example, *LaSalle National Bank v. Brodsky,* 51 Ill. App. (2d) 260, (1964). See also American Law Institute, *Restatement of the Law Second. Agency,* 2d., American Law Institute Publishers, St. Paul, Minn., 1958, Vol. 1, p. 226, S 88.

17. *Goodison Thresher Co. v. Doyle* (1925), 57 O.L.R. 300; *Peterson v. Dominion Tobacco Co.* (1922), 52 O.L.R. 598.

18. *Farrell & Sons v. Poupore Lumber Co.,* [1935] 4 D.L.R. 783.

19. *Bolton and Partners v. Lambert* (1889), 41 Ch.D. 295.

Doe" where Mary Smith is the principal, and Jane Doe the agent. The use of the term **per** is a short form of ***per procurationem*** which means "on behalf of another," or in agency law, "by his agent." It is also possible to specifically state in the agreement that a party is only acting as agent for another; that is, John Doe may sign the contract as follows: "John Doe as agent for John Smith."

Where the agent has revealed to the third party that he or she is acting as an agent only, and acts in accordance with the given authority, the principal alone is liable to the third party. The agent has no rights and duties under the contract with respect to the third party, nor may the agent claim any of the benefits that flow to the principal. If the principal does not wish to have his or her identity revealed, and instructs the agent to enter into an agreement without revealing the principal's identity, the agent may proceed in either of two ways. The agent may enter into the agreement in the agent's own name, without revealing that he or she is acting as an agent, or the agent may enter into the agreement as agent for an unnamed principal.

Where the agent enters into an agreement without disclosing the fact that he or she is an agent, the third party may assume that the agent is acting as a principal. If the agreement is reduced to writing, and if the agent in the negotiations holds himself out as a principal, describing himself and signing as principal, then the agreement from the third party's point of view will be one of direct contractual relations with a principal, rather than with an agent. The agent alone in this case would be liable.[20] Under these circumstances, the third party may look to the agent for damages if the contract is not performed, because the agent under the contract would be personally responsible for performance. The agent, by the same rule of law, would be entitled to enforce the agreement against the third party if the third party should fail to perform the agreement in accordance with its terms.

A different liability would fall upon the agent if the agent contracts on behalf of a fictitious or non-existent principal, and the third party discovers the non-existence of the principal. The third party may sue the agent for **breach of warranty of authority**.[21] The same right would also be available to the third party if the agent entered into the agreement on behalf of a principal for whom the agent did not have authority to act.[22] In each of these cases, the agent would not be liable on the contract, but would be liable to the third party for damages arising from the agent's warranty that he or she had authority to act for the named principal.[23] In the first instance, where the principal was fictitious or non-existent, if the intention of the agent was to deceive the third party, the agent's actions would amount to fraud. An action for deceit would be available to the third party as well.

In the case of an agreement negotiated by an agent (where the agent neither describes himself as a principal or agent), if the principal should decide to come forward and reveal his or her identity, the principal may enforce the contract. However, if the principal should do so, the third party may then bring an action against the principal instead of the agent if a breach should occur. The third party, however, is restricted in this regard. The third party may sue either the principal

---

20. *Lawson v. Kenny* (1957), 9 D.L.R. (2d) 714; *Collins v. Associated Greyhound Racecourses, Ltd.,* [1930] 1 Ch. 1.

21. *Gardiner v. Martin and Blue Water Conference Inc.,* [1953] O.W.N. 881.

22. *Wickberg v. Shatsky* (1969), 4 D.L.R. (3d) 540.

23. *Austin v. Real Estate Listing Exchange* (1912), 2 D.L.R. 324.

or the agent, but not both.[24] A particular exception to this rule does exist with respect to a contract under seal in which the agent signs as a contracting party. In this case, only the agent may enforce the agreement, and only the agent would be liable under it.[25]

If the agent enters into a contract with a third party in which the agent expressly describes himself as an agent, but without disclosing the identity of the principal, the agent will not be personally liable. The fact that the agent describes himself as an agent, and that the third party is willing to enter into a contract with the agent on that basis, protects the agent from personal liability. However, if the agent simply does not disclose that he or she is acting as an agent, and enters into a contract with the third party, the third party may elect to hold either the principal (if the third party discovers the principal's identity) or the agent liable. Of importance, in the case of an undisclosed principal, is the position of the principal. If the principal makes his or her existence known after the contract has been made by an agent who did not disclose the principal's existence, the principal may be in a position somewhat analogous to that of an assignee of a contract. The principal may take the agent's place, but in doing so, the principal would also be obliged to accept the relationship as it stands between the agent and the third party. If the third party had contracted in the belief that the agent was in fact a principal, then any defence that the third party might have had against the agent may be raised against the principal. For example, Smith entered into a contract with Jones without disclosing that she was acting as an agent for Brown. If Brown should come forward after the contract is made and sue on it when Jones defaults, any defence that Jones might have against Smith could be raised against Brown. If Smith owed Jones a sum of money, Jones might legitimately claim the right to deduct Smith's debt with him from any sum owing under the contract.[26]

LIABILITY OF PRINCIPAL AND AGENT TO THIRD PARTIES IN TORT

The general rule in agency law is that a principal may be held liable for a tort committed by the principal's agent, if the tort is committed by the agent in the ordinary course of carrying out the agency agreement. A tort that an agent might commit is sometimes based upon fraudulent misrepresentation. This constitutes the tort deceit. If a third party should be induced to enter into a contract by an agent as a result of a fraud on the part of the agent, then both principal and agent will be liable if the tort was committed in the ordinary course of the agent's employment. However, if the tort is committed outside the scope of the agent's employment, only the agent will be liable. Also, the principal will not be liable for damages for a failure to perform such an agreement, unless the principal adopts the contract or accepts benefits under it.

If a third party is induced to enter into a contract on the basis of a false statement that the agent innocently makes, the third party may repudiate the contract on the basis of innocent misrepresentation. Similarly, if the third party is in a position to prove that the principal knew the statement was false, but allowed the agent to innocently convey it to the third party, the principal may be liable for fraud.[27]

---

24. *M & M Insulation Ltd. v. Brown* (1967), 60 W.W.R. 115; *Phillips v. Lawson*, [1913], 4 O.W.N. 1364.

25. *Pielstricker and Draper Dobie & Co. v. Gray*, [1947] O.W.N. 625.

26. *Campbellville Gravel Supply Ltd. v. Cook Paving Co.*, [1968] 2 O.R. 679.

27. *Campbell Motors Ltd. v. Watson* (Crescent Motors), [1949] 2 W.W.R. 478.

TERMINATION OF THE PRINCIPAL-AGENT RELATIONSHIP

In many cases, agency relationships created by express agreement also provide for termination. If the agreement specifies that either party may terminate the agency relationship by giving the other party a particular period of notice and, if such notice is given, the agency will then terminate on the expiry of the notice period. If no specific time for termination is fixed in the agreement, the right to terminate may be implied, and either party may give notice to end the relationship. An agency may also terminate in other ways. Agency agreements may be made for the purpose of accomplishing a particular task. When the task is complete, the agency relationship will automatically terminate. For example, B Co. may own a quantity of wood, and engage D Co. to sell it as its agent. Once the wood is sold, the task is complete, and the agency ends.

The incapacity of the principal or of the agent (by way either of death or insanity) has the effect of terminating the relationship, but the general legal incapacity of an agent or principal if the agent or principal is a minor, may not. As with infant's contracts in general, in some jurisdictions the agency contract, in which one party is a minor, may only be voidable at the option of the infant or minor.

The bankruptcy of the principal terminates the agency agreement. The principal would not be bound by any agreement negotiated by the agent after the point when the bankruptcy took place. The agent is expected to be in constant touch with the principal, and therefore aware of the principal's financial state. Consequently, a contract negotiated by an agent after the principal becomes bankrupt may render the agent liable to the third party for damages for breach of warranty of authority.

In all cases where the agency relationship is for more than a specific task, it is of the utmost importance that the principal inform all third parties that had dealings with the agent that the agency has been terminated. If the principal fails to notify the third parties of the termination of the agency, the agent may still bind the principal in contract on the basis of the agent's apparent authority. For example, for many years Joliet, as Alford's agent, purchased goods on Alford's credit from Clayton. Alford terminated the agency relationship, but did not notify Clayton. Joliet later purchased goods from Clayton on Alford's credit and sold them. Alford would be liable to Clayton for the payment, as Joliet had the apparent authority to purchase goods as Alford's agent in the absence of notice to the contrary.[28]

SUMMARY

The law of agency is concerned with the relationship that exists when one person, either expressly or impliedly, uses the services of another to carry out a specific task on his or her behalf. This relationship may be created by express agreement, through conduct, or by necessity. If the agent has negotiated a contract on behalf of the principal within the scope of the agent's authority, only the principal and the third party will be bound by the contract. An infant may be an agent and still bind the principal if the principal is of full age; but for a contract negotiated on behalf of an infant, the infant principal would not be bound except for necessaries. If an agent should negotiate a contract on behalf of a principal without the authority

---

28. *Consolidated Motors Ltd. v. Wagner* (1967), 63 D.L.R. (2d) 266; *Watson v. Powell* (1921), 58 D.L.R. 615.

to do so, it may be possible for the principal to ratify the agreement. By ratification, the contract would be effective from the date that it was entered into by the agent.

Ordinarily, if a contract is negotiated by an agent within the scope of the agent's authority, only the principal will be liable on the agreement and entitled to enforce the rights under it. However, if the agent negotiated a contract on behalf of a fictitious or non-existent principal, the agent would be liable to the third party on the basis of breach of warranty of authority. Similarly, if the agent negotiated an agreement on behalf of a principal and had no express or apparent authority to do so, the agent, and not the principal, would be liable. In cases where the agent did not disclose the identity or existence of the principal to the third party, depending upon the circumstances, the third party may elect to hold one or the other liable. If a fraud is involved in the contract negotiated, both the principal and agent may be liable, provided that the agent acted within the scope of the agency agreement.

Agency may be terminated on the death or insanity of either the principal or the agent. It may also be terminated in the case of bankruptcy of the principal. Agency may automatically end on the completion of the task for which it was formed or by notice, either as specified in the agreement, or at any time, if no notice period is required. Where an agency agreement is terminated (other than by death, insanity or bankruptcy), notice to third parties is important. Otherwise the agent may still bind the principal in contract with an unsuspecting third party.

DISCUSSION QUESTIONS

1. What is the role of an agent?
2. What types of agency relationships may arise or be formed?
3. Is a written document setting out the terms of an agency relationship always necessary? If not why not?
4. Why do the courts sometimes recognize the existence of agency relationships as based upon the conduct of parties?
5. How does the implied authority of an agent differ from express authority? Give examples of each.
6. Define an "agent of necessity." Explain how this agency might arise.
7. Describe briefly the duties of an agent to his or her principal.
8. Explain "agency by estoppel."
9. Under what circumstances would a principal be entitled to ratify a contract made by an agent?
10. If an agent exceeds his or her authority in negotiating a contract, under what circumstances would the agent alone be liable?
11. When would a principal be liable for the acts of an agent who exceeded his or her authority?
12. List the various ways that an agency relationship may be terminated.
13. Is a principal liable for the torts of his or her agent? Under what circumstances would the principal not be liable?

MINI-CASE PROBLEMS

1. Alice engaged Kelly as her agent to negotiate a contract for the purchase of a large quantity of china for her shop. Before Kelly completed his negotiations, Alice became insolvent and was declared a bankrupt. Kelly completed the transaction for the purchase of the supplies some day later. What are the supplier's rights?

2. The Acme Co. frequently sold goods through B Company, as its agent. The Acme Co. terminated the agency agreement, but failed to pick up goods at B Company's warehouse. B Company later sold the goods to D Company. However, before D Company took delivery, Acme Co. demanded return of the goods from B Co. Discuss.

JUDICIAL DECISIONS

The judicial decisions in this chapter illustrate: (a) the liability of the principal where the agent has apparent authority to act on behalf of the principal and (b) the duty of the agent to the principal.

In the *Freeman & Lockyer* case, the agent had apparent, but not real authority, to bind his company in engaging the services of the plaintiffs. The company, however, permitted the plaintiffs to do their work. The judge considers the difference between "actual" and "apparent" authority in usual business settings. He concludes that, by allowing the agent to act as if he had actual authority, the principal had indeed given the agent authority to act in that manner.

The second case, *McNeel and McNeel* v. *Low et al.* provides an example of a business transaction where an agent placed his own interests ahead of those of his principal. The judge reviews the nature of the fiduciary relationship between a principal and agent, and the duty of the agent as set out in other legal decisions. The cases noted by the judge illustrate the agent's obligations to the principal. Applying this law the judge finds that the agent was in breach of his duty.

Apparent Authority of Agent — Liability of Principal

Freeman & Lockyer v. Buckhurst Park Properties (Mangal) Ltd. et al., [1964] 2 Q.B. 480.

K, a director of the defendant company, engaged the plaintiffs to do certain professional work on behalf of the company. The plaintiffs completed the work and submitted an account for their fees. When the company failed to pay, legal action was instituted to collect the account.

The defendants argued that the director K was not a managing director (the firm did not have one), and therefore he did not have authority to bind the company.

DIPLOCK, L.J.:

It is necessary at the outset to distinguish between an "actual" authority of an agent on the one hand, and "apparent" or "ostensible" authority on the other. Actual authority and apparent authority are quite independent of one another. Generally they co-exist and coincide, but either may exist without the other and their respective scopes may be different. As I shall endeavour to show, it is upon the apparent authority of the agent that the contractor normally relies in the ordinary course of business when entering into contracts.

An "actual" authority is a legal relationship between principal and agent created by a consensual agreement to which they alone are parties. Its scope is to be ascertained by applying ordinary principles of construction of contracts, including any proper implications from the express words used, the usages of the trade, or the course of business between the parties. To this agreement the contractor is a stranger; he may be totally ignorant of the existence of any authority on the part of the agent. Nevertheless, if the agent does enter into a contract pursuant to the "actual" authority, it does create contractual rights and liabilities between the principal and the contractor. It may be that this rule relating to "undisclosed principals," which is peculiar to English law, can be rationalised as avoiding circuity of action, for the principal could in equity compel the agent to lend his name in an action to enforce the contract against the contractor, and would at common law be liable to indemnify the agent in respect of the performance of the obligations assumed by the agent under the contract.

An "apparent" or "ostensible" authority, on the other hand, is a legal relationship between the principal and the contractor created by a representation, made by the principal to the contractor, intended to be and in fact acted upon by the contractor, that the agent has authority to enter on behalf of the principal into a contract of a kind within the scope of the "apparent" authority, so as to render the principal liable to perform any obligations imposed upon him by such contract. To the relationship so created the agent is a stranger. He need not be (although he generally is) aware of the existence of the representation but he must not purport to make the agreement as principal himself. The representation, when acted upon by the contractor by entering into a contract with the agent, operates as an estoppel, preventing the principal from asserting that he is not bound by the contract. It is irrelevant whether the agent had actual authority to enter into the contract.

In ordinary business dealings the contractor at the time of entering into the contract can in the nature of things hardly ever rely on the "actual" authority of the agent. His information as to the authority must be derived either from the principal or from the agent or from both, for they alone know what the agent's actual authority is. All that the contractor can know is what they tell him, which may or may not be true. In the ultimate analysis he relies either upon the representation of the principal, that is, apparent authority, or upon the representation of the agent, that is, warranty of authority.

The representation which creates "apparent" authority may take a variety of forms of which the commonest is representation by conduct, that is, by permitting the agent to act in some way in the conduct of the principal's business with other persons. By so doing, the principal represents to anyone who becomes aware that the agent is so acting, that the agent has authority to enter on behalf of the principal into contracts with other persons of the kind which an agent so acting into the conduct of his principal's business has usually "actual" authority to enter into.

| Agency — Fiduciary Relationship — Accountability for Secret Profit by Agent | ### McNeel and McNeel v. Low, Low & Renfrew Realty Ltd. (1962), 35 D.L.R. (2d) 226. |

A corporate real estate agent employed Low as a salesman. The appellants listed their property for sale with the agent for $78 000. The salesman found an offeror willing to purchase the property for the listed price, but the offeror could not raise sufficient funds. The salesman and the offeror then entered into an agreement to purchase the property from the appellants for $70 000 under an arrangement that allowed the salesman to make a secret profit of $8000.

When the appellants discovered the true facts, they brought an action for recovery of the secret profit.

TYSOE, J.A.:

There are innumerable kinds of fiduciary relationships and they exist in innumerable forms. They may arise from specific contract but they may and often do arise out of acts or relationship creating a duty. In the circumstances existing here, Low was in a fiduciary position in relation to the appellants. Renfrew

Realty Ltd. being a limited company, the exigencies rendered it necessary that its duties to the appellants be performed by and through the instrumentality of some person selected by it. In undertaking those duties, Low placed himself in a position of fiduciary relationship to the appellants. There rested upon him the same fiduciary obligations and responsibilities and duties to the appellants as rested upon the limited company. In this respect he was in the same position as he would have been had he himself been appointed the appellants' agent. The principles of equity do not allow him to do for himself that which the limited company could not do for itself.

In *Regal (Hastings), Ltd. v. Gulliver et al.*, [1942] 1 All E.R. 378, Viscount Sankey at p. 381 said:

"In my view, the respondents were in a fiduciary position and their liability to account does not depend upon proof of *mala fides*. The general rule of equity is that no one who has duties of a fiduciary nature to perform is allowed to enter into engagements in which he has or can have a personal interest conflicting with the interests of those whom he is bound to protect."

In the same case Lord Wright at p. 392 said:

"My Lords, of the six respondents, two, Gulliver and Garton, stand on a different footing from the other four. It is in regard to the latter that the important question of principle brought into issue by the decisions of Wrottesley, J., and the Court of Appeal call for determination. That question can be briefly stated to be whether an agent, a director, a trustee or other person in an analogous fiduciary position, when a demand is made upon him by the person to whom he stands in the fiduciary relationship to account for profits acquired by him by reason of his fiduciary position, and by reason of the opportunity and the knowledge, or either, resulting from it, is entitled to defeat the claim upon any ground save that he made profits with the knowledge and assent of the other person. The most usual and typical case of this nature is that of principal and agent. The rule in such cases is compendiously expressed to be that an agent must account for net profits secretly (that is, without the knowledge of his principal) acquired by him in the course of his agency. The authorities show how manifold and various are the applications of the rule. It does not depend on fraud or corruption."

In *Charles Baker Ltd. v. Baker & Baker*, [1954] 3 D.L.R. 432 [1954] O.R. 418, Mackay, J.A., delivering the judgement of the Court, at p. 440 D.L.R., p. 432 O.R. said:

"The onus is upon the agent to prove that the transaction was entered into after full and fair disclosure of all material circumstances and of everything known to him respecting the subject-matter of the contract which would be likely to influence the conduct of his principal. The burden of proof that the transaction was a righteous one rests upon the agent, who is bound to produce clear affirmative proof that the parties were at arm's length, that the principal had the fullest information upon all material facts, and that having this information he agreed to adopt what was done."

That these statements are correct statements of the law, there can be no doubt.

In *Dunne v. English* (1874), L.R. 18 Eq. 524, Sir G. Jessel, M.R., said at p. 533:

"It is not enough for an agent to tell the principal that he is going to have an interest in the purchase, or to have a part in the purchase. He must tell him all the material facts. He must make a full disclosure." And at pp. 534-5:

"I will only read a few words from another well-known case, *Lowther v. Lowther* (13 Ves. 95, 102), in which Lord *Erskine*, then Lord Chancellor, states the doctrine as Lord *Eldon* had laid it down: 'Considering the Defendant Bryan as an agent, the principle upon which a Court of Equity acts in cases of this kind is very properly admitted; having being settled in many instances, particularly in the time of Lord *Eldon*; resting upon grounds connected with the clearest principles of equity and the general security of contracts, viz., that an agent to sell shall not convert himself into a purchaser, unless he can make it perfectly clear that he furnished his employer with all the knowledge which he himself possessed.' So that the older authorities and the modern authorities agree.

"Now, what is the meaning of 'knowledge which he himself possessed' — 'full disclosure of all that he knows?' Is it sufficient to say that he has an interest? Is it sufficient to put a principal on inquiry? Clearly not. Upon that point I have before me the case of *Imperial Mercantile Credit Association v. Coleman* (L.R. 6 H.L. 189, 194). There is a passage in the argument of the counsel for the Appellants which, I think, very fairly and properly states the law: 'It is not enough to say that the directors were sufficiently informed to put upon inquiry. They ought in such a case to have the fullest information given to them, and ought not to be driven to inquiry;' for which two cases are cited: *Fawcett v. Whitehouse* (1 Russ. & My. 132) and *Hichens v. Congreve* (1 Russ. & My. 150, n.). I take it that it is a correct statement of the law."

Low was clearly in breach of his duty to the appellants.

CASE PROBLEMS FOR DISCUSSION

Case 1

A property owner listed her property for sale. She provided the agent with authority to sell the property on her behalf if the terms of any offer received met the terms set out in the listing agreement. A prospective buyer inspected the property during the period of time that the property was listed for sale, but did not make an offer to purchase.

After the agency agreement had expired, the prospective buyer made an offer to purchase the property that corresponded with the terms of the listing agreement. The agent accepted the offer on behalf of the property owner.

When the buyer discovered that the agency agreement had expired, he brought an action against the agent.

Explain the nature of the buyer's action and indicate how the case may be decided. Could the property owner ratify the agreement? What factors would affect the ratification?

Case 2

Race Motors, an automobile dealer, engaged Simple as its agent to sell its automobiles in a nearby city. In November, 1992, Hyde agreed to purchase a new 1993 model through Simple, with delivery to be made in May, 1993. The order was duly placed with Race Motors, and a vehicle was delivered to Simple in April, 1993.

Simple recognized the vehicle as a 1992 model. However, he urged Hyde to complete the sale in April rather than May, as the automobile was ready for delivery. Hyde did so, but a few weeks later discovered that the vehicle was a 1992 model, and not a 1993 model as he had ordered.

Hyde brought an action against Simple for damages. Then he brought a second action against Race Motors.

Explain the nature of Hyde's claim against Simple and Race Motors. What problems does the second action raise? On what basis will the litigation likely be resolved?

Case 3

Smith was interested in the purchase of the shares of a manufacturing firm that was in financial difficulties due to a high debt load. He contacted Jones, a business consultant, to provide him with an assessment of the firm. Jones was to negotiate the purchase on Smith's behalf if his investigation indicated that the purchase of the shares represented a good investment.

Jones suggested that Brown, a consulting engineer, be engaged to assess the condition and value of the manufacturing equipment. Brown was also to provide some advice on what might be done to improve the profitability of the operation. Smith agreed, so Jones and Brown proceeded with their assessment of the firm.

During their examination, Jones and Brown realized that the firm represented a good investment if the equity to debt ratio could be altered and some manufacturing processes changed to improve efficiency. The two then established a corporation. They indicated to the present owners of the manufacturing firm (whom they had met through Smith) that they also represented a corporation that might be interested in the purchase if Smith should decide against the investment.

Jones and Brown completed their assessment of the business that in their written opinion to Smith was worth approximately $1.1 million. They submitted accounts of $3000 and $3500 respectively, which Smith promptly paid.

A few days later, Smith presented the owners of the manufacturing firm with an offer to purchase the shares for $1 million. The offer was promptly rejected. Before Smith could submit a new offer, the corporation that Jones and Brown had incorporated made an offer of $1.1 million for the business. The second offer was accepted, and the shares transferred to the corporation for the $1.1 million.

When Smith discovered that Jones and Brown were the principal shareholders of the corporation that had made the $1.1 million offer, he brought an action against them for damages.

Describe the nature of Smith's action. Discuss the possible arguments that might be raised by both the plaintiff and the defendants. Identify the main issues and render a decision.

Case 4

Chelsey engaged Kent to act as his agent in the sale of 3000 live rabbits. Without disclosing the fact that he was only an agent, Kent offered the rabbits to Somerset at $2 each. Somerset agreed to purchase the lot, but at the conclusion of the discussion, reminded Kent that he owed him $1500. Kent responded, "When this sale is completed you will get your $1500."

Kent advised Chelsey of the sale. Chelsey delivered the rabbits to Somerset's farm and informed him that he was delivering the rabbits in accordance with the sale that Kent had negotiated on his behalf.

Somerset agreed to take delivery and offered his cheque in the amount of $4500. Chelsey demanded the full $6000. He threatened to sue Somerset if he did not pay the purchase price in full.

Advise Chelsey and Somerset in this case. Offer a possible outcome if Chelsey should carry out his intention to institute legal proceedings against Somerset.

Case 5

Johnson used Birkett as his stockbroker for most of his investments. Occasionally, when Johnson had spare funds, he would seek the advice of Birkett as to investments he should make. On one such occasion, Birkett recommended two companies as investments with potential for profit. At the time, Birkett indicated that he personally preferred stock "B" over stock "A" and intended to purchase some shares on his own account. Johnson ignored his advice, however, and purchased stock "A."

During the next few weeks, stock "A" dropped in value as a result of unexpected political upheaval in a Third World country where the company had extensive holdings. Stock "B," on the other hand, gradually increased in value during the same period. It reached a price approximately 20% above its value when Birkett recommended it as a possible investment.

Johnson discussed his investment with Birkett, and Birkett suggested he sell stock "A." Johnson did so and requested Birkett to invest the proceeds in stock "B." Birkett cautioned Johnson that the stock had already climbed in price and might not be as attractive an investment as it was some weeks earlier. Johnson, nevertheless, insisted that he buy the shares. Birkett then transferred some of his own shares to Johnson at the current market price, without disclosing the fact to Johnson.

The shares almost immediately declined in value for reasons unknown to both Johnson and Birkett.

A month later, Johnson discovered that the shares that he had acquired had been transferred to him by Birkett. He immediately brought an action against Birkett for the amount of his loss.

Explain the nature of the claim that Johnson might make against Birkett. Indicate how the case might be decided.

Case 6

John R. had been a successful businessman during his lifetime. When he died, he left his business to his son and daughter and, under the terms of his will, left his widow, Florence, a life annuity that paid her $40 000 per year. Florence was quite elderly at the time of her husband's death. Her son and daughter concluded that the $40 000 annuity might not be sufficient for her to maintain her home and cover her living expenses, since she required a housekeeper to look after the premises. To provide her with additional income, the two children placed $300 000 in the hands of the family stockbroker in their mother's name.

The funds were placed with Margaret L., a registered representative of the brokerage firm. She was instructed to invest the money in the shares of Canadian corporations only, in order to provide Florence with income and dividend tax credits. No part of the funds was to be placed in bonds or the securities of foreign corporations.

Florence had no investment experience, and so advised Margaret. She informed Margaret that she intended to leave the choice of investment with her, as she did not wish to have "the worry of making investment decisions."

During the next two years, Margaret invested the funds in the shares of Canadian corporations. The investment income was approximately $40 000 per year. Florence was pleased with the results and, at the end of the second year, wrote a note to Margaret that read: "Many thanks for your hard work and success to date. Invest as you see fit, until further notice from me."

During the third year, Margaret switched most of the Canadian shares to bonds, foreign currency holdings, and speculative issues, at a very high investment turnover rate. The high trading activity resulted in very high sales commissions for Margaret, but very little in earnings for Florence. By the end of the third year, Florence's income was down to $3000, and the net worth of her investment fund had diminished to $180 000.

At the end of the third year, Florence notified her son that "something seemed to be wrong" with her investment income. Her son immediately contacted the investment firm. At that point, Margaret's trading practices were discovered, and the value of the investment fund was determined. On the advice of her son, Florence brought an action against the stockbroker and Margaret, an employee of the firm.

Discuss the nature of the action that Florence might bring, and the issues involved. Render a decision.

Case 7

The R Corporation carried on business as a representative for investor groups that wished to acquire active business firms. PR, the President of R Corporation met with a group of business people who had recently established a small brewery, and who wished to purchase some of the assets of another brewery business, the ABC Brewery Ltd.

At the direction of the investor group, PR met with the president of the ABC Brewery Ltd. and negotiated a purchase price of $4.5 million for the assets. PR then prepared a "letter of intent" which set out the purchase price of the assets and the terms of payment. The letter called for the payment of a deposit of $450 000 within 48 hours of the signed acceptance of the offer by ABC Brewery Ltd. The "letter of intent" was signed: "R Corporation on behalf of an investor group. per PR."

PR delivered the letter to the president of the ABC Brewery Ltd. On receipt of the letter, the president inquired as to the identity of the group of investors, and PR arranged for G, a member of the investor group to telephone the president and assure him that R Corporation had authority to sign the letter on the investor group's behalf. G telephoned the president of ABC to assure him, but did not reveal the fact that he was a principal in the group that had established the competitor brewery. The president then wrote to PR advising him that the company would accept the offer.

The investor group was unable to arrange financing, and decided to abandon the purchase. When the investor group did not pay the deposit within the 48-hour period, the ABC Brewery Ltd. delivered a written notice of termination of the agreement to R Corporation. PR, however, felt that he could assemble another group of investors to acquire the assets, and decided to enforce the agreement. R Corporation then instituted legal proceedings against ABC Brewery Ltd. claiming for breach of the agreement and damages.

Explain the basis upon which R Corporation might bring the claim, and indicate the defences, if any, that the ABC Brewery Ltd. might raise. Render a decision.

CHAPTER 16

Law of Partnership

**HISTORICAL
DEVELOPMENT**

A **partnership** is a relationship that subsists between two or more persons carrying on business in common with a view to profit.[1] This definition represents a narrower delineation of the relationship than most people might realize, as it excludes all associations and organizations that are not carried on for profit. Social clubs, charitable organizations, and amateur sports groups are not partnerships within the meaning of the law, and many business relationships are excluded as well. For example, the simple debtor-creditor relationship and the ordinary joint ownership of property do not fall within the definition of a partnership.

The partnership is an ancient form of organization, and undoubtedly one that existed long before the advent of the written word and recorded history. The first associations had their roots in early trading ventures, where merchants banded together for mutual protection from thieves and vandals. The natural extension of these loose associations was for the merchants to join together in the trading itself and to share the fortunes of the ventures. The partnership form of organization has been used by merchants for thousands of years. References to early partnerships are found both in biblical writings[2] and in early Roman history. These sources indicate that partnerships were frequently used for many commercial activities.

By the time of the Roman Empire the partnership had developed into a common form of business organization that was subject to a number of different rules of law. The earliest partnerships tended to be joint ventures by merchants engaged in the purchase or sale of goods in distant places, or by merchants banding together to undertake an activity that required more capital than one merchant alone was prepared to risk or invest. These early associations were often informal and were

---

1. The Partnerships Act, R.S.O. 1990, c. P-5, s. 2. All common law provinces have similar legislation relating to partnership. Quebec partnership law is found in the Civil Code.
2. Ecclesiastes 4:9-10 (about 977 B.C.)

based upon mutual trust and confidence between the partners. These two characteristics of the relationship have remained as essential elements of the modern form of organization.

It was not until the discovery of distant markets and the New World in the fifteenth and sixteenth centuries that the capital requirements of the merchants demanded an alteration of the ordinary partnership organization. To meet these needs, the *société en commandite* was developed in Continental Europe. This form of organization allowed the contribution of capital by investors and a share of the profits from the venture, although no right to actively participate in the management of the organization was attached to the investment. As a result, the investors were given limited liability for the debts of the organization. The concept in a modified version found favour in England in the sixteenth century in the form of the **joint stock company**. This organization was essentially a partnership in which the investors, as partners, delegated the authority to manage the organization to a board of management. However, unlike the European *société en commandite*, unlimited liability of the individual partners remained.

By the late eighteenth century, the courts began to examine the partnership and its activities in the light of contract law. The expansion of trade, both domestic and foreign, during this period and throughout the nineteenth century increased the use of partnerships as a form of business organization. The inevitable litigation associated with such a large number of entities produced a large body of law concerning the relationship. By the latter part of the nineteenth century, the law had reached a stage of maturity where codification was both possible and desirable. In 1879, Sir Frederick Pollock was requested to prepare a draft bill for the English Parliament that would codify the law of partnership. The bill was duly prepared and presented, but did not come before Parliament until 10 years later. The act was carefully drawn to reflect the common law at the time. As a part of legislation, it retained the rules of equity and common law relating to partnerships, except where the rules were inconsistent with the express provision of the act.[3]

Since the Partnership Act was passed in England, it has been adopted with some minor modifications in all of the common law provinces of Canada and in many other countries that were part of the British Commonwealth. Partnership legislation permits the formation of partnerships for all commercial enterprises, except for a number of activities such as banking and insurance, where the corporate form (and special legislation) is necessary.[4] By definition, a partnership must consist of at least two persons. While some provinces restrict the number of partners to a specific maximum,[5] no limit is imposed in most.

NATURE OF A PARTNERSHIP

The essential characteristic of the partnership is that it is a relationship that subsists between persons carrying on business in common with a view to profit. The partnership, however, must be distinguished from other relationships, such as

---

3. Partnership Act, 1890 53 Vict. c. 39.

4. The Partnerships Act, R.S.O. 1990, c. P-5. Reference in this chapter will be made to specific sections of the Ontario Act, but most other provincial statutes are similar.

5. The Partnerships Act, R.S.O. 1990, c. P-5, s. 45. Reference in this chapter will be made to specific sections of the Ontario Act, but most other provincial statutes are similar.

joint or part ownership of property, profit-sharing schemes, the loan of money, and the sharing of gross receipts from a venture. The foregoing associations in themselves do not constitute partnerships. The existence of a partnership turns very much on the particular agreement made between the parties, but, as a general rule, the sharing of the net profits of a business is *prima facie* evidence of the existence of a partnership.[6] In contrast, the remuneration of a servant or agent by a share of the profits of the business would normally not give rise to a partnership,[7] nor would the receipt of a share of profits by the widow or child of a deceased partner.[8]

There must usually be something more than simply sharing profits before a partnership agreement exists. If the parties have each contributed capital and have each actively participated in the management of the business, then these actions would be indicative of the existence of a partnership. Even then, if the "business" simply represents the ownership of a block of leased land, the relationship may not be a partnership. It may, instead, be co-ownership of land; that is, a relationship that closely resembles a partnership, but that is treated in a different manner at law. Co-ownership, when examined carefully and compared to a partnership, is a distinct and separate relationship. The principal differences between the two may be outlined as follows:

— A partnership is a contractual relationship. Co-ownership may arise in several ways: it may arise through succession or through the inheritance of property from a deceased co-owner.

— A partnership is a relationship that is founded on mutual trust. It is a personal relationship that is not freely alienable. Co-ownership, on the other hand, may be freely alienable without the consent of the other co-owner. For example, Alexander and Bradley may jointly own a block of land. Alexander may sell his interest to Calvin without Bradley's consent, and Bradley and Calvin will then become co-owners. This is not possible in the case of partnership.

— A partner is generally an agent of all other partners in the conduct of partnership business. A co-owner is normally not an agent of other co-owners.

— A partner's share in partnership property is never real property. It is always personalty, as it is a share in the assets, which can only be determined (unless there is an agreement to the contrary) by the liquidation of all partnership property. In contrast, co-ownership may be of either personalty or realty. Two persons as co-owners, for example, may purchase an automobile or they may purchase a parcel of land. In each instance they would be co-owners of the property, but they would not be partners in the absence of an agreement to the contrary.

— A partnership is subject to the Partnerships Act in its operation, and dissolution is by the act. Co-ownership may be dissolved or terminated under legislation that provides for the division or disposition of property held jointly.[9]

6. The Partnerships Act, R.S.O. 1990, c. P-5, s. 3.

7. Ibid., s. 3(a).

8. Ibid., s. 3(b).

9. Ibid., s. 3(c).

A partnership may, in a sense, be established from the point of view of, and for purposes of, third parties by **estoppel**. If a person holds himself out as being a partner, either by words or conduct, or permits himself to be held out as a partner of the firm, that person may be liable as a partner if the third party, on the strength of the representation, advances credit to the firm. This would apply even where the representation or holding out is not made directly to the person advancing the credit.[10] For example, Oxford, an employee of a partnership, holds herself out as a partner and Baker, a merchant, sells goods on credit to the partnership on the faith of Oxford's representation. In this case, Oxford will be liable to Baker as if she were a partner. The same would hold true if the partnership held out Oxford as a partner and she permitted them to do so, even though she was only an employee. By allowing the firm to hold her out as a partner, she would become liable, as if she were a partner, for any debts where the creditor advanced money in the belief that she was a partner.

In the case of *Lampert Plumbing (Danforth) Ltd. v. Agathos et al.*[11] the court reviewed partnership law as it relates to "holding out" as a partner in the following terms:

> It is clear from s. 15 of the Partnerships Act and from the authorities that the person holding himself out as a partner "is liable as a partner" to one who has relied in good faith upon the representations made. Since in my view Agathos did hold himself out as the sole proprietor of the defendant construction company to Kreizman he incurs liability to the plaintiff company as if he were in fact a partner of the construction company or its sole proprietor.
>
> All persons with capacity to enter into contracts have the capacity to become partners. An infant or minor may become a partner, but if he or she should do so, the ordinary rules of contract apply. The contract is voidable at the infant's option. Since it is deemed to be a continuing relationship, the infant must repudiate the agreement either before or shortly after attaining the age of majority. If the infant fails to repudiate, then the infant would be bound by the agreement. The infant would also be liable for the debts of the partnership incurred after he or she reached the age of majority. Where repudiation takes place before the infant reaches the age of majority, then the infant will not normally be liable for the debts of the partnership unless he or she committed a fraud. Once repudiation takes place, the infant is not responsible for the liabilities of the partnership. However, the infant is not entitled to a share in the profits until the liabilities have been paid.

LIABILITY OF A PARTNERSHIP FOR THE ACTS OF A PARTNER

The persons who form a partnership are collectively called the **firm**, and the business is carried on in the firm name.[12] In a partnership, every partner is the agent of the firm in the ordinary course of partnership business. Every partner may bind the firm in contract with third parties, unless the person with whom the partner was dealing knew that he or she had no authority to do so.[13] The act that the partner performs (for example, where a partner enters into a contract to supply goods or to perform some service) must be related to the ordinary course of partnership business before his or her act binds the other partners. If the act is not something

---

10. For example, in Ontario under the Partition Act, R.S.O. 1990, c. P-4.

11. [1972] 3 O.R. 11; and see the Partnerships Act, R.S.O. 1990, c. P-5, s. 15(1).

12. Ibid., s. 5.

13. Ibid., s. 6.

that falls within the ordinary scope of partnership business, then only that partner would be liable.[14]

A firm may also be liable for a tort committed by a partner, if the tort is committed in the ordinary course of partnership business.[15] Examples of this situation might arise where the partner is responsible for an automobile accident while on firm business, or where the partner is negligent in carrying out a contract and, as a result, injures a third party. Another example would be where a partner fraudulently misrepresents a state of affairs to a third party to induce the third party to enter into a contract with the firm. The firm would also be liable where a partner, within the scope of his or her apparent authority, receives money or property either directly from a third party or from another partner, and, while it is in the custody of the firm, misappropriates it or takes it for personal use.[16]

As these examples illustrate, a partnership is generally liable for the acts of the individual partners if committed in the course of partnership business. It is in this respect that a partnership represents a risky form of business organization. For this reason alone, business persons who may wish to engage in business activities using the partnership form should carefully select their partners. In essence, partners expose their total assets to the claims of others who deal with the partnership or who may suffer some injury at the hands of a partner. Consequently, the partnership form of business organization should be supported by a carefully prepared written partnership agreement that clearly delineates the duties and responsibilities of each partner, as well as their rights. In addition, business procedures should also be established to reduce the possibility of one partner having the right to commit the partnership to contracts or agreements that could conceivably result in substantial partnership liability.

The admission of a new partner to a firm does not automatically render the new partner liable for the existing debts of the partnership. Under the Partnerships Act, a new partner is not liable for any debts incurred before the person becomes a partner.[17] However, a new partner may, if he or she so desires, agree to assume existing debts as a partner, by express agreement with the previous partners. Much the same type of judicial reasoning is applied to the case of a retiring partner. A retiring partner is not relieved of debts incurred while a partner,[18] but if proper notice of retirement is given to all persons who had previous dealings with the firm (and to the public at large) the retiring partner would not be liable for partnership debts incurred after the date of retirement.

RIGHTS AND DUTIES OF PARTNERS TO ONE ANOTHER

The rights and duties of partners are normally set out in a partnership agreement, since most partners wish to arrange their own affairs and those of the partnership in a particular manner. As with most agreements, the parties, within the bounds of the law of contract and the specific laws relating to partnerships, may establish their own rights and duties with respect to each other. They are free to fix their rights and duties in the contract, and they may vary them with the consent of all

14. Ibid., and see, for example, s. 8 where credit is pledged.

15. Ibid., s. 11.

16. Ibid., s.2.

17. Ibid., s. 18(1).

18. Ibid., s. 18(2).

partners at any time. They need not have a written agreement if they do not wish to have one; but if they do not, their rights and obligations to one another will be defined as in the act.

Under the act, all property and rights brought into the partnership by the partners, and any property acquired by the partnership thereafter, becomes partnership property. It must be held and used for the benefit of the partnership, or in accordance with any agreement of the partners.[19] Any land acquired by, or on behalf of, a partnership, regardless of how the title is held by the partners (or a single partner), is considered to be bought in trust for the benefit of the partnership, unless it is established to be otherwise.[20] Insofar as the partners themselves are concerned, the land is not treated as real property but as personal property, since an individual partner's interest in partnership property is only personalty.[21]

The act provides a number of rules that, in the absence of any express or implied agreement to the contrary, determine the partners' interests with respect to each other. The rules, as they appear in the Ontario statute,[22] provide as follows:

1. All the partners are entitled to share equally in the capital and profits of the business, and must contribute equally towards the losses, whether of capital or otherwise, sustained by the firm.
2. The firm must indemnify every partner in respect of payments made and personal liabilities incurred by him,
   (a) in the ordinary and proper conduct of the business of the firm; or
   (b) in or about anything necessarily done for the preservation of the business or property of the firm.
3. A partner making, for the purpose of the partnership, any actual payment or advance beyond the amount of capital that he has agreed to subscribe, is entitled to interest at the rate of 5% per annum from the date of the payment or advance.
4. A partner is not entitled, before the ascertainment of profits, to interest on the capital subscribed by him or her.
5. Every partner may take part in the management of the partnership business.
6. No partner shall be entitled to remuneration for acting in the partnership business.
7. No person may be introduced as a partner without the consent of all existing partners.
8. Any difference arising as to ordinary matters connected with the partnership business may be decided by a majority of the partners, but no change may be made in the nature of the partnership business without the consent of all existing partners.
9. The partnership books are to be kept at the place of business of the partnership, or the principal place, if there is more than one, and every partner may, when he or she thinks fit, have access to and inspect and copy any of them.

19. Ibid., ss. 21(1) and 22.
20. Ibid., ss. 21(2) and 22.
21. Ibid., s. 23.
22. Ibid., s. 24.

In addition to these general rules, the act also provides that in the absence of an express agreement to the contrary, a majority of the partners may not expel any partner from the partnership.[23] The only method that a majority may use if they wish to get rid of a partner would be to terminate the partnership, then form a new partnership without the undesirable partner. Of course, this method of expelling a partner has certain disadvantages, but it is the only procedure available to the partners if they have failed to make express provisions for the elimination of undesirable partners in an agreement.

Because a partnership is a contract of utmost good faith, the partners have a number of obligations that they must perform in the best interests of the partnership as a whole. Every partner must render a true account of any money or information received to the other partners,[24] and deliver up to the partnership any benefit arising from personal use of partnership property.[25] For example, a partnership owns a boat that is occasionally used for partnership business. One of the partners, for personal gain and without the consent of the other partners, uses the boat on weekends to take parties on sightseeing cruises. Any profits earned by the partner using the partnership boat must be delivered up to the partnership, as the earnings were made with partnership property. The same rule would apply where a partner, without the consent of the other partners, uses partnership funds for an investment, then returns the money to the partnership, but retains the profits. The other partners could insist that the profits be turned over to the partnership as well.

In addition to the unauthorized use of partnership property by a partner, the obligation of good faith extends to activities that a partner might engage in that conflict with the business interests of the firm. A partner, for example, may not engage in any other business that is similar to, or competes with, the business of the partnership, without the express consent of the other partners. If a partner should engage in a competing business without consent, any profits earned in the competing business may be claimed by the partnership. The partner may also be obliged to provide an accounting for the profits.[26]

A final important matter relating to the duties of a partner to the partnership arises where a partner may assign his or her share in the partnership to another, or change his interest. The assignment does not permit the assignee to step into the position of the partner in the firm. The assignee does not become a partner because of the personal nature of a partnership and only becomes entitled to receive the share of the profits of the partner who assigned the partnership interest. The assignee acquires no right to interfere in the management or operation of the partnership. He or she must be content with receipt of a share of the profits as agreed to by the partners.[27] If the assignment takes place at the dissolution of the partnership, the assignee would then receive the share of the assets to which the partner was entitled on dissolution.[28]

---

23. Ibid., s. 25.
24. Ibid., s. 28.
25. Ibid., s. 29(1).
26. Ibid., s. 30.
27. Ibid., s. 31(1).
28. Ibid., s. 31(2).

DISSOLUTION OF A PARTNERSHIP

The parties to a partnership agreement may provide for the term of the agreement and the conditions under which it may be dissolved. A common clause in a partnership agreement is one that provides for a period of notice if a partner wishes to dissolve the partnership. Another common practice is to provide for the disposition of the firm name on dissolution, if some of the partners should desire to carry on the business of the partnership following its termination. Coupled with this provision, the parties may also provide a method of determining the value of the business and the partners' shares if some should wish to acquire the assets of the dissolved business.

Apart from special provisions in a partnership agreement to deal with notice of dissolution, a partnership agreement drawn for a specific term will dissolve automatically at the end of the term.[29] If the agreement was to undertake a specific venture or task, then the partnership would dissolve on the completion of the task or venture.[30] Where the agreement is for an unspecified period of time, then the agreement may be terminated by any partner giving notice of dissolution to the remainder of the partners. Once notice is given, the date of the notice is the date of dissolution. However, if no date is mentioned, then the partnership is dissolved as of the date that the notice is received.[31]

A partnership may also be dissolved in a number of other ways. The death or insolvency of a partner will dissolve the partnership, unless the parties have provided otherwise.[32] The partners may, at their option, treat the charging of partnership assets for a separate debt as an act that dissolves the partnership.[33] A partnership will be automatically dissolved if it is organized for an unlawful purpose, or if the purpose for which it was organized subsequently becomes unlawful.[34]

In addition to these particular events that dissolve a partnership, there are instances when a partner may believe that a partnership for a fixed term should be terminated before the date fixed for its expiry. If a partner is found to be mentally incompetent or of unsound mind,[35] or if a partner becomes permanently incapable of performing his or her part of the partnership business,[36] the other partner may apply to the courts for an order dissolving the relationship. Relief is also available from the courts in cases where a partner's conduct is such that it is prejudicial to the carrying on of the business.[37] The same applies when the partner willfully or persistently commits a breach of the partnership agreement, or so conducts himself that it is not reasonable for the other partners to carry on the business with such a partner.[38] The courts may also dissolve a partnership if it can be shown that the business can only be carried on at a loss,[39] or where, in the opinion of the

29. Ibid., s. 32(a).
30. Ibid., s. 32(b).
31. Ibid., s. 32(c).
32. Ibid., s. 33(1).
33. Ibid., s. 33(2).
34. Ibid., s. 34.
35. Ibid., s. 35(a).
36. Ibid., s. 35(b).
37. Ibid., s. 35(c).
38. Ibid., s. 35(d).
39. Ibid., s. 35(e).

court, the circumstances were such that it would be just and equitable to dissolve the relationship.[40] This latter authority of the courts to dissolve a partnership has been included in the Partnerships Act. It provides for unusual circumstances that may arise that are not covered by specific provisions in the act, and that may be shown to work a hardship on the partners if they were not permitted to otherwise dissolve the agreement.

Once notice of dissolution has been given, either in accordance with the partnership agreement or the act, the assets of the firm must be liquidated, and the share of each partner determined. A partner's share is something that is distinct from the assets of the business and, unless otherwise specified in the agreement, cannot be ascertained until the assets are sold. However, until the share is determined and paid, each partner has an equitable lien on the assets.[41]

Unless the partnership agreement provides otherwise, the assets of the partnership must first be applied to the payment of the debts to persons who are not partners of the firm.[42] Then each partner must be paid rateably what is due for advances to the firm (as distinct from capital contributed).[43] The next step in the procedure is to pay each partner rateably for capital contributed to the firm,[44] and then to divide the residue (if any) amongst the partners in the proportion in which profits are divisible.[45] Any losses are to be paid first out of profits, then out of capital, and, if insufficient funds are available to cover the debts, out of contributions from the partners in the proportions in which they were entitled to share profits.[46] However, the procedure where one partner is insolvent represents an exception to this rule. This results from a case tried some years after the Partnership Act was passed in England. The judges in that case stated that if one partner should be insolvent, the remaining solvent partners would be obliged to satisfy the demands of the creditors — not in proportion to the manner in which they share profits, but in proportion to the ratio of their capital accounts at the time of dissolution.[47] The reasoning of the court in reaching this particular conclusion was rather obscure, but presumably was based upon the assumption that the ratio of the capital accounts represented a better indicator of the ability of the remaining partners to sustain the loss than the ratio in which profits were shared.

An example of how this would be applied may be illustrated by a hypothetical case. Suppose on the dissolution of the ABC partnership after disposing of all assets and paying all liabilities, the partnership had a loss of $30 000. At that time, the capital accounts of A, B, and C were as follows:

A	B	C
$5000	$20 000	$30 000

After dividing the $30 000 loss equally ($10 000 each) A's account would be in a deficit position, as A had only a $5000 capital balance. If A is insolvent and

---

40. Ibid., s. 35(f).
41. Ibid., s. 39.
42. Ibid., s. 44(2)(a).
43. Ibid., s. 44(2)(b).
44. Ibid., s. 44(2)(c).
45. Ibid., s. 44(2)(d).
46. Ibid., s. 44(1).
47. Ibid., and see *Garner v. Murray*, [1904] 1 Ch. 57.

cannot pay the remaining $5000, the $5000 deficit would have to be made up by the remaining partners.

According to the law, B and C would be obliged to make up the $5000 deficit in the ratio of their capital accounts *at the time of dissolution*; i.e., 2/5 for B and 3/5 for C. B would therefore be obliged to pay $2000 and C $3000 of C's $5000 deficit. The capital accounts of the partners after payment of the $30 000 would then look like this:

A	B	C
$ 0	$ 8000	$17 000

Once a partnership has been dissolved, it is necessary to notify all customers of the firm and the public at large. This is particularly important if some of the partners are retiring, and the remaining partners intend to carry on the business under the old firm name. If notice is not given to all customers of the firm, the retiring partners may be held liable by creditors who had no notice of the change in the partnership.[48] The usual practice is to notify all old customers of the firm by letter, and notify the general public by way of a notice published in the official provincial *Gazette*. The notice in the *Gazette* is treated as notice to all new customers who had no dealings with the old firm. Even if the new customers were unaware of the published notice, the retired partner could not be held liable for the debt.[49]

If a partner should die, and the firm thereby dissolve, no notice is necessary to the public. However, the deceased partner's estate would remain liable for the debts of the partnership to the date of that partner's death.

Once dissolution is under way, the business may be conducted by the partners only insofar as it is necessary to close down the operation. This right usually includes the completion of any projects under way at the time of dissolution, but does not include taking on new work. The individual partners may continue to bind the partnership, but only to wind up the affairs of the firm.[50]

After the partnership relationship has terminated, each partner is free to carry on a business similar to the business dissolved. Normally any restriction on the right to do so would be unenforceable unless it is a reasonable restriction limited to a particular term, and within a specified geographic area. Even then, all of the rules of law relating to restrictive covenants would apply.

LIMITED PARTNERSHIP

A **limited partnership** is one in which a partner under certain circumstances may limit his or her liability for partnership debts, and protect his or her personal estate from claims by the creditors of the partnership. The limited partnership bears a resemblance to the European *société en commandite,* which found its way into the Quebec Civil Code from French law and into the laws of other provinces by way of the laws of England. All of the common law provinces except Prince Edward Island have enacted legislation for the formation of limited partnerships. The provisions of each statute governing the relationship are somewhat similar.

While legislation exists for the formation and operation of limited partnerships

48. Ibid., s. 36(1).
49. Ibid., s. 36(2).
50. Ibid., s. 38.

(except where certain tax advantages exist), the limited partnership is seldom used for ordinary small business. The corporation has been found to be more suited to the needs of persons who might otherwise form a limited partnership. As a result, this type of entity is not commonly found in active small business organizations other than family business relationships. However, its use as a special-purpose organization for mining, oil exploration, hotel operations, and cultural activities such as television and film productions is not uncommon, particularly where some of the parties do not wish to engage in an active role in the undertaking.

The legislation pertaining to limited partnerships is not uniform throughout Canada. In general, it provides that every limited partnership must have at least one or more general partners with unlimited liability and responsibility, both jointly and severally, for the debts of the partnership.[51] In addition, the partnership may have one or more limited partners whose liability is limited to the amount of capital contributed to the firm.[52]

Only the general partners may actively transact business for the partnership and have authority to bind it in contract.[53] The name of the limited partner usually must not be a part of the firm name. If a limited partner's name should be placed on letterhead or stationery, in most jurisdictions he or she would be deemed to be a general partner.[54] The limited partner may share in the profits and may examine the partnership books, but must refrain from actively participating in the control of the business. Otherwise the limited partner will be treated as a general partner and lose the protection of limited liability.[55] The limited partner is further restricted with respect to the capital contributed. Once the limited partner has contributed a sum of money to the business, the limited partner may not withdraw it until the partnership is dissolved.[56]

To provide public notice of the capital contribution of the limited partners, and to identify the general partners in the business, information concerning the limited partnership must be filed in the appropriate public office specified in the provincial legislation. The registration of the notice is very important, as the partnership is not deemed to be formed until the partnership has been registered or the certificate filed.[57] A failure to file, or the making of a false statement in the documents filed, in some jurisdictions renders all limited partners general partners.

While the form of the document filed to register the limited partnership varies from province to province, the information contained generally provides the name under which the partnership operates, the nature of the business, the names of the general and limited partners, the amount of capital contributed by the limited partner, the place of business of the partnership, the date, and the term.[58] Changes

---

51. The Partnership Act, R.S.M. 1987, c. P-30, s. 52.

52. Ibid., s. 52 and 53.

53. Ibid., s. 54.

54. Ibid., s. 58(1).

55. Ibid., s. 63(1).

56. Ibid., s. 60 and 65.

57. Ibid., s. 55.

58. See, for example, The Business Names Registration Act, R.S.M. 1987, c. B-110, ss. 4(1) and 8(1).

in the partnership require a new filing, otherwise the limited partners may either lose their protection or the change is ineffective.

The document is designed to provide creditors and others who may have dealings with the limited partnership with the necessary information to enable them to decide if they should do business with the firm. Alternatively, it also provides information that they might need to institute legal proceedings against the firm if it fails to pay its debts or honour its commitments.

Changes in tax laws have also made certain types of investments attractive if the business is established in the form of a limited partnership. These partnership agreements normally provide for an organization or corporation to carry on the business activity on behalf of the partners, while providing the limited partners the special tax advantages associated with limited partnership ownership and entitlement to the assets and profits.

Notwithstanding the limited use of this type of partnership, some provinces have recently revised their legislation in an effort to clarify and expand the rights and duties of limited partners.[59] How useful these changes will be and whether they stimulate interest in this form of business organization remains to be seen.

REGISTRATION OF PARTNERSHIPS

Limited partnerships are not the only business entities subject to registration requirements. Most provinces require the registration of ordinary partnerships and of sole proprietorships if the sole proprietor is carrying on business under a name other than his own. Provincial legislation is not uniform with respect to registration, and some provinces exempt some types of partnerships from registration. For example, professions governed or regulated by provincial bodies are frequently exempt, and, in at least one province, farming and fishing partnerships need not be registered. The purpose of registration is the same as for limited partnerships, that is, to provide creditors and others with information concerning the business and the persons who operate it.

Declarations generally require the partners to disclose the name of the partnership, the names and addresses of all partners, the date of commencement of the partnership, and the fact that all partners are of the age of majority (or if not, the date of birth of the infant partners).[60] The declaration must normally be filed in a specified public office, usually the local Registry Office (or a central registry for the province), within a particular period of time after the partnership commenced operation.[61] Changes in the partnership usually require the filing of a new declaration[62] within a similar time period.

The provinces of Nova Scotia and Ontario provide in their legislation that no partnership or member may maintain any action or other proceeding in a court of law in connection with any contract, unless a declaration has been duly filed.[63] The significance of this particular section looms large in the event that an unregistered partnership wishes to defend or institute legal proceedings. The failure to register would act as a bar to any legal action by the partnership, until such time as registration is effected.

---

59. See, for example, the Limited Partnerships Act, R.S.O. 1990, c. L-15.
60. The Business Names Act, S.O. 1990, c. 5, s. 2.
61. See, for example, s. 3.
62. Ibid., s. 4(1).
63. Ibid., s. 7 and see the Partnership and Business Names Registration Act, R.S.N.S. 1989, c. 335, s. 20.

Sole proprietorships normally need not be registered in most provinces. However, a sole proprietor carrying on business under a name other than his or her own is usually required to register in much the same manner as a partnership, since persons doing business with such a business entity would be interested in knowing the identity of the true owner.

In a partnership, all partners required to register under registration legislation usually remain liable to creditors until a notice of dissolution is filed in the proper office. The declaration of dissolution acts as a public notice that a partnership has been dissolved. If afterwards the firm is to continue on, composed of the remaining or new partners, the old partners may still be deemed partners until the declaration of dissolution has been filed.

SUMMARY

The partnership is an ancient form of business organization. It is a relationship of utmost good faith that requires the partners to disclose to one another all information of importance to the firm. Partners are agents of the firm, and one partner acting within the apparent range of his or her authority may bind the partnership in contract with third parties. A partnership may also be liable for the torts of partners committed within the ordinary course of partnership business.

Partnership agreements are usually written contracts signed by the parties. A partnership agreement, however, need not be in writing, and need not specify the terms of the partnership. However, where no terms are set out, the provisions of the Partnerships Act apply to determine the rights and obligations of the partners.

Partners must not use partnership assets or funds to make secret profits at the expense of the partnership. Also the partners must not engage in other businesses that compete with the partnership, unless they have the express permission of all of the other partners.

A partnership may be dissolved by the completion of the specific venture for which the partnership was formed, or at the end of a specified term, or it may be terminated on notice if no term is specified. It may also terminate on the death or insolvency of a partner, or where the purpose for which it was organized is unlawful. The court under certain circumstances has the right to dissolve a partnership. Where a partnership is dissolved, all creditors and the public at large must be notified of the dissolution by the partners if the retiring partners wish to avoid liability for future debts of the partnership.

Subject to certain exceptions, partnerships must be registered. The limited partnership, which may be established in most provinces, depends upon registration to establish the limited liability of the limited partners.

DISCUSSION QUESTIONS

1. What essential characteristic distinguishes a partnership from other associations of individuals?
2. How is a partnership formed?
3. Why is a simple sharing of gross profits not conclusive as a determinant of the existence of a partnership relationship?
4. How does a partnership differ from co-ownership?
5. Under what circumstances may a minor be a member of a partnership? What is the extent of the minor's liability?

6. Explain how agency and partnership are related in terms of the operation of a partnership.

7. Under what circumstances would a partnership be liable for a tort committed by a partner?

8. What is the extent of the liability of the partners for the tort of a partner or for contracts entered into by a partner?

9. Under what circumstances may a partnership be dissolved?

10. Is it possible for a partner to sell his or her interest to another person? What is the status of the purchaser of the interest if it should be sold?

11. Explain the rights of creditors of a partnership when the partnership is dissolved.

12. If one partner should become personally bankrupt, and the partnership dissolved, how is the liability of each remaining partner for the debts of the partnership determined?

13. Why is registration of a partnership important in certain provinces?

14. What is a retiring partner obliged to do in order to avoid liability for future debts incurred by a partnership?

MINI-CASE PROBLEMS

1. A and B purchase a sailboat (which is in poor condition) with the intention of refurbishing it together and selling it when the work is completed. Are A and B partners?

2. X, Y, and Z agree to carry on business in partnership under the firm name XY Plumbing. Y, in the course of partnership business, carelessly injures T. T intends to take legal action against the partnership for the injury, but is unaware of Z being a partner, since his name is not included in the partnership name. Is Z liable if T sues only X and Y?

JUDICIAL DECISIONS

The first judicial decision in this chapter illustrates a problem that may arise when a partner retires from a partnership. In this case the issue was whether a creditor who knew that the partner had retired could hold the partner liable for partnership debts simply because the partnership had failed to register the change in the make-up of the partnership. As the judge notes in this case, the purpose of the registration is to notify the public of the names of the partners. However, where a creditor is aware of the partner's identity and aware of the fact that one of the partners that he had done business with had retired, he could not claim against that partner as a creditor for after-acquired debt incurred by the partnership. The judge, in effect, held that the person could not claim the estoppel created by the act where he knew the person was no longer a partner.

The second case in this chapter (*Garner* v. *Murray*) is an English case that established the way in which partners must deal with the payment of partnership debts on the dissolution of a partnership where one partner has become insolvent. In the case, the two remaining partners were solvent but had different amounts in their capital accounts in the partnership.

The issue in the case was whether the solvent partners should be liable on the basis of how they shared profits (and losses) or on the basis of their capital in the partnership. The court in this case decided that the remaining solvent partners would be obliged to satisfy the claims of creditors in proportion to the ratio of their capital accounts as they stood on dissolution.

Registration of Partnership — Liability of Retired Partner Who Failed to Register Dissolution

Clarke v. Burton, [1958] O.R. 489.

A partner retired from a partnership that had been registered in accordance with the provincial Partnership Registration Act. A creditor who was aware of the partner's retirement continued to do business with the remaining partners. He later attempted to hold the retired partner liable for partnership debts because the retired partner had not filed a declaration with respect to dissolution.

McRUER, C.J.H.C.:

Where customers have dealt with the firm prior to dissolution, registration of a certificate of dissolution is not enough. There must be notice. On the other hand, the law contemplates that a customer who deals with a firm for the first time after a notice of dissolution has been registered is taken to have notice, as the law contemplates that he should search before first supplying the firm with goods, but customers who supplied the firm with goods after the registration of the partnership are not required to continue to search from day to day to see if dissolution has taken place.

In *Re Merrick, Jamieson v. Trustee,* [1933] O.W.N. 295, two Merrick brothers and one Sims had registered a certificate under the Partnership Registration Act in March 1925. One Mrs. Jamieson advanced $7,500 to them. Sims retired from the partnership about the end of 1925 when the assets and liabilities of the firm were taken over by the Merrick brothers who carried on business until 1927 when a certificate of dissolution of the partnership of the two brothers was registered. No document had been registered when Sims retired. T.W. Merrick, one of the brothers, continued the business, assuming sole control and responsibility until his bankruptcy. The changes in the firm were known to and agreeable to Mrs. Jamieson and there was complete novation as far as the debt was concerned. The trustee in bankruptcy contended that Mrs. Jamieson could not rank against the estate until other creditors were paid in full, relying on s. 122 of the Bankruptcy Act and the Partnership Registration Act. He maintained that the partnership was still subsisting by reason of the failure to register a certificate of dissolution. Middleton, J.A. at page 297, said:—

"The contention as to the failure to register the certificate of dissolution is based upon an entire misconception of the purpose and meaning of the Partnership Registration Act. The effect of this Act is to impose a liability on the nature of an estoppel upon the partner who fails to record the dissolution of the partnership. Creditors may hold him liable as though he had continued to be a partner.... It is a very different thing to suggest that the failure to register a dissolution of partnership will operate in any way as an estoppel against the creditor."

It is to be noted that in this case Middleton, J.A., referred to the effect of the Partnership Registration Act as imposing a liability in the nature of an estoppel. It may be that what was said is *obiter* in view of the fact that the matter decided was that the failure to register a dissolution of partnership will not operate in any way as an estoppel against a creditor. However, I do not think this judgement can be interpreted that Middleton, J.A., intended to lay down any principle that creditors who had actual notice of the dissolution could nevertheless claim against a retired partner for goods supplied after the dissolution because no certificate of dissolution had been registered under the Act.

Of all the cases I think *Oakville v. Andrew* (1905), 10 O.L.R. 709, throws the most light on the problem that I have to solve. In this case a partnership in a private banking business which had existed between the defendant and one H. was dissolved, but the business continued to be carried on in the firm name and no notice of dissolution was given nor any certificate thereunder registered. After the dissolution H., who was also treasurer of the municipality, received as such, moneys belonging to the municipality out of which, and other moneys, he made certain payments for the municipality and deposited the balance in a bank where the firm kept its account, subsequently using it in the firm's business. On the death of H. the account was overdrawn and the municipality sought to hold the defendant liable on two grounds: (1) that he held himself out to be a partner or that the partnership in fact continued to exist; and (2) if the partnership was dissolved no declaration of dissolution had been filed. Moss, C.J.O., after stating that Falconbridge, C.J.K.B., had given judgement for the plaintiffs, chiefly on the ground that the defendant in consequence of his failure to file a declaration of dissolution of partnership must be deemed to be a partner, said, at p. 715:—

"It is not necessary to place a construction upon the provisions of the Act because the absence of any notice and the continued use of the defendant's name rendered him liable to be treated by all persons dealing with the firm as still a member of the firm. *The filing of a declaration was one mode of giving notice to the public,* and the defendant neglected this as well as the usual common law methods of freeing himself from the future liability to persons dealing with the firm. [Emphasis added]" The appeal was allowed on the ground that the plaintiff was not a customer and did not deal with the partnership in the transaction in question. It was contended, however, that the former partner, as treasurer of the municipality, was their agent to deal with the partnership. The learned Chief Justice said, at p. 716:—

"If he acted as the authorized agent of the plaintiff he knew at the time that the defendant was not a partner, and his knowledge should be attributed to the plaintiff."

These passages from the judgement of the learned Chief Justice appear to me to clearly indicate that in his opinion a creditor who continues to deal with the partnership with full notice of the dissolution cannot claim against a retired partner merely because a certificate of dissolution has not been registered.

If the liability imposed under the statute is in the nature of estoppel as Middleton, J.A., said in the *Merrick* case, the principles of law applicable to estoppel ought to apply. These principles can be no more clearly stated than in the language of Lord Brokenhead in *MacLaine v. Gatty*, [1921] 1 A.C. 376, at p. 386, where he said:—

"The learned counsel cited various authorities in which these doctrines have been discussed, but the rule of estoppel or bar, as I have always understood it, is capable of extremely simple statement. Where A has by his words or conduct justified B in believing that a certain state of fact exists, and B has acted upon such a belief to his prejudice, A is not permitted to affirm against B that a different state of facts existed at the same time. Whether one reads the case of *Pickard v. Sears* (1837), 6 A. & E. 469, or the later classic authorities which have illustrated this topic, one will not, I think, greatly vary or extend this simple definition of the doctrine."

If this is the doctrine of estoppel to be applied, I cannot see how one who has specific notice of the dissolution of the partnership can take advantage of an estoppel created by a statute. To come to any other conclusion would, in my opinion, reduce the law to an absurdity. Take, for example, in this case, if the solicitor that the defendant consulted had written the plaintiff and told him that the partnership was dissolved, that the defendant was no longer connected with it, and that he was commencing business for himself and the plaintiff continued to supply goods to the partnership, could any Court in good conscience give him judgement against the defendant simply because the formality of the registration of a dissolution had not been gone through, a formality that in no way affected the plaintiff? My conclusion is that there is no merit in the action and it should be dismissed on this ground alone.

Having arrived at this conclusion, it is not necessary for me to consider whether the persons involved were "associated in partnership for trading or manufacturing...purposes". The action will therefore be dismissed with costs.

Dissolution of Partnership — One Partner Insolvent — Liability of Other Partners for Deficiencies in Capital

Garner v. Murray, [1904] 1 Ch. 57.

Three persons carried on business in a partnership until it was necessary to dissolve the relationship. One partner had no assets, and the deficiency that resulted in payment of creditor's claims had to be covered by the two remaining partners. The parties had contributed unequal amounts of capital, but had agreed to share profits and losses equally.

The question put before the court was: How should the deficiencies be paid?

JOYCE, J.:

The real question in this case is how, as between two partners, the ultimate deficit, which arises in the partnership from the default of a third partner to contribute his share of the deficiency of the assets to make good the capital, is to be borne by them. We have now in the Partnership Act, 1890, a code which defines the mode in which the assets of a firm are to be dealt with in the final settlement of the accounts after dissolution.

Sect. 44 is plain. [His Lordship read the section, and continued:—] I do not find anything in that section to make a solvent partner liable to contribute for an insolvent partner who fails to pay his share. Sub-s.(b) of s. 44 proceeds on the supposition that contributions have been paid or levied. Here the effect of levying is that two partners can pay and one cannot. It is suggested on behalf of the plaintiff that each partner is to bear an equal loss. But when the Act says losses are to be borne equally it means losses sustained by the firm. It cannot mean that the individual loss sustained by each partner is to be of equal amount.

There is no rule that the ultimate personal loss of each partner, after he has performed his obligations to the firm, shall be the same as or in any given proportion to that of any other partner. I have to follow the Act, and see no difficulty in doing so in this case. The assets must be applied in paying to each partner rateably what is due from the firm to him in respect of capital, account being taken of the equal contributions to be made by him towards the deficiency of capital.

CASE PROBLEMS FOR DISCUSSION

Case 1

Sarah, aged 17 years, and Jane, aged 19 years, had been shopping in a large shopping mall. Jane wished to purchase a lottery ticket, but had only $1 in her purse. She turned to Sarah and said, "Do you have $4? They are selling lottery tickets here." Without a word, Sarah took the money from her pocket and gave it to Jane. Jane purchased a ticket that she and Sarah agreed bore a lucky number. The next week, the ticket that Jane had purchased was the winner of $25 000.

When news of the win reached Jane, she immediately visited her friend Sarah and attempted to pay her the $4 that she said she had borrowed. Sarah, who had also heard the good news, refused to accept the $4 and demanded her share of the winnings.

If the above dispute should be brought before a court, describe the arguments that might be raised by each of the parties in support of their respective positions. Indicate how the case might be decided.

Case 2

Henry, Able, Charlie, and Kim established a tree pruning business under the firm name of HACK Enterprises. Except for Henry, who was a minor, the partners had all reached the age of majority. Most of their equipment was acquired from their respective families, or by way of cash purchases at farm auction sales. The group, however, lacked funds to purchase a chain-saw that they required to cut large trees. The original capital of $400, which represented a $100 contribution from each partner, had already been used to acquire small tools. All that remained in the firm's account was $26.

Henry, without the consent of the remaining partners, went to a local hardware store and purchased a chain-saw that had been placed on sale for $300. The merchant was reluctant to sell the saw to him on credit because he was under age. When Henry told the merchant that he was buying it for HACK Enterprises, the merchant agreed to make the sale, because he had seen advertisements placed by the firm in the local newspaper.

Henry gave a cheque in the firm name for $25. He also signed an agreement whereby the firm would be obliged to make regular monthly payments of $25, until the balance of the purchase price had been paid.

The firm made several payments on the saw, then ceased to do so when the partners decided to disband the partnership. Henry took the saw as his part of the partnership proceeds when the four partners divided the assets.

A month later, the hardware merchant discovered that the partnership had dissolved and contacted Henry for payment. Henry refused to make payment and refused to return the saw.

Discuss the issues raised in this case and explain how the matter might be ultimately resolved if the merchant should take legal action to recover his loss.

Case 3

In 1979, Smith, who operated a business under the name "Downtown Grocery," employed Jones as a clerk in his store at a weekly salary of $175. Jones received regular salary increases in the years 1980 to 1993. By 1993, he was earning $500 per week.

Early in 1993, Jones approached Smith with a request for a further increase in his wages. Smith refused on the basis that low business profits limited his ability to pay more than $500 per week. A lengthy discussion followed and the two parties reached the following agreement:

> Jones would receive $500 per week and, in addition, would receive 20% of the net profits. He would continue to perform the duties of clerk, but would also assume responsibility for the Meat Department. He would make all management decisions concerning meat purchases and pricing.
>
> Smith would continue to handle the general management of the business. He would draw the amount of $800 per week and would be entitled to 80% of the net profits.

Jones would be permitted to examine the business account books, and would be consulted in all major business decisions by Smith.

A few weeks after the agreement was reached, Smith discovered that Jones was purchasing groceries (for his personal use) at a competitor's store. In a rage, he barred Jones from entering the store and told him that he would send him his severance pay by mail.

Shortly thereafter, Jones instituted legal proceedings for a declaration that he was a partner in Downtown Grocery.

Discuss the merits of the action taken by Jones and discuss the arguments that might be raised by the parties. How would you expect the matter to be decided?

Case 4

Harold Green and Herbert Green, who were unrelated persons with the same surname, carried on parcel delivery businesses in the same city. Each operated as a sole proprietor, under the name "Green Delivery," and carried on business from the same warehouse building. The two men were good friends. They frequently assisted each other by carrying parcels for the other in deliveries in outlying parts of the city. To complicate matters further, the two proprietors would sometimes use the spare truck owned by the other when their own vehicles had breakdowns or required service. Apart from the fact that each had a different telephone number, it was impossible to distinguish between the two firms. Over time, regular customers often referred to the two firms collectively as "Green Brothers Delivery," even though the two men were not related to each other.

Smith, an antique dealer, who frequently used the delivery services of both men, requested Harold Green to deliver an expensive antique chair to his country home. Harold Green, at the time of the request for pick up, advised Smith that he would send his truck out to pick up the chair. However, Herbert Green picked up the chair at Smith's place of business and took it to the warehouse for delivery. That day a fire of unknown origin destroyed the warehouse and its contents. The charred remains of the chair were found in the jointly used part of the warehouse after the fire.

The chair had a value of $3000. Each of the sole proprietors denied liability for the loss.

Advise Smith as to how he might proceed in this case.

Case 5

Williams, Oxford, Ogilvie, and Lennox carried on business in partnership for many years as wool merchants. The widespread use of synthetic materials, however, adversely affected the fortunes of the business. Eventually the partners found themselves at the point where the business could no longer be carried on at a profit. Before anything could be done to sell the business, Lennox became insolvent. It was then necessary to wind up the business in accordance with the partnership agreement.

The partnership agreement provided that the parties share losses and profits equally. On dissolution, the capital accounts of the partners were as follows:

Williams	$5000
Oxford	$3000
Ogilvie	$2000
Lennox	—

Creditors' claims at dissolution amount to $35 000; whereas the total assets of the firm were $25 000.

Explain the nature of the liability of the firm. Calculate the liability of each of the partners as between themselves with respect to creditor claims.

Case 6

Baker, Sims, and Toby carried on business for many years as clothing retailers under the firm name and style of "Family Clothing Market." The store premises were large and consisted of three separate smaller shops located side by side in the downtown shopping district of a large city. Different clothing lines were sold in each shop, and each shop was managed exclusively by one of the partners. Baker managed the children's clothing shop; Ms. Sims, the women's clothing store; and Toby, the men's clothing store. Each shop had its own distinctive name displayed on its shop window and entrance door.

Toby eventually grew tired of the business and decided to retire. He did so on March 1st. The two remaining partners purchased Toby's interest in the partnership and placed an employee (who had previously been the buyer for men's clothing) as manager in charge of the men's clothing store. This employee continued to act as the buyer for men's clothing and to deal with the clothing suppliers, without informing them of the change in the partnership. Nor was any notice of change in the make-up of the partnership filed under the provincial partnership registration legislation.

On April 1st, Baker died. Following his death, the auditors discovered that he had been systematically concealing the true state of the children's clothing operation from the other partners by creating fictitious assets to offset the losses. When the overall loss was calculated, the business was determined to be in serious financial condition.

News of the discovery soon leaked to the suppliers. When all the creditors' claims were presented, the liabilities of the business exceeded its assets by some $50 000.

Rogers, a suppler, brought an action against the partnership for payment of his account in the amount of $5000.

Discuss the status and liability of the partners, indicate any defences that might be raised, and render a decision.

Case 7

Sandra is a successful real estate agent with HomeBase Realty Inc. (HBRI). Sandra acts for, among many other people, a struggling small contractor, Herbert Homes Limited (HHL). HHL buys land, builds a home on it in the hope of attracting a buyer, and uses Sandra and HBRI as its agent to list the property and make the sale.

HHL was short on cash when a desirable vacant acre of land came on the market. Sandra was to loan HHL $30 000 (the full price of the lot). Rather than take a mortgage on the land for security, as that could interfere with HHL's ability to borrow bank funds to finance construction, Sandra and HHL agreed that her name would go on the deed as well as that of HHL. They further agreed that when the property was sold with a house on it, she would get her usual 6% commission on the sale, together with her original $30 000 loan, plus interest of 12% to the sale date.

The property was purchased; Sandra carried on with her other commitments; and HHL built a house, which two months after competition was sold for $100 000. On the sale, Sandra and HHL signed off on the deed to the new owners, and payment was made directly to the lawyer for the vendors. The lawyer for the vendors split up the money, $6000 to HBRI, $30 600 to Sandra personally, and the balance to HHL.

As matters turned out, HHL had not built the house up to standard. The roof leaked, and cost the purchasers $7000 in damages. The purchasers sued HHL and Sandra as the vendors. Conclusive evidence was presented that they received a faulty house from the vendors. The Provincial Government New Home Warranty Board was advised of the matter, and its investigation showed that while HHL was a registered builder, as one must be under the law to sell a new home, Sandra was not. She has now been charged with a violation of the law. Such an offense usually results in a $500 fine for a first offence.

Consider the aspects of partnership law as they may apply, and advise Sandra as to how she should proceed. Consider how she is exposed to risk, and what defences or claims she may raise in civil court against HHL or the purchasers, and against the Crown in Provincial Offences Court. If you were in a position to advise the judge in Provincial Offences Court, what would you do?

CHAPTER 17

Corporation Law

INTRODUCTION

A **corporation** is an entity that has an existence at law that is separate from those who form it. It is also separate from those who from time to time possess shares in it, or who are responsible for its direction and control. A corporation is a creature of the state, and owes its continued existence to the legislative body responsible for its creation. One of its principal uses is as a vehicle by which large amounts of capital may be accumulated for business purposes. Throughout its history, the corporation has represented a means by which a large number of persons could participate in business transactions requiring more capital than one individual or a small group possessed, or cared to risk in a venture.

HISTORICAL DEVELOPMENT OF THE CORPORATION

The corporation is not a new form of business organization. Its history dates back to the time of the first city states when trade became an important activity. Since the earliest times, its creation and operation have generally remained under the control of the sovereign or state. Most of the early corporations were formed for the purpose of carrying out public or quasi-public functions or to provide essential services or goods to the community. It was not until the nineteenth century that modern English trading corporations were generally permitted to incorporate. Even then, it was only during the last half of the century that limited liability was available to the shareholders. The modern form of corporation, incorporated by simply following the procedure set out in a general statute, did not emerge until the middle of the century. Even then, its introduction was decades behind a similar change in the United States and Canada.

In the United States, the War of Independence severed ties between the colonies and England, and the royal prerogative was replaced by special legislation for the incorporation of companies. In 1811, the state of New York passed a statute that in form was a general incorporation act. It was alleged to have furnished the model for the first incorporation act in the United Provinces of Upper and Lower Canada in 1848-49. Some years later, the British North America Act, 1867 established the rights of both the provinces and the federal government to incorporate companies. As a result, legislation at both the federal and provincial levels was introduced to provide for the incorporation and control of corporations. The legislation, unfortunately, was not uniform, with the result that considerable variation existed from province to province. The newer provinces, as they joined Confederation, passed their own legislation. This again was subject to some variation and, consequently, no uniform legislation exists in Canada today.

NATURE OF A CORPORATION

A corporation is neither an individual nor a partnership. It is a separate legal entity in the sense that it has an existence at law, but no material existence. A corporation possesses many of the attributes of a natural person, but it is artificially created and never dies in the natural sense. Its rights and duties are delineated by law, and its existence may be terminated by the state. It has a number of important characteristics that may be summarized as follows:

(a) a corporation is separate and distinct from its shareholders, and it acts not through them, but through its authorized agents;

(b) a properly authorized agent may bind the corporation in contract with third parties;

(c) the shareholders of a corporation possess limited liability for the debts of the corporation, and the creditors may look only to the assets of the corporation to satisfy their claims.

This latter characteristic particularly distinguishes the corporation from the ordinary partnership or sole proprietorship where the parties have unlimited liability for debts incurred in the course of business.

The management of a corporation is vested in a small group of shareholders chosen by the general body of shareholders at an annual meeting held for the purpose of electing the management group. This group, known as **directors of the corporation**, in turn selects from their number the principal **officers** of the corporation. These individuals are normally charged with the responsibility to bind the corporation in formal contracts with third parties.

The directors of the corporation are free to carry out the general management functions of the corporation in accordance with the corporation's objects, but their powers are limited by any restriction imposed on them in the **articles of incorporation** or the **charter.** To keep the shareholders informed of their activities, the directors are obliged to report to them on a regular basis. The shareholders normally do not participate in the management of the corporation, except where major changes in the corporation are proposed. In these cases, the shareholders usually must approve the proposal before it becomes effective.

Except for private or closely held corporations that do not offer their shares to the public, the shareholders may freely dispose of their interests in the corporation. This is permitted because the relationship is not of a personal nature. The fortunes of the corporation are not dependent upon the personal relationship between shareholders, nor are the creditors of the corporation normally concerned with the shareholders' identity. The shareholders' liability is limited to the amount that they paid or agreed to pay for the shares that they purchased from the corporation.

In general, the corporate form of business organization overcomes many of the disadvantages associated with the partnership. We can compare the differences between these two forms of organization by an examination of each under three major headings: **control, liability,** and **transfer of interests.**

Control

In a partnership, every partner is an agent of the partnership as well as a principal. All of the partners have input into how the business may be operated, and on important matters all parties must agree before a change can be made. In a large partnership, these particular rights of each partner often render decision-making awkward and time-consuming, and make general control difficult.

In a corporation, management is delegated by the shareholders to an elected group of directors. The ordinary shareholder does not possess the right to bind the corporation in contract. Only the proper officers designated by the directors may do so. The directors have the authority to make all decisions for the corporation, although the shareholders may periodically be called upon to approve major decisions at meetings held for that purpose.

Limited Liability

In an ordinary partnership, every general partner has unlimited liability for the debts incurred by the partnership. Since any partner may bind the other partners in contract by his or her actions, the careless act of one partner may seriously affect all. The personal estates of each partner, then, are exposed to the creditors in the event of a loss that exceeds the partnership assets.

The corporate form eliminates this particular risk for ordinary shareholders. Shareholders' losses are limited to their investment in the corporation, and their personal estate may not be reached by creditors of the corporation. The creditors of a corporation must be content with the assets of the corporation in the event of a loss, as creditors are aware at the time (when extending credit to a corporation) that the only assets available to satisfy their claims are those possessed by the corporation.

Transfer

A partnership is a contractual relationship that is personal in nature and based upon the good faith of the parties in their dealings with each other. The right of each partner to bind the partnership in contract, coupled with the unlimited liability of each of the partners, precludes the unfettered right of a partner to transfer his or her interest in the partnership to another. The retirement of a partner raises a similar problem. Since the retiring partner's interest is not freely transferable, the remaining partners must either acquire the retiring partner's share in the partnership or wind up the business. Neither of these solutions may be entirely satisfactory to either the retiring partner or those who remain. The death of a partner represents another disruptive event that also raises the problem of transfer of interests in the partnership. Unless special provisions are made in the partnership agreement (such as provision for the payment of a deceased partner's share by way of insurance), the retirement or death of a partner will generally have a serious effect on the relationship and the business associated with it.

The corporate form of organization differs substantially in this regard. The rights of the shareholders in a corporation do not include the right to bind the corporation in contract, nor may creditors look to the personal assets of the shareholders in determining whether or not credit should be extended to the corporation. Under these circumstances, the identity of the shareholder, to some extent, becomes unimportant, as does the shareholder's personal worth. Once a corporation issues a share to a shareholder and receives payment for it, no further contribution may be demanded from the shareholder. If the shareholder should desire to transfer the share to another, it has no real effect upon the corporation except for a change in the identity of the person holding the share. For these reasons, shares may be freely transferred in a public company, thus overcoming one of the main drawbacks of the partnership.

The corporation has a number of other advantages over the partnership. These are subsequently noted.

Term of Operation of the Business

A partnership's existence is limited by the life of its members. If a partner should die, the partnership is dissolved, but it may be reformed by the remaining parties if the agreement so provides. A partnership may continue as long as its partners wish it to do so, but the death of a partner, or the partner's retirement, is disruptive to the operation.

A corporation, on the other hand, theoretically has an unlimited term of operation. It never dies, even though the persons who own shares in it may do so. The death of a shareholder has no effect on the continued existence of the corporation. A corporation may be dissolved by the state or it may voluntarily be wound up; but in each case, the act is not dependent upon the life or death of a shareholder. Some corporations have been is existence for many hundreds of years. For example, the Hudson's Bay Company was incorporated in 1670 and remains in existence today. No partnership (at least with original unincorporated members) is likely to match this record.

Because a corporation's existence is not affected by the fortunes of the shareholders, a corporation is free to accumulate or acquire large amounts of capital — either through the issue of shares, or by the issue of bonds and debentures. These latter forms are special types of security instruments, issued by a corporation, that can be used where large sums of money are required.

Operation of the Business Entity

A partnership is governed by an agreement that establishes the rights and duties of the partners and the manner in which the partnership is to operate. In the absence of an agreement (or where the agreement is silent), the partnership is governed by the Partnerships Act[1] and a number of other related statutes.

In contrast, the corporation is governed by the statute under which it is incorporated (as well as a number of other statutes such as securities legislation) that sets out the conditions and rules that apply to its operation. The rights and duties of the shareholders and directors with respect to the corporation are statutory rather than contractual in nature, although both the corporation and partnership are subject to statute.

Separate Existence of the Corporation

At law, the partnership is in a sense indistinguishable from the partners, yet it does possess many of the attributes of a separate entity. Contracts are made in the firm name, and a partnership in most jurisdictions may be sued in the firm name. However, the fact remains that the parties individually as well as collectively are responsible for its operation. The corporation in contrast has a clearly defined separate existence at law.

This particular issue was established in a case that came before the English courts in 1896.[2] The case dealt with the principal shareholder and a corporation that he had incorporated to take over his successful shoe and leather business. The principal shareholder had taken back a debenture from the corporation. When the corporation later became insolvent, the principal shareholder claimed priority in payment of the debenture over the claims of the general creditors. In the litigation that followed, the court held that the corporation was an entity separate and distinct from its shareholders. It permitted the principal shareholder to obtain payment of the debenture from the money available, before claims of the general creditors could be satisfied.

Corporate Name

The corporation name is an asset of the business.[3] The name must not be the same as the name of any other existing corporation. In the case of a corporation incorporated to carry on a business (other than a corporation incorporated under a special statute), the last word in the name must be a word that identifies it as a corporation. A corporation in some jurisdictions may have a number name. The last word that may be used varies from jurisdiction to jurisdiction, but generally must be **Limited** or **Ltd., Incorporated** or **Inc.**, or **Corporation** or **Corp.** (or the French equivalent). The purpose of the identifying word is to distinguish a corporation from a partnership and/or sole proprietorship. Partnerships are not permitted to use any word reserved for corporation identification or any word that might imply corporate status.

As a general rule, the corporation's name may not be one that denotes any connection with the Crown; nor may the name be obscene, too general, or such that it would cause confusion with other existing names, or the names of well known incorporated or unincorporated organizations.[4]

---

1. All provinces have legislation governing this relationship. See, for example, the Partnerships Act, R.S.O. 1990, c. P-5.
2. *Salomon v. A. Salomon & Co. Ltd.,* [1897] A.C. 22.
3. *Hunt's Ltd. v. Hunt* (1924), 56 O.L.R. 349.
4. *Tussaud v. Tussaud* (1890), 44 Ch.D. 678.

A corporation must clearly indicate its name and its place of business on all printed letterhead and business forms. Where required, it must formally execute documents by the use of a seal (which contains the corporation name). The authorized officers of the corporation impress this seal upon all written documents that require the formal "signature" of the corporation.

METHODS OF INCORPORATION

Royal Charter

The original method of incorporation was by a **royal charter.** The issue of the charter was for the purpose of creating a legal existence for the entity, to permit it to either operate as a monopoly or to own land. The Hudson's Bay Company, for example, was granted rights to all of the land drained by the rivers flowing into Hudson's Bay. The British South Africa Company was granted a similar type of charter with respect to large amounts of land in South Africa.

The royal charter was an exercise of the king's prerogative, and the issue of the charter gave the entity all the rights at law of a natural person (subject to certain exceptions). The charter, however, did not generally give those persons connected with the corporation limited liability if the corporation was a trading company. The royal charter method of incorporation has not been used to incorporate ordinary trading corporations for many years.

Letters Patent

The **letters patent** system of incorporation is a direct development of the royal charter form. When the Crown ceased the issue of royal charters for trading corporations, a new system was developed whereby legislation was passed that set out the criteria for the issue of letters patent by a representative of the Crown.[5] The application for incorporation would then be prepared and submitted in accordance with the legislation, and the Crown's representative would issue the incorporating document.

Letters patent is a government document that grants a special right or privilege. In the case of a corporation, it represents the creation of a legal entity. A corporation created by letters patent acquires all the powers of a royal charter corporation, and has, as a result, all of the usual rights at law of a natural person.[6] The federal government, and the provinces of Manitoba, New Brunswick, Ontario, Prince Edward Island, and Quebec used the letters patent system for many years. However, after 1970, some of the provinces and the federal government adopted a different system, and, by 1993, only Quebec and Prince Edward Island still retained the letters patent system.

Third parties dealing with a letters patent corporation may assume that the corporation has the capacity to enter into most ordinary contracts. If the officers of the corporation, with apparent authority to bind the corporation, enter into a contract of a type prohibited by the objects or by-laws of the corporation, the corporation

---

5. For example, prior to 1970, under the Corporations Act of Ontario, R.S.O. 1960, c. 71, the Provincial Secretary issued the letters patent. At the federal level, the Secretary of State issued letters patent prior to 1976.

6. *Bonanza Creek Gold Mining Co. v. The King,* [1916] 1 A.C. 566.

would still be bound. The exception would be if the third party had actual notice of the lack of authority in the offices of the corporation.

Special Act

The third type of incorporation represents a quite different form. Parliament may use its powers to create corporations by way of special statute, and these corporations are known as **special act corporations.** Instead of the broad powers possessed by a corporation incorporated under royal charter, the special act corporation has only the powers specifically granted to it by the statute. Special act corporations, as the name implies, are corporations incorporated for special purposes. Many are for public or quasi-public purposes, such as for the construction of public utilities, or for activities that require a certain amount of control in the public interest. Banks, telephone companies, railroads, and Crown corporations (such as the Canadian Broadcasting Corporation) are examples of corporations incorporated under special legislation. Special act corporations as a general rule do not use the words limited, incorporated, or their abbreviations in the corporate name. For example, chartered banks use no corporate identification at all in the corporation's name.

The legislation sets out the rights and obligations of the corporation. If the corporation should attempt to perform an act that it is not authorized to do under the statute, the act is *ultra vires* (beyond the powers of) the corporation and a nullity. For example, in a case that involved an English corporation that was limited by special act to borrowing £25 000, the corporation exceeded the amount and eventually borrowed £85 000. When a secured creditor attempted to recover money loaned to the corporation, the court held that the plaintiff creditor could not enforce the security because the corporation had no authority to issue it. In rejecting the claim, the court held that all the security issued in excess of the £25 000 authorized by statute was a nullity.[7] The judge in the case described the powers of the special act corporation and its limitations in the following terms:

> ...there is a large difference between (an ecclesiastical) corporation and a corporation such as we are dealing with here, called into existence by statute, the creature of statute for specific purposes, and armed with specific powers which must not be exceeded for the fulfillment of those particular purposes. Looking at the exercise of any alleged power on behalf of a corporation of that kind we must see whether it is either expressly given by the statute, or is necessarily implied in order to the fulfillment of its powers. If we cannot bring it within that — and a necessary implication in such a case differs not at all from expression — then the company cannot exercise the alleged power.

General Act

In Canada, a few of the provinces patterned their legislation after the English general act system. As a result, Canadian business corporations may be incorporated under either letters patent (in some provinces) or two forms of general act incorporation. In those provinces that patterned their legislation after the English general act, the incorporators need only comply with the preparation and filing

---

7. *Baroness Wenlock v. River Dee Co.* (1887), 36 Ch.D. 674 at p. 685.

requirements to form a corporation. Alberta, British Columbia, Newfoundland, Nova Scotia, and Saskatchewan adopted the English registration system for their incorporation acts. The document filed in these jurisdictions is referred to as the **memorandum of association**. The memorandum contains the details of the corporation as required by the act and, on filing, the corporation comes into existence.

The federal government, Ontario, and Manitoba used the letters patent system for many years. In 1970, Ontario introduced a general act for the incorporation of business corporations. This act borrowed some of its terminology from the United States model, rather than the English one. In Ontario, the document filed is called the **articles of incorporation** and the document issued by the government is referred to as a **certificate of incorporation.**

In 1975, the federal government introduced legislation for the incorporation of business corporations that also was patterned after the United States model and comparable in some respects to the Ontario statute. Shortly thereafter, Manitoba introduced a similar statute, using the Canada Business Corporations Act as a model. Since that time, a number of other general act provinces (including Ontario) have either introduced new legislation based upon the Canada Business Corporations Act, or modified their corporations acts to incorporate many of the provisions of the federal statute. While the provincial laws relating to corporations are by no means identical, a pattern has emerged in Canada, whereby provincial corporations' legislation is moving in the direction of the Canada Business Corporations model. Only Quebec and Prince Edward Island remain as exceptions to the general act system, and only Newfoundland and Nova Scotia continue to follow the English general act pattern. Alberta, Manitoba, New Brunswick, Ontario, Saskatchewan, and British Columbia, as well as the federal government, now use the certificate of incorporation as a method of incorporation. There is, however, some variation in the legislation governing the operation of the corporations falling under the legislation in each province.

The general act corporation, like the special act corporation, is a creature of statute, and its powers are limited to those powers specifically granted under the act. Unlike the royal charter and letters patent corporations, it does not necessarily have all the powers of a natural person, but only those powers set out in the statute and its memorandum of association. To provide flexibility and greater latitude provincial jurisdictions in some cases have attempted to extend to a general act corporation the powers of a natural person.

The provinces of British Columbia, Alberta, Manitoba, Saskatchewan, Ontario, New Brunswick, and the federal government, for example, have specifically set out in their legislation that a business corporation incorporated under their legislation has all of the powers of a natural person.[8] Currently,[9] only Nova Scotia and Newfoundland have continued to follow the general act system without expanding the rights of corporations. Consequently, in those two provinces the powers of a corporation are limited to those established by the statute and the powers set out in the memorandum of association filed under the statute.

---

8. See for example, Business Corporations Act, 1990, c. B-16 s. 15; Canada Business Corporations Act, R.S.C. 1985 c. C-44, s. 15(1); Business Corporations Act. Consolidated Stat. Alberta, c. B-15 s. 15(1); Corporations Act, 1987 (Man.) c. 225 s. 15(1); Business Corporations Act, R.S.S. 1979 c. B-10 s. 15(1).

9. As at May, 1993.

The courts treat both the statute and the memorandum of association as the body of law that delineates the powers of the corporation. Any act of a corporation incorporated by memorandum of association that is beyond or outside the powers set out in either the statute or the memorandum is considered *ultra vires* and a nullity. The harshness of the **doctrine of ultra vires**, however, is generally avoided by incorporators taking special care in the drafting of their memorandum of association. By stating their objects and powers as broadly as possible in the document, problems that may develop as a result of lack of capacity are less likely to be encountered.

The limited capacity of the general act corporation carries with it a danger for those who deal with it. Because the statute and the memorandum of association are treated as public documents the public is deemed to be aware of any limitations on the power of the corporation to contract or to do specific acts. For example, if the memorandum of association prohibits the directors of the corporation from engaging in a particular type of business activity, and the directors proceed to do so, any contract negotiated in that respect would be *ultra vires* the corporation and could not be enforced by the other contracting party. This rule would apply even though the contracting party was unaware of the limitation on the power of the corporation. This rule is known as the **doctrine of constructive notice.** To avoid this problem, most of the general act provinces and the federal government have specifically given corporations incorporated in their jurisdictions the powers of a natural person. All general act jurisdictions except Newfoundland have either abolished the doctrine of constructive notice, or provided in their legislation that third parties are not deemed to have notice of any unusual limitations on the rights or powers of directors or officers of a corporation. This is simply because the limitations or restrictions are set out in documents filed under the act.[10]

The general effect of this clause is to protect third parties from any unusual limitations on the powers of directors or on the corporation itself. It provides that a third party contracting with the corporation is not deemed to have notice of any limitation on the rights or powers of the corporation or its officers. When this clause is coupled with the clause that provides that the corporation has the capacity of a natural person, third parties acquire protection similar to that which they would have in contracts with natural persons. However, in those general act provinces where the legislation does not do away with the doctrine of constructive notice, the third party dealing with a corporation must use extreme care. The third party in those circumstances would be obliged to ascertain not only that the officers of the corporation had the authority to bind the corporation, but that the corporation had the power to do the particular act contemplated in the contract.

In all cases where a third party is dealing with a corporation, once the corporation is determined to have the power to enter into a particular type of contract, the third party is entitled to rely on what is known as the **indoor management rule** for the validity of the acts of the officers of the corporation. If the officers of the corporation, for example, are required to obtain the approval of the shareholders before a contract may be effected, the third party may accept the evidence submit-

---

10. See, for example, the Canada Business Corporations Act, R.S.C. 1985, c. C-44, s. 17.

ted by the officers that shareholder approval was obtained. The third party may rely on this evidence if it appears to be regular, and need not inquire further into the internal operation of the corporation. It would not apply, of course, where a third party is deemed to have notice of a limitation on the powers of the corporation contained in its memorandum of association or in the statute. The application of the rule is directed to the internal operation of the corporation, of which the third party normally would have no actual knowledge.

The duties of third parties dealing with a corporation were considered in the early case of *Biggerstaff v. Rowatt's Wharf, Ltd.,*[11] where the court summarized the responsibilities in the following terms:

> What must persons look to when they deal with directors? They must see whether according to the constitution of the company the directors could have the powers which they are purporting to exercise. Here the articles enabled the directors to give to the managing director all the powers of the directors except as to drawing, accepting, or indorsing bills of exchange and promissory notes. The persons dealing with him must look to the articles, and see that the managing director might have power to do what he purports to do, and that is enough for a person dealing with him bona fide. It is settled by a long string of authorities that where directors give a security which according to the articles they might have power to give, the person taking it is entitled to assume that they had the power.

THE INCORPORATION PROCESS

In most jurisdictions, the incorporation process begins with the preparation of an **application for incorporation** (see Appendix A Documents) that sets out the name of the proposed corporation, the address of the head office and principal place of business, the names of the applicants for incorporation (usually called the **incorporators**), the object of the corporation (although this is not required in most jurisdictions that have followed the Canada Business Corporations Act pattern), the share capital, any restrictions or rights attached to the shares, and any special powers or restrictions that apply to the activities of the corporation. The applicants for incorporation usually must also indicate whether the corporation will offer its shares to the public or whether it will remain "private," in the sense that it will not make a public offering of its securities. This last matter is generally quite important from the point of view of the incorporating jurisdiction. Corporations that intend to offer their shares to the public usually must follow elaborate procedures under the jurisdiction's securities legislation or corporations act. This is to ensure that the public is properly advised of all details of the corporation and the purpose for which the shares are offered to the public. A corporation that does not offer its shares to the public, but that may offer them to investors by private negotiation, is usually relieved of many of the special formalities imposed by the legislation to protect shareholders and the public at large. For example, the shareholders of such a corporation may, if they so desire, dispense with the formal audit of the corporation's books each year. The reason is that a small group of shareholders (as few as one in most jurisdictions) may not require the elaborate examination of the financial records of the corporation that is necessary for a public corporation. A corporation that does not offer its shares to the public may also impose restrictions on the transfer of shares in the corporation. This is

11. *Biggerstaff v. Rowatt's Wharf Ltd.,* [1896] 2 Ch. 93.

to enable the remaining shareholders to exercise some control over persons who become a part of the small group. Corporations that offer their shares to the public must not place restrictions on the transfer of their shares. A number of other differences exist between the two forms of incorporation. The distinction is made to relieve the closely held corporation of many of the onerous obligations imposed on the large public corporation for the protection of its shareholders.

The complete application for incorporation must be submitted to the appropriate office in the incorporating jurisdiction, together with the fee charged for the incorporation. In the case of a jurisdiction that issues letters patent, the company will be incorporated when the letters patent are issued. In general act provinces, where a memorandum of association is filed, the filing date becomes the date of incorporation. In those general act provinces where articles of incorporation are filed and a certificate of incorporation issued, the corporation comes into existence when the certificate is issued.

Following incorporation, the incorporators, as first directors, proceed in the case of letters patent and certificate corporations with the remaining formalities of establishing by-laws and passing resolutions. These rules for the internal operation of the corporation set out the various duties of the officers and directors. They also provide for banking, borrowing, the issue of shares, and perhaps for the purchase of an existing business, if the corporation was incorporated for that purpose.

If the incorporators are not the permanent directors of the corporation, they usually hold a special meeting to resign as first directors. The shareholders then elect permanent directors to hold office until the next annual meeting. The permanent directors will, among themselves, elect the officers of the corporation to hold the offices of president, secretary, treasurer, etc. Once under way, the directors carry on the operation of the corporation until the annual meeting of the shareholders. At the annual meeting, the directors and officers report to the shareholders on their performance since the previous meeting.

CORPORATE SECURITIES

Corporations may issue a variety of different securities to acquire capital for their operations. One of the most common forms of acquiring capital is to issue shares in the organization. A **share** is simply a fraction of the ownership of the corporation. It represents a part-ownership equal to one part of the total number of shares issued. For example, if a corporation has issued 1000 shares, each share would represent a one-thousandth part-ownership of the corporation. Unfortunately, corporations may issue many different kinds of shares at different values, and with different rights attached to them. To determine the actual value of the part-ownership that a share represents is sometimes difficult.

Shares may be designated as having either a fixed value or **par value**, or **no par value**. In the latter case the value is not fixed, but is the issue price of the share established by the board of directors at the time of the sale of the share. Par value shares have diminished in importance in recent years, and in many of the provinces and federally, par value shares have been abolished.[12] Shares may also be classed as either **common** or **preference** shares. All corporations must have some voting common shares, as these are the usual form of shares issued to the

---

12. See for example, the Canada Business Corporations Act, R.S.C. 1985 c. C-44, s. 24(1); Business Corporations Act, R.S.S. 1979 c. B-10 S. 24(1); Business Corporations Act, R.S.O. 1990 c. B-16 s. 22.

shareholders who will elect the directors of the corporation. Corporations some-times issue preference shares. As the name denotes, these will have special rights attached to them, such as the right to a fixed rate of return in the form of divi-dends, special voting privileges, or a priority in payment over the common share-holders in the event that the corporation should be wound up.

A corporation may also issue securities that do not represent a share of the ownership of the corporation, but a debt. The debt may be either secured by a **fixed charge** attaching to specific assets of the corporation or a **floating charge**, which does not usually attach to any particular assets of the corporation but sim-ply to the assets in general. Corporate securities that represent a charge against specific assets of the corporation are generally called **mortgage bonds.** Those that are normally subordinate to mortgage bonds in priority are usually called **debentures.** The degree of security that each type represents depends to a consid-erable degree on the priority of the rights that it has to the corporation's various assets in the event that the corporation should default on its debts. The rights of these security holders are examined in Chapter 31, "Security for Debt" and in Chapter 32, "Bankruptcy."

DIVISION OF CORPORATE POWERS

Duties and Responsibilities of Directors

Every corporation must have at least one director. In some jurisdictions, notably Quebec and Prince Edward Island where the letters patent method of incorpora-tion is used, the minimum number is three. The directors of a corporation are, in effect, the managers of the business. Unlike a partnership where all partners may bind the partnership, in a corporation this right is limited to the directors, and in most cases to certain directors who may be officers of the corporation. Thus, in a corporation, the directors, once elected by the shareholders, are responsible for its operation. The various corporation acts attempt to separate ownership from man-agement insofar as it is practicable, in order to clearly identify the particular rights and duties of shareholders and directors. Most rights with respect to man-agement have been given exclusively to the directors. For example, the right to declare dividends and to conduct the business of the corporation fall exclusively to the directors. Major changes in the nature of the corporation, although initiated by the directors, must generally be referred to the shareholders to confirm. For example, the shareholders must be the ones to ultimately decide if the corporation is to change its objects, wind up, or alter its capital structure. The purpose of the division of powers between shareholders and the directors is essentially one of balancing the need for shareholder protection with the need for freedom to man-age on the part of the directors. This balance is reflected in the rights and duties of each group.

The directors are responsible for the day-to-day operations of the corporation. Once the shareholders have elected a board of directors, they have little more to do with the management of the corporation until the next annual general meeting. The ultimate responsibility rests with the shareholders, however, as they are free to elect new and different directors at the next annual meeting if the directors fail to per-form satisfactorily. Under extreme circumstances the shareholders may also take steps to terminate the appointment of directors before the next annual meeting.

A director, once elected, has a duty to conduct the affairs of the corporation in the best interests of the corporation as a whole, rather than in the interests of any particular group of shareholders. This distinction is most important because the directors may be held accountable at law for a breach of their duty to the corporation. Usually the shareholders' interests and the interests of the corporation are the same, but this is not always so. Where they are divergent, the directors must concern themselves with the interests of the corporation alone.

The relationship between a director and the corporation is **fiduciary** in nature. It requires the director to act in good faith at all times in his dealing with, and on behalf of, the corporation. At common law, the duty on the part of the director to act in good faith is augmented by a duty to use care and skill in carrying out corporation business. Some jurisdictions have imposed an additional statutory duty on directors to exercise the powers and duties of their office honestly with the care and skill of a reasonably careful and prudent person in similar circumstances.[13]

The fiduciary relationship that a director has with the corporation precludes the director from engaging in any activity that might permit the director to make a profit at the corporation's expense. For example, the director must not use the corporation's name to acquire a personal benefit, nor must he or she use the position in the corporation to make a personal profit that rightfully belongs to the corporation.

A director may, under certain circumstances, engage in a business transaction with the corporation. However, considerable care is necessary, otherwise the director will be in violation of this duty as a director. As a general rule, in any transaction with the corporation, the director must immediately disclose his or her interest in the particular contract or property and refrain from discussing or voting on the matter at the directors' meeting.[14] Also, in some jurisdictions, shareholder approval of contracts in which a director has an interest is required.[15]

It should be noted, however, that as a general rule, if a director has a conflict of interest, the conflict does not prevent the director from exercising his or her rights as a shareholder at any shareholder's meeting called for the purpose of considering any matters related to the conflict of interest. However, the actions of the shareholder at the shareholders meeting must be such that they are not illegal, fraudulent, or oppressive towards the shareholders that may oppose the decision related to the conflict of interest. For example, in the case of *North-West Transportation v. Beatty*[16] a director and shareholder of the company entered into an agreement with the company to sell it a steamship. The directors approved the purchase, and the purchase was then directed to the shareholders for approval. At the shareholders' meeting, the owner of the steamship voted in favour of the purchase, and because of his shareholding, the purchase was approved. In the case, the court set out the general rule in the following words:

> The general principles applicable to cases of this kind are well established. Unless some provision to the contrary is to be found in the charter or other instrument by which the company is incorporated, the resolution of a majority of the shareholders, duly convened, upon any question with which the company is legally competent to

13. See, for example, the Canada Business Corporations Act, R.S.C. 1985 c. C-44, s. 122(1).
14. The Canada Business Corporations Act, R.S.C. 1985 c. C-44, s. 120.
15. The Business Corporations Act, R.S.O. 1990, c. B-16, s. 134.
16. *North-West Transportation Co. v. Beatty* (1887) 12 App. Cas. 589.

deal, is binding upon the minority, and consequently upon the company, and every shareholder has a perfect right to vote upon any such question, although he may have a personal interest in the subject-matter opposed to, or different from, the general or particular interests of the company.

A director may not normally engage in any business transaction with a third party that might deprive the corporation of an opportunity to make a profit or acquire a particular asset. For example, a director might become aware of an opportunity to acquire a valuable property through his or her position as a director. That property must not be acquired for personal use if the corporation might be interested in obtaining it. To do so would be a violation of the director's duty of loyalty to the corporation. In an instance of this nature, the courts would apply the principle or **doctrine of corporate opportunity,** and find that the director's acquisition of the property was in trust for the corporation. They would treat the corporation as the beneficial owner. If the director had already disposed of the property, the court might require him or her to deliver up any profit made on the transaction to the corporation.

A similar situation may arise where a director trades in shares of the corporation. Directors may lawfully buy and sell shares of the corporation on their own account and retain any profit that they might make on the transactions. However, if directors use information that they acquire by virtue of their position in the corporation, and buy or sell shares using that information to the detriment of others, they may be liable for the losses that those persons suffer as a direct consequence of their actions. In most jurisdictions, the legislation pertaining to corporations requires **"insiders"** (such as the directors, officers, and persons usually holding over 10% of the shares in a public corporation) to report their trading each month to a government regulatory body or official. This information is then made available to the public as a deterrent to directors who might be tempted to use inside information for their own profit.

For example, the issue concerning the particular fiduciary duties of directors and officers of a corporation came before the courts for consideration in the case of *Canadian Aero Service Ltd. v. O'Malley et al.*[17] Two directors of the corporation used information available to them as directors for the purpose of gaining a benefit for a new corporation that they incorporated after resigning their positions. The court considered the extent of their duty to the corporation from which they resigned in the following manner:

> ...the fiduciary relationship goes at least this far: a director or a senior officer like O'Malley or Zarzycki is precluded from obtaining for himself, either secretly or without the approval of the company (which would have to be properly manifested upon full disclosure of the facts), any property or business advantage either belonging to the company or for which it has been negotiating; and especially is this so where the director or officer is a participant in the negotiations on behalf of the company.
>
> An examination of the case law in this Court and in the Courts of other like jurisdictions on the fiduciary duties of directors and senior officers shows the pervasiveness of a strict ethic in this area of the law. In my opinion this ethic disqualifies a director or senior officer from usurping for himself or diverting to

17. *Canadian Aero Service Ltd. v. O'Malley et al.* (1973), 40 D.L.R. (3d) 371.

another person or company with whom or with which he is associated a maturing business opportunity which his company is actively pursuing; he is also precluded from so acting even after his resignation where the resignation may fairly be said to have been prompted or influenced by a wish to acquire for himself the opportunity sought by the company, or where it was his position with the company rather than a fresh initiative that led him to the opportunity which he later acquired.

Personal Liability of Directors

Over the years, there has been a general trend towards holding the directors liable for different events that might take place as a result of their actions. Many of these responsibilities have been imposed on directors as a result of their use of their position or the corporation in such a way that it causes hardship to third parties, employees, or shareholders.

As a general rule, the directors may be held liable for any loss occasioned by the corporation itself, if the directors commit the corporation to an act that is clearly *ultra vires* regarding the corporation's objects clause or contrary to its by-laws. The corporation usually is the body that suffers a loss in such a case, and the shareholders may take action against the directors to recover the loss. The directors would also be liable to the company if they should sell shares at a discount contrary to the statute, or declare a dividend that impairs the capital of the corporation.

More so today than in the past, directors are expected to play a greater and more active role in the operation of the corporation itself. Governments have increasingly imposed obligations on business corporations with respect to activities that have an environmental impact or where economic losses of the corporation result in plant closures and job losses. Penalty or liability provisions in these statutes often are directed at not only the corporation, but the directors as well. For example, a shoe manufacturing company stored a number of containers of industrial waste of a toxic nature in an outside location without protection from the weather. Some of the containers leaked toxic waste into the soil and ground water. The company was charged under the provincial environmental protection statutes as were the directors of the corporation. The directors were obliged under the statute to prove that they were not negligent, and only one director was successful in doing so. The corporation and the remaining two directors were convicted and personally fined for their breach of the law.[18]

In some jurisdictions, a special liability is imposed on directors with respect to employee wages in the event of bankruptcy of the corporation. The law imposes a duty on the directors to satisfy the amounts owing to employees for unpaid wages if the corporation lacks the funds to do so. The liability for unpaid wages is, in a sense, a contingent liability, because it would only come into play if the assets of the corporation were insufficient to satisfy the employee wage claims.

In addition to these particular liabilities, the directors are exposed to a number of penalties and fines if they should fail to comply with the legislation concerning the filing of notices, or if they should fail to make returns to the various government agencies that monitor corporation activity.

---

18. *Regina v. Bata Industries Ltd., Bata, Marchant and Weston* (1992), 9 O.R. (3d) 329.

Shareholders' Rights

The shareholders, as owners of the corporation, are entitled at regular intervals to a full disclosure by the directors of the corporation's business activities. In addition to the right to information, the shareholders have the right to elect the directors at general meetings of the shareholders and to approve the actions of the directors since the previous annual meeting. Shareholders must also approve all important matters that concern the corporation. These usually take the form of special by-laws. Generally these special by-laws do not become effective until shareholders' approval has been received. In this fashion, the shareholders have ultimate control over all major decisions of the directors affecting the corporation's structure or purpose.

Each year the shareholders review the management of the directors at the **annual general meeting** of the corporation. At that time they elect directors for the ensuing year. All common shareholders have a right to vote at the meeting with the number of shares held determining the number of votes that a shareholder might cast.

At the general meeting, the president of the corporation usually explains the activities of the corporation over the past year and may discuss the general plans for the firm's next year. The president or the treasurer may present the financial statements of the corporation and comment on them, as well as answer questions raised by the shareholders. The financial statements are prepared by a public accounting firm that is engaged as an auditor, and the auditor's report is attached to them. The auditor's report is discussed by the shareholders. If necessary, the auditor may be present to explain matters of a financial nature that pertain to the audit. The shareholders also appoint an auditor for the next year at the annual meeting. The auditor's duty is to the shareholders, not to the directors of the corporation. The auditor is responsible for the examination of the books and financial affairs of the corporation on the shareholders' behalf. In order to perform the audit the auditor has access to all financial accounts and books, but the shareholders do not. The shareholders are only entitled to the financial reports provided by the directors' and auditor's report at the year end. The shareholders, however, do have access to certain other corporation records. A shareholder may, for example, examine the minute-books of shareholders' meetings, the shareholder register, the list of directors, the incorporating documents, and the by-laws and resolutions of the corporation. However, a shareholder may not examine the minute-books for directors' meetings.

Special meetings of shareholders may be convened for a variety of purposes relating to the corporation if a number of shareholders[19] believe that the meetings are necessary. The group of shareholders usually request the directors to call the meeting. But if the directors should fail to do so within a fixed period of time, the shareholders may do so themselves, and the corporation will be obliged to reimburse them for the expenses incurred.[20] At the meeting, the shareholders may deal with the subject-matter of the requisition, and where appropriate, take action in the form of a by-law or resolution. An example of a special meeting called by

---

19. The number is usually presented as a small percentage of the total number of shares outstanding. See, for example, Canada Business Corporations Act, R.S.C. 1985 c. C-44, s. 143, where the percentage is set at 5%.

20. The Canada Business Corporations Act, R.S.C. 1985 c. C-44, s. 143.

shareholders may be to remove an auditor, or to object to a particular course of action that the directors have taken that might be reversed by a special resolution or by-law of the shareholders.

The fact that shareholders must approve all important decisions of the directors prevents the directors from engaging in certain activities that might be contrary to the interests of the majority of the shareholders. Unfortunately, it does little to protect minority shareholders if the majority of the shares are held by the directors or those who support them. Because "the majority rules" for most decisions within a corporation, a minority shareholder has only limited rights where there is a misuse of power by the majority. At common law, it is normally necessary for the complainant to show some injury has occurred as a result of the decision of the majority. This is particularly difficult in the case of a minority shareholder of a corporation, because the corporation, and not the shareholder, is usually wronged by the misuse of power or the breach of duty.[21] Where the corporation is controlled by the very majority that has committed the breach of duty or misused its power, the corporation is not likely to take action against that particular group.

To overcome this difficulty, the common law courts have recognized a number of exceptions to the "majority rule." They have permitted minority shareholders to take action on behalf of the corporation against the majority (or the directors) in the following instances:

(a) where the act objected to is *ultra vires* the corporation,
(b) where the act personally affects the rights of the minority shareholders;
(c) where the corporation has failed to comply with the procedural requirements for approval of the act;
(d) or where the act of the majority constitutes a fraud on the minority shareholders.

The last exception to the general rule includes cases where the majority attempt to appropriate the minority interests for themselves, or where they attempt to acquire corporate property at the expense of the corporation.

Unfortunately, a common law action taken against the directors by a shareholder who believes that the directors have acted improperly is not an easy matter to bring before the courts. The difficulty lies in the fact that the corporation is the body injured by the alleged improper action of the directors, and the shareholder is only one of perhaps a great many persons indirectly injured or affected. Thus, the shareholder must take action for the corporation on behalf of all persons indirectly injured by the injury to the corporation, using a type of class action known as a **derivative action.**

The common law courts, however, will not proceed with derivative actions of this nature unless the shareholder can first satisfy the court that all internal attempts to have the matter resolved have been exhausted, and that all reasonable demands to rectify the problem were refused by the directors. Then the shareholder must establish that the actions or decisions of the directors were improper, and did in fact cause injury to the corporation. Finally, the shareholder is usually required by the court to provide some security for the costs of the action should the claim fail, as derivative actions tend to be very lengthy and expensive cases.

---

21. This situation arose in the case of *Foss v. Harbottle,* [1834] 2 Hare 461; 67 E.R. 189.

To overcome the difficulties associated with the common law derivative action, corporations legislation patterned after the Canada Business Corporations Act[22] usually provides some relief for the shareholder who believes that the corporation has been injured through some act or omission of the directors. For example, under the Canada Business Corporations Act,[23] a shareholder may apply to the court for permission to institute the action by satisfying the court that (1) reasonable notice was given to the directors of the shareholder's intention to apply to the court if the directors failed to do so, and the directors refused to act; (2) it would appear to be in the interests of the corporation that the matter be dealt with; and (3) the complainant shareholder is acting in good faith in making the application to the court.

If a shareholder satisfies these conditions, the court may then permit the action to be brought before it. The court may also, if it so desires, order the corporation to pay reasonable legal fees incurred by the complainant as well.[24]

Minority shareholders, particularly those in corporations that do not offer their shares to the public, are also protected in a similar manner by the Canada Business Corporations Act[25] and comparable provincial legislation. A minority shareholder, for example, who believes that actions taken by the majority are repressive of the minority shareholders' rights, may apply to the court for relief. If the court is satisfied that the actions of the corporation are oppressive, unfairly prejudicial, or unfairly disregard the interests of any security holder, the court may rectify the matter under the broad powers given to it under the statute. These powers include the right of the court to order the corporation to purchase the securities of the aggrieved shareholder, to restrain the improper conduct, or, in an extreme situation, to order the liquidation or dissolution of the corporation.

The remedial powers of the courts have been examined briefly here in connection with shareholder rights, but it is important to note that complaints may also be brought by others who might be affected as well. For example, a director or officer of the corporation or one of its affiliates, or any other person the court deems a proper person to make an application, may be considered a complainant under the act.[26]

Dissolution

Theoretically, a corporation has an infinite life span. However, in reality, events may occur that have the effect of limiting the existence of the entity. While these events may take many forms, the most common, at least with respect to the business corporation, is undoubtedly the inability of the corporation to carry on its affairs in a profitable manner. When this situation arises, the corporation, if it is solvent, may wind up its operations and **surrender its charter** or apply for a **certificate of dissolution**. If the corporation is in the unfortunate situation of being

---

22. Certificate of incorporation provinces as well as the federal government have this type of provision in their statutes. British Columbia provides for a similar procedure in its legislation.

23. Canada Business Corporations Act, R.S.C. 1985 c. C-44, s. 239.

24. Ibid., s. 240.

25. Ibid., s. 241.

26. Ibid., s. 238.

insolvent, then it may be involuntarily dissolved through corporation winding-up proceedings.

The procedure in both instances is complex, but the result is the same. The corporation ceases to exist when the process is completed. However, where the directors of a solvent corporation make a conscious decision to cease operations and dissolve the entity, the shareholders must approve the proposal. An application may then be made to the incorporating jurisdiction to have the corporation's existence cease. The corporation must follow a specific procedure set out in the statute, depending upon whether it has been operational or not. This usually includes the filing of **articles of dissolution** (in the case of a certificate of incorporation jurisdiction) along with the appropriate approval of the shareholders, or filing a notice of intention to dissolve. The appropriate procedures are then resumed. They normally include the publication of notice of the intention. When the procedure is completed, a certificate of dissolution is issued, formally putting an end to the existence of the corporation. A somewhat different procedure must be followed for letters patent corporations and memorandum corporations under general act legislation.

SUMMARY

A corporation is a legal entity that has an existence separate from its owners. The powers that the corporation may acquire vary from something close to the powers possessed by a natural person to very restricted and narrow powers, where the corporation is incorporated by a legislature under a statute for a very specific purpose.

The method of incorporation varies from province to province. It may take a number of different forms, each granting a corporation different rights and powers. In some provinces, incorporation is by the issue of letters patent, which is very similar to the royal charter form of incorporation and gives the corporation virtually all of the powers of a natural person. Other provinces provide for incorporation under a general statute, which limits the powers of the corporation to those powers acquired under the statute and contained in the memorandum of association filed under it. The federal government and several provinces use a general act for incorporation, but they use a slightly different terminology and have given corporations incorporated under the legislation all the powers of a natural person.

Regardless of the form of incorporation, the corporate body takes on a separate existence from its incorporators and continues in existence until it is wound up, or it surrenders its charter.

A corporation acts through its agents and is liable to its creditors for all corporation debts. The shareholders who own the corporation have limited liability for the debts of the corporation. Their limit is the value of the shares that they purchased in the corporation.

In a corporation, the shareholders elect directors annually to manage the affairs of the corporation. The directors, once elected, have a general duty to operate or manage the business in the best interests of the corporation. They owe a duty of loyalty and good faith to the corporation in all of their dealings on its behalf. The shareholders, on the other hand, do not participate in the active day-to-day management of the business, but are entitled to information from the directors on the corporation's performance. If the shareholders disapprove of the directors' management, they may remove the directors at the annual general meeting of shareholders and elect other directors in place of those that previously held the office.

Corporation legislation, in general, attempts to balance the powers of the directors to manage the corporation with the protection of the investment of the shareholders. To some extent, it also considers the rights of the public. It does this through the imposition of special duties and obligations on the directors. It permits the shareholders to take action either within the corporation or through the courts, when the directors fail to comply with the duties and responsibilities imposed upon them.

DISCUSSION QUESTIONS

1. What is the legal nature of a corporation?
2. How does a corporation differ from a partnership?
3. What is a special act corporation? For what purpose would it be formed? Give two examples.
4. Explain the term "letters patent." In what way or ways would a letters patent corporation differ from a general act corporation?
5. Define *corporate ultra vires*. Explain why most provinces have attempted to eliminate the doctrine as it applies to third parties dealing with a corporation.
6. What drawbacks commonly associated with partnerships are overcome by the use of the corporate form?
7. Describe briefly the relationship between a corporation and its shareholders. How does a shareholder's relationship with the corporation change if the shareholder becomes a director?
8. Explain the *doctrine of corporate opportunity.*
9. Define the *indoor management* rule and, by way of example, explain how it is applied.
10. What are the obligations of a director of a corporation in an instance where the director has a financial interest in a firm with which the corporation wishes to do business?
11. Indicate how the principle of "majority rule" is applied in the decision-making process of a corporation. What protection is available to a dissenting minority shareholder where a fundamental change in the corporation's object is proposed?
12. Distinguish a "public" corporation from a "private" corporation. Why is this distinction made? What other terms are used for each of these types of corporations?
13. Where a corporation wishes to sell its securities to the public, what requirements are imposed upon the promoters, directors, and others associated with the sale and distribution of the securities?

MINI-CASE PROBLEMS

1. A, B, and C are the directors of ABC Corporation. At a directors' meeting, B suggests that the corporation consider the purchase of a block of land owned by the RST Corporation. C is a principal shareholder in the RST Corporation. What are C's obligations to B, A, and the ABC Corporation?
2. X, a director of the DC Corporation, is informed by the corporation's accountant that the decline in the corporation's sales has resulted in a large fourth quarter loss. Before the corporation's financial results for the year are announced to the public, X sells a large block of his shareholding in the corporation. When the news of the corporation's loss is announced, the price of the shares on the stock exchange falls by $10 per share. What are the rights of Z, who purchased 1000 shares from X at the higher price?

**JUDICIAL
DECISIONS**

The judicial decisions in this chapter represent two classic cases on corporation law. The first one, *Salomon v. A. Salomon & Co. Ltd.* is an old English case that established that a corporation has an existence at law that is separate from its shareholders, and that the liability of the shareholders is essentially limited to their investment in the corporation.

In the Salomon case the creditors attempted to establish that the company was really a "front" for the principal shareholder, and that he should be responsible for the debts of the company. The various arguments raised by the creditors in their case are discussed. But the final conclusion reached by the court was that the corporation was a separate entity and that the creditors' dealings were with the corporation, rather than the principal shareholder.

The second judicial decision, *Gluckstein v. Barnes* illustrates the duty of disclosure imposed upon persons who act as promoters of a corporation. Persons, such as directors who are responsible for the issue and sale of shares to the public, have a duty to disclose any secret profits they might make as a result of their positions in the company. In the case, the court reviews the obligations of disclosure that the law imposes on them.

**Nature of a
Corporation —
Limited
Liability —
Existence Separate
from Shareholders**

Salomon v. A. Salomon & Co. Ltd., [1897] A.C. 22.

A. Salomon operated a successful leather and footwear business. He incorporated a company and sold the business to the company in return for 20 000 shares and certain debentures. Members of his family each held one share to meet the requirements of the Companies Act, which required seven shareholders. The company later became insolvent, and both the unsecured creditors and Salomon claimed the remaining assets that were allegedly secured by Salomon's debentures.

Lord Herschell:

It is to be observed that both Courts treated the company as a legal entity distinct from Salomon and the then members who composed it, and therefore as a validly constituted corporation. This is, indeed, necessarily involved in the judgement which declared that the company was entitled to certain rights as against Salomon. Under these circumstances, I am at a loss to understand what is meant by saying that A. Salomon & Co., Limited, is but an "alias" for A. Salomon. It is not another name for the same person; the company is ex hypothesi a distinct legal persona. As little am I able to adopt the view that the company was the agent of Salomon to carry on his business for him. In a popular sense, a company may in every case be said to carry on the business for and on behalf of its shareholders; but this certainly does not in point of law constitute the relation of principal and agent between them or render the shareholders liable to indemnify the company against the debts which it incurs. Here, it is true, Salomon owned all the shares except six, so that if the business were profitable he would be entitled, substantially, to the whole of the profits. The other shareholders, too, are said to have been "dummies," the nominees of Salomon. But when once it is conceded that they were individual members of the company distinct from Salomon, and sufficiently so to bring into existence in conjunction with him a validly constituted corporation, I am unable to see how the facts to which I have just referred can affect the legal position of the company, or give it rights as against its members which it would not otherwise possess.

The Court of Appeal based their judgement on the proposition that the formation of the company and all that followed on it were a mere scheme to enable the appellant to carry on business in the name of the company, with limited liability, contrary to the true intent and meaning of the Companies Act, 1862. The conclusion which they drew from this premiss was, that the company was a trustee and Salomon their cestui que trust. I cannot think that the conclusion follows even if the premiss be sound. It seems to me that the logical result would be that the company had not been validly constituted, and therefore had no legal existence. But, apart from this, it is necessary to examine the proposition on which the Court have rested their judgement, as its effect would be far reaching. Many industrial and banking concerns of the highest standing and credit have, in recent years, been, to use a common expression, converted into joint stock companies, and often into what are called "private" companies where the whole of the shares are held by the former partners. It appears to me that all these might be pronounced "schemes to enable" them "to carry on business in the name of the company, with limited liability," in the very sense in which those words are used in the judgement of the Court of Appeal. The profits of the concern carried on by the company will go to the persons whose business it was before the transfer, and in the same proportions as before, the only difference being that the liability of those who take the profits will no longer be unlimited. The very object of the creation of the company and the transfer to it of the business is that, whereas the liability of the partners for debts incurred was without limit, the liability of the members for the debts incurred by the company shall be limited. In no other respect is it intended that there shall be any difference: the conduct of the business and the division of the profits are intended to be the same as before. If the judgement of the Court of Appeal be pushed to its logical conclusion, all these companies must, I think, be held to be trustees for the partners who transferred the business to them, and those partners must be declared liable without limit to discharge the debts of the company. For this is the effect of the judgement as regards the respondent company. The position of the members of a company is just the same whether they are declared liable to pay the debts incurred by the company, or by way of indemnity to furnish the company with the means of paying them. I do not think the learned judges in the Court below have contemplated the application of their judgement to such cases as I have been considering; but I can see no solid distinction between those cases and the present one.

It is said that the respondent company is a "one man" company, and that in this respect it differs from such companies as those to which I have alluded. But it has often happened that a business transferred to a joint stock company has been the property of three of four persons only, and that the other subscribers of the memorandum have been clerks or other persons who possessed little or no interest in the concern. I am able to see how it can be lawful for three or four or six persons to form a company for the purpose of employing their capital in trading, with the benefit of limited liability, and not for one person to do so, provided, in each case, the requirements of the statute have been complied with and the company has been validly constituted. How does it concern the creditor whether the capital of the company is owned by seven persons in equal shares, with the right to an equal share of the profits, or whether it is almost entirely owned by one person, who practically takes the whole of the profits? The creditor has notice that he is dealing with a company the liability of the members of which is limited, and the register of shareholders informed him how the shares are held, and that they are substantially in the hands of one person, if this be the fact. The creditors in the present case gave credit to and contracted with a limited company;

the effect of the decision is to give them the benefit, as regards one of the shareholders, of unlimited liability. I have said that the liability of persons carrying on business can only be limited provided the requirements of the statute be complied with; and this leads naturally to the inquiry, What are those requirements?

The Court of Appeal has declared that the formation of the respondent company and the agreement to take over the business of the appellant were a scheme "contrary to the true intent and meaning of the Companies Act." I know of no means of ascertaining what is the intent and meaning of the Companies Act except by examining its provisions and finding what regulations it has imposed as a condition of trading with limited liability. The memorandum must state the amount of the capital of the company and the number of shares into which it is divided, and no subscriber is to take less than one share. The shares may, however, be of as small a nominal value as those who form the company please: the statute prescribes no minimum; and though there must be seven shareholders, it is enough if each of them holds one share, however small its denomination. The Legislature, therefore, clearly sanctions a scheme by which all the shares except six are owned by a single individual, and these six are of a value little more than nominal.

It was said that in the present case the six shareholders other than the appellant were mere dummies, his nominees, and held their shares in trust for him. I will assume that this was so. In my opinion, it makes no difference. The statute forbids the entry in the register of any trust; and it certainly contains no enactment that each of the seven persons subscribing the memorandum must be beneficially entitled to the share or shares for which he subscribes. The persons who subscribe the memorandum, or who have agreed to become members of the company and whose names are on the register, are alone regarded as, and in fact are, the shareholders. They are subject to all the liability which attaches to the holding of the share. They can be compelled to make any payment which the ownership of a share involves. Whether they are beneficial owners or bare trustees is a matter which neither the company nor the creditors have anything to do: it concerns only them and their cestuis que trust if they have any. If, then, in the present case all the requirements of the statute were complied with, and a company was effectually constituted, and this is the hypothesis of the judgement appealed from, what warrant is there for saying that what was done was contrary to the true intent and meaning of the Companies Act?

It may be that a company constituted like that under consideration was not in the contemplation of the Legislature at the time when the Act authorizing limited liability was passed; that if what is possible under the enactments as they stand have been foreseen a minimum sum would have been fixed as the least denomination of share permissible; and that it would have been made a condition that each of the seven persons should have a substantial interest in the company. But we have to interpret the law, not to make it; and it must be remembered that no one need trust a limited liability company unless he so please, and that before he does so he can ascertain, if he so please, what is the capital of the company and how it is held.

Promoters of Corporation — Duty of Disclosure of Any Secret Profit Earned

Gluckstein v. Barnes, [1900] A.C. 240

A number of promoters acquired property, then incorporated a limited company to purchase the property from them. The promoters elected themselves as first directors of the company and then solicited applications for the purchase of shares by way of a prospectus. The prospectus did not disclose the fact that the promoters would earn a secret profit of £20 000 on the sale.

EARL OF HALSBURY, L.C.:

My lords, in this case the simple question is whether four persons, of whom the appellant is one, can be permitted to retain the sums which they have obtained from the company of which they were directors by the fraudulent pretence that they had paid £20,000 more than in truth they had paid for property which they, as a syndicate, had bought by subscription among themselves, and then sold to themselves as directors of the company. If this is an accurate account of what has been done by these four persons, of course so gross a transaction cannot be permitted to stand. That that is the real nature of it I now proceed to shew.

In the year 1892 the freehold grounds and buildings known as "Olympia" were the property of a company which in that year was being wound up. That company had issued debentures of the extent of £100,000 as a first charge, and a mortgage as a second charge for £10,000. The four persons in question knew that the property would have to be sold, and they combined to buy it in order that they might resell it to a company to be formed by themselves. The combination, which called itself the Freehold Syndicate, but which, perhaps, the common law would have described by a less high-sounding title, proceeded to buy up so far as they could the incumbrances on the property called "Olympia." They expended £27,000 in buying debentures. These, of course, were very much depreciated in value, and they gave £500 for the mortgage of £10,000. As soon as this transaction had been completed they, partners in it, proceeded to form a company, and it was of course necessary that the company should be willing to help, and accordingly the four persons in question were made by the articles of association the first directors.

The property was sold on February 8 by the chief clerk of North J. for £140,000 and the syndicate purchased nominally for that sum, but, by reason of the arrangement to which I have referred, that sum was less by £20,734 6s. 1d. than what they appeared to give. On March 29 they completed as directors the purchase of the property for £180,000 and they as directors paid to themselves as members of the syndicate £171,000 in cash and £9000 in fully paid-out shares — in all £180,000.

The prospectus by which money was to be obtained from the public disclosed the supposed profit which the vendors were making of £40,000, while in truth their profit was £60,734 6s. 1d., and it is this undisclosed profit of £20,000, and the right to retain it, which is now in question.

My Lords, I am wholly unable to understand any claim that these directors, vendors, syndicate, associates, have to retain this money. I entirely agree with the Master of the Rolls that the essence of this scheme was to form a company. It was essential that this should be done, and that they should be directors of it, who would purchase. The company should have been informed of what was being done and consulted whether they would have allowed this profit. I think the Master of the Rolls is absolutely right in saying that the duty to disclose is imposed by the plainest dictates of common honesty as well as by well-settled principles of common law.

Of the facts there cannot be the least doubt; they are proved by the agreement, now that we know the subject-matter with which that agreement is intended to deal, although the agreement would not disclose what the nature of the transaction was to those who were not acquainted with the ingenious arrangements which were prepared for the entrapping the intended victim of these arrangements.

In order to protect themselves, as they supposed, they inserted in the prospectus, qualifying the statement that they had bought the property for £140,000 payable in cash, that they did not sell to the company, and did not intend to sell, any other profits made by the syndicate from the interim investments.

Then it is said there is the alternative suggested upon the agreement that the syndicate might sell to a company or to some other purchaser. In the first place, I do not believe they ever intended to sell to anybody else than a company. An individual purchaser might ask inconvenient questions, and if they or any one of them had stated as an inducement to an individual purchaser that £140,000 was given for the property, when in fact £20,000 less had been given, it is a great error to suppose that the law is not strong enough to reach such a statement; but as I say, I do not believe it was ever intended to get an individual purchaser, even if such an intention would have had any operation. When they did afterwards sell to a company, they took very good care there should be no one who could ask questions. They were to be sellers to themselves as buyers, and it was a necessary provision to the plan that they were to be both sellers and buyers, and as buyers to get the money to pay for the purchase from the pockets of deluded shareholders.

My Lords, I decline to discuss the question of disclosure to the company. It is too absurd to suggest that a disclosure to the parties to this transaction is a disclosure to the company of which these directors were the proper guardians and trustees. They were there by the terms of the agreement to do the work of the syndicate, that is to say, to cheat the shareholders; and this, forsooth, is to be treated as a disclosure to the company, when they were really here to hoodwink the shareholders, and so far from protecting them, were to obtain from them the money, the produce of their nefarious plans.

I do discuss either the sum sued for, or why Gluckstein alone is sued. The whole sum has been obtained by a very gross fraud, and all who were parties to it are responsible to make good what they have obtained and withheld from the shareholders.

I move your Lordships that the appeal be dismissed with costs.

CASE PROBLEMS FOR DISCUSSION

Case 1

Acme Forwarding Company leased docking and warehouse facilities at a harbour. The lease gave the company exclusive use of the pier and the buildings, but held the company responsible for the maintenance and repair of the pier.

Baker, a director of the Acme Forwarding Company, was responsible for the authorization of use of the pier by ships bringing cargo for off-loading at the company warehouse. The company policy was that only ships handling goods destined for the company warehouse were to use the pier. No authorization would be given unless the shipowners carried adequate insurance to cover any damage that might be done to the pier by careless docking.

Baker also held an interest in a shipping firm that wished to off-load a small cargo at the city where the Acme Forwarding Company pier was located. The shipping company, however, wished to place the cargo directly onto two trucks, rather than use the facilities of Acme Forwarding Company. Baker, with the intention of accommodating the shipping company, authorized the docking of the ship at the pier.

When the ship attempted to dock with its cargo, it collided with the pier, causing extensive damage to both the ship and the pier. Under the terms of the lease that Acme Forwarding Company had with the property owner, it was obliged to repair the pier. Acme Forwarding Company did so, at a cost of $120 000. Then it looked to the shipping company to recover the cost of the damage caused by the ship.

The shipping company, which had suffered damage to its only ship, was unable to pay for the damage to the pier. Its insurance would cover only a part of the $120 000 cost of the pier repairs. When the directors of Acme Forwarding Company were informed of the shipping company's inability to pay for the damaged pier, they were also informed that Baker was a shareholder in the shipping company.

Discuss the rights of the parties in this case and explain how these rights might be enforced.

Case 2

Model T Motors Ltd. was indebted to Simple Finance for a substantial sum of money. The finance company held a number of mortgages on the corporation's assets, but pressed the corporation for a blanket demand chattel mortgage as additional security. Under pressure from the finance company, one of the principal shareholders, who was also one of the signing officers of the corporation, executed a blanket chattel mortgage to the creditor. The mortgage was not made under the corporation seal, and only one of the two signatures required by the corporation's by-laws was placed on the document.

Some time later, the finance company obtained the corporate seal of Model T Motors for another purpose and affixed it to the chattel mortgage. A few weeks later, when a payment on the loan was overdue, Simple Finance seized the assets of Model T Motors under the blanket chattel mortgage.

Advise Model T Motors of its position in this case. If the matter came before the courts how would you expect the case to be decided?

Case 3

A corporation owned a parcel of vacant land on which it stored its construction equipment. The land was not large enough for the requirements of the company. When the adjoining landowner expressed a desire to purchase the property from the company, the directors informally considered the offer and agreed to sell the land for $150 000. No directors' meeting was held to formally deal with the matter. However, the secretary-treasurer, on the basis of the informal agreement amongst the directors, contacted the offeror and advised him of the price. The price was acceptable to the purchaser, so the secretary-treasurer then drew up a written purchase agreement that he signed on behalf of the corporation in his capacity as secretary-treasurer. The purchaser also signed the document.

The directors later decided not to carry through with the sale, and the purchaser brought an action against the corporation for specific performance of the contract.

What defences might be raised by the corporation in this case? What legal principles are involved? Render a decision.

Case 4

Ritchie owned 13 shares of the Vermilion Mining Co. Three other shareholders held four shares each. The remainder of the 2400 shares of capital stock was held by the three directors of the company. The company owned certain mining claims on which some preliminary exploration work had been done, but that required the investment of a large amount of capital in order to establish a mine. Because the company had not been in a position to proceed with the development of the properties, the company faced the prospect in the near future of forfeiture of the mining claims as a result of their forced inaction.

The directors, who were shareholders in another mining company, entered into an agreement to sell the mining claims to that company in exchange for shares in the second company. The share exchange for the mining claims would give Vermilion a 10% interest in the other company.

A meeting of shareholders was called to approve the transaction. At that time the directors declared their interest in the other mining company. The directors explained that in their opinion, the transfer represented fair market value for the claims and they urged approval of the transaction. The directors voted in favour of the sale over the objections of Ritchie, who was the only dissenting shareholder.

He accused the directors of attempting to confer a benefit on a company in which they had an interest, to the detriment of the company in which they were directors. He eventually brought an action to restrain the directors from completing the sale of the mining claims to the other company.

Discuss the issues raised in this case and render a decision.

Case 5

Cinema Ltd. owned a theatre that it wished to sell. To make the property more attractive to a prospective purchaser, the directors decided to acquire a second theatre in the same city and offer the two properties as a "package deal."

Some inquiries were made as to the purchase price of a second theatre, and a price of $300 000 was determined for the property. A subsidiary company was incorporated to acquire the second theatre, with the intention that the shares in the subsidiary would be wholly owned by Cinema Ltd. Unfortunately, the lending institutions would only advance Cinema Ltd. $180 000 on its assets. In order to effect the purchase of the second theatre, the three directors of the corporation and a lawyer (who frequently acted for the corporation) each agreed to invest $30 000 to make up the necessary $120 000. The subsidiary corporation issued 300 000 shares valued at $1 each to the parent company and the four investors in return for the $300 000 in cash. It then proceeded with the purchase of the second theatre.

Some time later, a purchaser was found for the two theatres, and a purchase agreement completed. The purchaser, however, insisted on acquiring the second theatre by way of a purchase of the shares in the subsidiary company. The share price was determined at $1.25. This netted Cinema Ltd. a profit on the sale of $45 000, and each of the four investors a profit of $7500. When details of the sale were revealed to the shareholders, one shareholder demanded that the four individuals pay over their profits to the corporation. When the three directors and the lawyer refused to do so, the shareholders instituted legal proceedings to have the funds paid to the corporation.

Discuss the various legal arguments that might be raised in this case by the parties. Indicate how the case might be decided.

Case 6

High Rise Apartments Ltd. expressed an interest in the purchase of a large block of land suitable for development as an apartment site. The board of directors requested Harris, one of the directors who was also a real estate broker, to investigate the possibility of the corporation purchasing the land for a reasonable price.

Harris, without revealing that he was a director of High Rise Apartments Ltd., contacted the president of Land Assembly Ltd., the corporation that owned the land. He inquired as to the price the corporation was asking for the property. The president replied that the price was $500 000. Harris then offered to sell the land for Land Assembly Ltd. for his "usual commission" as a real estate broker. The president of the corporation agreed to have Harris attempt to sell the property on its behalf, so Harris reported back to the board of directors at High Rise Apartments Ltd. that the land was for sale at $525 000.

Unknown to the remaining members of the board of directors, the following events occurred before discussion took place as to whether the corporation should purchase the land at the price of $525 000.

(1) Black and Jones, both directors of High Rise Apartments Ltd., became interested in the land as a site for a shopping centre. They had incorporated a company of the purpose of buying the land if High Rise Apartments Ltd. should decide not to purchase the property.

(2) Green, a director of High Rise Apartments Ltd., was urged by her spouse, who was a minority shareholder in Land Assembly Ltd., to speak and vote against the purchase because he felt that Land Assembly Ltd. was selling the land for less than its true worth.

(3) Olsen, a director of High Rise Apartments Ltd., who was also a principal shareholder in Condominium Construction Company (a corporation interested in the parcel of land as a condominium site), was busy attempting to make an offer to purchase the property. When she heard of the offer from the president of Land Assembly Ltd. to sell the property for $525 000, Olsen slipped out of the directors' meeting and telephoned the president of Condominium Construction Company, urging him to call Land Assembly Ltd. with a higher offer.

A meeting of the Board of Directors of High Rise Apartment Ltd. was called for the purpose of considering the purchase of the property at a price of $525 000. Davis, the Chairman of the Board, called for a vote on the purchase. Only Davis and Harris voted in favour. The remaining members of the board (Olsen, Green, Black, and Jones) voted against the motion.

After the purchase was rejected by the Board of Directors at High Rise Apartments Ltd., both the company incorporated by Black and Jones and Condominium Construction Company attempted to purchase the land. When they contacted the president of Land Assembly Ltd., he advised them to contact Harris, who was the real estate broker engaged to sell the property. Eventually, the property was sold to Condominium Construction Company at a selling price of $560 000. Harris received a real estate commission on the sale of $26 000, which was paid to him by Land Assembly Ltd. After the sale was completed,

Davis discovered the facts surrounding the sale and the actions of the directors of High Rise Apartments Ltd.

Advise Davis of the legal issues raised in this case and the course of action he might follow. Indicate the arguments that might be raised if the matter came before the court, and render a decision.

Case 7

Henri Boucher and his son, Gaetan, lived in the same city where Gaetan ran a small business, an unincorporated restaurant. Henri had operated a small strip plaza comprising a convenience store, a gas station, and a pizzeria/arcade. Under pressure from creditors, Henri had sold the plaza for the amount of his debts, and began anew with his son's assistance.

They formed a corporation to develop a roadside piece of land into a 10-unit commercial plaza near a residential area.

Otherwise unemployed, and with Gaetan busy in his restaurant, Henri looked after contracting the majority of the work. This included considerable construction work to build the plaza. As construction progressed there were disturbing signs of discontent among the contractors who were building the plaza. On occasion, they would call the restaurant, asking Gaetan for payment. Gaetan would call his father, who would in turn pay them. Often, however, the calls persisted and Gaetan would find himself paying bills out of his own pocket and keeping a tally of the bills he had paid on behalf of the company.

Eighteen months after incorporation, and fifteen months after breaking ground on the project, the plaza had acquired a bad reputation in the town, and suppliers were unwilling to deliver materials. It quickly foundered when the bank called for repayment of the $290 000 that had been borrowed (on demand) by the company. The land had been bought with bank funds for $175 000. Invoices totalling $87 000 had been paid, but the company had no more money in its account. Gaetan's tally showed that he had paid bills out of his own pocket totalling $11 000. Unfortunately, with a half-built plaza and a bad reputation, the only offers for purchase of the site were in the order of $145 000. Henri was despondent, and soon left the province, leaving behind Gaetan with the restaurant.

The company lawyer showed Gaetan a resignation that had been sent to him a month before in which Henri had resigned as an officer and director of the company, and had turned in his shares. This left Gaetan as sole officer, director, and shareholder. The lawyer thought Gaetan had known of his father's resignation.

Advise Gaetan with respect to the issues that the company creditors will raise. Discuss Gaetan's rights and/or liabilities, and explain any steps he could have taken to protect himself.

PART V

Special Contractual Relationships

Special contractual relationships cover a number of business-related areas of the law that have the law of contract as their basis or that represent statutory control of business activities. For text purposes, employment at common law is examined first, then the labour relations law alternative to the common law employment relationship. This is followed by bailment, which is a special relationship concerning the loan or lease of a chattel or the storage or transport of goods.

The sale of goods is examined in terms of the application of the Sale of Goods Act to the contract of sale. Consumer protection laws, as they affect the contract of sale and related business activities, follows the sale of goods. This is then expanded to review the control of business activities, not only related to the sale of goods, but to business practices generally, by an examination of restrictive trade practices legislation. Restrictive trade practices for the most part fall under the Competition Act, a federal statute designed to promote greater competition between firms.

Risk reduction, which is essential in any business activity, is examined in the chapter on insurance law. This chapter places this important special type of contract in a business perspective.

The final topic in Part V is concerned with the law as it relates to negotiable instruments. Negotiable instruments, which include cheques, promissory notes and bills of exchange, represent the most widely used forms of debt payment both domestically and internationally. The law pertaining to these instruments is statutory, and the most important provisions of the legislation are considered with emphasis on the business uses of negotiable instruments.

CHAPTER 18

Employment Relationship

CONTRACT OF EMPLOYMENT

The origins of the employment relationship have their roots in antiquity, and it is impossible to know at what point the first individual voluntarily consented to do the bidding of another in return for a wage. The employment relationship of master and servant developed in early England as slavery declined, and the rise of towns and guilds fostered the climate for the new form of servitude. By the middle of the fourteenth century there were sufficient numbers of workmen and craftsmen employed in England to warrant legislation to fix their wages.[1]

The first English act that dealt specifically with the contract of employment was the Master and Servant Act of 1867, which was subsequently adopted in Canada by a number of provinces.[2] This statute modified the common law contract of employment by imposing limits on the length of time a written contract of employment might bind the parties and specified many of the terms and conditions that relate to the relationship. Legislation that protected workmen from injury arising out of work accidents in England took the form of a Workmen's Compensation Act in 1897. It, too, was introduced in a number of Canadian provinces some time later.

Apart from legislation that had a direct bearing on employment, the common law over a long period of time gradually established the relationship as one of contract. The courts saw the relationship as a form of "bargain," struck between the master and the servant, in which the servant (in return for a wage) agreed to submit to the direction of the master in the performance of his work. The relationship, however, was never considered to be one of pure contract in which the parties, both vested with equal bargaining power, devised an agreement to their

---

1. 23 Edw. III. (1349). The statute was apparently not a true statute, as Parliament had been prorogued because of the Plague. It was, however, treated as such.
2. For example, the Master and Servant Act, R.S.O., 1897, c. 157, and R.S.M. 1891, c. 96.

mutual satisfaction. The law of master and servant had been around too long to abandon all of the law that had developed over many centuries, and as a result, the relationship was never treated as being strictly contractual. Masters, for example, had historically been held liable for the torts of their servants committed in the performance of the masters' business, and the breach of a master's contract by a servant at law was the master's default. Since it was first recognized, the relationship has been modified by case-law and by statutes that have generally imposed additional duties or limitations on the master. Nevertheless, the basic concept of employment as a contract has remained for the most part intact.

NATURE OF THE RELATIONSHIP

The common law contract of employment involves the payment of wages or other remuneration by the employer to the employee in return for the services of the employee. As with other forms of contract, the agreement must contain the essential elements of a contract to be enforceable. The basic characteristic of the relationship, which determines whether a person is an employee or not, is generally considered to be the **degree of control** that one person exercises over the other. For many years, the courts considered the relationship to be one of employment where the employer had the right to direct what work was to be done and the manner in which it was to be done.[3] This basic test proved to be inconclusive, however, as employment relationships in the twentieth century took on a wide variety of forms. The courts gradually came to realize that control in itself was insufficient to determine the relationship. Eventually, a more complicated test was devised to meet the complex interpersonal relationships that had arisen in modern business. The test was essentially a **fourfold** one, of which only one of the factors considered was control. The courts added to this three other factors: the ownership of tools, the chance of profit, and the risk of loss.

The fourfold test was described by the court in the following terms:

> In earlier cases a single test, such as the presence or absence of control, was often relied on to determine whether the case was one of master and servant, mostly in order to decide issues of tortious liability on the part of the master or superior. In the more complex conditions of modern industry, more complicated tests have often to be applied. It has been suggested that a fourfold test would in some cases be more appropriate, a complex involving (1) control; (2) ownership of the tools; (3) chance of profit; (4) risk of loss. Control in itself is not always conclusive.[4]

More recently, the courts have recognized the limitations of their fourfold test and appear to be groping their way toward an **organization test,** which examines the relationship in relation to the business itself. This latter test is based upon the services of the employee, and whether they represent an integral part of the business or something that is adjunct or accessory to the normal business activities of the employer.[5] In recent cases that have come before the courts, its principal application has been to distinguish between employees and independent contractors — not an easy task in today's complex business world.

The independent contractor has usually been distinguished from the employee

3. *Harris v. Howes and Chemical Distributors, Ltd.,* [1929] 1 W.W.R. 217.

4. *City of Montreal v. Montreal Locomotive Works Ltd. et al.,* [1947] 1 D.L.R. 161; [1946] 3 W.W.R. 748.

5. *Co-operators Ins. Ass'n v. Kearney* (1964), 48 D.L.R. (2d) 1; *Armstrong v. Mac's Milk Ltd.* (1975), 7 O.R. (2d) 478; *Mayer v. J. Conrad Lavigne Ltd.* (1979), 27 O.R. (2d) 129.

on the basis that the initiative to do the work and the manner in which it is done are both under the control of the contractor. This has been generally characterized by the right of the contractor to exercise his or her own discretion with respect to any matter not specifically stipulated in the contract.[6] However, in recent years this distinction has become blurred in situations where the contractor acts alone.

Where the contractor also employs others to do the work, the relationship is generally that of an independent contractor rather than employment, because the independent contractor exercises the function of an employer as well.[7] It was, however, the difficulties associated with the determination of the true relationship, in cases where no employees were engaged by the independent contractor, that required the courts to devise an organization test to identify the nature of the contract. The test examines the contractor's role in the context of the employer's business, and the relationship is determined on the basis of whether the work done is a part of the business or something outside it.

The same test might be applied to distinguish the agency relationship from that of the employer-employee. Generally, the principal has the right to direct the work that the agent is to perform, but not the manner in which it is to be done.[8] Again, this is not always so, particularly where the agent acts only for a single principal, and the principal exercises a substantial degree of control over the agent. Other characteristics of the principal-agent relationship may also apply that may distinguish a case of agency from employment in given circumstances, but the application of the organization test represents a useful tool to identify and distinguish the two relationships.[9]

FORM OF THE CONTRACT

A contract of employment need not be in writing to be valid and binding on the parties, but a contract that is to run for a fixed term of more than one year is subject to the Statute of Frauds and must be in writing to be enforceable. If the contract may be terminated on proper notice in less than one year, or if the agreement has no fixed term of duration, then it has generally been held to be a **contract of indefinite hiring** and not subject to the statute.[10]

The impact of the Statute of Frauds on employment contracts was examined in the case of *Campbell v. Business Fleets Ltd.*[11] where the court considered the relationship between an employer and an employee where no written agreement existed. The judge in that case observed:

> In the case at bar, in accordance with the findings of the learned trial judge, the agreement was to continue in force as long as the plaintiff was satisfied with the salary and bonuses, but if not so satisfied the plaintiff could terminate the employment at any time. Therefore, the plaintiff could terminate his employment within the space of one year. Moreover, the contract (if there was no wrongdoing on the part of the plaintiff, and such wrongdoing was not suggested) was to continue for his (the plaintiff's) life, which might or might not be for a period of one day, one

---

6. *McAllister v. Bell Lumber Co. Ltd.,* [1932] 1 D.L.R. 802.

7. *Re Dominion Shipbuilding & Repair Co. Ltd.; Henshaw's Claim* (1921), 51 O.L.R. 144.

8. *Mulholland et al. v. The King,* [1952] Ex. C.R. 233.

9. *Co-operators Ins. Ass'n v. Kearney* (1964), 48 D.L.R. (2d) 1.

10. *Campbell v. Business Fleets Ltd.,* [1954] O.R. 87.

11. Ibid.

month, one year or twenty years. It is to me manifest that this contract must have
come to an end at any time the plaintiff was not satisfied with his salary and bonus
or on the death of the plaintiff, which might or might not be within the year: *Glenn
v. Rudd* (1902), 3 O.L.R. 422.

We are of opinion that on the above authorities the law is that the statute has no
reference to cases in which the whole contract may be performed within one year,
but there is no definite provision as to its duration, even although it may appear as
a fact that the performance has extended beyond that time; that where the contract
is such that the whole may possibly be performed within a year and there is no
express stipulation to the contrary, the statute does not apply; and that the same
principle has been applied to promises in terms of unlimited duration made by or
to a corporation when performance of the promise is by the nature thereof limited
to the life of the corporation or to the life of the individual... The Court is of the
opinion, therefore, that in the case at bar this verbal contract is without the provisions of s. 4 of The Statute of Frauds...

Where evidence in writing is required to render the contract enforceable, the
courts are prepared to accept informal, rather than formal, written evidence. For
example, in one case the writing requirement was satisfied by an exchange of letters between the employer and the employee, offering and accepting the employment, but without mention of wages.[12] In another case, the entry of details of the
hiring in the corporation minute-book, which had been signed by the corporation
officers, was held as sufficient evidence to satisfy the statute.[13]

Employment contracts are often verbal agreements of indefinite hiring,
although most employment relationships where the employee is likely to have
access to secret processes or confidential information of the employer are reduced
to writing and subject to a restrictive covenant. An employer may insert a restrictive covenant in an employment contract in an effort to protect his or her business
secrets, but the ability to enforce such a restriction on the employee is limited to
those situations where the restriction is reasonable and necessary to protect the
employer from serious loss. Restrictive covenants usually may not restrict an
employee from exercising skills learned on the job, but may limit the employee's
use of secret or confidential information if the employee should leave his or her
employment.[14] Apart from these few provisions, most employment contracts tend
to be informal documents.

DUTIES OF THE EMPLOYER

The duties of the employer have been the subject of much of the labour legislation since the beginning of the nineteenth century. Laws relating to minimum
wages, hours of work, and working conditions have been largely directed against
employer abuses in the employment relationship and override contract terms
made contrary to them. For example, each province has passed laws frequently
referred to as employment standards or industrial standards laws that regulate the
terms and conditions of employment and the conditions under which work may
be performed. These laws may be divided into two separate classes: those that
deal with employee safety and working conditions, and those that deal with the
terms of the employment contract.

---

12. *Goldie v. Cross Fertilizer Co.* (1916), 37 D.L.R. 16.

13. *Connell v. Bay of Quinte Country Club* (1923), 24 O.W.N. 264.

14. *Management Recruiters of Toronto Ltd. v. Bagg*, [1971] 1 O.R. 502.

The former class of laws usually deal with the physical aspect of employment, such as sanitary facilities, control of dust, fumes, and equipment that might affect employee health and safety in a plant or building. Government inspectors enforce these laws and visit an employer's premises from time to time to make certain that these work hazards are minimized.

Health and safety legislation frequently dictates that the employer must provide employees with safety equipment where hazards are associated with a particular job. The failure on the part of the employer to provide safety equipment normally entitles the employee to refuse to do the work until the equipment is made available. Employers are also obliged to train employees in the safe handling of equipment and substances that pose a safety or health hazard. In addition, the legislation usually imposes stiff penalties on the employer if he or she should violate the safety requirements. In many provinces, occupational health and safety legislation also imposes fines or penalties on supervisory staff personally if they allow breaches of the legislation to occur.

Employment standards laws, dealing with the employment contract, generally impose minimum terms of employment on the parties and allows them to negotiate more favourable terms (from the employee's point of view) if they wish to do so. Most of these provincial statutes establish minimum wage rates, fix maximum hours of work, set conditions under which holiday and vacation pay must be given, and impose minimum conditions for termination of the contract by the parties. While some similarity exists in the legislation, the provinces have generally written their laws to meet their own particular employment needs. Consequently, the laws relating to working conditions, wage rates, and other aspects of employment vary somewhat from province to province.

Human rights legislation in most provinces also dictates that employers must not discriminate in their hiring practices on the basis of a person's race, creed, colour, place of origin, nationality, sex, age, or, in some cases, on the basis of physical disabilities or past criminal record. What this usually means to employers is that the selection process they follow must consider factors other than those mentioned in the statute. In jurisdictions where the age of the employee is included (such as Ontario) a minimum and a maximum age are usually set out in the legislation. The employer must not consider the age of the employee if the employee falls within the boundaries set by the statute. Where physically handicapped persons are covered by the human rights legislation, the handicap may only be considered as a factor where it would affect performance of the job. For example, an employer may reject an applicant for a position that requires a great deal of climbing over and around operating equipment, if the person's handicap would prevent him or her from performing the work in an efficient manner. Apart from these limitations, at common law, an employer is normally free to select the person whom the employer believes to be best suited for the position.

Human rights considerations also apply to the workplace and the employer's obligation to maintain a discrimination free work environment. In particular, employers are obliged to control discrimination by employees against other employees in the firm. In one case, an employee was the subject of racial harassment by other employees and complained to the employer. The employer did not investigate the matter, and the harassment continued until the employee lodged a formal complaint under the applicable human rights legislation. The human rights tribunal held the employer vicariously liable for the employees' racially discriminating remarks because the employer had failed to investigate the complaint of discrimination.

Employers must also avoid work practices that would constitute discrimination under the act or code. While employers are not obliged to eliminate bona fide or legitimate work requirements of a job, or incur costs to satisfy a particular employee, the employer must demonstrate that the job requirement or action is not intentional discrimination. For example, employers are expected to make reasonable efforts to accommodate the religious and other creed-related activities of employees in the scheduling of work, holidays, and vacation time. However, they would not be obliged to close down operations on a normal business day simply because it represented a religious day for certain employees.

Employers are not permitted to pay female employees a lesser wage rate than male employees, where both employees are performing the same job. In 1988, the Province of Ontario carried this equal pay requirement a step further and introduced legislation to provide for equal pay for work of equal value. This legislation required all public sector employers, and over a time frame, most medium to large private sector firms to ensure that certain types of positions that have been traditionally filled by women would be assessed vis-à-vis positions traditionally filled by men in terms of their value, using job-related criteria such as skill, ability, education, working conditions, and effort. Salaries and wages would then be determined on the basis of values assigned to these factors rather than allowing market forces to determine the wage rates for the respective positions.

In addition to the terms of employment imposed by statute, many duties of the employer are implied by common law. The most important of these relate to compensation. The employer must pay wages or other remuneration to the employee in return for the employee's services, and generally must indemnify the employee for any expenditures or losses that the employee might incur in the normal course of his or her employment, if made at the employer's direction.[15] For example, if the employer requires the employee to travel to a neighbouring community to carry out some duty on behalf of the employer, the employer would be expected to reimburse the employee for the employee's travel and other expenses associated with the assignment unless customs of the trade or the terms of employment provided otherwise.

Two further duties of the employer are implied in the employment relationship: the employer is obliged to provide the employee with sufficient tools to do the work where it is not the custom of the trade for the employee to provide his or her own, and the employer must provide the employee with sufficient information to allow the employee to calculate the remuneration due where the employee is paid on some system other than a salary or hourly rate. For example, the employer who operates an iron mine would be obliged to provide a group of employees with sufficient information to calculate the bonuses due to them for mining over and above a stipulated minimum amount of ore, where the bonus is based upon the tonnage mined.

---

15. *Dugdale et al. v. Lovering* (1875), L.R. 10 C.P. 196.

DUTIES OF THE EMPLOYEE

Apart from specific duties that may be set out in a contract of employment, an employee is subject to a number of implied duties that arise out of the employment relationship. As a general rule, the employee has a basic duty to obey all reasonable orders of the employer that fall within the scope of the employment.[16] In addition, the employee has an obligation to use the property or information of the employer in a careful and reasonable manner.[17] Any confidential information that the employee obtains from the employer must be kept confidential during the course of employment,[18] and afterwards.[19] The employee is also under an obligation to devote the agreed hours of employment to the employer's business, and the employer is entitled to the profits earned by the employee during those intervals of time.[20] The employee's spare time, however, is the employee's own.[21]

If the employee should inform the employer that he or she has a special skill or professional qualification, then it is an implied term of the employment contract that the employee will perform the work in accordance with the standard required of the skill or profession.[22] An employee that professes to be skilled and is negligent in the performance of a skilled task may be liable for damages suffered by the employer as a result of the employee's negligence, provided that there are no intervening factors or special controls exercised over the employee by the employer.[23]

In Ontario, the courts have recently expressed the opinion that senior employees, the executives of a corporation, have a higher duty to their employer than do ordinary employees. According to this opinion, senior executives are in a sense in a fiduciary position vis-à-vis their employer. Therefore they owe a clear duty to their employer to devote all of their energy, initiative, and talents in the best interests of the corporation. If they should fail to do so, the employer may treat this failure as grounds for termination. For example, in a case where a senior executive was hired to help improve the profitability of a group of companies, he did so by way of an invention that both improved material handling practices and reduced accounting costs. He then engaged in a protracted disagreement with the employer over the ownership rights to the invention and the right to produce and market it for his own benefit. The employer dismissed the employee. In the legal action that followed, the Court of Appeal, in upholding the employer's right to dismiss the executive without notice, stated that senior employees have an added obligation to make the corporation more profitable. This responsibility consequently requires the employee to place the interests of the corporation before his own.[24]

Employees have a duty at law to act in the best interests of the employer in the performance of their duties. If they use their position to earn secret profits for

16. *Smith v. General Motor Cab Co. Ltd.,* [1911] A.C. 188.

17. *Lord Ashburton v. Pape,* [1913] 2 Ch. 469.

18. *Bents Brewery Co. Ltd. et al. v. Luke Hogan,* [1945] 2 All E.R. 570.

19. *Robb v. Green,* [1895] 2 Q.B. 315.

20. *William R. Barnes Co. Ltd. v. MacKenzie* (1974), 2 O.R. (2d) 659; *Bennett-Pacaud Co. Ltd. v. Dunlop,* [1933] 2 D.L.R. 237.

21. *Sheppard Publishing Co. v. Harkins* (1905), 9 O.L.R. 504.

22. *Lister v. Romford Ice & Cold Storage Co. Ltd.,* [1957] A.C. 555.

23. *Harvey v. R.G. O'Dell Ltd. et al.,* [1958] 1 All E.R. 657.

24. See *Helbig v. Oxford Warehousing Ltd. et al.* (1985), 51 O.R. (2d) 421.

themselves, the court may require them to turn over their profits to the employer. The dishonesty associated with such an act would also entitle the employer to dismiss the employee without notice. In the case of *William R. Barnes Co. Ltd. v. MacKenzie*[25] the court described this obligation in the following manner:

> The principle that a dishonest agent is not entitled to a commission from his principal is well recognized as is the right of a principal to any secret profit earned by his dishonest agent. An agent stands in a fiduciary relationship with his principal with his remuneration usually attributable to separate transactions. If he is dishonest in one transaction he forfeits his commission thereon but not on other transactions faithfully performed. In the instant case the relationship is basically that of master and servant rather than principal and agent and the remedy of a master against his defaulting servant is restricted to a right of instant dismissal and to damages which flow from the default. I do not consider wages paid to be such an item of damages and disagree with that part of the judgment in *Protective Plastics Ltd. v. Hawkins* which appears to hold otherwise.

> I adopt the view of the trial Judge that wages cannot be recovered if one allows to the plaintiff all secret profits made by the delinquent employee and also holds the employee liable for any loss sustained by the employer as a result of the employee's breach of his employment contract. The argument is that the damages awarded the employer place him in the same position as if the delinquent employee had in fact been performing his duties as a faithful employee and that since all benefits ultimately accrue to the employer, the employee should be compensated for his time and labour in producing such benefits. The employer has already received the fruit of the employee's efforts, honest or otherwise, and cannot repudiate his obligation to pay. I recognize that in an agency situation the principal may take the benefit and refuse to pay the commission, but I am not aware of any binding authority which requires me to extend that principle to a master and servant situation.

TERMINATION OF THE CONTRACT OF EMPLOYMENT

The notice required to terminate a contract of employment has been the subject of legislation in most provinces. Many of these statutes provide a minimum period of notice that varies depending upon the length of service of the employee. This period of notice is generally the minimum requirement, but in some cases, it may replace the common law rule that reasonable notice of termination is required to terminate the contract.

At common law, unless the contract stipulates a specific termination date, or a period of notice for the termination of the agreement, both parties are obliged to provide reasonable notice of termination.[26] The adequacy or "reasonableness" of the notice is a matter of fact to be determined from a number of factors, including the nature of the contract, the method of payment, the type of position held by the employee, the length of service, the customs of the business, and even the age of the employee. All of these factors would be considered in the determination of what would constitute a reasonable time period. In some of the older cases, where the employee was unskilled and employed for only a short period of time at an hourly rate, the length of notice was often very short. The trend, however, has been away from short notice since the middle of the current century. A one-week

---

25. *William R. Barnes Co. Ltd. v. MacKenzie* (1974), 2 O.R. (2d) 659.
26. *Harvard v. Freeholders Oil Co.* (1952), 6 W.W.R. (N.S.) 413.

notice period is commonly determined as the minimum for an employee, and as much as a year or more as reasonable notice for a long-service employee or an employee engaged in a senior position in the firm.[27]

DISMISSAL AND WRONGFUL DISMISSAL

In the absence of an agreement to the contrary, an employer has the right to dismiss an employee without notice where the employee is incompetent or grossly negligent in the performance of his or her duties. The employer would also be entitled to do so where the employee concurs in a crime against the employer, or where the employee's actions are such that they would constitute a serious breach of the contract of employment. As noted earlier, the failure of a senior executive to devote his or her energies to the exclusive benefit of the employer may also be considered grounds for dismissal in some cases. In each case, however, the onus would be on the employer to establish that the employee's actions were not condoned by the employer, and that termination of the employment relationship was justified. Otherwise, the employee would be entitled to damages against the employer for wrongful dismissal.

More recently, the courts have considered other grounds to justify the dismissal employees. The **disruption of the corporate culture**, which encompasses improper employee behaviour towards other employees and customers, may be just cause for the dismissal of an employee. For example, a trust company was held to be entitled to dismiss a branch manager where the manager had treated customers in a rude manner and had berated staff to the extent that the branch had a higher than normal employee turn-over.

The courts may also consider the activities of employees both on and off the job that have a negative impact on the firm as just cause for dismissal. This basis for termination tends to be character related, and while the courts do not establish a moral standard for the behaviour of employees, if an employee exhibits a serious lack of judgement or integrity in activities off the job that affect the ability of the employee to carry out his or her duties or the employer's dealings with customers or clients of the firm, the activities may be just cause for dismissal.

Some provinces have attempted to clarify the matter of dismissal and termination without notice by setting out in their legislation conditions that permit an employer to terminate an employee without notice. Ontario, for example, provides in its legislation that the notice provisions do not apply to "an employee who has been guilty of willful misconduct or disobedience or willful neglect of duty that has not been condoned by the employer."[28]

Employees may also terminate their employment without notice under certain circumstances. The grounds, however, are for the most part limited to those situations where the work has an element of danger attached to it that has caused the employee to believe that it poses a threat to the employee's health or life, where the employer has seriously mistreated the employee, or where the employer has failed to perform the employer's part of the employment contract.

Where an employee believes that he or she has been wrongfully dismissed, the employee may bring an action against the employer for the failure to give

---

27. *Campbell v. Business Fleets Ltd.*, [1954] O.R. 87; *Bardal v. The Globe & Mail Ltd.* (1960), 24 D.L.R. (2d) 140.

28. The Employment Standards Act, R.S.O. 1990, c. E-14, s. 57. It should be noted, however, that this section of the act does not apply to employees in certain trades, businesses, and professions: see s. 57(10)(e).

reasonable notice of termination. If the employee should decide to pursue this course, it is important that the employee do everything that a reasonable person might be expected to do to minimize his or her loss. The employee would be expected to seek other employment immediately, and take whatever other steps that may be necessary to mitigate financial loss. The employee's actual loss would be the loss that the employee incurred between the time when he or she was terminated and the end of a reasonable notice period. For example, if Able was employed by Baker in a responsible position where reasonable notice might be determined as six months, and Baker should wrongfully dismiss Able, Able would be obliged to seek new employment immediately. If Able could not find suitable employment within a six-month period, then his damages would be the lost wages and benefits that he would ordinarily have received from the employer during that period. Had he found employment during the six-month interval, his actual loss would be reduced by the income he received during the period, and that amount would be deducted from the damages to which he would be entitled as a result of the wrongful dismissal.

The purpose of damages for wrongful dismissal is to place the injured employee in relatively the same position that the employee would have been in had the employee been given proper notice of termination of the contract. The courts will normally not award punitive damages, nor will they compensate the employee for any adverse effects that the wrongful dismissal might have on the employee's reputation or stature in the business community.[29] Judges, however, have recently awarded extra compensation where the actions of the employer were such that they caused the employee undue mental distress as a result of the termination.

Employers who terminate employees by these novel or different ways leave themselves open to the possibility of punitive damage awards if the employee successfully maintains a wrongful dismissal action. For example, in a 1992 case, a branch manager of a bank discovered that he was terminated when he attempted to use his bank credit card at an automated teller machine. The machine would not allow the manager access to his bank account, and flashed a message to him to contact the bank. When he did so, he was informed that the machine was informing him that he had been discharged. Based upon this evidence, the court found that the employee had been wrongfully dismissed and awarded the employee 12 months salary and $30 000 in punitive damages.[30]

Harsh or callous treatment coupled with sudden termination, in a situation where an employee was led to believe at the time of hiring that the position would be permanent and secure, may result in the employee making a claim for mental distress. To succeed, however, it would appear that the employee would be obliged to establish that the distress was brought on by the failure of the employer to give reasonable notice of termination.[31]

---

29. See for example, *Wardell v. Tower Co. (1961) Ltd.* (1984), 49 O.R. (2d) 655. *Peso Silver Mines Ltd. v. Cropper,* [1966] S.C.R. 673.

30. *Francis v. Canadian Imperial Bank of Canada* (1992), Ontario Court General Division (Hollett J.) unreported.

31. See, for example, *Pilon v. Peugeot Canada Ltd.* (1980), 29 O.R. (2d) 711, where the plaintiff was awarded damages to cover the mental distress associated with termination from what he was led to believe was a life-time position with the company. See also *Brown v. Waterloo Regional Board of Police Commissioners* (1983), 43 O.R. (2d) 112.

In some cases, the employer need not discharge or terminate an employee directly to constitute dismissal. Unilateral change in an employee's contract or employment may be considered **constructive dismissal** if the change radically alters the terms of employment or the conditions under which the work of the employee would be performed. Normally, changes instituted by the employer that represent the employee's promotion to a position of greater responsibility and a higher wage are acceptable to the employee, but changes constituting a "demotion" to a lower-paying or undesirable position may represent constructive dismissal if the employee is unwilling to accept the change. This may permit the employee to bring an action for wrongful dismissal. For example, if the employer unilaterally and without good reason moves a senior manager from a position of responsibility to that of an ordinary salesperson, with an accompanying substantial reduction in salary, the employee need not accept the new position, but may treat the change as constructive dismissal.

Constructive dismissal may also occur where the employer changes the employee's work environment or facilities so as to render it impossible for the employee to do his or her job. This might take many forms, but in one case, where the employer re-arranged the office and removed the employee's desk, the court held that the change constituted constructive dismissal, because, by removing the desk, the employer indicated to the employee that his services were no longer required. An adjudicator appointed under the Canada Labour Code reached a similar conclusion in another instance, where an employee's desk was removed and replaced with a small table after he had several altercations with his supervisors. Even though the employer had grounds for dismissal, the adjudicator held that the harassment and unusual treatment of the employee by the supervisors constituted wrongful dismissal.

EMPLOYER LIABILITY TO THIRD PARTIES

A general rule with respect to third party liability is that an employer may be held liable for any loss or damage suffered by a third party as a result of an employee's failure to perform a contract in accordance with its terms, or for any negligence on the part of the employee acting within the scope of his or her employment that causes injury or loss to the third party. This rule imposes **vicarious liability** on the employer for the acts of the employee that occur within the scope of the employee's employment.[32] For example, if Arthurs takes her automobile to Gordon's Garage for repairs, and an employee, Smith, negligently performs the repairs, Arthurs would be entitled to recover from Gordon's Garage for the breach of contract. Similarly, if an employee is sent to a customer's home to repair a defective boiler, and the employee negligently damages the equipment, causing it to explode, the customer would be entitled to look to the employer for the loss on the basis of the employer's vicarious liability for the acts of the employee.

The reason for the imposition of liability on the employer for the acts of the employee has a historical perspective and justification. In the past, employees seldom possessed the financial resources to compensate third parties for any loss suffered as a result of their negligence, and the third party would be unlikely to

---

32. See *McKee et al. v. Dumas et al.*; *Eddy Forest Products Ltd. et al.* (1975), 8 O.R. (2d) 229, for the difficulty in determining which employer may be vicariously liable where an employee is also under the direction of a temporary employer.

obtain compensation, even if a judgement was obtained against the employee. However, most employers did have the financial resources sources to cover a loss that a third party might suffer. In view of the fact that the employee was under the control of the employer, the courts simply carried the liability through the employee to the party primarily responsible for the employee's actions.

Employer liability is limited to those acts of the employee that fall within the ordinary scope of the employee's duties, but does not include acts of negligence that take place outside the employer's normal duties. For example, an employer sends an employee to another city to perform certain services on his behalf for a customer. After the work has been completed, the employee decides to spend the evening in the city, and rents a hotel room for the night. The employee's careless smoking sets fire to the carpet in the room, and results in a loss to the hotel. If the work had been completed in time for the employee to return, and if the employee had been instructed to do so but failed to heed his employer's instructions, the employee would be personally liable for the loss. However, if the employer had required the employee to use the room to display goods to prospective customers and to remain overnight in the room, the employer might be held liable for the loss suffered by the hotel, if it could be established that the employee's occupancy of the room was at the employer's direction and in the course of employment.

EMPLOYER LIABILITY FOR AN EMPLOYEE'S INJURIES

At common law, an employee injured while working for an employer was generally faced with a dilemma. If the injury occurred as a result of the negligence of another employee, it would be necessary to bring an action against the employer for that employee's negligence. The recovery of damages from the employer under such circumstances would be unlikely to enhance the employee's advancement or career with the particular employer. Nor was the prospect of bringing an action against the employer any more promising if the employee was injured by equipment or machinery that the employee was using. If the employee was successful, the employer would be obliged to pay for the injury, but, the legal action would likely result in termination of the employee by reasonable notice. On the other hand, if the employer could prove negligence on the part of the employee, or if the employer could establish that the employee had voluntarily assumed the risks that resulted in the injury, the employee would not be successful in the action for damages.

In spite of a number of attempts by the courts to accommodate the injured employee, the law relating to employee on-the-job injury remained unsatisfactory. It was not until the close of the nineteenth century that legislation in England remedied the situation. In 1897, the Workmen's Compensation Act was passed to provide compensation to workmen injured in the course of their employment. In essence, the act was an insurance scheme similar in concept to ordinary accident insurance. All employees covered by the act were entitled to compensation without the need to take legal action to prove fault if they were injured in the course of their employment. All employers subject to the legislation were required to contribute to a fund from which the compensation was paid, and the employee was not entitled to take action against the employer if the employee received compensation from the fund. Similar legislation was eventually passed in all provinces and territories in Canada, and in many states of the United States. The legislation has also been further refined since its introduction into England at the end of the last century. It has virtually eliminated actions against employers for injuries suffered by employees.

SUMMARY

The common law contract of employment is a special type of agreement that sets out the rights and duties of the employer and employee. It need not be in writing unless subject to the Statute of Frauds. The essential characteristic of the employment relationship is the control of the employee by the employer. Originally, the relationship was that of employment if the employer had the right to direct the work to be done, and the manner in which it was to be done. However, modern forms of business organization have required the courts to look beyond the simple control aspect to other determinants, and have included consideration of the ownership of tools, the chance of profit, the risk of loss, and in some cases, the relationship of the employee's work to the overall operation of the employer. The courts also consider the nature of the work done by the employee in terms of the role of the work in the employer's operation. This latter test is known as the organization test for employment.

Under the contract of employment both the employer and employee have a number of implied duties, the most important being the employer's obligation to pay wages in return for the employee's services, and the employee's obligation to obey all reasonable directions of the employer. If an employee acts in breach of his or her duty, the employer may be entitled to dismiss the employee. However, if the dismissal is unwarranted, the employee may bring an action against the employer for wrongful dismissal. A failure to give reasonable notice of termination, where such is required, would also be grounds for wrongful dismissal and entitle the employee to damages. The employee, however, must act promptly to mitigate loss by seeking employment elsewhere.

An employer may be vicariously liable for the acts of his or her employees, if the acts are done within the scope of the employee's employment. The employer, however, may have a right over and against a skilled or professional employee if the employee was negligent in the exercise of a professional skill in the performance of professional duties.

DISCUSSION QUESTIONS

1. How is an employment relationship established? What elements of the relationship distinguish it from agency or partnership?
2. Explain the fourfold test for employment. Why did the courts find it necessary to establish this test?
3. Distinguish a *contract of service* from a *contract for services.*
4. Must a contract of employment always be in writing to be enforceable? If not, under what circumstances would writing be required?
5. Outline the general or implied duties of an employee under a contract of employment.
6. What duties of an employee extend beyond the period of employment? In what way would a breach of these duties be enforced?
7. Why are employers, under certain circumstances, vicariously liable for the torts of their employees? Identify the circumstances under which vicarious liability would arise.

8. Identify the conditions or circumstances under which an employer would be justified in terminating a contract of employment without notice.

9. What factors must be considered in determining reasonable notice, if an employee or employer should decide to give notice of termination of a contract of indefinite hiring.

10. If an employee is wrongfully dismissed, explain how a court would determine the money damages that should be paid by the employer for the wrongful act.

11. Why must an employee mitigate his or her loss when wrongfully dismissed?

MINI-CASE PROBLEMS

1. Marie was employed by Rigney as bookkeeper and office manager in her sales agency for over 10 years. Without notice or explanation, Rigney informed Marie that her services were no longer required and requested her to leave the premises. At the time, Marie was earning an annual salary of $35 000. What additional information would you wish to know if Marie were to ask your advice as to whether she should take legal action against Rigney for wrongful dismissal?

2. Jones, who was earning an annual salary of $30 000, was summarily dismissed by Smith, his employer. A week later, Jones obtained a new position with another firm at an annual salary of $30 000. If Jones were to take legal action against Smith for wrongful dismissal, what would his damages be if he were able to prove his claim successfully?

3. A hired B as a sales clerk in her fabric shop, with a promise that the position would be "permanent" employment. Later, A overheard B arguing with a customer about the quality of some cloth the customer wished to buy. When questioned as to why she argued with the customer, B replied that no one was going to insult her by challenging the truth of any statement she made about the goods she was selling. A then dismissed B for her "attitude" toward customers. Advise A and B.

JUDICIAL DECISIONS

The judicial decisions in this chapter illustrate two important aspects of the employment relationship. The case of *Mayer v. J. Conrad Lavigne Ltd.* (1979), 27 O.R. (2d) 129 provides a judge's description of the test for the employment relationship. The judge reviews the "fourfold test" as described by Lord Wright in the *Montreal v. Montreal Locomotive Works Ltd.* case, then goes on to examine the "organization test." He concludes his judgement by applying the test to the case before him.

The *Bardal v. The Globe & Mail Ltd.* case illustrates the factors considered by a judge in determining the reasonable notice period in a wrongful dismissal case where no notice of termination was given. The judge first reviews the basis for the reasonable notice requirement, then outlines the factors that should be considered. The obligation on the employee to mitigate his loss is also noted by the judge.

Master and Servant — Test for Employment Relationship

Mayer v. J. Conrad Lavigne Ltd. (1979), 27 O.R. (2d) 129.

The plaintiff sold television time for the defendant on a straight commission basis. He was required to attend regular sales meetings of the defendant each day and file sales reports. Some direction of the plaintiff's activity was carried out by the sales manager, but this was generally limited to where and to whom to sell. When the defendant failed to pay the salesman vacation pay, the salesman instituted legal proceedings.

MACKINNON, J.A., A.C.J.O.:

The law and cases were much canvassed before us, but as the determination of whether a particular individual is a servant or an independent contractor is completely dependent on the facts, it would serve no useful purpose to review them all only to distinguish them on their facts. The emphasis in the earlier authorities was on the extent of the "control" that the master had over the servant to determine whether there was, indeed, a master-and-servant relationship. The concept of this relationship has, however, been an evolving one, changing with the changes in economic views and conditions. As Lord Wright put it in the leading case of *Montreal v. Montreal Locomotive Works Ltd. et al.,* [1947] 1 D.L.R. 161 at p. 169, [1946] 3 W.W.R. 748: "In the more complex conditions of modern industry, more complicated tests have often to be applied." He postulated a fourfold test involving: (1) control, (2) ownership of the tools, (3) chance of profit, and (4) risk of loss. This test has been enlarged by the more recent "organization test" which was approved and applied by Spence, J., in *Co-operators Ins. Ass'n v. Kearney* (1964), 48 D.L.R. (2d) 1. In that case (pp. 22-3), he quoted with approval the following passage from Fleming, *The Law of Torts,* 2nd ed. (1961), at pp. 328-9:

"Under the pressure of novel situations, the courts have become increasingly aware of the strain on the traditional formulation [of the control test], and most recent cases display a discernible tendency to replace it by something like an "organization" test. Was the alleged servant part of his employer's organization? Was his work subject to coordinational control as to 'where' and 'when' rather than 'how'? [citing Lord Denning in *Stevenson, Jordan & Harrison Ltd. v. MacDonald,* [1952] 1 T.L.R. 101, 111.]"

Lord Denning in *Stevenson, Jordan & Harrison Ltd. v. MacDonald et al.,* [1952] 1 T.L.R. 101, referred to by Fleming, said this:

"One feature which seems to run through the instances is that, under a contract of service, a man is employed as part of the business, and his work is done as an integral part of the business; whereas, under a contract for services, his work, although done for the business, is not integrated into it but is only accessory to it."

In my view, the facts as recited satisfy whichever test is used. The appellant had and exercised the control necessary to establish a master-and-servant relationship. The "when" and "where" was within the master's control, and to a certain extent, the "how" when clients were transferred from one salesman's list to another. Because of the training, skill, and experience of the respondent, one would not expect that the appellant would control "how" the respondent sold the air-time, any more than any other skilled or professional servant would be directed how to do his work. Equally, the relationship satisfies the "organization" test. The respondent's work was a necessary and integral part of the appellant's business. It supplied the financial life-blood of the appellant, and his work was subject to the co-ordinational control of management. His work was clearly integrated into the business and not merely accessory to it. In my view, applying the common law tests, the facts establish that the respondent was a servant and employee of the appellant.

Wrongful Dismissal — Reasonable Notice — Considerations — Duty to Mitigate Loss

Bardal v. The Globe & Mail Ltd. (1960), 24 D.L.R. (2d) 140.

The plaintiff was employed by the defendant newspaper on a contract of indefinite hiring. He was first hired as advertising manager. Sixteen years later, by which time he had become Director of Advertising, he was terminated without notice.

The plaintiff immediately sought other employment, and some months later, found a new position that paid substantially less in salary and benefits.

An action for wrongful dismissal was instituted against his previous employer.

McRUER, C.J.H.C.:

In every case of wrongful dismissal the measure of damages must be considered in the light of the terms of employment and the character of the services to be rendered. In this case there was no stipulated term during which the employment was to last. Both parties undoubtedly considered that the employment was to be of a permanent character. All the evidence goes to show that the office of advertising manager is one of the most important offices in the service of the defendant. In fact, it is by means of the revenue derived under the supervision of the advertising manager that the publication of a newspaper becomes a profitable enterprise. The fact that the plaintiff was appointed to the Board of Directors of the defendant goes to demonstrate the permanent character of his employment and the importance of the office.

It is not argued that there was a definite agreement that the plaintiff was employed for life but the case is put on the basis of an indefinite hiring of a permanent character which could be terminated by reasonable notice.

In *Carter v. Bell & Sons,* [1936] 2 D.L.R. 438 at p. 439, O.R. 290 at p. 297, Mr. Justice Middleton concisely and with great clarity stated the law applicable to this case in this way: "In the case of master and servant there is implied on the contract of hiring an obligation to give reasonable notice of an intention to terminate the arrangement."

On this branch of the case the only remaining matter to be considered is what should be implied as reasonable notice in the circumstances of the contract in question. In *Carter v. Bell* Middleton J.A. went on at p. 439 D.L.R., p. 297 O.R. to say: "This notice in a case of an indefinite hiring is generally 6 months, but the length of notice is always a matter for inquiry and determination, and in special circumstances may be less."

The contractual obligation is to give reasonable notice and to continue the servant in his employment. If the servant is dismissed without reasonable notice he is entitled to the damages that flow from failure to observe this contractual obligation, which damages the servant is bound in law to mitigate to the best of his ability.

In *Grundy v. Sun Printing & Publishing Ass'n* (1916), 33 T.L.R. 77, the plaintiff was an editor of a newspaper earning a salary of £20 a week. The jury awarded the plaintiff damages based on the failure to give 12 months' notice of termination of contract. On appeal to the Court of Appeal this award was sustained. In delivering the judgment of the Court Lord Justice Swinfen Eady said at p. 78: "In cases which had come before this Court a custom has been proved that an editor was entitled to 12 months' notice, and a sub-editor to six months' notice. In the absence of evidence of custom it could not be said that the view of the jury in this case was unreasonable."

There is no evidence of custom in the case before me and I think I must determine what would be reasonable notice in all the circumstances and proper compensation for the loss the plaintiff has suffered by reason of the breach of the implied term in the contract to give him reasonable notice of its termination.

There can be no catalogue laid down as to what is reasonable notice in particular classes to cases. The reasonableness of the notice must be decided with reference to each particular case, having regard to the character of the employment, the length of service of the servant, the age of the servant and the availability of similar employment, having regard to the experience, training and qualifications of the servant.

Applying this principle to this case, we have a servant who, through a lifetime of training, was qualified to manage the advertising department of a large metropolitan newspaper. With the exception of a short period of employment as manager of a street car advertising agency, his whole training has been in the advertising department of two large daily newspapers. There are few comparable offices available in Canada and the plaintiff has in mitigation of his damages taken employment with an advertising agency, in which employment he will no doubt find useful his advertising experience, but the employment must necessarily be of a different character.

I have come to the conclusion, as the jury did in the *Sun Printing & Publishing Ass'n* case and as the Court of Appeal agreed, that 1 year's notice would have been reasonable, having regard to all the circumstances of this case.

That being true, the next question to decide is what damages have flowed from the failure of the defendant to give a year's notice and how far have those damages been mitigated by the receipt by the plaintiff of a salary from another employer.

The plaintiff's salary with the defendant was $17,750 per year. In his new employment he has been receiving $15,000 per year since July 1, 1959. He is therefore entitled to recover $3,254.15 for loss of salary from April 25th to July 1st and $2,245.20, being the difference between the salary which would have been received from July 1, 1959, to April 24, 1960, and the salary actually received in his new employment during that time.

Upon the termination of the plaintiff's employment with the defendant his pension rights were said to have been valued as an employee with 16 to 17 years' service. According to ex. 7 the pension allowed to the plaintiff was based on the defendant's contribution to his pension at 40%. If he had been continued in the service for another year, pursuant to proper notice, the defendant's contribution would have been on a higher basis. The matter of what the dollar value of the plaintiff's pension would have been had he been employed for another year is a matter for actuarial computation. This aspect of the case was not developed in the argument. It is, however, quite clear that had the plaintiff been given proper notice according to the implied term of the contract he would have had another year's service with the defendant which would have increased his pension allowance. In view of the unsatisfactory condition of the evidence, I am unable to make a proper assessment of what damage the plaintiff has suffered in loss of pension by reason of his employment having been terminated a year sooner than it ought have been terminated. If the parties cannot agree as to these damages, I would direct a reference to the Master to ascertain these damages.

Three other aspects of damage remain to be considered: the alleged loss of the Christmas bonus, participation in the profit-sharing plan and loss of director's fees. I do not think the plaintiff is entitled to recover under any of these heads. The Christmas bonus was a purely voluntary gift distributed among the employees as a matter of good will between employer and employee. I do not think this case comes within the principles applied in *Manubens v. Leon*, [1919] 1 K.B. 208. In that case Lush J. allowed a plaintiff who was a hairdresser's assistant damages for loss of tips that he might reasonably have expected to have received from his customers, if his employment had not been wrongfully terminated. It was held that it was within the contemplation of the parties at the time of the engagement that the assistant would receive gratuitous payments from his customers. I think that is quite different from the case before me where the bonus was something that came from the employer and was not within the contemplation of the parties at the time that the plaintiff entered the service.

The case for claiming damages for loss of any share in the distribution of profits is still weaker. The profit-sharing plan was not founded on contract. It was instituted by the chief shareholder of the defendant and was not applicable to all employees but only those who were selected by a committee appointed by him. There was no obligation to put anyone on the list of those who should receive benefits in this way. It would appear to me that it would have been very improbable that the committee would have distributed profits to an employee who had received notice of the termination of his contract. I therefore allow no damages under this heading.

The appointment of the plaintiff to the Board of Directors of the defendant was an appointment at the will of the shareholders of the company and they were under no obligation to continue him on the Board for any period of time. There is no foundation for a claim for loss of director's fees.

It was argued that in his new employment the plaintiff is entitled to certain stock option rights and some allowance should be made in assessing damages in this account. I do not think it has been established in evidence that any allowance should be made in mitigation of the damages by reason on these alleged benefits. In the first pace, the value of the stock option rights is purely speculative. There is no evidence that any events have happened to entitle the plaintiff to stock under the agreement nor is there evidence that the stock would be worth anything if he did become entitled to it under the provisions of the agreement.

The plaintiff will therefore be entitled to judgment for $5,499.35, with a reference to the Master to ascertain the amount by which the dollar value of the plaintiff's participation in the pension plan was reduced by reason of the termination of his employment before April 24, 1960. The plaintiff will have the costs of the action.

CASE PROBLEMS FOR DISCUSSION

Case 1

Martin was employed by Chemical-Cosmetic Distributors to sell its products in a defined territory on a commission basis. Martin was not subject to strict hours of work, but signed a devotion to business agreement with Chemical-Cosmetic Distributors whereby she agreed to devote her time to the sale of their products, subject to her right to sell other non-competing lines of goods, provided that they did not interfere with her promotion of those of Chemical-Cosmetic Distributors. Under the terms of the agreement she was required to visit each retail outlet in her territory at least once a month and report the sales of each establishment to Chemical-Cosmetic Distributors.

One day Martin was travelling along a country road in her automobile en route to a retail customer of Chemical-Cosmetic Distributors when a young man on a bicycle suddenly appeared in front of her car. She attempted to brake the car, but could not do so in time to avoid a collision. The young man was seriously injured as a result of the accident and, some time later, brought an action for damages against Martin and Chemical-Cosmetic Distributors. Evidence of the police officer, who investigated the accident, indicated that the accident was largely the fault of Martin.

Advise Chemical-Cosmetic Distributors of their liability in this case and indicate how the matter might be decided by the court.

Case 2

Willard had been well known as a racing-car driver for many years. He had driven a number of different types of racing cars during his racing career, either under the sponsorship of automobile manufacturers or as an "independent."

Following a spectacular race in which Willard had won first prize, a sports car distributor offered him a position in his organization as director of marketing. The offer included a starting salary of $40 000 per year, participation in a profit-sharing plan open only to senior management, a generous pension plan, and a variety of other benefits including the use of a company-owned automobile. The position also gave him a place on the board of directors of the company.

As a part of his duties, Willard was expected to enter and drive company racing cars in a number of highly publicized race events held each year.

During his first year with the company, Willard won four of the five races that he had entered and worked hard at all other times to boost sales for the company. As a result of his efforts, sales increased by 20%. Willard received a year-end bonus of $5000 in addition to his salary and share of profits, and was advised by the president of the company that his salary for the next year would be raised to $50 000.

The second year of Willard's employment did not match the previous year. Willard won only two of the five races, and, in spite of spending extra time promoting the employer's sports cars, sales decreased by 3%. At a year-end directors' meeting, a bitter argument occurred between Willard and the company president over the poor sales performance of the company. The president blamed the drop in sales on Willard's poor showing on the race circuit, and Willard blamed the unreliability of the new model of the car for his poor performance. The argument ended with the president dismissing Willard.

The next day, Willard received a cheque from the company to cover his salary to that date, along with a formal notice of his termination.

Prior to his dismissal, Willard had arranged for a two-week holiday in Europe. He decided to follow through with these plans, then look for other employment on his return.

Willard searched diligently for a similar position when he returned from his holiday, but could find nothing. Eventually, some six months after his termination, he found a position as a staff writer for a sports car magazine at an annual salary of $28 000.

Under the terms of his employment at the time of his dismissal, Willard was entitled to receive (in addition to his salary of $50 000 per year) pension contributions by the company on his behalf of $3000 per year, director's fees of $2000 per year, a profit-sharing plan payment of approximately $6000, and the use of a company automobile.

He eventually brought an action for wrongful dismissal against the company and, in addition, alleged damage to his reputation as a professional driver as a result of his summary dismissal by his employer. He claimed $100 000 for damage to his reputation.

Indicate the arguments that might be raised by the parties to this action. Discuss the factors that would be taken into consideration by the court. Render a decision.

Case 3

McKenzie was a qualified and licensed driver of tractor trailers and other heavy types of trucks. He was first employed by FMP Company in 1963, and was steadily employed by the company as a truck driver until 1988. At that time he was voluntarily placed "on loan" to Timber-Hall Trucking under an agreement which provided as follows:

(1) Timber-Hall will provide and maintain trucks and equipment to haul logs from FMP Company logging sites to the FMP Mill.

(2) FMP Company will provide any qualified truck drivers required by Timber-Hall. Drivers will continue to be paid their regular wage rates and benefits by FMP Company.

(3) Timber-Hall will have the right to direct and supervise the work of the drivers, but will not have the right to discharge or discipline drivers provided by FMP Company.

Timber-Hall operated a fleet of 36 trucks used for hauling timber from various logging sites to the FMP mill. Of the drivers, 32 were employees of Timber-Hall and four were "on loan" from FMP Company. All drivers were under supervision of Timber-Hall management at both the loading and unloading points, and the drivers were directed to specific locations by Timber-Hall supervisors.

McKenzie was directed to a particular loading area by Timber-Hall and told to deliver the load to the FMP Company mill some 100 km away. McKenzie picked up the load of timber and set out for the FMP mill. En route, McKenzie encountered an icy road condition as he descended a long hill. Before he could bring the heavy truck under control, it careened from the road and collided with a road-side cabin owned by McGee.

The cabin was demolished, and McGee brought an action against McKenzie, Timber-Hall, and FMP Company for damages. Both Timber-Hall and FMP Company alleged in their defence that they were not the employer of McKenzie.

Discuss the arguments that may be put forward by the defendants and the issues raised by the case. Render a decision.

Case 4

Harkin entered into a contract of employment with the Periodical Publishing Company. Under the terms of his contract he agreed to devote his time to the advertising interests of the employer's business, and to engage in no other business in competition with the employer during the term of his employment.

Harkin assumed the position of "advertising agent" for the company and worked in that capacity for a number of years. During that time, however, he entered into an arrangement with a business acquaintance to publish an "Elite Directory" that contained brief biographical sketches and pictures of prominent individuals who resided in the city. The directory, which was printed by a competitor of Periodical Publishing Company, contained no advertising, but was sold at a profit by Harkin and his associate.

Some time later, Harkin's employer brought an action against him for an accounting of the profits made on the sale of the directory. The basis of the complaint (apart from the breach of the covenant) was that the directory competed with a weekly "society magazine" that the company produced.

Harkin argued that the directory was done in his spare time and that it did not conflict with his position of advertising agent. He admitted, however, that some of the information that came to his attention was obtained from reading his employer's weekly society magazine.

Indicate the legal issues and the arguments relating to them. Render a decision.

Case 5

Lynne and Leroy were employed as commission salespersons by a large computer and electronic company. Each received a basic salary of $500 per week and a commission on gross sales they made on behalf of the company. In addition, the company paid their reasonable travel and living expenses on all authorized business trips involving travel of more than 25 km from the head office building where their own offices were located.

Both Lynne and Leroy were highly productive sales representatives, and earned substantial sales commissions that placed their average earnings close to the $75 000 mark each year. While each was responsible for a specific territory, the two of them took on a proposal of the company concerning a new, remote-community computerized communications system that a government agency had opened to tender. The particular tender required extensive research and preparation, as well as presentation of the proposal for review and approval by several related government agencies before it could be submitted. A number of companies were interested in the project, and Lynne and Leroy put in long hours at their offices to prepare their presentations to the various agencies. Eventually, after much work and effort, they managed to obtain approval for the company project from each agency. A tender on the project was then prepared for submission to senior management for approval. Both Lynne and Leroy were optimistic that their tender would be successful, in spite of the fact that four other manufacturers were preparing tenders as well.

During the two weeks before Lynne and Leroy submitted the tender for senior management approval, the company initiated a minor reorganization of its marketing department. Then, several days after the submission was in the hands of senior management, both Lynne and Leroy were advised that they would each be promoted to the position of regional manager, a position carrying with it an annual salary of $80 000.

Regional managers were responsible for a number of salespersons who reported to them and were also expected to negotiate some of the larger contracts with customers. However they received no commissions, since their salaries were designed to cover their efforts as well as their responsibility.

The two employees were initially delighted with the thought of promotion. However, on reflection, they decided that, by accepting it, they would perhaps deny themselves the large commission they would earn if their tender was accepted by the government agency. To clarify their position, they met with the vice-president of marketing, who informed them that the company intended to include their old sales territories with those of other salespersons and that, if they refused to accept the promotions, no sales territory would be open for them. The rationale was that, since, as a result of the reorganization, the sales force would consist of persons with greater service with the company, those salespersons with less service would be terminated or moved to positions of less responsibility and lower salary rates. The vice-president urged both to accept the promotion, since they each had only three years' service with the company, and the company was anxious to retain them. The vice-president also stated that he believed that the two employees would likely have a bright future if they remained with the company.

At this point in the discussion, Leroy demanded to know if they would be entitled to the commission on the government sale if the tender was accepted. The vice-president responded that they would not be entitled to commissions in their new positions. Both Lynne and Leroy then became angry and accused the company of robbing them of what was rightfully theirs. The discussion quickly degenerated into a shouting match, until Lynne ended it by striking the vice-president with her heavy handbag. Both employees were then told to leave the office and "clean out their desks," as they were terminated.

Discuss the possible arguments of the two employees and the employer if the employees were to bring an action for wrongful dismissal. Render a decision, and in it consider the effect of the success or failure of the company to secure the government contract.

Case 6

Mall Merchandising Co. operates a department store in a shopping centre located near the outskirts of a large metropolitan city. The store employs a permanent and part-time staff of approximately 120 persons, and is open to the public from 10:00 a.m. to 10:00 p.m. on a six day per week basis. The store is closed on Sundays. Full-time employees work on a shift basis that requires each employee to work on two Saturdays each month, with an equivalent day off during the week that a Saturday shift was scheduled.

Mary K. was first employed by Mall Merchandising Co. in 1985. She was a good employee and had worked in the Giftwares Department since 1986. Her attendance record was above average, and she seldom lost time due to illness, Until very recently, she willingly worked her Saturday shift.

Some months ago, Mary K. joined a religious sect that considered Saturdays as their holy day. Saturdays were devoted to religious activities at the sect's place of worship, and Mary K. refused to work her scheduled Saturday shifts. The store manager was made aware of Mary K.'s refusal to work, and she informed Mary that no employee could be excused from the Saturday work, as it would be unfair to all of the other employees who were required to work. When Mary K. refused to comply with the manager's direction to work on Saturdays, the manager discharged her for insubordination. Mary K. was paid her wages and benefit entitlement up to and including her last day of work.

Advise Mary K. of her rights at law and the course of action (if any) that she might take. If she should decide to take action against her employer, what defences (if any) might the employer raise? How would you expect the case to be resolved?

Case 7

Harold B was employed as an installer and repairman for a cable television company. His work involved the installation of cable lines to customer's houses, and the repair and maintenance of the equipment installed. He worked out of the one of the company's branch establishments located in a small municipality. In that community, the company serviced approximately 5000 customers. The staff consisted of Harold, another repair/installer, an office manager and a receptionist/clerical employee. Harold and the other installer divided "on call" evening hours between them, but only responded to customer's service requests in the evening if a total breakdown of equipment occurred. Evening service calls were screened by an answering service, and only emergency service relayed to the installer on call for that evening.

Harold's performance during his first year of employment had been satisfactory, but by the end of the second year was causing concern for the employer. On several occasions he had quit work at the 5:00 p.m. end of his normal work day, leaving a customer's unit only partially installed when the job could have been completed by a few minutes extra time. In each case when he was reminded by the receptionist of the company policy to complete the installation in only one visit to the customers home, he became angry and informed the receptionist that he would decide if the work could be done in one visit. On another occasion, a customer reported that Harold's breath smelled of alcohol when he attended at her home one evening to repair the cable equipment.

Shortly after the last incident, Harold, on an evening when he was not on call, attended at a local tavern, and was involved in a brawl with several other patrons. The police were called, and Harold, along with several others, was charged and convicted of creating a disturbance. Harold was given a $100 fine and placed on probation. The incident and the subsequent conviction were duly reported in the local newspaper.

At this point, the company decided to dismiss Harold. He was paid his wages to that date, and given his accumulated vacation pay.

Discuss the issues raised in this case, and the various arguments that may be raised by the parties if Harold should decide to take legal action against the company. Render a decision.

Case 8

Jim and John were engineers with a mining company which frequently sent employees to remote job sites for long periods of time while a new property was being developed. Because of the long periods of time during which employees were required to stay at the remote sites, the company paid extremely well and attracted a large number of unmarried, young men to both its professional and labour positions.

The company had discovered, however, that it had difficulty attracting and keeping more senior and experienced personnel at the job sites. These employees were always in demand for the supervisory tasks and inevitable problems which arose that required the expertise of experienced professionals. After discovering that one of the main factors that discouraged senior employees from accepting such positions was their reluctance to be absent from their families, the company offered to pay all costs of a return flight home once each month for married staff at remote sites.

When Jim and John were interviewed for positions with the company they were told of this policy for married staff. Neither man was married and, when both were offered positions a short time later, they understood that they would not be eligible to receive the travel allowance.

One evening Jim and John were talking with some of the other employees at the job site about the travel policy. A colleague said that he would like to be able to get home to see his ill father more often, but that he could not afford the cost of a commercial flight on a regular basis and, since he was not married, he was not entitled to the company allowance. Overhearing this, one of the more senior employees commented, "I don't think that policy is very fair. Come to think of it, isn't there some law against that? You guys should go talk to management about it. They're pretty good guys and might make some changes."

Discuss the legal issues raised in this case and the arguments that the respective parties might raise. Explain the factors that a court would consider and what its decision might be.

CHAPTER 19

Labour Law

LABOUR LAW DEFINED

Labour law is an area of law concerned with the employment relationship. By strict definition, it would include all laws that touch on employment, including the common law and statutes. In the previous chapter, the common law contract of employment, employment standards legislation, and worker's compensation laws were mentioned. However, it is worthwhile to note that many other laws have been passed at both the federal and provincial levels of government that affect the employment relationship as well.

Canada does not have a national labour policy because employment falls for the most part within the jurisdiction of the individual provinces. Nevertheless, the federal government has jurisdiction in labour relations matters in some areas, because a number of business activities and industries (such as banking, navigation and shipping, aviation, interprovincial railways, and communications) are federal matters under the Constitution Act, 1982.[1] As a result of the split jurisdiction, all provincial governments and the federal government exercise control over the employment relationship within their respective spheres.

At the federal level, nation-wide employment-related legislation includes a contributory pension plan for most employees and a number of employment assistance schemes in the form of national unemployment insurance, manpower training, and placement programs. In addition, the federal government has implemented employment standard's laws and collective bargaining legislation that apply to firms operating within those defined industries and businesses that come under its jurisdiction.

The provinces generally are responsible for the establishment of labour

---

1. Proclaimed in force April 17, 1982.

legislation applicable to most business activities, as employment (except in those areas within the control of the federal government) is considered to be a matter of "property and civil rights." Consequently, it is under the jurisdiction of the provinces.2 As a result, all of the provinces have introduced legislation concerning many aspects of the employment relationship.

In addition to the broad definition of labour law, a second and narrower definition is sometimes used to describe a particular type of legislation relating to collective bargaining. This body of law is concerned with most aspects of employment where employees have decided to negotiate their terms and conditions of employment on a collective basis through a trade union.

DEVELOPMENT OF LABOUR LEGISLATION IN CANADA

Little more than a century ago, collective bargaining and labour unions were still looked upon with disfavour, and their activities treated as restraint of trade and contrary to public policy. Since that time, statute law has legitimized many of their actions, and permitted collective bargaining to take place by way of statutory authority and regulation. The process, however, was a slow and, for the most part, evolutionary one, rather than a sudden reversal of public policy. During this period of time, most of the legislation was introduced as a response to the growth and activities of the labour movement, rather than as an attempt to lead labour in a new direction. The laws have simply attempted to deal with the growth of the labour movement and the impact of its activities, as it gradually acquired a prominent position in the conduct of economic activity in Canada.

In Canada, the earliest significant legislation related to the labour movement was introduced at the federal level of government. In 1872 (following a similar change in the law in England), Canada amended its criminal laws to recognize trade unions as lawful entities.3 As a result of this change, unions and their membership were free from criminal prosecution in the conduct of their collective bargaining activities, provided that their actions were otherwise lawful in nature. The change in status permitted the union movement to expand rapidly in the industrialized areas of Canada, particularly in the skilled trades and, later, in the forestry and mining fields.

The first meaningful collective bargaining legislation was introduced in the United States:4 the law established a National Labour Relations Board to determine the right of a union to represent employees, and to require the employer to bargain with the union with respect to wages and working conditions of the employees.5 This legislation produced a rapid organization of the mass production industries by labour unions. The spillover of enthusiasm to Canada produced a similar interest in organization for collection bargaining purposes by Canadian employees in the mass production industries. Canadian provinces, however, lacked the legislative and administrative machinery to deal with rapid unionization of the workforce. The result was much labour unrest and disruptive recognition strikes in the years that preceded the outbreak of World War II.

---

2. The matter was determined by the case of *Toronto Electric Com'rs v. Snider,* [1925] A.C. 396.

3. The Trade Unions Act, 35 Vict., c. 30; Criminal Law Amendment Act, 35 Vict., c. 31.

4. The National Labor Relations Act, 49 Stat. 449 (1935) U.S.

5. This legislation was first introduced in 1933 as a part of the National Industrial Recovery Act, 48 Stat. 195 (1933) U.S., and later embodied in the National Labor Relations Act (Wagner Act), 49 Stat. 449 (1935) U.S.

The onset of World War II in 1939 brought with it a need for uninterrupted war production. Under the War Measures Act,[6] Orders in Council eventually established a legislative collective bargaining framework that bore some similarity to the United States' laws.[7] The new laws applied to all industries engaged in war production, and they provided for recognition of trade unions and the right of employees to bargain collectively. Administrative machinery was set up to determine the rights of unions to represent employees, and a procedure was set out to assist the parties in their collective bargaining.

The wartime legislation tended to encourage the unionization of industry. When the war ended, most of the major firms in the manufacturing, mining, and forestry sections of the economy were unionized. Since labour relations fell generally under the jurisdiction of the provinces, all provincial governments found it necessary to introduce collective bargaining legislation when the federal government wartime controls were removed. As with most provincial laws, each province introduced labour legislation to suit its own particular needs. As a consequence, the law relating to collective bargaining varied from province to province. Some basic aspects of the laws, nevertheless, were similar. This was due in part to the fact that many of the procedural aspects of the new legislation were adaptations of the rules and regulations set down by the labour relations boards under the wartime legislation.

COLLECTIVE BARGAINING LEGISLATION

The general approach taken to labour relations law federally and in each province has been to remove the collective bargaining relationship from the common law and the courts (insofar as possible) and deal with it administratively. The laws normally place employee selection of a union as a bargaining agent, the negotiation of the collective agreement, and the resolution of disputes relating to negotiations (unfair practices and bargaining in bad faith) under the jurisdiction of an administrative tribunal. The rights and duties of the employer, the union, and the employees are also set out in the legislation.

Each of the provinces and the federal government have enacted labour legislation that provides for the control of labour unions and collective bargaining in their respective jurisdictions, and each has established a labour relations board to administer the law. Labour legislation in each jurisdiction generally assigns a number of specific duties to the respective labour relations boards established under it. The boards normally have the authority to determine the right of a labour union to represent a group of employees, the nature and make-up of the employee group, the wishes of the employees to bargain collectively through a particular union, the certification of a union as a bargaining agent, and the enforcement of the rights and duties of employers, employees, and unions under the legislation. In some jurisdictions, the board is given the power to deal with strikes and lockouts as well.

The general thrust of the legislation is to replace the use of economic power by unions and employers with an orderly process for the selection of a bargaining representative for the employees, and for the negotiation of collective agreements.

---

6. The War Measures Act, 5 Geo. V, c. 2.

7. See: Order in Council P.C. 1003 (1944) under the War Measures Act.

The use of the strike or lockout is prohibited with respect to the selection and recognition of the bargaining agent, and severely restricted in use as a part of the negotiation process. In most jurisdictions the right to strike or lockout may not be lawfully exercised until the parties have exhausted all other forms of negotiation, and compulsory conciliation or other third party assistance has failed to produce an agreement.

The Certification Process

Collective bargaining usually begins with the desire on the part of a group of employees to bargain together, rather than on an individual basis with their employer. To do this, they must first establish an organization to act on their behalf. This may be done by the employees themselves forming their own organization, or more often, by calling upon an existing labour union for assistance. Most large labour unions have trained organizers whose job consists of organizing employees into new unions or locals affiliated with the larger union organization. These persons will assist the group of employees in the establishment of their own local union. Once the organization is in existence, with its own constitution and officers, its executive and members will then attempt to interest other employees of the firm to join. When the organization believes that it has the support of a majority of the employees in the employer's plant, shop, or office, it may then approach the employer with a request to be recognized as the bargaining representative of the employees. If the employer agrees to recognize the union as the bargaining representative, he or she may meet with representatives of it and negotiate a collective agreement that will contain the terms and conditions of employment that will apply to the group of employees represented by the union. On the other hand, if the employer refuses to recognize the union as the bargaining representative of the employees, the union is obliged to be **certified** as the bargaining representative by the labour relations board before the employer is required to bargain with it. This process is known as the **certification process.**

The process formally begins with the submission of a written application (by the labour union), to the labour relations board of the correct jurisdiction, for certification as the exclusive bargaining representative of a particular group of employees. On receipt of the union's application, the labour relations board will usually arrange for a hearing. At that time it will normally require a new union to prove that it is a bona fide trade union that is neither supported financially (or otherwise) nor dominated in any way by the employer. Once this has been accomplished by the union, the labour relations board will then determine the unit of employees appropriate for collective bargaining purposes.

The group of employees, or the **bargaining unit,** is usually determined by the board in accordance with the legislation or regulations setting out the kinds of employees eligible to bargain collectively. While variation exists from province to province and federally, only "employees" are entitled to bargain collectively. Within this group some professionals employed in a professional capacity, management employees, and persons employed in a confidential capacity with respect to labour relations are usually excluded. As well, the legislation does not apply to certain employee groups. Most provinces have special legislation to deal with collective bargaining by persons engaged in essential services and in the employ of government. In some provinces, persons employed in certain activities (such as hunting and trapping) may be excluded from collective bargaining entirely.

Labour relations boards at their hearings will usually receive the representations of the employer, the union, and the employees, if the parties cannot agree upon an appropriate bargaining unit. The determination of the bargaining unit, however, is a board decision. When the decision is made, the board will then proceed with the determination of employee support for the union in the particular unit. It may do this by an examination of union membership records and the examination of union witnesses at a hearing. However, if any doubt exists, the board will usually hold a representation vote to determine the true wishes of the employees.[8] If a majority of the votes are cast in favour of collective bargaining through the union, then the board will certify the union as the exclusive bargaining representative of all of the employees in the bargaining unit. Certification gives the union the right to negotiate on behalf of the employees the terms of their employment and the conditions under which their work will be performed. It also permits the union to demand that the employer meet with its representatives to negotiate the collective agreement that will contain these provisions.

The Negotiation Process

The **negotiation process** begins when the certified trade union gives written notice to the employer of its desire to meet with representatives of the employer to bargain for a collective agreement. On receipt of the notice, the employer must arrange a meeting with the union representatives and bargain in good faith with a view to making a collective agreement. This does not mean that the employer is obliged to accept the demands of the union, but it does mean that the employer must meet with the union and discuss the matters put forward by it. Nor does it mean that the demands are always one-sided. Employers often introduce their own demands at the bargaining table. For example, employers generally insist upon the insertion in the collective agreement of terms that set out the rights of management to carry on specified activities without interference by the union or employees.

Where the parties reach an agreement on the terms and conditions of employment, and on the rights and duties of the employer, the union, and the employees, the agreement is put in writing and signed by the employer and representatives of the union. When approved by the employees, the agreement then governs the employment relationship during the term specified in the agreement.

Collective agreements must normally be for a term of at least one year. Either the employer or the union may give notice to bargain for a new agreement, or for changes in the old agreement, as the expiry date of the agreement approaches. The minimum term is generally dictated by the governing legislation, and usually cannot be reduced without the consent of the labour relations board. The purpose of the minimum term is to introduce an element of stability to collective bargaining by requiring the parties to live under the agreement they negotiate without stoppage of work for at least a reasonable period of time.

If the parties cannot reach agreement on the terms and conditions of employment,

8. Some provinces (e.g., Ontario) require the Labour Relations Board to hold a vote where the support of the employees falls within a certain percentage range.

or the rights and duties of the employer and the union, most jurisdictions provide for third party intervention in the negotiations to assist the parties. This intervention may take the form of conciliation, mediation, or in some cases, fact-finding. The purpose of the intervention is to assist the parties by clarifying the issues in dispute and (in the case of mediation) by taking an active part in the process through offers of assistance in resolving the conflict. Only when third party intervention is exhausted are the parties permitted to strike or lockout to enforce their demands.

The law in most jurisdictions does not permit employers to alter working conditions or the work relationship during the negotiation process. Unions also may not unilaterally alter the relationship. For example, in one case where negotiations had reached an impasse, and before third party assistance was requested, some of the union members decided to picket at the employer's premises during off-duty hours. The employer then sought an injunction to prohibit the picketing. In handing down its decision the court observed:

> Either party has a definite course to follow if negotiations break down. A request for conciliation services is available to them. I repeat that any act by an employer or a union which at that stage in the negotiations is not in conformity with the "rules" set out in the Act to achieve agreement between the parties, allows drawing an inference of bad faith as it is not pursued by legal and peaceful steps as contemplated by statute. It then becomes an attempt to circumvent the Act and the use of parading, picketing, or in any way affecting the business of the employer or the liberty of the employees is a process or substitute to foster the contract by a procedure not contemplated nor within the purview of the Act.[9]

Where the parties are unable to reach an agreement, and the negotiations are for a first agreement between the employer and the union, if the employer's actions or unreasonableness in negotiations have prevented the parties from reaching an agreement, some provinces (for example, Manitoba, Newfoundland, Ontario, and British Columbia) have made provision in their legislation for the imposition of the first agreement on the parties. This is usually done by way of a process whereby either an arbitrator or the labour relations board (depending upon the jurisdiction) will hear the arguments of both sides to the dispute, then impose a collective agreement on the parties. The agreement will normally include the terms agreed upon by the parties plus terms to complete the agreement that address the issues in dispute. The imposed first collective agreement binds the parties for a term of up to two years.

Strikes and Lockouts

A **strike** is considered to be a concerted refusal to work by the employees of an employer, although in some jurisdictions, any slow-down or concerted effort to restrict output may also be considered a strike.[10] A lawful strike under most labour legislation may only take place when a collective agreement is not in effect and after all required third party assistance has failed to produce a collective

---

9. *Nipissing Hotel Ltd. and Farenda Co. Ltd. v. Hotel & Restaurant Employees & Bartenders International Union C.L.C., A.F. of L., C.I.O., et al.* (1962), 36 D.L.R. (2d) 81.

10. See, for example, the Labour Relations Act, R.S.O. 1990, c. L-2, s. 1(1).

agreement. A strike at any other time is usually an unlawful strike, regardless of whether it is called by the union, or whether it is a spontaneous walk-out by employees (i.e., a wildcat strike).

A **lockout** is, in some respects, the reverse of a strike. It is the closing of a place of employment or a suspension of work by an employer. It is lawful when a collective agreement is not in effect and after all required third party intervention has failed to produce an agreement.

Lawful strikes and lockouts must normally be limited to the premises of the employer that has a labour dispute with his employees. Under a lawful strike, the employees may withhold their services from their employer and, if they so desire, they may set up picket lines at the entrances of the employer's premises to inform others of their strike. Lawful picketing is for the purpose of conveying information.[11] Any attempt by pickets to prevent persons from entering or leaving the plant may be actionable by law. Where property is damaged or persons injured while attempting to enter or leave the employer's premises, the usual action on the part of the employer is to apply for a court order limiting the number of pickets to only a few. In this fashion the lawful purpose of picketing is served, and the likelihood of damage or injury is substantially diminished.

Striking employees are normally not permitted to picket the premises of strangers to the labour dispute, such as the customers of the employer or the employer's suppliers. These individuals are innocent bystanders to the dispute. They are entitled to protection at law if the strikers attempt to injure them in an effort to pressure the employer into a collective agreement by such tactics.[12] This form of picketing, which is known as **secondary picketing,** is unlawful, except in certain cases where the customer or supplier is so closely related to the employer that the supplier or customer might be considered to be involved in the dispute as a part of the employer's overall operation.[13]

Compulsory Arbitration

The strike or lockout, however, is not available to all employee groups when negotiations break down. Persons employed in essential services, such as hospitals, firefighting, and police work, are usually denied the right to strike. **Compulsory arbitration** is used to resolve the issues that they cannot settle in the bargaining process.

Where compulsory arbitration is imposed, an arbitration process replaces the right to strike or lockout and permits work to continue without interruption. Under this system, if the employer and union cannot reach an agreement, they are generally required to have the issues in dispute decided by a representative tribunal called an **arbitration board.** The tribunal is usually made up of one representative each, chosen by the employer and the union, and an impartial third party, chosen by the representatives (or appointed by the government) who becomes the chairperson of the board. The tribunal will hold a hearing where the

---

11. Criminal Code, R.S.C. 1985, c. C-34, s. 381. See also *Smith Bros. Construction Co. Ltd. v. Jones et al.,* [1955] O.R. 362.

12. *Hersees of Woodstock Ltd. v. Goldstein et al.* (1963), 38 D.L.R. (2d) 449.

13. See, for example, *Canadian Pacific Ltd. v. Weatherbee et al.* (1980), 26 O.R. (2d) 776.

arguments of both sides concerning the unresolved issues may be presented. At the conclusion of the hearing the board will review the presentations and the evidence, then make a decision. The parties will be bound by the decision of the arbitration board. The decision of the board, together with the other agreed upon terms, will become the collective agreement that will govern the employment relationship for the period of its operation.

While compulsory arbitration is normally applied to employers and employees engaged in activities where the disruption of services by a strike or lockout would be injurious to the public, some jurisdictions have provided for the use of arbitration as an optional means of settling outstanding issues in those industries and services that are not treated as essential. This method of settlement is generally available as a procedure that may be adopted by the parties as a part of their negotiations, or it may be employed as a means of resolving a labour dispute where the parties have been engaged in a lengthy strike or lockout.

The Collective Agreement and Its Administration

The **collective agreement** differs from the ordinary common law contract of employment in a number of fundamental ways. The collective agreement sets out the rights and duties, not only of the employer and the employees, but of the bargaining agent as well. It is also an agreement that is sometimes negotiated under conditions that would render an ordinary common law contract voidable. The imposition of economic sanctions, or the threat of their use, is treated as a legitimate tactic in the negotiation of a collective agreement, but one that would not be tolerated by the courts in the case of a common law contract.

Most jurisdictions require the parties to insert special terms in their collective agreement that will govern certain aspects of their relationship. The agreements must usually include a clause whereby the employer recognizes the union as the exclusive bargaining representative of the employees in the defined bargaining unit. This has a twofold purpose. Firstly, it is a written acknowledgment by the employer that the union is the proper body to represent the employees. Secondly, recognition of the union as the exclusive bargaining representative prevents the employer from negotiating with any other union purporting to act on behalf of the employees while the collective agreement is in existence.

Most jurisdictions also require the parties to provide in their agreement that no strike or lockout may take place during the term of the agreement, should a dispute arise after the agreement is put into effect. Coupled with this requirement is the additional requirement that the parties provide in their agreement some mechanism to settle disputes that arise out of the collective agreement during its term of operation.

The most common method of dispute resolution is **arbitration.** This is generally compulsory under most collective bargaining legislation. The law frequently sets out an arbitration process that is deemed to apply if the parties fail to include a suitable procedure in their collective agreement. As a rule, any dispute that arises out of the interpretation, application, or administration of the collective agreement, including any question as to whether a matter is arbitrable, is a matter for arbitration. The procedure would also be used where a violation of the collective agreement is alleged.

Collective agreements usually provide for a series of informal meetings between the union and the employer concerning these disputes (called **grievances**) as a possible means of avoiding arbitration. The series of meetings, which involve progressively higher levels of management in both the employer and union hierarchy, is referred to as a grievance procedure. It is usually outlined as a series of steps in a clause in the collective agreement. If, after the grievance procedure is exhausted, no settlement is reached, either the employer or the union may carry the matter further and invoke the arbitration process.

The parties under the terms of their collective agreement may provide for the dispute to be heard by either a **sole arbitrator** or an **arbitration board.** If the procedure calls for a board, it is usually a three-person board, with one member chosen by the union, and one by the employer. The third member of the board is normally selected by the two persons so nominated and becomes the impartial chairperson. If the parties cannot agree on an independent chairperson, the Minister of Labour usually has the authority to select a chairperson for the arbitration board.

An arbitration board (or sole arbitrator) is expected to hold a hearing where each party is given the opportunity to present their side of the dispute, and to introduce evidence or witnesses to establish the facts upon which they base their case. When all of the evidence and argument has been submitted, the arbitrator (or arbitration board) renders a decision called an **award** that is binding upon the parties.

Arbitrators and arbitration boards are usually given wide powers under the legislation to determine their own procedure at hearings, to examine witnesses under oath, and to investigate the circumstances surrounding a dispute. However, they are obliged to deal with each dispute in a fair and unbiased manner. If they fail to do so, or if they exceed their jurisdiction, or make a fundamental error of law in their award, their award may be quashed by the courts.

While arbitration is used as a means of interpreting rights and duties of the employer and the union under the collective agreement, it may also be used by the union to enforce employee rights. Employees who are improperly treated by the employer under the terms of the collective agreement, or who believe that they have been unjustly disciplined or discharged, may file grievances that the union may take to arbitration for settlement.

The rights of employees under collective bargaining differ to some extent from the rights of persons engaged in employment under the common law. The common law right of an employee to make a separate and different contract of employment with the employer is lost insofar as the collective agreement is concerned, but this is balanced by way of new collective bargaining rights. For example, employees under a collective agreement are subject to different treatment in the case of disciplinary action by the employer. An employer may suspend or discipline an employee (usually for just cause) under a collective agreement in cases where discharge is perhaps unwarranted. This represents an approach to discipline that is not found at common law. Where the right is exercised, however, the employer's actions may be subject to review by an arbitrator, as they might also be if the employee is discharged by the employer without good reason.

A difference also exists between the remedies available to an arbitrator and the remedies available to the courts in the case of discharge. In most jurisdictions, an arbitrator has the authority to substitute a suspension without compensation where discharge is too severe a penalty or is unwarranted. The arbitrator may also order the reinstatement of an employee wrongfully dismissed, with payment of compensation for time lost. The courts, on the other hand, are unwilling to order the reinstatement of an employee wrongfully dismissed. They limit the compensation of the employee to monetary damages.

THE UNION-MEMBER RELATIONSHIP

As a party to a collective agreement, and as an entity certified by a labour relations board as the exclusive bargaining agent for a group of employees, a trade union is unique. It was initially an illegal organization at common law, whose lawful existence was made possible only by legislation. In some provinces, such as Ontario, it is not a suable entity by virtue of statute law.[14] However, in other provinces the courts have held that trade unions have acquired a legal existence through legislation that has clothed them with special rights and powers. As a result, in some provinces their actions may be subject to legal action, except in matters directly related to collective bargaining.[15]

Apart from its special status as a bargaining agent under labour legislation, a trade union is similar to any club or fraternal organization. As an unincorporated entity, it has no existence separate from its members, and its relationship with its members is contractual in nature.[16] In concept, it consists of a group of individuals who have contracted with one another to abide by certain terms embodied in the organization's constitution (and which form a part of each member's contract) in order to carry out the objects or goals of the organization. The rights of each member, then, are governed by the contract. If a member fails to abide by the contract, the remainder of the members may expel the offending member from the organization.

Most jurisdictions in their collective bargaining legislation have imposed certain limits on the rights of trade unions to refuse membership or to expel existing members, because of the effect that denial of membership has on an individual's ability to find employment in unionized industries. This is due to the fact that many unions have required employers to insert in their collective agreements a term whereby the employer agrees to hire only persons who are already union members (a **closed shop** clause), or a clause whereby continued employment of an employee is conditional upon union membership (a **union shop** clause). In both of these cases, a loss of union membership would either prevent an employer from hiring the person, or oblige the employer to dismiss the employee. To safeguard the rights of individuals, and to protect them from arbitrary action by labour unions, the right to refuse membership or expel an existing member must be based upon legitimate and justifiable grounds. Membership, for example, generally may not be denied on the basis of race, creed, colour, sex, nationality, place of origin, or other discriminatory factors. Nor may membership normally be

---

14. See the Rights of Labour Act, R.S.O. 1990, c. R-33.

15. *Int'l Brotherhood of Teamsters, Chauffeurs, Warehousemen & Helpers, Building Material, Construction & Fuel Truck Drivers, Loc. No. 213 v. Therien* (1960), 22 D.L.R. (2d) 1.

16. *Astgen v. Smith*, [1970] 1 O.R. 129.

denied or revoked simply because a person belongs to a rival union. Once membership is granted, it may not be withdrawn at the whim of a union officer or union executive.

Membership for the union member, like the membership in any club or organization, involves adherence to the rules and obligations set out in the organization's constitution. If the member fails to abide by the terms of the contract made with the rest of the organization, the membership may take steps to end its relationship with the offending member. The expulsion of the member must not, however, be made in an unfair or arbitrary way. The courts generally require that the rules of natural justice be followed by the organization, and the accused be given an opportunity to put his or her case before the membership before any decision is made. This would involve giving the accused member full details of the alleged violation, an opportunity to prepare his case, and the conduct of a hearing before the membership that would allow the accused to face his or her accusers and answer their charges by way of evidence and cross-examination.[17] Only then may the decision of the membership be made on the question before them.

It is the obligation of a trade union to treat its members fairly and its duty to only expel a member after giving the member an opportunity to be heard and defend himself or herself before the membership. This may be exemplified by an English case where a long-time member of a union was expelled and then complained to the courts. The court, in reviewing the actions of the union, summarized the duties in the following manner:

> The jurisdiction of a domestic tribunal, such as the committee of the Showmen's Guild, must be founded on a contract, express or implied. Outside the regular courts of this country, no set of men can sit in judgment on their fellows except so far as Parliament authorizes it or the parties agree to it. The jurisdiction of the committee of the Showmen's Guild is contained in a written set of rules to which all the members subscribe. This set of rules contains the contract between the members and is just as much subject to the jurisdiction of these courts as any other contract.
>
> Although the jurisdiction of a domestic tribunal is founded on contract, express or implied, nevertheless the parties are not free to make any contract they like. There are important limitations imposed by public policy. The tribunal must, for instance, observe the principles of natural justice. They must give the man notice of the charge and a reasonable opportunity of meeting it. Any stipulation to the contrary would be invalid. They cannot stipulate for a power to condemn a man unheard....
>
> The question in the present case is: To what extent will the courts examine the decisions of domestic tribunals on points of law? This is a new question which is not to be solved by turning to the club cases. In the case of social clubs the rules usually empower the committee to expel a member who, in their opinion, has been guilty of conduct detrimental to the club, and this is a matter of opinion and nothing else. The courts have no wish to sit on appeal from their decisions on such a matter any more than from the decisions of a family conference. They have nothing to do with social rights or social duties. On any expulsion they will see that there is fair play. They will see that the man has notice of the charge and a reasonable opportunity of being heard. They will see that the committee observe the

---

17. *Evanskow v. Int'l Brotherhood of Boilermakers et al.* (1970), 9 D.L.R. (3d) 715.

procedure laid down by the rules, but will not otherwise interfere ... It is very different with domestic tribunals which sit in judgment on the members of a trade or profession. They wield powers as great, if not greater, than any exercised by the courts of law. They can deprive a man of his livelihood. They can ban him from the trade in which he has spent his life and which is the only trade he knows. They are usually empowered to do this for any breach of their rules, which, be it noted, are rules which they impose and which he has no real opportunity of accepting or rejecting. In theory their powers are based on contract. The man is supposed to have contracted to give them these great powers, but in practice he has no choice in the matter. If he is to engage in the trade, he has to submit to the rules promulgated by the committee. Is such a tribunal to be treated by these courts on the same footing as a social club? I say: "No." A man's right to work is just as important, if not more important, to him than his rights of property. These courts intervene each day to protect rights of property. They must also intervene to protect the right to work.[18]

Duty of Fair Representation

A union has a responsibility towards its members to fairly represent them not only in the collective sense, but on an individual basis as well. The Canada Labour Code and the legislation in most provinces imposes a duty upon unions to act in good faith and in a non-arbitrary, non-discriminatory manner towards individual members in their representation of them and the enforcement of their rights under collective agreements. The duty also extends to services that unions may provide for their members. For example, where a union operates a "hiring hall" (that sends unemployed members to employers who require workers), the union must treat all members fairly in the filling of job openings. It must not give certain members priority over others in the allocation of work.

The most common type of case to arise relates to the right of the union under most collective agreements to process grievances on behalf of employees in the bargaining unit. Because an employee normally does not have the individual right to take a grievance to arbitration, the union has a duty to act in good faith towards an employee with a grievance in any decision to carry a grievance on to the arbitration stage. For example, in a Manitoba case, an employee was accused of theft, but no charges were laid. The employee sought the assistance of his union in the dispute with the employer over the alleged theft. The union reluctantly did so, but made no effort to investigate the charge, nor did it press the employee's grievance. The employee filed a complaint against the union. The labour board held that the union had failed in its duty to fairly represent the employee, and ordered the union to take the employee's grievance to arbitration. The board also ordered the union to pay the employee's legal costs and expenses.[19]

It is important to note, however, that the duty of fair representation does not oblige a union to carry every employee grievance to arbitration. A union is entitled to assess each grievance in terms of its merits, and provided that the assessment is made in good faith and not in an arbitrary or discriminatory manner, it may properly decide against proceeding to arbitration without violating its duty of fair representation.

---

18. *Lee v. Showmen's Guild of Great Britain,* [1952] 1 All E.R. 1175.
19. *Shachtay v. Creamery Workers Union, Local 1* (1986), 86 CLLC 16,033 (Man. L.R.B.)

SUMMARY

While labour law in the broad sense refers to all law relating to the employment relationship, it is a term that is often used to refer to the area of employment law concerned with collective bargaining. Collective bargaining is concerned with the negotiation of the terms and conditions of employment by a group of employees with their employer, using a trade union as their bargaining agent. Collective bargaining is conducted under legislation that sets out procedures for the selection of a bargaining agent (the certification process), the negotiation of the collective agreement (the negotiation process), and for the administration of the negotiated agreement (the administration process).

Unlike the common law contract of employment, the collective agreement is a special contract of employment that applies to unionized employees. It is not a contract brought before the courts for interpretation, but an agreement that falls within the jurisdiction of a tribunal. The law relating to the collective agreement is administrative law, rather than common law. Labour legislation, of which the law relating to collective bargaining is a part, represents a body of statute law that has grown substantially during the last century to meet the needs of employees in more complex industrial and commercial employment settings.

DISCUSSION QUESTIONS

1. Explain briefly the role of a union in collective bargaining.
2. Why was a collective agreement unenforceable at common law?
3. Indicate the reasons why early trade union activities were considered unlawful.
4. Define a collective agreement.
5. What legislation determines the rights and duties of the parties engaged in collective bargaining?
6. What effect does collective bargaining have on the common law employment relationship?
7. Explain how a union acquires bargaining rights.
8. What is a bargaining unit? How is it determined?
9. Outline the steps in the negotiation process and its purpose.
10. Why is "third party assistance" sometimes necessary in the negotiation process? What is the role of the third party?
11. How are disputes between the parties resolved during the negotiation process if third party assistance fails?
12. If a collective agreement is negotiated, what methods may be used to resolve disputes that arise out of the collective agreement?
13. Explain compulsory arbitration.
14. What powers do arbitrators possess? What duties must they perform?
15. Explain the legal nature of a trade union, and explain how it differs from other types of voluntary association.
16. Describe the legal obligations a union has towards its members.

MINI-CASE PROBLEM

1. ABC Company is a supplier of goods for the XYZ Company. A lawful strike takes place at the XYZ Company plant, and the picketing employees refuse to allow a truckload of goods sent by ABC Company to enter the XYZ Company plant gates. What are the rights of ABC Company? Suppose that, the next day, the ABC Company finds striking employees of the XYZ Company picketing the ABC Company plant because it is a supplier of XYZ Company. What are the rights of ABC Company?

JUDICIAL DECISION

The case of *Astgen v. Smith et al.* examines the legal nature of a trade union. The case involves the merger of two unions. The court was called upon to decide if the merger was possible since the constitution of one contained no merger procedure. The judge was required to examine the precise legal status of a trade union. He compares the organization to a club or fraternal organization and then turns to the relationship between the union and its members. He determines the relationship to be one of contract between the members since the organization itself has no legal existence separate from its members.

Trade Union — Nature of Organization

Astgen et al. v. Smith et al., [1970] 1 O.R. 129.

Two trade unions agreed to a merger, but the constitution of one of the unions made no provision for a merger procedure. When some of the employees objected to the merger, the question arose: Was the merger invalid because some of the members objected to it? The case turned on the legal nature of the particular union.

EVANS, J.A.:

Prior to dealing with the merger agreement I consider it desirable to determine the precise legal status of a trade union or labour union, the relationships existing among the membership *inter se* and the relationships of each member to the totality of the persons associated together. I concede at the outset that a labour union under the *Labour Relations Act,* R.S.O. 1960, c. 202, and allied legislation has a "status" conferred by such legislation which makes it somewhat different from a fraternal organization or an athletic club but apart from such statutes a labour union is essentially a club, a voluntary association which has no existence, apart from its members, recognized by law. A club is basically a group of people who have joined together for the promotion of certain objects and whose conduct in relation to one another is regulated in accordance with the constitution, by-laws, rules and regulations to which they have subscribed.

The proposition that a trade union has a special status, that it is a sort of hybrid corporation, has no foundation in law. This is fostered by the "legal entity" character which labour legislation has thrust upon trade unions but is not legally supportable outside the purview of those statutes. While trade unions have historically strenuously opposed and rejected any movement toward corporate status with its attendant strictures, there has evolved a concept, which has no basis in law, that unions have a *quasi*-legal entity; that they have a peculiar status which clothes them with the advantages of corporations but shields them from the restrictions and liabilities attaching to corporate entities. This misunderstanding, and it is a fundamental one, must not be allowed to becloud the issues herein.

We are not concerned in this appeal with the pseudocorporate status bestowed on labour unions by statute; nor are we assisted by English case law in view of the fact that under various Trade Union Acts, trade unions in England may be registered and upon registration are vested with certain powers and responsibilities. Ontario has no comparable legislation and resort must be had to the common law to determine both status and capacity. Mine Mill is not a corporation, individual or partnership, and is accordingly not a legal entity; it is an unincorporated group or association of workmen who have banded together to promote certain objectives for their mutual benefit and advantage and in law nothing is recognizable other than the totality of members related one to another by contract. The objects and purposes of the association are spelled out in the memorandum of association usually referred to as the "constitution"; the by-laws or rules provide the machinery for the proper carrying out of activities intended to advance the objectives and purposes of the voluntary association. Each member of Mine Mill, upon being granted membership, subscribed to those purposes and objects and in so doing entered into a contractual relationship with every other member of Mine Mill. Rand, J., in *Orchard et al. v. Tunney,* [1957] S.C.R. 436 at p. 445, 8 D.L.R. (2d) 273 at p. 281, stated:

"...each member commits himself to a group on a foundation of specific terms governing individual and collective action ... and made on both sides with the intent that the rules shall bind them in their relations to each other."

I adopt also the proposition stated by Thompson, J., in *Bimson v. Johnston et al.,* [1957] O.R. 519 at p. 530, D.L.R. (2d) 11 at p. 22, which was affirmed on appeal [1958] O.W.N. 217, 12 D.L.R. (2d) 379: "...that a contract is made by a member when he joins the union, the terms and conditions of which are provided by the union's constitution and by-laws... The contract is not with the union or the association as such, which is devoid of the power to contract, but rather the contractual rights of a member are with all others members thereof."

The prevalence in our society of the corporate entity has led to the adoption with reference to unincorporated associations of terms strictly applicable to the incorporated corporations. Particularly is this so with respect to the term *ultra vires.* Apart from those accustomed to the strict observance of accurate terminology, *ultra vires* is applied both — to purported corporate acts beyond the statutory capacity of the corporation and — to the purported exercise by the officers and directors of an authority to bind the corporation which they do not possess.

In this jurisdiction where generally upon incorporation the incorporated body is given the status equivalent to that of a person at common law, no act otherwise legal is *ultra vires* in the sense that it is beyond the capacity of the corporation; *ultra vires* properly refers only to the exceeding of authority of the persons purporting to act on behalf of the corporation.

There is no limit to the lawful objects for the furtherance of which men may associate voluntarily, and in my view, provided it is properly authorized by every member of the association, there is no restriction upon the powers of the members to alter the objects for which they became associated or to terminate the relationship *inter se* of those associated, or to agree individually to become bound by other contractual relationships to the members of the same or some other group of associates. In this sense of the meaning of *ultra vires* I do not consider that the realization of what was contemplated by the provisions of the merger agreement would be beyond the capacity of the members of Mine Mill provided that there was unanimous approval individually or by means of some procedure which all of the members had agreed upon.

The contract of association is not between the member and some undefined entity which lacks the capacity to contract; it is a complex of contracts between each member and every other member of the union. These are individual contracts impressed with rights and obligations which cannot be destroyed in the absence of the specific consent of each person whose rights would be affected thereby.

CASE PROBLEMS FOR DISCUSSION

Case 1

Cleaning Company employs a number of employees in its office cleaning business. The company is known as a demanding employer that is reluctant to pay more than the statutory minimum wage unless forced to do so.

Six of the ten employees decide to organize a union. They wish to bargain collectively in an effort to pressure their employer into improving working conditions and wage rates. The employees are aware that the company would not likely recognize their union once it was formed. They decide to follow whatever procedures are necessary in order to enable them to compel the company to bargain collectively with them.

What advice would you offer the employees? How should they proceed? Explain the various steps that the employees must follow.

Case 2

Gear Manufacturing Company carries on business in a part of a factory building in an industrial park located at the outskirts of a large municipality. The remainder of the building is leased by Gear Warehousing Company, a wholly owned subsidiary of Gear Manufacturing Company. Gear Warehousing Company is essentially the storage and marketing subsidiary of Gear Manufacturing Company. It purchases and markets all standard types of gears manufactured by the parent company, even though it is a separate entity.

The employees of Gear Manufacturing Company are represented by the Gear Makers' Union. In the previous year, the union negotiated a collective agreement that expired some months ago. Collective bargaining took place before the expiry of the old agreement, but Gear Manufacturing Company and the union could not agree on the terms of a new collective agreement. They requested conciliation services offered by the Ministry of Labour (which were required before a strike or lockout could take place), but the services failed to produce an agreement. Eventually, the employees went out on strike and set up picket lines at the entrances of the plant of Gear Manufacturing Company. They also set up picket lines at the entrance to Gear Warehousing Company to prevent the shipment of goods from the warehouse.

A few days later, the employees set up a picket line at Transmission Manufacturing Company, an important customer of Gear Warehousing Company, even though the company's only connection with Gear Manufacturing and Gear Warehousing was as a purchaser of Gear products. The pickets prevented Transmission Manufacturing from shipping a large truckload of transmissions to another manufacturer. As a result, the company suffered a loss of $5000 by its failure to make delivery on time.

Advise Gear Warehousing Company and Transmission Manufacturing Company of their rights (if any), and suggest a course of action that they might take.

Case 3

Bonsor was a member of the Piano Players' Union. He was 55 years old and had been a professional musician for most of his working life. He had joined the union some time before 1957 and, by so doing, worked regularly at the union wage scale in the years that followed.

Regular payment of union dues was a requirement for maintenance of membership in the union. Mr. Bonsor was a regular contributor up to a particular time, when, through oversight or neglect, he failed to pay his weekly contribution. Under the union rules, a failure to pay union dues was a cause for expulsion, and the union secretary, acting in accordance with the rules, promptly erased Bonsor's name from the membership register.

The effect of the secretary's act was catastrophic for Bonsor. Because the musicians were highly organized and employed the closed shop as a union security measure, Bonsor was unable to find employment as a musician. He appealed to the secretary for reinstatement, but was refused. As a result, he was reduced to working at a variety of unskilled jobs to earn a meagre living.

Some time later, he brought an action against the union for wrongful expulsion and damages.

Discuss the arguments that might be raised by Bonsor and the union in this case. Render a decision.

Case 4

Smith was employed as a taxi-driver by the Rapid Cab and Cartage Company. On May 23rd, while driving his taxi, he was involved in a serious collision with a train at a level crossing. The taxi was demolished as a result of the accident, and three passengers riding in the rear seat of the taxi were seriously injured. Smith, by some miracle, escaped injury.

An investigation of the accident revealed that Smith had been racing the train to the level crossing and had collided with the side of the engine when the train and the vehicle reached the crossing at the same instant. As a result of the investigation, Smith was charged with criminal negligence and released on bail pending his trial.

The employees of the company worked under a collective agreement and were represented by a truck drivers' union. The company manager and the union representatives met on May 27th, to discuss Smith's accident. At the request of the union, the company agreed to allow Smith to continue to drive until his trial.

Smith had been employed by the company for five years prior to the accident, and had an accident-free driving record until April of that year. During April, Smith was involved in four minor accidents that were clearly his fault. On May 9th (only two weeks before the accident on May 23rd) he had crashed his vehicle into the side of the taxi garage, causing extensive damage to both the vehicle and the building. On that occasion, and the two previous occasions, he had been given verbal warnings by the supervisor that he would be dismissed if he continued to drive in a careless manner.

Smith's case came before the courts on June 10th. He was convicted and given a six-month jail term. His driving privileges, however, would be reinstated on his release. Following his conviction, the union, on his behalf, arranged for a six-month leave of absence from the company, subject to the right of the company to review the matter on his return to work.

Before Smith was released from jail, several large damage claims were made against the company as a result of the accident, and the insurer expressed concern over Smith's accident frequency rate. The company management thereupon notified the union of its intention to dismiss Smith, and advised Smith that his services would no longer be required on his release.

Upon receipt of the notice of dismissal, Smith immediately filed a grievance through the union, requesting reinstatement. The grievance was filed in accordance with the time period and procedure outlined in the collective agreement.

The collective agreement contained the following clause:

12.01 The company shall have the right to establish reasonable rules of conduct for all employees, and shall have the right to discipline or discharge employees for just cause, subject to right of grievance as set out in this agreement.

The company had posted the following rule on the office bulletin board in September of 1990:

Rule 6 Any failure on the part of a driver to place the comfort and safety of passengers before his (or her) own convenience shall be cause for discipline or dismissal.

As the sole arbitrator in this case, how would you deal with this grievance? Prepare an award and give reasons for your decision.

Case 5

ABC Manufacturing Ltd. was a large producer of automotive parts and supplies and employed a workforce of over 400 employees. The employees had been represented by the local of a large international union for several years.

An unexpected upturn in consumer demand forced ABC to schedule additional production shifts to meet backlogged orders. This necessitated most employees working at least one overtime shift per week, on either Saturday or Sunday, for which the collective agreement provided that employees be paid time-and-a-half. When the new work schedule was posted, Susan, who was a parts painter, found herself scheduled to work the overtime shifts on Saturdays. Susan belonged to a religious order which observed Saturday as its day of worship and, as a result, Susan did not wish to work this particular shift.

She went to see the production scheduler to explain her situation and to suggest that he schedule her for the Sunday shift but at the normal, non-overtime rate of pay. Susan felt that her offer was a fair compromise and would be accepted by management. Her suggestion was, in fact, quite acceptable to management which promised to accommodate her request. The union shop steward was informed of Susan's request and the arrangement which she had made with management. Shortly thereafter the union sent a memo to management stating that it would not permit management to schedule Susan for the Sunday shift without paying her the time-and-a-half rate stipulated by the collective agreement. When management approached Susan about the memo, she stated that she knew nothing about it and that it had not been sent at her request. She also stated that her offer still stood since that arrangement worked out very well for her.

Management took the position that if the union would not waive the overtime pay provision for Susan on Sunday, thereby effectively barring her from that shift, it would have no choice but to require her to work on the Saturday shift. Susan refused to do this and was subsequently dismissed by ABC.

What recourse and rights, if any, does Susan have against the parties in this case? Discuss the arguments each might employ and what remedies might be imposed by a court or arbitrator.

CHAPTER 20

The Law of Bailment

NATURE OF BAILMENT

Bailment is a special arrangement between a person (a **bailor**) who owns or lawfully possesses a chattel, and another person (a **bailee**) who is given possession of the chattel for a specific purpose. In a business setting, many business activities involve the transfer of possession of chattels. For example, the leasing of trucks or automobiles by a business constitutes a bailment transaction because the ownership of the vehicles remains with the leasing company, and the persons who have the use of the vehicles only have possession under the lease agreement and not legal title. Similarly, where goods are shipped by a common carrier such as a highway truck transport company, the carrier of the goods has possession of them only as a bailee. The carrier assumes responsibility for the goods until they are delivered to the designated receiver. Other examples of business transactions that include a bailment would be those transactions that require goods to be left with repair services, such as motor vehicle repair garages, jewellery shops, and appliance repair services.

By definition, bailment consists of the delivery of an article on the express or implied condition that the article will be returned to the bailor or dealt with according to the bailor's wishes as soon as the purpose for which the article was bailed is completed.[1]

A bailment consists of three elements:
(1) the delivery of the goods by the bailor;
(2) possession of the goods by the bailee for a specific purpose;
(3) a return of the goods to the bailor at a later time, or the disposition of the goods according to the bailor's wishes.

---

1. Osborn, P.G., *The Concise Law Dictionary,* 4th ed. (London: Sweet & Maxwell Ltd., 1954), p. 45.

410

Sub-bailment

Under certain circumstances, a second or **sub-bailment** may take place. In this case the bailee becomes the **sub-bailor,** and the person who takes delivery of the goods from the sub-bailor becomes the **sub-bailee.** Sub-bailment, however, must normally only be by special agreement between the bailor and bailee, or be a custom or practice of the trade relating to the particular type of bailment. The right to make a sub-bailment is not a part of every trade activity. However, the courts have held that bailments involving automobile repairs, the carriage of goods, or the storage of goods are trade activities in which a sub-bailment may customarily be made by the bailee.[2]

In each case, however, the right of sub-bailment may only be made where the bailor is not relying on the special skill of the bailee to perform the work or service. If the bailee makes a sub-bailment under such circumstances, then the bailee would do so at his or her own risk. If a sub-bailment is permissible, either by custom of the trade or by express agreement, the terms of the sub-bailment must be consistent with the original bailment; otherwise it will have the effect of terminating the original bailment. The bailor will then have a right of action against the bailee if the bailee cannot recover the goods from the sub-bailee. In addition, the bailee may be liable to the bailor for any loss or damage to the goods while in the hands of the sub-bailee.

Bailor-Bailee Relationship

Because the essence of a bailment is the delivery of possession of a chattel by one person to another, delivery must take place before the bailor-bailee relationship may come into existence. Where the goods are physically placed in the hands of the bailee by the bailor, delivery is apparent. For example, if Smith delivers a book to Jones on the condition that it be returned at a later time, the transfer of possession creates the bailment. The element of delivery becomes less clear, however, where the bailee takes only constructive possession of the goods. For example, a businesswoman enters a restaurant and places her coat on a coat-rack located beside her table. Has she created a bailment by the act of placing her coat on the rack that the proprietor has obviously placed there for that specific purpose? The basic requirement for a bailment is delivery of possession. If the coat has not been placed in the proprietor's charge, then no bailment may exist. Clearly, if the bailee is unaware of the delivery, and has not consented to it, there may be no bailment. But if the proprietor has either expressly or impliedly requested that the coat be placed upon the rack, then a bailment may have been created by the proprietor's actions. The proprietor under such circumstances may be said to have constructive possession of the goods.[3]

An important characteristic of a bailment is the retention of the title to the goods by the bailor. The bailee receives possession only, and at no time does the title to the goods pass. The rights of the bailee, nevertheless, once delivery has taken place, are much like those of the owner. The bailee has the right to institute

---

2. *Edwards v. Newland*, [1950] 1 All E.R. 1072.
3. *Murphy v. Hart* (1919), 46 D.L.R. 36.

legal proceedings against any person who interferes with the property or the bailee's right of possession, even though the bailee does not have the legal title to the goods. The bailee may also recover damages from any person who wrongfully injures the goods, but the money recovered that relates to the damage must be held for the bailor.

The third aspect of bailment is the return of the goods or chattel to the bailor, or the disposition of the goods according to the bailor's directions. The same goods must be returned to the bailor, except **fungibles,** which are interchangeable commodities such as grain and other natural foodstuffs, fuel oil, gasoline, or similar goods that are frequently stored in large quantities in elevators or tanks. Fungibles of the same grade or quality, and in the same quantity, must be returned in that case. If the bailee refuses to return the bailed goods, the bailor is entitled to bring an action against the bailee for **conversion.**

Liability for Loss or Damage

The law of bailment is a very old area of the law that dates back to the Middle Ages in England. It developed as a result of the problems that persons had when they entrusted goods to others, or when their goods were at the mercy of a stranger, such as an innkeeper. As the law developed, the courts determined different standards for each of the forms of bailment that they were required to consider. As a result, the liability of a bailee for loss or damage to goods while they are in the bailee's possession varies significantly from one type of bailment to another. There are many different general bailment relationships that the courts recognize, and the liability of the bailee differs for each.

Regardless of the standard of care fixed for a bailee, if the bailor can establish that the bailee failed to return the goods, or if the goods when returned were damaged or destroyed (reasonable wear and tear excepted) if the bailee was entitled to use the goods, then the onus shifts to the bailee. He or she must satisfy the court that the standard of care fixed for the particular kind of bailment was maintained, and that the loss or damage was not a result of his or her culpable negligence.

The reason for the placement of the onus on the bailee to show that he or she was not negligent, rather than the normal legal practice of requiring the plaintiff to prove the defendant negligent, is based upon the respective knowledge of the parties. While the goods are in the hands of the bailee, only the bailee is likely to know the circumstances surrounding any damage to the goods. The bailor during the period of time would be unlikely to have any knowledge of how the loss or damage came about, and the courts have accordingly recognized this fact. If the bailee is unable to offer any reasonable explanation for the loss, or if the bailee is unable to establish no negligence, then responsibility for the loss is likely to fall on him or her. In this sense, the bailor's position is much like that of a person claiming *res ipsa loquitur* in an ordinary tort action: the bailor need only prove the existence of the bailment, and the subsequent loss. The onus then shifts to the bailee to satisfy the court that he or she was not negligent.

Because of the obligation imposed upon bailees to maintain a relatively high standard of care in most bailment relationships, it is not uncommon for bailees to attempt to limit their liability in the event of loss. The usual method used by bailees to limit their liability is to insert a clause that is known as an **exculpatory**

clause in the bailment agreement. An exculpatory clause (or **exemption clause** as it is sometimes called), if carefully drawn and brought to the attention of the bailor before the bailment is effected, generally has the effect of binding the bailor to the terms of the limited liability (or no liability at all) as set out in the clause.[4] Recent cases, however, have tended to reduce the protection offered by exemption clauses. If the clause is so unreasonable that it amounts to a clear abuse of freedom of contract, the exemption may not be enforced.[5]

TYPES OF BAILMENT

Gratuitous Bailment

A gratuitous bailment is a bailment that may be for the benefit of either the bailor or the bailee, or both, and that, as the name implies, is without monetary reward. In the case of gratuitous bailment, the liability for loss or damage to the goods varies with the respective benefits received by the parties to the bailment, unless the parties have fixed the standard of care by agreement. If the bailment is entirely for the benefit of the bailor, such as where the bailee agrees to store the bailor's canoe or sailboat without charge during the winter months, then the bailee's liability is minimal. The bailee in such a case is only obliged to take reasonable care of the goods by protecting them from foreseeable risk of harm. The actual standard, unfortunately, appears to vary somewhat, depending upon the nature of the goods delivered. Some years ago, in an English case, the court held that the bailee, in a gratuitous bailment that was entirely for the benefit of the bailor, would only be liable for gross negligence — a degree of carelessness that would constitute neglect in the eyes of a reasonable person.[6] More recent cases, however, have tended to require a somewhat higher standard of care in similar circumstances.[7]

Conversely, where the bailment is entirely for the benefit of the bailee (for example, where a bailor gratuitously loans the bailee his automobile), the bailee would be liable for any damage caused to the goods by the bailee's negligence, reasonable wear and tear being the only exception.

The liability for loss or damage to the goods tends to fall between the two extremes where the bailment is for the benefit of both the bailor and the bailee. For example, Adams stores his sailboat at Burley's cottage, and grants Burley permission to use the boat if he wishes to do so. If the boat should be damaged, the standard that might apply would be that of the ordinary prudent person, and how that person might take care of his own goods.[8]

Bailment for Reward

Bailment for reward includes a number of different bailment relationships. The bailment may be for storage (or deposit) such as in the case of a warehouse operator, or it may take the form of the delivery of goods to a repair shop for repairs. It may also take the form of a rental of a chattel, the carriage of goods, or the pledge

---

4. *Samuel Smith & Sons Ltd. v. Silverman* (1961), 29 D.L.R. (2d) 98.
5. *Gillespie Bros. & Co. Ltd. v. Roy Bowles Transport Ltd.,* [1973] Q.B. 400; *Davidson v. Three Spruces Realty Ltd.* (1978), 79 D.L.R. (3d) 481.
6. *Master v. London County Council,* [1947] 1 K.B. 628.
7. *Desjardins v. Theriault* (1970), 3 N.B.R. (2d) 260.
8. *Roy v. Adamson* (1912), 3 D.L.R. 139; *Chaing v. Heppner* (1978), 85 D.L.R. (3d) 487.

of valuables or securities as collateral for a loan. It would apply as well, to the safekeeping of goods by an innkeeper. Again, the liability of each of these particular bailees varies, due to the nature of the relationship that exists between each type of bailee and the bailor.

Storage of Goods

The storage of goods for reward may take on many forms, but each represents a bailment if possession and control of the goods passes into the hands of the party offering the storage facility. The bank or trust company that rents a safety deposit box to a customer, the marina that offers boat storage facilities, or the warehouse operator that offers storage space for a person's furniture are bailees for reward. So, too, are the operators of grain elevators, fuel storage facilities, and parking lots, if the parking lot operator obtains the keys to the vehicle.

Warehouse Storage

The bailee is expected to take reasonable care of the goods while they are in his or her possession, and the standard is normally that which would be expected of a skilled storekeeper.[9] In other words, the bailee would be expected to protect the goods from all foreseeable risks. If the goods have a particular attribute that requires special storage facilities, and the warehouse operator holds himself out as possessing those facilities, then the failure to properly store the goods would render the warehouse operator liable for any loss. For example, if a company holds itself out as the operator of a cold storage warehouse, and a bailor delivers to it a quantity of frozen meat that requires the temperature of the goods to be held at some point below freezing, the failure to store the meat at the temperature would render the company (as bailee) liable for any loss if spoilage should occur.

It is important to note that the liability of a bailee for storage is not absolute. The bailee is generally only liable if the bailee fails to meet the standard of care fixed by the courts for the nature of the business that the bailee conducts. The bailee firm may be liable for the negligence of its employees if the goods are damaged through their carelessness. However, the courts are unlikely to hold the bailee responsible in cases where the loss or damage could not, or would not, have been foreseen by a careful and vigilant shopkeeper.[10]

The extent of a bailee's liability for loss arose in a case[11] where a fur storage company agreed to take a valuable fur coat into storage. The coat was subsequently stolen from the company premises by thieves who broke into the building. The company had taken precautions to secure the building from forced entry. The issue before the court was whether the company, as a bailee, was liable for the loss in spite of the safety precautions taken. The judge hearing the case made the following comment on the standard of care required:

> There can I think be no doubt that the Mitchell Fur Co. Ltd. was a bailee for reward and as such owed a duty to the bailor to take such due and proper care of the bailed goods as a prudent owner, in similar circumstances, might reasonably be

---

9. *Brabant & Co. v. King*, [1895] A.C. 632.

10. *Bamert v. Parks* (1964), 50 D.L.R. (2d) 313.

11. *Longley v. Mitchell Fur Co. Ltd.* (1983), 45 N.B.R. (2d) 78.

expected to take of his or her own goods. In other words, a bailee must, in safe-guarding the property of a bailor, do what a reasonably prudent person would do to safeguard his or her own property. And the onus is upon the bailee to show that any loss which occurs did not result from his neglect to use the required degree of care and diligence. However, a bailee is not an insurer. Therefore, if bailed goods are stolen and the bailee can establish that he took reasonable care of the goods, and that he was not guilty of any negligence which was the proximate cause of their loss, the bailee will not normally be held liable.

In another case,[12] where the standard of liability of the bailee for reward was in issue, the judge reviewed the authorities and established the standard of care in the following manner:

> The question to be determined here is whether any responsibility for the loss of the watch rests with Heppner as a result of his accepting, for reward, the possession of the watch for repair, there being no contract with special provisions and conditions between the parties.
>
> In *Heriteau et al. v. W.D. Morris Realty Ltd.*, [1944] 1 D.L.R. 28, [1943] O.R. 724, it was held that where goods are lost or damaged while in a bailee's posses-sion, the onus is on him to prove that it occurred through no want of ordinary care on his part.
>
> *Leck et al. v. Maestaer* (1807), 1 Camp. 138, 170 E.R. 905, states that a work-man for hire is not only bound to guard the thing bailed to him against ordinary hazards, but likewise to exert himself to preserve it from any unexpected danger to which it may be exposed and further, in effect, that where there is need for precau-tion, the defendant would be answerable for defects of this deficiency.
>
> In essence, what emerges from the authorities is: that the defendant was a bailee for consideration and owed a duty to the plaintiff to exercise that care and diligence which a careful and diligent man would exercise in the custody of his own goods in the same circumstances; that there being loss of the goods bailed the onus is on the defendant (bailee) to show that he exercised a proper degree of care; that failure to observe that duty is negligence; that the unexpected and accidental destruction of the goods while in the possession of the defendant (bailee) for reward, may still render the defendant liable if during his possession of the goods he did not exercise to a reasonable extent the skill or ability which he held out as an expected duty of his calling; and that while no specific period of time may be arranged for the completion of the work to be done, the defendant must perform it within a reasonable time, and if delay in the performance is caused by the defen-dant's negligence, he is liable.

Contracts for the storage of goods frequently involve what is known as a **warehouse receipt,** or evidence of the contract of bailment. The receipt entitles the bearer to obtain the goods from the bailee. Often the original bailor of the goods sells the goods while they are in storage and, as a part of the sale transac-tion, provides the purchaser with the warehouse receipt. The presentation of the receipt by the new bailor would entitle him or her to delivery of the goods from the bailee. The **bill of lading** used by carriers of goods performs a similar func-tion when goods are shipped to a purchaser.

At common law, in the absence of a specific right contained in an agreement, the ordinary bailee for storage is not entitled to retain the goods until storage

---

12. *Chaing v. Heppner et al.* (1978), 85 D.L.R. (3d) 487.

charges are paid. However, all provinces have passed legislation that provide for statutory lien that may attach to the goods in the warehouse operator's possession.[13] The legislation generally provides that the warehouse operator may retain the goods until payment is made, and may sell the goods by public auction if the bailor fails to pay the storage charges. The statutes generally require special care be taken by the bailee with respect to notice and advertisement of the sale to ensure that the bailor has an opportunity to redeem the goods. The statutes also require that the sale of the goods be conducted in a fair manner. The right to a lien, however, is based upon the possession of the goods by the bailee. If the bailee voluntarily releases the goods to the bailor before payment is made, the right to claim a lien is lost.

Parking Lots

The bailment of a motor vehicle for the purpose of parking the vehicle represents one of the most common short-term bailment relationships. However, it is important to distinguish the true bailment of an automobile for the mere use or rental of space for parking. Again, the transfer of possession by the driver of the vehicle to the parking lot operator is essential to create the bailment. If the operator of the lot accepts the keys to the automobile and parks the vehicle, a bailment is created. The operator has possession of the bailor's property. Similarly, if the operator of the parking lot directs the person to place the vehicle in a certain place on the parking lot, and requests that the keys be deposited with the attendant, the deposit of the keys would also create a bailment. The simple act of parking a vehicle as a "favour" for the patron, however, may not create a bailment that would render the parking lot operator liable as a bailee if the car should subsequently be damaged or stolen.[14]

If the agreement between the parking lot operator and the patron is one of rental of a space for parking purposes, and if the patron parks his or her own vehicle and retains the keys, possession does not pass from the patron to the operator of the lot. The retention of the keys by the vehicle owner precludes any control over the vehicle by the parking lot operator, and, consequently, a bailment does not arise. In these cases, the courts generally view the transaction not as a bailment, but as an arrangement whereby the parking lot operator licenses the use of the parking space by the vehicle driver on a contractual basis.[15]

The enforcement of exculpatory clauses arises frequently in cases concerning the bailment of vehicles. The success of a bailee in avoiding liability by way of an exculpatory clause depends in no small measure on the steps taken to bring the limitation on the bailee's liability to the attention of the bailor either before or at the time that the bailment takes place. The simple printing of a limitation of liability on the back of the parking lot ticket is clearly not enough.[16] The limitation must be forcefully brought to the attention of the bailor, either by direct reference to

---

13. See, for example, Warehousemen's Lien Act, R.S.S. 1978, c. W-3, s. 3; Warehouser's Lien Act, R.S.N. 1990, c. W-2, s.3; R.S.M. 1987, c. W-20, s. 2.

14. *Palmer v. Toronto Medical Arts Building Ltd.* (1960), 21 D.L.R. (2d) 181; *Martin v. Town N'Country Delicatessen Ltd.* (1963), 45 W.W.R. 413.

15. *Palmer v. Toronto Medical Arts Building Ltd.* (1960), 21 D.L.R. (2d) 181.

16. *Spooner v. Starkman,* [1973] 2 D.L.R. 582.

the limitation or by placing clearly marked signs in conspicuous places where they will not fail to catch the eye of the bailor.[17]

Bailment for Repair or Service

Where chattels require repair or service, a bailment takes place if the owner delivers the goods to the repair shop and leaves them with the proprietor. The bailee is expected to protect the goods entrusted to him or her for repair. Even though no charge is made for the bailment separate from the repair charge, the bailment is nevertheless a bailment for reward, and the bailee is expected to take reasonable care of the automobile while it is in his or her possession. If the goods are lost or damaged while they are in the bailee's possession, the bailee may be liable if the loss is due to his or her negligence. If the goods are sub-bailed to a sub-bailee in accordance with the customs of the trade, then the bailee may also be liable for loss or damage to the goods by the neglect or willful acts of the sub-bailee. For example, Smith delivers her automobile to Baker for repairs, and Baker, by way of a sub-bailment, places the car in Carter's possession to have some specialized work done on the vehicle. If Carter negligently damages the automobile while it is in his possession, Baker may be liable to Smith for the damage. However, if Baker has held himself out to be skilled in the performance of the task, and Smith contracts with Baker for personal performance, the sub-bailment would be improper. Baker would become liable for any damage to the goods, whether caused by Carter's negligence or not. The particular reason for this additional liability for an improper bailment is that Smith, in placing the vehicle in Baker's possession, is accepting a particular set of circumstances or risks relating to the repair of her vehicle, but an unauthorized sub-bailment would be a change in the risk without her consent. To protect the bailor in such cases, the courts have simply imposed liability for any loss or damage to the goods on the bailee.

The bailee who professes to have a particular repair skill is expected to execute the repairs in accordance with the standards set for the skill. The bailee is expected to exercise the duty of care attendant with the skill in the protection or handling of the goods while in his or her possession. For this service, the bailee is entitled to compensation that may be either agreed upon at the time the goods are placed in his or her possession, or to a reasonable price for the services when the work is completed. If the bailor refuses to pay for the work done on the goods, at common law, the bailee has a right of lien and may retain the goods until payment is made. If payment is not made within a reasonable time, subject to any statutory requirements that set out the rights of the bailee, the bailee may have the goods sold (usually by public auction) to satisfy his or her claim for payment.[18]

Should the bailee be negligent in the repair of the goods, or not possess the particular skill that he or she professed to have, the bailor would be entitled to institute legal proceedings for damages to cover the loss suffered. This claim may cover not only the value of the chattel damaged, but any other loss that would

---

17. *Samuel Smith & Sons Ltd. v. Silverman* (1961), 29 D.L.R. (2d) 98.

18. Most provinces and territories have legislation covering this type of bailment: see, for example, Mechanics' Lien Act, R.S. Nfld. 1990, c. M-3, s. 45.

flow from the bailee's breach of the agreement to repair, if the loss was foreseeable at the time the agreement was made.

Hire or Rental of a Chattel

The hire of a chattel is a bailment for reward in which the bailor-owner delivers possession of a chattel for use by the bailee-hirer in return for a monetary payment. This type of bailment is usually in the form of a written agreement with each party's rights and duties set out. However, it need not be in writing to be enforceable, unless by its terms it falls subject to the Statute of Frauds.

Under a bailment for the hire of a chattel the bailee is required to pay the rental fee for the use of the chattel that the parties have agreed upon. Or if no fee was specified at the time the agreement was entered into, then the bailee is required to pay the reasonable or customary price for the use of the goods. If the bailment is for a fixed term, the bailee is usually liable for payment for the full term, unless the bailor agrees to take back the chattel and clearly releases the bailee from any further obligation to pay. Apart from the payment of the rental fee, and except for any specific obligations imposed upon the bailee, the bailee is entitled to possession and use of the goods for the entire rental period.

The bailee at common law must not use the goods for any purpose other than the purpose for which they were intended. The bailee must not sub-bail the goods, or allow strangers to use them, unless permission to do so is obtained from the bailor. In the event that the bailee should do any of these things without permission, the bailee would become absolutely liable for any loss or damage to the chattels. Otherwise, the bailee will only be liable if he or she fails to use reasonable care in the operation or use of the goods.[19] The bailee would not be liable for ordinary "wear and tear" that may result from use of the chattel unless the agreement specifically holds the bailee responsible. The maintenance of the equipment in fit condition for the use intended is usually the responsibility of the bailor.

Under an agreement for the hire of a chattel, the prime responsibility of the bailor is to provide the bailee with goods that are reasonably fit for the use intended. The goods must be free from any defects that might cause damage or loss to the bailee when the equipment is put into use. If the bailor knew or ought to have known of a defect when the goods were delivered, the bailor may be liable for the damage caused by the defective equipment. For example, Lyndsey hired a truck from Foster for the purpose of delivering crates of eggs to market. If Foster knew or ought to have known that the truck had defective brakes and, as a result of the defect, the truck swerved off the road when the brakes were applied and destroyed Lyndsey's load of eggs, Foster would be liable for Lyndsey's loss. However, if the defect was hidden and would not be revealed by a careful inspection, Foster may not be liable.

Where the goods hired have an inherent danger or risk associated with their use, the bailor is normally under an obligation to warn the bailee of the danger, or possible dangers, associated with the use. However, where the bailee is licensed or experienced in the use of the equipment, any loss or damage that may result from the use of the equipment may be assessed in part against the bailee.[20]

19. *Morris v. C.W. Martin & Sons Ltd.,* [1965] 2 All E.R. 725.
20. *Hadley v. Droitwich Construction Co. Ltd. et al.,* [1967] 3 All E.R. 911.

Carriage of Goods

The carriage of goods may include a number of different forms of bailment. The carriage of goods involves the delivery of goods by the bailor to the bailee for the purpose of delivery to some destination by the bailee. As with all bailments, the goods are in the possession of the bailee for a particular purpose, but the title is in someone else.

A carrier of goods is normally a carrier for reward, but this is not always the case. A carrier may be a gratuitous carrier who transports goods without reward, such as a person who agrees to deliver a parcel to the post office for a friend. With a gratuitous carrier, if the service provided is entirely for the benefit of the bailor, the bailee is only expected to use reasonable care in the carriage of the goods.

There are two classes of carriers for reward: **private carriers** and **common carriers.** The standard care differs for each. A private carrier is a carrier that may occasionally carry goods, but who is normally engaged in some other business activity. A company that is a private carrier is free to accept or reject goods as it sees fit. However, if it should decide to act as a carrier of goods for reward, then it would have a duty to take reasonable care of the goods while they are in its possession.

The common carrier, unlike the gratuitous carrier and the private carrier, carries on the business of carriage of goods for reward. It offers to accept any goods for shipment if it has the facilities to do so. For example, a trucking company or railway company that engages in the carriage of goods would be classed as a common carrier. Common carriers are to some extent controlled by statute. The statute generally limits the carrier's ability to escape liability in the event that the goods that are carried are lost or damaged. The common carrier is essentially an insurer of the goods, and is liable for any damage to the goods except in certain circumstances.

The principal reason for the very high standard of care required of the common carrier is that the goods are totally within the control of the carrier for the entire period of time that the bailment exists. Unlike other forms of bailment where the bailor could presumably check on the goods, once the goods are in the hands of the carrier, they are no longer open to inspection by the bailor until they reach their destination. Under the legislation pertaining to common carriers, the carrier is usually permitted by contract to limit the amount of compensation payable in the event of loss or damage to the goods. The carrier may also avoid liability if the damage to the goods was caused by an act of God, the improper labelling or packing of the goods by the shipper, or if the nature of the goods was such that they were subject to self-destruction during ordinary handling. The carrier would also be exempt from liability if the damage resulted from the actions of the Queen's enemies in time of war.

Most common carriers are subject to legislation that imposes certain responsibilities on their operation. These statutes usually either set out the liability of the carrier, or set out the carrier's rights and duties in the carriage of goods. In many cases, the rights and duties must be included in the contract of carriage, and these terms are frequently found in small print on the back of the contract. Since separate legislation governs railways, trucking firms, and air carriers, the specific liability tends to vary somewhat for each. The basic liability, however, remains the same.

Under a contract of carriage, the bailor also has certain responsibilities. The bailor is obliged to pay the rates fixed for the shipping of the goods. If the bailor fails to pay, the carrier may claim, or receive under the terms of the contract, the right of lien on the goods until payment is made. If the charges are not paid within a reasonable length of time, the goods normally may be sold to cover the carrier's charges. The bailor is also required to disclose the type of goods shipped, and must also take care not to ship dangerous goods by carrier unless a full disclosure of the nature of the goods is made.

A common occurrence in the carriage of goods is a change of ownership of the goods while in the hands of the carrier. The original bailor is not always the recipient at the destination where goods are to be shipped. Indeed, in most cases, the goods are shipped by the bailor to some other person. The contract with the carrier (sometimes called a **bill of lading**) names the person to whom the goods are consigned, and the carrier will deliver the goods to the person named as consignee. Goods may be shipped under a second type of contract of carriage, called an **order bill of lading**. This is essentially a contract combined with a receipt and document of title, that may be endorsed by the consignee, if the consignee so desires, to some other person. An order bill of lading must be surrendered to obtain the goods from the carrier.

Pledge or Pawn of Personal Property as Security for Debt

Bailment may be associated with debt transactions in the sense that personal property may be delivered to a creditor to be held as security for a loan. The particular personal property may take the form of such securities as bonds, share certificates, or life insurance policies. These securities may be held by the creditor as collateral to the loan. Because the creditor takes possession of the securities, the transaction represents a bailment, and the creditor as a bailee would be responsible for the property while in his or her possession. When the debt is paid, the same securities must be returned to the bailor. The delivery of securities or similar personal property to the creditor as security for a loan is called a **pledge**. If the bailor-debtor should default on the loan, the bailee-creditor may look to the securities pledged to satisfy the debt. Any surplus, however, from the sale of the securities would belong to the debtor, and must be paid over to the debtor by the creditor.

A **pawn** is similar to a pledge, but is confined to a transaction between a debtor and a pawnbroker. It is concerned with the delivery of goods to the pawnbroker as security for a loan. Pawnbrokers are licensed in Canada. They may accept goods as security under loan agreements that entitle them to sell the goods if default on the debt occurs. While the goods are in the possession of the pawnbroker a bailment exists, and the pawnbroker must take reasonable care of the goods. As with other forms of bailment, the pawnbroker has only possession of the goods, and the bailor-debtor retains the title. The bailment, however, is made on the express condition that the goods may be sold by the creditor if default should occur. At that time the creditor may give a good title to the goods to a third party. Any surplus from the sale would belong to the debtor and, conversely, any deficiency would remain as an obligation.

INNKEEPERS

The liability of the innkeeper or hotel keeper extends back to the Middle Ages in England to a time when a traveller's goods were at the mercy of the innkeeper. The early English inns (and for that matter, many of the inns in both Canada and the United States until as late as the nineteenth century) provided a large single room for sleeping purposes. There were only a few separate bedchambers, so the guests were easy prey for thieves while they slept. The innkeeper was seldom unaware of the pilfering and was often an accomplice in the act. To discourage theft, and to ensure that the innkeeper was not a party to the crime, the common law imposed a very high standard of care on the innkeeper with respect to goods brought on the premises by guests. At common law, the innkeeper was held to be responsible for any loss, even if it was not the innkeeper's fault. The only exception was where the loss was due to the guest's own negligence. The innkeeper, in effect, was someone who closely resembled an insurer of the goods in the event of loss. This was so in spite of the fact that the goods were not in the innkeeper's possession, and the guests exercised some control over the goods as well.

While the liability of the innkeeper to guests of the hotel was similar to a bailment, the innkeeper's liability at common law was essentially based upon "custom of the realm." Later this was established by statute. This rather unique form of responsibility for the goods of the guest was described by the court to be as follows:

> At common law an innkeeper was responsible to his guests if any of their goods were lost or stolen while on his premises. In *Shacklock v. Ethorpe Ltd.*, [1939] 3 All E.R. 372, Lord MacMillan, whose opinion was concurred in by all of the other Law Lords, applies the words of Lord Esher M.R. in *Robins & Co. v. Gray,* [1895] 2 Q.B. 501 at 503, who said:
>
> "The duties, liabilities, and rights of innkeepers with respect to goods brought to inns by guests are founded, not upon bailment, or pledge, or contract, but upon the custom of the realm with regard to innkeepers. Their rights and liabilities are dependent upon that, and that alone; they do not come under any other head of law ... the innkeeper's liability is not that of a bailee or pledgee of goods; he is bound to keep them safely. It signifies not, so far as that obligation is concerned, if they are stolen by burglars, or by the servants of the inn, or by another guest; he is liable for not keeping them safely unless they are lost by the fault of the traveller himself. That is a tremendous liability: it is a liability fixed upon the innkeeper by the fact that he has taken the goods in..."[21]

An innkeeper, however, must be distinguished from other persons who offer accommodation to guests, as the special liability applies only to innkeepers. Persons who offer only room accommodation to travellers, or who are selective in offering room and meals (for example, a rooming-house), are not usually innkeepers by definition. A restaurant that offers only meals and no sleeping accommodation would not be classed as an "inn." To be treated as an innkeeper, it would appear that a person must offer both meals and room accommodation to the public.[22]

An innkeeper has a public duty to accept any transient person and their belongings as a guest — provided that accommodation exists, and also that the

---

21. *Hansen v. "Y" Motor Hotel Ltd.,* [1971] 2 W.W.R. 705.
22. *King v. Barclay and Barclay's Motel* (1960), 24 D.L.R. (2d) 418.

traveller is "fit and orderly" and has the ability to pay. An innkeeper is defined in the Innkeepers Acts of most provinces and territories as a person who offers accommodation and meals to the travelling public. Once the proprietor of the establishment falls within the definition, the liability under the statute also applies. Each province has legislation that sets out the rights and obligations of innkeepers, but unfortunately the legislation is not uniform. In general, with respect to the protection of the goods and belongings of travellers, the innkeeper may in most provinces limit his or her liability to a fixed sum that varies from $40 to $150. This limit applies where the loss or damage is not due to the negligence of, or the willful or deliberate act of, the innkeeper or the innkeeper's employees, or where the goods are not placed in the innkeeper's custody for safe keeping. The legislation in most provinces provides that to obtain the protection of the act, the innkeeper must post the relevant sections in all bedrooms and public rooms in the inn.[23]

Because the innkeeper and the guest to some extent share responsibility for the protection of the guest's goods, the liability of the innkeeper is not absolute. If the innkeeper can establish that the loss of the guest's goods was due entirely to the guest's negligence, the innkeeper may be able to avoid liability.[24] Full liability applies where the goods have been placed in the hands of the innkeeper for safe keeping. In most provinces, full liability will also apply if the innkeeper refuses to accept the goods when requested to do so by a guest.[25]

SUMMARY

A bailment is created by the delivery of possession of a chattel by the bailor (who is usually the owner) to a bailee. Bailment involves the transfer of possession and not title, but a bailee may exercise many of the rights normally exercised by an owner while the goods are in his or her possession. Bailment may be either gratuitous or for reward. Liability is least for a gratuitous bailee who receives no benefit from the bailment. It is highest for special forms of bailment for reward such as the common carrier of goods, where the bailee is essentially an insurer for any loss or damage. If the agreement between the parties permits a sub-bailment, the bailee may make such a bailment. The bailee may also do so in some cases where sub-bailment in the absence of an agreement to the contrary, may be made by custom of the trade.

Bailment for reward may take the form of bailment for storage, for the carriage of goods, the deposit of goods for repair, the hire of a chattel, and the pledge or pawn of goods to secure a loan. The liability of the bailee in each of the bailment relationships arises if the bailee fails to take reasonable care of the goods while in his or her possession. However, in the case of the common carrier and the innkeeper (who is similar to a bailee) a much higher standard prevails. A

23. Saskatchewan requires only that the sections of the Act be placed in the hall and entrance: Hotel Keepers Act, R.S.S. 1978, c. H-11, s. 11. The Manitoba Act does not require the posting of a notice as the Act does not hold the innkeeper liable for loss except as set out in the statute: see the Hotel Keepers Act, R.S.M. 1987, c. H-150.

24. *Loyer v. Plante*, [1960] Que.Q.B. 443; *Laing v. Allied Innkeepers Ltd.*, [1970] 1 O.R. 502; *Hansen v. "Y" Motor Hotel Ltd.*, [1971] 2 W.W.R. 705.

25. See, for example, Innkeepers Act, R.S.O. 1990, c. I-7, s. 6.

bailee may limit his or her liability by an express term in the contract. However, legislation governing such bailees as warehouse operators, carriers of goods, and innkeepers contain specific provisions and limitations that generally govern these special relationships.

DISCUSSION QUESTIONS

1. Define a bailment.
2. Explain the term *constructive bailment.*
3. How is the standard of care of a gratuitous bailee determined?
4. What rights over a bailed chattel does a bailee possess? Why are these rights necessary?
5. Why do the courts impose a greater responsibility for the care of goods on a common carrier than upon a gratuitous carrier?
6. Indicate the "defences" available to a common carrier in the event of loss or damage to goods in the carrier's possession.
7. What standard of care is imposed on a bailor in a hire of a chattel?
8. What essential element distinguishes the rental of space in an automobile parking lot from a bailment of the vehicle? How does this affect the liability of the owner of the parking lot?
9. In what way or ways is the responsibility of an innkeeper for the safe keeping of the goods of guests similar to that of a bailee for reward?
10. Why should an innkeeper be responsible for the goods of a guest that are brought into the guest's hotel room?
11. Indicate the effectiveness of an exemption clause in a bailment contract for the storage of an automobile. How do the courts view these clauses?
12. To what extent is a bailee for reward entitled to claim a lien for storage costs against the goods?
13. Explain: (a) fungible, (b) pawn, (c) pledge, (d) sub-bailment.

MINI-CASE PROBLEMS

1. Simple took his power lawn-mower to a repair shop to have it repaired. At the shop he signed an "authorization to repair" sheet that directed the repair shop to "repair the engine." The shop did so, but apparently found it necessary to replace most of the internal parts of the engine. The repair bill was $250, almost the price of a new machine. Simple refused to pay the account when he realized the cost of the repairs, and the repair shop refused to release the mower to him.

   Discuss the rights of the parties.

2. Smith entered a clothing shop to purchase a new coat. The clerk was busy, and Smith placed her purse on a table located near the coat racks while she examined several coats for size and fit. Her purse was stolen while she was examining the coats.

   Discuss the question of liability for the stolen purse.

JUDICIAL DECISION

The judicial decision in this chapter deals with the bailment of an automobile in a parking lot situation. The judge notes that the relationship is one of bailment because the owner of the automobile left the car and the keys with the attendant. The "contract" of bailment was included on the ticket/receipt that the automobile owner received when the bailment was arranged. The liability in this case turns on the question of whether the terms of the bailment that essentially released the bailee of responsibility for the damage were enforceable. The judge examines the law relating to exculpatory clauses and signs, then applies the law to the case before him. He then concludes that the clause and sign does allow the bailee to avoid liability because the bailor had sufficient notice of the limited liability of the bailee at the time the contract was entered into between the parties.

Bailment — Storage for Reward — Car Parking Lot — Signs and Ticket Excluding Liability for Loss

Samuel Smith & Sons Ltd. v. Silverman (1961), 29 D.L.R. (2d) 98.

The plaintiff parked his car in a parking lot and left the keys with the lot attendant. He received a ticket in return for payment of the parking fee. The ticket contained a statement that the owner of the parking lot was not responsible for damage to the car or its contents. Several large signs at the entrance to the lot contained the same message. When the plaintiff returned to the lot some time later, he found his car damaged.

An action was brought against the owners of the parking lot for damages.

SCHROEDER, J.A.:

It is conceded by counsel for the appellant that this is a true case of bailment since Sussman had been requested by the parking attendant to leave the keys in the motor car in order that it could be driven as required to a suitable place on the lot. It was therefore received into the custody of the defendant and a contract of bailment for reward has been made out. At the time of the delivery of the car to the defendant's servant Sussman was given a parking ticket containing the following terms:

"WE ARE NOT RESPONSIBLE FOR THEFT OR DAMAGE OF CAR OR CONTENTS HOWEVER CAUSED."

These terms are spelled out in bold black type and in letters large enough to dispel any suggestion of an attempt on the part of the defendant to conceal the limiting conditions from the recipient. Had the defendant looked at this ticket he could not possibly have failed to see the terms quoted.

When a chattel entrusted to a custodian is lost, injured, or destroyed, the onus of proof is on the custodian to show that the injury did not happen in consequence of his neglect to use such care and diligence as a prudent or careful man would exercise in relation to his own property. Counsel for the appellant admits that the plaintiff having proved that its motor car was damaged while in the care and custody of the defendant, it made out a *prima facie* case, subject to any special conditions in the contract, limiting or relieving the appellant from his common law liability. At the trial no attempt was made to show how or when the loss or damage in question occurred, and apart from such conditions, the plaintiff would be entitled to succeed. It is well settled that a custodian may limit or relieve himself from his common law liability by special conditions in the contract, but such conditions will be strictly construed and they will not be held to exempt the bailee from responsibility for losses due to his negligence unless the words of limitation are clear and adequate for the purpose or there is no other liability to which they can apply: *Can. Steamship Lines v. The King,* [1952] 2 D.L.R. 786 at p. 793, A.C. 192 at pp. 207-8.

In *Olley v. Marlborough Court Ltd.*, [1949] 1 All E.R. 127, Lord Justice Denning stated at p. 134:

"People who rely on a contract to exempt themselves from their common law liability must prove that contract strictly. Not only must the terms of the contract be clearly proved but also the intention to create legal relations — the intention to be legally bound — must also be clearly proved. The best way of proving it is by a written document signed by the party to be bound. Another way is by handing him before or at the time of the contract, a written notice, specifying certain terms and making it clear to him that the contract is in those terms. A prominent public notice which is plain for him to see when he makes the contract would, no doubt, have the same effect, but nothing short of one of these three ways will suffice."

The learned trial Judge accepted the evidence of the plaintiff to the effect that he had not parked a car on this property before. He testified that he had not seen any signs erected on the premises, and that he had not read the conditions set out on the parking ticket which he had been given at the time the contract was made. There was evidence given on behalf of the defendant by the defendant's manager who stated that there were four signs erected on the defendant's lot, two of them at the front near the Victoria St. entrance, and the other two on the rear parking lot. They were at a height of approximately 8 to 10 ft. from the ground, 2 1/2 by 3 ft. in dimension, and contained the following words:

"WE ARE NOT RESPONSIBLE FOR THEFT OR DAMAGE OF CAR OR CONTENTS HOWEVER CAUSED."

The learned Judge accepted this evidence. He found as a fact that there were signs on the lot in the four places indicated, which were lighted at the time in question, and which bore the words set out above. The point to which the Court should address itself in a case where the defendant relies upon signs of this nature is clearly stated in the judgment of Baron Alderson in the old case of *Walker et al. v. Jackson* (1842), 10 M. & W. 160, 152 E.R. 424, from which I quote at p. 173:

"The acts proved by the plaintiffs, upon which they relied to substantiate the existence of a contract, were those done with respect to persons bringing carriages. These notices were stuck up in the way for foot passengers, and it appeared that the plaintiff did not go by that way; neither was it shewn that any person with a carriage ever went by it. No reasonable probability, therefore, existed that the plaintiff, or any other parties going with carriages, ever saw them."

It may well be that if the defendant were forced to rely solely upon the limiting conditions set out on the parking ticket given to the plaintiff's agent, the reasoning in *Spooner v. Starkman* and in *Appleton et al. v. Ritchie Taxi* might prevail against his defence. Here, however, notice of the limiting condition was also provided in four prominently displayed signs, two of which were placed near the entrance on Victoria St. which any reasonably attentive person should have seen.

In *Brown v. Toronto Auto Parks Ltd.*, [1955] 2 D.L.R. 525, O.W.N. 456, this Court had to consider a defence based on limiting conditions contained on signs displayed on the custodian's premises. Laidlaw, J.A., delivering the judgment of the Court there stated [p. 527 D.L.R., p. 457, O.W.N.]:

"In the instant case we are all satisfied that the signs displayed by the appellant were displayed with such prominence and in such a way that the respondent ought to have seen them and ought to have had knowledge of what was on the signs. We think that a person exercising reasonable care and diligence would have seen those signs and in particular he would have seen, first, that there was an attendant — the words were 'Attendant in charge', and that the car and contents were left at the owner's risk. But the appellant did not satisfy the learned trial Judge, nor has it satisfied this Court, that the loss sustained by the respondent did not happen in consequence of the appellant's breach of its duty to use such care and diligence as a prudent and careful man would exercise in relation to his own property. It has not discharged the onus of proof resting in law on it as a bailee for valuable consideration."

It was held that the exculpatory signs did not assist the defendant, for while the plaintiff should reasonably have seen them, the words "car and contents at owner's risk" did not suffice clearly to relieve the defendant for liability for negligence. The Court applied the strict rule of construction to which I have referred and supported the judgment for the plaintiff on that ground alone.

The words printed on the ticket and the signs in question are not susceptible of this criticism. The clear declaration that the defendant was not responsible for theft or damage of car or contents however caused, is sufficiently broad in its terms to extend to a case where the damage occurred through the negligence either of the defendant or his servants, or the negligence or carelessness of a third party whether lawfully on the premises or not.

CASE PROBLEMS FOR DISCUSSION

Case 1

Hart operated a restaurant and bakery shop that was located on a busy downtown street. The front portion of the premises contained the bakery shop, and the rear part of the building housed the restaurant. Patrons entering the building were required to pass through the store portion to reach the restaurant. In the store area, near the entrance to the restaurant, the owner had installed a number of coat hooks in a recess in the wall of the building. Employees of the shop and restaurant used the alcove to store their overcoats and hats.

Murphy, a stranger to the community, entered the shop for the purpose of dining, and proceeded through the shop to the restaurant area. Along the way he noticed the clothing in the alcove and placed his overcoat and hat on one of the unused hooks. He then entered the restaurant and ordered a meal. Some time later, when he was about to leave the restaurant, he discovered that his overcoat and hat were missing.

Hart denied responsibility for the loss. Murphy brought an action against him for the value of the hat and coat.

Discuss the arguments that the parties might raise in this case, and identify the legal issue involved. Render a decision. Would your decision differ in any way if the coat hooks were located in the restaurant beside Murphy's table?

Case 2

Harriet, a licensed pilot, rented an aircraft from Aircraft Rental Services at a local airport. The purpose of the rental was to fly a friend to a large metropolitan city some 500 km away and return before nightfall. At the time that she arranged for the use of the aircraft, she assured the owner that she would leave the city in ample time to return the aircraft before dark. She paid a deposit for the use of the aircraft and, accompanied by her friend, made an uneventful flight to the distant city. Before returning home, however, she spent some time shopping and lost track of time. Eventually, she realized that she was behind schedule and hurried to the airport.

The weather report for the return trip was not promising, but she nevertheless decided to chance the flight. She took off at 4:45 p.m. some two hours before official nightfall on that particular January night. En route, she discovered that the weather had deteriorated and that visibility was decreased by the combination of sundown and low cloud conditions.

At 7:05 p.m., some 20 minutes after official nightfall, she found that she could proceed no further, as the poor weather and semi-darkness made recognition of her route on the ground virtually impossible. To avoid further difficulties, she made a forced landing in a farmer's field, which resulted in extensive damage to the airplane's undercarriage.

Harriet assumed that the aircraft owner's insurance would cover the cost of the repairs. However, she was surprised to hear that the insurance covered only public liability and not damage to the aircraft itself. The cost of repairs amounted to $6165. When Harriet refused to pay for the damage, Aircraft Rental Services brought an action for damages against her for the amount of its loss.

In her defence, Harriet alleged no negligence on her part, as the landing was made in accordance with accepted forced landing procedures and skillfully executed on her part. She argued that in any forced landing, some damage to the undercarriage could be expected, and that the mere fact that damage occurred was not an indication of negligence.

The plaintiff brought out in the evidence that Harriet was licensed to fly under daylight conditions only. She did not have what was called a "night endorsement" on her licence that would permit her to fly after dark. The plaintiff alleged that her act of flying after official nightfall was a violation of Air Regulations under the Aeronautics Act.

Discuss the nature of the plaintiff's claim in this case, and the various other arguments that might be raised by the parties. Indicate the issues that must be decided by the court. Render a decision.

Case 3

Brown parked his automobile in a parking lot owned by Smith. At the request of the parking lot attendant, he left his keys at the attendant's office and received a numbered ticket as his receipt for the payment of the parking fee. Before leaving his keys with the attendant, he made certain that the doors of the vehicle were securely locked, as he had left a number of valuable books on the rear seat of the car.

Unknown to Brown, the attendant closed at midnight. Then he delivered the keys to the cars on the lot to the attendant of the parking lot across the street. This lot was also owned by Smith, but it remained open until 2:00 a.m.

Brown returned to the parking lot to retrieve his automobile shortly after midnight, only to discover no attendant in charge and his vehicle missing. By chance, he noticed the attendant on duty at the lot across the street. Brown reported the missing vehicle to him, and found the attendant in possession of his keys.

The police discovered Brown's automobile a few days later in another part of the city. The vehicle had been damaged and stripped of its contents, including Brown's rare books.

Brown brought an action against Smith for his loss. However, Smith denied liability on the basis that the ticket (which Brown received at the time of delivery of the keys) read: "Rental of space only. Not responsible for loss or damage to car or contents however caused." Smith also alleged that the attendant's office had a sign posted near the entrance that bore the same message.

Identify the issues in this case and prepare the arguments that Brown and Smith might use in their claim and defence respectively. Render a decision.

Case 4

The Frasers considered moving to western Canada from the city of Toronto on Mr. Fraser's retirement. In order to determine an appropriate community in which to reside, they visited a number of West Coast cities by automobile.

On their visit to one community, which appeared to be a delightful place to live, they met the owner of a warehouse business. The warehouse owner suggested that he would be prepared to receive their household goods if they wished to ship them to him. He would hold them in storage until such time as they found a permanent residence.

On their return to Toronto, the Frasers decided to move immediately. They dispatched their household goods to the warehouse operator that they had met on their visit to the city. Instead of taking up residence immediately, they planned an extensive vacation that would take them across the United States and eventually to that particular community.

While the Frasers were on vacation, the household goods arrived at the warehouse. The owner issued a warehouse receipt, which he mailed to the Frasers at the temporary address that they had given him. The warehouse receipt set out the terms and conditions of storage, one item being a condition that read: "All goods stored at owner's risk in case of fire (storage rates do not include insurance)."

On their return from their vacation, the Frasers found the warehouse receipt in their mail, but did not read the document. They proceeded to obtain a new home. However, before they could retrieve their goods from the warehouse, the building was burned by an arsonist who had apparently gained entry to the building by way of an open roof-top skylight window. The household goods that belonged to the Frasers were totally destroyed by the fire.

When the warehouse operator refused to compensate the Frasers for their loss, an action was brought claiming damages for the value of the goods.

Discuss the nature of the plaintiff's claim, and the defences that the warehouse operator might raise. Render a decision.

Case 5

The spouses of a number of business executives in a small northern community belonged to a social club. Each year they would plan a banquet dinner at a hotel in a large city some 160 km distant, in order to combine a shopping trip with club activities that marked their year-end.

In 1993, the club arranged for a banquet and overnight room accommodations for their members at the Municipal Hotel. Most of the members arrived early for the dinner in order to check into their rooms. One member, however, arrived late and, instead of checking in at the desk, went directly to the banquet room where the dinner was about to be served. Before entering the room, she noticed a coat room adjacent to the dining-room that contained a number of coats. She hung her fur jacket on a hanger in the coat room. No attendant was in charge of the coat room, although a person wearing a hotel porter uniform was standing near the doorway to the room.

The club member spent the evening in the banquet room, and at the end of the dinner meeting went to the coat room to retrieve her jacket. The jacket was missing.

As compensation the hotel offered her the sum of $40, the amount that an innkeeper was obliged to pay under the Innkeeper's Act of the province. The hotel explained that as a guest in the hotel, this was the extent of its liability to her. The hotel manager pointed out that the club member was aware of the limited liability of the hotel by virtue of the notice to that effect that was posted in all hotel bedrooms.

The club member refused to accept the sum offered as payment. She brought an action against the hotel for $2800, an amount that she alleged was the appraised value of the fur jacket.

Discuss the issues raised in this case and indicate how the courts might deal with them. Would your answer be any different if the club member's jacket had been stolen from a locked hotel room?

Case 6

Lacey inherited a large brooch from her grandmother. The brooch appeared to contain a number of large precious stones. She was curious as to the value of the piece of jewellery and took it to the B & S Jewellery Shop for examination. The jeweller was busy at the time. He asked Lacey to leave the brooch, saying he would examine it when he had a moment to do so. Lacey filled out a small claim check that required her to set out her name and address. She did so, and was given a portion of it bearing a claim number.

Lacey placed the claim check in her jewellery box when she returned home. She paid no further attention to the matter, believing that the jeweller would notify her when he had completed his appraisal of the brooch.

Some five years later, while cleaning out her jewellery box, Lacey noticed the claim stub in the bottom of it and remembered that she had left the brooch at the jewellers. She immediately went to the jewellery shop with the ticket to claim her jewellery, but the jeweller was unable to find the brooch. His records indicated that he had written Lacey three weeks after she had brought the brooch to him, to advise her that its value was $6500. Lacey, however, had not received the letter and, until her return to the jewellery shop, was unaware of its value.

When the jeweller could not produce the brooch, Lacey brought action for damages against the jeweller for the value of the piece.

Indicate the nature of Lacey's action, and the various arguments that both Lacey and the jeweller might raise. Render a decision.

Case 7

Central Ceramic China Ltd. was an importer of various lines of dishes and tableware that it sold in quantity to hotels and restaurants. Approximately 70% of its sales consisted of hotel grade dishes, 20% consisted of fine bone china dishes, and the remaining 10% consisted of cutlery and eating utensils.

For many years the firm used the services of Able Transport Co. to deliver its goods to customers who were located in various parts of the country. All goods were shipped in cartons marked: "FRAGILE. CONTENTS BREAKABLE IF ROUGH-HANDLED." The contents were normally packed in a strawlike material to provide some protection in the event of impact or careless handling. This reduced breakage of the shipped china to a minimum acceptable level. Only occasionally would a customer report breakage, and this usually consisted of only one or two pieces in a shipment of perhaps many hundreds of pieces.

Central Ceramic recently tested a new type of foam packing material, and decided that its use would permit the contents of a case to withstand a reasonable amount of impact if the case should accidentally be dropped. Management then decided to use the new packing material in cartons that were not marked with a "fragile" label in order to obtain a lower shipping rate. The company informed Able Transport of the removal of the "fragile" notice on the containers and requested a lower shipping rate. Able Transport agreed to handle the goods at a lower rate.

During the month that followed, management of Central Ceramic monitored the breakage rate and noted that it was approximately the same as when the other marked containers were used. The next month the company shipped a very large quantity of china to a distant hotel customer in the new containers. The china was shipped in 36 cases. When it was received by the hotel, almost half of the china was found to be either cracked or broken. An investigation by the carrier revealed that road vibration during the long trip had caused the packing material to shift, allowing the pieces of china to come in contact with each other and break, if the carton received any impact.

Central Ceramic took legal action against Able Transport for damages equal to the loss. Able Transport denied liability.

Discuss the arguments (if any) that the parties might raise in this case. Render a decision.

Case 8

Universal Paper Products Ltd. of Vancouver consigned three-and-a-half boxcar loads of goods to RapidMovve Transport Co. to take the goods from Vancouver to Le Havre, France. RapidMovve would normally have made direct arrangements with Canadian Atlantic Railways for the Vancouver–Montreal leg, but because there was a half carload involved, they engaged Railshippers Inc. to put together the Vancouver–Montreal leg. Railshippers could get a better rate from CAR as they specialized in making up full carloads from an assortment of partial carloads. RapidMovve engaged Maritime Containerways to ship from Montreal to France, and a French trucking firm for local delivery in France.

All would have gone well, had it not been for a derailment of the CAR train in Northern Ontario. Unseasonable rains had washed out a section of track and, in the dark, the train was derailed. Most of the product was probably in good shape after the accident, but unfortunately one of the welding crew pressed into service by CAR to clear the blockage of the main line in the emergency ignited the contents of one car as he cut away wreckage. The flames spread to the other cars, destroying $60 000 of paper products.

Three weeks later, Universal Paper became frustrated that RapidMovve could still only provide a garbled, contradictory explanation of what had happened. A newspaper account noted that there had been no salvage of any freight from the wreck. Universal Paper, knowing only that they had delivered goods to

RapidMovve, and that none had arrived in France, sued RapidMovve for the value of the goods.

Identify and discuss the legal issues raised in this case, and the liability (if any) of the parties. Render a decision.

CHAPTER 21

The Sale of Goods

CODIFICATION OF THE LAW

The law that relates to the sale of goods represents a direct response to the need for clear and precise rules to govern transactions that involve the exchange of money for goods. The existence of laws of this nature are indicative of the stage of development of a society. In a primitive society, where the individual members live at or near the subsistence level, no laws are necessary because the sale of goods seldom occurs. Any surplus production of one product is usually exchanged for other necessary products, usually by barter. It is only when a genuine surplus is produced that a basis for trade is established. Even then, a number of other conditions must be present before laws are necessary to govern the exchanges.

In England during the Middle Ages, most families and communities were relatively self-sufficient. Any goods that could not be produced within the family were usually acquired by way of exchange or barter with neighbours. Surplus goods of one community were often carried to nearby communities and exchanged for goods not available locally, as the same products were seldom concurrently in surplus supply. The rise of towns, however, set the stage for commerce. Not only did towns provide a ready market for agricultural products, but they also produced goods required by the agricultural community and represented a convenient place where exchanges might take place.

Trade was initially by barter at the market "fairs" held in each town, and was largely local. However, as the towns grew in size, foreign merchants began to appear, either with goods to sell, or with money to purchase the surplus goods of the community.

Transactions between merchants were first governed by the law merchant, and disputes concerning the sale of goods that arose were settled by the merchants themselves. Dealings between merchants and members of the community, however, were sometimes taken to the common law courts. Where the particular transaction involved the sale of goods, the courts would often apply the same rules that the merchants used in their own transactions. Over the years, a body of common law relating to the sale of goods gradually developed.

The law, unfortunately, was far from satisfactory. The methods that a plaintiff was obliged to use to obtain relief were cumbersome. In spite of a desire on the part of the merchants for change, the courts did not re-examine the nature of the transaction until the eighteenth century. At that time, the modern concept of contract emerged, and the sale of goods was treated as a contractual relationship between the buyer and seller.

During the next century, the rules of law relating to the sale of goods developed rapidly. By the late nineteenth century the law had matured to the point where the business community pressed for the law's organization into a simplified and convenient statute. The government responded in 1893 with the codification of the common law in the form of a single statute entitled the Sale of Goods Act.[1]

MacKenzie D. Chalmers, a prominent English county court judge, at the request of the government of the day, prepared the draft bill that set out the law relating to the sale of goods as a clear and concise body of rules. Chalmers was familiar with the common law relating to the contract of sale and, as a result, the statute became one of the best drafted laws on the English statute books. Other countries were quick to recognize the advantages of having a codification of this part of the law. It was soon after adopted by the common law provinces of Canada and a number of other jurisdictions in the British Empire.

The legal profession in the United States proposed similar legislation there, and a Uniform Sales Act was prepared, based upon the English Sale of Goods Act. This act was adopted by many of the states, occasionally with modifications. It eventually found its way into the U.S. Uniform Commercial Code, in a somewhat different form, as Article 2. At the present time, the Code has been adopted by all states except Louisiana. This widespread adoption of the English principles and rules relating to the sale of goods reflects the clarity and simplicity of the original law that Mr. Chalmers had so carefully drawn. It remains today in virtually unaltered form on the statute books of many jurisdictions.

NATURE OF A CONTRACT OF SALE

A contract of sale, as the name implies, is a type of contract. Consequently, the rules that relate to the formation, discharge, and impeachment of ordinary contracts also apply to the contract of sale, except where the Sale of Goods Act has specifically modified the rules.

A contract of sale, however, is something more than an ordinary contract, because the contract not only contains the promises of the parties, but often represents evidence of a transfer of the ownership of the property to the buyer as well. It must, therefore, operate in accordance with the act to accomplish this purpose.

---

1. Sale of Goods Act, 1893, 56 & 57 Vict., c. 71.

Under the act, "a contract of sale of goods is a contract whereby the seller transfers or agrees to transfer the property in goods to the buyer for a money consideration called the price...."[2] Two different contracts are contemplated by this definition. In the first instance, if the ownership is transferred immediately under the contract, it represents a **sale**. In the second, if the transfer of ownership is to take place at a future time, or subject to some condition that must be fulfilled before the transfer takes place, the transaction is an **agreement to sell**. Both the "sale" and the "agreement to sell" are referred to as a contract of sale under the act where it is unnecessary to distinguish between the two. An agreement to sell may apply to goods that are in existence at the time, or it may apply to a contract where the goods are not yet in existence. An example would be where a farmer enters into a contract with a food processor to sell his entire crop of fruit or vegetables before they are grown.

Application of the Act

The sale or agreement to sell must be for goods, as distinct from land and anything attached to the land. Buildings, for example, form a part of the land, because they are attached to it, and so, too, would any right to use the land or the buildings. Transactions concerning land are not covered by the Sale of Goods Act. The act, as its name indicates, concerns a sale of goods, but even then some "goods" are excluded. A sale of goods subject to the act would include tangible things such as moveable personal property; but the term "goods" would not include money or intangible things such as shares in a corporation, bonds, negotiable instruments, or "rights" such as patents or trade marks.

The contract itself must be for the sale of goods, and in this sense it is distinguished from a contract for work and materials. It is sometimes difficult to differentiate between a contract for work and materials and an agreement to sell, where the goods are not yet produced. However, as a general rule, if the contract is for a product of which the cost of the materials represents only a small part of the price, and the largest part of the cost is labour, the contract may be treated as a contract for work and materials. In that case the Sale of Goods Act would not apply. For example, if a person engages another to paint a house, or if a person takes a watch to the repair shop to be cleaned and to have a minor part replaced, the contracts would probably be treated as for work and materials rather than a sale of goods. In both cases, most of the purchase price would be represented by the "work" rather than the goods themselves.

A second distinction between a contract of sale and other forms of contract is the requirement that the property in the goods be transferred for a monetary consideration. By this definition, a barter or exchange of goods where no money changed hands would not be a contract of sale within the meaning of the act; nor would a consignment, where the title to the goods is retained by the owner, and the seller has only possession of the goods pending a sale to a prospective buyer.

No special form is required for either the sale contract or the agreement to sell. The contract may be in writing, under seal, verbal, or in some cases, implied

---

2. Sale of Goods Act, R.S.O. 1990, c. C-1, s. 2(1). Reference to the act in this chapter will refer to the Ontario act. While the name of the act and the numbering of the sections of the other provincial statutes may vary, the rules stated usually may be found in the laws of all provinces and the territories.

from the conduct of the parties. However, if the contract is for the sale of goods valued at more than a particular amount,[3] the agreement must be evidenced by a memorandum in writing, and signed by the party to be charged (or his or her agent) to be enforceable.

The requirement of writing was originally found in the Statute of Frauds, and later included in the English Sale of Goods Act. When the legislation was adopted by the Canadian provinces and territories the requirement of writing was included. Three exceptions are provided in the act, however, which permit the parties to avoid the requirement of writing. The agreement need not be in writing if the buyer:

(1) accepts part of the goods sold;

(2) makes a part-payment of the contract price; or

(3) gives something "in earnest" to bind the contract.[4]

In each of these cases, the actions of the buyer must relate specifically to the particular contract of sale. The acceptance of part of the goods has been interpreted by the courts to mean any act that would indicate acceptance or adoption of the pre-existing contract, including the ordinary inspection of the goods. The part-payment of the contract price must be just that: a payment of money that relates specifically to the particular contract. The third requirement, the giving of something "in earnest," refers to an old custom of giving something valuable for the purpose of binding the agreement. The object might be an article, or something of value, other than a part-payment of the purchase price. This practice is seldom followed today.

Transfer of Title

A final observation with respect to the nature of the contract of sale is that it represents an agreement to transfer property in the goods to the buyer. The "property in the goods" is the right of ownership to the goods, or the **title**. The ownership of the goods normally goes with possession, but this is not always the case. A person may, for example, part with possession of goods, yet retain ownership. It is this attribute that creates most of the difficulties with the sale of goods. The parties in their agreement may determine when the title will pass, and this may differ from the time when possession takes place. Since the risk of loss generally follows the title, in any agreement where the transfer of possession is not accompanied by a simultaneous transfer of ownership, any damage to the goods while the title is not in the person in physical possession of them can obviously raise difficulties.

Goods that are not in a deliverable state (i.e., goods that must be produced, weighed, measured, counted, sorted, or tested before they are identifiable as goods for a particular contract) unless otherwise provided, remain at the seller's risk until such time as they are "ready for delivery." Under the Sale of Goods Act, no property in the goods is transferred to the buyer until the goods are in this state.[5] In a contract for goods that are specific or ascertained, the property in the

---

3. The amount in Ontario, New Brunswick, and Nova Scotia is $40. Newfoundland and the three western provinces fixed the amount at $50, and Prince Edward Island placed the amount at $30. British Columbia, following the English example, repealed the requirement of writing in 1958.

4. Sale of Goods Act, R.S.O. 1990, c. S-1, s. 5(1).

5. Ibid., s. 17; *Harris v. Clarkson* (1931), 40 O.W.N. 325.

goods may be transferred to the buyer at such time as the parties intend the transfer to take place.[6] In most cases, this intention will be determined by an examination of the contract terms, the conduct of the parties, or the circumstances under which the contract arose.[7] If the parties specify when the title passes, then the parties themselves have decided who should bear the loss in the event that the goods should be destroyed or damaged before the transaction is completed. If they have not dealt with this matter in their agreement, or if it cannot be ascertained from their conduct (or the circumstances of the case), then the act provides a series of rules that are deemed to apply to the contract. These rules deal with a number of different common contract situations. The first rule deals with goods that are **specific** (i.e., identified and agreed upon at the time the contract is made) and in a deliverable state.

Rule 1. Where there is an unconditional contract for the sale of specific goods in a deliverable state, the property in the goods passes to the buyer when the contract is made, and it is immaterial whether the time of payment or the time of delivery or both be postponed.[8]

Example. Henderson enters Nielsen's shop and purchases a large crystal bowl that Nielsen has on display in her shop window. Henderson pays for the item and informs Nielsen that he will pick it up the next morning.

During the night, a vandal smashes the shop window and destroys the crystal bowl. The title passed in this case when the contract was made, because the goods were specific and in a deliverable state. Henderson, if he wished, could have taken the bowl with him at the time the contract was made, but he elected not to do so. Since loss follows the title, the destroyed goods belonged to the buyer and not to the seller. It is the buyer who must bear the loss.

The second rule is a variation of Rule 1. It is applicable to a contract where the seller must do something to the goods to put them in a deliverable state. Title in this case does not pass until the seller does whatever is necessary to put the goods in a deliverable state, and notifies the buyer that the goods are now ready for delivery. The rule states:

Rule 2. Where there is a contract for the sale of specific goods and the seller is bound to do something to the goods for the purpose of putting them in a deliverable state, the property does not pass until the thing is done and the buyer has notice thereof.[9]

Example. Leblanc entered into a contract with Ross to purchase a used car on display at Ross' car lot. The door lock on one door was inoperable, so Ross agreed to fix the lock as a term of the contract. Leblanc paid the entire purchase price to Ross. Ross repaired the lock, but before he notified Leblanc that the car was ready for delivery, the car was destroyed by a fire at Ross' garage. Leblanc would be entitled to a return of the purchase price in this case, as the title was still in

---

6. Ibid., s. 18(1): see also *Goodwin Tanners Ltd. v. Belick and Naiman,* [1953] O.W.N. 641.

7. Sale of Goods Act, R.S.O. 1990, c. S-1, s. 18(2).

8. Ibid., s. 18.

9. Ibid., s. 19; see also *Underwood Ltd. v. Burgh Castle Brick & Cement Syndicate,* [1921] All E.R. Rep. 515.

Ross' name. The title would not pass until Ross notified Leblanc that the car was ready for delivery, and the risk was his until the buyer received the notice.

The third rule is again a variation of Rule 1. It applies where the contract is for the sale of specific goods in a deliverable state, but where the seller must weigh, measure, test, or do something to ascertain the price. Under this rule, the property in the goods does not pass until the act is done and the buyer notified.

Rule 3. When there is a contract for the sale of specific goods in a deliverable state, but the seller is bound to weigh, measure, test, or do some other act or thing with reference to the goods for the purpose of ascertaining the price, the property does not pass until such act or thing is done, and the buyer has been notified thereof.[10]

Example. Grange agrees to purchase a quantity of grain that Thompson has stored in a bin in his warehouse. Thompson agrees to weigh the material and inform Grange of the price. If the grain should be destroyed before Thompson notifies Grange of the weight and price, the loss would be the seller's, as the property in the goods would not pass until the buyer has notice. If, however, Thompson weighed the grain and notified Grange of the weight and price, the title would pass immediately. If the goods were subsequently destroyed before Grange took delivery, the loss would be his, even though the goods were still in the seller's possession.

It is important to note with respect to Rule 3 that the seller must have the duty to weigh, measure, or otherwise deal with the goods. In the case where the buyer took the goods and agreed to weigh them on the way home, and then notify the seller, a court held that Rule 3 did not apply to transfer the property interest. The title passed to the buyer when he took the goods.[11]

The fourth rule for the transfer of ownership in goods deals with contracts for the sale of goods "on approval" or with return privileges. This rule is a two-part rule that provides that the title will pass if the buyer, on receipt of the goods, does anything to signify his or her acceptance or approval of the goods, or the adoption of the contract. If the buyer does nothing but retains the goods beyond a reasonable time, then the title will pass at the expiry of that period of time. The buyer must do some act that a buyer would only have the right to do as the owner in order to fall under the first part of this rule. The sale of the goods by the buyer, for example, would constitute an act of acceptance, as it would be an act that only a person who had adopted the contract would normally do. The same rule would hold if the buyer mortgaged the goods. In that case, the title would pass to the buyer the instant that the act of acceptance took place.

Under the second part of the rule, if the buyer simply does nothing after he or she receives the goods, the title will pass when the time fixed for return expires; or if no time is fixed, after a reasonable time. The purpose of this second part of the rule is to ensure that a buyer cannot retain "approval" goods beyond a reasonable time. The delivery of goods is frequently a courtesy extended by the seller. To allow the prospective purchaser to retain the goods an unnecessarily long time

---

10. Sale of Goods Act, R.S.O. 1990, c. S-1, s. 19.
11. *Turley v. Bates* (1863), 2 H & C 200, 159 E.R. 83.

would only increase the chance of loss or damage to the goods while the risk is still with the seller.

Rule 4. Where goods are delivered to the buyer on approval or "on sale or return" or other similar terms, the property therein passes to the buyer:

    (i) when he signifies his approval or acceptance to the seller or does any other act adopting the transaction;

   (ii) if he does not signify his approval or acceptance to the seller but retains the goods without giving notice of rejection, then if a time has been fixed for the return of the goods, on the expiration of such time, and if no time has been fixed, on the expiration of a reasonable time, and what is a reasonable time is a question of fact.

Example A. Baxter Construction Company purchased a small bulldozer on approval. A few days later the company pledged it as security for a loan at its bank. The machine was later damaged in a fire. In this case, the buyer, Baxter Construction Company, would be considered to have accepted the goods at the time it pledged the machine as security, and the resulting loss would be the buyer's.

The terms of the contract may alter the liability of the parties, however. In a case where goods were delivered "for cash or return, goods to remain the property of the seller until paid for" it was held that Rule 4 did not apply, as the seller had specifically withheld the passing of the title.[12]

Example B. A buyer ordered 140 bags of rice from a seller. The seller delivered 125, with 15 bags to follow. The buyer asked the seller to hold delivery of the remaining 15 bags. After the passing of a reasonable time, the seller asked the buyer if he was appropriating the 125 bags, but the buyer did not reply. The seller later sued the buyer for the price of the 125 bags of rice. In this case the court held that the buyer, in failing to reply within a reasonable time, had implied acceptance.[13]

The fifth rule applies to unascertained goods (or goods that are not as yet produced) and that would therefore be the subject-matter of an agreement to sell rather than a sale. Under this rule, as soon as the goods ordered by description are produced and in a deliverable state and are unconditionally appropriated to the contract, either by the seller or by the buyer (with the seller's consent), the property in the goods will pass. This rule again is in two parts that provide:

Rule 5. (i) Where there is a contract for the sale of unascertained or future goods by description, and goods of that description in a deliverable state are unconditionally appropriated to the contract, either by the seller with the assent of the buyer, or by the buyer with the assent of the seller, the property in the goods therein passes to the buyer, and such assent may be expressed or implied, and may be given either before or after the appropriation is made.

(ii) Where, in pursuance of the contract, the seller delivers the goods to the buyer or to a carrier or other bailee (whether named by the buyer or not) for the

---

12. *Weiner v. Gill,* [1905] 2 K.B. 172.

13. *Pignitaro v. Gilroy,* [1919] 1 K.B. 459.

purpose of transmission to the buyer, and does not reserve the right of disposal, he is deemed to have unconditionally appropriated the goods to the contract.[14]

Example A. A pipeline contractor ordered a quantity of special steel pipe from a manufacturer. When the pipe was produced, the contractor sent one of his trucks to the manufacturer's plant with instructions to have the pipe loaded. After the truck was loaded, it was stolen (through no fault of the manufacturer) and destroyed in an accident. The pipe, as a result of the damage suffered in the accident, was useless. Here, the goods were unconditionally appropriated to the contract and the title had passed to the contractor.

Again, the time at which the title passes is deemed to be when the buyer obtains possession of the goods either himself or through his agent, or when the seller loses physical control of the goods.

Example B. A buyer in England ordered certain dyes from a seller in Switzerland, knowing that the seller had them in stock. The seller sent the order by mail to the buyer in England, and in so doing was accused of infringement of the English patent. One of the issues in the case was: Where and when did title pass? The court held that, since the buyer had given his implied assent to delivery by mail, as soon as the seller filled the order and placed it in the mail the title passed to the buyer.[15]

This decision is consistent with cases dealing with the use of common carriers to deliver the goods to the buyer as provided in the second part of the rule. Unless the seller has reserved the right of disposal, goods delivered to the carrier have essentially been disposed of by the seller. Once delivered, the seller no longer has control of the goods, and usually only the buyer may recover the goods from the carrier. Since the seller has effectively transferred control over the goods to the buyer's agent, the rule is sensible in providing for the passing of ownership from the seller to the buyer at the moment when the seller parts with possession.

Withholding title by the seller, or reserving the right of disposal if goods are delivered to the buyer or a carrier, have important implications in the event that the buyer should become insolvent at some point in time during the sale. The general rule is that the trustee in bankruptcy is only entitled to claim as a part of the bankrupt's estate those goods that belong to the bankrupt at the time of the bankruptcy. If the seller has retained the title to the goods, the seller may, in many cases, be in a position to recover the goods or stop their delivery to the bankrupt if they are in the hands of a carrier. Hence the importance, for example, of reserving the title until the goods are paid for in full by the buyer.

CONTRACTUAL DUTIES OF THE SELLER

The Sale of Goods Act permits the parties to include in their contract any particular terms or conditions relating to the sale that they wish, and the seller is obliged to comply with these terms. Sometimes the contract is one that is not carefully drawn in terms of the particular rights and duties of the parties. In these cases, the act implies certain obligations. These obligations generally are imposed upon the seller in terms of warranties and conditions with respect to the goods. Under the act, these terms have particular meanings.

A **condition** is a fundamental or essential term of the contract that, if broken,

---

14. Sale of Goods Act, R.S.O. 1990, c. S-1, s. 19.

15. *Badische Analin and Soda Fabrik v. Basle Chemical Works, Bind Schedler,* [1898] A.C. 200.

would generally entitle the innocent party, if he or she so elects, to treat the breach as a discharge. The innocent party would then be released from any further performance.

A **warranty** is not an essential term in the contract, but rather a term that, if broken, would not end the contract, but would entitle the injured party to take action for damages for the breach. A warranty is usually a minor term of the contract, and not one that goes to the root of the agreement.

The Sale of Goods Act stipulates the particular terms in the contract of sale that constitute conditions and those that, if broken, would only be warranties. For example, the time for delivery of the goods is treated as a condition, and the promise of payment a mere warranty.

As to the title of the seller, unless the contract indicates otherwise, there is an implied condition that in the case of a sale, the seller has the right to sell the goods. In the case of an agreement to sell, the seller will have the right to sell the goods at the time when the property or the title in the goods is to pass to the buyer.[16] There is also an implied warranty that the goods are free from any charge or encumbrance (such as a chattel mortgage) in favour of a third party, unless the seller has informed the buyer of the charge or encumbrance, either before or at the time the agreement is made.[17] An additional implied warranty relates to the seller's title. It states that the buyer shall have quiet possession of the goods. The term "quiet possession" has nothing to do with solitude; it simply means that no person will later challenge the buyer's title to the goods by claiming a right or interest in them.[18]

Goods that are sold by description are subject to an implied condition that the goods will correspond with the description.[19] For example, if a buyer purchases goods from a catalogue, where the specifications are given and perhaps a picture of the goods is shown, the goods ordered by the buyer must correspond with the catalogue specifications. Otherwise the seller will be in breach of the contract, and the buyer will be entitled to reject the goods. If the goods are sold by description as well as by sample, then the goods must correspond to the description as well as the sample.[20]

Where goods are sold by sample alone, there is an implied condition that the bulk of the goods will correspond to the sample in quality,[21] and that the buyer will have a reasonable opportunity to examine the goods and compare them with the sample.[22] Even then, there is an implied condition that the goods will be free from any defect (apparent on reasonable examination of the sample) that would render them unmerchantable.[23] For example, a seller sold cloth by sample to a buyer to be resold by sample to tailors. However, unknown to both the seller and

---

16. Sale of Goods Act, R.S.O. 1990, c. S-1, s. 13(a). See also *Cehave N.V. v. Bremer Handelsgesellschaft*, [1975] 3 All E.R. 739; *Wickman Machine Tool Sales Ltd. v. L. Schuler A.G.,* [1972] 2 All E.R. 1173; affirmed, [1973] 2 All E.R. 39.

17. Sale of Goods Act, R.S.O. 1990, c. S-1, s. 13(c).

18. Ibid., s. 13(b).

19. Ibid., s. 13: see also *Beale v. Taylor*, [1967] 3 All E.R. 253.

20. Sale of Goods Act, R.S.O. 1990, c. S-1, s. 14.

21. Ibid., s. 16(2)(a). See also *Buckley v. Lever Bros. Ltd.,* [1953] O.R. 704.

22. Sale of Goods Act, R.S.O. 1990, c. S-1, s. 16(2)(b). See also *Godley v. Perry,* [1960] 1 All E.R. 36.

23. *Grant v. Australian Knitting Mills Ltd.*, [1935] All E.R. Rep. 209.

buyer, the cloth dye was such that perspiration would cause the colours to run. When the defect was later discovered, the tailors who manufactured the overcoats complained to the buyer, who in turn complained to the original seller. The defect was not apparent on ordinary examination of the cloth, but was in both the sample and the bulk of the cloth. When the seller refused to compensate the buyer, the buyer sued the seller for breach of contract. The court held that the examination need only be that which a reasonable person would make. There was no need to conduct elaborate chemical tests. The standard for the examination would be the same as that which a reasonable man buying an overcoat would have made of the material.[24]

In the case of *James Drummond & Sons v. E.H. Van Ingen & Co.*[25] the judge outlined the law as it relates to sale by sample:

> The sample speaks for itself. But it cannot be treated as saying more than such a sample would tell a merchant of the class to which the buyer belongs, using due care and diligence, and appealing to it in the ordinary way and with the knowledge possessed by merchants of that class at the time. No doubt the sample might be made to say a great deal more. Pulled to pieces and examined by unusual tests which curiosity or suspicion might suggest, it would doubtless reveal every secret of its construction. But that is not the way in which business is done in this country. Some confidence there must be between merchant and manufacturer. In matters exclusively within the province of the manufacturer the merchant relies on the manufacturer's skill, and he does so all the more readily when, as in this case, he has had the benefit of that skill before.
>
> Now I think it is plain upon the evidence that at the date of the transaction in question merchants possessed of ordinary skill would not have thought of the existence of the particular defect which has given rise to this action, and would not have discovered its existence from the sample. It appears to me, therefore, that the sample must be treated as wholly silent in regard to this defect, and I come to the conclusion that if every scrap of information which the sample can fairly be taken to have disclosed were written out at length, and embodied in writing in the order itself, nothing would be found there which could relieve the manufacturer from the obligation implied by the transaction.
>
> I prefer to rest my view on this broad principle. But it seems to me that the obligation of the manufacturer may be put in another way with the same result. When a manufacturer proposes to carry out the ideas of his customer, and furnishes a sample to show what he can do, surely in effect he says, "This is the sort of thing you want, the rest is my business, you may depend upon it that there is no defect in the manufacture which would prevent goods made according to that sample from answering the purpose for which they are required."

CAVEAT EMPTOR

As to quality and fitness for a particular purpose, the buyer is, to a certain extent, subject to *caveat emptor* ("let the buyer beware"). The law assumes that the buyer, when given an opportunity to examine the goods, can determine the quality and the fitness for his or her purpose. The Sale of Goods Act does, however, impose some minimum obligations on the seller. Where the seller is in the business of supplying a particular line of goods, and where the buyer makes the purpose for

24. *James Drummond & Sons v. E.H. Van Ingen & Co.* (1887), L.R. 12 H.L. 284.
25. *James Drummond & Sons v. E.H. Van Ingen & Co.* (1887), L.R. 12 H.L. 284.

which the goods are required known to the seller, and where the buyer relies on the seller's skill or judgement to supply a suitable product, there is an implied condition that the goods provided shall be reasonably fit for the use intended.[26] This rule, however, would not apply in a case where the buyer requests a product by its patent or trade name, as there would be no implied condition as to its fitness for any particular purpose.[27] This particular proviso means that any time that a purchaser orders goods by "name" rather than leaving the selection to the seller, the buyer will have no recourse against the seller if the goods fail to perform as expected, as the buyer was not relying on the seller's skill to select the proper product.

The importance of distinguishing between reliance on the skill of the seller and merely asking for goods by trade name was examined in the case of *Baldry v. Marshall*[28] where the judge noted:

> The mere fact that an article sold is described in the contract by its trade name does not necessarily make the sale a sale under a trade name. Whether it is so or not depends upon the circumstances. I may illustrate my meaning by reference to three different cases. First, where a buyer asks a seller for an article which will fulfil some particular purpose, and in answer to that request the seller sells him an article by a well-known trade name, there I think it is clear that the proviso does not apply. Secondly, where the buyer says to the seller, "I have been recommended such and such an article" — mentioning it by its trade name — "will it suit my particular purpose?" naming the purpose, and thereupon the seller sells it without more [sic], there again I think the proviso has no application. But there is a third case where the buyer says to a seller, "I have been recommended so and so" — giving its trade name — " as suitable for the particular purpose for which I want it. Please sell it to me." In that case I think it is equally clear that the proviso would apply and that the implied condition of the thing's fitness for the purpose named would not arise. In my opinion the test of an article having been sold under its trade name within the meaning of the proviso is: Did the buyer specify it under its trade name in such a way as to indicate that he is satisfied, rightly or wrongly, that it will answer his purpose, and that he is not relying on the skill or judgment of the seller, however great that skill or judgment may be?

In general, where goods are bought by description from a seller who deals in such goods, there is an implied condition that the goods shall be of merchantable quality. However, if the buyer has examined the goods, the implied condition would not apply to any defect in the goods that would have been revealed by the examination.[29]

The seller also has a duty to deliver goods as specified in the contract in the right quantity, at the right place, and at the right time. The time of delivery, if stipulated in the contract, is usually treated as a condition. If the seller fails to deliver the goods on time, the buyer may be free to reject them if delivery is late.[30] If no time for delivery is specified, the goods must usually be delivered within a reasonable time.[31]

---

26. Sale of Goods Act, R.S.O. 1990, c. S-1, s. 15(a). See also *Canada Building Materials Ltd. v. W.B. Meadows of Canada Ltd.,* [1968] 1 O.R. 469.

27. Sale of Goods Act, R.S.O. 1990, c. S-1, s. 15(a). See also *Baldry v. Marshall,* [1925] 1 K.B. 260.

28. *Baldry v. Marshall,* [1925] 1 K.B. 260.

29. Sale of Goods Act, R.S.O. 1990, c. S-1, s. 15(b).

30. Ibid., s. 27.

31. Ibid., s. 28(2).

Delivery of the proper quantity is also important. If the seller should deliver less than the amount fixed in the contract, the buyer may reject the goods, as this generally is a condition of the contract and a right of the buyer under the Sale of Goods Act.[32] If the buyer accepts the lesser quantity, then the buyer would be obliged to pay for them at the contract rate.[33] The delivery of a larger quantity than specified in the contract, however, does not obligate the buyer to accept the excess quantity. The buyer may reject the excess, or may reject the entire quantity delivered. However, if the buyer should accept the entire quantity, the buyer usually must pay for the excess quantity at the contract price per unit.[34]

The importance of exact performance in terms of delivery was described by the court in the following terms:[35]

> ...the right to reject is founded upon the hypothesis that the seller was not ready and willing to perform, or had not performed his part of the contract. The tender of a wrong quantity evidences an unreadiness and unwillingness, but that, in my opinion, must mean an excess or deficiency in quantity which is capable of influencing the mind of the buyer. In my opinion, this excess is not. I agree that directly the excess becomes a matter of possible discussion between reasonable parties, the seller is bound to justify what he has done under the contract; but the doctrine of de minimis cannot, I think, be excluded merely because the statute refers to the tender of a smaller or larger quantity than the contract quantity as entitling a buyer to reject.
>
> I wish to add this. The reason why an excess in tender entitles a buyer to reject is that the seller seeks to impose a burden on the buyer which he is not entitled to impose. That burden is the payment of money not agreed to be paid. It is prima facie no burden on the buyer to have 55 lbs. more than 4,950 tons offered to him, and there is nothing to suggest that these sellers would have ever insisted, or thought of insisting, upon payment of the 4s. over the 40,000£. The sellers' original appropriation appeared to be within the proper quantity. The excess of 55 lbs. appears when the quantity shipped is converted from kilos into tons. If the sellers had expressly or impliedly insisted upon payment of the 4s. upon their view of the contract, the case would have been different; but nothing of that kind can be supposed to have taken place here.

The place for delivery is usually specified in the contract. However, if the parties have failed to do so, the seller is only obliged to have the goods available and ready for delivery at his place of business if he has one, or if not, at his place of residence. If the parties are aware that the goods are stored elsewhere, then the place where the goods are located would be the place for delivery.[36] The place of delivery is often expressly or impliedly fixed when goods are sold. If this should be the case, or if by some custom of the trade the delivery takes place elsewhere than the seller's place, then the seller would be obliged to make delivery there.[37]

Where a contract calls for delivery by installments, and the seller fails to make delivery in accordance with the contract, the buyer is often faced with a dilemma. If a lesser quantity is delivered and the contract calls for separate

---

32. Ibid., s. 29(1).

33. Ibid., s. 29(1).

34. Ibid., s. 29(2).

35. *Shipton, Anderson & Co. v. Weil Brothers & Co.*, [1912] 1 K.B. 574.

36. Sale of Goods Act, R.S.O. 1990, c. S-1, s. 28(1).

37. Ibid., s. 28(1).

payments for each installment, the buyer may take delivery, if the buyer so desires, and pay for the goods delivered. If the buyer wishes to reject the goods, he or she must take care. The buyer may not treat the failure to deliver the proper amount on a particular installment as a basis for repudiation of the contract, unless the buyer is certain that he could satisfy the courts that the quantity delivered was significantly below the requirement set out in the contract, and that there was a high degree of probability that the deliveries would be equally deficient in the future.[38] This problem however, is normally limited to installment contracts requiring separate payments. If the contract does not provide for a separate payment for each installment, the contract is generally treated as being indivisible, and the buyer is free to repudiate the whole agreement.

In contracts of sale that are not sales to a consumer, the seller may, by an express term in the contract, exclude all implied conditions and warranties that are imposed under the Sale of Goods Act. Where this is done, however, the seller must comply exactly with the terms of the contract made. For example, a buyer entered into a contract with a seller for the purchase of a new truck for his business. The purchase agreement provided that "all conditions and warranties implied by law are excluded." The truck delivered by the seller was slightly used and did not correspond to the description. The buyer in this case was entitled to reject the truck, as he did not receive what he contracted for (a new truck).[39] The particular thrust of most cases on exemption clauses is to limit the extent to which a seller may avoid liability. Many cases of this nature are decided on the basis of fundamental breach, or on the basis of strict interpretation of the seller's duties under the agreement. Additional protection is afforded to consumers in most provinces and territories by limiting or eliminating entirely the seller's right to exclude implied conditions and warranties in contracts for the sale of consumer goods.[40]

The protection of the consumer has been carried one step further in some jurisdictions. Not only is the seller prevented from excluding implied warranties and conditions from the contract in a consumer sale, but any verbal warranties or conditions expressed at the time of the sale not included in a written agreement would also be binding on the seller.[41] In addition, consumer protection legislation often provides a **cooling-off period** for certain consumer sales contracts made elsewhere than at the seller's place of business. This allows the buyer to avoid the contract by giving notice of his or her intention to the seller within a specified period of time after the contract is made. The most common type of contract of this nature is one in which a door-to-door salesperson sells goods to a consumer in the consumer's home.[42] The purpose of the cooling-off period is to allow buyers to examine the contracts at their leisure after the seller has left. If, after reviewing their actions, the buyers decide that they do not wish to proceed with the contract, they may give the seller notice in writing within the specified period (usually 48 hours) and the contract will be terminated. In each case of this kind,

---

38. Ibid., s. 30(2).
39. *Andrews Bros. (Bournemouth) Ltd. v. Singer & Co. Ltd.,* [1934] 1 K.B. 17.
40. Consumer Protection Act, R.S.O. 1990, c. C-31, s. 44a(2).
41. Business Practices Act, R.S.O. 1990, c. B-18, s. 4.
42. Consumer Protection Act, R.S.O. 1990, c. C-31, s. 33(1).

where the legislation applies, the contract is essentially in suspension until the cooling-off period expires. It is only then that it becomes operative.

The general trend in consumer protection legislation in recent years has been to impose greater responsibility on the seller in the sale of goods. While the rule of *caveat emptor* is still very much alive, the right of the buyer to avoid a contract has been expanded beyond the normal rights of the commercial buyer. The justification for the change is based upon the premise that the buyer and seller are no longer the equals presumed by contract law. Many sales are offered on a "take it or leave it basis." In other instances, high pressure selling techniques or methods have placed the buyer at a particular disadvantage. The widespread use of exemption clauses has also been a factor that prompted legislation to redress the balance in negotiating power and to ensure honesty on the part of sellers in their dealings with buyers.

CONTRACTUAL DUTIES OF THE BUYER

Apart from the general duty of the buyer to promptly examine goods sent on approval, or to compare goods delivered to a sample, the buyer has a duty to take delivery and pay for the goods as provided in the contract of sale or in accordance with the Sale of Goods Act. The delivery of the goods and the payment of the price are concurrent conditions in a sale, unless the parties have provided otherwise.[43] For example, if the contract is silent on payment time and place, then the buyer would be obliged to pay a reasonable price at the time of the delivery of the goods.[44]

Payment is not a condition under the contract unless the parties specifically make it so. Under the act, payment is treated as a mere warranty.[45] As such, it would not entitle the seller to avoid performance if the buyer failed to pay at the prescribed time. The seller would, however, have the right to claim against the buyer for breach of the warranty and to recover any damages the seller might have suffered as a result of the buyer's default.[46]

REMEDIES OF THE BUYER

Rescission

The seller is subject to a number of conditions and warranties in addition to those that may be set out in the contract itself. The rights of the buyer under the contract are, for the most part, governed by the manner in which the seller fulfills the contract terms, and the manner in which the seller complies with the various implied warranties and conditions. If the seller's breach of the agreement is a breach of a condition or a breach that goes to the very root of the agreement (for example, something that the courts would treat as a fundamental breach), the buyer may be in a position to repudiate the contract and reject the goods. Where a buyer is entitled to repudiate the contract, the buyer also has the right to refuse payment of the purchase price; or if the buyer has already paid the price, or a part of it, the buyer may recover it from the seller. The buyer has an alternate remedy in a case where the seller fails to deliver the goods. The buyer may purchase the

---

43. Sale of Goods Act, R.S.O. 1990, c. S-1, ss. 26, 27.

44. Ibid., s. 9(2).

45. Ibid., s. 47.

46. Ibid., s. 47.

goods elsewhere then sue the seller for the difference between the contract price and the price paid in the market.[47]

Damages

In some cases, the seller may be in breach of contract, but only of a minor term, or one that does not go to the root of the contract. For example, in a contract where the seller is obliged to deliver goods according to sample by installments at a fixed price each, the seller may make one delivery that is slightly deficient. In that case the buyer would not be entitled to repudiate the contract as a whole, but only the particular installment.[48] "Microscopic" variation in deliveries, however, would not likely be treated as a breach of contract.[49] If the contract is not severable and the buyer has accepted the goods, or a part of them, or where the contract is for specific goods and the property in the goods has passed to the buyer, the breach of any condition by the seller may only be treated as a breach of warranty. Thus, the buyer would not be entitled to reject the goods or repudiate the agreement unless entitled to do so by an express or implied term in the agreement to that effect.[50] The buyer, if he or she elects to do so, may treat any breach of a condition as a breach of warranty. In that case the contract would continue to be binding on the buyer, but the buyer would be entitled to sue the seller for **damages** arising out of the breach.[51]

Specific Performance

A third remedy is available to the buyer on rare occasions. If the goods in question have some unique or special attribute or nature, and cannot be readily obtained elsewhere, monetary damages may not be adequate as a remedy if the seller refuses to make delivery. Under such circumstances, the remedy of **specific performance** may be available to the buyer at the discretion of the courts.[52] Unless the contract is for the sale of something in the nature of a rare antique or work of art, however, the courts are unlikely to award the remedy, as monetary damages are normally adequate in most sales transaction.

REMEDIES OF THE SELLER

Lien

The remedies available to the seller in the event of a breach of the contract of sale are to some extent dependent upon the passing of the title to the buyer, as well as the right of the seller to retain the goods. These rights may be exercised either against the buyer personally, or against the goods themselves, depending upon the circumstances and the nature of the remedy. The seller normally may not repudiate the contract in the event of non-payment by the buyer, unless payment has been made a condition in the contract. The seller, however, is not obliged under

---

47. Ibid., s. 49.
48. *Jackson v. Rotax Motor & Cycle Co.,* [1910] 2 K.B. 937.
49. *Shipton, Anderson & Co. v. Weil Bros. & Co.,* [1912] 1 K.B. 574.
50. Sale of Goods Act, R.S.O. 1990, c. S-1, s. 12(3). See also *O'Flaherty v. McKinlay,* [1953] 2 D.L.R. 514.
51. Sale of Goods Act, R.S.O. 1990, c. S-1, s. 12(1).
52. Ibid., s. 50.

the Sale of Goods Act to deliver the goods, unless payment is made or credit terms are granted by the seller for the purchase in question.[53] In this respect, the seller may claim a **lien** on the goods. This may be done if the sale is a cash sale, or if the sale is a credit sale and the period of credit has expired as, for example, where the goods are sold on a "lay-away" plan. The seller may also claim a lien on the goods if the buyer should become insolvent before the goods are delivered.[54] A seller's lien depends, of course, upon possession of the goods. If the seller should voluntarily release the goods to the buyer, the right of lien may be lost.

Action for the Price

If the seller has delivered the goods to the buyer, and the title has passed, the seller may sue the buyer for the price of the goods.[55] An **action for the price** would also lie where the title has not passed but the seller delivered the goods, and where delivery was refused by the buyer. In this case, the seller has no obligation to press the goods on the buyer, but may simply sue the buyer for the price.[56] The seller must, of course, be prepared to deliver the goods if the seller recovers the price.

Damages

A more common remedy available to the seller is ordinary **damages** for non-acceptance. This remedy permits the seller to resell the goods to another, and sue the buyer for the loss incurred.[57] The damages that the seller may recover would probably be the monetary amount necessary to place the seller in the same position as he or she would have been in had the transaction been completed. The amount would either be the profit lost on the sale, or perhaps the difference between the disposal price of the goods (if the seller sold them privately) and the contract price.

Retention of Deposit

A feature common of many contracts is a clause that entitles the seller to **retain any deposit** paid as liquidated damages if the buyer should refuse to perform the contract. A deposit is not necessary in a written agreement to render it binding on the parties. However, its advantages would be to circumvent the requirements of writing under the Sale of Goods Act if the contract is unwritten, and if it is for more than the stipulated minimum. The second advantage (from the seller's point of view) is that it represents a fund that the seller might look to in the event of a breach of the agreement by the buyer. If the agreement provides for the payment of a deposit by the buyer and also provides that, in the event of default by the buyer, the seller might retain the deposit as liquidated damages, then if the default

---

53. Ibid., s. 39(1). See also *Lyons (J.L.) v. May & Baker* (1922), 129 L.T. 413.
54. Sale of Goods Act, R.S.O. 1990, c. S-1, s. 39(1).
55. Ibid., s. 47(1).
56. Ibid., s. 47(2).
57. Ibid., s. 48.

should occur, the seller would possess funds sufficient to cover the estimated loss. The amount of the deposit required, however, must be an honest estimate by the parties of the probable loss that the seller would suffer if the buyer should default. If it does not represent an honest estimate, in the sense that the payment is a substantial part of the purchase price rather than a deposit, the seller may not retain the part-payment. However, the seller would be obliged to return the excess over and above the actual loss flowing from the buyer's default.[58]

Stoppage in Transitu

An additional remedy available to the seller, in cases where the seller has shipped the goods by carrier to the buyer, is **stoppage in transitu**. If the seller has parted with the goods, but discovers that the buyer is insolvent, he or she may contact the carrier and have delivery stopped. "Insolvent" does not mean in this instance the actual bankruptcy of the buyer. It means only that the buyer is no longer meeting his or her debts as they fall due. A particular difficulty associated with this remedy relates to this fact. If the seller should stop delivery, and if the buyer is not insolvent, the buyer may claim compensation from the seller for the loss caused by the wrongful stoppage of the goods. However, if the buyer should be insolvent, and the seller is successful in stopping the carrier before delivery is made, then the title will not pass to anyone who has notice of the stoppage. If the seller fails to contact the carrier in time, and the goods have been delivered to the buyer or the buyer's agent, it is too late, and the title will be in the buyer.[59] The same would hold true if the buyer had sold the goods to a bona fide purchaser for value and without notice of the stoppage.

Resale

The act of stopping the goods in transit does not affect the contract between the buyer and the seller. It simply represents a repossession of the goods by the seller. The seller is then entitled to retain the goods pending tender of payment of the price by the buyer. If the buyer does not tender payment, then the seller has the right to resell the goods to a second purchaser, and the second purchaser will obtain a good title to the goods.[60]

SUMMARY

The sale of goods represents one of the most common business and consumer transactions. The law of contract in general applies to the sale, but legislation entitled the "Sale of Goods Act" sets out the special rules that apply to this type of contract. Two forms of contract of sale are covered by the act: the sale and the agreement to sell. The former applies to specific goods, and the latter to goods that are not yet manufactured or not yet available for delivery. The property in the goods under a contract of sale passes when the parties stipulate that it will pass.

---

58. *Stevenson v. Colonial Homes Ltd.* (1961), 27 D.L.R. (2d) 698; see also *R.V. Ward Ltd. v. Bignall*, [1967] 2 All E.R. 449.

59. *Plischke v. Allison Bros. Ltd.*, [1936] 2 All E.R. 1009.

60. Sale of Goods Act, R.S.O. 1990, c. S-1, s. 46(2).

However, if no time is mentioned, then a series of rules in the act will apply to make this determination. Risk of loss follows the title and, as a result, the time that the title passes is important. Under a contract of sale, a buyer and seller may fix the terms. However, if the parties do not do so, the act contains a number of implied conditions and warranties that will apply to the contract and to the goods. Implied conditions and warranties, among other things, require the seller to provide goods of merchantable quality at the time for delivery, in the right quantity, and at the right place, and to provide a good title to the goods delivered.

In most provinces and territories, under consumer protection legislation, consumer goods contracts may not contain exemption clauses that would eliminate implied warranties and conditions. If a seller acts in breach of a condition (which is a fundamental or major term), under certain circumstances the buyer may treat the contract as at an end and be relieved from any further obligations to perform. A breach of a warranty, which, in contrast to a condition, is only a minor term, simply entitles the buyer to sue for damages. The buyer is not entitled to avoid the contract. The buyer may, at his or her option, treat the breach of a condition as a breach of a warranty if desired.

If a breach of contract on the part of the seller occurs, the buyer may, in the case of a breach of a condition, obtain either rescission or damages. But for a breach of a warranty, the buyer would only be entitled to damages. In rare instances, a buyer may be granted specific performance of the contract if the subject-matter is unique.

The seller has six possible remedies if the buyer refuses delivery or fails to pay the price. The seller is entitled to take action for the price or claim a lien on the goods until payment is made, if the goods are still in the seller's possession. If the buyer rejects the goods and the seller must resell them, the seller may sue for the loss, or the seller may retain any deposit paid as liquidated damages if the contract so provides. Finally, if the seller ships the goods to the buyer and then discovers the buyer is insolvent, the seller may stop delivery and hold the goods until payment is made, or resell them to a second buyer. If a resale is made, the second buyer will obtain a good title to the goods, notwithstanding the prior sale to the original buyer.

DISCUSSION QUESTIONS

1. Distinguish a *sale* from an *agreement to sell.* Why and when is this distinction important?
2. Why is the time of passage of title important in the sale of goods?
3. What are the implications of an unconditional contract for the sale of specific goods in a deliverable state?
4. Indicate the significance of *notice* in the sale of goods.
5. Outline the contractual duties of a seller under the Sale of Goods Act.
6. What implied warranties are part of a sale of goods?
7. Distinguish between a *warranty* and a *condition.* Why is this distinction important?
8. Explain the significance of *caveat emptor* in the sale of goods.
9. Under what circumstances would a buyer of goods be entitled to rescind the contract? Give an example.
10. Outline the remedies available to a seller of goods if the buyer fails to comply with the contract.
11. Explain *stoppage in transitu.*

12. Under what circumstances would the skill and judgement of the seller give rise to an implied warranty or condition upon which the buyer might rely?

13. If goods that are the subject matter of a contract for sale are stolen by a thief during the *cooling-off period,* who bears the loss — the buyer or the seller?

MINI-CASE PROBLEMS

1. A wished to buy paint for a dock he had built at his cottage, so he visited the local paint store to obtain something suitable. He asked the clerk for dock paint that would not peel under damp weather conditions. A mentioned that he had heard Brand X was good, but wished to have the clerk's opinion as to its suitability for use on a dock. The clerk said it was "Okay as a paint," and A purchased a quantity.

Several months after the paint was applied to the dock, it began to peel and fall off the surface.

If the paint supplier refused to accept responsibility for the suitability of the paint, outline the rights of A.

2. Fresh Fruit Juice Co. agreed to supply one hundred 250-litre drums of concentrated apple juice to the Institutional Food Produce Corporation, with delivery not later than October 31st.

On October 30th, the seller delivered one hundred and twenty-five 200-litre drums of the concentrate to the purchaser's plant. The purchaser rejected the goods because they were in the small drums rather than the 250-litre size.

Discuss the rights of the parties.

JUDICIAL DECISION

The judicial decision in this chapter illustrates the type of problem that may arise where a seller provides goods that are unfit for the use intended by the buyer.

The judge discusses the fact that the buyer relied on the skill of the seller to provide the appropriate equipment for the buyer's needs, and the equipment failed to do the work expected of it. The judge concludes that the failure of the equipment amounted to a fundamental breach of the contract.

Sale of Goods — Goods Unfit for Buyer's Purpose — Remedies of Buyer

Public Utilities Com'n for City of Waterloo v. Burroughs Business Machines Ltd. et al., [1973] 2 O.R. 472.

The treasurer of the plaintiff commission, D.J. Black, wrote a letter to the defendant for information concerning computers made by the defendant. Several conversations took place between Mr. Black and a Mr. Murdoch of the defendant corporation. Following this the defendant submitted a proposal for an equipment system that it alleged would perform a number of the billing and accounting services of the plaintiff commission.

The equipment was eventually purchased and installed, but failed to operate satisfactorily. The purchaser then brought an action for rescission of the contract.

DONOHUE, J.:

Mr. Black testified that in his invitation letter to manufacturers of business machines he specified unit record equipment.

When the Burroughs' man came to call on Waterloo Public Utilities Commission in answer to the invitation of March 1967, he told Mr. Black that Burroughs did not have unit record equipment but had something better, namely, the E4000 computer.

Mr. Black also states that in discussing Burrough's equipment there appeared to be no problem about who would programme the machine. Further, Mr. Murdoch stated that Burroughs had a lot of experience in public utilities requirements for business machine operators. Mr. Black denies that Burroughs asked that they be allowed to put one of their men into Waterloo Public Utilities Commission in order to survey the latter's needs.

I am satisfied that the machine or system called the E4000 and its complementary units supplied to the plaintiff was incapable of doing the work which the plaintiff specified. It was not faulty programming by the plaintiff's employees which was the real cause of the trouble and error. If there were such faulty work by such employees, it was part of Burroughs Company's responsibility in the matter to see to it that the programming was not faulty. As Jerry Thompson, one of Burroughs' employees, said in evidence "without a system the hardware is useless". The system was part of the package which Burroughs was selling to the plaintiff and, in my view, it was the responsibility of Burroughs to see to it that the programming was right and that the hardware would process the programmes efficiently.

If, as Burroughs Company asserts, there were faults in the programming done by the plaintiff's employees, it seems to me that evidence could have been put forward of specific instances of such faults. No such evidence was introduced. Further, computer programmes can be corrected or amended. As stated, I find against this contention on the part of Burroughs Company.

It is, I think, unnecessary for me to make findings as to the various causes of failures or breakdowns of the equipment. However, one such cause was referred to by witnesses both for the plaintiff and Burroughs Company as follows: part of the system's function was to print on a customer's bill the name and address of the customer and other data. This printing function involved such a large amount of movement in the machines that the wear and tear was excessive and brought on frequent breakdowns.

As I have already stated, the machine or machines or system supplied by Burroughs Company simply could not do the job which the plaintiff specified. Here the plaintiff was relying on the skill or judgment of Burroughs Company and there arose an implied warranty on the part of Burroughs Company that the equipment which was supplied was fit for the plaintiff's purposes.

The exclusionary clause in s. 15, para. 1 of the *Sale of Goods Act* which relates to the purchase of goods by their patented or trade name does not apply here because, first, it was not a single machine which was supplied but a combination of machines. Further, it would appear by Mr. Murdoch's own letter, ex. 28, that the machine had not even been designed at the time of the contract. Further, it appears that this machine or system was tailored to the plaintiff's requirements.

The failure to do the job amounts to a fundamental breach of warranty which entitled the plaintiff to an order for rescission of the contract which I grant. Damages arising upon a fundamental breach of contract are at large: *R.G. McLean Ltd. v. Canadian Vickers Ltd. et al.,* [1971] O.R. 207, 15 D.L.R. (3d) 15.

The rescission of the contract determines that Burroughs Company owns the equipment involved in the transaction and is, of course, at liberty to remove the same and has an obligation to do so.

CASE PROBLEMS
FOR
DISCUSSION

Case 1

Henderson contacted a local refrigeration contractor with a view to obtaining an air-conditioner for use in the beverage-room of his hotel. He explained to the contractor that he wished to install a device that would not only cool the room, but remove tobacco smoke as well. The contractor described a number of room air-conditioners (for which he was the local distributor). He recommended a particular model that he indicated was adequate for a room the size of Henderson's beverage-room. Henderson entered into a contract for the model suggested by the contractor and had the equipment installed.

After the equipment was put into operation, Henderson discovered that the equipment did an adequate job of cooling the room, but did not remove the smoke to any significant extent. He complained to the contractor, but the contractor was unable to alter the equipment to increase its smoke-removal capacity. When the contractor refused to exchange the air-conditioner for a larger model, Henderson refused to pay for the equipment. The contractor then brought an action against him for the amount of the purchase price.

Discuss the issues raised in this case and indicate how a judge might decide the matter.

Case 2

Grant planned to spend his winter vacation at a ski resort in the Rockies. In preparation for the holiday, he purchased a new ski outfit from a local sports clothing merchant.

The first time that he wore his new ski outfit he noticed that his wrists had become swollen and irritated where the knitted cuffs of the jacket contacted his skin. He wore the jacket the second day, but found that after skiing for a short time, he had to return to the lodge because his wrists had again become badly irritated and had blistered.

Grant required medical treatment for the injury to his wrists. The cause of the injury was determined to be a corrosive chemical that had been used to bleach the knitted cuffs of his jacket. The chemical was one that was normally used to bleach fabric. However, from the evidence, the chemical had not been removed from the material before the cloth was shipped to the manufacturer of the jacket. Neither the manufacturer nor the retailer were aware of the chemical in the cloth, and its existence could not be detected by ordinary inspection.

The injury to Grant's wrists ruined his holiday and prevented his return to work for a week following his vacation.

Discuss the rights (if any) and liability (if any) of Grant, the sports clothing merchant, the manufacturer of the jacket, and the manufacturer of the cloth.

Case 3

Small Parts Manufacturing Co. entered into an agreement with Foremost Forging Co. to have an automated stamping press made for it. The agreement called for the construction of the press and its preparation for pick-up by a carrier which Small Parts Manufacturing would designate, not later than March 1st. Payment terms were 50% payable at the time of signing the agreement, with the balance of the price payable on March 1st.

On February 25th, the construction of the press was complete. Foremost Forging informed Small Parts Manufacturing that the press was now ready for pick-up by the transport company. The parties agreed that the press would be turned over to the carrier as soon as pick-up could be arranged.

The press was placed in Foremost Forging's warehouse for the carrier to pick up. However, on February 26th, the press was destroyed when an unknown arsonist set fire to the warehouse building.

Discuss the rights (if any) and the liability (if any) of the parties in this case. Indicate the possible outcome of the case if legal action should be taken.

Case 4

A wholesaler in Toronto agreed to sell 2000 cases of walnut pieces to a buyer in Vancouver. The price was to be $1.10 a kilo with delivery F.O.B. Toronto. The goods were shipped by common carrier in accordance with the buyer's instructions.

The goods were subject to moisture and freezing during transit, and the buyer, on inspection of the goods, found them unfit for his purposes. The goods were then sold by the buyer for 66 cents a kilo in Vancouver, while the goods were still in the hands of the carrier. In the meantime, the carrier had found a buyer willing to purchase the 2000 cases of walnuts at 88 cents a kilo. However, the carrier was unable to complete the sale because of the buyer's actions.

The Vancouver merchant later brought an action against the Toronto wholesaler and the carrier for his loss calculated at 44 cents a kilo.

Indicate the nature of the plaintiff's claim in this action and the defences that might be raised by the defendants. Render a decision.

Case 5

Davy Crockett, a northern Alberta farmer, ordered a set of logs for the construction of a log home from a lumber company that advertised log houses for sale in a back-to-the-land magazine. The magazine advertisement stated that the house was in kit form, and claimed that any qualified builder could construct it in less than ten days. The advertisement recommended hiring a qualified builder. However, it indicated that any person who had experience in house construction could probably do the work, but the result would be his or her own responsibility.

Crockett ordered the log kit early in March for delivery in the second week of April. The logs did not arrive until late May, however, when Crockett was busy planting his crop. He was unable to begin construction during the summer months, due to an injured hand; and during the fall months he was busy with his harvest. When Crockett was ready to build in late October, he unwrapped the logs and discovered that a large number of them were warped and unsuitable for construction. The lumber company normally instructed buyers to construct the house promptly on delivery, or at least within 14 days of receipt, to avoid warping. However, they had failed to do so in Crockett's case because of the late delivery. The company refused to refund Crockett's money or take back the log kit.

Crockett continued to correspond with the company concerning the logs. Eventually, some months later, the company agreed to replace the logs that had warped. When Crockett was finally able to begin construction a few weeks later, he discovered that because the replacement logs had experienced a different drying or seasoning time, they would not fit properly with the remainder of the logs in the kit. He then brought an action for rescission against the lumber company.

Discuss the arguments that might be raised in this case. Render a decision.

Case 6

A Swiss corporation entered into a contract with the Canadian Dairy Commission to purchase anhydrous milk fat for the production of condensed milk. The contract was executed in Canada by a New York agent of the corporation, who provided that the goods be shipped to Algeria. The Commission was advised that it was to meet the import conditions of the Algerian government, and payment was to be made on presentation of a clean bill of lading and proper certificates of analysis of the goods.

While they met the contract stipulations in Canada, the goods were rejected by the Algerian authorities because the caps on the drums had not been sealed and some of the caps had loosened during shipment, allowing the contents to spoil.

The Swiss corporation then brought an action against the Commission for rescission and reimbursement of the contract price.

Discuss the arguments that the parties might raise and render a decision.

Case 7

Stubert operated a produce brokerage, buying agricultural produce and reselling it to any of 30 smaller independent regional distributors. Each distributor served an area no greater than a city, and some competed with one another. The distributors generally sold to the independent convenience stores, and vied for institutional sales such as hospital kitchens.

Stubert visited a farmers co-operative in an agricultural area, and after some discussion secured a truckload of tomatoes at the wholesale market price for Number 1 Grade Hothouse Tomatoes.

Three weeks later, a commercial freight company truck arrived in Stubert's part of the province, with the tomatoes. Stubert had the driver open the van, and he looked at the frames of cello-packed tomatoes visible from the door. They appeared fine, so he handed over his $4400 bank draft to the driver in return for the bill of lading.

He endorsed the bill of lading, and gave it back to the driver with instructions to him to carry on, as was often the case, to one of his bigger customers, a distributor in the next town. The driver was to turn over the bill of lading against a payment of $6700.

When the driver returned to Stubert's premises, he had no payment to deliver, but rather, he still had the entire load of tomatoes. The distributor had insisted on unloading the tomatoes before payment. He had found that while the tomatoes near the doors were Number 1 Hothouse, those beyond the doors were at best Number 3 Hothouse, or perhaps even Field Grade. The distributor rejected the shipment, packed it back on the truck, and sent the driver back to Stubert. Stubert demanded a return of his bank draft, and ordered the tomatoes to be returned to the co-operative. The driver said his company rule was that a driver is to always leave the load with the last person who pays, and that one never returns money once it is received. Accordingly, he off-loaded "Stubert's" tomatoes despite the protests of Stubert, and drove away.

Advise the parties, including a commentary on the trucking company's policy. Render a decision.

CHAPTER 22

Consumer Protection Legislation

INTRODUCTION

Business organizations for the most part attempt to establish sound and on-going relationships with their suppliers and customers. This is so because continuing relationships with customers and suppliers represent the most efficient and profitable way for a firm to operate in today's competitive market. To achieve this goal, most businesses follow policies of fair dealing and honesty in their contractual relationships with customers and the advertising of their goods or services. However, not all business organizations adhere to the high ethical standards of fairness and honesty, and some legislative control is necessary in order to protect the public from unscrupulous operators.

Unfortunately, consumer protection legislation is not uniform throughout Canada, as it falls partly within provincial jurisdiction, and in part within the federal sphere of legislative powers. The result has been a complex "mix" of federal and provincial statutes, each designed to redress some real or perceived unfairness in the marketplace.

HISTORICAL DEVELOPMENT

Laws protecting the consumer are not a new phenomenon. The state has always attempted to protect its constituents from both real and imaginary harm at the hands of unscrupulous merchants. Many of the early laws were concerned with the control of suppliers of food and clothing rather than durable goods. They reflected the particular concerns of the populace in the marketplace at that time. Bakers in Paris, France, for example, were subject to inspection as early as 1260. Any bread that they produced for sale that was of insufficient weight was subject to confiscation and distribution to the poor folk in the city. How uniform weights were determined undoubtedly raised some difficulties for the bakers. However, by 1439 under the reign of Charles VII, the problem was solved in part by an ordinance requiring the municipal magistrates to designate a place for the weights to be kept and grain and flour to be weighed. By 1710, the consumer information movement was under way, with the bakers required to mark each loaf of bread with its weight. Again, any loaf that failed to correspond to the actual weight was confiscated, and the baker subject to a fine.[1] Similar consumer protection laws were placed on the statute books in England, and later in the colonies. They were the forerunners of present-day consumer protection legislation, and serve to remind us that consumer protection is not something unique to our modern consumer society.

Governments have seldom been reluctant to pass legislation governing the activities of parties to commercial transactions where the safety or the welfare of the citizenry was concerned, but consumer protection has been subject to varying degrees of emphasis by lawmakers throughout English history. Merchants were subject to much control during the guild period, and after that, during the fifteenth to eighteenth centuries, to a somewhat lesser degree of control. The rise of *laissez faire* and the concept of a contract as a bargain struck between individuals, however, resulted in a shift to *caveat emptor* as a consumer rights philosophy. In general, the common law courts only attempted to inject an element of fairness into contracts between buyers and sellers where bargaining power was relatively unequal. What it did not do, however, was protect the careless buyer, as the courts saw (and to some extent still see) little reason why the law should do so.

Modern consumer protection legislation is essentially a response to changes in technology and marketing practice. The major changes in technology, manufacturing, and distribution that had their beginnings in the late nineteenth century brought with them fundamental changes in the sale of goods to consumers. To an increasing extent, throughout the first half of the twentieth century, goods became more complex. New scientific advances spawned a vast array of durable goods for household use, sometimes so complex that they were not easily understood and were not self-serviceable. As mechanical products became more technical, so too did the chances of breakdown and costly repairs. Concurrent with the development of new household goods was the widespread use of limited warranties and the use of exclusionary clauses to eliminate the warranty protection offered by the Sale of Goods Act.[2]

The change to large-scale manufacturing also removed the manufacturer from the immediate area where the consumer resided. It was no longer possible to seek out the maker for repairs, nor was it as important to the manufacturer to satisfy every consumer complaint. The retailer first provided the level of service required to satisfy consumers in order to protect his or her own reputation in the community. However, as the high service retailers were forced to compete with the discount sellers of the late 1950s and the 1960s (who offered no after-service), the situation changed. Service by retailers gradually declined, and with the decline, the frustration of consumers mounted. When consumer complaints to manufacturers went unheeded, the consumers turned to the legislators for assistance.

Political response was not uniform throughout Canada, rather it reflected the

1. An interesting account of the development of the ordinances under which bakers in Paris were obliged to carry on business may be found in P. Montague, *Larousse Gastronomique* (N.Y.: Crown Publishers Inc., 1961), pp. 78-80.
2. The Sale of Goods Act, R.S.O. 1990, c. S-1.

major complaints of consumers in particular jurisdictions. In most provinces, the initial changes took the form of laws that prevented sellers from excluding the implied warranties of the Sale of Goods Act in contracts for the sale of consumer goods.[3] Other legislation, particularly in Western Canada, required manufacturers to provide parts and service for equipment in the province and, in some provinces, to warrant that the equipment would last for a reasonable period of time in use.[4]

Concern for the safety of users of consumer products also resulted in legislation at both the federal and provincial levels in an attempt to protect consumers from products that had an element of hazard associated with their use. In addition, the 1960s and 1970s saw amendments to the Combines Investigation Act (now called the Competition Act) designed to control misleading advertising, double ticketing of consumer products, bait-and-switch selling, and a number of other questionable selling techniques.

During the same period, legislation was also introduced to deal with a number of other business practices that had developed with respect to credit reporting, credit selling, and selling door-to-door. All governments dealt with these problems, but again, unfortunately, not in a uniform fashion. As a result, considerable variation in consumer protection legislation exists in Canada today. The different laws, for the most part, have much the same general thrust in those jurisdictions where they have been introduced. They may be classified in terms of laws relating to product safety, laws relating to product quality and performance, laws relating to credit granting and credit reporting, and laws directed at business practices in general. Depending upon the nature of the protection required, the laws have generally taken five different approaches: (1) disclosure of information to the consumer; (2) expanded consumer rights at law; (3) minimum standards for safety, quality, and performance; (4) control of sellers and others by way of registration or licensing of the activities and individuals; and (5) the outright prohibition of certain unethical practices. In many cases the legislation may employ two or more of these approaches to protect the consumer. For example, consumer credit reporting organizations in Ontario and other jurisdictions must be licensed or registered and, in addition, are subject to certain disclosure rules for consumer credit information. Since only licensed or registered organizations may carry on consumer credit reporting activities, a failure to comply with the legislation could have as a consequence the loss of the licence to carry on the activity. The various methods of control are examined in greater detail with respect to each of the different types of consumer protection legislation.

CONSUMER SAFETY

Common law remedies are available to consumers injured by defective goods where the seller or manufacturer owes a duty not to injure, but the rights arise only after injury occurs. Governments long ago were quick to realize that consumer protection from hazardous products or services to be effective, must not only compensate for injury, but must contain an incentive for the manufacturer or seller to take care. Consequently, governments everywhere have generally con-

---

3. The Consumer Protection Act, R.S.O. 1990, c. C-31.

4. See, for example, the Consumer Products Warranties Act, R.S.S. 1978, c. 30.

trolled products injurious to the health of consumers, or imposed a duty on the manufacturer or seller of the products to warn the consumer of the hazards associated with the products' use or consumption.

In Canada, the provinces and the federal government have established legislation to control hazardous activities and products. The most notable legislation, however, has been passed at the federal level in the form of a number of statutes relating to consumer goods. These include the Food and Drugs Act[5] and the Hazardous Products Act.[6] Some overlap exists between the two statutes with respect to false or deceptive labelling of products, but the intent of the legislation in each case is to protect the consumer from injury. Both are regulatory in part, and quasi-criminal in nature. The Food and Drugs Act, for example, does not confer a civil right of action as a result of a breach of the statute,[7] but instead, imposes strict liability and penalties under the act where a breach occurs. A manufacturer, therefore, would be strictly liable in the case of false or deceptive labelling of a product.[8]

Both statutes are designed to enhance the public's safety. The Food and Drugs Act has, as a primary purpose, the control of harmful products that could cause injury or illness if improperly used or ingested by consumers. Under the act, many drugs are controlled in an effort to limit their possession and application to proper medical purposes. The legislation also safeguards the purity of food products and regulates matters such as packaging and the advertisement of food and drug products.

The Hazardous Products Act takes a slightly different approach to consumer safety. As the name implies, it is concerned with hazardous products. It either prohibits the manufacture and sale of products of an extremely dangerous character or regulates the sale of those that have the potential to cause injury. Hazardous products sold to the public are usually subject to regulation with respect to packaging, and must bear hazard warnings depending upon their particular nature. In addition to written warnings, most must depict the type of danger inherent in the product by way of warning symbols. Products that are stored under pressure, corrosive substances such as acids, and products that are highly flammable or explosive are required to have these warning symbols printed on their containers.

Some products are subject to a special legislation at the federal level in an effort to protect consumers from injury. The Motor Vehicle Safety Act[9] provides for the establishment of safety standards for motor vehicles and vehicle parts, and for notice to consumers when unsafe parts or other defects are discovered through use or testing. Similar legislation applies to aircraft in Canada,[10] with elaborate testing procedures that must be undertaken and satisfied before the aircraft may be certified as safe to fly. The statute also governs the use and maintenance of all powered and non-powered aircraft in an effort to protect the public from injury. The act not only deals with the safety of the product, but governs the qualifications and licensing of all persons associated with the flying or maintenance of aircraft,

---

5. The Food and Drugs Act, R.S.C. 1985, c. F-27.
6. The Hazardous Products Act, R.S.C. 1985, c. H-3.
7. See, for example, *Heimler v. Calvert Caterers Ltd.* (1974), 49 D.L.R. (3d) 36.
8. *R. v. Westminster Foods Ltd.,* [1971] 5 W.W.R. 300.
9. The Motor Vehicle Safety Act, R.S.C. 1985, c. M-10.
10. The Aeronautics Act, R.S.C. 1985, c. A-2.

since safety is related not only to the maintenance of the product itself, but to the skills of those engaged in its use.

CONSUMER INFORMATION

Consumer information is closely related to both consumer safety and consumer protection from deceptive or unfair practices. For this reason, much of the legislation designed to protect consumers is concerned with either the disclosure of information about the product or service, or the prohibition of false or misleading statements by sellers. Some laws, however, are designed to protect consumers by providing standards by which the consumer may make direct comparisons of products and prices. The **Weights and Measures Act**[11] is one such statute. It is designed to establish throughout Canada a uniform system of weights and measures that may be applied to all goods sold. This act fixes the units of measure that may be lawfully used to determine the quantity of goods and to calculate the price. The statute also provides for the testing and checking of all measuring devices used for such purposes.

A complementary statute at the federal level is the **Consumer Packaging and Labelling Act**[12] that, from a consumer protection point of view, has as its purpose the protection of the public from the labelling and packaging of products in a false or misleading manner.[13] This act provides penalties for violation, but does not provide a civil cause of action for consumers misled by the false labelling. The right to damages for any injury suffered as a result of the misleading label, however (depending upon the circumstances), may be available at common law, or under one of the provincial statutes that provide for such a right of action.

CONSUMER PRODUCT QUALITY AND PERFORMANCE PROTECTION

The first action to protect consumers in the product performance area took the form of consumer protection legislation to prohibit sellers from exempting sales of consumer goods from the implied conditions and warranties available under the Sale of Goods Act. While these moves helped to balance the rights of buyers with those of sellers at the point of sale, after-sale service and provision for repairs were not affected. The change also did nothing to provide persons who obtained consumer goods by way of gift with enforceable rights under the original sale agreement. Manufacturers of inferior goods continued to enjoy relative protection from consumer complaints through the rules relating to privity of contract. For the most part, only the sellers were directly affected in actions for breach of contract. To overcome some of the difficulties faced by consumers, any redress in the balance of rights between buyers and sellers had to clearly come through new legislation directed at specific abuses in the marketplace.

A comparatively recent trend in consumer protection legislation has been towards the expansion of buyers' rights and sellers' obligations with respect to consumer goods that fail to deliver reasonable performance, or that prove to be less durable or satisfactory than manufacturers' claims indicate. New Brunswick[14] and Saskatchewan[15] have both passed legislation of this nature, and other

---

11. The Weights and Measures Act, R.S.C. 1985 c. W-6.

12. The Consumer Packaging and Labelling Act, R.S.C. 1985, c. C-38.

13. *R. v. Steinbergs Ltd.* (1977), 17 O.R. (2d) 559.

14. The Consumer Protection Warranty and Liability Act, S.N.B. 1978, c. C-18.1.

15. The Consumer Products Warranties Act, R.S.S. 1978, c. 30.

provinces appear to be in the process of considering somewhat similar consumer protection.[16]

As a method of addressing consumer complaints about automobile warranties, some provinces have established dispute resolution mechanisms patterned after the U.S. state automobile "lemon laws." Ontario, for example, developed a motor vehicle arbitration plan[17] whereby the automobile manufacturers agreed to resolve consumer warranty complaints related to the operational or reliability qualities of their vehicles by a binding arbitration process. Under this process, if a new automobile has reliability problems which the manufacturer is unable to repair, or if the vehicle possesses numerous defects, the purchaser of the vehicle must first give the manufacturer the opportunity to repair, and if this proves unsuccessful, the dispute may be taken before an arbitrator. The arbitrator hears both sides of the dispute, and then renders a decision. The arbitrator has the authority to direct the manufacturer to repair the defects, take back the vehicle and repay all or a part of the purchase price to the buyer, or dismiss the complaint if it is frivolous or unwarranted. The program applies only to new vehicles during the warranty period, and for a fixed time thereafter. In the case of a vehicle that has so many problems or defects that a manufacturer buy-back is appropriate, the arbitrator is required to determine a usage charge as a deduction from the price if the vehicle has been in the buyer's possession for more than a year. This deduction recognizes the fact that the buyer has had the use of the vehicle during that period of time.

The Saskatchewan legislation, entitled the Consumer Products Warranties Act, substantially alters the contractual relationship between the consumer and the seller by expanding the class of persons entitled to protection under the act, and by imposing heavy burdens on sellers and manufacturers of consumer goods who fail to provide products capable of meeting advertised performance claims. The legislation applies to all sales of consumer goods, and in addition, many goods not normally considered to be products of a consumer nature.[18] It also covers used goods sold by "second-hand" dealers,[19] but permits dealers in used goods to exempt themselves from many of the obligations imposed on sellers under the act if they expressly exclude the warranties at the time of the sale.[20]

The Saskatchewan act defines a consumer in a very broad way in order that not only the immediate purchaser of a consumer product, but also persons who subsequently acquire the goods, may enforce statutory warranty rights under the act. For example, persons who obtain consumer goods by way of gift or inheritance would be entitled to enforce a breach of a statutory warranty, even though no consideration was given to acquire the goods and no direct contractual link may exist between them and the seller. In order to achieve this end, the act provides that a manufacturer may not claim a lack of privity of contract as a defence against a claim by an owner of goods where a breach of a warranty under the act is alleged.[21]

---

16. The Province of Ontario introduced the Consumer Products Warranties Act in 1979 (Bill 110), but the bill did not reach the third reading stage before the session ended.

17. Motor Vehicle Arbitration Plan (Ont. Min. Consumer and Commercial Relations).

18. For example, certain goods used in agriculture and fishing.

19. The Consumer Products Warranties Act, R.S.S. 1978, c. 30, c. 6.

20. Ibid., s. 6(2).

21. Ibid., s. 14.

The legislation sets out a number of statutory warranties that apply to all sales of consumer goods.[22] The majority of these resemble sections of the Sale of Goods legislation in most other provinces. They include a warranty that the retailer has the right to sell the goods and that the goods are free from any liens or encumbrances. Included, as well, are the usual sale of goods warranties as to fitness, etc. The legislation, however, goes beyond the usual types of warranties and includes a requirement that the goods be durable for a reasonable period of time. It also requires a warranty that spare parts and repair facilities will be available for a reasonable time after the date of the sale, if the product is one that normally may be expected to require repair.

In addition to the statutory warranties, the act imposes the obligation on the seller to comply with any or all other warranties or promises for performance made either through advertising, writing, or statements made at the time of sale.[23] These statements or representations are treated as express warranties and are actionable in the event of breach.

The act provides a number of different remedies, depending upon the nature of the breach, and includes exemplary damages as a remedy where the seller or manufacturer willfully acts contrary to the statute.[24] In an effort to reduce litigation arising as a result of the act, provision is made for mediation of disputes by officials of the Saskatchewan Department of Consumer Affairs,[25] and for binding arbitration where the parties agree to have the matter decided by an arbitrator.[26]

Consumers who wish to exercise rights under the act are obliged to do so within a relatively short time after a breach occurs. No action may be brought that alleges a violation of the act unless it is commenced within two years after the alleged violation took place.[27] However, since the rights set out in the act are in addition to any other rights that the person may have at law,[28] the time limit may not affect the ordinary common law remedies available to the consumer.

While consumer groups have advocated similar legislation in all provinces, some concern has been expressed over the introduction of laws if they should vary from province to province. Uniform legislation has been urged upon the provinces if only to provide common consumer rights throughout the country. Whether other provinces heed this admonition remains to be seen.

CONSUMER PROTECTION RELATED TO BUSINESS PRACTICES

Itinerant Sellers

Door-to-door sellers have always presented a special problem for consumers because of the conditions under which the selling takes place. The door-to-door seller conducts business in the prospective buyer's home, and, as a result, the sale is not initiated by the buyer, but rather by the seller. One of the particular difficulties with door-to-door selling is the fact that the buyer cannot leave the premises if the product is not what he or she needs or wants. As a consequence, the buyer

22. Ibid., s. 1
23. Ibid., s. 8.
24. Ibid., s. 28.
25. Ibid., s. 31.
26. Ibid., s. 31.
27. Ibid., s. 30.
28. Ibid., s. 3.

often feels uncomfortable or vulnerable. Under these circumstances, high-pressure or persuasive selling techniques may result in the buyer signing a purchase contract on impulse, or under pressure, simply to get rid of the seller.

While many products sold by door-to-door sellers are of high quality and are sold by reputable firms, the selling practices of the less reputable eventually resulted in consumer demands to have this form of selling brought under legislative control. Most provinces, as a part of their consumer protection legislation, now require door-to-door sellers to be licensed or registered in order to conduct their selling practices and to ensure compliance with the statute and regulations.[29] While variation exists from province to province, door-to-door sales are now usually subject to a "cooling-off period" after the purchase agreement is signed. During this period, the contract remains open to repudiation by the buyer without liability. It is only after the cooling-off period has expired that a firm contract exists between the buyer and the seller.[30]

In addition to the imposition of a cooling-off period, the contract negotiated for the sale of goods by door-to-door sellers, if it exceeds a specified sum, must be in writing. It must also describe the goods sufficiently to identify them, provide an itemized price, and give a full statement of the terms of payment. If a warranty is provided, it must be set out in the agreement, and if the sale is a credit sale, a full disclosure of the credit arrangement, including details of any security taken on the goods, must be provided.[31]

The general thrust of consumer protection legislation of this nature is to nullify or eliminate the use of questionable selling techniques, and to provide sufficient information to the consumer to allow the consumer to review the agreement during the cooling-off period. By providing the consumer with the necessary information, and an opportunity to contemplate the transaction without the presence of the seller, the law encourages the buyer to make a rational buying decision.

Unfair Business Practices

Honest sellers, as well as consumers, suffer when questionable practices are used by unethical merchants to induce consumers to purchase goods. As a result, consumer protection legislation is frequently designed to not only protect the consumer, but to maintain fair competition between merchants in the marketplace. Consumer protection legislation concerning unfair business practices may take the form of general legislation, or it may be directed at specific areas of business activity or sectors of business. Motor vehicle repairs are an example of a sector of business where legislation has been directed toward protecting consumers. Both the province of Quebec and Ontario have specifically targeted automobile repairs for control,[32] and require repair shops to provide written estimates (on request, in the case of Ontario). Repair charges cannot exceed the estimate by more than 10% and a detailed invoice must be provided. The work must also be guaranteed

29. For example, the Consumer Protection Act, R.S.O. 1990, c. C-31, s. 4(1).
30. Ibid., s. 33.
31. Ibid., s. 31.
32. Quebec included this legislation in its Consumer Protection Act. Ontario has separate legislation. See: Motor Vehicle Repair Act, R.S.O. 1990, c. M-43

for a period of time or mileage, and any breakdowns due to faulty work may be charged back to the shop.

While specific legislation is common, the general trend has been for provinces to pass broad legislation concerning all sectors of consumer related business. The Province of Ontario, for example, has a **Business Practices Act**[33] that sets out a list of activities deemed to be unfair practices. These activities include false, misleading, or deceptive representations to consumers as to quality, performance, special attributes, or approval that are designed to induce consumers to enter into purchases of consumer goods or services.[34] This act also covers the negotiation of unconscionable transactions that take advantage of vulnerable consumers, or that result in one-sided agreements in favour of the seller. The kinds of transactions that are considered unconscionable include: (1) those that take advantage of physical infirmity, illiteracy, inability to understand the language, or the ignorance of the consumer; (2) those that have a price that grossly exceeds the value of similar goods on the market; and (3) those contracts in which the consumer has no reasonable probability of making payment of the obligation in full.[35] In addition, transactions that are excessively one-sided in favour of someone other than the consumer, and those in which the conditions are so adverse to the consumer as to be inequitable, are treated in the same fashion. The same part of the act treats misleading statements of opinion upon which the consumer is likely to rely, and the use of undue pressure to induce a consumer to enter into a transaction, as unfair practices.[36]

The list of unfair practices is not limited to those set out in the act, for the legislation provides that additional unfair practices may be proscribed by regulation. The general thrust of the law, however, is to eliminate the specified unfair practices. The legislation provides that any person that engages in any of the enumerated practices commits a breach of the act.[37] While fines are provided as a penalty, the most effective incentive to comply may be found in the sections of the act that permit a consumer to rescind an agreement entered into as a result of the unfair practice, or to obtain damages where rescission is not possible.[38] The act also provides that the courts may award exemplary or punitive damages in cases where the seller has induced the consumer to enter into an unconscionable or inequitable transaction.[39]

The director responsible for the administration of the act has wide powers of investigation[40] and may issue cease-and-desist orders to prevent repeat violations. An added penalty, where violations persist, is the right to cancel the registration of the seller if the seller is engaged in a business that requires registration or a licence to carry on the activity. Safeguards are included in the act to prevent the arbitrary exercise of powers under the act, and limitation periods are included. These require action on the part of the consumer within a relatively short period

33. The Business Practices Act, R.S.O. 1990, c. B-18.

34. Ibid., s. 2(a).

35. Ibid., s. 2(b).

36. Ibid., s. 2(b).

37. Ibid., s. 3.

38. Ibid., s. 4(1).

39. Ibid., s. 4(2) provides for this form of penalty for unfair practices of the type found in s. 2(b) of the act.

40. Ibid., ss. 10 and 11.

of time after an unfair practice occurs, if the consumer wishes to obtain the relief provided by the legislation.[41]

The Ontario Business Practices Act approach has been incorporated in part in the legislation of a number of other provinces, but again, the provinces have not made a concerted effort to establish uniform laws in the area of unfair business practices. At the federal level, however, certain practices have been dealt with under the anti-combines legislation that has nation-wide application.

Restrictive Trade Practices

The **Competition Act**[42] specifically prohibits false and misleading advertising with respect to both price and performance. Provisions in the act also prohibit deceptive practices such as bait-and-switch selling techniques, referral selling, and the charging of the higher price where two price stickers are attached to goods. Resale price maintenance and monopoly practices detrimental to the public interest are also prohibited. A more complete description of these consumer protection measures, and others relating to restrictive trade practices, is presented in the next chapter.

Regulation by License or Registration

In most provinces, many business activities have been subject to licensing and special rules in an effort to control unfair practices that are contrary to the public interest. The sellers of securities, real estate and business brokers, mortgage brokers, motor vehicle dealers, persons dealing in hazardous products, to name a few, are groups that are often subject to laws regulating their activities and practices. By imposing a licensing requirement on the particular activity, compliance with the law becomes necessary in order to maintain the licence, and violations of the statute are accordingly minimized. As a result, most provinces provide for licensing or registration as a means of control of the particular activities in the public interest.

Collection Agencies

A particular business organization that has been singled out by most provinces for the purpose of consumer protection and control is the **collection agency**. Collection agencies play a useful role in the collection of debts, often from delinquent consumers, but many of their collection methods in the past aroused the ire of debtors. As a result of complaints to provincial governments, all provinces now regulate collection agencies by way of licences or registration, and their activities are subject to a considerable degree of control.[43]

In general, collection agencies are not permitted to harass or threaten the debtor in any way, nor are they permitted to use demands for payment that bear a resemblance to a summons or other official legal or court form. The legislation also prohibits the agency from attempting to collect the debt from persons not liable for the debt, such as the debtor's family, or by harassing persons other than

---

41. The act provides that steps to rescind the agreement must be taken by the consumer within six months of the date the transaction was entered into. See the Business Practices Act, R.S.O. 1990, c. B-18, s.s. 4(5), s. 4(5).

42. The Combines Investigation Act, (now called the Competition Act) R.S.C. 1985 c. C-34 as amended.

43. The Collection Practices Act, R.S.A. 1980 c. C-17, c. 47; the Collections Agencies Act, R.S.O. 1990, c. C-14.

the debtor in an effort to pressure the debtor into payment. As well, the agency is usually not permitted to communicate with the debtor's employer, except to verify employment, unless the debtor has consented to the contract. These are but a few of the limitations on collection techniques of the agencies, but they serve to indicate the attempts by the provincial legislatures to balance the legitimate rights of creditors to obtain payment with protection of the debtor from undue pressure to make payment. Again, the laws relating to this form of consumer protection lack uniformity, but in each case the method of control of the activity remains similar. Agencies that persistently violate the act may find that the province has revoked their licence to operate.

CREDIT GRANTING AND CREDIT REPORTING CONSUMER PROTECTION

The granting of credit by a lender or seller depends to a large extent upon the credit rating of the consumer who wishes to borrow or the buyer who wishes to purchase goods on credit.

For many years, lenders of money and sellers of goods on credit were not obliged to disclose to the borrower or buyer more than a minimum amount of information concerning the credit extended. Even then, it was usually only in the form of the promissory note, mortgage, or other documents that secured or evidenced the actual loan or credit sale. In many cases, the borrower was unaware of the true cost of credit, because the lender often made special charges for arranging or servicing the loan and added these to the amount that the debtor was obliged to pay. The lack of information, together with the inability to fully understand the documents signed to secure the loan, left the debtor bewildered and often at the mercy of the lender or seller.

The widespread use of consumer credit following the Second World War, along with consumer complaints, prompted governmental review of lending practices and credit selling. This resulted in legislation that requires the lender or seller to disclose the true cost of credit to the borrower or credit buyer at the outset of the transaction. During the last two decades, virtually all provincial legislatures have established the requirement that the borrower be provided with a written statement that discloses the total dollar cost of credit, including any charges, bonuses, or amounts that the borrower must pay in addition to the interest, as well as the interest amount. The cost of the credit must also be displayed as an annual percentage rate.

The general thrust of the legislation is toward consumer credit in the form of consumer loans and credit purchases. Consequently, long-term financing such as housing or other substantial purchases that utilize a land mortgage as security are treated as exempt transactions in a number of provinces.[44] The penalties imposed for a failure to comply with the disclosure requirements, unfortunately, vary from province to province. However, the legislation generally prevents the lender from collecting the full amount of interest set out in the loan document. Some provinces prohibit the lender from claiming other than the principal amount of the loan; one province limits the lender to an amount fixed by the courts if the lender should attempt to recover on the loan;[45] another province limits the lender to the legal rate.[46]

---

44. All provinces except Alberta, British Columbia, and Manitoba.

45. Consumer Reporting Act, R.S.N.S. 1989, c. 93, s.11 (1)(b).

46. The Consumer Protection Act, R.S.M. 1987, c. C-200.

Disclosure of a different nature that is nevertheless related to consumer credit is **credit reporting**. Credit reporting agencies for many years have provided an important service to lenders and credit sellers by supplying credit reports on borrowers or credit buyers. The widespread use of credit, coupled with the relatively impersonal nature of credit sales, created a need for quick and accurate information about prospective debtors to enable the lender or seller to decide promptly if credit should be extended. Agencies providing this type of service keep files on persons using credit. They generally include in the file all information that might have an effect on a person's ability to pay. The information is usually stored in a computer, and, through nation-wide hook-ups, credit reporting organizations are usually in a position to provide credit information on borrowers anywhere in the country on relatively short notice.

The potential for error, however, becomes greater as the amount of information on an individual increases. Concern over the uses made of the information, and its accuracy, have resulted in new laws designed to control the type and use of the collected information, and to enable the consumer to examine the information for accuracy. Once again, variation exists from province to province, but generally the laws are designed to license the consumer credit reporting agencies and limit access to the information to those persons who have the consent of the debtor, or to persons with a legitimate right to obtain the information. The nature of the information stored or revealed is also usually subject to the proviso that it be the best reasonably obtainable, and that it be relevant. If a consumer credit reporting agency has collected information on a person, it must permit the person to examine the file and challenge or counter any inaccurate information by way of insertion in the file of other information of an explanatory nature. In most provinces, the agency must also provide the person with the names of all persons who received credit reports during a particular interval of time, although the specifics of this obligation vary from province to province.

Persons who intend to obtain credit reports usually obtain the prospective debtor's permission to do so, but this is not always necessary in all provinces. In many cases, the creditor need only inform the prospective debtor of his or her intention, and the name and address of the agency that the creditor intends to use.[47]

Where credit is refused, or where credit charges are adjusted to reflect a poor credit rating, if the action is based upon a report received from a consumer credit reporting agency, the creditor must generally so advise the person and supply the name and address of the credit reporting agency. The purpose of this latter provision in the legislation is to enable the person refused credit the opportunity to determine if the report was inaccurate in any way, and take steps to correct it. The law is enforced by way of penalties, but serious repeated violations may be dealt with by the revocation of the agency's licence to operate.

SUMMARY

Laws to protect consumers from deceptive or unfair business practices are not new. At common law, for example, a contract entered into as a result of misrepresentation, whether innocent or fraudulent, is voidable at the option of the injured party. In addition, the law of torts provides a remedy where a person is injured as a

---

47. See, for example, the Consumer Reporting Act., R.S.O. 1990, c. C-33.

result of a breach of duty by the seller or manufacturer. The recent flood of legislation in Canada takes a different approach. It is designed to protect the consumer by regulations discouraging deception or unfair practices. The laws attempt to do this by way of penalties that may be imposed upon dishonest merchants who engage in such practices. The legislation also attempts to broaden the group of persons entitled to relief by protecting not only purchasers but the users or recipients of consumer goods as well.

The laws generally fall into a number of different classifications: those designed to protect consumers from hazardous or dangerous products, those designed to provide accurate and useful information and to prohibit deception, and those designed to control activities associated with the actual sale of goods, such as credit and credit information services. Control is generally exercised by licensing persons engaged in the particular activities where such control is considered necessary, or by way of penalties for violation of the legislation where licensing is impractical or unworkable as a means of control.

Unfortunately, there is much overlap in the various statues at the two levels of government, and a lack of uniformity in the approaches taken to consumer protection among the provinces themselves. As a result, in Canada, no uniform consumer protection legislation exists, and consumer rights and protection vary from province to province.

DISCUSSION QUESTIONS

1. Why was it necessary for provincial legislatures to introduce comprehensive consumer protection laws during the post-World War II period?
2. What form did the consumer protection laws take?
3. What controls were generally imposed on sellers of durable goods?
4. Describe the impact of much of the consumer protection legislation on exemption clauses in the sale of goods.
5. How has consumer protection legislation addressed exaggerated advertising claims?
6. Why was it necessary for the Province of Saskatchewan to introduce its Consumer Products Warranties Act?
7. Has consumer protection legislation carried consumer protection too far in terms of the onus it places on the seller? Does this not simply increase the cost of goods to the buyer?
8. Explain the need for legislative control over the selling practices of door-to-door sellers.
9. What is the purpose of the "cooling-off period" that the consumer protection legislation frequently imposes on contractual relations between buyers and door-to-door sellers?
10. Describe some of the practices of credit reporting agencies that resulted in legislative control over their activities.
11. What practices of some collection agencies led to legislation controlling the collection of debts generally?
12. The general thrust of consumer protection legislation has been to provide accurate information or disclosure of essential terms to the buyer. Has consumer protection legislation generally met this goal?
13. Assess the statement: "Consumer protection legislation has increased the cost of selling and, in turn, the price the buyer must pay for the goods purchased. It does nothing to protect the negligent or careless buyer."

**MINI-CASE
PROBLEM**

1. An automobile owner purchased a container of cleaning solvent that was designed for removing rust and dirt from corroded metal parts. The directions indicated that it should be dissolved with 10 parts water to 1 part solvent, and stated that it should not be used full strength. The label bore the symbol for corrosive material and the words: "For Industrial Use Only." The automobile owner diluted the solvent and applied it as directed but, in doing so, accidentally splashed the chemical into his eyes, causing him to lose the sight of one eye. He brought an action for damages against the manufacturer for his injury.

    Discuss and render a decision.

**JUDICIAL
DECISION**

The *Buchan v. Ortho Pharmaceutical (Canada) Ltd.* case examines consumer protection from the point of view that manufacturers have a duty to inform users of their products of any and all risks associated with the use of their products. In this case, the plaintiff was prescribed a birth control pill manufactured by the defendant. Some time later, while still using the drug the plaintiff suffered a stroke. The case examines the duty of care imposed on manufacturers and the issue of whether a warning required under the Food and Drugs Act satisfies the warning onus. The case also raised the issue of whether the duty to warn of dangers is limited to a notification to prescribing physicians or to the users of the prescription drug.

    The trial judge concluded that the duty of care extends beyond a warning as required by the Food and Drugs Act, and must inform the prescribing physician and the patient (user) as well, in order that an informed decision may be made by both the medical practitioner and the patient.

    The defendant appealed the case to the Court of Appeal, but the Court of Appeal in effect reached the same conclusions as the trial court.

**Consumer
Protection —
Duty to Warn
Consumer of
Risks Associated
with Use —
Extent of Duty**

Buchan v. Ortho Pharmaceutical (Canada) Ltd. (1986), 54 O.R. (2d) 92.

The plaintiff was prescribed a birth control drug manufactured by the defendant company. As a result of taking the drug, the plaintiff alleged that she suffered a stroke and was left partially paralysed. Medical evidence indicated a link between the drug and the injury suffered by the plaintiff. The excerpts from the judgement reproduced here deal with a number of the issues raised when the case came before the Court of Appeal.

HOLLAND, J.:

...The gravamen of the plaintiff's case is that Ortho failed to warn of the danger of stroke inherent in the use of the oral contraceptive and that that failure caused or materially contributed to her injuries. There is no question of any defect or impropriety in the manufacture of the oral contraceptive, nor of its efficacy when taken as prescribed.

In holding Ortho liable in negligence for breach of a duty to warn, the trial judge made a number of specific findings, including: (1) that Ortho knew of the association between oral contraceptive use and thromboembolism or stroke; (2) that Ortho was under a common law duty to warn consumers of the dangerous side-effects of the drug both directly (by including a warning on the pill package) and indirectly (by warning physicians of the risk); (3) that Ortho's duty to warn was not discharged merely by warning physicians; (4) that Ortho's compliance with the labelling requirements laid down in the *Food and Drugs Act,*

R.S.C. 1970, c. F-27, and regulations passed thereunder, did not relieve it of the duty to warn consumers and physicians of material risks of which it knew or should have known; (5) that the warning given by Ortho to both consumers and physicians was inadequate, and (6) that Ortho's breach of the duty to warn consumers was causative of the plaintiff's injuries.

While Ortho acknowledges that manufacturers of prescription drugs are subject to a common law duty to warn prescribing physicians of the material risks involved in using their drugs of which they know or should know, it denies any duty to warn consumers directly. In the alternative, Ortho argues that its compliance with the statutory standard of disclosure established under the *Food and Drugs Act* satisfies any duty to consumers, and it is under no obligation to provide consumers with supplementary information or to issue additional warnings. With respect to physicians, Ortho contends that the plaintiff's physician was aware of the then current medical information on the relationship between oral contraceptives and stroke when he prescribed the pill for the plaintiff, and any further warning by Ortho would have been redundant. In any event, Ortho says, in the circumstances any lack of warning on its part to prescribing physicians was not the proximate cause of the plaintiff's injuries. Furthermore, Ortho argues, a reasonable person in the plaintiff's position would have accepted her doctor's advice and taken the pill even if properly warned. Therefore, the argument concludes, the trial judge erred in finding the necessary causal link between Ortho's alleged breach of the duty to warn and the plaintiff's use of the pill.

III

Before considering the issues raised by Ortho it may perhaps be helpful to review briefly some general principles applicable in products liability cases involving a manufacturer's duty to warn consumers of dangers inherent in the use of a product.

As a matter of common law, it is well settled that a manufacturer of a product has a duty to warn consumers of dangers inherent in the use of its product of which it knows or has reason to know. The guiding principle of liability underlying the present law of products liability in this country was formulated by Lord Atkin in his classic statement in *M'Alister (or Donoghue) v. Stevenson,* [1932] A.C. 562 at p. 599 (H.L.):

"...a manufacturer of products, which he sells in such a form as to show that he intends them to reach the ultimate consumer in the form in which they left him with no reasonable possibility of intermediate examination, and with the knowledge that the absence of reasonable care in the preparation or putting up of the products will result in an injury to the consumer's life or property, owes a duty to the consumer to take that reasonable care."

This statement has been the source of subsequent developments in products liability law based on negligence. The rationale is that one who brings himself into a relation with others through an activity which foreseeably exposes them to danger if proper care is not observed must exercise reasonable care to safeguard them from the danger. It can now be taken as a legal truism that the duty of reasonable care which lies at the foundation of the law of negligence commonly comprehends a duty to warn of danger, the breach of which will, when it is the cause of injury, give rise to liability: see, generally, Fleming, *The Law of Torts,* 6th ed. (1983), at p. 459 ff., and Linden, *Canadian Tort Law,* 3rd ed. (1982), at p. 563 ff.

Once a duty to warn is recognized, it is manifest that the warning must be adequate. It should be communicated clearly and understandably in a manner calculated to inform the user of the nature of the risk and the extent of the danger; it should be in terms commensurate with the gravity of the potential hazard, and it should not be neutralized or negated by collateral efforts on the part of the manufacturer. The nature and extent of any given warning will depend on what is reasonable having regard to all the facts and circumstances relevant to the product in question.

IV

With those general observations in mind, I return to the facts of this case. Before examining the warnings actually given by Ortho to consumers and physicians, the role of the *Food and Drugs Act* in the marketing of oral contraceptives should be briefly outlined.

The *Food and Drugs Act* governs the standards for and distribution of drugs in Canada. The Act itself is general in nature; most of the detail is to be found in the regulations. The Act contains broad prohibitions against advertising to the general public:

3(3) Except as authorized by regulation, no person shall advertise to the general public any contraceptive device or any drug manufactured, sold or represented for use in the prevention of conception.

and against false, misleading or deceptive labelling or packaging:

9(1) No person shall label, package, treat, process, sell or advertise any drug in a manner that is false, misleading or deceptive or is likely to create an erroneous impression regarding its character, value, quantity, composition, merit or safety.

(2) A drug that is not labelled or packaged as required by the regulations, or is labelled or packaged contrary to the regulations, shall be deemed to be labelled or packaged contrary to subsection (1).

Before a new drug can be sold the manufacturer is required to file a submission with the Minister of Health and Welfare which must include all final labels, package inserts, product brochures and file cards to be used in conjunction with the drugs. If approval is granted, the Minister issues a notice of compliance with respect to, *inter alia,* the packaging and labelling of the drug. Any drug that is not labelled or packaged as required by the regulations or contrary to the regulations is deemed to be labelled and packaged contrary to s.9(1), and cannot be sold or advertised in Canada.

The manufacturer's new drug submission must also include detailed reports of tests made to establish the safety of the new drug and a statement of its contra-indications and side-effects. There is a continuing duty on manufacturers to report adverse drug experiences and to establish and maintain detailed records concerning each drug. If new information is obtained after the issuance of a notice of compliance indicating, for example, that a drug is not safe or that the labelling is false, misleading or incomplete in any particular, the drug may not be sold until the manufacturer files a supplementary submission and it is approved by the Minister. The Minister may suspend a notice of compliance if new information is received where, in the Minister's opinion, requires its suspension in the public interest.

Under the regulations, Ortho-Novum 1/50 was a drug which could not be advertised to the general public, nor could it be sold unless labelled and packaged as required by the regulations.

In late 1969, the Minister appointed a special advisory committee to advise the Food and Drug Directorate on all aspects of the safety and efficacy of oral contraceptives marketed in Canada. The committee, composed of seven eminent physicians, produced a 44-page report which was circulated in December, 1970, by the Minister to all practising physicians in Canada in the form of an RX Bulletin. The report (which I may sometimes refer to as the "RX Bulletin") is vital to Ortho's defence to the allegation that it improperly failed to warn of the risk of stroke inherent in the use of its product.

The advisory committee, under the heading "Information to the Public", recommended that the Food and Drug Directorate require manufacturers of oral contraceptives to include in the consumer package an explanatory pamphlet couched in suitable lay language along the following lines:

"As with all other types of potent and effective medication, complications can result from taking birth control pills. Your doctor is in the best position to decide whether or not any medical conditions are present which pose a special risk to you.

Take only on the advice of your doctor and follow his directions.

Contact your doctor at least once a year.

Contact your doctor immediately if you develop severe or persistent headache, blurred vision, pain in calves of the legs, pain in the chest, menstrual irregularities, or other unusual symptoms."

This recommendation was accepted by the Minister in December, 1970, and, thereafter, Ortho and other manufacturers of oral contraceptives in Canada were required to include that explanatory statement in their packages. Ortho complied with the direction and it can be accepted that the Ortho-Novum packages purchased by the plaintiff contained the statement. However, in the view of the trial judge, that statement "amounted to no warning at all". In his opinion, Ortho was under a common law duty to adequately warn the consuming public of material risks, whether or not such a warning was required by the Food and Drug Directorate. This statement was not an adequate warning and, therefore, Ortho was in breach of the duty.

Assuming that manufacturers of birth control pills are under a duty at common law to warn consumers and that that duty is not coextensive with the statutory duty imposed by the *Food and Drugs Act,* in my opinion, the trial judge's conclusion that the information provided to consumers did not satisfy the duty is undoubtedly correct. The duty to warn clearly necessitates a warning comprehensible to the average consumer which conveys the nature and extent of the danger to the mind of a reasonably prudent person. The warning given here fails by any reasonable stand to adequately apprise oral contraceptive users of the nature or extent of the risks inherent in the use of the drug: see *Ortho Pharmaceutical Corp. v. Chapman* (1979), 388 N.E. (2d) 541 (Ind.): *Seley v. G.D. Searle & Co.* (1981), 423 N.E. 831 (Ohio).

VI

In determining whether a drug manufacturer's warnings satisfy the duty to make adequate and timely warning to the medical profession of any dangerous side-effects produced by its drugs or which it knows, or has reason to know, certain factors must be borne in mind. A manufacturer of prescription drugs occupies the position of an expert in the field; this requires that it be under a continuing duty to keep abreast of scientific developments pertaining to its product through research, adverse reaction reports, scientific literature and other available methods. When additional dangerous or potentially dangerous side-effects from the drug's use are discovered, the manufacturer must make all reasonable efforts to communicate the information to prescribing physicians. Unless doctors have current, accurate and complete information about a drug's risks, their ability to exercise the fully informed medical judgment necessary for the proper performance of their vital role in prescribing drugs for patients may be reduced or impaired.

Whether a particular warning is adequate will depend on what is reasonable in the circumstances. But the fact that a drug is ordinarily safe and effective and the danger may be rare or involve only a small percentage of users does not necessarily relieve the manufacturer of the duty to warn. While a low probability of injury or a small class of endangered users are factors to be taken into account determining what is reasonable, these factors must be balanced against such considerations as the nature of the drug, the necessity for taking it, and the magnitude of the increased danger to the individual consumer. Similarly, where medical evidence exists which tends to show a serious danger inherent in the use of a drug, the manufacturer is not entitled to ignore or discount that information in its warning solely because it finds it to be unconvincing; the manufacturer is obliged to be forthright and to tell the whole story. The extent of the warning and the steps to be taken to bring the warning home to physicians should be commensurate with the potential danger — the graver the danger, the higher the duty.

A reading of Ortho U.S.'s warnings to physicians makes it manifest that Ortho was aware or should have been aware of the association between oral contraceptive use and stroke. Moreover, the expert testimony and the exhibits in this case disclose an abundance of published information in medial and scientific journals prior to and at the time the plaintiff was prescribed Ortho-Novum which linked the use of oral contraceptives with stroke. Ortho U.S. provided American physicians with data from and the conclusions of the studies in Britain and the United States, and warned of the risk of cerebral damage posed by the pill. Yet, in Canada, Ortho chose not to provide physicians with any similar warning. Why the medical profession in this country, and, through it, consumers in this country, should be given a less explicit and meaningful warning by the Canadian manufacturer of the same drug is a question that has not been answered. Be that as it may, I think it evident that Ortho failed to give the medical profession warnings commensurate with its knowledge of the dangers inherent in the use of Ortho-Novum; more specifically, it breached its duty to warn of the risk of stroke associated with the use of Ortho-Novum....

CASE PROBLEMS FOR DISCUSSION

Case 1

Green was employed by an aircraft maintenance and repair company to repair and modify aircraft airframes and interiors. Green possessed the necessary Department of Transport licences to perform the type of work for which he was engaged. Since much of the work involved metal repair and refinishing, a certain amount of the work consisted of grinding and polishing, using power grinders and finishers.

While engaged in the grinding of a metal seat bracket in a large jet aircraft, Green decided to change grinding wheels on his power grinder in order to speed up the shaping of the part. He replaced the fine grit wheel on his grinder with a coarse grit wheel that bore the following warning on the package: "DO NOT USE AT MACHINE SPEEDS IN EXCESS OF 6000 RPM."

Brown, a fellow employee, picked up the grinder after Green had completed the grinding work on the seat bracket, and began the grinding of a part of the wing assembly. He set the machine speed first at 5000 rpm, but later increased the speed to 9000 rpm, a common grinding speed. No sooner had the speed increased then the grinding wheel disintegrated, causing injury to Brown and a nearby worker.

What consumer protection issues are raised by this incident? What rights (if any) would Brown have at law?

Case 2

Hamilton admired a used car that Honest Harry had on display at his car lot. Hamilton took the car for a test drive and found the vehicle to be ideal for her purposes. When she inquired about the previous owner, the salesman told her that it was his understanding that the last owner had been an elderly school teacher, who usually used the automobile only on weekends. The odometer on the automobile indicated that the vehicle had been driven only 80 000 km.

Hamilton purchased the automobile, but discovered a few months later that the vehicle had been used as a taxi before it was purchased by the school teacher. The automobile, in effect, had been driven 100 000 km further than the odometer indicated, as it registered only five digits before returning to zero — the true distance that the vehicle had been driven was 180 000 km.

The automobile had given Hamilton no trouble during the time she had owned it, and she had driven the vehicle over 5000 km. She was annoyed, however, that the machine had had so much use, even though it still had a "like-new" appearance.

Hamilton brought an action for rescission of the contract when Honest Harry refused to take back the automobile and return the purchase price.

Discuss the argument that each party might raise in this case. Render a decision.

Case 3

Harvey purchased 1 kg of ground meat from Alice's Meat Market. The package was labelled "ground lean beef" and had been located in a freezer under a sign that advertised "Special sale: $1.99 for 1 kg."

Harvey's friend, who was a meat inspector at a local packing house, dropped by for a visit while he was preparing to barbecue patties made from the ground meat. His friend examined the meat and advised Harvey that in his opinion the meat was not ground lean beef, but ordinary "hamburg" that contained close to 40% fat.

Harvey checked with Alice's Meat Market, and was told that a clerk had mislabelled the meat as ground lean beef, and that the meat was actually hamburg. The special sale, however, was for hamburg at $1.99.

Discuss the issues raised in this case, and the legal position of Harvey and of Alice's Meat Market.

Case 4

Carter carried on a part-time business of lending money to his friends to enable them to purchase consumer goods. He would also lend money to strangers who had been directed to him by his friends. The loans were generally for a short term, and written up in a casual way. Usually the document set out the name of the party and referred only to the principal amount borrowed and the lump-sum interest amount payable on the due date.

On March 1st, John Doe approached Carter in order to borrow $800 for the purchase of a stereo system. Carter loaned him the money, and had him sign a document that read as follows:

March 1, 19—

I promise to pay S. Carter on the first day of each month the sum of $200 until the total amount of $1000 has been paid.

$800   principal
$200   interest
$1000

Value received
"J. Doe"

A few weeks later, Doe advised Carter that he had no intention of paying him the money, as the paper he signed was worthless and the debt unenforceable.

Advise Carter and Doe. What issues (if any) might arise if Carter should decide to institute legal proceedings against Doe?

Case 5

John Smith lived at 221 Pine Avenue in a large city. He had no debts and had never previously purchased goods on credit. He did, however, wish to purchase a particular power boat, so he entered into negotiations with the owner of a marina to obtain the boat on credit. He consented to the marina owner making a credit check before the transaction was completed, and was dismayed when the marina owner refused to proceed with the transaction because he was a "poor credit risk."

The credit reporting agency apparently had provided a credit report on a John Smith who some months before had resided at 212 Pine Street in the same city, and who had defaulted on a number of substantial consumer debts. John Smith knew nothing of the other John Smith, nor had he resided at 212 Pine Street.

What avenues are open to John Smith in this case to rectify the situation?

Case 6

Mary Dwight purchased a vacuum cleaner from a salesman who represented himself as a sales agent for Speedy Vacuum Cleaners. The salesman gave a demonstration of the vacuum in Mary's living room, and the machine appeared to do an excellent job of cleaning dust and dirt from her carpets. At the conclusion of the demonstration, the salesman produced a form contract that called for a deposit of $50, and monthly payments of $50 each until the full purchase price of $400 was paid. Mary paid the $50 deposit and signed the contract. Later that day, the salesman delivered the new vacuum to her residence. On his departure, he stated that he was certain that Mary would find the vacuum satisfactory, as the particular model was "the finest model that the company had produced."

The machine did operate in a satisfactory manner for some seven months. Then one day while Mary was using the vacuum to clean her automobile, she noticed a wisp of black smoke seeping from a seam in the casing. She immediately unplugged the machine and threw it in the swimming pool.

A few minutes later she retrieved the machine from the pool and returned it to the Speedy Vacuum Cleaner store. The repair man examined the machine and explained to her that the smoke had been caused by the melting of a small electrical part in the machine. He offered to replace the part free of charge even though the six-month written warranty had expired, but refused to provide free replacement for several other electrical parts that had been damaged by the machine's immersion in the swimming pool. The cost of repairs amounted to $80, and Mary paid the account. At the end of the month, however, she refused to make the final $50 payment under the purchase agreement, because she felt that the company should cover at least a part of the cost of the repairs to the machine.

Eventually, the company brought an action against her for the $50 owing under the purchase agreement.

Discuss the defences (if any) that Mary might raise in this case, and indicate the possible outcome.

Case 7

Wily Willie sold kitchen gadgets door-to-door. One of his products was a tomato slicer that he stated would slice tomatoes "paper thin." His sales display included a picture of a tomato cut into slices of a uniform 1 mm thickness. The caption on the picture stated: "Look at what our slicer does to a firm ripe tomato!" The photograph was of a very firm variety of tomato, noted for its uniformity. The instruction sheet that accompanied the gadget stated that the user should "select only firm tomatoes that have not fully ripened." Users were cautioned against using fully ripe or over-ripe tomatoes.

Charlie purchased one of the tomato slicers at a price of $9.95 and attempted to slice a tomato for his lunch. He ignored the instruction sheet and simply selected a tomato from his refrigerator. The gadget mashed the tomato instead of slicing it. Charlie tried to slice a second tomato and, when the machine mashed the second tomato as well, he became angry and smashed the slicer. He then sought out Willie, who was at the next house, attempting to sell his products to Charlie's neighbour. Charlie threw the smashed slicer at the salesman's feet and demanded his money back. When Willie refused, Charlie turned to the neighbour and said: "Don't buy anything from this crook! The junk he sells doesn't work!"

Discuss the legal issues raised in this case, and advise Charlie and Willie of their rights.

Case 8

Adrienne had been annoyed with the paint peeling from the iron railing on the stairs of her front porch. She had purchased some inexpensive paints in the past, and each time, after two or three months, rust had bubbled up from beneath the paint.

Exasperated, she returned to the hardware store. On this occasion, the store had a glossy cardboard end-of-aisle display of a premium-priced paint made by

Protecto Paints Ltd. Printed on the display were the words "stops rust," and on the labels of the cans were the words "prevents rust."

Adrienne bought the paint, and set out to apply it to the railing. The directions called for the removal of all prior paint and primer. For the most part, she was successful in removing the prior paint, but not the primer beneath.

After twenty-four months, the rust returned, flaking the paint. Adrienne informed the government consumer ministry, who brought suit against Protecto Paints.

An internationally recognized expert on paint gave evidence that no paint known to industry can stop rust indefinitely. The ability to stop rust ends when the seal is broken, and some paints keep a seal better than others. The expert advised the court that the Protecto formulation was the finest known to industry, using the finest possible ingredients.

Render a decision on behalf of the court.

CHAPTER 23

Restrictive Trade Practices

INTRODUCTION

The law relating to restrictive trade practices is based upon the premise that the forces of competition and the free market should regulate industry, rather than governments or dominant members of the business community. As a consequence, both the common law and restrictive trade practices legislation have as their main thrust the preservation or protection of competition. Only those activities that tend to restrict or interfere with competition are controlled by the law, and industry is left to regulate itself by the market forces that are created by the free enterprise system.

Restrictive trade practices were originally governed by the common law, and all restraints of trade that were considered unreasonable or contrary to the public interest were actionable at law. The common law, unfortunately, was not adequate to ensure that the forces of competition remained free from manipulation by those in industry who possessed substantial economic power, so protection of competition (in the form of legislation) was necessary.

Most of the control of anti-competition activity is now found in the **Competition Act**.[1] The law, in general, prohibits combinations or conspiracies that prevent or lessen competition unduly, and reviews mergers or monopoly actions that may operate to the detriment of the public. It establishes a number of unfair trade practices such as resale price maintenance (where manufacturers attempt to control or set retail prices), price discrimination (selling at different prices to different buyers), discriminatory promotional allowances, false advertising, and bid-rigging as criminal offences. The act applies to both federal and provincial Crown corporations, as well as those in the private sector.

---

1. The Competition Act, R.S.C. 1985, c. C-34 as amended by S.C. 1986, c. 26.

The current law represents an attempt by government to eliminate those forces that interfere with free competition and thereby minimize the need for direct government regulation of activities in the marketplace. The general thrust of anti-competition legislation represents a means of control of industry and trade by way of prohibition of only those activities that interfere unduly with free enterprise. The Competition Act describes the intent of the legislation in the following terms:

> The purpose of this Act is to maintain and encourage competition in Canada in order to promote the efficiency and adaptability of the Canadian economy, in order to expand opportunities for Canadian participation in world markets, while at the same time recognizing the role of foreign competition in Canada, in order to ensure that small and medium-sized enterprises have an equitable opportunity to participate in the Canadian economy in order to provide consumers with competitive prices and product choices.[2]

This philosophical approach was not always taken towards trade and commerce. The most significant change took place at the beginning of the industrial period in England when the country adopted the philosophy of *laissez faire*. Adam Smith's views of competition and its benefits were embraced by the courts and the populace. Restraint of trade at common law became *prima facie* void, unless circumstances could justify some "reasonable restraint." In general, the law as a matter of public policy prohibited any unjustified interference with a person's right to trade, and all conspiracies to willfully injure business became actionable at law.

While it was not unlawful at common law for an owner of a business to purchase a competitor's business, and lessen competition accordingly, the development of large trusts and businesses that had acquired monopoly powers did alarm the governments of the United States and Canada in the late nineteenth century. In both of these countries, the adverse effects on the public of large-scale business acquisitions by investment trusts, and the vertical integration of business activities that gave particular firms virtual monopolistic power over the supply of goods and services, prompted legislative action. The response by the governments took the form of the Sherman Act[3] in the United States, and a statute in Canada that prohibited any combination or conspiracy that had the effect of limiting competition unduly in a trade or manufacture.[4]

The new Canadian legislation was essentially criminal law. It made the conspiracy or combination an offence punishable on conviction. The statute became the foundation of restrictive trade practices legislation, and still remains as the core of the present act. Over time, various other practices that interfered with competition were added. Price fixing and price discrimination were prohibited, and predatory pricing designed to destroy competition was also declared contrary to public policy.

By 1960, it was necessary to consolidate the law pertaining to restrictive trade practices. The statute, entitled the Combines Investigation Act,[5] incorporated the

---

2. Competition Act R.S.C. 1985 c. 34 as amended by S.C. 1986, c. 26 s. 19 (new section 1.1 of the act).

3. The Sherman Act, 26 Stat. 209, as amended 15 U.S.C. §§ 1 and 2.

4. "An Act for the Prevention and Suppression of Combinations Formed in Restraint of Trade," 1889 (Can.), c. 41.

5. "An Act to Amend the Combines Investigation Act and the Criminal Code," 1960 (Can.), c. 45.

provisions of the Criminal Code in the new legislation. It added a number of additional trade practices to the prohibited list, and defined misleading price advertising and discriminatory promotional allowances as restrictive trade practices. No other major changes were made in the law until 1976, when the act was subjected to a thorough review and a number of major revisions made. The changes represented an attempt by Parliament to preserve and encourage free competition and was the first of a two-part overhaul of the law relating to restrictive trade practices. The changes were not finalized until 1986 when the second phase of the law was passed by Parliament. The complete legislation, now known as the Competition Act, represents the present law in Canada with respect to restrictive trade practices.

NATURE OF THE LEGISLATION

The Competition Act is an act of Parliament and, as such, applies throughout Canada. The law represents a blend of both criminal and administrative approaches to the regulation of restraint of trade, with certain trade practices prohibited and subject to criminal law proceedings and penalties, and others, subject to review and control. Included in the legislation are civil remedies that may be pursued by persons or businesses injured as a result of violations of the act or orders issued pursuant to it.

Prohibited trade practices (some 15 in number) are designated as criminal offences. The enforcement of the act with respect to these remains subject to the criminal law standard of proof that requires the Crown to prove beyond any reasonable doubt that the offence was committed by the accused. The onus in these instances was described in *R. v. British Columbia Sugar Refining Co. Ltd. and B.C. Sugar Refinery Ltd.*[6] in the following terms:

> As this is a criminal prosecution there are certain principles that I must apply to its consideration. They are: (1) The onus is on the crown throughout to prove its case and every essential part of it by relevant and admissible evidence beyond a reasonable doubt; (2) This onus never shifts; (3) There is no onus on the accused to prove their innocence; (4) To the extent that the guilt of the accused depends on circumstantial evidence, that evidence must be consistent with the guilt of the accused and inconsistent with any other rational conclusion; (5) In the construction of a penal statute, such as the Combines Act, if there are two or more reasonable interpretations possible, the interpretation most favourable to the accused must be adopted.

The **Director of Investigation and Research,** as the title implies, is primarily responsible for the investigation of any complaint that a violation of the Competition Act has taken place. While criminal law standards of proof apply to prohibited trade practices, the act provides for broad investigative powers that the Director of Investigation and Research may utilize in the gathering of evidence. These powers include very wide powers of search and seizure, and the right to compel parties to provide information. A complaint from a private individual to the director often results in an investigation, but the act provides that the director must investigate any allegation of a violation of the act that is brought to his or her attention in the form of an application for inquiry requested by six residents of Canada.[7]

---

6. *R. v. British Columbia Sugar Refining Co. Ltd. and B.C. Sugar Refinery Ltd.* (1960), 32 W.W.R. 577.
7. The Competition Act, R.S.C. 1985, c. C-34, s. 9 and s. 10.

The act permits the director or the director's agents to enter on the premises of any person that the director believes may have evidence related to the inquiry. However, usually the director or agent must first obtain a search warrant from the Federal Court or a Provincial Supreme or County Court to authorize the search and seizure of evidence.[8] The director cannot, however, use the search and seizure powers simply to engage in a "fishing expedition" for possible evidence of violation. The director must only do so in accordance with an inquiry pursuant to a complaint of an alleged violation. The director's powers extend beyond the mere right to search. The act empowers the director to apply to the court for an order to interrogate corporate officers or require them to furnish affidavit evidence relating to the inquiry.[9]

If at any time during the inquiry the director decides that further investigation is unwarranted, the director may discontinue the inquiry.[10] If, however, the director finds evidence of a violation of the act, he or she may either deliver the evidence to the Attorney-General of Canada for consideration of possible criminal charges, or the director may bring the matter before the Competition Tribunal.

The Competition Tribunal is the second component of the Competition Act enforcement process. The tribunal was established under the **Competition Tribunal Act**[11] in 1986. The tribunal is a rather unique court of record that consists of both lay members and judges of the Trial Division of the Federal Court. The tribunal is presided over by a chairperson who supervises the tribunal and assigns the work to its members. All matters brought before the tribunal are heard by a panel of between three and five members, presided over by one of the judges or the chairperson.

Proceedings before the tribunal are normally brought by the Director of Investigation concerning trade practices that are designated under the act as **reviewable practices**. In addition, the tribunal is empowered to deal with matters concerning foreign laws and judgements, foreign suppliers, and specialized agreements and mergers. The tribunal has the authority to issue appropriate orders after hearing all of the evidence and the submissions of the director and the parties involved. An order of the tribunal is similar to a judgement of the court, and the statute provides that a failure to comply with an order of the tribunal constitutes contempt of the order or a criminal offence. An appeal from an order of the tribunal lies with the Federal Court of Appeal.

The Competition Tribunal has the right to investigate and review certain business activities and make **rectification orders** to restore competition. Reviewable marketing activities include market restriction, exclusive dealing, "tied" selling, consignment selling, and the refusal to supply goods.[12] The tribunal also has the authority to investigate and deal with abuse of dominant position[13] and mergers.[14] In these cases, the tribunal may review the practices of persons in a dominant or monopoly position and make whatever order it deems necessary to restore

---

8. Ibid., s. 12(3).
9. Ibid., s. 14.
10. Ibid., s. 22.
11. Competition Tribunal Act, S.C. 1986, c. C-26.
12. The Competition Act, R.S.C. 1985, c. C-34 as amended by S.C. 1986, c. 26.
13. Ibid., s. 50-51.
14. Ibid., s. 64.

competition. In each of these situations, the director must first make an inquiry, then, if the circumstances warrant, recommend that a hearing be held into the practice. Again, a full opportunity to be heard must be given to any person affected. In addition to the right to be heard, the act also entitles such persons to cross-examine other witnesses. However, unlike an inquiry into an ordinary restrictive trade practice, the commission does not make recommendations. In the case of a reviewable practice, if the results of the hearing dictate some action on the part of the commission, it may make an order prohibiting the practice engaged in by the party, or it may establish procedures that the party must follow to restore competition. Under the act, a failure to obey the order would constitute contempt or a criminal offence.[15]

RESTRICTIVE TRADE PRACTICES

The Competition Act applies to both goods and services. Only those services or goods that fall under the control of a public regulatory body would appear to be exempt from the legislation. Any seller or supplier whose services or goods are sold at prices reviewed or determined by a government body or commission, even if the seller is in a monopoly position, would probably not be subject to prosecution under the Competition Act for any marketing activity carried on under the direct control of the regulatory body. The act, of course, would still apply to activities of the organization that fall outside the direct control of the regulatory body, and to any action designed to prevent the regulatory body from protecting the public interest.[16]

Restrictive trade practices subject to the act may be divided into three separate categories:

(1) practices related to the nature of the business organization itself;
(2) practices that arise out of dealings between a firm and its competitors;
(3) practices that arise out of dealings between a firm and its customers.

MERGERS AND FIRMS IN A DOMINANT POSITION

The first category is related to the nature of the firm, if the firm should become dominant in a particular field of business or industry. This may arise in one of two ways: a firm may gradually eliminate all competition by aggressive business activity, or it may merge with other competitors to assume a dominant position. Neither of these methods of growth or dominance is in itself improper. However, under the Competition Act, any merger or monopoly activity that is likely to lessen competition to the detriment of the public would be subject to review and intervention by the Competition Tribunal.[17] The rationale behind these provisions is that mergers or monopolies that substantially control the market have the potential for abuse, in that the price-reducing effects of free competition no longer apply to their product or service. While it is difficult to pinpoint when a merger becomes contrary to the public interest, or may have the effect of lessening competition to the detriment of the public, any merger that gives a single organization in excess of half the market for a particular product might very well come under scrutiny by the director. If the merger is found to be one that would

---

15. The tribunal has all the powers of a superior court. See: S.C. 1986, c. 26, s. 8(2).
16. See, for example, *R. v. Canadian Breweries Ltd.*, [1960] O.R. 601.
17. The Competition Act, R.S.C. 1985, c. C-34 as amended by S.C7

result in a substantial lessening of competition, the tribunal has the power to intervene and modify (or prohibit) the activity.[18]

In the past, when criminal prosecution was the only choice, the courts were reluctant to convict in the case of mergers and monopolies, because of the many factors that must be considered in the determination of what constitutes a lessening of competition "unduly." Apart from one case, in which a monopoly firm was so blatant in its conduct of restrictive trade practices that competition was clearly lessened "unduly" and the public interest adversely affected,[19] the Crown has had little success in the enforcement of the merger and monopoly sections of the act. Some of the reasons put forward by the courts in dismissing the Crown's cases have been the control or regulation of prices by a public body,[20] the potential for competition from large firms in other areas of the country,[21] and the fact that substitutes for the product were available.[22]

The new Competition Act, however, moves away from the criminal approach to the protection of competition. It provides the Competition Tribunal with the power to review the practices of business firms in a dominant position (such as a monopoly) on a non-criminal basis. After an examination of the practice, the tribunal may make an order that will restore competition if the practice is determined to be an abuse of the dominant position.[23] In the case of a merger, if after a review it should determine that the merger would result in a substantial lessening of competition, the tribunal may prohibit or modify the proposed change.[24]

The importance of preserving competition by intervention was noted in an early case[25] where the court expressed the need for control in the following manner:

> The right of competition is the right of every one, and Parliament has now shewn that its intention is to prevent oppressive and unreasonable restrictions upon the exercise of this right; that whatever may hitherto have been its full extent, it is no longer to be exercised by some to the injury of others. In other words, competition is not to be prevented or lessened unduly, that is to say, in an undue manner or degree, wrongly, improperly, excessively, inordinately, which it may well be in one or more of these senses of the word, if by the combination of a few the right of the many is practically interfered with by restricting it to the members of the combination.

CONSPIRACIES AND COMBINATIONS IN RESTRAINT OF TRADE

The general thrust of the present legislation is to prohibit conspiracies and combinations that unduly lessen competition. The relative seriousness of offences relating to these activities may be underscored by reference to the penalties imposed for contravention of this part of the act: a breach of any of the sections related to combinations and conspiracies carries with it a fine of up to ten million dollars, or imprisonment for up to five years.[26]

---

18. Ibid., s. 64.

19. Ibid., *R. v. Eddy Match Co. Ltd.* (1952), 13 C.R. 217; affirmed, (1954) 18 C.R. 357.

20. *R. v. Can. Breweries Ltd.,* [1960] O.R. 601.

21. *R. v. British Columbia Sugar Refining Co. Ltd. et al.* (1960), 32 W.W.R. (N.S.) 577.

22. *R. v. K. C. Irving Ltd.* (1974), 7 N.B.R. (2d) 360; affirmed, [1978] 1 S.C.R. 408.

23. *R. v. K.C. Irving Ltd.* (1974), 7 N.B.R. (2d) 360; affirmed, [1978] 1 S.C.R. 408.

24. Ibid., s. 64.

25. *R. v. Elliott* (1905), 9 O.L.R. 648.

26. The Competition Act, R.S.C. 1985, c. C-34 s. 45(1) as amended by S.C. 1986 c. 26 s. 30(1).

The "conspiracy and combination" (section 45) of the act[27] provides that:
everyone who conspires, combines, agrees or arranges with another person:

(a) to limit unduly the facilities for transporting, producing, manufacturing, supplying, storing or dealing in any product.

(b) to prevent, limit or lessen, unduly, the manufacture or production of a product, or to enhance unreasonably the price thereof,

(c) to prevent, or lessen, unduly, competition in the production, manufacture, purchase, barter, sale, storage, rental, transportation or supply of a product, or in the price of insurance upon persons or property, or

(d) to otherwise restrain or injure competition unduly, is guilty of an indictable offence and is liable to imprisonment for five years or a fine of ten million dollars or to both.

The obligation on the Crown to prove a violation of the act is alleviated to some extent by a requirement in the legislation. This provision states that it is not necessary to prove that the combination, conspiracy, or agreement if carried into effect would be likely to completely or virtually eliminate competition in the market to which it relates, or that it was the object of the parties to eliminate, completely or virtually, competition in that market.[28] However, the act would not apply if the combination or agreement between the parties relates only to one of the following activities:[29]

(a) the exchange of statistics;

(b) the defining of product standards;

(c) the exchange of credit information,

(d) the definition of terminology used in a trade, industry, or profession;

(e) co-operation in research and development;

(f) the restriction of advertising or promotion, rather than a discriminatory restriction directed against a member of the mass media;

(g) the sizes or shapes of the containers in which an article is packaged;

(h) the adoption of the metric system of weights and measures; or

(i) measures to protect the environment.

If the arrangement or agreement to carry out any of these activities restricts (or is likely to restrict) any person from entering the business, trade, or profession, or has the effect of lessening (or is likely to lessen) competition with respect to prices, markets or customers, channels or methods of distribution, or the quantity or quality of production, then the parties would still be subject to conviction under the act.[30]

The act normally applies only to conspiracies, combinations, or agreements in restraint of trade on a domestic basis. If the activity relates wholly to the export of products from Canada, the restraint of trade restrictions would not apply,[31] unless (1) the agreement or arrangement has resulted, or is likely to result in a reduction or limitation of the real value of exports of a product; (2) has restricted or injured, or is likely to restrict any person from entering into or expanding the

---

27. The Competition Act, R.S.C. 1985, c. C-34 s. 45.

28. Ibid., s. 46, and new s. 1.1.

29. Ibid., s. 45(2).

30. Ibid., s. 45(3).

31. Ibid., s. 45(4).

export business; or (3) has lessened or is likely to lessen competition unduly in the supply of service facilitating the export of products from Canada.[32] The purpose of the exception is to allow Canadian business firms maximum latitude in their activities with respect to the export of goods from Canada, and to limit their actions only where the activity would harm other Canadian firms or have a negative impact on the domestic market.

In the case of services, a further exception is made. The courts are not to convict an accused if the conspiracy, combination, agreement, or arrangement relates only to the standards of competence and integrity reasonably necessary for the protection of the public in either the practice of the trade or profession, or in the collection and dissemination of information relating to such services.[33] As a result, firms engaged in certain activities such as skilled trades (master electricians, etc.) or professions (such as accountants, lawyers) would not violate the act if they "conspired" to set professional standards for their services or to provide the public with information about their services.

Banks are also covered by the Competition Act. Any conspiracy or arrangement between banks to establish rates of interest for deposits on loans, the service charges to customers, the amount or kind of loan to a customer, or the classes of persons to whom loans or other services would be provided or withheld is a violation of the act. It constitutes an indictable offence subject to a penalty of up to five years in prison or a fine of up to five million dollars, or both.[34] Certain exceptions are made with respect to some bank activities to reflect the realities of banking and the making of loans to persons outside of Canada.[35]

The act exempts affiliated corporations from the conspiracy provisions. As a consequence, if a wholly owned subsidiary of a corporation enters into an agreement with that corporation that would otherwise be a conspiracy, it would not be subject to charges under this part of the act.[36] However, if the parent corporation is a foreign corporation and requires the Canadian subsidiary to enter into an agreement with another firm outside Canada that would constitute a violation of the conspiracy provisions of the act if the agreement had been made in Canada, the directors or officers of the Canadian corporation may be liable, even if unaware of the agreement.[37]

The practice of "bid-rigging," which is any agreement or arrangement among two or more persons where all but one undertakes not to submit a bid in response to a call for bids or tenders (and where the person calling for bids is unaware of the arrangement), is prohibited under the act.[38] The practice was made an offence under the act in 1976 in an effort to encourage greater competition by the elimination of secret arrangements. The offence differs to some extent from other restrictive trade practices in that it would not be necessary for the Crown to prove that the bid-rigging represents an undue restraint of trade. An important point to note with respect to this activity, however, is the fact that a bidding arrangement

---

32. Ibid., s. 45(5).
33. Ibid., s. 45(6).
34. Ibid., s. 49(1).
35. Ibid., s. 49(2).
36. Ibid., s. 45(7).
37. Ibid., s. 46(1).
38. Ibid., s. 47.

is only an offence if the fact is not revealed to the person calling for the bids, either before or at the time the bid is made. The purpose for this exemption is to allow parties to undertake projects jointly, provided that the nature of the arrangement is revealed beforehand to the other party.

The legislation also applies to services generally. For example, the Competition Act prohibits conspiracies relating to professional sports where the conspiracy is intended to limit unreasonably the opportunities for any person to participate as a player or competitor in a professional sport, or to impose unreasonable terms on persons who so participate. It also applies to any attempt to limit unreasonably the opportunity for any person to negotiate with and (if an agreement is reached) to play for the team or club of his or her choice in a professional league.[39] This provision in the legislation applies only to professional sport. It requires the courts to take into consideration the international aspects of the activity and the unique relationship that exists between teams or clubs that compete in the same league.[40] Nevertheless, the law has necessitated a change in a number of activities associated with professional sport, the most notable being the practice of tying a player to a club by way of a special reserve clause.

OFFENCES RELATING TO DISTRIBUTION AND SALE OF PRODUCTS

Offences relating to distribution are generally designed to prevent sellers from granting special concessions to large buyers and, conversely, to prevent large buyers from insisting upon special concessions from sellers. Special concessions, usually in the form of lower prices or special allowances would grant one buyer a particular competitive advantage over other buyers. They carry with them the potential for a restriction on competition. The act, consequently, has identified and prohibited a number of distribution activities that affect competition.

A seller, for example, must not make a practice of discriminating between competing purchasers with respect to the price of goods sold.[41] This activity only constitutes an offence where the seller makes a practice of price discrimination between competing firms, where the goods sold are of the same quality, in the same quantity, and are sold at approximately the same time.[42] Isolated sales to meet competition, or sales between affiliated firms, would probably not constitute offences under the act.[43]

In a similar fashion, a seller is prohibited from granting buyers special rebates, promotional allowances, or grants for the advertising or promotion of goods unless the allowance or amount is made on a proportional basis.[44] Once again, the purchasers must be in competition with one another, and the seller must not discriminate. Under the act, an allowance would be treated as proportional if it is based upon the value of sales to each competing purchaser, or, if it is in the form of services, in accordance with the kinds of services that purchasers at each level of distribution would ordinarily be able to perform.[45]

---

39. Ibid., s. 48.
40. Ibid., s. 48(2) and (3).
41. Ibid., s. 50(1)(a).
42. Ibid., s. 50(2).
43. Ibid., s. 45(7).
44. S.C. 1986 c. 26 s. 47 (new s. 51).
45. Ibid., s. 51(3).

A seller must not engage in a policy of selling products in any area of Canada at prices lower than those elsewhere if the sales would have the effect of substantially lessening or eliminating competition in that area,[46] or if the policy of low prices is established for the purpose of lessening or eliminating competition.[47] In both of these cases, the act is not attempting to prohibit lower prices, but rather to make it an offence if a seller uses lower prices to eliminate or lessen competition either on a regional or broader basis. The practice of selling goods at a low price normally would not offend the act, but if the price is unreasonably low for the purpose of lessening or destroying competition, then the practice would probably be in contravention of the act.

The underlying thought behind each of these prohibitions is that a seller must treat all competing buyers of his or her products in a fair and impartial manner, and that the selling of products must be done without some unlawful motive such as the elimination of competition. A seller is not obliged to treat non-competing buyers in the same fashion, however, and a seller may establish separate prices and discounts for each type of non-competing buyer.

A quite different sales activity is also covered by a section of the act that prohibits the seller from controlling the prices at which the seller's goods may be sold by others. A seller is prohibited from attempting, either directly or indirectly, by any threat or promise or any other inducement, to influence the price upwards of his or her products, or from discouraging price reductions by the purchasers of the products for resale.[48] The offence is not limited to cases where a seller attempts to fix the price at which the product may be sold, but also applies to any attempt to enhance the price or influence the price upwards. The practice by sellers of providing a "suggested retail price" for advertising, or for price lists or other material, would probably violate the act unless the seller clearly indicates that the buyer is under no obligation to resell the goods at the suggested price, and that the goods may be resold at a lower price.[49]

A seller may not refuse to supply goods to a buyer in an attempt to prevent the buyer from reselling the goods to others who maintain a policy of selling the goods at lower prices. However, a seller would have the right to refuse to supply goods if the buyers make a practice of selling the goods as "loss leaders" and not for the purpose of profit.[50] The same would be the case if the goods required certain services, and the person was not making a practice of providing the level of service that a purchaser would normally expect.[51]

The act also prohibits a number of schemes used by sellers to promote sales that tend to discourage competition. It contains a prohibition of "referral selling,"[52] a practice whereby a customer receives a rebate or commission on each additional customer obtained for the seller. There is also a prohibition of "pyramid selling," a practice involving the payment of fees or commissions not based upon the sale of a product, but upon the recruitment or sales of others.[53] In the latter case, where a

---

46. The Competition Act, R.S.C. 1985 c. C-34 s. 50(1)(b).

47. Ibid., s. 50(1)(c).

48. S.C. 1986 c. 26 s. 47 (new s. 61).

49. Ibid., s. 61(3).

50. Ibid., s. 61(9)(a).

51. Ibid., s. 61(9)(d).

52. The Competition Act, R.S.C. 1985 c. C-34 s. 56.

53. Ibid., s. 55.

province has legislation governing or controlling the activity, the practice is not subject to the Competition Act.[54]

REVIEWABLE ACTIVITIES

In addition to prohibited activities relating to the sale of goods and services, the Competition Tribunal may review a number of different selling methods. These include abuse of dominant position, a refusal to supply goods, consignment selling, exclusive dealing, "tied" selling, and market restriction. The tribunal may also review foreign directives to Canadian subsidiaries and foreign arrangements in restraint of trade that affect Canadian business.[55] A review that confirms that the activity has taken place, and that the activity is carried on for a purpose specified in the act, may be ordered stopped, or a remedy set out in the legislation for that particular activity may be applied. For example, the tribunal may order a major supplier to cease exclusive dealing arrangements if the arrangement is likely to: impede entry into or expansion of a firm in the market; impede the introduction of a product into the market; impede an expansion of sales of a product in the market; or have any other exclusionary effect in the market,[56] with the result that competition is or is likely to be lessened substantially. The tribunal is also permitted, in the case of exclusive dealing, to include in the order any other requirement necessary to overcome the effects of the exclusive dealing, or to include any other requirement that might be necessary to restore or stimulate competition.[57]

OFFENCES RELATING TO PROMOTION AND ADVERTISING OF PRODUCTS

Misleading or false advertising and a number of other promotional activities are subject to the Competition Act. The act makes any representation to the public that is false or misleading in any material respect,[58] or any materially misleading representation to the public concerning the price at which a product or products have been, are, or will be sold, an offence under the act.[59] The act, with respect to false or misleading advertising, is broadly written to include cases where the information may be technically correct but where the impression given would mislead the public in some material way.[60] The act also puts the onus on the advertiser to prove that any claims or promises made in the form of a warranty or guarantee of performance are valid and are substantiated in accordance with recognized testing procedures. While every article or service need not meet the claim, the percentage of articles that do must be high. Where claims are made as a result of recognized tests, the percentage of articles that meet the test has been suggested to be not less than 95%.[61]

Where a testimonial of a user is included in an advertisement to establish the performance of a product, or to attest to its usable life, it is essential that the performance test was made. Also, the person making the testimonial must approve the content of the report and grant permission to publish it prior to its use by the advertiser.[62]

---

54. Ibid., s. 55(4).
55. S.C. 1986 c. 26 s. 47 (new s. 55(1) and s. 54).
56. Ibid., s. 49(2).
57. Ibid.
58. The Competition Act, R.S.C. 1985 c. C-34 s. 52(1)(a).
59. Ibid., s. 52(1)(d).
60. Ibid., s. 52(4).
61. Canada, Department of Consumer and Corporate Affairs: Misleading Advertising Bulletin, 1976.
62. The Competition Act, R.S.C. 1985, c. C-34, s. 53.

Sales above the advertised price constitute an offence under the Competition Act, and a seller who advertises a product at a particular price in a geographic area would be expected to sell the goods to all persons in that general area at the advertised price. The act, however, recognizes that errors do occur in the advertisement of goods. It provides that where a false or misleading advertisement is made with respect to the price at which goods are offered for sale, prompt action by the advertiser to correct the error by placing another advertisement advising the public of the error would exempt the advertiser from prosecution under the act.[63]

A practice somewhat related to misleading price advertising is the "double ticketing" of goods for sale. This sometimes occurs in self-serve establishments. To discourage the practice, the act provides that the seller must sell the goods at the lowest of the marked prices; otherwise, the sale would constitute an offence.[64]

The act also discourages the rather dubious selling technique of "bait-and-switch," whereby the seller advertises goods at a bargain price for the purpose of attracting customers to the establishment when there is not an adequate supply of the low-priced goods to sell. The practice is an offence under the act[65] unless the seller can establish that he or she took steps to obtain an adequate supply of the product, but was unable to obtain such a quantity by reason of events beyond the seller's control. Another defence would arise where the seller did not anticipate the heavy demand for the advertised product. Here, to avoid a violation of the act, the seller would be obliged to prove that he or she obtained what was believed to be an adequate supply and, when the supply was exhausted, undertook to supply the goods (or similar goods) at the same bargain price within a reasonable time to all persons who requested the product.[66]

Under the act, a final promotion-related activity that should be noted is the use of promotional contests by sellers to increase the sales of a product. All promotional contests must make an adequate and fair disclosure of the number and approximate value of the prizes, the area or areas to which they relate, and any fact within the knowledge of the advertiser that might materially affect the chances of winning. The selection of participants or the distribution of prizes must also be made on the basis of skill, or on a random basis within the area where the prizes are to be awarded.[67] If the promoter fails to comply with the requirements set out in the act, the failure constitutes an offence punishable by a fine or imprisonment.

CIVIL ACTIONS UNDER THE COMPETITION ACT

Apart from the right to maintain a common law civil action for restraint of trade activities not covered by the legislation, the Competition Act provides that a civil action may be maintained by a party injured as a result of a breach of the Competition Act or the violation of a Competition Tribunal order. The party affected by the breach may claim damages suffered as a result of the breach of the act, but the amount that may be recovered is limited to the actual loss.[68] In this

63. Ibid., s. 60.
64. Ibid., s. 54(1).
65. Ibid., s. 57(2).
66. Ibid., s. 57(3).
67. Ibid., s. 59.
68. Ibid., s. 36(1).

sense, Canadian legislation differs from that of the United States, where triple damages may be recovered in restrictive trade practice cases.

The burden of proof that is imposed upon the private plaintiff in the civil action would not be the criminal burden of "beyond any reasonable doubt," but the lesser civil law burden based upon a balance of probability. The civil plaintiff, however, would be entitled to use the record of any criminal proceedings against the defendant as evidence in the civil action, provided that the action is commenced within two years of the final disposition of the criminal case.[69]

While some doubt was initially raised as to the validity of the part of the Competition Act[70] that creates a civil cause of action, Federal Court and Ontario Court of Appeal judgements have held the provisions of the act to be a valid exercise of federal powers under the constitution.[71] More recently, challenges were also made as to the constitutionality of the Competition Tribunal and its powers, but the Supreme Court of Canada has held that the Competition Tribunal is a constitutionally valid body with the power to enforce its orders by contempt proceedings.[72]

SUMMARY

The purpose of restrictive trade practice legislation is to maintain free competition. The law is designed to permit the forces of competition to regulate trade and industry rather than government or dominant members of an industry.

The general thrust of the law is to review mergers and monopolies and prohibit those that are contrary to the public interest, and to ban any combination or conspiracy that might unduly lessen competition. The law also prohibits certain activities (on the seller's part) designed to drive the prices of goods and services upward, as well as to prevent price discrimination, along with certain other practices that might restrict competition.

The Competition Act is, in part, criminal in nature. However, parts of the act are regulatory to cover a number of reviewable activities, and provide for the right of civil action for persons injured as a result of a breach of the act.

The legislation has worked reasonably well in controlling selling practices that are contrary to the public interest, but until recently has failed to deal adequately with mergers and monopolies. The particular problem with the merger-monopoly parts of the legislation was related to the criminal nature of the law, and the burden of proof that it imposes upon the Crown. Changes in this area of the law now permit the Competition Tribunal to review mergers and monopoly actions with power to protect the public interest by way of modification or prohibition of the activities.

---

69. Ibid., s. 36(4).

70. *Seiko Time Canada Ltd. v. Consumers Distributing Co. Ltd.* (1980), 29 O.R. (2d) 221; *Racois Construction Inc. v. Quebec Red-i-Mix Inc.* (1979), 105 D.L.R. (3d) 15; *Vapor Canada Limited et al. v. MacDonald et al.* (1977), 66 D.L.R. (3d) 1.

71. See, for example *City National Leasing v. General Motors of Canada Limited* (1986), 28 D.L.R. (4th) 158 n. *Attorney-General for Canada v. Quebec Ready Mix Inc. et al.* (1985), 25 D.L.R. (4th) 373.

72. See for example: *Canada (Competition Tribunal) v. Chrysler Canada Ltd.* S.C.C., June 25, 1992 (unreported); *R. v. Nova Scotia Pharmaceutical Society,* S.C.C. July 9, 1992 (unreported); See also *R. v. Wholesale Travel Group Inc.,* [1991] 3 S.C.R. 154.

**DISCUSSION
QUESTIONS**

1. Why did the Canadian government find it necessary to introduce restrictive trade practices legislation?
2. Why was it originally necessary to make the restrictive trade practices laws criminal in nature?
3. What effect has the criminal nature of the law had upon the ability of the Crown to control restrictive trade practices?
4. Mergers of corporations or businesses are not unlawful per se. Under what circumstances would a merger likely be subject to review under the Competition Act?
5. What activities are considered prohibited trade practices?
6. What activities are not "prohibited" but "reviewable" practices?
7. Under what circumstances would an investigation under the Competition Act be instituted?
8. Must a manufacturer of goods sell his or her products to all retailers? If not, why not? Give an example of a case where a manufacturer might lawfully refuse to do so.
9. Outline the implications of the Competition Act for an advertiser of goods. What types of advertising would likely be affected by the act?
10. Explain the following terms: bait-and-switch, loss leader, bid-rigging, exclusive dealing, predatory pricing, tied selling.
11. What is the significance of a price advertised by a manufacturer as a "maximum retail price"? How does this differ from a "suggested retail price"?

**MINI-CASE
PROBLEMS**

1. A retailer advertised television sets for sale with banner headlines that stated, "Special Sale! Brand X Model XX 20" colour TV Only $199 with trade-in!" At his store he had three model XX sets for sale at $199, but required an older working model of the same type of TV as a trade-in. At his shop he would also urge customers to buy a different brand of TV at $599, since brand X, in his opinion, was poor quality and not really worth buying. A and B went to the retailer's shop to buy a brand X TV set, but neither had a brand X TV set for trade-in purposes.

   Discuss the issues raised in this case.

2. Workers' Clothing Co. conducted a promotional contest in which the prize offered was described as a new motorcycle with a retail value of $12 995. Investigation revealed that the motorcycle had a suggested retail price of $12 495 and was a new, but previous year's model.

   Discuss the implications of this information in the light of the Competition Act.

**JUDICIAL
DECISION**

The case of *Regina* v. *Epson (Canada) Ltd.* deals with the issue of vertical price restraints under the Competition Act (formerly called the Combines Investigation Act). The offence concerns attempts by threats to maintain the prices at which distributors advertised the corporation's products. The corporation pleaded guilty to the charges.

The judge begins his judgement by pointing out that the company's printer was a high quality, well-known product, and competitors were few in number. He then notes that the company prepared a dealership agreement that contained an illegal clause requiring the dealers to advertise at prices not less than the company's suggested retail price.

The judgement continues with a review of the evidence and argument, and the findings of fact by the judge. The judge next states the law to be applied to the findings of fact, and then ends with a decision that the company violated the act.

**Competition Act —
Resale Price —
Maintenance —
Nature of Offence**

Regina v. Epson (Canada) Ltd. (1988), 19 C.P.R. (3d) 195.*

The accused corporation pleaded guilty to ten offences of attempting to maintain the price of its products by requiring its dealers to advertise its products at a price of not less than the retail price suggested by the manufacturer.

HUMPHREY, D.C.J.:

— Epson (Canada) Limited has pleaded guilty to 10 offences under the Combines Investigation Act, R.S.C. 1970, c. C-23 s. 38(1)(*a*). The gist of the offences is that the corporation, by threats attempted to influence upward the price at which its distributors advertised its products, particularly the QX-10 computer and the Matrix dot printer.

Before the offences were committed, the corporation, which is the Canadian corporation, 81% of whose shares were owned by Maurice LaPalme, was engaged in selling computer products to the public through a Canada wide network of dealers.

The company's computer printer was a leader in the industry. It was one of the first on the market, a quality product with a high degree of reliability, and this printer so dominated the market that at least a third of all printers sold in Canada were the Epson printer. Sale of the printer accounted for almost all of Epson sales which were in 1984, $26 million plus, and $40 million plus in 1985.

There were other manufacturer competitors, but they were few in number, and the largest of which sold only one half of the number of printers that Epson sold.

The company was about to introduce the QX-10 computer and as a policy decision decided that they wished to market the machine through their dealers, but wished to ensure that the dealers were prepared to give to the public the pre-sale advice and assistance that most members of the public required, and also the post-sale follow up and assistance that a very complicated new product would require.

Daniel LaPalme, a nephew of the owner, who was in the marketing division, approached the corporation's solicitor, one Mr. Thomas who practised in Unionville, Ontario. Mr. LaPalme told Mr. Thomas that the company wanted some term put into the dealer contract that would ensure integrity of the product and would allow the new computer to be sold in an atmosphere that was free from the free ride discounters who were to be discouraged. He felt that these discounters would sell in the market and for a fast, small profit, turn the machine over to the public in a way that was not compatible with their marketing ideas because they did not have sufficient profit to be able to give the type of service that the company felt that the public needed.

While I accept the statement of intent by the company, it must be remembered that it is the *raison d'être* of the company to make *profit* and the quest for profit, of course, is its ultimate object of any commercial corporation.

Lawyer Thomas was given copies of the dealer contracts in the United States, and he, with the company's marketing goals in mind, formulated the illegal restriction in the QX-10 dealer contract. Paragraph 10 of the EPSON QX-10 Certified Dealership Agreement concludes with these words: "Dealer agrees not to advertise the QX-10 for sale at a price lower than the Suppliers suggested Retail Price". Some 40 dealers were persuaded to sign this contract and it was in force for some six to seven months before the company's offices were searched pursuant to a search warrant and the illegality of this term was drawn to the company's attention, at which time this term was deleted from the contract.

As an out growth of the QX-10 agreement, and with the same proclaimed motivation, the company "in house" incorporated a similar clause in their general EPSON Dealership Agreement, where in para. 13 of sch. A, these words appear:

"Dealer agrees not to advertise EPSON products at a price lower than Epson's suggested retail list price as set out in the current price list hereinafter referred to as Schedule B."

This agreement was signed by some 222 dealers across Canada and was nominally at least, in force for three to four months before the execution of the search warrant after which the clause was deleted.

I am satisfied that because of the erroneous legal advice, that there is no evidence that any officer of the company *knew*, and I emphasize the word knew, that these vertical restrictive clauses were illegal, but I must say in passing, that for a national corporation of this size and with the very extensive experience that Mr. Maurice LaPalme had in this field, the company displayed an amazing degree of naïvety. Perhaps a little twinge of wilful blindness may be attributed to the company.

I recognize that all aggravating circumstances must be proven by the Crown and I therefore approach my consideration of an appropriate sentence with the idea that the company did not deliberately break the law.

I also believe that the company had no evil or criminal intent in mind and may have believed that it was in everybody's interest that these clauses be a condition of becoming an authorized dealer, which they were.

Even though agents of the company threatened dealers (and in fact a threatened dealer is the subject of each count of the indictment), with either cancellation of their authorized dealer status (and the company only sold to authorized dealers) or with non-delivery of products, especially during those times when demand exceeded supply, the fact is, not one dealer complied with the advertising constraint. The company advertised extensively, spending huge amounts of money to promote its product in different media, and in many instances advertised the suggested retail price.

Only one dealer did not advertise below the suggested retail price, and he mentioned no price at all. All other dealers advertised in a competitive way for the relatively short period of time that these dealer contracts were supposed to be in force.

During the hearing, a major issue was raised as to whether vertical price restrictions on advertising or even a programme of retail price maintenance was, if imposed by the manufacturer, good or bad for the public, particularly when there was a service component in the product.

Defence called Professor Mathewson who told us that there are two competing theories; the *per se* theory, where the restrictive practices are simply branded illegal as interfering with the free market-place and are detrimental to the public; and the other theory espoused by himself and supported by none other than Judge Bork whose recent nomination to the Supreme Court in the United States was rejected. The competing theory is that the public is better served by allowing, through restrictions on deep discounters, the full service dealer a profit sufficient to both allow and induce him to provide the service required by the public.

As interesting as this debate was, it is really irrelevant for two reasons; one, I am sure Daniel LaPalme knew of neither when he instructed Mr. Thomas, the lawyer, to create the phrase in question; and secondly, since parliament has branded the restricted advertising clause as illegal, it is *per se* criminal conduct and the law of the land.

I agree with the principles outlined in the authorities submitted to me as being at least a rough basis for formulating a just fine. In this regard, I make the following findings of fact:

(1) The corporation did not intend any harm to either the dealers or the public and in fact felt that trying to discourage deep discounters was in everybody's best interest.

(2) The company did not actually know the restrictive clauses were illegal and I emphasize the words *actually*, and *know*.

(3) No one lived up to the restrictive agreements and dealers advertised as though no agreement of this nature had been signed. This was in spite of numerous threats by the company to the dealers.

(4) I find that there was no reasonable inference to be drawn that one dollar of profit was made because of the illegal restrictions on advertising since in the market-place, the illegal restrictions were totally ignored. Not only that, once the illegal clauses were deleted, sales and profits increased.

Indeed, I go so far as to find that the market-place operated as though the illegal constraints never existed and, therefore, I find that there are no illegal, ill-gotten gains. Even though Mr. LaPalme made very substantial profits, they did not come from the illegal activity. It is not the company's fault that the alleged scheme did not become fully operational. The company did attempt, by threats, to enforce the illegal agreements. It says something for the strength of the market-place that those threats failed; but the potential for harm was there.

If the company had succeeded in its efforts, then the company and not the market-place would become the guardian of the public interest. This is something like the fox guarding the chicken coop. It goes without saying that the public's interest is better served by a free competitive market-place rather than one rigged by the company whose products are being sold to the public.

Not only was there a potential for harm to the public, I must also consider the expense of the investigation. Under officer John Grant of the investigative branch of the Department of Consumer and Corporate Affairs, a very extensive and costly investigation took place. To its credit, the company has pleaded guilty saving the expense of a longer trial.

As I have said before, Mr. LaPalme who had extensive experience in this industry, states that he, because lawyer Thomas drafted the first legal clause, believed it to be legal. Well, that is amazingly naïve. I would have thought that a man of his experience selling millions of dollars of goods across Canada might have doubted the company's ability to rig the market-place and to fool the public, and to do so for the stated reason that it was in the public's best interest. I believe there is a higher duty on an entrepreneur making millions of dollars, to know the limits of legal marketing.

In formulating the amount of the fine to be imposed, I have considered the principle of sentence in cases such as this by reviewing *R. v. A & M Records of Canada Ltd.* (1980), 51 C.P.R. (2d) 225; *R. v. Browning Arms Co. of Canada Ltd.* (1974), 15 C.P.R. (2d) 97; 18 C.C.C. (2d) 298, and other cases referred to me by counsel. I especially adopt the words of the late Judge Honsberger in the *A & M Records'* case where he had this to say at p. 229, and I quote: "It is equally beyond doubt that an inducement to advertise at a higher price creates an inducement to sell at higher prices."

I also, from a dealer point of view, consider the "bully" factor. The company dominated the printer market and dealers clamoured to be authorized to sell the company's product. To take advantage of that situation by bullying the dealers into agreeing not to engage in competitive advertising is obviously contrary to the public interest.

Giving the matter the best consideration of which I am capable, I assess a fine of $20,000 on each count for a total of $200,000. I have endorsed the indictment, "Sentence $20,000. Fine on each count total $200,000. Sixty days to pay or distress order to issue".

CASE PROBLEMS FOR DISCUSSION

Case 1

Prior to 1927, widgets were manufactured in Canada by three companies: World Widgets Ltd., Canadian Widgets Ltd., and E.M.C. Widgets Ltd. In 1927, the three firms merged to form the World Widget Co. Ltd., a new firm incorporated that year. As a result of the merger, World Widget Co. Ltd. became the only producer of widgets in Canada.

In January 1928, the company issued new price lists for its products to jobbers and distributors. The new lists raised the case price from $18 (the price before the merger) to $21.91.

In March 1928, Columbia Widgets Ltd. was incorporated in New Brunswick, and started widget production in October of that year. The price of its product (per case) to jobbers was $19.75.

In October of the same year, World Widget Co. Ltd. introduced its product under a new brand name at a very low price to jobbers in those areas where Columbia widgets were sold. World Widget also granted confidential prices or special rebates to large jobbers and distributors that agreed to handle only the World Widget product.

In 1932, Columbia Widgets Ltd. closed its doors and sold its assets to D. Widget, an American firm controlled by World Widget. A few weeks later, the Commonwealth Widget Company Ltd. was established by D. Widget on the site occupied previously by Columbia Widgets. Prices established by the new company were in line with those published by World Widget.

In 1931, Canada Widget Ltd., a competitor, was formed by a group of Quebec businessmen, and a plant to manufacture widgets was established in Quebec. World Widget gradually acquired control of this new firm by the acquisition of shares through its subsidiary, Widget Holdings Ltd. Prices of widgets sold by Canada Widget Ltd. were brought in line with World Widget prices following the acquisition of Canada Widget Ltd. by Widget Holdings Ltd.

In 1936, Federal Widget Ltd. was organized, and a plant established in Quebec. Following the establishment of this company, World Widget offered its regular product under another brand at a lower price in all areas where Federal widgets were sold. World Widget also established special prices and rebates on a confidential basis with jobbers prepared to carry World Widgets exclusively.

In the years that followed, World Widget maintained the selling price of its product sold in those areas where no competition existed. It entered into agreements with distributors whereby the distributor would receive special rebates if they would certify from time to time in writing that all widgets sold by them were sold above specified minimum prices.

In addition to these practices, World Widget established an elaborate network of "contacts" within the Federal Widget firm, and with individuals in the firm's channel of distribution. Information sent to World Widget gave World Widget a complete picture of the operation of Federal Widget. World Widget was aware of the quantities of goods received or shipped by the firm, the destination of shipments, the names of the recipients, and the selling prices of the goods shipped. Documentation of the internal operation of Federal Widget was so complete that world Widget was in possession of the Federal Christmas bonus list, and aware of the Christmas presents to be given by Federal to its employees and customers before the presentations were made.

Federal Widget found competition with World Widget difficult, and eventually came under the control of Widget Holdings Ltd. through the acquisition of shares of Federal Widgets by Widget Holdings Ltd.

In British Columbia, the Western Widget Company, a new competitor, was established. Western Widget was interested in the widget market west of Ontario and instituted an active campaign to enter this market.

World Widget, once aware of its new competition, flooded the western market with its product, using special brands and special discounts to distributors to encourage the exclusive handling and sale of World widgets.

Western Widget tried in vain to offset the activities of World Widget with its own discounts, but failed. Eventually, Western Widget was purchased by World Widget for $210 000.

World Widget continued aggressive marketing activity until complaints triggered an investigation of its past practices. The investigation confirmed the previous actions of the company and revealed the following information:

(1) On each "take-over" (purchase of assets or shares) World Widget Co. Ltd. or Widget Holdings Ltd. would obtain an agreement from the vendor company and its officers whereby the company and its officers would agree not to engage in the widget business in Canada either directly or indirectly, for a specified period of time (usually 20 years).

(2) World Widget Co. Ltd. restricted the distribution of its special brand name widgets to areas where competition existed. These products were priced lower than regular widgets bearing the World Widget name, and were offered to distributors at prices that gave the distributor a larger margin. World Widget also entered into agreements with distributors that required the distributor to offer the special brand name products to retailers at reduced prices.

Assuming that a widget is an essential consumer and industrial product of standard design, difficult to differentiate, and with a very limited useful product life (purchased frequently), discuss the legality of the activities carried on by the firm. Identify any difficulties that might arise with respect to interpretation and enforcement of the law.

Case 2

In an effort to increase sales, the marketing manager of the World Widget Co. Ltd. introduced a co-operative advertising campaign, in which it agreed to pay 50% of the widget advertising expense of any retailer selling World Widget products, provided that the retailer agreed to advertise widgets at the "suggested retail price." No assistance would be given to the retailer if the retailer did not include the price of the product in its advertisement. The 50% payment would be based upon the dollar cost of the advertising and would be open to all who sold the company product, regardless of sales volume.

The memorandum to retailers advised all retailers taking part in the campaign that they were free to sell the product at any price they wished to establish. The memorandum also stated that retailers were free to advertise at their own expense, if they wished to advertise widgets at a price different from the suggested retail price. The proclaimed purpose of the advertising campaign, according to the marketing manager, was to promote the product on a national basis, and not to advertise the product as a special sale item.

Assess the activities of the company in the light of current trade practices legislation.

Case 3

Retailers from time to time advertised widgets at extremely low prices as an advertising gimmick to attract customers to their stores, much to the annoyance of the marketing manager of World Widget Co. Ltd. To clarify its position on "loss leaders," the company decided to issue a price list and a memorandum to discourage the use of its product in this fashion. The new price list read as follows:

Standard Model	Distributor Net Price	Regular Dealer Price	Minimum Profitable Resale Price	Fair Retail Value
(case lot)	$21.07	$24.47	$29.95	$34.95

All widget distributors were advised by the company that the sale of widgets at prices lower than fair retail value would be investigated, and any sale at a price lower than the minimum profitable resale price might be considered a loss leader sale. The company indicated that it would "assess such a sale as it related to the marketing of World Widget Co. Ltd. products."

The memorandum further stated that it was the opinion of the company that a person "loss leads" widgets when he or she sells the product at a gross margin less than the average cost of doing business plus a reasonable profit.

In the months that followed the issue of the memorandum, the World Widget Marketing Manager noted that two retailers continued to sell widgets at very low prices. One of the retailers, a large retail chain, regularly advertised and sold widgets at a unit price that would amount to $21 a case. Since the retailer was a purchaser at the distributor price of $21.07, the product was sold at slightly less than actual cost.

The marketing manager stopped shipments to the retailer on the completion of his investigation. He advised the customer that no further shipments would be made until World Widget had some assurance that the retailer would not "loss lead" widgets. The retailer eventually agreed to notify all branch managers that widgets should be sold at the regular price, and loss leader selling would be discontinued. A copy of the memorandum was sent to World Widget, and on its receipt, shipments of widgets to the retailer resumed.

The other retailer, who purchased widgets at $24.47 a case, sold widgets at a price equivalent to $24.90 a case. World Widget considered this to be "loss leader" selling and refused to make further shipments until the retailer agreed to stop selling widgets as "loss leaders." The retailer eventually agreed to stop selling widgets in this manner, and further agreed to sell the product at a price not less than the "minimum profitable resale price." Shipments of widgets were resumed when this agreement was reached.

Assess the actions of the marketing manager in this case.

Case 4

In an attempt to diversify its product line, World Widget Co. Ltd. purchased all right, title, and interest in an automobile "jet ignition unit with transistors" from a Miami, Florida inventor. The unit consisted of a small metal container, two transistors, a small spring, and a blob of tar. The designer of the unit claimed that the device would give "better automobile gas mileage, easier starting, and better performance." In support of his claim, he provided 625 testimonial letters from users of the product who reported reduction in gas consumption ranging from 10% to 30%.

World Widget engineers were skeptical of the performance claims made for the jet ignition unit, but their concern was brushed aside by the general manager when he discovered that the selling price represented a 100% mark-up over cost.

During 1992, the "jet ignition unit with transistors" had been advertised in Canada by the previous manufacturer through several metropolitan television stations, and World Widget arranged for continued television advertising for 1993. The advertising indicated that the product would increase automobile gas mileage by up to 30% and would improve engine performance. It was sold under a money-back guarantee if the product was returned to the manufacturer within 30 days of purchase.

In January 1993, a motorist purchased a unit. When it was installed in his car, the engine would not start. He reported his experience to a government agency which then tested the motorist's unit in a number of its own vehicles. The tests indicated that the unit had no noticeable effect on engine performance or fuel consumption. The agency informed World Widget of its findings.

In the same month, another motorist wrote the company the following letter: "I purchased one of your jet ignition units recently, and I am very pleased with the change in performance of my automobile. Starting is much easier, and gasoline mileage has improved 10%. Two of my friends purchased ignition units and have obtained similar results. I heartily recommend your product."

The company received no complaints concerning its product from purchasers, and no user requested a return of the purchase price under the money-back guarantee.

Should the company continue to market the product?

Case 5

Retail Furs carried on business as a furrier in a large metropolitan city. The general manager attributed much of the company's sales volume to the use of extensive advertising and frequent "sales." As a general practice, the store held four sales a year: a Summer (off-season) Sale, a Fall Sale, a New Year's Sale, and a Spring Sale. In addition, the general manager would occasionally hold a special sale if sales volume was below expectations for the year. Each sale normally lasted for a month, although extensions were occasionally made to clear models that proved to be "poor sellers."

During the past year, the company held five sales, and each featured a standard type of mink jacket at 50% off the regular price. On the last day of the final sale for the year, a customer entered the store and wished to purchase one of the advertised jackets. The regular price was stated as $2000, and the sale price $1000. The customer, however, argued that the regular price was really $1000 for at least 5 of the previous 12 months.

The general manager denied that $1000 was the regular price and refused to sell the jacket for $500.

An investigation into the ordinary selling prices of similar jackets in the area found that prices ranged from $995 to $2300, depending upon the quality of the fur pelts, the cut, and the style.

Discuss the issues raised in this case.

Case 6

Best Appliance Company produces a complete line of small and large domestic kitchen appliances, about 30 different products in all, ranging from small electric toasters to automatic dishwashers and laundry appliances. Most of the small appliances are sold through wholesalers, while the larger appliances are sold directly to "authorized dealers." The authorized dealers normally carry only the larger appliance line consisting of about 12 different products, but the occasional dealer would carry the full line of both large and small appliances.

In recent years, the company experienced problems with retailers selling its smaller appliances as "loss leaders." It considered either selling only through "authorized dealers" who would agree to carry the full line of products, or to dealers on a consignment basis (whereby the company would control the retail price). A third alternative would be to notify all wholesalers who carried the small appliance lines that they must refrain from selling to retailers who used the company's products as loss leaders. Then, if the wholesaler failed to monitor retail sales and keep retailers from loss leader selling, the company would no longer supply them with stock.

The company officers, who wish to have the legal implications of these proposals examined, ask for advice. Prepare a response to their request and include suggestions as to how they might deal with their problem.

Case 7

Gargantuan Gravel Corporation carries on business as a producer and supplier of gravel and crushed rock for road construction and building construction purposes. It owns and operates pits and quarries located in a 160 km radius of its head office operation (which is located in a large metropolitan city). It supplies its products to approximately 55% of the users in that area.

Crushed Rock Corporation, the second largest producer in the area, owns most of the remaining quarries. It holds approximately 42% of the market. The remaining 3% of the market is controlled by 26 operators that own small gravel pits. These operators tend to service customers located in the immediate area of their pits, or supply only their own construction projects.

For many years, Gargantuan Gravel followed a practice of setting its prices for gravel and crushed rock on January 2nd in each year. Crushed Rock Corporation usually established its prices a few weeks later, and the prices were the same or slightly lower than those set by Gargantuan. The 26 smaller producers normally followed price structures of the two larger firms. The asset values of both of the larger firms are in the multi-million dollar range. Both firms have extensive aggregate holdings and operate large fleets of trucks. Sales are proportionally large for both firms, and fall in the multi-million dollar range for each.

The directors of the two large firms recently entered into negotiations whereby Gargantuan Gravel would acquire all of the shares of Crushed Rock Corporation. However, some of the customers of Gargantuan Gravel are concerned about the take-over of Crushed Rock Corporation, and the effect that it might have on them financially.

Advise the customers of their rights, and how their concerns might be dealt with if they elect to take action on their concerns.

Case 8

Hewson Jewellers Limited were agents for, among other famous names, one of the finest of the Swiss watchmaker-jewellers. As Hewson was undergoing rough financial times due to an economic downturn, it decided for the first time in its history to have a general 50% off sale. A newspaper advertisement was prepared, and to entice the public it mentioned by name a number of the product lines "to be slashed by half."

The advertisement ran for one day in a national daily newspaper before it was discovered by the Canadian business representative and wholesaler of the Swiss firm. The representative-wholesaler, CanJewel Ltd., telephoned Hewson, and threatened to stop shipment of further stock, and to call Hewson's debt for stock previously shipped, unless the ad was stopped and the name of the Swiss line dropped from the copy. CanJewel reminded Hewson that "image was everything," and the Swiss line must never appear to the public to be "on sale." CanJewel extracted a signed agreement from Hewson that all future advertising copy would be reviewed by CanJewel on behalf of the Swiss manufacturer. Hewson complied, and the second advertisement made no mention of the Swiss line.

When government authorities became aware if the matter, a charge was laid under the Competition Act. State what the charge would likely be, upon whom it would be laid, the possible defences, and render a decision on behalf of the court.

CHAPTER 24

Insurance Law

HISTORICAL DEVELOPMENT

The reduction of risk, and in particular the risk of loss from unforeseen dangers, has been a quest of humankind since the beginning of time. Originally, risk was reduced by members of a family banding together to protect one another and their possessions. However, as society developed, the community tended to act as an expanded family when misfortune struck one of its members. The loss of a limb or the destruction of a dwelling often triggered a community response to aid the unfortunate individual.

Protection from the financial loss that frequently accompanies a misfortune was recognized by the early guilds in England and Continental Europe during the Middle Ages. The benefits of protection from loss due to injury was not, however, the primary reason why craftsmen and merchants joined guilds, but it did represent an attractive advantage of membership. Originally the members of the group made a common pledge to compensate one another in the event of loss. Later, the individuals in the group contributed sums of money to form a pool or fund from which a loss incurred by a member would be paid. As the fund was gradually reduced by the payment of compensation for losses, additional levies were made on the group members to replenish the fund. Eventually, nearly all guilds used this method as a basis for their insurance. It should be noted, however, that insurance schemes were not restricted to the guilds alone. Some early merchants operated indemnity funds as well, and charged fees in return for a promise to indemnify a fund member in the event of loss.

In the late medieval period some forms of insurance developed that did bear a certain resemblance to the modern concept of insurance. The practice of spreading the risk of loss for maritime adventures among a number of individuals was apparently carried on in the early Middle Ages. By the twelfth century, merchants in the Lombard area of what is now Italy insured against some of the perils of navigation. Italian merchants that visited England to trade brought the custom with them, and, by the fourteenth century, a form of maritime insurance was available for English adventurers to cover loss at sea. Disputes between the parties were normally settled by the merchants themselves in accordance with the customs that had developed to deal with these early forms of insurance.

Throughout the early stages of development of the concept of insurance, the law did little to encourage the practice of reducing risk. The early merchants settled their own insurance disputes using their own law or custom, but non-members of the guilds had to be content with a common law and with a court system that was unsuited to the enforcement of insurance agreements. It was not until the middle of the eighteenth century that widespread use of insurance prompted the courts to examine the nature of insurance and to make the common law responsive to the legal problems associated with insurance and the enforcement of claims. By this time, the courts began to view the insurance relationship as one of contract, and treated it as such in their application of the law. The relatively favourable climate that existed after that permitted the creation of many types of insurance based upon this concept. A general body of law soon developed, based in part on the law of contract.

FORMS OF INSURANCE

There are many different kinds of insurance available to the business executive today. Nearly every conceivable form of risk may be insured, the only exception being certain activities that might encourage carelessness if insured, and deliberate acts that may cause injury or loss.

Modern insurance is based upon statistical calculation of the likelihood of a particular loss occurring. As a result of accurate recordkeeping over a long period of time, insurers can determine the frequency of occurrence of different types of losses. By these records they may establish the amount of money they require from each insured in order to maintain a fund sufficiently large at all times to cover losses as they occur. Because some of these funds are invested by the insurer, the income earned is included in the fund as well to cover the insurer's expenses, profits, and to reduce the amount that the insured must pay for the insurance coverage.

Life insurance differs, to some extent, from other forms of insurance, in that the insurer will eventually be obliged to pay the face value of all policies of insurance in force at the time of death of the insured person. Statistical data on the probable life span of individuals, called actuarial tables, are used to determine the likelihood of loss due to the premature death of policy holders, and to determine the premium required to cover this unexpected event. The tables are also used to calculate the expected pay-out of the value of the policy, if the policy holder dies at the end of a normal life span.

Some life insurance policies may be used for investment purposes, as well as for protection of the beneficiaries in the case of the unexpected death of the insured. For life insurance of this type, the premiums include not only an amount to cover the cost of coverage for an unexpected loss of life, but also an amount to provide the insured a sum of money at the end of a specified period of time.

Fire Insurance

This type of insurance is designed to indemnify a person with an interest in property for any loss that might occur as a result of fire. Normally, any person with an interest in the property may protect that interest by fire coverage. The owner of the property, and any secured creditors or tenants (to the extent of their interest), may obtain this form of protection. Fire coverage is not limited to buildings only, as chattels contained in a building may also be insured. Fire policy protection is normally extended to damage caused as a result of the fire, as in the case of smoke and water damage. Insurance policies usually only indemnify the insured against loss from "hostile" fires, i.e., a fire that is not in its proper place. In contrast, a fire in a fireplace, for example, would be classed as a "friendly" fire, rather than a "hostile" one, as it is a fire deliberately set in its proper place. Insurers distinguish between the two types of fires, because a friendly fire is usually not insured. If a friendly fire becomes a hostile fire, the resultant loss is usually covered by fire insurance, unless the actions of the insured with respect to the fire were such that the fire may be classed as arson, or as a deliberate attempt to destroy the insured premises by that fire.

Life Insurance

As the name indicates, life insurance is insurance on the life of a person, be it one's own life, or that of another person in which one has an **insurable interest.** Life insurance, in its simplest form, is payable on the death of a particular person. Unlike other forms of insurance, it is based upon an event that will eventually occur. The only uncertainty attached to life insurance is the timing of the death that will render the policy payable. It differs from other forms of insurance in that the person upon whose life the insurance is placed does not receive the proceeds of the insurance, although they may be made payable to the deceased's estate if no specific beneficiary is named in the policy.

Life insurance policies usually include an application for the insurance, in which the insured sets out all the information required by the insurer to determine if the risk should be accepted, and if so, the premium payable for assuming the risk. The application is usually incorporated in the policy and becomes a part of the contract. Fraudulent statements by the applicant generally permit the insurer to avoid payment under the policy when the fraud is discovered.

Under provincial legislation, a life insurance policy may take on a variety of different forms, from simple **term insurance** to special purpose policies. The legislation generally does not determine the specific kinds of policies that a life insurer may issue but, rather, the terms that must be contained in the policy respecting such matters as lapse, renewal, time for payment of proceeds, and the proof of death of the insured. The legislation also covers other aspects of life insurance, such as life insurers themselves and the operation of their businesses. As with most insurers, life insurers are required to follow strict rules regarding the investment of their funds, in order to make certain that the company remains solvent, and that it is in a position to pay all claims under the policies.

Sickness and Accident Insurance

Insurance for sickness and accident represents a type of insurance that protects against or reduces the loss that a policy holder might incur through sickness or accident. The amounts payable usually vary, but upper limits on sickness benefits are normally set at an amount less than a person's normal income, payable on presentation of proof of the illness. Accident benefits that cover loss of limb, eyesight, or other permanent injuries are generally fixed in the policy at specific dollar amounts. As with other forms of insurance (other than life), this type of insurance is designed to provide indemnity for the loss incurred.

Liability and Negligence Insurance

Liability and negligence insurance is designed to indemnify persons for liability for losses due to negligence in the performance of their work, profession, or actions, or the use of their premises. The policy, by nature, covers specific losses such as those that may arise from negligence in the operation of a motor vehicle, the operation of a business establishment, or even a residence. These policies are designed to compensate for losses due to the torts of the individual, rather than for direct losses that an individual might suffer through no fault of his or her own. Of the many forms of negligence or liability insurance, automobile insurance has become so important, and its use so widespread, that it is treated separately under insurance legislation in most provinces. A standard policy form has also been devised as a result of interprovincial cooperation by those provinces that do not maintain their own compulsory government administered automobile insurance scheme.

Apart from automobile insurance, liability insurance is normally used to protect against claims of loss arising out of the use of premises (i.e., occupier's liability), manufacturer's product liability, professional negligence, and third party liability for the acts of servants or agents.

More recently, many firms have turned to insurance as a means of protection from claims under new environmental laws. Policies may be obtained to cover environmental accidents such as product spills causing ground or water pollution, pollution damages caused by customer use of products manufactured by the insured, or the insured's negligence in the design of products for others which in turn causes environmental damage. Of these types of policies the most important is probably the policy that covers the cost of clean-up in cases where the government orders a business to remove contaminants from soil or water.

Special Types of Insurance

In addition to these general forms of insurance coverage, insurance is also available for many specialized purposes. For example, insurance policies may be obtained to protect an employer from an employee's dishonesty, for theft or loss of goods, for business interruption, for ships and cargo, and for a variety of other business activities. All of these have one characteristic in common, i.e., they are designed to indemnify the insured in the event of a loss, or in a claim for compensation.

THE NATURE OF THE INSURANCE CONTRACT

The contract of insurance, as the name implies, is a contractual relationship to which the general rules of contract, and a number of special rules, apply. It is treated by the courts as a contract of **utmost good faith**. This means that the applicant for insurance must disclose all information requested by the insurer to enable the insurer to decide if it should assume the risk. The insurer-insured relationship has also been the subject of much control through legislation. Each province has legislation governing the contract of insurance in its various forms and, with the exception of the Province of Quebec, the legislation has tended to become uniform for most types of insurance. A number of provinces have special legislation that provides for provincially controlled automobile insurance, or for "no-fault" insurance for automobile accident cases. For the remainder, the general legislation and the common law rules apply. Changes in standard form contracts are effected by riders or endorsements that represent changes or additions to the standard terms and coverage in the agreement. While these two terms are frequently used to refer to changes made to a standard form contract, a **rider** is an additional clause attached to the contract that adds to, or may alter, standard form coverage. A rider is normally included in the agreement at the time the contract is written. An **endorsement**, on the other hand, is a change the parties agree to make to an existing contract and that, to save rewriting the contract, is simply attached to it.

The contract of insurance is a special type of contract called a **policy** that is made between an insurer and an insured, whereby the insurer promises to **indemnify** the insured for any loss that may flow from the occurrence of any event described in the agreement. In return for this promise, the insured pays, or agrees to pay, a sum of money called a **premium**.

The contract of insurance bears a resemblance to a simple wagering agreement, in that the insurer must pay out a sum of money on the occurrence of a particular event. The resemblance, however, is only superficial because there are substantial differences between the two types of agreements — the most important difference being the interests of the parties. In the case of a simple wager, the basis of the agreement is generally the occurrence of an event that will not directly result in a loss to either party (except for the amount of the wager that each party has pledged). In contrast to this, under an insurance policy, the insured receives nothing until he or she suffers some loss. Even then, the insured will only receive a sum that will theoretically place the insured in the same position that he or she was in before the loss occurred. The exception here is life insurance, where the insured must die to collect. However, even here, payment is not made unless the insured suffers the loss.

The loss that the insured suffers must relate to what is known as an **insurable interest**. This interest must be present in every insurance contract. It may be defined as anything in which the insured has a financial interest that on the occurrence of some event might result in a loss to him. An insurable interest may arise from ownership or part-ownership of a chattel or real property, or a security interest in either of them, or it may be one's own life, the life of one's spouse or child, or the life of a debtor or anyone in whom a person may have a pecuniary interest (for example, a partner or a key employee). It may also arise out of a person's profession, or activity to protect income or assets. Most insurers, however, will not insure persons against the willful acts that they commit against themselves or against their insured interests. For example, an insured person may not obtain fire coverage on a home, then deliberately burn the premises to collect the insurance proceeds. Nor would an insurer normally be obliged to pay out life insurance on the life of an insured who committed suicide. However, it should be noted that under insurance legislation in some jurisdictions, the beneficiaries may be entitled to the insurance proceeds in the case of a suicide where the policy has been in effect for some time.[1] In general, an insurable interest is anything that stands to benefit the insured person by its continued existence in its present form, and that, if changed, would represent a loss. With the exception of life insurance, the insurable interest must exist both at the time the contract of insurance is made and when the event occurs that results in a loss. For example, if Arthurs places a policy of insurance on a house she owns, then later sells the house to Bond for cash, and the house is subsequently destroyed by fire, Arthurs would not be permitted to collect the insured value of the house. By selling the house she divested herself of the interest she had in the property, and she no longer had an insurable interest in the property at the time of the loss. Nor would Bond be entitled to recover under the policy, because he was not a party to the insurance contract.[2]

In the case of life insurance, the person who takes out a policy of insurance on the life of another need only establish an insurable interest in the life of that person at the time the policy of insurance was issued. For example, if a creditor arranged for the issue of a policy of life insurance on the life of a person indebted to him, the creditor could show an insurable interest at the time of issue of the policy. The creditor, however, need not establish an insurable interest at the time of the debtor's death to receive the proceeds of the policy.

In addition to the requirement that the insured possess an insurable interest, the contract of insurance, being a contract of utmost good faith, requires full disclosure on the part of the applicant for the insurance of all material facts that might affect the decision of the insurer to accept the risk and determine the appropriate premium. With respect to disclosure, the courts have reasoned that the insurer knows nothing, and the applicant everything; hence, the obligation on the part of the applicant to disclose all material facts.

The right of the insurer to be apprised of all material facts is important. The insurer is undertaking a risk that is frequently determined from the information supplied by the applicant. Consequently, honesty on the part of the applicant is essential. If the applicant fails to disclose material facts, then the insurer may later refuse to compensate the insured if a loss occurs. For example, if the true owner of a motor vehicle arranges with a friend to have the vehicle registered in his name for the purpose of obtaining insurance, the insurance protection may not extend to the true owner if the true owner was driving the vehicle at the time of an accident that involved him, and for which he was responsible.[3]

The question of what represents an innocent misrepresentation of a material fact or non-disclosure was discussed by the courts in the case of *Mutual Life Ins. Co. of N.Y. v. Ontario Metal Products Co.*[4] where the judge commented:

---

1. Ontario, for example, provides that payment shall be made if the policy has been in force for more than two years.
2. *Rowe v. Fidelity Phoenix Fire Insurance Co. of New York,* [1944] O.W.N. 387, 600.
3. *Minister of Transport et al. v. London & Midland General Ins. Co.,* [1971] 3 O.R. 147.
4. *Mutual Life Ins. Co. of N.Y. v. Ontario Metal Products Co.,* [1925] 1 D.L.R. 583.; [1925] A.C. 344; [1925] 1 W.W.R.

The main difference of judicial opinion centres round the question what is the test of materiality? Mignault, J., [1924] 1 D.L.R., at p. 145, thought that the test is not what the insurers would have done but for the misrepresentation or concealment but "what any reasonable man would have considered material to tell them when the questions were put to the insured". Their Lordships are unable to assent to this definition. It is the insurers who propound the questions stated in the application form, and the materiality or otherwise of a misrepresentation or concealment must be considered in relation to their acceptance of the risk. On the other hand, it was argued that the test of materiality is to be determined by reference to the questions; that the Insurance Company had, by putting the question, shown that it was important for them to know whether the proposer had been in the hands of a medical man within 5 years of his application, and, if so, to have had the opportunity of interviewing such medical man before accepting the risk. The question was therefore, they contended, a material one, and the failure to answer it truthfully avoids the contract. Now if this were the true test to be applied there would be no appreciable difference between a policy of insurance subject to s. 156 of the Ontario Insurance Act, and one in the form hitherto usual in the United Kingdom. All of the questions may be presumed to be of importance to the insurer who causes them to be put, and any inaccuracy, however unimportant in the answers, would, in this view, avoid the policy. Suppose, for example, that the insured had consulted a doctor for a headache or a cold on a single occasion and had concealed or forgotten the fact, could such a concealment be regarded as material to the contract? Faced with a difficulty of this kind, the appellants' counsel frankly conceded that materiality must always be a question of degree, and therefore to be determined by the Court, and suggested that the test was whether, if the fact concealed had been disclosed, the insurers would have acted differently, either by declining the risk at the proposed premium or at least by delaying consideration of its acceptance until they had consulted Dr. Fierheller. If the former proposition were established in the sense that a reasonable insurer would have so acted, materiality would, their Lordships think, be established, but not in the latter if the difference of action would have been delay and delay alone. In their view it is a question of fact in each case whether if the matters concealed or misrepresented had been truly disclosed, they would, on a fair consideration of the evidence, have influenced a reasonable insurer to decline the risk or to have stipulated for a higher premium.

At common law, the non-disclosure or misrepresentation of a material fact would entitle the insurer to later avoid liability when the non-disclosure or misrepresentation was discovered. This has been altered, to some extent, by statute in various provinces, but for the most part the rule still holds. The exception that the legislation makes relates generally to innocent misrepresentation or innocent non-disclosure. However, where the non-disclosure or the misrepresentation amounts to fraud, then the common law rule still holds.

The legislative modification of the common law position has, as its justification, the unfairness of an insurer refusing payment of a loss where the insured without intention to deceive failed to disclose a fact, or stated an untruth as something that he or she honestly believed to be true. In these cases, the common law requirements for a contract of utmost good faith have been modified to require the insurer to carry out the policy terms if the policy has been in effect for a considerable period of time before the loss occurs (usually several years). For example, Ontario legislation provides that innocent non-disclosure by an applicant for life or health and accident insurance may not be a basis for the insurer to avoid payment of a claim made after the policy issued on the basis of the application has been in force for a period of more than two years.[5]

A contract of insurance differs from an ordinary contract in a number of other ways as well. It tends to be an ongoing relationship that usually requires the insured to advise the insurer of any substantial changes in the risk covered by the policy. Fire insurance policies usually require the insured to notify the insurer if the insured premises will be left unoccupied for more than a specified period of time. Insured business people are expected to notify the insurer if the risks associated with the conduct of their business change substantially. For example, if a manufacturer of children's toys decides to change his product line to include the manufacture of fireworks or some other dangerous product, he would be obliged to notify the insurer that a new, higher risk activity was to take place on the premises.[6]

THE CONCEPT OF INDEMNITY FOR LOSS

The particular feature that distinguishes the contract of insurance from a wager is the fact that it is a contract of **indemnity**. With the exception of life insurance and, to some extent, accident insurance, all contracts of insurance prevent the insured from making a profit from a loss. A number of special insurance concepts ensure that the insured will only be placed in the position that he or she was in before the event occurred that caused the loss. For some forms of loss, which concerns third parties, no special protection is needed for the insurer. For example, if Smith should injure Jones by her negligence, Smith's insurer will compensate Jones for his loss, or pay any judgement that Jones might obtain against Smith for her carelessness. Only the injured party will be compensated, and then only for the actual loss suffered.

With respect to chattels or property owned by the insured, three special rights of the insurer apply in the event of loss in order to prevent the insured from receiving more than the actual loss sustained. If the property is not completely destroyed, the insurer has the option to repair the chattel, or pay the insured the full value of the property at the time of loss. If the insurer pays the insured the value of the chattel, then the insurer is entitled to the property. This particular right is known as **salvage**, and it gives the insurer the right under the policy to demand a transfer of the title to the damaged goods. For example, McKay owns an automobile insured by the Car Insurance Company. The automobile is involved in an accident and is badly damaged. If the Car Insurance Company compensates McKay for the value of the automobile, then McKay must deliver up the damaged automobile to the insurer in return for the payment. The insurance company may then dispose of the wreck to reduce the loss that it has suffered through the payment of McKay's claim.

The same principle would apply in the case of goods stolen from the insured. If the insurer pays the insured the value of the stolen goods, and if the goods are subsequently recovered, the goods will belong to the insurer and not the insured. By the terms of the policy of indemnity, the goods become the goods of the insurer on the payment of the claim. In a sense, the contract bears some resemblance to a purchase of the goods by the insurer.

---

5. Insurance Act, R.S.O. 1990 c. 1-8, s. 185 and s. 309.

6. *Poapst v. Madill et al.*, [1973] 2 O.R. 80; (1973) 33 D.L.R. (3d) 36.

A second form of protection for the insurer is the **doctrine of subrogation**. Subrogation concerns the right of the insurer to recover from another person that which the insured recovers from the insurer. The doctrine of subrogation arises where the insured is injured or suffers some loss due to the actionable negligence or deliberate act of another party. For example, if an insured automobile is damaged by the negligence of another driver, the owner would have a right of action against the other driver for the damage caused by the other driver's negligence. If the insurer compensates the owner for the damage to his or her automobile then, by the doctrine of subrogation, the insurer is entitled to benefit from the owner's right of action against the negligent party. Contracts of insurance may contain a subrogation clause that specifically provides that the insured cedes the right to proceed against the party causing the injury to the insurer, or it may require the insured to proceed against the wrongdoer on behalf of the insurer, if the insurer pays the insured for the loss that the insured suffered.

The doctrine of subrogation represents an important insurance concept. Without the right of subrogation, the insured would be entitled to payment twice: once from the insurer under the contract of insurance, and a second amount in the form of damages that the insured might obtain by taking legal action against the negligent party for the injury suffered. The right of subrogation precludes double payment to the insured, and places the liability for the loss upon the person responsible for it. Subrogation has an additional beneficial side-effect: the right of the insurer to recover losses from the negligent party substantially reduces the premiums that the insured must pay for insurance coverage.

A third factor that limits the insured's compensation to the actual amount of the loss is the right of **contribution** between insurers. Persons sometimes have more than one policy of insurance covering the same loss. However, if the policies contain a clause that entitles the insurer to contribution, then each insurer will only be required to pay a portion of the loss. For example, if an insured has insurance coverage with three different insurers against a specific loss and suffers a loss of $1000, the insured will not be permitted to collect $1000 from each of the insurers. He or she will only be entitled to collect a total of $1000 from the three (i.e., $333.33 each). Each insurer would only be required to pay its share of the loss suffered by the insured.

In some cases, if the policy so provides, the insured may become an insurer for a part of the loss if the insured fails to adequately insure the risks. With some risks, the likelihood of a total loss may sometimes be small. To prevent the insured from placing only a small amount of insurance to cover the risk, the insurer may, in the policy of insurance, require the insured to become a co-insurer in the event of a partial loss. Generally, a minimum amount of insurance will be specified in the policy. If the insured fails to maintain at least that amount, then the insured becomes a **co-insurer** for the amount of the deficiency. For example, if the policy contains an 80% **co-insurance clause**, then the insured must maintain insurance for at least that amount of the value of the property (or if the insurance is burglary insurance, not less than a stated sum). The formula applied in the event of a partial loss would be:

$$\frac{\text{actual amount of insurance carried}}{\text{minimum coverage required}} \times \text{ loss } = \text{ insurer's contribution}$$

Thus, if the property is worth $100 000, and the insurance coverage is $60 000, a loss of $10 000 would be calculated as follows if the policy contains an 80% co-insurance clause (80% of $100 000 = $80 000 minimum coverage required).

$$\text{insurer's contribution} = \$10\,000 \; \times \; \frac{\$60\,000}{\$80\,000} \; = \; \$7500$$

In this example, the insurer would only be obliged to pay $7500 of the $10 000 loss. Because the insured failed to maintain a minimum of 80% coverage, the insured would be required to absorb the remainder of the loss as a co-insurer. If the loss, however, had exceeded $80 000, then the full amount of the insurance would be payable by the insurer. Co-insurance only applies where the insured suffers a partial loss of less than the required amount of insurance coverage.

THE PARTIES ASSOCIATED WITH INSURANCE CONTRACTS

Apart from the insurer and the insured, a number of other parties may be involved in either the negotiation of the contract of insurance or the processing of claims under it. Most insurance is negotiated through **agents** or employees of the insurer, and these persons have varying degrees of authority to bind the insurer in contract. Agents are generally agents of the insurer and are liable to the insurer for their actions. However, in cases where the insured has relied on the statements of the agent that the policy written by the agent covers the risks that the insured wished to have insured, and this later proves not to be the case, the insured may have a cause of action against the agent if a loss should occur.[7]

This occurred in the case of *Fine's Flowers Ltd. et al. v. General Accident Assurance Co. of Canada et al.*[8] where the insured requested insurance coverage for specific risks from an agent of the insurers. The agent failed to obtain the required coverage in the insurance policy. When a loss occurred, the insured discovered that the policy did not cover the loss. The insured brought an action against the agent for the agent's failure to include the requested coverage in the policy. In finding the agent liable for the loss, the court stated:

> The agent's duty, counsel submits, is "to exercise a reasonable degree of skill and care to obtain policies in the terms bargained for and to service those policies as circumstances might require".
>
> I take no issue with counsel's statement of the scope of the insurance agent's duty except to add that the agent also has a duty to advise his principal if he is unable to obtain the policies bargained for so that his principal may take such further steps to protect himself as he deems desirable. The operative words, however, in counsel's definition of the scope of the agent's duty, are "policies in the terms bargained for".
>
> In many instances, an insurance agent will be asked to obtain a specific type of coverage and his duty in those circumstances will be to use a reasonable degree of skill and care in doing so or, if he is unable to do so, "to inform the principal promptly in order to prevent him from suffering loss through relying upon the successful completion of the transaction by the agent": *Ivamy, General Principles of Insurance Law,* 2nd ed. (1970), at p. 464.

7. *Fine's Flowers Ltd. et al. v. General Accident Assurance Co. of Canada et al.* (1974), 49 D.L.R. (3d) 641.
8. *Fine's Flowers Ltd. et al. v. General Accident Assurance Co. of Canada et al.* (1977), 81 D.L.R. (3d) 139.

But there are other cases, and in my view this is one of them, in which the client gives no such specific instructions but rather relies upon his agent to see that he is protected and, if the agent agrees to do business with him on those terms, then he cannot afterwards, when an uninsured loss arises, shrug off the responsibility he has assumed. If this requires him to inform himself about his client's business in order to assess the foreseeable risks and insure his client against them, then this he must do. It goes without saying that an agent who does not have the requisite skills to understand the nature of his client's business and assess the risks that should be insured against should not be offering this kind of service. As Mr. Justice Haines said in *Lahey v. Hartford Fire Ins. Co.,* [1968] 1 O.R. 727 at p. 729, 67 D.L.R. (2d) 506 at p. 508; varied [1969] 2 O.R. 883, 7 D.L.R. (3d) 315:

"The solution lies in the intelligent insurance agent who inspects the risks when he insures them, knows what his insurer is providing, discovers the areas that may give rise to dispute and either arranges for the coverage or makes certain the purchaser is aware of the exclusion."

I do not think this is too high a standard to impose upon an agent who knows that his client is relying upon him to see that he is protected against all foreseeable, insurance risks.

Brokers may also place insurance with insurers. They may act either for the insured or the insurer. Persons with complex insurance needs may use a broker to determine the various kinds of insurance that they require. The broker will determine the risks, then arrange for the appropriate coverage by seeking out insurers who will insure the risks for the client.

Insurance adjusters are persons employed by an insurer to investigate the report of loss by an insured and to determine the extent of the loss incurred. Insurance adjusters report their findings to the insurer, and, on the basis of the investigation, the insurer frequently settles insurance claims. When, as a result of the adjuster's investigation, the issue of liability is unclear, the insurer may carry the matter on to the courts for a decision before making payment for the loss.

SUMMARY

With the exception of life insurance, the contract of insurance is a special type of contract designed to indemnify an insured if the insured should suffer a loss insured against in the insurance policy. A contract of insurance differs from a wagering agreement in that it is only designed to indemnify the insured for the actual loss sustained. It differs also in that the insured must have an insurable interest in the property or activity before the loss becomes payable. The contract of insurance is a contract of utmost good faith. The full disclosure of all material facts must be made to the insurer if the insured wishes to hold the insurer bound by the policy. Life insurance differs from other forms of insurance in that it is not payable to the person on whose life it is placed.

Because insurance (except life and accident insurance) is designed only to indemnify the insured for losses suffered, the insurer is entitled to the rights of salvage, subrogation, and contribution to limit the loss that it suffers as an insurer. Where an insured underinsures, some policies also make the insured a co-insurer for partial losses.

DISCUSSION QUESTIONS

1. Explain the concept of insurance and indicate how it differs from wagering.
2. Explain an insurable interest as it applies to a contract of insurance.
3. Why is a contract of insurance a contract of utmost good faith?
4. At what point in time does a life insurance policy become effective?
5. What limitations or exceptions permit an insurer to avoid payment of loss claims caused by deliberate acts of the insured?
6. What right of the insurer prevents an insured party from making a profit by a loss?
7. Is it possible for a creditor to insure the life of a person indebted to him or her? Explain.
8. Explain the doctrine or concept of salvage. Give an example of how it might apply.
9. In what way does the right of subrogation ultimately benefit the insured?
10. Describe the right of contribution and, by way of example, show how insurance companies use it to determine their liability.
11. What mathematical principles are used to determine premium rates for life insurance policies?
12. A creditor insured the life of a debtor to cover the amount of the debt owed. Two years later the debtor died, having paid back over half the debt. Is the creditor entitled to the full amount of the policy?

MINI-CASE PROBLEMS

1. A homeowner insured her home for $50 000, knowing that its true value was $100 000. An accidental fire in her kitchen caused $10 000 damage. Her fire insurance policy contained an 80% co-insurance clause. Calculate the liability of the insurer.
2. Assume a situation identical to that described in the above question, except that damage caused by the fire exceeded $50 000. How would you calculate the liability of the insurer in this case?

JUDICIAL DECISION

The following judicial decision illustrates the importance of the disclosure requirements that the law imposes on persons who wish to acquire or maintain insurance protection. In this case, the insured, having obtained automobile liability coverage from an insurer, continued to renew his policy on the basis of his original application. He was required to notify the insurer of "any change in the risk." However, he did not reveal the suspension of his licence to operate a motor vehicle when he renewed his policy. When the insured was later involved in a motor accident, the insurer refused to pay the claim on the basis that the insured had withheld the change in the risk from the insurer. The issue in the subsequent court action was whether the insured had a duty to inform the insurer of the licence suspension.

In the decision, the judge discusses the statutory conditions of the policy. He notes that the conditions impose a duty to notify the insurer of "any change in the risk material to the contract." The judge then deals with the question of whether a licence suspension was material change in the risk. To answer this question, he reviews a number of other cases. Finally he concludes that the licence suspension did constitute a material change in the risk because it would influence the insurer's decision to renew the policy or the premium it would charge.

At the end of the case the judge finds that the failure to notify the insurer placed the insured in breach of the statutory condition of the policy. The judge released the insurer from liability.

**Motor Vehicle
Insurance Policy
Renewal —
Failure to Inform
Insurer of Change
Material to Risk —
Enforceability of
Policy Against
Insurer**

Swinimer et al. v. Corkum; Prudential Assurance Co. Ltd., Third Party (1978), 89 D.L.R. (3d) 245.

In 1968, the insured took out an automobile insurance policy in which he stated that his driver's licence had not been suspended during the previous three years. Each year he received a renewal statement that provided that the insurance would be renewed on the basis of the statements of the insured in the original application, subject to any amendments. The insured continued to renew the insurance without reading the renewal statements. The insured's licence was cancelled for a period of time in 1973, and in his renewals he did not disclose this fact. Several years later, the insured was involved in an automobile accident and the insurer took the position that the policy was not enforceable.

Macintosh, J.:

Was Corkum in breach of stat. con. 1 [enacted 1966, c. 79, s. 7] of the automobile insurance part of the Insurance Act?

Statutory condition 1 reads as follows:

"1 (1) Material Change in Risk — The insured named in this contract shall promptly notify the insurer, or its local agent, in writing, of any change in the risk material to the contract and within his knowledge.

" (2) Without restricting the generality of the foregoing the words 'change in the risk material to the contract' include:

(a) any change in the insurable interest of the insured named in this contract in the automobile by sale, assignment or otherwise, except through the change of title by succession, death or proceedings under the Bankruptcy Act (Canada);

and with respect to insurance against loss or damage to the automobile:

(b) any mortgage, lien or encumbrance affecting the automobile after the application for this contract;

(c) any other insurance of the same interest, whether valid or not, covering loss or damage insured by this contract or any portion thereof."

This statutory condition imposes a duty on the insured to notify his insurer of "any change in the risk material to the contract".

In order to show that the change of risk is material to the contract it must be shown that the facts which were not disclosed would have influenced a reasonable insurer to decline the risk or to have stipulated from a higher premium.

This question was dealt with by Cromarty, J., of the Ontario High Court, in *Poapst v. Madill et al.* (1973), 33 D.L.R. (3d) 36, [1973] 2 O.R. 80, wherein he was considering whether or not a change of the use of trucks from limited local use to long haul use by an insured constituted a change to the risk. His Lordship stated at pp. 41-2:

"I therefore hold that by making long-haul runs to Florida, as he did, there was a change in the operation of the vehicle material to the risk known to the insurer when the policy, ex. 1, and the alteration endorsement made part thereof, were issued by the defendant Lloyd's.

"This problem is discussed in several cases.

"*Henwood v. Prudential Ins. Co. of America,* [1967] S.C.R. 720, 64 D.L.R. (2d) 715. This case dealt with an application for life insurance in which the applicant failed to disclose that she had undergone an emotional disturbance some time prior to making the application.

"*Per* Ritchie, J., at p. 724 S.C.R., p. 718 D.L.R.:

"'There is, in my view, no doubt that the question of materiality is one of fact and, as the learned trial judge has pointed out, no evidence was called on behalf of the appellant to contradict the categorical statement made by the respondent's own doctor to the effect that if true information had been available to the respondent, the premium rate for the policy would have been a very high one.'

"and at pp. 727-8 S.C.R., p. 722, D.L.R.:

"'If the matters here concealed had been truly disclosed they would undoubtedly have influenced the respondent company in stipulating for a higher premium and as there is no evidence to suggest that this was unreasonable or that other insurance companies would have followed a different course, I am satisfied that, on the evidence before us, it has been shown affirmatively that untrue answers respecting the medical advisers consulted by the insured were material to the risk. This is enough to avoid the policy.'

"The same problem with respect to a life policy was considered in *Mutual Life Ins. Co. of New York v. Ontario Metal Products Co. Ltd.,* [1925] 1 D.L.R. 583, [1925] A.C. 344, [1925] 1 W.L.R. 362, where the headnote [A.C.] is as follows:

"'When statements made by an insured person upon his application for a policy of life insurance are not made the basis of the contract but are to be treated merely as representations, an inaccurate statement is material so as to vitiate the policy if the matters concealed or misrepresented, had they been truly disclosed, would have influenced a reasonable insurer to decline the risk, or to have stipulated for a higher premium; it is not sufficient that they would merely have caused delay in issuing the policy while further inquires were being made.'

"An automobile policy was considered in *Johnson v. British Canadian Ins. Co.,* [1932] S.C.R. 680 at p. 687, [1932] 4 D.L.R. 281 at p. 287, where Lamont, J., said:

"'Every fact is material which would, if known, reasonably affect the minds of prudent and experienced insurers in deciding whether they will accept the contract, or in fixing the amount of premium to be charged in case they accept it.'"

H. Mullane is an assistant branch manager of Prudential and responsible for the underwriting of this company in the Atlantic area. He testified that had Prudential knowledge of the suspension of Corkum his file would have then been automatically reviewed and if renewed would be at an increase in premium of 100%. He further stated that this was the practice of other insurance companies. There was no evidence to the contrary.

Corkum's suspension of his driving privileges for the reasons above mentioned was a "change in the risk material to the contract". His failure to notify the insurer of such change placed him in breach of stat. con. 1, thereby releasing Prudential from liability under its policy with Corkum.

CASE PROBLEMS FOR DISCUSSION

Case 1

Speedy Goliath had a poor driving record and found that insurers were reluctant to insure his automobile. Part of the reason for his high accident rate was the fact that he enjoyed using his automobile in car rally contests. By ignoring the driving rules in the races, he frequently became involved in minor accidents. When he purchased a new sports car, he decided that he might obtain a lower insurance rate if the ownership of the vehicle was placed in his friend's name. His friend consented to the arrangement, and insurance coverage on the vehicle was arranged.

A short time later, while Speedy was driving his friend to work, he carelessly backed up and collided with a parked car.

The owner of the parked car demanded damages in the amount of $1000 for Speedy's carelessness, but the insurer refused to make payment.

The owner of the damaged vehicle brought an action against Speedy as the driver of the automobile, and his friend as its owner. He obtained a judgement against them for $1000.

Discuss the position of Speedy, his friend, and the insurer in this case.

Case 2

Hepburn lived 40 km from the town in which he worked. The town was a northern lumbering community surrounded by forest.

A particularly dry summer increased the forest fire hazard; already a number of forest fires were burning in the general area. None of the fires were large or out of control, and all were some distance from the town.

A small forest fire was burning several kilometres from where Hepburn lived. One morning before leaving for work, he noticed that the wind was high. He became concerned that the fire might get out of control and move in the direction of his home. Hepburn warned his wife to call him by telephone at work if the fire reports indicated that the fire was spreading in their direction.

Later that afternoon, his wife called to tell him that the high winds were moving the fire towards their home, but the fire was still some kilometres away. On receiving the news, Hepburn called a local agent for a fire insurance company and asked for fire coverage. The agent asked him a number of questions concerning the type of construction of his home, its location, and the fire protection facilities in the area. Hepburn provided accurate information in answer to the questions.

As a final question, the agent asked, "Are there any fires in your area at the present time?" To this question, Hepburn replied, "There are forest fires everywhere at this time of year." The agent laughed at his response and told him that he could consider himself covered from that moment. That evening Hepburn mailed the agent a cheque for the amount of the premium.

Because high winds prevented the fire-fighters from containing the fire, it moved closer to Hepburn's home. Eventually, the fire swept through the area where his home was located, and the building was totally destroyed.

Hepburn claimed for the fire loss, but the insurer refused to pay the claim.

Discuss the defences that the insurer might raise, and the position of Hepburn. Indicate how this case might be decided if it came before the courts.

Case 3

Benton carried on a successful restaurant business in a large city. The restaurant had an excellent reputation. This was for the most part due to the skill of Benton's gourmet chef, Simmons.

Benton realized that his business would be adversely affected if he should lose Simmons through accident or injury. For that reason he arranged for a life insurance policy in the amount of $100 000 on Simmons' life, and named himself as the beneficiary. The annual premium in the amount of $500 was paid by Benton.

Some months later, at the end of a busy day, Benton and Simmons became involved in a violent argument. Simmons left the restaurant saying, "Don't expect me to work tomorrow. I quit. I'll be in to pick up my personal belongings at 8:00 a.m."

On his way home from the restaurant, Simmons was involved in a serious automobile accident and was killed. Benton claimed the $100 000 under the life insurance policy.

Should the insurer pay the claim? What defences might it raise to resist the demand for payment?

Case 4

Hector and Keech carried on a fishing business together as a partnership. Each partner's life was insured for $200 000 under an insurance policy that named the other partner as beneficiary.

One afternoon, while the two partners were in their boat fishing close to the shore, a sudden storm came up. Hector started the engine to run the boat back to harbour. Keech wished to remain and insisted that they ride out the storm. The two men exchanged words, and then both struggled for the controls of the boat. In the process, Hector was pushed overboard and into the water. Before Keech could turn the boat around, Hector had disappeared beneath the surface of the choppy water.

Keech was charged with criminal negligence causing the death of Hector and was convicted. Because of the circumstances surrounding the death, he was given only a light prison sentence.

On his release, Keech claimed the $200 000 under the insurance policy on Hector's life in which he was named beneficiary.

Should Keech be entitled to the insurance proceeds?

Case 5

Rosa Rugrosa carried on business as a florist. She operated a large greenhouse in which she grew most of her flowers during the cold winter months. To protect her business, she contacted her insurance agent for insurance coverage against loss or damage by fire, and for theft of stock. Because the building was largely glass and steel, the agent placed its value at $25 000; when in fact its actual value was approximately twice that amount. The contents, also covered by the policy, were similarly undervalued.

The insurance agent placed the insurance coverage, and a policy was issued that contained an 80% co-insurance clause in the event of fire damage.

A few months later, on a cold winter night, vandals broke into Rosa's greenhouse, smashed some of the panes of glass by throwing potted plants against the sides of the building, and pulled the furnace flue pipe from the chimney. Smoke from the furnace filled the greenhouse, damaging most of the flowers and other plants. The vandals took with them equipment valued at $1000.

Rosa claimed the following amount from her insurer:

Damage to building by vandals	$ 3 000
Smoke damage to plants, etc.	10 000
Equipment stolen	1 000
	$14 000

The insurer agreed to compensate Rosa for the stolen equipment in the amount of $1000 and to cover the damage to the building. However, pointing to the 80% co-insurance clause in the fire insurance policy, the insurer argued that it was only responsible for a part of the damage and the loss of the plants, as the damage was caused by fire.

A few days later, the vandals were apprehended by the police and admitted causing the damage. Unfortunately, they had sold the equipment and had spent the money before they were caught. The vandals had no personal assets.

Discuss the rights and obligations of the parties in this situation. Explain how the loss would be borne.

Case 6

Major Manufacturing Company produced a variety of children's toys in a small plant located in a multiple-unit industrial complex. Most of the products manufactured were either of a plastic composition or painted metal. Consequently, relatively large quantities of flammable solvents and paint products were stored on the premises.

As a tenant of the building, Major Manufacturing Company carried fire and liability insurance on its operations in the amount of $500 000, as well as business interruption insurance designed to compensate the company for any losses arising from the interruption of the operation due to fire damage. The fire policy agreement restricted the storage of flammable products to a single room of the plant area, and it prohibited smoking in that area. Containers of flammable products in the remainder of the plant were to be kept to a minimum, and no container was to be opened in the storage area.

Employees in the plant followed the insurer's directions by taking the large storage drums out of the storage room. Once outside the room, they would open them and fill smaller containers from them for distribution to the various painting areas, then return the drum to the storage area.

One day, while an employee was filling smaller containers from an open drum, he was visited by an executive of a company that purchased toys from Major Manufacturing Company. The executive was making a tour of the manufacturing facilities with the marketing manager of Major Manufacturing Company. At the moment when the marketing manager opened the fire door to show the visitor the storage area, the visitor, without thinking and without noticing the large NO SMOKING sign, took out a cigarette and lit it. The fumes in the area immediately ignited, and the resulting fire destroyed the entire complex. The visitor, the employee, and the marketing manager were all seriously burned in the accident, but there was no loss of life.

Discuss the ramifications of this incident. Speculate as to how the loss may be determined, assuming that the building owner, all tenants, and the visitor's company were insured for liability, fire, and business interruption losses.

Case 7

Jennifer and Suzanne were the sole equal shareholders in the operation of a company which owned a retail department store. The owner's equity in the store amounted to four million dollars.

At age 52, both Jennifer and Suzanne knew that no one in either of their families had any interest in taking over their shares in the business in the event that either Jennifer or Suzanne died. At the same time, neither wanted to see the other saddled with a new partner should the family of the deceased sell the inherited half share to someone undesirable. Accordingly, they made a buyout agreement, and resolved to buy insurance sufficient that, on the death of either of them, the survivor would have enough cash to buy up the deceased's shares in the company, and that survivor would then own the company outright.

Carlyle, an agent for Solid Life Insurance Co., had been Jennifer's agent for the better part of 25 years. Carlyle wrote two policies; one on each life, with the other named as the beneficiary in the amount of two million dollars. A medical exam was required, and in the course of Suzanne's examination, she was asked by the doctor if she had smoked in the last twelve months. She said that she had not.

A year later, Suzanne was killed in an auto accident. After investigation, Solid Life Insurance Co. refused to pay because it had discovered that Suzanne had, in fact, been a smoker at the time the policy was issued. There was a policy available for smokers at the time of original issuance, but it carried a higher premium.

Jennifer sued Carlyle (with Solid Life Insurance Co. as a co-defendant) in a suit for negligence. Identify the issues involved, and render a decision.

The Law of Negotiable Instruments

INTRODUCTION

Most business transactions are based upon the exchange of money for either goods or services. For example, goods are sold for a price that represents a money amount. Similarly, employees work for a wage or salary at an agreed upon money rate, payable at specific intervals of time. Except for the simplest transactions, these contracts are generally settled by some means other than the actual payment of money by one party to the other.

The most common form of payment used is the **negotiable** instrument, which for payment purposes is frequently in the form of a cheque, a generally accepted substitute for the actual payment of money. A cheque, however, is only one type of negotiable instrument. Business persons may use other types of negotiable instruments, depending upon the form of settlement specified in the contract or agreement. Negotiable instruments in their simplest form are written promises or orders to pay sums of money to the holders of the instruments. They are represented in today's business world by cheques, promissory notes, and bills of exchange. The widespread use of these documents is due to the convenience and reduced risk that has been attached to them since early times. The nature of these "money substitutes" and the rights that attach to them are governed for the most part by the **Bills of Exchange Act**,[1] a federal statute.

---

1. Bills of Exchange Act, R.S.C. 1985 c. B-4.

HISTORICAL DEVELOPMENT OF THE LAW

A **negotiable instrument** is a written document that passes a good title to the rights contained in the document from a transferor to a transferee if the transferee takes the instrument in good faith and for value, without notice of any defect in the transferor's title.[2] The law relating to this unique instrument has its roots in early mercantile customs that date back to, and perhaps beyond, the time of the Roman Empire. The law developed from the practices of merchants in their dealings with each other, and from the decisions made to settle their disputes, first by their own guild members, and later by the courts.

Negotiable instruments were first used in international transactions between merchants. During the Middle Ages, a European merchant who sold his goods at the various "fairs" held throughout Europe might be reluctant to carry on his person the gold he received for his goods. In that case, he would arrange with a merchant in the fair town who had a business connection with a merchant in his own town to provide a note or order authorizing the payment to him (on presentation) of the amount set out in the document. In return for the note, the foreign merchant would pay over his gold to the local merchant and carry the note with him until he returned home. There, he would present the note for payment to the merchant named in the document and receive from him the required amount of gold. Over time these notes became known as **bills of exchange.**

By the late nineteenth century, the law relating to negotiable instruments was relatively well settled, but found only in a myriad of court decisions, many being at slight variance with one another on the same point of law. To simplify and render certain the law, the English Parliament passed the Bills of Exchange Act in 1882.[3] The Parliament of Canada passed a statute in 1890 that was essentially the English statute of 1882 with a few minor modifications.[4]

THE BILLS OF EXCHANGE ACT

The Bills of Exchange Act sets out the general rules of law that relate to bills of exchange, cheques, and promissory notes. Since the legislation is a federal statute, it applies throughout Canada. Very few changes have been made in the act since its introduction in 1890. Its provisions are very similar to the laws relating to these instruments in both the United Kingdom and the United States.

Today, the important features of bills of exchange are the particular features that made them so attractive to merchants centuries ago. In particular, a bill of exchange reduces the risk involved in transporting money from one place to another. Merchants no longer carry gold coin from place to place. However, its modern counterpart, legal tender of the Bank of Canada, would be required if some of the more convenient forms of negotiable instruments were not available for use in its place. In a sense, it is a convenient substitute for money.

A second advantage of a negotiable instrument is that it may be used to create credit. A great deal of modern commercial activity is based upon credit buying. Without the ease attached to the creation of credit by way of a bill of exchange, credit buying would not be as widespread as it is today. For example, A Company wishes to purchase goods from B Company but will not be in a position to pay for the goods for several months. If it is agreeable to B Company, A Company may

---

2. P.G. Osborn, *The Concise Law Dictionary,* 4th ed. (London: Sweet & Maxwell Ltd., 1954), p. 230.
3. Bills of Exchange Act, 45 & 46 Vict., c. 61.
4. Bills of Exchange Act, 1890 (53 Vict.), c. 33, now R.S.C. 1985, c. B-4 as amended.

give B Company a promissory note payable in 60 days. A Company will receive the goods but must be prepared to honour the note later when B Company presents the note for payment.

A third advantage of a bill of exchange is its **negotiability,** a particular attribute that permits it to be more readily transferred than most contractual obligations. In addition, in some circumstances a transferee of a bill of exchange may acquire a greater right to payment than the transferor of the bill. In this respect the transferee of a bill encounters less risk in taking an assignment of the instrument than the assignee of an ordinary contract. Recent consumer protection amendments, however, have altered this particular attribute of a bill of exchange if it is issued in connection with a consumer purchase. The change was designed to prevent consumer abuse through the use of bills of exchange by unscrupulous businesses. However, apart from this limitation, it remains as a method of reducing risk in an ordinary business transaction.

The Bills of Exchange Act deals at length with three general types of negotiable instruments: the **promissory note,** the **cheque**, and the **bill of exchange**. A cheque, however, is essentially a special type of bill of exchange. As a result, much of what might be said in general about a bill of exchange would apply to a cheque as well. A promissory note, on the other hand, differs in form and use from both the cheque and the bill of exchange.

Each of these instruments has particular features that lend themselves to specific commercial uses. Because they developed as a separate branch of the common law, much of the legal terminology associated with the instruments differ from that used in the law of contract. For example, a contract at common law is assigned by an assignor to an assignee, usually by a separate contract. A negotiable instrument on the other hand, is negotiated by an endorser to an endorsee on the document itself. The **endorser** and **endorsee** are roughly the equivalent of the assignor and the assignee of a contract. The endorser is a person who holds a negotiable instrument and transfers it to another by signing his or her name on the back, and delivering it to the endorsee. The endorsement, together with **delivery,** gives the endorsee the right to the instrument. For example, Jones is indebted to Brown and gives Brown a cheque for the amount of the debt. Brown is named as the **payee** on the cheque (i.e, he is named as the person entitled to payment). If Brown is indebted to Smith he may endorse the cheque by signing his name on the back and delivering it to Smith. On delivery, Smith becomes the endorsee and the **holder** of the cheque. If Brown endorsed the cheque by signing only his name on the back, the cheque then becomes a **bearer cheque,** and Smith becomes the **"bearer,"** since Smith is in physical possession of the instrument. The same terminology would apply if the cheque had been made payable to "bearer" instead of to Brown, since the person in possession of a cheque made payable to bearer is also called by that name.

The person in possession of a negotiable instrument is sometimes called a holder, but to be a holder, the party must be either a bearer, a payee, or an endorsee. In addition to an ordinary holder, a person who paid something in return for the instrument is referred to as a **holder for value** to distinguish such a holder from one who received the instrument as a gift. Since every party whose signature appears on a bill or note is presumed to have acquired the instrument for value, unless it can be established to the contrary, a holder of the instrument is usually considered to be a holder for value.[5]

A third type of holder is one who obtains special rights under a negotiable instrument. If a holder takes an instrument that is complete and regular on its face, before it is overdue, without any knowledge that it has been previously dishonoured, and, if the holder took the bill in good faith and for value and, at the time, had no notice of any defect in the title of the person who negotiated it, the holder would be a **holder in due course**.[6] The particular advantage of being a holder in due course of a negotiable instrument is the greater certainty of payment. Many of the defences that may be raised against an ordinary holder claiming payment are not available against a holder in due course. The particular advantages of being this type of holder are examined in greater detail in the part of this chapter that deals with defences available to the parties to a negotiable instrument.

BILLS OF EXCHANGE

The modern bill of exchange bears a close resemblance to the early negotiable instruments of this type used by merchants. Until recently, it was used extensively in business transactions. Its use, however, has declined to some extent since the middle of this century as a result of the greater use of cheques and other forms of payment by merchants and the general public.

A bill of exchange is a useful device where a merchant may wish to sell goods on credit to a customer and at the same time have some assurance that the customer will pay for the goods when the credit period expires. A bill of exchange permits this. For example, if a merchant is prepared to sell the goods on 30 days credit in return for the buyer giving a bill of exchange payable in 30 days, the merchant can send the bill along to the customer with the invoice for the goods. The buyer will then **"accept"** the bill by signing it, and return it to the seller. The seller may then "cash" the bill at the buyer's bank when the bill of exchange becomes payable, or simply deposit it in his or her own bank account and have the bank collect on the bill in the same manner as a cheque.

Under the Bills of Exchange Act, *a bill of exchange must be an unconditional order in writing, addressed by one person to another, signed by the person giving it, and requiring the person to whom it is addressed to pay either on demand, or at a fixed or determinable future time, a sum certain in money to, or to the order of a specified person or to a bearer.*[7] The act is very specific that the document alleged to be a bill of exchange must meet these requirements. If the document fails to comply, or if it includes some other thing that a person must do in addition to the payment of money (except as provided in the act) then the document will not be a bill of exchange.[8] Because a bill of exchange is not used by ordinary business or individuals nearly as often as cheques or promissory notes, a sample follows.

The bill of exchange in the example shown is a document in writing. It is partly printed, partly handwritten, and partly typewritten. Each of these methods of writing is permissible, but it is essential that all of the important terms be evidenced in writing.

---

5. Bills of Exchange Act, R.S.C. 1985, c. B-4, s. 53(1).

6. Ibid., s. 55(1).

7. Ibid., s. 16(1).

8. Ibid., s. 16(2).

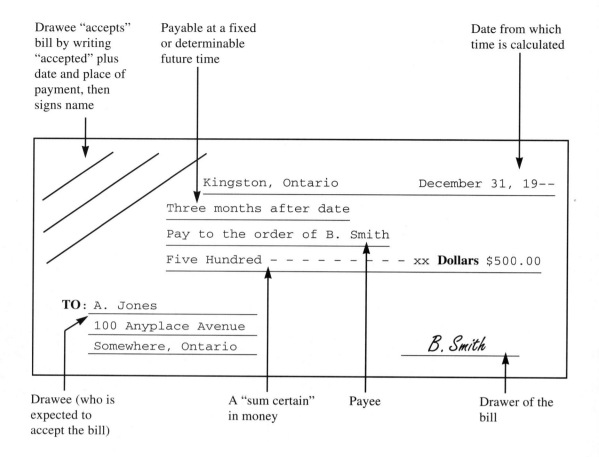

Drawee "accepts" bill by writing "accepted" plus date and place of payment, then signs name

Payable at a fixed or determinable future time

Date from which time is calculated

Kingston, Ontario   December 31, 19--

Three months after date

Pay to the order of B. Smith

Five Hundred - - - - - - - - - - xx **Dollars** $500.00

TO: A. Jones
        100 Anyplace Avenue
        Somewhere, Ontario

B. Smith

Drawee (who is expected to accept the bill)

A "sum certain" in money

Payee

Drawer of the bill

The bill is an unconditional order as indicated by the words, "Pay to the order of...," and it is addressed by one person to another ("To A. Jones, 100 Anyplace Avenue South, Somewhere, Ontario"). It is signed by the person giving it (B. Smith), and it requires the person to whom it is addressed to pay (in this case, at a fixed or determinable future time — "three months after date"). The bill is drawn for a sum certain in money ($500) and it is payable to the order of a specified person (in this case, B. Smith).

The person who prepares the bill is called the **drawer** (B. Smith), and the **drawee** (A. Jones) is the person to whom it is addressed. The payee named receives the money, and may be a bank or some person. However, the payee may be the drawer (as in this example), if the drawer wished to receive the money personally or negotiate the bill to someone else.

Once the bill is **drawn,** it is sent to the drawee for acceptance. The drawee "accepts" the bill by writing his or her **acceptance** of the bill across its face or in a corner of the bill set aside for acceptance. In this example, A. Jones would write "accepted" along with the date and where payable, then sign his name on the face of the bill. The drawee must deliver (i.e., return) the signed bill before acceptance is completed.[9] The drawee (who becomes the acceptor if he or she accepts the bill) is under no obligation to accept a bill drawn on him or her. However, if he or she does accept it, the drawee in effect promises to pay the bill when it falls due, and may be sued for payment if he or she defaults. If the drawee does not accept the bill, the drawee is said to have **dishonoured** the bill by non-acceptance.

Before the date for payment a bill may be negotiated to other persons, known as **holders.** A holder usually negotiates a bill by **endorsement.** This is the act of placing one's signature on the back of the note, then delivering it to the new holder. The act of endorsement in effect represents an implied promise to compensate the holder or subsequent endorsers in the event that the bill is dishonoured.

It should be noted that the time for payment of bills of exchange are subject to certain "rules" that may add three days to the time specified for payment, depending upon the type of bill drawn. In this example, the bill is payable at a particular time that may be calculated from the information given, but the bill may also be made payable on demand or at sight. If the bill is payable "on demand" or "on presentation" or if it does not set out a time for payment, it is considered to be a **demand bill.** It will be payable without acceptance by the drawee, unless it is payable other than at the drawee's place of residence or place of business.[10] A cheque is an example of a demand bill that is always drawn on a bank. In Canada, three days' **grace** is added to the payment date except in the case of a demand bill, which, like a cheque, is payable immediately on presentation. A **sight bill,** which is similar to a time bill, stated that it is payable "at sight" or at a specific number of days after "sight." Sight means "acceptance," and since three days' grace would be added in the case of a sight bill, the payment date in effect becomes three days after the date it is presented for acceptance. The bill may specify that the three days' grace will not apply, in which case it becomes payable on presentation.

It should be noted that a bill of exchange will not be invalid if it is not dated, has no place fixed for payment, no mention of consideration,[11] or if there is a discrepancy between words and figures.[12] However, if the bill is not dated, it must state when it is due, or it must contain the information necessary to calculate the due date. Under certain circumstances, the date may be added later if the bill is undated.[13]

The payee named in the illustration is also the drawer, but any person except the drawee may be named, or it may simply be made payable to the bearer. If the bill should be made payable to a fictitious person (such as Santa Claus or the Easter Bunny), the bill is still valid and becomes a bill payable to the bearer.[14]

LIABILITY OF THE PARTIES TO A BILL OF EXCHANGE

Acceptance of a bill of exchange by the drawee renders the drawee liable to pay the bill at the time and place fixed for payment, or in the case of a demand bill, within a reasonable time after its issue.[15] The bill must also be presented for payment by the holder or an authorized representative at a reasonable hour on a

---

9. Ibid., s. 16(2), s. 38.
10. Ibid., a. 74(2).
11. Ibid., a. 26.
12. Ibid., s. 27.
13. Ibid., s. 29.
14. Ibid., s. 20(5).
15. Ibid., s. 85(1)(b).

business day[16] at the place specified in the bill. However, if no place is specified, then it may be presented at the drawee's address. When payment is made, the drawee is entitled to a return of the bill from the holder in order that it might be cancelled or destroyed.

If payment is refused, then the holder must act quickly if he or she wishes to hold the drawer and any other endorsers liable on the bill. If the bill is dishonoured by non-payment, the holder can sue the drawer, acceptor, and endorsers.[17] However, in order to hold the parties liable, the holder must give them an opportunity to pay the bill by giving each of them (except the acceptor) **notice of the dishonour.**[18] To be valid, the notice must be given not later than the juridical or business day next following the dishonour of the bill.[19] The notice may be either in writing or by personal communication (such as telephone, or other verbal means) but it must identify the bill and indicate that it has been dishonoured by non-payment.[20] The drawer or any endorser who does not receive notice of the dishonour is discharged from any liability on the bill,[21] unless the holder is excused from giving immediate notice as a result of circumstances beyond his or her control.[22] As soon as the cause for the delay ends, however, notice must promptly be given.[23] As a result, it is in the interests of all parties to make certain that the person from whom they acquired the bill receive notice. Consequently all endorsers will generally give notice to prior endorsers to preserve their own rights.

Endorsers who receive notice have the same length of time as the holder to give notice of the dishonour to those liable to them,[24] but it is common practice to give notice to all parties liable as well. Notice of dishonour may also be dispensed with to certain parties under certain circumstances,[25] such as to the drawer where the drawer has countermanded payment,[26] or to an endorser where the endorser is the person to whom the bill is presented for payment.[27] If the bill is a foreign bill of exchange, a special procedure must be followed in the event of non-payment. A formal procedure called **protest** is used for notice, and the protest must generally be made on the same day that the dishonour occurs.[28]

CHEQUES

A **cheque** is a form of bill of exchange that is payable on demand, where the drawee is always a bank. The bank, however, is a special type of drawee in the case of a cheque, because it does not become liable to a holder in the same way that an ordinary drawee does when a bill is presented for payment. A bank need

16. Ibid., s. 77 for the time for presentation for acceptance. The time for payment would probably be somewhat similar.
17. Ibid., s. 94(2).
18. Ibid., s. 97.
19. Ibid., s. 96.
20. Ibid., s. 97(1)(d).
21. Ibid., s. 95(1).
22. Ibid., s. 104(1).
23. Ibid., s. 104(2).
24. Ibid., s. 100.
25. Ibid., ss. 106 and 107.
26. Ibid., s. 106(e).
27. Ibid., s. 107.
28. See, generally, Bills of Exchange Act, R.S.C. 1985, c. B-4, s. 111 et seq.

only honour the cheque when it is presented in proper form and sufficient funds of the drawer are on hand at the bank to cover the cheque. If the drawer has insufficient funds on deposit to permit the bank to make payment, it may refuse to honour the cheque, and the holder will be obliged to look to the drawer (or other endorsers) for payment. The only circumstances under which the bank might be liable would be if the cheque was properly drawn and the drawer had sufficient funds on deposit to cover payment. Even then, it would be liable to the drawer rather than to the holder.

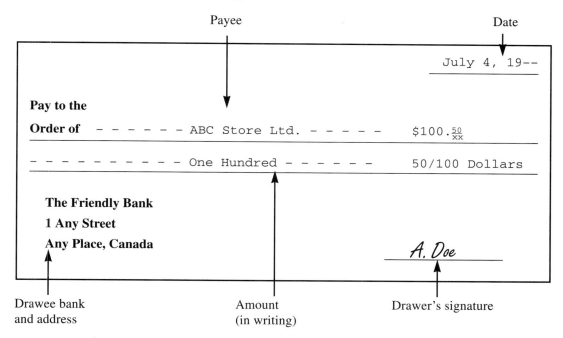

Note: *Drawer's account number normally is printed on cheque for electronic processing. If not, it is usually written on cheque by drawer in upper left corner.*

Cheques are sometimes presented to the bank for **certification.** The certification of cheques is a U.S. practice that is not covered by the Bills of Exchange Act, but one that has developed as a usage in Canada. As a result, the effect of certification on the rights of the parties to a cheque has for the most part been determined by the courts. This procedure alters the position of the bank with respect to the holder. The bank, on the presentation of the cheque, will withdraw the amount of the cheque from the drawer's account and place the funds in an account of the bank set aside for the purpose of payment. Once the funds have been removed, the bank is in a somewhat similar position to a person accepting a bill of exchange. Two forms of certification may take place: certification at the request of the drawer, and certification at the request of the payee or holder. If a bank is prepared to certify a cheque at the request of the drawer, the bank does so before delivery of the instrument, and in this sense it differs from ordinary acceptance of a bill of exchange. If the drawer should decide to return the cheque for cancellation before delivery, the drawer is entitled to do so, at which time the drawer may have the funds returned to his or her account. Countermanding the certified cheque before delivery would also have the effect of terminating the bank's obligation to honour the cheque.[29] However, if the cheque should be delivered to the payee, the right to countermand or stop payment on the cheque is not entirely clear, as delivery of the certified cheque to the payee may prevent the drawer from countermanding the cheque.[30]

Certification at the request of the holder places the bank in a different position. If the cheque is presented to the bank by the holder, the holder at that time would be entitled to payment. If the holder requests certification of the cheque instead, and the bank complies, the bank would become liable, and the drawer would be discharged from all liability. Since the drawer would in effect have made payment of the funds, the drawer would no longer be in a position to stop payment.[31] The bank, however, would be obliged to pay the cheque when presented for payment at a later time.

The Supreme Court of Ontario described the distinction between certification by the drawer and by the holder in the following terms:[32]

> The legal effect of certification of cheques is dealt with by Falconbridge in *Banking and Bills of Exchange,* 6th ed. (1956), at pp. 874-9. The learned author there draws a distinction between certification at the instance of the holder of the cheque and certification at the instance of the drawer. If a cheque is certified or marked by the drawee bank at the request of the payee or other holder, the amount of the cheque being charged by the bank to the account of the drawer, and if the holder does not then and there require payment, the drawer is discharged from all liability either on the cheque or on the original consideration for which it was given. On the other hand, in the case of a cheque which is certified by the drawer before delivery, no presentment at the time of the certification is made by the holder who alone is entitled to present the cheque for payment, and therefore he cannot be said (as he can in the first case) to have elected to accept the bank's undertaking to pay in place of actual payment. The holder or payee is still entitled to present for payment and if he so desires to receive the money.
>
> The reason why the drawer of the cheque is discharged in the first place but not in the second is stated to be as follows: The drawer's contract is that upon due presentment the cheque will be paid if the holder so desires. The holder's whole right is to present the cheque and to receive the money. The holder has no right as between himself and the drawer to present the cheque for any purpose except payment and if, when he presents the cheque and ascertains the bank is prepared to pay it, he elects not to draw the money at once, he thereby accepts the bank's undertaking to pay in place of payment. The drawer's whole obligation is performed and he is therefore discharged from liability on the cheque. The conditional payment by the giving and taking of the cheque becomes complete and the condition is fulfilled at that time.

---

29. *Gaden v. Newfoundland Savings Bank,* [1899] A.C. 281 (P.C.).

30. See *Gaden v. Newfoundland Savings Bank,* [1899] A.C. 281; but see also *Maubach v. Bank of Nova Scotia* (1987), 62 O.R. (2d) 220, and *Swartz v. Toronto-Dominion Bank* (1972), 27 D.L.R. (3d) 42.

31. *Commercial Automation Ltd. v. Banque Provinciale du Canada* (1962), 39 D.L.R. (2d) 316.

32. *Ontario Woodsworth Memorial Foundation v. Grozbord et al. Stone, Royal Bank of Canada and Bank of Nova Scotia, Third Parties* (1964), 48 D.L.R. (2d) 385.

An uncertified cheque, like a bill of exchange, is not legal tender and, if offered as payment to a creditor, represents only conditional payment of the debt. If the cheque should be dishonoured, the debt remains, and the creditor then may take action for payment on either the debt itself or the dishonoured cheque. A creditor or seller need not accept payment by way of a cheque. However, if the creditor or seller should decide to do so, and the cheque is honoured, the debt will be extinguished, and the drawer will have evidence of payment in the form of the creditor's endorsement on the back of the cheque. For this reason, a debtor giving a cheque in full or part-payment of a debt will often identify the purpose of the payment on the back of the cheque. The creditor's signature will then indicate that payment of the amount of the cheque had been received with respect to that specific account.

A cheque, being payable on demand, must be presented for payment within a reasonable time after its issue. This may vary depending upon the nature of the instrument, the customs of the trade, and the banks in the particular instance.[33] However, the fact remains that cheques should be promptly cashed on receipt; otherwise, circumstances could affect payment.[34]

Unless the cheque is made payable to bearer, it is negotiated by endorsement in the same manner as any other bill of exchange. The endorsement may be **in blank,** in which case the endorser would only sign his or her name on the back. The cheque then could be passed from one person to another without further endorsement in the same fashion as a bearer instrument. If, however, the endorser wishes to restrict the payment to one person only, the endorsement might, for example, take the form: "Pay to J. Brown only" followed by the endorser's signature below. This type of endorsement is called a **restrictive endorsement,** and would prevent any further endorsement. Only J. Brown would be permitted to present the cheque to the bank for payment. A person may also use a restrictive type of endorsement to prevent the theft and cashing of a cheque. By writing the words "for deposit only to the account of ..." followed by the person's name, the cheque may not be cashed. It may only be deposited to that person's bank account. A third general type of endorsement is called a **special endorsement.** This type requires the person named in the endorsement to endorse the cheque before it may be negotiated to anyone. A special endorsement would read "pay to the order of J. Brown" followed by the endorser's signature.

Other forms of endorsement exist as well. A person may endorse a cheque for the purpose of identifying the person or the signature of the person negotiating a cheque. In this case, the party would not incur liability on the cheque, since the endorsement would be for identification purposes only. A typical endorsement of this nature might read, "J. Brown is hereby identified," followed by the signature of the person making the identification.

An endorsement may be qualified, which would limit the liability of the endorser (provided that the other party should be willing to accept such an endorsement) if dishonour should later occur. This type of endorsement is usually called an

---

33. Bills of Exchange Act, R.S.C. 1985, c. B-4, s. 15(2). Most banks consider a "reasonable time" to be less than six months.

34. For example, the customer might die, in which case the duty of the bank to pay the cheque would have terminated. See Bills of Exchange Act, s. 167(b).

endorsement without recourse. It might read, "Without recourse" followed by the signature; or it might limit the time for recourse, "Without recourse unless presented within 10 days." The unwillingness of subsequent endorsers to accept this type of endorsement has limited its use, since subsequent endorsers must look to prior endorsers for payment in the event of non-payment by the drawer of the cheque.

An endorser, under the Bills of Exchange Act, by signing the back of a cheque or bill of exchange impliedly contracts that he or she will compensate the holder or any other subsequent endorser in the event that the cheque is not honoured when presented for payment, provided that the necessary proceedings are followed by the holder on dishonour.[35] Endorsement also precludes the endorser from denying to a holder in due course the regularity in all respects of the drawer's signature, and that of all previous endorsements.[36] In addition, an endorser is precluded from denying to immediate or subsequent endorsers that the bill was a valid bill at the time of the endorsement, and that the endorser had a good title to it.[37]

PROMISSORY NOTES

A promissory note differs from a bill of exchange or a cheque in that it is, as its name implies, a promise to pay, rather than an order. It differs also in its form and acceptance, as well. By definition, *a promissory note is an unconditional promise in writing, signed by the maker of the note, to pay to, or to the order of, a specific person or bearer on demand, or at a fixed or determinable future time, a sum certain in money.*[38]

From this definition, several differences between a promissory note and a bill of exchange are readily apparent. A note does not contain an order to pay, nor does it have a drawee that must accept the instrument. Instead, a note is a **promise** to pay, which is signed by the party who makes the promise. A simple promissory note might appear as in the sample that follows:

January 3, 19--

On demand after date, I promise to pay to *The Friendly Bank* or order,

– – – – – – Five hundred – – – – – – – – – ₓₓ/ₓₓ **DOLLARS**

At *The Friendly Bank* here, with interest at the rate of 10 percent per annum, as well after as before maturity, until paid.

Value Received

J. Smith

---

35. Bills of Exchange Act, R.S.C. 1985, c. B-4, s. 132.

36. Ibid., s. 132.

37. Ibid., s. 132.

38. Ibid., s. 176(1).

To be negotiable, the note must meet the essentials of negotiability as set down in the Bills of Exchange Act and outlined in the definition. It is important that the time for payment be clearly determined if the instrument is other than a demand note, and also that the promise to pay is unconditional, and for a sum certain in money. It cannot, for example, be payable "if I should win a particular lottery," nor can it be payable in merchandise or goods, as neither of these stipulations would meet the definition of time or payment.

A promissory note, then, is signed by the **maker,** and contains a promise to pay a sum certain in money on certain terms. The note is incomplete until it has been signed and delivered to the payee or bearer.[39] But once this act has been accomplished, the maker of the note (with legal capacity) becomes liable to pay the note according to its terms to the holder.

Like a bill of exchange or cheque, a promissory note that is payable on demand must be presented for payment within a reasonable time; otherwise, any endorser of the note may be discharged. But, if the note with the consent of the endorser is used as collateral or continuing security, then it need not be presented for payment as long as it is held for that purpose.[40]

The place of payment of a promissory note is normally set out in the body of the note, and, if so, presentation for payment must take place there if the holder of the note wishes to hold any endorser liable. If no place is specified, then usually the maker's known place of business or residence would constitute the place for payment. The time for payment is also important if the holder wishes to hold endorsers liable. As with bills of exchange, three days' grace would be added in the calculation of the time for payment for all promissory notes except those payable on demand.

Endorsers of promissory notes are in much the same position as endorsers of bills of exchange. The maker of a promissory note, by signing it, engages that he or she will pay the note according to its original terms, and is precluded from denying to a holder in due course the existence of the payee and the payee's capacity to endorse at the time.[41] If a promissory note is dishonoured when properly presented for payment at the date on which payment is due, the holder is obliged to immediately give notice of the dishonour to all endorsers if the holder wishes to hold the endorsers liable on the note. The Bills of Exchange Act provides for notice to the endorsers of a promissory note along the same procedural lines as set out for bills of exchange. The important difference is that the maker is deemed to correspond with the acceptor of a bill, and the first endorser of the note is deemed to correspond to the drawer of an accepted bill of exchange.[42]

Promissory notes, unlike bills of exchange or cheques, frequently provide for installment payments. An **installment note** is often used as a means of payment for relatively expensive consumer goods such as household appliances, automobiles, and boats. The seller may often take a security interest in the goods as collateral security to the promissory note, or may simply provide in the note that title not pass until payment is made in full. The advantage of using the promissory

39. Ibid., s. 178.
40. Ibid., s. 181.
41. Ibid., s. 185.
42. Ibid., s. 186.

note for this purpose is that the note initially facilitates the sale by the seller to the buyer. The buyer need not pay the full price at the time of purchase, but may spread the cost of the purchase over a period of time. The advantage to the seller of the promissory note is that it is a negotiable instrument, and the seller may negotiate the note to a bank or other financial institution and receive a payment of money immediately. This method permits the seller to avoid having large amounts of his or her own money tied up in credit transactions. Promissory notes of this nature normally provide for the payment of interest by the maker. Consequently the financial institution that receives the note collects the interest as its compensation for its investment.

A promissory note that provides for installment payments usually provides that each installment payment is a separate note for payment purposes. However, if default should occur, the whole of the balance immediately becomes due and payable. The reason for this special clause is that, in its absence, the holder would only be entitled to institute legal proceedings to recover overdue payments as they occurred. This clause, which is known as an **acceleration clause**, permits the holder to sue for the entire balance of the note if default should occur on any one installment payment.

DEFENCES TO CLAIMS FOR PAYMENT OF BILLS OF EXCHANGE

The holder of a negotiable instrument, whether it be a cheque, bill of exchange, or promissory note, is entitled to present the document for payment. If an instrument has two or more endorsers, each endorsement is deemed to have been made in the order in which it appears on the instrument unless an endorser can prove that the contrary is the case.[43] In the event of default, prior endorsers must indemnify subsequent endorsers. Liability to some extent follows the order of signing or endorsement, with the last person to receive the bill or note normally entitled to payment if the bill or note is properly presented for payment.

Not every holder may successfully receive payment when the instrument is presented, for instruments may be made from time to time under circumstances or contain defects that would entitle a party to the instrument to resist payment. Because a negotiable instrument is similar in many respects to a contract, the courts have applied many of the rules of contract to negotiable instruments. However, in spite of this, the rights of the holder differ substantially from those of an ordinary promisee in a contractual setting.

One of the advantages that a holder of a bill of exchange may have over an assignee of contractual rights is a right that is particular to bills of exchange in general. For reasons that are largely historical, and that arose out of the early merchants' need for certainty in payment, a holder of a bill of exchange may, under certain circumstances, obtain a better right to payment of a bill than an ordinary assignee of contractual rights would acquire.

An ordinary assignee of contractual rights takes the rights of the assignor, subject to any defects that may exist in the assignor's title. If the contract was obtained as a result of some fraud or undue influence, or if the promisor had a right of set-off against the assignor, the assignee's right to payment from the promisor might be thwarted by such a defence. With a negotiable instrument, this

43. Ibid., s. 64.

is not always so. If a negotiable instrument such as a bill of exchange, cheque, or promissory note is negotiated to a party for value and without notice of any defect in the instrument or the title of the prior holder, the holder who took the instrument under these circumstances may enforce the instrument against all prior parties in spite of any fraud, duress, undue influence, or set-off that may have existed between the original parties. The only case where such a holder (called a **holder in due course**) would be unsuccessful would be where the prior parties could establish that the instrument was essentially a nullity due to some defect such as forgery, or the minority of the maker.

These special rights and how they developed were described by the judge in the case of *Federal Discount Corp. Ltd. v. St. Pierre and St. Pierre*[44] in the following manner:

> The rights which accrue to a holder in due course of a bill of exchange are unique and distinguishable from the rights of an assignee of a contract which does not fall within the description of a bill of exchange. The assignee of a contract, unlike the holder in due course of a bill of exchange, takes subject to all the equities between the original parties, which have arisen prior to the date of notice of the assignment to the party sought to be charged.

> The special privileges enjoyed by a holder in due course of a bill of exchange are quite foreign to the common law and have their origin in the law merchant.

> There is little difficulty in appreciating how trade between merchants required that he who put into circulation his engagement to pay a specified sum at a designated time and place knowing that it was the custom of merchants to regard such paper much as we do our paper currency, should be held to the letter of his obligation and be prevented from setting up defences which might derogate from the apparently absolute nature of his obligation.

> At first the customs prevailing amongst merchants as to bills of exchange extended only to merchant strangers trafficking with English merchants; later they were extended to inland bills between merchants trafficking with one another within England; then to all persons trafficking and finally to all persons trafficking or not.

> Thus in time the particular conditions which were recognized as prevailing amongst merchants became engrafted onto the law generally applicable and came to be looked on as arising from the document itself rather than from the character of the parties dealing with the document. It is significant, however, that the transition did not affect the legal position as to one another of immediate parties and that as between any two immediate parties, maker and payee, or endorser and endorsee, none of the extraordinary conditions otherwise attaching to the bill, serve to affect adversely the rights and obligations existing between them as contracting parties. The document itself become irreproachable and affords special protection to its holder only, when at some stage of its passage from payee or acceptor to holder, there has been a bona fide transaction of trade with respect to it wherein the transferee took for value and without any notice of circumstances which might give rise to a defence on the part of the maker. Unless the ultimate holder or some earlier holder has acquired the instrument in the course of such a transaction the earlier tainting circumstances survive and the holder seeking to enforce payment of it must, on the merits, meet any defence which would have been available to the maker. Thus it appears that the peculiar immunity which the

---

44. (1962) 32 D.L.R. (2d) 86.

holding in due course arises not from the original nature of the document itself but from the quality which had been imparted to it by at least some one transfer of it.

The defences that may be raised on a negotiable instrument vary with the relationship that exists between the parties. Defences to an attempt to enforce a negotiable instrument may be divided into three separate classes, each good against a particular type of holder, if the defence can be proven.

Real Defences

Of the three classes of defences, the most effective are called **real defences.** Real defences are defences that go to the root of the instrument, and are good against all holders, including a holder in due course. These defences include the following:

Forgery

If the signature of a maker, drawer, or endorser is forged on a negotiable instrument, the holder may not enforce payment against any party through the forged signature unless the party claiming that it is forged is precluded from raising it as a defence either by conduct or negligence.[45] For example, White prepares a bearer cheque and forges Black's name as drawer, then negotiates it to Brown in return for goods sold to her by Brown. If Brown takes the cheque without knowledge of White's forgery of Black's signature, and presents it for payment, Black may raise the forgery of his signature as a defence to payment even though the holder Brown was innocent of the forgery. Brown's only right in this case would be to look to White for compensation.

Incapacity of a Minor

A minor cannot incur liability on a negotiable instrument; hence, it is a real defence against any holder, including a holder in due course.[46] If the party is insane, the same defence may apply in some circumstances, as the capacity to incur liability in the case of a negotiable instrument is co-extensive with the party's capacity to contract.[47]

Lack of Delivery of an Incomplete Instrument

If a drawer or maker signs an incomplete negotiable instrument, but does not deliver it, the lack of delivery of an incomplete instrument may be a real defence if another party should complete the instrument, and either negotiate it or present it for payment. Both elements must be present, however, as the lack of delivery alone does not constitute a real defence. For example, Smith signs a promissory note but does not fill in the amount. Later the note is stolen by Brown. If Brown fills in the amount and any other blanks, then negotiates it to Green, Smith may raise as a real defence the lack of delivery of an incomplete instrument. This defence would be good against all parties, even a holder in due course.[48]

Material Alteration of the Instrument

Under certain circumstances a person may be able to raise as a real defence the material alteration of the instrument. This defence is limited to the changes made,

---

45. Bills of Exchange Act R.S.C. 1985, c. B-4, s. 48(1). Note that an agent without express or apparent authority to sign a negotiable instrument would render the instrument void in so far as the principal is concerned.

46. Ibid., s. 46(1).

47. Ibid., s. 46(1).

48. J.D. Falconbridge, *The Law of Negotiable Instruments in Canada* (Toronto: Ryerson Press, 1923), p. 149.

however, and does not affect the enforcement of the instrument according to its original tenor. For example, if Martin draws a cheque payable to Baker for $100 and Baker alters the amount to $1100 and negotiates the cheque to Doe, Doe may only be entitled to enforce the cheque for its original amount. The material alteration may be raised as a real defence by Martin, unless Martin was negligent by drawing the cheque in such a way that Baker could easily alter it.[49]

Fraud as to the Nature of the Instrument

Fraud as a real defence to payment is limited to those cases where *non est factum* may be raised as a defence. Fraud is normally not a real defence because a person signing a negotiable instrument owes a duty of care to all others who may receive the instrument. However, if the fraud is such that the person signing the instrument is unable to ascertain the true nature of the instrument as a result of infirmity, advanced age, or illiteracy, and is induced to sign the instrument honestly believing it to be something else, then fraud might be raised as a real defence.[50]

Cancellation of the Instrument

Cancellation of an instrument, if the cancellation is apparent on the face of the instrument, would be a defence against a claim for payment by a holder.[51] If, however, payment should be made before the due date, and the cancellation is not noted on the instrument, the careless handling of the instrument may allow it to fall into the hands of another who may negotiate it to a holder for value. Under these circumstances, the holder may be able to require payment by the maker or drawer of the instrument a second time, and the defence of cancellation would not hold.

Defect of Title Defences

Real defences are good against all holders including a holder in due course. However, there are a number of other defences that are related to the title of a person that may be good against every holder except a holder in due course. A title may be defective where it is obtained by fraud, duress, or undue influence, or where the instrument is negotiated to another by way of a breach of trust or a promise not to negotiate the instrument after maturity. It may also arise where the consideration for the instrument is illegal, or where there is a total failure of consideration.[52] While fraud may be a real defence in cases where it is serious enough to constitute *non est factum*, it may be a defect of title defence as well, if the fraud is insufficient to constitute a real defence. For example, where a person is induced to sign a promissory note on the strength of false representations made by the payee, the defence of fraud may be raised by the maker as against the payee. However, it would not apply if the payee negotiated the note to a holder in due course. Duress and undue influence, as in the case of ordinary contract law, would be a good defence against a payee, or any other party to the instrument except a holder in due course.

A defect of title defence may also be available where a person charged with the responsibility for filling in the blanks on a negotiable instrument fills them in improperly, or releases an instrument to a holder when instructed not to do so.

---

49. See Bills of Exchange Act, R.S.C. 1985, c. B-4, ss. 144(1), 145 for examples of material alteration, but see *Will v. Bank of Montreal,* [1931] 3 D.L.R. 526, for negligence on the part of the drawer.
50. See, for example, *Foster v. MacKinnon* (1869), L.R. 4 C.P. 704.
51. Bills of Exchange Act, R.S.C. 1985, c. B-4, s. 142.
52. Ibid., s. 55(2).

Similarly, if a maker or drawer prepares and signs a bill or note, and it is stolen in completed form, the absence of delivery would constitute a defect of title defence good against a holder, but not against a holder in due course.

Personal Defences

A third type of defence is a defence that is effective only as against an immediate party, and not as against a remote party. The principal personal defence is **set-off**, which entitles a party to raise as a defence the indebtedness of the party claiming payment. For example, White owes Black $1000, and gives Black a note for that amount due in 30 days' time. In the interval, Black becomes indebted to White for $500. If, on the due date, Black claims payment of the $1000 note, White may set-off Black's indebtedness of $500 and pay only the remaining balance to Black.

A number of other personal defences also exist. The absence of **consideration** may be a defence that a drawer or maker may raise against a party who obtains the negotiable instrument. However, this may only be raised as a defence where the person holding the instrument has not given consideration for it, and no prior holder did so. If any prior holder gave consideration for the negotiable instrument, then the maker or drawer may not raise absence of consideration as a defence. The reason for this is that a holder, even though he or she personally did not give consideration, may enforce the instrument on the basis that the holder acquired all the rights of the prior holder.

Release or **payment before maturity** are also considered to be personal defences, where a release had been given or payment had been made before maturity. However, in each of these cases, the defences would only apply against the party who gave the release or who received the payment. The defence would not apply as against subsequent holders who had no notice of the release or payment.

DEFENCES TO CLAIMS FOR PAYMENT OF A BILL OF EXCHANGE

Defence	Defence Effective Against		
	Holder	Holder in Due Course	Endorser
Real Defences Forgery Incapacity of Minor Lack of delivery of an incomplete instrument Material alteration Fraud as to the nature* Cancellation of instrument	X	X	X
Defect of Title Defences fraud, duress, undue influence, total failure of consideration	X		X
Personal Defences set-off absence of consideration payment before maturity	X*		(if immediate party)*

*Subject to exception with respect to certain types of defences.

CONSUMER PROTECTION AND NEGOTIABLE INSTRUMENTS

In 1970, the Bills of Exchange Act was amended to provide for two new types of negotiable instruments called **consumer bills** and **consumer notes.** These instruments are ordinary bills of exchange or notes that arise out of a consumer purchase. According to the act, a consumer purchase is defined as one that is a purchase of goods or services other than a cash purchase from a person in the business of selling or providing consumer goods and services. It does not include the purchase of goods by merchants for resale, nor does it include the purchase of goods for business or professional use.[53]

The need for special legislation to govern negotiable instruments that arise from consumer purchases was recognized by the federal government in the 1960s. During that period, credit buying expanded rapidly, and companies that financed retail purchases frequently arranged with sellers to provide financing to consumers who purchased their goods. In those situations, the seller would agree to sell the goods on credit and, as a part of the sale, have the purchaser sign a promissory note to finance the purchase. The note would either be made payable directly to the finance company, or the seller would later sell the note to the finance company. In the latter case, the finance company would claim to be the holder in due course of the promissory note. In the event that the goods were defective or misrepresented by the seller, the purchaser could not withhold payment of the note to pressure the seller to correct the situation. Because the finance company was a remote party, and could enforce payment regardless of any breach of the contract of sale by the seller, the purchaser's only remedy was to take action against the seller (if the seller could be found).

Often, if the finance company took action against the purchaser, the courts would attempt to tie the seller and the finance company together in an effort to assist the hapless purchaser,[54] but in many cases, it could not do so. In the end, only legislation appeared to be the solution. In response to consumer demand, remedial legislation was introduced at the provincial and federal levels. The change at the federal level was reflected in the Bills of Exchange Act by identifying the particular negotiable instruments as consumer bills and consumer notes.

A **consumer bill** is a bill of exchange, including a cheque, that is issued in respect to a consumer purchase in which the purchaser or anyone signing to accommodate the purchaser is liable as a party. However, it does not include a cheque that is dated the day of issue (or prior thereto), or a cheque that is post-dated not more than 30 days.[55] A **consumer note** is a promissory note that is issued in respect of a consumer purchase on which the purchaser or anyone signing to accommodate the purchaser is liable as a party.[56] Both of these instruments are deemed to arise out of a consumer purchase if the funds secured by the note are obtained from a lender who is not dealing at arm's length with the seller.[57] In other words, if the seller directed the purchaser to a particular lending institution, or arranged the loan from the lending institution to enable the purchaser to make

---

53. Ibid., s. 188.

54. See, for example, *Federal Discount Corp. Ltd. v. St. Pierre and St. Pierre* (1962), 32 D.L.R. (2d) 86.

55. Bills of Exchange Act, R.S.C. 1985, c. B-4, s. 189(1).

56. Ibid., s. 189(2).

57. Ibid., s. 189(2).

the purchase, the note or bill signed by the purchaser would still be treated as arising out of a consumer purchase.

Under the act, every bill or note arising out of a consumer purchase must be marked with the words "consumer purchase" before or at the time that it is signed. A consumer bill or note that is not so marked is void except in the hands of a holder in due course who had no notice of the fact that the bill arose out of a consumer purchase.[58] The act provides penalties for violation, in addition to rendering the note void as against the purchaser. The principal thrust, however, is to eliminate collusion between sellers and lenders to avoid consumer protection legislation. The Bills of Exchange Act provides that the holder of a negotiable instrument arising out of a consumer purchase is subject to any defences by the consumer that might be raised against the seller of the goods if the goods prove to be defective or unsatisfactory.[59] This amendment to the Bills of Exchange Act also facilitates the operation of the provincial consumer protection laws by requiring the seller (or lender) in a consumer purchase to so identify the negotiable instrument.

SUMMARY

Negotiable instruments in the form of bills of exchange, cheques, and promissory notes are governed by the Bills of Exchange Act. Each of these instruments developed to meet the particular needs of merchants. Their operation was first governed by the law merchant; later, this body of law was absorbed into the common law. As a result, the law distinguished the negotiable instrument from an ordinary contract, particularly with respect to transfer. To be negotiable, an instrument must possess the essentials for negotiability. The instrument must be an unconditional order or promise in writing, signed by the maker or drawer, requiring the maker or the person to whom it is addressed to pay to a specific person or bearer, on demand, or at some fixed or determinable future time, a sum certain in money.

If an instrument meets the requirements for negotiability, it may be negotiated by the holder to another person by way of delivery (if a bearer instrument) or by endorsement and delivery. The endorsement of a negotiable instrument renders the person making the endorsement liable to the holder in the event that it is dishonoured by the maker, drawer, or acceptor. A holder acquires greater rights under a negotiable instrument than an ordinary assignee of a contractual right. This is particularly true if the person who holds the instrument is a holder in due course. A holder in due course generally is entitled to claim payment even though a defect of title may exist between prior holders. The only defences good against a holder in due course are defences that may be called real defences (forgery, incapacity of a minor, and others that render the instrument a nullity). Under the act, special instruments called consumer bills and notes must be so marked to distinguish them from other negotiable instruments. These particular instruments arise out of consumer purchases and, by marking them as a "consumer purchase," may limit the right of a holder to claim the rights of a holder in due course in the

58. Ibid, s. 190.
59. Ibid., s. 191.

event that payment is resisted by the maker or drawer for a breach of the contract of sale from which the instrument arose.

DISCUSSION QUESTIONS

1. Define a bill of exchange. Indicate how it is determined to be "negotiable."
2. How does a cheque differ from the usual type of bill of exchange?
3. Why is acceptance of a bill of exchange important?
4. What is the purpose of a bill of exchange in a modern commercial transaction?
5. Distinguish a sight bill from a demand bill.
6. Define a holder in due course. Explain how a holder in due course differs from an ordinary holder of a bill of exchange.
7. Outline the procedure to be followed when a bill of exchange is dishonoured by non-payment.
8. Indicate the different treatment at law that is given a cheque certified at the request of the holder as opposed to a cheque certified at the request of the drawer.
9. Define a promissory note. Distinguish it from a bill of exchange.
10. Explain how an endorsement in blank differs from a restrictive endorsement. Explain the circumstances under which each might be used.
11. Promissory notes that call for installment payments often contain acceleration clauses. Why is this so, and what is the purpose of such a clause?
12. When a holder in due course of a promissory note attempts to enforce payment, what types of defences might be raised by the maker named in the note?
13. What is a "defect of title" defence? What type of holder of a promissory note or bill of exchange would this type of defence be effective against?
14. Outline the various personal defences available. Indicate the type of holder that they might be raised against.

MINI-CASE PROBLEMS

1. X gave Y a post-dated cheque for $3000 as payment for a well that Y drilled on X's farm. The cheque fell due in 30 days' time. Y negotiated the cheque to Z for $2800, a few days after it was given as payment for the well drilling. Before the end of the month, the well ran dry, and X stopped payment on the cheque. Advise Z of his rights as the person in possession of the cheque.
2. B purchased an automobile from C for $500. B gave C a cheque for $500, that C, a minor aged 16, endorsed to D as payment for D's motorcycle that C had purchased. D presented the cheque for payment, only to discover that B had insufficient funds in the bank for payment, and the cheque was dishonoured. Advise D of the law in this instance.

JUDICIAL DECISION

The case of *Re Maubach and Bank of Nova Scotia* examines the legal position of a bank that certifies a cheque for a drawer and the cheque is subsequently lost before delivery to the payee. The issue taken before the judge was whether the bank was entitled to demand a bond of indemnity from the drawer before it issued a new cheque to replace the lost cheque.

In the case, the judge examines the nature of a cheque certified at the request of the drawer, and how it affects the liability of the bank. The judge refers to the Bills of Exchange Act and to the case law in order to define the liability of the bank. He then concludes that the bank would be obliged to pay the lost cheque if it was found and presented for payment. From this conclusion, he determines that the bank is entitled to a bond of indemnity if it is to issue a new cheque to replace the missing instrument.

The trial judge in his judgement concludes that the certification is not "acceptance" of the cheque under the Bills of Exchange Act, but it is equivalent to acceptance in terms of liability. However, on appeal, the Court of Appeal decided that certification in this case was equivalent to acceptance under the Bills of Exchange Act, and otherwise upheld the trial judgement set out here. See: *Re Maubach and Bank of Nova Scotia* (1988) 62 O.R. (2d) 220.

Re Maubach and Bank of Nova Scotia (1987) 60 O.R. (2d) 189.

The drawer prepared a cheque and had the cheque certified by the bank where he maintained his account. The bank certified the cheque. The drawer subsequently lost the cheque before it was delivered to the payee. The drawer requested the bank to issue a new cheque to replace the missing cheque, but the bank was not willing to do so unless the drawer was prepared to give the bank a bond of indemnity to cover the lost cheque in the event that it should be found and presented for payment. The drawer refused to do so.

GRAY J.:

...I am told by counsel for the respondent that there are, in general terms, two issues: first, whether the respondent is entitled to insist on an indemnity before issuing a second cheque; and secondly, whether in these particular circumstances, the respondent was unreasonable in insisting on an indemnity since, in the present mercantile practice, a certified cheque is equivalent to cash. I was further told that it was unnecessary for me to decide if certification is acceptance within the meaning of the *Bills of Exchange Act*. The respondent is liable whether there be acceptance or no acceptance and therefore I am urged to conclude that there is some potential risk of loss on the respondent.

Just to conclude this summary dealing with the respective positions of the parties, I should make it clear that in reply, counsel for the applicant put forward three points: (1) the court cannot take judicial notice of weight placed on mercantile practice because there was no evidence before the court in that regard; (2) the practice and custom between banks cannot ignore the law as set forth in the *Bills of Exchange Act;* and (3) legal authority is lacking to substantiate the conclusion of the writers who suggest that at the present time certification is acceptance.

To understand the applicant's position as to the necessity for acceptance, and the respondent's position that it faces possible liability if no indemnity is given, it is necessary to set out the four sections of the *Bills of Exchange Act* to which reference was earlier made. These sections are ss. 39, 127, 165 and 167:

• • • •

Delivery

39. Every contract on a bill, whether it is the drawer's, the acceptor's or an endorser's, is incomplete and revocable, until delivery of the instrument in order to give effect thereto, but where an acceptance is written on a bill, and the drawee gives notice to, or according to the directions of, the person entitled to the bill that he has accepted it, the acceptance then becomes complete and irrevocable.

• • • •

Liabilities of Parties

127. A bill, of itself, does not operate as an assignment of funds in the hands of the drawee available for the payment thereof, and the drawee of a

bill who does not accept as required by this Act is not liable on the instrument.

• • • •

CHEQUES ON A BANK

1965(1) A cheque is a bill of exchange drawn on a bank, payable on demand.

(2) Except as otherwise provided in this Part, the provisions of this Act applicable to a bill of exchange payable of demand apply to a cheque.

167. The duty and authority of a bank to pay a cheque drawn on it by its customer, are determined by

(a) countermand of payment;

(b) notice of the customer's death.

• • • •

I turn now to the case-law. In *Broadhead v. Royal Bank of Canada,* [1968] 2 O.R. 717, 70 D.L.R. (2d) 445, Grant J. tried an action by a trustee in bankruptcy to recover money paid out on a certified cheque by the bankrupt's banker after notice of the assignment into bankruptcy. The certification was at the request of the payee and the bank was entitled to reduce its indebtedness to the bankrupt and to credit what we have been calling the suspense account. At the time of the bankruptcy, there was no credit item of the bankrupt's with the bank which could vest in the trustee. The distinction is made with the situation of a cheque certified before delivery where the holder cannot be said to have elected to accept the bank's undertaking to pay in place of actual payment. The decision, however, does involve certification at the request of the payee.

The question remains as to the entitlement of the respondent to debit the applicant drawer's account when certification takes place at the request of the drawer. In the *Broadhead* case, reference was made to two other decisions: *Gaden v. Newfoundland Savings Bank,* [1899] A.C. 281, and *Commercial Automation Ltd. v. Banque Provinciale du Canada* (1962), 39 D.L.R. (2d) 316.

In the *Gaden* case, *supra,* the drawer had a cheque certified by her bank and then deposited it with the defendant Newfoundland Savings which credited her account. The drawee bank, the Commercial Bank which had initialled the cheque for certification failed. The appellant claimed a right to recover the amount from the respondent bank as the legal effect of the deposit and credit entry. The appellant was unsuccessful.

These words of Sir Henry Strong in the Judicial Committee of the Privy Council, at pp. 285-6, are to be noted according to counsel for the applicant: "It was contended on behalf of the appellant that the initialling of the cheque had the effect of making it current as cash. It does not, however, appear to their Lordships, in the absence of evidence of such usage, that any such effect can be attributed to this mode of indicating the acceptance of a cheque by the bank on which it is drawn. A cheque certified before delivery is subject, as regards its subsequent negotiation, to all the rules applicable to uncertified cheques. The only effect of the certifying is to give the cheque additional currency by showing on the face that it is drawn in good faith on funds sufficient to meet its payment, and by adding to the credit of the drawer that of the bank on which it is drawn."

We shall return to this judgment and the concluding words aforesaid in due course. The *Commercial Automation Ltd.* decision, *supra,* dealing with a bank liquidation, did not decide the exact legal status of the holder of cheques marked by the bank not at the request of the payee or drawee of the cheque but of the drawer himself. The distinction is made by Bain J. in *Re Commercial Bank of Manitoba* (1894), 10 Man. R. 187, between acceptance and certification. At p. 199, this is said:

> "In section 23 of The Bills of Exchange Act, it is said that no person is liable as the acceptor of a bill who has not signed it as such; and generally it will be found, I think, that when a banker marks or certifies a cheque, as these were, he does not intend to accept it but only to certify it, and there is a difference between "acceptance" and "certification". In *Daniel's Negotiable Instruments*, section 1605, it is said, "Frequently a depositor procures his own cheque to be certified before he offers it in payment. In such case it does not lose its character as a cheque in any particular, it only has the additional credit imparted to it by the certificate."

The applicant's submission is that certification at the drawer's request does not constitute acceptance notwithstanding the words "acceptance" on the cheque. The requirements of the *Bills of Exchange Act* (ss. 17, 127 and 165) as to acceptance not having been met, the respondent cannot be liable on the missing cheque so the respondent is not entitled to make the indemnity demand it is now making.

I now turn to the respondent's submission. It is put in para. 7 of the respondent's factum:

> 7. The mercantile expectation is that a certified cheque ought to be honoured by the drawee bank, whether certified at the request of the drawer or the payee, irrespective of either the drawer's state of account or termination of the drawee's authority to pay by virtue of the drawer's countermand of payment pursuant to s. 167 of the *Bills of Exchange Act.*

An article by Benjamin Geva, "Irrevocability of Bank Drafts, Certified Cheques and Money Orders", 65 Can. Bar Rev. 107 (1986), speaks to many of the arguments presented in this application. At p. 129, Geva makes this statement:

> "But whether the drawee bank merely accepts a cheque, or, in the case of a current cheque, certifies it, the legal nature of its liability on the instrument is quite the same. Debiting the drawer's account may create an added dimension to certification. It nevertheless falls short of affecting the nature of the drawee bank's undertaking. Certification is thus an acceptance plus something else. Nonetheless, it is still an acceptance."

And at p. 145:

> "Banker's instruments can broadly be described as payment instruments governed by the Bills of Exchange Act payable on demand, on which a bank or another financial institution is liable to the holder. They are mechanisms for the transmission of funds between individual as well as corporate debtors and creditors, which facilitate the avoidance of the risk of physical carriage of money as well as giving the creditor the assurance of payment in the form of the banker's credit attached to them.

• • • •

The binding effect of cheque certification is well established. The precise legal impact of certification is nevertheless quite controversial. The better view is to treat the certification of the cheque as an acceptance.

...I return again to the words of Sir Henry Strong at pp. 285-6 in the *Gaden* case, *supra,* after speaking of the effect of certification. "The only effect of certifying is to give the cheque additional currency by showing on the face that it is drawn in good faith on funds sufficient to meet its payment, *and by adding to the credit of the drawer that of the bank on which it is drawn.*" (Emphasis added by me.) After referring to the law in the United States, Lord Wright, at pp. 186-7 in *Bank of Baroda v. Punjab National Bank,* [1944] A.C. 176, speaks thus:

> "Certification makes the banker the debtor of the holder, and discharges the drawer altogether if the certification is not made by his procurement. Certification adds a new party, the bank, as primary debtor, and necessarily involves readjusting the legal position of the original parties, drawer and payee. A similar rule has been adopted, it seems, by the courts of Canada, on the basis of the custom in Canada judicially recognized by this Board in *Gaden v. Newfoundland Savings Bank.*"

The conclusion I have reached is that although certification by the drawee bank is not "acceptance" of the cheque by the drawee bank within the meaning of s. 35 of the *Bills of Exchange Act,* certification is equivalent to an acceptance with the result that the drawee bank is liable on a certified cheque to the payee and any holder thereof. This follows from the authorities I have quoted. By certification, the respondent upon presentation undertakes to pay the cheque: *Campbell v. Raynor* (1926), 59 O.L.R. 466 at p. 470; *Commercial Automation Ltd., supra,* at p. 321; *Boyd et al. v. Nasmith* (1888), 17 O.R. 40 at p. 46.

I remind myself that in this application, I am not adjudicating on the rights of some holder of the cheque and I also remind myself that the respondent which seeks the bond of indemnity is at risk. Examples were given to me of situations wherein the respondent might suffer at loss but no good purpose would be served by canvassing them in detail. If the cheque is certified, the respondent cannot simply honour the applicants' countermand.

CASE PROBLEMS FOR DISCUSSION

Case 1

Sugar Confectionery Ltd. borrowed a sum of money from its banker, the Big Business Bank, to purchase certain production equipment. The promissory note that the bank prepared and that John Smith, the president of the corporation, signed, reads as follows:

April 1, 1986

I hereby promise to pay on demand to the Big Business Bank, Metro Branch, the sum of Fifty Thousand Dollars ($50 000) together with interest thereon at 10% per annum calculated from April 1st, 1993, until the date of payment.

Value Received
"John Smith"
President

The bank placed the $50 000 in the Sugar Confectionary Ltd. bank account, and the corporation drew a cheque on the amount to pay the equipment supplier.

Some months later, the shareholders of Sugar Confectionary Ltd. removed John Smith as president of the company and elected Jane Doe in his place. Shortly thereafter, the Big Business Bank endorsed the note to Big Finance Company in return for the sum of $48 000.

On September 1st, Big Finance Company contacted Sugar Confectionery Ltd.

and demanded payment. Sugar Confectionery Ltd. refused to pay and stated that it was not indebted to Big Finance Company or, for that matter, to any other creditor.

Discuss this situation, evaluate the claim of Sugar Confectionery Ltd., and outline the nature of the arguments the parties might raise if the matter should come before a court. Render a decision.

Case 2

Ascot was in the process of negotiating the purchase of a valuable oil painting from a local art gallery. As a result of a number of telephone calls to the gallery owner, he eventually convinced the owner to sell the painting to him for $1000. He prepared a cheque in the amount of the purchase price and signed it. However, because he was uncertain as to the exact spelling of the gallery owner's name, he left that part of the cheque blank. He placed the signed cheque in his office desk drawer, with the intention of making a telephone call to the gallery later in the day for the information necessary to complete it.

Ascot determined the owner's name while at lunch, but when he returned to the office, he discovered that the cheque had been stolen.

Hines, a fellow employee of Ascot, had taken the cheque, filled in the cheque payable "to bearer," and used it to purchase items at a store where Ascot frequently shopped. The store owner accepted Ascot's cheque without question, as he was familiar with his signature, and later presented it to Ascot's bank for payment.

Within minutes after the bank had paid the cheque, Ascot telephoned to have the bank stop payment.

Advise the parties of their respective rights (if any) and liability (if any).

Case 3

James Baker found a wallet containing a cheque-book and a few other documents that identified the owner as one John Baker.

Using the name of John Baker, James Baker answered an advertisement that offered a small sailboat for sale. The price of the boat was $700. James Baker showed the owner John Baker's identification papers. Using one of the personalized cheques, he gave the owner of the boat a cheque for the full amount. He signed the cheque "J. Baker."

The boat owner, an infant, endorsed the cheque over to a local merchant as a part of the purchase price for a larger boat. When the merchant presented the cheque for payment, the bank refused to honour it on the basis that the signature was not that of John Baker.

Advise the merchant of his legal position.

Case 4

Casey purchased a small pick-up truck from Shady Sam's Used Car Lot. The vehicle was licensed as a commercial vehicle, but Casey intended to use it primarily as transportation to and from his employment at a local manufacturing plant. Apart from this type of driving, he expected to use it occasionally in his part-time work as a fishing guide.

As a part of the purchase price, he signed a promissory note to Shady Sam for $3000 that called for payments of principal and interest of $100 per month over a three-year term. Shady Sam immediately sold the note to Easy Payment Finance Co. for $2700. A few days later, Casey was notified by letter to make all payments on the note to Easy Payment Finance Co.

Before the first payment was due, Casey discovered that the truck was in need of extensive repairs and returned it to Shady Sam. Shady Sam refused to take back the truck and return Casey's money. Casey then refused to make payments on the promissory note.

Some months later, Easy Payment Finance Co. brought an action against Casey for the amount owing on the note.

On what basis would Easy Payment Finance Co. claim payment? What defences might be available to Casey? Render a decision.

Case 5

On May 1st, Sue agreed to purchase Henry's racing bicycle for $250. The understanding was that Henry would accept five post-dated cheques for the purchase price, the first payable on June 1st, the others monthly thereafter, until the full purchase price had been paid. Sue was still a minor, but her birthday was to fall on July 10th, at which time she would reach the age of majority. Sue gave Henry the five post-dated cheques, each for the sum of $50, and received the bicycle.

Henry cashed the first cheque on June 1st. He endorsed the remaining four cheques over to Carol as partial payment for a sailboard. Carol, who was a minor, endorsed the cheques to Denis, as payment for a loan she had received from him in order to purchase the sailboard she had later sold to Henry.

On July 1st, Denis endorsed the cheque post-dated August 1st to his wife, Alice, and endorsed the cheque post-dated September 1st to his brother George. He endorsed the cheque post-dated October 1st to Albert, as payment for a radio he purchased at Albert's Radio Shop.

On July 9th, Denis presented the cheque dated July 1st for payment, but was informed by the bank that Sue had insufficient funds in her account to honour it. On the due date of each remaining cheque, the holder presented the cheque at Sue's bank and was also advised by the bank that Sue had insufficient funds to honour the cheque.

Assume that all of the cheque holders consult you for advice on the day of dishonour. Advise them of their rights and recommend the course of action they should follow.

Case 6

Hanley sold Roberts a quantity of goods on 30 days' credit. As agreed, he drew a bill of exchange on Roberts, naming himself as payee. The bill was payable in 30 days' time. Roberts accepted the bill and returned it to Hanley. Hanley endorsed the bill to Smith to cover his indebtedness to him. Smith endorsed the bill in blank to Brown as a gift. Brown delivered the bill without endorsing it to Jones, whom he owed a sum of money. Jones, in turn, endorsed the bill and sold it to Doe. Doe presented the bill for payment, and it was dishonoured.

Advise Doe of his rights. Explain the liability (if any) of each of the parties.

Case 7

Edward bought a number of products from Scoville Limited in a single mail order, and enclosed a cheque for $130 with the order, drawn on the Bank of Hamilton. In the interval between mailing the order and the arrival of the products, Edward noticed a few of them (totalling $65) were available locally at a much lower price.

On the day the products arrived, he visited his bank and was pleased to see that his cheque had not yet been cashed. He placed a stop payment order on his cheque. In filling out the request slip, he placed the words "goods unsatisfactory" in the box allotted for the reason for the request. He decided he would send back the half of the order that he had now bought more cheaply elsewhere, and assumed that Scoville would send him a new invoice for $65.

The Bank of Hamilton failed to immediately enter the request into it's computer system, and as a result, on the arrival of the cheque a day later, it paid Edward's cheque out of his account in the normal manner. Edward discovered this error in the course of using an automated cash machine a few days later, and asked the bank to correct the error. The bank put $130 back into Edward's account and told him that they would collect back the $130 that they had paid Scoville's bank, The Bank of Manitoba. The Bank of Hamilton returned the cheque in the clearing system, now marked "Payment Stopped," and demanded $130 from the Bank of Manitoba.

The Bank of Manitoba refused the stopped cheque and would not make payment back, stating that by accepted banking convention, too much time had elapsed between acceptance by The Bank of Hamilton and the return of the item. While this had been going on, Scoville Limited had received the goods returned by Edward, and had mailed him a refund cheque for $65, for as far as they knew, they had been paid in full.

Edward was pleased. Clearly a computer error had sent him a $65 cheque rather than a $65 invoice, and he ignored the whole matter.

Assume another week passes. Discuss the events that follow, and the positions of the parties, with respect to the law of negotiable instruments as it is written. In advising the banks, what would you suggest that they add to their standard form account operation agreements?

PART VI

Real Property Law

The law relating to real property is of major importance to business. Virtually every business firm requires some space from which to operate or sell its wares. Real property is also an important asset of a business in the sense that it may be used as security for business debts. In addition, real property may also represent revenue-producing investments for business persons. This part of the text examines those areas of the law of real property that affect the business organization.

Chapter 26 provides an overview of property rights and interests in land. Chapter 27 examines the condominium, which represents a particular type of property interest used for residential as well as commercial/industrial occupancy, and a blending of individual and common ownership of the property. The third chapter in this series shifts to the financial aspects of property ownership and the use of mortgage security in real estate transactions.

Chapter 29 examines the lease as a means of acquiring possession of property for business and residential purposes. The final chapter in Part V details the steps that the parties must follow to establish and close a real estate purchase. It also outlines the various contributions which professionals such as surveyors, property appraisers, and lawyers make to a real estate transaction.

CHAPTER 26

Interests in Land

INTRODUCTION The right to hold property is central to the free enterprise system. However, even in those few countries that do not permit individuals to own land, the state is obliged to recognize certain basic property rights, if only to permit individuals to occupy some form of shelter or to allow state enterprises or co-operatives to utilize land or buildings free from interference by others. In Canada, business persons may acquire interests in land for virtually any type of business activity. Indeed, some businesses and landlords are largely concerned with the acquisition, use, and disposition of real property interests.

Interests in land may take on many forms, each designed to serve a particular purpose. For example, a business that only requires a small office space in a downtown location need not necessarily acquire land and building by purchase, but may acquire the necessary space by way of a lease of a part of a building. If the business person believes that ownership of a small amount of a space in a large building is desirable, then the acquisition of an office in a commercial condominium is an alternative form of property holding. These property rights are examined in this chapter, but at the outset it is important to note that most property rights are referred to as "estates" in land, which have attached to them specific rights and obligations.

HISTORICAL DEVELOPMENT Real property is a term used to describe land and everything permanently attached to it. At common law, the term real property includes buildings constructed on the land, the minerals or anything below the surface, and the airspace above. It may, in some instances, include chattels attached to the land in such a way that they have become **fixtures;** but as a general rule, the term does not include ordinary moveable property. Chattels are personal property. The distinction between real and personal property at law is significant, because the law relating to each form of property evolved in a distinctly different fashion.

The law that relates to land or real property is not unique to North America. It has its origins in the laws of England, dating back to the introduction of the feudal system. Much of the terminology used today in land law and the basic concept of Crown ownership of all land was developed during that time in England.

The feudal system was essentially a system under which land was held as long as the holder of the land complied with a promise to provide the necessary armed men or services in support of the Crown. If the holder of the land failed to comply, then the land would revert (or **escheat**) to the Crown. Since land was essentially the only source of wealth at the time, the holder of the land was generally always aware of the importance of providing the promised support. Not all grants, however, were made in return for military service; some grants of land were made in return for services such as the supply of agricultural produce, weapons, or administrative functions. Grants of estates in land were also made to the church or religious orders, but these were discouraged by the Crown because they were incompatible with the feudal system. In all cases where the land was granted, the Crown retained ownership and could recover the land from the person in possession. This was seldom done by the Crown, however, and the various estates in land gradually took on a degree of permanency that closely resembled ownership for all but the lowest forms of landholding.

The estates carried with them a **tenure** or right to hold the land that was either free or unfree. Estates that were **freehold** had fixed services attached to them. The type of service, the time, and the place were determined in the grant of the estate. For example, knight service was a form of freehold tenure in which the holder was usually obliged to provide the king with the services of a fully armed knight for 40 days each year, or make an equivalent payment of money.

While freehold estates could take on a number of different forms, the highest estate in land was one that permitted the holder to pass the estate along to heirs-at-law by way of inheritance. This was important at the time, because it meant that the wealth represented by the land could be passed to succeeding generations as long as there were heirs. This form of estate was known as an estate in **fee simple.** The term fee was a derivative of the Latin word feodum meaning fief or estate. Except for persons holding land directly from the Crown, the holder of an estate in fee simple was free to sell the estate if he so desired, or to devise it to another by way of a will or testamentary disposition.

As the feudal system declined in England, the practice of providing the Crown with personal services or particular quantities of produce declined with it. Instead, the services were generally satisfied by a monetary payment, which the Crown used to acquire the necessary services or goods. The development of trade and the gradual increase in importance of the production and sale of goods provided alternative methods of acquiring wealth. As these methods became more widespread, the value of land as a source of wealth and power declined. By the seventeenth century, the personal service aspects of the feudal system had all but disappeared. In 1660, Parliament passed a statute that eliminated the last vestiges of personal servitude feudal rights.[1] What remained however, was the system of

---

1. Statute of Tenures, 12 Car. II, c. 24.

landholding based upon Crown ownership of all land, and the holding of land by individuals in the form of estates based upon the estate in fee simple.[2]

ESTATES IN LAND

Fee Simple

In Canada, all land is still owned by the Crown, and estates of land in fee simple are granted by **Crown patent** to individuals.[3] The patent sets out the conditions subject to which the grant is made. It is not uncommon to find that the Crown in the right of the province has reserved either the right to all minerals or the rights to certain precious metals in the grant of the land. For example, in the past, the provinces of Ontario and some of the provinces in Eastern Canada frequently reserved all gold, silver, and precious metals. It also reserved all of the white pine trees standing on the property during the period when the British navy and merchant marine used these particular trees as material for the masts of their sailing ships. More recently, the Crown has followed the practice of reserving not only the mineral rights, but all timber standing on the property. The purchasers of the land generally purchase the timber rights separately, but the rights still represent a reservation of the Crown in the patent. In Western Canada, a Crown reservation of mineral rights is a common feature found in the patent of new lands.

Land that is granted by Crown patent seldom reverts to the Crown, because it is freely alienable by way of sale, will, or inheritance. As long as the land may be disposed of in one of these three ways, it does not escheat (revert) to the Crown. If a person, however, fails to dispose of the property during his or her lifetime and dies without heirs, or dies without a will devising the property to some other person, the land will revert to the Crown.[4] In addition, the Crown may re-acquire the land for public purposes by way of expropriation. Expropriation differs from an escheat of the lands to the Crown, because it constitutes a forceful taking of the property, for which the Crown must compensate the person in possession when land is expropriated. The taking usually must be justified as being for some public purpose, but it nevertheless represents the Crown exercising its right of ownership. Apart from expropriation, the land, once granted by Crown patent, remains in the hands of the public, unless it should, by some accident, escheat to the Crown through the failure of an owner without heirs-at-law to provide for its disposition upon the owner's death.

Generally, if a person grants land during his or her lifetime, the grant is by way of a formal document called a **deed** (see example in Document Appendix). The grant is embodied in the document in such a way that (1) the execution of the deed by the grantor (under seal in some provinces) and (2) the delivery of the document to the grantee passes the title to the land to the recipient. The receipt of the deed vests the title in the grantee, and the grantee, as the new freehold tenant, is entitled to exercise all the rights of "owner" with respect to the land. The owner of the land, for example, may use the land as he or she sees fit, subject only to the common law of nuisance and statutory enactments that restrict the use of

---

2. Some of the lesser forms of land tenures remained until the twentieth century; however, see Law of Property Act, 1922, 12 & 13, Geo. 5, c. 16.

3. In Ontario, for example, all property in the province was granted freehold after 1791. See The Canada Act, 1791, 31 Geo. III, c. 31.

4. See, for example, the Escheats Act, R.S.O. 1990, c. E-20.

property. For example, the owner may farm the land, cut down trees, construct buildings on the land, and use it for any purpose. The owner may also be granted lesser estates in the land.

Life Estate

The highest estate in land that the person in possession of the fee simple might grant (apart from the fee itself) is a **life estate.** A life estate is a freehold estate that may be held by a person other than the owner of the fee simple for a particular lifetime (usually the life tenant's own). This form of grant is frequently made within a family where the person who possesses the fee simple may wish to pass the property to younger members of the family, yet retain the use of the land during his or her lifetime. In this case, the landowner would prepare a deed that would grant the fee simple to the younger members of the family, but retain a life estate in the land. The effect of the conveyance would be that possession of the land would remain with the grantor during his or her lifetime. On death, possession would pass to the grantees. For example, Andrews owns a parcel of land in fee simple and conveys the fee simple to Brown, reserving a life estate to himself. Brown would be the grantee of the fee, subject to the life estate of Andrews. The interest in land that Brown receives in the conveyance would be the **remainder** or **reversion** interest. On Andrews' death the life estate would end. Brown would then possess the fee simple and the right to enter on and use the land.

The owner of the land in fee simple may grant many successive life estates in a particular parcel of land if desired. For example, Axleson might grant a parcel of land to Baker for life, then to Chapman for life, then to Dawson for life, and the remainder to Emmons. In this case, Baker would be entitled to the land during his lifetime, and then it would pass to Chapman for her lifetime, and then on to Dawson for her lifetime. On Dawson's death, the remainderman Emmons would acquire the land in fee simple.

A life tenant, while in possession of a life estate, is expected to use the land in a reasonable manner and not to commit **waste.** The life tenant is under no obligation to maintain any buildings in a good state of repair. However, the tenant cannot tear down buildings, nor is the life tenant permitted to deliberately destroy the property. Normally, a life tenant is not entitled to destroy trees planted to shelter the property from the wind, nor would the tenant be entitled to destroy trees planted for ornamental purposes. The tenant may, however, clear land for cultivation of crops or cut trees to obtain the wood for heating purposes. Where land is transferred to a life tenant subject to a mortgage, the life tenant is normally only obliged to pay the interest on the mortgage. The obligation to pay the principal amount rests with the person who holds the remainder or reversion interest. A life tenant is also usually obliged to pay land taxes, but not local improvement taxes charged to the land. Since the remainder interest reaps the benefits of the local improvements, the charge is his or her responsibility. However, the usual practice might be for the life tenant to pay the local improvement levy and recover it from the holder of the reversion interest.

Life estates are not without certain drawbacks or disadvantages. The existence of a life estate frequently renders the property unsaleable. A prospective purchaser of the reversion is unlikely to be willing to wait until the life tenant dies to gain possession. Unless both the life tenant and the holder of the remainder are willing to convey their respective interests in the land, the purchaser would probably not be interested in acquiring the property. The same would hold true for a sale of the life estate. A purchaser of a life estate only acquires the property for the remainder of the life tenant's lifetime. The uncertainty attached to the tenure would not prompt a purchaser to pay a high price for such an estate. More important than the sale of the property, however, is the fact that the life tenant cannot alter the property during the life tenancy, nor may the holder of the remainder, as the holder of the remainder has no right to the property until the life tenant dies. As a result, the life estate is seldom used, except to convey interests in land within families.

Leasehold Estate

A **leasehold estate** differs from a life estate or an estate in fee simple. It represents a grant of the right to possession of a parcel of land for a period of time in return for the payment of rent to the landowner. A leasehold estate, while an ancient form of tenancy, is contractual in nature, and given for a fixed term. The law has always treated leasehold interests as being distinctly different from freehold interests in land, and the body of law applicable to these interests in land remains separate from the law concerning leases. Since a lease is contractual in nature, the parties may insert in the agreement any rights or obligations they may wish, provided that they do not violate any law or regulation affecting leasehold interests in the jurisdiction where the land is located.[5]

A leasehold interest grants the tenant exclusive possession of the property for the term of the lease, provided that the tenant complies with the terms of the lease agreement. Specific legislation in each jurisdiction governs leasehold estates. These are examined in greater detail in Chapter 29.

The Condominium

Estates in land may also be "mixed" to create different forms of landholding. One such creation is the **condominium,** which represents exclusive ownership of part of the property and co-ownership of other parts. The condominium concept is used for a variety of different residential, commercial, and industrial uses, where the person or corporation may wish to have exclusive freehold ownership of part of the building or property for residential or business use and shared ownership of those parts of the property used in common with others. The "private-owned" parts of the building or structure would be the parts used as a residence or business premise. The shared parts would usually be and include the exterior building structure and walls, hallways, stairwells, elevators, lawn areas, and parking lots. The unique features of the modern condominium in Canada are examined in greater detail in the next chapter.

INTERESTS IN LAND

Easements

Persons other than the owner of land in fee simple may acquire a right or interest in land either by an express grant from the owner, by statute, by implication, or

---

5. Landlord and tenant legislation in most provinces specifies many of the duties and obligations of the parties. See, for example, The Landlord and Tenant Act, R.S.O. 1990, c. L-7.

by prescriptive right. The interests are usually acquired for the better use and enjoyment of a particular parcel of land called the **dominant tenement,** and represent an interest in a second parcel called the **servient tenement.**

Interests in the lands of another may be acquired for a wide variety of reasons. For example, a person may wish to travel across the lands of another in order to gain access to a body of water that is not adjacent to the person's own land, or a person may wish to drain water from his or her own land across the lands of another to a catch-basin. A person may also wish to place something such as a telephone line or gas pipeline on or under the lands of another for particular purposes. These rights are known as **easements.**

An easement may be granted by the owner of the fee simple (or servient tenement) to the owner of the dominant tenement by an express grant. This is often done where the owner wishes to obtain a permanent right that will run with the land and be binding on all future owners of the servient tenement. Similar rights may also be acquired by the owners of dominant tenements by way of expropriation rights granted under statute, where the legislation enables the owners to obtain rights of way across lands for public purposes, such as for a hydro power-line or a pipeline.

Easements may also be implied by law. These easements are sometimes referred to as **rights of way of necessity**. They usually arise where the grantor of a parcel of land has failed to grant access to the property sold. For example, if Adams buys a block of land from Baxter that is surrounded by land retained by Baxter, Adams would have no means of access to the land without trespassing on the land of Baxter. In such a case, the courts will imply a right of way for access to the land sold on the basis that a right of access was intended by the parties at the time that the agreement was made.

The same rule would also apply where a grantor sells a parcel of land, then realizes afterwards that the land retained is landlocked and without a right of access. In each situation, however, the land must be truly landlocked. If some other means of access exists, no matter how inconvenient it might be, then a right of way of necessity will not be implied.

An easement may also arise as a result of long, open, and uninterrupted use of a right of way over the lands of another. This type of easement is known as a **prescriptive right of easement,** and it may be acquired in most provinces.[6] A prescriptive right of this nature arises where the person claiming the easement uses the property openly and continuously as if by right, usually for a period of 20 years. The use, however, must be visible and apparent to all who might see it. The use by night, without the knowledge of anyone, would not create an easement by prescription, as the use must be open and notorious, and adverse to the owner's rights.

The exercise of the rights in the face of the owner's title is an important component of the acquisition of the prescriptive right of easement. The use must be with the knowledge of the owner of the property, or under circumstances where the owner would normally be aware of the use. If the owner fails to stop the use by the exercise of ownership rights during the 20-year period, the law assumes

---

6. All except Quebec, Alberta, and Saskatchewan, and lands under the Land Titles System in other provinces.

that the true owner is prepared to permit the use by the person claiming the prescriptive right. Any exercise of the right of the true owner to exclude the trespasser would have the effect of breaking the time period, provided that the user acknowledges the rights of the true owner and refrains from using the easement for a period of time.

Restrictive Covenants

A **restrictive covenant** is a means by which an owner of property may continue to exercise some control over its use after the property has been conveyed to another. The covenant that creates the obligation is usually embodied in the conveyance to the party who acquires the land. Normally this covenant takes the form of a promise or agreement not to use the property in a particular way. For example, a person owns two building lots. He constructs a dwelling-house on one lot and decides to sell the remaining lot. He is concerned that the prospective purchaser might use the land for the construction of a multiple-family dwelling. To avoid this, the vendor may include a term in the agreement of sale that the lands purchased may only be used for a single-family dwelling. If the purchaser agrees to the restriction, the vendor may include in the deed a **covenant** to be executed by the purchaser that the purchaser will not use the land for the construction of anything other than a single-family dwelling. Then, if the purchaser should attempt to construct a multiple-family dwelling on the property, the vendor may take legal action to have the restriction enforced.

Restrictive covenants may be used for a number of other purposes as well. They may be used to prevent the cutting of trees on property sold, control the uses of the land, require the purchaser to obtain approval of the vendor for any building constructed on the property, control the keeping of animals, or a variety of other limitations. Any covenant that attempts to prevent the purchase or use of land by any person of a particular race, creed, colour, nationality, or religion would be void as against public policy. But generally, any lawful restriction, if reasonable, and for the benefit of the adjacent property owner, may be enforced by the courts if it is described in terms that would permit the issue of an injunction.

Restrictive covenants are used for the better enjoyment and the benefit of the adjacent property owner, usually to maintain the value of the properties, or to maintain the particular character of the area. The widespread use of zoning and planning by municipalities has eliminated the use of restrictive covenants to a considerable degree. However, in many areas they are still used for special purposes where a landowner may wish to control the use of adjacent land in a particular manner.

Mineral Rights

The right to the minerals below the surface of land is possessed by the owners of the land in fee simple in most of the older provinces of Canada. In the past it was a practice of the Crown to include in the Crown patent a grant of the right to the minerals (except perhaps for gold and silver) along with the surface rights. More recent Crown patents in all provinces usually reserve the mineral rights to the

Crown, unless the patentee acquires the mineral rights at the time of issue by way of an express purchase. A person who acquires the mineral rights in the lands of another acquires an interest in land known as a ***profit à prendre*** that must be in writing, since it is a contract concerning land. In addition, the conveyance of the interest must be in deed form to be enforceable. Unless the owner of the mineral rights owns the surface rights as well, the mining of the minerals carries with it certain obligations to the owner of the surface rights. Since the extraction of minerals normally requires some disturbance of the surface, the owner of the mineral rights must compensate the owner of the surface rights for the interference with the property.

The documents that provide for the removal of the minerals and for the surface use by the persons with rights to the minerals are frequently referred to as "leases." However, they are much more than ordinary leases, even though they relate to the occupancy of a portion of the surface area. It should be noted that the right to remove water from the lands of another is not the same as the right to remove oil, gas, or other minerals. The right to remove water is generally considered to be an easement, rather than a *profit à prendre.*

Riparian Rights

A **riparian** owner is a person who owns land that is adjacent to a watercourse, or has land through which a natural stream flows either above or below the surface. A riparian owner has certain rights with respect to the use and flow of the water that have been established and recognized at common law. These rights include the right to take water from the stream or water course for domestic and commercial uses such as the watering of livestock, generation of power, or for manufacturing purposes. However, the landowner cannot interfere with the flow to downstream users and must return the quantity of water used to the stream (less the amount consumed in the use if it does not appreciably affect the quantity flowing to the downstream landowner). Some provinces control the amount of water that may be diverted from a watercourse for commercial or industrial use.

Riparian owners may erect dams on streams for the purpose of generating hydro-electric power or operating water-powered equipment or machinery. Any such structure, however, must not (except initially) restrict the flow of water downstream nor force water upon the upstream landowner by the ponding effect of the dam. The dam must not interfere with fish travelling upstream to spawn, etc. Some provinces (notably New Brunswick, Saskatchewan, British Columbia, and Ontario) control the erection of dams on watercourses and require the construction of "fishways" to ensure unobstructed upstream fish travel.

A riparian owner, while permitted to use water from a natural watercourse may not do anything to change the quality of the water used. The user may not do anything to raise the temperature of the water or add chemicals or sewage to the water, as the downstream owner is entitled to receive the water in its natural state.

A downstream owner may take legal action against an upstream owner who interferes with the flow or pollutes the water. No proof of damage is necessary, as the landowner need only establish a violation of his or her rights as a riparian owner. An injunction is the usual remedy granted by the court. It is important to note that a downstream landowner may not be successful in enforcing riparian rights if the upstream user or polluter can establish a prescriptive right at common law to pollute, due to long and uninterrupted use. Most provinces, however, have not passed legislation to control water pollution. This may be something of a mixed blessing to riparian owners, because the legislation frequently permits a certain amount of pollution if the manufacturing operations or use of the water is made in accordance with government standards. Pollution of water that endangers public health is, nevertheless, an offence under the Criminal Code.[7]

Possessory Interests in Land

Title to land may be acquired through the possession of land under certain circumstances. In some provinces, the exclusive possession of land for a long period of time — in open, notorious, visible, uninterrupted, and undisputed defiance of the true owner's title — will have the effect of creating a possessory title in the occupier of the land. The possessory title will be good against everyone, including the true owner, if the true owner fails to regain possession of the property by way of legal action within a stipulated period of time. In provinces where a possessory title may be acquired, the time period varies from 10 to 20 years. If the owner fails to take action within that period, the title in the occupier becomes **indefeasible.**

The period of possession must be continuous and undisputed, but it need not be by the same occupant. For example, one occupant may be in exclusive possession for a part of the time and may convey possession to another occupant for the remainder of the time period. As long as the period of possession is continuous, the time period will run. Any break in the chain of possession, such as where the true owner regains possession for a period of time, will affect the right of the occupant. The time period will begin again only when the possession adverse to the true owner commences for a second time.

Adverse possession requires the occupant in possession to do the acts normally required of an owner of the land. For example, the occupant would be expected to use the land, pay taxes, maintain fences, and generally treat it as the occupant's own. This must be done openly and with the knowledge of the person with title to the land.

The courts have laid down a number of general requirements that must be met before persons claiming adverse possession may succeed. As one judge described the obligation on the claimants, the claimants must establish:

(1) Actual possession for the statutory period by themselves and those through whom they claim;

(2) that such possession was with the intention of excluding from possession the owners or persons entitled to possession; and

(3) discontinuance of possession for the statutory period by the owners and all others, if any, entitled to possession.[8]

A tenant may acquire a possessory title to leased property if the tenant continues to possess the land for the statutory period of time after the lease has expired, provided that no act or acknowledgement of the lessor's title is made during the

---

7. Criminal Code, R.S.C. 1985, c. C-46, s. 180 (common nuisance endangering lives or safety).

8. See Pennell, J. in *Re St. Clair Beach Estates Ltd. v. MacDonald et al.* (1974), 50 D.L.R. (3d) 650.

period. The tenant, during the period of possession following the expiry of the lease, would be obliged to pay taxes and all other assessments usually imposed on the owner of the land, in addition to maintaining possession of the property to the exclusion of the owner for the statutory period. Any acknowledgement (such as the payment of rent) would terminate the possession time and cause it to begin again from that point. Continuous possession is the essential requirement for the acquisition of a possessory title. Unless continuous, open, and undisturbed possession can be proven, a possessory title may not be acquired.

Encroachments

An **encroachment** is also a possessory right to the property of another that may be acquired by the passage of time. It most often takes the form of a roof "overhang," where a building has been constructed too close to the property line, or where the building has actually been constructed partly on the lands of a neighbour. If the true owner of the land on which the encroachment is made permits it to exist for a long period of time, the right to demand the removal of the encroachment may be lost. In the case of a building constructed partly on the lands of another, after undisturbed possession for a period of 10 to 20 years (according to the province), the right to object to the encroachment is lost. Encroachments are normally rights in property that may be acquired only in those areas of Canada where land is recorded under the Registry System.

FIXTURES

Fixtures are chattels that are permanently or constructively attached to real property. Real property includes land and all things attached to it in some permanent fashion. For example, a building constructed on a parcel of land becomes a part of the land insofar as ownership is concerned. Some objects, however, are not normally a part of the land, but are sometimes affixed to it. Then the question arises: Did they become a part of the real property or are they still chattels that may be removed? In the early cases, the rule that developed to determine if a chattel had become a fixture and a part of the land was based upon the use and enjoyment of the particular item. Generally, it was thought that any chattel that was attached to the land to improve the land (or building), even if only slightly attached, became a part of the realty, but anything attached for the better use of the chattel did not.[9]

In the case of *Stack v. T. Eaton Co. et al.* (1902), 4 O.L.R. 335, the judge set out in the following manner the basic tests at common law that apply to fixtures:

(1) That articles not otherwise attached to the land than by their own weight are not to be considered as part of the land, unless the circumstances are such as shew that they were intended to be part of the land.

(2) That articles affixed to the land even slightly are to be considered part of the land unless the circumstances are such as to shew that they were intended to continue chattels.

(3) That the circumstances necessary to be shewn to alter the prima facie character of the articles are circumstances which shew the degree of annexation and object of such annexation, which are patent to all to see.

9. *Haggert v. Town of Brampton et al.* (1897), 28 S.C.R. 174; *Stack v. T. Eaton Co. et al.* (1902), 4 O.L.R. 335; *Re Davis*, [1954] O.W.N. 187.

(4) That the intention of the person affixing the article to the soil is material only so far as it can be presumed from the degree and object of the annexation.

(5) That, even in the case of tenants' fixtures put in for the purposes of trade, they form part of the freehold, with the right, however, to the tenant, as between him and his landlord, to bring them back to the state of chattels again by severing them from the soil, and that they pass by a conveyance of the land as part of it, subject to this right of the tenant.

These tests over the years have resulted in an unusually confusing series of cases that have failed to provide a clear rule as to what may constitute a fixture. For example, carpet in a hotel was held to be a fixture,[10] but a mobile home on a concrete foundation and attached to a septic tank and drainage field was held not to be a part of the land.[11] As a result of these and similar cases, what constitutes a fixture turns very much on the particular facts of the case. The degree of annexation to the land is generally important, as is the ability of the person in possession to remove the chattel without causing serious damage to either the chattel or the building. The particular use of the chattel is also important, since some obviously have little value except as a part of the land. Made-to-measure storm-windows, designed for a particular house, for example, would normally be constructively attached to the property as fixtures. These windows would be used specifically for the better use of the particular building, and in themselves, as chattels, would have very little value. The same would hold true for fences and trees planted on the land.

Where chattels are brought on the property and affixed by a tenant, the chattels are treated differently by the courts. Fixtures that are firmly affixed to the land or building become a part of the property and may not be removed, but items that are classed as **trade fixtures** may generally be removed by the tenant. Trade fixtures include chattels such as display cabinets, shelving, signs, mirrors, equipment, and machinery. These normally may be removed at the termination of the lease, provided that the tenant does so promptly and repairs any damage caused by their removal. Prompt removal, however, is important. Trade fixtures left on the premises for a long period of time may eventually become a part of the realty, and the tenant may not later claim them.

TITLE TO LAND

Estates in land may be held by either an individual or a number of persons. Where a number of persons hold title to property, the interests of each need not be equal, depending upon the nature of the conveyance.

Where land is conveyed to persons in **joint tenancy,** the interests of the grantees are always equal. Joint tenancy interests in land are identical in time, interest, and possession with respect to all joint tenants. A joint tenant acquires an undivided interest in the entire property conveyed. A joint tenancy must also arise out of the same instrument, such as a deed or will, and possession must arise at the same time. For example, two parties may be granted land as joint tenants in a

10. *La Salle Recreations Ltd. v. Canadian Camdex Investments Ltd.* (1969), 4 D.L.R. (3d) 549.
11. *Lichty et al. v. Voigt et al.* (1977), 80 D.L.R. (3d) 757, 17 O.R. (2d) 552.

deed or devised land under a will as joint tenants, but they cannot become joint tenants through inheritance in the sense that a person inherits the share of a joint tenant on his or her death. Joint tenancy interests vest in the surviving joint tenants on the death of a joint tenant. Consequently, a joint tenancy interest may not be devised by will to another to create a new joint tenancy. A joint tenancy may be terminated by the sale of the interest of a joint tenant to another party.

A second type of tenancy is a **tenancy-in-common,** which differs from a joint tenancy in that the right of survivorship does not attach to the interests of the tenants; nor do the interests necessarily need to be equal. For example, two individuals might receive a grant of land as tenants-in-common. The grant may be of equal interests, in which each would acquire an undivided one-half interest in the land. The grantor, however, could convey unequal interests in the property to each person, in which case the interests would be unequal but in the whole of the land. In the example above, one might receive an undivided three-quarters interest, and the other might receive an undivided one-quarter interest in the whole. It should also be noticed in the case of tenancy-in-common that a part of the tenancy may be inherited or may be devised by will. Since the right of survivorship does not exist, when a tenant-in-common dies the interest of the tenant passes by way of the tenant's will or by way of intestacy to the devisee or heirs-at-law. The interest does not vest in the surviving tenant-in-common.

If the tenants wish to divide the property and they cannot agree upon the division, the division may be made by the courts or under the Partition Act in those provinces with partition legislation.[12] The tenancy may also be dissolved by the acquisition by one tenant of the interest of the other tenant (or tenants), as the union of the interest in one person will convert the tenancy-in-common into a single fee simple interest.

REGISTRATION OF PROPERTY INTERESTS

In the past, it was necessary for the individual landowner to closely guard all documents related to the title of land in order to establish ownership rights to the property. The list of title documents began with the Crown patent and extended down through a chain of deeds from one owner to another to the deed granting the land to the present owner. If the list of deeds contained no flaws or breaks in the chain of owners, the present owner was said to have a "good title" to the land. If for some reason the title documents were destroyed through fire or were stolen, the landowner faced a dilemma. The documented legal right to the land in the form of a chain of title was gone, so a prospective purchaser was obliged to rely on the landowner's word (and perhaps the word of the neighbours) that he or she in fact had title to the lands that were being sold. The difficulties attached to this system of establishing land ownership eventually gave way to a system of land registration in which all of the land in a country or district was identified. A public record office was established to act as the recorder and custodian of all documents pertaining to the individual parcels of land. Then a prospective purchaser could simply go to the public record office to determine if the vendor had a good title to the property that was offered for sale.

Surprisingly, the widespread use of the public record office approach for the custody of documents pertaining to land and the recording of the instruments in

---

12. For example, Ontario and British Columbia.

land registers first took place in North America, rather than in England. In 1862 a Land Registry Office was established in London, but for many years the registration of title documents was voluntary. Registry offices were established in other areas of England as well, but it was not until comparatively recent times that compulsory registration was extended to all areas of England. In this respect, Canada and the United States were many years ahead of the country in which their system of land tenure developed.

In Canada, the registration system did not develop immediately, but evolved gradually, with the public office first acting as custodian of the title documents, then providing for the registration of documents. Over the years, this was refined further to the point where, in some provinces of Canada, the province itself now certifies the title of the owner of the land.

The purpose of the public registration system and the certification of titles is designed to reduce to an absolute minimum the chance of fraud in land transactions and to eliminate the need for safeguarding title documents by the individual. All provinces have a system for the registration of interests in land and have public record offices where a person may examine the title to property in the area.

All interests in property require registration to protect the interests. Otherwise, any person who does not have actual notice of the interest of another in the land may acquire an interest in the land in priority over the interest of the holder of an unregistered instrument or deed. All unregistered interests in land would therefore be void as against a person who registers a deed to the property and who had no actual notice of the outstanding interest.

Two distinct systems of registration of land interests exist in Canada. In the eastern provinces, and in parts of Ontario and Manitoba, the **Registry System** is used for land registration. In the western provinces, and parts of Manitoba and Ontario, the **Land Titles** or **Torrens System** is used.

The Registry System is the older of the two systems of land registration. Under the Registry System, a register is maintained for each particular township lot or parcel of land on a registered plan of subdivision. All interests in land that affect the particular parcel or lot are recorded in the register that pertains to the lot, and may be examined by the general public. Any person may present for registration an instrument that purports to be an interest in the land, and it will be registered against the land described in the document. For this reason, the prospective purchaser or investor must take care to ascertain that the person who professes to be the owner of the land has, in fact, a good title.

Under the Registry System, to determine the right of the person to the property, it is necessary to make a search of the **title** at the Registry Office to ascertain that a good "chain of title" exists. This means that the present owner's title must be traced back in time through the registered deeds of each registrant to make certain that each person who transferred the title to the property was in fact the owner of the land in fee simple at the time of transfer.

In Ontario, it is necessary to establish a good chain of title for a 40-year period before the title of the present owner may be said to be "clear." Each document registered against the land must be carefully examined to make certain that it has been properly drawn and executed, and that no outstanding interests in the land exist that are in conflict with the present registered owner's title. Under the

Registry System, the onus is on the prospective purchaser or investor to determine that the registered owner's title is good. Consequently, the services of a lawyer are usually necessary to make this determination. If a person fails to examine the title and later discovers that the person who gave the conveyance did not have title to the property, or that the property was subject to a mortgage or lien at the time of the purchase, the purchaser has only the interest (if any) of the vendor in the land. The only recourse of the purchaser under the circumstances would be against the vendor (if the person could be found) for damages.

The Land Titles System differs from the Registry System in a number of important aspects. Under the Land Titles System, the title of the present registered owner is confirmed and warranted by the province to be as it is represented in the land register. It is not necessary for a person to make a search of the title to the property to establish a good chain of title. This task has already been performed by the Land Registrar, and the title of the last registered owner as shown in the register for the particular parcel of land is certified as being correct. To avoid confusion, instruments pertaining to land under the Land Titles System are given different names. A deed, for example, is called a **transfer**, and a mortgage is referred to as a **charge.** The legal nature and the differences between these latter two instruments are dealt with in Chapter 28, The Law of Mortgages. As well, a number of other differences exist between the two systems. One of the more notable differences is that in land titles jurisdictions an interest in land may not normally be acquired by adverse possession.

The advantage of the Land Titles System over the older Registry System is the certainty of title under the newer system. If, for some reason, the title is not as depicted in the Land Titles Register, the party who suffered a loss as a result of the error is entitled to compensation from the province for the loss.

In an effort to streamline the land registration system in Ontario, under legislation entitled the Land Registration Reform Act, 1984,[13] the province established a new computerized system called Polaris (Province of Ontario Land Registration and Information System). The new system consists of two computerized databases: (1) a Title Index database and (2) a Property Mapping database.

The Title Index database is designed to provide a computerized version of the existing records, organized on a property ownership basis with immediate update of ownership registration. The index system will permit computer searching of the title to properties and provide print-outs of information on properties if the search person has a property identifier number, an address, the owner's name, or an instrument registration number.

The Property Mapping database provides a computerized property map file organized by property identifier number. Using these numbers, a search person may obtain a computer-generated map of a property showing survey and property lines to assist in searching the title to a property. This project, when completed, will improve the system by simplifying the methods of registration, certify the title to lands on plans of subdivision, and generally provide greater ease and certainty in the examination of the title to land in the province. The project of modernization also includes the extensive use of computerized information, storage,

---

13. Land Registration Reform Act, R.S.O. 1990, c. L-4.

and indexing, and completely new forms for deeds, mortgages, and all other documents used to convey or deal with interests in land.

New forms for conveying or dealing with property were introduced on a test basis in one Land Registry Division in 1984. When the test proved to be satisfactory, the forms were extended to the entire province in April of 1985. The new forms for deeds, mortgages, etc., provide the necessary data about each property for land registry office staff to compile the two databases. In addition, database information is collected from government surveys, map, and other databases to complete the records for each parcel of land in the province. Eventually, every parcel of land will be recorded with a property identification number and map. When the conversion is complete, the automated system will replace the present manual system of property registration. The change-over of the land registry system is expected to take approximately 15 years to complete, and be fully operational by the turn of the century.

SUMMARY

Real property includes land and everything attached to it in a permanent manner. The Crown owns all land, but has conveyed estates in land by way of Crown patents. The highest estate in land is an estate in fee simple. When someone states that he or she owns land, the estate to which the person refers is ownership in fee simple. A life estate is another estate in land that is limited to a particular lifetime, and afterwards reverts to the grantor or the person in possession of the remainder or reversion.

A condominium is a unique estate in land. A person who acquires a condominium acquires exclusive ownership of a part of it (a unit) and part of it in co-ownership with all other unit owners.

An individual may possess land either alone, or jointly. This may be either by a joint tenancy or tenancy-in-common. In both cases, the interests are in the entire property. However, in the case of the tenancy-in-common, the interests may be unequal.

Interests in land, other than estates, exist as well. A person may acquire an easement or right-of-way over the land of another, or a person may exercise control over land granted to another by way of a restrictive covenant in the conveyance. Restrictive covenants are generally used to protect adjacent property by controlling the use that the grantee may make of the property.

Land or interests in land may be acquired in some parts of Canada by way of adverse possession. This usually requires the open and undisputed adverse possession of the land or right for a lengthy period of time, but once the right has been established, the lawful owner can do nothing to eliminate it.

All instruments concerning land must be registered in order that the public may have notice of the interest in land and the identity of the rightful owner. Each province maintains public registry offices where the interests in land are recorded, either under the Registry System or the Land Titles System. The Registry System is used in most of Canada east of Saskatchewan, and the Land Titles System is found in Western Canada and parts of Manitoba and Ontario. Persons must satisfy themselves as to the title to lands under the Registry System. In contrast, under the Land Titles System, the province certifies the title to be correct as shown in the land register for the particular parcel. Under both systems, an unregistered conveyance or interest in land is void as against a person who has registered his or her interest without actual notice of the unregistered instrument.

DISCUSSION QUESTIONS

1. Describe briefly how landholding developed in Canada, and identify the system upon which it is based.
2. Explain the term *freehold estate*. How does this term apply to land?
3. What lesser estates may be carved out of an estate in fee simple?
4. Once land is granted by the Crown, how is it recovered?
5. Define the terms: *fee simple, escheat, life estate, tenants-in-common, and prescriptive right.*
6. How does a life estate differ from a leasehold estate?
7. In what way (or ways) would an easement arise?
8. Under what circumstances would a restrictive covenant be inserted in a grant of land? Give three common examples of this type of covenant.
9. What characteristic distinguishes a fixture from other chattels brought onto real property?
10. Explain the term *adverse possession,* and describe how it might arise.
11. What is the purpose of a land registry system?
12. Explain how the Land Titles or Torrens System differs from the Registry System.
13. What special advantages attach to the Land Titles System?
14. Why is a "good chain of title" important under the Registry System?
15. Distinguish joint tenancy from tenancy-in-common.

MINI-CASE PROBLEMS

1. S offered to sell T a small block of parkland in a large city for $1000 cash. S presented a deed describing the property and showing S as the owner in fee simple. What information should T obtain before delivering the $1000 to S?
2. A conveyed a parcel of land to his daughter B and son C. The deed recited, in effect: to B for life, and then to C in fee simple. C would like to sell the land to D. Advise C.

JUDICIAL DECISIONS

The judicial decisions in this chapter provide illustrations of two different property issues. In the case of *Credit Valley Cable TV/FM Ltd. v. Peel Condominium Corporation #95 et al.* the judge is required to decide if a community television antenna and the cable system installed in a condominium building belongs to the cable company or the building owner. The issue turns on whether the equipment has become a fixture and is attached to the property.

In the case, the judge sets out the test for when a chattel becomes a fixture by reference to the leading case on the point of law. He then refers to several other cases where the "rules" were applied. In the end he concludes that the cable remained a chattel and did not become a part of the building.

The second case provides an example of a life estate and adverse possession claims concerning property. In the case, a deceased property owner left the land to his widow for life, and then to his nine children. Only certain children, however, remained on the farm. They later claimed it by adverse possession against the other children.

The judge first sets out the law relating to adverse possession (the Limitations Act), then turns to the facts. He then reviews the elements of the law necessary to establish adverse possession by reference to a number of cases. Finally he concludes that the case for adverse possession has been established.

**Interests
in Land —
Test for Fixtures**

Credit Valley Cable TV/FM Ltd. v. Peel Condominium Corp. #95 et al. (1980), 27 O.R. (2d) 433.

The plaintiff entered into an agreement to supply community television antenna and cable services to the unit owners of a condominium. The agreement provided that the cable was to remain the property of the plaintiff. The cable was installed in conduits provided in the building. The defendant later entered into an agreement with another company for the same services using a different antenna, but hooked up to the cable installed by the plaintiff. The plaintiff sued the defendant for trespass to its cable by the second system. The issue was whether the cable had become a fixture or remained a chattel owned by the plaintiff.

GRANGE, J.:

The test for fixtures was set out in the judgment of Meredith, C.J.C.P., in the divisional court in *Stack v. T. Eaton Co. et al.* (1902), 4 O.L.R. 335. He formulated, at p. 338, five rules as follows:

"(1) That articles not otherwise attached to the land than by their own weight are not to be considered as part of the land, unless the circumstances are such as shew that they were intended to be part of the land.

"(2) That articles affixed to the land even slightly are to be considered part of the land unless the circumstances are such as to shew that they were intended to continue chattels.

"(3) That the circumstances necessary to be shewn to alter the *prima facie* character of the articles are circumstances which shew the degree of annexation and object of such annexation, which are patent to all to see.

"(4) That the intention of the person affixing the article to the soil is material only so far as it can be presumed from the degree and object of the annexation.

"(5) That, even in the case of tenants' fixtures put in for the purposes of trade, they form part of the freehold, with the right, however, to the tenant, as between him and his landlord, to bring them back to the state of chattels again by severing them from the soil, and that they pass by a conveyance of the land as part of it, subject to this right of the tenant."

The last rule is, of course, not relevant to the case at bar. Rule (2) certainly applies at least to much of the equipment, making it necessary to examine the circumstances to find out whether the articles were intended to be continued as chattels. Under rule (3) the only relevant circumstances are those which show the degree of annexation and object of such annexation "which are patent for all to see". Finally, under rule (4) the subjective intention of the affixer (which I suggest was manifestly to retain the articles as chattels) is immaterial.

Under the third rule in *Stack v. Eaton,* I must consider the degree of annexation. While it is clear that there was some affixing of the articles to the building, I think it is equally clear and more important that both equipment and cable could be readily removed with a minimum of injury to the building. Indeed that was precisely what Bertoni found to have been done by All-View to much of the equipment when he gained access to the building in early June. The removal of the cable might well cause damage to the cable but there is no evidence that the removal would cause any damage whatever to the building. The presence or absence of likelihood of damage in removal is an important factor in the determination of whether or not the article has become a fixture — see *Liscombe Falls Gold Mining Co. et al. v. James R. Bishop et al.* (1905), 35 S.C.R. 539. In my view there is not evidence of potential damage upon removal sufficient to affect the matter materially, as was said by Lord Macnaghten in *Leigh et al. v. Taylor et al.,* [1902] A.C. 157 at p. 162:

"The mode of annexation is only one of the circumstances of the case and not always the most important — and its relative importance is probably not what it was in ruder or simpler times."

What is important to me is the resolution of the intention question. It has been said more than once that the determination is based upon the facts of the particular case — see, for example, *Bing Kee et al. v. Yick Chong* (1910), 43 S.C.R. 334, *per* Davies, J., at p. 337, and Milvain, J., in *Re Burtex Industries Ltd. (in Bankruptcy); Elleker v. Farmers & Merchants Trust Co. Ltd. et al.* (1964), 47 W.W.R. 96 at p. 101, as follows:

"I have reached the conclusion that great confusion is created by courts which slavishly follow cases rather than principles. As I understand the law it is a question of intent as to whether chattels become part of the realty, and such intent is to be found in the circumstances of each case as a finding of fact."

The test (or as Milvain, J., would have it — the principle) that has been accepted is that found in *Haggert v. Town of Brampton et al.* (1897), 28 S.C.R. 174, quoted by Spence, J., in *Re Davis,* [1954] O.W.N. 187 at p. 190: "If the object of the affixing of chattels is to improve the freehold, then, even if the chattels are only slightly affixed to the realty, they may well become part of the realty. If, on the other hand, the object of the affixation of the chattels is the better enjoyment of the chattels, then the affixation does not make them part of the realty."

It is not an easy test to follow. In a sense every chattel affixed to a building could be said to improve the building or else it would not be affixed. The test has led to some apparently conflicting results — see *La Salle Recreations Ltd. v. Canadian Camdex Investments Ltd.* (1969), 4 D.L.R. (3d) 549, 68 W.W.R. 339 (carpeting in a hotel held to be a fixture); *Lichty et al. v. Voigt et al.* (1977), 17 O.R. (2d) 552, 80 D.L.R. (3d) 757 (a mobile home cemented to the ground complete with septic tank and field bed held not to be a fixture). In any event, I think that applying the test here one must inevitably find the cable and equipment remained a chattel. Its installation in no way improved the building; all it did was make it possible for Terra to provide its subscribers with cable television. Its presence did not make the service cheaper; indeed the cost of service is prescribed by federal Regulation. In my view the situation is governed by such cases as Re Davis, supra (bowling alleys); *General Steel Wares Ltd. v. Ford & Ottawa Gas,* [1965] 2 O.R. 81, 49 D.L.R. (2d) 673 (gas dryers). In both cases although one might assume the articles were well affixed, they were held to be chattels affixed for purposes of carrying on bowling or gas-drying and not for the benefit of the building.

The plaintiff alleges that Peel and All-View were engaged in a conspiracy to interfere with the plaintiff's contractual and economic relations with its subscribers. There is no direct evidence to support the allegation but I am asked to infer the conspiracy and the interference from the loss of custom. I am not prepared to do so. I suspect that the loss of business is a direct result of subscriber resentment at the frustration of their desire expressed in a vote of 106 to 8 to change to an MATV system; if so it is hardly actionable against the defendants.

The prayer for relief asks for an injunction prohibiting interference with the plaintiff's system, an injunction requiring the defendants to cease to operate an MATV system, a declaration that the agreement of April 22nd is in full force and effect and further asks damages for breach of contract, loss of goodwill, conspiracy and interference. As I see the matter, it is simply a trespass action by All-View with the encouragement and participation of Peel lasting for about seven days and terminating upon the granting of the interlocutory injunction. I have found that the system is the property of the plaintiff but I do now see why Peel should be required by injunction to respect the continued presence of the system in the building. The plaintiff is required to provide cable television to any subscriber who seeks it and obviously some of the subscribers do. It is a right, however, of the subscriber and not of the plaintiff; and the problem is one for resolution between the subscribers and the Condominium Corporation. It is no part of my judgment, but I should think Peel would hesitate to require the removal of the system until the consent of all subscribers had been obtained. While I would terminate the injunction, I do not, of course mean that the plaintiff thereby forfeits the system.

The plaintiff will be entitled to a declaration that it is the owner of the cable system installed pursuant to the agreement of April 22, 1974, and to damages against both defendants for trespass to that system in the amount of $1000.

Interests in Land — Adverse Possession — Life Estates

Re O'Reilly (No. 2) (1980), 28 O.R. (2d) 481.

A testator died leaving a will in which he devised his farm and all stock and implements to his wife for life, and on her death, to his nine children as remaindermen.

The testator's widow and three of the children remained on the farm from the testator's date of death (March 18, 1945) until May 11, 1957, when the widow died. The three children continued to reside on the farm and carry on a farming operation as owners of the property.

In 1978, one of the children, who had left the farm prior to 1945, claimed an interest in the farm as one of the remaindermen named in the will. The children who had remained on the farm claimed a possessory title to the property and argued that the interests of the other children had been extinguished.

RUTHERFORD, J.:

As s. 43 of the *Limitations Act* has no application to the facts of this case, the operative sections of the Act are ss. 4 and 7 which provide as follows:

"4. No person shall make an entry or distress, or bring an action to recover any land or rent, but within ten years next after the time at which the right to make such entry or distress, or to bring such action first accrued to some person through whom he claims, or if the right did not accrue to any person through whom he claims, then within ten years next after the time at which the right to make such entry or distress, or to bring such action, first accrued to the person making or bringing it."

The next matter to be considered is whether the plaintiffs have acquired a possessory title, so-called. The plaintiffs, to establish their claim to a possessory title, must prove:

(1) actual possession for the statutory period by themselves and those through whom they claim;

(2) the intention to possess the property to the exclusion of all others; and

(3) discontinuance of possession for the statutory period by the owners and all others, if any, entitled to possession.

With regard to the possession of the plaintiffs and the dispossession of the owners, I find as follows:

(1) Rupert, Lorne and Isabella O'Reilly entered into possession of the O'Reilly farm in May, 1957, on the death of their mother, the life tenant;

(2) That Rupert, Lorne and Isabella O'Reilly remained in possession of the property until Rupert's death in 1964, and thereafter to the present the plaintiffs have remained in possession of the property;

(3) that from 1957 to 1962, the plaintiffs and their brother Rupert carried on a beef and dairy products farming business on the property;

(4) that in 1962, they conducted an auction of much of the farm stock and equipment, and retained all proceeds for their own use;

(5) that from 1957 to the present, the plaintiffs have attended to the payment of all municipal taxes on the property;

(6) that during the period of their possession, the plaintiffs have suitably maintained the farm buildings and structures;

(7) that the plaintiffs have not accounted to anyone for any of the profits or income generated by the farming business;

(8) that from time to time during the period 1962 or 1964 to the present, the plaintiffs rented portions of the farm to neighbouring farmers, the plaintiffs acting as lessors in their own right, and that the plaintiffs have retained for their own use all rent moneys received;

(9) that from time to time during the period of their possession, the plaintiffs paid insurance premiums with respect to the farm;

(10) that the plaintiffs completed construction of the farmhouse on the property;

(11) that the plaintiffs have held themselves out as the owners of the property during the period of their possession;

(12) that the owners received no income, benefit, or enjoyment from the property during the period of the plaintiffs' possession.

Based on the above, I find as a fact that the plaintiffs were in actual possession of the farm during the period from 1957 to 1978, and that the owners were correspondingly dispossessed during the same period.

It now remains to consider whether the plaintiff had the *animus possidendi* required to establish a possessory title. The intention to exclude all other persons, including the true owner, may be presumed from a long period of undisturbed possession: see *Re Gibbins and Gibbins* (1977), 18 O.R. (2d) 45 at p. 48, 1 R.F.L. (2d) 352 [affirmed 22 O.R. (2d) 116, 92 D.L.R. (3d) 285]; *Re Strong and Colby et al.* (1978), 20 O.R. (2d) 356 at p. 359, 87 D.L.R. (3d) 589 at p. 592. In the instant case, I find the plaintiffs' undisturbed possession of the farm for a period in excess of 20 years to be more than sufficient to raise a presumption of the requisite *animus possidendi,* a presumption the defendant has failed to rebut.

Quite apart from this presumption, the plaintiffs' conduct over the 20-year period is of itself sufficient to establish the existence of the requisite intention. Their acts of possession are consistent with their claim to ownership and are inconsistent with the claim of any other person, including the true owner. The plaintiffs' mistaken belief that they were the true owners does not prevent the characterization of their acts as being acts of possession sufficient to establish a possessory title; Anger and Hongsberger, *Canadian Law of Real Property,* p. 791; *cf. Kosman et al. v. Lapointe* (1977), 1 R.P.R. 119. Such a belief in conjunction with acts of possession may support a claim of adverse possession;

McGugan et al. v. Turner et al., [1948] O.R. 216 at p. 221, [1948] 2 D.L.R. 338 at p. 342; *Smaglinski et al. v. Daly et al.,* [1970] 2 O.R. 275 at p. 282, 10 D.L.R. (3d) 507 at p. 514 [varied [1971] 3 O.R. 238, 20 D.L.R. (3d) 65]. The acts of possession in the instant case, when taken with the belief of ownership, albeit mistaken, establish the requisite possession by the plaintiffs.

Based on this and my other findings, the plaintiffs have established all the elements necessary to extinguish the title of the true owners. There will be a declaration that the titles of those beneficially entitled to the farm property of James O'Reilly, deceased, have been extinguished by virtue of the *Limitations Act,* ss. 4 and 15.

My judgment, in addition to being based on ss. 4 and 15 may be based on another footing, namely, s. 2 of the Act which provides as follows:

"2. Nothing in this Act interferes with any rule of equity in refusing relief on the ground of acquiescence, or otherwise, to any person whose right to bring an action is not barred by virtue of this Act."

In the event that the interests of the beneficiaries are not extinguished under the *Limitations Act* by virtue of the running of the limitation period, I find this an appropriate case to exercise this Court's equitable jurisdiction under s. 2 of the Act. Failure to do so would result in a manifest injustice to the plaintiffs. The unreasonable delay in seeking a grant of letters of administration and the failure of the beneficiaries to enforce their rights as against the plaintiffs induced the plaintiffs to occupy the farm as their own with all the rights and obligations attendant on ownership. At this late date, the defendant cannot be heard to claim the farm as being property belonging to the estate nor can the beneficiaries be heard to claim their interests. I find that by reason of laches and acquiescence, the defendant and the beneficiaries are estopped or otherwise barred from claiming their interests in the farm property of James O'Reilly, deceased.

CASE PROBLEMS FOR DISCUSSION

Case 1

Samuels, an elderly widower, conveyed his farm land to his son Peter for life, then to his grandson Paul in fee simple. In the deed, he reserved to himself the right to continue to live on the farm and to receive 50% of the income from the farm during the rest of his lifetime.

Peter operated the farm with the assistance of both Samuels and Paul for a number of years, during which time he paid his father 50% of the farm income. Eventually, Peter decided to seek employment in industry and took a job in a nearby manufacturing plant. At that point he decided to cease farming. A short time later, the barn was accidentally destroyed by fire and the farm machinery destroyed. Samuels, Peter, and Paul each claimed to be entitled to the proceeds of the fire insurance on the barn and the farm machinery.

Discuss the rights (if any) of each of the parties to the insurance funds in this dispute.

Case 2

Smith owned a large farm in eastern Ontario. Part of the farm, which consisted of a woodlot, fronted on an unimproved township road. In 1965, Crockett, a middle-aged bachelor, with Smith's permission, constructed a small log cabin in the woodlot for use as a fishing and hunting camp. For several years Crockett occupied the cabin on weekends, while fishing in the area in the summer months, and for a few weeks in the fall of each year during the hunting season.

During the summer of 1968, Crockett took a month's vacation and spent the time at the cabin. He planted a small vegetable garden and constructed a fence around both cabin and garden to keep animals away from his flowers and vegetables. During the hunting season of the same year he cut down a number of small trees and extended the fenced-in area to a parcel of land 23 m by 30 m, and built a gate in the fence where it faced the roadway.

Smith noticed the fence and gate shortly after it was constructed and asked Crockett why it was necessary. Crockett replied that the animals in the area were damaging the flowers that he had planted around the cabin, and he felt that the fence would probably keep them out.

The next year, Crockett decided to accept early retirement from the firm where he was employed. He spent the period from May 1st to November 30th at the cabin. Crockett planted a vegetable garden, fished, and helped Smith with the planting of his crops and his fall harvest. At the end of November, he left his belongings in the cabin and spent the winter in a warmer climate.

He returned to the cabin the next April, only to be met by the local tax assessor who asked him if the cabin was his. He replied in the affirmative, and some time later, received a municipal tax bill issued in his name. He paid the municipal taxes for that year (1970).

Crockett continued to live in the cabin, spending only the coldest of the winter months away from the premises. He paid the taxes on the land and building each year. In 1981, he moved the fences to include an area 30 m by 45 m in order to enclose a larger vegetable garden. Smith did not object to the new location of the fence, but warned Crockett not to cut down two large hickory nut trees in the enclosed area. Crockett agreed to leave the trees standing.

In the summer of 1989, during a thunderstorm, lightning struck and damaged one of the large hickory trees. Without consulting Smith, Crockett cut down the damaged tree.

Several months later, Smith noticed that the tree was missing. In a rage, he ordered Crockett from the property. Crockett refused to leave, claiming he was the owner of the parcel of land.

Discuss the rights of the parties. Evaluate the arguments and evidence that each might raise if the matter should be brought before the courts to determine the rights of the parties in the land. Render a decision.

Case 3

Barron owned a parcel of land fronting on a large lake. The lake was approximately 370 m from a road that represented one of the boundaries of the property. In 1966, Barron sold to Bulkley a parcel of land with a frontage of 185 m on the lake and a depth of 123 m. Included in the deed was a 6 m-wide access right of way that was described as follows: "...a free and uninterrupted right of way for the grantee, his heirs, assigns, and their agents, servants, workmen, and their animals and vehicles, provided that they maintain at their own expense a gate at each end of the said way."

The right of way was not specifically described in the deed, but an existing roadway some 2.5 m wide was used by Bulkley from 1966 until 1988 as a means to reach his property. Throughout the period he maintained the gates that existed at each end of the roadway. In 1989, Bulkley widened the road to 4 m and improved the surface by placing a few truck loads of gravel in low, marshy spots to permit the use of the road from early spring until late fall. The same year he allowed two of his friends to bring in their camping trailers and park them on his land for the summer.

Bulkley's two friends brought in their trailers again for the summer of 1990. In the summer of 1991, two other trailer owners rented space on Bulkley's property for the summer, and brought in their large trailers, bringing the total number of trailers to four. That summer Bulkley improved the roadway to the property by surfacing the entire distance (246 m) with gravel.

The next year, Bulkley rented trailer space to several others in addition to the four trailer owners of the previous year. He placed a small sign on the gate at the road side that read "Bulkley's Beach." The sign attracted a few holiday travellers, and Bulkley rented each of them trailer space, which they used for a few days before they moved on to other campgrounds. By the end of the summer of 1992, Bulkley discovered that he had earned over a thousand dollars from vacationers. He made plans for the opening of a trailer park the next year.

In the spring of 1993 he widened the roadway to 6 m, gravelled and rolled the roadway, then advertised his "beach" in a number of vacation magazines. The advertising attracted large numbers of tourists with trailers, and Bulkley's Beach became a busy tourist establishment.

When Barron, whose home was located near the roadway to the beach, realized that Bulkley had established a full-fledged trailer camp on his property, he objected to the use of the right of way for commercial purposes. He brought an action for an injunction on the basis that the right of way was intended only as a private right of access and not intended for use as a right of way by members of the public. He also claimed that the dust raised by the heavy use of the right of way by vehicles interfered with the enjoyment of his property on which the roadway was located.

Discuss the arguments of the parties in this dispute. Render a decision.

Case 4

Baxter owned a large block of forest land that surrounded a small lake. The lake was fed by a small stream that crossed the property, and another that drained the lake into a larger body of water several kilometres away.

With the intention of eventually constructing a cottage on the lot, Wilson purchased from Baxter a small parcel of land fronting on the lake. On the payment of the purchase price he received a deed to the land from Baxter. Without examining it, he placed it in his safety deposit box.

Wilson used the property as a campsite for several years. Because the lake was several hundred metres from the road, each time he visited the lake he would leave his automobile parked at the roadside and carry his camping equipment through the woods to his property.

Five years after he purchased the land from Baxter, he decided to build a cottage on his lot. No road access was available to the land, but Wilson assumed that the pathway that led to his property was his access route. He began cutting trees to widen the path in order that a truck carrying his building materials could reach his lot. No sooner had he cut the first tree, then Baxter appeared and ordered him to stop cutting. When Wilson refused, Baxter ordered him to leave the property.

Wilson protested that he was entitled the clear the trees from the access route to his land, but Baxter replied that he had sold him only the lot and not a roadway. According to Baxter, Wilson had water access by way of the stream if he wished to enter or leave his property. The surrounding land belonged to Baxter.

Wilson had travelled the stream with his canoe on a number of occasions. While it was possible to gain access to his lot in that fashion, it would not be possible to transport the heavy building materials into the property using a canoe, and the stream was too shallow to allow the use of any larger water craft. Rather than continue his argument with Baxter, Wilson decided to examine his deed to determine if Baxter was correct in his position on the access route. Wilson returned home and read the description of the property contained in the conveyance. It described the lot only and made no mention of a roadway to the property. According to the deed, Baxter owned all of the land surrounding Wilson's property. His only access appeared to be by way of the small stream to the lake.

Examine the rights of the two parties in this case. If either party should decide to take legal action to enforce his rights, explain the nature of the action and indicate the probable outcome.

Case 5

Suburban Land Development Ltd. owned a block of land that it wished to develop as a residential housing subdivision. The land was heavily treed and bordered the shore of a lake. To preserve the woodland setting of the area as each house lot was sold, the corporation inserted in the deed the following clauses:

The grantee agrees

(1) to construct a house on the premises with a floor space of not less than 237 m² and a construction value of not less than $200 000.

(2) Construction shall not begin until the grantor approves in writing the architectural drawings or plans for any proposed dwelling.

(3) No trees shall be cut on the property without the express consent in writing of the grantor.

(4) No pigs, chickens, or other domestic animals may be kept on the property.

(5) The above covenants shall run with the land for a period of 20 years, and shall be binding on the heirs, executors, and assigns of the grantee.

Casey purchased a large, heavily wooded lot in the subdivision. She received a deed to the lot in fee simple that was registered in the Land Registry Office and contained the above covenants. Without constructing a house or dealing in any way with the property, she sold it to MacGregor, who received a deed to the lot that did not contain the covenants. He registered that deed in the Land Registry office without examination of the title to the property.

Some time later, MacGregor attempted to cut some of the trees on the property to clear a place where he intended to build a small building to house his racing pigeons.

When Suburban Land Development Ltd. became aware of MacGregor's activity, it immediately informed him that he must stop cutting the trees until approval was given, and also that the company would not permit the construction of any building on the property except a dwelling-house.

MacGregor decided to ignore the prohibition, on the basis that he was unaware of the restrictions and had not agreed to them.

Advise MacGregor and Suburban Land Development Ltd. What might be the possible outcome, if legal action was taken by Suburban Land Development Ltd. to enforce the restrictions?

Case 6

The Golf and Country Club owns a large block of land at the edge of a municipality that the club uses as an 18-hole golf course. A small stream runs through the property and eventually drains into a lake some distance away. The stream also passes through the municipality that is located upstream from the Golf and Country Club property.

The municipality installed new storm sewers in an area of the city and constructed them in such a way that, in a heavy rain, overflow from the sewers would drain into the stream.

Shortly after the construction of the new sewers, several days of heavy rains resulted in a large quantity of water from the storm sewers being discharged into the stream. This in turn produced flooding of the stream and serious erosion of the banks of the stream where it passed through the golf course. Damage was estimated a $35 000.

The Golf and Country Club instituted legal proceedings against the municipality for the damage. Discuss the arguments that might be raised by each of the parties, and render a decision.

Case 7

Ivan owned a farm of 100 acres and a farmhouse on the land. An appraisal valued the land at $1000 per acre, and the house at $60 000. Ivan decided to give up farming. He mortgaged the farmstead to the bank for $140 000 and started what he thought would be a profitable venture in automobile repair. He used some of the money for the purchase of tools, the lease of a garage, and to pay himself a wage while he tried to make a success of the business.

Calamity rained upon Ivan. The business failed within a year, and he had to sell the tools to satisfy some of the creditors, leaving him with only the farm and house. House values, however, had fallen, and while the land was still worth $1000 per acre, the value of the house had dropped to $40 000. The property value now equalled the entire $140 000 he had borrowed. Ivan had paid his interest up to date, but nothing on the principal.

At that point, Ivan ordered a $2000 water conditioning unit and a $500 dishwasher from a local appliance store. After the dishwasher was hooked up and the water conditioner installed, Ivan told the installer that he would mail the company a cheque. He did not.

The appliance store then filed a claim for lien against the property in the amount of $2500.

That month, when the bank wanted to have the farm and house sold as a result of the unpaid mortgage, a survey revealed that a neighbouring farmer had fenced improperly, and for the past 12 years, a 10-acre strip had been fenced off and used by the other farmer.

CHAPTER 27

Condominium Law

INTRODUCTION

Condominium is a term used to describe a particular form of ownership of real property where the property is held in part by exclusive ownership, and in part by co-ownership. The term is usually applied to a multiple-unit dwelling or commercial building in which the occupant of each unit owns the unit exclusively, and also possesses ownership rights as a co-owner of the common use areas of the remainder of the building and the surrounding land. In concept, it differs from other forms of property ownership in that it represents two separate interests within the bounds of the same parcel — the right to exclusive possession and control over an individual unit of the condominium, and co-ownership rights over those parts of the property that are not exclusively owned units. For example, in a condominium constructed as a multiple-unit residential building similar in design to an apartment building, each dwelling-unit would be exclusively owned by the occupant. In addition, the unit owner would be a co-owner of the surrounding land and common areas of the building, and would have the right to use them in common with all other unit owners.

Modern condominium legislation usually provides that the land and building (excluding the individual units) be operated and maintained by a corporation that the owners of the individual units control and manage, but this was not always the case. Until comparatively recent times, the corporation was not used for such a purpose. In its earliest form, the forerunner of the modern condominium was simply exclusive ownership of a part of a building, and a part-ownership of the common elements, or a right to use them.

HISTORICAL DEVELOPMENT

The condominium as a method of property ownership was conceived long before the development of the feudal system. Legal historians have suggested that a condominium type of ownership of multiple-unit buildings existed as long ago as 500 B.C. in the Middle East, and as early as the twelfth century in parts of Western

Europe.[1] The condominium concept was essentially a response to the high cost or scarcity of land for dwelling construction in some of the ancient walled cities. When no space was available for the construction of separate family dwellings, each on its own parcel of land, the logical next step was to construct multiple-family dwellings, sometimes as multi-storied buildings. Separate ownership of each unit was a frequent development following construction of a multiple-dwelling unit structure, where the tenants desired the security of tenure associated with the ownership of property.

While the concept has ancient roots, it is essentially an urban phenomenon. Its use spread from the walled cities of Babylon to Greece, Italy, and on to the cities of Germany and France. By the sixteenth century, the condominium had found acceptance in Continental Europe, but not in England. Even though the system of land tenure in England did not prevent the possession of interests in land in condominium fashion, the concept failed to gain popularity there until very recent times. Instead, as a response to the crowded conditions of some English cities, the long-term lease and "flat" ownership were favoured over the condominium.

In North America, the low cost of land, and perhaps the general desire of the population for land ownership and a separate dwelling, discouraged interest in the concept even in the larger urban centres. Until World War II, the availability of inexpensive urban and suburban land made the need for condominiums a matter of low priority. The growth of urban centres following World War II, however, had an upward pressure on land prices in the cities. By the decade of the 1960s, rapidly rising prices for residential property prompted property developers to consider other forms of residential ownership in an effort to provide something in addition to the "apartment" as an alternative to expensive single-family dwellings. As a result of the sudden interest in this relatively new form of property ownership, legislation was introduced in most of the states of the United States and in many of the provinces in Canada. The legislation enabled the condominium to grow in popularity, and at the present time it represents a rapidly expanding segment of all new residential construction in urban areas.

CONDOMINIUM LEGISLATION

The common law in England and North America has long recognized the right of property ownership in either a horizontal or vertical plane, and of rights to property above and below ground. In England, the ownership of apartments or flats has been the equivalent of condominium ownership, and the rights of these property owners over time have become clearly defined by the law. Under the common law, the sale of a part of a building situated above the ground represents a sale of "air rights" or space, but, nevertheless, the sale of a recognized property right. The particular difficulty with the common law in this regard, however, is that the establishment of the necessary rights and obligations associated with the "strata title" are extremely complex. For example, to sell the second-storey of a three-storey building would require the parties to define with some degree of accuracy the right of access by the owner of the second-storey, the right of the owner of the remainder of the building to the support of the third-storey, the right to services, maintenance, and many other considerations.

---

1. See, for example, A. Ferrer and K. Stecher, *Law of Condominium*, vol. 1 (Orford, N.H.: Equity Publishing Corp., 1967), pp. 15-23.

While the condominium unit in the case of a multi-storey building is similar to an "air right" in property, the owner of the unit usually obtains part-ownership of the common areas of the entire building and the land on which it stands, as a tenant-in-common. Originally, this took the form of co-ownership, and the owners were obliged to jointly maintain the condominium. However, by the twentieth century, the corporation appeared as a more appropriate vehicle to manage and maintain the common elements of the property and to regulate the unit owners' exercise of their rights over those parts of the condominium. Modern condominium legislation in North America, as a result, has generally taken this route, although not universally. In Canada, all of the provinces (except Nova Scotia) provide for a corporation without share capital to come into existence when the condominium is created. While in the United States, the corporate form is used in some jurisdictions, and an association or uncorporated body is used in others.

NATURE OF A CONDOMINIUM

A condominium is essentially a property on which some type of multiple-occupancy building is erected. It may resemble a row-housing development, in which the units are connected horizontally on the land, or it may be a multi-storey building in which the occupancy units are connected horizontally and stacked vertically. It might also be erected for residential, commercial, or industrial use. In any event, regardless of its shape or purpose, it is characterized by individual ownership of units and some form of co-ownership of the non-unit remainder. A third element that distinguishes the condominium from other forms of ownership is the use of some type of administrative structure to manage the property.

Unfortunately, the documentation required for the creation of a condominium varies from province to province. In some provinces, the condominium comes into existence on the filing or registration of a **description and declaration** (drawn in accordance with the legislation) at the Land Registry or Land Titles office. In other provinces additional formalities are sometimes required. British Columbia, for example,[2] (where a condominium interest is referred to as a **strata title**) also requires the filing of a prospectus with the Superintendent of Insurance. In all cases, however, the creation of the condominium requires not only the intention to have the property used as a condominium, but the preparation of accurate surveyor's drawings of the overall project and the individual units in sufficient detail to allow the property interests to be identified and dealt with under the land registration system of the particular province. These documents are usually referred to as the **description.**

The document that embodies the details of the condominium is referred to by various names depending upon the jurisdiction. In Ontario, for example, it is called a **declaration,** in British Columbia, a **strata plan,** and in Alberta, a **condominium plan.** In each case, the document sets out the interests of the unit owners and provides the general outline for the management and operation of the condominium as a whole. It provides also for the creation of a corporation or society to manage the property for the use and enjoyment of the unit owners. The registration of this documentation in the land registry or land titles office automatically establishes the condominium.

---

2. Real Estate Act, R.S.B.C. 1979, c. 356, ss. 50-59.

A condominium frequently has its beginning as a project of a land developer. A parcel of land is acquired, then a building that is specifically designed as a condominium is erected on the land. The property is divided into units (sometimes called apartments), that are generally laid out so that exclusive ownership is confined to the area enclosed by the exterior walls of the unit. Usually the limits of the unit are described as being to the planes of the centre line of all walls, ceilings, and floors that enclose the space; although this need not always be the case. The developer is free to define it by the planes of the inside surfaces, or any combination of the two.[3] Sometimes the exclusive use area may include other parts of the building as well. In many buildings with underground parking or storage facilities, these are sometimes designated as exclusive use areas and included in the description of the unit. This permits the unit owner to have the exclusive ownership of a parking space or storage locker on the premises, but it has the disadvantage that the management organization loses control over the areas in question. Whatever the extent of the units or exclusive use areas may be, they must be so designated in the description.

The balance of the property, excluding the units (and exclusive use areas, if included), is the part of the property known as the **common elements** or common use area. All of the unit owners hold this part of the land jointly as tenants-in-common. Included in this part of the property are usually the exterior walls of the building, all hallways, stairwells and stairs, entrance areas, the building basement, heating plant, land, and facilities installed for use by all of the unit owners. In some cases, it also includes a unit set aside for use by the building supervisor or manager. All of these areas, however, must be so set out in the description as common elements.

In a condominium, the co-ownership rights to the common elements are tied to the ownership of the individual units. If the interest of a person in the unit is transferred to another, the interest in the common elements also will pass, as it is not possible to sever the two by way of a deed. The interest of the individual unit owner in the common element is usually related to the value of the unit owned in relation to the other units, the relative sizes of the units, or in accordance with a formula that the developer might use to establish the interest of each unit. Only two provinces[4] impose restrictions on the methods that may be used to calculate this value. As a result, the methods used may vary from province to province and, indeed, from condominium to condominium.

One of the simplest methods of determining the interest of the unit owner in the common elements is to divide the total cost of the condominium by the value of each unit. For example, if the cost of the condominium is $2 000 000 and the value of a particular unit $100 000, the interest of the unit owner in the common elements would be 5%. While this is an oversimplification of the method used, the percentage fixed as the interest of the unit owner would be the amount that the unit owner would receive from the proceeds of a sale should the property be sold on the termination of its use as a condominium.

The maintenance of the common elements is related to the exclusive use

---

3. Saskatchewan assumes the planes of the centre lines unless the boundaries are otherwise defined; see the Condominium Property Act, R.S.S. 1978, c. C-26, s. 7(2).

4. Quebec and British Columbia. See, for example, the Condominium Act, R.S.B.C. 1979, c. 61, s. 128.

units, usually by a calculation of the maintenance cost, and an apportionment of the cost to each unit on the basis of unit size or value. Included in this cost is usually the municipal property tax, insurance, property maintenance such as cleaning, snow removal, yard maintenance, elevators, building security, and the operating costs of special facilities for recreation and entertainment. While the cost or charge apportioned to each unit may be the same percentage amount as for the interest of the unit owner in the common elements, this need not necessarily be the case. Sometimes, for example, the cost allocation to unit owners located on the ground floor may recognize the fact that some above-ground floor services are not utilized by them, and their contribution to the operating expenses is correspondingly reduced.

The legal nature of the condominium and the various features that distinguish it from co-ownership of property in general was examined by the court in an early case[5] (in terms of modern condominium legislation) where the judge described a condominium in the following terms:

> A condominium project has two basic parts, the first being the individually-owned suites, usually referred to as the units, and the second, all the rest of the building, the land, and any auxiliary features simply defined in the Act, s. 1(1)(e), as "all the property except the units". These are owned by the unit owners as tenants in common and are usually referred to as the common elements.

Subsidiary to these two basic elements are other essential features:

1. A system of government, including an effective method of making each owner pay his share of the common expenses.

2. A method of transferring, leasing, or mortgaging the units and the owner's interest in the common elements or restricting the same.

3. A method of taxing the unit and the owner's interest in the common elements.

4. Devising means of handling the destruction of the whole or part of the project, winding-up, sale, obsolescence or additions to the common elements.

To bring the Act into force, a declaration and description must be registered:

"2(6) Upon registration of a declaration and description, the land and the interests appurtenant to the land described in the description are governed by this Act."

Certain things must be provided for the declaration. Those of concern in this action are:

(1) A declaration shall not be registered unless it is executed by the owner or owners of the land and interests appurtenant to the land described in the description and unless it contains,

(a) a statement of intention that the land and interests appurtenant to the land described in the description be governed by this Act;

(c) a statement, expressed in percentages, of the proportions of the common interests;

(d) a statement, expressed in percentages allocated to the units, of the proportions in which the owners are to contribute to the common expenses..."

Certain other things may be provided for:

"3(2) In addition to the matters mentioned in subsection 1, a declaration may contain,

(a) a specification of common expenses;

---

5. *Frontenac Condominium Corp. No. 1 v. Joe Macciocchi & Sons Ltd.* (1974), 3 O.R. (2d) 331.

(c) provisions respecting the occupation and use of the units and common elements;

(g) a specification of the majority required to make by-laws of the corporation;

(h) provisions regulating the assessment and collection of contributions towards the common expenses;

(o) any other matters concerning the property.

(3) The declaration may be amended only with the consent of all owners and all persons having registered encumbrances against the units and common interests.

"4(1) A description shall contain,

(c) a specification of the boundaries of each unit by reference to the buildings;"

The declaration prepared and filed by the defendant and which created the plaintiff contains, among other things:

"(a) statement of intention.

(b) a statement that the proportions of the common interests shall be as set out in a schedule which lists percentages opposite unit numbers.

(c) that each owner shall contribute to the common expenses in the proportions shown in the schedule.

(d) that common expenses, without limiting the definition of the Act, shall be realty taxes on the whole property until units are taxed separately, payment of any employees needed for the proper operation and maintenance of the property, and payments under any management contract between the plaintiff and a manager.

(e) a requirement that units be used for single family residences only.

(f) a provision that by-laws may be made by a vote of members who own sixty-six and two thirds per cent of the common elements, inter alia,

1. governing the management of the property
2. governing the use of the units
3. governing the use of common elements
4. regulating the maintenance of the units and the common elements
5. regulating the assessment and collection of contributions towards the common expenses."

It should be observed that the provisions of the Act take precedence. If the declaration does not comply with the Act, the Act prevails. Similarly the declaration prevails over the by-laws (s. 10(2)), and the by-laws prevail over the common element rules, if any (s. 11(2)).

Management

In all Canadian provinces, the general management of the condominium is in the hands of a board of directors or executive of a condominium corporation. The corporation is a corporation without share capital, but each unit owner has a say in its operation. This is done by way of a right to discuss matters and vote at general meetings held for the purpose of making major decisions affecting the condominium. It is also reflected through the election of members to the board of directors. The day-to-day management and operation of the condominium, however, is left with the board of directors.

Apart from the general duty to "manage" and to maintain the common elements of the condominium in a good state of repair, the corporation has the following specific obligations:

(1) to protect the premises from damage by way of insurance;

(2) to collect common element expenses from the unit owners in accordance

with the percentage liability of each unit;

(3) to enforce any rules established for the use and enjoyment of the common areas, and the condominium as a whole.

In addition to the rights granted to the corporation under provincial condominium legislation, the rights and duties of the corporation are governed by by-laws. The by-laws of the corporation delineate its powers and constitute the "rules" for its operation. Some provinces have specified that the buildings be regulated by by-laws and have set out the procedures for their implementation, amendment, and enforcement. Other provinces have simply provided that by-laws may be passed by the corporation without specifying details as to their nature, or implementation, other than in general terms.

Use of Common Elements

The by-laws and the rules govern the use that the unit owners may make of their individual units and of the common elements. For example, by-laws may prohibit alteration of the structure of the unit, restrict the occupancy to one family, prohibit commercial use, prohibit the keeping of animals, prohibit the erection of awnings or shades on the outside of windows, or prohibit the playing of musical instruments on the premises if they constitute a nuisance or disturbance to neighbouring units. Common element rules generally govern behaviour of unit owners and their guests in the common areas, or in the use of facilities such as swimming pools.

Most provinces have vested in the corporation the **right of lien**[6] against a condominium unit for unpaid expenses, and the right to enforce the lien in the event of non-payment. Provision is normally made in the legislation for the foreclosure or sale of the unit in a manner similar to that for mortgages or charges. The reason for the vesting in the corporation of this particular right is the importance of the contribution of each unit owner of his or her share of the common expenses. A failure on the part of one unit owner to pay shifts the burden of the expense to the remaining unit owners. To allow default to continue would not only burden the remaining unit owners, but would create a serious problem for the owners as a whole if a number of unit owners refused to honour their obligation.

In most other respects the corporations are not unlike other non-profit corporations. The officers of the corporation carry out their duties in accordance with the by-laws and the legislation for the general benefit of the property owners, and for the better use of enjoyment of the common elements. The right to vote for the election of directors provides a means whereby the unit owners might remove unsatisfactory directors and replace them with others more to the liking of the majority. As with most corporations, it remains in existence until the condominium is terminated, at which time it is dissolved, and any assets that it might hold are then transferred to the unit owners.

Using an Ontario example, the legal nature of the condominium corporation, the various powers granted to it, and the features that distinguish it from other corporations have been described as follows:[7]

---

6. All provinces except Saskatchewan; the Condominium Property Act, R.S.S. 1978, c. C-26, s. 22(2).

7. *Frontenac Condominium Corp. No. 1 v. Joe Macciocchi & Sons Ltd.* (1974), 3 O.R. (2d) 331.

It is quite unlike the usual share capital corporation or a corporation without share capital incorporated under either the Business Corporations Act, R.S.O. 1970, c. 53, or the Corporations Act, R.S.O. 1970, c. 89.

Section 9(1) creates a corporation upon the registration of a declaration and description.

Section 9(3) immediately brings out the above distinction by providing that the Corporations Act, the Corporations Information Act, R.S.O. 1970, c. 90, and the provisions respecting mortmain of the Mortmain and Charitable Uses Act, R.S.O. 1970, c. 280, do not apply to the corporation.

Some assistance in determining the nature of the corporation created under s. 9(1) may be found in the Interpretation Act, R.S.O. 1970, c. 225, which provides in part:

"26. In every Act, unless the contrary intention appears, words making any association or number of persons a corporation or body politic and corporate,

(a) vest in the corporation power to sue and be sued, to contract and be contracted with by its corporate name, to have a common seal, to alter or change the seal at its pleasure, to have perpetual succession, to acquire and hold personal property or movables for the purpose for which the corporation is constituted, and to alienate the same at pleasure;

(b) vest in a majority of the members of the corporation the power to bind the others by their acts; and

(c) exempt individual members of the corporation for personal liability for its debts, obligations or acts if they do not contravene the provisions of the Act incorporating them."

However, cl. (b) above has its applicability cut down by the Condominium Act, 1967, which requires unanimity of the owners, or members of the corporation, in some matters and, it appears, a two-thirds vote in others, and under s. 17 an 80% vote in favour of certain other acts.

Clause (c) above does not apply to a condominium corporation because of s. 9(17) which provides:

"9(17) A judgment for the payment of money against the corporation is also a judgment against each owner at the time the cause of action arose for a portion of the judgment determined by the proportions specified in the declaration for sharing the common expenses."

Section 9(16) provides that the corporation's assets are owned, not by the corporation, but by the unit owners.

"9(16) The members of the corporation share the assets of the corporation in the same proportions as the proportions of their common interests in accordance with this Act, the declaration and the by-laws."

There is no limited liability protection for the owners as this is normally understood. If a judgment is bad against the corporation, each unit owner is responsible for a percentage of the judgment which is the same as his percentage for sharing the common expenses. If, however, the percentage of the judgment exceeds the value of his unit and its appurtenant portion of the common elements, the owner will nevertheless be responsible to pay an amount greater than the value of his share in the property.

Conversely, if an action is brought with respect to the common elements and a judgment is obtained, this judgment belongs to the members.

"9(18) Any action with respect to the common elements may be brought by the corporation and a judgment for the payment of money in favour of the corporation in such an action is an asset of the corporation."

The result is that the corporation as such owns nothing, except in the sense of a conduit, because s. 9(16) has said the members share the assets.

The corporation is directed to repair the units and the common elements after damage and to maintain the common elements (s. 16(2) and (3)).

Termination of a Condominium

A condominium, once created, need not remain one forever. The unit owners may decide to terminate the condominium if the character of the building has changed or deteriorated over time, or if the property no longer serves its intended purpose. It cannot, however, be terminated by a simple majority vote of the unit owners, as provincial legislation usually requires either the unanimous consent of all unit owners (and encumbrancers) or a very high percentage (usually 80%) to signify approval. A few provinces leave the matter in the hands of the courts to decide.

A sale of the condominium is essentially the sale of a number of individual units and interests. As a general rule, after all expenses related to the condominium have been paid, the funds available for each property owner are distributed in accordance with the proportional ownership of the common elements, unless the sale agreement provides otherwise. Where less than unanimous consent of all unit owners is required to approve a sale (for example, 80%), dissenting owners are protected in some jurisdictions (such as Manitoba and Ontario) by a provision for arbitral determination of the fair market value of the particular interests at the time of the sale, and the payment of that amount to the dissenters. The remaining property owners would be expected to make up any deficiency in the event that the value determined by the arbitrator exceeded the sale price of the units.[8]

FUTURE OF THE CONDOMINIUM

Although it did not find favour in North America until very recently, the condominium, as a concept, is not a new or radical form of property ownership. Changes in society, however, have attracted many to this particular form of ownership, not only for residential, but for business purposes as well. The high cost of land was the initial attraction, but the general trend to smaller families, the desire to live close to work, and to have recreational facilities available in the same building, has prompted many individuals and small families to opt for this form of residential accommodation over apartment living. A major advantage is that a condominium provides security of tenure by ownership of the unit, as well as some degree of control over management of the building and grounds.

The concept also has a number of attractions to business organizations. Not only does it provide the commercial unit owner with the right to use the unit as he or she pleases (within limits), but it frequently reduces business costs by way of shared expenses for the maintenance and operation of the common elements. Only recently have business organizations recognized the significant advantages of the condominium as a means of housing their operations. Consequently, its current uses may be expanded to include a greater variety of commercial operations, in addition to its present application to office structures, shopping centres, parking garages, and light industrial complexes. If the cost of urban land and maintenance costs continue to rise, many more business organizations will undoubtedly be attracted to this form of housing for their facilities.

---

8. See, for example, Ontario, the Condominium Act, R.S.O. 1990, c. C-26.

SUMMARY

A condominium is a multiple-unit building in which each unit is subject to exclusive ownership and possession, and the remainder of the building and surrounding land is held by the unit owners in co-ownership as tenants-in-common. Condominiums may be for residential, commercial, or industrial use, and the units need not have ground contact to be subject to ownership. Units of a high-rise condominium may be held in the same manner as ground floor units. The interests in the property of a condominium are tied together in such a way that the ownership of a unit carries with it an inseparable co-ownership interest in the common elements as well. The percentage interest in the common elements is usually calculated in such a way that it reflects the value of the particular unit to which it is tied, relative to all other units in the condominium.

A condominium comes into existence when the owner or developer registers in the land registry or land titles office the required description and declaration that describe and set out the details of the nature of the condominium, the rights of the unit owners, and the rules governing its operation. Once established, a corporation society manages the common elements and protects the interests of the unit owners. It handles the payment of expenses related to the maintenance of the common areas and collects the charges from the co-owners. It also enforces all by-laws and rules established for the better enjoyment of the condominium.

When all, or a substantial majority, of the unit owners and encumbrancers (depending upon the province) desire to terminate the condominium, they may do so, provided that they comply with the procedure for termination set out in the condominium legislation for that province.

DISCUSSION QUESTIONS

1. What economic conditions gave rise to the condominium concept?
2. What special advantages does a condominium owner have over an apartment dweller?
3. How does "ownership" of a condominium differ from the fee simple ownership of a conventional house and lot?
4. Can an interest in property exist that does not include the land beneath it?
5. How are condominium unit interests defined?
6. In what way is a condominium development usually operated to ensure that the common elements are properly maintained?
7. How are condominiums normally established?
8. What method is generally used to determine the unit owner's interest in the common elements?
9. Indicate how a condominium organization deals with the problem of a unit owner who fails to contribute his or her share of the cost of maintaining the common elements of the condominium.
10. Explain how a condominium is terminated. Why is unanimous or near unanimous consent necessary to bring about termination?
11. What methods are usually used to protect the rights of unit owners who object to the termination of the condominium?

MINI-CASE PROBLEMS

1. Henrietta owned a large white Persian cat. She purchased a condominium unit in a high-rise building and moved in with her cat and other belongings. Unknown to her at the time of purchase, the condominium corporation had passed a rule that prohibited the keeping of pets in the building. If Henrietta did not permit the

cat to wander the hallway or other common element areas, would she lawfully be permitted to keep the cat in her unit?

2. Able acquired a condominium unit that included a parking space on a surface lot facing a sidewalk and street. Able leased the space to his friend Samantha who parked her chip wagon in the space. She sold french fries and soft drinks to the public from the location. The other residents of the condominium objected. Advise Able of his rights (if any).

JUDICIAL DECISIONS

The case of *Re York Condominium Corporation No. 52 and Melanson* illustrates an ever-present problem of condominium dwellers: the issue of keeping pets in units. In this case the Court of Appeal of Ontario dealt with the issue by first examining the by-law of the condominium corporation that prohibited the keeping of pets. The court then considered the need for such a restriction and the corporation's power to make such a by-law. In doing so, the court distinguished between the power to regulate and the power to prohibit.

The court also examined what constitutes an "occupant" and what falls within the definition of "animal." Finally, the court considered the "reasonableness" of the by-law.

In the second case, *Re Winnipeg Condominium Corp. No. 1 and Stechley*, the court was obliged to consider whether a condominium corporation declaration providing that a unit could only be used as a single family residence could be leased.

The court considered interpretations of the word "owner" and the rights of owners of property. The court also considered the type of restrictions that might reasonably be imposed on unit owners consistent with fundamental property rights of owners. The court concluded that the restriction was invalid because the act defines "owner" to include owner of a leasehold estate.

Condominium — By-Laws — Validity

Re York Condominium Corporation No. 42 and Melanson (1975), 59 D.L.R. (3d) 524.

A condominium passed a by-law prohibiting the keeping of animals on the property. An owner of a unit owned a dog and objected when the solicitor for the condominium directed him by letter to remove his dog from the premises.

At trial, the judge ordered the unit owner to remove the animal from his unit within 90 days. He appealed the judgement of the court.

HOWLAND, J.A.:

On August 19, 1971, By-law Number Two was enacted by the Corporation. It included the following provision:

"The following rules and regulations shall be observed by the owners and the term "owner" shall include the owner or any other person occupying the unit with the owner's approval:...

"14. No animal shall be allowed upon or kept in or about the property." Paragraph 14 is hereafter referred to as the "prohibitive paragraph".

By-law Number Two was duly registered and became effective on September 9, 1971. Both By-law Number One and By-law Number Two were enacted by Delzotto Enterprises Limited as the owner of all the units and the sole member of the Corporation.

Melanson is the owner of one of the units. By letter dated August 6, 1974, from the solicitors for the Corporation, Melanson was directed to remove his dog from the condominium complex on or before August 23, 1974. An application was then made by the Corporation to enforce compliance with By-law Number Two.

The issue in this appeal is whether the Corporation has exceeded its statutory powers in enacting the prohibitive paragraph, or if it did have the power, is the prohibitive paragraph enforceable? As the Corporation is a statutory creation, the relevant rights and duties of an owner and of the Corporation must be found in the Act. The following provisions are relevant:

"2(6) Upon registration of a declaration and description, the land and the interests appurtenant to the land described in the description are governed by this Act.

"6(2) Subject to this Act, the declaration and the by-laws, each owner is entitled to exclusive ownership and use of this unit.

"7(4) Subject to this Act, the declaration and the by-laws, each owner may make reasonable use of the common elements.

"9(12) The corporation has a duty to effect compliance by the owners with this Act, the declaration and the by-laws.

"12(1) Each owner is bound by and shall comply with this Act, the declaration and the by-laws.

"(3) The corporation...has a right to the compliance by the owners with this Act, the declaration and the by-laws."

In creating a condominium corporation, a developer has to consider carefully what restrictions it is going to impose on the user of the units and common elements because such restrictions will affect the character of the condominium and the marketability of its units. The prohibitive paragraph could have been included in the declaration pursuant to s. 3(2) of the Act, just as the declaration provided that each unit should be used only as a single-family residence. However, the objection to so doing is that under s. 3(3) of the Act the declaration may be amended only with the consent of all owners and all persons having registered encumbrances against the units and common interests. In the case of a restriction such as the prohibitive paragraph this could be a formidable task.

Here the prohibitive paragraph was embodied in a by-law. This provides greater flexibility. Since no higher percentage was specified in the declaration, under s. 10(1) of the Act the making of such by-laws only required the vote of members owning 66 2/3% of the common elements. If the prohibitive paragraph in question falls within the Corporation's power to make by-laws, the fact that it is described in By-law Number Two as a rule or regulation does not, in my opinion, affect its validity as a by-law. It is true that the prohibitive paragraph, whilst embodied in By-law Number Two, is referred to as a rule or regulation. In pursuance of s. 11(1) of the Act, By-law Number One authorized the owners, by a vote of members owning 51% of the common elements, to make rules, but such power was limited to rules respecting the use of the common elements. By-law Number Two draws a distinction between the units, the common elements and the property. The by-law does not contain a provision that the word "property" shall have the same meaning in the by-law as in the definition of property in s. 1(1)(*n*) of the Act, *i.e.:* "the land and interest appurtenant to the land described in the description". In my view, however, this is the only proper interpretation to be given to the word in the prohibitive paragraph. Consequently, the attempt to impose restrictions respecting the units would go beyond the powers of the members under By-law Number One to make rules.

Under s. 10(1) the Corporation has power to make by-laws:

"(b) governing the use of units or any of them for the purpose of preventing unreasonable interference with the use and enjoyment of the common elements and other units;

(c) governing the use of the common elements."

Under s. 10(2) such by-laws shall be reasonable and consistent with the Act and the declaration.

In order to fall within the Corporation's power to make by-laws under s. 10 of the Act, four matters have to be considered:

(i)   are the words "governing the use" in s. 10(1)(b) and (c) of the Act broad enough to include the making of a by-law regulating the allowing of animals upon or the keeping or animals in or about the property?

(ii) are the words "no animal" in the prohibitive paragraph so broad as to be beyond the powers of the Corporation under s. 10(1)(b) of the Act?

(iii) is the prohibitive paragraph reasonable and consistent with the Act and the declaration as required by s. 10(2) of the Act?

(iv) is the word "animal" in the prohibitive paragraph so broad that even if the Corporation had power to enact the prohibitive paragraph it is incapable of enforcement?

"Govern" is defined in *The Shorter Oxford English Dictionary,* 3rd ed., vol. 1, at p. 816, to mean: "To rule with authority...to regulate the affairs of (a body of men)."

A careful distinction has to be drawn between the power to regulate or govern and the power to prohibit. In *City of Toronto v. Virgo,* [1896] A.C. 88, the Judicial Committee of the Privy Council had to consider whether under a power to pass by-laws "for...regulating and governing hawkers or petty chapmen, and other persons carrying on petty trades", the Council might prohibit hawkers from plying their trade at all in a substantial and important part of the city. Lord Davey stated, at pp. 93-4:

"No doubt the regulation and governance of a trade may involve the imposition of restrictions on its exercise both as to time and to a certain extent as to place where such restrictions are in the opinion of the public authority necessary to prevent a nuisance or for the maintenance of order. But their Lordships think there is marked distinction to be drawn between the prohibition or prevention of a trade and the regulation or governance of it, and indeed a power to regulate and govern seems to imply the continued existence of that which is to be regulated or governed.

"Several cases in the English and Canadian reports were referred to in illustration of the respondent's argument...through all these cases the general principle may be traced, that a municipal power of regulation or of making by-laws for good government, without express words of prohibition, does not authorize the making it unlawful to carry on a lawful trade in a lawful manner."

In *Re Karry and City of Chatham* (1910), 21 O.L.R. 566, the Court of Appeal had to consider whether a by-law of the City of Chatham, stipulating the hours when eating houses should be closed, was a "regulation" authorized by the *Municipal Act* which provided that the Council could pass by-laws "limiting the number of and regulating such houses". Magee, J.A. pointed out at p. 573: "The partial prohibition, it has thus long been recognised, may well come within the powers of regulation."

In *Re R. v. Napier,* [1941] O.R. 30, [1941] 1 D.L.R. 528, 72 C.C.C. 191, the statute authorized the passing of by-laws "For licensing, regulating and governing bill posters..." A by-law had been passed prohibiting the distribution of bills by leaving them in or on parked motor-cars or by handing them to persons on the street. Hogg, J., concluded at p. 34 O.R., pp. 531-2 D.L.R., that:

"... the prevention of such activities in connection with this trade or calling is not of such a degree that it can be said to be practically a prohibition of the entire business or trade of bill distributors. There is still left to them the large field, which seems to constitute the greater part — or at least as great a part — of this business, namely, of leaving bills at the residences and other buildings in the municipality."

Here the power of the Corporation is to make by-laws "governing the use of units" and "governing the use of the common elements". In this appeal, the prohibitive paragraph as to allowing animals upon or keeping them in or about the units or common elements, is only a partial prohibition of the use of the units or the common elements. It would properly fall within the power to regulate the use of the units and common elements. In my view the word "governing" in s. 10(1)(b) is broad enough to include the restriction respecting animals in the prohibitive paragraph. It would be quite different if the power in s. 10(1)(b) and (c) of the Act had been to make by-laws governing the allowing or keeping of animals on the units or the common elements. In that even the prohibitive clause would have been *ultra vires* of the Corporation as it would have been a prohibition rather than a regulation.

It should be pointed out that the power to make by-laws under s. 10(1)(b) and under s. 10(1)(c) is with respect to "the use" of units and the common elements, whereas s. 3(2)(c) stipulates that the declaration may contain provisions respecting "the occupation and use" of the units and common elements.

As Lord Radcliffe pointed out in *Arbuckle Smith & Co. Ltd. v. Greenock Corp.*, [1960] 1 All E.R. 568 at p. 574:

"'Use' is not a word of precise meaning, but in general it conveys the idea of enjoyment derived by the user from the corpus of the object enjoyed."

Robertson, D.J.O., in *R. v. Lou Hay Hung*, [1946] O.R. 187, stated at pp. 191-2:

"The words 'occupy' and 'occupant' have a variety of shades of meaning. No doubt, we commonly speak of the 'occupants' of a dwelling-house, meaning thereby all persons who, at the time, live there. We use the word in even a wider sense when we speak of the 'occupants' of premises, meaning thereby all the persons who happen to be within them at the particular time. Primarily, however, 'to occupy' means 'to take possession'...."

Possession is a primary element but occupation includes something more. As Lord Denning explained in *Newcastle City Council v. Royal Newcastle Hospital*, [1959] A.C. 248 at p. 255: "Occupation is matter of fact and only exists where there is sufficient measure of control to prevent strangers from interfering...."

Under s. 3(2)(c-1) of the Act, the right to include a provision in the declaration respecting occupation of the units would embrace such matters as restricting the use to single-family residences. On the other hand, the right to restrict the keeping of animals in such units as incidental to such single-family use would seem properly to fall within the power to make by-laws governing the use of units.

It will also be noted that the power to make by-laws is more restrictive under s. 10(1)(b) of the Act than it is under s. 10(1)(c). Under s. 10(1)(b) the power can only be exercised "for the purpose of preventing unreasonable interference with the use and enjoyment of the common elements and other units". This brings me to a consideration of the second question, whether the words "no animals" in the prohibitive paragraph are so broad as to be *ultra vires* of the Corporation.

The word "animal" is very comprehensive. The definition in *The Shorter Oxford English Dictionary,* 3rd ed., at p. 68, includes: "1. A living being, endowed with sensation and voluntary motion, but in the lowest forms distinguishable from vegetable forms...2. One of the lower animals; a brute or beast, as distinguished from man." *Black's Law Dictionary,* 4th ed., defines "animal" as "Any animate being which is endowed with the power of voluntary motion. An animate being, not human." In *The Shorter Oxford English Dictionary, supra,* at p. 181, it is noted that the word "bird" is defined as "any feathered vertebrate animal" and at p. 705, that "fish" is defined as "In pop. language, any animal living exclusively in the water... In scientific language any vertebrate animal provided with gills throughout life, and cold-blooded; the limbs, if present, being modified into fins."

The words "no animal" in the prohibitive paragraph are wide enough to include not only cats and dogs but such animals as hamsters, canaries and goldfish. Can it be said that the broad prohibition against *any* animal being allowed upon or kept in or about the units is for the purpose of preventing unreasonable interference with the use and enjoyment of the common elements and other units? In my opinion it cannot. I am unable to conclude that goldfish, for example, would cause such unreasonable interference. Section 6(2) of the Act makes it clear that subject to the Act, the declaration, and the by-laws, each owner is entitled to exclusive ownership and use of his unit. One of the incidents of such ownership is the right to keep pets. The declaration does not contain any prohibition against the keeping of animals in the units. It is appreciated that it is important in a condominium development, particularly a condominium apartment building, to prevent the owner of a unit from unreasonably interfering with the use and enjoyment of others of their units and of the common elements. As Driver, Assoc. J., stated in *Sterling Village Condominium, Inc. v. Breitenbach* (1971), Fla., 251 So. (2d) 685 at p. 688: "Every man may justly consider his home his castle and himself as the king thereof; nonetheless his sovereign fiat to use his property as he pleases must yield, at least in degree, where ownership is in common or cooperation with others. The benefits of condominium living and ownership demand no less."

The owners of 66 2/3% or more of the common elements may wish to pass a by-law to protect themselves against unreasonable interference by way of vicious, malodorous, dirty or noisy animals, or pollution of the common elements. However, the prohibitive paragraph in question goes far beyond the limited powers in s. 10(1)(*b*) to govern the use of units and would have the effect of prohibiting animals in or about the units which could not be the cause of unreasonable interference.

In my view, the prohibitive paragraph in question, in so far as it governs the use of units, is beyond the powers of the Corporation.

It should be observed that the powers of the Corporation under s. 10(1)(*c*) are to govern the use of the common elements and there is no limitation on the exercise of this power as in the case of s. 10(1)(*b*). It would seem that under s. 10(1)(*c*) the Corporation could prohibit animals generally from being allowed upon the common elements.

If access to the units can only be obtained by passing through the common elements, then even if the portion of the prohibitive paragraph governing the use of the units were invalid, the owner of a unit might be prohibited from bringing animals into the units. The question arises whether the portion of the prohibitive paragraph which regulates the use of the units is severable from the portion which regulates the use of the common elements, or whether the entire prohibitive paragraph is *ultra vires* of the Corporation.

As Craies points out in his text on *Statute Law*, 6th ed. (1963) at p. 335, there is some difference of judicial opinion as to whether a by-law is severable or divisible. In *Strickland v. Hayes,* [1896] 1 Q.B. 290 at p. 292, Lindley, L.J., stated:

"There is plenty of authority for saying that if a by-law can be divided, one part may be rejected as bad while the rest may be held to be good."

On the question of severability, decisions respecting the exercise of the jurisdiction of the Supreme Court to quash a municipal by-law in whole or in part under s. 283(1) of the *Municipal Act,* R.S.O. 1970, c. 284, are of assistance. In *Re Morrison and City of Kingston,* [1938] O.R. 21 at p. 27, [1937] 4 D.L.R. 740 at p. 745, 69 C.C.C. 251, Middleton, J.A. said:

"It is not, I think, competent to the Court to quash part of a by-law, unless it is clearly severable from the provisions that remain."

This statement was approved by the Court of Appeal in *Re Musty's Service Stations Ltd. and Ottawa,* [1959] O.R. 342, 22 D.L.R. (2d) 311, 124 C.C.C. 85, where Aylesworth, J.A. in delivering the judgment of the Court, concluded that the invalid provisions of the by-law were integral and indispensable parts of the by-law and were not severable from the rest of the by-law.

In so far as the prohibitive paragraph itself is concerned, in view of the fact that the prohibition is made applicable to the property which includes both the units and the common elements, I do not think it is possible to sever the portion of the paragraph which deals with the units from the portion which deals with the common elements even if s. 10(1)(*c*) was wide enough to permit the restriction so far as the common elements were concerned.

Having reached this conclusion it is not necessary to consider the third question which arises as a result of s. 10(2) of the Act which provides:

"10(2) The by-laws shall be reasonable and consistent with this Act and the declaration."

Nor is it necessary to consider the fourth question, that the word "animal" in the prohibitive paragraph is so broad that even if the Corporation had power to enact the prohibitive paragraph it is incapable of enforcement.

Paragraph 14 of By-law Number Two is, in my view, beyond the powers of the Corporation in its entirety. It is not necessary to express any view as to the validity of the remaining provision of By-law Number Two, as para. 14 is severable from the remaining provisions of the by-law.

Author's Note: For a judicial decision where the judge reached the opposite conclusion on the right of the condominium unit owner to keep an animal on the premises see *Re Peel Condominium Corp. No. 78 and Harthen et al.* (1978), 20 O.R. (2d) 225.

Condominium Declaration — Whether It Prohibits Owner from Leasing Unit

Re Winnipeg Condominium Corp. No. 1 and Stechley (1979), 90 D.L.R. (3d) 703. A condominium corporation declaration restricted use of each unit to a single family residence. A unit holder leased his unit to a third party. The corporation took legal action to prohibit the lease.

SOLOMON, J.:

Applicant, a condominium corporation under the *Condominium Act,* R.S.M. 1970, c. C170, is applying for an order directing respondent to perform a duty imposed on him by a declaration duly registered, relating to the condominium

situated at 1052 Buchanan Blvd., in Winnipeg, Manitoba. Applicant maintains
that under para. 5(1) of said declaration respondent, who is the owner of suite
No. 2, must occupy the suite for his own use and has no right to lease it to a third
party.

The facts relating to the matter before this Court are not in dispute.
Respondent purchased suite No. 2 in applicant's condominium and became the
registered owner of an estate in fee simple of the said real property as shown by
certificate of title No. C66918, subject to a declaration registered as No. J86594
1/2. After purchasing the suite No. 2, respondent leased it to the tenant who is
now occupying it with his family as a one-family unit. Applicant asks this Court
to declare that the respondent has no legal right to lease his suite to a third person.

Paragraph 5(1) of the declaration provides:

> Each unit shall be occupied only as a one-family residence by the owner
> of the unit(s), his family and guests. For the purpose of these restrictions,
> "one-family residence" means a building occupied or intended to be occu-
> pied as a residence by one family alone and containing one kitchen, provided
> that no roomers or boarders are allowed. A "boarder" for the purpose of
> these restrictions is a person to whom room and board are regularly supplied
> for consideration.

and para. 1 of the declaration adopts the definition of the owner contained in the
Act and it "means the owner of the freehold estate or estates or leasehold estate
or estates in a unit and common interest, but does not include a mortgage unless
the mortgagee is in possession". Applicant argues that respondent, by taking title
subject to the said declaration, agreed not to lease his unit to a third party but to
occupy it as owner of a freehold estate.

If this Court were to accede to applicant's interpretation of its legal position
and find that respondent has purchased his unit subject to said prohibitions, it
would be placing a very great restriction on the rights of the owner who holds a
certificate of title for an estate in fee simple. Before this Court could accede to
applicant's submission it would have to be satisfied that the language in the declaration clearly prohibits the owner from leasing his freehold estate and that
there is a very clear provision in the *Condominium Act* to permit such a clause to
be included in the declaration.

I was not able to find any Manitoba judicial interpretations of these sections
of the *Condominium Act* which deal with the restrictions in the declarations, but
there is a reported decision by the Ontario High Court of Justice in the case of *Re
Peel Condominium Corp. No. 11 and Caroe et al.* (1974), 48 D.L.R. (3d) 503 at
p. 504, 4 O.R. (2d) 543 at p. 544, where Mr. Justice Galligan held:

> If the declaration is given the meaning which the applicant contends it
> ought to be given, then as a practical matter there would be a substantial
> restriction imposed upon the very nature of the ownership that rests in the
> owner. One of the fundamental incidents of ownership is the right to alienate
> the property that one owns. With respect to real property the right to freely
> alienate dates to 1290, when the Imperial Statute of *Quia Emptores,* 18 Edw.
> I, was enacted. The provisions of that statute were made part of the law of
> Ontario in 1897 [R.S.O. 1897, c. 330]. (See Anger and Honsberger, *Canadian
> Law of Real Property* (1959), p. 21.)

> Earl Jowitt, in the *Dictionary of English Law,* at p. 1284, considered the
> nature of ownership in the following terms:

"Ownership is essentially indefinite in its nature, but in its most absolute form, it involves the right to possess the use or enjoy the thing, the right to its produce and accessions, and the right to destroy, encumber, or *alienate it;*"
(The emphasis is mine.)

One of the important forms which alienation of one's property takes is leasing or renting of the property. As was said by Pearson, J., in *Re Rosher* (1884), 26 Ch.D. 801 at p. 818: "There are various modes of alienation besides sale; a person may lease, or he may mortgage, or he may settle." The right to lease one's property is therefore one of the important ingredients of absolute ownership.

A declaration under the *Condominium Act* is a creature of that statute and is therefore prescribed by it. In my view, a declaration may only restrict rights and impose duties if the statute authorizes it to do so.

The statutory provisions in the *Condominium Act* of Ontario contain similar provisions to the corresponding sections of the Manitoba *Condominium Act* and the relevant provision in the declaration with which the Ontario Court had to deal in the *Peel* case, is identical to para. 5(1) of the declaration which is the subject-matter before this Court. There is, however, a material difference between the two declarations. In the declaration with which the Ontario Court was dealing in the *Peel* case there was no definition of "owner", but in the declaration before this Court "owner" is defined to include not only the owner of the estate in fee simple but also mortgagee in possession and owner of a leasehold estate. According to the declaration the tenant who is leasing the unit from respondent has the right to occupy the premises as an owner of a leasehold estate. Despite these provisions in the declaration the applicant is asking this Court to find that it was applicant's intention to limit occupancy of unit No. 2 to the owner of the estate in fee simple. If it was the intention of applicant to limit occupancy of the unit to the owner of the estate in fee simple, the provisions in the declaration should have unequivocally provided for such prohibition. To prevent the owner of an estate in fee simple from having a right to lease his freehold estate to a third party is a very restrictive one and should be strictly construed. I cannot see how such prohibition could be construed from the language contained in the said declaration.

Even if the language in the declaration could be construed to limit occupancy of the units to the owners of estates in fee simple, I would hold that applicant would not have the right to enforce such a provision because there is nothing in the *Condominium Act* which would give it the right to include such a prohibition in the declaration. The relevant provisions in the Act are:

1....

• • • •

(p) "owner" means the owner of the freehold estate or estates or leasehold estate or estates in a unit and common interest, but does not include a mortgage unless the mortgagee is in possession:

• • • •

5(2) In addition to the matters mentioned in subsection (1), a declaration may contain

• • • •

    (c)   subject to subsection (3), provisions respecting the occupation and use of the units and common elements; or

    (d)   subject to subsection (3), provisions restricting gifts, leases and sales of the unit and common interests...

        I think that statutory provisions which may permit encroachment on the rights of individuals should be strictly interpreted. Obviously the above provisions authorized certain reasonable restrictions on occupation and use of the units to be included in the declaration. The very nature of condominium construction would indicate that some restrictions on the use and occupancy of the individual units, such as provisions for one-family occupancy, anti-commercial use and the like, should be permitted to be included in the declaration. I cannot see how the Legislature could have intended to take away such a fundamental right as an owner's right of alienation of his freehold estate by such language as is contained in s. 5(2)(c) and (d) of the Act. I would think the Legislature would have expressed its intention in very clear and unambiguous language had it intended to take away such an enshrined legal right from the owner of the estate in fee simple. Section 1(p) of the Act clearly provides that a tenant, as holder of a leasehold estate, may be the owner within the meaning of the Act. I cannot find any other provision in the Act which would permit applicant to include in the declaration a prohibition for a tenant to occupy the unit as owner of leasehold estate.

        I, therefore, find that even if the language in the declaration is capable of being construed as prohibiting the owner of the estate in fee simple to lease the unit to the third party, such provision is not authorized by the Act and is therefore invalid. The application therefore is dismissed with costs.

CASE PROBLEMS FOR DISCUSSION

Case 1

Wagner, an orchestra member, was the owner of a unit in a high-rise condominium that contained 210 units. The condominium corporation maintained a music room in the general recreational area of the building for use by unit owners and their guests. On Wednesday evenings, Wagner would invite the members of the orchestra to the condominium, where they would practice for several hours in the music room.

        Wagner's practice sessions were carried on for a number of months before several of the unit owners complained of the noise. Wagner ignored the complaints, and eventually a complaint was lodged with the manager employed by the corporation. The manager wrote a letter to Wagner in which he pointed out that the music room facilities were maintained for the use and enjoyment of the unit owners. He also included in the letter a copy of one of the by-laws related to the use of the common elements that read in part: "Unit owners shall not cause noise to be made or anything done that may annoy or interfere with any other owner."

        Wagner's response to the letter was that she had no intention of ceasing her practice sessions. She pointed out that users of the swimming pool in the adjacent room made substantially more noise than her orchestra and, in any event, the room was specifically designed as a place where "noise" should be made.

        When the corporation threatened legal action to restrain Wagner, she countered with a threat to have the swimming pool area closed under the same by-law.

If the dispute should come before the court, how should the matter be decided?

Case 2

Sampson purchased a ground floor unit in a large condominium that maintained all recreational and other facilities on the same floor where his unit was situated. After he had moved into the unit, he discovered that he was obliged to pay the same monthly common element expenses as the tenants on the upper floors who used the elevators.

At the next meeting of unit owners, he proposed that the common element expenses be adjusted to reflect the fact that he and a dozen other unit owners did not use the elevators in the building. His proposal was rejected.

Undaunted by his defeat, Sampson deducted what he calculated would be his share annual of the cost of maintenance of the elevators ($35) from his common element expenses for the next month. He sent his cheque in the lesser amount to the corporation.

Advise the corporation in this case. What principles are involved?

Case 3

A condominium consisting of 204 units had included in its declaration a provision that prohibited all owners from keeping dogs, cats, reptiles, or rodents in their units or in the common elements.

Lupus owned a large wolfhound and kept it in his unit. He exercised the dog each evening on the grounds of the condominium. He was unaware of the stipulation in the declaration that prohibited the keeping of dogs in the building, and he had been informed by the real estate agent at the time of purchase that pets would be permitted. Lupus also had a copy of the proposed declaration for the condominium, which had been given to him by the developer, that did not prohibit the keeping of pets.

Unknown to Lupus, the developer had revised the declaration before he registered the documents that created the condominium. The revised declaration contained the prohibition with respect to the keeping of dogs, cats, reptiles, and rodents. Lupus purchased the unit without knowledge of the change.

A short time after he had purchased his unit, Lupus was notified that he must remove his pet from the property.

In response, he raised two arguments:

(1) He was misled by the real estate agent and the developer in that the proposed declaration that contained no restriction on pets was changed immediately before it was registered, and the change constituted a manifest error that should be corrected to read in accordance with the proposed declaration.

(2) The particular proviso that prohibits pets is *ultra vires* the corporation as it is not a provision "respecting the occupation and use," but rather a proviso that attempts to "regulate the conduct of the owner." Hence, the proviso is void, as it is not permitted under the Condominium Act. In support of this position, Lupus cited a case in which the court held that a by-law prohibiting the keeping of pets on the property was inoperative.

The condominium corporation responded that there was no error in the declaration. It argued that the declaration was changed before it was registered to include the prohibition. The change was not done in error, but as a deliberate act that was subsequently supported by those who purchased units aware of the prohibition contained therein.

In response to the argument raised by Lupus that the provision attempted to regulate the conduct of the unit owner, the corporation argued that it was designed only to regulate occupation and use — something that was within its powers.

Assess the arguments raised by the parties. If the dispute should be taken before the courts, how might the case be decided?

Case 4

Simple and Simon were unit owners in the Happy Times Condominium complex, along with 95 other unit owners. Both Simple and Simon considered themselves to be creative cooks or bakers. Their cooking odours or the smoke from their burnt baked goods constantly filled the hallways and common elements, because both insisted on leaving the doors to their units open during the baking or cooking process to allow the air to circulate through their units.

The remaining unit owners objected to their cooking activities and demanded that the Happy Time Condominium Corporation prohibit Simple and Simon from engaging in their hobbies on the premises. The solicitor for the corporation, however, advised that cooking or baking as long as it was not for commercial purposes, could not be prohibited in the complex without affecting everyone else as well.

When the unit owners discovered that the cooking could not be stopped, a number of the unit owners suggested that the condominium be terminated by selling the complex to a buyer who was interested in operating it as a rental apartment building. Simple and Simon objected vigorously to the suggestion of terminating the condominium. However, in the end, all unit owners except Simple and Simon agreed that steps should be taken to do so.

Advise Simple and Simon of their rights. Describe the procedure that must be followed to terminate the condominium.

Case 5

Winston County Condominium Corp. No. 221 (WCCC #221) was formed in July of 1993, with all the usual condominium documentation. Contained in its declaration was a reference that common expenses included municipal water charges, unless the same were separately metered for each unit. There were 91 units in the building, one of which was a ground floor restaurant unit. The restaurant represented 10% of floor space, and therefore 10% of common expenses. Each of the other 90 dwelling units would bear 1% of common expenses.

After examination of the accounts for the first year of operation, WCCC No.221 found that the restaurant accounted for 47% of water charges, and the amount budgeted by the corporation of $50 000 would fall short of actual costs by $18 500. The directors passed a motion for a special levy on the restaurant unit, and a motion that a meter be installed on the pipes to and from the restaurant unit. The action was ratified by the unit holders 90 to 0, with one abstention in protest.

The owner of the restaurant unit came before the courts for relief, stating that water rates had figured into her calculations on whether to purchase the unit, and that the same calculations must have figured into WCCC #221's decision to sell the unit to her. WCCC #221 had the power to write what it wished into its declaration, and she now holds it to what it has written. The corporation had set the price for her commercial unit, knowing it would contain a restaurant. The restaurant owner acknowledged she was prepared to suffer her fate, should WCCC #221 on a vote decide to install meters to all units.

Elaborate on the issues in the arguments, and render a decision on behalf of the court.

CHAPTER 28

The Law of Mortgages

INTRODUCTION

A mortgage is a very old method of securing payment of indebtedness. In its simplest form, it involves the transfer of the debtor's title or interest in property to the creditor on the condition that the title or interest will be reconveyed to the debtor when the debt is paid. The **mortgage** is the formal agreement made between the parties, under which the debtor is referred to as the **mortgagor,** and the creditor, the **mortgagee** (see example in Appendix A: Documents). The written agreement effects the transfer of the mortgagor's interest in the property or title to the mortgagee, and contains the terms of the debt and the conditions under which the property interest will be returned to the mortgagor.

From a conceptual point of view, a modern mortgage has a number of distinct characteristics:

(1) It transfers the title of the mortgagor's property to the mortgagee.

(2) The mortgagor retains possession of the property until the debt is paid or default occurs.

(3) The document that transfers the title also contains a proviso that entitles the mortgagor to a reconveyance of the title to the property when the debt is paid.

(4) The document imposes certain obligations on the mortgagor to protect and maintain the property while the debt remains unpaid.

(5) The document also contains terms that permit the mortgagee to take steps to terminate the mortgagor's rights and interest in the property if the mortgagor defaults in payment.

Under the Land Titles System, a land or real property "mortgage" is called a **charge.** While similar to the mortgage in purpose, it does not transfer the title of the property to the creditor, but merely, as the name states, charges the land with payment of the debt. The obligations imposed on the debtor or chargor are much the same as those imposed on the mortgagor. If default occurs, the creditor in most provinces may take steps to acquire the title and possession of the land or have the land sold to satisfy the debt.

Under the Land Titles System, a mortgage in the ordinary sense of the word does not exist, as a charge does not involve the transfer of the title to the property to the mortgagee. Consequently, the remedies available to the mortgagee and the procedure that must be followed to realize on the debt in some provinces may differ from the procedure in provinces under the Registry System. At the present time, the charge under the Land Titles System may be found in parts of Ontario and Manitoba, and in Saskatchewan, Alberta, British Columbia, the Yukon, and the Northwest Territories. The Registry System and the mortgage are used in parts of Ontario,[1] Manitoba, and the provinces lying to the east of the Province of Quebec. Unfortunately, with both systems, substantial provincial and territorial variation exists, and the legislation of each jurisdiction must be consulted for the law applicable to the particular securities in question.

The mortgage is not found in the Province of Quebec. Instead, an instrument somewhat similar to the charge, which is called a **hypothec,** is used to secure debt. This particular instrument gives the creditor a security interest in the lands of the debtor and permits the debt to be satisfied by way of a sale of the land if the debtor defaults in payment.

Land is not the only form of property that may be used as security for debt. The mortgage may also be used to establish a security interest in personal property as well. Chattels such as automobiles, boats, aircraft, furniture, and equipment of all kinds are frequently used as security for indebtedness, in which case, the security instrument is called a **chattel mortgage.** Because of the many varied and specialized uses of this form of mortgage, it is treated separately along with a number of other forms of security for debt in Chapter 31.

HISTORICAL DEVELOPMENT

The fact that land has a value and represents a source of wealth is the principal reason why the mortgage has acquired widespread acceptance as a security instrument. When land is used for agricultural or silvicultural purposes, it provides income in the form of produce or timber. Where buildings are situated on the land, the buildings may be leased to provide income in the form of rents. Even in a raw state, land has value based upon the potential uses that may be made of it.

Land was particularly important as a source of wealth in the past. Until the Industrial Revolution, it represented one of the most important forms that wealth might take. As such, land was naturally considered by creditors and debtors alike as something that might be conveniently pledged as security for the payment of a debt. As a result, some legal mechanism for the pledge of land as security was considered soon after individual rights to property emerged in Western Europe

---

1. In Ontario, a mortgage under the Registry System does not transfer legal title to the mortgagee, but rather creates a charge on the land in the same manner as a Land Titles charge. See Land Registration Reform Act, R.S.O. 1990, c. L-4.

and England. The modern form of mortgage nevertheless differs substantially from its ancient predecessors, although the concept has changed very little. The first mortgages were conceived as a means of securing debt by way of a transfer of an interest in land, and this is essentially what a mortgage does today. The older forms of mortgages, however, were subject to different formalities in execution and effect.

Since the mortgage involved a change in title, the legal nature of the transaction had to comply with procedural requirements of the law. At common law, the agreement made between the mortgagor and mortgagee was strictly enforced. For the usual type of mortgage, the title passed to the mortgagee, subject to a condition subsequent that allowed the mortgagor to acquire the title back upon payment of the debt on the due date. From the point of view of the common law courts, a failure to pay on the due date would extinguish the rights of the mortgagor; after that the right to recover the property was forever lost. The debt, however, remained, and (unless the agreement provided otherwise) the mortgagor was still liable to the mortgagee for payment of the money owing.[2]

The strict approach to the agreement that the common law courts followed, and the inevitable hardships that it placed on unfortunate mortgagors, led many to seek relief from forfeiture in the Court of Chancery, where equitable relief might be had. This was done because, during the sixteenth century, the attitude of the Court of Chancery had changed with respect to mortgage actions. At the beginning of that century, the general rule was that the mortgagor must pay the mortgage debt by the date fixed for payment, otherwise a decree of foreclosure would be issued.[3] Later, the Court of Chancery was prepared to provide relief for the mortgagor who failed to make payment on the due date, if the mortgagor could satisfy the court that the failure to make payment on time was due to some unforeseen circumstance or delay. Eventually, the court was prepared to provide relief regardless of the mortgagor's reason for the delay, so long as the mortgagor offered payment to the mortgagee within a reasonable time after the due date.[4] By this time — towards the end of the century — the court recognized the fact that the true nature of the contract was that of debt, rather than that of a transfer of land. From that time on, the court treated the transaction as a form of contract in which the land was simply held as security and viewed as something that could be used to satisfy the debt if payment was not made by the debtor.[5]

The establishment of an equitable right to redeem in the mortgagor by the court also affected the mortgagee's rights. Having taken the position that a mortgagor had the right to redeem the property within a reasonable time after the contractual right was lost, the court unwittingly placed the mortgagee in a position of uncertainty with respect to the property. This in turn prompted mortgagees to seek relief from the same court. In response to petitions from mortgagees for recognition of their titles to mortgaged lands, the court engaged in a practice of granting decrees of foreclosure, which confirmed the mortgagee's absolute title and precluded the mortgagor from later demanding the right to redeem.[6]

---

2. See, for example, comments by Lord Haldane in *Kreglinger v. New Patagonia Meat & Cold Storage Co. Ltd.,* [1914] A.C. 25 at p. 35.

3. Holdsworth, vol. 3, p. 129.

4. See Holdsworth, vol. 5, (1st ed.) pp. 330-331.

5. Holdsworth, vol. 5, p. 331.

6. The right is described in *Cummins v. Fletcher* (1880), 14 Ch.D. 699.

Over time, a change also took place with respect to possession of the land by the mortgagee. The inconvenience of the mortgagor losing possession during the term of the mortgage was gradually replaced by an agreement that allowed the mortgagor to remain in possession of the property, provided that the mortgage terms were complied with and the mortgagor was not in default in payment. This change permitted the mortgagor to retain what was often the source of income necessary to pay the debt. It also reflected the true nature of the transaction: the use of the property as security for a debt.

The concept of a mortgage was further refined by the courts as a security instrument (rather than a transfer of title), by requiring the mortgagee to look first to the property mortgaged for payment of the debt. This relieved the mortgagor of the double disaster of not only losing the land, but remaining liable for the debt as well, and introduced the final element of fairness in the transaction. Thereafter, the mortgage as a form of security for debt changed little in its basic form and effect until the late nineteenth century.

In Canada and the United States, the mortgage arrived with the first settlers in the colonies. It developed along similar lines to those in England until the late nineteenth century with the introduction of the Land Titles (or Torrens) System of land registration. The adopting of this system by many of the states of the United States and some of the provinces of Canada further changed the form of mortgage to that of a charge on the land, rather than a transfer of title to the property. The late nineteenth and early twentieth century also saw the introduction of legislation relating to mortgages and charges, which clarified and modified the rights of the parties. As a result, the modern law of mortgages has become a blend of historic legal concepts, common law rules, equitable principles, and statute law.

THE NATURE OF MORTGAGES

The most common form that a mortgage may take is that of a **first mortgage** or **legal mortgage**. Only the first mortgage of a parcel of land may be the legal mortgage, since it represents a transfer of the title of the property to the mortgagee. Where the mortgagor holds an estate in fee simple, the mortgagee acquires the fee, leaving the mortgagor with possession of the property and the right to redeem the title in accordance with the terms of the instrument.

Assuming that a willing mortgagee may be found, a mortgagor may also pledge the same property as security for debt by a **second mortgage** or **equitable mortgage.** A second mortgage differs from a first or legal mortgage in the sense that the mortgagor does not have a title to transfer to the mortgagee as security. The mortgagor has only an **equity of redemption,** or the right to redeem the first mortgage. It is this right that the mortgagor mortgages, hence the name equitable mortgage. In essence, it is the equitable right of the mortgagor that the mortgage attaches as security, a right made possible because the Court of Chancery over time treated the right of redemption as an estate in land[7] and, hence, open to mortgage.

A second mortgagee, therefore, obviously assumes substantially greater risks with respect to the property than does the first mortgagee. The second mortgagee

---

7. See *Kreglinger v. New Patagonia, supra,* footnote 1. Comments by Lord Parker at pp. 47–48. See also *Casborne v. Scarfe* (1737), 1 Atk. 603 at p. 605, 26 E.R. 377 (Lord Hardwicke).

must be always vigilant and prepared for default on the part of the mortgagor. Default on the first mortgage would entitle the first mortgagee to take steps to foreclose the interests of not only the mortgagor, but the second mortgagee as well. The second mortgagee must, as a result, be in a position to make payment of the first mortgage if the mortgagor should fail to do so. This greater risk associated with second mortgages explains the reluctance on the part of some lenders to advance funds under this type of mortgage, and the reason why lenders, when they do agree to make such a loan, charge a higher rate of interest.

Mortgages subsequent to a second mortgage are also possible, as the mortgagor does not entirely extinguish his or her equity of redemption by way of the second mortgage. A mortgagor may, for example arrange a third mortgage on the same property, which would be essentially a mortgage of the right to redeem the prior mortgages. Again, the risk associated with a third mortgage would be correspondingly higher than that associated with the second mortgage, as the third mortgagee must make certain that the mortgagor maintains the first and second mortgages in good standing at all times. The third mortgagee must also be prepared to put the prior mortgages in good standing or pay them out if the mortgagor should default.

The number of equitable mortgages that might conceivably be placed on a single parcel of land is generally limited to the mortgagor's equity in the property. For example, if a person owns a building lot in fee simple with an appraised market value of $50 000, it might be encumbered up to its market value by any number of mortgages. Lenders rarely lend funds on the security of land that would exceed the value of the property, unless some other security is also provided for the loan. Many lenders are unwilling to lend up to the market value in the event that the property value might decline. It is not uncommon for lending institutions to limit the amount of a mortgage loan to 75% of the appraised value of the property, unless some other guarantee of payment is also associated with the loan. Where property is used as security for more than one mortgage, the mortgagor must, of course, maintain each mortgage in good standing at all times. Otherwise, the default on one mortgage would trigger foreclosure proceedings on that particular mortgage and produce a parallel reaction among all other mortgagees holding mortgages subsequent to it.

PRIORITIES BETWEEN MORTGAGES

Where a mortgagor encumbers a parcel of land with more than one mortgage, the priority of the mortgagees becomes important. Since, in theory, only the mortgage first in time constitutes a legal mortgage (and all subsequent mortgages are merely mortgages of the mortgagor's equity), it is essential that some system be used to establish the order of the instruments and the rights of the parties.

In all provinces, the order of priority is established for the most part by the time of registration of the mortgage documents in the appropriate land registry office.[8] Assuming that a bona fide mortgagee has no actual notice of a prior unregistered mortgage, the act of registration of a valid mortgage in the registry office would entitle a mortgagee to the first or legal mortgage with respect to the property. It should be noted, however, that a mortgagee must undertake a search

---

8. See, for example, the Registry Act, R.S.O. 1990, c. R-20, s. 74.

of the title to the property at the land registry office in order to determine the actual status of the mortgage, since the registration of a document, such as a mortgage, is deemed to be notice to the public of its existence.[9] Any prior mortgage of the same property, if registered, would take priority. Consequently, a mortgagee as a rule does not accept only the word of the mortgagor that the land is unencumbered, but makes a search of the title at the land registry office as well. This is done in advance of the registration to determine the status of the mortgage before funds are advanced under it.

RIGHTS AND DUTIES OF THE PARTIES

Under mortgage law, a mortgagor is entitled to remain in possession of the mortgaged property during the term of the mortgage, provided that the mortgagor complies with the terms and conditions set out in the mortgage. (If the mortgagor defaults in any material way, the mortgage usually provides that the mortgagee is entitled to take action for possession or payment.) A mortgagor also has the right to demand a reconveyance of the title to the property, or a discharge of the mortgage when the mortgage debt has been paid in full. In contrast to these rights, a mortgagor has a number of duties arising out of the mortgage itself.

A mortgage, apart from being an instrument that conveys an interest in land, is contractual in nature. It contains a number of promises or covenants that the mortgagor agrees to comply with during the life of the mortgage. While the parties are free to insert any reasonable covenants they may desire in the mortgage, the instrument normally contains four important covenants on the part of the mortgagor. These are:

(1) a covenant to pay the mortgage in accordance with its terms;

(2) a covenant to pay taxes or other municipal assessments;

(3) a covenant to insure the premises, if the property is other than vacant land; and

(4) a covenant not to commit waste, and to repair the property if any damage should occur.

Covenant of Payment

Both the mortgagor and the mortgagee are vitally interested in the payment of the debt. The mortgagee wants to receive back the principal and interest earned on the loan, and the mortgagor wishes to obtain a reconveyance of the title to the property.

Mortgage payment terms are negotiated by the parties and may take many forms. The most common arrangement calls for the repayment of the principal together with interest in equal monthly payments over the term of the mortgage. The particular advantage of this form of repayment over provisions that provide for quarterly, half-yearly, annual, or "interest only" payments during the life of the agreement is that any default on the part of the mortgagor will be quickly noticed by the mortgagee, and steps may then be taken to remedy the situation. Mortgages that call for periodic payments generally contain an **acceleration clause** that is triggered by default of payment of a single installment, thereby rendering the whole of the outstanding balance due and payable immediately.

---

9. See, for example, the Registry Act, R.S.O. 1990, c. R-20, s. 78.

This permits the mortgagee to demand payment of the full amount. Failing payment by the mortgagor, the default would entitle the mortgagee to take steps to realize the debt from the property by way of foreclosure or sale proceedings.

A mortgagee seldom demands payment in full simply because a mortgagor fails to make a monthly payment on the due date. However, a failure to make a number of payments would probably result in action taken by the mortgagee on the basis of the mortgagor's breach of the covenant to pay.

Payment of Taxes

Under most tax legislation, taxes on real property levied by municipalities (or in some cases by the province) provide that the claim of the municipality for unpaid taxes becomes a claim against the property in priority over all other encumbrances. To ensure that the municipality does not obtain a prior claim against the property, mortgages usually contain a covenant on the part of the mortgagor to pay all such taxes levied when due. Again, if the mortgagor fails to pay the taxes, he or she is treated as being in default under the mortgage for breach of the covenant concerning taxes, and the mortgagee may then take action under the mortgage.

In the recent past and, to some extent, today, mortgagees (especially lending institutions) inserted a clause in their mortgages requiring the mortgagor to make payments to the mortgagee over the course of the year (usually on a monthly basis) of sufficient funds to pay the municipal taxes on the property. The mortgagee would then use the funds to pay the taxes when levied by the municipality. In this fashion the mortgagee was in a position to maintain the mortgage free of any claims for taxes. As an alternative, mortgagees who do not collect tax payments and pay the taxes directly may still require the mortgagor to submit the paid municipal tax bill each year for examination in order to substantiate payment and to ensure that no claims for taxes may take priority over their mortgages.

Insurance

The obligation on the part of the mortgagor to insure only applies where a building or structure is erected on the mortgaged land. The purpose of the covenant to insure is obvious: much of the value of the property rests in the existence of the building or structure, and its loss, through damage by fire or other causes, in most cases would substantially lessen the security for the mortgagor's indebtedness.

Careful mortgagees generally arrange their own insurance on the mortgaged premises in order to satisfy themselves that the insurance is adequate and that it covers their interest in the event that loss or damage should later occur. Other mortgagees simply rely on the mortgagor to maintain the required insurance. The liability for the payment of the premium, however, remains with the mortgagor even though the insurance covers both the mortgagor and mortgagee. In the event of a loss, the proceeds of the insurance would be payable first to satisfy the principal and interest owing to the mortgagee, and the balance, if any, would then be payable to the mortgagor. The land, of course, would remain intact. If the insurance proceeds paid the mortgage in full, the mortgagor would be entitled to a discharge of the mortgage and a return of the title to the property.

Waste

Closely associated with insurance, but of a different nature, is the mortgagor's covenant not to commit waste. **Waste** is a legal term to describe any act that would reduce the value of the property. It would include, in the case of a mortgage, an act by a mortgagor to reduce the security available to the mortgagee. For example, a mortgagor that demolishes a building on the mortgaged property would be committing waste, because the building would represent part of the value of the property. Similarly, a mortgagor that strips and sells the top soil from the land would commit waste if the act was done without the consent of the mortgagee.

The covenant by the mortgagor not to commit waste is essentially a term that preserves the property intact during the time that the mortgage is in existence. It is inserted in the agreement to protect the mortgagee by requiring the mortgagor to maintain the property value. A violation of the covenant by the mortgagor would entitle the mortgagee to take action under the terms of the mortgage. Waste, however, does not include ordinary deterioration of property as a result of lack of repair. To cover this, mortgages may also include a term that obliges the mortgagor to maintain the property in a good state of repair while the mortgage is in effect.

SPECIAL CLAUSES

Not every term in a mortgage imposes an obligation on the mortgagor. Frequently the parties will agree that the mortgage should contain the privilege of prepayment. The parties will inset in the mortgage a provision whereby the mortgagor, while not in default, may pay the whole or any part of the principal amount owing at any time without notice or without the payment of a bonus to the mortgagee. This is often a valuable privilege for the mortgagor, as the mortgagee is not required to accept payment of the mortgage money owing except in accordance with the terms of the mortgage.[10]

A mortgagor may also have the privilege of obtaining discharges of parts of the mortgaged land on the part-payment of stipulated amounts of principal, if such a right is inserted in the mortgage. The particular advantage of this clause only arises where the mortgagor intends to sell parts of the mortgage land, either to pay the mortgage or as a part of a development scheme for the property.

DISCHARGE OF MORTGAGE

If the mortgagor complies with the terms and conditions set out in the mortgage and makes payment of the principal and interest owing as required and when due, the mortgagor is entitled to a discharge of the mortgage. Mortgage legislation, in provinces where the Registry System is in effect, generally provides that a mortgagee may release all right, title, and interest in the property subject to the mortgage by providing the mortgagor with a **discharge of mortgage**. This

---

10. See the Interest Act, R.S.C. 1985, c. I-15, s. 10. A mortgage, however, in a long-term mortgage is obliged to accept payment in full if a non-corporate mortgagor tenders full payment and an additional three months' interest at any time after the mortgage has been in effect for five years.

particular instrument, when properly executed and delivered to the mortgagor, along with the registered duplicate original copy of the mortgage, constitutes a receipt for payment. When registered, the discharge of mortgage acts as a statutory reconveyance of the title to the mortgagor. The document, in effect, releases all claims that the mortgagee may have in the land under the mortgage and acknowledges payment of the debt. In provinces where the Land Titles System is used, the discharge of mortgage is replaced by a **cessation of charge**, which has a somewhat different effect. This document acts as an acknowledgement of payment of the debt and removes the charge from the title to the property when it is registered in the land titles office where the land is situated. On receipt of the cessation of charge, the office amends the title to the parcel of land to reflect the change and to show the title free of the particular charge.

ASSIGNMENT OF MORTGAGE

A mortgagee may assign a mortgage at any time after the mortgage is executed by the mortgagor. A mortgage, however, is unlike an ordinary debt in that it represents an interest in land. Consequently, it must be made in a form that complies with the legislation pertaining to mortgages in the particular jurisdiction where the land is situated. This is due to the fact that the assignment must not only assign the debt, but also transfer the assignor's interest in the property. Consent to the assignment by the mortgagor is not required, but actual notice of the assignment to the mortgagor is essential if the assignee wishes to protect the right to demand payment of the balance owing on the mortgage from the mortgagor.

As with the assignment of any contract debt, if notice of the assignment is not given to the mortgagor, the mortgagor may quite properly continue to make payments to the original mortgagee (the assignor). All other rules relating to the assignment of debts normally apply to a mortgage assignment. The mortgage, for example, is assigned as it stands between the mortgagor and the mortgagee at the time of the assignment. Any defence that the mortgagor might raise to resist a demand for payment by the assignor would also be effective as against the assignee. The assignee must, therefore, be certain to promptly give the mortgagor notice of the assignment following the assignment, and determine the status of the mortgage between the mortgagor and the mortgagee immediately. In most cases, an assignee will determine this from the mortgagor prior to the assignment.

SALE OF MORTGAGED PROPERTY

A mortgagor is free to sell or otherwise dispose of the equity of redemption in mortgaged land at any time during the term of the mortgage, unless the mortgage provides otherwise.[11] The disposition of the property, however, does not relieve the mortgagor of the covenants made in the mortgage. In the event that the purchaser should default on the mortgage at some later time, the mortgagee may, if the mortgagee so desires, look to the original mortgagor for payment in accordance with the original covenant to pay. It should be noted, however, that this particular rule of law only applies to the original mortgagor, and not to a purchaser who subsequently sells the property subject to the mortgage before default occurs.

---

11. Occasionally, a mortgagee may insert a term in the mortgage that requires the mortgage to be paid in full if the mortgagor should desire to sell the property.

For example, Smith gives Right Mortgage Company a mortgage on a parcel of land that she held in fee simple. Smith later sells her equity in the land to Brown. If Brown defaults in payment of the mortgage, Right Mortgage Company may either claim payment from Smith under her covenant to pay the mortgage, or it may take steps to have the debt paid by way of foreclosure or sale of the property. If the mortgagee pursues the latter course, Brown would lose his interest in the land. However, if Brown does not default, but sells his equity in the land to Doe, and Doe allows the mortgage to go into default, Right Mortgage Company does not have a claim against Brown, but only against Smith on the covenant, or Doe, who is in possession of the land.

Mortgagees frequently require the purchaser of the mortgagor's equity to sign an agreement to assume the mortgage and all its covenants in order to increase the security for payment. A purchaser who covenants to pay the mortgage in accordance with its terms becomes liable on the covenants as a result. The purchaser is placed in much the same position as the original mortgagor with respect to payment.

DEFAULT, FORECLOSURE, AND SALE

If the mortgagor defaults in the payment of principal or interest under the terms of a mortgage, or causes a breach of a covenant (such as the commission of waste), the mortgagee may at his or her option call for the immediate payment of the full amount owing by way of the acceleration clause in the mortgage. The demand for payment in full, however, does not necessarily mean that the mortgagor has no choice but to find the full amount required to pay the mortgage. In most provinces, the legislation pertaining to mortgages permits the mortgagor to pay the arrears, or correct the breach of covenant along with the payment of all related expenses, and thereby put the mortgage in good standing once again.[12]

Where financial difficulties prevent the mortgagor from correcting the default, the mortgagee is usually obliged to take action in order to recover the debt secured by the property. In this respect, the mortgagee has a number of options open. The most common courses of action that the mortgagee may follow are:

(1) sale of the property under the power of sale contained in the mortgage;

(2) foreclosure;

(3) judicial sale;

(4) possession of the property.

Sale under Power of Sale

Mortgages drawn in accordance with most provincial statutory forms generally contain a clause that permits the mortgagee to sell or lease the property subject to the mortgage if the mortgagor's default in payment persists for a period of time.[13] To exercise the **power of sale** under the mortgage, the mortgagee must give written notice to the mortgagor and to any subsequent encumbrancers, then allow a specified period of time to elapse before the property may be sold. The purpose of the notice and the delay is to provide the mortgagor and any subsequent encum-

---

12. See, for example, the Mortgages Act, R.S.O. 1990, c. M-40, ss. 22 and 23. See also *Township of Scarborough v. Greater Toronto Investment Corp. Ltd.,* [1956] O.R. 823.

13. In Ontario, for example, the usual clause provides that the mortgagee may begin the exercise of the power of sale when default exceeds 15 days. See also the Mortgages Act, R.S.O. 1990, c. M-40.

brancers with an opportunity to put the mortgage in good standing once again, or to pay the full sum owing to the mortgagee.

If the mortgagor is unable to place the mortgage in good standing, the mortgagee is free to proceed with the sale and to use the proceeds first in the satisfaction of the mortgage debt, and the remainder in the payment of subsequent encumbrances and any execution creditors. Any surplus after payment to the creditors belongs to the mortgagor. Should the mortgagor be in possession prior to the sale, the mortgagee would be obliged to bring an action for possession in order to render the property saleable. If the mortgagee is successful in this action, the courts will render a judgement for possession, which in turn would enable the mortgagee to obtain a **writ of possession**. The writ of possession is a direction to the sheriff of the county where the land is situated, authorizing the sheriff to obtain possession of the property for the mortgagee.

Since the mortgagor is entitled to the surplus in a sale under a power of sale (and also liable for any deficiency), the mortgagee is under an obligation to conduct the sale in good faith and to take steps to ensure that a reasonable price is obtained for the property. The effort normally required would include advertising the property for sale, and perhaps obtaining an appraisal of the property to determine its approximate value for sale purposes. The mortgagee, however, is not obliged to go to great lengths to obtain the best price possible.[14]

Foreclosure

Except in Quebec, an alternative to sale under the power of sale contained in the mortgage is an action for foreclosure. While much procedural variation exists between provinces, this type of action, if successful, results in the issue by the courts of **final order of foreclosure** that extinguishes all rights of the mortgagor (and any subsequent encumbrancer) in the property. An action for foreclosure, however, gives the mortgagor and any subsequent encumbrancers the right to redeem. Also the courts will provide a period of time (usually six months) to enable any party who makes such a request the opportunity to do so. If the party fails to redeem the property within the time provided, or if no request for an opportunity to redeem is made, the mortgagee may then proceed with the action and eventually obtain a judgement and final order of foreclosure. In spite of its name, the final order of foreclosure is not necessarily final in every sense of the word. The mortgagor may, under certain circumstances, apply to have it set aside after its issue, if the mortgagor acquires the necessary funds to redeem and the mortgagee has not disposed of the property.

Sale

As an alternate method of obtaining payment of the mortgage, the mortgagee may apply to the court for possession, payment, and **sale** of the property. Under this procedure, the property would be sold and the proceeds distributed — first in the payment of the mortgage, then in payment of the claims of subsequent encumbrancers, and finally, the payment of any surplus to the mortgagor. The sale under

---

14. *Farrar v. Farrars, Ltd.* (1889), 40 Ch.D. 395.

this procedure differs substantially from a sale under the power of sale. However, the most common procedure is to have the property sold by tender or public auction, usually subject to a reserve bid. The method of sale does vary, since in most provinces the courts generally have wide latitude in this respect.

A sale may also be requested by the mortgagor where foreclosure action is instituted by the mortgagee. In this case, the mortgagor is usually expected to pay a sum of money to the courts to defray a part of the expenses involved in the sale. This is normally required at the time that the request for a sale is made. Once the request is received, however, the foreclosure action becomes a sale action, and the action then proceeds in the same manner as if a sale had been requested originally by the mortgagee. The advantage to the mortgagor of a sale is that the proceeds of the sale will also be applied to the payment of the claims of subsequent encumbrancers and not just to the claim of the first mortgagee. In this manner, the mortgagor is released from all or part of the claims of the subsequent encumbrancers, rather than only the claim of the first mortgagee.

Possession

When default occurs, the mortgagee has a right to **possession** of the mortgaged premises. If the premises are leased units, the mortgagee may displace the lessor and collect any rents that are payable by the tenants.

The rents collected, however, must be applied to the payment of the mortgage, and the mortgagor is entitled to an accounting of any monies collected. If the mortgagor has vacated the mortgaged property, the mortgagee may move into possession. But usually this is not the case, and the mortgagee must normally apply to the courts for an order for possession. This is generally done when the mortgagee institutes legal proceedings on default by the mortgagor. The usual relief requested by the mortgagee is either foreclosure, payment, and possession, or sale, payment, and possession.

BUSINESS APPLICATIONS OF MORTGAGE SECURITY

The purchase of real property represents a substantial investment by most purchasers, and they often do not have sufficient funds available to pay the purchase price in full. Many financial institutions and other investors are prepared to provide these funds by way of a mortgage, because a mortgage permits them to secure their investment in the property. Consequently, real property purchase transactions frequently involve three parties: a vendor, a purchaser, and a mortgagee.

A simple business transaction, such as the purchase of a dwelling-house by an individual, might be conducted in the following manner. The purchaser enters into an agreement with the vendor to purchase the property for a fixed amount, say $160 000, subject to the condition that the purchaser obtain suitable financing. The purchaser would then contact a mortgage lender such as a bank, trust company, mortgage corporation, or private investor to arrange for a loan to be secured on the land by way of a mortgage. If the lender agrees to provide financing (usually up to 75% of the property value), the purchase transaction would then proceed with the purchaser paying the vendor $40 000 (25%) and the lender advancing $120 000 (75%) for a total of $160 000. A mortgage to the lender securing the $120 000 would be registered against the property at the time that the purchaser's deed was registered. The purchaser would then have the property (subject to the mortgage) and would pay the mortgage amount to the lender over the period of time specified in the mortgage.

A more complex transaction using mortgage financing is represented by the **land development mortgage.** Land developers usually buy large tracts of land suitable for development as housing or for commercial buildings (an office or industrial condominium, for example). The developer may finance the development by way of a mortgage that contains a clause allowing the developer to obtain the release of parts of the land covered by the mortgage as the property is developed. For example, Land Development Corporation may purchase a 20 hectare parcel of land zoned for residential housing. If the purchase price is $1 500 000, the developer may finance the transaction by making a $500 000 cash payment and obtaining a mortgage for $1 000 000 from a financial institution. The mortgage could contain a term that allows the developer to obtain partial discharges of the mortgage at the rate of $25 000 per building lot.

Once the developer acquires the raw land, the developer would lay out the property into perhaps 150 building lots and obtain the necessary approvals for a housing subdivision. The developer would then build roads, install services, and generally prepare the parcels of land for sale as housing sites. As each lot was sold to a purchaser, the developer would pay the mortgagee the required $25 000 to obtain a **partial discharge** of the lot from the mortgage. This would allow the developer to convey a clear title in fee simple to the lot to the purchaser, and at the same time reduce the mortgage debt. In this case, when 40 lots were sold, the mortgage would be fully paid. The remaining lots in the development would be released from the mortgage when the mortgagee received payment for the last lot of the 40, and would give the developer a full discharge of the mortgage.

Mortgages may also be used to finance the construction of buildings, under a type of mortgage known as a **building mortgage.** With this type of mortgage, only a small portion is advanced initially to the property owner (usually an amount not exceeding the value of the building lot). As the building construction proceeds, the mortgagee would advance further sums to enable the property owner to pay for the construction work done. These **advances** are usually made at specific points in the construction process, such as when the foundation is completed, when the exterior walls and roof are finished, when plumbing and electrical work are completed, when the interior is finished, etc. The final payment would be made when the landscaping was completed and the building was ready for occupancy. Mortgage financing of a very large commercial building complex is usually handled in a somewhat different manner, but the general concept underlying the use of the mortgage as a means of financing the building project remains the same.

Mortgages may also be used as a means of providing security to support other debt instruments such as promissory notes. In these situations, the debtor under a promissory note may offer as collateral security a mortgage on real property. The mortgage given in this instance is related to the negotiable instrument and is called a **collateral mortgage**. If the debtor (mortgagor) defaults on payment of the promissory note, then the creditor (mortgagee) may look to the collateral security that is the mortgage on the land, as default on the note would constitute default on the mortgage. Payment of the debt could then be realized by taking action under the mortgage by way of sale or foreclosure.

SUMMARY

A mortgage is an instrument that utilizes land as security for debt. In most provinces, the mortgagee acquires an interest in the land by way of the mortgage, either in the form of a transfer of the title to the property as security (such as in Eastern Canada, and parts of Ontario and Manitoba under the Registry System) or in the form of a charge on the land in those provinces under the Land Titles System. Quebec law provides for a somewhat similar instrument (called a hypothec) that is in the nature of a lien on the land.

A mortgage, in addition to conveying an interest in the land, contains the details of the debt and the provisions for its repayment. In the instrument, the mortgagor covenants to protect the property by payment of taxes and insurance, and promises not to diminish the mortgagee's security by waste or non-repair. If the mortgagor defaults in payment, or fails to comply with the covenants in the mortgage, the mortgagee may institute legal proceedings to have the mortgagor's interest in the property foreclosed or sold. Foreclosure is not available in some provinces. However, in all provinces, if the mortgagor fails to pay the debt after default, the property may be sold, and the proceeds used to satisfy the indebtedness.

Where more than one mortgage is registered against a parcel of land, the mortgagees are entitled to payment in full in the order of their priority. This is usually determined by the time of registration of each instrument under the land registry system in the province. If a surplus is available after the claims of all mortgagees and other creditors with claims against the land are satisfied, the sum goes to the mortgagor.

Where no default occurs during the term of a mortgage, and the indebtedness is paid by the mortgagor, the mortgagee must provide the mortgagor with a discharge of the mortgage. This acts as a statutory reconveyance of the title and receipt for payment for a mortgage under the Registry System, or a release of the claim against the property in the case of a cessation of charge under the Land Titles System. In both instances, the discharge given to the mortgagor extinguishes the debt and releases the property as security from the mortgagee's claim against it.

Because mortgage law developed in a different fashion in each province, the nature of mortgage instruments and the rights of the parties vary substantially from province to province. The basic concept of land as security for debt, however, is common to all provincial systems.

Mortgages represent a very useful tool in the financing of many business transactions related to land, particularly in the field of land development and building construction.

DISCUSSION QUESTIONS

1. Define the term *mortgage* as an interest in land.
2. In what way does a mortgagee's interest differ from that of a person who holds land in fee simple?
3. In what way (or ways) does a mortgage differ from a charge?
4. Outline the nature of a mortgagor's interest in the mortgaged land.

5. How does a "first" mortgage differ from a "second" mortgage?

6. What factors must be considered by a person who wishes to extend a loan of money to another on the security of a second mortgage?

7. What is the nature of the covenants that a mortgagor agrees to in a mortgage?

8. Why do mortgages usually contain an acceleration clause? What is the effect of the clause if default occurs?

9. Explain the relationship that exists between a mortgagee and a person who acquires the mortgaged property from the mortgagor. Does the original relationship of mortgagor-mortgagee continue as well?

10. Indicate what the rights of a mortgagee would be if a mortgagor defaulted on the payment of the mortgage.

11. If the original mortgagor sold the mortgaged lands to a purchaser, and the purchaser failed to make payments on the mortgage, explain the possible courses of action that the mortgagee might take.

12. What are the rights of a mortgagor if, on default of payment, the mortgagee commences foreclosure proceedings?

13. How does a sale under a power of sale differ from a sale action?

14. What rights, if any, are available to a mortgagor after foreclosure takes place?

15. What is the normal procedure used to re-vest the legal title of a property in the mortgagor when the mortgage debt is paid? Does this differ in the case of a charge?

16. Outline the rights of an assignee of a mortgage from a mortgagee. What steps must be taken to ensure that the mortgagor makes payment to the assignee after the assignment takes place?

MINI-CASE PROBLEMS

1. B mortgages "Blackacre" to A for $10 000. Some time later, B defaults on payment, and A begins foreclosure proceedings. If "Blackacre" has a value of $50 000, what should B do?

2. If B did nothing in the above case until after foreclosure proceedings were completed, then wished to pay the amount owing, could B still do so to re-acquire the property? Would your answer be any different if A had sold the land to C?

JUDICIAL DECISIONS

The *Bank of Nova Scotia v. Dorval et al.* case concerns a collateral mortgage, and action taken by the bank after foreclosure on the mortgage. When the bank foreclosed and subsequently sold the land for less than the outstanding debt, the bank attempted to recover the balance from the mortgagors by taking legal action on the promissory notes.

On appeal, the court first examined the arguments advanced concerning the payment of deficiencies and the principles of law applicable to the arguments. The "rules" from the case-law were next considered, as was the distinction between "primary" and "collateral" security. Again, reference was made to other judicial decisions. The court finally concluded that the bank could not succeed in its action to recover the deficiency from the defendant on the promissory notes because it was not in a position to give back the security.

The second judicial decision, *Sterne v. Victoria & Grey Trust Co.,* examines the obligation of a mortgagee selling under a power of sale to obtain a fair price for the property. In this case the court reviewed the various judicial decisions that set out tests for duty owed by the mortgagee. The court then considered the unique nature of the property, and whether the mortgagee met the "test" of duty. The conclusion of the court was that the mortgagee failed to meet the duty, given the unique nature of the property.

Remedies of Mortgagee — Right of Mortgagee to Claim Deficiency When Property Sold after Foreclosure

Bank of Nova Scotia v. Dorval et al. (1979), 25 O.R. (2d) 579.

The defendants gave the plaintiff several promissory notes and a collateral mortgage to secure their indebtedness. They later defaulted on the debt, and the plaintiff sold the property, but the sale did not provide sufficient funds to satisfy the amount owing. The plaintiff then sued the defendants for the balance of the debt.

The trial judge gave the plaintiff judgement for the balance owing. The defendants then appealed the decision.

THORSON, J.A.:

The issue on this appeal brought by Suzanne Dorval from the above judgement is whether the Bank is precluded from suing on the promissory notes for the deficiency, by reason of its sale of the realty after obtaining the final order of foreclosure. The appellant contends that it is. The respondent Bank contends that the learned Weekly Court Judge correctly appreciated the right of the Bank, and the requirement upon it, to realize on the "collateral security" (*i.e.,* the mortgage) before seeking to realize upon what it termed the "primary security" (*i.e.,* the promissory notes) for the deficiency. In the Bank's submission, the principles of law which apply to foreclosure proceedings where the mortgage foreclosed upon represents the primary security taken to secure the loan, cannot apply to this case where the mortgage foreclosed upon represents "security collateral to and further securing the primary security represented by the promissory notes".

The arguments advanced by counsel on this appeal raise two basic principles of mortgage law. The first of these is that an action on the covenant in a mortgage may only be pursued as long as the mortgagee is able to reconvey the property. This principle was recently reiterated by Laskin, J. speaking for the majority of the Supreme Court of Canada in *Rushton v. Industrial Development Bank,* [1973] S.C.R. 552 at p. 562, 34 D.L.R. (3d) 582 at p. 589, as follows:

"I test the matter under well-recognized principles of mortgage law, applicable in Ontario, under which there has always been close regard for the rights of the mortgagor. Where a mortgagee forecloses upon mortgaged land, taking title, and then sells the land as its own, it cannot sue for the balance owing on the mortgage unless it is in a position to return the land: see *Davidson v. Sharp* (1920), 60 S.C.R. 72 at p. 82. The situation would be different if the mortgagee had exercised a power of sale under its mortgage or if it had sought a judicial sale in the foreclosure proceedings, thus obliging itself to give an accounting. Where, however, it proceeds to foreclosure only, a subsequent suit on the covenant for payment of the mortgage debt reopens for foreclosure and entitles the mortgagor to have the foreclosed property available to him as a condition of his liability. If it is not so available, the mortgagee is precluded from turning the matter into an accounting proceeding to enable it to sue for the debt when it cannot return the mortgaged land."

In an earlier case, *Mutual Life Ass'ce Co. of Canada v. Douglas* (1918), 57 S.C.R. 243, 44 D.L.R. 115, the Supreme Court of Canada stated this principle even more broadly, as one precluding not only action on the covenant but also any action to realize upon property held as collateral security to the mortgage. Idington, J., commented, in *obiter,* at p. 253 S.C.R., p. 122 D.L.R.:

"It was settled that he, seeking to impose common law right of suing upon a covenant for the debt, must be ready to reopen the foreclosure and ready to restore that property which had become his as absolutely as the English language could express it and further that if he had sold and conveyed away the property he had so acquired he should be restrained from proceeding to enforce that

common law right whether by suing upon the covenant or in any way of asserting a proprietary right over any property he had held by way of collateral security to his mortgage."

The second principle raised is that if a mortgagee holds collateral security
for the payment of the mortgage debt, he should realize the security before seeking to foreclose under the mortgage because, if he obtains foreclosure first, "he
deprives himself of the benefit of the security in the sense that the foreclosure
will be reopened if he subsequently realizes the security": *Falconbridge on
Mortgages,* 4th ed. (1977), p. 509. Falconbridge cites as authority the case of
Dyson v. Morris (1842), 1 Hare. 413 at p. 423, 66 E.R. 1094, in which it was
said:

"Again, in the case of a mortgagee, whose security was composed both of
land and stock, or personal chattels, or a policy simply assigned as a security, I
should probably experience little difficulty as to the decree to which the mortgagee would be entitled. In the case of securities so constituted the course usually recommended out of Court to a mortgagee is, first, to realize his collateral
securities, and then to proceed to foreclose the mortgage for so much of his debt
as the collateral securities may not satisfy.... [I]t is only by first realizing his collateral securities, and afterwards proceeding to foreclose the mortgage, that a
mortgagee can get a valid decree of foreclosure without foregoing the benefit of
the collateral securities which he cannot, as a matter or course, be required to do."

In my view the *rationale* behind both rules is the same; the sale of mortgaged property after final foreclosure, unlike a sale under power of sale or judicial sale, is not conducted under the auspices of the Court or in a manner
prescribed by the mortgage or by statute. Thus, there can be no assurance that
the mortgagee has obtained the full value of the property. The mortgagor has no
right to question the amount realized, nor the manner in which it was realized,
and if the property was sold for more than the mortgage debt the mortgager has
no right to the surplus. It would, therefore, be inequitable to allow the mortgagee
to claim for any deficiency either on the covenant or on other securities, since
the mortgagee, having disposed of the property without any accounting having
been taken, has placed it beyond any possibility of restoration to the mortgagor
and is thus no longer in a position to pursue an accounting to establish whatever
debt might remain. See Marriot and Dunn, *Practice in Mortgage Actions in
Ontario,* 3rd ed. (1971), at p. 16, and *Dewitt v. Simms,* [1924] 1 D.L.R. 592 at
pp. 596-7, 56 N.S.R. 515 at p. 523 (N.S.S.C.), where the following statement
was made, in *obiter:*

"Where the mortgagee simply forecloses the equity of redemption and then,
being clothed with the equitable as well as the legal estate, sells the property,
there is no assurance that he has obtained its full value and there is good reason
for saying that he should not have recourse to any other securities for his debt
unless he can surrender the pledge and that if he still retains the property his
recourse to other securities opens up the foreclosure giving the mortgager the
right to redeem."

In my view, this is all that is imported by two cases relied on by counsel for
the Bank, namely, *Miller et al. v. Budreau et al.,* [1954] O.W.N. 274 [affirmed
ibid., p. 560] and *Greenberg v. Rapoport,* [1970] 2 O.R. 349, 10 D.L.R. (3d) 737.
These cases do not, as contended by counsel for the Bank, stand for the proposition that the holder of both primary and collateral security must, as a matter of
law, realize upon the collateral security first; rather, they support a more general
proposition that where security is pledged for a debt and the lender has put it
beyond his power to restore the pledge, he must be taken to have elected to

accept the amount realized in satisfaction of the debt and to have foregone recourse to any other security *for that same debt,* whether that other security be characterized as secondary, additional, primary or collateral.

In *Miller et al. v. Budreau et al., supra,* a loan was made on a promissory note wherein the borrowers agreed to furnish, as collateral security, both a chattel mortgage and land mortgage. Subsequently, a chattel mortgage was given and a seizure was made thereunder. The lenders brought an action seeking a declaration that they were entitled to a mortgage on the lands and that such mortgage was in arrears and subject to foreclosure, since the mortgage had been promised but not actually given. It was held that the simple fact of the seizure under the chattel mortgage did not constitute a bar to the granting of the declaration. The act of seizing was not equivalent to an election to proceed only under the chattel mortgage by way of realization and an abandonment of the right to call for the security under the land mortgage, since the step toward one type of realization did not exclude the right to assert another type of realization. However, Gale, J., concluded at p. 276 that:

"...if the plaintiffs had appropriated the goods to their own use, which would of course include disposal or realization of the goods, they could not thereafter have the declaration here sought."

Gale, J., relied on *McDonald v. Grundy* (1904), 8 O.L.R. 113, where the *rationale* for the above proposition was stated to be, as discussed above, that where the lender is unable to restore the pledges he must be found to have taken them for the debt and cannot thereafter enforce the debt itself.

The second of the cases relied on by counsel for the Bank, *Greenberg v. Rapoport, supra,* is, in my view, likewise more supportive of the appellant's position. The facts of that case, simply stated, were that the mortgagee under a chattel mortgage and collateral land mortgage seized the chattels upon default of payment under the chattel mortgage, leased them to a third person with the consequent deterioration and depreciation of their value and ultimately sold them at a low price. In an application by the mortgagor for a declaration that the land mortgage given as collateral security be considered satisfied, the Court found that the mortgagee, in dealing with the chattels as he did, must be taken to have appropriated the goods to his own use so as to make himself their owner. The consequence of so doing, said Lieff, J., at p. 354 O.R., p. 742 D.L.R., is that:

"...the mortgage debt becomes extinguished and the right to pursue the original mortgagor either on his covenant to pay or under the terms of the collateral security is lost."

Counsel for the Bank contends that his holding supports the proposition advanced by him that:

"Where the holder of primary and secondary or additional security realizes against the primary security, he disentitles himself from realizing against the security given as further collateral to that primary security, and accordingly must at law realize upon the collateral security first." In my opinion, however, the issue turns not on which security was realized first but on whether the mortgagee has put it beyond his power to restore the property pledged as security. This was apparently the view of Lieff, J., who, in holding that the realty mortgage must be considered satisfied, stated the proposition thus at p. 354 O.R., p. 742 D.L.R.:

"[W]here collateral security is held and the prime security has been sold, so that the mortgagor can no longer redeem because the mortgagee has put it beyond his power to restore the prime security, therefore, in divesting himself of the prime security the rights of the mortgagee under the collateral security are extinguished."

If the Bank in the present case had sued first on the "primary security" (the promissory note) for payment, it would not, as I see it, have thereby disentitled itself from subsequently realizing upon the collateral security (although this is the proposition that the counsel for the Bank would have us accept). This is so because:

1. The action on the note would be analogous to an action on the covenant in the mortgage for payment, and it is clear law that a judgement on the covenant does not preclude the mortgagee from later enforcing his security upon the property in respect of the balance remaining due.

2. Such an action would not offend the basic principle that where a lender realizes upon security pledged for a debt and so puts it beyond his power to restore it, he must be taken to have accepted the property in satisfaction of the debt and may not thereafter assert a claim for any deficiency.

Indeed, on the facts of this case, it is not really helpful to speak of the "primary security" as distinct from the "collateral security" herein, or to attempt to apply cases which refer to that distinction to these facts. The promissory notes are more appropriately characterized, if they need be characterized at all, as the primary *obligation*, since they are not given as "security" in the ordinary sense. Strictly speaking, if there is a "primary security" in this case it is probably the realty, since it is the property pledged to secure the performance of the obligation evidenced by the notes. Thus the respondent Bank's contention that the "authorities cited [by the appellant] reflect upon the position of the holder of the primary security and the consequence of foreclosure upon that security" is not a valid basis for distinction. This, however, does not detract from the correctness of the characterization of the mortgage itself as a "collateral security" as that expression was defined by this Court in *Royal Bank of Canada v. Slack,* [1958] O.R. 262 at p. 273, 11 D.L.R. (2d) 737, at p. 746: "Collateral security is any property which is assigned or pledged to secure the performance of an obligation and as additional thereto, and which upon the performance of the obligation is to be surrendered or discharged."

However the promissory notes and the mortgage are characterized, I conclude that the issue in this appeal must be tested by recourse to "the well-recognized principles of mortgage law, applicable in Ontario" to which reference was made in the *Rushton* case, *supra*. An early illustration of the application of those principles in this Province is furnished by *Allison v. McDonald* (1894), 23 S.C.R. 635, in which the Supreme Court of Canada dealt with a fact situation bearing some substantial similarity to that of this case. There, two partners had borrowed money on the security of their joint promissory note and a realty mortgage. Subsequently, the lender gave one of the partners a discharge of the mortgage, but without receiving payment of his debt, and later brought an action against the other partner on the promissory note. The Supreme Court of Canada affirmed the decision of the Ontario Court of Appeal where [at p. 638] it was held that: "[T]he mortgage and promissory note having been given for the same debt, the appellant could not recover upon the note after having the mortgage inasmuch as...the respondent...on payment of the note, would have been entitled to a transfer of the mortgage which the appellant had, by discharging that security, put it out of his power to give him."

The Chief Justice of Canada at pp. 639-40 set out the rule and its *rationale* in so clear a manner that it merits quotation here at some length:

"The judgment of the Court of Appeal proceeds upon the point taken up in the first branch of the Chancellor's judgment, namely, that the appellant could not call upon the respondent to pay the mortgage debt without being prepared to re-convey to him the lands mortgaged to secure the debt which he had incapacitated himself from doing....

"So completely is the principal [*sic*] upon which they have decided the case supported by authority that it would, under the old system of procedure when law and equity were administered separately, have been of course to enjoin an action to recover on a promissory note brought under such circumstances as are disclosed by the evidence in this record. The rule is elementary and so well established that it is almost superfluous to quote authorities in support of it. *The principal is the plain and just one that he who gives a pledge in security for a debt is, upon payment, entitled to a return of that which he has given in security, from whence it follows that if the creditor is unable to return the pledge he will not be allowed to exact the debt.... Even if the mortgagee had obtained an absolute foreclosure by which he had made the mortgaged estate his own, and had then sold it for its fair value but for less than the mortgage debt, he could not sue the mortgagor on his bond, covenant, note or other collateral personal security for the unsatisfied residue, and that for the same reason, that he could not give him back the estate.*" (Emphasis added.)

Much more recently, the Alberta Court of Appeal, in *Clayborn Investments Ltd. v. Wiegert* (1977), 77 D.L.R. (3d) 170, 3 Alta. L.R. (2d) 295, dealt with a fact situation even more closely resembling that of this case, but which turned on certain legislation peculiar to Alberta. There the Court was concerned with the effect of the *Judicature Act*, R.S.A. 1970, c. 193, s. 34(17)(a), and the *Land Titles Act*, R.S.A. 1970, c. 198, s. 109(1), on the common law of mortgages. *Allison v. McDonald, supra*, and *Rushton v. Industrial Development Bank, supra*, were referred to as stating the applicable common law. Mr. Justice Clement said, at p. 173: "At common law, in the absence of statutory modification, *where the promissory note and the mortgage are given for the same debt and there are no circumstances to distinguish the obligation of payment under the note from that under the mortgage,* then a sale of the mortgaged premises by the mortgagee after foreclosure...will prevent a claim on the note for the deficiency since the mortgagee could not then reconvey the security." (Emphasis added.)

The Court then went on to deal with the case before it on the basis of the statutory provisions in question, after Morrow, J.A., noted with reference to the Land Titles Act provisions that they were "almost declaratory of the common law".

For the foregoing reasons I conclude that the Bank in this case is precluded from suing on the promissory notes for the deficiency, having proceeded in the way that it did with respect to the realty that was the subject of its collateral security.

I would therefore allow the appeal and set aside the judgment of the Weekly Court Judge, on the ground that the Bank has no cause by action against the appellant Suzanne Dorval.

**Power of Sale —
Duty of Care on
Mortgagee in
Exercising Power**

Sterne v. Victoria & Grey Trust Co. (1985), 14 D.L.R. (4th) 193.

When the mortgagor defaulted on payment, the mortgagee trust company sold the property under its power of sale. Appraisals indicated that the property was worth between $190 000 and $210 000. The mortgagee advertised in local newspapers only and accepted an offer for $185 000. The mortgagor objected to the sale on the basis that he had an offer for $210 000 that the mortgagee prevented the mortgagor from accepting.

RUTHERFORD, J.:

...I now consider what duty the defendant owed the plaintiff in exercising its power of sale. It has been suggested that there is some conflict in the case-law over the nature of the test to be applied in reviewing the exercise by a mortgagee of his power of sale.

One line of authority, which has as its touchstone the case of *Liquidation Estates Purchase Co. v. Willoughby,* [1896] 1 Ch. 726, affirmed [1897] A.C. 180 *sub nom. Kennedy v. De Trafford,* has it that the mortgagee's only obligation to the mortgagor is to exercise his power of sale in good faith: [1897] A.C. at p. 185, *per* Lord Herschell. The other line of authority, which finds its origin in cases earlier than *Kennedy v. De Trafford,* cases which were not discussed in the decision of either the Court of Appeal or the House of Lords in that case, imposes a much stricter duty on the mortgagee. He must use the same care and caution a prudent owner would use and take steps to carry out the sale under conditions that would produce the best possible price: see *Faulkner v. Equitable Reversionary Society* (1858), 4 Drew. 352 at p. 355, 62 E.R. 136; *Marriott v. Anchor Reversionary Co. Ltd.* (1860), 7 Jur. N.S. 155 at p. 156-7, 2 Giff. 457 at p. 469, 66 E.R. 191, affirmed 3 De G.F. & J. 177, 45 E.R. 846.

These two lines of authority were considered by the English Court of Appeal in *Cuckmere Brick Co. Ltd. et al. v. Mutual Finance Ltd.,* [1971] 1 Ch. 949, where it came to the conclusion that the duty was best set out in the second. As was said by Salmon L.J. at pp. 968-9:

"...a mortgagee in exercising his power of sale does owe a duty to take reasonable precautions to obtain the true market value of the mortgaged property at the date on which he decides to sell it."

This court has recently considered the question on at least two occasions and in both it has adopted the principal [*sic*] enunciated in *Cuckmere Brick: Wood v. Bank of Nova Scotia et al.* (1979), 10 R.P.R. 165, affirmed 29 O.R. (2d) 35, 112 D.L.R. (3d) 181, 14 R.P.R. 1, and *Bank of Nova Scotia v. Barnard* (1984), 46 O.R. (2d) 409, 9 D.L.R. (4th) 575, 32 R.P.R. 292. I note that, in the *Wood* case, Arnup J.A. at p. 37 O.R., p. 183 D.L.R., left open the question as to which formulation of the duty was the proper one.

With great respect to the learned judges who have considered this matter, I am of the opinion that the two "tests" laid down in the authorities cited above do not represent separate lines of development in the case-law. Rather they, in fact, represent two separate and distinct duties owed by the mortgagor to the mortgagee. I need not rationalize these duties as was done, for example, in *Cuckmere Brick, supra,* because they arise under different and mutually exclusive conditions. This is so because their application depends on the nature of the remedy sought by the mortgagor.

In my opinion, it is clear on an analysis of the case-law that, where the mortgagor brings an action against both the mortgagee and the purchaser to set aside the sale, the court will interfere only where fraud or bad faith is shown, even when the sale price is very disadvantageous to the mortgagor: *Jones v. Matthie* (1847), 11 Jur. 504, reversing 2 Coll. 465, 10 Jur. 347, 63 E.R. 817 *sub nom. Matthie v. Edwards; Warner v. Jacob* (1882), 20 Ch.D. 220 at p. 224; *Martinson v. Clowes* (1882), 21 Ch.D. 857 at p. 860; *Prentice v. Consolidated Bank* (1886), 13 O.A.R. 69 at p. 78; and, *Kennedy v. De Trafford, supra.* But, where the mortgagor seeks his remedy against the mortgagee alone and seeks only an accounting between them following the mortgagee's exercise of his power of sale, then the court will hold the mortgagee to a much higher standard and will require him to have adopted "such means as would be adopted by a prudent man to get the best price that could be obtained": *Prentice v. Consolidated Bank, supra, per* Osler J. at pp. 76-7; *Wolff v. Vanderzee* (1869), 20 L.T. 353 at p. 354; *Tomlin v. Luce* (1889), 43 Ch.D. 191 at p. 194; *Marriot v. Anchor Reversionary Co. Ltd., supra; Aldrich v. Canada Permanent Loan & Savings Co.* (1897), 24 O.A.R. 193 at p. 195; and *McHugh v. Union Bank* (1913), 10 D.L.R. 562 at p. 571, [1913] A.C. 299 at pp. 311-2, 3 W.W.R. 1052 (P.C. on appeal from S.C.C.).

I should emphasize that the second duty, that of reasonable care, was recognized by our own Court of Appeal long before the English Court of Appeal's decision in *Kennedy v. De Trafford* and *Prentice v. Consolidated Bank* and that the English court's decision was, subsequently, interpreted by the same court to mean no more than that the mortgagee could be liable in negligence. In *Aldrich v. Canada Permanent Loan & Savings Co., supra,* Maclennan J.A. says at p. 195:

"Recklessly means carelessly, negligently, and if there be negligence and want of proper care and precaution and if that is followed by a sacrifice of the interest of the mortgagor, then according to all the authorities, the mortgagee is answerable for the loss and must make it good..."

I should also note that the distinction I have drawn between the two duties and the circumstances of their application was, in fact, recognized by the Ontario Court of Appeal in *Prentice, supra,* by Osler J.A. at p. 78. It is, in my opinion, unfortunate that this distinction was lost sight of in subsequent decisions for I think it is an eminently reasonable one.

Where a mortgagee sought to set aside a sale to a third party who purchased for value and in good faith, the court was quite properly reluctant to intervene unless bad faith on the part of the mortgagor could be shown or unless some knowledge on the part of the purchaser could be shown such that he should have been put on notice to inquire further: *Jenkins v. Jones* (1860), 2 Giff. 99, 6 Jur. N.S. 391, 66 E.R. 43. But, where the only action is for an accounting, it seems to me equally proper that the mortgagor should have been entitled to require the mortgagee to exercise his sale in a prudent fashion. Such a requirement could not have prejudiced the mortgagee in any way since collateral to it was the right of the mortgagee to claim in accounting his reasonable expenses: *McHugh v. Union Bank, supra,* at pp. 570-1 D.L.R., p. 312 A.C. Nor do I see how this second duty is any different from that imposed on a mortgagee in possession in general. It is quite clear that a mortgagee in possession must take reasonable steps to preserve the property which is simply another way of saying that he must take steps to preserve its value. For the mortgagee to expose the property for sale in circumstances where anything like its full value would be unlikely to be realized — for example, by failing to advertise it or by listing it at a gross undervalue — is, in my mind, no different than the case where he allows the pipes to freeze in a mortgaged property. The loss to the mortgagor arises in both cases because the value of the security available to him to place as a credit against the amount of his debt to the mortgagee is lessened through the negligence of the mortgagee. In short, I cannot see any grounds for distinguishing between the mortgagee's duty to preserve the physical state of the property and a duty to preserve the value at which it could be sold by ensuring that the sale takes place under conditions reasonably calculated to secure the best price under the circumstances.

It is all very well to say, and often is, that a mortgagee is not a trustee for the mortgagor or that, since the mortgagor gave the mortgagee the contractual right to sell, he cannot be heard to complain if the exercise of that power is not to his liking: *Jones v. Matthie, supra,* at p. 505. But, such ritualistic repetition of unexamined formulas obscures the true nature and purpose of the contract between the two parties. The purpose of the power granted to the mortgagee by the mortgagor is to realize on the security to the extent necessary to diminish, if not eliminate, the mortgagor's debt. Since the mortgagor knows at the time he makes the contract that he will remain liable for any balance undischarged by the sale, it is reasonable to assume that he grants the power only in the expectation that the mortgagee will use his best efforts to achieve the best price for the security. But, if that is the case when the mortgage debt exceeds the value of the security, I fail to see why it should be any different when the reverse is true. This does not mean that the mortgagor must achieve the best price. He has his own interests to look after as well and the mortgagor is not entitled to require him to act against them as, for example, by waiting out a protracted slump in the market. It is the effort rather than the result to which the court looks. As was said by Salmon L.J. in the *Cuckmere Brick* case at p. 969, in deciding whether the mortgagee "has fallen short of that duty the facts must be looked at broadly, and he will not be adjudged to be in default unless he is plainly on the wrong side of the line".

Turning now to the facts of the case before me. The defendant says that it was not negligent. It secured two appraisals of the property, listed it with an experienced local realtor who specialized in rural properties and accepted an offer that was within the range of its appraised value. But while this procedure might well describe in principal [*sic*] the efforts of a prudent man, the facts do not support the defendant's position. First, as I have already found, the appraisals were not, in fact, accurate estimates of the true market value of the property at that time. The negligence of the defendant's agent is its own: *Bank of Nova Scotia v. Barnard, supra,* at p. 421 O.R., p. 586 D.L.R.

Secondly, the defendant knew, or should have known, that the property was a hobby farm; it was characterized as such by the Heynen appraisal. The value of this property would, accordingly, be most likely recognized in a somewhat more specialized market than the rural one in the vicinity of Milton. Yet neither the defendant nor its agent took any steps to ascertain how a hobby farm could be sold to the best advantage. In my opinion, advertising it in the local papers and treating it simply as another rural property were not calculated to reach the market that would be most interested in such a property. That potential market would more likely have been found in the large urban centres of Toronto and Hamilton. This failure itself constitutes negligence: *Aldrich v. Canada Permanent Loan, supra,* at p. 196 and *Bank of Nova Scotia v. Barnard,* at p. 421 O.R., pp. 586-7 D.L.R.

In the result, I find the defendant to have been negligent in failing to ascertain the true market value of the property and in failing to take the steps necessary to ensure that the best price possible was achieved. I calculate the plaintiff's damages to be $25 000, this being the difference between the property's market value and its sale price. The sale price was adjusted in favour of the vendor on February 28, 1984, by $304.92 (ex. 14) and I allow that as a credit to the defendant.

CASE PROBLEMS FOR DISCUSSION

Case 1

Hambly was the owner of a block of land in fee simple. He arranged a mortgage on the property with Blake for $50 000, and the mortgage was duly registered in the appropriate Land Registry Office. Hambly used the funds for the renovation of an existing building on the premises, but discovered that he had insufficient funds to complete the changes he wished to make.

A few months later, he borrowed the sum of $10 000 from his friend Clark and gave a second mortgage on the property as security. Clark did not register the mortgage; instead, she placed it in her safety deposit box, with the intention of registering it at some later date.

When the renovations to the building were completed, Hambly decided to install a swimming pool on the grounds. He borrowed $5000 from Simple Finance Co. to pay the pool contractor for the installation. Simple Finance, as security for its loan to Hambly, took a mortgage on the property. The mortgage was registered the same day that the funds were given to Hambly.

Shortly thereafter, Hambly arranged a party to celebrate the completion of the swimming pool and invited his many friends to attend. At the party, Clark mentioned to Anderson, another friend of Hambly, that she held a mortgage on Hambly's property, and that she would like to dispose of it in order to have the funds available for another more attractive investment.

Anderson expressed an interest in the purchase of the mortgage and, after some discussion, agreed to give Clark $9000 for it. The next day, Anderson paid Clark the $9000 for the mortgage (on which the full $10 000 principal was owing) and received an assignment of the mortgage. When Anderson realized that the mortgage itself had not been registered, he had the documents registered immediately. Unfortunately, he failed to notice the mortgage to Simple Finance in his examination of the title to the property.

Hambly was killed in an automobile accident a few days before he was scheduled to make his first payments on the mortgages. His only asset was his interest in the property. Blake instituted foreclosure proceedings when the first payment required under the mortgage became overdue. An appraisal of the property indicated that it had a market value of approximately $60 000.

Discuss the position of the parties in this case. Indicate their rights in the foreclosure action. Comment on the possible outcome of the case.

Case 2

Parker, a building contractor, constructed a single family dwelling on a building lot in a suburban area. To obtain the necessary funds to build the house, Parker had entered into a mortgage with Green Mortgage Co. for the principal amount of $85 000, repayable in monthly installments of $900 each.

Some time later, Parker sold the property subject to the mortgage to Baker at a purchase price of $155 000. Baker paid Parker $70 000 cash and assumed the mortgage. He continued to make payments on the mortgage while he possessed the house, but two years after he had purchased the property, he was transferred to another city by his employer. He sold the property at that time to Brown, who assumed the mortgage and paid Baker $160 000 for the property. The mortgage had a principal balance outstanding of $81 500 at the date that the property was sold.

Brown, unfortunately, found herself over-extended financially soon after she had purchased the property. She was forced to let the monthly mortgage payments fall into arrears in order to pay more pressing debts. In spite of repeated requests for payment by the mortgage company, Brown refused to do so. Eventually, Green Mortgage Co. was obliged to take action. Instead of foreclosure, however, it brought an action against Parker for payment.

Discuss the possible reasons why the mortgage company decided to take action against Parker rather than institute foreclosure proceedings. On what basis could it do so? Discuss the rights and obligations of the parties in the light of this action by the mortgagee.

Case 3

Agricola sold his farm to Ambrose for $100 000. Ambrose arranged for a purchase money mortgage from the Agricultural Loan Company for $60 000, and Agricola agreed to take back a mortgage in the amount of $20 000 in order that Ambrose could acquire the property. On the date fixed for closing, Agricola gave Ambrose the deed to the property and received a cheque from Ambrose in the amount of $20 000. He also received a cheque from the loan company for $60 000 when the company registered its mortgage immediately after the registration of the deed to Ambrose. Agricola then registered his mortgage for $20 000. At the time, Agricola transferred the fire insurance policy (which covered the buildings) to Ambrose. The policy transfer named Ambrose as the new owner, subject to the interest of Agricola as mortgagee. Through an oversight, Agricultural Loan Company was not named as an insured on the policy.

Some time later, Ambrose defaulted on the mortgage to Agricola, and it was necessary for Agricola to foreclose on the mortgage. Agricola continued to make the mortgage payments each month to Agricultural Loan Company and allowed Ambrose to remain on the property to work the farm on a crop-sharing basis.

Not long after Agricola had foreclosed on his mortgage and taken back the property, a serious fire destroyed a large barn on the premises. The barn had a value of $50 000. The insurer noted that the fire insurance policy listed Ambrose as the owner of the property, and Agricola as the mortgagee. However, before the insurance company made payment, all three parties — Agricola, Ambrose, and the Agricultural Loan Company — claimed the insurance proceeds.

Discuss the nature of the rights that each party might raise. Discuss the possible outcome.

Case 4

An elderly woman who could only read with difficulty operated a rooming-house for students. Her home was large and in close proximity to the college. As such, it was a valuable piece of residential property.

Her nephew, Herman, had on numerous occasions urged her to retire and suggested that she sell the property. For many years she refused to consider the idea. However, as a result of Herman's insistence, she eventually agreed that she would list the property with a local real estate agent to see what the market might be. A few days later, Herman appeared at her home with some papers that he said were the forms that he had obtained from the real estate agent for the listing of her property. In reality the forms were mortgage forms. Herman represented the forms as "only a formality, to let the real estate agent have authority to show the house to prospective buyers." His aunt signed the forms, believing them to be copies of the real estate listing agreement.

Herman later registered the mortgage, which was drawn for $50 000, and assigned it to a finance company for $45 000. He intended to use a part of the money to make the payments on the mortgage himself; the balance, he planned to use for a trip to Monte Carlo where he expected to make a fortune by employing a new system for placing bets at the gambling tables in a casino.

Herman's scheme failed, however, and he returned to Canada penniless. He soon spent the funds, which he had originally set aside to make a few payments on the mortgage, and again found himself without funds. The mortgage, as a result, went into default, and the finance company instituted foreclosure proceedings against the property. At that point his aunt suddenly became aware of the mortgage.

Indicate the action that the aunt might take in this case. Discuss the position of the finance company. What might be the outcome of its foreclosure proceedings?

Case 5

Zalinski was the owner in fee simple of a house and lot. He mortgaged the property to the Home Bank for $50 000. Then he sold the house and lot to Steele for $75 000, of which $50 000 represented the mortgage Steele assumed and the remaining $25 000 was payment to Zalinski for his equity.

Shortly after that Steele borrowed $10 000 from Gray, giving Gray a $10 000 second mortgage on the property as security for the loan. Steele then sold the property to Allen for $80 000, of which $50 000 was the first mortgage to the Home Bank, $10 000 the mortgage to Gray, and $20 000 cash payment for Steele's equity.

The house caught fire and burned to the ground a few days after Allen acquired the property. The house was insured for $45 000. The policy named Allen as the insured, the Home Bank as first mortgagee, and Gray as second mortgagee. After the fire, Allen abandoned the property and left the country.

Advise the Home Bank and Gray as to their legal rights. Speculate as to how the parties might proceed to protect their respective interests.

Case 6

Penfield owned property which he mortgaged to The Bank of Regina for $100 000 on a term of three years, amortized over 25 years, at a rate of 10% per annum. His payments were $894.49 monthly.

At the end of one year he sold the property to Carson, who assumed the Bank of Regina mortgage. At the end of two more years, when the mortgage came up for renewal, Carson renewed the mortgage for another three years, at the going rate of 11% per annum, amortized over 25 years. The monthly payments became $962.53.

Two years later, Carson defaulted on the mortgage, and the bank sued not only Carson (who was penniless) but Penfield as well. In defence, Penfield claimed novation.

What is the source of the bank's claim against Penfield, and how does Penfield construct novation as a defence?

Who is likely to be successful?

CHAPTER 29

Leasehold Interests

**LEASEHOLD
INTEREST**

A leasehold interest in land arises when a person who owns an estate in land grants, by way of either an express or implied contract, possession of the land to another for a fixed period of time. The owner of the estate in land holds the "lordship" over the particular parcel of land and is known as the **landlord** or **lessor.** The person granted possession of the property is called the **tenant** or **lessee,** and the contract between the landlord and tenant, a **lease** or **tenancy.** While the contract may be verbal, written or sometimes implied, the terms of the tenancy may vary from a simple verbal agreement giving the tenant possession in return for a periodic rent, to a complex and lengthy lease of shopping centre premises that grants the landlord a percentage of the profits of the tenant's business and substantial control over a number of aspects of the tenant's activities.

The contract is, in a sense, more than an ordinary contract, because it amounts to a conveyance of a part of the landlord's interest in the land to the tenant for the term of the lease. The lease creates a **privity of estate** between the landlord and tenant, since each has an interest in the same land. In addition, the contract itself creates a **privity of contract** between the parties. If the landlord and tenant retain their interest for the entire period of the tenancy, privity of estate and privity of contract would remain between them. However, if either party should assign his or her interest in the land, the privity of estate ceases to exist when the new party acquires the interest in the land. The contract between the landlord and tenant may continue to be bound by the covenants in the contract if it is expressly set out, even though the tenant has parted with the estate or interest in the land.

Privity of estate in itself creates certain rights in the landlord and in the tenant. For example, where a lease is assigned to a new tenant, by virtue of the privity of estate that exists between the landlord and tenant, the new tenant would be obliged to pay the rent and also perform all covenants that run with the land.

The creation of a tenancy gives rise to two concurrent interests in land: the **leasehold** and the **reversion.** The tenant acquires the exclusive possession of the land under the tenancy, and the landlord retains the reversion or the title to the property until the lease terminates. At the expiration of the term of the lease, the two interests (possession and title) merge, and the landlord's original estate becomes whole once again. In the interval, however, the tenant has exclusive possession of the property. Unless an agreement is made to the contrary, the tenant may exclude everyone from the land, including the landlord.

A leasehold interest is an interest in land. Consequently, anything that is attached to the land becomes a part of the leasehold interest during the currency of the lease. For example, if a person leases a parcel of land that has a building upon it, the building becomes the possession of the tenant for the time. Also any rents or benefits that the building produces would belong to the tenant, unless the parties had agreed that the rents would be used or applied in a different manner.

Commercial leases, in particular, tend to be negotiated leases where the parties include in the lease those terms specific to their relationship and needs. For example, a commercial tenant may wish to make extensive changes to the interior or exterior of the building to suit its business operations, and the commercial lease will be written to permit such changes to the building or premises. Similarly, a landlord may enter into an agreement with a tenant to construct a building on a parcel of land that is designed specifically for the tenant's business. The tenant under these circumstances will usually agree in return to lease the property for a lengthy period of time. A variation of this type of lease arrangement is the **sale and lease-back,** where a firm will acquire land and construct a building on the land suitable for its business activities. In order to free up the capital investment in the new building for use in the business, the firm may sell the property to an investor and in turn lease the property back from the investor under a long-term lease.

HISTORICAL DEVELOPMENT

A lease is a very old method of acquiring an interest in land. Long before the modern concept of contract was developed, the leasehold interest was recognized, and the rights and duties attached to it defined. Many changes have naturally taken place over the years that have altered the relationship of landlord and tenant, but the basic concept has remained the same.

Leases existed in Europe and England long before the feudal system of land tenure was adopted, and the leasehold interest was never (in England at least) a feudal tenure. It was always an interest in land that was based upon an agreement between the parties, and seldom considered to be something permanent in nature.

When the further subdivision of estates in England became impossible in the late thirteenth century, the lesser lords turned to leases as a means of creating interests in land that would, in turn, provide them with benefits. The leasehold interest, while it lacked the permanency of a tenured estate in land, did have certain advantages. Since it was for a fixed term, the land would eventually return to the landlord. Thus the wealth associated with the land remained with the lord. In the meantime, the land produced revenue in the form of rents or a share of the produce. It also provided the landlord with some protection against inflation (particularly after the mid-fourteenth century), because the rents could be renegotiated at the end of the term of the lease. The advantage to the tenant under a lease, apart from the right to possession of the land, was the fact that the land did not carry with it the burdens or restrictions of feudal duties that accompanied some grants of feudal estates.

A significant change in leases took place in 1677 with the passing of the Statute of Frauds. The statute affected leases as well as other interests in land. It required all leases to be in writing and made under seal unless the term was for a period of less than three years.[1] Under the act, a lease for more than three years that had not been made in writing was void.[2] The requirements imposed by this statute have continued to the present time in most common law provinces of Canada, and remain in England in the form of another statute, the Law of Property Act.[3]

In Canada, the law relating to the landlord and tenant relationship followed the English law, but, due to the availability of much low-cost land, was less concerned with agricultural leases. The Canadian legislation, as a consequence, has tended to be more streamlined, with the emphasis on leases of land for business or residential purposes rather than agriculture. As in England, much of the law relating to landlord and tenant has been incorporated into provincial statutes that set out the nature of the relationship and the rights and duties of the parties.[4]

CREATION OF A TENANCY

A lease is a contract made between a landlord and a tenant that gives the tenant exclusive possession of the property for a specified period or term. A lease is distinct from a licence in that a lessee is entitled to exclusive possession of the property, whereas a licence grants the licensee the right to use the property in common with others, but does not create an interest in land. For example, a property owner may permit certain persons to use property from time to time for the purpose of hunting, but the permission to do so would not create an interest in land. It would only give the licensee the right to lawfully enter on the property for the particular purpose set out in the licence. A lease, on the other hand, would give the tenant exclusive possession of the property and an interest in land. The extensive use of licences for various purposes has, unfortunately, made the distinction between a lease and a licence unclear with regard to the question of when rights granted under a licence become an interest in land. The courts generally look at the intention of the parties in order to distinguish between the two, since possession alone is no longer a deciding factor.[5] Nevertheless, where the agreement gives the occupier of the land exclusive possession of the property and the right to exclude all others, including the owner, the courts generally conclude that the relationship established by the agreement is one of landlord and tenant.[6]

---

1. The Statute of Frauds. See, for example, R.S.O. 1990, c. S-19, s. 3.
2. Ibid., s. 1(2).
3. The Law of Property Act, 1925, 15 & 16 Geo. V., c. 20.
4. See, for example, the Landlord and Tenant Act, R.S.O. 1990, c. L-7; R.S.M. 1987, c. L-70.
5. *Errington v. Errington,* [1952] 1 All E.R. 149; *Lippman v. Yick,* [1953] 3 D.L.R. 527.
6. *Re British American Oil Co. Ltd. and De Pass* (1959), 21 D.L.R. (2d) 110.

A lease is contractual in nature, and may be either an express agreement (verbal or written) or it may be implied from the conduct of the parties. The terms of the lease may set out the specific rights and duties of the parties. In that case (provided that they are lawful), they will be binding on the lessor and lessee and delineate the tenancy. If specific terms are not set out, then the rights of the parties and their duties may be determined by statute or the common law. The nature of the relationship being contractual, the law of contract, as modified by the common law and statutes relating to leasehold interests, will apply. A lease then must normally meet the requirements for a valid contract to be enforceable. It must contain an offer and acceptance, consideration (in the form of rent and premises), and legality of object. The parties must also have capacity to contract and the intention to create a legal relationship.

Where the Statute of Frauds (or similar legislation pertaining to leases) applies to lease agreements, it requires any lease for a term of more than three years to be made in writing and under seal, otherwise it is void.[7] Leases for a term of less than three years need not be in writing, provided that the tenant goes into possession.

An infant may enter into a lease as a tenant, but unless the accommodation is necessary, the lease would be voidable at the infant's option. The infant, however, must repudiate the lease promptly on attaining majority, as the contract of lease is an agreement of a continuing nature, and to continue to acknowledge the relationship may render the lease binding.[8]

A lease by a drunken or insane person is generally held to be binding, unless the person in that state at the time of the execution of the lease is in a position to prove that he or she was drunken or insane and that the other party knew of his condition.[9] This rule is simply the application of the ordinary contract rule with respect to agreements made by persons incapable of appreciating the nature of their acts. However, it is generally necessary to show as well that the person of sound mind took unfair advantage of the person with the disability in cases where the leased premises would be treated as a necessary. As with the ordinary law of contract, leases must be repudiated promptly by drunken or insane persons on their return to sanity or sobriety.[10]

Legislation in a number of provinces has distinguished between residential and other tenancies in the determination of the rights and duties of the parties to a lease. To some extent the legislation has changed the nature of the lease itself. The general thrust of the new legislation with respect to residential tenancies has been to provide greater security of tenure for the tenant and to put additional obligations on the landlord to maintain safe premises for the tenant. The particular rights and obligations generally apply to all residential tenancies, and the parties usually may not contract out of the statutory requirements. Commercial and other tenancies are subject to the ordinary common law rules for landlord and tenant and to the general provisions of the legislation pertaining to the tenancy relationship. Many of the rules relating to the relationship are the same, but the

7. For example, the Statute of Frauds, R.S.O. 1990 c. S-19, ss. 1-3.

8. *Sturgeon v. Starr* (1911), 17 W.L.R. 402.

9. See, for example, *Hunt v. Texaco Exploration Co.*, [1955] 3 D.L.R. 555.

10. *Seeley v. Charlton* (1881), 21 N.B.R. 119.

special provisions concerning residential tenancies have substantially altered the rights of the parties.

A characteristic of a lease is that it is a grant of exclusive possession for a term certain. The lease itself must stipulate when the lease will begin, and when it will end. If it is for a term that begins at some future time, it is said to be an **agreement for a lease** rather than a lease and, with the exception of Ontario, it must be in writing to be enforceable. In Ontario, the requirement of writing would only appear to apply if the agreement to lease relates to a period of more than three years.[11] In addition to the requirement of writing for long-term leases, leases that run for more than three years must be registered in most provinces if the tenant wishes to retain priority over subsequent purchasers or mortgagees.[12]

Where the lease does not specify a definite term, the tenancy may be a **periodic tenancy,** in which the lease period may be yearly, monthly, or weekly. A periodic tenancy automatically renews at the end of each period, and continues until either the landlord or the tenant gives the other **notice to quit.** The type of periodic tenancy is usually determined from the agreement of the parties; but, in the absence of evidence to the contrary, the tenancy is usually related to the rent payment interval. For example, unless otherwise indicated, if the rent is paid monthly, the tenancy is generally considered to be a monthly tenancy. A periodic tenancy may also arise on the expiration of a lease for a term certain. If the tenant continues to occupy the premises and the landlord accepts the rent, the lease will become a periodic tenancy that will continue until either party gives notice to terminate.

A tenancy for a term certain may also give rise to another form of tenancy that is not a tenancy in the true sense, but an occupancy of the property only. If a tenant at the end of the term remains in possession after notice to quit has been given and the notice period expired, then the occupancy of the premises is known as a **tenancy at sufferance.** Under this form of occupancy, no rent is payable, since a tenancy does not exist. However, if the landlord so desires, the landlord may demand compensation for the overholding tenant's possession of the property.

A form of tenancy may also be established by a landowner who permits another to enter on premises and occupy them where no express lease is made, and where the purpose of the occupancy is usually related to another transaction. This tenancy is known as a **tenancy at will,** and no rent is payable. The occupier remains on the premises at the pleasure of the landlord, and the landlord may at any time order the occupier from the property. It frequently arises where a property owner permits a purchaser to occupy the land pending the completion of some aspect of the sale.

A special form of tenancy arises where a tenant enters into a lease with another for a term that is less than the tenancy that the tenant holds. A lease of a leasehold interest of this nature is called a **subtenancy** (or under-tenancy), and the tenant in the subtenancy, a **subtenant.** The lease creating the subtenancy is called a **sublease**. It may contain terms and obligations that differ substantially from

11. The Statute of Frauds, R.S.O. 1990, c. S-19, s. 3; *Manchester v. Dixie Cup Co. (Canada) Ltd.,* [1952] 1 D.L.R. 19.

12. In Ontario, a lease for more than seven years must be registered to preserve priority under the Registry System. Under the Land Titles System, notice of a lease must be registered if drawn for a term of more than three years. A copy of the lease is usually deposited with the notice. See the Land Titles Act, R.S.O. 1990, c. L-5, s. 116.

those of the lease under which the tenant-in-chief is bound. A subtenancy, never-theless, must be consistent with the term of the original tenancy in the sense that it is for a lesser term. To have a subtenancy, the tenant-in-chief must possess a reversion that would entitle the tenant-in-chief to regain possession before the expiry of the original lease with the landlord. For example, a tenant may lease premises for a term of five years, then immediately enter into a lease with a sub-tenant to sublet the premises for a period of three years. The tenant-in-chief would be liable to the landlord under the original lease, and the subtenant would be liable to the tenant under the sublease. Each would be obliged to perform their particular obligations to their respective "landlords." On the termination of the sublease, the tenant-in-chief would regain possession of the premises and, in turn, would deliver up possession to the landlord on the expiry of the original lease.

RIGHTS AND DUTIES OF THE LANDLORD AND TENANT

The landlord and tenant usually specify their rights and duties in the lease agreement, which they agree will be binding upon them for the duration of the lease. Most writ-ten leases set out these rights and duties in the form of promises or **covenants** that apply to the tenancy. However, where the lease is merely verbal, the common law and the statutes pertaining to landlord and tenant in most provinces will incorpo-rate in the verbal lease a number of implied terms to form the basis for the tenancy. As previously indicated, residential tenancies in a number of provinces are now subject to special rights and obligations that have been imposed on landlords and tenants, and that distinguish residential tenancies from the ordinary landlord-ten-ant relationship. Some of the more important differences are noted under the fol-lowing topics that deal with the general rights and duties of the parties to a lease.

Rent

The covenant that comes to mind first when a lease is suggested is the covenant to pay rent. Rent is usually paid in the form of legal tender or a cheque of a mon-ey amount, but rent is not restricted to money only. Rent may take the form of goods in the case of an agricultural lease where the landlord is to receive a share of the crop grown on the land,[13] or it may be in the form of services, such as where a person living in an apartment building agrees to provide cleaning or jani-torial services in return for an apartment in the building.[14] In rare circumstances, such as a tenancy at will, no rent may be payable at all.

Commercial and industrial leases usually have their rental amounts deter-mined upon the basis of the square footage leased, with the rent calculated at a dollar amount per square foot. For example, a small accounting or law firm may lease 2000 square feet of office space in a building at a rental rate of $5/sq. ft. This would represent a yearly rental of $10 000 for the premises. Residential ten-ancies, on the other hand, are usually based upon a "flat rate" rental for the prop-erty leased. For example, a residential tenant might lease an apartment at a rental of $800 per month.

Commercial leases are often drawn for lengthy periods of time, and it is difficult under these circumstances to establish a rental amount for the full term.

13. *Kozak v. Misiura,* [1928] 1 W.W.R. 1.
14. *Robertson v. Millan* (1951), 3 W.W.R. (N.S.) 248.

A common method of determining the rental amount on a long-term lease is to provide for periodic adjustments (for example, at five-year intervals). The parties will, in effect, negotiate a new rental amount, based upon the rental market at the time the new rental rate becomes negotiable. If the parties are unable to agree upon a new rental rate for the next period, the lease will usually provide that the dispute may be submitted to arbitration, where the arbitrator will fix the rent payable, based upon the current market for such a property.

The method expressed for the payment of rent may indicate the nature of the tenancy, if the parties have not expressly agreed on the term. For example, the rent may be expressed as a lump sum for the entire lease period, or it may be expressed as an annual amount. In the former example, the payment method would indicate a lease for the term, and in the latter (if no agreement to the contrary), an annual lease. If the parties agree to a periodic tenancy with the rent payable monthly, a monthly tenancy will generally be inferred. If the rent is payable weekly, it usually indicates a weekly tenancy. Tenancies for longer terms than a month often specify a total rent amount or lump-sum payment, then break the amount down into monthly rent payments. However, in this type of lease agreement the requirement for monthly payments would not change the term of the lease to a monthly tenancy.

At common law, the time for payment of rent may be either express or implied from the agreement of the parties, or it may be determined by custom. If the rent is to be paid in advance, the parties must generally agree to the advance payment either expressly or by their conduct.[15] In the case of residential tenancies, the landlord may demand rent in advance, but in some provinces the practice of demanding the equivalent of several months' rent as a "security" or "damage" deposit has been prohibited. Instead, the landlord may retain an amount equal to the last month's rent under the lease as a deposit, but must pay interest on the sum for the period of time that the funds are in the landlord's possession.[16]

As a general rule, if no place for the payment of rent is specified, the tenant must seek out the landlord on the day on which the rent is due and make payment as required under the lease.[17] If, however, the landlord is in the habit of collecting the rent at the leased premises, the tenant is not in default so long as he or she is ready and willing to make payment on demand.[18]

The covenant to pay rent affects both the landlord and the tenant. During the term of the tenancy, unless the lease provides otherwise, the rent is fixed and may not be raised by the landlord. The tenant at common law is generally liable for the payment of rent for the entire term in cases where the land is leased, even if some of the buildings on the land may be destroyed by an act of God, or through no fault of the tenant. Where residential tenancies are concerned, some provinces have included in their legislation that the **doctrine of frustration** applies where the property is seriously damaged or destroyed by fire. In these jurisdictions, the lease may be terminated.[19] In other provinces, the doctrine of frustration would

15. *Brunner v. Pollock*, [1941] 4 D.L.R. 107.

16. See, for example, Ontario, the Landlord and Tenant Act, R.S.O. 1990, c. L-7, ss. 82 and 83.

17. *Chemarno v. Pollock*, [1949] 1 D.L.R. 606.

18. *Browne v. White*, [1947] 2 D.L.R. 309.

19. See, for example, Ontario, the Landlord and Tenant Act, R.S.O. 1990, c. L-7, s. 86.

not apply. However, the courts have suggested that in apartment buildings and other multi-storied buildings, where the landlord is responsible for parts of the building, if there is destruction of a part of the building, the rent would cease until repairs were completed; or if the landlord did not repair, then the lease would be terminated.[20] Some attempts have been made to clarify the law in this area, but only residential tenancies in some provinces would appear to be fully protected, and then only where the premises are totally destroyed.[21] No great pressure for legislative reform has taken place in this regard, probably because most commercial leases specifically provide for this, as do most formal leases for residential tenancies. The only leases that might not cover this eventuality would be short-term leases, and monthly or weekly periodic tenancies. In each of these situations, only a small amount of money would be in issue if the premises should be destroyed, and the question of the tenant's continued liability for rent would not likely be a matter that would come before the courts.

Quiet Possession

In return for the payment of rent, the tenant is entitled to possession of the premises undisturbed by any person claiming a right to the property through or under the landlord. This entitlement is in the form of an express or implied covenant by the landlord that the tenant will have quiet possession of the leased premises. In the case of a leasehold, the landlord covenants that he or she has a right to the property that is such that he or she is entitled to make the lease. The landlord also promises not to enter on the premises or interfere with the tenant's possession, except as authorized by law. The covenant extends as well to any activities of the landlord that would be actionable in nuisance. For example, if the landlord uses neighbouring premises in the same building in such a way that it interferes with the tenant's use and enjoyment, the tenant may have a right of action against the landlord for breach of the covenant.

Repairs

The obligation to repair is usually set out in the lease, because at common law neither the landlord nor the tenant would be liable to make repairs, unless the lease specifically required one or the other to do so. Where neither party is obliged to make repairs, the landlord has an obligation to warn the tenant at the time the tenancy is made of any dangers that exist as a result of the non-repair of the premises. However, if the tenant causes any subsequent damage to the property, the tenant must repair it and must not deliberately commit waste (such as the demolition of buildings, or the cutting of shade or ornamental trees).[22]

If the premises are leased as furnished, the property must be fit for habitation at the beginning of the tenancy, but at common law, the landlord is under no obligation to maintain the property in that state. Landlord and tenant legislation in many provinces has altered the common law rule, however, and landlords are normally required to maintain the safety of the premises. This is particularly true

---

20. *Dunkelman v. Lister,* [1927] 4 D.L.R. 612.

21. See, for example, Ontario Law Reform Commission, Report on Landlord and Tenant Law, 1976, pp. 209-211.

22. *McPherson v. Giles* (1919), 45 O.L.R. 441.

where provinces have imposed an obligation to repair on the landlord with respect to residential tenancies.[23] The landlord's obligation, even under recent legislation, does not extend to damage caused to the premises by the tenant's deliberate or negligent acts, but only to ordinary wear and tear or structural defects. Even then, the landlord would only be obliged to repair those defects brought to the landlord's attention by the tenant.

Sublet and Assignment of Leasehold Interests

Most commercial leases provide for the tenant's right to assign or sublet leased premises. Unless the lease contains an express prohibition, a tenant may assign or sublet if he or she wishes. At common law, the tenant is entitled to assign a lease, as the assignment does not affect the tenant's liability under the lease agreement. The tenant is still liable under the express covenants in the lease. The normal practice for leases is to include a right to assign the lease with the consent of the landlord, and to provide further that the landlord may not unreasonably withhold the consent. A number of provinces have included this change in their landlord and tenant legislation. Where special legislation with respect to residential tenancies is in force, the right to assign or sublet with the landlord's consent is usually expressly provided.[24]

Taxes and Insurance

Most leases also provide for the payment of municipal taxes and insurance by the tenant, but unless the lease so provides, there is no obligation on the tenant to be concerned with either of these expenses. In the absence of an express covenant to pay taxes, the landlord is usually obliged to cover the cost; but if the tenant pays the taxes, depending upon the province, the tenant may deduct the expenses from the rent payable. Municipal charges assessed for property improvements — such as sewer and water lines, sidewalks, or road paving — however, are improvements to the lands. Generally these charges are a responsibility of the landlord, regardless of any obligation on the tenant in the lease to pay ordinary municipal taxes. Municipal business taxes, which may be levied against a business occupying leased premises, are the responsibility of the tenant and represent a tax separate from the property tax itself.

Insurance may be an obligation on the tenant by an express term in the lease, but apart from an express requirement, there is no obligation on the tenant to insure the premises. Most tenants, if careful and prudent, would at least insure their own chattels and provide for liability insurance in the event of an injury to a guest on the premises. Landlords similarly insure their buildings to protect themselves from loss or damage through the negligence of the tenant in possession.

Fixtures

A tenant may bring chattels on leased premises during the currency of a lease, and unless the chattels become a part of the realty, the tenant may remove them

---

23. See, for example, Ontario, the Landlord and Tenant Act, R.S.O. 1990, c. L-7, s. 86.
24. The Landlord and Tenant Act, R.S.O. 1990, c. L-7, s. 89.

on departure. If the chattels have become attached to the realty in the form of improvements to the building, such as walls, plumbing fixtures, or similar permanently attached chattels, they may not be removed on the expiry of the lease. Some fixtures, called **trade fixtures,** may be removed by the tenant, provided that any minor damage to the premises that occurs during removal is repaired. The nature of a fixture is dealt with in some depth in Chapter 26. It is sufficient to note with respect to the tenant's fixtures that goods that are normally considered trade fixtures may be removed, if the tenant does so either on, or immediately after, vacating the premises.

RIGHTS OF A LANDLORD FOR BREACH OF THE LEASE

The rights of a landlord in the event of a breach of the lease depend to some extent on the nature of the breach committed by the tenant. The most common breach by a tenant is the breach of the covenant to pay rent. If the tenant fails to pay rent, the landlord has three remedies available. However, as a general rule, the breach of a term or covenant in the commercial lease by the landlord will not entitle the tenant to withhold payment of rent. Residential tenancies legislation does permit tenants to withhold rent under certain circumstances, but unless a term in a commercial lease expressly permits the tenant to withhold rent, the tenant must continue to make rental payments and select an appropriate available remedy for redress.

The first remedy is the right to institute legal proceedings to collect the rent owing. This is known as an **action on the covenant.** The landlord may also **distrain** against the goods of tenants until the rent is paid, or if the rent is not paid, have the goods of the tenant sold to cover the rent owing. The right of **distress** is very similar to a claim for lien in the sense that the landlord may seize the chattels of the tenant (subject to certain exceptions) and hold them as security for payment of the rent owing. If it is necessary to sell the goods to cover the arrears of rent, and the proceeds are insufficient to pay the arrears, the landlord may then take action on the covenant against the tenant for any difference in the amount.[25] In some jurisdictions,[26] the right to distrain against the goods of the tenant is no longer applicable to residential tenancies.

A third right that may be exercised by the landlord in the event of non-payment of rent is the **right of re-entry.** Under landlord and tenant legislation, in a number of provinces, the landlord's right to re-enter arises when rent is in arrears for a period of time. On the expiry of the time, the landlord may repossess the premises. The exercise of the right of re-entry has the effect of terminating the tenancy, since the tenant no longer has possession. It should be noted, however, that the right of re-entry in a sense is an alternative to the right of distress. A landlord may not distrain against the goods and re-enter at the same time. The act of re-entry terminates the tenancy, and with it the right of distress. Consequently, the landlord must distrain first, then later re-enter or choose between the two remedies.

If the tenant's breach is of a covenant or term other than the covenant to pay rent, the landlord may give notice to the tenant to correct the breach (if possible) within a reasonable time. If the tenant fails to do so, the landlord may take action

---

25. *Naylor v. Woods,* [1950] 1 D.L.R. 649.

26. See, for example, Ontario, Landlord and Tenant Act, R.S.O. 1990, c. L-7, s. 89.

to regain the premises. The legislation in most provinces provides that the courts may relieve against forfeiture. If the matter comes before the courts, the courts may order the tenant to correct the breach or pay damages to the landlord for the breach of the covenant. A court may also issue an injunction to restrain any further breach by the tenant.[27] A landlord may also have the tenant evicted by court order if the court believes that such an order should be issued. In the case of residential tenancies (in some provinces) the right of re-entry for breach of a covenant is restricted, and the landlord may only regain possession by way of an order of the court. For example, in Ontario, in the case of a residential tenancy, the landlord must not only notify the tenant of a breach (other than non-payment of rent), but give the tenant seven days to correct the matter. If the tenant fails to do so, the landlord may then apply to the courts for an order to have the tenant evicted. The grounds upon which the landlord may evict the tenant at the present time are limited to undue damage, overcrowding the premises, disturbing or interfering with the enjoyment of the premises of the landlord or other tenants, and interfering with the safety or the rights of other tenants.[28]

RIGHTS OF A TENANT FOR BREACH OF THE LEASE

A tenant is entitled to enforce all covenants made for the tenant's benefit in the lease. If the landlord fails to comply with the covenants, the tenant may take advantage of three possible remedies available. A tenant may bring an action for damages against the landlord if the landlord's actions constitute a breach of the lease. For example, if a landlord wrongfully evicts a tenant from farm property, the tenant may be entitled to damages as compensation for summer fallow work done, crops planted, and the estimated future profits for the term of the lease.[29] If the interference does not constitute eviction from the premises, the tenant may obtain relief from the courts in the form of an injunction to restrain the landlord from interfering with his or her possession and enjoyment of the property. This remedy might, for example, be sought where the landlord conducts an operation on premises adjacent to the tenant's land that creates a nuisance.

A third remedy is also available to a tenant where the landlord's breach of the lease is such that the interference with the tenant's possession amounts to eviction: the tenant may seek to terminate the lease. For example, in the case of a residential tenancy, the landlord's refusal to repair the building and maintain it in a safe condition would constitute a breach that would entitle the tenant to apply to the courts to have the lease terminated.[30]

TERMINATION

A lease may be terminated in a number of different ways. A commercial lease for a fixed term will terminate when the term ends, or when the landlord and tenant agree to terminate the lease before the date on which it is to expire. Where the parties agree to terminate the lease, the agreement is called a **surrender.** If the lease is made in writing and under seal, the surrender normally must take the same form.[31] A lease may also terminate if the parties agree to replace the existing lease with a

---

27. See, for example, the Landlord and Tenant Act, R.S.O. 1990, c. L-7, ss. 19(2) and 20.
28. Residential Rent Regulation Act, R.S.O. 1990, c. L-7, s. 94.
29. *Haack v. Martin,* [1927] 3 D.L.R. 19.
30. The Landlord and Tenant Act, R.S.O. 1990, c. L-7. s. 94.
31. By virtue of the requirements of the Statute of Frauds in most provinces. See, for example, Ontario, R.S.O. 1990, c. S-19, c. 2.

new lease, or if the tenant, at the landlord's request, voluntarily gives up possession to a new tenant, and the new tenant takes possession of the premises.[32]

In the case of a periodic tenancy, a lease may be terminated by the giving of proper **notice to quit.** It should be noted, however, that recent legislation in a number of provinces has limited the right of a landlord to obtain possession on the expiry of a lease, or to give effective notice to quit in the case of residential tenancies. Generally, such legislation limits the landlord's rights to enforce the termination (apart from non-payment for rent) to those cases where the tenant has damaged the premises, or where the landlord requires possession for his or her own use, or to change the nature of the property. In some provinces, the landlord is obliged to obtain possession through the courts even under these circumstances, if the residential tenant refuses to deliver up possession.

For commercial tenancies, the point in time when the notice to quit is given is important and must be carefully adhered to, if the notice is to be effective in terminating the tenancy at the time required by the person giving the notice. In the absence of a term in a lease that specifies the notice period, a party who wishes to terminate a periodic tenancy must give notice equal to a full tenancy period. In other words, notice must be given before the end of one tenancy period to be effective at the end of the next tenancy period. For example, if a monthly periodic tenancy runs from the first day of the month to the last day of the month, notice to terminate must be given not later than the last day of one month to be effective on the last day of the next month. To give notice on the first day of the month would be too late to terminate at the end of that month, and would not be effective until the end of the following month. The reasoning here is that the tenancy would have renewed on the first day, and notice on that day would not give the other party the required full notice period.

Where a periodic tenancy is yearly in nature, a full year is not required as notice. Instead, most provincial statutes provide for a lesser period of time. Quebec and the Maritime provinces of New Brunswick, Nova Scotia, and Prince Edward Island require three months' notice, Alberta requires only 60 days' notice, and the remainder of the provinces specify six months' notice. Residential tenancies in most provinces have different notice requirements and procedures for termination.

The breach of a covenant may give the landlord the right to treat the lease as being at an end. For example, if the tenant is in arrears of payment of rent, the landlord may, by complying with the statute, move into possession of the property and terminate the tenancy. Similarly, if the tenant abandons the property during the currency of the lease, the lease is not terminated. However, any act of the landlord that would indicate that the landlord has accepted the abandonment as a surrender on the part of the tenant would constitute termination. For example, if the landlord moved into the premises abandoned by the tenant, or if the landlord leased the premises to another tenant without notice to the original tenant that the premises were re-let on the tenant's account,[33] the lease would be treated as at an end.

---

32. *Wallis v. Hands,* [1893] 2 Ch. 75.
33. *Green v. Tress,* [1927] 2 D.L.R. 180.

SHOPPING CENTRE LEASES

In contrast to the typical commercial lease of an office, plant, or warehouse, the shopping centre lease is usually more complex, since it frequently provides for greater landlord involvement in the tenant's business activities. The complexity of the lease, however, varies depending upon the type of shopping centre premises that are the subject matter of the lease. For small neighbourhood shopping plazas the lease may not differ substantially from the ordinary commercial lease of retail store premises. On the other hand, for premises in large shopping centres that contain major department stores, supermarkets, and chain retail outlets, the leases generally require the tenant to contribute toward the cost of maintenance of the parking and common areas, to play an active part in the centre's merchant's association, and to participate in all promotional activities of the centre.

Landlords who build large shopping centres actively seek a desirable mix of retailer tenants in order to provide the widest variety of goods and services possible for the type of consumer that the centre wishes to attract. Because these tenants are often large retail chains, the landlord and tenant generally have equal bargaining power, which is reflected in the leases that the parties negotiate. Certain clauses in the lease must nevertheless remain uniform for all tenants, but apart from these many of the terms of the lease are negotiated on an individual basis.

The shopping centre lease varies from the ordinary commercial lease in that it must cover the use of premises outside the retailing area. Most shopping centre leases will cover parking area maintenance, the use of storage, shipping and receiving areas, maintenance of the common areas of the centre, participation in the advertising and promotional activities of the centre, and a contribution to their cost. Shopping centre leases normally provide for landlord participation in the profits of the tenant as well. This latter term in the lease usually requires the tenant to pay a minimum rent, plus an additional **percentage rent** if the tenant's sales exceed a certain dollar amount in a specified time period (usually a monthly time frame).

Shopping centre leases generally require all tenants to remain open for business during the hours that the landlord designates as hours of operation of the centre. This type of lease frequently contains a clause that prohibits a tenant from operating a similar retail outlet using the same business name within a specified distance of the shopping centre. The lease may also contain a **use clause** that sets out the use and type of products that the tenant may sell in the leased premises, in order to avoid tenant disputes and maintain as wide a variety of goods as possible for the consumer.

In addition to these specific clauses in shopping centre leases, most of the more common commercial lease provisions may also be present. These would include the term of the lease and the options to renew, a description of the area leased, payment of taxes, insurance and utilities, repairs to premises, assignment of the lease and the right to sublet, notice requirement, and such provisos as tenant guarantees and landlord responsibilities.

The negotiation of shopping centre leases usually requires the assistance of legal counsel due to the complexity and long-term nature of the lease.

SUMMARY

The landlord and tenant relationship is a contractual relationship that gives rise to two concurrent interests in land: exclusive possession of the property by the tenant, and a reversion in the landlord. A leasehold is an interest in land for a term, and at the end of the term, possession reverts to the landlord. During the term of the lease, however, the tenant is entitled to exclusive possession, and the tenant may then exercise many of the rights that are normally possessed by a landowner.

A lease being contractual in nature may contain express terms that delineate the relationship and the rights and duties of the parties; but where the lease is silent, some terms may be implied by law. The most common terms or covenants are the covenants to pay rent, to repair, to pay taxes, the covenant of quiet enjoyment, and the right to assign or sublet. In most provinces leases for more than three years must be in writing and be under seal to be enforceable. In addition, the lease or a notice of lease must normally be registered to protect the tenant's interest as against subsequent mortgagees or purchasers without notice.

A failure to perform the covenants in a lease by either party may give rise to an action for damages or injunction, or perhaps permit the injured party to terminate the relationship. The particular rights of the parties, and in particular those of the landlord, have been altered in some provinces by legislation to protect tenants under leases of residential property. These changes have granted tenants greater security of tenure and have imposed a number of statutory duties on landlords to maintain residential premises in a good state of repair. In most cases, these new laws permit the landlord to repossess residential property only through court order if the tenant refuses to deliver up possession.

Apart from termination arising out of a breach of the lease, a lease may be terminated automatically at the end of its term, by surrender, abandonment, or by notice to quit in the case of a periodic tenancy. Again, residential tenancies in some provinces may only be terminated for limited reasons and with the permission of the courts.

DISCUSSION QUESTIONS

1. What is the legal nature of a leasehold interest, and how does it arise?
2. In what way (or ways) does a tenancy differ from a licence to use property?
3. Explain the legal nature of a covenant of quiet enjoyment as it pertains to a leasehold. Give an example of a case where breach of the covenant would arise.
4. What is a reversion in a lease?
5. Explain how the term of a tenancy may be determined where the tenancy agreement is not specifically set out in writing.
6. Define or explain the term *tenancy at will* and indicate how it differs from a *tenancy at sufferance.*
7. How does a subtenancy differ from an assignment of a lease by a tenant? What rights are created in the sub-tenant by the granting of a subtenancy by the tenant?
8. Distinguish *privity of estate* from *privity of contract.* Explain how the rights of the assignee and the landlord are affected when an assignment of lease is made by a landlord.
9. Outline the covenants that a tenant makes in an ordinary lease. Explain the effect of a tenant's non-compliance with these terms.
10. What are the rights of a landlord if a tenant abandons the leased property?

11. What remedies are available to a landlord where a tenant fails to comply with the terms of the lease?
12. How do residential tenancies differ from commercial tenancies in most provinces? Why was this change in the law necessary?
13. Explain the legal significance of "surrender of a lease." How is this effected?
14. In a commercial lease, in most provinces, landlords may distrain against the chattels of the tenant for non-payment of rent. What does this mean, and how is it accomplished?

MINI-CASE PROBLEMS

1. X entered into a verbal monthly tenancy with Y, on June 1st, to rent Y's shop. X paid Y the first month's rent and also moved into possession on the same day. Some months later, on November 1st, X gave Y notice of his intention to vacate the premises on November 30th and paid Y the November rent. Y demanded an additional month's rent in lieu of notice. Is Y entitled to the additional rent?
2. ABC Co. leased a large commercial building for its business. The lease called for monthly payments of $5000 per month on a two-year lease. At the end of the first year, ABC Co. fell into arrears on its monthly rent payments. Three months' rent is now due and owing. What action might the landlord take against the ABC Co.?

JUDICIAL DECISION

The case of *Klein v. Savon Fabrics Ltd.* concerns the formation of a tenancy relationship, and a subsequent attempt by the tenant to avoid the tenancy by vacating the premises. The issue is whether innocent misrepresentation took place and, if so, did it constitute grounds for rescission of the lease by the tenant. The tenant argued that it did, while the landlord argued that no representation of fact was made, only an opinion was expressed. The trial judge reached the conclusion that innocent misrepresentation had taken place, and the tenant was entitled to rescind the lease agreement. The landlord appealed.

The Court of Appeal first considered the nature of the relationship and concluded that the parties had established a monthly periodic tenancy. Consequently, a month's notice was required for its termination. The court then turned to the alleged misrepresentation and, with reference to other judgements, concluded that the landlord's comment was a mere expression of opinion. The appeal was allowed and the court found in favour of the plaintiff landlord.

Rights of Landlord and Tenant — Rescission of Lease for Innocent Misrepresentation

Klein v. Savon Fabrics Ltd., [1962] O.W.N. 199.

A landlord and tenant entered into a tenancy agreement that provided for a rental payment of $138 per month, with the lease being terminable on one month's notice. The tenant moved into possession, but moved out shortly thereafter when it was discovered that the tenant's goods stored on the premises could not be insured.

The landlord afterwards commenced an action for one month's rent in lieu of notice and the costs of cleaning the premises.

At trial, the plaintiff's action was dismissed. The case was then appealed by the plaintiff to the Court of Appeal.

SCHROEDER, J.A.:

It was important for the Judge to determine, first, the nature of the tenancy which was brought into being. It is unquestionably true that in the instrument setting out the terms of the lease the parties carried informality very far. It was nevertheless the duty of the Court to endeavour to place a reasonable and a proper construction upon the agreement which the parties had reduced to writing. It is well settled that a demise of property at a monthly or weekly rental affords a presumption of a monthly or weekly tenancy: *Huffell v. Armistead* (1835), 7 C. & P. 56. In *Semi-Ready v. Tew* (1909), 19 O.L.R. 227, Boyd, C., stated at p. 230:

"In the absence of other controlling circumstances implying a different intention, the payment of monthly rent is deemed to indicate a monthly tenancy."

That proposition is so well settled that it requires no further elaboration. The agreement, on a fair and reasonable construction thereof, does not create a lease for a definite period of one month as contended, but evidences a renting for an indefinite period at a monthly rent of $130. The conclusion is inescapable that the parties intended to create and did enter into a monthly tenancy. If there were any doubt upon that point it would be dispelled by the terms of cl. 2. Clearly, therefore, the plaintiff has established that a monthly tenancy was created, and under the Landlord & Tenant Act, R.S.O. 1960, c. 206, s. 27, a month's notice to quit was required. Such notice not having been given, the plaintiff is entitled to succeed and should have judgment against the defendant for the sum of $138 as claimed.

It was argued on behalf of the defendant that the document in question did not set out all terms of the lease and that it was entered into upon a condition that the defendant's goods stored on the premise would be insurable, in that Klein had falsely and fraudulently represented to the defendant in the course of negotiations that the defendant's goods would be insurable while stored in this building. We are concerned here not with an executory contract, but with an executed contract. The lease, such as it was, was duly executed, the rent for the first month was paid, and possession of the premises had been taken by the defendant. In these circumstances it was not open to the defendant to make a claim for rescission of the written lease unless the alleged condition or warranty was expressed therein, or there was *error in substantialibus,* or fraud. The problem presented for solution must be approached from the standpoint that the contract between the parties has been executed. That being so, no action can be maintained for damages or compensation arising from errors as to quantity or quality of the thing sold or leased except in particular cases not material here, nor unless the sale or leasing has been induced by a fraudulent, as distinguished from an innocent, misrepresentation. The governing authority on that point in Canada is *Redican v. Nesbitt,* [1924] S.C.R. 135, which was followed in *Shortt v. MacLennan,* [1957] O.W.N. 1, and *Dalladas v. Tennikat,* [1958] O.W.N. 169.

In *Angel v. Jay,* [1911] 1 K.B. 666, it was held that a Court of equity would not grant rescission of an executed lease on the ground of an innocent misrepresentation. Darling, J., stated, at p. 671:

"On the contrary, one of the cases cited, *Legge v. Croker* (1811), 1 Ball & B. 506, was a case of a lease, and it was there held that a lease deliberately executed cannot be set aside for a misrepresentation which is not wilful. This doctrine has not been confined to cases of conveyances, whether of freeholds or leaseholds; in *Seddon v. North Eastern Salt Co.,* [1905] 1 Ch. 326, it was applied in the case of a sale of shares in a company, and I have come to the conclusion that, there being here an executed contract and no suggestion of fraud, the County Court Judge was wrong in ordering rescission of this lease. That might have been done if the contract had not been executed; but here there had been completion, the plaintiff had gone into possession under the lease, and nothing remained to be done. That being so, on the authority of the cases cited for the appellant, we must come to the conclusion that the County Court Judge was wrong."

The trial Judge made an express finding that the representation alleged had been made, but he also found that it was not false and misleading. Thus, if it was a misrepresentation at all it was an innocent one. On a consideration of the evidence as a whole it is plain that what is alleged by the defendant by way of defence cannot even be regarded as an innocent misrepresentation, since it was not a representation of a fact but a mere expression of opinion which proved to be unfounded. So viewed, it neither affords ground for rescission of the lease nor support for the defendant's counterclaim.

The appeal will be allowed, the judgment at trial set aside, and there will be substituted therefore a judgment in favour of the plaintiffs for $138 and costs with a counsel fee at trial fixed at $25. The defendant's counterclaim will be dismissed with costs. The plaintiffs shall have the costs of the appeal fixed at $25 together with the taxable disbursements.

CASE PROBLEMS FOR DISCUSSION

Case 1

The Washa-Matic Company carried on business as the owner of coin operated-washing machines. The company entered into an agreement with "108 Suite Apartments" to provide washing machines for use by tenants of the apartment building.

The agreement was entitled "Lease Agreement" and provided that the landlord "demise and lease the laundry room on the ground floor of the building to the tenant for a monthly rental equal to $1 per machine installed." The agreement was drawn for a five-year term and provided for free access to the room by all tenants. The agreement also allowed employees of Washa-Matic the right of access to the premises "at all reasonable times" to repair or service the machines.

Some time after the machines were installed, the owner of the building sold the premises to a new owner, and the new owner requested Washa-Matic to remove the washing machines. Washa-Matic refused and argued that it was the lessee of the laundry room under the lease agreement.

The new owner removed the washing machines owned by Washa-Matic and installed new equipment. Washa-Matic Company then brought an action against 108 Suite Apartments for damages for breach of the lease and for lost profits.

Discuss the legal issues raised in this case. Render a decision.

Case 2

The Youngs leased an apartment suite from Broughton Rd. Apartments for a one-year term, commencing July 1st. The Youngs were particularly attracted by the location of the apartment building, since it was a long, low building of Tudor design, surrounded by rather spacious grounds. The grounds were important to them because they required a place where their two-year-old child might have a safe place to play.

A few weeks after the tenants moved into their apartment, the owner of the building decided to remove the roof of the building and replace it with new roofing boards and shingles. The noise of the construction work, which was carried on from approximately 8:00 a.m. to 4:00 p.m., interfered with the normal sleeping hours of Mr. Young, who worked a second shift as a night security guard at a nearby industrial plant. It also interfered with their child's customary afternoon nap.

In addition to the noise of the construction, the Youngs discovered that another tenant in the building owned a large pet snake, which was permitted to roam at will over the lawns of the property.

The Youngs protested to the landlord that the noise of the roof repairs interfered with Mr. Young's sleep, and the presence of the snake made the use of the grounds impossible, since they both feared the reptile, even though it was of a harmless species.

When the landlord refused to limit the construction and failed to control the snake, the Youngs moved from the apartment. They had been in possession for less than two weeks. The landlord then brought an action to recover apartment rent and other expenses that were alleged to be owing as a result of the breach of the lease by the tenants.

Discuss the arguments that the defendants might raise in this action and determine the issues that the court must deal with before a judgement might be given. Render a decision.

Case 3

Bingham leased a small shop from Wright under a tenancy agreement that provided for a three-year term at a monthly rental of $300 per month. The lease did not contain an option to renew, but following the expiry of the lease on October 31, 1976, Bingham continued to pay the monthly rental of $300 to Wright.

The term of the tenancy was never discussed between the parties, nor was the lease arrangement discussed until June 1988, when Wright gave Bingham a written notice that read: "I have sold the property in which you presently occupy space, and the purchaser will require vacant possession on December 31, 1988. This letter gives you written notice to vacate in six months' time."

In response, Bingham wrote Wright and advised her that he was in possession under a lease that did not expire until October 31, 1989, and that the notice given did not apply to his present tenancy.

Wright gave Bingham a second written notice on October 25, 1988, demanding vacant possession of the premises by November 30, 1988.

When Bingham refused to vacate the shop, Wright brought an action for a writ of possession.

Outline the arguments that might be raised by the parties in this case. Render a decision.

Case 4

Quinn leased a small retail shop from Chaplin for the purpose of establishing a fruit and vegetable market. The lease was drawn for a three-year term, commencing May 1, 1993, and provided for a total rental of $18 000, payable at $500 per month. The first and last month's rent were due on May 1st. Quinn paid the two months' rent and moved into possession.

A month later, and a few days after the rent for the month was due, Chaplin discovered that Quinn had sold the business to Rizzoto. The sale was contrary to the terms of the lease, which permitted assignment of the lease only on consent. Chaplin immediately went to the shop and, when Rizzoto arrived, Chaplin told him that he was not willing to have anyone but Quinn operate a shop on the premises. Chaplin advised Rizzoto that Quinn was in breach of the lease by assigning it without his consent and suggested that Rizzoto seek out Quinn to get his money back.

Chaplin then contacted a licensed bailiff and gave him authority to collect the rent owing. The sheriff went to the store and made an inventory of the stock and equipment that he valued at $5000 and $6000 respectively. He then changed the locks on the door and posted a notice on the premises that informed the public that the landlord had taken possession for non-payment of rent. The next day he notified Quinn and Rizzoto that he had distrained the chattels in the shop on behalf of the landlord. He advised the two parties that they had five days to redeem the chattels by payment of the arrears of rent, otherwise the chattels would be sold. Quinn and Rizzoto made no attempt to pay the rent.

The bailiff later attempted to sell the business, but was unsuccessful. Eventually his services were terminated by Chaplin.

Chaplin did not attempt to rent the premises and retained the stock and equipment. In December 1993, he brought an action against Quinn for damages for breach of the lease.

Discuss the particular issues that are raised by this case, and indicate the arguments that the parties might present with respect to each. Render a decision.

Case 5

Sheila verbally agreed to lease Beverly's furnished apartment from her for the months of May through to August, while Beverly would be in another city attending a university summer program. Under the agreement, Sheila would pay the rental payments to the landlord at the beginning of each month and "take good care of the apartment" in Beverly's absence. Sheila was expected to vacate the apartment on August 30th.

Sheila moved into the apartment on May 1st and lived in it until July 30th, when she found a new apartment located closer to her place of employment. On July 30th, she permitted several of her friends to move into Beverly's apartment on the condition that they paid the August rent and vacated before the end of the month, when Beverly was expected to return to the city.

The "new" tenants did not pay the rent as they had agreed to do. On August 25th they held a party at the apartment that resulted in $1000 damage to the premises and $800 damage to Beverly's furniture. The new tenants vacated the apartment the next day, leaving no forwarding address.

When Beverly returned to the city on August 31st, she discovered her apartment in ruins. A few days later, she received a notice from her landlord demanding the overdue rent for the month of August.

Advise Beverly of her rights and outline a course of action for her to follow.

Case 6

The Acme Co. leased the second floor of a three-storey office building to the High Finance Company for a three-year term. The lease contained a clause in which the tenant acknowledged that the building was in a good state of repair. The lease, however, made no mention of responsibility to repair subsequent damage to the rental premises.

Before moving into the premises, the High Finance Company made extensive changes in the leased premises by adding several partition walls, special electrical wiring for its computer operation, and an air conditioning system. Three months later, a fault in the electrical wiring caused a serious fire that destroyed the interior of the High Finance Company's rental premises, and caused serious damage to the third floor of the building and water damage to the first floor tenant's equipment and merchandising business.

High Finance Company agreed to pay for the damage to the part of the premises that it had leased, but refused to pay for the general damage to the building on the basis that the landlord had agreed to the changes in the electrical wiring that had resulted in the fire. High Finance Company also refused to pay rent for its part of the building until the premises were again fit for occupation.

Discuss the rights of The Acme Co., the third floor tenant, and the first floor tenant. On what basis, if any, might the High Finance Company refuse to pay its rent?

Case 7

New Tomorrows Inc. is a registered non-profit charitable corporation which runs a group home, allowing ex-convicts, homeless persons, and others who are down on their luck a chance to "get on their feet" in an understanding environment. Applicants sign a rehabilitation agreement, and receive the use of a bedroom and common kitchen space. Failure to pay any month's modest fee on time was to be taken, under the agreement, to be notice by the resident of his or her intention to leave the home in five days time. The point was driven home each month, as those who had given their notice were quickly replaced by other people from the streets.

After residing for three months, Henry was late in the payment of his fees on the first day of the new month. Five days later, he and his belongings were "helped" to the street, and as was so often the case, he was replaced by someone else. Henry went to the provincial ministry responsible for tenancies to complain.

Discuss the legal issues in this case, and the arguments and principles which the parties may rely upon. What rights, if any, does Henry have?

Real Estate Transactions

INTRODUCTION   The purchase of real property — whether it involves vacant land, a house and lot, cottage property, or business premises — has, in recent years, become a complex transaction for which the advice and services of a member of the legal profession is not only desirable, but virtually a necessity. In one sense, the transaction has now turned full circle. In the past, the transfer of property was characterized by much formality and ritual and required the services of a person not only literate, but knowledgeable of the process of transfer. Over the years, the process has remained so in England; but in North America, by the nineteenth century and early twentieth century, the transaction acquired a large degree of informality, particularly in rural areas. During this period of time, in many localities, deeds were drawn by persons with only a limited knowledge of the formalities required to transfer title. Often the transaction consisted of little more than the preparation and delivery of a deed to the property, with no thought given to the examination of the vendor's title to the property or the accuracy of the boundaries of the land transferred.

    The informality of real estate transactions during this period may be easily explained. In rural North America, land was relatively inexpensive, and where a sale of property did occur, the parties were generally familiar with the land and its past owners. All dealings with the property were frequently common knowledge to the community at large, and the boundaries of the lands were usually settled and known. It was also a simpler age, when government planning and interference with the use of property was virtually non-existent. By the middle of the twentieth century, however, the introduction of planning legislation and land use control gradually increased the complexity of real estate transactions to the point where, today, expert assistance is usually essential to properly carry out the necessary searches, clearances, and formalities required to effect the transfer of a good title to a purchaser.

The sale of freehold land in England was originally characterized by a formal ceremony, without a written conveyance. The ceremony known as **livery of seisin** could take one of two forms: **livery in law** or **livery in deed.** Livery in law simply involved the owner of the freehold, in the presence of witnesses, pointing to the land and stating to the intended recipient that it was his intention to give the recipient the particular property for himself and his heirs. The transfer would be complete when the party would enter into possession of the land.[1] Livery in deed followed a slightly different pattern, which required an act (or deed) on the part of the owner of the land. The event was usually ceremonial and symbolic, with the owner, in the presence of witnesses, delivering to the intended recipient some element of property associated with the land itself, as well as providing vacant possession of the property for the new owner.[2]

Gradually, documentary evidence of the transaction also became a part of the ceremony, first in the form of a written record of the ceremony itself, and then as a written statement of the transaction in which the grantor described the property and the grantee to whom the property was delivered, accompanied by the expression of the intention to transfer and deliver up the land. The written document gradually assumed a greater significance in the ceremony. Eventually the document became an important part of the transfer itself.

The execution of the document under seal has a long history in connection with the transfer of land. After the Norman Conquest, the practice of affixing a seal as a means of execution became a common method used by grantors to evidence their intention to be bound by the covenants in the conveyance. Literate persons would sign their names as well.

For many years, the written document was used as a symbolic element in the ceremony by a practice that required the grantor in the presence of the witnesses to sign, seal, and deliver the deed to the grantee at the property site. Gradually, this too changed, as the written document assumed greater importance, and the ceremonial aspects became a mere formality. Eventually, the written document became the essential element of the transfer of the title to property, but not to the total exclusion of the ceremonial component. Even today, in some provinces that call for registration under the Registry System the deed must be "signed, sealed, and delivered" to transfer the title to the property. The role of witnesses (although not absolutely essential at common law) remains, since in those provinces the execution of the document by the grantor must be in the presence of a witness, and the witness must, by a sworn affidavit, attest to the fact to enable the grantee to register the deed.[3] It should be noted, however, that under the Land Titles System in a number of provinces, the conveyance need not be under seal, but the document must be executed in the presence of a witness.[4] The formality of delivery to the grantee also remains as an essential act before the interest in the land passes.[5] The modern real estate transaction, therefore, is concluded by a ceremo-

---

1. P.G. Osborn, *The Concise Law Dictionary 4th ed.* (London: Sweet & Maxwell Ltd., 1954), p. 206.

2. The significance of the ceremonial aspects associated with the transfer of property are described in W.S. Holdsworth, A *History of English Law,* 3rd ed., vol. 3 (London: Methuen & Co. Ltd., 1923), pp. 222-225.

3. This is required by statute in most provinces. See, for example, the Registry Act, R.S.O. 1990, c. R-20, s. 28, 29.

4. See, for example, the Land Titles Act, R.S.O. 1990, c. L-5, ss. 88 and 89.

5. It should be noted, however, that under the Land Titles System, registration of the transfer is necessary to vest the title in the grantee. See the Land Titles Act, R.S.O. 1990, c. L-5, ss. 90 and 91.

ny that includes some remnants of the ancient livery of seisin, in spite of continuing efforts to streamline the process.

MODERN REAL ESTATE TRANSACTIONS

The purchase and sale of real property takes place with much greater frequency at present than it did in the past. Until very recently, property (and in particular agricultural lands) often remained in the hands of families for many generations, but with the mobility that developed in the twentieth century as a result of technological advances, this is not so today. Current employment and business practices often require persons to move regularly. As a result, residential property may change hands every few years. This change in lifestyle has created a need for the services of a large number of persons with expertise in the negotiation and completion of land transactions. Some of these experts, such as land surveyors and members of the legal profession, have long been associated with this type of activity. But more recently, others, such as real estate agents, property appraisers, and (in some cases) public accountants, now play an important role in the purchase and sale of property.

The Role of the Real Estate Agent

The complexity of the modern real estate transaction virtually obliges the vendor and purchaser to obtain the services of professionals in order to transfer the property interest. For example, some services, such as those of the real estate agent, are often essential to initiate the transaction. Most property owners rarely have the time to search for a prospective purchaser if they should desire to sell their property. Consequently, the successful sale is often dependent upon the efforts of persons whose expertise lies in the area of seeking out interested buyers and bringing such parties into a contractual relationship with the property owner. This, in essence, is the role of the real estate agent.

A real estate agent (or **broker,** as he or she is sometimes called) is a particular type of agent who (except in special circumstances) normally acts for the vendor of the property. The relationship between the property owner and the real estate agent is usually established by a contract between the two that is called a **listing agreement.** Under the terms of this agreement, the agent agrees to seek out prospective buyers for the owner and bring the two parties together in contract. In return for this service, the property owner usually agrees to pay the agent a commission (based upon a percentage of the sale price, usually in the 5-10% range, or a fixed sum) for the agent's services, if a sale is negotiated. Sales of commercial and industrial properties usually command a higher commission rate than residential property, and usually fall in the 8-10% range.

The services that a real estate agent is expected to provide under a typical listing agreement are as follows:

(1) inspect and value the property or, where an expert opinion as to the value is required, arrange to have an evaluation made by a professional appraiser;

(2) actively seek out prospective purchasers of the property by way of advertisement (paid for at the agent's expense), by personal contact, and, in some cases, by way of notification to other agents of the availability of the property for sale;

(3) arrange to have prospective purchasers inspect the property and advise the purchasers of the vendor's terms of sale;

(4) prepare a written offer to purchase for execution by the prospective purchaser and deliver it to the owner for consideration;

(5) in extremely rare cases, execute the purchase agreement on behalf of the owner under a grant of express authority (a power of attorney); and

(6) hold all deposits paid by the prospective purchaser in trust pending the completion or termination of the transaction, and either pay the funds over to the vendor on completion of the sale, or return the money to the prospective purchaser, if the offer is rejected by the vendor.

It is important to note that the real estate agent, under a listing agreement, is expected to act at all times in the best interests of the vendor who engaged the agent to sell the property. The rules of law pertaining to agency (subject to a few minor exceptions) generally apply to the relationship. The agent is not a "middle man" who is used simply to bring the parties together, but is the agent of the vendor.[6] For example, a real estate agent must never act for both parties in a transaction without the express consent of both (a rare situation) and, while engaged by the owner of the property as his or her principal, must never attempt to obtain a benefit for the purchaser that would be to the vendor's detriment. If the agent should attempt to obtain a benefit for the purchaser that is detrimental to the agent's principal, the agent would not only be liable for the amount of the loss, but would also not be entitled to claim a commission from the vendor on the sale. This would arise from the fact that the agent would be in breach of duty to the client.[7]

Assuming that the real estate agent brings together a willing vendor and purchaser, the agent's duties are generally completed when the written offer, which the agent draws and the purchaser signs, is accepted by the vendor. At that time, the parties are bound in contract for the purchase and sale of the property that is the subject-matter of the agreement. The contract, however, only establishes the contractual relationship. It does not effect a transfer of the title to the purchaser, as the parties must both carry out a number of duties under the agreement before the title documents change hands. In addition, the offer to purchase usually provides the purchaser with a period of time to make a number of searches and determinations in order to be satisfied that the title to the property is in order.

Appraisal

Property value is often determined by the real estate agent at the time that the vendor enters into a listing agreement. The valuation of an ordinary residential property is usually well within the expertise of the experienced real estate agent. However, in the case of a commercial or industrial property, the services of a professional property appraiser are usually obtained in order to fix a value for sale purposes. Appraisers are frequently engaged by purchasers as well, especially for commercial or industrial purchases. The appraisal, from the purchaser's point of view, is important for two reasons:

6. See, for example, *D'Atri v. Chilcott* (1975), 55 D.L.R. (3d) 30; *Len Pugh Real Estate Ltd. v. Ronvic Construction Co. Ltd.* (1973), 41 D.L.R. (3d) 48.

7. *Len Pugh Real Estate Ltd. v. Ronvic Construction Co. Ltd.* (1973), 41 D.L.R. (3d) 48.

(1) The appraisal provides the purchaser with an expert opinion as to the value of the property and provides some guidance in the negotiation of a price.

(2) The appraisal will provide the purchaser with a general estimate of the amount of financing that might be obtained from a lending institution to assist in the financing of the purchase, since most lending institutions will fix the mortgage principal amount that they will lend as a percentage of the appraised value of the property.

Unlike the real estate agent, a property appraiser charges a fixed fee for appraisal services. This service usually consists of an examination of the property and the formulation of an opinion as to its market value based upon a number of factors. The most important factors are the condition of the building, the value of the land, the zoning of the property, the present rate of return (in the form of rents, etc.), the potential for development, and the known market value of similar properties. The ultimate value placed on the given property depends a great deal upon the expertise of the appraiser, but the report is particularly useful for the purchaser in the determination of the purchase price to include in the offer.

Offer to Purchase

The offer to purchase is only an offer until such time as the vendor accepts it. At that point, the agreement becomes a binding contract. Nevertheless, the usual offer to purchase generally contains a number of provisions that, if unsatisfied by the vendor, render the agreement null and void at the option of the purchaser. For example, a standard form of an offer to purchase usually provides that the purchaser will have a period of time following the acceptance of the offer by the vendor in which to examine the title to the property at his or her own expense. If any valid objection to the vendor's title is raised within that time that the vendor is unable or unwilling to correct, the agreement will then become null and void, and any deposit paid by the purchaser must be refunded. The right to rescind the agreement may also be available to the purchaser if the property itself is not as described. This may arise, for example, where the purchaser discovers that the vendor does not have title to all the lands that he or she has agreed to sell. This latter discrepancy is frequently determined by way of a survey of the property and a comparison of the surveyor's description of the property with the description of the land contained in the vendor's deed.

Other provisions in the offer to purchase that the purchaser is given time to confirm usually relate to the zoning of the property, the existence of special rights attached to the land, the suitability of the building or land for a specific purpose or use, and the confirmation of the ownership of chattels and fixtures sold with the property.

Most properties are unique, and the circumstances that surround the negotiation of the purchase agreement consequently reflect the particular concerns of each of the parties. Thus, as a general rule, the purchase agreement for each transaction is as unique as the property itself. For this reason, both the purchaser and the vendor normally seek the services and advice of experts other than the real estate agent and appraiser before the agreement is executed. As a result, real estate contracts frequently include additional clauses, conditions, and assurances that must be satisfied before the transaction may be finalized and the title transferred.

Examples of these clauses include conditions precedent with respect to financing; the sale of some other property owned by the purchaser; tests made to determine the quality and quantity of water supply (if in a rural area); the acquisition of special licences for the use of the property in a particular fashion; the right to sever the property from a larger parcel under planning legislation; the successful application for a change in the zoning of the lands; or the issue of a building permit to erect a particular type of structure on the lot.

All of the conditions and terms of the agreement must be complied with in a real estate transaction. The failure on the part of either party to fully perform the agreement would entitled the injured party (usually at the purchaser's option) to terminate the agreement, or bring an action for either specific performance or for damages. To satisfy themselves that the terms of the agreement are complied with, and to carry out their own duties and responsibilities, most parties to real estate transactions engage the services of legal experts. The experts should be engaged before the offer to purchase is signed. However, if this is not done, it is wise to do so immediately after the contract is made to ensure that rights are protected during the course of the transaction.

Survey

While an appraisal of the property is frequently obtained by a prospective purchaser before the purchase agreement is entered into, a survey is not usually obtained until after the parties have signed the contract. The reason for this procedural difference is due to the nature of the transaction. Most purchase agreements provide that the vendor must have a good title to the lands described in the agreement. A survey is used to determine if the vendor's land as described in the deed actually coincides with the boundaries and area of land that the vendor claims to possess.

Surveys are prepared by persons trained and licensed to perform the service pursuant to provincial legislation. Statutes govern not only the procedure for the conduct and preparation of surveys, but the licensing of persons who may perform the work. One statute usually governs the technical aspects of survey work, and another, the training and licensing of the profession.

The importance of obtaining a survey (from the purchaser's point of view) is that it will uncover any encroachments on the vendor's property by adjoining property owners, and any easements or rights of way that might affect the land. It will also establish the accuracy of the boundaries of the property as described in the deed. This will not only be determined by the surveyor from the vendor's title, but by "ground reference," because the surveyor generally marks the boundaries of the property by driving steel bars or pins into the ground at each of the corners of the parcel of land. In this fashion, the legal description of the property is translated into ground area for the purchaser to examine.

If the survey reveals a boundary discrepancy, the vendor is usually obliged to have the discrepancy corrected in order that the purchaser will receive the amount of land described in the purchase agreement. If the discrepancy is significant and the vendor cannot correct the title, the purchaser may agree to take the property, but with some abatement of the purchase price to compensate for the deficiency. However, if the difference should be substantial, the purchaser would be in a position to avoid the transaction. In this regard, the survey is used by the purchaser's solicitor to assess the vendor's title to the property and to determine the vendor's right to the property described in the agreement.

The Role of the Legal Profession

The class of lawyers who engage in the practice of law concerning land transactions have historically been solicitors. Both the vendor and the purchaser usually require the services of a solicitor to perform the many searches and duties associated with the transfer of the title in a sale of land. The services vary substantially depending upon whether they are for the vendor or the purchaser, and whether the transaction is one that involves the sale of residential or commercial property.

In the sale of a property, the purchaser's solicitor (depending upon the province where the land itself is situated) will usually be called upon to make the following searches:

(1) A search of the title to the property at the land registry office in the county or district where the land is located. If the land is under the Registry System, then the solicitor is obliged to prepare an abstract of the title to the property in order to establish a good chain of title for a lengthy period of time.[8] This search would involve an examination of all deeds, mortgages, discharges of mortgage, and other documents registered against the title to the property to determine that the vendor's title, when traced back, represents a right in the vendor to convey a good title to the purchaser that would be free of any claims adverse to the vendor's interest in the land.

Under the Land Titles System, the solicitor's search is much easier, as the province certifies the title of the vendor as being as it stands on the register. Any charges, liens, or other instruments that might affect the title of the vendor would be recited, and the solicitor might then ascertain their status and call on the vendor's solicitor to take steps to have the encumbrances or interests cleared from the title before it is transferred to the purchaser.

On the completion of the search (under both systems) the purchaser's solicitor notifies the vendor's solicitor of any problems concerning the title by way of a **letter of requisition,** which requires the vendor to clear the rights or encumbrances from the title before the closing date. The vendor's solicitor on receipt of the letter must make every effort to satisfy requisitions that represent valid objections to the vendor's title. If the objection cannot be satisfied, the purchaser under the terms of the contract is usually free to reject the property, and the purchase agreement becomes null and void.

(2) The purchaser's solicitor also undertakes a series of searches at the local municipal office to determine

(a) if the municipal taxes on the property have been paid and that no arrears of taxes exist;

(b) the zoning of the property is appropriate for the existing or intended use of the property;

(c) the property conforms to the municipal building and safety standards, and that no work orders are outstanding against the property;

---

8. In Ontario, for example, under the Registry System, the chain of title must cover a 40-year period. See the Registry Act, R.S.O. 1990, c. R-20, s. 112.

(d) in the case of land under development, that any obligations that the builder-developer may have under any subdivision or development agreement have been fully satisfied, or funds deposited with the municipality to cover the completion of the work;

(e) where services (such as electric power) are provided by the municipality, a careful solicitor will also inquire to determine if the payment for these services is in arrears. For this and other municipal searches, the solicitor will obtain a certificate, or some other written confirmation, as to the status of the property.

(3) In some provinces, where the vendor is a corporation, or where one of the vendor's predecessors in title was a corporation, a search for liens for unpaid corporation taxes is required, and the solicitor will contact the appropriate government office to obtain this information. If a lien for the unpaid tax is claimed by the province, the purchaser's solicitor will require the payment of the taxes before the transaction is closed in order to clear the lien from the property. This is not a universal requirement, however, as in some provinces the lien does not attach to the land unless a notice of the lien is registered against the title to the property in the appropriate land registry office.

(4) Where a province has a new housing warranty scheme in effect, a solicitor will make a search to determine if the building is registered under the scheme, and that the particular dwelling-unit is enrolled under the program. Not all provinces provide this form of consumer protection, but where the transaction concerns the sale of a new housing unit, and such a scheme is in operation, the solicitor for the purchaser would be anxious to ensure that the property was properly covered by the building warranty under the program.

(5) A search for any claims or encumbrances against chattels or fixtures sold with the property would be made by the purchaser's solicitor in the appropriate government office. Depending upon the province, this might be maintained in the local land registry office, the county or district court office, or in a central registry for the entire province. A certificate is usually obtained by the solicitor that would indicate any creditor claims against the goods in question.

(6) The purchaser's solicitor would also make a search for any judgements or writs of execution in the hands of the sheriff of the county or district that might attach to the lands of the vendor. Again, a certificate would be obtained by the solicitor from the sheriff if no writs of execution were in the sheriff's hands. Because a writ of execution can attach to the property under the Registry System as soon as it is filed with the sheriff, it is essential that this particular search be made as close to the time of transfer of the property as possible. As a result, the purchaser's solicitor normally makes a second or final search for executions immediately prior to the registration of the conveyance of the property to the purchaser. Under the Land Titles System, the execution does not affect the land until it is placed in the hands of the Land Titles office. Nevertheless, careful solicitors make the search to avoid the problems that might be created by the delivery of an execution at or before the closing.

In addition to the many searches that the purchaser's solicitor makes (some of which are outlined above), the solicitor attends to a number of other duties associated with the transaction itself. Insurance coverage for the property is obtained for the purchaser; the status of any mortgage or charge to be assumed by the purchaser is determined; draft copies of the conveyance and other title documents are checked; a mortgage back to the vendor (if a part of the transaction) is prepared; and the funds are obtained for the closing of the transaction.

While the purchaser's solicitor is busy with the many searches and preparations for the closing, the vendor's solicitor usually prepares[9] draft copies of the deed or transfer (see example in Appendix A: Documents) and a statement of adjustments (setting out the financial details of the transaction). These documents are then sent to the purchaser's solicitor for approval. The vendor's solicitor is obliged to answer any requisitions that the purchaser's solicitor may raise concerning the title to the property. The vendor's solicitor must also attempt to correct them in order that the vendor may pass a good title to the purchaser. If the transaction involves the assumption of an existing mortgage by the purchaser, the vendor's solicitor must obtain a mortgage statement from the mortgagee at the time that it is assumed by the purchaser. The vendor's solicitor must also collect all title documents, surveys, tax bills, keys, proof of ownership of chattels to be transferred, and other documents pertaining to the sale for delivery to the purchaser on closing. The solicitor must also prepare a bill of sale for any chattels to be sold as a part of the transaction. This document, along with the deed or transfer, must then be properly executed by the vendor in the presence of a witness. These documents are collected together in preparation for delivery on the date fixed for the closing of the transaction. If the property to be sold is occupied by tenants, the vendor's solicitor will attend to preparing assignment of the leases to the purchaser and to obtaining from the tenants an acknowledgement as to the status of the lease agreements. Copies of these documents will also be examined by the purchaser's solicitor, and the lease agreements verified. Notices to the tenants of the change of ownership of the property would also be prepared by the vendor's solicitor for delivery to the tenants on or after the closing of the sale transaction.

The Closing of the Transaction

The actual closing of the real estate transaction today lacks much of the ceremony associated with a transfer of property in the past. The transaction is usually completed by the solicitors for the vendor and the purchaser on the appointed day at the land registry office. There, the purchaser's solicitor examines the deed and other documents of title, makes a last minute subsearch of the title to the property to make certain no changes have taken place in the register since the previous search was made, obtains a sheriff's certificate, and makes a final check for encumbrances or claims against any chattels to be transferred. If the final searches reveal that all is in order, the two solicitors are then ready to exchange the documents and complete the closing. The vendor's solicitor usually delivers to the purchaser's solicitor the signed deed or transfer and a bill of sale for chattels (if

---

9. This is not a universal practice, however, as the practice varies. It is not uncommon to have draft documents prepared by the purchaser's solicitor.

any), along with copies of old title documents and the keys. In return, the vendor's solicitor receives the purchase monies and any mortgage or charge that the purchaser has given back to the vendor. The purchaser's solicitor attends to the registration of the title documents, following which, the vendor's solicitor registers the mortgage or charge, if any. The delivery and registration of the documents completes the transaction, and the title at that point is registered in the purchaser's name. Vacant possession of the property is normally a part of the transaction, and the delivery of the keys to the premises is symbolic only of the delivery of possession to the purchaser. In most cases, the vendor and purchaser arrange between themselves the time when the vendor will vacate the premises, and when the new purchaser will move into possession. This is usually on the same day that the transaction closes.

Following the closing of the transaction in the land registry office, the solicitors attend to the many final tasks associated with the change of ownership. These tasks usually take the form of providing notice of the change of ownership to municipal tax offices, assessment offices, mortgagees, public utilities, insurers, and any tenants. When these duties have been completed, the solicitors make final reports to their respective clients.

Where a purchase and sale agreement involves the sale of a commercial building or a business, the transaction is considerably more complicated, for the purchaser had contracted for not only the purchase of land and a building, but stock-in-trade, trade fixtures, goodwill, and other assets of the business. Such a sale frequently involves the transfer or acquisition of special licences, as well as compliance with legislation governing the sale of business assets "in bulk." Because most businesses have trade and other types of creditors, a sale of a business "in bulk" (which means a sale of stock and/or the assets of a business such as equipment, trucks, furnishings, etc.) requires the vendor's solicitor to notify the seller's creditors of the sale, and make arrangements for the payment of their accounts out of the proceeds of the sale. This procedure may be either simple or lengthy depending upon the number of creditors and the nature of their claims, but the bulk sales legislation must be complied with, otherwise the sale may be overturned by the creditors. For this reason, the sale of a business or business assets tends to be more complex, and the solicitors' work under the circumstances includes additional duties and responsibilities on behalf of their clients in order to effect the transfer of ownership of the business in accordance with this special legislation. The legislation concerning the sale of business assets is the subject-matter of a part of the next chapter.

SUMMARY

The transfer of the title to real property was effected originally by way of ceremony and the expression of intent. This took the form of livery of seisin. Over time, the embodiment of the grantor's intentions in a written document gradually replaced the ceremony. Today, the preparation of a deed or transfer that (in most provinces) has been signed and sealed by the grantor in the presence of a witness and delivered to the grantee, effects the transfer of the interest in the land between the parties. The registration of the deed (or transfer) in the proper land registry office completes the transaction in terms of public notice and, in the case of a transfer under the Land Titles System, places the grantee's name on the register as the person whom the province certifies as the registered owner of the particular parcel of land.

Real estate agents assist the owner of land by providing a service that brings together the owner and prospective purchasers in an effort to establish a purchase and sale agreement. Where property is listed with a real estate agent, the agent must act in the best interests of the principal at all times. The general rules of agency normally apply to the relationship between the principal and the agent.

In any sale of real property, it is essential that the lands described in a deed or transfer correspond with the land actually occupied by the title holder. To determine this relationship, a survey is used to identify the land to ascertain if any discrepancy exists between the two. Surveys are prepared by persons trained and licensed under provincial legislation, and surveys must be prepared in accordance with statutory requirements as well.

Land ownership is presently subject to a great many controls and regulations that, if ignored, can adversely affect the owner. For this reason, the parties to real estate transactions usually engage the services of members of the legal profession to assist in the completion of the transfer of title to the purchaser. In addition to the preparation of the formal documents associated with the transaction, the lawyers involved (called solicitors) perform the many services necessary to carry out the terms of the contract. On the purchaser's part, this usually involves a number of searches in addition to an examination of the title to the property, in order that the title passed to the purchaser will be good and marketable in the future. The ceremonial aspects of the transfer (insofar as they exist) are mainly performed by the solicitors at the land registry office.

DISCUSSION QUESTIONS

1. Why were the ceremonial aspects of the transfer of land important in early real estate transactions in England?
2. Explain the significance of the vendor providing vacant possession at the time of transfer of ownership. Is this also important today?
3. What role does a real estate broker or agent play in a modern real estate transaction?
4. How is the agency relationship established?
5. What are the duties of a real estate agent? Do they differ in any way from that of an agent in an ordinary principal-agent relationship?
6. Explain the purpose and use of an exclusive listing agreement.
7. In what way (or ways) does an appraiser assist in a real property transfer?
8. Outline the role of a land registration system in modern real estate transactions.
9. How does the land registration system aid a prospective purchaser of real property?
10. What constitutes a good and marketable title to real property? How is this determined under the Registry System?
11. In what way or ways does the Torrens or Land Titles System simplify the determination of the vendor's title to lands offered for sale?
12. Why is a survey important in a land transaction? What does it establish?
13. Describe the role of a lawyer or solicitor in a land transaction.
14. What other searches in addition to a title search are necessary in a land transaction in order to protect the purchaser? How are these searches usually made?

15. Explain the significance of the process whereby a deed of land is "signed, sealed, and delivered."

16. Why must a purchaser make certain that no writs of execution are attached to the property to be purchased?

17. Indicate the importance of registration of a transfer of land in the proper land registry office as soon as possible after the documents of ownership change hands.

MINI-CASE PROBLEMS

1. A agreed to sell B a building lot for $25 000. Without searching the title, B gave A the $25 000, and received a deed to the property in fee simple. B then discovered that the property was registered in A's wife's name and not in A's name. What are B's rights?

2. The ABC Co. intends to offer to purchase a large parcel of vacant land from D, a farmer. The company plans to erect a manufacturing plant on the land after the purchase is completed. What conditions or provisos should the company include in the offer to purchase, and what searches should it make to ensure that it may use the land for its intended purpose?

JUDICIAL DECISION

The case of *George W. Rayfield Realty Ltd. et al. v. Kuhn et al.* provides an example of the law as it relates to real estate agents and their duty to act in good faith with respect to their principal's interests.

In the judgement, the court reviews the obligation of the agent to the principal as set out in s. 42 of the legislation governing the agent's conduct. The judge next reviews the facts (the events that occurred) and whether the notice given by the agent was adequate in terms of the legislation and the common law.

The judge concludes that while the notice given might technically meet the requirements of the legislation, it fell short of the full disclosure required of an agent to his or her principal. The agent was found to be in breach of the duty, and action by the agent for the commission on the "sale" was dismissed.

Real Estate Agent with Interest in Purchaser — Notice of the Interest to Vendor — Fiduciary Relationship

George W. Rayfield Realty Ltd. et al. v. Kuhn et al. (1980), 30 O.R. (2d) 271.
The real estate agent acting for a vendor had a personal interest in the corporation that offered to purchase the parcel of land owned by the vendor. The agent gave written notice of his financial interest in the purchase to the vendor before the purchase agreement was made. The agent later brought an action for a commission on the sale.

GALLIGAN, J.:

I turn now to consider the problems arising from the fiduciary responsibility which Woods had to the defendants and the provisions of s. 42 of the *Real Estate and Business Brokers Act*. Since there was no licensing agreement, only s-s. (1) of that section is applicable. That statutory provision reads as follows:

"42(1) No broker or salesman shall purchase, lease, exchange or otherwise acquire for himself or make an offer to purchase, lease, exchange of otherwise acquire for himself, either directly or indirectly, any interest in real estate for the purpose of resale, unless he first delivers to the vendor a written statement that he is a broker or salesman, as the case may be, and the vendor has acknowledged in writing that he has received the statement."

As I mentioned earlier, Woods, the salesman for Cathcart, was a principal in Bambi at the time the offer resulting in the agreement exs. 1 and 7 was made. He remained a principal in Bambi throughout the whole time that that company had contractual arrangements with the defendants. In my opinion s. 42(1) applies to him and applies to Cathcart.

I find as a fact that on September 12, 1973, Woods delivered to Kuhn the following notice:

"Please be advised that Mr. David Woods has a financial interest in Bambi Developments Limited and is purchasing the above property for the purpose of developing and/or resale. Mr. David Woods is a real estate agent and will be receiving part of the commission from the above sale."

I find as a fact that Kuhn signed an acknowledgement on September 12, 1973, that he received that notice on that day. I do not accept Kuhn's evidence that he signed it months later. Mr. Kuhn is an experienced real estate developer. He had been in that business for almost 20 years at the time this transaction developed. I think it is utterly preposterous for him to expect anybody to believe that he would sign a document such as this, months after the event. I accept that the date September 12, 1973, was probably written in by Woods, but I am quite satisfied that Kuhn would not have signed such a document in blank and I accept that that date was in there at the time he signed it.

I am not persuaded, on the reasonable balance of probability that any notice required by s. 42 was given to Petrullo at or prior to the time he executed exs. 1 and 7. Mr. Warne argued that there is no pleading of that section as a defence, nor is there any pleading about breach of fiduciary responsibility on the part of Woods as a defence. In my opinion, compliance with s. 42 is a statutory condition precedent to any right of action for commission, and it is part of a plaintiff's case to prove compliance with that section. In my opinion, there is no need for a defendant to plead it.

Likewise, in my opinion, the requirement of conforming with the obligations resting on a person in a fiduciary capacity is so important that it, too, is part of a plaintiff's case and it is not necessary for the defendant to plead breach of fiduciary responsibility, when an agent is bringing an action against his principal for a commission.

In my view, the simple failure on the part of the plaintiff Cathcart to comply with the provisions of s. 42 of the *Real Estate and Business Brokers Act* in so far as Petrullo is concerned disentitles Cathcart to any commission against Petrullo. Cathcart's claim against Petrullo must be dismissed.

It remains to be considered whether notice given to Kuhn is sufficient compliance with s. 42 and sufficient performance of Woods' fiduciary responsibility to the defendants to entitle Cathcart to claim commission against Kuhn. I think the decision of the Court of Appeal in *Christie et al. v. McCann,* [1972] 3 O.R. 125, 27 D.L.R. (3d) 544, is relevant to this case. That case involved what was then s. 49 of the *Real Estate and Business Brokers Act.* Section 49 is not exactly the same as s. 42(1). In that case the Court of Appeal held that an acknowledgement, which was substantially similar to the notice in this case, was held to comply neither with s. 49, nor to fulfil the obligations of an agent to disclose material matters to his principal.

It may be that the notice in this case does amount to technical compliance with the provisions of s. 42(1) of the Act as it now exists. However, in my opinion, it does in no way amount to compliance with or fulfilment of the high fiduciary responsibility that a real estate agent owes to his principal. The conflict between a purchaser's interest and that of a vendor is so great that, in my opinion, there must be the most complete disclosure by a real estate agent purchasing from his principal before it can be said that he has fulfilled his fiduciary responsibility to his principal.

In such a case, it is my opinion that the agent must give his principal the fullest disclosure of his knowledge of the real estate market in the area where the subject lands were situate. For example, if an agent had information that a property might even possibly be sold to some other purchaser at a higher price than that offered by the agent then that information must be brought to the attention of the principal so that the profit would be that of the principal rather than of the agent. I do not know whether, at the material time, Woods had any such knowledge, but whatever his knowledge was of the market at that time and in that place and any other factor that might affect the value of the property at the time ought to have been brought to the attention of his principals so that they could judge whether the price offered by Bambi was the most advantageous one possible.

A real estate agent dealing with his own client may not simply enter the market-place. The agent is in a position of great trust and he owes great trust to his principal. In my view, the simple disclosure that he was an agent, discloses the most abysmal ignorance of, or misconception of the very fundamental duties arising from the fiduciary relationship of a real estate agent to his principal. In my opinion, this agent was simply greedy. He wanted to purchase the property and he wanted to get a commission from the vendor as well.

In my view, it would be under the most extraordinary circumstances that an agent would be entitled to purchase from his principal and as well obtain a commission from him. In my opinion the notice given in this case is not worth the paper it is written on. It is far from amounting to a fulfilment of the duties arising from the fiduciary relationship that existed between them. In my opinion, Woods has disentitled Cathcart to any commission from anyone. Cathcart's action is dismissed.

CASE PROBLEMS FOR DISCUSSION

Case 1

Brown was the registered owner of several adjoining parcels of vacant land that he had purchased some 12 years before. During that period of time the property had appreciated substantially in value.

Recently, Brown was approached by a real estate agent who suggested that the property might be of interest to a number of developers who had just begun construction in the immediate area. After some discussion, Brown entered into a listing agreement with the agent, and the agent agreed to seek out prospective purchasers for the property. Brown established $200 000 as the selling price he would accept for the land.

For several months, the agent attempted to find a buyer for the property, but without success. When the developers in the area were not interested in the property, the agent returned to Brown and suggested that a corporation in which he had an interest might be willing to purchase the land. To this suggestion Brown replied that it did not matter to him who the purchaser was, so long as the purchaser was prepared to pay his price for the land.

A week later, the agent returned with an offer to purchase from the corporation in which he had an interest. The offer price was $200 000, and was described by the agent as a "clean deal — all cash." The offer was prepared on a standard real estate offer-to-purchase form and contained a clause that read: "Any severance or impost fee plus any expenses for water and sewer connections to be included in the purchase price." Brown queried the clause, and the agent explained that it meant that the cost of obtaining permission to use the three parcels of land as separate building lots, and the hook-up costs of water and sewer lines to them, would be deducted from the purchase price. He added that this "usually did not cost much."

At the agent's urging, Brown signed the offer. Some weeks later, Brown discovered to his sorrow that the severance fees and the water and sewer connections would cost close to 10% of the sale price. The municipality required the payment of 5% of the value of the property as part of the severance fee, and the water and sewer connections accounted for the remainder. When Brown refused to proceed with the transaction, the purchaser instituted legal proceeds for specific performance, and Brown, on the advice of his solicitor, settled the action. As a result, he received only $180 000 for the property, from which the real estate agent demanded a selling commission of 5% based upon the $200 000 selling price.

Brown refused to pay the agent and demanded that the agent compensate him for the $20 000 loss that he had suffered. Eventually, the agent brought an action against Brown for the commission that he claimed was due and owing. Brown, in turn, filed a counter-claim for payment of the $20 000 loss that he had suffered.

Discuss the arguments that might be raised by the parties in this case. Render a decision.

Case 2

Abernathy was the registered owner of a building lot in a residential area of a large city. He entered into an agreement of purchase and sale with Jones, who wished to build a house on the land.

Following the execution of the agreement, Jones engaged a land surveyor to prepare a survey of the property. When the survey was completed, it disclosed that the building lot had a frontage of only 18.15 m. The agreement of sale stated that the lot had "frontage of approximately 18.46 m and a depth of 38.46 m, more or less." Abernathy's deed described the lot as being 18.46 m × 38.46 m.

The discrepancy between the two measurements was apparently due to the fact that the owner of the adjacent lot had erected a fence that encroached on Abernathy's property. The fence had been erected some 15 years before and was taken by the surveyor as the property line.

Determine the rights of the parties in this case. Indicate how the problem might be decided if Jones should refuse to proceed with the agreement.

Case 3

In December of 1993, Fanshawe agreed to purchase a house and lot from Bradley for a purchase price of $158 000. The property was in an area under the Registry System, and Fanshawe determined from the registry office that Bradley had what appeared to be a good title to the land. Unfortunately, he had failed to notice a mortgage that had been registered against the property to secure the indebtedness of Williams, Bradley's predecessor in title. The mortgage had been assumed by Bradley as a part of his purchase from Williams, but that fact had not been revealed to Fanshawe at the time that the offer was drawn.

The offer to purchase that Fanshawe had accepted contained the following clause that read in part: "The purchaser shall have 10 days to examine the title at his own expense.... Save as to any valid objections made to the vendor's title within that time, the purchaser shall be conclusively deemed to have accepted the title of the vendor."

Without knowledge of the existing mortgage, Fanshawe proceeded to pay over to Bradley the $158 000 and received a deed to the property. He registered the deed on January 6, 1993. Some time later, Fanshawe was contacted by the mortgagee and advised that the sum of $35 000 remained due and owing on the mortgage. As Fanshawe was the new owner of the property, the mortgagee would look to him for payment.

To compound Fanshawe's problems, a finance company that had obtained a judgement for $2000 against Bradley in October of 1990 had filed a writ of execution with the sheriff of the county where the property was located. Fanshawe had not searched in the sheriff's office at the time of closing of the transaction. He was surprised to discover that the finance company now claimed that the execution had attached to the land that he had purchased.

Advise Fanshawe of his legal position in this case. What are the rights of the mortgagee and the execution creditor? What action could they take against Fanshawe or the property?

Case 4

Samuel Reynolds was the registered owner of a 200-hectare farm. In July 1981, he retired from farming and gave his son Jacob a deed to the farm property. Jacob did not register the deed, but instead placed it in a safety deposit box that both he and his father rented at a local bank.

Samuel Reynolds died in 1993. His will, dated, May 3, 1978, devised the farm to his daughter, Ruth, who was living on the farm at the time, and who maintained the house for her father. The will also named Ruth as the sole executrix of his estate. When the contents of the will were revealed, Jacob announced to Ruth that their father had given him a deed to the farm some years before, and that he was the owner of the property.

No further discussion of the farm took place between the brother and sister. However, after the debts of the estate were settled, Ruth had a deed to the farm prepared and executed in her capacity as the executrix of her father's estate. Then Ruth delivered the deed to the registry office. The deed conveyed the farm property to her in her personal capacity.

Some months later, Jacob entered into an agreement of purchase and sale for the farm with Smith. Smith made a search at the registry office and discovered that the title to the property was not registered in the name of Jacob, but in the name of his sister, Ruth. Smith refused to proceed with the transaction.

Discuss the rights of the parties in this case. Indicate, with reasons, the identity of the lawful owner of the property. If Jacob should show his deed to Smith and insist that he has title to the property, what argument might Smith raise to counter Jacob's claim?

Case 5

Abner, who was quite elderly, owned a large number of vacant building lots in different parts of a city. He was approached by Bartlett to purchase a particular lot that Abner agreed to sell for $25 000. After making certain that Abner had a good title to the property, Bartlett paid over the purchase price to Abner and received a deed to the land in fee simple. Bartlett didn't register the deed, but placed it in his safety deposit box instead, as it was his intention to sell the lot himself at a later date.

A year later, Abner was approached by Carol's Construction Corporation with an offer to purchase the lot he had sold to Bartlett. The price was $35 000, and Abner, who had forgotten that he had previously sold the lot to Bartlett, agreed to sell it to Carol's Construction Corporation.

The solicitor for Carol's Construction Corporation made the appropriate searches in the land registry office and, from the records there, determined that Abner was the owner of the land in fee simple. The money was then paid to Abner, and Abner delivered a deed to the property, which the lawyer registered at the land registry office.

Some time later, Bartlett entered into an agreement with Davis to sell her the lot for $38 000. When Davis searched the title to the property, she discovered that the lot was registered in the name of Carol's Construction Corporation. Davis then demanded that Bartlett obtain a conveyance of the land from Carol's Construction Corporation to enable him to provide her with a good title in fee simple.

If Davis brought an action for specific performance against Bartlett, discuss the arguments that the parties might raise. Explain the respective positions of Abner and Carol's Construction Corporation in relation to the claim. Speculate as to the ultimate outcome of the situation.

PART VII

The Debtor-Creditor Relationship

Credit transactions play a very important part in the conduct of business in Canada. While some transactions by their very nature do not lend themselves to the use of security for payment, many may be secured by the various types of security instruments that have been developed to provide creditors with some security for payment. The many and varied forms of security available to creditors are outlined in Chapter 31. They include such devices as chattel mortgages, conditional sale agreements, the assignment of book debts, and such specialized rights as mechanics' and construction liens.

Chapter 32, which provides an overview of bankruptcy legislation, is concerned with creditor and debtor rights when a debtor is unable to pay his or her creditors. Because business persons and firms must take risks in the conduct of their affairs in a competitive marketplace, a series of poor business decisions might quickly reduce a financially sound business firm to a firm unable to meet its obligations. When this situation arises, an orderly and fair system to dispose of the debtor's assets is necessary. Bankruptcy legislation provides this framework and procedure.

CHAPTER 31

Security for Debt

INTRODUCTION

The extension of credit or the loan of money by a lender on the strength of the borrower's unsupported promise to repay carries with it considerable risk and a blind faith in the integrity of the borrower. Because debtors have not always been as good as their word, creditors have looked beyond the assurances of the debtors to their lands and goods in order to ensure payment.

One of the earliest methods of securing payment of a debt was the mortgage transaction in which an interest in the debtor's lands would be transferred to the creditor, on the condition that it would be returned when the debt was paid. In this arrangement, the creditor could retain the property in satisfaction of the debt if the debtor failed to pay. Many debtors, however, did not possess land. In those instances, creditors were obliged to consider the debtor's chattels (such as stock-in-trade, furniture, animals, tools, jewellery, etc.) as security for the debt. Security for the debt was effected by either the physical transfer of possession of the goods to the creditor, or by the grant of an interest in the property by way of a transfer of title. Both of these methods are in use today.

The possession of the debtor's property by the creditor forms the basis for the **pledge** or **pawn** bailment situation. However, as a debt relationship, possession is for the most part limited to smaller, expensive chattels such as jewellery and other valuables. The second type of security relationship, the transfer of an interest in the goods, is perhaps the most versatile from a business point of view in that it may use virtually any type of identifiable chattel to secure debt. Of these two methods, the transfer of physical possession of the goods to the creditor is probably the oldest, and one of the first to fall subject to statutory control in England.[1]

---
1. An Act against Brokers (1604), 1 Jac. I, c. 21.

The expansion of commerce during the nineteenth century created a greater demand for credit and for new means to protect the interests of creditors. During this period, the courts came to recognize the different interests of the debtor and creditor in chattels, and of the need to utilize goods as security for debt. This change in attitude was reflected in the development of a variety of legal instruments designed to create security interests in chattels as well as real property.

In England, the chattel mortgage was the first security instrument (apart from the pledge or pawn) to receive statutory recognition and general acceptance. Closely following the **chattel mortgage** was the hire-purchase agreement. Unlike the chattel mortgage, which was similar in purpose and effect to the land mortgage, the **hire-purchase agreement** represented a means of facilitating the sale of goods on credit, whereby the seller retained title to the goods until the goods were paid for, but the buyer acquired possession. While the chattel mortgage could also be used for this purpose, the hire-purchase agreement provided a much simpler procedure for the seller to follow in the event of default by the buyer.

During this same period, economic activity of a rapidly growing business community in Canada produced a demand for additional means of securing credit, and a parallel desire by creditors for means whereby the payment of the debts might be secured. The various security instruments used in England were quickly adopted by Canadian debtors and creditors, occasionally in modified form. The hire-purchase agreement, in particular, found favour in a slightly modified form known as the **conditional sale agreement.** In addition, new security instruments were developed to facilitate the expansion of business and the sale of goods on credit. Chartered banks in Canada were permitted, under the Bank Act,[2] to acquire a security interest in the present and future goods of a debtor in priority over subsequent creditors by following a simple filing procedure set out in the legislation. Laws were also passed to give workmen, suppliers, and building contractors security interests in land by way of **mechanics' lien** legislation. Shortly after the turn of the present century, creditor protection in the form of a **Bulk Sales Act** was introduced to protect the interests of unsecured trade creditors, where a sale "in bulk" was made of business assets.

The rapid growth of commerce during the present century and the tremendous expansion of consumer credit, coupled with the mobility of the population, particularly after 1950, eventually created a need for more modern legislation to deal with security interests. The registration of security interests and the notice protection afforded by most of the statutes, while adequate for a relatively stationary population, proved to be totally inadequate where secured goods moved frequently with a jurisdiction, and from one jurisdiction to another.

The provinces of Ontario and Manitoba were the first to recognize the fact that the security registration and notice requirements, and indeed many of the security instruments themselves, were outmoded with regard to the needs of creditors and debtors in a credit-oriented, mobile society. In Ontario, a draft **Personal Property Security Act,** modelled after the United States' Uniform Commercial Code, Article 9, was prepared in 1964. It was eventually passed by the legislature in June 1967.[3] The act required the establishment of a province-wide registration

---

2. The Bank Act, 1890, 53 Vict., c. 31, s. 74 (Can.).
3. The Personal Property Security Act, 1967 (Ont.), c. 73; now R.S.O. 1990, c. P-10.

system for chattel security interests using a single, computer-based registry. The development of the new system and its implementation required almost six years, with a further three years necessary to complete the change-over from a document file to a notice file system. The new act finally came into force on April 1, 1976. Manitoba, with the benefit of the Ontario experience, introduced somewhat similar legislation in 1973[4] that was proclaimed in force in 1978. More recently, the province of Saskatchewan introduced its own legislation,[5] based upon the United States' Uniform Commercial Code rather than the Ontario and Manitoba legislation. As a result, the modernization of the law in Canada appears once again to show signs of jurisdictional preferences, rather than uniformity. At the present time, the laws with respect to security for debt vary quite substantially — with the provinces of Ontario, Manitoba, Saskatchewan and Alberta, British Columbia and the Yukon territories each with a modified version of the United States' Uniform Commercial Code, Article 9, in place. The remaining common law provinces and the territories continue with the older forms of legislation. The province of Quebec also has provision for the recognition and protection of security interests in chattels under its Civil Code. It is against this backdrop of confusion that creditors must attempt to protect their interests.

FORMS OF SECURITY FOR DEBT

Apart from the mortgage of real property (which is examined in Chapter 28), there are a number of methods that may be used by the parties to credit transactions in order to provide security for the debt. The most common forms of security with respect to chattels are the chattel mortgage, the conditional sale agreement, and the bill of sale. These may be used in appropriate forms for commercial and consumer credit transactions. In addition, a creditor of a commercial firm may take an assignment of book debts to secure the indebtedness of the merchant; while a chartered bank, under the Bank Act, may acquire a security interest in the inventory of wholesalers, retailers, manufacturers, and other producers of goods. Corporations may pledge their real property and chattel assets as security by way of bonds and debentures (including a floating charge). Each of these instruments creates or provides a security interest in the property that a creditor might enforce to satisfy the debt in the event that the debtor should default in payment.

Other special forms of security are available to certain types of creditors, or to creditors in certain circumstances. These include the right of lien available to workers, suppliers, and contractors in the construction industry, and the statutory protection of unsecured trade creditors of a business where the merchant makes a sale in bulk. All of these forms of security are subject to legislation in each province or territory. Although variation exists with respect to each under the different statutes, the nature of the particular security is usually similar in purpose and effect.

Chattel Mortgage

Before the development and judicial recognition of the validity of the chattel mortgage, the most common method of using chattels as security for debt was for the creditor to take physical possession of the goods until payment was made.

---

4. The Personal Property Security Act, 1973 (Man.), c. 5. Now Re-enacted Statutes of Manitoba, 1987, c. P-35.

5. The Personal Property Security Act, 1979-80 (Sask.), c. P-6.1. Proclaimed in force May 1, 1981.

This early form of security involved the transfer of possession, but not title, to the creditor, with an arrangement whereby the creditor might keep the goods or dispose of them if the debtor should default. This form of security for debt has been subject to statutory regulation since as early as 1604 in England, and remains so today. The obvious drawback of this method is that the debtor is deprived of the use of the goods, and the creditor is obliged to care for and protect the goods while they are in his or her possession. To overcome the disadvantages of this form of security, the chattel mortgage was devised. This permitted the debtor to retain the goods, but granted the creditor title until the debt was paid.

In concept, the chattel mortgage is essentially the same as the real property mortgage after which it was designed. Under a chattel mortgage, the debtor transfers the entire interest in the property to the creditor, subject to the right to possession while not in default, and the right to redeem. In Canada, chattel mortgages are subject to legislation in all of the common law provinces and territories. In Ontario, Manitoba, Saskatchewan, Alberta, British Columbia and the Yukon where Personal Property Security Acts are in force, the rights of the parties with respect to chattel security interests are governed by these statutes; the remaining jurisdictions have their own legislation pertaining to this form of security interest. Though provincial variation exists, the nature of the instrument is similar in each province and territory, and the mortgage form itself is largely standardized.

Under a chattel mortgage, the title to the property is transferred to the chattel mortgagee, and the mortgagor retains possession. The mortgage sets out the covenants of the mortgagor, the most important being the covenant to pay the debt and the covenant to insure the goods for the protection of the mortgagee. The mortgage also sets out the rights of the parties in the event of default.

If the mortgagor fails to pay the debt as provided in the chattel mortgage, the mortgagee normally has the right to take possession of the mortgaged goods, and either sell the goods by public or private sale, or proceed with foreclosure.[6] In most jurisdictions, the mortgagee, after taking possession of the goods, must give the mortgagor an opportunity to redeem the goods before the sale or foreclosure may take place. If the goods are sold, any surplus after payment of the debt and the costs of the sale belongs to the mortgagor. However, if the proceeds of the sale are insufficient to cover the debt, the mortgagor remains liable for any deficiency.

The mortgagee's right to foreclosure in the case of a chattel mortgage is much like that of a mortgagee under a land mortgage, but the procedure is less formal.[7] The mortgagor is entitled to an opportunity to redeem under the foreclosure procedure. However, if the mortgagor fails to redeem, the mortgagee then obtains foreclosure, which vests the ownership of the property absolutely in the mortgagee. Foreclosure is seldom used by mortgagees, not only because the procedure is more involved than sale proceedings, but also because the mortgagee is generally interested in receiving payment of the debt rather than acquiring the chattel.

The use of a chattel mortgage as a means of securing debt required the provinces to put in place a number of procedures to protect the creditor and other interested parties. Since a chattel mortgagor retains possession of goods and has

---

6. *Rennick v. Bender,* [1924] 1 D.L.R. 739.

7. *Carlisle v. Tait* (1882), 7 O.A.R. 10. See also, *Warner v. Doran* (1931), 2 M.P.R. 574.

the equity of redemption, it was necessary to provide third parties with notice of the mortgagee's interest in the goods.

To make this information available to the public at large, all jurisdictions have established either a central registry for the province or regional registries (usually at the County Court Office), where a chattel mortgagee might register the mortgage. The registration must be made within a short time after the mortgage is executed. This registration has the effect of giving public notice of the creditor's security interest. The failure to register renders the chattel mortgage void as against any person who purchases the goods for value and without notice of the mortgage, or as against any subsequent encumbrancer who has no actual notice of the prior chattel mortgage. It does not, however, affect the validity of the mortgage as between the mortgagor and the mortgagee.

Unlike the real property mortgagor, who is usually free to sell or dispose of the mortgaged property without the consent of the mortgagee, the chattel mortgagor may not sell the mortgaged chattels without consent. If a mortgagor should sell the goods without the mortgagee's consent, and the chattel mortgage had been properly registered to provide notice to the buyer, the buyer of the goods takes them subject to the mortgage. For this reason, a person who purchases goods from other than a merchant should make certain that the goods are free from encumbrances, and that the seller is the lawful owner before the purchase is effected. This may be done by way of a search in the appropriate public office where registers of chattel mortgages and other security interests in chattels are maintained.

A chattel mortgage may be assigned by a chattel mortgagee if the mortgagee so desires, and this may be done without the consent of the mortgagor. The formalities associated with assignments must, however, be complied with, and the mortgagor must be properly notified of the assignment to the assignee. The assignment of a chattel mortgage in this regard is much like the assignment of a real property mortgage.

Registration requirements usually call for the renewal of the registration from time to time if the mortgage is to run for a long period of time. If a chattel mortgagee fails to renew the registration as required under the statute, the effect is similar to a failure to register initially. A subsequent mortgagee could obtain priority over the initial mortgagee, or a bona fide purchaser for value without notice could obtain a good title to the goods in spite of the outstanding mortgage interest. The fact that the registration of a chattel mortgage expires after a specific time interval has limited the use of discharges of chattel mortgages. However, where a chattel mortgagor has paid the mortgage debt in full, a chattel mortgagee is obliged to provide the mortgagor with a discharge of the mortgage if the mortgagor so desires. This discharge may be registered in the office where the chattel mortgage was registered.

Conditional Sale Agreement

The conditional sale agreement differs from a chattel mortgage in that it is a security interest that arises out of a sale rather than a conventional debt transaction. The conditional sale agreement had its beginnings in the English hire-purchase agreement. The hire-purchase agreement was devised in the early nineteenth century[8]

---

8. See, for example, *Hickenbotham v. Groves* (1826), 2 C. & P. 492, 172 E.R. 223 where reference is made to hotel furniture purchased under a hire-purchase agreement.

to permit a prospective purchaser of goods to acquire possession of the goods immediately under a lease agreement, with an option to purchase the goods at a later date. If the option was exercised, the payments made under the hire agreement were applied to the purchase price, and the title to the goods then passed to the buyer. This type of agreement was developed in the mid-nineteenth century, but it was the adoption of the hire-purchasing agreement by the Singer Manufacturing Company for the purpose of selling sewing machines to the general public that publicized its use as a method of securing debt. It was adopted not long after by the sellers of wagons, carriages, furniture, and most other durable goods.

The conditional sale agreement differs from the hire-purchase agreement in one important aspect. Under the hire-purchase agreement, the "hirer" has the option to purchase the goods. It is only when the option is exercised that the title passes to the hirer, who at that point becomes the buyer. The conditional sale agreement contains no such option. Instead, the installment payments are applied to the purchase price from the outset, but the title does not pass to the buyer until the final payment under the agreement had been made. Under the early conditional sale agreements, if the buyer defaulted on an installment payment, the seller was free to treat the payments as rent for the use of the goods and to recover the goods from the purchaser, since the title had never passed. The passage of legislation governing the use and application of conditional sale agreements altered the rights of the parties and imposed certain duties on sellers in the event of default by the buyer. As has been the case with most matters within the jurisdiction of the provinces, each province established legislation for its own perceived needs. Consequently, the law relating to conditional sale agreements is not uniform throughout the country. More recently, some provinces have introduced new legislation of an all-encompassing nature with respect to personal property security, and have repealed their legislation that dealt specifically with conditional sale agreements.

In those provinces that have legislation governing conditional sale agreements,[9] the legislation provides that the agreement must be in writing and signed by the parties. The agreement need not be in any special form, but must set out a description of the property and the terms and conditions relating to the sale. Since a conditional sale agreement is by definition a sale in which the goods are paid for over time, consumer protection legislation, which, for example, requires the true interest rate and the cost of credit to be revealed, must be complied with in the preparation of the sale agreement. As with chattel mortgages, the conditional buyer has possession of the goods, but not the title. To protect the creditor against subsequent creditors' claims or against a sale of the property to an unsuspecting purchaser, the conditional sale agreement must normally be registered in a public record office (usually the County Court Office) in order that the public be made aware of the seller's title to the property. The legislation, with certain exceptions, provides that a failure to register the agreement renders the transaction void as against a bona fide purchaser for value of the goods without notice of the seller's interest, or as against a subsequent encumbrancer without notice of the prior claim. The failure to register the agreement, however, does not render it void as

---

9. All provinces except Ontario, British Columbia, Manitoba, Quebec, and Saskatchewan. The territories also have legislation for conditional sales agreements.

between the buyer and the seller. It should also be noted that some provinces have exempted the conditional seller from the requirement of registration for certain kinds of goods where the seller's name is affixed to the goods. In some cases, these provinces have provided special registration procedures for conditional sale agreements for specific chattels such as automobiles and farm machinery.

Registration of a conditional sale agreement must usually be made within a relatively short period of time after the sale is made, failing which, the seller must usually obtain a judge's order to permit registration. The time interval for registration varies from province to province and ranges from 20 to 30 days, with the latter being the most common. Once registered, the conditional sale agreement is usually protected for a period of three years.[10] If the goods are moved to another county, or to another province or territory, the registration of the conditional sale agreement would also be necessary in the new location in order to provide continued protection for the seller's interest and rights.

The registration of a conditional sale agreement between a manufacturer (or wholesaler) and a retailer is not effective against a purchaser of the goods from the retailer. A retailer who sells goods in the ordinary course of business would give a good title to the goods to the purchaser, because the retailer had purchased the goods from the manufacturer for the purpose of resale. This particular rule makes good sense from the purchaser's point of view. Where a purchaser makes a purchase of goods from a retailer who deals in the goods, the purchaser should not be obliged to look behind the transaction to make certain that the retailer has good title. Instead, the law provides that the retailer gives a good title if the sale is in the ordinary course of business, and if the goods had been acquired for resale. An exception to this rule exists, however, with used goods. A seller, even though a retailer, may not give a good title to used goods if the goods acquired were subject to the conditional sale made between a retailer and a person who had sold the used goods to a second retailer. For example, a manufacturer of snowmobiles sells a snowmobile to a retailer of snowmobiles under a conditional sale agreement that was subsequently registered. A purchaser of the snowmobile would acquire a good title to the snowmobile from the retailer, even though the conditional sale agreement existed between the manufacturer and the retailer. This is the case because the retailer had purchased the goods for resale. If we assume further that the sale by the retailer to the purchaser was by a registered conditional sale agreement, and the purchaser then traded the used snowmobile to another retailer for a different type of machine, the sale by the second retailer to a subsequent purchaser would not be protected. The purchaser of the used snowmobile would not get a good title to the machine, as the title would still be in the first retailer, who was the conditional seller. The reason why the second sale falls within the exception is that the sale by the first retailer of the snowmobile was an "end sale" and not for the purpose of resale, so the title would not pass from the conditional purchaser to the second retailer. The second retailer, as a result, could not pass a good title to a purchaser of the used machine. It should be noted, however, that the seller under the sale of goods of the province would be subject to the implied warranty that the goods were free from encumbrance. The buyer

---

10. The time period in Nova Scotia is five years. See The Conditional Sales Act, R.S.N.S. 1989, c. 84, s. 13(1).

would therefore be in a position to demand that the seller pay off the secured creditors' claim, and recover the goods.

A conditional seller may assign to a third party the title to goods covered by a conditional sale agreement. The rules applicable to the assignment of ordinary contracts also apply to conditional sale agreements. A common practice of merchants who sell goods by way of conditional sale agreements is to arrange with a financial institution (usually a finance company) to purchase the agreements once signed by the buyers, and to collect the money owing. The merchant with this type of arrangement assigns the agreements to the financial institution that would then register the agreements, give notice to the conditional buyers of the assignment, and collect the installments as they fall due. As with all contracts, the assignee takes the agreement as it stands between the conditional buyer and the seller. Any defence that the buyer might have against the seller could also be raised against the assignee.

Apart from the protection of the seller's interest in the goods, conditional sale agreement legislation is generally designed to provide the buyer with relief against sellers who place onerous terms in the agreement itself. This usually takes the form of providing the buyer with time to redeem after default, since sellers frequently provide in their conditional sale agreements that they are entitled to repossess and sell the goods immediately on default.

Except in those provinces with consumer protection legislation that prohibits repossession where a substantial portion of the purchase price has been paid,[11] or where the goods are exempt from repossession,[12] the seller is generally free to repossess the goods when default occurs. Again, this is subject to qualification, as some provinces require that a "notice of intention to repossess" be first given, or a judge's order be obtained before the goods may be taken. However, in no case may force be used to acquire possession of the goods. Once acquired however, the seller may then proceed with the sale of the chattels to recover the amount owing on the debt. To provide relief from a seller's right of immediate sale, and to introduce an element of fairness in the relationship, a buyer in default is given a period of time to find the funds necessary to complete the payment. Most provincial statutes require the seller who repossesses goods on default to hold the goods for a period of time before selling them. The time interval varies depending upon the province and method of repossession,[13] and ranges from 14 to 30 days, with 20 days being the most common time period for the buyer to redeem the goods.

A seller who repossesses goods with the intention of resale must comply strictly with the resale procedure requirements of the statute. For example, depending upon the particular province, the seller must provide written notice to the buyer of his or her intention to sell the goods. The notice must contain a detailed description of the goods, the amount owing and required in order for the buyer to redeem, and the time period in which the buyer has to make payment. In

---

11. New Brunswick, Nova Scotia, and Ontario, for example, prohibit repossession after two-thirds of the purchase price has been paid unless a court order is obtained. Manitoba fixes the amount at 75% of the selling price.

12. Saskatchewan, for example, restricts the right to repossess certain goods such as agricultural implements and certain household goods. See The Exemptions Act, R.S.S. 1978, c. E-14, s. 2.

13. Alberta provides that the sheriff must repossess and hold the goods for 14 days. See the Seizures Act, R.S.A. 1980, c. S-11, s. 28.

order to conduct a valid sale, the seller must carefully comply with the notice requirements, then wait the full statutory period before proceeding with the sale.

If the buyer fails to pay the balance owing within the prescribed time period, the seller may then proceed with the sale, and the proceeds obtained would be applied to the outstanding indebtedness. In some provinces, the seller may look to the buyer for any deficiency if the proceeds of the sale fail to pay the balance owing in full. However, this right is only available when the seller has expressly established the right in the conditional sale agreement. Any surplus that the conditional seller may receive as a result of the sale, must be turned over to the buyer. All of the common law provinces and territories, except Saskatchewan, provide an alternate remedy to the conditional seller in the event of default by permitting the seller to take legal action on the contract to recover the amount owing.

Bills of Sale

A bill of sale is a contract in which the title to goods passes to the buyer. However, it is important from the buyer's point of view that certain formalities be followed where goods are purchased, and possession of the goods remains with the seller. Under these circumstances, if the buyer wishes to protect his or her interest in the goods, the bill of sale must be registered in accordance with the requirements of the provincial legislation relating to this type of transaction.

The territories and all provinces except Quebec have legislation that requires a buyer of goods who takes title but not immediate possession to register the bill of sale in a designated public registry office (usually the County Court Office) within a specified time after the bill of sale is executed. The time for registration varies from province to province, and ranges from 5 days to 30 days. Most statutes require that the bill of sale be accompanied by affidavit evidence of the buyer to the effect that the sale was a bona fide sale, and not for the purpose of defeating the claims of the seller's creditors. In addition, most provinces require affidavit proof that the seller signed the bill of sale, and some provinces impose special requirements on the parties where the bill of sale concerns the sale of an automobile.

The purpose of the legislation requiring the registration of the bill of sale is two-fold. First, it protects the interest or title of the buyer in the goods in the event that the seller should attempt to sell the goods a second time to another, unsuspecting buyer. Second, the registration provides public notice that the title has passed to the buyer, and creditors of the seller will be made aware that the ownership of the goods in the hands of the seller lies elsewhere. The affidavit of bona fides attached to the bill of sale is designed to discourage sellers from transferring the ownership of goods in their possession to a third party by way of a bill of sale to defeat their creditors. The fact that the document is registered in a public record office represents notice to the public at large of the transaction that has taken place.

Registration is generally effective for three years.[14] A failure to register would permit an innocent third party who purchases the goods from the seller to obtain a

---

14. Registration in Prince Edward Island is effective for five years. See the Bills of Sale Act, R.S.P.E.I. 1974, c. B-3, s. 11(1).

good title to the goods, leaving the unregistered owner with only a right of action against the seller.

Assignment of Book Debts

The assignment of book debts is a method whereby a creditor of a merchant might take an assignment of the accounts receivable of the merchant and collect what is owed to the merchant from customers. The assignment is similar in many respects to the ordinary assignment of a contract in the sense that the debtors must be notified to make payment to the assignee, if the assignee should decide to have the debts paid directly to him or her. Because merchants are not enthusiastic at the thought that their customers will be notified by the creditor to make payments of their accounts directly to the creditor, the creditor and the merchant frequently agree that the general assignment of book debts will not be acted upon by the creditor while the merchant is not in default under the debt payment arrangement between them.

The assignment of book debts is subject to registration requirements under provincial legislation, in order that the creditor might preserve his or her claim to the book debts as security.[15] Ontario, for example, requires an assignment of book debts to be registered within 21 days of the date upon which the assignment was executed.[16] Most other provinces have similar registration provisions. Registration is usually in the same public office where chattel mortgages and conditional sale agreement registers are maintained. Ontario, Manitoba, and Saskatchewan provide for registration of the security interest in a province-wide central registry under their personal property security legislation.[17] The mere fact that the assignment has been registered, however, does not give the creditor under a general assignment priority over a subsequent creditor who obtained an assignment of a specific debt and gave notice to the debtor of the merchant to make payment of the debt to him or her.[18] A particular advantage of the properly executed and registered assignment of book debts, however, is that the assignee will acquire a secured claim to the book debts over the trustee in bankruptcy should the merchant become insolvent.

Personal Property Security Legislation

By 1990, Ontario the four western provinces,[19] and the Yukon Territory had modernized their legislation concerning the use of chattels and other personal property as security for debt by the introduction of personal property security legislation. In addition, a number of other provinces were considering similar legislation.

---

15. This is provided under personal property security legislation in some provinces. See, for example, Ontario, the Personal Property Security Act, R.S.O. 1990, c. P-10, s. 47(3).
16. Personal Property Security Act, R.S.O., 1990, c. P-10, s. 2(b).
17. See, for example, Ontario, the Personal Property Security Act, R.S.O. 1990, c. P-10.
18. *Snyder's Ltd. v. Furniture Finance Corp. Ltd.* (1930), 66 O.L.R. 79.
19. Alberta, Ontario, Manitoba and Saskatchewan. The Yukon Territory introduced personal property security legislation in 1982, which became fully effective on May 31, 1985. For some years, Alberta maintained a central registry for motor vehicles and certain chattel registrations, and in 1988 introduced the Personal Property Security Act, S.A., 1988, c. P. 40.5.

The province of Ontario was the first Canadian province to implement the new system, which is based upon the United States' Uniform Commercial Code, Article 9. In concept, the act represents a complete overhaul of the older systems of registration of security interests and the elimination of a number of conflicting rules with respect to creditor's rights. The general thrust of the new legislation is to simplify transactions associated with securing debts, and to provide a simple system for the registration of all personal property security interests. The act recognizes the fact that all of the older security devices had a common purpose: to provide the creditor with a security interest in personal property. To simplify the process of establishing the security interest, the legislation abolishes the registration requirements of the older security devices and replaces them with a single registration procedure for the security interest. This interest would represent, for example, the rights of the mortgagee under a chattel mortgage, or the rights of a conditional seller under a conditional sale agreement. The property to which this security interest attaches is called the **collateral,** which may be almost any type of personal property.

Under the act, the proper registration of the security agreement (usually called a financing statement) **perfects** the security interest in the creditor. The registration establishes the creditor's priority right to the security interest in the personal property.

The Ontario statute establishes a procedure whereby security interests are registered at county land registry offices in Ontario, and the information is then transmitted to a central, computer-based storage system. This enables any person to make a search to determine if a security interest is claimed in personal property located anywhere in the province. A failure to register, as required under the act, would allow a subsequent bona fide purchaser to obtain a good title to the goods, or a subsequent creditor to obtain a security interest in the goods in priority over the unregistered security interest.

If a debtor defaults under a security agreement, depending upon the nature and provisions of the security agreement, the creditor may seize the collateral and dispose of it by public or private sale in accordance with the procedure set out in the statute. In the case of consumer goods, the creditor must normally proceed with the sale within 90 days of repossession where the debtor has paid at least 60% of the amount owing. If the sale provides a surplus after all expenses have been paid, the balance must be paid over to the debtor. The right to redeem, however, unless otherwise provided in writing, is available to the debtor until the collateral is sold by the creditor, or until the creditor signifies in writing his or her intention to retain the goods in full satisfaction of the debt.

Secured Loans under the Bank Act, s. 178

In addition to ordinary secured loans that a bank may make under the Bank Act,[20] the legislation gives a bank the right to lend money to wholesalers, retailers, shippers, and dealers in "products of agriculture, products of the forest, products of the quarry and mine, products of the sea, lakes, and rivers, of goods, wares and merchandise, manufactured or otherwise" on the security of such goods or products,

---

20. The Bank Act, R.S.C. 1985, c. B-1.

and to lend money to manufacturers on their goods and inventories. The act also makes special provision for such loans to farmers, fishermen, and forestry producers on their equipment and goods as well as their crops and products.[21]

The Bank Act provides that the borrower must sign a particular bank form and deliver it to the bank in order to vest in the bank a first and preferential lien on the goods or equipment similar to that which the bank might have acquired if it had obtained a warehouse receipt or bill of lading for the particular goods.[22] The bank usually extends the security interest to include after-acquired goods of a similar nature. To perfect its security interest, the bank need only register with the Bank of Canada a notice of intention to take the goods as security for the loan at any time within the three years prior to the date on which the security is given.[23] The registration is designed to give the bank priority over subsequent creditors and persons who acquire the goods (except for bona fide purchasers of goods) or equipment, and over the trustee in bankruptcy in the event that the debtor should become insolvent. However, the priority is not absolute. The failure to register the notice of intention as required under the act would render the transaction void as against subsequent purchasers and mortgagees in good faith and for value.

The obvious advantage of the procedure under the Bank Act is the ease by which the security interest is established, and the broad reach of the claim to after-acquired goods. It use, however, is limited only to those lenders set out in the legislation. Although this type of loan is available to a large group in terms of the commercial or business community, it represents only a small number, when compared to the consumer-borrower group who are not eligible for loans under this particular section of the act.

Bank Credit Cards

Credit cards issued by charter banks and other financial institutions represent a type of payment instrument frequently used in consumer purchase of chattels and services. While not security instruments in themselves, credit cards provide for security of payment to the merchant that sells goods to the cardholder. A credit card transaction is supported by two separate agreements:

(1) a contract between the bank and the merchant whereby the merchant agrees to accept the credit cards issued by the bank (when offered by the cardholder) as payment for purchases;

(2) a contract between the bank and the applicant of a credit card which provides that the applicant, when issued a credit card, will pay the bank for all debts incurred by the cardholder through the use of the card.

The contract between the bank and the merchant assures the merchant of prompt payment of all purchases made by the cardholder using the bank card, as the bank in effect guarantees payment of the bank card amounts. In return for this security of payment the merchant pays the bank a small percentage charge based upon the amount of the bank card sales.

---

21. Ibid., s. 178(1).
22. Ibid., s. 178(2).
23. Ibid., s. 178(4).

In the contract or agreement between the bank and the cardholder, the cardholder agrees to compensate the bank for all purchases made using the bank card. The bank usually issues monthly statements listing card purchases, and if the cardholder pays the statements promptly (usually within a stipulated time period of 10 to 21 days) no interest is charged on the amount of the statement. Amounts unpaid are subject to interest charges and cardholders are expected to make certain minimum payments on account of their outstanding indebtedness on a monthly basis. Most credit cards have an established upper limit on the amount of credit the bank will extend or allow to be charged against the credit card.

While security of payment is provided to merchants who agree to honour the bank's credit cards, the credit extended by the bank to the cardholder is normally unsecured, as the cardholder does not pledge any particular security as collateral for what is essentially a loan extended to the cardholder. For this reason, credit limits for cardholders are often fixed at relatively low amounts (for example, $5000). The credit limit, however, may vary substantially depending upon the credit worthiness of the cardholder or the type of card issued by the financial institution.

Bonds, Debentures, and Floating Charges

Corporations may use a variety of different methods of acquiring capital using the assets of the corporation as security for the debt. A corporation may, for example, mortgage its fixed assets, or it may pledge its chattels as security under a chattel mortgage. In addition to these various methods, a corporation has open to it the opportunity to raise funds by way of the issue of bonds and debentures.

Bonds and **debentures** are instruments issued by corporations that represent a pledge of the assets of the corporation or its earning power as security for debt. The two terms are used interchangeably to refer to debt obligations of the corporation, since no precise legal definition exists for either of these terms. Nevertheless, the term *bond* is generally used to refer to a debt that is secured by way of a mortgage, as charge on the assets of the corporation. Such bonds are sometimes referred to as **mortgage bonds.**

The term *debenture* is frequently used with reference to debt that is unsecured or secured to the extent that it takes priority over unsecured creditors, but subsequent to secured debt such as first mortgage bonds. The practice, however, of issuing bonds that secure debt by way of a mortgage on the fixed assets and chattels, and a floating charge on all other assets, leaves subordinate security holders with very little security in the event that the corporation becomes insolvent. As a result, holders of subordinate obligations are sometimes in much the same position as ordinary unsecured creditors.

Where the security is given to a single creditor, such as a bank or other financial institution, a single instrument is prepared and executed. However, where the amount of capital desired through the issue of the bonds or debentures is substantial, and the terms of the debt obligation lengthy, the common practice is to prepare a **trust indenture** that embodies all of the terms and conditions of the indebtedness. Then shorter, less detailed debentures are issued that incorporate the terms of the trust indenture by reference. These are then sold to the public as a means of acquiring capital for the corporation, and the purchasers of the securities become creditors of the corporation.

The practice of including a floating charge in the debt instrument provides the bond or debenture holders with added security. A **floating charge** is a charge that does not affect the assets of the corporation or its operation so long as the terms and conditions of the security instrument are complied with. But in the event that some breach of the terms of the debt instrument occurs (such as a failure to make a payment on the debt) the charge ceases to "float" and crystallizes. At that point it becomes a fixed charge and attaches to the particular security covered by it. For example, finished goods of a manufacturer may be covered by a floating charge. While the charge remains as an equitable charge, the corporation is free to sell or dispose of the goods, as it has the title and the right to do so. Default, however, will crystallize the charge, and it will immediately attach to the remaining goods in possession of the corporation. The goods will then become a part of the security that the holders of the debt obligation may look to for the purpose of satisfying their claims.

The nature of the floating charge and its operation as security both before and after default was succinctly described in the case of *Evans v. Rival Granite Quarries Ltd.*[24] where the court said:

> A floating security is not a future security; it is a present security, which presently affects all the assets of the company expressed to be included in it. On the other hand, it is not a specific security; the holder cannot affirm that the assets are specifically mortgaged to him. The assets are mortgaged in such a way that the mortgagor can deal with them without the concurrence of the mortgagee. A floating security is not a specific mortgage of the assets, plus a licence to the mortgagor to dispose of them in the course of his business, but is a floating mortgage applying to every item comprised in the security, but not specifically affecting any item until some event occurs or some act on the part of the mortgagor is done which causes it to crystallize into a fixed security. Mr. Shearman argued that it was competent to the mortgagee to intervene at any moment and to say that he withdrew the licence as regards any particular item. That is not in my opinion the nature of the security; it is a mortgage presently affecting all the items expressed to be included in it, but not specifically affecting any item till the happening of the event which causes the security to crystallize as regards all the items. This crystallization may be brought about in various ways. A receiver may be appointed, or the company may go into liquidation and a liquidator be appointed, or any event may happen which is defined as bringing to an end the licence to the company to carry on business. There is no case in which it has been affirmed that a mortgagee of this description may at any moment forbid the company to sell a particular piece of property or may take it himself and keep it, and leave the licence to carry on the business subsisting as regards everything else. This would be inconsistent with the real bargain between the parties, which is that the mortgagee gives authority to the company to use all its property until the licence to carry on business comes to an end.

Legislation in each province requires corporations, which issue securities or pledge their assets by different forms of debt obligations, to file the particulars of the bond or debenture and a true copy of the debt instrument with the office of the Minister responsible for the administration of the act or under the personal property security legislation of the province.[25] The failure to do so within the prescribed time (usually 30 days) renders the bonds or debentures void as against

---

24. *Evans v. Rival Granite Quarries Ltd.,* [1910] 2 K.B. 979.

25. In Ontario, for example, the filing must be made under the Personal Property Security Act, R.S.O. 1990, c. P-10, s. 84.

any subsequent purchasers or encumbrancers for value and without notice of the prior debt obligations.

STATUTORY PROTECTION OF CREDITOR SECURITY

In addition to the secured rights that a creditor might obtain by taking a security interest in the property of the debtor, most provinces have provided the creditors of certain debtors with special statutory rights in cases where the actions of the debtor could seriously affect the rights of the creditors to payment. The first of these statutes is the Bulk Sales Act, and the second, the Mechanics' Lien Act or Construction Lien Act. Both are designed to protect the rights of creditors in transactions in which the creditor may not be a party, and both provide the creditor with rights that were not originally available at common law.

Bulk Sales Act

Statutes pertaining to sales "in bulk" refer to the sale of all or large quantities of stock by a merchant in a transaction that is not in the ordinary course of business, or the sale of assets and equipment of the business itself to a purchaser. The purpose of the legislation is to protect the creditors of a merchant by requiring the merchant to comply with the procedure set down in the act for all sales not in the ordinary course of business.

Canadian bulk sales legislation had its origins in the laws of the United States, rather than the laws of England. The first bulk sales statute was enacted in Ontario in 1917,[26] and most other provinces have since followed the Ontario example. At the present time, all provinces and the territories have bulk sales legislation in place. Provincial variation exists, in spite of attempts to draft uniform legislation.

Under the statutes of most provinces, a prospective buyer of the goods or assets of a business is obliged to follow the procedure set out in the act, otherwise the sale may be declared void, and the buyer perhaps unable to recover the purchase price from the seller. The procedure set down for bulk sales generally permits the prospective buyer to make only a small deposit or down payment on the goods or equipment. The buyer must withhold the balance until the seller in bulk either provides an affidavit to the effect that all creditors have been paid, or that arrangements have been made to pay the creditors in full from the proceeds of the sale. In the latter case, unless the creditors waive their rights in writing, the prospective buyer is obliged to have the proceeds paid to a trustee, who will arrange for the payment of the creditors.[27]

In some provinces, a statement of indebtedness must also be provided to the prospective buyer, showing the amounts owing to each creditor of the seller. If the creditors' claims do not exceed a stipulated amount (in Ontario, unsecured and secured creditor claims must each be less than $2500)[28] the buyer may then pay over the balance. In some provinces, it is also possible to obtain an order from the court to complete a sale in bulk if the court can be convinced that the transaction is in the best interests of the creditors.[29]

---

26. The Bulk Sales Act, 1917 (Ont.), 7 Geo V, c. 33.
27. See, for example, Ontario, the Bulk Sales Act, R.S.O. 1990, c. B-14, s. 9.
28. The Bulk Sales Act, R.S.O. 1990, c. B-14, s. 8.
29. See, for example, Ontario, the Bulk Sales Act, R.S.O. 1990, c. B-14, s. 3.

If the buyer fails to comply with the act, an unpaid creditor may within a stipulated time, which ranges from 60 days in Saskatchewan[30] to 6 months in most
other provinces,[31] attack the sale in bulk and have it declared void. The effect of
such a declaration would be to make the goods purchased by the buyer available
to satisfy the creditor's claims, and leave the buyer only with recourse against the
seller who may, under the circumstances, be difficult to find.

Mechanics' or Construction Liens

A mechanics' lien (which may be referred to as a builder's or construction lien) is
a statutory right of a worker or contractor to claim a security interest in property
to ensure payment for labour or materials applied to land or a chattel. A mechanics' lien is a creature of statute. Hence, it is not a right available to a party except
as provided under the legislation responsible for its creation and application. The
lien takes two forms: a lien against real property, and a lien against chattels. Each
is distinct and separate in the manner in which it is claimed and enforced.
Consequently, some provinces have established separate legislation to govern the
two distinct types of liens. Other provinces, however, have incorporated both in
the same statute, but distinguished the procedure applicable to each.[32] Where separate legislation has been enacted, the law related to chattels is usually described
as a mechanics' lien act, and the real property lien legislation as a construction
(or builder's) lien act.

A mechanics' lien, like a sale in bulk, is subject to legislation that found its
way into the common law provinces of Canada by way of the United States. The
right of lien under the circumstances provided in mechanics' lien statutes is not of
common law origin, but rather has its roots in Roman law, and later, in the civil
codes of European countries. As a result, the province of Quebec was the first
Canadian province to possess legislation similar to the Mechanics' Lien Acts that
were eventually enacted by the common law provinces. Manitoba and Ontario
were the first common law provinces to adopt mechanics' lien legislation,[33] and
the other provinces, over time, followed suit. At present, all provinces and territories in Canada have legislation that provides workers with a right of lien against
land. Although the legislation is not uniform, the general thrust and application of
the law is similar everywhere.

A right of lien to protect the labour and materials of workers and contractors
was found to be necessary in the latter part of the nineteenth century, when the
vulnerability of persons engaged in the construction industry became evident. The
construction of buildings, regardless of size, usually requires large quantities of
materials and the special skills of many craftspeople and professionals. At the
time, these parties were tied together by a series of contracts under which each
was required to invest labour or materials in a property in which they had no
security interest to protect their investment. If the owner sold the property and
failed to pay the contractor, the contractor's only recourse was legal action for

---

30. The Bulk Sales Act, R.S.S. 1978, c. B-9, s. 39.

31. See, for example, Ontario, the Bulk Sales Act, R.S.S. 1990, c. B-14, s. 19.

32. The legislation of Saskatchewan, for example, covers both types of liens in the same statute. See the Mechanics'
Lien Act, R.S.S. 1978 c. M-7 s. 61.

33. The Mechanics' Lien Act of 1873. 36 Vict. c. 27 (Ont.); the Mechanics' Lien Act. 36 Vict. c. 31 (Man.) (1873).

breach of contract against the owner. Subcontractors were equally vulnerable. If the principal contractor became insolvent during the course of construction, the subcontractors and workers had no recourse against the owner of the property for payment, because their contract was with the principal contractor. In order to protect all parties who expended labour and materials on property, the Mechanics' Lien Acts were passed to give each worker or contractor a right to claim a lien against the property as security for payment, regardless of the relationship between the party and the property owner.

Mechanics' lien legislation as it pertains to chattels varies to some extent from province to province, but the general thrust of the various statutes is to allow a person who repairs a chattel to lawfully retain possession of the goods until payment is made. The legislation usually provides that where the owner does not pay for the repairs within a specific time (usually a number of months) the repair person on notice may advertise the goods for sale by public auction. If the public auction sale does not provide sufficient money to cover the repair account, the owner may still be liable for the shortfall in the amount payable for the repairs.

With respect to building construction and similar land based projects, the construction or builder's lien statutes of all provinces broadly define the term "owner" to include not only the person who holds property in fee simple, but persons with lesser legal or equitable interests in property. They may also include a mortgagee or a tenant who enters into a construction contract. The broad definition of the term "owner" is compatible with the intent of the act: to prevent the person entitled to an interest in the real property from obtaining the benefit of the labour and materials expended upon the land without providing compensation for the benefit received.

The class of persons entitled to claim a lien is equally as broad in most jurisdictions. It includes wage earners, subcontractors, material suppliers, suppliers of rental equipment used for construction purposes (in some provinces), the principal or prime contractor and, under certain circumstances, the architect.[34] In addition to providing the right of lien to persons who expend labour and materials to enhance the value of real property, the legislation also provides a simplified procedure for the enforcement of lien rights. Low cost and general compliance with formalities are emphasized in the enforcement procedure, but certain aspects, such as the time-limits set out in the act, are rigidly enforced.

The right to claim a lien arises when the first work is done on the property by the claimant, or when the material supplier delivers the first supplies to the building site. Thereafter, the worker, subcontractor, or material supplier may claim a lien at any time during the performance of the contract, and until a stipulated time after the work has been substantially performed. The time-limit following the date on which the last work was done (or material supplied) varies from province to province, and ranges from 30 days to 60 days, depending upon the nature of the work and the province. For example, in British Columbia, the time for registration of a lien is 31 days from the date on which the last work was done; but in the case of a mine or quarry, the time-limit is extended to 60 days.[35] In Ontario,

---

34. *Re Computime Canada Ltd.* (1971), 18 D.L.R. (3d) 127.
35. Builders Lien Act, R.S.B.C. 1979, c. 40, s. 22(1).

the time-limit is 45 days.[36] In order to preserve the right to a lien, a lien claim must be registered in the Land Registry Office in the jurisdiction where the land is situated, and notice of the lien claim given to the owner of the property.[37] In some provinces, however, a lien claimant's rights may be protected if another claimant has instituted lien proceedings and filed a certificate of action within the time-limits appropriate to protect the unregistered claimant. The registration of a lien gives the lien claimant priority over subsequent encumbrancers and subsequent mortgages of the lands.

Following the registration of a lien claim, a lien action must be commenced within a relatively short period of time based upon the date when the last work was done, materials supplied, or lien filed (depending upon the province). An informal legal procedure then follows to determine the rights of the lien claimants and the liability of the contractor and "owners" of the property. Lien claimants are treated equally in a lien action and, with the exception of wage earners who are entitled to all or a part of their wage claims in priority over other lien claimants, all are entitled to a share pro rata in the funds or property available.

In order to avoid disputes that may arise between the contractor and subcontractors, or others, the owner may avoid liability for payment of lien claims by complying with the **hold-back** provisions of the act. These sections require the owner to withhold a certain percentage of the monies payable to the contractor (10% in the case of Ontario)[38] for a period of time following the completion of the contract (45 days in the case of Ontario).[39] The hold-back replaces the land for lien purposes. If claims for lien should be filed within the period that the "owner" is obliged to hold back the funds, the owner may pay the lien claims (or pay the money into court if the claims exceed the hold-back) and obtain a discharge of the lien or a **vacating order** to clear the liens from the title of the property. The failure of an owner to hold back the required funds would oblige the owner to pay the amount necessary to clear the liens (up to the amount of the required hold-back) in order to free the property from lien claims. If the "owner" should be insolvent or unable to pay the hold-back, the lien claimants may proceed with the lien action and have the property sold by the court to satisfy their claims.

Some provinces, notably British Columbia, Manitoba, New Brunswick, Ontario, and Saskatchewan, provide additional protection to subcontractors and wage earners by declaring in their legislation that all sums received by the contractor from the "owner" constitute trust funds for the benefit of the subcontractors, workers, and material suppliers. These funds must be used first for the payment of the suppliers of labour and materials before the contractor is entitled to the surplus. A failure to distribute the funds in this fashion would constitute a breach of trust on the part of the contractor.

The trust provision of the various lien acts has been the subject of much litigation in order to establish the rights of creditors and other parties to the funds. Nevertheless, the provision remains as an added security for the payment of those who depend on the contractor for payment for their goods or services.

---

36. Construction Lien Act, R.S.O. 1990, c. C-30 s. 3.

37. Ibid., s. 34.

38. Ibid., s. 22(1).

39. Ibid.

SUMMARY

The desire of creditors to reduce risk in debt transactions is reflected in the development of the large and varied assortment of debt instruments available to the business community today. With the exception of the land mortgage and the pledge of goods as security for debt, most of these instruments have been developed within the past few centuries. The chattel mortgage was one of the first security instruments to be developed and recognized as a means of securing debt against chattels by way of a transfer of the title to the creditor. The conditional sale agreement was used in a somewhat similar fashion, but the seller simply retained the title and gave the conditional buyer possession. When the price was paid, title passed to the buyer. Both of these instruments were used to facilitate purchases of goods.

Corporations are permitted to use a number of different methods of raising capital on the security of their assets. These take the form of bonds and debentures, which may represent charges on specific assets by way of mortgage, or they may be simply unsecured debentures or debentures secured by way of a floating charge.

The need for business to finance purchase of goods resulted in the development of other security interests. The assignment of book debts permitted creditors to obtain security for debt on loans to merchants. Also, under the Bank Act, banks were entitled to make loans to wholesalers, manufacturers, lumber businesses, farmers, and fishermen on a security interest in inventories, equipment, crops, and machinery. In addition to these forms of creditor security, statutory protection for unsecured creditors also developed in the form of legislation designed to establish creditors' rights to payment when a sale of the assets of a business was made in bulk, or where subcontractors, workers, and material suppliers increased the value of property by their labour and materials. In the former case, unsecured creditors in a bulk sale were given the right to have a sale declared void if they were not paid. In the latter case, mechanics' lien legislation established a statutory right of lien against the property to secure payment of the claim of subcontractors and workers.

Apart from legislation designed to establish special rights for unsecured creditors and persons in the construction industry, all security interests are designed to protect creditors' claims to the debtor's assets in the event of default. Because of the many confusing procedures and security instruments associated with these interests, attempts have been made by some provinces to streamline and simplify the procedures. These statutes, which are commonly referred to as Personal Property Security Acts, are already in place in British Columbia, Ontario, Manitoba, Alberta, the Yukon, and Saskatchewan.

DISCUSSION QUESTIONS

1. How does a chattel mortgage differ from a pledge or pawn of a chattel?
2. What procedure must a chattel mortgagee follow to preserve the security of the mortgage against subsequent encumbrancers or purchasers?
3. Describe the procedure that a chattel mortgagee may follow to recover the debt, if default should occur.
4. How does a conditional sale agreement differ from a chattel mortgage?

5. Explain how a conditional seller may realize on the security if default in payment occurs.
6. Describe the effect of personal property security legislation on chattel mortgages and conditional sales agreements in those provinces where such legislation has been introduced.
7. What is the purpose and effect of an assignment of book debts? Identify the circumstances where registration must take place.
8. Why must a bill of sale be registered in certain circumstances? Identify the circumstances where registration must take place.
9. Outline the special types of security instruments that may be issued by corporations as security for debt.
10. Define: bond, floating charge, debenture.
11. What types of assets may be used as security by chartered banks for loans made under section 178 of the Bank Act?
12. Describe the procedure that a bank must follow to secure a loan under section 178 of the Bank Act.
13. What is a bank credit card? In what way does it secure a debt?
14. Explain the purpose of the procedure set down in the Bulk Sales Act. What is the effect of a sale that does not comply with the act?
15. Why was legislation for mechanics' lien (sometimes referred to as construction lien) necessary?
16. Outline the general procedure that a subcontractor would follow to secure payment under mechanics' lien legislation.
17. What must an "owner" of property under construction do to protect against mechanics' lien claims attaching to the property?

MINI-CASE PROBLEMS

1. X purchased an automobile under a conditional sale agreement from Y. Y registered the agreement in accordance with the provincial security registration requirements. X sold the automobile to Z without revealing the fact that it was subject to a conditional sale agreement. X defaulted on the payments to Y. Advise Y of his rights at law.
2. A engaged B to build a garage for her on her property. B constructed the garage with materials purchased on credit from C Co. A paid B. B did not pay C Co. Advise C Co. of their rights.

JUDICIAL DECISION

This case of *Dolan v. Bank of Montreal* illustrates the distinction that the law makes between a chattel mortgage and a mortgage of real property (land). The principal issue in this case is whether a mobile home is a chattel (and hence covered by a chattel mortgage) or whether, by the acts of the owner, the mobile home became a part of the realty upon which it was located.

The court is obliged to examine the nature of a chattel such as a mobile home, and the case first sets out the law pertaining to when a chattel becomes attached to land. A number of other cases are examined by the court in reaching the conclusion that because the owner of the mobile home also owned the land, the improvements made to make it permanent on the site resulted in the chattel becoming a part of the realty. This conclusion led the court to decide that the seizure rights of the bank under the chattel mortgage could not be executed.

Chattel Mortgage on Mobile Home — Whether Mobile Home Attached to Land is a Chattel

Dolan et al. v. Bank of Montreal (1985), 5 P.P.S.A.C. 196.

Dolan was the owner of a lot and he purchased a mobile home as a residence. The mobile home was moved to the lot, its wheels and undercarriage removed, and a porch added. The bank later took a chattel mortgage on the mobile home as security for a loan. Dolan defaulted on the loan, and the bank attempted to seize the mobile home. The issue before the court was whether the mobile home was a chattel subject to seizure under the chattel mortgage.

The Saskatchewan Court of Appeal reviewed the judgement of the trial court (set out in part below), then followed with its judgement that dismissed the appeal by the bank.

MATHESON, J.:

...The mobile home has had its wheels and undercarriage removed, and it rests on concrete blocks and is skirted with wood panelling. A porch addition was built onto the side of the mobile home and concrete steps were connected into place, as was a concrete patio. Sewer, water and power services were trenched and connected with the mobile home in May 1976, and there has been extensive landscaping of the lot. Photographs of the mobile home convey an impression of permanence. Nevertheless, the bank has asserted that all of these facts cannot be distinguished from those recited in *Burlington Administration Group Ltd. v. Nikkel* (1979), 17 B.C.L.R. 229 (B.C.S.C.); *Dunwoody Ltd. v. Farm Credit Corp.,* [1982] 1 W.W.R. 190, 15 Man.R. (2d) 208 (*sub nom. Re Plett and Plett*), 41 C.B.R. (N.S.) 209 (Man.Q.B.); *Royal Bank v. Beyak* (1981), 8 Sask. R. 145 (Sask.Q.B.). It was concluded in each of these cases that a mobile home had not become affixed to real property. The opposite conclusion was reached, based on similar facts, in *Plaza Equities Ltd. v. Bank of N.S.,* [1978] 3 W.W.R. 385 (Alta. T.D.).

All of the decisions involving the question of whether a chattel has become annexed to realty referred to the principles enunciated in *Haggert v. Brampton* (1897), 28 S.C.R. 174 (S.C.C.); summarized in *Stack v. T. Eaton Co.* (1902) 4 O.L.R. 335 (Ont. C.A.); and confirmed in *LaSalle Recreations Ltd. v. Cdn. Camdex Investments Ltd.* (1969), 68 W.W.R. 339, 4 D.L.R. (3d) 549 (B.C.C.A.). The application of these principles is stated, in each decision, to ultimately depend on the facts. The reason therefor is the nature of the principles as summarized in *Stack v. Eaton, supra,* at p. 338, as follows:

"I take it to be settled law:—

(1) That articles not otherwise attached to the land than by their own weight are not to be considered as part of the land, unless the circumstances are such as to shew that they were intended to be part of the land.

(2) That articles affixed to the land even slightly are to be considered part of the land unless the circumstances are such as to shew that they were intended to continue chattels.

(3) That the circumstances necessary to be shewn to alter the *prima facie* character of the articles are circumstances which shew the degree of annexation and object of such annexation, which are patent to all to see.

(4) That the intention of the person affixing the article to the soil is material only so far as it can be presumed from the degree and object of annexation.

(5) That, even in the case of tenants' fixtures put in for the purposes of trade, they form part of the freehold, with the right, however, to the tenant, as between him and his landlord, to bring them back to the state of chattels again by severing them from the soil, and that they pass by a conveyance of the land as part of it, subject to this right of the tenant."

An additional factor to be considered was also referred to in *Reynolds v. Ashby & Son,* [1904] A.C. 466, namely, the positions of the rival claimants to the property alleged to be a chattel. In that case the dispute was between the vendor of equipment pursuant to a hire-purchase agreement and the assignee of a mortgagee of the real property. Some concern was expressed that if the equipment should be held to be affixed to the real property the real property mortgagee would be obtaining title to equipment without paying anything therefor. It was nevertheless concluded that the equipment formed part of the realty.

In all of the other decisions mentioned above the dispute was between a chattel mortgagee and a real property mortgagee, with the exception of *Dunwoody,* which involved a real property mortgagee and a trustee in bankruptcy.

It is significant in this instance that Dolan owns both the mobile home and the lot on which it is located. This was also the situation in *Royal Bank v. Beyak, supra,* although the electricity was connected in that case only by a cable; the plumbing was only connected to a septic tank; and there were only wooden steps. It was apparently considered significant that the mobile home was in no way embedded or bolted to the land or to any permanent structure.

The fact that a mobile home, from which the wheels and substructure have been removed, is not affixed to a substructure implanted in the real property would appear to be relevant only to the extent that a substructure would ordinarily be required in the particular circumstances, such as to accommodate heating equipment. There is no evidence in this instance that a substructure, or even bolts, would have served any useful purpose except to provide additional factors to support the conclusion in law that the motor vehicle was affixed to the real property. Conversely, utilizing bolts merely to secure the chattel to the real property, because the weight of the chattel alone was not sufficient for proper stabilization, should not be decisive in determining that the chattel became part of the realty.

In many instances the owner of a mobile home may not desire that the mobile home be deemed to be affixed to the real property, lacking a long term proprietary interest in the real property. Nevertheless, some degree of annexation may be required to permit adequate use of the housing facility. In that circumstance it would be necessary to proceed to examine the other factors enumerated in *Stack v. Eaton* to avoid the application of the second factor involving slight affixation to the land.

The Dolan mobile home is affixed to the real property, albeit slightly, by the attachment thereto of a porch and concrete steps. A somewhat greater degree of annexation exists by virtue of the connections to the entrenched water, sewage and electrical services. But the slight degree of annexation, which *prima facie* permits a conclusion that the mobile home is part of the realty, must be examined in light of all other relevant factors, both objective and subjective.

The fact that the property may be easily removed from the realty without causing significant damage is only one factor. Many buildings which were initially quite clearly annexed to realty are now moved to different sites. After removal from the original site the building becomes a chattel until affixed once again to realty. But the law has always recognized that a chattel may become affixed to realty and yet regain its status as a chattel after removal. Section 36 of the Personal Property Security Act, S.S. 1979-80, c. P-6.1 contains extensive provisions relating to rights and chattels which become fixtures, perfection of security interests therein and priorities, and the removal of fixtures upon default.

The Dolan mobile home was placed on real property owned by Dolan at the time of acquisition thereof. The subsequent improvements and development of the property, together with the length of time that the mobile home has been located on the site, and the appearance of the home was similar to a bungalow, of the owner do not permit of any other conclusion but permanence.

When the chattel mortgage was executed on July 14, 1983 the witness to the signature of the mortgagors was the loans officer of the bank, who deposed that the mortgage was executed in Saskatoon, which is a fair distance from Perdue, Saskatchewan. Although the property was still described as a mobile home, it does not appear that any effort was made by the bank to determine, at that time, whether it was still a chattel. After the sheriff's officer had formally seized the mobile home, the same loans officer deposed that she had been informed by the sheriff's officer the mobile home was resting on blocks and not on a permanent foundation.

There is no evidence that Dolan informed the bank, when the chattel mortgage was executed, that the mobile home was, or was not, still a chattel. It would have been relatively simple for the bank to obtain a declaration that the mobile home was not affixed to realty. Perhaps even an undertaking could have been obtained that the mobile home would not be affixed to realty as long as the security interest existed. When many house trailers and mobile homes are acquired for the express purpose of being installed more or less permanently on real property, it would seem that it would in the interest of a proposed secured party to ensure that it was obtaining the proper type of security agreement by examining the proposed security, or obtaining some type of undertaking as to the status in law of the property offered as security.

As a result of the foregoing, there will be an order that the mobile home owned by Dolan is affixed to the real property on which it is located. The warrant issued by the bank to seize the mobile home is therefore invalid.

There will be no costs to any of the parties.

CASE PROBLEMS FOR DISCUSSION

Case 1

Hazel purchased a sewing machine from the Easy-So Company under a conditional sale agreement that required her to make 36 equal monthly payments of $15 each in order to fully pay for the machine. Easy-So Company assigned the conditional sale agreement to Easy Finance immediately after the agreement was signed by Hazel. Easy Finance registered the agreement in accordance with the provincial legislation pertaining to security instruments of this type, and notified Hazel of the assignment.

Hazel used the machine for several months, during which time she found that the machine required constant adjustment by the seller. Eventually, Hazel came to realize that the sewing machine was unsuitable for her purpose. She arranged with Easy-So to take back the machine as a trade-in on a different type of sewing machine that the dealer also sold. Hazel paid the cost difference of $100 and took the new machine home.

Without advising Easy Finance of the change in the transaction, Easy-So Company sold the trade-in model to Henrietta for $350 cash.

Some time later, Hazel defaulted in her payments to Easy Finance, and the finance company repossessed her sewing machine. When the finance company indicated that it intended to sell the machine to satisfy the debt, Hazel demanded the return of the machine on the basis that it was not the sewing machine described in the conditional sale agreement. When Easy Finance confirmed the error, it traced the machine covered by the conditional sale agreement to Henrietta, then seized the proper sewing machine.

Both Hazel and Henrietta brought a legal action against Easy Finance for a return of their respective sewing machines. Advise all parties of their legal position in this case and indicate the possible outcome. What is the legal position of Easy-So Company?

Case 2

Casey, a resident of the United States, visited Canada with his sailboat. While in Canada, he sold the boat to his friend Donald, who resided in Toronto, Ontario. The friend purchased the sailboat for $10 000. Some time later, Donald purchased a power boat from a dealer and used the sailboat as a trade-in to cover part of the purchase price. The dealer made a search for security interests under the provincial Personal Property Security Act and found no claims against the sailboat. The boat dealer sold the sailboat some time later to Morgan, under a conditional sale agreement, and registered the security interest. Morgan later sold the sailboat to Kidd for $8000 and moved to the province of Alberta.

Kidd did not make a search for creditor claims at the time of the purchase. He had paid over the money unaware of the boat dealer's registered security interest in the property.

The conditional sale agreement went into default when Morgan neglected to make a payment to the boat dealer. However, before the dealer could find the boat, Customs and Excise claimed that the sailboat had been illegally brought into Canada, and the property in the goods, as a result, had vested in the Crown.

Discuss the rights of the parties, including the Crown, in this case.

Case 3

Smith & Co. carried on business as a wholesaler and operated a fleet of delivery trucks to supply its customers. The company found the cost of maintaining the delivery equipment excessive and decided to sell its fleet of trucks. The company arranged to have all delivery work handled by a local cartage company and advertised for a buyer for its delivery equipment.

Eventually, Smith & Co. found a buyer willing to purchase the trucks for $180 000, and the sale was immediately completed.

Some months later, a creditor of Smith & Co. discovered that it no longer possessed a fleet of trucks. The creditor complained that the trucks should not have been sold without his permission, even though he was only an unsecured creditor to whom Smith & Co. owed $6000 on a trade account.

What are the rights of the parties in this case? What steps should Smith & Co. have taken to avoid creditor complaints?

Case 4

Baxter owned a block of land that fronted on a large lake. On May 1st, he entered into a contract with Cottage Construction Company to have a custom-designed cottage constructed on the site. Cottage Construction Company fixed the contract price at $50 000, payable $10 000 on the signing of the agreement, and the balance on the completion of the contract. Baxter signed the contract and urged the building contractor to begin construction immediately. On May 1st, he gave the contractor a cheque in the amount of $10 000.

Cottage Construction Company entered into the following subcontracts for the construction work:

(a) A $3000 contract with Abe Excavation to excavate and prepare the foundation, the work to be completed on June 1st.

(b) A $15 000 contract with Larch Lumber Company for materials, the last to be delivered by July 1st.

(c) A $10 000 contract with Ace Framing Contractors to provide labour only to erect and close in the cottage by July 20th.

(d) A $5000 contract with Roofing Specialty Company to install and shingle the building roof by July 20th.

(e) A $5000 contract with Volta Electrical for wiring and electric heating equipment, the work to be completed by August 1st.

Cottage Construction Company agreed in its contract to have the cottage completed and ready for occupancy by August 6th. Work progressed on schedule, and each subcontractor completed the subcontract on the agreed finish date. By August 1st, the cottage was almost ready for occupancy; only the door trim and eavestroughing remained unfinished.

On August 1st, the proprietor of Cottage Construction Company approached Baxter and asked him if he might receive the balance of the contract price, as he wished to use the funds to pay his subcontractors. Baxter gave him a cheque for the remaining $40 000, confident that the contract would be completed.

On August 2nd, a dispute arose between Cottage Construction and Ace Framing Contractors over the terms of the contract between them, and Cottage Construction refused to make payment. Ace Framing Contractors registered a construction lien against the cottage lot later the same day. All of the other subcontractors immediately became aware of the lien claim, and registered liens on August 3rd.

The next day, Cottage Construction Company was found to be insolvent without having paid the subcontractors.

Discuss the legal rights (if any) of the various subcontractors, Baxter, and Cottage Construction Company. Indicate the probable outcome of the case.

Case 5

The Mamouth Housing Corporation required capital in order to finance certain land acquisitions for its proposed housing projects. The corporation made a $2 000 000 bond issue to acquire the funds necessary for working capital and to cover a 20% down payment on the purchase of a large block of land that it purchased for $5 000 000. The balance of the land transaction was in the form of a first mortgage back to the vendor for $4 000 000.

Once the land was acquired, Mamouth Housing Corporation entered into a building contract with High Rise Construction Company to construct a large apartment building on the site. The contract was for the sum of $15 000 000, which Mamouth Housing Corporation expected to finance by a construction loan of $18 000 000 from Apartment Finance Limited. The money was to be advanced as construction of the building progressed. The building mortgage was registered as a second mortgage, on the understanding that the part of the funds remaining after the building was constructed (plus the corporation's working capital) would be used to discharge the first mortgage.

After the contractor had completed $1 000 000 worth of work on the building, and after Mamouth Housing Corporation received a $1 000 000 advance on the building mortgage, Mamouth Housing Corporation decided to stop construction due to a sudden decline in demand for apartment units in the city.

Assuming that the bonds issued contain a floating charge, and assuming that the contractor files a construction lien against the property for $1 000 000, discuss the rights of the various creditors if Mamouth Housing Corporation decides to abandon the project and allow its bonds and mortgage obligations to go into default, even though it has cash in the amount of $1 000 000 and assets (excluding land) in the amount of $500 000.

Case 6

Betty's Typing Service Ltd. acquired five new computers and two laser printers from Computing Supplies Inc., a major wholesale supplier of word processing equipment to business and institutions. Each piece of equipment was acquired pursuant to a lease that Betty signed on behalf of her company. The cost of each computer was $2700, and the printers were $3600 each. Betty was required to pay $75 monthly for each computer lease and $100 monthly for each printer for three years.

In addition to the monthly payments Betty's company was to make, Betty was required by Computing Services Inc. to sign a personal guarantee for payment on each lease in the event that her company should default. The wording of the guarantee stated that Betty would be liable to make payments under the lease even if the lease turned out to be void or voidable against her company or its creditors.

Shortly after the acquisition of the computing equipment, Betty borrowed a sum of money from the bank for some improvements to her offices. As security for the bank, she executed a general security agreement over all assets of her business.

After about a year of making regular payments on the computer leases and to the bank, Betty's business began to slow down considerably. She struggled to make the payments for a few more months, but eventually found herself unable to continue. First, Betty failed to make payments on the leases. The following month she defaulted on her bank loan. The bank immediately seized the computing equipment, and the other assets of the business, pursuant to the terms of its general security agreement.

In the legal argument that followed, it became apparent that the bank had registered its security agreement under provincial personal property security legislation, but Computing Services Inc. had not registered any of its leases.

Identify the legal issue or issues that have arisen, and the arguments that each party will rely upon, including the legal principles upon which they are based. Render a decision.

CHAPTER 32

Bankruptcy and Insolvency

INTRODUCTION

Bankruptcy and insolvency are matters of concern to both debtors and creditors. Persons who carry on business must accept the risk that their business venture may prove unsuccessful, either through their own poor management decisions or through the actions of their competitors. When a business fails, not only do the operators of the business frequently suffer economic loss, but their creditors may do so as well if insufficient assets remain to pay the debts. Bankruptcy legislation is designed to provide a procedure whereby the assets of the unfortunate debtor are divided in a fair and orderly way amongst the creditors. It promotes commerce as well, in the sense that it is a means by which a failing business may be ended, and the entrepreneur permitted to start again. Because the assets on bankruptcy seldom cover the full amount of creditors' claims, most creditors will attempt to minimize their risk in extending credit while a business is in operation.

The debt transaction carries with it a risk that the loan or debt will not be repaid, either as a result of some misfortune that may fall upon the debtor, or as a result of the debtor's deliberate refusal to make payment. The secured transaction is essentially an attempt by a creditor to ensure repayment, regardless of the circumstances that might affect the debtor's ability to repay the debt in the future. However, secured transactions, in terms of time, are relatively recent phenomena. The more common forms of security such as chattel mortgages, conditional sale agreements, and mechanics' liens did not receive judicial or statutory (in the case of mechanics' liens) recognition until the nineteenth century. While these forms of security assist creditors in many instances, a great many trade debt transactions are unsecured because the very nature of business often involves an element of trust. Consequently, the decision to extend credit is frequently based upon the reputation of the debtor. Nevertheless, debtors with the best of intentions sometimes

encounter financial difficulties due to unforeseen illness or injury, loss of employment, or a decline in business, and find themselves unable to pay their debts. To
compound the problems of creditors, persons who deliberately set out to defraud
creditors still seem to be ever present.

**HISTORICAL
BACKGROUND**

Roman law recognized the distinction between the honest but unfortunate debtor
and the debtor who obtained credit by fraud or deception. The law established
separate remedies for the creditor in each case. The debtor who could establish
that his inability to repay the debt was due to matters beyond his control could
avoid execution by delivering up his assets to his creditors. The dishonest debtor,
on the other hand, was not granted this privilege.

The term **bankruptcy** did not appear until the Middle Ages and was of Italian
origin. With the rise of trade and the general increase in commercial activity,
many small businesses developed. Invariably, some tradesmen and artisans
encountered financial difficulties. The solution adopted by creditors during that
period was to go to the place of business of the debtor and break up his work-
bench. The term *bankruptcy* was derived from the Italian *bankarupta* that literally
translated means "broken bench."

While the *bankarupta* process of the early Italian creditors was no doubt an
effective method of demonstrating their displeasure with the debtor's default, it
did little to satisfy their financial loss. The Roman law, however, still applied, and
the debtor's assets (other than his work-bench) presumably remained open to
seizure by the creditors to satisfy their debts.

In England, the expansion of trade, particularly during the nineteenth century,
carried with it an expansion of credit and the inevitable problem of default by
debtors (either by accident or design) to the sorrow of their creditors. The common law at the time did not address itself to the problems of trade creditors. It
provided only a rather complex procedure that a creditor was obliged to follow in
order to attach the property of a debtor. The only effective remedy was through
legislative enactment of procedures to deal with a bankrupt debtor's property.

Canada introduced its own insolvency legislation in 1869.[1] Then some years
later it repealed the act,[2] leaving the problems of insolvency and debt with the
provinces until 1919, when it once again occupied the field.[3]

The **Bankruptcy Act** of 1919 provided for the liquidation of the debtor's assets
and the release of the honest debtor, with no protection for the debtor in cases of
fraud or willful wastage of assets. Over the next 30 years, the act proceeded through
a series of amendments, with greater official supervision of the liquidation and
disposition process added by each change. By 1949, however, an overhaul of the
legislation was necessary in order to clarify and simplify the procedures and the
application of the act. The revisions became the Bankruptcy Act in 1949.[4] In
1992, the act was extensively revised again to reflect and recognize the changes
that have taken place in business. The new Bankruptcy and Insolvency Act[5]

1. The Insolvent Act of 1869, 32-33 Vict., c. 16 (Can.).
2. "An Act To Repeal the Acts Respecting Insolvency Now in Force in Canada," 43 Vict., c. 1 (Can.).
3. The Bankruptcy Act, 9-10 Geo. V, c. 36 (Can.) (1919).
4. The Bankruptcy Act, 1949, 13 Geo. VI, c. 7 (Can.).
5. Bankruptcy and Insolvency Act, R.S.C. 1985, c. B-3, as amended by S.C. 1992 c. 27.

constitutes the principal bankruptcy and insolvency legislation in Canada at the present time.

BANKRUPTCY LEGISLATION IN CANADA

Purpose and Intent

The bankruptcy legislation is multi-purpose. It is designed first of all to provide honest but unfortunate debtors with a release from their debts if the debtors deliver up all of their assets to their creditors in accordance with the act. The second general thrust of the legislation is to eliminate certain preferences and provide a predictable and fair distribution of the assets of the debtor amongst the creditors in accordance with the priorities set out in the statute. A third purpose of the law is to uncover and punish debtors who attempt to defraud creditors by various means. The legislation, being federal law, has the added benefit of providing a uniform system for dealing with bankruptcy throughout Canada.

The general thrust of the new legislation is to promote the survival of the debtor's business rather than simply provide a procedure for its dissolution and the distribution of the debtor's assets to its creditors. The shift in emphasis from creditors to debtors represents a marked change from past legislation. The new act contains additional measures to preserve business firms and the employment they support in the economy. The change, nevertheless, significantly reduces creditor's rights and their security interests in the course of bankruptcy proceedings. The new act does, however, enhance the rights of certain unsecured creditors, particularly unsecured trade creditors, by giving them a greater role in the process. In the past, these creditors frequently suffered the most when their customers became insolvent. These groups, along with the debtors, benefit most under the new legislation.

The importance of the release of the honest but unfortunate debtor and the underlying reasoning for the release was described by the court in the following terms:

> I think it is a fair statement to say that originally bankruptcy and insolvency legislation was designed to enable the assets of an honest debtor to be equitably distributed among his creditors, and to enable him to have a livelihood, in business or otherwise, which he might have difficulty in doing unless he was freed of the burden of his debts, and, with respect to a debtor who was not engaged in business but who had been imprisoned for non-payment of his debts, that he might be released from imprisonment. Bankruptcy laws are now of wider application and provide for the right of persons who are not engaged in business to make assignments of their property to trustees for distribution among their creditors and for discharge from further liability with respect to their debts, subject, of course, to certain rules and conditions. But, as has been said, The Bankruptcy Act should not be regarded as a clearing-house for the liquidation of debts solely, irrespective of the circumstances in which they were incurred. As to the position of the debtor, if it is a case of a person being so weighed down by his debts as to be incapable of properly earning a living or of performing the ordinary duties of citizenship, including the support of a wife and family, that is one thing; but where the only object to be served is the comfort and convenience of the debtor and his being freed from the necessity for using his earning-capacity or any property he may acquire or be able to acquire in the future for the discharge or partial discharge of his debts, it is quite another.[6]

6. *Re Buell*, [1955] O.W.N. 421

Application

The **Bankruptcy and Insolvency Act** is administered by a Superintendent of Bankruptcy who appoints and exercises supervision over all trustees who administer bankrupt estates under the act. In 1966,[7] the Superintendent was given additional powers to investigate suspected violations of the act, particularly in the case of complaints concerning fraud, and this provision was carried over to the new legislation.

The act designates a particular court, usually the highest trial court in each province or territory, as the court to deal with bankruptcy matters in that jurisdiction.[8]

Bankruptcy falls within the jurisdiction of the federal government under the Canadian constitution and, as a consequence, the law applies to all parts of the country. The Bankruptcy and Insolvency Act is not, however, the only statute that pertains to bankruptcy and insolvency, nor does it apply to all persons and corporations. Proceedings under the **Winding Up Act**[9] are available to creditors of a corporation, and the **Companies' Creditors Arrangement Act**[10] is available to corporations with bondholders, if the corporation is in financial difficulties.

The Companies' Creditors Arrangement Act applies only to corporations that have outstanding issues of bonds or debentures and find themselves in financial difficulty. If a corporation cannot meet its client obligations to its creditors, it may apply to the court for time to submit a plan for its reorganization and restructuring of its financial obligations. If the court grants the order, the order usually will stay any action by creditors until the corporation's plan for reorganization has been brought before the creditors and the creditors given the opportunity to deal with the plan. If the required number of creditors in each class approve the plan, then the plan becomes binding on all creditors, and all must accept the rescheduled debt payment arrangements.

The Companies' Creditors Arrangement Act is a very broadly worded statute that allows the courts a great deal of latitude in dealing with the debt problems of corporations in financial difficulty. The act differs substantially from the Bankruptcy and Insolvency Act, and is normally used only by very large corporations as the process is usually much more expensive than under the Bankruptcy Act. It should be noted, however, that corporations entitled to use the Companies' Creditors Arrangement Act are also free to use the Bankruptcy and Insolvency Act if they are in financial difficulty, as are their creditors. More debtor corporations may now use the Bankruptcy and Insolvency Act not only because it will probably be less expensive to do so, but because the new act places greater emphasis on the preservation of businesses that may be viable if their debts are restructured. Proceedings, once underway under the Companies' Creditors Arrangement Act would probably forestall action under bankruptcy legislation pending the completion of the process.

---

7. "An Act to Amend the Bankruptcy Act," 14-15 Eliz. II, c. 32 (Can.) (1966).

8. For example, in Newfoundland, the court is the Trial Division of the Supreme Court; in Alberta it is the Court of Queen's Bench, and in Ontario, it is the Ontario Court (General Division) Bankruptcy and Insolvency Act, R.S.C. 1985, c. B-3, s. 2, as amended by S.C. 1992, c. 27.

9. Winding Up Act, R.S.C. 1985, c. W-11.

10. Companies' Creditors Arrangement Act, R.S.C. 1985, c. C-36.

The Bankruptcy and Insolvency Act does not apply to certain persons or to corporations of special kinds. For example, the act at the present time does not apply to farmers or fishermen, or any wage-earner or commission salesperson whose income is less than $2500 per annum, although these persons may make a voluntary assignment in bankruptcy. Nor does the act apply to any chartered bank, trust or loan company, insurance company, or railway, as special provision is made in the legislation governing each of these if they should become insolvent. Farmers also have special legislation available to them in the case of financial difficulties in the form of the Farm Debt Review Act.[11] The Bankruptcy and Insolvency Act, however, does apply to most persons and corporations and takes precedence over the Winding Up Act in its application.

Acts of Bankruptcy

The failure on the part of a debtor to pay a creditor does not automatically render the debtor bankrupt, nor does it establish that the debtor is insolvent. A debtor may have good reason not to pay a particular creditor, or circumstances may prevent the debtor from doing so. For example, a debtor may, through oversight, fail to have sufficient funds available when a debt falls due. Nevertheless, the debtor may possess assets worth many times the value of the indebtedness. Under such circumstances, the debtor's problem would be one of liquidity rather than bankruptcy.

Under bankruptcy law, a distinction is made between insolvency and bankruptcy, even though the former may be a part of the latter. **Insolvency** is essentially the inability of an individual or corporation to pay debts as they fall due. It frequently represents a financial condition that precedes bankruptcy. **Bankruptcy,** on the other hand, is a legal condition that arises when a person has debts exceeding $1000, and has committed one of the 10 acts of bankruptcy set out in the act within six months prior to a creditor filing a petition in bankruptcy against the debtor. The particular activities that the act[12] defines as acts of bankruptcy are as follows:

> *42(1) A debtor commits an act of bankruptcy in each of the following cases:*
> *(a) if in Canada or elsewhere he makes an assignment of his property to a trustee for the benefit of his creditors generally, whether it is an assignment authorized by this Act or not;*
> *(b) if in Canada or elsewhere he makes a fraudulent conveyance, gift, delivery, or transfer of his property or of any part thereof;*
> *(c) if in Canada or elsewhere he makes any conveyance or transfer of his property or any part thereof, or creates any charge thereon, that would under this Act be void as a fraudulent preference;*
> *(d) if with intent to defeat or delay his creditors he does any of the following things: namely, departs out of Canada, or being out of Canada, remains out of Canada, or departs from his dwelling-house or otherwise absents himself;*
> *(e) if he permits any execution or other process issued against him under which any of his property is seized, levied upon or taken in execution to remain unsatisfied until within four days from the time fixed by the sheriff for the sale thereof or for fourteen days after such seizure, levy or taking in execution, or if the property has been sold by the sheriff, or if the execution or other process has*

---

11. Farm Debt Review Act, S.C. 1986, c. 33.
12. Bankruptcy and Insolvency Act, R.S.C. 1985, c. B-3 s. 42(1).

been held by him for fourteen days after written demand for payment without seizure, levy or taking in execution or satisfaction by payment, or if it is returned endorsed to the effect that the sheriff can find no property whereon to levy or to seize or take, but where interpleader proceedings have been instituted in regard to the property seized, the time elapsing between the date at which such proceedings were instituted and the date of which such proceedings are finally disposed of, settled or abandoned shall not be taken into account in calculating any such period of fourteen days;

(f) if he exhibits to any meeting of his creditors any statement of his assets and liabilities that shows that he is insolvent, or presents or causes to be presented to any such meeting a written admission of his inability to pay his debts;

(g) if he assigns, removes, secretes or disposes of or attempts or is about to assign, remove, secrete or dispose of any of his property with intent to defraud, defeat or delay his creditors or any of them;

(h) if he gives notice to any of his creditors that he has suspended or that he is about to suspend payment of his debts;

(i) if he defaults in any proposal made under this Act;

(j) if he ceases to meet his liabilities generally as they become due.

Bankruptcy Proceedings

The Bankruptcy and Insolvency Act distinguishes between commercial and consumer bankruptcies, and provides a somewhat more streamlined process for the latter. Commercial debtors, on the other hand, are given the opportunity if they so desire to restructure their financial affairs. There are essentially three routes that debtors in financial difficulties may follow to resolve their financial problems. A debtor may (1) make a proposal to his or her creditors; (2) make a voluntary assignment in bankruptcy; (3) permit the creditors to petition for a receiving order. Of the three methods, only the first two may be undertaken by a debtor as a voluntary act; the third represents an involuntary procedure from a debtor's point of view.

In the case of a commercial business, if the business finds itself in financial difficulty, or if secured creditors have notified the debtor of their intention to realize on their security, the debtor may file with the Official Receiver a notice of intention to make a **proposal** to its creditors.[13] The filing then provides the debtor with a 30-day period during which time a plan for the restructuring of debts may be prepared for presentation to the creditors. If the debtor is unable to prepare a proposal within the 30-day period, 45-day extensions may be obtained from the court (up to a maximum of five months) to allow time for the preparation of the proposal. Secured creditors may oppose extensions of the time if the extension will jeopardize their security. The court, however, is free to impose conditions on the creditors in limiting the debtor's time to prepare a proposal.

Once the proposal is prepared, it is filed and presented to the creditors for approval. A meeting of creditors must be held within 21 days after the proposal is filed, and both secured and unsecured creditors are entitled to vote on the proposal. Each group of creditors votes as a separate group or class, but the votes of the unsecured creditors are the most important. The emphasis on the wishes of the

---

13. Bankruptcy and Insolvency Act, R.S.C. 1985, c. B-3, s. 50, as amended by S.C. 1992, c. 27, s. 18, 19.

unsecured creditors is recognition of the fact that these creditors as a group usually have the most to lose if the business in closed. Secured creditors may look to specific assets to recover their money, but the unsecured creditors in many cases have few unencumbered assets to cover their debt, and would receive little or nothing if the business terminated. If the unsecured creditors as a class vote two-thirds or more in favour of the proposal, then the proposal will be binding on the creditors and the debtor.

The approval by the court has the effect of binding the parties to the terms of the proposal. Compliance with the proposal by the debtor will preclude any creditor from taking independent proceedings against the debtor. The successful performance of the agreement by the debtor would have the same force and effect as if the debtor had paid the debts in full. If the proposal is rejected by the unsecured creditors, the debtor is deemed to have made an assignment in bankruptcy, and proceedings for the administration of the debtor's estate begins.

An insolvent person may make a **voluntary assignment**[14] in bankruptcy as an alternative to a proposal. A voluntary assignment differs from creditor-instituted proceedings only at the outset. Under a voluntary assignment, the debtor files with the Official Receiver an assignment of his or her property for the general benefit of the creditors, with the assignee's name left blank.[15] The Official Receiver then selects a trustee to accept the debtor's property and to proceed with the bankruptcy. Once this is done, the Bankruptcy and Insolvency Act procedure comes into play, and the administration of the bankrupt's estate begins.

The third method of instituting proceedings under the act is through the action of a creditor. Where a debtor, as defined in the act, has debts owing to one or more creditors in excess of $1000 and has committed an act of bankruptcy, a creditor may at any time, within the six months after the act of bankruptcy occurred, file a **petition** for a receiving order with the Registrar in Bankruptcy of the provincial or territorial court designated under the Bankruptcy and Insolvency Act to hear such matters.[16] If the debtor does not object to the petition (or consents), a **receiving order** is issued by the registrar that determines the debtor to be bankrupt and that permits the appointment of a Licensed Trustee to administer the estate of the bankrupt. If the debtor objects, the matter is heard by a judge, and the debtor may then present evidence to satisfy the court that he or she is not bankrupt. If the debtor is successful, then the judge will dismiss the petition; if not, the receiving order is issued.

Provision is made under the act for the appointment of an interim receiver if it should be necessary to preserve the assets or the business of the debtor pending the hearing of the petition by the court. The interim receiver usually becomes the trustee who administers the debtor's estate if the receiving order is later issued by the court.

Following the issue of the receiving order, the appointed trustee has a duty to call together the creditors of the bankrupt. At that time the trustee's appointment is affirmed or a new trustee is appointed. The trustee then reports the assets of the debtor and determines the amount of the creditors' claims. The debtor must be

---

14. Ibid., s. 49.

15. Ibid., s. 42(1)(a). An assignment for the general benefit of creditors constitutes an act of bankruptcy.

16. Ibid., s. 43(5).

present at the first meeting of creditors. At that time the creditors are free to examine the debtor as to the state of his or her affairs and the reasons for the insolvency. At the first meeting the creditors also appoint inspectors (not exceeding five), who assume responsibility for the supervision of the trustee on behalf of the rest of the creditors. The inspectors usually meet with the trustee following the first meeting of creditors and instruct the trustee on all matters concerning the liquidation of the bankrupt debtor's estate. The trustee, even though an officer of the court and subject to its direction, must act in accordance with the inspectors' instructions, as they must authorize all important decisions concerning the realization of the assets. This is so, provided that their decisions are consistent with the Bankruptcy and Insolvency Act.

Unpaid suppliers are entitled to reclaim goods supplied to the bankrupt business if the goods are recognizable in inventory, and were delivered within 30 days preceding the bankruptcy. Farmers, fishermen, and aquaculturalists who have supplied a bankrupt business with their goods during a 15-day period prior to the bankruptcy may claim a special priority security interest on the debtor's inventory for the value of the goods so delivered.[17]

The trustee usually collects all assets of the bankrupt and converts them to cash. Assets that are subject to security interests such as land mortgages, chattel mortgages, or conditional sale agreements (to name a few) must be made available to the secured creditor. If the goods are sold, any surplus goes to the trustee to be included in the estate for distribution to the creditors. If the proceeds from the disposition of the particular security are insufficient to satisfy a secured creditor's claim, the secured creditor is entitled to claim the unpaid balance as an unsecured creditor. The assets not subject to secured creditors' claims, and any surplus remaining from the disposition of assets subject to security interests when liquidated are distributed by the trustee in accordance with the priorities set out in the Bankruptcy and Insolvency Act. The legislation provides that certain preferred creditors be paid before the unsecured general creditors in the following order:[18]

> *136(1) Subject to the rights of secured creditors, the proceeds realized from the property of a bankrupt shall be applied in priority of payment as follows:*
> *(a) in the case of a deceased bankrupt, the reasonable funeral and testamentary expenses incurred by the legal personal representative of the deceased bankrupt;*
> *(b) the cost of administration, in the following order,*
> *(i) the expenses and fees of the trustee,*
> *(ii) legal costs;*
> *(c) the levy payable under section 147; (costs paid to the court).*
> *(d) wages, salaries, commissions or compensation of any clerk, servant, travelling salesman, labourer or workman for services rendered during six months immediately preceding the bankruptcy to the extent of two thousand dollars in each case, together with, in the case of a travelling salesman, disbursements properly incurred by that salesman in and about the bankrupt's business, to the extent of an additional one thousand dollars in each case, during the same period, and for the purposes of this paragraph commissions payable when goods are*

17. See S.C. 1992, c. 27, s. 38(1).
18. Ibid., s. 136(1).

shipped, delivered or paid for, if shipped, delivered or paid for within the six-month period, shall be deemed to have been earned therein;

(e) municipal taxes assessed or levied against the bankrupt within two years next preceding his bankruptcy and that do not constitute a preferential lien or charge against the real property of the bankrupt, but not exceeding the value of the interest of the bankrupt in the property in respect of which the taxes were imposed as declared by the trustee;

(f) the landlord for arrears of rent for a period of three months next preceding the bankruptcy and accelerated rent for a period not exceeding three months following the bankruptcy if entitled thereto under the lease, but the total amount so payable shall not exceed the realization from the property on the premises under lease, and any payment made on account of accelerated rent shall be credited against the amount payable by the trustee for occupation rent;

(g) the fees and costs referred to in subsection 70(2) but only to the extent of the realization from the property exigible thereunder;

(h) in the case of a bankrupt who became bankrupt before the prescribed date, all indebtedness of the bankrupt under any Act respecting workers' compensation, under any Act respecting unemployment insurance or under any provision of the Income Tax Act creating an obligation to pay to Her Majesty amounts that have been deducted or withheld, rateably;

(i) claims resulting from injuries to employees of the bankrupt in respect to which the provisions of any Act respecting workers' compensation do not apply, but only to the extent of moneys received from persons guaranteeing the bankrupt against damages resulting from such injuries; and

(j) in the case of a bankrupt who became bankrupt before the prescribed date, claims of the Crown not mentioned in paragraphs (a) to (i), in right of Canada or of any province, rateably notwithstanding any statutory preference to the contrary.

The unsecured creditors, being at the bottom of the list, share pro rata in any balance remaining. This amount is usually calculated in terms of "cents on the dollar." For example, if after the payment of secured and preferred creditors in a bankruptcy, the sum of $4000 remains, and unsecured creditors' claims amount to $10 000, the creditor's individual claims would be paid at the rate of 40 cents for each dollar of debt owing to the creditor.

Discharge

Until a bankrupt is discharged by the court, the bankrupt is not released from his or her debts. In effect, any earnings or other income received by the debtor before the discharge may be applied to the payment of the creditors if the court so orders. Apart from this, the bankrupt must not engage in any business without disclosing that he or she is an undischarged bankrupt. Also the bankrupt must not purchase goods on credit except for necessities (and then only for amounts under $500 unless the bankrupt discloses the undischarged bankrupt status).

Bankruptcy also places certain limitations on the activities of the bankrupt until a discharge is obtained. The debtor may not become a director of any limited liability corporation, nor may the debtor accept an appointment to the Senate (a matter unlikely to be of concern to most bankrupts in any event).

The trustee will generally arrange for the discharge of the bankrupt shortly after bankruptcy proceedings are under way. In most cases, if the bankrupt was an honest but unfortunate debtor who had done nothing to defraud the creditors and who had complied with the act and the debtor's duties and obligations under it during the course of the proceedings, a discharge will normally be granted on application by the trustee. This usually occurs from three to six months after proceedings were instituted, but normally not later than 12 months. A debtor may, however, make an application for discharge on his own behalf and at his own expense if he so desires. However, the debtor is not likely to succeed unless he or she can satisfy the court that the creditors have received at least 50 cents on the dollar as payment of their debts, and that no fraud existed. Whether the bankruptcy was the debtor's first, and whether the debtor carried out the debtor's duties under the act, are also factors considered by the court in reaching a decision. Even then, the court has wide powers to impose conditions on the bankrupt. The conditions to some extent are governed by the circumstances that led to the bankruptcy and the debtor's conduct thereafter. A debtor who has never been declared bankrupt before is entitled to an automatic discharge nine months after bankruptcy proceedings were instituted unless creditors, the superintendent, or the trustee objects to the discharge.

A discharge releases the bankrupt from all debts and obligations except those arising from the debtor's wrongdoing and those associated with the debtor's marital obligations. All fines and penalties imposed by law and any obligation that arose out of the fraud of the debtor or a breach of trust would remain, as would any personal obligation arising out of a maintenance or alimony agreement or order.[19] Any debts incurred for necessaries would not be released, if the court so ordered.

"Necessaries" have been described by the court in the following terms:

> Unfortunately there is no definition of the term "necessaries of life" in the Bankruptcy Act. Rarely has the judicial mind placed so many and varied interpretations on a particular phrase in its attempts to determine the intention of the legislators. The legion of cases in no way restricts the term to mean the basic necessaries of life, such as food, shelter, clothing and the like, but would stretch its coverage to such things as "gas for the family Cadillac". Perhaps this is a reflection of the regional disparity that exists in this country of ours. In any event the general judicial consensus appears to be that the term envisions all goods appropriate to a person according to his or her particular lifestyle.[20]

A corporation, unlike an individual, is not entitled to a discharge unless all of the creditors' claims are paid in full.[21]

Consumer Bankruptcy Summary Proceedings

The 1949 Bankruptcy Act provided a simplified procedure for the administration of small estates where the assets of the bankrupt debtor amounted to $500 or less. This procedure was frequently used by consumer or non-trader bankrupt debtors as a means of making a fresh start, as the procedure provided for a prompt discharge. Under the 1992 act, non-trader or consumer insolvencies where the individual

---

19. Ibid., s. 178(1).

20. *Amherst Central Charge Limited v. Hicks* (1979), 29 C.B.R. 313.

21. Ibid., s. 169(4).

has assets of less than $5000 may be eligible for a summary administration procedure. This procedure may be used where the consumer debtor has total debts excluding those secured by the person's principal residence of less than $75 000.

Under the consumer proposal provisions of the act, the consumer begins the process by obtaining the assistance of an **administrator** (a person designated to act in this capacity by the superintendent or a trustee) to assist in the preparation of a proposal to creditors. The proposal must provide for its performance to be completed in not more than five years, and also provide for the priority payment of certain debts and of the fees and expenses of the administrator and debt counselling services. If the proposal is accepted by the creditors, and no objection is raised, the proposal is deemed to be approved by the court. The administrator then proceeds to receive all moneys payable under the proposal, pays the expenses and distributes funds in accordance with the proposal. When the proposal has been fully performed by the debtor, the administrator provides the debtor with a certificate to that effect.

In an effort to reduce the possibility of debtors falling into financial difficulties in future, consumer debtors are expected to attend financial counselling sessions, and this requirement is usually included in the proposal.

Bankruptcy Offences

The Bankruptcy and Insolvency Act is not only designed to provide an orderly procedure for the distribution of a debtor's assets to his or her creditors, but it is designed to identify and punish debtors who attempt to take advantage of their creditors by fraud or other improper means. The legislation therefore addresses the problem by establishing a series of offences punishable under the act by way of fine or imprisonment, as well as by the withholding of discharge from the bankrupt.

Under the act, the superintendent has wide powers to investigate fraudulent practices and allegations of violation of the act by bankrupt debtors. For example, if a debtor, once aware of the serious state of her finances, transfers or conveys assets to members of her family in an effort to hide the assets from her creditors, she would in effect have committed a bankruptcy offence by making a fraudulent conveyance of her assets. The principal offences under the legislation include:[22]

> *198. Any bankrupt who*
> *(a) fails, without reasonable cause to do any of the things required of him...*
> *(b) makes any fraudulent disposition of his property before or after bankruptcy;*
> *(c) refuses or neglects to answer fully and truthfully all proper questions put to him at any examination held pursuant to this Act;*
> *(d) makes a false entry or knowingly makes a material omission in a statement or accounting;*
> *(e) after or within twelve months next preceding his bankruptcy conceals, destroys, mutilates, falsifies, makes an omission in or disposes of or is privy to the concealment, destruction, mutilation, falsification, omission from or disposition of a book or document affecting or relating to his property or affairs unless he proves that he had no intent to conceal the state of his affairs;*
> *(f) after or within twelve months next preceding his bankruptcy obtains any credit or any property by false representations made by him or made by some other person to his knowledge;*

---

22. Ibid., 198.

(g) after or within twelve months next preceding his bankruptcy fraudulently conceals or removes any property of a value of fifty dollars or more or any debt due to or from him; or

(h) after or within twelve months next preceding his bankruptcy pawns, pledges or disposes of any property which he has obtained on credit and has not paid for, unless in the case of a trader such pawning, pledging or disposing is in the ordinary way of trade and unless in any case he proves that he had no intent to defraud; is guilty of an offence punishable on summary conviction and is liable to a fine not exceeding five thousand dollars or to imprisonment for a term not exceeding one year or to both, or is guilty of an indictable offence and is liable to a fine not exceeding ten thousand dollars or to imprisonment for a term not exceeding three years or to both.

As a general rule, investigations are conducted by an official receiver under the direction of the Superintendent of Bankruptcy. These investigations are usually to determine the cause of the bankruptcy; but in a case where fraud or a criminal act is suspected, the investigation may extend to those matters as well.[23] If the court suspects that the debtor might attempt to leave Canada with assets to avoid paying his or her debts, or to take other similar action to avoid creditors, the court has the power to order the debtor's arrest.[24]

SUMMARY

Bankruptcy legislation is a federal statute and, in its present form, is an attempt to provide an honest but unfortunate debtor with an opportunity to reorganize his or her debts or to start afresh and free of debts. The procedure requires the debtor to deliver up his or her property to a receiver or court-appointed trustee for the purpose of distribution to the creditors in accordance with certain specified priorities. The act also deals with fraudulent and improper actions by debtors who attempt to defraud their creditors. Penalties are provided in the statute for persons found guilty of these bankruptcy offences.

Before persons may be subject to bankruptcy proceedings, they must first commit an act of bankruptcy. The commission of any one of the acts by a debtor would entitle a creditor (or creditors), owed at least $1000 by the debtor, to petition for a receiving order at any time within six months after the commission of the act of bankruptcy. If the debtor fails to convince the court that he or she is not bankrupt, the receiving order is issued, and a trustee establishes control of the debtor's assets for liquidation and distribution to the creditors. Inspectors, appointed by the creditors, supervise the trustee until the estate has been fully distributed. The debtor, if he or she has acted without fault, is entitled to a discharge of all debts except such debts as fines, court maintenance orders for support or alimony, and funds acquired by fraudulent means or by breach of trust.

A voluntary procedure and two summary procedures are available to debtors, in addition to the creditor-initiated process. Recent changes in the legislation, permit debtors to make proposals for the restructuring of the debtor's business rather than the immediate division of its assets amongst the creditors.

---

23. Ibid., s. 161, 162.
24. Ibid., s. 168(1).

DISCUSSION QUESTIONS

1. Why is an insolvent person not necessarily a bankrupt?
2. Under what circumstances could a person have assets in excess of liabilities, yet be bankrupt?
3. What should a person do who finds it impossible to carry on business any longer without incurring further losses?
4. Describe the acts of bankruptcy that would entitle a creditor to institute bankruptcy proceedings.
5. Outline the requirements a creditor must satisfy in order to institute bankruptcy proceedings against a debtor.
6. If a debtor makes a proposal to his or her creditors, then fails to comply with the proposal at a later date, what steps may be taken by the creditors?
7. Under what circumstances would a debtor be permitted to make a voluntary assignment for the benefit of his or her creditors?
8. Why are "inspectors" appointed by creditors at their first meeting in bankruptcy proceedings?
9. In what way (or ways) does bankruptcy affect the rights of secured creditors? How would they recover their debts if the security they held was insufficient to cover the amount owing?
10. What is a "preferred" creditor, and how does this status affect the right to payment?
11. Outline the order of priority to payment of preferred creditors in a bankruptcy.
12. Explain the duties of an undischarged bankrupt.
13. What is the effect of a discharge on a bankrupt debtor's obligation to pay his or her creditors?
14. Describe the role of the Superintendent of Bankruptcy in bankruptcy proceedings.

MINI-CASE PROBLEM

1. A was insolvent and attempted to hide from his creditors his only asset, a valuable painting worth $10 000. Assuming that he is two months in arrears on his apartment rent of $1000 per month, owes his housekeeper back wages of $1000 for one month's work, and owes unsecured creditors $12 000, what would the unsecured creditors receive in cents on the dollar if the trustees' fees and the costs of the bankruptcy were $2000?

JUDICIAL DECISIONS

The case of *Re 536646 Ontario Inc.* illustrates a situation where a creditor attempts to place a debtor into bankruptcy simply because the debtor has refused to pay the debt.

In this case the judge first determines if the refusal to pay a debt is an act of bankruptcy. The judge here must decide if the debtor has failed to pay its debts generally to its creditors. He concludes that all other creditors have been paid, leaving only the petitioner, and finds that the debtor has not committed an act of bankruptcy.

The second case raises a somewhat different issue under the Bankruptcy Act.

The case of *Briscoe v. Molsons Bank* deals with a creditor-debtor relationship where the bank was aware that the debtor was insolvent, yet took payment and securities that placed it at an advantage over other unsecured creditors. The court was obliged to consider whether these acts created a fraudulent preference.

In the judgement, the court first considers the relevant sections of the Bankruptcy Act, then poses two questions concerning the actions of the bank. The court answers the questions by reference to the Bankruptcy Act and the facts of the case.

At the end of the case, the court concludes that the debtor had given a fraudulent preference to the bank.

A footnote to the case refers to the appeal, where the Court of Appeal upheld the decision of the trial court.

Refusal To Pay a Creditor— Whether an Act of Bankruptcy

Re 536646 Ontario Inc. (1987), 63 C.B.R. 222.

The debtor corporation failed or refused to pay a creditor a debt. When default occurred, the creditor petitioned the court to have the debtor declared bankrupt.

McRAE, J.:

Hasty Market Inc. petitions that the numbered company, 536646 Ontario Inc., as it should be styled, be adjudged bankrupt. The facts are the numbered company operates two convenience stores both in the metropolitan area of Toronto, a Mini Mart and a Hasty Market, under franchises; the same principals are franchises of these stores through different companies.

The Hasty Market at 895 Lawrence Avenue East has not been a profitable operation. On 11th November 1986 the principal of the numbered company, Mr. Shamon, complained to agents of the petitioner that his store was not doing as well as they had suggested it would at the time he bought the franchise and he asked them for help, that is, that they delay requiring payment of some of his obligations. At the same time he explained the problems he was having. The principals made some encouraging noises and extracted payment from him of a sum in excess of $15 000 which was due on an N.S.F. cheque he had previously sent them. To use his expression, they told him "the payment would show good faith". The principals of the petitioner went back to their office, discussed his problems and decided that they would not help him.

It is Mr. Shamon's evidence that three days later he was required to pay cash on delivery for all merchandise that he obtained. Shortly thereafter, about ten days later, he was served with a notice cancelling his franchise effective in mid-December 1986.

With respect to the numbered company and the Hasty Market store on Lawrence Avenue East, Mr. Shamon has not communicated with the petitioner since, has not paid rent except for one payment in February 1987, paid into court pursuant to an order of Judge Whealy, made pursuant to the Landlord and Tenant Act. The numbered company has a substantial liability to the petitioner, certainly more than $1000 and, at best, has a rather tenuous counterclaim for misrepresentation.

The question I have to determine is whether an act of bankruptcy has been committed pursuant to s. 24(j). That is, has the numbered company ceased to meet its liabilities generally as they become due. I have decided that the onus on the petitioner has not been satisfied for these reasons: there is only one unpaid creditor, the petitioner. All other creditors, I accept the evidence of Mr. Shamon, are paid to date. They number about 16; and include newspaper publishers, provincial and federal tax departments; and, most importantly, all the obligations that the numbered company has with respect to the Mini Mart are current.

The Bankruptcy Act should not be used by a creditor to collect a debt. Declaration of bankruptcy is for the benefit of creditors generally, not for the benefit of a single creditor. While there are cases where a single creditor may successfully petition, I am not satisfied this is such a case. The onus is on the petitioner to strictly prove the act of bankruptcy complained of. In this case the facts do not suggest any other act of bankruptcy.

I have reviewed the case of *Re Holmes and Sinclair* (1975), 9 O.R. (2d) 240, 20 C.B.R. (N.S.) 111 at 113, 60 D.L.R. (3d) 82 (H.C.), a decision of my brother,

Henry J., and I am not satisfied that the circumstances of this case satisfy the test that he has therein set out. The creditor here is not the only creditor of the debtor; all other creditors are being paid. There has not been any evidence of repeated demands by the petitioner. There are not special circumstances such as fraud on the part of the debtor and the debtor does not admit that he is unable to pay his creditors generally.

For those reasons the petition is refused. The application is dismissed. Costs to the respondent.

**Bankruptcy —
Fraudulent
Preferences —
Payment to
Creditor Aware of
Insolvency**

Briscoe v. Molsons Bank (1922), 69 D.L.R. 675.

A bank that was aware of the insolvency of a customer accepted payments on account and took securities as payment even though the securities could not be chased until after the bankruptcy. The payments to the bank were alleged to be a fraudulent preference given to one creditor.

At trial, the judge found that a fraudulent preference had been made.

MEREDITH, C.J.C.P.:

The question involved in this issue is: whether certain payments, or any of them, made by the bankrupt to the defendants in the issue, are "fraudulent and void as against the trustee" in bankruptcy of the bankrupt's estate.

Section 31 of the *Bankruptcy Act* provides, among other things, that every payment made by an insolvent person in favour of any creditor with a view to giving such creditor a preference over other creditors, or which has the effect of giving such creditor a preference over the other creditors, shall, if the person paying the same make an authorised assignment within three months after the date of paying, if made with such view as aforesaid, be deemed fraudulent and void as against the trustee. The enactment then goes on to provide for the case of payment, etc., which has the effect of giving such a preference, creating a *prima facie* presumption only that such payment, etc., was made, etc., with a view to giving the creditor a preference over other creditors.

All that seems plain enough, but Parliament did not deem it sufficient and added another section — 32 — in which, subject to some provisions of the Act not applicable to this case, it is provided that nothing in the Act shall invalidate any payment by the bankrupt to any of his creditors provided that certain conditions are complied with, one of which is: that the payment "is in good faith" and takes place before the date of the receiving order or authorised assignment; and the other is: that the person (other than the debtor) to whom the payment is made has not at the time of the payment notice of any available act of bankruptcy committed by the bankrupt or assignor.

This somewhat roundabout way of expression does not at all dim the meaning of the enactment in its effect upon this case: there are just two questions involved in it, either of which, being answered in the plaintiff's favour, concludes the case against the defendants upon the main point involved in it.

The questions are: (1) Were the payments in question payments made in good faith before the date of the assignment to the plaintiff? and (2) Had the defendants, at the time of payment, notice of any available act of bankruptcy committed by the bankrupt?

As I deem that the second question must be answered in favour of the defendants, I shall consider it first.

At the time of all these transactions, an available act of bankruptcy was: "an act of bankruptcy available for a bankruptcy petition at the date of the presentation of a petition on which a receiving order is made:" sec. 2(*h*) of the Act. How can that be applicable to this case, which is one of an authorised assignment only? The amendment to the Act in this respect was made after all these transactions: *The Bankruptcy Act Amendment Act,* 1921, 11 & 12 Geo. V, ch. 17, sec. 3.

The act of bankruptcy alleged relates to a writ of execution in a sheriff's hands; I do not consider whether or not an act of bankruptcy has been proved in respect of it, because that is unnecessary: as I am unable to find that the defendants had notice of it. It is strange that they did not, if in very truth they had not; but I am unable, in view of the positive denial of their manager in the witness-box, to find that they had, whichever way the onus of proof may lie.

But, on the whole evidence, I cannot but find in favour of the plaintiff on the first question.

However it might seem under sec. 31 alone, it is tolerably plain — though not nearly as plain as it might and should have been made — that both parties must be implicated in the want of good faith which invalidates a transaction.

It is not needful either to consider what "good faith" is, because the facts of this case prove the want of it, whatever reasonable, definite meaning may be given to the words "good faith."

The payments in question with two exceptions were by the bankrupt, when in a hopeless state of insolvency, for the one purpose of preferring his creditors, the defendants, so that his guarantors to them might be relieved from their obligations, under their guaranties held by the defendants, as much as possible; and the defendants, when the moneys were paid to them, knew that.

The bankrupt was so insolvent that the trustee's estimation is that his estate shall pay only about 10 cents in the dollar; for about a writ of execution lay in the sheriff's hands against him in full force and virtue, binding all his property; and all the payments in question were made within a few days of his voluntary assignment in bankruptcy; indeed it is contended and is literally a fact that some were paid after it.

The defendants' manager knew that judgment had been entered up against his debtor in the sum of over $4000 at the suit of a competing bank; he learned then that his customer had gone to and was dealing with the other bank without having informed him and without his knowledge; he knew that that judgment had been reported by the mercantile agencies; and that thereby the debtor's credit should be ruined, and that his creditors should come down upon him "like a thousand of bricks," and he had had a conversation with the debtor's bookkeeper, who had gone to see him with a view to "all getting together to pull Hanning out of the hole," and he knew that she on finding how much the indebtedness to the bank was, had given up the effort "to pull Hanning out of the hole," as hopeless. On that occasion they discussed the Standard Bank affair, and the defendants' manager seemed to know all about it. He was of course complaisant, knowing that the defendants were fully secured and that all payments really should enure to the debtor's relative, connection, and friend, and who were his guarantors to the defendants.

Therefore, generally, the plaintiff succeeds; but there are some minor points yet to be considered; some actual present consideration was given for some parts of the payments in question; the plaintiff cannot recover the whole payments, the value so given must be deducted: sec. 32(1)(*d*). This affects two items.

For the plaintiff it was contended: that the four payments credited to the bankrupt in the defendants' books on and after the date of the assignment should go to the plaintiff under any circumstances, not having been made before the date of the assignment: sec. 32(1)(*i*).

These amounts were the proceeds of sales by the defendants of Victory bonds given to them by the bankrupt before the date of the assignment, the proceeds of which were not received and credited until after that date. But I find that the bonds were intended to be treated as cash, and the fact that they had to be sold before the exact amount of the payment could be known and credited did not, under or for the purposes of the Act, prevent the transaction being then and now treated as a "payment" at the time when the bonds were delivered as and for that purpose. It, however, is further evidence of the intention to feather the nest of the guarantors with all kinds of material that could be made available for that purpose.

The parties can, no doubt, readily calculate and agree upon the amount that the plaintiff should recover from the defendants, and should do so; but, if they will not, the local registrar should ascertain and state it in the presence of or after notice to the parties; and in that case the matter is to be mentioned to me again, otherwise it need not.

The guarantors of the defendants are parties to the issue and joined with the defendants in resisting the plaintiff's claim and so are bound by this judgment; but no other judgment or order affecting them can rightly be made here; it is nothing like a case for indemnity or contribution; the defendants can recover against them only on their guaranties, and any such action is quite foreign to these bankruptcy proceedings.

The bank appealed this decision and the Ontario Supreme Court, Appellate Division (at p. 678) dealt with the matter as follows:

Mulock, C.J.Ex.:

This appeal must fail, because the learned trial Judge found that there was a lack of good faith on the part of the bank. It was successfully contended at the trial by the trustee in bankruptcy that there was a fraudulent preference, and that the bank knew that the payment to it was illegal, because it had notice. There is sufficient evidence to support the view taken by the learned judge at the trial.

CASE PROBLEMS FOR DISCUSSION

Case 1

Simple purchased a small business from a well-established proprietor for $100 000. To finance the transaction, he borrowed $80 000 by way of a mortgage on the premises, and prevailed upon the proprietor to accept a chattel mortgage on the equipment for the balance. Both mortgages were duly registered. He then arranged with the trade suppliers to sell him his inventory on credit.

The business was a high volume, low mark-up type of business. A large amount of money passed through Simple's hands each day, even though the portion that represented his profit was small. During the first few months of operation, he purchased a new, expensive automobile, refurnished his apartment, and took a quick four-day holiday to Las Vegas where he lost several thousand dollars at the gambling tables.

When his suppliers began pressing him for payment of their accounts, he managed to pacify them by staggering payments in such a way that each received the payment of some accounts, but their total indebtedness remained about the same. He accomplished this in part by seeking out other suppliers and persuading them to supply him with goods on credit.

A few months later, it became apparent to Simple's creditors that he was in financial difficulty, and several creditors threatened to institute bankruptcy proceedings. To forestall any action on their part, Simple paid their accounts in full. The threats of the creditors brought his desperate financial position forcefully to his attention, however. He promptly transferred $10 000 to his wife, and placed a further $10 000 in a bank account that he opened in another city.

A few days later, Simple purchased two one-way airline tickets for a flight to Brazil that was scheduled for the next week. Before the departure date, a creditor, to whom Simple owed a trade account in excess of $5000, became aware of his plans and instituted bankruptcy proceedings against him.

Discuss the actions of Simple and indicate how the provisions of the Bankruptcy Act would apply. What steps may be taken to protect the creditors in this case?

Case 2

Able carried on business as a service station operator. In addition to repairing automobiles, he maintained a franchise for the sale of a line of new automobiles. He also sold gasoline and the usual lines of goods for the servicing of vehicles. Business was poor, however, and Able made a voluntary assignment in bankruptcy in which he listed as assets:

Land and building	$50 000
New automobiles (3)	24 000
Gasoline & oil	3 000
Parts, supplies, and equipment	3 000
Accounts receivable	2 000
Bank	100
Personal assets (furniture, etc.)	1 900
	$84 000

His creditors' claims were as follows:

1st registered mortgage	$40 000
2nd registered mortgage	7 000
Registered conditional sale agreements on automobiles	22 000
Due and owing to fuel supplier	5 000
Due and owing to other trade creditors	18 000
Municipal taxes owing	1 000
Personal debts (unsecured)	10 000
	$103 000

When the trustee went to Able's place of business he discovered that: (a) the new cars had been taken by the manufacturer; (2) the fuel tanks had been emptied by the fuel supplier; and (3) Baker, an employee of Able's, was on the premises and in the process of removing an expensive set of tools that he maintained had been given to him by Able in lieu of wages for his previous week's work.

Discuss the steps that the trustee might take as a result of the discoveries.

Case 3

For many years the Acme Company carried on business as a manufacturer of consumer products. In 1988, it embarked on an ambitious program of expansion that involved the acquisition of a new plant and equipment. Financing was carried out by way of real property mortgages, chattel mortgages, and conditional sale agreements, with very few internally generated funds being used for the expansion.

The general decline in demand for its product line as a result of the energy crisis and poor economic climate placed the company in a serious financial situation by 1993. As a result of a failure to pay a trade account to one creditor, bankruptcy proceedings were instituted. Acme did not object to the proceedings, and did not make a proposal to its creditors.

The trustee disposed of the assets of the company and drew up a list of creditors entitled to share in the proceeds. His preliminary calculations were as follows:

Sale of assets, etc.	
Sale of land and buildings	$350 000
Sale of production equipment	35 000
Sale of trucks & automobiles	25 000
Sale of inventory of finished goods, etc.	30 000
Accounts receivable	45 000
Cash	3 000
	$488 000

Expenses and Creditor claims (all secured claims properly registered)	
1st mortgage on land and buildings	$290 000
2nd mortgage on land and buildings	45 000
3rd mortgage on land and buildings	40 000
1st chattel mortgage on trucks & automobiles	22 000
2nd chattel mortgage on trucks & automobiles	40 000
Bank claim under s. 178 of Bank Act	25 000
Unsecured trade creditors	60 000
Unpaid wages (12 employees @ $250 each)	3 000
Unpaid commissions to salespeople 1 @ 1 500	1 500
Bankruptcy expenses, fees & levy	39 000
Unpaid municipal taxes	9 000
Production equipment conditional sale agreement	10 000
	$584 500

Calculate the distribution of the funds to the various creditors and calculate the cents per dollar amount that the unsecured trade creditors would receive.

PART VIII

Special Legal Rights

Special legal rights include not only the exclusive rights to intellectual and industrial property, but the various forms of organization and legal rights available to business firms that engage in international trade.

Chapter 33 provides an overview of the laws that relate to patents, trade marks, copyright, and registered designs, the four principal forms of protection available for intellectual and industrial property. Chapter 34 examines some of the particular laws and procedures that are of concern to business firms that carry on business on an international basis.

Chapter 35, Environmental Law, is concerned more with the obligations of business firms than their rights at law. It is, nevertheless, an important area of the law that requires the attention of all persons engaged in business activities that may impact on the environment in a negative way.

CHAPTER 33

Patents, Trade Marks, and Copyright

INTRODUCTION

Patents, trade marks, and copyright are essentially claims to the ownership of certain types of industrial and intellectual property. A **patent** is a right to a new invention; a **trade mark** is a mark used to identify a person's product or service; and a **copyright** is a claim of ownership and the right to copy a literary or artistic work. Bridging trade marks and copyright is a fourth form of protection, known as an **industrial design,** that is simply the right to produce in quantity some artistic work such as a piece of furniture or article of a unique design.

The authority to pass legislation concerning these rights falls under the exclusive jurisdiction of the federal government by virtue of the division of powers under the Canadian constitution.[1] Statutes have been passed concerning each of these rights that apply uniformly throughout Canada. In addition, Canada has signed a number of international "conventions" that provide procedures by which the owner of a patent, trade mark, or copyright work may obtain protection for the work in the various convention countries.

From a public policy point of view the purpose and intent of each statute is somewhat different. However, each statute attempts to balance the right of public access to, and the use of ideas and information, with the need to foster new ideas and new literary and artistic works. As a result, the legislation incorporates special benefits or rights to promote the particular activities, along with appropriate safeguards to protect the public interest.

---

1. The authority is vested in the federal government by virtue of the Constitution Act, 1867. Formerly the authority was under The British North America Act 1867, 30 Vict., c. 3 s. 91. Patents falls under s. 91(22); copyright under s. 91(23); trade marks would presumably fall under s. 91(2) or (29) since they are not specifically covered in s. 91.

Patent legislation is designed to encourage new inventions and the improvement of old ones by granting the inventor monopoly rights (subject to certain reservations) for a period of time. Copyright laws are also designed to encourage literary and artistic endeavour by vesting in the author or creator of the artistic work the ownership and the exclusive right to reproduce the work over a lengthy period of time. Registered design legislation has a similar thrust. Trade mark legislation, on the other hand, has a slightly different purpose and intent. It is designed to protect the marks or names that persons use to distinguish their goods or services from those of others, and to prevent unauthorized persons from using them.

Originally, the rights associated with intellectual and industrial property were not subject to legislation. Inventors, authors, and artists had very little or no protection for their creative efforts. The general need for protection, however, did not arise until the invention of printing and the Industrial Revolution in England. These two changes created an economic environment in which the creators of industrial and intellectual property were in a position to profit from their creativity. The changes also created an opportunity for others to reap the rewards of an inventor's or author's endeavours without providing the creators with compensation for their loss. The common law proved unequal to the task of establishing and enforcing ownership rights to inventions and creative works of a literary or artistic nature. It was eventually necessary for the English Parliament to deal with each specific property right by way of legislation.

PATENTS

Historical Development of Patent Law

Early patents in England were essentially monopoly rights granted by the Crown under letters patent. These rights were granted to individuals or guilds that gave them exclusive rights to deal in the particular commodity, or the right to control a particular craft or skill. Most of these grants were made ostensibly for the purpose of fostering the trade or the skill. However, in many cases they were simply privileges bestowed upon a subject by the Crown for the general enrichment of the individual.

The issue of monopoly rights to encourage the production of new products was justified on the basis of public policy generally, since England lacked the special skills and equipment necessary to produce the many kinds of goods available on the Continent, especially cloth and metal wares. To encourage English and foreign entrepreneurs to bring in artisans with the necessary skills to produce similar goods in England, monopoly rights were frequently granted. The justification was that the new skills would be learned by native craftsmen, and the country as a whole would benefit. Most of the early "patents" stipulated that the holders of the patent must provide particular quality products in sufficient supply to satisfy the market. The patentees, as a consequence, were obliged to establish production facilities and train their workers in order to comply with the stipulations in the patents. The incentive to do so, in many cases, was a proviso in the patent to the effect that a failure to comply with the conditions set out in the document would result in a revocation of the grant.

The province of Lower Canada introduced legislation in 1823 relating to patents by the statutory recognition of the right of inventors to the exclusive making, use, and selling of their new inventions, provided that they were British subjects and residents of the province.[2] The province of Upper Canada established similar legislation three years later.[3] In 1869, two years after Confederation, the first federal law was introduced that took a different approach to patent rights. This was due, in part, to events that occurred in the United States and, in part, to the fact that patents in England at the time were still issued under the Great Seal of the Crown.

As a result of the severance of its ties with England by the Revolutionary War, the United States had introduced its own patent law in 1790.[4] The statute blended the right of the individual to the fruits of his or her labours with the right of the state to permit free trade for the benefit of the public. The product of this blend was essentially a bargain struck between the state and the inventor, whereby the inventor, by revealing the secrets of the invention, would obtain monopoly rights to its use and manufacture for a fixed period of time. When the time period expired, the invention became public property.

Canada adopted the procedure outlined in the United States' law, but retained the common law for the interpretation and expression of patent rights. In this sense, it incorporated English case-law as authoritative for the exercise of the patent rights. The Canadian act[5] was subsequently amended on a number of occasions, the most important ones being the introduction of a compulsory licence requirement in 1903,[6] and the complete revision of the act in 1923 to set out the rights and duties of the patentee and to prevent abuse of the system.[7] These amendments were based upon the 1919 English Patents and Designs Act, with the result that the Canadian law became a unique blend of both English and United States' laws.[8] Since that time, the statute has been subject to numerous amendments that were designed to change the rights of the patentees or protect the public interest. Amendments that became effective in 1989 moved the Canadian patent law closer to the laws of the European Patent Convention countries and Japan.

The Patent Act

The present patent legislation is available to inventors of any "new and useful art, process, machine, manufacture, or composition of matter, or any new or useful improvement of the same."[9] To *invent,* however, means to produce something new and different — something that did not exist before.[10] What is created must be more than what a skilled worker could produce, in the sense that it must be something more than mere mechanical skill that is the subject-matter of the patent.[11] It must also be new in terms of time as well. As a general rule, an

---

2. "An Act to Encourage the Progress of Useful Arts In This Province," 4 Geo. IV, c. 25 (Lower Canada).

3. "An Act to Encourage the Progress of Useful Arts Within the Province," 7 Geo. IV, c. 5 (Upper Canada).

4. The Patent Act, 1790, 1 Stat. at L. 109 (U.S.).

5. The Patent Act of 1869, 32-33 Vict., c. 11 (Can.).

6. "An Act to Amend the Patent Act, 1903," 3 Edw. VII, c. 46 (Can.).

7. The Patent Act, 13-14 Geo. V, c. 23 (Can.).

8. Patent Act, R.S.C. 1985, c. P-4, s. 2.

9. Ibid., s. 2.

10. Ibid., ss. 2 and 27.

11. *Can. Raybestos Co. Ltd. v. Brake Service Corp. Ltd.,* [1927] 3 D.L.R. 1069.

invention must be kept secret from the public before the filing of the application for a patent takes place. Any invention that has been described or disclosed by the inventor more than a year before the date of application for the patent is not patentable, as it is deemed to be in the public domain. In general, it is not possible to patent something that is only a vague idea or an abstract theory, nor is it possible to patent a very slight improvement in an existing invention.[12] It should also be noted that any invention that has an unlawful purpose is not subject to patent protection. For example, a new "five-in-one burglary tool" would not be granted a patent, no matter how handy or useful it might be for a burglar.

The legal nature of a patent and the justification for its issue was described by the court in the case of *Barter v. Smith*[13] in the following terms:

> It is universally admitted in practice, and it is certainly undeniable in principle, that the granting of letters-patent to inventors is not the creation of an unjust or undesirable monopoly, nor the concession of a privilege by mere gratuitous favor; but a contract between the State and the discoverer.
>
> In England, where letters-patent for inventions are still, in a way, treated as the granting of a privilege, more in words however than in fact, they, from the beginning, have been clearly distinguished from the gratuitous concession of exclusive favors, and therefore were specially exempted from the operation of the statute of monopolies.
>
> Invention being recognized as a property, and a contract having intervened between society and the proprietor for a settlement of rights between them, it follows that unless very serious reasons, deduced from the liberal interpretation of the terms of the contract, interpose, the patentee's rights ought to be held as things which are not to be trifled with, as things sacred in fact, confided to the guardianship and to the honor of the State and of the courts.
>
> As it is the duty of society not to destroy, on insufficient grounds, a contract thus entered upon, so it is the interest of the public to encourage and protect inventors in the enjoyment of their rights legitimately, and sometimes painfully and dearly, acquired. The patentee is not to be looked upon as having interests in direct opposition to the public interest, an enemy of all in fact.

Patent Procedure

An application for a patent may be made by the inventor or the inventor's agent[14] at the Patent Office. Under present legislation,[15] the first inventor to file for a patent is entitled to the patent. Foreign inventors, as well as Canadians, may apply for patent protection for their inventions, as it is always possible that someone in Canada or elsewhere in the world may become aware of an inventor's invention, or may develop essentially the same device or process. Consequently, a prompt application for a patent is important.

The usual practice in a patent application is for the inventor to engage the services of a **patent attorney** (or **patent agent** as they are called in Canada) to assist in the preparation of the documentation and in the processing of the patent. Patent agents are members of the legal profession who specialize in patent work. In

---

12. *Lightning Fastener Co. v. Colonial Fastener Co.,* [1932] Ex. C.R. 89, reversed on appeal, [1937] 1 D.L.R. 21.

13. *Barter v. Smith* (1877), 2 Ex. C.R. 455.

14. Patent agents (or attorneys) are registered with the Patent Office under the Patent Act, R.S.C. 1985, c. P-4.

15. Patent Act, R.S.C. 1985, c. P-4.

addition to training in the area of law, most agents usually have a specialized professional background. Patent agents frequently possess professional engineering degrees, or advanced training in another field of science, and are skilled in the assessment of inventions in terms of their being new and useful.

The patent agent will generally make a search at the Patent Office for any similar patents before proceeding with an application on behalf of the inventor. This search is a useful first step in the patent process, because any patents already issued that cover a part of the invention (or possibly all of it) would indicate that the invention may not be patentable at all, or subject to patent for only those parts that are new. The same would hold true if the search revealed that the same invention had been patented some time ago and the invention was now in the public domain. Patent agents frequently conduct a similar search at the U.S. Patent Office to determine if a patent has been issued there for all or a part of the invention.

If the search reveals that the invention is in fact something new and open to patent, the next step is that the inventor makes an application for patent protection for the invention. This is done by the preparation of an application or **petition** for the patent, which the inventor must submit, along with detailed **specifications** of the invention. A part of this must be a **claims statement** that indicates what is new and useful about the invention. A drawing of the invention is usually required if the invention is something of the nature of a machine, product, etc., that has a shape or parts that must be assembled. To complete the application, the inventor must submit the patent filing fee and a short abstract of the disclosure written in simple language, capable of being understood by the ordinary technician. Each of these documents is important from the applicant's point of view and must be carefully prepared.

The most important document is the specifications and claims statement that describes the invention in detail and sets out what is new and useful about the discovery. It must contain a description of all important parts of the invention in sufficient detail to enable a skilled worker to construct the patented product from the information given when the patent protection expires. If the inventor intentionally leaves out important parts of the invention in order to prevent others from producing it, the patent may be void. Hence, accuracy is important to obtain patent protection.

The claims statement is equally as important, as it sets out the various uses of the invention and what is new in the product or process that would entitle the inventor to a patent. The claim must also be accurate, as too broad a claim could cause difficulties for the inventor later if the invention should fail to live up to its "claims."

The abstract that accompanies the application is simply a brief synopsis of the detailed submission to enable a person searching later to determine the general nature of the invention and its intended uses. It is written in non-technical language and seldom exceeds a few hundred words in length.

Once the material filed is in order, the staff of the Patent Office proceed with a detailed examination of the material and the Patent Office records to determine if the invention infringes on any other patent. If the patent staff determine that the invention is indeed new and different, then a patent is issued to the inventor. In the past, the search and issue sometimes took long periods of time. For example, a patent for the manufacture of a type of plastic dinnerware was applied for in 1935, but the patent was not issued until 1956, some 21 years later. Today, however, the period of protection is from the date of application, and the process is expected to take only a short period of time. Delay in issue, however, is seldom a serious matter, as most manufacturers of the product for which the patent has been applied may institute a special process for rapid examination and issue of the patent if some other manufacturer should produce the product without the inventor's consent. The prompt issue of the patent under these circumstances would place the other manufacturer in the position of infringing on the patent and liable to the inventor for damages once the patent is issued. As a result, few manufacturers would likely trouble themselves to tool up for the manufacture of goods knowing that a patent has been applied for. The making of goods "patent pending" or "patent applied for" has no other purpose than to notify others that the application has been made for the patent. It has no special significance at law, as the rights of the inventor only arise on the issue of the patent.

The issue of a patent under the present act provides the inventor with exclusive right to the invention and its manufacture and distribution for a period of 20 years from the date of the application.[16] Inventors granted a patent are required to pay both an issuing fee and an additional annual fee to maintain the patent. To enable others to know how long the patentee's rights run, the article or product must be marked with the date of issue of the patent. If the product cannot be so marked, then a label must be attached containing the information.[17]

Patents for medical drug products are subject to special provisions under the patent act that protect the public from excessive prices being set for the products by patent holders. A Patent Medicines Prices Review Board may review drug prices to ensure that medical drugs are available at the lowest cost to the public yet still recognize the research and development costs of the drug manufacturers. The purpose of the board is to attempt to balance these interests and provide an incentive for manufacturers to undertake the high cost of research to develop new drug products.

Foreign Patent Protection

During the nineteenth century, patent protection was the subject of discussion at a number of meetings held by industrialized countries in an effort to devise a system whereby inventors might obtain patent protection for their inventions in countries other than that of their place of residence. Eventually, at the meeting in Paris, France, in 1883, agreement was reached whereby an inventor, who had applied for patent protection in his or her own country, could make an appropriate application in any other country that was a party to the agreement within 12 months after the original application. The application in the foreign country would have the same filing date as that of the first filing. This permitted any inventor residing in a country that belonged to the Union Convention of Paris, 1883, to obtain a uniform filing date in all countries where patent protection was applied for. For example, if an inventor applied for a patent in Canada on

---

16. Patent Act, R.S.C. 1985, c. P-4, s. 46.

17. Ibid., s. 24.

February 1st and applied for a patent on the same invention in the United Kingdom on June 1st, the effect of the convention would be that the inventor's application in the United Kingdom would be back-dated to the date of the original filing in Canada (i.e., February 1st). Proposed amendments to the Patent Act would require a foreign applicant to claim treaty priority within six months of filing, and provide the Commissioner of Patents with information concerning the foreign application.[18]

Compulsory Licences

One of the obligations of a patentee is that he or she must work the invention to satisfy public demand for the new product or process. This is essentially a public duty that the patentee must perform in return for the grant of monopoly rights to his or her discovery. Most inventors are usually only too happy to perform this duty, either by the production of the product themselves or by licensing others to manufacture the product in return for a royalty payment. If the patentee so desires, he or she might also assign the patent rights to another, in which case the obligation to work the patent would shift to the assignee.

The act provides that for certain inventions, a **compulsory licence** may be in order for the general benefit of the public. Compulsory licensing, for example, may arise where the work of the patent is dependent upon the right to produce a part covered by an earlier patent. If such a licence is required to work the later patent (usually an improvement in some part of the original patent), the patentee of the improvement may apply to the Commissioner of Patents for the issue of a compulsory licence.

If a patentee fails to work a patent to meet public demand for the invention, or if the price for the product is unreasonably high, any interested party may apply to manufacture the invention under licence at any time after the patent has been in effect for three years. If the patentee cannot refute the claim that he or she cannot supply the demand for the invention, a licence may be issued to the applicant on whatever terms would appear reasonable in the circumstances. This usually means the issue of a licence to manufacture on a royalty basis. However, depending upon the circumstances, a failure or refusal to work a patent in the face of demonstrated public demand for the invention could also result in a revocation of the patent.

Infringement

The issue of a patent is essentially a grant of a monopoly to the patentee for a fixed period. During this time the patentee, subject to certain public interest limitations, has the exclusive right to deal with the invention. The production of a product or use of the process covered by the patent by any person not authorized to use it would constitute **infringement** and would entitle the patentee to take legal action against the unauthorized producer, user, or seller. Infringement is very broad in its application. It includes not only unauthorized production of the invention but the importation of the product, or any other working of the patent without the consent or payment of royalties to the patentee.

---

18. Patent Amendment Act, S.C. 1987, c. 41.

To succeed against the unauthorized producer or importer of the invention, the patentee (assignee or licensee) must prove that infringement has taken place, since damages do not automatically flow from the production of an invention that is subject to a patent. For example, a defence against a claim for infringement might be that the patent is invalid, or that the patent had expired before the goods were produced. A patentee may also be faced with the defence of estoppel if the validity of the patent was successfully attacked by another person prior to the patentee's claim of infringement, or if the patentee had allowed the infringement to take place with tacit approval for some time before claiming infringement. Infringement cases tend to be very complex, and infringement itself very much a question of fact; consequently, the defences can be many and varied.

TRADE MARKS

Historical Development of the Law

A trade mark is a mark that may be used by a producer or merchant to distinguish his or her goods or services from those of others. It may take the form of either a trade mark or a trade name, but the purpose of the mark or name is the same: to identify the goods or services of the owner of the mark.

The use of trade marks to distinguish or identify the wares of a producer or seller would appear to be a practice with a long history. Early craftsmen, such as the brickmakers of early Babylon and the water pipe manufacturers of ancient Rome, marked their wares with their distinctive symbols or signatures. Later, members of some of the early guilds established their own special marks for the goods that they produced.

In England, one of the first recorded cases dealing with trade mark infringement concerned an action in which a manufacturer of cloth claimed damages for deceit from another who had passed off his goods by marking the cloth with the plaintiff's mark.[19] The court found in favour of the plaintiff, but some doubt existed as to whether the plaintiff was in fact the cloth manufacturer or a purchaser of the cloth who was deceived by the improper use of the mark. At common law, if the plaintiff was the purchaser, the action was an ordinary action of deceit; but if the plaintiff was the manufacturer, the case would be common law recognition of the right of action for infringement. The matter remained confused for over two centuries following this initial case. However, the need for legislation to establish ownership of trade marks was finally recognized by 1875, when the **Trade Marks Registration Act**[20] was introduced to remedy the situation.

The act provided that, by registration, the owner of a trade mark would establish the prima facie right to use the mark exclusively. After five years, the right became absolute, so long as the owner used the mark in business. The act set out the various requirements for registration and a general outline of the type of marks that were registrable.

Trade marks legislation in Canada followed a similar pattern of development, with the first statute introduced in 1868.[21] The act provided for the registration of marks under a procedure that gave the registered user the right to exclusive use of

---

19. *Southern v. How* (1618), Popham 143, 79 E.R. 1243.

20. Trade Marks Registration Act, 1875, 38 & 39 Vict., c. 91.

21. The Trade Mark and Design Act of 1868, 31 Vict., c. 55 (Can.) (1868).

the mark. An unusual feature of the act was the sharing of the fine for infringement on a 50-50 basis between the Crown and the party injured by the infringement. The act, along with legislation pertaining to patents and copyright at the time, was placed under the administration of the Department of Agriculture.[22]

Trade marks legislation passed through a number of amendments and changes during the latter part of the nineteenth century, with a complete revision of the act in 1879.[23] The revision repealed and replaced the prior legislation except for those acts dealing with the marking of timber,[24] and the law dealing with the fraudulent marking of merchandise.[25] While not following the English legislation in detail, the law in Canada underwent a number of changes to expand the nature of the protection available to users of marks by including **certification marks** (marks used to identify goods or services produced or performed under controlled conditions, or of a certain quality), the importation of trade-marked goods, the licensing of users of trade marks by the "owner," and a revision of the penalties for unfair practices and infringement. The last major overhaul of the act was in 1953, but more recently the legislation has been subject to study and proposed revision.[26]

Trade Marks Act

The present Trade Marks Act[27] is a federal statute that governs the use of all trade marks and trade names in use in Canada. The act defines a trade mark as any mark "used by a person for the purpose of distinguishing or so as to distinguish wares or services manufactured, sold, leased, hired or performed by him from those manufactured, sold, leased, hired or performed by others."[28] The act also provides for the registration of trade marks and maintains a register of marks at the Trade Marks Office. Protection under the act is provided by a registration process, and any mark that is not descriptive, not in use by another prior user, not confusing with existing marks, and not contrary to the public interest, may be registered.

At the present time, there are a number of different types of marks that may be registered under the act:

(1) Service marks: marks that are used by service industries such as banks, airlines, and trucking companies, where the principal business is that of providing a service to the public. The mark, however, may also be applied to any product that the user might sell, such as an airline that sells flight bags or toy models of its aircraft.

(2) Certification marks: marks used to distinguish goods or services of a certain quality that, in the case of goods, are produced under certain working conditions; or in the case of services, performed by a certain class of persons;

---

22. 31 Vict., c. 53 (1868) (Can.).

23. The Trade Mark and Design Act of 1879, 42 Vict., c. 22 (Can.).

24. An Act Respecting the Marking of Timber, 33 Vict., c. 36 (Can.).

25. "The Trade Mark Offences Act, 1872," 35 Vict., c. 32 (Can.).

26. See, for example, Working Paper Trade Marks Law Revision (Ministry of Consumer and Corporate Affairs, 1974).

27. Trade Marks Act, R.S.C. 1985, c. T-13.

28. Trade Marks Act, R.S.C. 1985, c. T-13, s. 2.

or goods or services produced in a particular area. Most certification marks are used for franchise operations where the owner of the mark does not produce the goods or perform the services directly, but merely sets and enforces the standard for the goods or services to which the mark is applied. Certification marks are essentially "quality marks."

(3) Distinctive guise: a trade mark that takes the form of a particular shape to distinguish it from the products of others. Distinguishing guises are generally in the form of the package, or the shape of the product itself, and may be protected by the act. Utilitarian features of the guise, however, may not be protected, for example, a moulded or built-in handgrip on a bottle or box.

(4) Trade name: generally a name coined or chosen to describe a business. It must not be a name that might be confused with any other name. As a rule, a person is not prohibited from using his or her own name, simply because it is the same as that of a well-known establishment.

A classic case on the right to a trade name or mark was *Singer Mfg. Co. v. Loog* [29] where the judge described the right to mark goods in the following language:

> ...no man is entitled to represent his goods as being the goods of another man; and no man is permitted to use any mark, sign or symbol, device or other means, whereby, without making a direct false representation himself to a purchaser who purchases from him, he enables such purchaser to tell a lie or to make a false representation to somebody else who is the ultimate customer. That being, as it appears to me, a comprehensive statement of what the law is upon the question of trade-mark or trade designation, I am of opinion that there is no such thing as a monopoly or a property in the nature of a copyright, or in the nature of patent, in the use of any name. Whatever name is used to designate goods, anybody may use that name to designate goods; always subject to this, that he must not, as I said, make directly, or through the medium of another person, a false representation that his goods are the goods of another person. That I take to be the law.

Registration Requirements

A trade mark must be distinctive and used in order to be registrable under the act. However, special provision is made for proposed marks that may be cleared as suitable trade marks, then later registered, once they are put in use. The act does not permit all marks to be registered that are distinctive and used, as certain marks are prohibited by the statute. **Prohibited marks** are usually associated with royalty, governments, or internationally known agencies, and may not be used without their consent. A mark must also be such that it cannot be associated with any famous or well-known living person (or a person who has died within the previous 30 years), and it cannot be an offensive symbol. The "distinctive" requirement is often the most difficult to meet, as the mark must be such that it cannot be confused with the mark of another.

Marks that are searched in the register and found to be acceptable are advertised in the *Trade Marks Journal* to advise the public of the intended registration

---

29. *Singer Mfg. Co. v. Loog* (1880) 18 Ch.D. 395.

of the mark. If no objections arise as a result of the public notice, the mark may then be registered. If its distinctiveness is not challenged within the next five years, it becomes incontestable unless it can be shown that the applicant knew of other users prior to the application for registration. A mark that should not have been registered in the first place would, of course, be open to challenge as well. An example of the latter objection would be a mark that was later discovered to be an offensive symbol. Registration is valid for a period of 15 years, and the registration may be renewed, as long as the mark is in use.

Enforcement

A person who has registered a trade mark is entitled to protect the mark by taking legal action to prevent the use of the mark by another. The usual remedy is an injunction. However, where unauthorized goods or services were sold under the registered mark, an accounting for the lost profits due to the use of the mark may be had. The forgery of a trade mark, or the passing off of goods as being the goods of another, is also a criminal offence.[30] Criminal penalties may be imposed if criminal proceedings are taken against the unlawful user of the trade mark.

If the trade mark is no longer used, or has lost its distinctiveness because the product has become so successful that the name has become generic, the user may no longer claim exclusive rights to the use of the name. The trade mark "Linoleum," for example, became the generic word through public use of the term to mean all floor coverings of that type, and the word lost its distinctiveness with respect to its user's product. The name "Aspirin" suffered the same fate in the United States, but to date it is a registered trade name in Canada. Users of well-known trade marks, as a result, are careful to guard their trade marks and names to prevent the word from being used by the news media as a generic term for all products of a similar type.

Foreign Trade Marks

As with patents, Canada is a member of an international convention concerning trade marks that permits a user of a trade mark in a foreign country to apply for registration there. If an application is also made in Canada within six months thereafter, the application in Canada will be dated as of the date of application in the foreign country. Special filing requirements, however, are imposed upon the foreign trade mark applicant.

COPYRIGHT   Copyright is a term that means what it says: it is the "right to copy." The law pertaining to copyright is concerned with the control of the right to copy. It recognizes the right of the original creator of any writing or artistic work to control the reproduction of the work. Included in the type of work that copyright covers is all writing in the form of books, articles, and poems, as well as written work of every description, including musical compositions (both music and lyrics), dance choreography, and dramatic works. The right also covers all forms of artistic work in the nature of sculpture, paintings, maps, engravings, sketches, drawings, photographs, and motion pictures. Because reproduction in the case of music and

---

30. Criminal Code, R.S.C. 1985, c. C-46, ss. 406-411.

dramatic works involves, in many cases, the recording of the music or work on phonograph record, tape, or film, the right extends to the right to record the work by electronic or mechanical means. The same holds true for the reproduction of any literary or other work photocopied or stored in a computer retrieval system. Copyright protection also extends to computer programs that may not be reproduced (except for the making of a single back-up copy by the owner of the copy of the program).[31] Subject to certain exceptions, the law protects the original author's right to control all reproduction of his or her work.

Historical Development of the Law

At common law, the right of the author of a literary or artistic work was not entirely clear. This was due in part to the fact that reproduction of a literary or artistic work prior to the invention of printing was a laborious undertaking. It was not a matter likely to be of much concern before the courts. After the invention of the printing press, written work acquired a special commercial value, and the question of ownership of written work and the right to reproduce it became important (at least from the author's point of view). The establishment of a printing press and the printing of the first book in England in 1477 by William Caxton, in a sense, created the need for a law that would determine the right of an author to control the reproduction of his work.

At common law, the right of an author to control unpublished work was generally settled: the author was entitled to do as he wished with the material, because it was his, and his alone.[32] The right to control the copy of the work once published, however, was another matter. On this point, the law was unclear, so much so that many legal authorities believed that the right did not exist once the work was published, as publication was, in a sense, placing the work in the public domain.

In 1709, the first statute was passed to establish the rights of authors in their published works.[33] A series of statutes followed that extended copyright to musical and dramatic works, and later to photographs and other products of the advancing technology of the nineteenth and early twentieth centuries. By 1909, copyright in England was covered by a number of different statutes, and rationalization was clearly in order. To clear away the confusion, a new act was introduced in 1911 to clarify and consolidate the law.[34]

The law pertaining to copyright in Canada (apart from the laws of England) had its beginnings in a statute of Lower Canada,[35] that recognized an author's rights in all literary work. The law, however, related only to what is now the province of Quebec. The remainder of Canada was subject to the English law, beginning with the act of 1709. The passage of the British North America Act, 1867, however, transferred the legislative authority to the federal government.

---

31. S.C. 1988 c. 15, s. 5.

32. *Jefferys v. Boosey* (1854), 4 H.L. Cas. 815, 10 E.R. 681.

33. "An Act for the Encouragement of Learning by Vesting Copies of Printed Books in the Authors and Purchasers of Such Copies," 8 Anne, c. 19.

34. Copyright Act, 1911, 1 & 2 Geo. V, c. 46.

35. "An Act to Protect Copy Rights," 2 Will. IV, c. 53 (Lower Canada).

The first **Copyright Act** was passed the next year.[36] Legislation pertaining to copyright was passed from time to time in the years that followed, but it was not until 1921 that a comprehensive law was introduced.

The 1921 act,[37] which came into force in 1924, covered virtually all literary and artistic endeavour, and provided for a Registrar of Copyrights and a Copyright Office. The act provided for the registration of copyrights and set out an elaborate list of material that was subject to copyright. It also included penalties for the infringement of copyright.

In 1988, new legislative changes were introduced that updated the law pertaining to copyright. The new changes addressed some of the technological advances that have had an impact on the reproduction of copyrighted work, and included new types of work that required protection under the act.

The Copyright Act

The present legislation[38] provides that the sole right to publish or reproduce an original work of a literary or artistic nature is in the original author of the work. The protection of the right extends for the life of the author and for 50 years after the author's death. Work not published during the author's lifetime is subject to a copyright for a period of 50 years. In the case of recorded works, it runs for a period of 50 years from the date the recording is cut or first made. Registration of the copyright is not essential in order to claim copyright. However, registration is public notice of the copyright. It becomes proof of ownership of the work if the author should be required to bring an action for damages against a person who copies the work without permission.

It is important to note that the author is the first owner of the work and entitled to claim copyright in it, unless the author was employed by another for the purpose of producing the work, painting, photograph, etc., provided that the parties did not agree to the contrary. However, only the arrangement of the words or the expression of the idea is subject to copyright; the idea or the subject-matter of the work is not subject to protection. For example, two authors might each write an article for a magazine dealing with energy conservation, each article containing the same ideas or suggestions. Each would be entitled to claim copyright in the arrangement of the words, but the ideas contained in the articles, although identical, would not be subject to a claim of copyright by either of the writers.

Protection of copyright usually takes the form of registration of the work and the marking of material by the symbol © . This is followed by words to indicate the date of first publication and the name of the author. Canada has been a member of the **Universal Copyright Convention** since 1962,[39] and the marking of the published material in this manner is notice to all persons in those countries that are a part of the convention that copyright is claimed in the marked work. The enforcement or protection of the copyright, however, is the responsibility of the owner.

An author or artist is entitled to assign a copyright, either in whole or in part to another. However, to be valid, the assignment must be in writing. Assignments

---

36. The Copyright Act of 1868, 31 Vict., c. 54 (Can.).

37. The Copyright Act, 1921, 11 & 12 Geo. V., c. 24.

38. Copyright Act, R.S.C. 1985, c. C-42.

39. Canada is also a member of the Berne Copyright Convention that provides an author with protection in member countries.

of copyright are normally registered as well, to give public notice of the assignment. The act also provides for the issue of licences to print published works in Canada where a demand exists and the author has failed to supply the market. Where a licence is issued, the publisher is expected to pay a royalty to the author as compensation. If a work is printed or copied without either the permission of the author or a licence, the reproduction of the work may constitute **infringement.** It may also expose the unauthorized publisher to penalties under the act and/or an action for infringement by the holder of the copyright.

Infringement consists of unauthorized copying of the protected work except for "fair dealing" with the work by others for the purpose of private study, research, criticism, review, or newspaper summary. Certain other exceptions exist as well, such as the reading in public of short excerpts from a copyright work, the performance of a musical by a church, school, or charitable body (if the work is performed for educational or charitable purposes by unpaid performers), and a number of other uses of the material.[40] In the case of infringement, the copyright owner is usually entitled to an injunction and an accounting, as well as damages.

Infringement action may also arise where the moral rights of the author have been affected by persons dealing with the author's work.[41] In particular, the author has a "moral right" to have his or her name associated with the work. Under the act this is described as a "right to the integrity of the work." The author also has the moral right to have a pseudonym associated with the work or to remain anonymous. The right to integrity also encompasses a right of action where distortion or mutilation of works would prejudice the honour or reputation of the author.

Moral rights may not be assigned by the author, but may be waived and pass on the author's death to the author's beneficiaries under a will or to heirs-at-law. Infringement of a moral right of the author would entitle the author to take legal action against the violator for damages.

REGISTERED DESIGNS

Registered design legislation applies to certain artistic works produced by an industrial process. A registered design is normally a design that would be the subject-matter of copyright if it was not for the fact that it is reproduced by an industrial process. For example, new furniture designs would require registration under the Industrial Designs Act[42] in order to be protected. Not all products must be registered, as the act does not apply to some "artistic" products produced by industrial processes. The act also does not apply to features that are purely utilitarian, such as a handle on a container. However, the design of the handle may be protected if it is unique in appearance.

Registration gives the owner of the design exclusive rights to produce the design for a period of five years, renewable for a further term of five years. The design, however, must be original, and not something that is likely to be taken for the design of another. In this respect, the requirements for registration are similar to those for a patent, but the investigative process is not nearly so exhaustive. The design must also be registered within 12 months of its first publication in Canada in order to acquire protection.

40. See, for example, Copyright Act, R.S.C. 1985, c. C-42, s. 27(2).
41. S.C. 1988 c. 15, s., 12.1, 18.2.
42. Industrial Design Act, R.S.C. 1985, c. I-9.

Once the design is registered, the owner of the design is obliged to notify the public of the rights claimed in the design by marking the goods (or by printing a label with "Rd." The date and the design owner's name should also appear.

The ownership of the design, as with patents or copyright, may be assigned, or rights to manufacture may be granted under licence. Any unauthorized manufacture, however, would entitle the owner of the design to take legal action for infringement.

SUMMARY

The protection of rights to intellectual and industrial property are covered by a number of federal statutes. Each act recognizes and protects a special property right and confirms ownership rights in it. A patent, which is the exclusive right of ownership granted to a first inventor of a new and useful product, lasts for 20 years from time of filing. During this time the holder of the patent (subject to certain exceptions related to the public interest) is granted monopoly rights in the invention. Patents, in some cases, are subject to compulsory licensing requirements, and may also be revoked if they are not "worked" to meet public demand. Once a patent is issued, unauthorized production of patented works constitutes infringement and would entitle the patentee or those claiming rights through the patentee to bring an action for damages against the unauthorized producer.

Trade marks are rights to the exclusive use of marks that distinguish the wares or services of one person from the wares or services of another. Under the Trade Marks Act distinctive marks used to identify a person's product or service may be protected by registration. Registration permits the user of the name or mark to prevent others from using the mark without express permission. The unauthorized marking of goods by a person, for the purpose of passing them off as being those of the authorized owner of the trade mark, constitutes the criminal offence of "passing off." It would also leave that person open to an action for damages and an injunction by the owner of the mark.

Copyright is the "right to copy" original literary or artistic work. Copyright legislation recognizes the author or composer of the work as the owner of the copyright and the person entitled to benefit from any publication of the material. The statute provides the exclusive right in the owner for the owner's lifetime plus 50 years; but in the case of some types of copyright material, the right is limited to only 50 years. A copyright may be assigned or licences may be granted for copyright work. However, any unauthorized publication or performance of the work (subject to certain exceptions) constitutes infringement and would entitle the owner of the copyright to receive the profits on the unauthorized publication, damages, and an injunction, depending upon the circumstances.

A registered design is somewhat similar to copyright in the sense that it is an artistic work that is reproduced by an industrial process. Registration of the design protects the owner from unauthorized reproduction of the same design by others. A registered design is protected for five years from the date of registration, but the registration may be renewed for a further five years.

DISCUSSION QUESTIONS

1. For what public purpose did the Crown originally grant monopolies for certain products?
2. Under modern patent legislation, what is the purpose of granting a patent for a new product?
3. How is the public interest protected under patent legislation?
4. What steps must an inventor follow in order to acquire patent protection for an invention?
5. Explain the meaning of *patent pending*.
6. If an inventor had reason to believe that someone was producing a product that infringed on his or her patent, what would the inventor's rights be? What remedies are available for infringement?
7. Outline the steps that a Canadian inventor must follow to obtain patent protection for an invention in a foreign country.
8. Describe briefly the purpose of trade mark legislation. Why has it been necessary?
9. How does a trade mark differ from a trade name?
10. Distinguish between a service mark and a certification mark.
11. Explain the term *distinguishing guise*.
12. What must a person who has a proposed mark do in order to establish rights to the mark?
13. What constitutes infringement of a trade mark? What steps must the owner of a trade mark take in order to prevent further infringement?
14. Outline the purpose of copyright legislation. What type of work is it intended to protect?
15. How is notice of copyright usually given?
16. What defences may be available to a person who is accused of infringing on a copyright work?
17. Where infringement is established, what remedies are available to the owner of the copyright?
18. What is a registered design? How does it differ from copyright?
19. Explain the protection that a registered design offers the owner of the design. How is this enforced?

MINI-CASE PROBLEMS

1. A engaged the services of B, a professional photographer, to take a series of photographs of his power boat. B did so and was paid $200 for his services. Some time later, A discovered that B had sold the negative of one of the pictures to a boating magazine for the cover of one of its issues. B received $500 from the magazine for the picture. Is A entitled to the $500?
2. X produced a cola beverage that he sold for many years under the trade name Krazy Kola. If Y decided to produce and sell a cola beverage in the same area under the name Crazy Cola, would Y's actions constitute a violation of X's trade name?

JUDICIAL DECISIONS

The case *Coca-Cola Co. of Canada Ltd. v. Pepsi-Cola Co. of Canada Ltd.* is a classic case on trade marks. The case illustrates the problem of confusing marks and the test that the court developed to determine when a mark might be confusing to the public. The common word in both trade names is the word "cola" that the court examines with reference to a number of other trade marks or names that include "cola" as well. The court concludes that the distinctive words are the words that precede the word "cola," and "pepsi" is sufficiently different from "coca" to distinguish the two wares.

The *Reckitt & Colman (Overseas) Ltd. v. Brass Magic Inc.* case also deals with the issue of confusing marks. In this case, in contrast to the Coca-Cola case, the court concludes that the words "Brasso" and Brass Magic are sufficiently similar to be confused, and the trade mark requested by Brass Magic is refused.

The third judicial decision concerns industrial design registration and the issue of whether an industrial design may be used to protect a method of construction. The case hinges on whether the design of the overshoe meets the criteria for registration. The court reviews these requirements for registration and applies them to the design before the court. In the end, the court decides that the action should fail because the design is not appropriate for registration.

Trade Mark — Test for Determining Confusion with Other Names

Coca-Cola Co. of Canada Ltd. v. Pepsi-Cola Co. of Canada Ltd., [1942] 2 D.L.R. 657.

The plaintiff sued the defendant for infringement of its registered trade mark because its name was written in a script similar to that of the plaintiff's; it was a hyphenated word using the same word "cola," and applied to a similar soft drink product. The defendant argued that the words were not confusing to the public.

LORD RUSSELL OF KILLOWEN:

The plaintiff's mark consists of the words Coca and Cola joined by a hyphen and written, not in block letters, but in a script form with flourishes. It was applied to beverages and syrups, and was used for that purpose in Canada from the year 1900 (or perhaps earlier) by a company formed in the State of Georgia and called the Coca-Cola Company. It was registered by that company under the Trade Mark and Design Act of Canada on November 11, 1905. The mark was assigned in the year 1922 by the Georgia company to a company formed in the State of Delaware, and called also the Coca-Cola Company. The Canadian business of the last mentioned company was acquired in the following year by the plaintiff, and an assignment by the Delaware company of the mark to the plaintiff was registered on March 7, 1930. The plaintiff then renewed the registration of the mark for a period of 25 years from November 11, 1930. There is no doubt that the plaintiff has carried on and is carrying on in Canada under its registered mark a large business in the manufacture and sale of a non-alcoholic beverage known as Coca-Cola. The scale of its trade is sufficiently indicated by the fact that in the year 1936 it owned some 20 bottling plants, and in addition had contracts with some 80 independent bottlers.

The defendant was incorporated on May 29, 1934, and began to sell in Canada a non-alcoholic beverage called Pepsi-Cola, under a mark consisting of the words Pepsi and Cola joined by a hyphen and written in a script form with flourishes. Whether the defendant had acquired the goodwill of any business, and whether the defendant was properly on the register in respect of a mark which differs slightly from the mark actually in use by the defendant, were matters much discussed by plaintiff's counsel. These matters however seem to be irrelevant to the only question which their Lordships have to decide *viz.,* whether the mark which the defendant uses infringes the plaintiff's registered mark. The respective rights of the parties are now governed by the *Unfair Competition Act, 1932* (Can.), c. 38, to which more detailed reference must be made.

By s. 3(c) of the Act it is provided that no person shall knowingly adopt for use in Canada in connection with any wares any trade mark which is similar to any trade mark which is in use in Canada by any other person and which is registered pursuant to the provisions of that Act as a trade mark for the same or simi-

CHAPTER 33 Patents, Trade Marks and Copyright 723

lar wares. There is no dispute that the mark which the defendant uses is subject to the above prohibition if it is "similar" to the plaintiff's registered mark. The other requirements as to "knowingly" and similarity of wares are admittedly fulfilled.

The word "similar," in relation to trade marks is defined by the Act (unless the context otherwise requires) thus:

"2(*k*) 'Similar,' in relation to trade marks ... describes marks ... so resembling each other or so clearly suggesting the idea conveyed by each other that the contemporaneous use of both in the same area in association with wares of the same kind would be likely to cause dealers in and/or users of such wares to infer that the same person assumed responsibility for their character or quality, for the conditions under which or the class of persons by whom they were produced, or for their place of origin." The contemporaneous use of both marks in the same area in association with wares of the same kind is not in dispute. The actual question for decision in the present case may, therefore, in the light of the above definition by stated thus: — Does the mark used by the defendant so resemble the plaintiff's registered mark or so clearly suggest the idea conveyed by it, that its use is likely to cause dealers in or users of non-alcoholic beverages to infer that the plaintiff assumed responsibility for the character or quality or place of origin of Pepsi-Cola?

The President of the Exchequer Court answered the question in the affirmative; the Supreme Court answered it in the negative. Their Lordships are in agreement with the Supreme Court.

The case appears to them to be one which is free from complications, and which raises neither new matter of principal [*sic*] nor novel question of trade mark law. The only peculiar feature of the case is the dearth of evidence, attributable doubtless to the procedure adopted by the plaintiff at the trial. The only matters proved before the plaintiff's case was closed were (1) the plaintiff's registered mark and (2) the use by the defendant of the mark alleged to be an infringement. No evidence of (to put it shortly) confusion either actual or probable was adduced. It was contended that a statement by a witness called by the defendant (one Charles Guth) was proof of actual confusion. Guth was general manager of a United States company which owns the capital stock of the defendant. He was also President of a New York company called Loft Incorporated which own a large number of candy stores in New York at which Coca-Cola was sold. Subsequently the sale of Coca-Cola was discontinued, and Pepsi-Cola was sold at the stores. A passing-off action was brought by the Delaware Coca-Cola Co. against Loft Incorporated [(1933), 167 Atl. 900]. The Judge of the Court of Chancery, Delaware, dismissed the action holding that Loft Incorporated was not responsible for the acts of its agents of which evidence had been given. In the course of his cross-examination in the Exchequer Court, Guth was asked "Then you have no quarrel with the Chancellor's decision as to the facts expressed in his opinion?" and he answered "None at all." It was argued that this answer proved the fact found in the judgment of the Chancellor *viz.* (as quoted by the President of the Exchequer Court [1938] 4 D.L.R. at p. 167, from a report of the case) that "the 'uncontradicted evidence shows that substitutions were made by employees of the defendants of a product other than Coca-Cola for that beverage when calls for the same were made.'"

The learned President [p. 169] relied on this judgment as "very formidable support to the plaintiff's contention, that ... there is a likelihood of confusion"; but in their Lordships' opinion he was not entitled to refer to or rely upon a judgment given in proceedings to which neither the plaintiff nor the defendant was a party, as proving the facts stated therein. Those facts are in no way proved thereby, nor are they in any way proved by the answer of Guth which has been quoted above. Guth could not of his own knowledge either quarrel or agree with the Chancellor's decision as to what it was that had happened in the numerous stores, and that was described by the word "substitutions". There was accordingly no evidence before the Exchequer Court of confusion actual or probable.

In these circumstances the question for determination must be answered by the Court, unaided by outside evidence, after a comparison of the defendant's mark as used with the plaintiff's registered mark, not placing them side by side, but by asking itself whether, having due regard to relevant surrounding circumstances, the defendant's mark as used is similar (as defined by the Act) to the plaintiff's registered mark as it would be remembered by persons possessed of an average memory with its usual imperfections.

In the present case two circumstances exist which are of importance in this connection. The first is the information which is afforded by dictionaries in relation to the word "Cola." While questions may sometimes arise as to the extent to which a Court may inform itself by reference to dictionaries there can, their Lordships think, be no doubt that dictionaries may properly be referred to in order to ascertain not only the meaning of a word, but also the use to which the thing (if it be a thing) denoted by the word is commonly put. A reference to dictionaries shows that Cola or Kola is a tree whose seed or nut is "largely used for chewing as a condiment and digestive" (Murray), a nut of which "the extract is used as a tonic drink" (Webster), and which is "imported into the United States for use in medical preparations and summer drinks" (Encyclopaedia Americana). Cola would therefore appear to be a word which might appropriately be used in association with beverages and in particular with that class of non-alcoholic beverages colloquially known by the description of "soft drinks". That in fact the words "Cola" or "Kola" has been so used in Canada is established by the second of the two circumstances before referred to.

The defendant put in evidence a series of 22 trade marks registered in Canada from time to time during a period of 29 years, *viz.,* from 1902 to 1930, in connection with beverages. They include the mark of the plaintiff and the registered mark of the defendant. The other 20 marks consist of two or more words or a compound word, but always containing the word "Cola" or "Kola". The following are a few samples of the bulk: — "Kola Tonic Wine", "La-Kola", "Cola-Claret", "Rose-Cola", "Orange Kola", "O'Keefe's Cola", "Royal Cola". Their Lordships agree with the Supreme Court in attributing weight to these registrations as shown that the word Cola (appropriate for the purpose as appears above) had been adopted in Canada as an item in the naming of different beverages.

The proper comparison must be made with that fact in mind.

Numerous cases were cited in the Courts of Canada and before the Board in which the question of infringement of various marks has been considered and decided; but except when some general principle is laid down, little assistance is derived from authorities in which the question of infringement is discussed in relation to other marks and other circumstances.

The plaintiff claimed that by virtue of s. 23(5) (*b*) of the *Unfair Competition Act* 1932 its registered mark was both a word mark and a design mark; and their Lordships treat it accordingly.

If it be viewed simply as a word mark consisting of "Coca" and "Cola" joined by a hyphen, and the fact be borne in mind that Cola is a word in common use in Canada in naming beverages, it is plain that the distinctive feature in this hyphenated word, is the first word "Coca" and not "Cola". "Coca" rather than

"Cola" is what would remain in the average memory. It is difficult, indeed impossible, to imagine that the mark Pepsi-Cola as used by the defendant, in which the distinctive feature is, for the same reason, the first word "Pepsi" and not "Cola", would lead anyone to confuse it with the registered mark of the plaintiff. If it be viewed as a design mark, the same result follows. The only resemblance lies in the fact that both contain the word "Cola", and neither is written in block letters, but in script with flourishes. But the letters and flourishes in fact differ very considerably, notwithstanding the tendency of words written in script with flourishes to bear a general resemblance to each other. There is no need to specify the differences in detail; it is sufficient to say that in their Lordships' opinion, the mark used by the defendant, viewed as a pattern or picture, would not lead a person with an average recollection of the plaintiff's registered mark to confuse it with the pattern or picture represented by that mark.

Trade Marks — Opposition Based upon Confusion of Marks

Reckitt & Colman (Overseas) Ltd. v. Brass Magic Inc. (1988), 20 C.P.R. (3d) 382.*

Brass Magic Inc. applied for the trade mark "Brass Magic" for a brass polish. The opponent, as owner of the mark "Brasso," opposed the registration.

On July 18, 1985, the applicant, Brass Magic Inc., filed an application to register the trade mark BRASS MAGIC based on use in Canada since April of 1985 in association with: "cleaning compound for brass, copper and bronze; polishing cloth". The application was amended to include a disclaimer to the word "brass" and was subsequently advertised for opposition purposes on April 16, 1986.

The opponent, Reckitt & Colman (Overseas) Limited, filed a statement of opposition on July 16, 1986, a copy of which was forwarded to the applicant on August 15, 1986. The grounds of opposition include *inter alia* that the applied for trade mark is not registrable pursuant to the provisions of s. 12(1)(*d*) of the *Trade Marks Act,* R.C.S. 1970, c. T-10, because it is confusing with the opponent's trade mark BRASSO registered under No. 121,850 for "metal polish".

The applicant filed and served a counterstatement. As its evidence, the opponent filed the affidavit of Frederick D. Keenan, vice-president of the opponent's registered user. The applicant did not file evidence. Both parties filed written arguments but no oral hearing was conducted.

As for the opponent's ground of opposition based on s. 12(1)(*d*) of the Act, the material time for considering the circumstances is as of the filing of the opposition. Furthermore, the onus or legal burden is on the applicant to show no reasonable likelihood of confusion. Finally, in applying the test for confusion set forth in s. 6(2) of the Act, regard must be had to all the surrounding circumstances including those specifically set forth in s. 6(5) of the Act.

The applicant's trade mark BRASSO, being a coined word, is inherently distinctive. However, it is not inherently strong since it is somewhat suggestive of metal polishes that could be used for polishing brass objects. On the other hand, the opponent has evidenced fairly significant sales of its BRASSO product and fairly substantial advertising expenditures. Thus, I am able to conclude that the opponent's mark had become known to some extent in Canada as of the material time.

The applicant's mark is inherently weak in that it comprises the non-distinctive word "Brass" modified by the somewhat laudatory word "magic". The applicant's mark strongly suggests that its product will clean brass objects like

---

*Reproduced with the permission of Canada Law Books Inc., 240 Edward Street, Aurora, Ontario L4G 3S9.

magic. The applicant having filed no evidence, I must conclude that its mark had not become known at all in Canada.

The length of time the marks have been in use overwhelmingly favours the opponent. The wares of the parties are either identical or similar. The trades of the parties would also be identical or similar.

The marks of the parties bear a fair degree of resemblance in all respects. The applicant argues that this only arises as a consequence of the common use by both parties of the non-distinctive word "brass" as the initial component of the trade marks. That may be true but it does not lessen the actual degree of resemblance between the marks and the applicant has done nothing to evidence third party use and adoption of similarly prefixed marks for the same type of wares. In fact, Mr. Keenan states that he is unaware of any other such marks in the Canadian market-place.

In applying the test for confusion, I have considered that it is a matter of first impression and imperfect recollection. In view of the foregoing, and particularly in view of the similarity between the wares of the parties, the acquired reputation of the opponent's mark, the degree of resemblance between the marks and the absence of evidence from the applicant, I find that the applicant has failed to satisfy the onus on it to show that its mark is not confusing with the opponent's registered mark. It is therefore unnecessary to consider the remaining grounds of opposition.

In view of the above, I refuse the applicant's application.

Use of Industrial Design to Protect Method of Construction — Improper Use

Kaufman Rubber Co., Ltd. v. Miner Rubber Co., Ltd., [1926] 1 D.L.R. 505. The plaintiff held two registered designs for overshoes and claimed infringement of the designs by the defendant. One design illustrated an ordinary overshoe with two straps and buckles and two straps with dome fasteners. The other design was of an overshoe with three straps with dome fasteners and one strap with a buckle. The designs were described as a "novel configuration of overshoes or galoshes."

MACLEAN, J.:

Part II of the Trade Mark and Design Act relates to industrial designs and the registration of the same. No definition of industrial designs is contained in the Act, and there has been no litigation in our Courts upon the point so far as I know, and consequently no assistance is available from judicial decisions, in determining what constitutes an industrial design, under the statute.

A review of some sections of the statute should however furnish some light, as to what was intended to be the principal characteristics of an industrial design, and what are the necessary elements to be found in a design to sustain its registration.

Section 24 requires that the design be one not in use by any other person than the proprietor, at the time of his adoption thereof. Section 27(3) would indicate that originality of the design was necessary. Then s. 31 is to the effect that no person shall, without the licence of the registered proprietor, apply a design to the ornamentation of any article of manufacture or other article to which an industrial design may be attached or applied, or to sell or use any article to which such design may be applied. Section 34 provides that the name of the proprietor of a design shall appear upon the article to which his design applies. Section 36 is the penalty clause for violation of this part of the Act, and s-s (a) states, that any person applying a design to the ornamenting of any article of manufacture or other article, without licence, is subject to a money penalty.

The sections of the statute to which I have just referred, would therefore seem to indicate that "industrial designs" is there intended to mean some design or mark, which is to be attached to a manufactured article. The use of the word "ornamenting," in 2 different sections of the Act, would clearly indicate that a design might be adapted to purposes of ornamentation. In dealing with designs, the Legislature had I think primarily before it, the idea of shape or ornamentation involving artistic considerations. Clearly a design cannot be an article of manufacture, but something to be applied to an article of manufacture, or other article to which an industrial design may be applied, and capable of existence outside the article itself; nor do I think that the registration of a design would afford any protection for any mechanical principle or contrivance, process or method of manufacture, or principle of construction. Then there must be something original in a registered design, and it must be substantially novel or original, having regard to the nature and character of the subject-matter to which it is applied.

A design to be registrable must therefore be some conception or suggestion as to shape, pattern or ornament applied to any article, and is judged solely by the eye, and does not include any mode or principle of construction. What would constitute a registrable design, is I think admirably and comprehensively expressed in *Pugh v. Riley*, [1912] 1 Ch. 613, at pp. 619-20, by Parker, J., and is I think quite applicable to the provisions of our statute. There he said: — "A design, to be registrable under the Act, must be some conception or suggestion as to shape, configuration, pattern or ornament. It must be capable of being applied to an article in such a way that the article to which it has been applied will shew to the eye the particular shape, configuration, pattern, or ornament the conception or suggestion of which constitutes the design. In general any application for registration must be accompanied by a representation of the design — that is, something in the nature of a drawing or tracing by means of which the conception or suggestion constituting the design may be imparted to others. In fact, persons looking at the drawing ought to be able to form a mental picture of the shape, configuration, pattern, or ornament of the article to which the design has been applied. A conception or suggestion as to a mode or principle of construction though in some sense a design, is not registrable under the Act. Inasmuch, however, as the mode or principle of construction of an article may affect its shape or configuration, the conception of such a mode or principle of construction may well lead to a conception as to the shape or configuration of the completed article, and a conception so arrived at may, if it be sufficiently definite, be registered under the Act. The difficulty arises where the conception thus arrived at is not a definite conception as to shape or configuration, but a conception only as to some general characteristic of shape or configuration necessitated by the mode or principle of construction, the definite shape or configuration being, consistently with such mode or principle of construction, capable of variation within wide limits. To allow the registration of a conception of such general characteristics of shape or configuration might well be equivalent to allowing the registration of shape or configuration of a conception relating to the mode or principle of construction.

In the case before me, the design covers the shape or configuration of the whole overshoe, together with the buckles and straps, the means of fastening. That this is a registrable design within the contemplation of the statute, is not I think to be seriously considered. To hold that it is so registrable would be as said by Bowen, L.J., in *Le May v. Welch* (1884), 28 Ch. D. 24, at p.34, "to paralyse industry, and to make the *Patents, Designs, and Trade-marks Act* a trap to catch honest traders." The registrations are but an attempt to protect a mode of construction.

There is nothing original or novel in the configuration of an overshoe as shown by the plaintiff's designs, or any part of them. The form or configuration of the overshoe, and the fastenings, whether with buckles or dome fasteners or both, are old and disclose no originality. The addition of straps with buckles or straps with dome fasteners, whether concealed or exposed, or the substitution of the one for the other, or the variation in the respective number of each, merely represent a change in the mode of construction of the article. Such variations are mere trade variants, and do not represent invention, originality or novelty. The introduction or substitution of ordinary trade variants in a design, is not only insufficient to make that design new or original, but it does not even contribute to give it a new or original character.

For the reasons which I have above given, I am of the opinion that the registered designs in question are not proper subject-matters for registration within the spirit and intendment of the Trade Mark and Design Act, and in any event neither of them possess the originality or novelty necessary to warrant registration. If it were necessary to dispose of this matter upon other grounds, I might say that the evidence does not establish, that the idea of applying the dome fasteners with a strap beneath the flap of the overshoe, which is admittedly the only original suggestion in the configuration of the overshoe, originated not with the plaintiff, but with Beddoe, who does not claim any invention for it, or the authorship of it. Then again, the statute and the rules require a description of the design, to accompany the drawing upon the application for registration. This was not done, the only description being the mere statement that the design consists of the novel configuration of an overshoe, which is no description at all. If the plaintiff's case is rested upon the contention that the design was intended to cover only a part of the configuration of the overshoe and its fastenings, then the registration is void by virtue of the absence of a description. If it was intended to comprehend the whole of the overshoe and all its parts, then the registration is also void for want of description.

The plaintiff's action therefore fails. There will be judgment directing that the 2 industrial designs mentioned in the pleadings, be expunged from the register of industrial designs. The judgment will also contain an order allowing the defendant his costs of the action.

CASE PROBLEMS FOR DISCUSSION

Case 1

Holdsworth produced a beautiful drawing of a French Provincial love-seat at the request of Classical Furniture Manufacturing Company. Classical Furniture paid Holdsworth $500 for the drawing and used it as the design for its love-seat in a current furniture collection. Six months after it acquired the drawing, and several months after it produced its first production models of the love-seat, the company applied for registration of the design.

Shortly after Classical Furniture registered its design for the love-seat, it discovered that Antique Furniture Co. had a similar love-seat on display in its collection at a furniture exhibit. Classical Furniture immediately accused Antique Furniture of copying its design.

As a defence, Antique Furniture argued that the design was not original. It also came out in the course of discussion that it had acquired its own design by purchasing it from a designer by the name of Holdsworth.

If Classical Furniture should institute legal proceedings against Antique Furniture, what arguments might the parties raise on their own behalf. What is the position of Holdsworth, and what are his rights (if any) or liability (if any)? Speculate as to the outcome of the action.

Case 2

The Cod Oil Drug Company produced a concentrated vitamin product that it sold in capsule form to its customers. To identify its products, it produced its capsules with three broad red bands — the first bearing the letter "C," the second, an "O," and the third, a "D." Each letter was printed in white against the red background to identify the company and its product that was derived from cod liver oil. The centre red band, bearing the letter "O," also acted as a seal that held the two parts of the capsule together. The Cod Oil Drug Company applied for a patent on the method of sealing the two parts of the capsule together, and for registration of the three bands with the letters imprinted as a trade mark for its product.

In the course of its application for a trade mark, Cod Oil Drug Company was faced with an objection to its use of the trade mark by Careful Drug Company, a competitor that produced its product in capsule form bearing two blue bands, one on each part of the capsule, the first bearing a white "C" and the second, a white "D" against the blue bands. A thin blue band was used to join the capsule together, but it bore no letter. The design had been used by Careful Drug for many years before Cod Oil Drug developed the marking of its capsules.

On what basis would Careful Drug argue that the trade mark should not issue? What might Cod Oil Drug argue in response? How successful would the patent application likely be?

Case 3

Denton, an electronics engineer, worked at the development of a miniature hearing aid in his spare time. After much experimentation, he was successful in developing what he wanted. Denton was a member of a local service club that frequently assisted persons with hearing problems. For a special meeting of the club, he was invited to give the members a short lecture on hearing aids and a demonstration of how his device operated. At the meeting, he described how the device was constructed and demonstrated its effectiveness even though it was still in the experimental stage. The meeting was later reported in the local newspaper, along with some general information on Denton's presentation at the meeting. Another member of the club, who was also an electronics engineer, wrote a brief note on Denton's presentation and submitted it to a scientific journal that subsequently printed the note in its "New Developments Section."

Several years later, Denton finally perfected his hearing device and applied for a patent. He then set up facilities for its production, marking each unit produced with the words "patent pending." The product sold well in all parts of the country except British Columbia. When Denton investigated the market in that area, he discovered that a west coast manufacturer was producing hearing aid units that incorporated the particular design that he had developed. His competitor had been selling the similar models for almost a year before Denton had gone into production. Unknown to Denton, the manufacturer had apparently developed his own hearing aid model from information that he had read in the scientific journal report of Denton's presentation to his service club.

Denton had the Patent Office expedite his patent application. On its issue, he instituted legal proceedings against the west coast manufacturer for infringement.

Discuss the arguments that might be raised by the parties in this case. Render a decision.

Case 4

Brown, a part-time news writer for a local newspaper, attended an air show at a local airport. While watching two aircraft performing synchronized aerobatics, she noticed that the wings of the two aircraft were exceptionally close to each other. She photographed the aircraft at the instant that the two aircraft collided and took a second photograph of the pilots as they parachuted to the ground. Brown wrote a brief résumé of the accident and submitted the two pictures and the written material to the local newspaper for publication. The pictures and the report were published in the next edition of the newspaper, in which she received credit for the pictures and the story in a "byline." She was paid her regular rate for the written material, and $50 for each picture. Brown later submitted the same pictures and story to an aviation magazine, and the material was subsequently published. Brown was paid $300 for the pictures and story by the magazine.

When the newspaper discovered the magazine article it instituted legal proceedings against the magazine and Brown for copyright infringement, claiming that the copyright belonged to it.

Discuss the arguments that might be raised by the parties. Indicate how the case might be decided.

Case 5

Holtzkopf, a furniture manufacturer, engaged the services of Adrienne, a professional photographer, to attend a furniture exhibit and take a number of photographs of a particular chair that Larsen, a competitor, had on display. Adrienne did so and delivered the photographs to Holtzkopf, along with her account for $100. Holtzkopf paid the account and began the production of a chair that was very similar in appearance to the competitor's chair, but that had a different structural design beneath the fabric outer cover.

Holtzkopf advertised his chair in a trade magazine. He used several of Adrienne's photographs (which were black and white prints) because, although the chairs were similar in appearance, the exact design and colour of the fabric could not be ascertained from the photographs to identify the chair as Larsen's.

Larsen noticed Holtzkopf's advertisement and brought an action against him for violation of the registered design that he held on the chair. Holtzkopf's defence was that he did not copy the design, he only used Adrienne's photograph of the chair, which was too small to permit him to make an exact reproduction of the design. He also argued that the structural design of his chair was completely different as well.

When Larsen discovered that Adrienne had photographed his chair, he included her as a co-defendant with Holtzkopf, claiming that she was a part of a conspiracy to infringe on his registered design.

Adrienne had also noticed the advertisement in the trade magazine and determined that Holtzkopf had used her photographs of the chair in the advertisement.

She immediately brought an action against Holtzkopf for infringement of her copyright in the pictures that she had taken of Larsen's chair.

Discuss the issues raised by the facts and the arguments that the parties might raise. Indicate how the court might decide the matter.

Case 6

For several years, the residents of Smallville had been served by one prominent pizza franchise, Lotza Pizza, which had operated in Smallville with the telephone number 456-1010. This telephone number corresponded to that of the parent company which was 123-1010 and was a registered trade mark of the company. The telephone number figured prominently in the company's advertising and jingles.

A rival franchise of a competing pizza company then moved into Smallville and established a similar operation. That company, Better Pizza, also had a trade-marked telephone number which was 222-0234. Just like Lotza Pizza, the telephone number played a large role in the company's promotions and was one of the major factors of customer recognition. In Smallville, Better Pizza had obtained the number 457-0234. Smallville had only two exchanges 456 and 457.

Jones, a resident of Smallville, who had the telephone number 456-0234 for almost 15 years, began to receive a large number of inadvertent calls intended for Better Pizza. Jones soon tired of receiving these calls, and approached the local Lotza Pizza franchise. He told the manager about his telephone number and the recurring problem. Shortly thereafter, the Smallville Lotza Pizza franchise acquired Jones' telephone number 456-0234 and used it in its business.

The local franchise of Better Pizza, upon discovering the use by Lotza Pizza of the number 456-0234, brought legal action against both the Smallville Lotza Pizza franchise and its parent company.

Discuss the nature of the action and the rights and liabilities, if any, of the various parties involved. What arguments and/or defences may be used, and what would be the likely outcome?

CHAPTER 34

International Business Law

INTRODUCTION

Canada is a trading nation that depends to a large extent upon foreign trade for its economic well-being. Initially, as a colony, Canada was a supplier of furs and fish. Later, as a fledgling Dominion, it was a source of a wide variety of raw materials. After the turn of the century, Canada gradually developed a manufacturing base, and eventually moved into the export of manufactured goods. Today, raw materials, agricultural products, and lumber continue to represent a substantial part of Canadian exports; but manufactured goods, particularly those in the high-tech fields, represent a growing segment of Canada's foreign trade.

Canadian businesses that engage in the export and import of goods operate in a different legal environment from those firms that carry on business in the domestic market. The laws that affect a Canadian firm trading on an international basis fall roughly into two categories: (1) Canadian laws, and those negotiated between nations to control or facilitate international trade, and (2) private laws that govern the transactions between the parties where one contracting party is not a domestic firm.

THE IMPORTATION OF GOODS INTO CANADA

The import (and export) of goods is subject to a number of federal statutes. The most important of these acts are the **Customs Act**[1] and the **Customs Tariff Act.**[2] The Customs Act is an administrative statute that sets out the various powers and duties of customs officers, the procedures for the importation of goods, and the rules for the collection of customs duties and the payment of refunds. The act also provides appeal procedures that may be taken by importers who disagree with

---

1. Customs Act, S.C. 1986, c. 1 as amended.
2. Customs Tariff Act, R.S.C. 1985, c. C-54 as amended.

alleged customs violations or duty rate decisions. Included in the act are penalties that may be imposed upon persons who violate the customs rules or who attempt to avoid payment of duty properly imposed.

The Customs Tariff Act sets out the various duty rates applicable to goods brought into Canada. This statute sets out not only the generally applicable rates, but preferential rates that may apply to goods imported from certain countries. It also contains a list of goods that may not be imported into Canada (prohibited commodities).

Canadian industries and businesses are protected from the "dumping" of foreign goods into Canada by the **Special Import Measures Act.**[3] Under this statute a special duty is levied on goods that are imported at a lower price than the price that the same commodities are sold for in the normal course of business in the country of origin. The statute is also intended to prevent foreign sellers from selling goods produced under government subsidy to the Canadian market, where the sales would cause injury to Canadian producers of similar goods, or where the subsidized goods would prevent or retard the development of the production of the goods in Canada. Dumping must be established before the special duty rates would apply to the goods.

In an effort to protect Canadian industries from competition from countries with extremely low production and labour costs, the importation of certain types of goods is subject to control under the **Export and Import Permits Act.**[4] In contrast, to the Special Import Measures Act, which is designed to deal with dumping situations, the Export and Import Permits Act attempts to control the flow of goods into Canada from those countries where goods may be produced at prices so low that Canadian firms would be unable to meet such competition on a fair basis. In an effort to provide Canadian firms with some protection, the statute essentially imposes limits on the quantities of certain goods brought into Canada by requiring importers to obtain import permits for specific goods that have been identified under the act. The act also requires exporters to obtain permits before they may export certain controlled goods from Canada. Goods subject to export permit requirements are generally goods of military importance, or goods classed as "strategic" commodities. The sale of these goods to countries that the government may list from time to time under Orders-in-Council is usually prohibited or, where export is permitted, may only be exported with a permit.

Canadian businesses engaged in the importation of goods from foreign countries are obliged to carry on their business within the framework of these four statutes. Because a special knowledge of the legislation is often necessary to import goods with a minimum of time and effort, many firms will use the services of business firms that specialize in dealing with customs officers and persons who administer the legislation affecting the importation of goods. Those firms are generally known as **customs brokers**, and they play an important role in the importation of goods into Canada.

THE EXPORT OF GOODS FROM CANADA

Canadian firms that engage in the export of goods to foreign purchasers face many trade and tariff barriers, not unlike those that have been erected by Canada to control the flow of goods and protect domestic industry. Apart from the Export

---

3. Special Import Measures Act, R.S.C. 1985, c. S-15.

4. Export and Import Permits Act, R.S.C. 1985, c. E-19.

and Import Permits Act, there are few Canadian laws that restrict Canadian exporters from selling Canadian goods abroad. Indeed, the export of goods is encouraged by the Canadian government. Some Canadian laws that would normally control or prohibit particular business practices for domestic firms would not apply to foreign or export operations. For example, the Competition Act specifically prohibits combination in restraint of trade domestically, but permits such combinations formed to engage in export market activities, provided that the combination does not adversely affect the domestic market.[5]

Many of the challenges faced by Canadian exporters are related to the trade barriers that foreign countries have erected to protect their own manufacturing and production sectors. The movement of goods into foreign countries often requires the services of foreign firms not unlike Canadian customs brokers. Efforts have been made, however, to reduce international trade barriers and provide a common structure or framework for the consideration of tariff rates and the control of such activities as dumping. These international agreements have been an important factor in the growth of international trade over the past few decades.

INTERNATIONAL TRADE REGULATION

Most countries control the import and export of goods to some degree. They have laws in place that either regulate trading in particular goods or impose duties or taxes on goods moving across their borders. However, because of the use of tariff barriers and controls by virtually all nations, a number of important international agreements have been established, whereby the signing nations have agreed to limit their controls and duties on goods in accordance with the terms of the particular treaties. For example, the **General Agreement on Tariffs and Trade** (GATT) represents a **multinational agreement** signed by over 90 countries. It has as its initial thrust the reduction of trade restrictions between countries. The GATT seeks to accomplish this purpose by the establishment of a number of rules to govern the various duties and import charges that a country may fairly impose on imports. It also provides a procedure for the determination of the fair value of goods subject to duty and charges and sets out rules to prevent the dumping of goods in export markets. The GATT agreement provides a general framework for the reduction of barriers to the free movement of goods between nations. At the same time it attempts to accommodate the particular economic and political goals of the individual countries.

Canada signed the GATT and, as a member nation, has an obligation to follow the rules that the agreement sets down in the determination of Canada's own customs duties and tariffs. As well, Canada is expected to abide by the GATT rules with respect to any restrictions that it may impose on imports and exports of goods. Canadian business firms engaged in international trade must, of course, comply with the Canadian laws that may impose restrictions on the importation or the export of goods, and must be aware of the various duties and controls imposed as a part of their overall business planning and decision-making. In addition to GATT, Canada has also negotiated a number of other agreements with other nations or groups of nations that have an impact on international trade. These agreements may be either **multinational** (like the General Agreement on Tariffs and Trade) or **bilateral agreements.**

---

5. Competition Act, R.S.C. 1985, c. C-34, s. 45(5) as amended.

It is important to note, however, that some multinational agreements to which Canada is not a signatory nation may also affect Canadian firms. The Organization of Petroleum Exporting Countries (OPEC) for example, which resembles an oil cartel, had a significant trading impact on Canadian firms in the oil import business during the 1970s. However, more recently the organization has been unable to maintain an effective price/production agreement due to the internal problems of its own member states. Consequently, familiarity with all laws of foreign nations and their agreements with nations trading in similar products is essential for Canadian firms trading on the international scene, if only to assess their own trading position in the market.

Bilateral agreements represent regulatory rules that may affect international trade in specific types of goods. While some bilateral agreements may establish a general framework for trade regulation or tariffs between two countries, bilateral agreements often deal with specific types of goods or sectors of trade. The agreement between Canada and the United States with respect to the trade in automotive products (the "Autopact") is an example of the latter. Bilateral agreements are frequently used to regulate the quantity or flow of specific goods. Consequently, these agreements frequently call for export licences or permits in order that the governments may monitor compliance with the agreement. Where such permits or licences are required, dealing in the specific goods for which a licence or permit is required is essentially contingent on the government. Entry into a particular market or the importation of the controlled goods may or may not be possible, depending upon the necessary approval. Information and advice on licences and permits is generally available from the federal government ministries concerned with international trade and commerce.

A further example of a bilateral agreement is the Canada/United States Free Trade Agreement that, when fully implemented, will provide a broad agreement concerning trade between the two countries. The agreement covers specific goods, services, business travel and investment, financial services, dispute settlement provisions, the protection of industries adversely affected by the agreement, procedures to deal with dumping, and countervailing duties. The agreement is quite lengthy, but the general thrust of the various provisions is to promote trade and create an expanded market for an extensive range of goods and services of both countries. The basic principle underlying the agreement is that each country will treat the other country's goods, services, investors, and investments in the same manner as their own with respect to the goods and services covered by the agreement. The agreement is expected to be fully operational by 1998.

Apart from legislation regulating the import and export of goods, a number of federal government agencies or bodies have been established to assist Canadian firms that may wish to establish export markets. These agencies or government departments may provide assistance in one of a number of ways:

(1) by providing financial assistance to Canadian firms that may wish to explore the possibility of export selling. This may take the form of organizing trade missions abroad, or the cost sharing of feasibility studies, or marketing research by firms interested in a particular export market or country.

(2) by providing security for the payment for goods sold under certain export transactions, and

(3) by providing loan guarantees to enable Canadian exporters to fund sales or operations internationally.

The Canadian International Development Agency (CIDA) and the Department of External Affairs under its Program for Export Market Development (PEMD) offer trade assistance to firms through the organization of trade missions and travel abroad to international trade fairs where Canadian firms may either display their wares or contact foreign buyers or sellers. Financial assistance in the form of cost sharing for market studies and similar activities may also be provided by these agencies. Government involvement for the latter usually consists of some form of dollar-for-dollar sharing of the costs.

At the present time the Export Development Corporation, a Crown corporation, provides Canadian firms with insurance against many of the risks associated with foreign business transactions. These may range from protection from loss on export transactions to compensation where the foreign government seizes the Canadian firm's foreign assets or prevents the transfer of money or property from the country in question. Loss from war or revolution are also covered by the Export Development Corporation. In general, the Crown corporation's mandate is to encourage foreign trade by offering a wide range of protective services to reduce many of the risks associated with international business transactions.

INTERNATIONAL TRADING RELATIONSHIPS

International trade in its simplest form may consist of a single transaction whereby a Canadian retailer may import goods for resale to the Canadian public. More often, however, international trade takes in the form of established business relationships with foreign buyers or sellers, or the establishment of business organizations in other countries to carry on trading operations alone or in concert with others. While we tend to think of foreign trade in terms of Canadian firms selling goods abroad, it is also important to note that international trade is essentially "two-way" in its nature, and includes foreign sellers establishing business relationships with Canadian firms as well. Canadian firms operating foreign automobile dealerships represent examples of the latter type of business relationship.

Foreign Distribution Agreements

Apart from the single transaction type of purchase of goods from a foreign seller, most international trading arrangements tend to be undertaken by manufacturers or wholesalers of goods where an ongoing relationship with the foreign firm (or firms) is established. These relationships may take on many forms, but the most common are probably the foreign distribution agreement, the foreign branch plant or sales office, the joint venture to sell or manufacture abroad, and the licensing of a foreign firm to use patents or technological information to produce goods in the foreign country. Many variants of these four basic relationships also exist, as do many purely service-oriented activities, such as the management of foreign businesses and the provision of advice on the manufacture or preparation of goods for sale in the Canadian market.

Foreign distribution agreements are essentially contracts between the Canadian exporters and firms that undertake the marketing of the exporters' products on an international basis or in a particular country. This form of distribution is frequently used by smaller Canadian firms that lack the necessary funding to support an international sales staff, or firms that believe that their interests in those markets are best served by distributors native to the particular countries. Foreign distribution agreements may also be negotiated by Canadian exporters with Canadian or foreign firms that specialize in the marketing of products in many foreign countries, or they may be negotiated with wholly owned subsidiary organizations. In the latter case, the subsidiary distribution firm would essentially be the international marketing organization of the parent manufacturing firm, but charged with the responsibility for foreign sales.

Since foreign distribution agreements are essentially contractual, considerable care is required in their negotiation. Such agreements will normally very clearly set out the product or products subject to the agreement, and the area or territory in which the foreign distributor has the right or exclusive rights (if permitted under the foreign country's restrictive trade practices laws) to sell the products. These agreements will usually include the obligation on the distributor to provide a sales staff of a particular size, and the efforts that the distributor will make to develop a market in the territory for the products. An obligation to keep information and special "know how" confidential, both during and after termination of the agreement, is usually included as well. Where the product requires servicing, the agreement may also set out the distributor's obligation to provide parts inventories of a particular size and service facilities or service depots where warranty work and the general service needs of the product may be satisfied. Most agreements of this type would also set out the terms and conditions under which the goods might be sold in the territory.

Foreign distribution agreements are seldom one-sided. They will also include the Canadian exporter's obligations. These usually include the obligation to supply the goods (with perhaps certain quality standards specified) and replacement parts, and to supply technical advice, advertising material, or catalogues. The right of the distributor to use the manufacturer's or exporter's trade names for the duration of the agreement is generally a term of the contract.

Most agreements are negotiated for a fixed term with provision for renewal or termination on notice. A common provision permits termination if sales volume fails to meet or be maintained at a specified minimum level. It also provides for the disposition of the distributors' inventories if termination takes place. A *force majeure* clause that would permit termination of the agreement in the event of major strikes, riots, or social disorder is often included in the agreement.

Foreign distribution agreements are generally complex agreements that will also set out the precise relationship between the Canadian firm and the foreign distributor. Due to their complexity and international nature, the agreement will usually set out the governing law that will apply in the event of a dispute between the parties. Most international agreements of this type will usually provide that the disputes be resolved by way of arbitration rather than the courts, and an arbitration procedure will usually be set out in the agreement.

Foreign Branch Plants or Sales Offices

The foreign branch plants or sales organizations represent two distinct alternatives to foreign distribution agreements, but both frequently require a commitment of

Canadian resources and personnel to the international venture. Both also require a more intimate knowledge of the laws of the particular countries where the plants or sales offices will be established, but permit the Canadian firm to exercise a greater measure of control over the product and its marketing abroad. A knowledge of the laws of the particular jurisdiction before the venture is begun is essential because, once committed to the project, the branch plant or sales office must operate subject to all of the laws of the particular country, both national and local. These laws often control capital flow as well as impose restrictions on technology that might conceivably have an adverse future effect on the Canadian firm. As a result, foreign branch plants often take the form of assembly facilities rather than full-scale manufacturing operations because the capital commitment is usually substantially less. Foreign laws that must be considered are those controlling the flow of capital, technology, and material both into the country and out, employment laws that may impact on the staffing and the health and safety of employees, and laws relating to business transactions, including consumer protection and the pricing of goods. The complexity of these laws tend to vary in terms of both the economic sophistication and the political orientation of the country in question.

International Joint Ventures

Problems associated with the wholly owned foreign branch plant or subsidiary may be reduced, or to some extent avoided, by way of a joint venture with a foreign national firm. Joint ventures of this type may take the form of unincorporated joint ventures (where the relationship would be based upon an agreement) or incorporated joint ventures (where a corporation would be created in the foreign jurisdiction and each of the parties to the venture would acquire a share interest in the corporation). The corporation so formed would carry on the manufacturing operations or the business activity. Share interests in the corporation and, indeed, the corporation itself would be subject to the laws of the foreign country. In many cases where foreign ownership is of national concern, shareholding requirements imposed by the law may fix the share interests of the parties to certain percentages that would give the national party or parties in the joint venture effective control over the corporation. In these instances, supporting agreements are normally required to ensure that the joint venture corporation has its full energies directed to the production and sale of products in such a way that the objectives of the Canadian shareholders' interests would be achieved and protected. This may sometimes be accomplished in part by the Canadian party to the joint venture licensing the joint venture corporation to produce products that the Canadian firm has protected by patent or design rights on an international basis.

Licence Agreements

The licensing of production of protected products in foreign countries is also an alternative to the joint venture. Where the Canadian manufacturer has protected the product by way of a patent or trade mark, or has a copyright or design right on a work, foreign firms with the facilities to produce and market the product may be licensed to do so. The particular product must, of course, be protected by patent or otherwise if the licence agreement is to be effective. But where, for example, a

Canadian firm has acquired patent protection for its product in a foreign country, the Canadian firm may license a foreign manufacturer to produce the product, usually on a royalty basis.

Licensing agreements for foreign manufacture usually include or address the following matters:

(1) the names of the parties,

(2) the ownership of the patent, design, trade mark, or other rights subject to the licence, and an acknowledgement of the ownership by the other party to the agreement,

(3) the royalty rate and its method of calculation,

(4) the quantities to be produced and the quality standards,

(5) the duration of the licence agreement,

(6) the method of dispute resolution should a dispute arise,

(7) the disposition of stock and special equipment used in the production of the product on termination of the agreement, or the ownership of plates, moulds, or masters for copyright works when termination arises,

(8) technical or other assistance provided to the licensee,

(9) the right to assign or sub-license by the licensee,

(10) the territorial boundaries where the licence covers sale as well as manufacture (to protect both the domestic market and other licensees),

(11) the protection of confidential information and manufacturing "know how" not protected by the patent, and

(12) right to improvements in the product made by both the licensor and the licensee.

The licensing arrangement has become an attractive means by which Canadian firms may expand into the international market because it usually requires a minimum investment in time and expertise on the part of the Canadian firm. Apart from the negotiation and legal work associated with the preparation of the licensing agreement, the licensor's obligations are generally limited to monitoring the agreement and the provision of technical assistance to the licensee. The capital investment in plant and equipment, recruitment of personnel, and compliance with foreign laws are the responsibility of the foreign licensee. Nevertheless, licence agreements are not without some disadvantages. Royalty arrangements may not produce the same levels of profits for the licensor that might otherwise be obtained (such as through a joint venture) because the licensee may not operate an efficient manufacturing facility or sales force. Under these circumstances, the Canadian licensor would be unable to directly control or correct the problems affecting the overall profitability of the venture.

INTERNATIONAL CONTRACTS OF SALE

The law of contract plays an important role in international trade in the sense that a contract is the heart of the export sale. Indeed, a basic export sale generally consists of four documents, each serving a distinct purpose in the overall transaction. These are: (1) the contract of sale, (2) the bill of lading, (3) the contract of insurance, and (4) the commercial invoice. While these four contracts are the core documents, other contracts, such as bank financing agreements and guarantee agreements with the Export Developing Corporation, frequently form a part of the contract package associated with the transaction.

Contract of Sale

International or export sale agreements frequently differ from domestic contracts for the sale of goods in that they must address a number of elements of the sale that have international importance. For example, trade terms and terminology must be clearly understood to have the same meaning to both parties. To avoid misunderstanding, contracts will often make reference to published interpretations of international trade terms such as those available from the International Chamber of Commerce. Export contracts will also usually refer to the governing law, as well as the time when title to the goods will pass. Apart from special terms, international sale agreements tend to be more detailed in that they will clearly set out the quantities of the goods and their quality, the unit prices (as well as total price), delivery dates, mode of shipping, type of packaging, the time and method of payment and currency to be used, financing arrangements, insurance, provision of any required licences or permits applicable to the sale, a *force majeure* clause, and usually an arbitration clause to resolve disputes.

Export sales are generally the result of a series of negotiations that often take the form of inquiries, quotations, orders and acknowledgements, and may include a variety of other forms of correspondence. Because each of these documents may have a different legal significance in each of the countries, export sellers often clearly define what may or may not constitute an offer, and the conditions under which it may be revoked or expire. From the outset then, the international sale is conducted in a manner different from that of the domestic sale where the Sale of Goods Act would apply.

Bill of Lading

The bill of lading is an essential part of an international sale. It is a contract between the seller of the goods and the carrier of the goods that sets out the carrier's responsibilities to protect and deliver the goods to the purchaser. The bill will generally set out the name of the seller (shipper) and the consignee (usually the buyer or the buyer's agent), a description of the goods, the aircraft (or vessel's name if by ship), export licence numbers or permit numbers, and any other information that the particular entry state may require on the bill. Apart from the use of the bill of lading as a contract between the shipper and carrier, the bill of lading also represents a title document. Once the goods are placed in the hands of the carrier, the carrier, as a bailee, has a duty to deliver up the goods only to the consignee named in the bill. In this sense the bill of lading becomes a title document, as the shipper will send a copy of the bill of lading to the consignee (assuming financing or payment has been settled between the parties), and the consignee on receipt of the bill of lading may present it to the carrier to receive the goods. Because the contract of sale usually provides that title will pass upon delivery of the bill of lading, the risk of loss generally follows with the bill. Since the bill of lading essentially represents the title to the goods, a buyer on receipt of the bill of lading may use the bill to acquire financing by using the bill as security for the loan.

The bill of lading may also be coupled with a sight draft if the seller wishes to retain title or perhaps maintain control of the goods until payment is assured. This procedure allows the seller to obtain a negotiable instrument (the sight draft) from the buyer in return for the title documents to the goods. Sellers who may wish to do this will usually use a negotiable bill of lading and send it to the buyer's bank along with the sight draft and other documents required under the terms of the sale agreement. The bank will acknowledge receipt of the documents and will not release the bill of lading and documentation until the amount of the sight draft has been paid to the seller.

Insurance

The third type of contract generally associated with an international sale is the contract of insurance. Because of the hazards associated with the shipment of goods, most agreements will provide for insurance against the loss or damage to the goods while in transit. The cost of insurance will normally vary according to the risks that the seller or buyer may wish to protect against. Insurers that specialize in insuring international trade agreements offer cargo insurance that covers either a specific shipment or insures on a blanket or open basis, covering all cargo that may be shipped by the particular seller. Because the contract of sale will usually specify that either the buyer or seller will arrange for the insurance, the party not required to provide the coverage may often acquire contingency coverage in the event that the other party neglects or fails to obtain cargo insurance. Contingency insurance is usually obtained by the seller, where the buyer has responsibility for obtaining insurance under the contract of sale. Sellers may also obtain political risk insurance in some instances where goods are shipped to buyers on a consignment or deferred payment basis, where the country in question is politically or economically unstable.

Commercial Invoice

In addition to the contracts related to the export sale, a commercial invoice is usually necessary or required by the buyer's customs office. The invoice form and content may vary from country to country, and in some cases must be prepared in the language of the particular foreign country. The commercial invoice frequently represents both an invoice for the goods sold and a customs document that sets out details of goods to enable the customs officials to set the tariff classification and rate applicable to the goods. As noted previously, other documentation may also be required by the government of Canada, the buyer's government, or the buyer. These documents may include export permits or licences, or certificates relating to purity or analysis with respect to certain types of goods (such as some prepared food products or chemicals).

Sellers may also require the delivery of certain documents as well. If an export sale provides for payment before shipment, acceptance of a time draft or sight draft, or provision of a letter of credit, these matters must be attended to and provided by the buyer in accordance with the terms of the contract of sale.

ARBITRATION OF INTERNATIONAL TRADE DISPUTES Agreements pertaining to international trade present a number of problems for the contracting parties because of the complexity of the transaction in terms of enforceability. In many cases, the parties each operate under different political systems, and, not infrequently, a government or state organization may be one of the contracting parties or a direct player in the negotiations. These differences, in an international trade context, often dictate some form of dispute resolution mechanism other than the courts of one country or the other. Commercial arbitration is frequently the method that the parties incorporate in their agreements to resolve any disputes that may arise.

Commercial arbitration, by definition, is a method of resolving disputes arising out of an agreement made by two or more parties. This method employs one or more third parties who impartially decide the dispute by rendering an interpretation of the agreement or a decision that becomes binding on the parties to the agreement. The authority of the third party decision-makers arises out of the agreement; although the procedural methods the third parties may use and the enforcement of their decision may either be incorporated in the agreement by reference to statute or code, or by state adoption of a particular international model arbitration law.

Commercial arbitration generally involves the resolution of commercial disputes by persons experienced in the particular branch of the trade or business where the dispute arose. Business persons have used this method of dispute resolution since the early years of commercial trading to quickly and effectively resolve their differences. It is also a means whereby the disputes would be resolved largely in private. Today, it represents a common form of dispute resolution utilized by business persons in Canada and other countries that have legislation pertaining to the arbitration of business disputes.[6] In recent years, efforts have also been made to establish international arbitration laws to facilitate the use of arbitration on an international basis and to enforce international arbitration awards.[7]

Arbitration is a method the parties at any time may mutually agree upon to resolve a dispute that arises out of a contract. However, to make arbitration a required method of resolution of future disputes that may arise out of the agreement, the arbitration process must be included in the agreement. For international trade agreements it is also necessary to set out the process in some detail in order that the arbitration itself will represent an appropriate and effective dispute resolution mechanism. This is so because a number of issues must be addressed in the preparation of the agreement clause to avoid problems with the implementation of the process and to confirm matters of a procedural and legal nature. For example, many international trade transactions involve not only private organizations but state or state agencies as well. A Canadian firm that engages in a transaction with a foreign state agency must ensure that its rights under the transaction may be enforced if the foreign country should attempt to exercise its sovereign power to revoke the particular trading rights or confiscate/expropriate the property of the Canadian firm or its assets in the foreign country. To protect itself in this example, the Canadian firm might insist at the time of negotiation that the agreement shall be subject to arbitration in a country other than the foreign state under internationally recognized arbitration rules. The firm might also provide in the agreement itself that unilateral actions by the foreign state such as expropriation, new controls on repatriation of capital, more onerous customs duties, and other changes be subject to arbitration.

6. See for example, for domestic disputes, Ontario: Arbitration Act, S.O. 1991, c. 17.

7. See: United Nations Commission on International Trade Law — Model Arbitration Law.

Because the effectiveness of an arbitration clause is dependent upon its terms, most clauses will include reference to the composition of the arbitration board, the place or country where the arbitration would be held, the applicable law, the language to be used in the proceedings, the procedure to be followed by the arbitration board, and its powers or jurisdiction. The enforcement of the arbitration award may also be addressed, depending upon the particular laws relating to arbitration in the jurisdictions involved.

As a general rule, arbitration boards usually consist of three persons, with each of the parties to the agreement appointing one member of the board. The two appointees then select the third member who may be characterized as a truly impartial member. The third person so selected is usually designated as the chairperson of the tribunal. If the parties are unable to agree on the third member, the agreement should provide a mechanism for the selection or appointment of a third member, or reference should be had to a statute or code that does provide for the selection. Unless specified in the agreement, the language of the arbitration is usually the language of the chairperson selected (or the single arbitrator, as the case may be), even if the language is not the native language of either of the parties to the arbitration.

Most arbitration agreements will state the place where the arbitration will take place and the governing law. This is an important term in the arbitration clause, as the governing law provides the procedural rules applicable to the arbitration. In the absence of specific reference to the governing law, the laws of the place where the arbitration is held will normally apply. The contracts, however, may specify one of the internationally recognized arbitration laws such as the UNCITRAL[8] rules for arbitrations prepared by the United Nations (see Appendix B).

ENFORCEMENT OF ARBITRATION AWARDS

The arbitration process as a means of international trade dispute resolution is essentially a creature of the contract negotiated by the parties. In a sense, the parties may, within bounds, determine in their agreement the powers of the arbitrator or board of arbitration, and the manner in which the award may be enforced. However, for the most part, the enforcement of the award is something that most developed countries have dealt with by statute. Enforcement of an award, then, will generally fall outside the agreement and may vary from state to state, depending upon their legislation.

In the early times when international trade was conducted as "fairs," the merchants resolved their disagreements by peer adjudication of the disputes, a process not unlike modern commercial arbitration. At that time, the enforcement of the decision was largely by the merchant guild or organization itself, with the threat of expulsion from the group as the principal sanction. Over time, however, merchants sought other means of enforcement with rather limited success, and it has fallen to the governments to establish enforcement mechanisms by statute. Canada adopted the United Nations Commercial Arbitration Code in 1986.[9] The code defines an arbitration agreement, provides for the appointment of arbitrators in cases where one party fails to act, sets out the jurisdiction of the arbitration

---

8. United Nations Commission on International Trade Law.

9. Commercial Arbitration Act, S.C. 1986, c. 22.

tribunal, the place and procedure, the recognition of the award, recourse against it, and its enforcement. Under the code, the award may be enforced by applying to the designated court and then proceeding on it through the court process against the defaulting party.

Canada also adopted the United Nations convention on the recognition and enforcement of foreign arbitral awards in 1986.[10] Enforcement of an arbitration award is effected by application to the designated court. In Canada, the designated courts are the Federal Court, and any superior, district or county court of a province.[11]

In 1992, Canada joined the Vienna Sales Convention, an international agreement that establishes a single set of rules that automatically apply to international trade contracts for the sale of a wide variety of goods. The convention also deals with the forum and law that will be applied in the event of a dispute. Business firms are not obliged to follow the convention, but may opt out of the rules if they so desire, and specify in their sale contracts the particular nation's laws that they wish to have govern their agreement and its enforcement.

In many jurisdictions, the most logical enforcement mechanism has been the court system, which not infrequently has also been charged with the duty of ensuring that the arbitration process itself has been conducted fairly and in accordance with the applicable law. For example, the enforcement process may consist of a filing of the arbitration award with the office of a designated court of the country, and on this basis obtaining a judgement of the court. The same court may also be called upon to review the arbitration process itself if some misconduct or unfairness is alleged on the part of an arbitrator or member of the arbitration board. Judicial review may also take place in some jurisdictions where the arbitrators have made an error in law or exceeded their authority.

The enforcement of arbitration awards in international trade transactions continues to remain complex in many jurisdictions. However, the adoption of model laws by many countries in recent years has generally reduced the enforcement process and made the process itself more uniform.

SUMMARY

Canada has become increasingly involved in international trade. Business firms engaged in this trade must be familiar with not only the Canadian laws that affect their business, but the laws of those countries with which they trade. This is particularly important where the Canadian firm has established a manufacturing facility or sales office in a foreign country.

The import or export type of transaction usually involves custom tariff legislation or laws requiring special permits to import or export certain goods. The purchase or sale itself is by contract, but the contract normally must address a number of aspects of the sale often unimportant in a domestic sale. The international contract usually includes not only the complete details of the transaction,

10. Foreign Arbitral Awards Convention Act, S.C. 1986, c. 21.
11. Ibid., s. 6.

but a clause whereby the parties agree to resolve any dispute arising out of the transaction by binding arbitration. Other documentation is also required, including a bill of lading, insurance, and a commercial invoice. Where required, special permits for customs clearance and certificates as to purity or analysis may also form a part of the transaction.

Where a firm decides to do business in another country it may do so by establishing a manufacturing facility or sales office, either on its own or as a joint venture with a local partner. A knowledge of local laws of the foreign country is essential in either case, but the advantage of a local partner might be its familiarity with its national laws. An alternative approach might be to license a foreign manufacturer to produce or sell the goods.

Where a dispute arises between the parties, arbitration is the usual method of resolving the matter. Arbitration clauses in the contract usually set out the procedural details or refer to arbitration in accordance with a particular internationally recognized procedure or set of rules.

DISCUSSION QUESTIONS

1. What is the effect of Canadian laws on the importation of goods into Canada?
2. Explain the difference between the Customs Act and the Customs Tariff Act.
3. How does the Special Import Measures Act affect foreign sellers?
4. Why was it necessary for Canada to pass an Export and Import Permits Act?
5. What is the role of a customs broker in a transaction whereby goods are imported by a Canadian firm?
6. Outline the general thrust and purpose of the General Agreement on Tariffs and Trade (GATT).
7. Distinguish a bilateral trade agreement from a multinational trade agreement.
8. What assistance does the Canadian government provide to Canadian firms that may wish to enter the international market?
9. Explain the different ways in which a Canadian firm may establish an international trading relationship.
10. What are the advantages and disadvantages of a foreign trading relationship in the form of a joint venture?
11. Outline the general provisions of a foreign licence agreement. Does this type of agreement have any advantages over a joint venture agreement?
12. Identify the usual documents required for an international contract of sale. What is the purpose of each of these documents?
13. Explain why commercial arbitration is used as a means of dispute resolution in international agreements.
14. Why do most international trade contracts provide that arbitration will take place in a country other than the country of either of the contracting parties?
15. How are arbitration awards enforced?

JUDICIAL DECISION

The *Canada Packers Inc. v. Terra Nova Tankers Inc.* case deals with the question of whether the International Commercial Arbitrations Act (which incorporates the UNCITRAL Model Law on Commercial Arbitration) would apply to a dispute between parties that includes a claim in tort. The court held in this case that the act applies to commercial disputes whether contractual or non-contractual in nature, and this may extend to claims in tort as well. The court directed the matter to arbitration.

International Dispute — Application of International Commercial Arbitrations Act — Dispute Includes Tort as well as Contract Complaint

Canada Packers Inc. et al. v. Terra Nova Tankers Inc. et al. (1992), 11 O.R. (3d) 382.

Day J. (orally):

By a voyage charter-party made as of April 30, 1991, Canada Packers Inc., as charters, agreed with "Cob Shipping Canada Inc., as agents for Terra Nova Tankers Inc.", as owner, to charter the ship "Tove Cob" to carry vegetable oils from East Asian ports for discharge at Montreal and Toronto.

The voyage charter-party included an arbitration clause which provided: "Any dispute arising from the making, performance or termination of the Charter Party shall be settled" by arbitration as further provided in s. 31 of the voyage charter-party clause.

The respondents have pleaded that the applicants in this motion, but not the defendant DMD Enterprises Pte. Ltd., were parties to the voyage charter-party. This is not disputed. The respondents have pleaded that the applicants are in breach of contract under the voyage charter-party. Whether or not they are in breach of contract is not the subject of this application.

The respondents have also pleaded against all applicants the following tort causes of action:

a) failure to disclaim liability as principal;
b) deliberate or negligent misrepresentation;
c) breaches of collateral warranties;
d) failure to warn; and
e) wrongful preference of commercial interest.

The respondents have, in addition, pleaded wrongful interference with contractual relations against all applicants and the defendant DMD Enterprises Pte. Ltd.

In respect of all those tort allegations regarding all parties except DMD Enterprises Pte. Ltd., the genesis would appear to come from the contract itself.

The *International Commercial Arbitration Act,* R.S.O. 1990, c. I.9, incorporates into Ontario law as its schedule the UNCITRAL Model Law on International Commercial Arbitration, including art. 8(1) as follows:

8(1) A *court* before which an action is brought in a matter which is the subject of an arbitration agreement *shall,* if a party so requests not later than when submitting his first statement on the substance of the dispute, *refer* the parties to arbitration *unless* it finds that the agreement is *null and void, inoperative or incapable of being performed.*

(Emphasis added)

Section 8 of the said Act provides:

8. *Where,* pursuant to article 8 of the Model Law, a *court refers* the parties to arbitration, the *proceedings of the court are stayed with respect to the matters to which the arbitration relates.*

(Emphasis added)

Counsel for the respondent referred to *Stancroft Trust Ltd. v. Can-Asia Capital Co.* (1990), 67 D.L.R. (4th) 131, 43 B.C.L.R. (2d) 341 (C.A.), Southin, J.A., to support the position that the potential application of art. 8(1) of the Model Law must be considered against each party individually. In this respect I understand his argument to be that DMD could not be included in such an order. I agree with this position.

It is not disputed between counsel in their arguments that Mr. Gilje is a principal charter-party and as such he will be bound by the order given herein.

I refer to the decision of *Kaverit Steel & Crane Ltd. v. Kone Corp.* (1992), 87

D.L.R. (4th) 129, 85 Alta. L.R. (2d) 287 (C.A.), Kierans J.A., and particularly at p. 133 D.L.R., p. 293 Alta. L.R., as follows:

> The extra claims also include allegations against all the defendants of conspiracy to harm all plaintiffs, Mr. Redmond for the distributor says that this pleading relies on tort, not contract, and offers two alternatives: conspiracy to harm by unlawful acts and conspiracy to harm by lawful acts.

And further at p. 134 D.L.R., p. 293 Alta. L.R.:

> The mere fact that a claim sounds in tort does not exclude arbitration Section 2 of the *International Commercial Arbitration Act* limits its scope to "...differences arising out of commercial legal relationships, whether contractual or not". This is permitted by art. 1, s. 3, of the Convention, which leaves to signatory states the decision whether the Convention applies to just those differences, as opposed to all manner of differences.

> The Convention and Act thus covers both contractual and non-contractual commercial relationships. They thus extend their scope to liability in tort so long as the relationship that creates liability is one that can fairly be described as "commercial". In my view, a claim that a corporation conspired with its subsidiaries to cause harm to a person with whom it has a commercial relationship raises a dispute "arising out of a commercial legal relationship, whether contractual or not".

Counsel for the applicant pointed out that the word "commercial" while in the Alberta Act is not included in the Ontario statute. Nonetheless, I take it that the concept "commercial" is picked up in the Convention and I would ascribe the same basis as if the word "commercial" were included in the Ontario Statute in order for consistency in the Convention.

For the above mentioned reasons, I order that any dispute arising from the making, performance or termination of the charter party be referred to arbitration in New York in accordance with s. 31 of the charter-party dated April 30, 1991. In making this finding, it shall apply to the parties of this action with the exception of DMD Enterprises Pte. Ltd. for the reasons above set out.

As a result, this action is stayed to the extent necessary to give effect to this order.

The plaintiffs shall be at leave to reapply to this court for further determination if there should be a finding that the arbitration tribunal lacks jurisdiction with respect to any of the parties to which this order applies or on any of the causes of action pleaded in the statement of claim dated June 15, 1992 in this action.

Costs to the moving parties in the arbitral cause provided that if the arbitration tribunal finds that it does not have jurisdiction as to these costs then party-and-party costs shall be paid to the applicant on assessment.

CASE PROBLEM FOR DISCUSSION

Case 1

Kyoto Mfg. Inc. was a producer of sensitive measuring equipment for the steel industry. Kyoto was a Japanese company and had its principal place of business in Japan. Kyoto had no assets in Canada.

A Canadian firm, Concepts Mfg. Limited, located in Vancouver, entered into a licensing agreement with Kyoto for the right to manufacture and market several of Kyoto's products in Canada. Concepts was to pay a royalty to Kyoto based upon a formula set out in the contract, and Kyoto was to provide technical support and "know how." Concepts was further entitled under the licence to receive information and support promptly whenever Kyoto made improvements to the products as the result of technological advances.

Two of the clauses contained in the agreement stated, in part, the following:

4.1 The validity and interpretation of this Agreement and of each clause or part thereof shall be governed by the laws of Japan...

5.1 Any and all disputes arising from this Agreement shall be amicably and promptly settled upon consultation between the parties hereto, however, in case of failure of settlement, the disputes shall be settled by arbitration in Tokyo, Japan, in accordance with the rules of the Japan Commercial Arbitration Association and the award shall be final and binding upon both parties. In no case shall any award against Concepts Mfg. Limited exceed all royalty fees due by Concepts Mfg. Limited at the date of commencement of the arbitration hearing.

The parties co-operated under the agreement for several years, then a dispute arose as to the entitlement of Kyoto to certain royalties. Concepts alleged that Kyoto had failed to provide adequate technical support and advice concerning certain improvements it had made to its technology. Kyoto denied this allegation and insisted on receiving its royalty payments. Concepts responded by alleging fundamental breach of the contract by Kyoto.

Following an unsuccessful attempt to resolve the matter, Kyoto submitted the dispute to the Japan Commercial Arbitration Association for arbitration. Both parties were sent notices concerning the names of the arbitrators appointed to the arbitration tribunal and the date, place, and time of the hearing. On the day set for the hearing, only Kyoto attended and made submissions. There was no correspondence from Concepts Mfg. before or during the proceedings.

The arbitration tribunal awarded Kyoto the sum of $150 000 in royalties to be paid by Concepts, together with interest and a portion of the costs of the arbitration process. Although Concepts was sent a copy of the award, it neither acknowledged its receipt nor made any payments in accordance with it.

After six months of unanswered communication, Kyoto brought an action in the British Columbia courts for a declaration that the Japanese arbitration award was valid and enforceable in Concepts' jurisdiction. Kyoto argued that it had complied with all procedures necessary to have the award enforced in Canada. Moreover, the parties had a written contract to submit disputes to arbitration, that the subject matter of the dispute was not outside that contemplated to be settled by arbitration and further, that Concepts had never taken any steps to dispute either the jurisdiction of the arbitration or the merits of Kyoto's claim.

Concepts argued that the award could not be enforced against it since the subject-matter of the dispute, namely fundamental breach of contract, is not a matter that can be settled by arbitration in its province. Rather, this is a question that could only be determined by a court. It further argued that to enforce the Japanese award would be contrary to public policy since it would allow a foreign company to receive benefits under the contract while, at the same time, preventing the Canadian company from seeking any remedy for its damages caused by the fundamental breach by the foreign company.

If you were the judge hearing this case, how would you decide and why? On what legal principles would you base your decision? What international laws would assist you in making your decision?

CHAPTER 35

Environmental Law

The Common Law	**Discussion Questions**
Environmental Legislation	**Mini-Case Problems**
Environmental Responsibility	**Judicial Decision**
Summary	**Case Problems for Discussion**

THE COMMON LAW

At common law, injury to the environment has generally been considered by the courts on a relatively personal level in the sense that actions of one individual that interfere with the property or rights of another are actionable at law. If a property owner pollutes a water course and causes injury to the downstream user, the downstream user (or riparian owner) may take action against the upstream owner for the injury caused. Similarly, where someone interferes with the lands of his or her neighbour by contaminating the neighbour's soil or ground water, the contamination may be an actionable tort of nuisance. Creating contaminated smoke where the particles fall on neighbouring properties and cause injury would also be actionable.[1] Even making excessive noise that interferes with a neighbour's enjoyment of his or her property may be treated as a tort.[2]

In one case, a foundry operated for many decades, producing smoke from its operations without complaint from its industrial neighbours. An automobile transport company then acquired vacant lands next to the foundry for the purpose of storing new automobiles pending shipment. Particles from the smoke caused damage to the finish of the stored automobiles, and the transport company took legal action against the foundry for the damage caused by its smoke emissions. The foundry argued that it had acquired the right to emit the smoke on the basis of the passage of time. In finding against the foundry, the court addressed the various defences raised in the following way:[3]

(1) A defendant cannot claim that the plaintiffs came to the nuisance.

(2) A defendant cannot claim that even though the nuisance caused injury to the plaintiff, it is a benefit to the public at large.

(3) A defendant cannot claim as a defence that the place where the nuisance operates is a suitable one for carrying on the operation in question, and that no other place that is suitable would result in less of a problem.

(4) The defendant may not claim that all possible care and skill were used to

---

1. *Russell Transport Ltd. v. Ontario Malleable Iron Co. Ltd.*, [1952] 4 D.L.R. 719.
2. *340909 Ontario Ltd. v. Huron Steel Products (Windsor) Ltd. and Huron Steel Products* (1990), 73 O.R. (2d) 641.
3. *Russell Transport Ltd. v. Ontario Malleable Iron Co. Ltd.*, [1952] 4 D.L.R. 719.

prevent the operation from being a nuisance, because nuisance is not a part of the law of negligence.

(5) The defendant cannot argue that its actions would not amount to a nuisance because other firms acting independently of it were doing the same thing as well.

(6) A defendant cannot say as a defence that it is merely making a reasonable use of its property, as no use of property is reasonable if it causes substantial discomfort to others or causes damage to their property.

In this case, the polluter was held responsible for the damages caused by the smoke particles, and given a brief period of time to correct the pollution problem. While the case effectively ended the environmental damage caused by the foundry, the cumulative damage to the environment was not, and could not be addressed by the court in its judgement. This was so because the common law relief was limited to those individuals who could show damage and establish their right to compensation in court. In effect, the common law and the relief it offered could only address injury to property or persons on an individual basis. Protection of the public from damage to the environment in general, in so far as the courts were concerned, was a matter for the government to address by legislation.

A further drawback of the common law in cases of damage to the environment was the matter of standing before the courts. In this type of situation the applicable law was the law related to nuisance, as manifested by interference with a person's enjoyment of their property. Environmental groups concerned about pollution of air or water could seldom establish that they suffered injury or damage, as in most cases the injury (if it could be established) was to the property of the Crown, and not directly to the individuals in question. In this regard, the common law was limited for the most part to an individual, rather than public action as a means of controlling or eliminating pollution to the environment.

In a case heard in 1917, the limitations of the common law vis-à-vis broader public policy issues were raised by the court. In that case,[4] a mining company used an open roasting method for the smelting of its ore. The smoke and fumes from its operations damaged the crops of neighbouring farmers, and a farmer who suffered damage applied to the court for an injunction to stop the damage. The mining company was clearly at fault, but the court faced a dilemma. To issue an injunction to stop the damage to the farmer's crops would essentially eliminate the employment of the majority of the residents of the city that had developed around the mine. The court recognized the broader economic issue raised by the case, and awarded money damages to the farmer, but refused to grant an injunction to stop the smoke damage. The provincial government responded with legislation shortly thereafter which dealt with the need for ongoing compensation for the smoke damage caused by the smelter. The legislation, however, did nothing to address the problem of ongoing environmental pollution caused by the smelting operation itself. This approach was typical of the response by governments at the time. While recognizing that environmental damage was broader than the individuals involved, the tendency was for the legislators of the day to treat environmental damage as a localized matter rather than a broader public policy problem.

---

4. *Black v. Canada Copper Company* (1917), 12 O.W.N. 243.

Attitudes changed following World War II, as the magnitude of the problem of damage to the environment began to unfold.

The necessities of war produced a host of new products and chemical compounds that had peace-time uses and applications. In addition, many new developments in the years that followed were later discovered to have harmful effects on the environment either through their manufacturing processes or when the products were discarded. Under common law it was not easy to provide relief to those affected by these products or processes because it was often difficult to pinpoint the source of the pollution. In many cases the pollution may have originated in a number of sources. For example, a downstream user of water might be affected by contaminants in the water supply, but may not be in a position to identify the particular polluter if the same water supply was used by numerous upstream commercial or industrial users. Long-forgotten waste disposal sites might also be leaking into the stream, or municipal storm sewer run-off allowed to enter the water supply may compound the problem. The run-off from farmlands adjacent to the stream may contain harmful chemicals that had been used by farmers for weed control or fertilizer. In some cases, the discharge of chemicals not harmful in themselves might combine to form pollutants with an unidentifiable source. In these situations, the common law could not adequately address the problem, and perhaps more importantly, not provide an appropriate remedy.

A further difficulty of the common law was the limitation of the remedy to address the problem of clean-up of the polluter's own lands. The landowner injured by the pollution would receive compensation for the damage suffered, but the court would not be in a position to order a clean-up of the polluter's own property, and the source of the pollution would remain.

Governments recognized the limitations of the common law as a means of control and abatement of environmental damage, and began a pro-active role in environmental protection. The common law, nevertheless, has continued to be a useful and effective means of dealing with individual and localized instances of injury to property. Its use, however, has largely been overshadowed by legislative regulation and control measures.

The legislative approach overcomes most of the difficulties related to identification of source, control and abatement (or prohibition) of pollution, and provides protection for the environment in general. Environmental protection laws recognize that a great many human endeavours produce some form of pollution of the air, water, or land. They also recognize that many necessary business activities can only be carried out through the production of waste, and in some cases, hazardous waste. What environmental protection legislation attempts to do is minimize the pollution through control and monitoring procedures, and where necessary, prohibition of former production or waste disposal practices.

ENVIRONMENTAL LEGISLATION

The protection of the environment falls within the legislative spheres of both the federal government and the provincial legislatures. All of the provincial governments and the federal government have passed legislation to either control or prohibit activities that have a negative impact on the environment in their respective areas of jurisdiction. The limits of these areas are far from clear in environmental law matters, and in some cases, an overlap of authority may exist. As a case in point, the government of Alberta's decision to construct a dam on the Oldman River in that province appeared to be a decision that fell within provincial jurisdiction. The Supreme Court of Canada,[5] however, held that the project was subject to the federal government's Environmental Assessment and Review Process Guidelines Order because the federal government's Navigable Waters Protection Act applied to the project.

The *Oldman River* case illustrates the complexity of the process in terms of environmental legislation when a government undertakes a major project that has an impact on the environment. The Oldman River was first considered as a potential site for a dam in 1958. Numerous water supply studies and public hearings and consultations took place in the years that followed, and eventually, in 1984, a decision was made to construct the dam. Before the announcement was made, the project was screened by the federal Department of the Environment. Following the announcement, the Province of Alberta conducted further environmental studies. Finally, in 1986, the province applied for federal government approval under the Navigable Waters Protection Act. The minister approved the project, but failed to make an environmental assessment under the federal government's Environmental Assessment and Review Process Guidelines Order. The project was challenged on this basis by an environmental group, and the issue was put before the courts. The Supreme Court decided that the minister was bound by the Guidelines Order, and was obliged to follow it before ministerial approval could be granted for the construction of the dam.

Apart from the "grey areas" of jurisdiction, for many business activities, provincial legislation is the applicable law, and it is this legislation that must be carefully adhered to in the conduct of business activity. Each province has addressed environmental protection in its own way, but the legislation has a common thrust and purpose: to limit or prohibit those business (or individual) activities that either harm or degrade the environment. The laws, therefore, deal with the discharge of harmful substances into the air, water and ground, and in some cases also address the clean-up of past pollution of ground and water. For example, under the Fisheries' Act[6] private landowners who damage fish habitat even inadvertently, may be subject to severe penalties. Nevertheless, environmental protection legislation recognizes that economic activity in many cases cannot be carried out without causing some environmental damage. As a consequence, rather than prohibiting the business activity entirely, the legislation takes a **regulatory** approach. These laws for the most part are concerned with the discharge of environmentally harmful substances into the air or water. They tend to be specific about the quantity of a pollutant that may be discharged in a certain period of time. The amounts may be expressed in parts per million of the specific substance in a specific volume of water or air. Some laws also require that the business carrying out the activity that causes the pollution monitor and record the discharge to ensure that the pollution does not exceed the allowable limits. In some jurisdictions, devices that cause pollution (such as equipment for burning materials) are subject to **licensing** requirements, and if the operators fail to contain the levels of pollutants produced to within the limits set out in the legislation, the license to

5. *Friends of the Oldman River Society v. Canada* (1991), 88 D.L.R. (4th) 1 (S.C.C.).

6. Fisheries' Act, R.S.C. 1985, c. F-14.

operate the equipment may be revoked. As an example of pollution regulation on a more individual level, automobile engines must be equipped with air pollution control devices that limit pollutants in engine exhaust to specific levels, and the vehicle owners may not alter or remove the equipment as long as the vehicle is licensed.

The general approach taken in the enforcement of this regulatory type of legislation is inspection and monitoring for **compliance**. In order to ensure compliance, enforcement officers are generally given wide powers of inspection, and the authority to examine and seize records where a violation of the act is suspected. Offenders are punished by fines where damage to the environment is established that contravenes the act or where the allowable pollution limits have been exceeded without excuse. In some cases, where pollution is serious, or where immediate action is required to prevent environmental damage, environmental enforcement officers have the authority to order the polluter to cease operations until the pollution problem can be corrected.

Environmental protection laws may also require governments, organizations, or businesses to engage in **environmental assessments** of certain kinds of activities if the activity has the potential for causing environmental damage. The proposed construction of power dams; the use, draining, or filling of wetlands; the use of large quantities of water from a waterway and the construction of waste disposal sites may be required to go through an approval process before the project may be undertaken. This process is frequently lengthy, and it requires considerable technical expertise, as the activity must be thoroughly examined in order to assess its impact in the light of the environmental damage that it might cause. The process usually provides for detailed studies and public input by interested parties or groups before approval is granted.

The storage and transportation of hazardous products or other materials that would cause environmental damage is generally subject to legislation that directs care in storage and handling, and in most cases requires notification to the appropriate government body (usually the Ministry of Environment or its designated agency) in the event that hazardous products or contaminants are spilled or released causing air, ground, or water contamination. In most cases, the legislation requires the person or business that caused the pollution to pay the cost of the clean-up, either by assuming responsibility of the cost directly, or by compensating the government authority that performed the clean-up for the costs that it incurred.

The legislation is often non-specific in terms of how parties must ensure the protection of the environment. The method of storage of products that may contaminate ground or water is not always specified, but a very high standard of care is imposed on the user. Products that are improperly stored or allowed to leak into the ground or water may result in charges under most environmental laws dealing with hazardous materials, as the laws tend to be couched in terms of a **prohibition** of certain types of pollution. In some provinces, the legislation holds the directors and officers personally responsible for allowing the pollution to occur, unless they can show that they used **due diligence** in their efforts to prevent the pollution from taking place. The Environmental Protection Act[7] of the Province

---

7. Environmental Protection Act, R.S.O. 1990, c. E-19, s. 194(1).

of Ontario, for example, places a heavy responsibility on officers and directors in the following terms:

> *Every director or officer of a corporation that engages in an activity that may result in a discharge of a contaminant into the natural environment contrary to this act or the regulations has a duty to take all reasonable care to prevent the corporation from causing or permitting such unlawful discharge.*

A number of federal government laws related to environmental protection also hold directors and officers of corporations personally liable. The Canadian Environmental Protection Act [8] provides that:

> *Where a corporation commits an offence under this Act, any officer or agent of the corporation who directed, authorized, assented to, acquiesced in or participated in the commission of the offence is a party to and guilty of the offence, and is liable to the punishment provided for the offence, whether or not the corporation has been prosecuted or convicted.*

The Transportation of Dangerous Goods Act [9] and the Hazardous Products Act, [10] both federal statutes related to environmental matters, contain director and officer liability provisions similar to the above-noted section of the Canadian Environmental Protection Act. As with the Ontario Environmental Protection Act, the violations tend to be strict liability offences, where intent is not a factor that permits a corporation or its directors to avoid liability. The only defence for a director would appear to be **due diligence**.

To be effective as a defence in this kind of situation, due diligence means much more than the directors or officers of the company issuing directives to management to carefully store hazardous products or potential contaminants. It requires follow-up efforts to ensure that employees are properly trained in the safe use, handling, and storage of potentially hazardous products. It probably also means the careful personal monitoring or inspection of the premises from time to time to ensure that the directives are enforced, and that no potentially risky conditions exist. In effect, due diligence probably requires the directors to satisfy the court that control and responsibility were not simply delegated to management on the assumption that compliance would take place, but that the policies were monitored by the directors on an ongoing basis. [11]

ENVIRONMENTAL RESPONSIBILITY

Environmental damage has generally been considered to be the responsibility of the party that caused the damage, but this is not always the case, particularly where the contamination involves land or water. Where contamination is found to exist on land, the legislation in most provinces permits the government agency or ministry to order the current owner to clean up the premises. The discovery of contamination on a land site may in some circumstances result in an order to clean the site, and the clean-up costs may exceed the value of the property. Consequently, careful legal practitioners will strongly recommend to a client interested in a land purchase that an **environmental audit** be made of the property before the purchase is finalized. Most commercial transactions of this nature

---

8. Canadian Environmental Protection Act, R.S.C., 1985 (4th supp.) s. 122, as amended.

9. Transportation of Dangerous Goods Act, R.S.C., 1985, c. T-19.

10. Hazardous Products Act, R.S.C., 1985, c. H-3.

11. *Regina v. Bata Industries Ltd., Bata, Marchant and Weston* (1992), 9 O.R. (3d) 329.

now include a "clean" environmental audit as a condition precedent to the purchase of the land. Even when an environmental audit concludes that a property is clean, some risk remains, as no standards have been determined for many contaminants, and the government may later require a higher standard of cleanliness. Nevertheless, the audit is a useful tool in reducing the risks associated with commercial property purchases. An audit may reveal long-forgotten buried fuel storage tanks, waste disposal sites, and sometimes soil contaminated with hazardous products produced in the distant past by previous owners of the site.

Contamination of property also poses a risk (in some jurisdictions) to lenders who look to land and buildings as security for debt, because a mortgagee may be required to move into possession of the property to realize on its security, and in doing so, it may fall within the definition of owner, and become responsible for clean-up costs.[12] To avoid this danger, banks and other financial institutions may require environmental audits before making a secured loan on property. A "clean"environmental audit would allow the mortgagee to seize the property of the debtor business on default without undue concern about hidden environmental risks associated with the land.

Environmental legislation in some cases may create situations where the risk is so great that no business, lender, or lower level government would be willing to acquire or deal with properties that have become seriously contaminated. In one instance, an old foundry operation went into receivership. The property remained vacant for many years as it could not be sold, and the mortgagee was unwilling to move into possession because of suspected land contamination from the foundry operations. Municipal tax arrears entitled the municipality to dispose of the land by tax sale, but the municipality was unwilling to do so, as it did not wish to assume any responsibility for clean-up. As a result, the property remained unsaleable and unusable. Environmental legislation does not effectively address this scenario, nor does it provide for government clean-up at public expense in this type of situation — other than through a direct government initiative to resolve an environmental problem.

The complex web of government regulation of business activities that have an environmental impact complicate the conduct of business, and undoubtedly add to the cost of operation. Provincial governments are beginning to recognize the fact that some streamlining of legislation is necessary, and the trend appears to be moving in the direction of consolidation of the laws into fewer statutes, or in some cases, a single omnibus law. Nova Scotia, for example, has announced that it intends to consolidate its 16 environmental statutes into a single piece of legislation with a view to its introduction in 1994.

SUMMARY

Protection of the environment was initially left with the individual to enforce through tort laws, but this was only satisfactory where the contamination was localized and directly affected the person bringing the action. Even then, the remedies were limited to damages and an injunction, and did not address pollution problems that caused more fundamental damage to the environment. The problem required legislative initiative and more effective solutions than the common law could offer.

---

12. *Ontario (Attorney-General) v. Tyre King Tyre Recycling Ltd.* (1992), 9 O.R. (3d) 318.

Most environmental legislation is designed to control or eliminate pollution and environmental hazards by either regulation of the quantity of pollutants produced or prohibition of their production. The legislation generally shifts the responsibility for pollution of the environment to the person causing environmental damage by requiring the polluter to cover the cost of the clean-up. It encourages compliance by holding directors and officers of corporations personally responsible for any pollution violations by their corporation.

Polluted or contaminated property represents a serious risk for purchasers and mortgagees unless they take steps to ensure that the lands are free from contaminating substances. Environmental audits are usually used to determine the "cleanliness" of lands before purchase.

DISCUSSION QUESTIONS

1. "At common law, damage to property or the environment is actionable, but restricted in terms of the type of case that may be brought before the court." Explain.
2. Identify the remedies available to the court to control damage to a person's property by his or her neighbour's actions.
3. Why was it necessary for governments to introduce legislation to control environmental damage?
4. Outline the various ways that legislation addresses environmental pollution.
5. To what extent does the legislation recognize the fact that environmental damage cannot be eliminated from certain industrial processes?
6. Where environmental damage is prohibited under legislation, what defence may be available to the directors and officers of the corporation?
7. Why does the purchase of lands previously used for industrial purposes pose a risk to the purchaser?
8. What steps may be taken by prospective purchasers of property to reduce the risk of facing an environmental clean-up order?
9. Why should mortgagees of industrial property be concerned when securing their mortgages on such property?
10. Outline the method used by governments to ensure that large industrial projects such as hydroelectric dams or large land development undertakings result in a minimum of environmental damage?

MINI-CASE PROBLEMS

1. ABC Company stored steel drums of contaminated waste products behind its plant. Some of the drums leaked contaminants into the soil, and these contaminants eventually found their way into a neighbour's drinking water supply.

    What are the rights of the neighbour?

2. C was a director of the ABC Company in the above example. As a director, C rarely visited the plant, and was unaware of the storage of the waste product behind the plant. However, a year previous, at a directors' meeting, he raised the issue of establishing a company directive to management that would require managers to ensure the safe storage of contaminants at all company plants.

    Advise C on whether a government examination of the plant site should take place.

JUDICIAL DECISION

The *Regina v. Bata Industries Ltd.* case illustrates the responsibility that the provincial Environmental Protection Act places not only on a business firm, but upon the persons who operate the business. In this case, the company improperly stored waste chemicals that leaked into the soil and ground water. The company and three directors were charged with violation of the act. Two of the three directors failed to establish their defence of due diligence and were fined. In the case, the judge discussed the standard required to successfully claim due diligence as a defence.

Environmental Law — Liability of Directors — Defence of Due Diligence

Regina v. Bata Industries Ltd., Bata, Marchant and Weston (1992), 9 O.R. (3d) 329.

The company, a shoe manufacturer, stored chemical waste at an outside site, and allowed the chemicals to leak into the ground, causing contamination of the ground water. The company was charged and found guilty of a violation of the Ontario Water Resources Act. Three directors were also charged with failing to take all reasonable care to prevent the spillage. The judge deciding the case discusses the charges against the directors in the following part of his judgement:

ORMSTON, PROV. DIV. J.:

In *R. v. Sault Ste. Marie,* at pp. 1324–25 S.C.R., p. 181 D.L.R., Justice Dickson (as he then was) addressed the issue:

> It may be suggested that the introduction of a defense based on due diligence and the shifting of the burden of proof might better be implemented by legislative act. In answer, it should be recalled that the concept of absolute liability and the creation of a jural category of public welfare offences are both the product of the judiciary and not of the Legislature. The development to date of this defense... has also been the work of judges. The present case offers the opportunity of consolidating and clarifying the doctrine.

> The correct approach in my opinion, is to relieve the Crown of the burden of proving *mens rea...* and to the virtual impossibility in most regulatory cases of proving wrongful intention. In a normal case, the accused alone will have knowledge of what he has done to avoid the breach and it is not improper to expect him to come forward with the evidence of due diligence. This is particularly so when it is alleged... that pollution was caused by the activities of a large and complex corporation.

Justice Cory, in *R. v. Wholesale Travel Group Inc.,* at p. 248 S.C.R., p. 259 C.C.C., said:

> Regulated actors are taken to understand that, should they be unable to discharge this burden, and interference of negligence will be drawn from the fact that the *proscribed result* has occurred.

> The Crown must still prove the *actus reus* of regulatory offences beyond a reasonable doubt. Thus, the Crown must prove that the accused polluted the river, sold adulterated food or published a false advertisement. However, once having established this beyond a reasonable doubt, the Crown is *presumptively relieved* of having to prove anything further. Fault is presumed from the bringing about of the *proscribed result,* and the onus shifts to the defendant to establish reasonable care on a balance of probabilities.

In my opinion, the *actus reus* of these sections is "engaging in an activity that may or does discharge." This would be consistent with the analysis of Mr.

Justice Cory and thereby leave the burden of proof of due diligence in the traditional way upon the defendants. This would also be consistent with the legislative attempt to provide for the defense of due diligence in terms suggested by Justice Dickson in *R. v. Sault Ste. Marie*...

I ask myself the following questions in assessing the defense of due diligence:

(a) Did the board of directors establish a pollution prevention "system" as indicated in *R. v. Sault Ste. Marie. i.e.*, was there supervision or inspection? was there improvement in business methods? did he exhort those he controlled or influenced?

(b) Did each director ensure that the corporate officers have been instructed to set up a system sufficient within the terms and practices of its industry of ensuring compliance with environmental laws, to ensure that the officers report back periodically to the board on the operation of the system, and to ensure that the officers are instructed to report any substantial non-compliance to the board in a timely manner?

I reminded myself that:

(c) The directors are responsible for reviewing the environmental compliance reports provided by the officers of the corporation, but are justified in placing *reasonable* reliance on reports provided to them by corporate officers, consultants, counsel or other informed parties.

(d) The directors should substantiate that the officers are promptly addressing environmental concerns brought to their attention by government agencies or other concerned parties including shareholders.

(e) The directors should be aware of the standards of their industry and other industries which deal with similar environmental pollutants or risks.

(f) The directors should immediately and personally react when they have notice the system has failed.

Within this general profile and dependent upon the nature and structure of the corporate activity, one would hope to find remedial and contingency plans for spills, a system of ongoing environmental audit, training programs, sufficient authority to act and other indices of a pro-active environmental policy.

THE BATA ORGANIZATION

The Bata Shoe Organization comprises some 80 companies around the world. Thomas G. Bata is the chief executive officer. The one company which is located in Canada and headquartered at Toronto is Bata Industries Limited. This company has four divisions. Each division operates autonomously under a general manager and each general manager is a vice-president and director of Bata Industries Limited. The president, also a director, of Bata Industries Limited during the material time, was Douglas Marchant. Thomas G. Bata, who functioned chiefly in an advisory capacity, was chairman of the board and a director of Bata Industries Limited.

The division of Bata Industries Limited that this case involves was the shoe manufacturing division located at Batawa, Ontario. The general manager/director/vice-president on site was Keith Weston.

The prosecution involves only three directors of Bata Industries Limited, namely Thomas G. Bata, the chief executive officer, Douglas Marchant, the president, and Keith Weston, vice-president of Bata Manufacturing, a division of Bata Industries Limited located in Batawa, Ontario.

In my opinion, the principle of delegation in environmental matters is aptly summarized as follows [McLeod, "Environmental Protection Legislation," *supra*]

Delegation is a fact of life. The Environmental Enforcement Amendment Act is not intended to prevent a reasonable degree of delegation. However, the Legislature has clearly declared that environmental protection is too important to delegate entirely to the lower levels of a corporation. Although the Legislature does not expect the Board of Directors or the officers of the Corporations to make all environmental decisions, it is not acceptable for them to insulate themselves from all responsibility for environmental violations by delegating all aspects of compliance to subordinates.

RE THOMAS G. BATA

Thomas G. Bata was the director with least personal contact with the plant at Batawa. His responsibilities were primarily directed at the global level of the Bata Shoe Organization. It was established in the evidence that TAC 298, the environmental alert, had been distributed to his companies throughout the world.

He attended on site in Batawa once or twice a year to review the operation and performance goals of the facility. He was a walk-around director while on the site. The evidence of Mr. Riden establishes that the plant managers could not orchestrate a visit for Mr. Bata: "You never knew where Mr. Bata was going to go, believe me. He had a habit of trying to outguess where you wanted him to go". There is no evidence that he was aware of an environmental problem.

Mr. Riden also established that when the Bata Engineering chemical storage problem was brought to Mr. Bata's attention, he immediately directed the appropriate resources ($20,000) to minimize the effect on the environment. The evidence also establishes that when a water problem was identified and funds were required to construct the water treatment plant for the town of Batawa, he (the family) authorized the expenditure of $250,000.

In short, he was aware of his environmental responsibilities and had written directions to that effect in TAC 298. He did personally review the operation when he was on site and did not allow himself to be wilfully blind or orchestrated in his movements. He responded to the matters that were brought to his attention promptly and appropriately. He had placed an experienced director on site and was entitled in the circumstances to assume that Mr. Weston was addressing the environmental concerns. He was entitled to assume that his on-site manager/director would bring to his attention any problem as Mr. Riden had done. He was entitled to rely upon his system as evidenced by TAC 298 *unless he became aware the system was defective.*

Bata Industries Limited is a privately held Ontario corporation. It complied with the minimal statutory requirements. However, unlike a public company, much of the business done at directors' meetings or between the board and the divisions was informal with no record kept. It is very difficult in the ordinary course for a director to establish due diligence if there is no contemporary written record.

Although the burden of establishing due diligence was onerous in the absence of more recorded corporate documentation, he has done so in my opinion and is not guilty of the offences charged.

RE DOUGLAS MARCHANT

Mr. Marchant presents another variation in directors' liability. His responsibility is more than Mr. Bata, but less than Mr. Weston's. This "doctrine of responsible share" is well accepted in American jurisprudence (*United States v. Park, supra*) and is applicable in this case.

He was appointed to the Board as president on January 26, 1988. Mr. Richer testified that Mr. Marchant was "down in Batawa once a month" and these visits included a tour of the plant. Mr. Richer brought the storage problem to his *personal attention* around February 15, 1989.

The evidence, therefore, establishes that for at least the last six months of the time alleged in the charges (February 15, 1989 to August 31, 1989), *he had personal knowledge.* There is no evidence that he took any steps after having knowledge to view the site and assess the problem. There is no evidence that the system of storage was made safer or temporary steps were taken for containment until such time as removal could be affected.

The evidence established that $100,000 had been reserved for disposal in March 1988. On January 25, 1989, Mr. De Bruyn wrote to Tricel requesting quotes for disposal. By April 14, 1989, all the quotes were received. There was still no action until August 11 when the Ministry officials were on site, Tricel was contacted and told "to get the waste out as soon as possible."

In the circumstances, it is my opinion that due diligence requires him to exercise a degree of supervision and control that "demonstrate that he was exhorting those whom he may be normally expected to influence or control to an accepted standard of behaviour": *R. v. Sault Ste. Marie, supra,* and *R. v. Southdown Builders Ltd.* (1981), 57 C.P.R. (2d) 56 (Ont. G.S.P.), p. 59.

He had a responsibility not only to give instruction but also to see to it that those instructions were carried out in order to minimize the damage. The delay in clean-up showed a lack of due diligence: *R. v. Canadian Cellulose Co.* (1979), 2 F.P.R. 256 (B.C. Co. Ct.) and *R. v. Genge* (1983), 44 Nfld. & P.E.I.R. 109 (Nfld. T.D.). There is no corporate documentation between February 15, 1989 and August 31, 1989 to assist him in his defense of due diligence on the balance of probabilities and is therefore guilty as charged.

There will be a conviction registered pursuant to s. 75(1) of the *OWRA*. The charges under s. 147a of the *EPA* are stayed for reasons previously given.

RE KEITH WESTON

I have considered the fact that during Mr. Weston's tenure at Batawa, the company committed $250,000 to the building of a water treatment system for the village. This would seem inconsistent with the commission of the environment offense on the site of the plant. However, I note from the evidence that in this circumstance, Mr. Weston advised the Bata *family* of the village's needs. The Bata *family* agreed to donate the land, then established further financial limits for assistance over the period of five years. Why Mr. Weston did not pursue this course of action with the environmental problem on site has not been explained. The evidence establishes that Mr. Riden had no difficulty receiving such approval from Mr. Bata.

In my opinion, this evidence in not evidence of Mr. Weston's personal attention to environmental concerns, but rather an example of the personal and sentimental attachment that the Bata family had to the area.

Keith Weston's responsibilities as an "on-site" director make him much more vulnerable to prosecution. He demanded the authority to control his work environment before he took the job. He had experience in the production side and was aware toxic chemicals were used in the process. He was reminded of his environmental responsibilities by TAC 298. In my opinion, Keith Weston has failed to establish that he took all reasonable care to prevent unlawful discharge.

In *addition* to the evidence previously related in respect to the due diligence of Bata Industries, it is my opinion, red flags should have been raised in his environmental consciousness when the first quote of $58,000 was obtained. Instead of simply dismissing it out of hand, he should have inquired why it was so high and investigated the problem. I find that he had no qualms about accepting the second quote of $28,000 and he had no further information other than it was cheaper. This was not an *informed* business judgement, and he cannot rely upon the business judgement rule, which at its core recognized that a business corporation is profit-oriented and that an honest error of judgement should not impose liability *provided* the requisite standard of care is met:

I find confirmation in this opinion by the fact that when he was transferred in November, he allotted $100,000 to waste disposal, again without any further knowledge. One cannot help but wonder if his diminished incentive package was a motivating factor in the allotment of $100,000 at this time. This expense would only affect him personally to the amount of $500 because the company was now in a profit position and his salary incentive based on reducing losses was minimal.

It is my finding that Keith Weston cannot shelter behind the advice he received from Mr. De Bruyn. As Bata was "cut to the bone" by Mr. Weston, the additional responsibilities fell upon Mr. De Bruyn and grossly overloaded him. The problem was aggravated by the inference from the evidence that Mr. De Bruyn was not given the authority to expend the $58,000 or $28,000 on his own. He required the approval of Mr. Weston who stands in sad comparison to Mr. Riden who occupied the same position and responsibilities at the plant next door.

As the "on-site" director Mr. Weston had a responsibility in this type of industry to personally inspect on a regular basis, *i.e.,* "walk-about". To simply look at the site "not too closely" 20 times over his four-year tenure does not meet the mark. He had an obligation if he decided to delegate responsibility to ensure that the delegate received the training necessary for the job and to receive detailed reports from that delegate.

There will be a conviction registered pursuant to s. 75(1) of the *OWRA*. The charges under s. 147a of the *EPA* will be stayed for reasons previously given.

Judgments accordingly.

CASE PROBLEMS FOR DISCUSSION

Case 1

Gerry and Janet Smith had been married for 15 years, and had operated a family business from their home. They lived on 50 acres of land just outside a small town, and their business consisted of breeding, training, and boarding German shepherd dogs. Formally, Gerry was the sole owner of the property and of the business. Janet, however, had been active throughout their marriage in the management and daily activities of the business.

Since the Smiths frequently transported their dogs to shows, to the veterinary or to handlers, they maintained three vans for this purpose. They also had a gasoline pump with an underground storage tank installed on their farm to fuel the vehicles as a convenience for their business.

The Smiths were having trouble maintaining the lawn above the tank. For several years the grass above the tank died despite repeated efforts to reseed and water the area each spring. They sought the advice of a landscaper who suggested that the problem might be gasoline spillage from the pump nozzle when the fuel tanks of the vehicles were being filled. This would cause the soil to be soaked with gasoline at the surface and would burn the grass roots.

Gerry eventually called a pump equipment service company who sent a representative out to the farm. On inspection of the equipment he discovered a crack in the underground tank which appeared to have been leaking leaded gasoline into the surrounding soil for quite some time. The company representative notified environmental authorities who came to the Smith's farm to test the surrounding soil. They found levels of soil contamination far in excess of approved standards, and ordered the Smiths to remove the damaged tank and clean up the site.

Partly as a result of the strain and financial burden that this incident placed on them, Gerry and Janet separated several months later. In the arguments that followed concerning the division of their property, the farmland and the business played a prominent role.

Under the applicable family law legislation, all the property of the husband and wife, whether jointly owned or not, was to be pooled for the purpose of valuation, and the value then divided equally between the spouses. Assets were generally valued at fair market value as at the date of separation. The division of assets often required that some be liquidated in order to ensure that equal shares could be given to each spouse.

The farm property was Gerry's primary asset. A year before the soil contamination had been discovered, Gerry had had the farm appraised at $175 000. After the separation, Gerry engaged the services of an environmental expert to prepare a report estimating the cost of cleaning up the site. The expert reported that a cost of at least $200 000 would have to be incurred in order to meet approved standards.

Janet then engaged her own environmental specialist who reported that the clean-up could be done at much less cost by using older technology. Her expert quoted a figure around $50 000.

There was no question that the farm would have to be sold in order to equally distribute the value of the couple's property. Gerry's shares in the business were his only other substantial asset and had been valued two years earlier at approximately $25 000.

Discuss the legal issues that arise in this case. Identify the arguments that the various parties may rely on and discuss their significance in the context of both environmental and business law. How would you resolve this matter?

Case 2

Hazardous Waste Trucking Company carried on business as a transporter of industrial waste products to licensed waste disposal sites. Liquid Waste Disposal Company carried on a similar type of business, but handled only liquid waste. On a clear winter day, a transport truck owned and operated by Hazardous Waste Trucking Company collided on an icy patch of highway with a truck operated by Liquid Waste Disposal Company. The drivers of both vehicles had been operating their respective vehicles in accordance with the provincial highway traffic act, and the patch of ice on the highway was totally unexpected. Both drivers had lost control of their vehicles on the ice, and their trailers that carried the waste products collided, causing their contents to spill on the highway.

The contents of each trailer did not constitute a toxic waste in itself, but the mixing of the two products produced a toxic compound hazardous to fish and animals. A local fire department answered the accident call, and flushed the substance from the highway, instead of simply containing the waste mixture. As a result, a small stream was contaminated by the run-off.

Environmental inspectors ordered a clean-up, but both companies refused to do so, blaming each other and the fire department. The government arranged for the clean-up at a cost of $135 000.

Discuss the issues raised in this case on the basis that the "owners" of a contaminant under the environmental protection legislation are responsible for any environmental damage that it may cause and the cost of any clean-up required.

Case 3

The Smiths purchased a rural house and lot located near the intersection of two highways. Adjacent to the intersection, ABC Fuels had operated a gas bar and service station for many years. Over time, spilled gasoline and other petroleum products may have seeped into the soil. The fuel tanks, however, had been removed some years before the Smith's purchased their home, and the service station property had been sold to a plumbing supply company that used the buildings and grounds to store plastic pipe and copper plumbing fittings.

Some time after the purchase of their home, the Smiths began to notice a strange taste and odour in their drinking water. Their water supply was obtained from a well on their premises. Tests of the water supply indicated that the water was contaminated by gasoline.

Advise the Smiths of their rights at law and the possible course of action open to them.

Case 4

McDonald operated a small farm where he raised pigs for market. The farm was located at the outskirts of a small city, and was surrounded on three sides by rural housing developments. McDonald stored pig manure in the corner of one field until late in the autumn of each year when he would use it to fertilize his crop fields. The manure pile was located behind Black's lot, and attracted an enormous number of flies and insects during the summer months. In addition, the pungent odour of fresh pig manure prevented Black from using his backyard for any kind of social or recreational purpose.

Black complained to McDonald about the storage of manure next to his lot, but McDonald refused to change the location, as it was the most convenient storage place from his point of view. Black then took his complaint to the office of the Ministry of the Environment in the city, but was told that manure was not considered a hazardous waste in a farm setting, and was apparently being handled and stored in accordance with standard agricultural practices.

Advise Black of his rights (if any) and the possible responses of McDonald to any action on Black's part.

APPENDIX A

Documents

CANADA BUSINESS CORPORATIONS ACT FORM 1 ARTICLES OF INCORPORATION (SECTION 6)	▮✦▮	LOI SUR LES SOCIÉTÉS COMMERCIALES CANADIENNES FORMULE 1 STATUTS CONSTITUTIFS (ARTICLE 6)

1 – Name of Corporation   Dénomination de la société

2 – The place in Canada where the registered office is to be situated   Lieu au Canada ou doit être situé le siège social

3 – The classes and any maximum number of shares that the corporation is authorized to issue   Catégories et tout nombre maximal d'actions que la société est autorisée à émettre

4 – Restrictions if any on share transfers   Restrictions sur le transfert des actions, s'il y a lieu

5 – Number (or minimum and maximum number) of directors   Nombre (ou nombre minimum et maximum) d'administrateurs

6 – Restrictions if any on business the corporation may carry on   Limites imposées quant aux activités commerciales que la société peut exploiter, s'il y a lieu.

7 – Other provisions if any   Autres dispositions s'il y a lieu

8 – Incorporators   Fondateurs

Names – Noms	Address (include postal code) Adresse (inclure le code postal)	Signature

FOR DEPARTMENTAL USE ONLY	À L'USAGE DU MINISTÈRE SEULEMENT
Corporation No. – No de la société	Filed – Déposée

NEWSOME AND GILBERT, LIMITED LF1388 (3/87)

Reprinted forms provided by Newsome and Gilbert Limited and reproduced with their kind permission.

Transfer/Deed of Land

Form 1 — Land Registration Reform Act, 1984

A

FOR OFFICE USE ONLY

(1) Registry ☐	Land Titles ☐	(2) Page 1 of ____ pages

(3) Property Identifier(s)   Block   Property   Additional: See Schedule ☐

(4) Consideration   Dollars $

(5) Description   This is a: Property Division ☐   Property Consolidation ☐

New Property Identifiers   Additional: See Schedule ☐

Executions   Additional: See Schedule ☐

(6) This Document Contains   (a) Redescription New Easement Plan/Sketch ☐   (b) Schedule for: Description ☐   Additional Parties ☐   Other ☐   (7) Interest/Estate Transferred Fee Simple

(8) Transferor(s) The transferor hereby transfers the land to the transferee and certifies that the transferor is at least eighteen years old and that

....

Name(s)   Signature(s)   Date of Signature Y M D

(9) Spouse(s) of Transferor(s) I hereby consent to this transaction
Name(s)   Signature(s)   Date of Signature Y M D

(10) Transferor(s) Address for Service

(11) Transferee(s)   Date of Birth Y M D

(12) Transferee(s) Address for Service

(13) Transferor(s) The transferor verifies that to the best of the transferor's knowledge and belief, this transfer does not contravene section 49 of the Planning Act, 1983.   Date of Signature Y M D   Date of Signature Y M D

Signature ....   Signature ....

Solicitor for Transferor(s) I have explained the effect of section 49 of the Planning Act, 1983 to the transferor and I have made inquiries of the transferor to determine that this transfer does not contravene that section and based on the information supplied by the transferor, to the best of my knowledge and belief, this transfer does not contravene that section. I am an Ontario solicitor in good standing.   Date of Signature Y M D

Name and Address of Solicitor   Signature ....

(14) Solicitor for Transferee(s) I have investigated the title to this land and to abutting land where relevant and I am satisfied that the title records reveal no contravention as set out in subclause 49 (21a) (c) (ii) of the Planning Act, 1983 and that to the best of my knowledge and belief this transfer does not contravene section 49 of the Planning Act 1983. I act independently of the solicitor for the transferor(s) and I am an Ontario solicitor in good standing.

Name and Address of Solicitor   Signature ....   Date of Signature Y M D

Planning Act — OPTIONAL

Affix Solicitor for Transferee(s) Statement by Solicitor for Transferee(s) here if necessary

(15) Assessment Roll Number of Property	Cty.	Mun.	Map	Sub.	Par.		Fees and Tax
						Registration Fee	
(16) Municipal Address of Property				(17) Document Prepared by:		Land Transfer Tax	
						Total	

FOR OFFICE USE ONLY

Newsome and Gilbert, Limited
Form LF1327 (1/85)   April, 1985

Newsome and Gilbert, Limited
Form LF1090 (2/85)

Offer to Purchase

AGREEMENT OF PURCHASE AND SALE

I/We ....

of the .... of ....(as Purchaser), having inspected the property, hereby

agree to and with ....(as Vendor)

through .... Agent for Vendor

to purchase All and Singular the premises on the .... side of ....

in the .... of .... known as

.... having a

frontage of .... more or less, by a depth of .... more or less, being

Lot No. .... according to Plan No. .... registered in the Land Registry Office for the Registry/

Land Titles Division of .... (herein called the "real property")

at the price of .... Dollars ($)

of lawful money of Canada, payable cash
cheque .... Dollars ($)

to the said Agent/Vendor on this date as a deposit to be held in trust pending completion or other termination of this Agreement and to be credited
on account of the purchase price on closing, and agree to

The Vendor represents that as at the date of acceptance hereof the Vendor has not received from any municipal or other governmental
authority any deficiency notice or work order affecting the real property pursuant to which any deficiencies are required to be remedied or
any demolition, repairs or replacements are required to be carried out. If the Vendor receives any such deficiency notice or work order after
the date of acceptance hereof, the Vendor shall forthwith produce same to the Purchaser for inspection. If by the date of closing the Vendor has
not either (a) complied with such deficiency notice or work order, or (b) settled with the Purchaser any question of an abatement of the
purchase price arising out of such deficiency notice or work order, the Purchaser may at his option either (a) accept the real property subject
to such deficiency notice or work order or (b) terminate this Agreement. In the event of termination as aforesaid, all moneys paid hereunder
shall be returned to the Purchaser without interest or deductions.

The spouse of the Vendor shall consent to this Agreement, and shall agree to consent to the transaction evidenced by the deed or transfer.

Tenancy, if any

The purchase price herein shall include the following, free and clear of encumbrances:
All fixtures, which shall remain affixed to the real property, except the following fixtures which may be removed by the Vendor prior to
closing:

The following chattels all of which are owned by the Vendor:

This Offer shall be irrevocable by the Purchaser until   p.m. on the   day of   19
after which time, if not accepted, this Offer shall be null and void and the deposit returned to the Purchaser without interest or deduction.

Provided the title is good and free from all encumbrances, except as aforesaid, and except local rates, and except as to any registered
restrictions or covenants that run with the land provided that such are complied with, and except for any minor easements for hydro, gas,
telephone or like services. Purchaser to accept the real property subject to municipal and other governmental requirements, including building
and zoning by-laws, regulations and orders, provided the same have been complied with. Vendor agrees to authorize municipal and other
governmental authorities to release unto the Purchaser or his solicitor any information on file pertaining to such requirements.

The Purchaser to be allowed   days from the date of acceptance hereof to investigate the title at his own expense, and to satisfy
himself that there is no breach of municipal or other governmental requirements affecting the real property, and that its present use may be
lawfully continued. If within the time allowed for examining title, the Purchaser shall furnish the Vendor in writing with any valid objection
to title, or to any breach of municipal or other governmental requirements, or as to the fact that the present use may not lawfully be continued,
which the Vendor shall be unable or unwilling to remove, remedy or satisfy and which the Purchaser will not waive, this Agreement shall,
notwithstanding any intermediate acts or negotiations, be null and void and the deposit money returned to the Purchaser, without interest or
deductions and the Vendor and the Agent shall not be liable for any costs or damages. Save as to any valid objection so made within such
time, the Purchaser shall be conclusively deemed to have accepted the Vendor's title to the real property.

Newsome and Gilbert, Limited
Form LF1091 (10/86)

Offer to Purchase
Page 2

The Purchaser shall not call for the production of any title deed, abstract, survey or other evidence of title except such as are in the possession or control of the Vendor. The Vendor agrees that he will deliver any existing survey to the Purchaser so soon as possible and prior to the last day allowed for examining title.

This Agreement shall be completed on or before the   day of   , 19   on which date vacant possession of the real property shall be given to the Purchaser unless otherwise provided for herein.

Until completion of sale all buildings and equipment on the real property shall be and remain at the risk of the Vendor, and the Vendor will hold all policies of insurance effected on the property and the proceeds thereof in trust for the parties hereto, as their interests may appear. In the event of damage to the said buildings and equipment before the completion of this transaction, the Purchaser shall have the right to elect to take such proceeds and complete the purchase, or cancel this Agreement, whereupon the Purchaser shall be entitled to the return, without interest or deduction, of all moneys theretofore paid on account of this purchase. Vendor agrees to furnish Purchaser with copies of existing fire insurance policies within seven days of the date of acceptance hereof.

Unearned fire insurance premiums, fuel, taxes, interest, rentals, and all local improvement and water rates and other charges for municipal improvements to be apportioned and allowed to the date of completion of sale (the day itself to be apportioned to the Purchaser). Provided Purchaser may elect not to accept assignment of fire insurance in which case no adjustment for insurance premiums.

The deed or transfer, save for Land Transfer Tax Affidavit, to be prepared at the expense of the Vendor in a form acceptable to the Purchaser and if a mortgage or charge is to be given back, it shall be prepared at the expense of the Purchaser in a form acceptable to the Vendor.

Provided that this Agreement shall be effective only if the provisions of Section 49 of the Planning Act, as amended, are complied with.

The deed or transfer shall contain the statement of the Vendor and the Vendor's solicitor referred to in section 49 (21a) of the Planning Act, 1983 as amended.

The Vendor represents and warrants to the Purchaser that the buildings on the property have not been, and will not be at the date of completion, insulated with urea formaldehyde foam insulation. This warranty shall survive the completion of this transaction.

The Vendor represents and warrants that no consent to this transaction is required pursuant to section 21(1) of the Family Law Act, 1986 unless the Vendor's spouse has executed this agreement to consent thereto, and that the Transfer/Deed shall contain a statement by the Vendor as required by subsection (3) of section 21 or the spouse of the Vendor shall execute the Transfer/Deed to consent thereto.

Vendor further agrees to produce evidence that he is not now and that on closing he will not be a non-resident of Canada within the meaning of Section 116 of the Income Tax Act, or, in the alternative, evidence that the provisions of said Section 116 regarding disposition of property by a non-resident person have been complied with at or before closing.

This Offer, when accepted, shall constitute a binding contract of purchase and sale, and time in all respects shall be of the essence of this Agreement.

It is agreed that there is no representation, warranty, collateral agreement or condition affecting this Agreement or the real property or supported hereby other than as expressed herein in writing.

Any tender of documents or money hereunder may be made upon the Vendor or Purchaser or upon the solicitor acting for the party on whom tender is desired, and it shall be sufficient that a cheque certified by a chartered bank or trust company be tendered instead of cash.

Each party to pay the costs of registration and taxes on his own documents.

This Offer and its acceptance to be read with all changes of gender or number required by the context.

DATED at   this   day of   19

     IN WITNESS WHEREOF   have hereunto set   hand   and seal.

SIGNED, SEALED AND DELIVERED
In the presence of:

.... (Affix Seal)
Purchaser

.... (Affix Seal)
Purchaser

I/We, hereby accept the above offer, and covenant, promise and agree to and with the above-named Purchaser to duly carry out the same on the terms and conditions above mentioned, and hereby accept the deposit of $ out of which the agent hereby authorized to retain   commission of   per cent of an amount equal to the above mentioned sale price. Commission payable only if, as and when transaction is completed.

AND I,   , spouse of the said Vendor, hereby consent to this Agreement and agree to consent to the transaction evidenced by the deed or transfer.

DATED at   this   day of   19

     IN WITNESS WHEREOF   have hereunto set   hand   and seal.

SIGNED, SEALED AND DELIVERED
In the presence of:

.... (Affix Seal)
Vendor

.... (Affix Seal)
Vendor or Vendor's Spouse

Name, address and telephone number of Vendor's Solicitor:

Name, address and telephone number of Purchaser's Solicitor:

The undersigned Vendor hereby acknowledges receipt of a copy of the accepted Offer to Purchase herein.

DATED the　　　　day of　　　　19　　.

The undersigned Purchaser hereby acknowledges receipt of a copy of the accepted Offer to Purchase herein.

DATED the　　　　day of　　　　19　　.

A.D. 19

—TO—

Dated

Offer to Purchase

Newsome and Gilbert, Limited—Form 1090

Newsome and Gilbert, Limited
Form LF 221 (2/85)

Page 1 of 3
Revised February, 1985

THIS CHATTEL MORTGAGE SECURITY AGREEMENT

made B E T W E E N:

(Name)

Birth Date (Individuals only):

Day/month/year

of

hereinafter called the "Debtor",

- and -

(Name)
of

hereinafter called the "Secured Party",

WITNESSES that the Debtor in consideration of the principal sum of

($) Dollars loaned to the Debtor by the Secured Party (the receipt of which the Debtor hereby acknowledges), the Debtor hereby enters into this Chattel Mortgage Security Agreement with the Secured Party, as security for payment of the said principal sum of $, interest thereon and all other amounts now or hereafter owing by the Debtor to the Secured Party hereunder (collectively, the "Indebtedness").

1.   The Debtor hereby agrees that it will pay to the Secured Party the Indebtedness and observe and comply with all of the provisions hereof.

2.   The Debtor hereby grants to the Secured Party a security interest in the chattels which are more particularly described in Schedule "A" hereto together with all additions and accessions thereto and substitutions therefor (all of which chattels and additions and accessions thereto and substitutions therefor and hereinafter collectively called the "Collateral").

3.   The Debtor represents and warrants to the Secured Party that:

(a)   it is the sole legal and beneficial owner of the Collateral and there are no liens, mortgages, charges or other encumbrances thereon; and

(b)   the Collateral is located in the premises at

4.   If the Collateral is at the time of the making of the loan, or thereafter becomes, subject to any charge or security interest in favour of any person other than the Secured Party, the Secured Party may pay all amounts owing under such charge or security interest and the amount so paid shall, together with interest thereon at the rate payable by the Debtor to the Secured Party with respect to the principal of the loan, become a charge on the Collateral in favour of the Secured Party and be part of the Indebtedness, and the Indebtedness secured hereby shall, at the option of the Secured Party, forthwith become due and payable.

5.   The Debtor shall insure the Collateral in an amount equivalent to its full insurable value against loss or damage by fire or theft, or if the Collateral includes a motor vehicle, collision, and hereby assigns to the Secured Party all such policies of insurance and all insurance proceeds and other amounts payable thereunder. If the Debtor fails to effect or maintain such insurance, the Secured Party may effect and maintain the same and all monies expended by it for such purpose, together with interest thereon at the rate payable by the Debtor to the Secured Party with respect to the principal of the loan, from the time the same has been expended, shall become a charge on the Collateral and part of the Indebtedness.

6.   The Debtor shall not sell or dispose of or part with the possession of the Collateral or any part thereof and shall not permanently remove it from the premises where it now is located without the prior written consent of the Secured Party.

Full names and full addresses of both parties are required

Insert full street address

Newsome and Gilbert, Limited
Form LF 223 (2/85)

SCHEDULE "A"

(Description of articles)

Newsome and Gilbert, Limited
Form LF 222 (2/85)

7.   The Debtor shall be in default under this Chattel Mortgage Security Agreement upon the occurrence of any of the following events:

(a)   the Debtor shall fail to pay any of the Indebtedness when due or to observe or perform any of the covenants contained herein;

(b)   the Collateral or any part thereof shall be seized or taken in execution;

(c)   the Debtor shall become insolvent or commit an act of bankruptcy or make an assignment in bankruptcy or a bulk sale of its assets or a bankruptcy petition shall be filed or presented against the Debtor and not be bona fide opposed by the Debtor;

(d)   the Debtor shall be wound-up (if the Debtor is a corporation), or shall die (if the Debtor is an individual);

(e)   the Secured Party shall be of the opinion that the Collateral is in danger of being sold or removed from the premises where it now is located without the prior written consent of the Secured Party.

Upon any default under this Chattel Mortgage Security Agreement, the Indebtedness shall, at the option of the Secured Party, forthwith become due and payable and the Secured Party, its servants or agents, may, with or without legal process, take possession of the Collateral (and may for that purpose enter upon the premises where the Collateral is located) and sell the same at public auction or private sale, with or without notice to the Debtor unless such notice is required by law. The net proceeds of such sale shall be applied consecutively to (i) all such reasonable costs, charges, expenses and fees incurred by the Secured Party and its agents and servants in connection with the recovery or enforcement of payment of the Indebtedness, including, without limiting the generality of the foregoing, legal fees on a solicitor and client basis, of or incurred by the Secured Party or agent or agents appointed by the Secured Party, all of which costs, charges, expenses and fees are secured hereby, and (ii) the payment of the Indebtedness. Any balance of proceeds shall be paid to whomever is entitled to such balance. If the net proceeds of sale are not sufficient to pay the Indebtedness, the Debtor shall pay the deficiency to the Secured Party on demand by the Secured Party.

8.   The Secured Party may, in order to recover any amount owing to it hereunder, pursue either singly or concurrently the remedy of action and the remedy of taking possession and selling given to it hereby and shall not be precluded by the exercise of either remedy from proceedings to exercise the other or any other remedy.

9.   The Debtor shall pay all reasonable costs, expenses, charges and fees, including legal fees on a solicitor and client basis, incurred by the Secured Party in the preparation, execution, registration and enforcement of this Chattel Mortgage Security Agreement and the payment of such costs, expenses, charges and fees shall be part of the Indebtedness and secured hereby.

This Chattel Mortgage Security Agreement shall enure to the benefit of and be binding upon the heirs, executors, administrators, successors and assigns of the parties hereto respectively; if there is more than one Debtor, all covenants and agreements of the Debtor shall be joint and several and when the context so requires the singular number shall be read as if the plural were expressed.

This Chattel Mortgage Security Agreement was executed on the   day of   , 19

Witness:

_____Seal

(Name in full)

(Address)

Newsome and Gilbert, Limited
Form LF 343 (1/85)

Bill of Sale
Revised January, 1985

THIS BILL OF SALE

made in duplicate this   day of   19

BETWEEN

*Full names
(not initials)
of both parties*

whose address is:

hereinafter called the "Seller"

and

whose address is:

hereinafter called the "Buyer"

WHEREAS the Seller is possessed of the goods hereinafter set forth, and has contracted and agreed with the Buyer for the absolute Sale to him thereof, for the consideration hereinafter mentioned:

NOW THEREFORE THIS BILL OF SALE WITNESSETH, that in pursuance of the said agreement, and in consideration of the sum of

Dollars of lawful

money of Canada, paid by the Buyer to the Seller at or before the sealing and delivery of this Bill of Sale (the receipt whereof is hereby acknowledged), the Seller doth bargain, sell, assign, transfer and set over unto the Buyer ALL THOSE goods described as follows:

Newsome and Gilbert, Limited
Form LF 344 (1/85)

Bill of Sale
Page 2
Revised January, 1985

all of which goods are in the possession of the Seller and are located at

AND all the right, title, interest, property, claim and demand whatsoever of the Seller of, in, to, and out of the same, and every part thereof.

TO HOLD the said goods and all the right, title and interest of the Seller therein and thereto, unto and to the use of the Buyer.

AND the Seller doth hereby covenant, promise and agree with the Buyer in the manner following, that is to say: THAT the Seller is now rightfully and absolutely possessed of and entitled to the said goods; AND that the Seller now has good right to assign the same unto the Buyer in the manner aforesaid and according to the true intent and meaning of this Bill of Sale; AND that the Buyer shall and may from time to time, and at all times hereafter, peaceably and quietly have, hold, possess, and enjoy the said goods to and for his own use and benefit, free and clear and freely and absolutely released and discharged, at the cost of the Seller from all former and other bargains, sales, gifts, grants, charges and encumbrances whatsoever, and the Seller hereby indemnifies the Buyer with respect thereto;

AND that the Seller and all persons rightfully claiming any estate, right, title or interest in or to the said goods or any of them shall and will from time to time, and at all times hereafter upon every reasonable request and at the cost and charges of the Buyer, make, do and execute, or cause to be made, done and executed, all such further acts, deeds and assurances for the more effectually assigning and assuring the said goods unto the Buyer in the manner aforesaid, as by the Buyer or his counsel in the law shall be reasonably advised or required.

IT IS AGREED that this Bill of Sale and everything herein contained shall enure to the benefit of and be binding upon the heirs, executors, administrators and assigns, or successors and assigns, as the case may be, of the parties hereto respectively.

IT IS FURTHER AGREED that wherever the singular and masculine are used throughout this Bill of Sale, they shall be construed as if the plural or feminine or the neuter had been used, where the context or the party or parties hereto so require, and the rest of the sentence shall be construed as if the grammatical and terminological changes thereby rendered necessary had been made.

IN WITNESS WHEREOF, the Seller has executed this Bill of Sale

this   day of   , 19   .

SIGNED, SEALED AND DELIVERED
     In the presence of

Newsome and Gilbert, Limited
Form LF 345 (1/85)

Bill of Sale
Page 3
Revised January, 1985

AFFIDAVIT OF EXECUTION BY INDIVIDUAL

I,

of the

in the

make oath and say:

1. I am a subscribing witness to the attached Bill of Sale and I was present and saw it executed

    at   on the   day of

    19   by

2. I verily believe that each person whose signature I witnessed is the party of the same name referred to in

    the Bill of Sale.

SWORN before me at

)
}
)

A COMMISSIONER FOR TAKING AFFIDAVITS, ETC.

AFFIDAVIT OF EXECUTION BY CORPORATION

I,

of the

in the

make oath and say:

1. I am a subscribing witness to the attached Bill of Sale and I was present and saw it executed

    at   on the   day of

    19   on behalf of
                                    (name of corporation)

    by   and

    the   and   respectively,

    of the said corporation.

2. I know the said   and the said

    and know them to be the   and

    respectively, of the said corporation.

SWORN before me at

)
}
)

A COMMISSIONER FOR TAKING AFFIDAVITS, ETC.

AFFIDAVIT OF BONA FIDES

See Section 12 of the Bills of Sale Act, R.S.O. 1980, C. 43. Note that if the Buyer is a corporation, the officer or agent thereof who makes this affidavit must be authorized to do so by resolution of the directors, and that for registration purposes, a certified copy of the resolution must be attached to the Bill of Sale.

I,

of the

in the

Describe capacity if agent or officer

the Buyer named in the attached Bill of Sale, make oath and say:

1. That the sale therein made is bona fide and for good consideration, namely the sum of
   dollars,
   as set forth in the said Bill of Sale, and is not for the purpose of holding or enabling the Buyer to hold the goods mentioned therein against the creditors of the Seller therein named.

2. And that I am aware of the circumstances connected with the said Bill of Sale and have personal knowledge of the facts therein deposed to.

SWORN before me at

}

A COMMISSIONER FOR TAKING AFFIDAVITS, ETC.

Dated   19

AND

BILL OF SALE

Newsome and Gilbert, Limited, Form LF343

Newsome and Gilbert, Limited
Form 693

Mortgage
Page 2

SCHEDULE A

(Description of property)

Newsome and Gilbert, Limited
Form 692

Mortgage
Page 1
Revised April, 1981

This Mortgage

made this   day of   , A.D. 19

Between

hereinafter called the "MORTGAGOR"

OF THE ONE PART

— and —

hereinafter called the "MORTGAGEE"

OF THE OTHER PART

— and —

hereinafter called the "RELEASOR"

OF THE OTHER PART

WITNESSETH that in consideration of the sum of

Dollars ($),

the Mortgagor hereby mortgages to the Mortgagee the lands described in the Schedule "A"

hereto annexed.

PROVIDED THIS MORTGAGE SHALL BE VOID upon payment to the Mortgagee of the

said full sum of   **Dollars**

with interest at   per centum (%) per annum,

Delete, if
blended
payments

calculated half-yearly, not in advance,

The Mortgagor covenants with the Mortgagee THAT:

1.   The Mortgagor will pay the mortgage money and interest aforesaid, and on default the Mortgagee may enter and have quiet enjoyment of the lands.

2.   The Mortgagor will pay all taxes, rates and assessments and show receipts on demand

3.   The Mortgagor has a good title in fee simple to the said lands and the right to convey the lands as hereby conveyed, and that the said lands are free from encumbrances, and that the Mortgagor will procure such further assurances as may reasonably be required.

4.   The Mortgagor will insure the buildings on the lands against fire to the amount of not less than   Dollars for the benefit of the Mortgagee, and in default thereof the Mortgagee may effect insurance and charge it against the Mortgagor.

5.   The Mortgagor will keep the said lands and buildings and improvements now thereon or hereafter bought or erected thereon in good condition and repair according to the nature and description thereof respectively and if said lands, buildings or improvements are not kept in good condition and repair or any act of waste is committed thereon, or if the Mortgagor defaults after any part of the principal has been advanced the Mortgagee may enter and complete, repair or manage the property and recover all reasonable costs with interest as part of this mortgage.

PROVIDED that in default of the payment of any instalment of the principal or interest hereby secured or on breach of any covenant or proviso herein contained or if waste be committed or suffered on said lands the whole of the monies hereby secured remaining unpaid shall become payable but the Mortgagee may waive his right to call in the principal and shall not be therefore debarred from subsequently asserting and exercising his right to call in the principal by reason of such waiver or by reason of any future default and the Mortgagor agrees that neither the execution nor registration of this mortgage nor the advancing of any part of the mortgage money shall bind the Mortgagee to advance said money or any unadvanced portion thereof but that the advance of the money or any part thereof shall be in the sole discretion of the Mortgagee;

PROVIDED that the Mortgagee may pay the amount of any encumbrance, lien or charge now or hereafter existing or to arise or be claimed upon the said lands, having priority over this mortgage, including any arrears of taxes or other rates on the said lands or any of them, and may pay all costs, charges and expenses, which may be incurred in taking, recovering and keeping possession of the said premises and all solicitor's charges or commissions for or in respect of the collection of any overdue interest, principal, insurance premiums or any other monies whatsoever payable by the Mortgagor hereunder, as between solicitor and client, whether any action or other judicial proceeding to enforce such payment has been taken or not and the amounts so paid shall be added to the debt hereby secured and be a charge on the said lands and shall bear interest at the same rate and shall be forthwith payable by the Mortgagor to the Mortgagee and the non-payment of such amount shall entitle the Mortgagee to exercise the powers exercisable for breach of the covenant first hereinbefore contained. In the event of the Mortgagee paying the amount of any such encumbrance, lien or charge, taxes or rates, either out of the monies advanced on this security or otherwise, they shall be entitled to all the rights, equities and securities of the person or persons, company, corporation or Government so paid off.

Newsome and Gilbert, Limited
Form 695

Mortgage
Page 4
Revised April, 1981

The taking of a judgment on any covenant herein shall not operate as a merger of the said covenant or affect the Mortgagee's right to interest at the rate and times herein provided and such judgment shall provide that interest thereon shall be computed at the same rate and in the same manner as herein provided until the said judgment shall have been fully paid and satisfied.

THE Releasor hereby consents, pursuant to the Matrimonial Property Act, to the within Mortgage and hereby conveys any and all right, title and interest which the Releasor may have with respect to the lands described in Schedule 'A'.

AND it is agreed and declared that the terms "Mortgagor" and "Mortgagee" used in this Mortgage shall be construed to include the plural as well as singular and the masculine, feminine or neuter genders where the context so requires. All covenants, liabilities and obligations entered into or imposed hereunder upon the Mortgagor shall be joint and several.

IN WITNESS WHEREOF, the said parties to these presents have hereunto their hands and seals set and affixed, the day and year first above written.

SIGNED, SEALED AND DELIVERED
        in the presence of

PROVINCE OF NOVA SCOTIA
COUNTY OF

ON THIS   day of   , A.D. 19   , before

me, the subscriber personally came and appeared

                                                              , a subscribing witness to the foregoing

Indenture, who having been by me duly sworn, made oath and said that

                                                                                                    of the

parties thereto, signed, sealed and delivered the same in h   presence.

A Barrister of the Supreme Court
of Nova Scotia.

Newsome and Gilbert, Limited
Form 640

Warranty Deed (Short Form)
Page 1
Revised April, 1981

This Indenture

made this   day of   , A.D. 19   ,

Between

being the Owner of the lands described in Schedule 'A' herein
hereinafter called the "GRANTOR"

OF THE ONE PART

— and —

hereinafter called the "GRANTEE"

OF THE OTHER PART

— and —

being the spouse of the Grantor who holds no title to the said lands
hereinafter called the "RELEASOR"

OF THE OTHER PART

WITNESSETH THAT in consideration of One Dollar and other good and valuable consideration :

THE GRANTOR hereby conveys to the GRANTEE the lands described in Schedule 'A' to this Warranty Deed and hereby consents to this disposition, pursuant to the Matrimonial Property Act of Nova Scotia.

THE GRANTOR covenants with the Grantee that the Grantee shall have quiet enjoyment of the lands, that the Grantor has a good title in fee simple to the lands and the right to convey them as hereby conveyed, that they are free from encumbrances and that the Grantor will procure such further assurances as may be reasonably required and it is agreed and declared that the terms "Grantor" and "Grantee" used in this Deed shall be construed to include the plural as well as singular and the masculine, feminine or neuter genders where the context so requires.

THE RELEASOR hereby consents to the within conveyance and releases any claim that the RELEASOR had, has or may have pursuant to the Matrimonial Property Act of Nova Scotia and hereby conveys any and all right, title and interest which the RELEASOR may have with respect to the lands described in Schedule 'A'.

IN WITNESS WHEREOF, the Grantor and Releasor have signed and sealed these presents on the day and year first above written.

SIGNED, SEALED AND DELIVERED
in the presence of

_____

_____

Newsome and Gilbert, Limited
Form 641

Warranty Deed (Short Form)
Page 2
Revised January, 1980

SCHEDULE A

(Description of property)

PROVINCE OF NOVA SCOTIA
COUNTY OF   }

       I CERTIFY that on this   day of

A.D. 19   ,

of the parties mentioned in the foregoing and annexed Indenture, signed and executed the

said Indenture in my presence and I have signed as a witness to such execution.

....
          A Barrister of the Supreme Court
               of Nova Scotia.

PROVINCE OF NOVA SCOTIA
COUNTY OF   }

ON THIS   day of   , A.D. 19   , before

me, the subscriber personally came and appeared

               , a subscribing witness to the foregoing

Indenture, who having been by me duly sworn, made oath and said that

               one of the

parties thereto caused the same to be executed in its name and on its behalf and its corporate

seal to be thereunto affixed in h   presence.

         _____
          A Barrister of the Supreme Court
               of Nova Scotia.

Deed

Newsome and Gilbert, Limited—Form 640

Dated   19

PROVINCE OF NOVA SCOTIA
COUNTY OF   }

ON THIS   day of   , A.D. 19   , before

me, the subscriber personally came and appeared

               , a subscribing witness to the foregoing

Indenture, who having been by me duly sworn, made oath and said that

               of the

parties thereto, signed, sealed and delivered the same in h   presence.

....
          A Barrister of the Supreme Court
               of Nova Scotia.

APPENDIX B

United Nations Commission on International Trade Model Law on International Commercial Arbitration (UNCITRAL)

(Adopted June 21, 1985)

Note on UNCITRAL

The term "commercial" as found in Article 1 is intended to have a very broad meaning, and should be interpreted to include all commercial relationships whether established by contract or otherwise.

CHAPTER I.   GENERAL PROVISIONS

Article 1. Scope of Application

(1) This Law applies to international commercial arbitration, subject to any agreement in force between this State and any other State or States.

(2) The provisions of this Law, except articles 8, 8, 35 and 36, apply only if the place of arbitration is in the territory of this State.

(3) An arbitration is international if:

    (a) the parties to an arbitration agreement have, at the time of the conclusion of that agreement, their places of business in different States; or

    (b) one of the following places is situated outside the State in which the parties have their places of business:

(i) the place of arbitration if determined in, or pursuant to, the arbitration agreement;

(ii) any place where a substantial part of the obligations of the commercial relationship is to be performed or the place with which the subject-matter of the dispute is most closely connected; or

(c) the parties have expressly agreed that the subject-matter of the arbitration agreement relates to more than one country.

(4) For the purposes of paragraph (3) of this article:

(a) if a party has more than one place of business, the place of business is that which has the closest relationship to the arbitration agreement;

(b) if a party does not have a place of business, reference is to be made to his habitual residence.

(5) This Law shall not affect any other law of this State by virtue of which certain disputes may not be submitted to arbitration or may be submitted to arbitration only according to provisions other than those of this Law.

Article 2. Definitions and Rules of Interpretation

For the purposes of this Law:

(a) "arbitration" means any arbitration whether or not administered by a permanent arbitral institution;

(b) "arbitral tribunal" means a sole arbitrator or a panel of arbitrators;

(c) "court" means a body or organ of the judicial system of a State;

(d) where a provision of this Law, except article 28, leaves the parties free to determine a certain issue, such freedom includes the right of the parties to authorize a third party, including an institution, to make that determination;

(e) where a provision of this Law refers to the fact that the parties have agreed or that they may agree or in any other way refers to an agreement of the parties, such agreement includes any arbitration rules referred to in that agreement;

(f) where a provision of this Law, other than in articles 25 (a) and 32 (2) (a), refers to a claim, it also applies to a counter-claim, and where it refers to a defence, it also applies to a defence to such counter-claim.

Article 3. Receipt of Written Communications

(1) Unless otherwise agreed by the parties:

(a) any written communication is deemed to have been received if it is delivered to the addressee personally or if it is delivered at his place of business, habitual residence or mailing address; if none of these can be found after making a reasonable inquiry, a written communication is deemed to have been received if it is sent to the addressee's last-known place of business, habitual residence or mailing address by registered letter or any other means which provides a record of the attempt to deliver it;

(b) the communication is deemed to have been received on the day it is so delivered.

(2) The provisions of this article do not apply to communications in court proceedings.

Article 4. Waiver of Right to Object

A party who knows that any provision of this Law from which the parties may derogate or any requirement under the arbitration agreement has not been complied with and yet proceeds with the arbitration without stating his objection to such non-compliance without undue delay or, if a time-limit is provided therefore, within such period of time, shall be deemed to have waived his right to object.

Article 5. Extent of Court Intervention

In matters governed by this Law, no court shall intervene except where so provided in this Law.

Article 6. Court or Other Authority for Certain Functions of Arbitration Assistance and Supervision

The functions referred to in articles 11 (3), 11 (4), 13 (3), 14, 16 (3) and 34 (2) shall be performed by ... [Each State enacting this model law specifies the court, courts or, where referred to therein, other authority competent to perform these functions.]

CHAPTER II.   ARBITRATION AGREEMENT

Article 7. Definition and Form of Arbitration Agreement

(1) "Arbitration agreement" is an agreement by the parties to submit to arbitration all or certain disputes which have arisen or which may arise between them in respect of a defined legal relationship, whether contractual or not. An arbitration agreement may be in the form of an arbitration clause in a contract or in the form of a separate agreement.

(2) The arbitration agreement shall be in writing. An agreement is in writing if it is contained in a document signed by the parties or in an exchange of letters, telex, telegrams or other means of telecommunication which provide a record of the agreement, or in an exchange of statements of claim and defence in which the existence of an agreement is alleged by one party and not denied by another. The reference in a contract to a document containing an arbitration clause constitutes an arbitration agreement provided that the contract is in writing and the reference is such as to make that clause part of the contract.

Article 8. Arbitration Agreement and Substantive Claim Before Court

(1) A court before which an action is brought in a matter which is the subject of an arbitration agreement shall, if a party so requests not later than when submitting his first statement on the substance of the dispute, refer the parties to arbitration unless it finds that the agreement is null and void, inoperative or incapable of being performed.

(2) Where an action referred to in paragraph (1) of this article has been brought, arbitral proceedings may nevertheless be commenced or continued, and an award may be made, while the issue is pending before the court.

Article 9. Arbitration Agreement and Interim Measures by Court

It is not incompatible with an arbitration agreement for a party to request, before or during arbitral proceedings, from a court an interim measure of protection and for a court to grant such measure.

CHAPTER III. COMPOSITION OF ARBITRAL TRIBUNAL

Article 10. Number of Arbitrators

(1) The parties are free to determine the number of arbitrators.

(2) Failing such determination, the number of arbitrators shall be three.

Article 11. Appointment of Arbitrators

(1) No person shall be precluded by reason of his nationally from acting as an arbitrator, unless otherwise agreed by the parties.

(2) The parties are free to agree on a procedure of appointing the arbitrator or arbitrators, subject to the provisions of paragraphs (4) and (5) of this article.

(3) Failing such agreement,

    (a) in an arbitration with three arbitrators, each party shall appoint one arbitrator, and the two arbitrators thus appointed shall appoint the third arbitrator; if a party fails to appoint the arbitrator within thirty days of receipt of a request to do so from the other party, or if the two arbitrators fail to agree on the third arbitrator within thirty days of their appointment, the appointment shall be made, upon request of a party, by the court or other authority specified in article 6;

    (b) in an arbitration with a sole arbitrator, if the parties are unable to agree on the arbitrator, he shall be appointed, upon request of a party, by the court or other authority specified in article 6.

(4) Where, under an appointment procedure agreed upon by the parties,

    (a) a party fails to act as required under such procedure, or

    (b) the parties, or two arbitrators, are unable to reach an agreement expected of them under such procedure, or

    (c) a third party, including an institution, fails to perform any function entrusted to it under such procedure,

any party may request the court or other authority specified in article 6 to take the necessary measure, unless the agreement on the appointment procedure provides other means for securing the appointment.

(5) A decision on a matter entrusted by paragraph (3) or (4) of this article to the court or other authority specified in article 6 shall be subject to no appeal. The court or other authority, in appointing an arbitrator, shall have due regard to any qualifications required of the arbitrator by the agreement

of the parties and to such considerations as are likely to secure the appointment of an independent and impartial arbitrator and, in the case of a sole or third arbitrator, shall take into account as well the advisability of appointing an arbitrator of a nationality other than those of the parties.

Article 12. Grounds for Challenge

(1) When a person is approached in connection with his possible appointment as an arbitrator, he shall disclose any circumstances likely to give rise to justifiable doubts as to his impartiality or independence. An arbitrator, from the time of his appointment and throughout the arbitral proceedings, shall without delay disclose any such circumstances to the parties unless they have already been informed of them by him.

(2) An arbitrator may be challenged only if circumstances exist that give rise to justifiable doubts as to his impartiality or independence, or if he does not posses qualifications agreed to by the parties. A party may challenge an arbitrator appointed by him, or in whose appointment he has participated, only for reasons of which he becomes aware after the appointment has been made.

Article 13. Challenge Procedure

(1) The parties are free to agree on a procedure for challenging an arbitrator, subject to the provisions of paragraph (3) of this article.

(2) Failing such agreement, a party who intends to challenge an arbitrator shall, within fifteen days after becoming aware of the constitution of the arbitral tribunal or after becoming aware of any circumstance referred to in article 12(2), send a written statement of the reasons for the challenge to the arbitral tribunal. Unless the challenged arbitrator withdraws from his office or the other party agrees to the challenge, the arbitral tribunal shall decide on the challenge.

(3) If a challenge under any procedure agreed upon by the parties or under the procedure of paragraph (2) of this article is not successful, the challenging party may request, within thirty days after having received notice of the decision rejecting the challenge, the court or other authority specified in article 6 to decide on the challenge, which decision shall be subject to no appeal; while such a request is pending, the arbitral tribunal, including the challenged arbitrator, may continue the arbitral proceedings and make an award.

Article 14. Failure or Impossibility to Act

(1) If an arbitrator becomes *de jure* or *de facto* unable to perform his functions or for other reasons fails to act within undue delay, his mandate terminates if he withdraws from his office or if the parties agree on the termination. Otherwise, if a controversy remains concerning any of these grounds, any party may request the court or other authority specified in article 6 to decide on the termination of the mandate, which decision shall be subject to no appeal.

(2) If, under this article or article 13 (2), an arbitrator withdraws from his office or a party agrees to the termination of the mandate of an arbitrator, this does not imply acceptance of the validity of any ground referred to in this article or article 12(2).

Article 15. Appointment of Substitute Arbitrator

Where the mandate of an arbitrator terminates under article 13 or 14 or because of his withdrawal from office for any other reason or because of the revocation of his mandate by agreement of the parties or in any other case of termination of his mandate, a substitute arbitrator shall be appointed according to the rules that were applicable to the appointment of the arbitrator being replaced.

CHAPTER IV. JURISDICATION OF ARBITRAL TRIBUNAL

Article 16. Competence of Arbitral Tribunal to Rule on its Jurisdiction

(1) The arbitral tribunal may rule on its own jurisdiction, including any objections with respect to the existence or validity of the arbitration agreement. For that purpose, an arbitration clause which forms part of a contract shall be treated as an agreement independent of the other terms of the contract. A decision by the arbitral tribunal that the contract is null and void shall not entail *ipso jure* the invalidity of the arbitration clause.

(2) A plea that the arbitral tribunal does not have jurisdiction shall be raised not later than the submission of the statement of defence. A party is not precluded from raising such a plea by the fact that he has appointed, or participated in the appointment of, an arbitrator. A plea that the arbitral tribunal is exceeding the scope of its authority shall be raised as soon as the matter alleged to be beyond the scope of its authority is raised during the arbitral proceedings. The arbitral tribunal may, in either case, admit a later plea if it considers the delay justified.

(3) The arbitral tribunal may rule on a plea referred to in paragraph (2) of this article either as a preliminary question or in an award on the merits. If the arbitral tribunal rules as a preliminary question that it has jurisdiction, any party may request, within thiry days after having received notice of that ruling, the court specified in article 6 to decide the matter, which decision shall be subject to no appeal; which such a request is pending, the arbitral tribunal may continue the arbitral proceedings and make an award.

Article 17. Power of Arbitral Tribunal to Order Interim Measures

Unless otherwise agreed by the parties, the arbitral tribunal may, at the request of a party, order any party to take such interim measure of protection as the arbitral tribunal may consider necessary in respect of the subject-matter of the dispute. The arbitral tribunal may require any party to provide appropriate security in connection with such measure.

CHAPTER V.   CONDUCT OF ARBITRAL PROCEEDINGS

Article 18. Equal Treatment of Parties

The parties shall be treated with equality and each party shall be given a full opportunity of presenting his case.

Article 19. Determination of Rules of Procedure

(1) Subject to the provisions of this Law, the parties are free to agree on the procedure to be followed by the arbitral tribunal in conducting the proceedings.

(2) Failing such agreement, the arbitral tribunal may, subject to the provisions of this Law, conduct the arbitration in such manner as it considers appropriate. The power conferred upon the arbitral tribunal includes the power to determine the admissibility, relevance, materiality and weight of any evidence.

Article 20. Place of Arbitration

(1) The parties are free to agree on the place of arbitration. Failing such agreement, the place of arbitration shall be determined by the arbitral tribunal having regard to the circumstances of the case, including the convenience of the parties.

(2) Notwithstanding the provisions of paragraph (1) of this article, the arbitral tribunal may, unless otherwise agreed by the parties, meet at any place it considers appropriate for consultation among its members, for hearing witnesses, experts or the parties, or for inspection of goods, other property or documents.

Article 21. Commencement of Arbitral Proceedings

Unless otherwise agreed by the parties, the arbitral proceedings in respect of a particular dispute commence on the date on which a request for that dispute to be referred to arbitration is received by the respondent.

Article 22. Language

(1) The parties are free to agree on the language or language to be used in the arbitral proceedings. Failing such agreement, the arbitral tribunal shall determine the language or languages to be used in the proceedings. This agreement or determination, unless otherwise specified therein, shall apply to any written statement by a party, any hearing and any award, decision or other communication by the arbitral tribunal.

(2) The arbitral tribunal may order that any documentary evidence shall be accompanied by a translation into the language or languages agreed upon by the parties or determined by the arbitral tribunal.

Article 23. Statements of Claims and Defence

(1) Within the period of time agreed by the parties or determined by the arbitral tribunal, the claimant shall state the facts supporting his claim, the points at issue and the relief or remedy sought, and the respondent shall state his defence in respect of these particulars, unless the parties have otherwise agreed as to the required elements of such statements. The parties may submit with their statements all documents they consider to be relevant or may add a reference to the documents or other evidence they will submit.

(2) Unless otherwise agreed by the parties, either party may amend or supplement his claim or defence during the course of the arbitral proceedings, unless the arbitral tribunal considers it inappropriate to allow such amendment having regard to the delay in making it.

Article 24. Hearings and Written Proceedings

(1) Subject to any contrary agreement by the parties, the arbitral tribunal shall decide whether to hold oral hearings for the presentation of evidence or for oral argument, or whether the proceedings shall be conducted on the basis of documents and other materials. However, unless the parties have agreed that no hearings shall be held, the arbitral tribunal shall hold such hearings at an appropriate stage of the proceedings, if so requested by a party.

(2) The parties shall be given sufficient advance notice of any hearing and of any meeting of the arbitral tribunal for the purposes of inspection of goods, other property or documents.

(3) All statements, documents or other information supplied to the arbitral tribunal by one party shall be communicated to the other party. Also any expert report or evidentiary document on which the arbitral tribunal may rely in making its decision shall be communicated to the parties.

Article 25. Default of a Party

Unless otherwise agreed by the parties, if, without showing sufficient cause,

(a) the claimant fails to communicate his statement of claim in accordance with article 23(1), the arbitral tribunal shall terminate the proceedings;

(b) the respondent fails to communicate his statement of defence in accordance with article 23(1), the arbitral tribunal shall continue the proceedings without treating such failure in itself as an admission of the claimant's allegations;

(c) any party fails to appear at a hearing or to produce documentary evidence, the arbitral tribunal may continue the proceedings and make the award on the evidence before it.

Article 26. Expert Appointed by Arbitral Tribunal

(1) Unless otherwise agreed by the parties, the arbitral tribunal

(a) may appoint one or more experts to report to it on specific issues to be determined by the arbitral tribunal;

(b) may require a party to give the expert any relevant information or to produce, or to provide access to, any relevant documents, goods or other property for his inspection.

(2) Unless otherwise agreed by the parties, if a party so requests or if the arbitral tribunal considers it necessary, the expert shall, after delivery of his written or oral report, participate in a hearing where the parties have the opportunity to put questions to him and to present expert witnesses in order to testify on the points at issue.

Article 27. Court Assistance in Taking Evidence

The arbitral tribunal or a party with the approval of the arbitral tribunal may request from a competent court of this State assistance in taking evidence. The court may execute the request within its competence and according to its rules on taking evidence.

CHAPTER VI.   MAKING OF AWARD AND TERMINATION OF PROCEEDINGS

Article 28. Rules Applicable to Substance of Dispute

(1) The arbitral tribunal shall decide the dispute in accordance with such rules of law as are chosen by the parties as applicable to the substance of the dispute. Any designation of the law or legal system of a given State shall be construed, unless otherwise expressed, as directly referring to the substantive law of that State and not to its conflict of laws rules.

(2) Failing any designation by the parties, the arbitral tribunal shall apply the law determined by the conflict of laws rules which it considers applicable.

(3) The arbitral tribunal shall decide *ex aequo et bono* or as *amiable compositeur* only if the parties have expressly authorized it to do so.

(4) In all cases, the arbitral tribunal shall decide in accordance with the terms of the contract and shall take into account the usages of the trade applicable to the transaction.

Article 29. Decision Making by Panel of Arbitrations

In arbitral proceedings with more than one arbitrator, any decision of the arbitral tribunal shall be made, unless otherwise agreed by the parties, by a majority of all its members. However, questions of procedure may be decided by a presiding arbitrator, if so authorized by the parties or all members of the arbitral tribunal.

Article 30. Settlement

(1) If, during arbitral proceedings, the parties settle the dispute, the arbitral tribunal shall terminate the proceedings and, if requested by the parties and not objected to by the arbitral tribunal, record the settlement in the form of an arbitral award on agreed terms.

(2) An award on agreed terms shall be made in accordance with the provisions of article 31 and shall state that it is an award. Such an award has the same status and effect as any other award on the merits of the case.

Article 31. Form and Contents of Award

(1) The award shall be made in writing and shall be signed by the arbitrator or arbitrators. In arbitral proceedings with more than one arbitrator, the signatures of the majority of all members of the arbitral tribunal shall suffice, provided that the reason for any omitted signature is stated.

(2) The award shall state the reasons upon which it is based, unless the parties have agreed that no reasons are to be given or the award is an award on agreed terms under article 30.

(3) The award shall state its date and the place of arbitration as determined in accordance with article 20(1). The award shall be deemed to have been made at that place.

(4) After the award is made, a copy signed by the arbitrators in accordance with paragraph (1) of this article shall be delivered to each party.

Article 32. Termination of Proceedings

(1) The arbitral proceedings are terminated by the final award or by an order of the arbitral tribunal in accordance with paragraph (2) of this article.

(2) The arbitral tribunal shall issue an order for the termination of the arbitral proceedings when:
   (a) the claimant withdraws his claim, unless the respondent objects thereto and the arbitral tribunal recognizes a legitimate interest on his part in obtaining a final settlement of the dispute;
   (b) the parties agree on the termination of the proceedings;
   (c) the arbitral tribunal finds that the continuation of the proceedings has for any other reason become unnecessary or impossible.

(3) The mandate of the arbitral tribunal terminates with the termination of the arbitral proceedings, subject to the provisions of articles 33 and 34 (4).

Article 33. Correction and Interpretation of Award; Additional Award

(1) Within thirty days of receipt of the award, unless another period of time has been agreed upon by the parties:
   (a) a party, with notice to the other party, may request the arbitral tribunal to correct in the award any errors in computation, any clerical or typographical errors or any errors of similar nature;
   (b) if so agreed by the parties, a party, with notice to the other party, may request the arbitral tribunal to give an interpretation of a specific point or part of the award.

If the arbitral tribunal considers the request to be justified, it shall make the correction or give the interpretation within thirty days of receipt of the request. The interpretation shall form part of the award.

(2) The arbitral tribunal may correct any error of the type referred to in paragraph (1)(a) of this article on its own initiative within thirty days of the date of the award.

(3) Unless otherwise agreed by the parties, a party, with notice to the other party, may request, within thirty days of receipt of the award, the arbitral tribunal

to make an additional award as to claims presented in the arbitral proceedings but omitted from the award. If the arbitral tribunal considers the request to be justified, it shall make the additional award within sixty days.

(4) The arbitral tribunal may extend, if necessary, the period of time within which it shall make a correction, interpretation or an additional award under paragraph (1) or (3) of this article.

(5) The provisions of article 31 shall apply to a correction or interpretation of the award or to an additional award.

CHAPTER VII. RECOURSE AGAINST AWARD

Article 34. Application for Setting Aside as Exclusive Recourse Against Arbitral Award

(1) Recourse to a court against an arbitral award may be made only by an application for setting aside in accordance with paragraphs (2) and (3) of this article.

(2) An arbitral award may be set aside by the court specified in article 6 only if:

(a) the party making the application furnishes proof that:

    (i) a party to the arbitration agreement referred to in article 7 was under some incapacity; or the said agreement is not valid under the law to which the parties have subjected it or, failing any indication thereon, under the law of this State; or

    (ii) the party making the application was not given proper notice of the appointment of an arbitrator or of the arbitral proceedings or was otherwise unable to present his case; or

    (iii) the award deals with a dispute not contemplated by or not falling within the terms of the submission to arbitration, or contains decisions on matters beyond the scope of the submission to arbitration, provided that, if the decisions on matters submitted to arbitration can be separated from those not so submitted, only that part of the award which contains decisions on matters not submitted to arbitration may be set aside; or

    (iv) the composition of the arbitral tribunal or the arbitral procedure was not in accordance with the agreement of the parties, unless such agreement was in conflict with a provision of this Law from which the parties cannot derogate, or, failing such agreement, was not in accordance with this Law; or

(b) the court finds that:

    (i) the subject-matter of the dispute is not capable of settlement by arbitration under the law of this State; or

    (ii) the award is in conflict with the public policy of this State.

(3) An application for setting aside may not be made after three months have elapsed from the date on which the party making that application had received the award or, if a request had been made under article 33, from the date on which that request had been disposed of by the arbitral tribunal.

(4) The court, when asked to set aside an award, may, where appropriate and so requested by a party, suspend the setting aside proceedings for a period of time determined by it in order to give the arbitral tribunal an opportunity to resume the arbitral proceedings or to take such other action as in the arbitral tribunal's opinion will eliminate the grounds for setting aside.

CHAPTER VIII.   RECOGNITION AND ENFORCEMENT OF AWARDS

Article 35. Recognition and Enforcement

(1) An arbitral award, irrespective of the country in which it was made, shall be recognized as binding and, upon application in writing to the competent court, shall be enforced subject to the provisions of this article and of article 36.

(2) The party relying on an award or applying for its enforcement shall supply the duly authenticated original award or a duly certified copy thereof, and the original arbitration agreement referred to in article 7 or a duly certified copy thereof. If the award or agreement is not made in an official language of this State, the party shall supply a duly certified translation thereof into such language.

Article 36. Grounds for Refusing Recognition or Enforcement

(1) Recognition or enforcement of an arbitral award, irrespective of the country in which it was made, may be refused only:

(a) at the request of the party against whom it is invoked, if that party furnishes to the competent court where recognition or enforcement is sought proof that:

  (i) a party to the arbitration agreement referred to in article 7 was under some incapacity; or the said agreement is not valid under the law to which the parties have subjected it or, failing any indication thereon, under the law of the country where the award was made; or

  (ii) the party against whom the award is invoked was not given proper notice of the appointment of an arbitrator or of the arbitral proceedings or was otherwise unable to present his case; or

  (iii) the award deals with a dispute not contemplated by or not falling within the terms of the submission to arbitration, or it contains decisions on matters beyond the scope of the submission to arbitration, provided that, if the decisions on matters submitted to arbitration can be separated from those not so submitted, that part of the award which contains decisions on matters submitted to arbitration may be recognized and enforced; or

  (iv) the composition of the arbitral tribunal or the arbitral procedure was not in accordance with the agreement of the parties or, failing such agreement, was not in accordance with the law of the country where the arbitration took place; or

(v) the award has not yet become binding on the parties or has been set aside or suspended by a court of the country in which, or under the law of which, that award was made; or

(b) if the court finds that:

(i) the subject-matter of the dispute is not capable of settlement by arbitration under the law of this State; or

(ii) the recognition or enforcement of the award would be contrary to the public policy of this State.

(2) If an application for setting aside or suspension of an award has been made to a court referred to in paragraph (1)(a)(v) of this article, the court where recognition or enforcement is sought may, if it considers it proper, adjourn its decision and may also, on the application of the party claiming recognition or enforcement of the award, order the party to provide appropriate security.

GLOSSARY

The following list contains brief definitions of many of the legal terms used in the text. For a full and complete definition of each term, reference should be made to the appropriate chapter of the text, or to a legal dictionary.

ab initio: "from the beginning."

acceleration clause: a clause in a debt instrument (e.g., a mortgage or promissory note) that requires the payment of the balance of the debt on the happening of a specific event such as default on an installment payment.

act: a law enacted by a legislature. See: statute.

action: legal proceedings instituted in a court of law.

act of God: an unanticipated event that prevents the performance of a contract or causes damage to property.

ad hoc tribunal: a tribunal established to deal with a particular dispute between parties.

ad idem: to be of the same mind, or in agreement (*consensus ad idem*).

administrative law: a body of rules governing the application of statutes to activities regulated by administrative tribunals or boards.

adverse possession: a possessory title to land under the Registry System acquired by continuous, open, and notorious possession of land inconsistent with the title of the true owner for a period of time (usually 10 to 20 years).

agent: a person appointed to act for another, usually in contract matters.

alternate dispute resolution (ADR): an informal process for resolving disputes between parties (usually by arbitration). An alternative to the use of the courts.

anticipatory breach: an advance determination that a party will not perform his/her part of a contract when the time for performance arrives.

arbitration: a process for the settlement of disputes whereby an impartial third party or board hears the dispute, then makes a decision that is binding on the parties. Most commonly used to determine grievances arising out of a collective agreement, or in contract disputes.

assault: a threat of violence or injury to a person.

assumpsit: an old common law action brought for the breach of a promise or covenant.

attorney: a lawyer.

bailee: the person who takes possession of a chattel in a bailment.

bailment: the transfer of a chattel by the owner to another for some purpose, with the chattel to be later returned or dealt with in accordance with the owner's instructions.

bailor: the owner of a chattel who delivers possession of the chattel to another in a bailment.

bargaining unit: a group of employees of an employer represented by a trade union recognized or certified as their exclusive bargaining representative.

barrister-at-law: a lawyer who acts for clients in litigation or criminal court proceedings.

battery: the unlawful touching or striking of another.

bid-rigging: a practice whereby contractors in response to a call for bids or tenders agree amongst themselves as to the price or who should bid or submit a tender. A restrictive trade practice, unless the person calling for the bids is advised of the arrangement.

bill of exchange: an instrument in writing, signed by the drawer and addressed to the drawee, ordering the drawee to pay a sum certain in money to the payee named therein (or bearer) at some fixed or determinable future time, or on demand.

bill of lading: a contract entered into between a bailor and a common carrier of goods (bailee) that sets out the terms of the bailment and represents a title document to the goods carried. It also requires the bailee to deliver up the goods to the consignee named in the bill.

bond: a debt security issued by a corporation in which assets of the corporation are usually pledged as security for payment.

breach of contract: the failure to perform a contract according to its terms.

bulk sale: a sale of the stock or assets of a merchant other than in the ordinary course of business.

canon law: the law developed by the church courts to deal with matters that fell within their jurisdiction.

capacity: the ability at law to enter into an enforceable contract.

caveat emptor: "let the buyer beware."

certification: of a cheque, an undertaking by a bank to pay the amount of the cheque on presentation. In a labour relations context, the term is used for the procedure whereby a labour union acquires bargaining rights for a group of employees.

certification process: a process under labour legislation whereby a trade union acquires bargaining rights and is designated as the exclusive bargaining representative of a unit of employees.

charge: a secured claim (similar to a mortgage) registered against real property under the Land Titles System.

chattel: moveable property.

chattel mortgage: a mortgage in which the title to a chattel owned by the debtor is transferred to the creditor as security for the payment of a debt.

cheque: a bill of exchange that is drawn on a banking institution, and payable on demand.

chose in action: a paper document that represents a right or interest that has value, (e.g., a share certificate).

civil code: a body of written law which sets out the private rights of the citizens of a state.

co-insurance: a clause that may be inserted in an insurance policy that renders the insured an insurer for a part of the loss if the insured fails to maintain insurance coverage of not less than a specified minimum amount or percentage of the value of the property.

collateral agreement: an agreement which has its own consideration, but supports another agreement.

collective agreement: an agreement in writing made between an employer and a union certified or recognized as the bargaining representative of a bargaining unit of employees. It contains the terms and conditions under which work is to be performed and sets out the rights and duties of the employer, the employees, and the union.

commercial arbitration: method of resolving disputes arising out of a commercial agreement using the arbitration process.

common carrier: a carrier of goods that offers its services to the public.

common law: the law as found in the recorded judgements of the courts.

condition precedent: a condition that must be satisfied before a contract or agreement becomes effective.

condition subsequent: a condition that alters the rights or duties of the parties to a contract, or that may have the effect of terminating the contract if it should occur.

conditional sale agreement: an agreement for the sale of a chattel in which the seller grants possession of the goods, but withholds title until payment for the goods is made in full.

condominium: a form of ownership of real property, usually including a building, in which certain units are owned in fee simple and the common elements are owned by the various unit owners as tenants-in-common.

consideration: something that has value in the eyes of the law which a promisee receives in return for a promise.

conspiracy: an agreement between two or more persons to carry out an unlawful act.

constitution: the basis upon which a state is organized, and the powers of its government defined.

constructive dismissal: employer termination of a contract of employment by a substantial unilateral change in the terms or conditions of employment.

contempt of court: refusal to obey a judge's order.

contingent liability: a liability that will arise only on the happening of a particular event or state of affairs.

contract: an agreement made by two or more parties that consists of an exchange of promises or acts and may be either written or oral.

conversion: the refusal to deliver up a chattel to its rightful owner by a bailee.

copyright: the right of ownership of an original literary or artistic work and the control over the right to copy it.

corporation: a legal entity created by the state.

covenant: a written agreement that establishes an obligation to be performed by one of the parties.

damages: a money payment awarded by the court as compensation for injury suffered as a result of a breach of duty or breach of contract by a defendant.

debenture: a debt security issued by a corporation that may or may not have specific assets of the corporation pledged as security for payment.

deceit: a tort which arises where a party suffers damage by acting upon a false representation made by a party with the intention of deceiving the other.

de minimis rule: "The law is not concerned with minor matters" (de minimis non curat lex).

director: under corporation law, a person elected by the shareholders of a corporation to manage its affairs.

discharge: the release from an obligation.

distress: the act of seizing moveable property to compel performance of an obligation. A right (in some provinces) which allows a landlord to seize a tenant's goods if rent is not paid.

doctrine of constructive notice: the deemed notice to the public of some fact or information as a result of registering or filing the information in a public record office.

dominant tenement: a parcel of land to which a right-of-way or easement attaches for its better use.

double ticketing: a practice of attaching several different price tickets to goods. Under the Competition Act, only the lowest price may be charged for the goods.

dower: the right of a widow to hold for her lifetime one-third of the real property owned by her husband at the time of his death.

due diligence: an obligation to make every effort to satisfy a directive or perform a particular duty.

duress: the threat of injury or imprisonment for the purpose of requiring another to enter into a contract or carry out some act.

easement: a right to use the property of another, usually for a particular purpose.

endorsement: the signing of one's name on the back of a negotiable instrument for the purpose of negotiating it to another.

environmental assessment: a procedure undertaken to determine the effect on the physical environment of a particular undertaking or activity (e.g., the assessment of the effect on the environment of the construction of a dam on a river).

equitable mortgage: a mortgage subsequent to the first or legal mortgage. A mortgage of the mortgagor's equity.

equity of redemption: the equitable right of a mortgagor to acquire the title to the mortgaged property by payment of the debt secured by the mortgage.

escheat: the reversion of land to the Crown when a person possessed of the fee dies intestate and without heirs.

estoppel: a rule whereby a person may not deny the truth of a statement of fact made by him or her where another has relied and acted on the statement.

ex delecto: an action in tort arising out of a wrong that has been committed.

execution: the post-judgement stage in a legal action whereby the judgement is enforced against the defendant.

exemplary damages: punitive damages awarded to "set an example" or discourage repetition of the act.

expropriation: the forceful taking of real property by the Crown (or its agents) or by a corporation that has been granted expropriation rights (such as a municipality).

fee simple: an estate in land that represents the greatest interest in land that a person may possess, and that may be conveyed or passed by will to another, or that on an intestacy would devolve to the person's heirs.

fiduciary interest: an interest in property held in trust for the benefit of another.

fiduciary relationship: a relationship of utmost good faith in which a person in dealing with property must act in the best interests of the person for whom he or she acts, rather than in one's own personal interest.

fixture: a chattel that is constructively or permanently attached to land.

floating charge: a debt security issued by a corporation in which assets of the corporation such as stock-in-trade are pledged as security. Until such time as default occurs, the corporation is free to dispose of the assets.

force majeure: a major, unforseen or unanticipated event that occurs and prevents the performance of a contract.

fraudulent misrepresentation: a false statement of fact made by a person who knows, or should know, that it is false, and is made with the intention of deceiving another.

frustrated contract: a contract under which performance by a party is rendered impossible due to an unexpected or unforeseen change in circumstances affecting the agreement.

fundamental breach: a breach of the contract that goes to the root of the agreement.

General Agreement on Tariffs and Trade (GATT): an international agreement on tariffs and trade.

grace: for certain negotiable instruments, a three-day extension in the time for payment beyond the payment date specified in the instrument itself.

grievance: an alleged violation of a collective agreement.

guarantee: a collateral promise (in writing) to answer for the debt of another (the principal debtor) if the debtor should default in payment.

holder: the person in possession of a negotiable instrument.

holder in due course: a person who acquires a negotiable instrument before its due date that is complete and regular on its face and who gave value for the instrument, without any knowledge of default or defect in the title of prior holders.

hypothec: an instrument used to secure debt in the province of Quebec that creates a security interest in land somewhat similar to a lien.

implied term: a standard or usual term that the courts will include in a contract on the assumption that the parties had intended the term to be included, but through some oversight had failed to include it.

indenture: a written document between two or more parties that was originally prepared in duplicate on a single page, and divided in such a way that the parts could be fitted together to prove its authenticity.

indictment: a written accusation of a crime committed by a person (or persons).

infant: a person who has not reached the age of majority.

infringement: the unlawful interference with the legal rights of another.

injunction: an equitable remedy of the court that orders the person or persons named therein to refrain from doing certain acts.

in statu quo: "in the original or former position."

insurable interest: an interest in property or in another person's life that would result in a loss to the person if the property should be damaged or destroyed, or the other person's life ended.

invitee: a person who enters upon the lands of another by invitation, usually for the benefit of the person in possession of the land.

judgement: a decision of the court.

laches: an equitable doctrine of the court that provides that no relief will be granted where a person delays bringing an action for an unreasonably long period of time.

law: a rule of conduct that is obligatory in the sense that sanctions are normally imposed if the rule is violated.

law merchant: the customs or rules established by merchants to resolve disputes that arose between them, and that were later applied by common law judges in cases that came before their courts.

lease: an agreement that constitutes a grant of possession of property for a fixed term in return for the payment of rent.

legal mortgage: a first mortgage of real property whereby the owner of land in fee simple transfers the title of the property pledged as security to the creditor on the condition that the title will be reconveyed when the debt is paid.

legal tender: money. The offer of payment which the creditor is obliged to accept in settlement of an account or debt.

lessee: a tenant.

lessor: a landlord.

libel: defamation in some permanent form, such as in writing, print, cartoon, etc.

licence: a right granted to someone to do something or to use property in a particular way.

lien: the right to hold or look to the property of another person as security for payment or performance of an obligation.

life estate: an estate in land in which the right to possession is based upon a person's lifetime.

liquidated damages: a bona fide estimate of the money damages that would flow from the breach of a contract.

lock-out: in a labour relations setting, the refusal of employee entry to a workplace by an employer when collective bargaining with the employees fails to produce a collective agreement.

loss leader selling: a practice of selling goods not for profit but to advertise or to attract customers to a place of business.

master: an employer.

mechanics' lien: a lien exercisable by a worker, contractor, or material supplier against property upon which the work or materials were expended.

mens rea: a guilty state of mind or intention to commit a crime.

misrepresentation: a statement of fact (or in some cases, conduct) that conveys a wrong or false impression to another.

mistake: a state of affairs where a party (or both parties) have formed an erroneous opinion as to the identity or existence of the subject-matter, or of some other important term.

mortgage: an agreement made between a debtor and a creditor in which the title to property of the debtor is transferred to the creditor as security for payment of the debt.

necessaries: goods that infants may require (such as food, clothing, shelter, and education) in order to maintain their station in life.

negotiable instrument: an instrument in writing that when transferred in good faith and for value without notice of defects passes a good title to the instrument to the transferee.

non est factum: a defence which may allow illiterate or infirm persons to avoid liability on a written agreement if they can establish that they were not aware of the true nature of the document, and were not careless in its execution.

novation: the substitution of parties to an agreement, or the replacement of one agreement by another agreement.

nuisance: interference with the enjoyment of real property or, in some cases, material interference with a person's physical comfort.

offer: a promise subject to a condition.

officer: a person elected or appointed by the directors of a corporation to fill a particular office (such as president, secretary, treasurer, etc.).

partnership: a legal relationship between two or more persons for the purpose of carrying on a business with a view to profit.

patent: the exclusive right granted to the inventor of something new and different to produce the invention for a period of 20 years in return for the disclosure of the invention to the public.

pawn: the transfer of possession (but not ownership) of chattels by a debtor to a creditor who is licensed to take and hold goods as security for payment of debt.

petition: a written request for a remedy from the Crown in certain kinds of proceedings such as bankruptcy, divorce, etc.

picketing: the physical presence of persons at or near the premises of another for the purpose of conveying information.

plagiarism: the passing-off of the writing or work of another as one's own.

pleadings: Written statements prepared by the plaintiff and defendant that set out the facts and claims of the parties in a legal action, and are exchanged prior to the hearing of the case by the court.

pledge: the transfer of securities by a debtor to a creditor as security for the payment of a debt.

POLARIS: a land title registration system used in the province of Ontario entitled Province of Ontario Land Registration and Information System.

power of attorney: a legal document usually signed under seal in which a person appoints another to act as his or her attorney to carry out the contractual or legal acts specified in the document.

predatory pricing: the practice of pricing goods at a very low price for the purpose of destroying competition. An offence under the Competition Act.

presumption at law: inferences drawn from facts which are considered true or conclusive until disproved by contrary evidence.

prima facie: "on first appearance."

principal: a person on whose behalf an agent acts.

procedural law: the law or procedures that a plaintiff must follow to enforce a substantive law right.

promissory note: a promise in writing, signed by the maker, to pay a sum certain in money to the person named therein, or bearer, at some fixed or determinable future time, or on demand.

provocation: acts that deprive a reasonable person of self-control and that may negate malice in an otherwise criminal act.

punitive damages: damages awarded by a court which are intended to punish a wrongdoer. See also: exemplary damages.

quantum meruit: "As much as he has earned." A quasi-contractual remedy that permits a person to recover a reasonable price for services and/or materials requested, where no price is established when the request is made.

ratification: the adoption of a contract or act of another by a party who was not originally bound by the contract or act.

real property: land and anything permanently attached to it.

referral selling: a practice whereby a customer receives a rebate or discount on a purchase by referring other customers to the seller. A prohibited practice under the Competition Act.

regulation: a procedural rule made under a statute.

release: a promise not to sue or press a claim, or a discharge of a person from any further responsibility to act.

remainderman: a person who is entitled to real property subject to a prior interest (e.g., a life estate), and who acquires the fee when the prior estate terminates.

replevin: court action which permits a person to recover goods unlawfully taken by another.

repudiation: the refusal to perform an agreement or promise.

rescission: the revocation of a contract or agreement.

res ipsa loquitur: "the thing speaks for itself."

respondeat superior: the liability or responsibility imputed to one person for the actions of another who acts under the direction of that person.

restitutio in integrum: to restore or return a party to an original position.

right-of-way: a right to pass over the land of another, usually to gain access to property.

salvage: under insurance law, the right of an insurer to the damaged, lost, or stolen property of the insured, if the insurer compensates the insured for the value of the property damaged, lost, or stolen.

seal: a formal mode of expressing the intention to be bound by a written promise or agreement. This expression usually takes the form of signing and affixing a wax or gummed paper wafer beside the signature, or making an engraved impression on the document itself.

servant: an employee.

servient tenement: a parcel of land subject to a right-of-way or easement.

set-off: where two parties owe debts to each other, the payment of one may be deducted from the other, and only the balance paid to extinguish the indebtedness.

share: the ownership of a fractional equity interest in a corporation.

share certificate: a certificate issued by a corporation that is evidence of a person's share ownership in the corporation.

shareholder: a person who holds a share interest in a corporation; a part owner of the corporation.

solicitor: a lawyer whose practice consists of the preparation of legal documents, wills, etc., and other forms of non-litigious legal work.

specific performance: an equitable remedy of the court that may be granted for breach of contract where money damages would be inadequate, and that requires the defendant to carry out the agreement according to its terms.

stare decisis: "to stand by previous decisions." The practice of a court to adhere to precedent in deciding the same issue as in a previous case.

statute: a law passed by (and within the legislative jurisdiction of) a properly constituted legislative body.

strike: in a labour relations setting, a cessation of work by a group of employees.

subrogation: the substitution of parties whereby the party substituted acquires the rights at law of the other party, usually by way of contractual arrangement.

tender: the act of performing a contract or the offer of payment of money due under a contract.

tenure: a method of holding land granted by the Crown.

title: the legal right to or ownership of property (goods or land).

tort: a civil wrong.

trade mark: a mark to distinguish the goods or services of one person from the goods or services of others.

trespass: a tort that may consist of the seizure or the injury of a person, the entry on the lands of another without permission, or the seizure or damage of goods of another without consent.

trial court: the court where a legal action is first brought before a judge for a decision.

trust: an agreement or arrangement whereby a party called a trustee holds property for the benefit of another, (called a beneficiary, or *cestui que* trust).

uberrimae fidei: "utmost good faith." A term applied to certain contractual relationships in which full disclosure is required on the part of both parties to the agreement.

ultra vires: beyond the legal authority or power of a legislative or corporate body to do an act.

UNCITRAL: United Nations Commission on International Trade Law.

undue influence: a state of affairs whereby a person is so influenced by another that the person's judgement is not his or her own.

vicarious liability: the liability at law of one person for the acts of another.

volenti non fit injuria: the voluntary assumption of risk of injury.

waiver: an express or implied renunciation of a right or claim.

warranty: in the sale of goods, a minor term in a contract. The breach of the term would allow the injured party to damages, but not rescission of the agreement.

REFERENCE LIST

The following texts and writing may be used to provide additional information on the various topics covered in the text.

GENERAL REFERENCE

Bird, Roger. Osborn's *Concise Law Dictionary.* 7th ed. London: Sweet & Maxwell Ltd., 1983.

Holdsworth, Sir William S. *A History of English Law.* London: Methuen; Sweet & Maxwell Ltd. (several editions; multiple volumes)

James, S. Philip. *Introduction to English Law.* 10th ed. London: Butterworths, Ltd., 1979.

Maitland, Frederick W. and Sir Frederick Pollock. *The History of English Law.* 2d ed., re-issued. London: Cambridge University Press, 1968.

AGENCY

Bowstead, William. *Bowstead On Agency.* 15th ed. (F.M. Reynolds and B.J. Davenport). London: Sweet & Maxwell Ltd., 1985.

Fridman, Gerald H.L. *The Law of Agency.* 5th ed. London: Butterworths Ltd., 1983.

BAILMENT

Palmer, N.E. *Bailment.* Sydney, Australia: Law Book Co., 1979.

BANKRUPTCY

Houlden, Lloyd W. and C.H. Morawetz. *The Annotated Bankruptcy and Insolvency Act 1993.* Toronto: The Carswell Company, 1992.

CONDOMINIUMS

Rosenberg, Alvin B. *Condominium in Canada.* Toronto: Canada Law Book Co., 1969. (update series)

CONSUMER PROTECTION

O'Grady, M.J., ed. *Consumers' Rights.* Toronto: The Law Society of Upper Canada, 1976.

CONTRACTS

Anson, Sir William R. *Anson's Law of Contract.* 26th ed. (A.G. Guest). Oxford: Clarendon Press, 1984.

Cheshire, G.C., Fifoot, C.H.S., and M.P. Furmston. *The Law of Contract.* 11th ed. London: Butterworths Ltd., 1986.

Waddams, Stephen M. *The Law of Contracts.* 3d ed. Toronto: Canada Law Book Co., 1993.

CORPORATIONS

Buckley, F.H. and M.Q. Conelly. *Corporations: Principles and Policies.* Toronto: Emond Montgomery Publications, 1988.

EMPLOYMENT AND COLLECTIVE BARGAINING

Adams, George W. *Canadian Labour Law.* 2d ed. Toronto: Canada Law Book, 1993.

Christie, I.M. *Employment Law in Canada.* Toronto: Butterworths Ltd., 1980.

ENVIRONMENTAL LAW

Saxe, Dianne. *Canadian Environmental Legislation.* Toronto: Canada Law Book, 1993.

Thompson, Geoffrey. *Environmental Law and Business in Canada.* Toronto: Canada Law Book, 1993.

INSURANCE

Brown, Craig, and Julio Menezes. *Insurance Law in Canada.* Toronto: The Carswell Company, 1982.

INTERNATIONAL BUSINESS LAW

August, Ray. *International Business Law.* Englewood Cliffs, N.J.: Prentice-Hall Inc., 1993.

MORTGAGES

Falconbridge, John D. *Falconbridge on Mortgages.* 4th ed. (W.B. Rayner and R.H. McLaren). Agincourt: Canada Law Book, 1977.

NEGOTIABLE INSTRUMENTS

Falconbridge, John D. *Crawford and Falconbridge: Banking and Bills of Exchange.* 7th ed. (B. Crawford). Toronto: Canada Law Book, 1986.

PARTNERSHIP

Lindley, N. *Lindley on The Law of Partnership.* 5th ed. (E. Scammell and R.C.I. Anson Banks). London: Sweet & Maxwell Ltd., 1984.

PATENTS, TRADE MARKS, COPYRIGHT	Hughes, Robert T., and John H. Woodley. *Hughes and Woodley on Patents*. Toronto: Butterworths Canada Ltd., 1984. (update series)
	Fox, Harold G. *The Canadian Law of Trade Marks and Unfair Competition*. 3d ed. Toronto: The Carswell Company, 1972.
REAL PROPERTY	Haber, Harvey M. *The Commercial Lease*. Toronto: Canada Law Book, 1989.
	Megarry, Sir Robert E., and W.H.R. Wade. *The Law of Real Property*. 5th ed. London: Stevens & Sons Ltd., 1984.
	Reiter, Barry, Risk, R.C.B., and Bradley N. McLellan. *Real Property Law*. 3d ed. Toronto: Emond Montgomery Publications Limited, 1986.
RESTRICTIVE TRADE PRACTICES	Khemani, R.S., and W.T. Stanburg, ed. *Canadian Competition Law and Policy at the Centenary*. Halifax, N.S.: The Institute for Research on Public Policy, 1991.
SALE OF GOODS	Fridman, Gerald H.L. *Sale of Goods in Canada*. 3d ed. Toronto: The Carswell Company, 1986.
SECURITY FOR DEBT	Macklem, Douglas N., and David I. Bristow. *Construction and Mechanics' Liens in Canada*. 6th ed. Toronto: The Carswell Company, 1985.
	MacLaren, Richard H. *Secured Transactions in Personal Property in Canada*. Toronto: The Carswell Company, 1979. (update series)
TORTS	Fleming, John G. *The Law of Torts*. 7th ed. Sydney, Australia: The Law Book Company, 1987.
	Linden, Allen M. *Canadian Tort Law*. 4th ed. Toronto: Butterworths Canada Ltd., 1988.
	Waddams, S.M. *Products Liability*. Toronto: The Carswell Company, 1980.

INDEX

— — — — — — — — — — cut here — — — — — — — — — — —

STUDENT REPLY CARD

CONTEMPORARY CANADIAN BUSINESS LAW 4/E By John A. Willes

You can help us to develop better textbooks. Please answer the following questions and return this form via Business Reply Mail. Your opinions matter: thank you in advance for sharing them with us!

Name of your college or university: _____

Major program of study: _____

Course title: _____

Were you required to buy this book? _____ yes _____ no

Did you buy this book new or used? _____ new _____ used ($_____)

Do you plan to keep or sell this book? _____ keep _____ sell

Is the order of topic coverage consistent with what was taught in your course?

Are there chapters or sections of this text that were not assigned for your course? Please specify:

— — — — — — — — — — · fold here — — — — — — — — — —

Were there topics covered in your course that are not included in the text? Please specify:

What did you like most about this text?

What did you like least?

Please add any comments or suggestions:

- - - - - - - - - - - - - - *cut here* - - - - - - - - - - - - - ┐
                                                                 ╎
                                                                 ╎ *cut here*
- - - - - - - - - - - - - *fold here* - - - - - - - - - - - - - ╎

Postage will be paid by

0183560299-L1N9B6-BR01

Attn.: Sponsoring Editor
College Division

MCGRAW-HILL RYERSON LIMITED
300 WATER ST
WHITBY ON   L1N 9Z9

tape shut